ngs gardens open for charity

GW01186514

The Yellow B

A GUIDE TO VISITING **THOUSANDS** OF GARDENS IN ENGLAND AND WALES

Published by
The National Gardens Scheme

A company limited by guarantee
Registered in England & Wales
Charity No. 1112664 Company No. 5631421
Registered & Head Office
Hatchlands Park East Clandon Guildford Surrey GU4 7RT
T 01483 211535 F 01483 211537 W www.ngs.org.uk
© The National Gardens Scheme 2008

Front cover: Coton Manor Garden, Northamptonshire.
Photograph: Clive Nichols. This page, above: Hutton-in-the-Forest,
Cumbria. Photograph: Val Corbett. Inset: 21 Lode Road, Cambridgeshire.
Photograph: Brian & Nina Chapple

Whether it's a single blade of grass or that imposing lawn, we're simply dedicated to ensuring you get the most out of your garden.

That's why we've been busy innovating and putting our technological know-how into the new range of HRX lawnmower models.

Take for instance our new HRX 537 VY variable-speed Versamow model that helps you go quicker in straight lines and slow down when negotiating a tree…or even a pink flamingo.

Furthermore we've shushed our engines by 30%, meaning less noise for you and your neighbours.

In fact, we're so green it's like we're part of the garden.

For more details on the new HRX 537 VY and our full range of Lawn & Garden equipment please visit **www.honda.co.uk** or call **0845 200 8000.**

ngs gardens open for charity

THE**CONTENTS**

The Yellow Book 2008

Above left: Winton Park, Cumbria. Photograph: Val Corbett. Above right: Springhead, Dorset. Photograph: Rosalind Simon. Inset: Teversal Manor Gardens, Nottinghamshire. Photograph: Mike Vardy

| Production team: Caroline Anderson, Elna Broe, Valerie Caldwell, Julia Grant, Tracey Layzell, Lisa Lewis, Kali Masure, Elizabeth Milner, Wendy Morton, Janet Oldham, Valerie Piggott, Sue Reeve, Jane Sennett. With thanks to our NGS county volunteers | Copyright of the photographs belongs to the individual photographers. Design by James Pembroke Publishing | Maps designed and produced by Mapworld | Data manipulation and image setting by utimestwo | Printing and binding by William Clowes Limited |

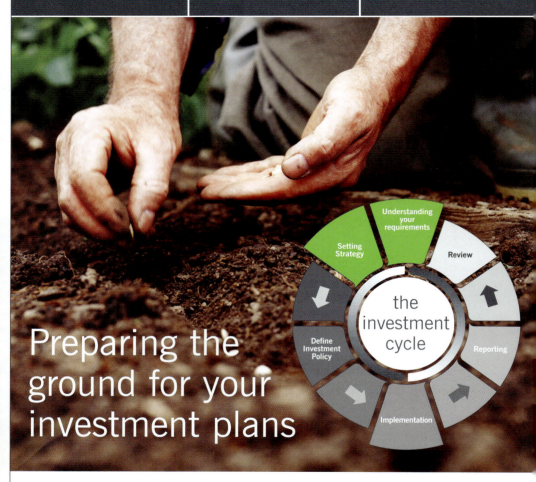

Rensburg Sheppards

Investment Management

the investment cycle

- Understanding your requirements
- Review
- Reporting
- Implementation
- Define Investment Policy
- Setting Strategy

Preparing the ground for your investment plans

Rensburg Sheppards Investment Management – we're with you all the way

www.rensburgsheppards.co.uk

Professional but entirely personal investment management

About us

Discover the wonders of private gardens, and help raise money for good causes at the same time, with *The Yellow Book 2008*

Manor House, Hampshire. Photograph: Nicola Stocken Tomkins

80 years young

The NGS keeps up with garden trends

The NGS was founded in 1927 to raise money for community nurses by opening private gardens to the public. In the first year 609 " Pioneer" gardens opened and over £8,000 was raised by charging 'a shilling a head'. Now the NGS welcomes over half a million visitors every year. Through this we have raised £40 million since we began for nursing, caring and gardening charities. In the last 10 years alone the gardens of the NGS have raised £22 million.

"The Yellow Book has everything from allotments to exotic gardens"

The range has also increased – everything from allotments to exotic gardens, without losing quality. Many people are adopting sustainable or organic techniques in some form and that is changing the way they garden.

Whatever you are looking for, from information to inspiration, tea and cake in a glorious setting or a plant bargain to bring back home, you can find it within the pages of *The Yellow Book*.

CHAIRMAN'S MESSAGE

When garden owners are asked why they would like to go into *The Yellow Book,* they frequently answer that (a) they find this a reward and recognition that they have created a work of quality, (b) they like the idea of sharing their creation with others and (c) they enjoy raising money for excellent charities. I am sure that you visitors can empathise with these thoughts.

The NGS is always developing. Over recent years the gardens have changed in size and style and, while we still have the larger and grander gardens in our Scheme, we now have thousands of smaller gardens that visitors can relate to more. This year we are starting a Friends organisation that you can read about on p17 – hopefully you might become a Friend.

I hope that you all have a busy and enjoyable garden-visiting season in 2008.

Nicholas Payne

Rensburg Sheppards

Investment Management

Attending to your changing needs

the investment cycle

- Understanding your requirements
- Setting Strategy
- Review
- Define Investment Policy
- Reporting
- Implementation

Rensburg Sheppards Investment Management – we're with you all the way

www.rensburgsheppards.co.uk

Professional but entirely personal investment management

Green Lane garden in Devon, one of those selected for The Yellow Book via the BBC2 Open Gardens series
Photograph: Nicola Stocken Tomkins

The NGS welcomes record number of new gardens

Every year The National Gardens Scheme is delighted to welcome gardens new to *The Yellow Book*. They are easy to spot as they have a pale green background and the **NEW** symbol next to the garden number. In 2008 there are record numbers of debutantes across the counties for visitors to enjoy alongside old favourites.

Amongst the diverse range you will find Whalton Manor in Northumberland with its magnificent walled garden designed by Sir Edwin Lutyens and Gertrude Jekyll, plus an imposing 30-yard peony border.

At the other end of the country on the River Thames in London are Downing Road Mooring Barge gardens, open at the height of the summer and showcasing a series of seven floating barge gardens with an eclectic range of plants, all connected by walkways and bridges.

With warmer weather continuing longer, there are more and more gardens opening at both ends of the season. Trefgarne Hall in Carmarthenshire is one such entry, new to this year's book, and which has open days in May and September.

Two gardens that featured on the BBC2 *Open Gardens* series are Fulvens Hanger in Surrey and Green Lane in Devon. The latter has some interesting features amongst the packed flowerbeds including a wooden staircase to a pergola of antique carved pillars from Turkistan.

More conventionally, Fulvens Hanger is an exciting new 3-acre woodland garden in the early stages of development featuring a bluebell walk and many new specimen plantings to be enjoyed through May, June and July.

There isn't room here to describe more than a handful of these wonderful gardens – but try a 'keyword' search on GardenFinder on the NGS website www.ngs.org.uk. You'll discover all types of garden – Borough Farm in Hampshire, which allows self-seeding to add many 'surprises' to an otherwise traditional farmhouse garden; the scented garden at Hough Cottage in Cheshire, or the totally organic garden at Gwyndy in Gwynedd.

There's (almost!) as much fun in the planning as in the visiting. Enjoy!

Rensburg Sheppards

Investment Management

Maximising the potential at every stage

the investment cycle

- Understanding your requirements
- Setting Strategy
- Review
- Define Investment Policy
- Reporting
- Implementation

Rensburg Sheppards Investment Management – we're with you all the way

www.rensburgsheppards.co.uk

Professional but entirely personal investment management

Some of the creative cakes submitted to the NGS, from Norfolk (below) and Bedford (right)

The NGS celebrates 80 years of garden visiting

Owners join in the birthday party fun

There is nothing NGS garden owners enjoy more than an excuse to have a party! And what could be better than 80 years of raising money for good causes? The 10th of June 2007 was the designated day and garden owners from across England and Wales came up with a variety of ways to add to the fun.

"…over 200,000 people turned out on the busiest day of the NGS year"

Down in Somerset every visitor was treated to a free piece of cake, from the famous NGS lemon drizzle to gloriously gooey chocolate cake. In Surrey and Bedfordshire visitors enjoyed huge plant fairs, jazz bands, flower arranging demonstrations and much more. Of course there was much 'friendly' competition to create a truly original birthday cake.

The sun shone all day (something we would not recognise for most of the summer) and over 200,000 people turned out on the busiest day of the NGS year to enjoy the gardens and take part in the celebrations – all true to the spirit of the original garden owners in 1927.

Many happy returns NGS!

CENTENARY CELEBRATIONS FOR MOLLY

Just four days after joining in the NGS birthday celebrations, gardener Molly Mills celebrated a special anniversary of her own – her 100th birthday.

Molly is a long-standing supporter of the NGS, who first opened her garden in 1976, originally for the Queens' Nursing Institute which evolved into The National Gardens Scheme. The entrance fee then for the six gardens open in Dorsington was 30p. She moved away from Dorsington briefly but returned and has opened her garden at 'Windrush' for the past 23 years, latterly with the help of her daughter Barbara.

Happy birthday Molly, and thanks for all your support!

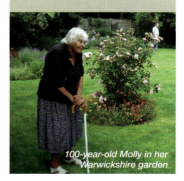

100-year-old Molly in her Warwickshire garden

More BBC fame for NGS gardeners

Open Gardens returns to the TV

The second series of *Open Gardens* returned in September 2007 for a new 30-part BBC2 daytime series. Each programme follows two gardens as their owners wait to win a place in the legendary *Yellow Book*.

Carol Klein is joined by Joe Swift (both of *Gardeners' World* and the Chelsea Flower Show), to offer advice and practical support to each of the 60 gardens from all over the country, which are featured in the series.

"Some incredibly talented gardeners have turned challenging sites into beautiful, show-stopping gardens."

Joe Swift

"I have met some incredibly talented gardeners who, against all the odds, have turned the most challenging sites into beautiful, show-stopping gardens," said Joe Swift. "It's fantastic that this series means that even more people can share gardens open to the public under The National Gardens Scheme."

The new series travels to gardens in every kind of situation and style. There's a sensory garden designed to be enjoyed by both sighted and unsighted; a neglected garden being restored with an Italian theme; huge gardens with big ideas but mountains to climb to achieve them; a windswept garden transformed into a fusion of planting styles; the tiniest garden ever to open to the public...

Open Gardens exemplifies Britain's unique talent for gardening and shows how The National Gardens Scheme provides a means for many people to share their private passion for plants and garden design with like-minded horticultural enthusiasts.

Look out for repeats on BBC2 and cable channels throughout the spring and summer.

CLARENCE HOUSE

Since 1927, members of the National Gardens Scheme have thrown open their gates to the public, inviting inspection, admiration and, most flattering of all, imitation of their gardens. As Patron, I know that this distinguished record of service could not have been achieved without the hard work and support of countless volunteers, staff and garden owners – to whom we owe an enormous debt of gratitude.

MARIE CURIE CANCER CARE

Marie Curie Nurses deliver high-quality nursing care, totally free, to give terminally ill people the choice of dying at home and provide support for their families. Did you know that funding from the NGS covers eight Marie Curie Nurses in eight patients' homes every night. Over the last 11 years the NGS has funded care for more than 4,600 cancer patients.

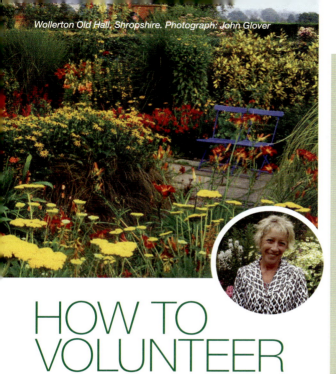

Wollerton Old Hall, Shropshire. Photograph: John Glover

HOW TO VOLUNTEER

Come to work for The National Gardens Scheme

The NGS is run by a team of volunteers based in each county. Over 350 people share the fun and work involved in organising thousands of garden events. Help and training is given so that new volunteers can make a start. Although knowledge of gardens is always helpful, the main requirement is for good organisational skills and for people who enjoy working as part of a team.

"As a *Yellow Book* veteran, I know just how much hard work is involved in preparing a garden for the NGS. It's fantastic that even more people can share gardens open to the public under The National Gardens Scheme." Carol Klein

- For more information about becoming a volunteer with the NGS go to www.ngs.org.uk or contact your local County Team, (details in the listings section of this book).

Rensburg Sheppards

SUPPORTING OUR FRIENDS

friends of the ngs

We at Rensburg Sheppards have sponsored *The Yellow Book* for the past 15 years, and subsequently the NGS website. We are now pleased to extend our sponsorship to include the launch of the 'Friends of the NGS' (see page 17).

In our opinion, there are many similarities between the vision, patience and hard work involved in looking after a garden and the way in which we, as investment managers, look after our clients.

We are conscious of the pleasure the gardens give to so many people and the increasing sums of money raised in aid of the charities which benefit from The National Gardens Scheme.

We are proud to sponsor *The Yellow Book*, the website and now the 'Friends of the NGS', and to be associated with an organisation which does so much good.

Steve Elliott

**Steve Elliott
Chief Executive,
Rensburg Sheppards**

Local volunteers will assess your garden to see if it is suitable to be in the scheme

26 Northumberland Avenue, Somerset. Photograph: Julia Phillips

Can my garden be in The Yellow Book?

How your garden can win the NGS seal of approval

Our local volunteer teams visit new gardens to advise them on whether they should open for the NGS. Their experience is the most important factor in determining whether or not gardens are likely to attract visitors and raise money.

Advice on opening

County teams visit all potential new gardens to discuss the practicalities of opening with the owner. Here are Carol Klein's tips to gain acceptance into the NGS:

- Your garden must provide enough interest to engage the visitor for at least 45 minutes.

- Plant interest – a wide range of interesting and well-grown plants are among the most important elements in an NGS garden.

- Design – nine out of ten county organisers say plants are more important than design. However, design should enhance the planting.

- Your garden must be made with love and care – money doesn't buy you love!

Other questions to ask yourself

- Are you happy to welcome and chat with visitors?

- Can you offer plant sales?

- Do you support our charities and are you happy to donate the money that you raise to the NGS?

The county team will also help with the paperwork and brief you on health and safety, insurance and publicity.

We welcome all contact from potential garden openers.

PROTECT THE FUTURE

It takes a special kind of person to look after National Trust gardens. A passion for plants and the outdoor life, a love of history and knowledge of traditional skills are just some of the requirements.

In 1991, The National Trust set up a three-year training scheme, known as 'Careership', to provide a much-needed pool of qualified gardeners equipped with an understanding of historic gardens and the specialist skills to care for them.

Twelve Careership posts are advertised each spring on the Trust's website. Training gardeners to this level is a huge financial commitment for the Trust – it costs around £50,000 to put each student through the course. None of this would be possible without the NGS, which has been supporting Careership since the beginning. In recent years the NGS has donated around £190,000 annually from the income it raises through opening gardens for charity.

Stourhead Garden, Wiltshire.
Photograph: National Trust Photo Library.
Inset: Zac Goldsmith.
Photograph: The Ecologist Magazine

An ecologist's view

It's clear climate change is affecting gardens now, but what might happen in the future is less predictable, says Zac Goldsmith, President of the NGS

"There's no doubt the climate is changing and that necessarily means our gardens and farms are going to change. It's already happening. English wine – for so long a poor but patriotic alternative to French wine – is beginning to gain followers. Olive groves are appearing and people are experimenting with fruits and trees that they wouldn't have considered a few years ago. On top of this, increasing numbers of gardeners are actively developing gardens to attract wildlife and encourage biodiversity. It's impossible to predict what our climate will be like in the future – but we know it will be different, and our farmers and gardeners are at the forefront."

Flourishing success
with country properties

Humberts combines local insight with a powerful national presence to produce the results its clients and their properties deserve

Humberts Residential

From our expanding network of over 80 offices Humberts provides expert advice on the sale, purchase and rental of all types of residential property.

Country Department

Based in the flagship Mayfair office in South Audley Street, the country department has a highly experienced team which is dedicated to helping clients buy and sell prime country houses, farms and estates throughout England.

If you are thinking of buying or selling in the country call the country department on **020 7290 2810** or visit our website for further information.

To request a copy of our latest property catalogue or one of our service brochures please call **01273 354800** or email brochures@humberts.co.uk

Humberts is delighted to support The National Gardens Scheme

Please visit our new website at humberts.co.uk

Join our community
of garden lovers!

Become a Friend of the NGS for just £25 a year in our new scheme

More than half a million of you visit our wonderful gardens every year; we'd love to keep you up to date with news from the NGS. In 2008 we will launch our long-anticipated Friends Scheme, which will see the NGS community grow from garden owners and county volunteers to include you, the garden visitor.

As a Friend of the NGS, you'll be helping us to raise more money for nursing, caring and gardening charities and there's a lot in it for you too. You will enjoy priority mailing of *The Yellow Book* in February, an exclusive programme of Friends events, invitations to special gardens not usually open to the public, twice-yearly Friends newsletters taking you behind the scenes of the NGS and regular e-news.

All this for just £25 per year.

Become a Benefactor

Another way to support our work is to become a Benefactor; as well as having all the Friends benefits extended to you, you'll also be acknowledged in *The Yellow Book* and on the NGS website and receive an exclusive NGS pin. NGS Benefactors make a special commitment to the work of the NGS.

To find out more...

- Visit www.ngs.org.uk
- Email friends@ngs.org.uk
- Phone us on 01483 213910

We look forward to welcoming you to our community of garden lovers and plant enthusiasts and seeing you at our Friends events throughout 2008.

friends
of the ngs

Spetchley Park Gardens, Worcestershire.
Photograph: Val Corbett

Visit an NGS garden and help raise millions for charity

Since 1927, visitors to the gardens in our scheme have helped us raise almost £40 million to support many charities, including the current beneficiaries

Most of the 3,500 gardens which open for the NGS are privately owned. More than half a million people visit the gardens each year, and through this more than £2 million is raised every year for national nursing, gardening and other charitable causes.

Since 1927 we have raised almost £40 million to support these charities, £22 million in the last 10 years. We keep overheads low, so most of the money from the garden gate goes straight to the beneficiary charities.

Donations are 'unrestricted' which means money can be invested in areas which the beneficiaries consider vital to future development, and which might be difficult to fund from other sources.

As well as funding nursing posts at **Macmillan Cancer Support**, the NGS's annual donation helps to provide financial advice, physiotherapy and counselling. In fact 130 different services are supported and the NGS is proud to be Macmillan's biggest ever donor.

Over the last decade, contributions from the NGS have funded **Marie Curie Cancer Care** nurses in each of the NGS counties. These nurses deliver high-quality care, totally free, to give terminally ill people the choice of dying at home, as well as providing support for their families.

Did you know that 83% of carers suffer increased stress and anxiety coupled

with isolation, and poor health? Through **Crossroads**, the NGS increased support to young and older carers and reduced waiting lists for carer support by 8% in 2006.

Through the NGS's longstanding support, **Help the Hospices** has helped with the training of over 1,400 hospice nurses, helping them gain new specialist skills and qualifications and enabling them to give the best possible care for patients with terminal illness, along with their families and friends.

"Every visitor makes a vital contribution"

The NGS keeps up its tradition of funding nursing care through **The Queen's Nursing Institute**.

The annual donation to **The Royal Fund for Gardeners' Children** enables ongoing support to orphaned and needy horticulturists' children, and through **Perennial** the NGS helps retired horticultural workers.

Each year the money donated to **The National Trust** helps fund trainee gardeners, a vital element in ensuring the long-term provision of professional skills and techniques. Many graduates continue with The National Trust.

In short, every visitor to an NGS garden is making a vital contribution to people who need care or support.

Quality Garden Tours 2008

Brightwater Holidays is the UK's leading specialist Garden Tour Operator.

Our fully inclusive itineraries combine the famous and grand gardens with the small and private gardens – most tours also visit specialist nurseries. Travel by coach, air, ferry and rail from a variety of local pick up points throughout the UK.

Tours include a full programme of UK garden tours, continental European holidays and exotic far-away places. If you have your own group and are looking for a tailor made itinerary we are happy to work to suit your interest and budget.

Please contact us for a copy of our comprehensive brochure for 2008.

Brightwater Holidays Brochure out now....

01334 657155

Brightwater Holidays Ltd
Eden Park House, Cupar, Fife KY15 4HS
info@brightwaterholidays.com
www.brightwaterholidays.com

Bartlett Science

We protect one of the most important growth investments you own.

Their beauty may be priceless, but the market value that trees add to your home is very tangible. Your investment in Bartlett tree care delivers one of the most reliable returns in your portfolio. Bartlett Science has been improving the landscape of tree care and growth investments since 1907.

For your nearest branch, call us at 0845 600 9000. Or visit us at www.bartlett.com.

BARTLETT TREE EXPERTS

SCIENTIFIC TREE CARE SINCE 1907

Principal Offices

Bedford	Cirencester	Guildford	Radlett
Beaconsfield	Crawley Down	London	Sevenoaks
Bristol	Glossop	Macclesfield	York

Thinking forward

The eco garden is all about giving something back to the environment, and compost bins and recycling tanks are the new must-haves

Following the drought of 2006 and floods of 2007, the NGS commissioned award-winning garden designer Andy Sturgeon to come up with a concept for the garden of the future. Andy's design reflects changing attributes to the environment, driven by rising energy prices and changing weather patterns. For example, large, paved driveways and patios which can raise local temperatures and increase the risk of flooding, may be dug up and replaced with porous gravels and paving interspersed with plants. Rammed earth walls could be used to make raised plant beds instead of CO_2-producing concrete. In addition, photovoltaic cells could use the sun's power to light gardens and pump water.

"The next 80 years," says Andy, "will see the biggest change in gardening ever, as we move from a temperate climate towards a sub-tropical one. We need cold winters to stimulate flower buds on

Dolly Barn, Derbyshire.
Photograph: Lu Jeffery

Durrance Manor, Sussex.
Photograph: Jonathan Need

fruits such as blackberries and cherries. Rhododendrons and birch, which need cool summers, will gradually die out, and traditional cottage-garden favourites such as delphiniums and phlox, which need a moist, fertile soil, will also disappear." Many NGS gardeners have already changed the way they garden. Some have stopped growing cottage-garden plants, or moved them to shadier areas because of drought. Tender plants such as dahlias are being left to over-winter in the ground, and more sub-tropical plants such as tree ferns and olives are being planted.

"A pond will be an essential breeding site and drinking hole for wildlife." Andy Sturgeon

Our homes are extending into the garden too, and changes to planning regulations will encourage that. Green roofs can be used to attract wildlife, they have good insulation properties and don't harm the visual environment.

With urbanisation will come displaced wildlife. The garden of the future will feature a pond as an essential breeding site and drinking hole for wildlife as water becomes scarce in summer months.

NATURAL BEAUTIES

A selection of environmentally friendly gardens in this year's *The Yellow Book*

Braxted Place
Essex
This mature organic garden has something for everyone. Approximately 1 acre, with attached Victorian chapel (open with garden). Walled kitchen and herb garden, conservatory and gravel garden. Informal lawns, borders, wild areas and mature trees give a romantic feel, especially in spring.
Photograph: Mike Howes

Chesters Walled Garden

Durham and Northumberland
Enjoy this garden with its wild flowers mingling with unusual perennials and extensive collection of herbs. Three National Collections: marjoram, sanguisorba and thyme. Roman garden, knot garden, ponds and vegetables. Organically run, the walled garden is a haven for wildlife including red squirrels.
Photograph: Suzie White

Littleham House Cottage
Devon
A secret garden full of colour. Winding paths lead you to horticultural surprises round every corner; spring bulbs, camellias and other treasures abound in this cottage garden. Organically grown vegetables, herbs and a variety of fruit trees.
Photograph: Julia Phillips

www.ngs.org.uk

Hotel Maes-Y-Neuadd
Gwynedd

For a relaxing weekend visit the gardens
and grounds of this country-house
hotel with views towards Snowdon,
Cardigan Bay and Lleyn Peninsula.
80 acres, meadows, woodland walks,
two working walled gardens, unusual
cultivars, cut flower borders; innovative,
intensive, organic gardening methods
with aesthetic appeal.
Photograph: Owner
Inset: Ian Gowland

Moors Meadow
Herefordshire

Enchanting, unique, organic 7-acre haven
overlooking the beautiful Kyre valley and
brimming with trees, shrubs, flowers,
ferns, grasses and bulbs from around
the world. Comprising several gardens
ingeniously created within one including
intriguing features and sculptures, potager
and pools, myriad wildlife, eccentric
plantswomen, nursery.
Photograph: Andrea Jones

Hallowarren
Cornwall

The ethos of this garden is harmony with
nature, run on organic lines. 2-acre garden and
orchard leading to 6-acre beautiful wooded
valley and bordering stream. Walk along the
valley through old woodland full of native
bluebells. Ducks, geese and chickens.
Photograph: Val Corbett

South Newington House
Oxfordshire

This wonderful garden with 5 acres of paddocks and garden is created for year-round interest. Tumbling rambling roses, softly coloured herbaceous borders. Ponds, organic fruit and vegetables. Walled garden with parterre and box topiary.

Photograph: Owner

Stillingfleet Lodge
Yorkshire

Visit this organic garden, also a plantsman's garden subdivided into smaller gardens, each based on colour theme with emphasis on use of foliage plants. Wild-flower meadow and natural pond. 55 yards of double herbaceous borders.

Photograph: Rosalind Simon

Knitson Old Farmhouse
Dorset

Enjoy the views through the new moon arch in this mature cottage garden. Herbaceous borders, rockeries, climbers, shrubs, 40 hostas. Large organic kitchen garden for self-sufficiency in fruit and vegetables including kiwis! Ancient stone cottage.

Photograph: Dianna Jazwinski

10 Chestnut Way
Derbyshire

Meander through an acre of natural borders, spring bulbs, mature trees, and intimate woodland to a stunning butterfly bed and wild-flower meadow. Behind the natural look, a pair of passionate, practical, organic gardeners gently manage the vast range of plants.

Photograph: Owner

How to be a
greener gardener

Organic gardening guru Bob Flowerdew gives a few tips
to help your plot become even more eco-friendly

We all want our plants and gardens to flourish, our wildlife to burgeon and for us to cause less pollution in doing so. The answer's simple – help nature's systems and everything works better in the garden. Encourage wildlife; from the almost microscopic all the way to birds, frogs and hedgehogs, especially with organic methods. Use hand labour rather than powered tools risking little lives and worse accidents. Cut down water usage and mowing; replace lawns with, for example, stepping stones amongst low growing perennial ground cover. Buy purchases wisely; and abstain from pesticides.

Don't just make compost, grab anything you see going that you can add to your compost bins. Learn to make more and better compost and apply it liberally. Recycling comes naturally to gardeners who are the world's most persistent 'bodgers' and 'make do'ers' – I don't need tell you how to do it.

Be cunning – we all need more water storage so hide butts away in 'dead spaces' connected by hoses to butts by down pipes, or even to butts where you want the water. Be sensible – if you can't turn down the temperature in your greenhouse or conservatory then insulate more effectively. And I hardly need say don't install huge pumped water features or get a Chelsea tractwor.

Bob's Best Tips

- Compost everything you can

- Recycle anything you can

- Have more water butts

- Have at least one informal, fish- and duck-free, pond, pool, sunken bath or even just a sink. As well as a bird bath

- Have a multiplicity of bird boxes, wildlife nests and hidden away piles of stones and bundles of prunings

- Use more mulches, organic and gravel etc

- Plant more perennial and less annual bedding

- Choose low watering options and plantings

- Plant more trees, evergreens, dense shrubs and native plants

- Reduce machine grass mowing – either have less sward or cut less often

- Add clover to your swards to make them self-fertilising, and add chamomile, thyme and daisies too.

- Use less, or no, unsustainable resources such as peat, water-worn limestone, or seeds, bulbs and plants collected from the wild

- Use timber from sustainable forestry or recycled, peat dredged from clogged waterways and recycled stone and brick

- If local byelaws permit recycle your grey water to established plants

- Be careful not to apply fertilizers or feeds which your plants do not clearly need

- Give up smoking bonfires. If you must burn then burn cleanly with no plastics, paints or man made junk – and bag the ashes to add back to your compost before they get wet

- Be careful in your choice of paints, preservatives and cleaners

- Don't use poisonous, or even 'safe' chemicals unless absolutely necessary. If you really must use something nasty then employ a professional to do the job properly and safely – and probably more effectively!

From the world's best tea gardens to the best gardens in Britain

The growers we buy from take extra time and care to cultivate their top quality teas for our Yorkshire Gold blend. We pay more for these special teas, and visit the gardens to build stronger and lasting partnerships with them.

Does this mean it's the best cup of tea in Britain? Tell us what you think at **www.bestteainbritain.co.uk**.

Yorkshire Tea. Try it. You'll see.

10 FAMILY-FRIENDLY GARDENS

Some *Yellow Book* entries designed to keep the kids entertained

Ashton House
Cheshire and Wirral

Lots of interest for the children in this country garden, with stream, natural pond, interesting trees, including an old monkey puzzle tree and many other unusual species of trees and shrubs. Children's garden with vegetables, herbs, living willow maze, tunnels and woodland area.

Photographs: Owner

6 Methuen Park
London

With a tree house providing hours of entertainment, this garden is for all the family. Across the formal pond, the beach grows into a path. An arch doubles as a swing. Flowing curves and unique planting create an enchanting, peaceful space.
Photograph: Owner

Holly Grove
Shropshire

A great opportunity for children to see rare White Park cattle and Soay sheep in this 3-acre garden. Yew and beech hedges enclosing 'rooms', box parterres, pleached limes, vegetable garden, rose and herbaceous borders containing many rare plants.
Photographs: Val Corbett

St Brides C/W Primary School
Glamorgan

Developed and maintained by children, individual gardens within the school grounds include the Warm Welcome Garden, Woodland, Organic Fruit and Vegetable Garden, Easter Garden, Jewish Garden, Sensory Garden, Patchwork Garden, Butterfly Garden, Flower Diary Garden, Woven Willow playground, maze, nature reserve and wild-flower meadow.
Photograph: St Brides C/W Primary School

Little Court
Hampshire

A garden for all the family, with bantams and newts for everyone to enjoy and also a quiz for the children. A tree house with spectacular views appeals to all ages. Carpets of crocuses and cowslips in the labyrinth.
Photograph: Sunniva Harte

Flaxbourne Farm
Bedfordshire

Bring the whole family and discover many inspirational features in this beautiful and entertaining garden of 2 acres. Lovingly developed with numerous water features, windmill, modern arches and bridges, a small moated castle, lily pond and herbaceous borders. Newly constructed Greek temple ruin.
Photograph: Owner

Llowes Court
Powys

With roaming ducks and hens, the family will enjoy a visit to this garden. Large low-lying garden of walled courtyards, lawns, woodland and meadows. Deep pools and stream. Grotto, rill, mounts, box, yew alley. Formal garden in reclaimed farmyard, rose tunnel and vegetables
Photograph: Rowan Isaac

13 Queen Elizabeth's Walk
London
The children will love the quirky
front garden with leaf sculpture fence.
A garden for all seasons with emphasis
on foliage, textures and unusual plants
from China, Australia and Mexico.
Interest for children without
encroaching on the plants or design.
Photograph: Owner

Yews Farm
Somerset and Bristol
The whole family will enjoy the
theatrical planting in the walled
gardens. Sculptural combinations
of shape, leaf and texture. Tall
plants, strange seed heads and
12ft-high echium in the jungle
garden. Working organic vegetable
garden feeds the growing family.
Pigs and hens in the farmyard
Photographs: Carol Drake

Poulton Hall
Cheshire and Wirral
This garden is a definite must with
its child-friendly features including
a surprising new approach to the
walled garden and redesigned
nursery rhyme area. Wood sculptures
of Robin Hood and the Jabberwock
by Jim Heath and other reminders
of Roger Lancelyn Green's retellings.
Photograph: Owner

GET THE INSIDE STORY ON OUR GREAT OUTDOORS

From beautiful spring bulbs to spectacular shrubs, pretty cottage gardens to working kitchen gardens, scent-filled summer displays to frosted winter wonderlands, the National Trust look after more than 200 of the most-loved and celebrated gardens. And every one has it's own tale to tell. Enlightening tours are available around many of our gardens and you can enjoy a delicious home-made lunch or cream tea to turn an ordinary day into something quite extraordinary.

To find your nearest National Trust houses and gardens visit www.nationaltrust.org.uk For National Trust membership enquiries, please call 0844 800 1895.

Registered Charity Number 205846

THE NATIONAL TRUST

Making her debut

Helen Newport explains how she was delighted when her garden, Old Pines in Berkshire, was included in this year's *Yellow Book*, at her first attempt

Old Pines, Berkshire

Until the summer of 2007 I had no thought of opening my garden until the local church formed a committee to open gardens in the area for one afternoon to raise money. They couldn't understand why I wasn't in *The Yellow Book*. I made a tentative approach to the NGS and thought it would be interesting to receive some constructive criticism. I was amazed and delighted when I was immediately invited to open for them.

"Since then there has been a flurry of activity geared to open day. My years of just doing it for me have been transformed into 'show time'."

Always something new

"My hobby is garden projects so there is always something on the go. Now we have a pond, stream, bridges, arches and footpaths. There's a variety of planting in the garden; we have woodland, vegetables, tulips in their hundreds, daffodils in their thousand and bluebells. I've introduced some new Grape Hyacinths and rare Fritillary pudica Golden Snow Drops, plus we have topiary, climbers, bits of statuary, a herb bed and five huge compost bays.

"There is a lot to see, including sheep and two miniature Shetland ponies. To make things even more enticing, we are going to introduce teas and plant sales. My next projects are to construct a pebble mosaic and a new shed to house my favourite bit of kit – the digger.

"I am not trained but I love 'painting with plants' and love showy colours; I am trying to make the garden interesting all year round.

"We had over 500 visitors for the church so hope to have lots more for the NGS."

Far left and left: If you like 'painting with plants', try visiting The Plant Specialist, Buckinghamshire, photograph: Fiona McLeod; or Grafton Cottage in Staffordshire, photograph: Marianne Majerus.

Bankton Cottage, above and inset. Photograph: Leigh Clapp

An old favourite

Rosie Lloyd explains how her garden, a regular in *The Yellow Book* for some years, has developed since it first opened and outlines her plans for its future

"When we arrived at Bankton Cottage 25 years ago the garden was boring and depressing: we couldn't wait to get started, especially as our previous garden was in central London and now we had 3 and a half acres to play with," recalls Rosie Lloyd.

"But we had no grand plan and obeyed the golden rule of waiting a year before doing a thing. During that time we tested the soil, worried about the drainage, shivered in the frost pockets and watched how the sun circumnavigated the garden. When we could, we visited other gardens to inspire us, avidly watched anything to do with gardens on the telly, and bought countless books by the likes of Rosemary Verey, Penelope Hobhouse and Christopher Lloyd, whose wit, wisdom and invention, both in his writing and his wonderful garden at Great Dixter, really got me going.

Cottage garden

"Over the years,
our walled garden has
developed a cottage garden
look, because that's the way
I plant: too much, too close, but bursting
with colour and with a shaggy casual look
that seems somehow to get everywhere.

"An atmosphere of peace and romance"

Outside the brick walls is a one-acre lake and
extensive woodland: once well stocked, it reverted
over the years to ponticum, birch, sycamore and
so on, so we have gradually tidied and planted
more interesting shrubs and trees. Now that we
have more time (the NGS notwithstanding) we are
improving the links between
the flowery area and the wilder
part, inspired by some of the
East Sussex gardens we've visited.

"A love affair with Italy, with the Medici
gardens of Florence high on the list, has resulted
in an outbreak of hedging, topiary and a parterre,
while my husband is determined to build a grotto
somewhere in the bossco.

"Hidden corners, views to entice you to explore,
an atmosphere of peace and romance and places
to sit to enjoy a glass of wine...that's what I'm trying
to create in our little bit of paradise."

*Above: Christopher Lloyd's wonderful garden at Great Dixter,
Sussex. Photograph: Jerry Harpur. Top right: Eastgrove
Cottage Garden, Worcestershire. Another garden with
a Lloydian influence. Photograph: Marcus Harpur.*

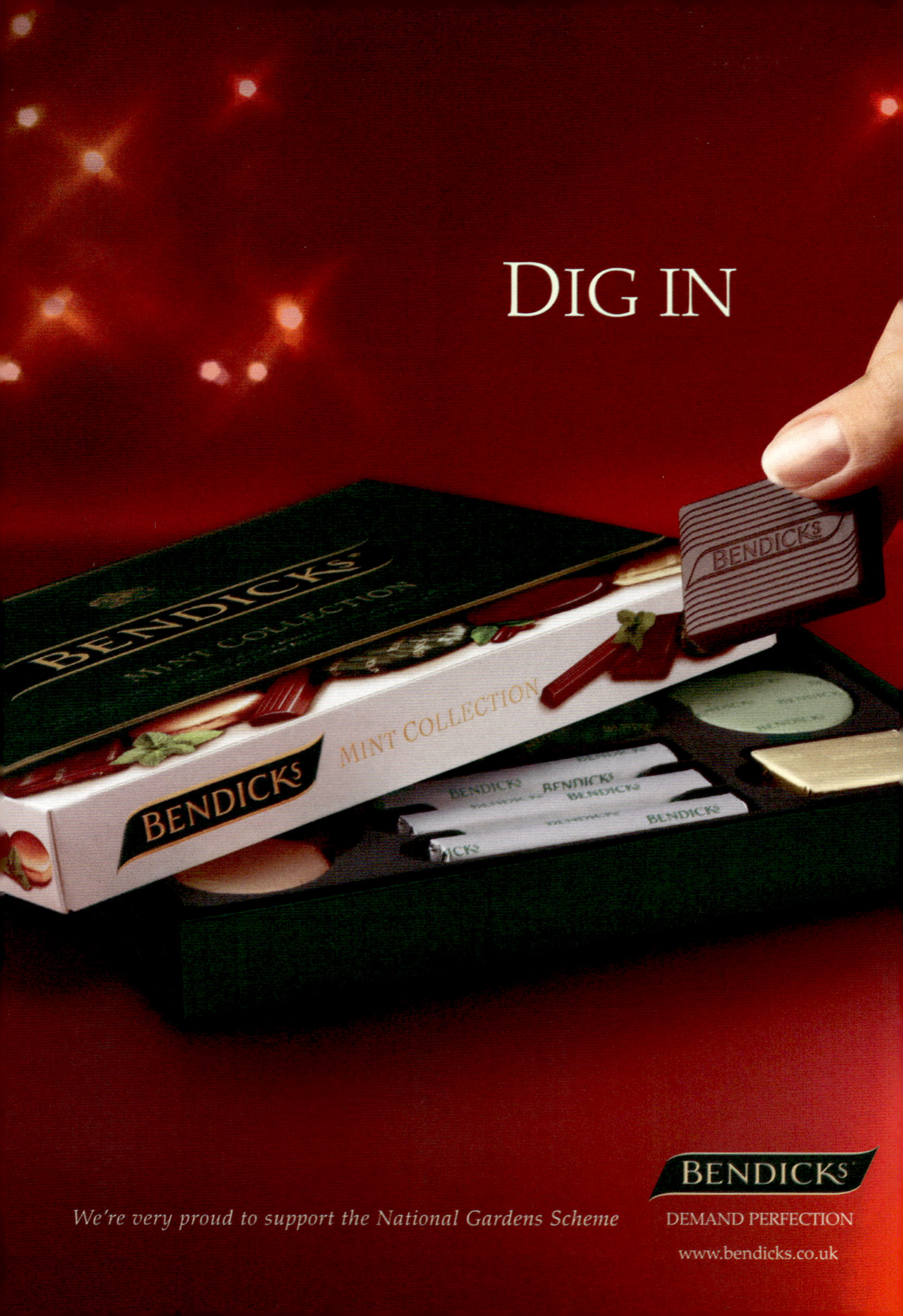

TIM WONNACOTT'S
Pick OF THE *Best*

As an Ambassador of the NGS, I was set the task of selecting three of my favourite gardens. I have to say it has proved incredibly difficult making the selection! The vast number and variety of gardens on offer, many of which are unique and very special in their own individual way, does not help. The only way forward was to weed out a garden from the three geographic regions in England that I have lived in and know well.

I was born and brought up in **North Devon** and of the 114 gardens on offer in the county, the one I have chosen (with great difficulty) I have felt associated with for nearly 40 years and that is **Marwood Hill, Devon**. The late Dr James Smart was a fanatical gardener and traveller. He created this garden from scratch, at first on the steep side of a valley opposite his Georgian House in the sleepy hamlet of Marwood.

As time went by, more and more acres were cultivated until both the sides and the bottom of

the valley were planted with classic camellias, rhododendrons and shrubs. Unusually there is a collection of Australian native plants and eucalyptus because Jimmy Smart often visited his nephew in Australia and could not resist bringing back seeds and plants to Marwood!

I remember him as a generous, sociable and most interesting man. How nice that his garden is now owned by his nephew with the Australian connection, John Snowdon, and continues to be open to the public, just as Jimmy would have wished.

Above and right: Marwood Hill, Devon

Having left Devon as a newly qualified Chartered Auctioneer I got a job at Sotheby's in London and in due course was 'posted' to the **North West** to Chester where I met my wife; we settled at first near Malpas and latterly in Macclesfield.

Cheshire has no fewer than 82 gardens listed in the 2007 *Yellow Book* and the choice of one garden as a favourite is nigh impossible. I have so many happy memories of the owners and their gardens: the late Viscountess Ashbrook in her impeccable herbaceous border at Arley with trowel forever to the fore; playing tennis in the rose garden at Cholmondeley Castle and being assailed by the scents; the late John Posnett at Houghton Hall, my rival at Christie's Ricky Roundell at Dorfold; old Mr Fildes at Manley Knoll – all with great gardens and bags of enthusiasm.

So a rich county where gardeners are spoilt for choice but if I have to chose a favourite, I guess I would go for **The Mount, Whirley, Nr Macclesfield, Cheshire.** NGS Chairman Nick Payne and his wife Mo have been friends of ours for more than 20 years and during that time I have marvelled at Nick creating the most delightful corner of Cheshire. Despite many hilarious moments when we were both developing our gardens, I suspect Nick's fingers were greener than mine!

The Mount, Whirley, Cheshire

Borde Hill, Sussex

My next big move was to the Sunny South and **Sussex** when I was appointed Chairman of Sotheby's saleroom in Billingshurst.

"Andrew John and his wife Eleni energetically manage the 200 acres and are endlessly coming up with new ideas for the enjoyment of their garden visitors"

After a lot of scratching about we eventually bought a house near Turner's Hill which luckily, apart from one of the finest unspoilt views in the South East, sits astride the fabled greens and loam of Nymans, High Beeches and Leonardslee fame.

Incredibly good for camellias and rhododendrons, the epitome for me of the larger local garden is **Borde Hill Nr Haywards Heath, Sussex.**

Owned and loved by generations of the Stephenson Clarke family, Andrew John and his wife Eleni energetically manage the 200 acres and are endlessly coming up with new ideas for the enjoyment of their garden visitors. Well worth a visit.

Gardens guaranteed to make you think

The following gardens from *The Yellow Book* 2008 have been selected by garden specialists and contributors to ThinkinGardens (www.thinkingardens.co.uk) for their inspiring if controversial designs

Photographs: Charles Hawes

Veddw House, Gwent

Here's an ambitious garden indeed; a fine, cleverly planted cottage garden, a flower meadow and winding perfumed shrubberies, but it's the garden's relationship to the landscape and landscape history that makes it so fascinating – it's hillside 'field system' filled with ornamental grasses, its memorials to lost settlements, its hidden but audible fountain garden. But why the lonely television in the oak wood, and what do the tree plaques mean? And how does it feel to sit on the pink wave-form bench looking over wave-shaped yew hedges to an amphitheatre of dark trees, and see the whole place and sky reflected in the still, oil-dark pool at your feet? Why this grim core to a joyous country garden? But then, what if you find it serene, not grim...?

Stephen Anderton is an award-winning journalist, author, lecturer and broadcaster; he writes weekly in The Times and for many magazines.

Photographs: RHS/Tim Sandall

Lyveden New Bield, Northamptonshire

Few gardens in this country are possessed of such strength of presence as the gardens of Lyveden New Bield. To modern eyes, the simple design of Sir Thomas Tresham's unfinished project might be dismissed as a fanciful Tudor period piece devoid of relevance for our digital age. And yet it bids us to experience its uncomplicated pleasures – the spiral mounts, moated walks, orchards of fruit trees and a cruciform stone lodge of astounding craftsmanship.

But it is here that true intention is unveiled. The allegorical and symbolic motifs etched into each wall are a powerful reminder of the mind games beloved of a bygone age and an unswerving devotion to an all-powerful Deity. Gardens need to do far more than simply appeal to the senses; they can and should reflect and express our humanity.

Centuries old it may be, but Tresham's unswerving vision remains just as fresh and vital as the day work stopped at news of his passing. It remains a poignant icon for a world waking to the realisation of our earthly vulnerability.

Ian Hodgson became editor of The Garden in 1993 and has overseen evolution of the title and the development of other aspects of the RHS's publishing.

Photographs: Clearbeck House

Clearbeck House, Lancashire

Although curiously neglected by the garden world, Peter Osborne's sculptural sensibility has informed his shaping of this 4-acre garden and its dialogue with the surrounding Lancashire moors.

The engagement between eye and mind, as described by Sara Maitland in *Gardens of Illusion*, continues in the use of allegory in a garden based on Christian symbolism: the Garden of Life and Death. Our last nod to expression in a garden,

the 18th-century landscape garden, is evoked and freshly revisited in the sculptures, maze and follies.

This is a garden where a man has expressed his feelings, thoughts, sense of humour, art, love of nature and his religion: a rare treasure.

Anne Wareham is a garden writer for newspapers and garden magazines and, together with her husband, Charles Hawes, the garden photographer, has designed and created the garden at Veddw House.

Photographs: Denmans Garden

Denmans Garden, Sussex

The beauty of this garden is that it is living proof of so many facets of John Brookes' style: open spaces, dense planting, views and vistas, gravel gardening, 'hard' and 'soft' landscaping. As one of the leading garden designers of our time, John has shown, through the example of Denmans, that many of his principles are viable and totally realistic – the walk from his Clock Tower into the lawned area; the paths

down to the natural-looking pond; the connection of spaces; the contrast and combination of foliage and flowers. Together, they make learning from, and experiencing this garden a lesson in design, creativity – and most of all the owner's ability.

Chris Young is the Deputy Editor of The Garden and a trained landscape architect, with a specific interest in garden design.

Bonhams ¹⁷⁹³

Bonhams conducts over 700 sales a year, more than any of its rivals worldwide
Our specialists are always on hand to provide free and confidential advice on buying and selling at auction

Bonhams is pleased to announce the opening of new offices in Hong Kong and Dubai. Along with recent European expansion in Paris, Amsterdam, Stockholm and Vienna and new gallery space in New York's famous Fuller building on Madison Avenue, Bonhams is the fastest growing international auction house.

In the UK, Bonhams has an extensive network of 33 offices and salerooms and continues to focus on bringing you the most convenient and personal auction service available.

For further information about buying or selling at Bonhams, or to find out the location of your nearest Bonhams office, please call +44 (0) 20 7447 7447 or visit www.bonhams.com

Bonhams
101 New Bond Street
London W1S 1SR
+44 (0) 20 7447 7447
+44 (0) 20 7447 7400 fax
www.bonhams.com

Whether it's the middle of winter or the height of summer, you'll find gardens at their best in *The Yellow Book*

SOMETHING FOR ALL SEASONS

Godmersham Park
Kent

You don't have to go to Cumbria to see a host of golden daffodils. This 24-acre garden contains superb daffodils in a restored wilderness. Also formal and landscaped gardens, topiary and rose beds as well as herbaceous borders.

Photograph: Suzie Gibbons
Inset: Ian Gowland

Ulting Wick
Essex

Visit this 4-acre garden set around a 16th-century farmhouse. Flower beds give a colourful display for spring. Natural pond and stream bordered by mature willows and beds containing moisture- and shade-loving plants. Peaceful woodland garden. Also an opportunity to explore the 17th-century barn.
Photograph: Jerry Harpur

East Bergholt Place
Suffolk

This garden is particularly beautiful in spring when the rhododendrons, magnolias and camellias are in flower. Full of many fine trees and shrubs, some of which are rarely seen in East Anglia. National collection of deciduous euonymus.
Photograph: Sarah Lee

Spring

Pennyholme
Yorkshire

Enchanting 10-acre country garden. Unique river and dale setting. Extensive collection of magnificent rhododendrons and azaleas in mature oak wood. Currently developing traditional rose/mixed borders, water features, wildlife garden and tree garden.
Photograph: Val Corbett

Early Summer

Elm Tree Cottage
London

A lovely cottage garden that has been transformed into an oasis of sharp gardening! There are 50 varieties of agaves as well as grasses, yuccas, olives, kniphofia, iris, alliums, phormiums, phlomis and figs. Topiary boxwood, taxus and much more.
Photograph: Leigh Clapp

Highnam Court
Gloucestershire

Everything you could wish for in this 40 acres of Victorian landscaped gardens set out by the artist Thomas Gambier Parry. Lakes, shrubberies and listed Pulhamite water gardens with grottos and fernery. Exciting ornamental lakes, and woodland areas. New extensive 1-acre rose garden.
Photograph: Suzanne Shacklock

Summer

Homelands
Buckinghamshire

This stunning three-quarter-acre garden on chalk with adjoining wild-flower meadow is definitely worth a visit. Wildlife pond, rockery, bog garden, water features. Gazebo and pergola walk, wide range of mixed shrub and herbaceous borders. Hidden corners, sitting-out areas, gravel bed and vegetable plot.
Photograph: Fiona McLeod

Camers
Somerset

As well as spectacular views over the Severn Vale, this lovely 4-acre garden and young woodland has something for everyone. Surrounding an Elizabethan farmhouse, there are formal and informal areas, a wide range of planting and lots of surprises!
Photograph: Owner
Inset: Rowan Isaac

Bourton House Garden
Gloucestershire

For inspiration, visit this exciting 3-acre garden which positively fizzes with ideas. Featuring flamboyant borders, imaginative topiary, profusions of herbaceous borders and exotic plants and, not least, a myriad of magically planted pots. A plantsman's paradise.
Photograph: Mandy Bradshaw

Autumn

Blossoms
Buckinghamshire
Open by appointment throughout the year, this garden has all the colours of autumn, with one acre of beechwood and many other trees. At other times there are bluebells, wild daffodils, spring bulbs and climbing roses to give something of interest all year round.
Photograph: Owner
Inset: Ian Gowland

Winter

Lake House
Norfolk
Situated on the edge of the Norfolk Broads and close to Norwich, the beautiful gardens at Lake House are a naturalist's paradise. There are two acres of water gardens set among magnificent trees in a steep cleft in the river escarpment.
Photograph: Owner

Let Ireland grow on you

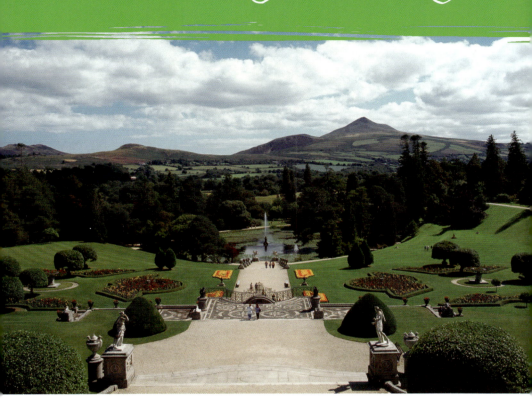

Discover over 300 wonderful gardens.

With gardening styles from many different periods you'll find a wonderful array of plants. Many 18th and 19th century gardens have been restored to their original splendour as part of the Great Gardens of Ireland Scheme. At the same time, stunning new 'designer' gardens showcase the best that modern planting and styling has to offer.

Inspiration blossoms at Ireland's gardens.

Your very own Ireland
Discover it at discoverireland.com

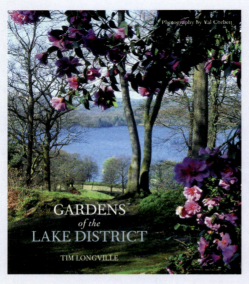

GARDENS
of the
LAKE DISTRICT

Tim Longville
Photography by Val Corbett

Hardback 256 pages
Full colour photography
throughout

Available now from all
good bookshops or visit
www.franceslincoln.com
£25

FRANCES LINCOLN LIMITED
PUBLISHERS

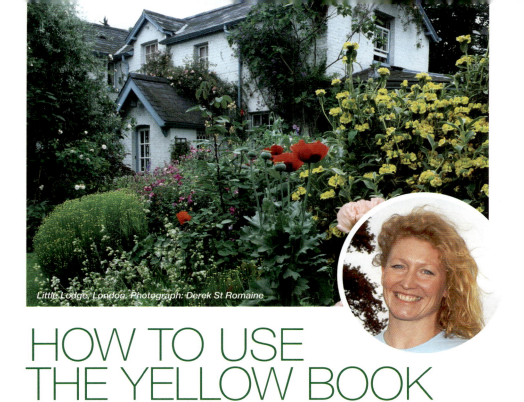

Little Lodge, London. Photograph: Derek St Romaine

HOW TO USE THE YELLOW BOOK

Whether you make an impromptu phone call or plan a visit in advance, come alone or in a group, *The Yellow Book* is so clearly laid out, it's easy to find what you're looking for, says Charlie Dimmock

Enjoying a visit to an NGS garden couldn't be easier. If you're like me, you'll grab hold of *The Yellow Book* as soon as it appears at the bookshop and look through the garden descriptions, new ones and old favourites, and mark the opening dates on your calendar.

"Some gardens welcome visitors by appointment."
Charlie Dimmock

Then, of course, there's the more opportunistic way when you know the weather's going to be great or you have some spare time. Then it's easy to go the start of the county section and see what's open by date – check the directions in the garden details and off you go.

More and more of the gardens also welcome visitors by appointment. Wherever you see the new telephone symbol at the top of the garden details, you know that all you have to do is give the owner a call and arrange a convenient time for your visit. The owners are happy to see small numbers of visitors but some are also able to accept minibuses and even coaches if you're planning a visit with a group of friends or local organisation.

Don't forget the website, www.ngs.org.uk. Many of the gardens have photographs and some even have extended descriptions, giving more of an insight into the garden and, often, the gardener too! You'll find detailed maps, the nearest NGS garden with accommodation and even the local weather at the end of each entry. The website also keeps you up to date on NGS news and changes to opening details. So now you're all set – enjoy the gardens!

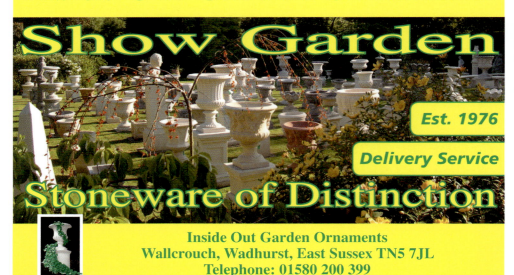

Geographical Area Guide
Visit a garden near you

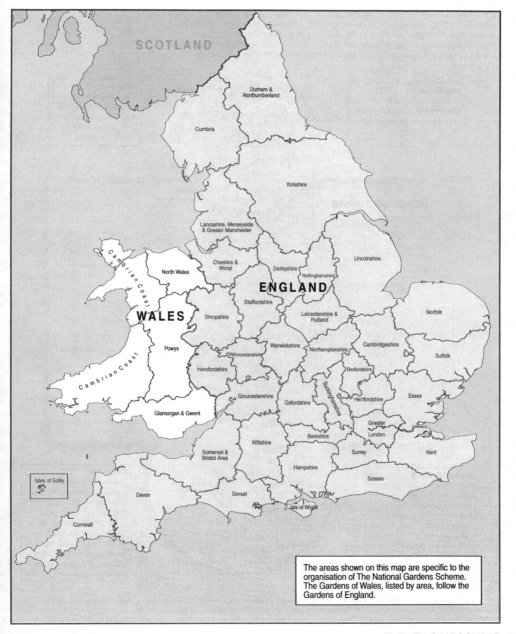

The areas shown on this map are specific to the organisation of The National Gardens Scheme. The Gardens of Wales, listed by area, follow the Gardens of England.

Understanding this book

A simple guide for getting the most out of the listings section

Overview

The Yellow Book 2008 lists all gardens opening between January 2008 and early 2009. The listings pages include opening dates, admission prices and directions as well as a description of the main features of the garden. Garden entries are listed by county (see map on page 57) and are ordered alphabetically in each county. A map at the start of each county section shows the location of the gardens.

Green oval
A green oval indicates a garden within the county with a number that corresponds to the number in the listings.

Grey oval
A grey oval indicates gardens located in the neighbouring counties. Refer to the relevant county for details.

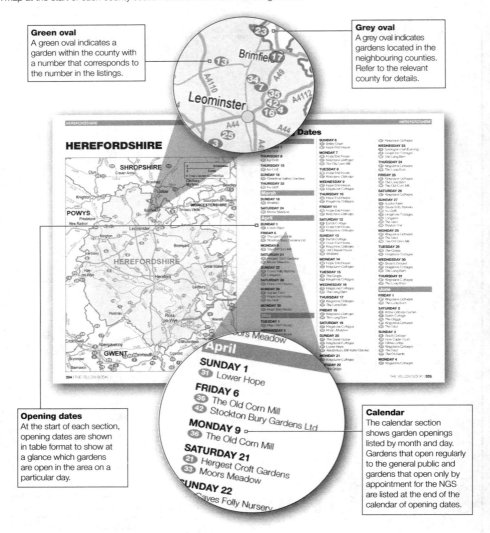

Opening dates
At the start of each section, opening dates are shown in table format to show at a glance which gardens are open in the area on a particular day.

Calendar
The calendar section shows garden openings listed by month and day. Gardens that open regularly to the general public and gardens that open only by appointment for the NGS are listed at the end of the calendar of opening dates.

All distances and sizes are approximate. **Coach parties** Only by appointment, please contact the garden direct to make arrangements. **Children** Must be accompanied by an adult. **Toilets** Not usually available at private gardens. **Updates** While every effort is made to ensure that entries are accurate, with so many gardens there will inevitably be last-minute changes. These will be publicised locally, and shown on the website.

County sections

Each county section includes a map, a calendar of opening dates and then an alphabetical listing of each garden. Further information, including contact details for local volunteer teams, is at the end of each section.

Description
A short description of each garden covers the main landscape and planting features. This is written by garden owners and reviewed each year.

County name
The county name appears in the top corner of each page of the listings. Gardens in England are listed first, followed by gardens in Wales.

Index
To find a particular garden within a county please refer to the index at the back of the book.

Directions
A simple set of directions to each garden from the nearest major road is at the start of each section. Most gardens also list postcodes for use with computer or satellite navigation systems.

Admission price
The admission price applies to all visitors unless exceptions are noted eg, child free, concessions, etc.

Website
Details of many NGS gardens and information about special events are on the NGS website
www.ngs.org.uk

Symbols
Symbols at the end of each entry indicate features and items of special interest at the garden. The key to each symbol is given in detail below.

Symbols explained

4 The garden's position on the county or area map.

NEW Garden opening this year for the first time or reopening after a long break or under new ownership.

◆ Denotes a garden that is open to the public on a regular basis. Gardens which carry this symbol contribute to the NGS either by opening on a specific day or days and/or by giving a guaranteed contribution to the Scheme.

& Wheelchair access to at least the main features of the garden. Often disabled parking is available close by, or in the owner's driveway.

✖ No dogs except guide dogs. Where dogs are allowed they must be on leads.

❀ Plants usually for sale, often propagated by the garden owners. If proceeds go elsewhere, this is shown at the garden opening.

NCCPG Garden that holds a NCCPG National Plant Collection.

⊫ Gardens that offer accommodation. For a detailed listing see the Accommodation index beginning on page 638.

☕ Refreshments are available, normally at a charge. Detailed information is given in the garden's entry. Wine is often available at Evening Openings. If proceeds go elsewhere, this is shown at the garden opening.

☎ Gardens showing this symbol welcome visitors by prior arrangement. These gardens are now also conveniently listed at the start of each county or area section. Some can accommodate clubs, some only small parties and some have limited parking. Please telephone, email or write to make an appointment. You will be very welcome.

PHOTOGRAPHS
Where taken at a garden opening, photographs must not be used for sale or reproduction without prior permission of the owner.

SHARE TO
If 'share to' is shown in a garden text, it indicates that a proportion of the money collected will be given to the nominated charity.

BEDFORDSHIRE

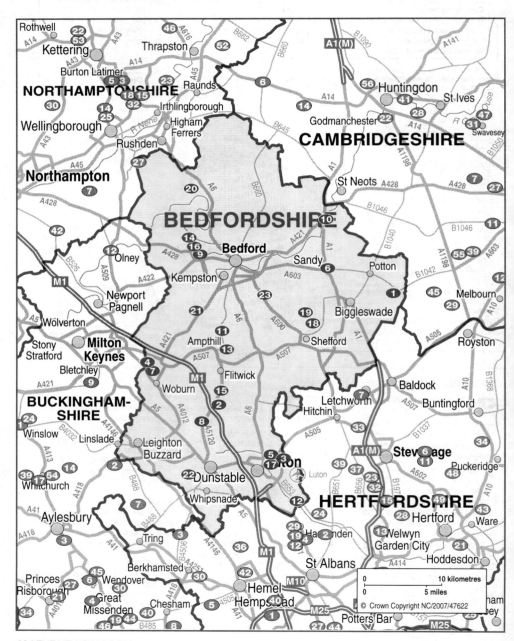

Opening Dates

March

SUNDAY 23
⑬ King's Arms Path Garden

SUNDAY 30
⑮ The Old Vicarage

April

SUNDAY 6
⑪ How End Cottage

SUNDAY 20
⑲ Swiss Garden

May

SATURDAY 10
⑫ The Hyde Walled Garden

SUNDAY 11
⑧ The Folly

SUNDAY 25
② Briarwood

June

SUNDAY 1
⑱ Southill Park

SUNDAY 8
⑥ The Firs
⑦ Flaxbourne Farm

SUNDAY 15
⑮ The Old Vicarage

SUNDAY 22
⑭ The Manor House
㉒ Valley Forge

SUNDAY 29
① Beck House
⑪ How End Cottage
⑫ The Hyde Walled Garden
⑯ Park End Thatch

July

SATURDAY 5
⑩ 8 Great North Road

SUNDAY 6
③ Conifers
⑦ Flaxbourne Farm
⑩ 8 Great North Road
⑰ Seal Point
㉓ 16 Wood Lane

SUNDAY 13
⑳ Tofte Manor Labyrinth & Garden
㉑ Treize

SUNDAY 27
⑤ 14 Fairford Avenue

August

SUNDAY 10
⑦ Flaxbourne Farm

October

SUNDAY 26
⑬ King's Arms Path Garden

Gardens open to the public

⑬ King's Arms Path Garden
⑭ The Manor House

By appointment only

④ Dawnedge Lodge
⑨ 59 Grange Lane

Also open by appointment ☎

③ Conifers
④ Dawnedge Lodge
⑤ 14 Fairford Avenue
⑥ The Firs
⑦ Flaxbourne Farm
⑨ 59 Grange Lane
⑩ 8 Great North Road
⑯ Park End Thatch
㉒ Valley Forge

The Gardens

ASCOTT
See Buckinghamshire.

① NEW **BECK HOUSE**
Water End, Wrestlingworth,
Sandy SG19 2HA.
Donal & Victoria McKenna.
*Wrestlingworth is ¹/₂ way between
Cambridge & Bedford. From High
St, Wrestlingworth turn into Water
End (opp 8 High St). Garden at far
end of Water End.* Home-made
teas. **Adm £3.50, chd free.**
Sun 29 June (2-5.30).
1¹/₂ acre garden created over 20yrs
with various formal and informal
areas divided by hedges and shrub
borders. features incl topiary yew
avenue, circular dahlia garden,
parterre with English roses,
herbaceous borders, white,
courtyard, herb and vegetable
gardens, rose and clematis pergola
walk. Some gravel paths and
slopes.
 ♿ 🐾 ⊗ ☕

Walled garden with Victorian
greenhouse . . .

② NEW **BRIARWOOD**
Toddington Road, Harlington
LU5 6LA. Jenny & Andrew
Asbury. *From M1 J12 take A5120
heading towards Flitwick, bear R at
1st mini roundabout signed for
Harlington Stn. Double gates
500yds on L. Ample parking
available. Disabled parking in drive.*
Light refreshments & teas. **Adm
£3.50, chd free (share to
BDSSG). Sun 25 May (9-4).**
In years gone by this 7-acre plot
would have been a hive of activity
being the remains of old brickworks. The 2 lakes are now a
haven for wildlife. Features incl
stunning boardwalks, walled
garden with Victorian greenhouse,
bridges, summerhouse and
thatched willow. Disabled access
to boardwalk.
♿ ☕

CHEDDINGTON GARDENS
See Buckinghamshire.

③ NEW **CONIFERS**
40 Sowerby Avenue, Luton
LU2 8AF. June & Richard Giles,
01582 415846. *3¹/₂ m NE of Luton
town centre. Take A505 towards
Hitchin. R at Jansell House
roundabout (Stopsley) into Ashcroft
Rd. After 200yds L into Wigmore
Lane, Sowerby Ave 3rd on L.*
**Combined with Seal Point adm
£5, chd free. Sun 6 July (2-5).
Visitors also welcome by appt
June, July, adm £3, groups
max 15.**
Interesting mature garden created
over 10yrs and set within ¹/₄ acre
plot featuring large colourful
borders with trees, shrubs and
herbaceous planting. Japanese-
style garden, pergola walk with
climbers, rockery surrounding
ornamental fish-pond with
waterfall. Rose arch and rose beds,
greenhouse and vegetable garden.
♿ 🐾 ⊗ ☕ ☎

**COWPER & NEWTON MUSEUM
GARDENS**
See Buckinghamshire.

Newly constructed Greek temple ruin, fernery and crow's nest. Bring the whole family and discover many more inspirational features . . .

CUBLINGTON GARDENS
See Buckinghamshire.

4 DAWNEDGE LODGE
Woburn Lane, Aspley Guise
MK17 8JH. Phil & Lynne Wallace,
01908 582233,
lynnewallace@hotmail.co.uk. *5m W of Ampthill. 3m from J13 M1. In Aspley Guise, turn L in centre of village at Moore Place Hotel.* Home-made teas. **Adm £2.50, chd free. Visitors welcome by appt May, June & July, also groups.**
1-acre garden on top of a hill with great views to Woburn. Victorian walled garden, rescued 9yrs ago, with colour themed island beds, pergolas, terracotta pots on stone patio. Cutting garden, Alitex greenhouse and woodland garden (2003). Alliums and agapanthus good.
👪 ⊗ ☕ ☎

THE DEERINGS
See Hertfordshire.

5 14 FAIRFORD AVENUE
Luton LU2 7ER. Brian & Ann Biddle,
01582 735669. *2m N of Luton town centre. Fairford Ave leads directly from Bradgers Hill Rd, past Luton VI college situated off the Old Bedford Rd parallel to A6.* Teas. **Adm £2.50, chd free. Sun 27 July (2-6). Visitors also welcome by appt throughout the year.**
1/4-acre hillside garden, with many changes of level, twists and turns, disguising the long, narrow plot and giving some surprise views. Variety of shrubs, trees and herbaceous plants which will tolerate poor, chalky soil give yr-round interest from snowdrops and hellebores to autumn flowering perennials.
👪 ⊗ ☕ ☎

6 THE FIRS
33 Bedford Road, Sandy SG19 1EP.
Mr & Mrs D Sutton, 01767 691992.
7m E of Bedford. On B1042 towards town centre. On rd parking. Home-made teas. **Adm £2.50, chd free. Sun 8 June (2-5). Visitors also welcome by appt, individuals May to Aug, groups welcomed all yr-round.**

1/4-acre town garden with many different features. This garden has been designed and created from scratch since 2000 and is productive in fruit, flowers, vegetables and wildlife. Run organically, this garden has everything from shrubs, trees, perennials, to water features. Featured in 'Real Homes'. Gravel drive at front of house.
♿ 👪 ⊗ ☕ ☎

7 FLAXBOURNE FARM
Salford Road, Aspley Guise
MK17 8HZ. Geoff & Davina Barrett,
01908 585329. *5m W of Ampthill. 1m S of J13 of M1. Turn R in village centre, 1m over railway line.* Home-made teas. **Adm £3.50, chd free (share to St Botolph Church). Special Opening Sun 8 June (10-5); Suns 6 July; 10 Aug (2-6). Visitors also welcome by appt groups or 10 or more, Coaches permitted.**
A beautiful and entertaining fun garden of 2 acres, lovingly developed with numerous water features, windmill, modern arches and bridges, small moated castle, lily pond, herbaceous borders. Shrubs and trees recently established, newly constructed Greek temple ruin, fernery and crow's nest. Bring the whole family and discover many more inspirational features. Former finalist of BBC Garden of the Year. **Plant Fair and Party Day adm £5 Sun 8 June.** Woburn Sands Band play throughout openings.
♿ ⊗ ☕ ☎

8 NEW THE FOLLY
69 Leighton Road, Toddington
LU5 6AL. Gillian & Edward Ladd.
5m N of Dunstable. J12 M1 follow B5120 to village. Turn R at Bell PH. Garden 0.2m on L. Light refreshments & teas. **Adm £3, chd free. Sun 11 May (12-5).**
Wheelchair friendly 1/4-acre created over 13yrs. Many mature shrubs and trees with various foliage. Small woodland walk, orchard and vegetable garden. Greenhouse and potting shed with cacti garden. Many interesting features incl numerous old farmimg implements.
♿ 👪 ⊗ ☕

9 59 GRANGE LANE
Bromham MK43 8PA. Mrs Mary
Morris, 01234 822215,
mary@gardenartist.freeserve.co.uk.
3m W of Bedford. A428 to Bromham, sign Oakley, into Village Rd. 3rd turning on L (Grange Lane), 59 is opp Springfield Drive on L. Home-made teas. **Adm £3, chd free. Visitors welcome by appt April & May.**
An informal 150ft organic garden developed over 25yrs. Herbaceous border with colour groupings; mixed border; small woodland garden with camellias and many spring flowers and bulbs. Gravel areas. Some unusual plants; hardy geraniums; pulmonarias. Formal pond and white border. Vegetable garden using raised beds and companion planting.
♿ 👪 ⊗ ☕ ☎

10 NEW 8 GREAT NORTH ROAD
Chawston MK44 3BD. D G
Parker, 01480 213284. *2m S of St Neots. Between Wyboston & Blackcat roundabout on S-bound lane of A1. Turn off at McDonalds, at end of filling station forecourt turn L.* Light refreshments & teas. **Adm £3, chd free. Sat 5, Sun 6 July (2-6). Visitors also welcome by appt, Apr to Sept, no coaches.**
1 acre garden, 1/2 acre young trees and shrubs. Cottage garden of 1/2 acre crammed with bulbs, herbaceous, water and bog plants, ferns, grasses, shrubs and trees. Rare, exotic and unusual plants abound, large pond, level grass paths. Yr round interest where plants provide structure and form.
♿ 👪 ⊗ ☕ ☎

11 HOW END COTTAGE
How End Cottage, Houghton
Conquest MK45 3JT. Jeremy & Gill
Smith. *1m N of Ampthill. Turn R 1m from Ampthill off B530 towards Houghton Conquest. How End Rd 300yds on RH-side. Garden at end of rd, approx 1/2 m.* Home-made teas. **Adm £2.50, chd free, concessions £1.50. Suns 6 Apr; 29 June (2.30-5.30).**
Approx 1 acre garden with 2 ponds, large vegetable garden, greenhouse and orchard. Large lawn gives an uninterrupted view of Houghton House. The garden contains mature trees and beds with many types of slow growing fir trees. Flower beds

contain home grown bedding plants and roses. 3 acres of paddocks, wood and further pond. Many spring bulbs.

 ⅃ ⋊ ☕

⑫ THE HYDE WALLED GARDEN
East Hyde, Luton LU2 9PS. D J J Hambro Will Trust. *2m S of Luton. M1 exit J10/10a. A1081 S take 2nd L. At E Hyde turn R then immed L. Junction entrance on R. From A1 exit J4. Follow A3057 N to roundabout, 1st L to B653 Wheathamstead/Luton to E Hyde.* Home-made teas. **Adm £3, chd free. Sat 10 May; Sun 29 June (2-5).**
Walled garden adjoins the grounds of The Hyde (house not open). Extends to approx 1 acre and features rose garden, seasonal beds and herbaceous borders, imaginatively interspersed with hidden areas of formal lawn. An interesting group of Victorian greenhouses, coldframes and cucumber house are serviced from the potting shed in the adjoining vegetable garden. Bluebell walk in season. Gravel paths.

 ⅃ ⋊ ✿ ☕

⑬ ◆ KING'S ARMS PATH GARDEN
Ampthill MK45 2PP. Ampthill Town Council, 01525 755648, bryden.k@ntlworld.com. *8m S of Bedford. Free parking in town centre. Entrance opp old Market Place, down King's Arms Yard.* **Adm £2, chd free. Last Sun of month from 27 Jan, please check for details. For NGS: Sun 23 Mar (2.30-5); Sun 26 Oct (2-4).**
Small woodland garden of about 1½ acres created by plantsman the late William Nourish. Trees, shrubs, bulbs and many interesting collections. Maintained since 1987 by 'The Friends of the Garden' on behalf of Ampthill Town Council.

 ⅃ ⋊ ✿ ☕

⑭ ◆ THE MANOR HOUSE
Church Road, Stevington, nr Bedford MK43 7QB. Kathy Brown, 01234 822064, www.kathybrownsgarden.homestead.com. *5m NW of Bedford. Off A428 through Bromham.* **Adm £4, chd free. Suns 3, 10 Feb (12-4); 25 May; 27 July (2-6). For NGS: Sun 22 June (2-6).**
Great swathes of roses and then late flowering clematis abound in this modern country garden designed and cared for by owners Simon and Kathy

Brown. The French Garden with its jury scene, cottage garden, wild flower meadow, and several major container displays, offer contrasting areas of interest with ornamental grass borders echoing works of art by Hepworth and Hokusai. Topiary Rothko rooms add to the living art theme. Featured in & on 'Beautiful Britain Magazine', 'Independent on Sunday' BBC Look East & Breakfast TV. Some gravel paths.

 ⅃ ⋊ ✿ ☕

⑮ THE OLD VICARAGE
Church Road, Westoning MK45 5JW. Ann & Colin Davies. *4m S of Ampthill. Off A5120, 2m N of M1 J12. ¼ m up Church Rd, next to church.* Cream teas at church. **Adm £2.50, chd free. Suns 30 Mar; 15 June (2-5).**
Traditional 2 acre vicarage garden with formal lawn, box and laurel hedges, large magnolia grandiflora, mature shrubs and trees, colour co-ordinated herbaceous beds, rose garden, pond and wild garden. Small vegetable garden. Spring interest with hellebores and daffodils.

 ⅃ ⋊ ☕

⑯ NEW PARK END THATCH
58 Park Road, Stevington MK43 7QG. Susan Young, 01234 826430. *5m NW of Bedford. Off A428 through Bromham.* **Adm £2.50, chd free. Sun 29 June (11-5). Visitors also welcome by appt, July, Aug, groups 6-10, no coaches.**
½-acre cottage garden set within old orchard. View of Stevington windmill. Sunny borders of flowering shrubs with herbaceous planting. Fragrant roses and climber covered pergola. Winding paths shaded by trees. Trellice border featuring colour and texture groupings. Fruit production and herbs. Garden cultivated to be drought tolerant. Wildlife friendly. Gravel path on slight slope, some uneven surfaces.

 ⅃ ⋊ ✿ ☕ ☎

RAGGED HALL
See Hertfordshire.

⑰ SEAL POINT
7 Wendover Way, Luton LU2 7LS. Mrs Danae Johnston, 01582 611567. *2m from Luton town centre. In NE Luton, turning N off Stockingstone Rd A505 into Felstead Way then 2nd L Wendover Way.* **Combined adm with Conifers £5.00, chd free. Sun 6 July (2-5).**
A garden of delight, incls wildlife spinney, lovely grasses, unusual trees and shrubs; 3 water features and tree-top balcony on which to enjoy refreshments. Danae won Gardener of the year E and SE 1999. We both love visitors to see our clipped topiary cats, dogs and King Kong! In 2007 the garden had an upgrade and is looking super. Access only in dry weather - grassy hill slippery.

 ⅃ ⋊ ✿

⑱ SOUTHILL PARK
nr Biggleswade SG18 9LL. Mr & Mrs Charles Whitbread. *3m W of Biggleswade. In the village of Southill. 3m from A1 junction at Biggleswade.* Cream teas. **Adm £3.50, chd free. Sun 1 June (2-5).**
Large garden, with mature trees and flowering shrubs, herbaceous borders, rose garden and wild garden. Large conservatory with tropical plants. The parkland was designed by Lancelot 'Capability' Brown in 1777.

 ⅃ ⋊ ✿ ☕

⑲ SWISS GARDEN
Old Warden Park SG18 9ER. Shuttleworth Trust in Partnership with Bedfordshire County Council, www.shuttleworth.org. *2m W of Biggleswade. Signed from A1 & A600.* **Adm £5, chd free, concessions £4 (share to Friends of the Swiss Garden). Sun 20 Apr (10-4).**
Designed in 1820s. 9-acre miniature landscape garden with winding paths, intertwining ponds, wrought iron bridges, fernery grotto and tiny buildings. Peacocks wander around splendid trees and shrubs, with daffodils, rhododendrons and roses in season. Adjacent further acres of native woodland.

 ⅃ ⋊ ✿

We both love visitors to see our clipped topiary cats, dogs and King Kong! . . .

⑳ TOFTE MANOR LABYRINTH & GARDEN

Souldrop Road, Sharnbrook MK44 1HH. Mrs Suzy Castleman, www.toftemanor.co.uk. *8m N of Bedford. Off A6 between Bedford and Rushden. Exit at roundabout signed Sharnbrook, through village towards Souldrop. At Y-Junction take R fork; house is 400yds on L, through large black wrought-iron gates.* Home-made teas. **Adm £3.50, chd free. Sun 13 July** (2-5).

5 acres of mature and beautifully laid out garden restored and modernised to blend with C17 manor house. Beautiful mature trees, colour themed herbaceous borders. Sunken area with central arbour and crystal ball like water feature. Modern statued parterre garden, unusual swings and crystals throughout garden. Walks and wild areas abound. Grass labyrinth in the design of Chartres Cathederal, France, incorporating crystals and sacred geometry. Water which has travelled the path of the labyrinth can be drunk. This is an unusual spiritual garden for those in search of tranquillity.

🍴 ⊛ 🛏 ☕

㉑ TREIZE

Cranfield Road, Wootton Green, Bedford MK43 9EA. Roger & Anna Skipper. *5m SW of Bedford. 10m NE of Milton Keynes. C70 Kempston to Cranfield rd, 1/2 m SW of Wootton. Private Lane on R opp Wootton Green Hamlet sign. Bungalow 100yds along lane on R. Car parking on open day in adjacent meadow (depending on weather).* Home-made teas. **Adm £3.50, chd free. Sun 13 July** (2-6).

1-acre plantsman's garden set out for yr-round interest on heavy clay. Hidden gardens and established herbaceous borders; formal pond; rockery, gravel beds. Many varieties of established and younger trees, shrubs and vast collection of perennials, incl over 150 varieties and species of penstemon.

♿ 🍴 ⊛ ☕

Wildlife area with folly and chickens, also facade of an old water mill . . .

㉒ VALLEY FORGE

213 Castle Hill Road, Totternhoe LU6 2DA. Pat & Mike Sutcliffe, 01525 221676, sutcliffes@leylandman.co.uk. *2m W of Dunstable. Turn R off B489 Aston Clinton rd, 1/2 m from Dunstable centre, signed Totternhoe. Fronting main rd, corner of Chapel Lane, 1m through village. On rd parking.* Teas. **Adm £3.50, chd free. Sun 22 June** (2-5). **Visitors also welcome by appt May & June, groups of 10+.**

Garden to rear of C17 grade 2 listed thatched cottage (not open). 1/2 -acre sloping site planted from scratch by owners 15yrs ago. Imaginatively landscaped, terraced on 4 levels, long pergola, archways and steps connecting to meandering pathways that lead intriguingly through the foliage. Small gravel garden, new 'sun trap' garden planted with an orange /yellow theme. Ponds on 2 levels connected by small cascade. Large range of shrubs, perennials and trees compatible with chalk, including the indiginous Aylesbury Prune. The site also houses The Mike Sutcliffe Collection of early Leyland buses (1908-1934). Featured in 'Amateur Gardening' & WI Life.

🍴 ⊛ ☕ ☎

㉓ 16 WOOD LANE

Cotton End MK45 3AJ. Lesley Bunker-Nixon & Eddie Wilkins. *2m S of Bedford. A600 signed Shefford from Bedford, 2nd L at The Bell PH, into Wood Lane, past Hall Way on RH-side.* Light refreshments & teas. **Adm £2.50, chd free. Sun 6 July** (12-5).

150ft garden consisting of cottage style garden, containers and bygones. Formal garden with large koi pond with beautiful fish, borders and lawns. Japanese garden with bonsai trees, wooded area with stream. Vegetable garden based on an allotment. Wildlife area with folly and chickens, also facade of an old water mill.

♿ 🍴 ⊛ ☕

Bedfordshire County Volunteers

County Organisers
Mike & Pat Sutcliffe, Valley Forge, 213 Castle Hill Road, Totternhoe, Dunstable LU6 2DA, 01525 221676, sutcliffes@leylandman.co.uk

County Treasurer
David Johnston, Seal Point, 7 Wendover Way, Luton LU2 7LS, 01582 611567

Publicity
Geoff & Davina Barrett, Flaxbourne Farm, Aspley Guise, Milton Keynes MK17 8HZ, 01908 585329, carole@boa.com

Mark your diary with these special events in 2008

EXPLORE SECRET GARDENS DURING CHELSEA WEEK

Tue 20 May, Wed 21 May, Thur 22 May, Fri 23 May
Full day tours: £78 per person, 10% discount for groups
Advance Booking required, telephone 01932 864532 or
email pennysnellflowers@btinternet.com

Specially selected private gardens in London, Surrey and Berkshire. The tour price includes transport and lunch with wine at a popular restaurant or pub.

FROGMORE – A ROYAL GARDEN (BERKSHIRE)

Tue 3 June 10am - 5.30pm (last adm 4pm)
Garden adm £4, chd free. Advance booking recommended telephone 01483 211535
or email orders@ngs.org.uk

A unique opportunity to explore 30 acres of landscaped garden, rich in history and beauty.

FLAXBOURNE FARM – FUN AND SURPRISES (BEDFORDSHIRE)

Sun 8 June 10am - 5pm Adm £5, chd free
No booking required, come along on the day!

Bring the whole family and enjoy a plant fair and garden party and have fun in this beautiful and entertaining garden of 2 acres.

WISLEY RHS GARDEN – MUSIC IN THE GARDEN (SURREY)

Tue 19 August 6 - 9pm
Adm (incl RHS members) £7, chd under 15 free

A special opening of this famous garden, exclusively for the NGS. Enjoy music and entertainment as you explore a range of different gardens.

For further information visit www.ngs.org.uk or telephone 01483 211535

BERKSHIRE

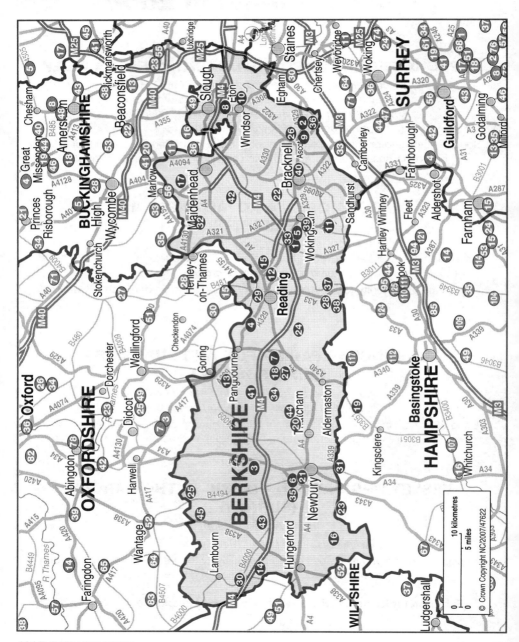

Opening Dates

March

WEDNESDAY 5
35 Stockcross House

April

WEDNESDAY 2
35 Stockcross House

SUNDAY 13
12 The Harris Garden

SUNDAY 20
25 The Old Rectory Farnborough

SUNDAY 27
17 Little Harwood

MONDAY 28
17 Little Harwood

WEDNESDAY 30
14 Inholmes
30 Rooksnest

May

SUNDAY 4
22 Moor Close Gardens

WEDNESDAY 7
35 Stockcross House
42 Waltham Place Gardens

SUNDAY 11
23 Old Pines House
25 The Old Rectory Farnborough

WEDNESDAY 14
42 Waltham Place Gardens

SUNDAY 18
1 Bearwood College
34 Stanford Dingley Gardens
40 Two Bracknell Gardens
44 Winchcombe Farm

WEDNESDAY 21
42 Waltham Place Gardens

SUNDAY 25
22 Moor Close Gardens

MONDAY 26
36 Sunningdale Park

WEDNESDAY 28
42 Waltham Place Gardens

June

SUNDAY 1
28 The Priory
33 21 Simons Lane

TUESDAY 3
10 Frogmore House Garden

WEDNESDAY 4
42 Waltham Place Gardens

SATURDAY 7
29 The RISC Roof Garden, Reading

SUNDAY 8
13 Hook End Farm
29 The RISC Roof Garden, Reading
35 Stockcross House

TUESDAY 10
43 Welford Park

WEDNESDAY 11
13 Hook End Farm
42 Waltham Place Gardens

SATURDAY 14
8 Eton College Gardens

SUNDAY 15
18 Mariners
22 Moor Close Gardens
31 Sandleford Place
45 Woolley Park

WEDNESDAY 18
42 Waltham Place Gardens

SUNDAY 22
16 Kirby House
25 The Old Rectory Farnborough

WEDNESDAY 25
14 Inholmes
30 Rooksnest
42 Waltham Place Gardens

SUNDAY 29
21 The Mill House

July

WEDNESDAY 2
42 Waltham Place Gardens

SUNDAY 6
3 Chieveley Manor

WEDNESDAY 9
42 Waltham Place Gardens

FRIDAY 11
6 Donnington Castle House

SATURDAY 12
4 17 Clevedon Road
29 The RISC Roof Garden, Reading

SUNDAY 13
4 17 Clevedon Road
29 The RISC Roof Garden, Reading
37 Swallowfield Horticultural Society
38 Thrive's Trunkwell Garden Project

WEDNESDAY 16
42 Waltham Place Gardens

WEDNESDAY 23
42 Waltham Place Gardens

SUNDAY 27
9 Fairacre
24 The Old Rectory Burghfield

WEDNESDAY 30
42 Waltham Place Gardens

August

SUNDAY 3
2 Boxwood House
39 Timberlea

WEDNESDAY 6
42 Waltham Place Gardens

SATURDAY 9
29 The RISC Roof Garden, Reading

SUNDAY 10
29 The RISC Roof Garden, Reading

WEDNESDAY 13
42 Waltham Place Gardens

SUNDAY 17
23 Old Pines House
32 Scotlands

WEDNESDAY 20
42 Waltham Place Gardens

SUNDAY 24
26 Old Waterfield

WEDNESDAY 27
42 Waltham Place Gardens

September

WEDNESDAY 3
42 Waltham Place Gardens

WEDNESDAY 10
42 Waltham Place Gardens

SATURDAY 13
29 The RISC Roof Garden, Reading

SUNDAY 14
29 The RISC Roof Garden, Reading

WEDNESDAY 17
42 Waltham Place Gardens

WEDNESDAY 24
42 Waltham Place Gardens

Gardens open to the public

7 Englefield House
42 Waltham Place Gardens
43 Welford Park

By appointment only

5 6 Crecy Close
11 Glenmere
15 Ivydene
19 Meadow House
20 Miles's Green House
27 Potash
41 Two Gardens at Ashampstead Common

Also open by appointment ☎

- **34** Bradfield Farm, Stanford Dingley Gardens
- **40** Devonia, Two Bracknell Gardens
- **13** Hook End Farm
- **18** Mariners
- **22** Moor Close Gardens
- **25** The Old Rectory Farnborough
- **28** The Priory
- **30** Rooksnest
- **31** Sandleford Place
- **32** Scotlands
- **40** 10 Shaftesbury Close, Two Bracknell Gardens
- **39** Timberlea

The Gardens

1 BEARWOOD COLLEGE
Winnersh RG41 5BG. *5m SE of Reading. Off B3030, 1m S of A329/ B3030 intersection at Winnersh, midway between Reading and Wokingham. Look for Bearwood Rd & College sign.* Cream teas. **Adm £3, chd free. Sun 18 May (2-5).**
Late C19 mansion and parkland now an independent school. Walks through mature woodland, pinetum, rhododendrons and grassland. Lake and natural margins. Pulham water garden under restoration. Some mansion rooms open.
⊛ ☕

Planted with
a mix of
English and
Mediterranean
horticultural
delights . . .

2 BOXWOOD HOUSE
Heathfield Avenue, Sunninghill SL5 0AL. Mr J P H Morrow & Mr R E G Beard. *6m S of Windsor. From A30 at Sunningdale, take Broomhall Lane, after 1/2 m follow signs to car park. From A329 turn into Silwood Rd and R to Larch Ave.* Home-made teas. **Adm £3, chd free (share to Terrence Higgins Trust). Sun 3 Aug (1-5.30).**
3/4 -acre designer's, plantsman's and flower arrangers garden in woodland setting with emphasis to plant and colour association. Large range of herbaceous perennials, large leaved hostas, acers, grasses, topiary, climbers, interesting foliage plants with pergola, woodland garden, natural style pond and many tender plant combinations in pots. Featured in 'The English Garden Calendar'.
✕ ⊛ ☕

3 CHIEVELEY MANOR
RG20 8UT. Mr & Mrs C J Spence. *5m N of Newbury. Take A34 N, pass under M4, then L to Chieveley. After 1/2 m L up Manor Lane.* Home-made teas. **Adm £3, chd free. Sun 6 July (2-5).**
Large garden with fine views over stud farm. Walled garden containing borders, shrubs and rose garden. Listed house (not open). Newly planted bed.
&. ✕ ⊛ ☕

4 NEW 17 CLEVEDON ROAD
Tilehurst RG31 6RL. G Emmerick & G Preston. *3m W Reading centre. A329 to Tilehurst stn, L into Carlisle rd, R into Clevedon rd.* Light refreshments & teas. **Adm £2.50, chd free. Sat 12; Sun 13 July (1-5).**
1/4 -acre yr-round town garden on 3 levels featuring a circular lawn and octagonal vegetable plot, planted with a mix of English and Mediterranean horticultural delights, incl grasses, climbers, shrubs, fruit and trees. A tranquil oasis with views to Arthur Newbery Park.
⊛ ☕

5 6 CRECY CLOSE
Wokingham RG41 3UZ. John & Anne Massey, 0118 9019099, anne.massey@ntlworld.com, www.acorngardenservices.co.uk. *Take A329 towards Reading. 1m after town centre, L at Woosehill roundabout, end of dual carriageway*

turn R, take 1st L and 5th on L. **Adm £2.50, chd free. Visitors welcome by appt, Sat & Sun, June to Sept, groups 10+.**
Lovely award winning garden, designed by the owner, offering many ideas for the small garden together with interesting and unusual plants.
&. ✕ ☎

DIPLEY MILL
See Hampshire.

6 DONNINGTON CASTLE HOUSE
Castle Lane. RG14 2LE. Mr & Mrs B Stewart-Brown. *1m N of Newbury. Follow signs to Donnington Castle. Entrance on R towards top of main castle entrance. Car park through wooden gates.* Home-made teas. **Adm £4, chd free. Fri 11 July (10-5).**
Large mature garden with additional planting during last 5yrs. Attractive herbaceous borders, roses, mixed borders, fine mature trees, lawns, woodland and garden walks.
&. ✕ ⊛ ☕

7 ♦ ENGLEFIELD HOUSE
RG7 5EN. Mr & Mrs Richard Benyon, www.englefield.co.uk. *6m W of Reading. 11/2 m from J12 M4. 1m from Theale. Entrance on A340 3m S of Pangbourne.* **Adm £3, chd free. Mon all yr, Mon to Thurs incl from 1 Apr to 31 Oct (10-6).**
9-acre woodland garden with interesting variety of trees and shrubs, stream, water garden descending to formal terraces with stone balustrades making background for deep borders. Small enclosed gardens of differing character incl children's garden with joke fountains. All enclosed by deer park with lake.
&. ✕ ⊛

8 ETON COLLEGE GARDENS
SL4 6DB. Eton College. *1/2 m N of Windsor. Parking off B3022 Slough to Eton rd, signed to R, S of junction with Datchet Rd (Pocock's Lane), walk across playing fields to entry. Or continue S on B3022 through T-lights in Eton, then signed 50yds on L (called Barnes Pool and suitable for wheelchairs). 100yds walk to entry.* Cream teas. **Adm £3, chd free. Sat 14 June (2-5.30).**
A delightful selection of college gardens which surround ancient school buildings incl Provost's Garden, Fellows' Garden, Headmaster's Garden and Luxmoore's garden (an

island in the Thames, created by a housemaster about 1880 and reached across an attractive bridge). Gravel paths, mown grass to Luxmoore's.

 ♿ ✕ ☕

⑨ FAIRACRE
Ravensdale Road, South Ascot SL5 9HJ. David & Mary Nichols. *6m E of Bracknell. On A330 ½ m S of Ascot Racecourse, turn R into Coronation Rd, 2nd R to Woodlands Ride, Ravensdale Rd 150yds on R. No cars except disabled in unmade Ravensdale Rd.* Home-made teas. **Adm £3, chd free (share to All Souls Church). Sun 27 July (2-5).**
1½ acres. Banks of large rhododendrons and azaleas, sunken garden with mix of annuals and perennials, beds of flowering shrubs, herbaceous borders, collection of conifers, kitchen garden. Some re-planting and new additions each year.

♿ ✕ ⊗ ☕

Atmospheric garden with a wild natural look . . .

⑩ FROGMORE HOUSE GARDEN
Windsor SL4 2HT. Her Majesty The Queen, www.royal.gov.uk. *1m SE of Windsor. Entrance via Park St gate into Long Walk (follow AA signs). Visitors are requested kindly to keep on the route to the garden & not stray into the Home Park. Stn & bus stop in Windsor (20 mins walk from gardens), Green Line bus no 701, from London. Limited parking for cars only (free). Coaches by appointment only.* Light refreshments & teas. **Garden only Adm £4, chd free, House Adm £4.50, child £2.50, concessions £3.50. Tue 3 June (10-5.30 last adm 4pm).**
30 acres of landscaped gardens rich in history and beauty. Large lake, fine trees, lawns, flowers and flowering shrubs. Gravel paths. For tickets apply to NGS, Hatchlands Park, East Clandon, Guildford, Surrey GU4 7RT, Tel 01483 211535, www.ngs.org.uk.

♿ ✕ ☕

⑪ NEW GLENMERE
246 Nine Mile Ride, Finchampstead RG40 3PA. Heather Bradly & John Kenney, 01189 733274. *7m J10 M4. 3m Crowthorne or Wokingham. On B3430 E of California Crossroads roundabout.* Home-made teas. **Adm £2.50, chd free. Visitors welcome by appt, April to August.**
Japanese style garden with waiting arbour, raked gravel area, tea house, Torii gate, dry stream bed with bridge and pond. Vegetable garden, greenhouse and soft fruit area.

✕ ☕ ☎

GRANGE DRIVE WOOBURN
See Buckinghamshire.

⑫ THE HARRIS GARDEN
Whiteknights RG6 6AS. The University of Reading, School of Biological Sciences, www.friendsoftheharrisgarden.org. uk. *1½ m S of Reading town centre. Off A327, Shinfield Rd. Turn R just inside Pepper Lane entrance to campus.* Home-made teas. **Adm £3, chd free. Sun 13 Apr (2-6).**
12-acre research and teaching garden. Rose gardens, herbaceous borders, winter garden, herb garden, jungle garden. Extensive glasshouses. Many plants labelled. Some uneven (but manageable) paths.

♿ ✕ ⊗ ☕

HEARNS HOUSE
See Oxfordshire.

HIGHER DENHAM GARDENS
See Buckinghamshire.

⑬ NEW HOOK END FARM
Upper Basildon RG8 8SD. David & Fiona Ambler, 01491 671255, fiona@hookendfarm.com. *3m W of Pangbourne. From A329 L into Hook End Lane, 1m on R.* Home-made teas. **Adm £3, chd free. Sun 8 (2-6); Wed 11 June (11-5). Visitors also welcome by appt 9th - 30 June.**
2-acre hillside walled garden and orchard in a tranquil rural valley with outstanding views. Atmospheric garden with a wild natural look. Over 250 varieties of roses, other interesting plants and shrubs filling box parterres, secret corners and arbours.

⊗ ☕ ☎

⑭ INHOLMES
Woodlands St Mary RG17 7SY. Lady Williams. *3m SE Lambourn. From A338 take B4000 towards Lambourn, Inholmes signed.* Teas. **Adm £4, £6 combined with Rooksnest, chd free. Weds 30 Apr; 25 June (11-4).**
Newly re-established, incl large walled garden, colour co-ordinated herbaceous border, cutting garden, tulip display, formal gardens, parkland walk with specimen trees leading to bluebell wood. Featured in 'GGG'. Gravel & stone paths.

♿ ✕ ⊗ ☕

⑮ IVYDENE
283 Loddon Bridge Road, Woodley RG5 4BE. Janet & Bill Bonney, 0118 969 7591, janetbonney2003@aol.com. *3½ m W of Reading. A4 from Reading towards Maidenhead. Woodley lies midway between. Loddon Bridge Rd is the main rd through the small town. Garden about 100yds S of the 'Just Tiles' roundabout. Parking is in adjacent rd.* **Adm £2, chd free. Visitors welcome by appt, for groups 5+.**
Small urban gardener's garden approx 120ft x 30ft, specialising in ornamental grasses with over 50 varieties integrated into both front and back gardens. Autumn viewing shows grasses to best advantage. New cottage garden and stained glass features.

☎

⑯ KIRBY HOUSE
Inkpen RG17 9DE. Mr & Mrs R Astor. *3½ m SE of Hungerford. A4 to Kintbury. L at Xrds in Kintbury (by Corner Stores) towards Coombe. 2m out of Kintbury turn L immed beyond Crown & Garter PH, turn L at junction, house at bottom of hill on R.* **Adm £3.50. Sun 22 June (2-5).**
6 acres in beautiful setting with views of S Berkshire Downs across lawn and parkland. C18 Queen Anne House (not open). Formal rose borders, double herbaceous border in kitchen garden, colour themed border between yew buttress hedges. Lily pond garden, reflecting pond with fountain, lake. Newly designed and planted walled garden.

✕

⑰ LITTLE HARWOOD
Choke Lane, Pinkneys Green SL6 6PL. Mr & Mrs David Harrold. *2½ m NW of Maidenhead. A308 towards Marlow from Maidenhead. At*

Pinkneys Green turn R into Winter Hill Rd signed to Winter Hill & Cookham Dean. Where rd forks continue on main rd towards Cookham Dean, now Choke Lane. 500yds along Choke Lane you reach a Z bend & SLOW sign. Little Harwood is on the L. Home-made teas or morning coffee. **Adm £3.50, chd free. Sun 27 (2-5); Mon 28 Apr (10.30-1).**
2-acre mature, formal and informal, terraced gardens, incl water garden, rock garden, herbaceous border completely redesigned spring 2007, herb bed and contemporary garden buildings. Large specimen trees and clipped yew and hawthorn hedges. 16-acre bluebell woodland walk and wild flower meadow. Bluebell walk. Plant sale in aid of Compassion in World Farming Trust, 10% NGS.

⊗ ☕

THE MANOR HOUSE, HAMBLEDEN
See Buckinghamshire.

18 MARINERS
Mariners Lane, Bradfield RG7 6HU. Anthony & Fenja Anderson, 0118 974 5226. *10m W of Reading. M4 J12 take A4 direction Newbury 1m. At roundabout exit A340 direction Pangbourne. 400yds turn L direction Bradfield. After 1m, turn L direction Southend Bradfield. After 1m opp signpost direction Tutts Clump turn R into Mariners Lane.* **Adm £3.50, chd free. Sun 15 June (2-6). Visitors also welcome by appt, 16th June-15 July.**
1½ -acre sloping site with creative feature made of slopes. Rich mixture of herbaceous planting incl unusual plants and grasses arranged in colour themes with emphasis on plant form and texture. Garden of old varieties of shrub roses, species and climbing roses. Streamside walk, orchard, sundial garden and 1-acre wild flower meadow. Featured in 'GGG*'.

♿ ✂ ⊗ ☎

19 MEADOW HOUSE
Ashford Hill RG19 8BN. Mr & Mrs G A Jones, 0118 981 6005. *8m SE of Newbury. On B3051. Take turning at SW end of village signed Wolverton Common & Wheathold. House on R approx 350yds down unmade track.* **Adm £2.50, chd free. Visitors welcome by appt.**
Approx 1¾ -acre plantsman's garden in beautiful rural surroundings. Designed by owners to create a feeling of tranquillity and space. Pond with

waterside planting, mixed shrub, rose and herbaceous borders. Trellis with wisteria, roses and clematis.

♿ ✂ ☎

20 NEW MILES'S GREEN HOUSE
Briff Lane, Bucklebury RG7 6SH. Mr & Mrs Eric Lloyd, 01635 862574, lloydmgh@googlemail.com. *6m NE of Newbury, off A4. From Thatcham take Harts Hill Rd N to Bucklebury.* **Adm 3.50, chd free. Visitors welcome by appt, 29 May - 12 Jun, no coaches.**
3-acre tranquil valley garden in a woodland setting with small lake, bog garden and adjacent pool. Specimen trees and shrubs feature on well-maintained sloping lawns with island beds of choice and unusual plants. Herbaceous beds combine shrubs, roses and perennials with a subtle blend of colours. Meadow with grass paths.

✂ ☎

21 THE MILL HOUSE
Oxford Road, Donnington RG14 2JD. Dr & Mrs Jane Vaidya. *1m N of Newbury. On B4494. Mill House on L immed after Donnington Alms Houses. M4 J13, A34 S towards Newbury. Take 1st exit follow signs to Donnington. Approx 2m (B4494 Oxford Rd) pass Castle PH on L. Mill House 50yds on R. Please park with consideration in Donnington village.* Home-made teas. **Adm £3.50, chd free. Sun 29 June (2-6).**
2¾ acres of secluded gardens set around the Mill House (not open) and surrounded by the R Lambourn. Small lake, stream and millrace, herbaceous borders, lawns, woodland and bog garden, wild area. Art exhibition.

✂ ⊗ ☕

22 MOOR CLOSE GARDENS
Popeswood Road, Binfield RG42 4AN. Newbold College, 01344 452427/407583, harryleonard@beeb.net/pdyckhoff@newbold.ac.uk. *2m W of Bracknell. Off B3408. From Bracknell turn R at Binfield T-lights, from A329(M) take B3408, turn L at Binfield T-lights. Follow signs.* **Adm £2.50, chd free. Suns 4, 25 May; 15 June (2-5). Visitors also welcome by appt Sun-Fri, May-July.**
A small Gll listed garden designed 1911-13 by Oliver Hill and a rare

example of his early work. Lavender garden, water parterre, remains of Italianate garden. Undergoing long-term restoration, it currently offers most interest in its historical architecture rather than planting. Garden history tours by appointment.

✂ ☎

> Divided into smaller sections with topiary and woodland paths . . .

23 NEW OLD PINES HOUSE
Ball Hill, Newbury RG20 0NN. Miss Helen Newport. *4m S of Newbury, off A343. From Newbury turn W off A343 past small bridge to Ball Hill on Washwater Rd with Woodpecker PH on R. 3m past Furze Bush PH to Ball Hill Garage, past 1st L turn into drive on L.* Light refreshments & teas. **Adm £3.50, chd free. Suns 11 May; 17 Aug (2-6).**
A beautiful setting for a Gll listed cottage and tithe barn, within 2 acres, planted for yr-round interest. Background of mature trees, lawns, herbaceous and mixed borders, fruit trees and vegetable garden. Stream running into large pond with waterfall. Garden divided into smaller sections with topiary and woodland paths. Sheep and Shetland ponies. Some paths scalpings.

♿ ✂ ⊗ ☕

24 THE OLD RECTORY BURGHFIELD
RG30 3TH. Mr A R Merton. *5m SW of Reading. Turn S off A4 to Burghfield village, R after Hatch Gate Inn, entrance on R.* Tea 50p. **Adm £3, chd free. Sun 27 July (12-4).**
4½ -acre plantsman's garden. Snowdrops, hellebores, old roses, shrub borders, woodland area, ponds, orchard, kitchen garden, terrace pots and late summer flowering double herbaceous borders. Georgian house (not open).

✂ ⊗ ☕

25 THE OLD RECTORY FARNBOROUGH

Wantage OX12 8NX. Mr & Mrs Michael Todhunter, 01488 638298 or letter. *4m SE of Wantage. Take B4494 Wantage-Newbury Rd, after 4m turn E at sign for Farnborough.* Home-made teas. **Adm £3.50, chd free (share to Farnborough PCC). Suns 20 Apr; 11 May; 22 June (2-5.30). Visitors also welcome by appt, Mar - Aug, any number.**

In a series of immaculately tended garden rooms, incl herbaceous borders, arboretum, boules, rose, pool and vegetable gardens, there is an explosion of rare and interesting plants, beautifully combined for colour and texture. With stunning views across the countryside, it is the perfect setting for the C1749 rectory (not open), once home of John Betjeman, in memory of whom John Piper created a window in the local church.

OLD THATCH
See Buckinghamshire.

26 OLD WATERFIELD

Winkfield Road, Ascot SL5 7LJ. Hugh & Catherine Stevenson. *6m SW of Windsor. On A330 (Winkfield Rd) midway between A329 and A332 to E of Ascot Racecourse. Parking on Practice Ground (by kind permission of Royal Ascot Golf Club) adjacent to house.* Home-made teas. **Adm £3, chd free (share to Thames Hospice Care). Sun 24 Aug (2.30-5.30).**

Nestling in 4-acres adjacent to Ascot Race Course the original cottage garden has attractive herbaceous borders and lovely views. Large productive kitchen garden full of fruit and vegetables, natural pond, specimen trees, a young orchard and mixed hedging.

27 POTASH

Mariners Lane, Southend Bradfield RG7 6HU. Mr & Mrs J W C Mooney, 0118 9744264, john@potash.plus.com. *10m W of Reading. From M4 J12 take A4 W 1m. At roundabout exit A340 direction Pangbourne, turn L after 400yds direction Bradfield. After 1m turn L direction Southend Bradfield. 1m opposite Southend Bradfield sign turn R. Potash is 400yds on L by Beech Hedge.* **Adm £3.50, chd free. Visitors welcome by appt, all year inc groups.**

5-acre garden. Wide range of plants, many unusual specimens and interest throughout the yr from snowdrops to autumn colour. Daffodils a feature, shrubs, tea roses, herbaceous borders, bog garden feeding a clay-lined pond, young woodland and space to sit and contemplate the view. Children and dogs very welcome.

THE PRIORS FARM
See Hampshire.

28 THE PRIORY

Beech Hill RG7 2BJ. Mr & Mrs C Carter, 01189 833146, tita@getcarter.org. *5m S of Reading. M4 J11. Follow signs to A33, then L at roundabout signed Swallowfield. After 1¼ m, R by Murco garage to Beech Hill. When in village turn opp church into Wood Lane, then R down Priory Dr - house at end of drive.* Home-made teas. **Adm £3.50, chd free. Sun 1 June (2-5.30). Visitors also welcome by appt.**

Extensive gardens in grounds of former C12 Benedictine Priory (not open), rebuilt 1648. Beside the R Loddon, the mature gardens are being restored and re-developed. Large formal walled garden with espalier fruit trees, lawns, extensive mixed and recently replanted herbaceous borders, vegetables and roses. Woodland, lake and new Italian style water garden in progress. Fine trees. A lot of gravel paths.

29 THE RISC ROOF GARDEN, READING

35-39 London Street. RG1 4PS. Reading International Solidarity Centre, www.risc.org.uk/garden. *5 mins walk from Oracle shopping centre.* Home-made teas. **Adm £2.50, chd free (share to WEB/RISC). Sats & Suns 7, 8 June; 12, 13 July; 9, 10 Aug; 13, 14 Sept (12-4).**

Small town centre roof forest garden developed to demonstrate sustainability and our dependance on plants. All plants in the garden have an economic use for food, clothing, medicine etc, and come from all over the world. Water harvesting and irrigation systems powered by renewable energy. Garden accessed by external staircase. Featured in '1001 Gardens You Must See Before You Die'.

30 ROOKSNEST

Ermine Street, Lambourn Woodlands RG17 7SB. Dr & Mrs M D Sackler, 07766 130398, lisa.rooksnest@hotmail.co.uk. *2m S of Lambourn. From A338 Wantage rd, along B4000. Rooksnest signed.* Light refreshments & teas. **Adm £4, £6 combined with Inholmes, chd free. Weds 30 Apr; 25 June (11-4). Visitors also welcome by appt.**

Approx 10-acre exceptionally fine traditional English garden. Sunken garden recently restored with help from Arabella Lennox-Boyd. Terraces, rose garden, lilies, pond, herbaceous border, herb garden, organic vegetable garden. Many specimen trees and fine shrubs.

Large productive kitchen garden full of fruit and vegetables . . .

31 SANDLEFORD PLACE

Newtown RG20 9AY. Mr & Mrs Alan Gatward, 01635 40726, melgatward@bigfoot.com. *1½ m S of Newbury. On A339. House is at W side of Swan roundabout.* Home-made teas. **Adm £3, chd free. Sun 15 June (2-6). Visitors also welcome by appt, inc coaches.**

4-acre grounds, more exhuberant than manicured, around a former old mill and granary. Many varied shrub and herbaceous borders crammed with plants for romantic, naturalistic effect. Walled garden with a wide range of plants arranged for yr-round interest, flowers, foliage and scent. Kitchen garden and herb bed. Wild flowers in meadow and along river. Unusual plants for sale, some seen in the garden. Weeping tree water feature.

32 SCOTLANDS
**Cockpole Green, Wargrave
RG10 8QP. Mr Michael Payne &
family, 01628 822648.** *6m W of
Maidenhead, 4m E of Henley. In centre
of triangle formed by A4130, A321 to
Wargrave & A4 at Knowl Hill - midway
between Warren Row Village &
Cockpole Green.* **Adm £3.50, chd
free. Special Open Day on Sun 17
Aug (2-5) in partnership with
MacMillan Cancer Support. Visitors
also welcome by appt.**
4-acre garden surrounding C17
farmhouse (not open). Clipped yews
surrounding oval swimming pool,
shrub borders, grass paths through
trees to woodland and pond-gardens,
within brick and flint partly walled
garden. Rocks with waterfall and
gazebo of C18 design. Come to our
special day! Featured in 'GGG'.
&. ☎

33 21 SIMONS LANE
**Wokingham RG41 3HG. Jill
Wheatley.** *Off A329. Between
Woosehill roundabout and Sainsburys.*
Home-made teas. **Adm £2.50, chd
free. Sun 1 June (2-5).**
Organically-run small garden,
developed since 1996, intensively
planted with wide variety of shrubs,
herbaceous perennials, climbers and
fruit. Rear garden is designed around
pond with water lilies. Paved area
features herbs and, in courtyard
garden, hosta collection. HDRA
information available on organic
methods. Some gravel paths.
&. ⊛ ☕

34 STANFORD DINGLEY GARDENS
RG7 6LS. *5m SW of Pangbourne.
From A4 take A340 (Pangbourne Rd),
1st L to Bradfield, after Bradfield, L at
Xrds, 2½ m, L into village.* Home-made
teas. **Combined adm £4, chd £1
(share to St Denys Church). Sun 18
May (2-6).**
One of Berkshire's most beautiful
villages set within the valley of the R
Pang, river walks in all gardens.
☕

BRADFIELD FARM
**Mrs Anna Newton, 01189
744113.** *Pink house in centre of
village.* **Visitors also welcome by
appt, groups 30 max, £5 ea incl
tea.**
½ -acre plantsman's garden with
wide variety of plants. Driveway
behind leading across fields to 6-
acre wild garden beside R Pang.

Long undisturbed ground and
mown walks, enjoy native flora
and fauna. Spring rising in pond
flowing into river. Dogs welcome in
wild garden. Gravel paths, slight
slopes.
&. ⊛ ☎

INGLE SPRING
David & Indra Townsend
2½ -acre garden beside R Ingle,
with beautiful views and a wide
range of different plantings.
Restored by present owners over
the past 5yrs. Partial wheelchair
access. Narrow bridge over river.
⊛

THE SPRING
Mr & Mrs Mark Hawkesworth.
Opp The Old Boot PH.
Cottage garden with spring-fed
pond and stream, mature tree
specimens, fruit trees and
vegetable area, herbaceous
borders, views over water
meadow. Newly planted green
oak rose pergola.

Spring rising in pond flowing into river . . . dogs welcome in wild garden . . .

35 STOCKCROSS HOUSE
**Church Road. RG20 8LP. Susan &
Edward Vandyk, 07764 180922
(Gardener).** *3m W of Newbury. 1m W
of A4/A34 (Newbury bypass) junction
on B4000. From M4, J14, take B4000
to Stockcross.* Home-made teas 8th
June only. **Adm £2.50, chd free
(share to Sutton Hall & Newbury
Symphony Orchestra). Weds 5 Mar;
2 Apr; 7 May (11-4); Sun 8 June
(2-5.30).**
1½ -acre garden developed over past
14yrs with an emphasis on plant
partnerships and colour combinations.
Winter bulbs and hellebores,
herbaceous borders, shrubs, roses,
pergola and pond, vegetable and
cutting gardens, all maintained to a
high standard. Music in the garden,
members of Newbury Symphony
Orchestra, 8th June. Gravel courtyard
to cross, slope to lower garden.
&. ⋇ ⊛ ☕

STOKE POGES MEMORIAL GARDENS
See Buckinghamshire.

36 SUNNINGDALE PARK
**Larch Avenue, Ascot SL5 0QE.
National School of
Government/Verve Venues.** *6m S of
Windsor. On A30 at Sunningdale take
Broomhall Lane. After ½ m turn R into
Larch Ave. From A329 turn into
Silwood Rd towards Sunningdale.*
Home-made teas. **Adm £4, chd free.
Mon 26 May (2-5).**
Over 20 acres of beautifully
landscaped gardens reputedly
designed after Capability Brown.
Terrace garden and Victorian rockery
designed by Pulham incl cave and
water features. Lake area with paved
walks, extensive lawns with specimen
trees and flower beds, impressive
massed rhododendrons. Beautiful 1m
woodland walk. Grade II listed building
(not open). Free garden history tour,
3.30pm.

37 SWALLOWFIELD HORTICULTURAL SOCIETY
RG7 1QX. *5m S of Reading. M4 J11 &
A33/B3349, signed Swallowfield.
Tickets and maps at village hall in
centre.* Light refreshments & teas.
**Combined adm £4, chd free. Sun 13
July (11-5).**
Swallowfield has survived as a real
village beside the Blackwater
meadows and offers a min of 8
gardens to visit, ranging from tiny and
perfect to large and shaggy (some
immaculate ones too). Some are full of
special plants, others developed in a
variety of styles. Model trains, donkeys
and views to love.

38 THRIVE'S TRUNKWELL GARDEN PROJECT
**Beech Hill, Reading RG7 2AT.
Thrive, www.thrive.org.uk.** *7m S of
Reading. M4 J11, follow signs to A33,
L at roundabout signed Swallowfield.
After 1¼ m, R by Murco garage to
Beech Hill. From S keep through
Swallowfield on B3349, after Mill
House restaurant turn L, bear R, then L
at Xrds to Beech Hill. Signs in village.*
Home-made teas. **Adm £2.50, chd £1
(share to Thrive). Sun 13 July
(2-4.30).**
3-acre site with Victorian walled garden
run by Thrive, a national charity which
uses gardening to support and inspire
disabled people. Formal and informal
interest, nature trail, pond, butterfly

garden, trained fruit and cut flower areas, potager, glasshouse, sensory and cottage gardens.

39 TIMBERLEA
**17 Oaklands Drive, Wokingham RG41 2SA. Mr & Mrs F Preston, 0118 978 4629,
nina.fred@tinyonline.co.uk.** *1m SW of Wokingham. M4 J10 or M3 J3. From Wokingham take A321 under 2 railway bridges, Tesco store is between. Immed turn R at mini roundabout, Molly Millars Lane. 3rd rd on L is Oaklands Drive. After 100yds, R into cul-de-sac.* Cream teas. **Adm £2, chd free. Sun 3 Aug (2-6). Visitors also welcome by appt, individuals and groups, 30 max, May to Sept. Refreshments.**
Something of interest at every turn! Triangular plot lends itself to hidden corners. Different levels, arches and pergolas lead to new vistas, re-planted perennial borders in 2007, kitchen garden with raised beds, fruit cage and greenhouses. Front garden includes waterfall, stream and pond with private decked seating area. New shady area with water feature. Locally crafted original garden ceramics. Wheelchairs limited by woodchip & shallow steps.

40 TWO BRACKNELL GARDENS
RG12 9BH. *1m S of Bracknell town centre. From M4 take A329(M), from M3 take A322, towards Bracknell and follow each garden directions.* Teas at Shaftesbury Close. **Combined adm £3, chd free. Sun 18 May (2-5).**

DEVONIA
Broad Lane. Andrew Radgick, 01344 450914, aradgick@aol.com. *From A329M take 3rd roundabout, 2nd exit into Broad Lane, 3rd house on L after railway bridge. From A322, Horse & Groom roundabout, take 4th exit into Broad Lane.* **Visitors also welcome by appt, adm £2.50, chd free.**
$1/3$ -acre plantaholic's garden designed for all seasons and planted to require minimal watering. Divided into several areas to provide appropriate conditions for over 1000 different shrubs, perennials, bulbs and alpines, incl many rare and unusual. Hot and dry front garden, shady and sheltered corners to

the rear. Awarded 'Best Front Garden in Bracknell '.

10 SHAFTESBURY CLOSE
Harmanswater. Gill Cheetham, 01344 423440. *At sports centre roundabout exit to Harmanswater. L on 2 mini roundabouts into Nightingale Crescent. Shaftesbury Close is 2nd on R.* **Visitors also welcome by appt, adm £2.50, chd free.**
Woodland garden, at its best during winter and spring. Many different ericaceous shrubs and plants. Walled garden, scree and alpine beds. Beds planted to reflect climatic changes.

41 TWO GARDENS AT ASHAMPSTEAD COMMON
**RG8 8QT, 01635 210399/202993, baggchute@aol.com/jacqaranda@bt
internet.com.** *2m E of Yattendon along Yattendon Lane. L into Sucks Lane, $1/2$ m, R opp common.* Home-made teas. **Combined adm £5, chd free. Visitors welcome by appt, Apr-Oct, groups 10+.**
2 gardens linked by pretty walk through medieval woodland. Stunning bluebells in May. No wheelchair access.

BAGGAGE CHUTE
Colin & Caroline Butler.
Lower terraced garden with colourful mix of shrubs and perennials leading to large informal pond. Vegetable and cutting garden. Hillside slopes feature prairie style mix of flowers and grasses with long views over surrounding countryside.

FARRIERS COTTAGE
Jackie Lomas.
Small immaculate cottage garden designed and planted by owner. Formal front garden in woodland setting leading to colourful mix of shrubs and herbaceous planting at the back.

TYLNEY HALL HOTEL & TYLNEY HOUSE
See Hampshire.

THE VYNE
See Hampshire.

Two gardens linked by pretty walk through medieval woodland . . .

42 ◆ WALTHAM PLACE GARDENS
**Church Hill, White Waltham SL6 3JH. Mr & Mrs N Oppenheimer, 01628 825517,
www.walthamplace.com.** *3$1/2$ m S of Maidenhead. From M4 J8/9 take A404. Follow signs for White Waltham. Pass airfield on RH-side. Take L turn signed Windsor/Paley St. Pass the church, follow signs for parking. From Bracknell/Wokingham A3095 to A330 direction Maidenhead. Turn L at Paley St B3024 to White Waltham. Follow parking signs.* **Adm £4, chd £1.50. Tues & Thurs, May-Sept, for groups, by appointment. For NGS: Weds 7 May to 24 Sept (10-4).**
New style naturalistic gardens (Henk Gerritsen) where weeds meet garden plants in an ancient framework of wonderful specimen trees. With organic kitchen garden and farm, several walled gardens, grasspath maze, lake and woodland with bluebells, camellias and rhododendrons. Explore the boundaries between nature and garden in our 170-acre nature inspired paradise.

43 ◆ WELFORD PARK
**Newbury RG20 8HU. Mrs J H Puxley, 01488 608203,
www.welfordpark.co.uk.** *6m NW of Newbury. On Lambourn Valley Rd. Entrance on Newbury-Lambourn rd. Please use clearly marked car park.* **House and Garden Adm £8 (advance booking for Queen Anne House), Garden only Adm £3.50, chd free, £2.50. See website for details. For NGS: Tue 10 June (2-6).**
Formal garden with herbaceous and rose pergolas. Spacious parkland and wonderful trees. Woodland walk by R Lambourn. Gravel paths, slope to tea rooms.

WEST SILCHESTER HALL
See Hampshire.

124 WHITE GABLES
See Hampshire.

44 NEW WINCHCOMBE FARM
Briff Lane, Bucklebury RG7 6SN.
Mr & Mrs N LeRougetel. *6m NE of Newbury, off A4. From Thatcham take Harts Hill Rd N, from Bucklebury take Little Lane N, keep R at fork, house on L approx ¹/₂ m.* **Adm £5, chd free. Sun 18 May (12-5).**
Best in late spring with wisteria, rhododendrons, azaleas and camellias. Wildflower meadow planted 12 yrs ago along with a large variety of trees, lovely formal garden and small orchard. Natural spring used to create a pond and bog garden.

1 WOGSBARNE COTTAGES
See Hampshire.

45 WOOLLEY PARK
Wantage OX12 8NJ. **Mrs P Wroughton.** *5m S of Wantage. A338. Turn L at sign to Woolley.* Home-made teas. **Adm £2.50, chd free. Sun 15 June (2-5).**
Large park, fine trees and views. Two linked walled gardens sensitively planted with a wide variety of interesting plants. Gravel paths.

For Bristol see Somerset

Berkshire County Volunteers

County Organiser
Heather Skinner, 5 Liddell Close, Finchampstead, Wokingham RG40 4NS, 0118 9737197, heatheraskinner@aol.com

County Treasurer
Hugh Priestley, Jennets Hill House, Southend, Reading RG7 6JP, 0118 974 4349, hughpriestley1@aol.com

Publicity
Fenja Anderson, Mariners, Mariners Lane, Southend, Reading RG7 6HU, 0118 974 5226, fenjaanderson@aol.com

Assistant County Organiser
Nigel Evans, 21 Cottrell Close, Hungerford RG17 0HF, 01488 681405, mandn21@onetel.com
Nina Preston, Timberlea, 17 Oaklands Drive, Wokingham RG41 2SA, 0118 978 4629, nina.fred@tinyonline.co.uk
Christopher Verity, Boundary House, Brimpton Common, Reading RG7 4RT, 0118 981 4849

ng's gardens open for charity

Old-fashioned roses, fragrant perennials and herbs grown together with wild flowers to provide habitat for birds, bees, butterflies and small mammals.
It has been described as 'organised chaos'!

Rustic Cottage, Yorkshire

BUCKINGHAMSHIRE

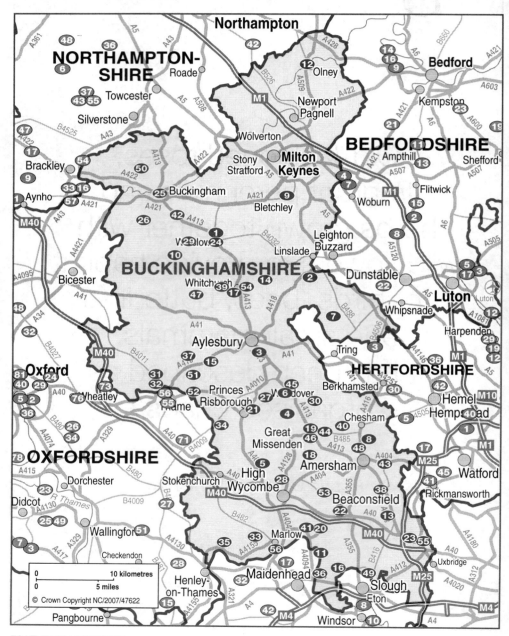

Opening Dates

February

SUNDAY 24
47 Quainton Gardens

March

SUNDAY 2
17 Fielding House
39 The Old School

SATURDAY 8
49 Stoke Poges Memorial Gardens

SUNDAY 23
44 Overstroud Cottage

SUNDAY 30
8 Chesham Bois House

April

SUNDAY 6
49 Stoke Poges Memorial Gardens

SUNDAY 13
31 Long Crendon Spring Gardens
43 6 Oldfield Close
48 Rivendell

SATURDAY 19
42 The Old Vicarage

SUNDAY 20
42 The Old Vicarage
44 Overstroud Cottage
56 Whitewalls

WEDNESDAY 23
19 Gipsy House
46 The Plant Specialist

SUNDAY 27
54 Whitchurch Gardens

May

SUNDAY 4
34 The Manor House, Bledlow

MONDAY 5
2 Ascott
51 Turn End

WEDNESDAY 7
49 Stoke Poges Memorial Gardens

SUNDAY 11
8 Chesham Bois House

WEDNESDAY 14
16 Dorneywood Garden

THURSDAY 15
19 Gipsy House
46 The Plant Specialist

SUNDAY 18
18 Fressingwood
44 Overstroud Cottage
55 The White House

THURSDAY 22
36 Maryfield

FRIDAY 23
36 Maryfield

SATURDAY 24
41 Old Thatch

SUNDAY 25
40 The Old Sun House
29 3 Jubilee Cottages

WEDNESDAY 28
16 Dorneywood Garden

SATURDAY 31
29 3 Jubilee Cottages

June

SUNDAY 1
14 Cublington Gardens
23 Higher Denham Gardens

SUNDAY 8
5 Bradenham Manor
28 Hughenden Manor
32 Long Crendon Summer Gardens
48 Rivendell

WEDNESDAY 11
19 Gipsy House
46 The Plant Specialist

THURSDAY 12
27 Homelands
33 Lords Wood

SATURDAY 14
12 Cowper & Newton Museum Gardens

SUNDAY 15
12 Cowper & Newton Museum Gardens
13 Craiglea House
34 The Manor House, Bledlow
35 The Manor House, Hambleden
52 Tythrop Park

SATURDAY 21
45 11 The Paddocks

SUNDAY 22
7 Cheddington Gardens
15 Dinton Gardens
20 Grange Drive Wooburn
37 Nether Winchendon House
45 11 The Paddocks

WEDNESDAY 25
21 Greenways

THURSDAY 26
21 Greenways

FRIDAY 27
29 3 Jubilee Cottages (Evening)
45 11 The Paddocks (Evening)

SUNDAY 29
25 Hill House
26 Hillesden House

July

WEDNESDAY 2
16 Dorneywood Garden

SATURDAY 5
45 11 The Paddocks

SUNDAY 6
3 Aylesbury Gardens
8 Chesham Bois House

FRIDAY 11
27 Homelands (Evening)

SUNDAY 13
56 Whitewalls

THURSDAY 17
19 Gipsy House
46 The Plant Specialist

SATURDAY 19
11 Cliveden
50 Stowe Landscape Gardens

SATURDAY 26
16 Dorneywood Garden

August

SUNDAY 3
55 The White House

THURSDAY 14
27 Homelands

MONDAY 25
2 Ascott

September

THURSDAY 4
33 Lords Wood

SUNDAY 7
10 Claydon House
56 Whitewalls

SATURDAY 20
11 Cliveden

Gardens open to the public

2 Ascott
10 Claydon House
11 Cliveden
12 Cowper & Newton Museum Gardens
28 Hughenden Manor
37 Nether Winchendon House
41 Old Thatch
46 The Plant Specialist
49 Stoke Poges Memorial Gardens
50 Stowe Landscape Gardens

By appointment only

1 Abbotts House
4 Blossoms
6 Cedar House
9 100 Church Green Road
22 Hall Barn
24 19 Highfield Road
30 2 Kingswood Cottages
38 North Down
53 Watercroft

Also open by appointment ☎

8 Chesham Bois House
13 Craiglea House
32 Croft House, Long Crendon
Summer Gardens
16 Dorneywood Garden
25 Hill House
26 Hillesden House
27 Homelands
34 The Manor House, Bledlow
42 The Old Vicarage
43 6 Oldfield Close
44 Overstroud Cottage
54 Priory Court, Whitchurch
Gardens
47 The Vine, Quainton Gardens
56 Whitewalls

The Gardens

1 ABBOTTS HOUSE
10 Church Street, Winslow
MK18 3AN. Mrs Jane Rennie, 01296
712326. *9m N of Aylesbury. On A413
into Winslow. From town centre take
Horn St & R into Church St.* Adm
£2.50, chd free. Visitors welcome by
appt, groups max 20, best May-July.
Garden on different levels divided into
4. Courtyard near house with arbour
and pots, woodland garden (planted
3yrs ago) with rose arbour, swimming
pool garden with grasses. Walled
Victorian kitchen garden with glass
houses, potager, fruit pergola, wall
trained fruit and many mediterranean
plants.
✗ ✿ ☎

2 ◆ ASCOTT
Wing LU7 0PS. Sir Evelyn de
Rothschild, The National Trust,
01296 688242,
info@ascottestate.co.uk. *2m SW of
Leighton Buzzard, 8m NE of Aylesbury.*
Adm £4, chd £2. Phone or see
website for other openings. For
NGS: Mons 5 May; 25 Aug (2-6).
Combining Victorian formality with early
C20 natural style and recent plantings

to lead it into the C21, with a recently
completed garden designed by
Jacques and Peter Wirtz who
designed the gardens at Alnwick
Castle, and also a Richard Long
Sculpture. Terraced lawns with
specimen and ornamental trees,
panoramic views to the Chilterns.
Naturalised bulbs, mirror-image
herbaceous borders, impressive
topiary incl box and yew sundial.
& ✗

Well stocked lodge greenhouse . . .

3 AYLESBURY GARDENS
HP21 7LR. *¾ m SE of Aylesbury
Centre. 4 town gardens off A413.*
Home-made teas at 2 Spenser Road.
Combined adm £4, chd free. Sun 6
July (1-6).
☕

NEW 16 MILTON ROAD
Mr & Mrs R King
Established town garden with a
variety of plants, shrubs and trees.
Grasses and fern area and a
mature wildlife pond.
✗

2 SPENSER ROAD
Mr & Mrs G A Brown
Tranquil cottage style garden with
many ornamental trees raised
from seed. Victorian greenhouse
with original features containing a
collection of pelargoniums and
tender plants.
✗ ✿

90 WALTON WAY
Mr & Mrs R Lewis-Smith
Established garden with wide
variety of unusual hardy and
tender perennials. Wildlife pond
and larger pond with koi carp.
Also features utilising an old air
raid shelter. Allotment area
containing large collection of
perennials.
& ✗ ✿

7 WESTMINSTER DRIVE
Mr & Mrs B J Ferguson
Formal town garden with
interesting features incl mixed
borders, shrubs and annuals.
Pergola with hanging baskets,
also vegetable parterre and pond.
✗ ✿

4 BLOSSOMS
Cobblers Hill HP16 9PW. Dr & Mrs F
Hytten, 01494 863140. *2½ m NW of
Great Missenden. By Rignall Rd,
signed Butler's Cross, to Kings Lane
1½ m on R, then to top of Cobblers
Hill. Turn R at yellow stone marker &
after 50yds turn R again at stone,
marked Blossoms.* Home-made teas.
Adm £3, chd free. Visitors welcome
by appt, no coach access.
4 acres began as hill-top fields, plus 1-
acre beechwood. Lawns, old apple
orchard, small lake, water, troughs,
scree and patio gardens. Large areas
of bluebells, wild daffodils and other
spring bulbs. Large climbing roses,
flowering cherries and many other
interesting trees incl acers, eucalyptus
and willows. Foliage effects throughout
yr.
& ☕ ☎

5 BRADENHAM MANOR
HP14 4HF. The National Trust, 07989
390940, len.bernamont@national
trust.org.uk. *2½ m NW of High
Wycombe, 5m S of Princes
Risborough. On A4010, turn by Red
Lion Pub, car park signed on village
green.* Adm £3.50, chd free. Sun 8
June (1-4.30).
Unique opportunity to see the ongoing restoration of the C17 gardens,
with views of the village and
countryside. Reinstated victorian
summer border, yew hedges, parterre
and wilderness at various stages of
restoration. Guided tour at 2pm.
Refreshments on village green at
cricket pavilion. Gravel & cobble paths,
steep slopes.
&

6 NEW CEDAR HOUSE
Bacombe Lane, Wendover
HP22 6EQ. Sarah Nicholson,
01296 622131. *5m SE Aylesbury.
From Gt Missenden take A413 into
Wendover. Take 1st L before row
of cottages, house at top.* Adm
£3.50, chd free. Visitors
welcome by appt, May-Sept for
groups 10+, no coaches, parking
for 10 cars only.
Chalk garden with beautiful views.
Lawn leads to new swimming
pond with aquatic plants. Shaped
borders contain a great variety of
perennial plants and shrubs. In
summer, colour co-ordinated half
hardy plants in pots, well stocked
lodge greenhouse. Steep grass
slope.
& ✗ ☎

7 CHEDDINGTON GARDENS

LU7 0RQ. *11m E of Aylesbury, 7m S of Leighton Buzzard. Turn off B489 at Pitstone. Turn off B488 at Cheddington stn, turn off Cheddington/Long Marston rd.* Home-made teas at Methodist Chapel on the green. **Combined adm £4, chd free (share to Cheddington Chapel & Church). Sun 22 June (2-6).**
Long village with green. Maps for visitors.

GENERALS YARD
Trefor Hamer
Formerly stables to the manor house and home to a horse called General. The gardens which were landscaped from sloping fields provide an eclectic mix of herbaceous borders, quiet corners and cameos of the English countryside with stunning views.

THE OLD POST OFFICE
Alan & Wendy Tipple
Cottage-style garden, softly planted with lavender, roses, clematis, herbaceous borders, shaded area and a small pond. Interesting low maintenance gravel garden to front.

ROSE COTTAGE
Mrs Margery Jones
$1/2$ -acre cottage garden filled with small rooms with max use of space. A balance of evergreens and deciduous resulting in a garden for all seasons, incl a late border with herbs, vegetable parterre and wildlife pond. Gravel paths.

21 STATION ROAD
Mr & Mrs P Jay
$1/2$ -acre informal garden with wild flower and wildlife conservation area, herbaceous and shrub borders, trees, herbs and kitchen garden.

WOODSTOCK COTTAGE
Mr & Mrs D Bradford
Front garden laid to gravel with assorted shrubs. Back courtyard and patio with small fountain at base of ancient elder tree.

8 CHESHAM BOIS HOUSE
85 Bois Lane, Chesham Bois HP6 6DF. Julia Plaistowe, 01494 726476, julia.plaistowe@yahoo.co.uk, www.cheshamboishouse.co.uk. *1m N of Amersham-on-the-Hill. From Amersham-on-the-Hill follow Sycamore Rd, over double mini roundabout, which turns into Bois Lane. Past village shops, house is $1/2$ m on L. Parking in road or on R at school & at scout hut.* Home-made teas. **Adm £3, chd free. Suns 30 Mar; 11 May (2-5.30); 6 July (2-6). Visitors also welcome by appt.**
Up a drive of mostly old lime trees, a late Georgian house (not open) surrounded by 3-acre garden of yr-round interest. Walled garden, small ornamental canal and rill with gazebo, lovely herbaceous borders with some tender and unusual plants, clipped trees and wide lawns. Winding walks through old orchard and over ancient bowling green. In spring, fine display of primroses, daffodils and hellebores. Featured on CH4 'Time Team Dig'. Gravel drive to front.

> A balance of evergreens and deciduous resulting in a garden for all seasons . . .

9 100 CHURCH GREEN ROAD
Bletchley MK3 6BY. Rosemary & Gordon Farr, 01908 379289, rosemary.farr@virgin.net. *13m E of Buckingham, 11m N of Leighton Buzzard. Off A421. Turn into Church Green Rd, take L fork. House is half way down.* Home-made teas. **Adm £2.50, chd free (share to Willen Hospice). Visitors welcome by appt in June & July.**
Established garden packed full of plants, interest and ideas. Innovative use of a very long narrow site that has been divided into rooms. Patio area, several water features, mixed herbaceous and shrub borders, fern collection and wildlife area. Milton Keynes Garden of the Year, winner Large Garden.

10 ◆ CLAYDON HOUSE
Middle Claydon MK18 2EX. Sir Edmund & Lady Verney, 01296 730252, www.claydonestate.co.uk. *4m S of Buckingham. Signed, nr village, adjacent to church.* **Adm £3.50, chd free. Sat to Wed, Apr-Oct (12-5). For NGS: Sun 7 Sept (2-5).**
Large country house garden under gradual redevelopment and redesign. Herbaceous borders, mixed plantings, shrubs, annuals and tender perennials. 2-acre Victorian kitchen garden planted with vegetables and flowers and adjacent walled flower garden with large pond, borders, and a restored Victorian glasshouse. Home grown vegetables, jams & chutneys for sale. Featured in 'Garden News', 'Kitchen Garden', and local press.

11 ◆ CLIVEDEN
Taplow SL6 0JA. The National Trust, 01628 605069, cliveden@nationaltrust.org.uk. *2m N of Taplow. Leave M4 at J7 or M40 at J4 & follow brown tourism signs.* **Adm £7.50, chd £3.70. For NGS: Sats 19 July (2-6); 20 Sept (11-6).**
Separate gardens within extensive grounds first laid out in C18. Water garden, secret garden, topiary, herbaceous borders, woodland walks and views of R Thames. Timber steps lead down yew tree walk to river. Guided garden tours.

12 ◆ COWPER & NEWTON MUSEUM GARDENS
Market Place, Olney MK46 4AJ. Mrs E Knight, 01234 711516. *5m N of Newport Pagnell. 12m S of Wellingborough. On A509. Please park on Market Place, Cattle Market Car Park or in High Street.* **Adm £2, chd free, concessions £1.50. Tues to Sat, 1 Mar to 23 Dec (10.30-4.30). For NGS: Sat 14, Sun 15 June (10.30-4.30).**
Restored walled flower garden with plants pre 1800, many mentioned by C18 poet, William Cowper, who said of himself 'Gardening was, of all employments, that in which I succeeded best'. Summerhouse garden in Victorian kitchen style with organic, new and old vegetables. Herb and medicinal plant borders in memory of the garden's original use by an apothecary.

13 NEW CRAIGLEA HOUSE

Austenwood Lane, Gerrards Cross SL9 9DA. Jeff & Sue Medlock, 01753 884852, jeffmedlock@hotmail.com. *6m SE Amersham. From Gerrards Cross take B416 towards Amersham. Take L fork after 1/2 m into Austenwood Lane, garden 1/3 m. Park at St Joseph's Church or Priory Road.* Cream teas. **Adm £4, chd free. Sun 15 June (2-5). Visitors also welcome by appt, Jun & July, groups 10+.**
1 acre landscaped to reflect the Edwardian house. Formal white garden bordered by pleached hornbeam and trellis with central fountain. Lawns edged by herbaceous and mixed borders, separated from rose garden by a pergola underplanted with lavender. Less formal area with wildlife pond, vegetables and beds of mixed planting.

14 CUBLINGTON GARDENS

LU7 0LQ. *5m SE Winslow, 5m NE Aylesbury. From Aylesbury take A413 Buckingham Rd. After 4m, at Whitchurch, turn R to Cublington.* Light refreshments & teas at The Old Rectory. **Combined adm £4, chd free. Sun 1 June (2-6).**

LARKSPUR HOUSE

Wing Road. Mr & Mrs S I Jenkins
S-facing family garden planted in 1996 to create a mix of moods and style, eclectic planting suggests a Mediterranean patio, moving to a tropical shade garden then to a cottage garden. Small kitchen garden.

THE OLD RECTORY

High Street. Mr & Mrs J Naylor
2-acre country garden with herbaceous border, rose beds, shrubs and mature trees, vegetables, ponds and climbing plants.

15 DINTON GARDENS

HP17 8UN. *4m SW Aylesbury, 4m NE Thame. 1/4 m off A418. Park in parish field, signed.* Home-made teas in village hall. **Combined adm £5, chd free. Sun 22 June (2-6).**
8 varied gardens in picturesque secluded village with many pretty thatched whitewashed cottages and Chiltern views. Conservation area. Lovely C11/12 G1 Norman church with outstanding S doorway. Village maps given to all visitors. Village used for TV 'sets'.

FRANCKLINS COTTAGE

Mr & Mrs S L Gooch
1/3 -acre garden surrounding C17 thatched cottage (not open). Courtyard, organic vegetable plot, wildlife pond.

GRAPEVINE COTTAGE

Anne & Mark Seckington
Very small spontaneous cottage garden with informal flower beds, herb garden, new water feature, terracotta patio and pots galore.

GREENDALE

S A Eaton
Small, colourful and informal. Clematis and rose covered pergola, small pond, shrubs giving yr-round shape and form. Benches for quiet contemplation.

HERMIT'S COTTAGE

Mr & Mrs M Usherwood
Nr green at Westlington, 3/4 -acre garden surrounding old thatched cottage (not open). Mature trees in open front and walled rear gardens, walled kitchen garden, mixed borders with open and shaded areas. Re-landscaped natural pond with bog garden.

ORCHARD COTTAGE

Harry & Barbara Bingham
Sculpted lawns, patios, pergola, arbour and fish pond. Wide variety of shrubs and trees, densely planted. Mixed borders giving perfume, interest and colour all yr.

STONEMEAD

Andrew & Helen Wild
1/3 -acre, totally organic, plot in the heart of the village. Small front and larger rear garden with views over open countryside. Informal planting incl drought tolerant plants. Small pond and vegetable garden.

WESTLINGTON FARM

Shaun & Catherine Brogan
400 yr-old thatched farmhouse with wildlife friendly garden surrounded by walls and hedges. Large trees, an old orchard, vegetable garden, 'secret' white garden, pond, trellises and flower beds. Gravel drive, wheelchair may need a 'push'.

WILLOW COTTAGE

Philip & Jennifer Rimell
Surrounded by fields from which it was developed, the garden is a series of diverse effects with established borders incl round herbaceous, rose and delphinium. Fruit and vegetable garden. 2 small slopes.

16 DORNEYWOOD GARDEN

Burnham SL1 8PY. The National Trust, 01628 665361, secretary. dorneywood@btopenworld.com. *1m E of Taplow, 5m S of Beaconsfield. From Burnham village take Dropmore Rd, at end of 30mph limit take R fork into Dorneywood Rd. Entrance is 1m on R. From M40 J2, take A355 to Slough then 1st R to Burnham, 2m then 2nd L after Jolly Woodman, signed Dorneywood Rd. Dorneywood is about 1m on L.* **Adm £4, chd under 5 free, NT members £3. Admission only by written application, or e-mail (to the Secretary) 2 weeks in advance for all dates and private visits. Weds 14, 28 May; Wed 2, Sat 26 July (2-5). Visitors also welcome by appt.**
7-acre country house garden on several levels with herbaceous borders, greenhouses, rose, cottage and kitchen gardens, lily pond and conservatory. Gravel paths.

Benches for quiet contemplation . . .

⑰ FIELDING HOUSE

31 High Street, Whitchurch HP22 4JA. Mrs Anne Fraser. *4m N of Aylesbury, 4m S of Winslow. On A413.* Light refreshments & teas. **Combined with The Old School, Oving, Adm £2.50, chd free. Sun 2 Mar (12-4).** Designed and planted by the present owner, this long narrow free draining partly sloping garden is exposed to the full force of SW winds and is dominated by a large old walnut tree. Gravel beds, mixed shrub and herbaceous borders, with a large collection of hellebores, burgeoning collection of snowdrops, erythronium, species tulips and other spring bulbs. Far reaching views over the vale.

&. ❀ ☕

Magnificent copper beech and magnolia reaching the rooftop . . .

⑱ FRESSINGWOOD

Hare Lane, Little Kingshill HP16 0EF. Mr & Mrs J & M Bateson. *1m S of Gt Missenden, 4m W of Amersham. From A413 Amersham to Aylesbury rd, turn L at Chiltern Hospital, signed Gt & Little Kingshill. Take 1st L into Nags Head Lane. Turn R under railway bridge & 1st L into New Rd. At top, turn into Hare Lane, 1st house on R.* Home-made teas. **Adm £2.50, chd free. Sun 18 May (2-6).** Thoughtfully designed garden with yr-round colour. Shrubbery with ferns, grasses and hellebores, small formal garden, herb garden, pergolas with wisteria, roses and clematis, topiary and landscaped terrace. Formal lily pond and bonsai collection. Many interesting features.

✕ ❀ ☕

⑲ GIPSY HOUSE

Whitefield Lane, Gt Missenden HP16 0BP. Mrs Felicity Dahl. *5m NW Amersham. Take A413 to Gt Missenden. From High St turn into Whitefield Lane, and under railway bridge. Small Georgian house on R. Park in field opp house.* Home-made teas. **Combined with The Plant Specialist, Adm £4, chd free. Wed 23 Apr; Thur 15 May; Wed 11 June; Thur 17 July (2-5).**

Home of the late Roald Dahl. York stone terrace, pleached lime walk to writing hut bordered with hosta, hellebore and allium. Sunken garden with water feature, sundial garden with topiary oaks, borders planted with herbaceous perennials and assorted roses in themed colours. Small walled vegetable garden with terraced beds, espalier fruits, herbs and greenhouse with vine, peaches and nectarines. Re-planted front garden with yews, roses and perennials. Wild-flower meadow.

✕ ☕

⑳ GRANGE DRIVE WOOBURN

Wooburn Green HP10 0QD. *On A4094, 2m SW of A40, between Bourne End & Wooburn. From the church, heading to Maidenhead, Grange Drive is on the L.* Home-made teas at Magnolia House. **Combined adm £3.50, chd free. Sun 22 June (2-5).** Private tree-lined drive which forms the entrance to a country house.

☕

MAGNOLIA HOUSE
Alan & Elaine Ford
1/2 acre containing 24 mature trees incl magnificent copper beech and magnolia reaching the rooftop. Small cactus bed, ferns, stream leading to pond overlooked by acers, small vegetable garden and greenhouses.

✕ ❀

THE SHADES
Pauline & Maurice Kirkpatrick
Drive approached through mature trees, area of shade-loving plants, beds of shrubs, roses and herbaceous plants. Rear garden with working well surrounded by shrubs, conifers and acers. Original green slate water features and scree garden with alpine plants.

✕ ❀

㉑ GREENWAYS

Whiteleaf HP27 0LY. Mr & Mrs K Muras. *3m E Princes Risborough. 4m NW Gt Missenden. From A4010 take Gt Missenden turn, 1st R into Upper Icknield Way, 1/2 m 1st L, follow signs.* Cream teas. **Adm £2.50, chd free. Wed 25, Thur 26 June (2-6).** Pretty cottage garden on thin chalk surrounding a C16 thatched cottage with climbing roses, delphiniums and lavender hedges. Stunning views across the Chilterns in an area of outstanding natural beauty.

✕ ❀ ☕

㉒ HALL BARN

Windsor End, Beaconsfield HP9 2SG. The Hon Mrs Farncombe. *1/2 m S of Beaconsfield. Lodge gate 300yds S of St Mary and All Saints' Church in Old Town centre.* **Adm £3, chd free. Visitors welcome by appt, apply in writing to the owner as above.** Historical landscaped garden laid out between 1680-1730 for the poet Edmund Waller and his descendants. Features 300-yr-old 'cloud formation' yew hedges, formal lake and vistas ending with classical buildings and statues. Wooded walks around the grove offer respite from the heat on sunny days. One of the original gardens opening in 1927 for the NGS. Open-air theatre in the garden, performing Shakespeare, 2 weeks June.

&. ☎

㉓ HIGHER DENHAM GARDENS

Higher Denham UB9 5EA. *6m E of Beaconsfield. From A40 take A412. 1/4 m from the junction turn L at part-time traffic lights into Old Rectory Lane. 1m on turn into Lower Rd signed Higher Denham.* Cream teas at community hall. **Combined adm £4, chd free (share to Higher Denham Community Association). Sun 1 June (12-5).** Small semi-rural village nestling in the delightful Misbourne Valley with its idyllic chalk stream.

☕

DRUMALEE
7 Lower Road. Moira & Len Smith
Small garden backing onto the R Misbourne with lawn and gravel, a variety of shrubs, climbers, perennials and annuals.

19 LOWER ROAD
Helene White
Flower arranger's garden backing onto stream. Shrubs, perennials and bulbs planted to create a garden with all-yr interest and plenty of cutting material for arrangements.

✕

19 MIDDLE ROAD
Sonia Harris. *From Lower Rd turn into Middle Cresent, becomes Middle Rd*
Small garden with terrace looking down onto a lawn and borders of shrubs, climbers, vegetables and fruit bushes. Terrace leading to ornamental pond has many pots.

WIND IN THE WILLOWS
Ron James
3-acre wildlife-friendly garden comprising informal, woodland and wild areas separated by streams. Over 300 shrubs and trees, many variegated or uncommon, marginal and bog plantings incl a collection of 80 hostas.

 ♿ ✕

24 19 HIGHFIELD ROAD
Winslow MK18 3DU. Mrs Gwladys Tonge, 18002 01296 713489 (type talk relay), mail@gwladystonge.co.uk. *5m SE of Buckingham, 9m N of Aylesbury. On A413 Winslow to Buckingham, take last turning L, 200yds after garage, 50yds before turning to Great Horwood.* **Adm £4 inc tea & homemade cake, chd free. Visitors welcome by appt, snowdrop time to autumn.**
Very small garden with extensive range of attractive hardy plants providing beauty and excitement for each season. Trees, shrubs, rose pergola, clematis and other climbers, bulbs, incl interesting snowdrop collection, ferns, grasses, evergreen and herbaceous perennials demonstrate ingenious use of space and grow happily together. Experimenting with growing fruit and vegetables in containers.

✕ ✿ ☕ ☎

25 HILL HOUSE
Castle Street, Buckingham MK18 1BS. Mr & Mrs P Thorogood, 07860 714758, llt@pjt.powernet.co.uk. *Town centre. On L of vehicle entrance to Parish Church (spire very visible). Castle St clearly marked as you face Old Town Hall at central town roundabout.* Teas. **Adm £2.50, chd free. Sun 29 June (12-6). Visitors also welcome by appt, May-Sept.**
1/3 -acre town garden on old castle walls, aiming at ease of maintenance, yr-round interest and colour. Limited wheelchair access, some steps & slope.

♿ ✕ ☕ ☎

26 HILLESDEN HOUSE
Church End, Hillesden MK18 4DB. Mr & Mrs R M Faccenda, 01296 730451, suefaccenda@aol.com. *3m S of Buckingham. Next to church in Hillesden.* Home-made teas. **Adm £3.50, chd free. Sun 29 June (2-5). Visitors also welcome by appt in June & July, groups 10+.**
By superb perpendicular church

'Cathedral in the Fields'. Lawns, shrubberies, rose, alpine and foliage gardens. Clipped hedges, conservatory. Surrounded by park with red deer. Large lakes with ornamental duck and carp. Large wild flower areas. Views over countryside and wonderful walks. Many birds and other wildlife.

♿ ✕ ✿ ☕ ☎

> Perennials demonstrate ingenious use of space and grow happily together . . .

27 HOMELANDS
Springs Lane, Ellesborough HP17 0XD. Jean & Tony Young, 01296 622306. *6m SE of Aylesbury, 4m NE of Princes Risborough. On B4010, 1¹/2 m W of Wendover. Springs Lane is between the Village Hall at Butlers Cross and St. Peter and St. Paul's Church. Narrow lane, uneven surface.* Home-made teas. **Adm £3, chd free. Thurs 12 June; 14 Aug (2-5). Evening Opening wine, Fri 11 July (6-9). Visitors also welcome by appt, June to Sept.**
3/4 -acre garden on chalk with adjoining wild flower meadow. Wildlife pond, rockery, bog garden, water features. Gazebo and pergola walk, wide range of mixed shrub and herbaceous borders. Hidden corners, sitting out areas, gravel bed and vegetable plot.

♿ ☕ ☎

28 ◆ HUGHENDEN MANOR
High Wycombe HP14 4LA. The National Trust, 01494 755573, www.nationaltrust.org.uk. *1¹/2 m N of High Wycombe. On W side of Gt Missenden Rd A4128, past church, into NT woodland car-park.* **House and Garden adm £7, chd £3.50, Garden only adm £2.90, chd £2.10. 1 Mar to 31 Oct, Wed to Sun. For NGS: Sun 8 June (11-5).**
Mary Anne Disraeli's colour schemes inspire spring and summer bedding in formal parterre. Unusual conifers, planted from photographs taken at time of Disraeli's death. Old English apple orchard with picnic area. Beech woodland walks. Mediterranean border. The walled garden under re-

development will be open too. Walled garden open with tours. Meet the Gardener in the formal gardens. Tracker packs to help children explore. Access to main features but slopes require help.

♿ ✕ ✿ ☕

29 3 JUBILEE COTTAGES
Verney Junction MK18 2JZ. Robert & Jane O'Connell. *2¹/2 m SW of Winslow. Turn in High Street by Windmill Vets and follow rd out of Winslow.* Home-made teas. **Adm £2.50, chd free. Sun 25 ; Sat 31 May; (2-6). Evening Opening, wine, Fri 27 June (6-9).**
Established but continually evolving mid-terrace garden. Ornamental garden divided into rooms linked by a boardwalk. Large vegetable garden, greenhouses, small orchard with summerhouse and further borders.

✕ ✿ ☕

30 2 KINGSWOOD COTTAGES
Swan Lane, The Lee HP16 9NU. Jon & Trish Swain, 01494 837752, swaino@talk21.com. *3m SE Wendover, 3m N of Gt Missenden. From A413, Gt Missenden to Wendover, take 3rd R up Rocky Lane. After 2m turn L at 1st X-rds. 200yds turn L down unmade road, 1st drive on R.* Teas, wine if required. **Adm £3, chd free. Visitors welcome by appt in May & June, groups 10+.**
2-acre garden on top of the Chiltern Hills in and area of natural beauty surrounded by meadows. Winding paths weave through the garden leading to sculptures and hidden surprises. Slate herb garden, sundial table, wildlife pond, beehives, chickens and possibly rare breed pigs.

✕ ☕ ☎

31 LONG CRENDON SPRING GARDENS
HP18 9AN. *2m N of Thame. On B4011 Thame-Bicester rd.* Teas at Church House. **Combined adm £4, chd free (share to (10%) between Scout Assoc & Day Centre). Sun 13 Apr (2-6).**
Attractive large village with many old and listed buildings.

☕

BAKER'S CLOSE
Mr & Mrs Peter Vaines
2 acres on SW slope. Partly walled with courtyard, terraced lawns, rockery with pond, roses, shrubs, herbaceous plantings and wild area.

BARRY'S CLOSE
Mr & Mrs Richard Salmon
2-acre sloping garden with interesting collection of trees and shrubs. Herbaceous border, spring-fed pools and water garden.

MANOR HOUSE
Mr & Mrs West
4-acre garden, lawns sweep down to 2 ornamental lakes each with small island, walk along lower lake with many varieties of willow. Large herbaceous borders, fine views towards Chilterns. Partial wheelchair access.

THE OLD CROWN
Mr & Mrs R H Bradbury
1$^1/_4$ -acre on SW slope. More than 250 assorted roses, colourful annual and perennial plants in numerous beds, incl 50-60 clematis, flowering shrubs, assorted colourful pots and containers, statues, 2 sizable vegetable plots. Great variety and very many spring bulbs.

32 LONG CRENDON SUMMER GARDENS
HP18 9AN. *2m N of Thame. On Thame/Bicester rd B4011.* Home-made teas at Church House & Croft House. **Combined adm £5, chd free (share to (10%) between Scout Assoc & Day Centre). Sun 8 June (2-6).**
Attractive large village with many old/listed buildings. Maps available for all visitors. Flower Festival at St Mary's Church.

BRADDENS YARD
Mr & Mrs P Simpson
$^1/_2$ -acre walled garden largely created over past 15yrs. Collection of roses, herbaceous and climbing plants. Arched walk with clematis, honeysuckle and roses, pond and small bothy garden.

CROFT HOUSE
**Cdr & Mrs Peter Everett, 01844 208451,
peverett@nildram.co.uk.
Visitors also welcome by appt.**
$^1/_2$ -acre walled garden with a variety of plants and shrubs, some unusual and of interest to flower arrangers. Water

feature, greenhouse and conservatory.

KETCHMORE HOUSE
Mr & Mrs C Plumb
Very attractive wildlife friendly cottage garden laid out in 3 sections; courtyard with raised pond, entertaining area with bog garden and lawn and vegetable area. Great variety of plants and shrubs.

MANOR HOUSE
Mr & Mrs N West
4-acre garden, lawns sweep down to 2 ornamental lakes, each with small island, walk along lower lake with many varieties of willow. Large herbaceous borders, fine views towards Chilterns. Partial wheelchair access.

MULBERRY HOUSE
Mr & Mrs C Weston
1-acre, old vicarage garden, recently restored. Set amongst mature trees, now incl formal knot garden, woodland walk, pond, vegetable garden, numerous beds and lawns, a notable monkey puzzle tree and a mulberry tree.

THE OLD CROWN
Mr & Mrs R H Bradbury
1$^1/_4$ acre on SW slope. More than 250 assorted roses, colourful annual and perennial plants in numerous beds, incl 50-60 clematis, flowering shrubs, assorted colourful pots and containers, statues, 2 sizeable vegetable plots. Great variety and very many spring bulbs.

NEW TOMPSONS FARM
Mr D Tye
Large woodland garden with mature trees and lawns sweeping down to an ornamental lake.

33 LORDS WOOD
Frieth Road, Marlow Common SL7 2QS. Mr & Mrs Messum. *1$^1/_2$ m NW Marlow. Off A4155, turn at Platts Garage into Oxford Rd, towards Frieth, 1$^1/_2$ m. Garden is 100yds past Marlow Common turn, on L.* Home-made teas. **Adm £4, chd free (share to NSPCC). Thurs 12 June; 4 Sept (11-5).**
Family home to the Messums since 1976, Lords Wood boasts fantastic

views over the Chilterns. 5-acre garden, large orchard, woodland and meadow. Varied planting styles throughout, extensive borders, large water garden and rockery. This garden never stands still, with something new to enjoy on each visit. Gravel, steep slopes.

Courtyard with raised pond, entertaining area with bog garden . . .

34 THE MANOR HOUSE, BLEDLOW
Bledlow HP27 9PB. The Lord & Lady Carrington. *9m NW of High Wycombe, 3m SW of Princes Risborough. $^1/_2$ m off B4009 in middle of Bledlow village.* Teas (May), Home made teas (Jun). **Adm £5, chd free. Suns 4 May; 15 June (2-6).** Visitors also welcome by appt, groups 10+, incl coaches, by written application only to 32a Ovington Street, London SW3 1LR.
Paved garden, parterres, shrub borders, old roses and walled kitchen garden. Water garden with paths, bridges and walkways, fed by 14 chalk springs. Also 2 acres with sculptures and landscaped planting. Church open. No wheelchair access to Lyde Garden.

35 THE MANOR HOUSE, HAMBLEDEN
Hambleden RG9 6SG. Maria Carmela, Viscountess Hambleden. *3$^1/_2$ m NE Henley-on-Thames, 8m SW High Wycombe. 1m N of A4155.* **Adm £3.50, chd free. Sun 15 June (2-6).**
Informal garden, sweeping lawns, mature trees and an exceptional rose garden designed by Peter Beales with a profusion of old fashioned scented roses. Large terrace on the S side of the house takes you to a magnificent conservatory with stunning plants climbing 30ft.

36 **NEW** **MARYFIELD**
SL6 0EX. Jacqueline & Roger
Andrews. *1m S Cliveden, 1/2 m E
Maidenhead. From M4 J7 or M40
J4 follow signs for Taplow. House
on bend of High St.* Light
refreshments & teas. **Adm £3.50,
chd free (share to Thames Valley
Adventure Playground). Thur 22,
Fri 23 May (2-6).**
2-acres wrapped around our
Victorian home in the heart of
Taplow Village. New walled
vegetable and herb garden
bordered by fruit trees, over-looked
by a mature lime walk, extends into
herbaceous planting, mature yew
hedging, pond area, orchard and
Japanese inspired garden. Cake
sale.
✂ ❀ ☕

Difficult stony
soil, designed
with scenic
effect in mind
and interest
throughout
the year . . .

37 ◆ **NETHER WINCHENDON
HOUSE**
Nether Winchendon HP18 0DY. Mr
Robert Spencer Bernard, 01844
290101,
www.netherwinchendonhouse.com.
6m SW of Aylesbury, 6m from Thame.
**Adm £3, chd free. For NGS: Sun 22
June (2-5.30).**
5 acres of fine and rare trees and
shrubs, a variety of hedges,
herbaceous borders and naturalised
spring bulbs. Founder garden (1927)
Medieval and Tudor manor house (not
open) in picturesque village with
beautiful church. Unfenced river bank.
♿ ✂ ❀

38 **NORTH DOWN**
Dodds Lane, Chalfont St Giles
HP8 4EL. Merida Saunders, 01494
872928. *4m SE of Amersham, 4m NE
of Beaconsfield. Opp the green in
centre of village. At Crown Inn turn into*
*UpCorner, on to Silver Hill. At top of hill
fork R into Dodds Lane. N Down is 6th
opening on L. Limited parking in
Dodds Lane.* **Adm £3, chd free.
Visitors welcome by appt, May to
Oct, groups welcome, no coaches.**
3/4 -acre sloping N-facing
compartmentalised site with mature
trees. Difficult stony soil. Designed with
scenic effect in mind and interest
throughout the yr. Large grassed areas
with island beds of mixed perennials,
shrubs and some unusual plants.
Variety of rhododendrons, azaleas,
acers, 70+ clematis and other
climbers. Displays of sempervivum
varieties, alpines, grasses and ferns.
Small patio/water feature. Greenhouse.
Italianate front patio to owner's design.
✂ ❀ ☎

39 **THE OLD SCHOOL**
Church Lane, Oving HP22 4HL. Mr &
Mrs M Ryan. *Off A413, 1m W of
Whitchurch, between pub & church.*
Light refreshments & teas. **Combined
with Fielding House, Whitchurch
Adm £2.50, chd free. Sun 2 Mar
(12-4).**
Playground now a walled lawn backed
by herbaceous borders. Fine views
from old orchard planted with roses
and spring bulbs, enclosed patio with
collection of scented-leaf geraniums,
hellebore collection.
✂ ☕

40 **THE OLD SUN HOUSE**
Pednor HP5 2SZ. Mr & Mrs M
Sharpley. *3m E of Gt Missenden, 2m
W of Chesham. From Gt Missenden
take B485 to Chesham, 1st L & follow
signs approx 2m. From Chesham
Church St (B485) follow signs approx
11/2 m.* Home-made teas. **Adm £3,
chd free. Sun 25 May (2-6).**
5-acre garden, abundant with wildlife,
set on a Chiltern ridge giving superb
views. The garden is surrounded by
mature trees with inner plantings of
unusual trees and shrubs. Features incl
large ornamental pond with walkway,
vegetable and herb garden, interesting
woodland walk, white peafowl, guinea
fowl, pheasantry and chickens.
♿ ❀ ☕

41 ◆ **OLD THATCH**
Coldmoorholme Lane, Well End
SL8 5PS. Jacky & David Hawthorne,
01628 527518,
www.jackyhawthorne.co.uk. *3m E
Marlow, 1m W Bourne End. Off A4155.
Thatched house on L just before the
Spade Oak PH. Public car park 100yds*
on, towards the R Thames. **Adm £3,
chd £1. 24 May-25 Aug, Sat, Suns &
BH Mons.** For NGS: Sat 24 May (2-
5.30).
Listed thatched cottage (not open),
famous home of Enid Blyton and
source of many of her stories. 2 acres,
re-designed by Jacky Hawthorne in
2000, now contain beautiful palettes of
colour, stunning ornamental grasses
and wonderful design features.
Cottage garden, lavender terrace, rose
arbour, formal garden, water circle.
Teas in room claimed by EB to be Dick
Turpin's stable, containing secret
treasures. Featured in 'GGG*'.
♿ ✂ ❀ ☕

42 **THE OLD VICARAGE**
Thornborough Road, Padbury
MK18 2AH. Mr & Mrs H Morley-
Fletcher, 01280 813045,
belindamf@freenet.co.uk. *2m S of
Buckingham, 4m NW of Winslow. On
A413, signed in village.* Home-made
teas. **Adm £3, chd free. Sat 19, Sun
20 Apr (2-6). Visitors also welcome
by appt.**
21/2 acres on 3 levels, flowering
shrubs and trees. Vegetable garden,
pond and sunken garden, parterre
and millennium arch. Magnolias and
trilliums. Sunken garden can be
viewed from above by wheelchair
users.
♿ 🛌 ☕ ☎

43 **6 OLDFIELD CLOSE**
Little Chalfont HP6 6SU. Jolyon &
Phyllis Lea, 01494 762384. *3m E of
Amersham. Take A404 E through Little
Chalfont, 1st R after railway bridge, R
again into Oakington Ave.* **Adm
£2, chd free. Sun 13 Apr (2-5).
Visitors also welcome by appt.**
Mature 1/6 -acre garden of shrub
borders, peat beds, rock plants,
troughs and alpine house. Over 2,000
species and varieties of rare and
interesting plants, incl spring bulbs,
cyclamen and dwarf rhododendrons.
Wide range of plants for sale.
✂ ❀ ☕ ☎

44 **OVERSTROUD COTTAGE**
The Dell, Frith Hill, Gt Missenden
HP16 9QE. Mr & Mrs Jonathan
Brooke, 01494 862701,
susie@jandsbrooke.co.uk. *1/2 m E Gt
Missenden. Turn E off A413 at Gt
Missenden onto B485 Frith Hill to
Chesham rd. White Gothic cottage set
back in lay-by 100yds up hill on L.
Parking on R at church.* Cream teas at
Parish Church. **Adm £2.50, chd 50p.**

Suns 23 Mar; 20 Apr; 18 May (2-6). **Visitors also welcome by appt, Apr to June, groups 15+, £3.**
Artistic chalk garden on 2 levels. Collection of C17/C18 plants. Potager/herb garden, spring bulbs, hellebores, succulents, primulas, pulmonarias, geraniums, species/old fashioned roses and lily pond. Garden studio with painting exhibition. Cottage was once C17 fever house for Missenden Abbey.

45 11 THE PADDOCKS
Wendover HP22 6HE. Mr & Mrs E Rye. *5m from Aylesbury, on A413. At Wendover after approx ½ m, turn L at mini-roundabout into Wharf Rd. Entrance is 2nd on L. From Gt Missenden, turn L at Clock Tower, then R at next mini-roundabout.* **Adm £2, chd free. Sat 21, Sun 22 June; Sat 5 July (2-6). Evening Opening,** wine, Fri 27 June (5.30-8).
Small peaceful garden with mixed borders of colourful herbaceous perennials and a special show of David Austin roses and delphiniums. Cool hosta walk and tremendous variety of plants in a small area. White garden with peaceful arbour 'The Magic of Moonlight'. Many unusual plants.

PATCHWORK
See Hertfordshire.

46 ◆ THE PLANT SPECIALIST
Whitefield Lane, Gt Missenden HP16 0BH. Sean Walter, 01494 866650, www.theplantspecialist.co.uk. *5m NW Amersham. A413 to Gt Missenden. Whitefield Lane opp Missenden Abbey. Under railway bridge on the L.* **Combined with Gypsy House Adm £4, chd free. Apr to Oct, Wed to Sat (10-5) Sun (10-4). For NGS: Wed 23 Apr; Thurs 15 May; Wed 11 June; Thurs 17 July (2-5).**
Plant nursery with herbaceous perennials and grasses, container grown bulbs and half hardy perennials in attractive garden setting and display garden. Featured on 'Gardeners' World'. Gravel paths on gentle slope.

47 QUAINTON GARDENS
HP22 4BW. *7m NW of Aylesbury, 7m SW of Winslow. Nr Waddesdon turn off A41.* Light refreshments & teas at Thorngumbald. **Combined adm**

£2.50, chd free. Sun 24 Feb (12-4). Charming village with green and windmill.

CAPRICORNER
Mrs Davis
Small garden planted for yr-round interest with many scented plants, winter flowering shrubs and bulbs, small woodland glade with interesting trees.

THORNGUMBALD
13 Station Road. Jane Lydall
Small heavily planted cottage garden designed for yr-round interest and to please all the senses. Drifts of snowdrops, hellebores and crocus form carpet under clipped evergreens and shrubs. Partial wheelchair access.

NEW THE VINE
Upper Street. Mr & Mrs D A Campbell, 01296 655243, david@dacampbell.com. Visitors also welcome by appt anytime.
Lying at the foot of the Quainton Hills, a stream runs through the bog garden into a pond, many exotic plants particularly from the Himalayas and China. Winter flowering shrubs and spring bulbs.

RAGGED HALL
See Hertfordshire.

48 NEW RIVENDELL
13 The Leys. HP6 5NP. Janice & Mike Cross. *Off A416. From Amersham take A416 N towards Chesham. The Leys is on L ½ m after Boot & Slipper PH. Park at Beacon School, 100yds N.* Teas. **Adm £3, chd free. Suns 13 Apr; 8 June (2-5).**
S-facing garden featuring a series of different areas with wide variety of perennials, especially hellebores. Alpine bed, box-edged herbaceous beds, sedum and thyme path leading to rose and clematis arbour. Raised woodland bed under mature trees, bog garden, gravel area with grasses and pond, vegetable plot, developing topiary.

Many exotic plants from the Himalayas and China . . .

49 ◆ STOKE POGES MEMORIAL GARDENS
Church Lane. SL2 4NZ. South Bucks District Council, 01753 537619, graham.pattison@southbucks.gov.uk. *1m N of Slough, 1m S of Stoke Poges. From Stoke Poges, B416 towards Slough, R at Church Lane. From Slough, Stoke Poges Lane, leads into Church Lane. By St Giles Church.* **Adm £3.50, chd free, concessions £3. Normally open daily. For NGS: Sat 8 Mar; Sun 6 Apr; Wed 7 May (2-5).**
Unique 20-acre Grade II registered garden constructed 1934-9. Rock and water gardens, sunken colonnade, rose garden incl 500 individual gated gardens. Spring garden, bulbs, wisteria, rhododendrons. Recently completed £1m renovation. Guided tours, 2,3,4pm. Gravel paths.

50 ◆ STOWE LANDSCAPE GARDENS
MK18 5DQ. The National Trust, www.nationaltrust.org.uk/stowegardens. *3m NW of Buckingham. Via Stowe Ave. Follow brown NT signs.* **Adm £6.20, chd £3.15, Family (2+3) £15.50. For NGS: Sat 19 July (10.30-5.30).**
Fine Georgian landscape garden made up of valleys and vistas, narrow lakes and rivers. More than 30 temples and monuments designed by many of the leading architects of C18. Programme of restoration is ongoing with many temples having been conserved. Guided tours. Access guide available, some unsuitable areas.

SUMMERLAWN
See London.

51 TURN END
Townside, Haddenham HP17 8BG. Peter Aldington. *3m NE of Thame, 5m SW of Aylesbury. Turn off A418 to Haddenham. Turn at Rising Sun to Townside. Please park at a distance with consideration for neighbours.* Home-made teas. **Adm £3, chd £1. Mon 5 May (2-5.30).**

Architect's own post-war listed house (not open). Garden less than 1 acre, space used to create illusion of size. Series of enclosed gardens, sunken or raised, sunny or shady, each different yet harmonious, contrast with lawns, borders and glades. Spring bulbs, irises, old roses and climbers. Courtyard with fish pool. Some gravel paths & steps.

Large natural old pond with diving ducks . . .

TURWESTON MILL
See Northamptonshire.

VERSIONS FARM
See Northamptonshire.

52 TYTHROP PARK
Kingsey HP17 8LT. Nick & Chrissie Wheeler. *2m E of Thame, 4m NW of Princes Risborough. Via A4129, lodge gates just outside Kingsey.* Home-made teas. **Adm £4.50, chd free (share to St Nicholas' Church).** Sun 15 June (2-6).
7 acres, formal gardens with many fine trees and shrubs, intricate dwarf box parterre with fountains. Large walled garden with wide variety of fruit trees, soft fruits and vegetables, divided by rows of roses and flowers. Magnificent greenhouse containing Black Hamburgh and Muscat Hamburgh vines propagated from vine at Hampton Court 150yrs ago. Secluded water garden with attractive walks and old roses. Nut grove, wilderness area, arboretum.

53 WATERCROFT
Church Road, Penn HP10 8NX. Mr & Mrs Paul Hunnings, 01494 816535. *3m NW of Beaconsfield, 3m W of Amersham. On B474, 600yds on L past Holy Trinity Church.* Home-made teas. **Adm £4, chd free.** Visitors welcome by appt.
Mature 3-acre chalk and clay garden. Unusual spring bulbs and hellebores. Large weeping ash. Rose walk with 350 roses. Courtyard with summer pots and box topiary. Large natural old pond with diving ducks, newly extended and replanted. Italianate garden with 14yr-old yew hedges and fine view. Wild flower meadow with wild roses. Formal herb garden with culinary herbs, small vegetable garden with hebe hedge. Glasshouse with unusual pelargoniums.

54 WHITCHURCH GARDENS
HP22 4JS. *4m N of Aylesbury, 4m S of Winslow.* On A413. Home-made teas at Priory Court. **Combined adm £3.50, chd free.** Sun 27 Apr (2-6).
Large village with many thatched cottages in the quieter older parts, down small lanes. Maps provided.

PARK HOUSE BARN
John & Mary Amos
Very small walled garden, gravel area, raised beds with herbaceous plants, roses and clematis. Many pots and containers.

PRIORY COURT
52 High Street. Mr & Mrs Ian Durrell, 01296 641563, marion.durrell@btconnect.com. Visitors also welcome by appt, Mar to Nov, groups 10+, incl coaches.
Approx 2/3 -acre, split-level, all-season walled garden with bulbs, rose beds, shrubbery, herb bed, fruit cage and herbaceous borders. Water feature, decking

and summerhouse and lawns. Gravel path and crazy paving.

THATCHINGS
Mr & Mrs S Cole
Traditional cottage garden with informal flower beds, vegetable garden, pond area and meadow with fruit trees.

55 THE WHITE HOUSE
Village Road, Denham Village UB9 5BE. Mr & Mrs P G Courtenay-Luck. *3m NW of Uxbridge, 7m E of Beaconsfield. Signed from A40 or A412. Parking in village rd. The White House is in centre of village.* Cream teas. **Adm £4, chd free.** Suns 18 May; 3 Aug (2-5).
Well established 6-acre formal garden in picturesque setting. Mature trees and hedges, with R Misbourne meandering through lawns. Shrubberies, flower beds, rockery, rose garden and orchard. Large walled garden with Italian garden and developing laburnum walk. Herb garden, vegetable plot and Victorian greenhouses.

56 WHITEWALLS
Quarry Wood Road, Marlow SL7 1RE. Mr W H Williams, 01628 482573. *1/2 m S Marlow. From Marlow cross over bridge. 1st L, 3rd house on L, white garden wall.* **Adm £2.50, chd free.** Suns 20 Apr; 13 July; 7 Sept (2-5). Visitors also welcome by appt, incl coaches.
Thames-side garden approx 1/2 acre with spectacular view of weir. Large lily pond, interesting planting of trees, shrubs, herbaceous perennials and bedding, large conservatory.

WOODCHIPPINGS
See Northamptonshire.

Buckinghamshire County Volunteers

County Organiser
Maggie Bateson, Fressingwood, Hare Lane, Little Kingshill HP16 0EF, 01494 866265, jmbateson@btopenworld.com

County Treasurer
Trish Swain, 2 Kingswood Cottages, Swan Lane, The Lee, Great Missenden HP16 9NU, 01494 837752, swaino@talk21.com

Publicity
Sandra Wetherall, Holydyke House, Little Missenden, Amersham HP7 0RD, 01494 862264, sandra@robertjamespartnership.com

Assistant County Organisers
Rosemary Brown, 2 Spenser Road, Aylesbury HP21 7LR, 01296 429605, grahama.brown@virgin.net
Judy Hart, Kingswood House, The Lee, Great Missenden HP16 9NU, 01494 837328, judy.hart@virgin.net
Mhairi Sharpley, The Old Sun House, Pednor, Chesham HP5 2SZ, 01494 782870, mhairisharpley@btinternet.com

ngs gardens open
for charity

Big leaves, giant grasses,
ferns, meat-eaters and
spiky things all come
together evoking a strange
and faraway land . . .

23 Woodville Road, London

CAMBRIDGESHIRE

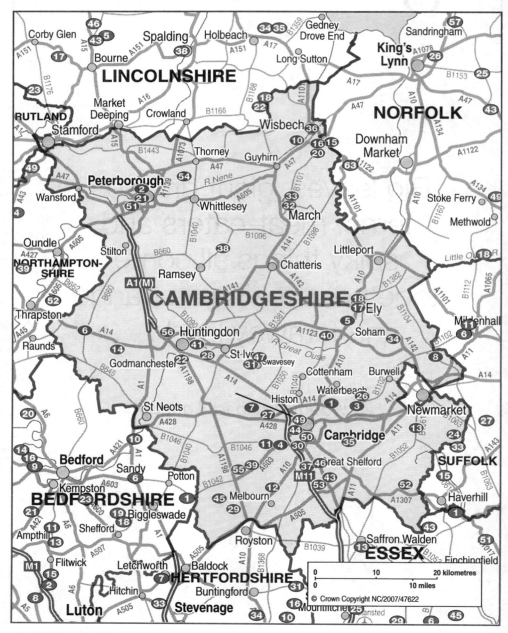

© Crown Copyright NC/2007/47622

Opening Dates

March

SUNDAY 16
- **20** Florence House

SUNDAY 23
- **34** Netherhall Manor

SUNDAY 30
- **8** Chippenham Park
- **49** Trinity Hall - Wychfield
- **54** Willow Holt

April

SUNDAY 6
- **4** Barton Gardens
- **24** Kirtling Tower
- **48** Trinity College, Fellows' Garden

SUNDAY 13
- **24** Kirtling Tower

SUNDAY 27
- **54** Willow Holt

May

SUNDAY 4
- **34** Netherhall Manor
- **50** Upwater Lodge

MONDAY 5
- **17** Ely Gardens 1
- **50** Upwater Lodge

SUNDAY 11
- **2** Almora
- **12** Docwra's Manor
- **25** Leckhampton

SUNDAY 18
- **4** Barton Gardens
- **20** Florence House

SUNDAY 25
- **10** Clearview
- **22** Island Hall
- **54** Willow Holt

June

SUNDAY 1
- **14** Easton Gardens
- **18** Ely Gardens II
- **37** Priesthouse
- **46** Stapleford Gardens

SATURDAY 7
- **15** Elm & Walsoken

SUNDAY 8
- **15** Elm & Walsoken
- **16** Elm House
- **26** Lode Gardens
- **51** The Village, Orton Longueville

SATURDAY 14
- **39** Rectory Farm House

SUNDAY 15
- **6** Catworth, Molesworth & Brington Gardens
- **30** The Mill House, Grantchester
- **39** Rectory Farm House
- **53** Whittlesford Gardens

WEDNESDAY 18
- **44** 4 Selwyn Gardens (Evening)

THURSDAY 19
- **44** 4 Selwyn Gardens (Evening)

SUNDAY 22
- **1** 15 Abbots Way
- **2** Almora
- **3** Anglesey Abbey, Gardens & Lode Mill
- **8** Chippenham Park
- **41** River View
- **43** Sawston Gardens

SUNDAY 29
- **10** Clearview
- **11** Comberton Gardens
- **19** Emmanuel College Garden & Fellows' Garden
- **31** 5 Moat Way
- **47** Sycamore Farm
- **54** Willow Holt
- **56** Wytchwood

July

SUNDAY 6
- **9** Clare College Fellows' Garden
- **26** Lode Gardens

SUNDAY 13
- **23** King's College Fellows' Garden
- **26** Lode Gardens
- **27** Madingley Hall
- **38** Ramsey Forty Foot

WEDNESDAY 16
- **55** Wimpole Hall

SATURDAY 19
- **36** Peckover House

SUNDAY 27
- **54** Willow Holt

August

SUNDAY 3
- **34** Netherhall Manor

SUNDAY 10
- **34** Netherhall Manor

SUNDAY 17
- **5** Breakaway

SUNDAY 24
- **3** Anglesey Abbey, Gardens & Lode Mill

SUNDAY 31
- **54** Willow Holt

September

SUNDAY 21
- **20** Florence House

SUNDAY 28
- **54** Willow Holt

October

SUNDAY 12
- **8** Chippenham Park

SUNDAY 26
- **54** Willow Holt

February 2009

SUNDAY 1
- **30** The Mill House, Grantchester

Gardens open to the public

- **3** Anglesey Abbey, Gardens & Lode Mill
- **12** Docwra's Manor
- **28** The Manor
- **36** Peckover House
- **55** Wimpole Hall

By appointment only

- **7** Childerley Hall
- **13** Dullingham House
- **21** 39 Foster Road
- **29** Mill House, Bassingbourn
- **32** Mosspaul
- **33** 88 Nene Parade
- **35** The Old House
- **40** Redlands
- **45** South Farm & Brook Cottage
- **52** Weaver's Cottage

Also open by appointment

- **6** The Poplars, Catworth, Molesworth & Brington Gardens
- **10** Clearview
- **11** Greystones, Comberton Gardens
- **18** 12 Chapel Street, Ely Gardens II
- **20** Florence House
- **22** Island Hall
- **26** Carpenters End, Lode Gardens
- **26** 21 Lode Road, Lode Gardens
- **26** Wild Rose Cottage, Lode Gardens
- **38** First Cottage, Ramsey Forty Foot
- **18** Rosewell House, Ely Gardens II
- **44** 4 Selwyn Gardens
- **47** Sycamore Farm
- **54** Willow Holt
- **56** Wytchwood

The Gardens

❶ 15 ABBOTS WAY
Horningsea CB25 9JN. Sally & Don Edwards. *4m NE of Cambridge. 1/2 m off A14. No access from Abbots Way. Follow signs in Horningsea to garden & car park*. Home-made teas. **Adm £2.50, chd free. Sun 22 June (2-5).** 1 1/4 -acre garden with interesting plants and colour, pergola, clematis, roses and natural pond. Overlooking R Cam and water meadows.

❷ NEW ALMORA
91 Thorpe Road, Peterborough PE3 6JQ. Dr Robert Stebbings & Sheila Stebbings. *1/2 m W of railway stn. W of Thorpe Lodge Hotel. 2nd house (red brick)*. **Adm £2.50, chd free. Sun 11 May; Sun 22 June (10-4).**
Small town garden 11m x 23m with pond, rockery and mix of native and exotic species. Created in 2004/5 with 120yr old Bramley and first project to replace a Leylandii hedge with native evergreens by inter-planting. Over 30 species of ferns in shade, all planned to attract native wildlife. Art exhibit will show how the garden was created.

❸ ◆ ANGLESEY ABBEY, GARDENS & LODE MILL
Cambridge CB25 9EJ. The National Trust, 01223 810080, www.nationaltrust.org.uk. *6m NE of Cambridge. From A14 turn N on to B1102 through Stow-cum-Quy.* **House and Garden £9.25, chd £4.65, Garden only £5.50, chd £2.75. For opening dates & times, please tel or see website. For NGS: Suns 22 June; 24 Aug (10.30-5.30).**
100 acres surrounding an Elizabethan manor created from the remains of a priory founded in reign of Henry I. Garden created during last 80yrs; avenues of beautiful trees; groups of statuary; hedges enclosing small intimate gardens; herbaceous border, wild flower meadows (June); dahlia beds (August).

❹ BARTON GARDENS
Cambridge CB23 7AY. *3 1/2 m SW of Cambridge. M11 J12. Take A603 towards Sandy, in village turn R for Comberton Rd*. Home-made teas at village hall. **Combined adm £5, chd free. Suns 6 Apr; 18 May (2-5).** Delightful group of gardens of wide appeal and expertise.

DORMERS
4 Comberton Road. Nigel & Jean Hobday. *Adjacent to village pond.* Not open 6 Apr.
Large lawn with mature trees and herbaceous borders.

FARM COTTAGE
18 High Street. Dr R M Belbin. *On corner of Ivy Field & High St* A landscaped feel in a cottage garden with woodland walk and walled herbaceous beds. Courtyard garden.

GLEBE HOUSE
1 High Street. David & Sue Rapley. *Top of High St*
1-acre mature, partly wooded and walled garden with large (unfenced) duck pond and timber decking, formal fruit/herb garden. Italiante style courtyard garden. Landscaped secret garden with gazebo.

114 HIGH STREET
Meta & Hugh Greenfield
Unusual shape garden surrounded by trees. Cottage garden with mature shrubs and herbaceous plants. Some gravel paths.

31 NEW ROAD
Dr & Mrs D Macdonald
Wildlife friendly cottage garden with good show of spring flowers, mature shrubs and trees. Kitchen garden. Featured in 'Garden News'.

THE SIX HOUSES
33-45 Comberton Road. Perennial (GRBS). *Last property on LH-side going to Comberton* Renovated garden, incl winter and dry gardens. Many new plants and trees. Lovely spring bulbs and small wood.

247 WIMPOLE ROAD
Ray & Nikki Scrivens
Established country garden and small paddock with room for animals and birds, wild, domestic and ornamental.

WINDY CORNER
245 Wimpole Road. Mike & Jules Webber
An adventurous bustling array of shrubs and perennials in a long, narrow country garden setting.

❺ NEW BREAKAWAY
Old Stretham Station Road. CB6 3QD. Mr & Mrs Grey. *3m S of Ely. From Ely follow A10 S 3m. Turn R (signed NGS). Garden 1m from A10 on L. From Cambridge 1 1/2 m N Stretham roundabout turn L (signed NGS)*. Home-made teas. **Adm £2, chd free. Sun 17 Aug (2-6).**
Medium sized garden containing wide range of interesting plants, shrubs, trees, and knot gardens, gravelled, grass and palm areas. Water features, summerhouse, exotic jungle area featuring bananas, gingers, tree ferns, bamboos and colocasia to name a few.

❻ CATWORTH, MOLESWORTH & BRINGTON GARDENS
nr Huntingdon PE28 0PF. *10m W of Huntingdon. For Catworth & Brington turn off A14 onto B660 (Catworth S bound) approx 7m W of A14 junction with A1. Village is on the N side of A14 flyover. Molesworth is on the A14, 8m W of the A1.* Home-made teas at Molesworth House & Yew Tree Cottage. **Combined adm £3, chd free. Sun 15 June (2-6).**

32 HIGH STREET
Catworth. Colin Small
Long narrow garden approx 1/4 - acre. Large informal patio, pergola with herbaceous borders and containers of unusual foliage plants; lawn with herbaceous borders either side, native woodland area. Many rare plants, collection of salvias and ferns. Featured in 'Garden News'.

MOLESWORTH HOUSE
Molesworth. John Prentis. *Next to the church in Molesworth* Classic Victorian rectory garden of approx 2½ acres. Bit of everything; old-fashioned and proud of it. Also rather groovy new tropical house.
&

THE POPLARS
Molesworth. Nick Frost, 01832 710539, tommaasss@aol.com. *By willow tree, opp Barnsby footpath.* **Visitors also welcome by appt.**
Garden on hillside set in terraces, wonderful ponds and waterfall surrounded by excellent planting. Created over the last 3yrs. Long low steps to pond areas.
& ✖ ☎

YEW TREE COTTAGE
Brington. Mr & Mrs D G Eggleston. *After village sign continue past school, up hill, Yew Tree Cottage is thatched cottage on L*
Informal garden, approx 1 acre, complements the C17 building (not open) and comprises flower beds, lawns, vegetable patch, boggy area, copses and orchard. Plants in pots and hanging baskets. Gravel drive.
& ❀

7 CHILDERLEY HALL
Dry Drayton CB23 8BB. Mrs Jenkins, 01954 210271. *6m W of Cambridge. Off A428 ½ m W of Caldecote turn.* **Adm £3. Visitors welcome by appt May to July.**
Romantic 4-acre garden (grade II historic garden) surrounds part Tudor house (not open). Winding paths lead through herbaceous borders to secret areas. Large collection shrub roses and good variety of plants and trees.
✖ ☎

8 CHIPPENHAM PARK
Chippenham, nr Newmarket CB7 5PT. Mr & Mrs Eustace Crawley. *5m NE of Newmarket. 1m off A11.* **Light refreshments. Adm £4, chd free (share to local village charity).**
Suns 30 Mar; 22 June; 12 Oct (11-5). The house (not open), gardens, lake, canals and 350-acre park enclosed by wall 3½ m long, built after Admiral Lord Russell petitioned William III in 1696 for permission to make a park. Gardens have been extended and restocked by Anne Crawley, descendant of John

Tharp who bought the estate in 1791. Superb display of narcissus and early flowering shrubs followed by extensive summer borders and dramatic autumn colours. Many plants stalls.
& ✖ ❀ ☕

> ## The surprise is a large hidden rear garden around mature willow tree . . .

9 CLARE COLLEGE FELLOWS' GARDEN
Trinity Lane, Cambridge CB2 1TL. The Master & Fellows, www.clare.cam.ac.uk. *Central to city. From Queens Rd or city centre via Senate House Passage, Old Court & Clare Bridge.* **Adm £3, chd free.** Sun 6 July (2-6).
2 acres. One of the most famous gardens on the Cambridge Backs. Herbaceous borders; sunken pond garden and fine specimen trees.
& ✖

10 NEW CLEARVIEW
Cross Lane, Wisbech St Mary PE13 4TX. Margaret & Graham Rickard, 01945 410724, magsrick@hotmail.com. *3m SW of Wisbech, off Barton Rd. Leave Wisbech on Barton Rd towards Wisbech St Mary. L at Cox Garage Xrds into Bevis Lane. 1st L into Cross Lane. Garden 4th on R with iron gates.* Home-made teas. **Adm £3, chd free.** Suns 25 May; 29 June (10-5). **Visitors also welcome by appt Apr to July. no coaches please.**
Approx 1-acre with lake incorporating large wildlife area - incl beehives. Secluded cottage garden with many old fashioned plants, herbaceous border, gravel garden with raised bed and pond. Large rose bed, allotments and small orchard. Plenty of secluded seating. Dixieland Jazz Band playing in June. Featured in 'Garden Monthly'. Wildlife Garden of the Year Wisbech in Bloom.
& ✖ ❀ ☕ ☎

11 COMBERTON GARDENS
CB23 7EF. *5m W of Cambridge. 2m from MII J12, via Barton on B1046. Parking at 58 Green End & the Three Horseshoes.* Home-made teas at Three Horseshoes. **Adm £3.50, chd free.** Sun 29 June (2.30-5.30).

NEW 60 GREEN END
Dr & Mrs A Hosking
Country garden approx 1 acre with irregular outline, divided into 'rooms' by diverse hedging. Many interesting and unusual trees and shrubs, with colour provided by shrub roses, cultivated and wild flowers.
✖

GREYSTONES
Swaynes Lane, Comberton. Dr & Mrs L Davies, 01223 262686. *5m SW of Cambridge.* **Visitors also welcome by appt.**
Artistically designed plantswoman's garden of ½ acre. Colourful borders with yr-round interest, productive summer potager.
& ✖ ☎

NEW THE THREE HORSESHOES
South Street. Lindsay & Colin Browne
Typical rural pub with colourful frontage of trailing hanging baskets and planters. The surprise is a large hidden rear garden around mature willow tree, S-facing border backed by climbers. Spacious patio with huge pots of hostas.
& ✖

12 ♦ DOCWRA'S MANOR
Meldreth Road, Shepreth SG8 6PS. Mrs Faith Raven, 01763 260235, www.docwrasmanorgarden.co.uk. *8m S of Cambridge. ½ m W of A10. Cambridge-Royston bus stops at gate opp the War Memorial in Shepreth. King's Cross-Cambridge train stop 5 min walk.* **Adm £4, chd free. All yr Weds, Fris (10-4.30), 1st Sun in month Apr to Oct (11-4).** For NGS: Sun 11 May (2-5.30).
2½ acres of choice plants in series of enclosed gardens. Tulips and Judas trees. Opened for NGS for more than 40yrs. Featured in 'Daily Telegraph' (Saturday).
& ✖ ❀ ☕

13 DULLINGHAM HOUSE
nr Newmarket CB8 9UP. Sir Martin & Lady Nourse, 01638 508186, lavinia.nourse@btinternet.com. *4m S of Newmarket. Off A1304 & B1061.* **Adm £3, chd free.** Visitors welcome by appt.
The grounds were landscaped by Humphrey Repton in 1799 and the view remains virtually intact today. To the rear there is a substantial walled garden with magnificent long shrub/herbaceous borders. The garden encompasses a fine claire voie and historic bowling green.
♿ ✝ ☏

Three delightful gardens all within easy walking distance of the cathedral . . .

14 EASTON GARDENS
PE18 0TU. *7m W of Huntingdon. On A14. Car parking in playing field.* Home-made teas. **Combined £4, chd free.** Sun 1 June (2-5.30).
Thatched cottages and C12 church form a conservation area in this typical small Cambridgeshire village. Exhibition of historic photographs of Easton and other local villages in the church.
☕

BROOK HOUSE
Church Road. Beth & Brian Davis. *Thatched cottage opp the brook and next to churchyard*
Garden of 1-acre created from farmyard. Mature trees, herbaceous borders, rock garden and potager. Wild garden in old orchard with mown paths. Gravel entrance drive to lawns.
♿ ⊛

THE GRANGE
Church Road. Alison & Peter Gould. *Opp church*
Walled garden, interesting perennial borders with emphasis on C18 plants at front, newly planted side garden, herb, fruit and vegetable garden.
♿ ✝ ⊛

15 NEW ELM & WALSOKEN
PE14 0DL. Home-made teas at Walnut Lodge. **Combined adm £3 (Sat), combined with Elm House £3.50 (Sun), chd free.** Sat 7, Sun 8 June (10-4).
☕

24 ELMFIELD DRIVE
Kathleen & Tony Price. *Off A47 towards Downham Market, 1st turning L on bend opp Blacksmith's Arms PH*
Approx 1/3 acre containing a variety of herbaceous plants, spring, summer and autumn bulbs together with flowering shrubs, incl over 90 clematis. Plus small arid garden and fish pond. Wheelchair access: most of garden on grass - no concrete paths.
♿

NEW WALNUT LODGE
Shirley Lakey. *Off A47 towards Walsoken, nr Walsoken Aquatics*
Approx 1-acre of secluded reclaimed derelict orchard, with raised herbaceous beds. Rockery overlooking 2 large ornamental fish ponds containing large koi etc. Rose garden, shrubbery, bulbs and mature trees. Adjacent to 4-acre wildlife orchard.
♿ ✝ ⊛

16 NEW ELM HOUSE
Main Road, Elm PE14 0AB. Mrs Diana Bullard. *2½ m SW of Wisbech. From A47 take A1101 towards Downham Market, take B1101 towards March, garden approx ¼ m on L.* Home-made teas. **Combined with Elm & Walsoken** adm £3.50, chd free (share to Independant Age). Sun 8 June (2-5).
Walled garden with arboretum, many rare trees and shrubs, mixed perennials C17 house (not open).
♿ ✝ ☕

17 ELY GARDENS 1
CB7 4HZ. *14m N of Cambridge. Follow signs to cathedral, from A10. and yellow signs to Barton Rd. Car park on Barton Rd. Map given at first garden visited.* Home-made teas at The Old Fire Engine House. **Combined adm £3, chd free.** Mon 5 May (2-5).
Historic city with famous cathedral. Three delightful gardens all within easy walking distance of the cathedral. Teas at The Old Fire Engine House.
☕

THE BISHOP'S HOUSE
The Rt Reverend the Bishop of Ely & Mrs Russell
(see Ely II Gardens entry).

HAZELDENE
36 Barton Road. Mike & Juliette Tuplin. *Nr Barton Rd car park*
Organic garden reflecting an interest in wildlife. Interesting planting and structures incl kitchen garden with raised beds, living roofs, courtyard garden - small ponds.
✝ ⊛

THE OLD FIRE ENGINE HOUSE
St Mary's Street. Mr & Mrs M R Jarman
Delightful walled country garden within the shadow of Ely cathedral. Cottage garden plants in beds and borders around old fruit trees. Described by those who see it as 'an oasis of peace'.
✝

QUANEA HILL
Quanea Drove, Ely. Nigel Wood & Claire Nicholl. nigel_e_wood@hotmail.com. *From Ely take A142, direction Newmarket. 2nd L Quanea Drove. Quanea Hill is at the end 1½ m rd. Visitors also welcome by appt , please apply to Quanea Farm, Quanea Drove, Ely CB7 5TJ.*
Quanea is on a small clay hill surrounded by fen. Extensive rural garden planted for constant interest throughout the yr. Short woodland walks with spectacular views of Ely Cathedral across the open fen. This exposed location is protected from the cold fen winds by closely planted woodland with poplar, beech, walnut and oak. Gardens, woods and meadows cover more than 8 acres.
♿ ☏

18 ELY GARDENS II
CB7 4TX. *14m N of Cambridge. Approaching Ely from A10 follow signs to the cathedral, or yellow signs in Prickwillow Rd. Maps given at first garden visited.* Home-made teas at Rosewell House. **Combined adm £4, chd free.** Sun 1 June (2-6).
Historic city with famous cathedral and river frontage. Delightful group of gardens with wide appeal and expertise.
☕

ALTON HOUSE
46 Prickwillow Road. Judy & Tim Graven
Enclosed town garden, mature trees, good selection of shade tolerant shrubs. Alpine and grass areas. Domed aviary.
&

THE BISHOP'S HOUSE
The Gallery. The Rt Reverend the Bishop of Ely & Mrs Russell
Walled garden adjacent to cathedral, former cloisters of monastery. Rose garden in June; box hedging. Mixed herbaceous and kitchen garden. Gravel paths, but wheelchairs can use lawn area.
& ✗

12 CHAPEL STREET
Ken & Linda Ellis, 01353 664219, ken.ellis1@ntlworld.com. Visitors also welcome by appt June/Sept.
Small town garden with lots of interesting corners. The plants reflect the eclectic outlook of the gardeners towards plants. Themes from alpine to herbaceous border. All linked by a railway! At least, that's the excuse...
& ✗ ⊗ ☎

50A PRICKWILLOW ROAD
CB7 4QT. Mr & Mrs J Hunter
Enthusiast's small walled garden.
✗

ROSEWELL HOUSE
60 Prickwillow Road. Mr & Mrs A Bullivant, 01353 667355. Visitors also welcome by appt in June. Ample parking.
Herbaceous borders with old roses and shrubs. Pond and kitchen garden. Secluded 'sitting areas'. Splendid views of Ely cathedral and surrounding fenland. Meadow being developed to encourage wildlife and wild flowers, with area of cornfield planting. Wheelchair access through sidegate.
& ✗ ⊗ ☎

⑲ EMMANUEL COLLEGE GARDEN & FELLOWS' GARDEN
St Andrews Street, Cambridge CB2 3AP. *Car parks at Parker's Piece & Lion Yard, within 5 mins walk.* **Adm £2, chd free. Sun 29 June (2-5).**
One of the most beautiful gardens in Cambridge. Buildings of C17 to C20

surrounding 3 large gardens with pools, herb garden, herbaceous borders, fine trees incl dawn redwood. Access allowed to Fellows' Garden (NGS day only) with magnificent oriental plane and more herbaceous borders. Gravel paths.
& ✗ ⊗

⑳ FLORENCE HOUSE
Back Road, Fridaybridge, Wisbech PE14 0HU. Mr & Mrs A Stevenson, 01945 860268. *3½ m S of Wisbech. On B1101. In Fridaybridge centre turn R in front of Chequers PH on to Back Rd.* Cream teas. **Adm £2.50, chd free. Suns 16 Mar; 18 May; 21 Sept (12-4). Visitors also welcome by appt for groups & individuals.**
Large sweeping borders in this 30yr-old 1-acre garden, growing a modern mix of trees, shrubs, perennials and grasses in C21 style. The ½ acre paddock borders planted in 2000, start bold and exotic building to a climax in the late summer. Shrubs and trees with spring bulbs and plants, winter flowering perennials shrubs and climbers. Vegetable and fruit garden. Some gravel areas.
& ✗ ⊗ ☕ ☎

㉑ NEW 39 FOSTER ROAD
Campaign Avenue, Sugar Way, Woodston PE2 9RS. Robert Marshall & Richard Handscombe, 01733 555978, robfmarshall@btinternet. *1m SW of Peterborough City Centre. From Oundle Rd turn N into Sugar Way at T-lights, L at 2nd roundabout onto Campaign Ave, R at next roundabout still on Campaign Ave, 2nd R at Foster Rd. Continue to very end of rd. Entrance via rear gate in green fence.* **Adm £3 incl tea & biscuits. Visitors welcome by appt Feb to Sept. Day & Evening.**
Plant enthusiasts' garden within typical, small, new estate plot. Informal and formal areas incl: mixed herbaceous border, woodland and shade, vestibule garden, exotic and ferns, kitchen garden, espaliered fruit trees, pergola, patio, pond, containers and octagonal greenhouse. Unusual snowdrops, over 100 hostas plus daphnes, acers and other choice plants.
✗ 🛏 ☎

HOLLY TREE FARM
See Lincolnshire.

㉒ ISLAND HALL
Godmanchester PE29 2BA. Mr Christopher & Lady Linda Vane Percy, 01480 459670, cvp@cvpdesigns.com. *1m S of Huntingdon (A1). 15m NW of Cambridge (A14). In centre of Godmanchester next to free car park.* Home-made teas. **Adm £3, chd free. Sun 25 May (12-5). Visitors also welcome by appt.**
3-acre grounds. Mid C18 mansion (not open). Tranquil riverside setting with mature trees. Chinese bridge over Saxon mill race to an embowered island with wild flowers. Garden restored in 1983 to mid C18 formal design, with box hedging, clipped hornbeams, parterres, topiary and good vistas over borrowed landscape, punctuated with C18 wrought iron and stone urns. Gravel paths.
& ✗ ⊗ ☕ ☎

Chinese bridge over Saxon mill race to an embowered island with wild flowers . . .

㉓ KING'S COLLEGE FELLOWS' GARDEN
Queens Road, Cambridge CB2 1ST. Provost & Scholars of King's College, domus.bursar@kings.cam.ac.uk. *In Cambridge, the Backs. Entry by gate at junction of Queens Rd & West Rd. Parking at Lion Yard 10mins walk, or some pay & display places in West Rd.* Cream teas. **Adm £3, chd free. Sun 13 July (2-5.30).**
Fine example of a Victorian garden with rare specimen trees.
& ✗ ☕

㉔ KIRTLING TOWER
Newmarket Road, Kirtling, nr Newmarket CB8 9PA. The Lord & Lady Fairhaven. *6m SE of Newmarket. From Newmarket head towards Saxon Street village, through village to Kirtling, turn L at war memorial, entrance is signed on L.* Light refreshments & cream teas. **Adm £4, chd free (share to All Saints Church, Kirtling). Suns 6, 13 Apr (11-4).**
Kirtling Tower is surrounded on 3 sides

by a moat. The garden of 5 acres was started by the present owners 7yrs ago. Main features are the spring garden, secret, walled and cutting gardens. Original Tudor walk. The spring garden is planted with 70,000 bulbs - daffodils, narcissus and camassias in memory of The Hon Rupert Broughton (1970-2000). Last yr 30,000 bulbs of muscari and chionodoxa planted along the 150m church walk. Cards and wrapping papers for sale.

25 LECKHAMPTON
37 Grange Road, Cambridge CB2 1RH. Corpus Christi College. *Runs N to S between Madingley Rd (A1303) & A603. Drive entrance opp Selwyn College. No parking available on site.* Home-made teas. **Adm £4, chd free.** Sun 11 May (2-6).
10 acres comprising formal lawns and extensive wild gardens, featuring walkways and tree-lined avenues, fine specimen trees under-planted with spring bulbs, cowslips, anemones, fritillaries and a large area of lupins. Grass and gravel paths.

26 LODE GARDENS
CB5 9ER. *10m NE of Cambridge. Take B1102 from Stow-cum-Quy roundabout, NE of Cambridge at junction with A14, Lode is 2m from roundabout.* Teas at 21 Lode Road. **Combined adm £4, chd free.** Suns 8 June; 6, 13 July (11-5).
Picturesque village to the E of Angelsey Abbey Garden.

CARPENTERS END
10 High Street. Mr & Mrs Paul Webb, 01223 812646. Visitors also welcome by appt.
³/₄ acre recently developed garden. Shrubs, trees with fine lawn, next to church yard.

21 LODE ROAD
Mr Richard P Ayres, 01223 811873. Visitors also welcome by appt.
Small garden, designed by the owner (retired head gardener at Anglesey Abbey NT) adjoining C15 thatched cottage (not open). Planted with bold groups of herbaceous plants complemen-ting a fine lawn and creating an element of mystery and delight.

NEW THE OLD VICARGE
Mr & Mrs Hunter
Recently designed and planted formal garden. Intricate designed layout with box, yew and pleached lime.

WILD ROSE COTTAGE
Church Walk. Joy Martin, 01223 812990, joy@wildrosegarden.co.uk. Visitors also welcome by appt.
An overflowing cottage garden, with rose tunnel, wildlife pond, circular vegetable garden edged with lavender and sage, wild flower spiral all entered through arches of roses and clematis.

Wildlife features strongly in the design . . .

27 MADINGLEY HALL
nr Cambridge CB23 8AQ. University of Cambridge, www.cont-ed.cam.ac.uk. *4m W of Cambridge. 1m from M11 Exit 13.* Cream teas. **Adm £3, chd free (share to Madingley Church Restoration Fund).** Sun 13 July (2.30-5.30).
C16 Hall (not open) set in 8 acres of attractive grounds. Features incl landscaped walled garden with hazel walk, alpine bed, medicinal border and rose pergola. Meadow, topiary, mature trees and wide variety of hardy plants. St Mary Magdalene Church open. Featured in & on various publications, BBC TV & radio.

28 ◆ THE MANOR
Hemingford Grey PE28 9BN. Mrs D S Boston, 01480 463134, www.greenknowe.co.uk. *4m E of Huntingdon. Off A14. Entrance to garden by small gate off river towpath. No parking at house except for disabled by arrangement with owner. Park in village.* **House and Garden £6, concessions £4.50, Garden only £3, chd free, £2 off season. Open daily throughout the yr 11-5.**
Garden designed and planted by author Lucy Boston, surrounds C12 manor house on which Green Knowe books were based (house open only by appt). 4 acres with topiary; over 200 old roses, bearded iris collection and

large herbaceous borders with mainly scented plants. Enclosed by river, moat and wilderness. Featured on Anglia TV 'Castles in the Country'.

29 MILL HOUSE
22 Fen Road, North End, Bassingbourn SG8 5PQ. Mr & Mrs A Jackson, 01763 243491, millhouseval@btinternet.com. *2m N of Royston. On the NW outskirts of Bassingbourn. 1m from Church, on the rd to Shingay. Take North End at the war memorial in the centre of Bassingbourn which is just W of the A1198 (do not take Mill Lane).* **Adm £3.50, chd free.** Visitors welcome by appt **May to Sept and Snowdrop time.**
Garden created over many years by retired garden designer owners and divided up into interesting enclosures, providing unusual formal and informal settings for many rare trees, shrubs, herbaceous plants, clematis and topiary whiich provide yr round interest. Wonderful elevated view over countryside and garden. New winter garden with snowdrop collection.

30 NEW THE MILL HOUSE, GRANTCHESTER
79 Mill Way. CB3 9ND. Dr Alan Smith. *M11 J12 A603 follow signs to Grantchester. Through the village, garden last house before river bridge. From A10 Trumpington turn off to Grantchester, garden 1st R after river bridge.* **Adm £3.50, chd free.** Sun 15 June (2-4.30). 2009 Sun 1 Feb.
Created 4yrs ago, this 125 acre garden was designed by Chelsea Gold Medalist Marney Hall. Situated on bank of R Cam. Walled garden featuring 2 long summer herbaceous borders. spring woodland, autumn border, winter garden and potager with central water feature. Wildlife features strongly in the design.

31 NEW 5 MOAT WAY
Swavesey CB24 4TR. Mr & Mrs N Kybird. *10m N of Cambridge. 2m E off A14. Off School Lane/Fen Drayton Rd. Access via adjoining field off Fen Drayton Rd.* Teas at Sycamore Farm. **Combined with Sycamore Farm adm £4, chd free.** Sun 29 June (2-5).

Small Japanese style garden filled with unusual collection of trees and shrubs, incl acers and pines with hostas, many grown in terracotta pots, summerhouse.

32 MOSSPAUL
6 Orchard Road, March PE15 9DD. Dinah Lilley, 01354 653396. *18m E of Peterborough. A605/A141. Nr Town Centre. Take 3rd turning on L off Elwyn Rd, straight down, 4th house on R.* **Adm £2, chd free. Visitors welcome by appt May to Aug.**
Large secluded garden with variety of mature shrubs, ornamental trees and specimen conifers. Lawns and mixed borders, Ponds. Fruit garden with cordon trees and soft fruit.

33 NEW 88 NENE PARADE
March PE15 8TA. Doreen & Neville Patrick, 01354 657796. *8m S of town centre take Creek Rd, past Sainsburys, after 1/2 m turn R into Wigstoner Rd, then L at end into Nene Parade.* **Visitors welcome by appt Weekends in August (10-5).**
Large garden approx 20yds x 40yds, mainly with hardy fuchsia over 100 planted around the beds and borders, with a mixture of lawn, flowers and shrubs. Highly Commended - March Garden in Bloom.

An elegant garden touched with antiquity . . .

34 NETHERHALL MANOR
Soham CB7 5AB. Timothy Clark. *6m Ely, 6m Newmarket. Enter Soham from Newmarket, Tanners Lane is 2nd R 100yds after cemetery. Enter Soham from Ely, Tanners Lane is 2nd L after War Memorial.* Home-made teas. **Adm £2, chd free. Suns 23 Mar; 4 May; 3, 10 Aug (2-5).**
'An elegant garden touched with antiquity' Good Gardens Guide. This is an unusual garden worth seeing for its

individual collections of genera and plant groups. Owner has contributed on gardening to Country Life since 1980.

35 NEW THE OLD HOUSE
2 Home End, Fulbourn CB21 5BS. Mr & Mrs Charles Comins, 01223 882907, comins@ntufton.co.uk. *4m SE of Cambridge. Opp Townley Village Hall, next to recreation ground, Home End.* **Adm £3, chd free. Visitors welcome by appt mid May to end July.**
1/3 -acre garden surrounded by high flint walls, mature trees, large formal pond with many fish, plants and centre fountain. Well stocked border round central lawn. Rockery with dwarf conifers. Close to centre of village and Fulbourn Nature Reserve.

36 ◆ PECKOVER HOUSE
North Brink, Wisbech PE13 1JR. National Trust, 01945 583463, www.nationaltrust.org.uk. *Centre of Wisbech on N banks of R Nene. Within easy walking distance of town bus stn. Nearest car park in Chapel Rd - no parking on property. Disabled blue badge parking outside property.* **House and Garden £5.50, chd £2.75, Garden only £3.50, chd £1.75. Sats to Weds 15 Mar to 2 Nov. For NGS: Sat 19 July (12-5).**
Said to be one of the best examples of a Victorian town house garden, Peckover is a 2-acre site offering many areas of interest. These incl herbaceous borders, bedding, roses, trees, ponds, lawns cut flower border, ferns, summerhouses and orangery with 3 very old fruiting orange trees and colourful display of pot plants throughout the season. Display and information about the NGS Careership scheme, and on-hand advice about the training scheme from our current careership student.

37 PRIESTHOUSE
33 Church Street, Little Shelford CB2 5HG. Mr & Mrs R Lury. *4m S of Cambridge. On R of village church.* Home-made teas. **Adm £3.50, chd free. Sun 1 June (2-5.30).**
1-acre garden of lawns, shingle paths and drives, clipped trees and shrubs, long borders designed to offset a listed

neo-gothic rectory (not open). Separate rose, herb, kitchen and courtyard gardens and orchard. Exhibition of C19 oil paintings (Cambridge Fine Art) open in The Coach House.

38 RAMSEY FORTY FOOT
nr Ramsey PE26 2YA. *3m N of Ramsey. From Ramsey (B1096) travel through Ramsey Forty Foot, just before bridge over drain, turn R, First Cottage 300yds on R, next door to The Elms.* Home-made teas at First Cottage & The Willows. **Combined adm £3, chd free. Sun 13 July (2-6).**

THE ELMS
Mrs J Shotbolt & Mr R Shotbolt, www.shotbolt.com
1 1/2 -acre water garden around C19 clay pit backed by massive elms. Beautifully landscaped with shrubs, perennials, ferns and large collection of bog and aquatic plants. 3 lakes full of wildlife.

FIRST COTTAGE
Hollow Road. Mr & Mrs R Fort, 01487 813973. Visitors also welcome by appt June & July only.
150ft x 40ft garden with herbaceous borders, shrub beds; natural pond. Miniature steam railway.

THE WILLOWS
Jane & Andrew Sills. *Turn L down private rd opp George PH. Park in Hollow Rd*
1/3 -acre cottage garden with riverside location. Old roses, herbaceous beds; shrubs, ferns; pond; vegetable garden.

39 RECTORY FARM HOUSE
Orwell SG8 5RB. Mr & Mrs Pinnington. *8m W of Cambridge. On & north of A603, towards Wimpole from Cambridge.* Cream teas. **Adm £3, chd free. Sat 14, Sun 15 June (2-5).**
2 acre garden on exposed site developed from a field in 1998. Enclosed spaces filled with roses, lavender and herbaceous plants, surrounded by box and hornbeam hedges. Garden designed and planted by Peter Reynolds. Some gravel paths.

40 REDLANDS

Twenty Pence Road, Wilburton CB6 3PU. Mrs Francis-Wood & Mr Wood, 01353 740073. *4m SW of Ely. Wilburton stands on the A1123 and the B1049. At Wilburton PO take Twenty Pence Rd. Redlands 300yds on L.* **Adm £3.50, chd free.** Visitors welcome by appt **for groups of 15+, May & June. Please ring in May for dates of June openings and events.**
2-acre garden where trees, shrubs, climbers and roses mingle informally. Paths wind through different areas and scent and colour predominate. Undisciplined and exuberant but also very tranquil. Come and enjoy it. Finalist in BBC Radio Cambs' Gardener of the Year.
&. ⚔ ☎

41 RIVER VIEW

Wyton PE28 2AA. John Meeks. *2m E of Huntingdon. Opp Hartford Marina.* **Adm £3, chd free.** Sun 22 June (2-6).
4-acre garden. Unusual trees and shrubs, water features, ponds, topiary and much more.
&. ⚔

42 NEW ROBINSON COLLEGE

Grange Road, Cambridge CB3 9AN, 01223 339100, www.robinson.cam.ac.uk. *Grange Rd runs N to S between Madingley Rd (A1303) & Barton Rd (A603). Turn S on Madingley Rd down Grange Rd, on R. N from Barton Rd on L, opp University Library. Park on st, (parking may be limited). Please report to the Porters Lodge on arrival.* **Adm £2.50, chd free. Open all year for NGS, please tel or see website for details.**
10 original Edwardian gardens are linked to central wild woodland water garden focusing on Bin Brook with small lake at heart of site. This gives a feeling of park and informal woodland, while at the same time keeping the sense of older more formal gardens beyond. Central area has a wide lawn running down to the pond, framed by many mature stately trees with much of the original planting intact. More recent planting incl herbaceous borders and commemorative trees. No picnics. Children must be accompanied at all times.
&. ⚔

Undisciplined and exuberant but also very tranquil. Come and enjoy it . . .

43 SAWSTON GARDENS

CB2 4LA. *5m SE of Cambridge. 3m from M11 J10. A505 follow signs to Sawston.* Home-made teas at Sawston Parish Church. **Combined adm £4, chd free.** Sun 22 June (1-6). Large village with several Grade II listed buildings.
☕

1A CHURCH LANE

Mr & Mrs M Carpenter
Bungalow with garden on 4 sides, with selection of roses, trellis arches, pond, annual and perennial plants. Opp church where teas are available.
&. ⚔ ⊛

30 CHURCHFIELD AVENUE

CB22 3LA. Mr & Mrs I Butler
Medium-sized garden. Circular lawns surrounded by shrubs, annual and perennial plants. Decking area covered by a grapevined pergola. Small pond with waterfall, secluded mirror to give effect of another garden, mixture of shrubs climbers, annual and perennial plants.
⚔ ⊛

DRIFT HOUSE

19a Babraham Road. Mr & Mrs A Osborne
1960's architect designed house (not open) set in $1/3$ acre. Mixture of shrubs, trees, climbers, bulbs and annuals. Vegetable garden and fruit trees, pond and lawns.
&. ⊛

NEW 12 ELDER CLOSE

Mrs Liz McManus. *Via Mill Lane, layby, back gate entrance only. No parking in Elder Close*
Typical long narrow modern garden with herbaceous borders, pots-a-plenty, pergola and modern water feature. Modern use of paving in small garden.

54 HIGH STREET

Dr & Mrs Maunder
C16/18 farmhouse (not open) with lawns and flowerbeds, kitchen garden with chickens, rose garden and paved area where once the goats were housed.
&.

NEW 35 MILL LANE

Doreen Butler. *Via Mill Lane next to firestation*
Bungalow with waterfall, ponds and lots of shrubs and border plants in back garden. Front garden, lawn, shrubs and plants.
&. ⚔

NEW 30 QUEENSWAY

John & Tessa Capes
Mainly perennials, incl approx 50 varieties of hardy geraniums, mixed with hardy fuchsias and shrubs. Selection of hostas in pots. Greenhouse with fuchsias and pelargoniums. Except for new plants and containers a no watering policy has been adopted for the last 2yrs.
⚔

VINE COTTAGE

Hammonds Road. Dr & Mrs T Wreghitt
C17 house (not open) surrounded by mature garden. Contemporary garden featuring Japanese courtyard adjacent to recent extension.
&.

44 4 SELWYN GARDENS

Cambridge CB3 9AX. Mr & Mrs A Swarbrick, 01223 360797, louiseswarbrick@yahoo.co.uk. *Grange Rd runs N to S between Madingley Rd (A1303) & Barton Rd (A603).* Light refreshments & teas. **Adm £5, chd free. Evening Openings** wine, Wed 18, Thur 19 June (6.30-8). **Visitors also welcome by appt.**
Family garden. Walled so no vista. Attempted to create space and interest through dense planting and areas within the garden itself. Lots of traditional cottage plants with a splash of exotic colour to catch the eye.
⚔ ☕ ☎

45 SOUTH FARM & BROOK COTTAGE

Shingay-cum-Wendy, Royston SG8 0HR. Philip Paxman, 01223 207581, philip@south-farm.co.uk, www.south-farm.co.uk. *12m W of*

Cambridge. Off A603. 5m N of Royston off A1198. **Adm £3, chd free. Visitors welcome by appt May to Sept incl, groups of 10+.**
Garden established over 30yrs on farmland site. 8 acres ring fenced by hardwood planting. Eco-garden with reed bed, wild flowers, ponds. Extensive vegetable garden. Restored listed barnyard (open). Also Private Nature Reserve with lake, otters, beautiful dragon flies and native crayfish, wild flowers. Neighbouring Brook Cottage (Mr & Mrs Charvile) Countryman's cottage garden. Abundant yr-long mixed colour, spilling over boundary stream, inter-mixed with traditional vegetables and poultry. Caterer of the Year. Greene King National Exellence award.

& ⅍ ⌸ ☎

46 STAPLEFORD GARDENS
CB2 5DG. Home-made teas at 59-61 London Road. **Combined adm £3, chd free (share to East Anglia Childrens Hospice). Sun 1 June (2-6).**
Contrasting gardens, showing a range of size, planting and atmosphere in this village just S of Cambridge. Home-made jams and marmlade.

☕

59 - 61 LONDON ROAD
Dr & Mrs S Jones. *On A1301 next to Church St*
Medium sized garden arranged in 'rooms'. Gravel garden, herbaceous beds, kitchen garden, fruit cage, alpine, pit and summer houses, sculptures. Access to 5 Priams Way.

⅍

57 LONDON ROAD
Mrs M Spriggs. *on A1301 next to Church St*
Garden integrated with that of 59 - 61, access to 5 Priams Way forming a series of garden rooms.

⅍

5 PRIAMS WAY
Mr Anthony Smith. *Off London Rd, easiest access via 59 - 61 London Rd*
Small garden with herbaceous beds and pergola.

⅍

THE STONE HOUSE
40 Mingle Lane. Sir James & Lady Mirrlees. *5 mins fron Shelford Stn, opp the church in Mingle Lane*
Lawns, trees and shrubs.

& ⅍

47 NEW SYCAMORE FARM
New Road, Over CB24 5PJ. Dr & Mrs R Hook, 01954 231371, rob@sycamorefarm.org. *10m N of Cambridge. 4m E of A14. Disabled parking on-site, other vehicles please park considerately along New Road.* Home-made teas. **Combined with 5 Moat Way adm £4, chd free. Sun 29 June (2-5). Visitors also welcome by appt for groups of 10+.**
2-acre garden incl dry garden, lily pond herbaceous border, old fashioned rose garden, white border, wild life pond with rill, and short woodland walk.

& ⅍ ☕ ☎

48 TRINITY COLLEGE, FELLOWS' GARDEN
Queen's Road, Cambridge CB2 1TQ. Trinity College. *City centre.* **Adm £3, chd free. Sun 6 Apr (2-5).**
Garden of 8 acres, originally laid out in the 1870s by W B Thomas. Lawns with mixed borders, shrubs and specimen trees. Drifts of spring bulbs. Recent extension of landscaped area among new college buildings to W of main garden. Gravel paths.

& ⅍

49 NEW TRINITY HALL - WYCHFIELD
Storeys Way, Cambridge CB3 0DZ. The Master & Fellows. *1m NW of city centre. Turn into Storeys Way from Madingley Rd (A1303).* **Adm £3, chd free (share to Breast Cancer Care). Sun 30 Mar (11-4).**
First-ever opening for this 18 acre site formed within the grounds of the Edwardian Wychfield House, now also containing sports accomodation facilities for Trinity Hall. Established lawns, majestic trees and beautiful borders complement recently completed accomodation set in newly laid out gardens. Some gravel paths.

& ⊛ ☕

50 UPWATER LODGE
23 Chaucer Road, Cambridge CB2 7EB. Mr & Mrs G Pearson. *1m S of Cambridge. Off Trumpington Rd (A1309), nr Brooklands Ave junction.* Home-made teas. **Adm £4, chd free. Sun 4, Mon 5 May (2-5).**
2 gardens - 1st, 6 acres with mature trees, fine lawns, old wisterias, colourful borders, network of paths

through bluebell wood leading down to water meadows and small flock of rare breed sheep. 2nd, adjoining (from same family) has rose and wisteria covered pergolas, colourful borders and plentiful bulbs. Waterproof footwear advised. Art card stalls. Some gravel paths, small incline.

& ⅍ ⊛ ☕

Majestic trees and beautiful borders . . .

51 THE VILLAGE, ORTON LONGUEVILLE
Peterborough PE2 7DN. *2m W of Peterborough. Off A605 Oundle Rd.* Light refreshments & teas at Holy Trinity Church. **Combined £3, chd free. Sun 8 June (1-5).**
Small village within the city of Peterborough. Church Fete.

☕

10 ENGAINE
Jane & Simon Smith
With wildlife in mind - variety of habitats and planting incl woodland garden, pond, vegetable and cottage-style gardens. Sand dunes and beach. Plus problem solved! Garden and wildlife experts on hand for advice. Gravel driveway.

& ⅍ ⊛

HEMINGDALE
16 The Village. Mr & Mrs J P Wilkinson
A cottage garden.

&

1A THE VILLAGE
Christine & George Stevenson
Garden featuring shrubs, herbaceous beds and arches supporting varieties of rose, honeysuckle and clematis. Gravel paths/drive.

& ⅍

52 WEAVER'S COTTAGE
35 Streetly End, West Wickham, Cambridge CB21 4RP. Miss Sylvia Norton, 01223 892399. *8m NW of Haverhill. On A1307 between Linton & Haverhill turn N at Horseheath towards W Wickham. Weaver's Cottage is 9th on R after 40 sign.* **Adm £2, chd free. Visitors welcome by appt anytime,**

any numbers - incl coaches.
½ -acre garden exuberantly planted for fragrance with spring bulbs; shrubs; herbaceous; climbers; old roses. Scree garden. NCCPG National Collection of *Lathyrus*.

WELL CREEK ROAD
See Norfolk

53 WHITTLESFORD GARDENS
CB22 4NR. *7m S of Cambridge. 1m NE of J10 M11 & A505. Parking nr church.* **Combined adm £3.50, chd free. Sun 15 June (2-6).**
Flowers in Parish Church C11. Maps of gardens given on arrival.

THE GUILDHALL
Professors P & M Spufford
Knot garden.

NEW 4 MIDDLEMOOR ROAD
Mr & Mrs A Osborne
Informal country garden, mixed herbaceous/vegetable area with lawn and stream.

23 NEWTON ROAD
Mr F Winter
Cottage garden, herbaceous plants, shrubs, fish pond. Allotment consisting of vegetables, fruit, flowers and bird aviary.

14 NORTH ROAD
Mr & Mrs R Adderley
Shady secluded garden with rockery and pond.

5 PARSONAGE COURT
Mrs L Button. *Please park on rd*
Trees, shrubs and large pond.

RAYNERS FARM
North Road. Mr & Mrs C Morton
Medieval-style herb beds in walled garden of C15 timber-framed farmhouse (not open). Restored barns, large pond and free-range poultry.

RYECROFT
1 Middlemoor Road. Mr & Mrs P A Goodman
Paddock; shrubs and compost making.

11 SCOTTS GARDENS
Mr & Mrs M Walker
Shady walled garden with shrub borders; pond and waterfall.

A treat for plant lovers and wildlife watchers . . .

54 WILLOW HOLT
Willow Hall Lane, Thorney PE6 0QN.
Angie & Jonathan Jones, 01733 222367, janda.salix@virgin.net. *4m E of Peterborough. From A47, between Eye & Thorney turn S into Willow Hall Lane. 2m on R. NOT in Thorney Village.* Teas. **Adm £2.50, chd free. Suns 30 Mar; 27 Apr; 25 May; 29 June; 27 July; 31 Aug; 28 Sept; 26 Oct (11-5). Visitors also welcome by appt.**
2-Acre corner of mature woodland, water-filled dells and tree-fringed flower meadow, with paths that meander among quirky structures and sculpted surprises. A treat for plant lovers,

wildlife watchers and anyone who appreciates the unhurried peace of a garden on the border of wilderness. Featured in & on 'The Independent', BBC Radio Cambs.

55 ◆ WIMPOLE HALL
Arrington SG8 0BW. The National Trust, 01223 206000, www.wimpole.org. *7m N of Royston (A1198). 8m SW of Cambridge (A603). J12 off M11, 30 mins from A1(M).* **Adm £3.50, chd £1.85. Open daily except Thurs & Fris (house (1-5), (gdn 10.30-5). For NGS: Wed 16 July (10.30-5).**
Part of 350-acre park. Restored Dutch garden and Victorian parterres on N lawns. Fine trees, marked walks in park. National Collection of walnuts. Walled vegetable garden. Chance to see the recreated Sir John Soane glasshouse financed with the help of the National Gardens Scheme.

56 WYTCHWOOD
7 Owl End, Great Stukeley PE28 4AQ. Mr David Cox, 01480 454835. *2m N of Huntingdon. On B1043. Parking at village hall, Owl End.* Home-made teas. **Adm £3.50, chd free. Sun 29 June (1.30-5.30). Visitors also welcome by appt, May to July.**
2-acre garden. Brightly planted borders of perennials, annuals and shrubs, lawns and ponds. Dry garden planted 2001. 1 acre of wild plants, grasses set among rowan, maple and birch trees leading to spinney. Planted with native trees, ferns, hostas and foxgloves. Plenty of seats and shade. Haven for wildlife. Gravel drive. Featured in 'Garden News'.

Cambridgeshire County Volunteers

County Organiser
George Stevenson, 1a The Village, Orton Longueville, Peterborough, Cambridgeshire PE2 7DN, 01733 391506, ChrisGeorge1a@aol.com

County Treasurer
Dr Lyndon Davies, 19 Swaynes Lane, Comberton, Cambridge CB23 7EF, 01223 262 686, lyndon@ldassoc.demon.co.uk

Publicity
Clare Foggett, 22 Mead Close, Peterborough, Cambridgeshire PE4 6BS, 01733 762042, clare.foggett@emap.com

Assistant County Organisers
Pam Bullivant, Rosewell House, 60 Prickwillow Road, Ely, Cambridgeshire CB7 4TX, 01353 667355, pam.bullivant@talk21.com
John Drake, Hardwicke House, Fen Ditton, Cambridgeshire CB5 8TF, 01223 292246
Patsy Glazebrook, 15 Bentley Road, Cambridge CB2 8AW, 01223 301302, glazebrc@doctors.net.uk
Christine Stevenson, 1a The Village, Orton Longueville, Peterborough, Cambridgeshire PE2 7DN, 01733 391506

Mark your diary with these special events in 2008

EXPLORE SECRET GARDENS DURING CHELSEA WEEK

Tue 20 May, Wed 21 May, Thur 22 May, Fri 23 May
Full day tours: £78 per person, 10% discount for groups
Advance Booking required, telephone 01932 864532 or
email pennysnellflowers@btinternet.com

Specially selected private gardens in London, Surrey and Berkshire. The tour price includes transport and lunch with wine at a popular restaurant or pub.

FROGMORE – A ROYAL GARDEN (BERKSHIRE)

Tue 3 June 10am - 5.30pm (last adm 4pm)
Garden adm £4, chd free. Advance booking recommended telephone 01483 211535
or email orders@ngs.org.uk

A unique opportunity to explore 30 acres of landscaped garden, rich in history and beauty.

FLAXBOURNE FARM – FUN AND SURPRISES (BEDFORDSHIRE)

Sun 8 June 10am - 5pm Adm £5, chd free
No booking required, come along on the day!

Bring the whole family and enjoy a plant fair and garden party and have fun in this beautiful and entertaining garden of 2 acres.

WISLEY RHS GARDEN – MUSIC IN THE GARDEN (SURREY)

Tue 19 August 6 - 9pm
Adm (incl RHS members) £7, chd under 15 free

A special opening of this famous garden, exclusively for the NGS. Enjoy music and entertainment as you explore a range of different gardens.

For further information visit www.ngs.org.uk or telephone 01483 211535

CHESHIRE & WIRRAL

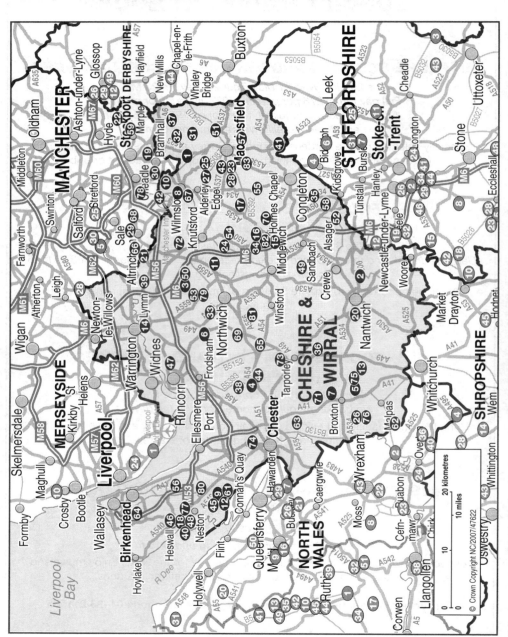

Opening Dates

April

SUNDAY 6
16 Dane Mount
47 Norton Priory Museum & Gardens
53 Parm Place
63 Saighton Grange
82 Woodcroft

SUNDAY 13
56 Poulton Hall

WEDNESDAY 16
73 Tirley Garth

SUNDAY 20
9 Briarfield
37 Lyme Park
73 Tirley Garth

SATURDAY 26
5 Bank House
55 Pikelow Farm

SUNDAY 27
5 Bank House
21 Dunham Massey
36 Long Acre
46 Newton House
52 Orchard House
70 Swettenham Village

WEDNESDAY 30
72 Tatton Park

May

SUNDAY 4
6 Bluebell Cottage Gardens
77 69 Well Lane

MONDAY 5
77 69 Well Lane

WEDNESDAY 7
29 35 Heyes Lane

SUNDAY 11
7 Bolesworth Castle
27 Hare Hill Gardens
29 35 Heyes Lane
39 Mayfield
51 One House Nursery

FRIDAY 16
4 Ashton House (Evening)

SATURDAY 17
8 9 Bourne Street
54 Peover Hall Gardens

SUNDAY 18
8 9 Bourne Street
15 Croco Brook Farm
20 Dorfold Hall
25 Glynleigh
28 Henbury Hall
38 Manley Knoll
54 Peover Hall Gardens

80 Willaston Village Gardens

WEDNESDAY 21
13 Cholmondeley Castle Garden

SUNDAY 25
23 Far Hills
43 The Mount
44 Mount Pleasant

MONDAY 26
44 Mount Pleasant

THURSDAY 29
50 The Old Hough (Evening)

SATURDAY 31
48 The Old Parsonage
67 68 South Oak Lane

June

SUNDAY 1
24 Free Green Farm
30 73 Hill Top Avenue
40 Maylands
48 The Old Parsonage
57 Ridgehill House
67 68 South Oak Lane

WEDNESDAY 4
52 Orchard House

THURSDAY 5
50 The Old Hough (Evening)

SATURDAY 7
5 Bank House

SUNDAY 8
1 Adlington Hall
5 Bank House
11 Bucklow Farm
69 Stonyford Cottage
78 West Drive Gardens

WEDNESDAY 11
72 Tatton Park

THURSDAY 12
50 The Old Hough (Evening)

FRIDAY 13
4 Ashton House (Evening)
79 Westage Farm (Evening)

SATURDAY 14
75 The Valve House
79 Westage Farm

SUNDAY 15
26 Grafton Lodge
68 199 Stockport Road
75 The Valve House
79 Westage Farm

THURSDAY 19
50 The Old Hough (Evening)

FRIDAY 20
26 Grafton Lodge (Evening)

SUNDAY 22
2 Alma Villa
36 Long Acre
71 Tattenhall Hall

SATURDAY 28
41 Millpool
51 One House Nursery

SUNDAY 29
12 Burton Village Gardens
31 Hillside Cottage
32 Holmcroft
41 Millpool
51 One House Nursery
76 The Well House

July

THURSDAY 3
81 Wood End Cottage (Evening)

SATURDAY 5
34 Lawrence Close Gardens

SUNDAY 6
21 Dunham Massey
34 Lawrence Close Gardens
65 Sandymere

THURSDAY 10
30 73 Hill Top Avenue (Evening)

SATURDAY 12
14 68 Cranborne Avenue

SUNDAY 13
10 Brooke Cottage
14 68 Cranborne Avenue
22 Edith Terrace Gardens
39 Mayfield
53 Parm Place

WEDNESDAY 16
52 Orchard House

SATURDAY 19
21 Dunham Massey (Evening)
35 Little Moreton Hall
37 Lyme Park
62 The Rowans
66 The School House

SUNDAY 20
55 Pikelow Farm
62 The Rowans
66 The School House
81 Wood End Cottage

SUNDAY 27
19 19 Dorchester Road

August

SATURDAY 2
3 Arley Hall & Gardens

SUNDAY 3
2 Alma Villa

42 31 Moss Lane
68 199 Stockport Road
70 Swettenham Village

THURSDAY 7
31 Hillside Cottage (Evening)

FRIDAY 8
31 Hillside Cottage (Evening)

SATURDAY 9
59 Rose Hill Gardens (Afternoon & Evening)

SUNDAY 10
6 Bluebell Cottage Gardens
30 73 Hill Top Avenue
49 The Old Farm
59 Rose Hill Gardens (Afternoon & Evening)
69 Stonyford Cottage

SATURDAY 23
33 2 Hough Cottage

SUNDAY 24
33 2 Hough Cottage

WEDNESDAY 27
52 Orchard House

September

SATURDAY 6
83 3 Woodhouse Lane

SUNDAY 7
83 3 Woodhouse Lane

SATURDAY 27
44 Mount Pleasant

SUNDAY 28
44 Mount Pleasant

October

SUNDAY 5
21 Dunham Massey

Gardens open to the public

1 Adlington Hall
3 Arley Hall & Gardens
6 Bluebell Cottage Gardens
13 Cholmondeley Castle Garden
21 Dunham Massey
27 Hare Hill Gardens
35 Little Moreton Hall
37 Lyme Park
44 Mount Pleasant
45 Ness Botanic Gardens
47 Norton Priory Museum & Gardens
54 Peover Hall Gardens
58 Rode Hall
69 Stonyford Cottage
72 Tatton Park

By appointment only

17 Deans Rough Farm

18 29 Dee Park Road
61 Rosewood
64 St Davids House
74 80 Upton Park

Also open by appointment ☎

2 Alma Villa
4 Ashton House
9 Briarfield
15 2 Claremont Avenue, Rose Hill Gardens
19 19 Dorchester Road
22 Edith Terrace Gardens
23 Far Hills
26 Grafton Lodge
30 73 Hill Top Avenue
32 Holmcroft
36 Long Acre
39 Mayfield
40 Maylands
41 Millpool
43 The Mount
48 The Old Parsonage
50 The Old Hough
52 Orchard House
53 Parm Place
55 Pikelow Farm
56 Poulton Hall
57 Ridgehill House
62 The Rowans
63 Saighton Grange
67 68 South Oak Lane
76 The Well House
81 Wood End Cottage
82 Woodcroft

Lavender hedge, densely planted mixed borders with ornamental trees . . .

The Gardens

1 ♦ ADLINGTON HALL
Macclesfield SK10 4LF. Mrs Camilla Legh, 01625 829206, www.adlingtonhall.com. *4m N of Macclesfield. Well signed off A523 at Adlington.* **Adm £4.50, chd free. House & Gardens Sun to Wed July.** For NGS: Sun 8 June (2-5).
6 acres of formal gardens with herbaceous borders, rose garden; rockeries; yew maze; water garden. Lawns with open views across ha-ha. 32-acre wilderness with mature plantings, various follies incl a 'Temple to Diana'; woodland walk. Yew and ancient lime walks. Flower parterre. Limited wheelchair access.
✗ 🍵

2 NEW ALMA VILLA
73 Main Road, Shavington, Crewe CW2 5DU. Rosemary & Roger Murphy, 01270 567710. *2m E of Nantwich. From J16 M6 take A500 towards Nantwich, at 3rd roundabout turn L signed Shavington, L at T-lights into village approx 1/2 m take 2nd R into Main Rd, garden approx 300yds on R. From Nantwich follow Shavington signs to Elephant PH turn 1st L into Main Rd, garden approx 400yds on L. Home-made teas.* **Adm £3, chd free. Suns 22 June; 3 Aug (1-6). Visitors also welcome by appt, June, July & Aug, groups of 4+.**
Beautifully presented country garden, created by plantswoman. Incl various hanging baskets and containers. Lavender hedge, densely planted mixed borders with ornamental trees, shrubs and perennials. Complemented by arches supporting roses and clematis. Structural planting with phormiums and yucca, vegetable plot, mature fruit trees and much more.
♿ ❀ 🍵 ☎

3 ♦ ARLEY HALL & GARDENS
Northwich CW9 6NA. The Viscount Ashbrook, 01565 777353, www.arleyhallandgardens.com. *4m W of Knutsford. Well signed from M6 J19 & 20, & M56 J9 & 10.* **Adm £5.50, chd £2, concessions £5. Fri 21 March - Sun 28 Sept; weekends in Oct.** For NGS: Sat 2 Aug (11-5).
One of Britain's finest gardens, Arley has been lovingly created by the same

family over 250yrs and is famous for its yew buttressed herbaceous border, avenue of ilex columns, walled garden, pleached lime avenue and Victorian Rootree. A garden of great atmosphere, interest and vitality throughout the seasons. Specialist nursery adjacent. NW's Visitor Attraction of the Year.

Children's garden with vegetables, herbs, living willow maze and tunnels, woodland area . . .

④ ASHTON HOUSE
Church Road, Ashton Hayes CH3 8AB. Mrs M Sheppard, 01829 752761, margaret@sheppard61.fsnet.co.uk. *7m E of Chester. Off A54, take B5393 to Ashton. 200yds past Golden Lion, R into Nursery car park.* **Adm £3, chd free. Evening Openings** wine, Fris 16 May; 13 June (6-9). **Visitors also welcome by appt May & June only.** Country garden with stream, natural pond and interesting trees, incl old monkey puzzle and many other interesting and unusual species of trees and shrubs. Children's garden with vegetables, herbs, living willow maze and tunnels, woodland area.

⑤ BANK HOUSE
Goldford Lane, Bickerton SY 14 8LL. Dr & Mrs M A Voisey. *4m NE of Malpas. 11m S of Chester on A41 turn L at Broxton roundabout to Nantwich on A534. Take 5th R (1¾ m) to Bickerton. Take 2nd R into Goldford Lane. Bank House is nearly 1m on L. Field parking.* Home-made teas. **Adm £3.50, chd free. Sats, Suns 26, 27 Apr; 7, 8 June (2-5.30).** 1¾ -acre garden at the foot of Bickerton Hill, in area of outstanding

beauty, with extensive views to Derbyshire and the Marches. Sheltered, terraced borders stocked with a wide range of shrubs, trees and herbaceous plants; established wild garden, Millennium garden with water features and productive vegetable garden. Unfenced swimming pool and ponds. Gravel paths, and some steep slopes.

BIDDULPH GRANGE GARDEN
See Staffordshire & part of West Midlands.

⑥ ◆ BLUEBELL COTTAGE GARDENS
Lodge Lane, Dutton WA4 4HP. Sue & Dave Beesley, 01928 713718, www.lodgelane.co.uk. *5m W of Northwich. From M56 (J10) take A49 (Whitchurch) turn R at T-lights towards Runcorn. Then 1st turning L.* Home-made teas. **Adm £4, chd free. For opening details please tel or see website. For NGS: Suns 4 May; 10 Aug (12-5).** The 1½ -acre garden is on a quiet rural lane in the heart of Cheshire and is packed with thousands of rare and familiar hardy herbaceous perennials, shrubs and trees. The wild flower meadow and bluebell woods are a delight in spring timed to coincide with spring openig and summer. Unusual plants available at the adjacent nursery.

⑦ BOLESWORTH CASTLE
Tattenhall CH3 9HQ. Mrs A G Barbour. *8m S of Chester. Enter by lodge on A41.* Home-made teas. **Adm £4.50, chd free (share to Burwardsley Church). Sun 11 May (2-5).** One of the finest collections of rhododendrons, camellias and acers in any private garden in the NW set on a steep hillside, accessed by a gently rising woodland walk and overlooking spectacular view of the Cheshire plain. Formal lawn beside castle with well stocked herbaceous borders. Terraces with lawn, rose gardens and many other plants. Partial wheelchair access. Dogs on leads.

⑧ 9 BOURNE STREET
Wilmslow SK9 5HD. Lucille Sumner & Melanie & Keith Harris, www.wilmslowgarden.co.uk. *¼ m W of central Wilmslow. Take A538 from Wilmslow towards Manchester Airport.*

Bourne St 2nd on L after fire stn. Or from M56 (J6), take A538 to Wilmslow. Bourne St on R. Home-made teas. **Adm £3, chd free. Sat 17, Sun 18 May (11-5).** ¼ -acre organic garden, evolved over three generations of one family. Mature trees incl ginkgo biloba, azaleas, rhododendrons and exotic foliage. Fish pond; greenhouse; water features and hens. Peaceful and secret garden with a surprise around every corner. Children and adults alike really enjoy this garden, whatever the weather.

⑨ BRIARFIELD
The Rake, Burton, Neston CH64 5TL. Liz Carter, 0151 336 2304, carter.burton@virgin.net. *9m NW of Chester. Turn off A540 at Willaston-Burton Xrds T-lights & follow rd for 1m to Burton village centre.* **Adm £3, chd free (share to Claire House Children's Hospice). Opening with Burton Village Gardens Sun 29 June. Visitors also welcome by appt.** Sheltered S facing sandy slope, home to many specialist plants, some available in plant sale. Colourful shrubs, bulbs, alpines and several water features compete for your attention as you wander through the four distinctly different gardens. Exciting new developments following spring 2007 storm damage.

⑩ BROOKE COTTAGE
Church Road, Handforth SK9 3LT. Barry & Melanie Davy. *1m N of Wilmslow. In the centre of Handforth Village, behind the Health Centre and Library. Turn off Wilmslow Rd next to St Chads Parish Church and follow Church Rd round to R. Garden last on L. Ample parking in Health Centre car park.* Home-made teas. **Adm £2.50, chd free. Sun 13 July (12-5).** Small garden separated into 3 areas. Woodland garden, tree ferns, hydrangeas, hellebores, hostas and astrantias. Patio featuring many large leaved plants incl banana, canna, ligularia, bamboo, dahlias, hemerocallis and small pond. Long mixed border and island beds with grasses and late flowering perennials.

BROOKFIELD
See Lancashire, Merseyside & Greater Manchester.

There's a unique atmosphere you'll want to embrace and amazing artefacts to bring smiles to the face . . .

⑪ BUCKLOW FARM

Pinfold Lane, Plumley WA16 9RP. Dawn & Peter Freeman. *2m S of Knutsford. M6 J19, head to Chester A556. L at 2nd set of T-lights by Smoker PH. In 1¼ m L at concealed Xrds, 1st R. From Knutsford A5033, L at Sudlow Lane. Follow rd, becomes Pinfold Lane.* Home-made teas. **Adm £3, chd free (share to Knutsford Methodist Church). Sun 8 June (2-5).** Country garden with shrubs, perennial borders, rambling roses, herb garden, vegetable patch, wildlife pond/water feature and alpines. Landscaped and planted over the last 18yrs with recorded changes. Free range hens. Wheelchair access, cobbles in the yard and entrance but reasonably flat in the garden area.

  ♿ ⚞ ❀ ☕

⑫ BURTON VILLAGE GARDENS

Wirral CH64 5SJ. *9m NW of Chester. Turn off A540 at Willaston-Burton Xrds T-lights & follow rd for 1m to Burton.* Home-made teas at Burton Manor. **Combined adm £4, chd free (share to Claire House Children's Hospice). Sun 29 June (2-6).** Gardens in centre of village, maps given to all visitors. Teas on Burton Manor terrace, glorious view across gardens to Cheshire countryside. Each garden has a unique character.

  ☕

BRIARFIELD

The Rake, Burton. Liz Carter. (See separate entry).

  ⚞ ❀

BURTON MANOR

Burton. College Principal, Keith Chandler
Three geometric gardens on E, S and N sides of house, essentially as designed by Thomas Mawson in 1906, with mature trees;

sunken parterre; yew hedges; formal flower beds and deep lily ponds. Delightful setting for afternoon tea on the terrace.

  ⚞ ❀

NEW MAPLE HOUSE

The Village. Ingrid & Neil Sturmey
Medium-sized garden, recently converted from field grass to create an attractive yr-round appearance with minimal maintenance. Wild area with pond, lawn and mixed borders of shrubs, herbaceous plants and grasses blending into local countryside. Deep ponds.

  ⚞

⑬ ◆ CHOLMONDELEY CASTLE GARDEN

Malpas SY14 8AH. The Marchioness of Cholmondeley, 01829 720383, penny@cholmondeleycastle.co.uk. *4m NE of Malpas. Off A41 Chester-Whitchurch rd & A49 Whitchurch-Tarporley rd.* **Adm £5, chd £2. Weds, Thurs, Suns & Bank Hols 21 Mar to 28 Sept; Suns 12 - 26 Oct (autumn tints). For NGS: Wed 21 May (11.30-5).** Romantically landscaped gardens. Azaleas, rhododendrons, flowering shrubs, rare trees, herbaceous borders and water gardens. Lakeside picnic area; rare breeds of farm animals and aviary breeds, incl llamas. Private chapel in the park.

  ♿ ❀ ☕

CLOUD COTTAGE

See Derbyshire.

COURTWOOD HOUSE

See Staffordshire & part of West Midlands.

⑭ 68 CRANBORNE AVENUE

Warrington WA4 6DE. Mr & Mrs J Carter. *1m S of Warrington Centre. From Stockton Heath N on A49 over swing bridge. L at 2nd set of T-lights into Gainsborough Rd, 4th L into Cranborne Ave.* **Adm £2.50, chd free. Sat 12, Sun 13 July (11-6).** Luxuriant planting makes this a secret place. An oasis of calm from life's busy pace. Colour and scent enhance and grace, with water and glass expanding the space. There's a unique atmosphere you'll want to embrace and amazing artefacts to bring smiles to the face.

  ⚞ ❀

⑮ NEW CROCO BROOK FARM

Selkirk Drive, Holmes Chapel CW4 7DR. John & Linda Clowes. *½ m W of Holmes Chapel centre. From M6 J18 take A54 towards Holme Chapel. After Texaco garage turn R A54 Congleton (Chester Rd). After 200yds R into Selkirk Drive, garden entrance 20yds on L. From T-lights in Holmes Chapel village take A54 towards Middlewich, Selkirk Drive 500yds on L. Park along Selkirk Dr.* Home-made teas. **Adm £3.50, chd free. Sun 18 May (2-5.30).** 2/3-acre garden developed over last 27 yrs. Containing a wide range of trees, shrubs and herbaceous plants arranged to create interest all yr round. The garden encircles the old farm house (not open) providing the opportunity to create areas with different characteristics.

  ♿ ⚞ ❀ ☕

⑯ DANE MOUNT

Middlewich Road, Holmes Chapel CW4 7EB. Mr & Mrs D Monks. *4m E of Middlewich. Approx 1m E of M6 J18.* Light refreshments & teas. **Combined with Woodcroft adm £4, chd free. Sun 6 Apr (1-5).** ¼ -acre garden full of colourful spring bulbs, camellias and early flowering clematis. Interesting layout with features incl pottery and garden sculptures.

  ♿ ⚞ ❀ ☕

⑰ DEANS ROUGH FARM

Lower Withington SK11 9DF. Mr & Mrs Brian Chesworth, 01477 571414, drumipn@aol.com. *3m S of Chelford. 5m N of Holmes Chapel. A535 nr Jodrell Bank turn into Catchpenny Lane. 1½ m turn R into no through rd (opp bungalow), 400yds turn L into Deans Rough Farm.* **Adm £3.50, chd free. Visitors welcome by appt April - Aug.** Area of 1½ acres; informal cottage garden around house. Herbaceous and mixed borders and old roses. Potager; large natural pond with wild flowers. Woodland area with bog garden.

  ♿ ⚞ ❀ ☎

⑱ 29 DEE PARK ROAD

Gayton CH60 3RG. E Lewis, 0151 342 5893. *7m S of Birkenhead. SE of Heswall. From Devon Doorway/Glegg Arms roundabout at Heswall, travel SE*

in Chester direction on A540 for approx ¼ m. Turn R into Gayton Lane, 5th L into Dee Park Rd. Garden on L after ¼ m. **Adm £2.50, chd free. Visitors welcome by appt.**
Mature trees and shrubs, climbing roses, clematis, mixed shrub, herbaceous borders and island beds provide yr-round interest. Set around gravel areas with thymes and alpines. A mirror in the secret garden reflects many shade-loving plants. A new attraction is the gated entrance by an arbour leading to a garden room with more climbing roses and clematis. Visitor comment 'I only popped in for 5 mins - I have been here 2 hours'.

🍴 ☎

19 **19 DORCHESTER ROAD**
Hazel Grove SK7 5JR. John & Sandra Shatwell, 0161 440 8574, john.shatwell@firenet.ws. *4m S of Stockport. On A5143 at junction of Dorchester Rd and Jacksons Lane. From Stockport take A6 S for approx 1m, R on A5102 for 2m, L at roundabout on A5143. Garden on L after mini-roundabout. Parking at shops or school (further up Jacksons Lane).* Home-made teas. **Adm £3, chd free. Sun 27 July (1-5). Visitors also welcome by appt, groups of 10+. Early June (roses) or week preceeding garden opening.**
Suburban garden redesigned and planted in 2003. 150sq yd front garden with David Austin and hybrid tea roses around a central gazebo. 400sq yd back garden with pond and waterfall, pergola, lawn. Colour-themed borders with perennials, annuals and small trees set against a background of beech trees.

♿ 🍴 ⊗ ☕ ☎

20 **DORFOLD HALL**
Nantwich CW5 8LD. Mr & Mrs Richard Roundell. *1m W of Nantwich. On A534 between Nantwich & Acton.* Home-made teas. **Adm £5, chd £2.50. Sun 18 May (2-5.30).**
18-acre garden surrounding C17 house (not open) with formal approach; lawns and herbaceous borders; spectacular spring woodland garden with rhododendrons, azaleas, magnolias and bulbs.

🍴 ⊗ ☕

21 ♦ **DUNHAM MASSEY**
Altrincham WA14 4SJ. The National Trust, 0161 941 1025, www.nationaltrust.org.uk. *3m SW of Altrincham. Off A56. Well signed.*

House and Garden adm £8.50, chd £4.25, Garden only adm £6, chd £3. Daily 8 Mar to 2 Nov. For NGS: Suns 27 Apr; 6 July; 5 Oct (11-5.30).
Evening Opening Sat 19 July (6.30-9.30).
Great plantsman's garden. Magnificent trees reflected in moat; richly planted borders vibrant with colour and subtle textures. The Orangery, Mount and Bark House give a sense of the garden's long history. Sweeping lawns, lush borders, shady woodland, a formal parterre set the stage while collections of shade-, moisture- and acid-loving plants such as blue poppies, Chinese lilies and hydrangeas contribute to an ever-changing scene. Special Evening Opening for NGS. Bring a picnic and dine at dusk in Dunham Massey Garden.

♿ 🍴 ⊗ ☕

Victorian terrace; described by BBC 'Gardeners' World' magazine as 'a colourful and beautiful living space' . . .

22 **EDITH TERRACE GARDENS**
Compstall, nr Marple SK6 5JF. The Edith Terrace Group, 0161 449 0981, alandannell@talktalk.net. *6m E of Stockport. Take Bredbury junction off M60. Follow Romiley-Marple Bridge sign on B6104. Turn into Compstall on Etherow Country Park sign. Take 1st R, situated at end of Montagu St. Parking in village public car parks - short walk to Edith Terrace.* Tea/coffee & home-made cake. **Adm £4.50, chd free. Sun 13 July (10-5). Visitors also welcome by appt.**
Series of gardens in mixed style from cottage to formal, situated to front and rear of Victorian terrace; described by BBC 'Gardeners' World' magazine as 'a colourful and beautiful living space'. Mixed herbaceous perennials, ornamental backyards and back alleyway. In lakeside setting in the conserved mill village of Compstall, adjacent to Etherow Country Park.

🍴 ☕ ☎

23 **FAR HILLS**
Andertons Lane, Henbury SK11 9PB. Mr & Mrs Ian Warburton, 01625 431800. *2m W of Macclesfield. Along A537 opp Blacksmiths Arms. At Henbury go up Pepper St. Turn L into Church Lane then Andertons Lane in 100yds.* Home-made teas at The Mount. **Combined with The Mount adm £5, chd free. Sun 25 May (2-5.30). Visitors also welcome by appt.**
Mixed ½-acre garden; planted for yr-round interest with regard for wildlife. Trees; shrubs; herbaceous perennials; small pond; fruit and vegetable area; native copse.

🍴 ⊗ ☕ ☎

10 FERN DENE
See Staffordshire & part of West Midlands.

24 **FREE GREEN FARM**
Free Green Lane, Lower Peover WA16 9QX. Sir Philip & Lady Haworth. *3m S of Knutsford. Free Green Lane connects A50 with B5081. From Holmes Chapel on A50 turn L after Drovers Arms. From Knutsford on B5081 turn L into Broom Lane, then L into Free Green Lane.* Home-made teas. **Adm £4, chd free. Sun 1 June (2-6).**
2-acre garden with pleached limes, herbaceous borders, ponds, parterre; collection of hebes, garden of the senses and British woodland. Collection of ferns. Topiary.

♿ 🍴 ⊗ ☕

GAMESLEY FOLD COTTAGE
See Derbyshire.

25 **GLYNLEIGH**
Withinlee Road, Prestbury SK10 4AU. Mr & Mrs C Hamilton. *3m NW of Macclesfield. Take A538 from*

Wilmslow to Prestbury pass Bulls Head on R, after 1m turn R into Withlee Rd. From Prestbury follow A538 towards Wilmslow, turn L after top of Castle Hill into Withinlee Rd. **Adm £4.50, chd free. Sun 18 May (2-5).**
Unique garden designed to create views through the use of a wide variety of unusual planting combinations. Hundreds of mature and recent plantings of rhododendrons and spring-flowering shrubs, trees and groundcovers make this garden strikingly colourful and inspiring. A deep water pond, rockery, rhododendron cone and pergola give added interest.

Set on a hillside, 1/4-acre garden with panoramic vistas, over the treetops, of the Cheshire Plain . . .

26 GRAFTON LODGE
Tilston, Malpas SY14 7JE. Simon Carter & Derren Gilhooley, 01829 250670, simoncar@aol.com. *12m S of Chester. A41 S from Chester turning towards Wrexham on A534 at Broxton roundabout. Past Carden Park Hotel & turn at Cock-a-Barton PH towards Stretton & Tilston. Through Stretton, garden on R before reaching Tilston.* **Adm £4, chd free. Sun 15 June (1-5.30). Evening Opening** wine, Fri 20 June (5-8.30). Visitors also welcome by appt.
Colourful garden of 2 acres with lawns, natural and formal ponds, specimen trees, many mature shrubs and several garden rooms incl herb garden, standard rose circle, large pergola with varied climbers, herbaceous beds, perfumed gazebo, orchard, roof terrace with far reaching views over garden and countryside. Gravel drive.

27 ◆ HARE HILL GARDENS
Over Alderley SK10 4QB. The National Trust, 01625 828836, mike.scott@nationaltrust.org.uk. *2m E of Alderley Edge. Between Alderley Edge & Prestbury. Turn off N at B5087 at Greyhound Rd.* **Adm £3.20, chd £1.50. For NGS: Sun 11 May (10-5).**
Attractive spring garden featuring a fine

display of rhododendrons and azaleas; good collection of hollies and other specimen trees and shrubs. 10-acre garden incl a walled garden which hosts many wall shrubs incl clematis and vines; borders are planted with agapanthus and geraniums. Partially suitable for wheelchairs.

28 HENBURY HALL
nr Macclesfield SK11 9PJ. Sebastian de Ferranti Esq. *2m W of Macclesfield. On A537. Turn down School Lane Henbury at Blacksmiths Arms. East Lodge on R.* Home-made teas. **Adm £6, chd £3. Sun 18 May (2-5).**
Large garden with lake, beautifully landscaped and full of variety. Azaleas, rhododendrons, flowering shrubs; rare trees; herbaceous borders.

29 35 HEYES LANE
Timperley, Altrincham WA15 6EF. Mr & Mrs David Eastwood. *1½ m NE of Altrincham. Heyes Lane, a turning off Park Rd (B5165) 1m from junction with A56 Altrincham-Manchester rd. Or from A560 turn W in Timperley Village for ¼ m. Newsagents shop on corner.* **Adm £3, chd free. Wed 7, Sun 11 May (2-5).**
Small mature suburban garden 30ft x 90ft on sandy soil, maintained by a keen plantswoman member of the Organic Movement (HDRA). Improved accessibility with several changes to this yr-round garden; trees; small pond; greenhouses; many kinds of fruit with a good collection of interesting and unusual plants. A true plantspersons garden with many environmentally friendly features. Featured in 'The Garden' & 'Cheshire Life'. Partial wheelchair access.

HIGH ROOST
See Derbyshire.

30 73 HILL TOP AVENUE
Cheadle Hulme SK8 7HZ. Mr & Mrs Martin Land, 0161 486 0055. *4m S of Stockport. Turn off A34 (new bypass) at roundabout signed Cheadle Hulme (B5094). Take 2nd turn L into Gillbent Rd, signed Cheadle Hulme Sports Centre. Go to end, small roundabout, turn R into Church Rd. 2nd rd on L is Hill Top Ave. From Stockport or Bramhall turn R or L into Church Rd by The Church Inn. Hill Top Ave is 1st rd on R.* Home-made teas. **Adm £3, chd**

free **(share to Arthritis Research Campaign). Suns 1 June; 10 Aug (2-6). Evening Opening** wine, Thur 10 July (6-9). Visitors also welcome by appt, for groups of 4+.
¹/₆ -acre plantswoman's garden. Well stocked with a wide range of sun-loving herbaceous plants, shrub and climbing roses, many clematis varieties, pond and damp area, shade-loving woodland plants and small unusual trees, in an originally designed, long narrow garden. Featured in 'The Garden'.

31 HILLSIDE COTTAGE
Shrigley Road, Pott Shrigley SK10 5SG. Anne & Phil Geoghegan. *6m N of Macclesfield. On A523. At Legh Arms T-lights turn into Brookledge Lane signed Pott Shrigley. After 1½ m signed Shrigley Hall turn L signed Higher Poynton. After 1m turn R at Methodist Chapel. Field parking with short walk to garden.* Home-made teas. **Adm £3.50, chd free (share to Great Dane Adoption Society). Sun 29 June (1-6). Evening Openings** wine, Thur 7, Fri 8 Aug (5-8.30).
Set on a hillside, ¹/₄ -acre garden with panoramic vistas, over the treetops, of the Cheshire Plain and beyond. Filled with colour, texture and the scent of roses. Landscaped on several levels with a wide variety of shrubs, small trees and 'cottage garden' perennials. Water features and walled patio garden with container planting. Featured in 'Amateur Gardening'.

32 NEW HOLMCROFT
Wood Lane North, Adlington SK10 4PF. Iain & Karen Reddy, 01625 877317, iainreddy@mac.com. *6m N of Macclesfield. From Poynton head towards Macclesfield, turn L opp The Little Chef. Stay on Street Lane until T-junction. Turn L until Minors Arms PH, Holmcroft is opp pub car park.* Light refreshments & teas, wine. **Adm £3.50, chd free. Sun 29 June (2-5).** Visitors also welcome by appt June/July only.
The garden is cottage style with mature shrubs, trees and perennial borders. 4 sections incl pond garden, small courtyard, vegetable garden and front garden, approx ¹/₂ acre. The gardens are on multiple levels. Limited access for wheelchairs.

A snail inspired
design for
a modern
small sized
garden . . .

33 **NEW** **2 HOUGH COTTAGE**
Hough Lane, Comberbach
CW9 6AN. Carole Hough. *1m W
of Anderton Lift. From Lift -
towards Comberbach - 1st L
Cogshall Lane 1m. From A49 take
A533 Northwich, after 2m turn L
Stone Heyes Lane, twice after 1m
turn R Hough Lane for ¹/₂ m.*
Home-made teas. **Adm £3, chd
free. Sat 23, Sun 24 Aug (11-5).**
Countryside cottage garden with
secluded secret areas, scented
garden and many tranquil places to
sit. Well stocked with late flowering,
unusual perennials and grasses
within herbaceous borders. Pond
with some unusual plants, cyperus
eragrostis.

34 **NEW** **LAWRENCE CLOSE
GARDENS**
Cranage CW4 8FA. *1m N of
Holmes Chapel. M6 J18. Car
parking courtesy of Cranage Hall
Byley Lane - 3mins walk from car
park to Lawrence Close.* Light
refreshments & teas outside no.
46. **Combined adm £5, chd free.
Sat 5, Sun 6 July (2-5).**
'Skips to Style' Lawrence Close
celebrates 10yrs of gardening.
Come and see 3 different
approaches to design and planting
on a small scale. Enjoy strolling
through the formal to the informal,
exotic and unusual. Each garden
uses containers, water features
and specimen planting to create its
own unique style.

NEW **12 LAWRENCE CLOSE**
Sue & Pete Hughes
An Italianate style garden, formal
design with infomal planting, incl
water features, statues, containers
and specimen trees.

NEW **14 LAWRENCE CLOSE**
Tony & Vera Hitchen
A small informal design for a
modern small sized garden, which
incls pergola, water feature,
container planting, herbaceous
perennials, shrubs and specimen
trees.

NEW **40 LAWRENCE CLOSE**
Ian & Romaine Bowman
Lush informal but structured
planting style, with pond, mature
trees and a conservatory thats
very much part of the garden.
Planting on a small scale with big
ideas.

35 ♦ **LITTLE MORETON HALL**
**Congleton CW12 4SD. The National
Trust, 01260 272018, www.national
trust.org.uk.** *4m S of Congleton. On
A34.* **Adm £6.40, chd £3.20. Weds to
Suns Mar to Oct, 11.30-5 last entry
4.30. For NGS: Sat 19 July (11.30-5
last entry 4.30).**
1¹/₂ -acre garden surrounded by a
moat, next to finest example of timber-
framed architecture in England. Herb
and historic vegetable garden, orchard
and borders. Knot garden. Adm
includes entry to the Hall with optional
free guided tours. Wheelchairs
available. Picnic lawn at front of hall.

36 **LONG ACRE**
**Wyche Lane, Bunbury CW6 9PS. Mr
& Mrs M Bourne, 01829 260944.**
*3¹/₂ m SE of Tarporley. On A49. Turn
2nd L after Wild Boar Hotel to
Bunbury. L at 1st rd junction then 1st R
by Nags Head PH 400yds on L. From
A51 turn to Bunbury until Nags Head.
Turn into Wyche Lane before PH car
park. 400yds to garden. Disabled
parking in lane adjacent to garden.*
Home-made teas. **Adm £3.50, chd
free (share to Horses & Ponies
Protection Assoc & St Boniface
Church Flower Fund). Suns 27 Apr;
22 June (2-5). Visitors also welcome
by appt for groups of 10+.**
Plantswoman's garden of approx 1
acre with unusual plants and trees.
Roses, pool gardens, small vineyard.
Exotic conservatory; herbaceous;
specialise in proteas, S African bulbs,
clivia and streptocarpus. Spring garden
with camellias, magnolias, bulbs.
Newly planted area with rare trees.
Gravel drive.

37 ♦ **LYME PARK**
**Disley SK12 2NX. The National
Trust, 01663 762023,
lymepark@nationaltrust.org.uk.** *6m
SE of Stockport. Just W of Disley on
A6.* **House and Garden adm £7.60,
chd £3.80, Garden only adm £4.80,
chd £2.80. Sats, Suns March 12-3,
Daily Apr to Oct. For NGS: Sun 20
Apr; Sat 19 July (11-4.30).**
17-acre garden retaining many original
features from Tudor and Jacobean
times. High Victorian style bedding,
Dutch garden, Gertrude Jekyll style
herbaceous border, Edwardian rose
garden, Wyatt orangery and many
other features. Also rare trees, lake,
ravine garden, lawns, mixed borders
and rare Wyatt garden.

38 **MANLEY KNOLL**
**Manley Road, Manley WA6 9DX. Mr
& Mrs R Fildes.** *3m N of Tarvin. On
B5393, via Ashton & Mouldsworth. 3m
S of Frodsham, via Alvanley.* Home-
made teas. **Adm £3.50, chd free. Sun
18 May (2-5).**
Terraced garden with rhododendrons,
azaleas etc. Quarry garden with
waterfalls and an air of mystery. Far
reaching views over Cheshire Plain.

39 **MAYFIELD**
**The Peppers, Lymm WA13 0JA.
Janet Bashforth & Barrie Renshaw,
01925 756107,
janetbashforth@talktalk.net.** *In Lymm
village turn by Lloyds TSB Bank into
Pepper St. Follow NGS signs, take 2nd
R leading into The Peppers.* Home-
made teas. **Adm £3, chd free. Suns
11 May; 13 July (12-5). Visitors also
welcome by appt.**
Constantly evolving plantswoman's
garden, approx ¹/₃ acre with mature
trees, mixed borders containing
herbaceous perennials, shrubs and
bulbs, dry shaded border. The S-facing
garden has a large number of grasses.
Interesting structures and features
throughout, designed to give maximum
seasonal interest.

40 **MAYLANDS**
**Latchford Road, Gayton CH60 3RN.
John & Ann Hinde, 0151 342 8557,
john.hinde@maylands.com,
www.maylands.com.** *7m S of
Birkenhead. SE of Heswall. From
Devon Doorway/Glegg Arms
roundabout at Heswall travel SE in
Chester direction on A540 approx ¹/₄*

m. Turn R into Gayton Lane, take 3rd L into Latchford Rd. Garden on L. Park on rd or at 69 Well Lane. Home-made teas. **Adm £3.50, chd free. Sun 1 June (1-5.30). Visitors also welcome by appt, groups of 5 - 25 anytime.**
Approx 1/2 acre with maturing plantings against background of mature oaks and elegantly curving lawn. Range of growing conditions and long season. Incl rhododendrons, wisteria, magnolia, pond, rockery, herbaceous borders. Continually evolving planting now incls grasses and scree area. Some gravel and bark paths, plus steps.

& ⚲ ✕ ⊗ ☕ ☎

41 MILLPOOL
Smithy Lane, Bosley SK11 0NZ. Joe & Barbara Fray, 01260 226581. *5m S of Macclesfield. Just off A523 at Bosley. Turn L 1m S of A54 T-lights. From Leek, turn R, 2½ m N of The Royal Oak PH at Rushton. Please follow direction to parking areas. No parking at garden.* Light refreshments & teas. **Adm £3, chd free. Sat 28, Sun 29 June (1-5). Visitors also welcome by appt, June & July only, groups 10+.**
Garden designed to extend the seasons with colour, texture and scent. Lush herbaceous borders and areas of deep shade. Small stream, pond and bog garden. Gravel plantings; containers and a fine collection of bonsai trees. Come and sit awhile and share our pleasure. Discovery sheet for children.

⊗ ☕ ☎

42 31 MOSS LANE
Styal SK9 4LF. Anne & Stephen Beswick. *2m N of Wilmslow. From M56 J5 towards Airport Terminal 1 then Cheadle, continue to T-junction. Turn R at T-lights then next R to Moss Lane. No 31 is 200yds on L.* Home-made teas. **Adm £3, chd free. Sun 3 Aug (1-5).**
Designer's evolving garden balancing enthusiasm with the need for low maintenance. Ground cover, mixed borders, wild flower area, wildlife pond, secret garden and fruit arch. N-facing front garden specialising in shady planting and ferns.

& ✕ ⊗ ☕

43 THE MOUNT
Andertons Lane, Whirley, Henbury, nr Macclesfield SK11 9PB. Mr & Mrs Nicholas Payne, 01625 422920, ngs@themount1.freeserve.co.uk. *2m due W of Macclesfield. Along A537*

opp Blacksmiths Arms. At Henbury go up Pepper St. Turn L into Church Lane then Andertons Lane in 100yds. Home-made teas. **Combined with Far Hills £5, chd free. Sun 25 May (2-5.30). Visitors also welcome by appt.**
Approx 2 acres with interesting trees incl *Eucryphia x nymansensis,* fern leaved beech and *Sciadopitys.* Shrubberies; herbaceous border and short vista of Irish yews. Water features and landscaped swimming pool. Far views to Wales.

& ✕ ⊗ ☕ ☎

Approx 1/2 acre with maturing plantings against background of mature oaks and elegantly curving lawn . . .

44 ◆ MOUNT PLEASANT
Yeld Lane, Kelsall CW6 0TB. Dave Darlington & Louise Worthington, 01829 751592, www.mountpleasantgardens.co.uk. *8m E of Chester. Off A54 at T-lights into Kelsall. Turn into Yeld Lane opp Farmers Arms PH, 200yds on L. Do not follow Sat Nav directions.* **Adm £3.50, chd free. Weds, Sats, Suns 2 Apr to 28 Sept. For NGS: Sun 25, Mon 26 May; Sat 27, Sun 28 Sept (12-5).**
10 acres of landscaped garden and woodland started in 1994 with impressive views over the Cheshire countryside. Steeply terraced in places. Specimen trees, rhododendrons, azaleas, conifers, mixed and herbaceous borders; 4 ponds, formal and wildlife. Vegetable garden, stumpery with tree ferns, sculptures, wild flower meadow and Japanese garden 2007. Exhibition of sculpture in the garden, stone carving demonstration. Featured in 'Cheshire Life'. Wheelchair access, please call prior to visit.

✕ ⊗ ☕

46 NEWTON HOUSE
18 Well Lane, Heswall CH60 8NF. John & Eileen Harsant. *7m S of Birkenhead. SE of Heswall. From Devon Doorway/Glegg Arms roundabout on A540, take E exit directly opp Devon Doorway into Well Lane. This forks L from Dawstone Rd in 1/4 m. Garden is approx 50yds on R down Well Lane after fork. There is no parking at garden. Park in Dawstone Rd or Well Lane before the fork, avoiding driveways.* Home-made teas. **Adm £3.50, chd free. Sun 27 Apr (2-5.30).**
Wide range of rhododendrons - hybrid species, unusual and tender varieties, Japanese and deciduous azaleas, magnolias. Growing collection of unusual camellias together with spectacular old favourites. Closely planted borders around sweeping lawns on light acid soil, will interest the general visitor and specialist plantsman. Productive vegetable area, which incl extensive fruit plantings. Selected wheelchair routes only.

& ✕ ☕

47 ◆ NORTON PRIORY MUSEUM & GARDENS
Tudor Road, Runcorn WA7 1SX. Norton Priory Museum Trust, 01928 569895, www.nortonpriory.org. *2m SW of Runcorn. From M56 J11 turn for Warrington & follow signs. From Warrington take A56 for Runcorn & follow signs.* **Prices not yet confirmed please tel, or see website. Walled Garden March to Oct, special winter tours. For NGS: Sun 6 Apr (1.30-4.30).**
16 acres of gardens. Georgian summerhouses, rock garden and stream glade, 3-acre walled garden of similar date (1760s) recently restored. Rosewalk, colour borders, herb and cottage gardens. National Collection of Tree Quince, (*Cydonia oblonga*).

& ✕ ⊗ NCCPG

49 THE OLD FARM
Gayton Farm Road, Gayton CH60 8NN. A Gamon. *7m S of Birkenhead. SE of Heswall. From Devon Doorway roundabout on A540, take the exit directly opp the Devon Doorway into Well Lane. Parking on Well Lane in approx 1/2 m. Garden entrance is up cobbled rd which is L as the main rd takes a R.* Home-made teas. **Adm £3, chd free. Sun 10 Aug (2-5.30).**
1/3 -acre, in 3rd generation ownership, set on slopes of Dee estuary, against

mid C18 farm building (not open). Main garden has 3 tiers, created from old sloping, cobbled farmyard with pond, roses, vegetables, soft fruit and bedding. Rose parterre completes the garden.

50 THE OLD HOUGH
Forge Mill Lane, Warmingham CW10 0HQ. Mr & Mrs D S Varey, 07976 381996, jdm@oldhough.co.uk. *3m from Middlewich. 4m from Sandbach. From Middlewich take A530 to Nantwich. At Wimboldsley School turn L to Warmingham L again at T-junction. Garden 1/2 m on R. From Sandbach take A533 to Middlewich, 1/2 m after Fox Inn on L turn into Mill Lane. At T-junction on canal bridge turn R. Stay on this rd. Garden 2m on. Ample parking.* **Adm £4, chd free. Evening Openings** wine, Thurs 29 May; 5, 12, 19 June (5.30-9). **Visitors also welcome by appt late May & June, groups by arrangement, ample parking for coaches.**
Gracious gardens surround a beautiful farmhouse (not open). Extensive lawns, long flower borders, choice trees incl paulownias, ginkgo and others with lovely bark, large lily pond. A more formal pond is fed by a sparkling rill and guarded by two naked maidens! Over 250 metres of climber-covered walls, incl many roses and the spectacular hedge festooned with tropaeolum speciosum are coveted features. WCs. Steps at end may mean retracing route, otherwise, small area of gravel.

48 THE OLD PARSONAGE
Arley Green, via Arley Hall & Gardens CW9 6LZ. The Viscount & Viscountess Ashbrook, 01565 777277, ashbrookarleyhall@btinternet.com. *5m NNE of Northwich. 3m Great Budworth. M6 J19 & 20 & M56 J10. Follow signs to Arley Hall & Gardens. From Arley Hall notices to Old Parsonage which lies across park at Arley Green.* Cream teas. **Adm £4, chd free (share to Save The Children Fund). Sat 31 May; Sun 1 June** (2-5.30). **Visitors also welcome by appt, May & June, groups of 10+.**
2-acre garden in attractive and secretive rural setting in secluded part of Arley Estate, with ancient yew hedges, herbaceous and mixed borders, shrub roses, climbers, leading

to woodland garden and unfenced pond with gunnera and water plants. Rhododendrons, azaleas, meconopsis, cardiocrinums, some interesting and unusual trees. Wheelchair access over mown grass.

51 ONE HOUSE NURSERY
Rainow SK11 0AD. Louise Baylis, www.onehousenursery.co.uk. *2 1/2 m NE of Macclesfield. On A537 Macclesfield to Buxton rd. 2 1/2 m from Macclesfield stn.* Home-made teas. **Adm £3, chd free. Sun 11 May; Sat 28, Sun 29 June** (10-5).
1/2 -acre plantswoman's garden featuring hostas, rare and unusual woodland and sun-loving perennials, rockery, gravel garden, sculptures and hornbeam arbour. Stunning views over Cheshire Plain. A short walk away is an atmospheric 1/3 -acre historic early C18 walled kitchen garden, hidden for 60yrs and recently restored. Heritage vegetables, gardening and farming bygones, orchard with rare-breed pigs. Sculpture trail (11 May).

52 ORCHARD HOUSE
72 Audley Road, Alsager ST7 2QN. Mr & Mrs J Trinder, 01270 874833. *6m S of Congleton. 3m W of Kidsgrove. At T-lights in Alsager town centre turn L towards Audley, house is 300yds on R beyond level Xing. Or M6 J16 to North Stoke on A500, 1st L to Alsager, 2m, just beyond Manor House Hotel on L.* Home-made teas. **Adm £2.50, chd free. Sun 27 Apr; Weds 4 June; 16 July; 27 Aug** (12-5). **Visitors also welcome by appt May/Sept.**
Fascinated by plants from an early age, we have an unusual collection of diverse plants. Our long narrow garden is organised to accomodate shrubs, herbaceous plants, alpines, grasses, ferns and specialising in bulbs and irises.

OTTERBROOK
See Derbyshire.

53 PARM PLACE
High Street, Great Budworth CW9 6HF. Peter & Jane Fairclough, 01606 891131, pfair@btinternet.com. *3m N of Northwich. Great Budworth on E side of A559 between Northwich & Warrington, 4m from J10 M56, also 4m from J19 M6. Parm Place is W of village on S side of High Street.* Home-

made teas. **Adm £3.50, chd free (share to Great Ormond Street Hospital). Suns 6 Apr; 13 July (1-5).** **Visitors also welcome by appt.**
Well-stocked 1/2 -acre garden with stunning views towards S Cheshire. Curving lawns, shrubs, colourful herbaceous borders, roses, water features, rockery, gravel bed with grasses. Fruit and vegetable plots. In spring large collection of bulbs and flowers, camellias, hellebores and blossom.

A more formal pond is fed by a sparkling rill and guarded by two naked maidens!

54 ◆ PEOVER HALL GARDENS
Knutsford WA16 6SW. Randle Brooks Esq, 01565 830395 (weekdays only). *4m S of Knutsford. Turn off A50 at Whipping Stocks Inn, down Stocks Lane. Follow signs to Peover Hall & Church. Entrance off Goostrey Lane clearly signed.* **Adm £4, chd free. Mons, Thurs except Bank Hols May - Aug. For NGS: Sat 17, Sun 18 May (2-5).**
15 acres. 5 walled gardens; C19 dell, rhododendrons, pleached limes, topiary. Grade II Carolean Stables and C18 park.

55 PIKELOW FARM
School Lane, Marton SK11 9HD. David & Ann Taylor, 01260 224231. *3m N of Congleton. In Marton Village take rd signed Marton Heath Trout Pools; 3/4 m down School Lane on R.* Home-made teas. **Adm £3, chd free. Sat 26 Apr; Sun 20 July (2-5).** **Visitors also welcome by appt, evenings only during spring & summer.**
Peace and tranquillity of a private Nature Reserve with 3 beautifully landscaped lakes bordered by wild flowers; native trees and plants. Typical

farm garden with traditional spring flowers, herbaceous borders and ponds. Echiums in the spring with amazing displays of non-stop begonias throughout the summer. A Nature Lovers Paradise. Teas, cakes, gifts, bird food etc by Macclesfield RSPB.

 ♿ ✂ ❀ ☕ ☎

56 POULTON HALL
Poulton Lancelyn, Bebington CH63 9LN. The Lancelyn Green Family, 0151 334 2057, www.poultonhall.co.uk. *2m S of Bebington. From M53, J4 towards Bebington; at T-lights R along Poulton Rd; house 1m on R. Home-made teas.* **Adm £4, chd free.** Sun 13 Apr (2-5.30). **Visitors also welcome by appt.**
3 acres; front lawns with view of the house, wild flower meadow and shrubbery. Child-friendly features incl a surprising new approach to the walled garden, redesigned Nursery Rhyme area, wood sculptures of Robin Hood and Jabberwocky by Jim Heath and other reminders of Roger Lancelyn Green's retellings. Sundial garden for the visually impaired is sponsored by Bebington Rotary club. As a powerful memorial to Richard Lancelyn Green, new monumental, stainless steel sculpture of enigmatic contemporary form has been created by Sue Sharples, who designed the bronze Viking head. Music: organ and choir recital. Art Exhibition.

✂ ❀ ☕ ☎

QUARRYSIDE
See Derbyshire.

57 RIDGEHILL HOUSE
Ridgehill, Sutton SK11 0LU. Mr & Mrs Martin McMillan, 01260 252353. *2m SE of Macclesfield. From Macclesfield take A523 to Leek after Silk Rd look for t-lights signed Langley, Wincle & Sutton turn L into Byron's Lane, under canal bridge 1st L to Langley at junction Church House PH. Ridgehill Rd is opp turn up Ridgehill Rd, garden on R. Coffee/Home-made teas.* **Adm £4.50, chd free.** Sun 1 June (10-4.30). **Visitors also welcome by appt May & June.**
Country garden set in 4 acres overlooking the Cheshire plain. Ponds and water features, shrubbery with rhododendrons, azaleas, camellias etc. Herbaceous borders, blue and winter gardens, topiary areas.

❀ ☕ ☎

One or two surprises at the bottom of the garden . . .

58 ◆ RODE HALL
Church Lane, Scholar Green ST7 3QP. Sir Richard & Lady Baker Wilbraham, 01270 882961, www.rodehall.co.uk. *5m SW of Congleton. Between Scholar Green (A34) & Rode Heath (A50).* **House and Garden adm £5, concessions/chd over 12 £4, Garden only adm £3, concessions/chd over 12 £2.50.** Snowdrops walks Sat 2 Feb - 2 Mar daily except Mons (12-4). Tues, Weds, Thurs & Bank Hols 24 Mar to 25 Sept (2-5).
Nesfield's terrace and rose garden with view over Humphry Repton's landscape is a feature of Rode gardens, as is the woodland garden with terraced rock garden and grotto. Other attractions incl the walk to the lake, restored ice house, working walled kitchen garden and new Italian garden. Fine display of snowdrops in February.

❀ ☕

59 ROSE HILL GARDENS
Marple SK6 6JE. *4m SE of Stockport. Marple Hall Drive. Claremont Ave is off Maple Hall Drive which is off Stockpot Rd, Marple. Please park on Marina Drive or Claremont Ave for 305 Stockport Rd. Home-made teas at 35 Claremont Avenue.* **Combined adm £4.50, chd free. Afternoon & Early Evening Openings** Sat 9, Sun 10 Aug (1-7).
Three gardens of different charactors. Each one is within 5 mins walk of each other. Chance to try your hand at silk painting, or making a hand-painted silk scarf in 30 mins. Other attractions to be arranged, please see NGS website.

☕

2 CLAREMONT AVENUE
Eric & Maggie Britten, 0161 427 5182, marple.brittenfamily@ cwctv.net. Visitors also welcome by appt July, Aug & Sept.
Stuffed with plants, many unusual, this artist and plantaholic's garden provides a different 'feel' and quirky surprise round every corner. A fun garden where plants are allowed a certain amount of licence.

✂ ❀ ☎

NEW 35 CLAREMONT AVENUE
Barry & Hazel Meakin
Herbaceous perennials and shrubs with mature trees and lawn give the garden a natural and tranquil atmosphere. S-facing but with areas of shade, and one or two surprises at the bottom of the garden.

✂ ❀

NEW 305 STOCKPORT ROAD
Rita & Barry Ware
Immediate impact provided by colourful side/front borders. Rear garden backed by wood and, steeply terraced (access by wide descending steps). Dramatic, colourful, informal planting of herbaceous perennials, flowering shrubs, ferns with pretty patio area.

✂ ❀

61 ROSEWOOD
Puddington CH64 5SS. Mr & Mrs C E J Brabin, 0151 353 1193, angela.brabin@tesco.net. *6m N of Chester. Turn L (W) off Chester to Hoylake A540 to Puddington. Park by village green. Walk to Old Hall Lane, 30yds away then through archway on L to garden. Owner will meet you at green by appt.* **Adm £3, chd free.** Visitors welcome by appt.
1-acre garden incl small wood, approx 100 rhododendron species and 50 camellias, both spring and autumn flowering, mature flowering dogwoods incl Cornus kousa, kousa chinensis and capitata. Very rare *Michelia yunnanensis* growing and flowering outside. Most of the above raised from seed by owner, some of which are available for sale. A wide range of other species, most of flowering size, in garden.

♿ ❀

62 THE ROWANS
Oldcastle Lane, Threapwood
SY14 7AY. Paul Philpotts & Alan
Bourne, 01948 770522. *3m SW of
Malpas. Leave Malpas by B5069 for
Wrexham, pass church on R, continue
for 3m, take 1st L after Threapwood
PO. 1st L into Oldcastle Lane, garden
1st bungalow on R.* Home-made teas.
**Adm £3.50, chd free. Sat 19, Sun 20
July (2-5.30). Visitors also welcome
by appt.** A very interesting garden
through all seasons.
Garden restored after many years of
neglect, it has been redesigned with an
Italian theme, with new borders and
beds with roses, perennials and
numerous magnolias, rhododendrons
and feature trees. Woodland dell,
secret garden, formal ponds and many
seating areas to sit and enjoy the
garden and its numerous statues.
Featured on BBC 2 Open Gardens.
Runner-up - Chester in Bloom.

63 SAIGHTON GRANGE
(Abbey Gate College), Saighton
CH3 6EN. The Governors of Abbey
Gate College, 01244 332077,
alan.kift@abbeygatecollege.co.uk,
www.abbeygatecollege.co.uk. *4m
SE of Chester. Take A41 towards
Whitchurch. At far end of Waverton
turn R to Saighton. Grange is at the
end of village.* Home-made teas. **Adm
£3, chd free (share to Deeside
House Educational Trust Ltd). Sun 6
Apr (12-4). Visitors also welcome by
appt.**
The gardens at Abbey Gate College
are a little masterpiece of garden
design. From the symmetrical vista
through the clipped yews hedges,
which are undergoing restoration, to
the Japanese garden, which is
beginning to blossom, all provide a
tantalising glimpse of what has been
and what is yet to come. This garden is
still in the process of restoration.

64 ST DAVIDS HOUSE
St Davids Lane, Noctorum
CH43 9UD. Ian Mitchell, 0151 652
5236. *3¹/₂ m SW of Birkenhead Town
Hall. Take A553 then A502 through
Claughton Village. After 2 sets of T-
lights, 1st L (Noctorum Lane). After
Xrds, St Davids Lane is 1st on R.* **Adm
£3.50, chd free. Visitors welcome by
appt any time of year.**
Victorian garden of 1¹/₂ acres recently
restored to original 1864 probable
planting. Azaleas, camellias,

rhododendrons, herbaceous and
mixed borders, rockeries, pond,
pine and silver birch copse with
winding steep paths. Excellent views
of Clwyd Hills, Snowdonia and Irish
Sea.

65 SANDYMERE
Cotebrook CW6 9EH. John & Alex
Timpson. *5m N of Tarporley. On A54
about 300yds W of T-lights at Xrds of
A49/A54.* Home-made teas. **Adm
£4.50, chd free. Sun 6 July (2-5).**
16 landscaped acres of beautiful
Cheshire countryside with terraces,
walled garden and amazing hosta
garden. Long views, native wildlife and
tranquillity of 3 lakes. Elegant planting
schemes, shady seats and sun-
splashed borders, mature pine woods
and rolling lawns accented by graceful
wooden structures. Different every
year: witness the evolution of a 5yr
plan that is now in its 20th yr.

Enjoy tranquility
and peace
on this plant-
packed garden
'journey' . . . .

66 THE SCHOOL HOUSE
School Lane, Dunham Massey
WA14 4SE. Andrew Bushell & Peter
White, 0161 928 3909. *1¹/₂ m SW of
Altrincham. From M56 J7 follow signs
for Dunham Massey Hall (NT). Turn into
Woodhouse Lane becoming School
Lane 100yds after Axe Cleaver PH. Car
park available from 1pm.* Home-made
teas. **Adm £3, chd free. Sat 19, Sun
20 July (1-5).**
Cottage garden divided into rooms. In
picturesque setting attached to village
hall and beside the Bridgewater canal.
Incl herbaceous borders, rose and bog
garden. Ideal start for local walks.
Village attractions incl maize maze,
lavender farm and stately home. Some
gravel paths.

SMITHY COTTAGE
See Staffordshire & part of West
Midlands.

**67 NEW 68 SOUTH OAK
LANE**
Wilmslow SK9 6AT. Caroline &
David Melliar-Smith, 01625
528147. *³/₄ m SW of Central
Wilmslow. From M56 take A528 to
Central Wilmslow. Turn R onto
B5086, follow Knutsford, take 1st
R into Gravel Lane (after Kings
Arms roundabout) then 4th R into
South Oak Lane. Park by
recreation ground.* **Adm £2.50,
chd free. Sat 31 May; Sun 1
June (1-5). Visitors also welcome
by appt July, Aug, mid Sept, max
group 12.**
With all yr round colour, scent and
interest, this attractive, small,
hedged cottage garden has
evolved over the years into 5
natural 'rooms'. As keen members
of the Hardy Plants Society, the
owners passion for plant is
reflected in shrubs, trees, flower
borders and pond, creating havens
for birds, bees and wildlife. Enjoy
tranquility and peace on this plant-
packed garden 'journey'. Featured
in 'Cheshire Life'.

SOUTHLANDS
See Lancashire, Merseyside &
Greater Manchester.

68 199 STOCKPORT ROAD
Timperley WA15 7SF. Eric & Shirley
Robinson. *1¹/₂ m NE of Altrincham.
Take A560 out of Altrincham, in 1m
take B5165 towards Timperley. B5165
is Stockport rd.* Home-made teas.
**Adm £2.50, chd free. Suns 15 June;
3 Aug (1-5).**
Overstuffed, cottage-style garden
owned by 2 plantaholics, one an
enthusiastic gardener, the other a very
keen flower arranger. The garden is full
of colourful herbaceous perennials,
shrubs and hostas, and has a small
brick-built pond complete with small
koi and goldfish. You will not believe
how many plants there are in such a
small garden. Newly designed front
garden with water feature.

69 ◆ STONYFORD COTTAGE
Stonyford Lane, Oakmere CW8 2TF.
Janet & Tony Overland, 01606
888128, tony_overland@
yahoo.co.uk. *5m SW of Northwich.*

Turn R off A556 (Northwich to Chester). At Xrds ¾ m past A49 junction (signpost Norley-Kingsley NB not Cuddington signs). Entrance ½ m on L. **Adm £3, chd free. Tues - Suns & Bank Hol Mons April - Sept 12-5 Guided tours for groups. For NGS: Suns 8 June; 10 Aug (1.30-5.30).** Set around a large pool this Monet style landscape has, a wealth of moisture loving plants, incl iris and candelabra primulas. Drier areas feature unusual perennials and rarer trees and shrubs. Newly planted woodland walk gives, hitherto unseen, vistas across the pool to the cottage gardens. Adjacent nursery.

Mid April brings a profusion of cherry blossom, magnolias, camellias and early rhododendrons

70 SWETTENHAM VILLAGE
CW12 2LD. 5m NW of Congleton. Turn off A54 N 2m W of Congleton or turn E off A535 at Twemlow Green, NE of Holmes Chapel. Follow signs to Swettenham. Parking at Swettenham Arms PH. Entrance at side of PH. Home-made teas at Dane Edge £2.50. **Combined adm £5, chd free. Suns 27 Apr; 3 Aug (12-4).**

DANE EDGE
Mr & Mrs J Cunningham.
Garden approx 5 mins walk from car park
Steep riverside garden of 10½ acres leading down to a beautiful and partially wooded wildlife haven with pleasant walks by R Dane. Peacocks roaming the garden. Spring opening for bluebell, wild garlic, summer opening for lavender meadow at Swettenham Arms.

◆ **THE QUINTA ARBORETUM**
Swettenham. **Tatton Garden Society, www.tattongardensociety.co.uk. Daily (not Christmas Day) 9 to dusk.**
Arboretum on a 28-acre site established since 1948 with over 2,000 species of trees incl collections of birch, pine, oak and flowering shrubs. Bluebell bank and snowdrops. 40 camellias and 64 rhododendrons planted 2004. Collection of 120 hebes. Lake. Guided tours available.

71 NEW TATTENHALL HALL
High Street, Tattenhall CH3 9PX. **Jen & Nick Benefield, Chris Evere & Jannie Hollins.** *S of Chester on A41. Turn L to Tattenhall, through village, turn R at Letters PH, past war memorial on L through Sandstone pillared gates. Park on rd or in village car park.* **Adm £3.50, chd free. Sun 22 June (2-5).**
Shared garden developed over 14yrs, around Jacobean house (not open). 4½ acres, incl wild flower meadows, with interesting trees, large pond, stream, walled garden with well stocked herbaceous borders, planted for succession, yew terrace overlooking meadow with views to hills. Glasshouse, vegetable garden. A relaxed garden style. Limited wheelchair access, gravel and cobbled paths, slope to field.

72 ◆ TATTON PARK
Knutsford WA16 6QN. **The National Trust, leased to Cheshire County Council, 01625 374400, www.tattonpark.org.uk.** *2½ m N of Knutsford. Well signed on M56 J7 & from M6 J19.* **House and Garden adm £5, chd £3, park entry £4.20, Garden only adm £3.50, chd £2. For opening details please tel or see website. For NGS: Weds 30 Apr; 11 June (10-6).**
Features include orangery by Wyatt, fernery by Paxton, restored Japanese garden, Italian and rose gardens. Greek monument and African hut. Hybrid azaleas and rhododendrons; swamp cypresses, tree ferns, tall redwoods, bamboos and pines. Fully restored productive walled gardens.

---

73 TIRLEY GARTH
Utkinton CW6 0LZ. *2m N of Tarporley. 2m S of Kelsall. Entrance 500yds from village of Utkinton. At N of Tarporley take Utkinton rd.* Home-made teas. **Adm £4, chd free. Wed 16, Sun 20 Apr (1-5).**
40-acre garden, terraced and landscaped. Designed by Thomas Mawson, it is the only Grade II* Arts & Crafts garden in Cheshire that remains complete and in excellent condition. The garden is considered an exceptionally important example of an early C20 garden laid out in both formal and informal styles. Mid April brings a profusion of cherry blossom, magnolias, camellias and early rhododendrons. Partial wheelchair access.

74 80 UPTON PARK
Upton by Chester CH2 1DQ. **Lynne & Phil Pearn, 01244 390326, lynnepearn@hotmail.com.** *1½ m NE of Chester. From A41 ring rd NE of Chester turn towards Chester at Gulf garage T-lights at Upton Heath. ½ m down Heath Rd (traffic calming) to mini roundabout, Upton Park is 2nd on L after roundabout. Please discuss parking arrangements when booking visit.* Home-made teas. **Adm £3, chd free. Visitors welcome by appt, groups up to 30, evening visits possible.**
'A Country garden in suburbia'. Plantswoman's garden designed for yr-round interest but 'peaking' in July/early Aug, featuring mixed beds with interesting metal and willow work sculptures (created by the owners) mingling with the flowers, colourful banked herbaceous beds, small vegetable plot, greenhouses, pond, ferns and hostas. Courtyard with ancient espalier pear tree, numerous pots, well and Victorian conservatory with vine and bouganvillea. Featured in 'Amateur Gardening'.

75 THE VALVE HOUSE
Egerton Green, nr Malpas SY14 8AW. **Nicola Reynolds.** *4m NE of Malpas. From Chester take A41 S, at Broxton roundabout turn L onto A534, 1st R after Coppermine PH (to Bickerton). Fork L at Bickerton School. Garden 1st on L. On A49 turn opp Cholmondeley Arms to Cholmondeley Castle. Garden opp Manor Farm.* Home-made teas. **Adm £3, chd free. Sat 14, Sun 15 June (2-6).**

$^1/_2$ -acre plantswoman's garden with many interesting features, well stocked herbaceous borders with an abundance of unusual plants. Wildlife pond with Monet-style bridge, productive vegetable and fruit gardens and rare breed chickens. Gravel paths.

♿ ✖ ◈ ☕

WEEPING ASH
See Lancashire, Merseyside & Greater Manchester.

76 THE WELL HOUSE
Tilston SY14 7DP. Mrs S H French-Greenslade, 01829 250332. *3m NW of Malpas. On A41, 1st turn R after Broxton roundabout, L on Malpas Rd through Tilston. House & antique shop on L.* Cream teas. **Adm £3.50, chd free (share to Cystic Fibrosis Trust).** Sun 29 June (1.30-5.30). **Visitors also welcome by appt, Apr to end of July, coaches permitted.**
1-acre cottage garden, bridge over natural stream, spring bulbs, perennials, herbs and shrubs. Triple pond and waterfall feature. Adjoining $^3/_4$ -acre field being made into wild flower meadow; first seeding late 2003. Large bog area of kingcups and ragged robin. Featured in 'The English Garden' magazine, Prize winner - Chester in Bloom.

✖ ◈ ☕ ☏

77 69 WELL LANE
Gayton CH60 8NH. Angus & Sally Clark. *7m S of Birkenhead. SE of Heswall. From the Devon Doorway/Glegg Arms roundabout at Heswall, travel SE in the direction of Chester for approx $^1/_4$ m. Turn R into Gayton Lane for about $^1/_2$ m then L into Well Lane. Garden approx 200yds on L. Park on rd.* Tea & Cakes. **Adm £3, chd free.** Sun 4, Mon 5 May (2-5).
This undulating established 1-acre garden has a stunning rear setting and is surrounded by a natural woodland backdrop. Many spring flowering shrubs (rhododendron, azalea, magnolia, cornus ... etc) with surprises at every corner. Restored old farm buildings with roofless area containing climbers and fronted by cobblestones. Summer wild flower area. Limited wheelchair access.

♿ ✖ ◈ ☕

78 WEST DRIVE GARDENS
4, 6, 9 West Drive, Gatley SK8 4JJ. Mr & Mrs D J Gane, Mr & Mrs K L Marsden & Mrs T Bishop & Mr J Needham. *4m N of Wilmslow. On*

B5166. From J5 (M56) drive past airport to B5166 (Styal Rd). L towards Gatley. Pass over T-lights at Heald Green. West Drive is last turn on R before Gatley Village. Cul-de-sac, please do not park beyond the notice. Home-made teas. **Combined adm £5, chd free (share to New Start).** Sun 8 June (10.30-4.30).
Here are three hidden gems in a suburban setting, each with its individual character. Surrounded by mature trees and incl woodland walk, wildlife pond, unusual containers and ceramics, these gardens are a plantperson's delight. Fantastic plant stall as usual. New developments in all gardens.

✖ ◈ ☕

79 WESTAGE FARM
Westage Lane, Great Budworth CW9 6HJ. Jean & Peter Davies. *3m N of Northwich. 4m W of Knutsford. Gt Budworth is on E side of A559 between Northwich & Warrington, 4m from J10 M 56, and 4m from J19 M6. Garden is 400yds to E of village. Follow Gt Budworth signs.* Home-made teas. **Adm £3.50, chd free. Evening Opening** wine, Fri 13 June (7-10); Sat 14, Sun 15 June (11-5).
2 acre cottage garden with herbaceous and mixed borders with architectural planting, a new interest around every corner. Large vegetable and soft fruit area, orchard and wild flower woodland garden with interesting trees. You can walk in the field to the well and see donkeys, hens, ducks and other rare breed poultry. There are many amusing light hearted features and raised colour themed plots. We have a small vine yard and Peter will talk about his wine making. The garden is totally child friendly and Jean will meet and greet each time. Featured in 'Cheshire Life'.

♿ ✖ ◈ ☕

80 WILLASTON VILLAGE GARDENS
Willaston CH64 1TE. *8m N of Chester. Take A540 Chester to West Kirby rd; turn R on B5151 to Willaston; at village centre turn R into Hooton Rd. Change Lane is $^3/_4$ m on R opp garage. All 3 gardens are entered from Change Hey garden. Parking available in field at bottom of Change Lane on RH-side. 15 mins walk from Hooton Stn along B5133 in direction of Willaston. Change Lane on LH-side opp garage. Leave M53 J5. Join A41, travel in direction of Queensferry, N Wales.*

$^1/_4$ m at T- lights turn R B5133. Along Hooton Rd, after $^3/_4$ m Hooton Stn on L. Then as from Hooton Stn. Home-made teas at Change Hey. **Combined adm £4, chd free.** Sun 18 May (2-5).
☕

CHANGE HEY
Change Lane. Keith & Joan Butcher
2-acre garden with mature trees, developing woodland area underplanted with rhododendrons and azaleas.

♿ ✖ ◈

THE DUTCH HOUSE
Joan & Michael Ring
$^1/_3$ -acre cottage-style garden with some formality. The rear garden vista, terminating with a 1920 Boulton & Paul revolving summerhouse, is surrounded on 2 sides by mature beech, oak and pine trees. Some gravel paths.

♿ ✖

SILVERBURN
Prof M P & Dr A M Escudier
Just under $^1/_2$ -acre garden designed by garden owners. A plantsman's garden with interesting herbaceous beds and mixed borders, species and old-fashioned roses, rhododendrons, azaleas, attractive trees, vegetable garden and small orchard. Bridge linking Silverburn and Change Hey not designed for wheelchairs. Alternative (separate) access possible.

♿ ✖

Many spring flowering shrubs (rhododendron, azalea, magnolia, cornus ... etc) with surprises at every corner . . .

81 WOOD END COTTAGE
Grange Lane, Whitegate CW8 2BQ.
Mr & Mrs M R Everett, 01606
888236. *4m SW of Northwich. Turn S off A556 (Northwich bypass) at Sandiway PO T-lights; after 1¾ m, turn L to Whitegate village; opp school follow Grange Lane for 300yds.* Home-made teas. **Adm £3.50, chd free (share to The Macular Disease Society). Evening Opening** wine, Thur 3 July (6-8.30); Sun 20 July (2-5). Visitors also welcome by appt, May, June & July only.
Plantsman's traditional country garden of ¹/₂ acre in attractive setting, gently sloping to a natural stream. Shade and moisture-loving plants. Well-stocked herbaceous borders with many unusual plants particularly featuring delphiniums (3 July) and many varieties of phlox (20 July). Red border, roses and clematis. Background of mature trees.

82 WOODCROFT
1 Oakfield Rise, Holmes Chapel
CW4 7DY. Mr & Mrs R Spencer,
01477 533482, renes@fish.co.uk. *4m E of Middlewich. In Holmes Chapel at roundabout take A54 to Middlewich. Parking available at County Primary School, ¹/₂ m on L, turn L into Brookfield Dr, next R. Limited parking at 1 Oakfield Rise.* Home-made teas at Dane Mount. **Combined with Dane Mount** adm £4 free. Sun 6 Apr (1-5). Visitors also welcome by appt.
Medium sized garden incorporates maturing spring flowering shrubs, conifers and heathers with an array of different bulbs. A large raised bed is a feature in the back garden which also contains fruit trees, vegetable patch, rose bed and herbaceous planting.

> Country garden in attractive setting, gently sloping to a natural stream . . .

83 3 WOODHOUSE LANE
Gawsworth SK11 9QQ. Shirley
Campbell & John Helm. *3m SW of Macclesfield. Take A536 from Macclesfield, after approx 3m turn L at Xrds into Church Lane (signed Gawsworth Hall). Take 1st L into Woodhouse Lane garden on L.* Home-made teas. **Adm £3, chd free. Sat 6, Sun 7 Sept (2-5).**
Gently sloping ¹/₃ -acre garden in the pretty village of Gawsworth, designed for yr-round interest. Perennials, annuals, dahlias and cannas provide plenty of late summer colour. Pond, greenhouses, small vegetable garden.

WROXHAM GARDENS
See Lancashire, Merseyside & Greater Manchester.

Cheshire & Wirrall County Volunteers

ngs gardens open for charity

6 acres of landscaped
cottage garden relying entirely
on the threat of visitors
to motivate the owners to
maintain it. We look forward
to seeing you . . .

Sotts Hole Cottage, Kent

CORNWALL

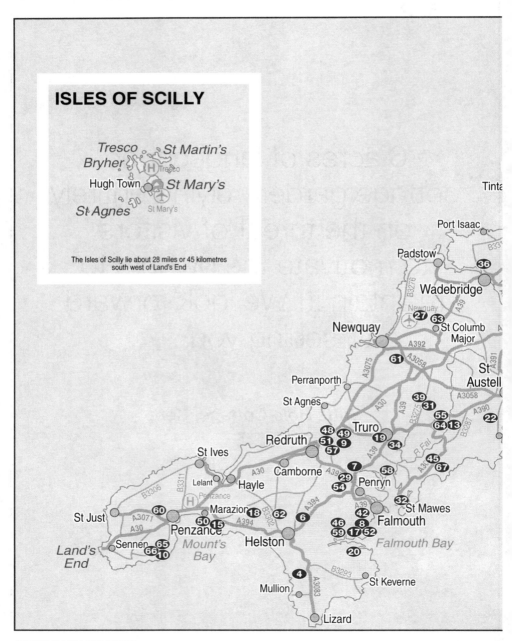

ISLES OF SCILLY

Tresco · St Martin's
Bryher
Hugh Town · St Mary's
St Agnes

The Isles of Scilly lie about 28 miles or 45 kilometres
south west of Land's End

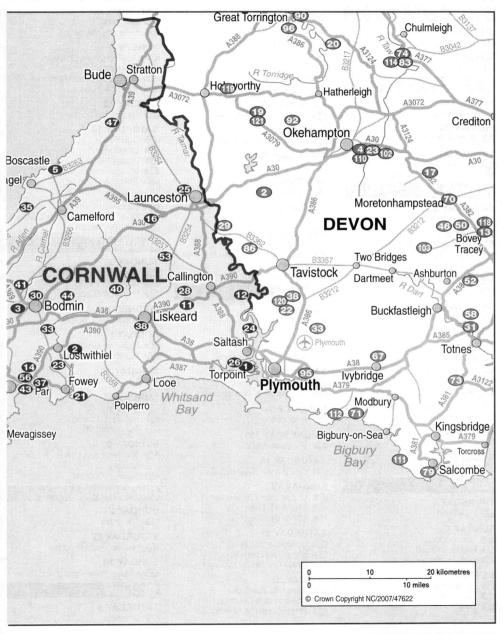

Opening Dates

January
SUNDAY 27
55 Tregoose

February
SUNDAY 10
55 Tregoose

SUNDAY 24
55 Tregoose

March
SUNDAY 16
26 Ince Castle

SUNDAY 23
60 Trengwainton

SUNDAY 30
7 Carclew Gardens
47 Poundstock Gardens

April
SATURDAY 5
58 Trelissick

SUNDAY 6
45 Poppy Cottage Garden
56 Tregrehan
67 Trist House

WEDNESDAY 9
41 Pencarrow

SATURDAY 12
17 Glendurgan

SUNDAY 13
26 Ince Castle

SUNDAY 20
42 Penjerrick Garden
51 Scorrier House

SUNDAY 27
13 Creed House
39 Nansawsan House

MONDAY 28
61 Trerice

WEDNESDAY 30
50 St Michael's Mount

May
THURSDAY 1
21 Headland

SUNDAY 4
2 Boconnoc
25 Higher Truscott
31 Ladock House

MONDAY 5
20 Hallowarren
38 Moyclare
57 Tregullow

TUESDAY 6
33 Lanhydrock

THURSDAY 8
21 Headland

SATURDAY 10
32 Lamorran House

SUNDAY 11
26 Ince Castle
63 Trewan Hall

THURSDAY 15
21 Headland

SATURDAY 17
44 Pinsla Garden & Nursery

SUNDAY 18
44 Pinsla Garden & Nursery

THURSDAY 22
21 Headland

SATURDAY 24
10 Chygurno

SUNDAY 25
10 Chygurno

MONDAY 26
20 Hallowarren
27 The Japanese Garden & Bonsai Nursery
40 Northwood Farm Water Gardens

June
SUNDAY 1
25 Higher Truscott
35 Long Hay

FRIDAY 6
23 Hidden Valley Gardens

SATURDAY 7
1 Antony
23 Hidden Valley Gardens

SUNDAY 8
53 Trebartha

WEDNESDAY 11
4 Bonython Manor

SATURDAY 14
9 Chacewater Garden Safari

SUNDAY 15
9 Chacewater Garden Safari
34 Little Park Farm
37 Marsh Villa Gardens

SATURDAY 21
5 Boscastle Gardens
35 Long Hay (Evening)
44 Pinsla Garden & Nursery

SUNDAY 22
5 Boscastle Gardens
36 Lower Amble Gardens
44 Pinsla Garden & Nursery

SATURDAY 28
48 Primrose Farm

July
SATURDAY 5
10 Chygurno
65 Trewoofe House

SUNDAY 6
6 Bowling Green Cottage
10 Chygurno
16 Ellis Gardens and Nurseries
65 Trewoofe House

SUNDAY 13
54 Tregonning Lodge

SATURDAY 19
12 Cotehele
17 Glendurgan
18 Godolphin
33 Lanhydrock
58 Trelissick

SUNDAY 27
15 Ednovean Farm
40 Northwood Farm Water Gardens
46 Potager Garden

August
SUNDAY 3
16 Ellis Gardens and Nurseries
19 Grey Stones
24 Highcroft Gardens

WEDNESDAY 6
47 Poundstock Gardens

SUNDAY 17
24 Highcroft Gardens
37 Marsh Villa Gardens

MONDAY 18
61 Trerice

SUNDAY 24
30 Kingberry
49 Roseland House
60 Trengwainton

MONDAY 25
27 The Japanese Garden & Bonsai Nursery
49 Roseland House

September
SUNDAY 21
53 Trebartha

SATURDAY 27
23 Hidden Valley Gardens

SUNDAY 28
23 Hidden Valley Gardens

October
SATURDAY 4
12 Cotehele

February 2009

SATURDAY 7
⑪ Coombegate Cottage

SUNDAY 15
⑪ Coombegate Cottage

Gardens open to the public

① Antony
② Boconnoc
④ Bonython Manor
⑧ Carwinion
⑩ Chygurno
⑫ Cotehele
⑬ Creed House
⑭ Eden Project
⑯ Ellis Gardens and Nurseries
⑰ Glendurgan
⑱ Godolphin
㉑ Headland
㉒ The Lost Gardens of Heligan
㉓ Hidden Valley Gardens
㉗ The Japanese Garden & Bonsai Nursery
㉘ Ken Caro
㉜ Lamorran House
㉝ Lanhydrock
㊲ Marsh Villa Gardens
㊳ Moyclare
㊶ Pencarrow
㊷ Penjerrick Garden
㊸ Pine Lodge Gardens & Nursery
㊹ Pinsla Garden & Nursery
㊺ Poppy Cottage Garden
㊻ Potager Garden
㊾ Roseland House
㊿ St Michael's Mount
52 Trebah
56 Tregrehan
58 Trelissick
60 Trengwainton
61 Trerice
62 Trevarno Gardens and the National Museum of Gardening
64 Trewithen
65 Trewoofe House
67 Trist House

By appointment only

③ Bodwannick
㉙ Kennall House
59 Trenarth

Also open by appointment ☎

⑪ Coombegate Cottage
⑮ Ednovean Farm
⑲ Grey Stones
⑳ Hallowarren
㉔ Highcroft Gardens
㉛ Ladock House
39 Nansawsan House

40 Northwood Farm Water Gardens
47 The Barn House, Poundstock Gardens
47 Southfield, Poundstock Gardens
48 Primrose Farm
54 Tregonning Lodge
66 Trewoofe Orchard

The Gardens

ALDER
See Devon.

① NEW ◆ ANTONY
Torpoint PL11 2QA. The National Trust, 01752 812191, www.nationaltrust.org.uk. *6m W of Plymouth. 2m from Torpoint town centre. Take main rd (Antony Rd) out of Torpoint and follow signs to Antony House and Gardens.* **Adm £5.20, chd £1.50. Tues, Weds, Thurs, 24 Mar to 31 Oct (1.30-5.30). For NGS: Sat 7 June (12.30-5.30).**
Beautiful garden set in 35 acres of Cornish countryside. Home to the Carew-Pole family, primarily a spring and summer garden but a visit any time between April and end Oct will delight as you walk around the National Collection of hemerocallis, summer and knot garden, specimen shrubs and trees. Humphrey Repton-designed views down to R Lymer. Carew Pole museum open. Gravel paths.
  ♿ ✕ ⊛ ☕

② ◆ BOCONNOC
Lostwithiel PL22 0RG. Mr Anthony Fortescue, 01208 872507, adgfortescue@btinternet.com. *4m E of Lostwithiel. 2m E of A390. Turn off A390 at Middle Taphouse.* **Garden only adm £4.50, chd free, house £4, under 12 free. Suns 13, 20, 27 Apr; 4, 11, 18, 25 May (2-5.30). For NGS: Sun 4 May (2-5).**
Gardens covering some 20 acres, surrounded by parkland and woods. Magnificent trees, flowering shrubs and views. Set in C18 picturesque landscape which surrounds the church and Boconnoc House (both open). Teas in the stable yard designed by Sir John Soane. Stalls in stable yard.
  ♿ ⊛ ☕

③ BODWANNICK
Nanstallon PL30 5LN. Mr P M Appleton, 01208 831427. *2½ m W of Bodmin. A389 turn at Pottery signed*

Nanstallon, L at Xrds signed Hoopers Bridge then sharp R. **Adm £2.50, chd free (share to FLEET). Visitors welcome by appt.**
Approx 1-acre compact garden incl water garden, herbaceous, granite Cornish cross, roses, shade garden and shrubs. Over 50 varieties of daffodils and narcissi. Large stone circle. Plantsman's garden.
  ♿ ☎

④ ◆ BONYTHON MANOR
Cury Cross Lanes TR12 7BA. Mr & Mrs Richard Nathan, 01326 240234, sue@bonythonmanor.co.uk. *5m S of Helston. On main A3083 Helston to Lizard Rd. Turn L at Cury Cross Lanes (Wheel Inn). Entrance 300yds on R.* **Adm £6, chd £2. Tues to Fri incl, 1 Apr to 30 Sept (closed Good Fri & Public Holidays). For NGS: Wed 11 June (2-4.30).**
Magnificent 20-acre colour garden incl sweeping hydrangea drive to Georgian manor (not open). Herbaceous walled garden, potager with vegetables and picking flowers; 3 lakes in valley planted with ornamental grasses, perennials and South African flowers. A 'must see' for all seasons colour.
  ♿ ✕ ⊛ ﹏ ☕

⑤ BOSCASTLE GARDENS
PL35 0BJ. *5m N of Camelford. Park in doctor's surgery car park at top of village (clearly signed). Limited parking for disabled at both gardens. Maps provided.* Home-made teas. **Combined adm £3, chd free. Sat 21, Sun 22 June (1.30-6).**
Boscastle Harbour is well-known to visitors. Both gardens are in older part of village, overlooking cliff, land and sea. Both gardens featured in Cornwall Gardens Guide.
  ☕

HALF ACRE
Carole Vincent
Sculpture in an acre of 3 gardens: cottage; small wood; the Blue Circle garden, constructed in colour concrete with Mediterranean planting. Studio open, painting exhibition.
  ✕ ⊛

WILDWOOD
Alex & Ian Stewart
Garden of magic deception. Front traditional, rear - lawns leading to wood with pond, tree ferns and shade-loving shrubs.
  ✕

6 NEW BOWLING GREEN COTTAGE

Wendron TR13 0NB. Stephen & Carol Lay. *2m from Helston. Signed from Helston - Redruth rd (B3297) and Helston - Falmouth rd (A394).* Cream teas. **Adm £3, chd free. Sun 6 July (2-5).**
Creating the 2½ acres of gardens and woodlands has been a battle against the elements. On top of a hill, 2 windswept fields have been transformed, incl wetland areas. Evidence of mining heritage has been retained around the property. Children's nature trail. Featured on BBC2 Open Gardens and Radio Cornwall and in local press. 1st prize for woodlands, Kerrier district garden competition. Partial wheelchair access, mostly grass paths which may be difficult if wet.

 ♿ ⊛ ☕

Many gardens in pretty mining village . . .

7 CARCLEW GARDENS

Perran-ar-Worthal TR3 7PB. The Chope Family. *5m SW of Truro. From A39 turn E at Perran-ar-Worthal. Bus: alight Perran-ar-Worthal 1m.* Home-made teas. **Adm £3.50, chd free. Sun 30 Mar (2-6).**
One of the original NGS gardens first opened in 1927 and home to the 'Sir Charles Lemon' rhododendron. 200 years of history are reflected in this large private garden with rare and mature specimen trees and shrubs, 'listed' walls, fine terraces and ornamental water.

 🍴 ☕

8 ◆ CARWINION

Mawnan Smith TR11 5JA. Anthony & Jane Rogers, 01326 250258, www.carwinion.co.uk. *3m W of Falmouth. 500yds from centre of Mawnan Smith.* **Adm £4, chd free, disabled free. Daily (10-5.30).**
Luxuriant, traditional, 14-acre Cornish valley garden with delightful walk running down to R Helford. Home of UK's premier collection of bamboos. Hardy fern nursery. Ferns and wild flowers abound. A garden of yesterday and tomorrow. Limited wheelchair access, some gravel paths. Steep slopes in lower garden.

 ♿ ⊛ 🛏 ☕

9 NEW CHACEWATER GARDEN SAFARI

Chacewater TR4 8QB. *4m W of Truro. On old Redruth rd, accessed from A390. Parking free in village car park.* Home-made teas at Roseland House. **Adm £4, chd free (share to 1st Redruth Guides). Sat 14, Sun 15 June (1-6).**
Many gardens in pretty mining village. Small cottage gardens, riverside retreats, 1-acre gardens, all full of surprises. Maps and tickets from Sunny Corner adjacent to car park.

 ☕

10 ◆ CHYGURNO

Lamorna TR19 6XH. Dr & Mrs Robert Moule, 01736 732153. *4m S of Penzance. Off B3315. Follow signs for The Cove Restaurant. Garden is at top of hill, past Hotel on LH side.* **Adm £4, chd free. Weds only Mar to Sept; Weds & Suns July, Aug (2-5). Other days by arrangement. For NGS: Sats, Suns 24, 25 May (2-5); 5, 6 July (11-5).**
Beautiful, unique, 3-acre cliffside garden overlooking Lamorna Cove. Planting started in 1998, mainly S-hemisphere shrubs and exotics with hydrangeas, camellias and rhododendrons. Woodland area with tree ferns set against large granite outcrops. Garden terraced with steep steps and paths. Plenty of benches so you can take a rest and enjoy the wonderful views. Well worth the effort. Featured on West Country News and Cornwall Today.

THE CIDER HOUSE

See Devon.

11 NEW COOMBEGATE COTTAGE

St Ive PL14 3LZ. Michael Stephens, 01579 383520, mike@coombegate.wanadoo.co.uk. *4m E of Liskeard. From A390 at St Ive take turning signed Blunts. Village car park immed on L, then take 2nd L for 400metres. Limited parking at house for less mobile.* Home-made teas in Village Hall. **Adm £2.50, chd free. Sat 7 Feb 2009 (11-4), Sun 15 Feb 2009 (1-4). Visitors also welcome by appt Jan/Feb 2008 only.**
1-acre garden full of winter colour and scent. Witch hazels, daphnes, hellebores, early rhododendrons and interesting collection of more unusual seasonal plants. Drifts of snowdrops. Sloping site with steps. Open weather permitting - check if in doubt. 7 Feb 2009 combined with art exhibition and plant sale in village hall.

 🍴 ⊛ ☕ ☎

12 ◆ COTEHELE

Saltash PL12 6TA. The National Trust, 01579 351346, www.nationaltrust.org.uk. *2m E of St Dominick. 4m from Gunnislake. (Turn at St Ann's Chapel); 8m SW of Tavistock; 14m from Plymouth via Tamar Bridge.* **House and garden adm £8.80, chd £4.40, garden only adm £5.20, chd £2.60. Garden open all yr (10-dusk). For NGS: Sats 19 July; 4 Oct (11-4).**
Formal garden, orchard and meadow. Terrace garden falling to sheltered valley with ponds, stream and unusual shrubs. Fine medieval house (one of the least altered in the country); armour, tapestries, furniture. 19 July tours of the garden; 4 Oct apple pruning demonstrations and identifications, displays and information. Gravel paths throughout garden, some steep slopes. Map available at reception for wheelchair users.

 ♿ 🍴 ⊛ ☕

13 ◆ CREED HOUSE

Creed TR2 4SL. Mr & Mrs W R Croggon, 01872 530372. *6m SW of St Austell. From the centre of Grampound on A390, take rd signed to Creed. After 1m turn L opp Creed Church & garden is on L.* **Adm £3.50, chd free. Open daily Feb to Oct (10-5). For NGS: Sun 27 Apr (2-5).**
5-acre landscaped Georgian rectory garden; tranquil rural setting; spacious lawns. Tree collection; rhododendrons; sunken cobbled yard and formal walled herbaceous garden. Trickle stream to ponds and bog. Natural woodland walk. Restoration began 1974 - continues and incl recent planting.

 ⊛ 🛏

14 ◆ EDEN PROJECT

Bodelva PL24 2SG. The Eden Trust, 01726 811911, www.edenproject.com. *4m E of St Austell. Brown signs from A30 & A390.* **Adm £15, chd £5, concessions £10, family £36. Mar to Oct (10-6, last adm 4.30); Nov to Feb (10-4.30, last adm 3).** Late night opening summer and Christmas. See website for full details.

The world's largest greenhouses nestle in a giant 50-metre deep crater the size of 30 football pitches, the centrepiece of a spectacular global garden. Eden is a gateway into the fascinating world of plants and people and a vibrant reminder of how we need each other for our mutual survival.

& ✕ ❀ ☕

⓯ EDNOVEAN FARM
Perranuthnoe TR20 9LZ. Christine & Charles Taylor, 01736 711883, www.ednoveanfarm.co.uk/gardens. *3m E of Penzance. From A394 ½ m E of Marazion, turn seawards at Perran Xrds beside Dynasty Restaurant. Continue towards Perranuthnoe, parking in field beside Perranuthnoe sign. Up hill to garden.* Teas. **Adm £4, chd free. Sun 27 July (1-5). Visitors also welcome by appt July/Aug/ Sept for groups of 2+, £5pp.**
Above Mounts Bay with sweeping sea views incl St Michael's Mount. A garden of contrasts. Formal parterres and courtyards around a converted barn, opening to flowing lawns, finishing with Italian and gravel gardens. Box, date palms, olive trees and figs in the courtyards, grasses, phormiums, cordalines beyond. Sculpture exhibition.

❀ ⛺ ☕ ☎

⓰ ◆ ELLIS GARDENS AND NURSERIES
Polyphant PL15 7PS. Tim & Sue Ellis, 01566 86641, timellis@ellisnursery.wanadoo.co. uk. *6m W of Launceston. From A30 take turning to Blackhill Quarry. Proceed up hill to village green. L at bottom of green and keep to L round bend. Garden 4th on R.* **Adm £3, chd free. Wed to Sat, Mar to Sept (9-5). For NGS: Suns 6 July; 3 Aug (10-5).**
Newly-created and developing ¾ acre perennial flower garden with deep herbaceous borders, willow tunnel, wildlife pond and white garden. Large collection of euphorbias planted through the gardens, many for sale in the nursery. Full of colour from May to Sept. A delight to behold. Featured on BBC2 Open Gardens. If wet, wheelchair access is difficult. Deep, unfenced pond.

& ❀ ☕

THE GARDEN HOUSE
See Devon.

⓱ ◆ GLENDURGAN
Mawnan Smith TR11 5JZ. The National Trust, 01326 250906, www.nationaltrust.org.uk. *5m SW of Falmouth. Take rd to Helford Passage. Follow NT signs.* **Adm £6, chd £3. Tues to Sat, 10 Feb to 31 Oct (last entry 4.30). For NGS: Sats 12 Apr; 19 July (10.30-5.30).**
Valley garden running down to Durgan village on R Helford. In spring large displays of rhododendrons, camellias and magnolias with drifts of primroses, bluebells and aquilegia below. Many specimen trees, laurel maze dating from 1833 and giant's stride.

✕ ❀ ☕

⓲ NEW ◆ GODOLPHIN
Godolphin Cross. TR13 9RE. The National Trust, 01326 561407, www.nationaltrust.org.uk. *5m NW of Helston. From Helston follow A394 towards Penzance, then B3302 to Hayle, turning L signed Godolphin Cross.* **Adm £3, chd free. Sun to Fri, Mar to Oct. For NGS: Sat 19 July (10-5).**
A near-miraculous survival from C14 and C16, unchanged by fashions through the centuries. The garden is not about flowers and plants but about the surviving remains of a medieval pattern. Acquired by the National Trust in 2007. Guided tours of garden £6, booking essential.

Walk along valley through old woodland full of native bluebells . . .

⓳ GREY STONES
15 Trethowan Heights, off Penwethers Lane, Truro TR1 3QQ. Roddy & Rachel Macpherson-Rait, 01872 261140. *¼ m W of County Hall Truro. On A390 Truro to Redruth rd. 1st L after County Arms PH, down Penwethers Lane.* Cream teas. **Adm £3, chd free. Sun 3 Aug (1-5). Visitors also welcome by appt July/Aug only.**

½ -acre plant-lovers' garden created over last 8yrs. Winding paths lead to 2 ponds and adjoining rill. Herbaceous borders, rockery, box beds, green and white tranquil garden; bamboo/restio area complements large number of grasses, lilies and exotics. Well-stocked, colourful summer garden. Partial wheelchair access, gravel paths.

& ✕ ❀ ☕ ☎

⓴ HALLOWARREN
Carne, Manaccan TR12 6HD. Mrs Amanda Osman, 01326 231224. *10m E of Helston. 1m out of the centre of Manaccan village. Downhill past inn on R, follow sign to Carne. House on R.* Home-made teas. **Adm £2.50, chd free. Mons 5, 26 May (2-6). Visitors also welcome by appt throughout yr.**
2-acre garden and orchard leading to 6-acre beautiful wooded valley and bordering stream. Mixture of the natural and cultivated, bog and cottage garden with primulas, lilies and kitchen herbs, unusual shrubs and trees. Walk along valley through old woodland full of native bluebells. The ethos of this garden is harmony with nature and it is run on organic lines. Ducks, geese and chickens. Prizewinner Kerrier Woodland Garden.

✕ ❀ ⛺ ☕ ☎

HARTLAND ABBEY
See Devon.

㉑ ◆ HEADLAND
Battery Lane, Polruan-by-Fowey PL23 1PW. Jean Hill, 01726 870243, www.headlandgarden.co.uk. *½ m SE of Fowey across estuary. Passenger ferry from Fowey, 10 min walk along West St & up Battery Lane. Or follow signs to Polruan (on E of Fowey Estuary). Ignore first car park, turn L for second car park (overlooking harbour), turn L (on foot) down St Saviour's Hill.* **Adm £2.50, chd £1. Thurs only 29 May to 28 Aug (2-6). For NGS: Thurs 1, 8, 15, 22 May (2-6).**
1¼ -acre cliff garden with magnificent sea, coastal and estuary views on 3 sides. Planted to withstand salty gales yet incls subtropical plants with intimate displays to sit and savour the views. Paths wind through the garden past rocky outcrops down to a secluded swimming cove. Featured in 'Country Life'. Some paths steep, rocky and narrow.

✕ ❀ ☕

22 ◆ THE LOST GARDENS OF HELIGAN

Pentewan PL26 6EN. Heligan Gardens Ltd, 01726 845100, www.heligan.com. *5m S of St Austell. From St Austell take B3273 signed Mevagissey, follow signs.* **Adm £8.50, chd £5, senior citizens £7.50, family £23.50. Daily all year except 24, 25 Dec (10-6; 10-5 in winter; last adm 1½ hrs before close).**
'The Nation's Favourite Garden' offers 200 acres for exploration, which include productive gardens, pleasure grounds, a lush 22-acre subtropical jungle, and walks through sustainably managed ancient woodlands, wetlands and farmland. Access info available in advance/on arrival.

  ♿ ✕ ⊕ ☕

23 ◆ HIDDEN VALLEY GARDENS

Treesmill, Par PL24 2TU. Tricia Howard, 01208 873225, www.hiddenvalleygardens.co.uk. *2m SW of Lostwithiel. From St Austell, take A390 towards Lostwithiel. After 6m turn R on to B3269 signed Fowey, after 200yds turn R signed Treesmill. After 1m turn L, signed to the gardens (½ m). At end of lane after Colwith Farm. Cream teas on NGS days only.* **Adm £2.50, chd free. Daily 20 Mar to 31 Oct (10-6). For NGS: Fri 6, Sat 7 June; Sat 27, Sun 28 Sept (10-6).**
4-acre colourful garden in secluded valley with nursery. Cottage-style planting with herbaceous borders, grasses, ferns and fruit. Gazebo with country views. Fishpond and courtyard area. New Japanese garden and vegetable potager. Irises flowering at June opening, dahlia display in Sept. Children's quiz.

  ⊕ 🛏 ☕

24 HIGHCROFT GARDENS

Cargreen PL12 6PA. Mr & Mrs B J Richards, 01752 842219. *5m NW of Saltash. 5m from Callington on A388 take Landulph Cargreen turning. 2m on, turn L at Landulph Xrds. Parking by Methodist Church. Cream teas in Methodist Church.* **Adm £3, chd free. Suns 3, 17 Aug (1.30-5.30). Visitors also welcome by appt July, Aug & early Sept only for groups of 10+.**
3-acre garden in beautiful Tamar Valley. Japanese-style garden, hot border, pastel border, grasses, arboretum with hemerocallis and new blue borders. Prairie planting containing 2,500 plants of herbaceous and grasses. Buddleia and shrub rose bank. Pond. All at their best in July, Aug and Sept. Featured in 'House Beautiful' and 'NFU Countryside' magazines.

  ✕ ⊕ ☕ ☎

25 HIGHER TRUSCOTT

St Stephens, Launceston PL15 8LA. Mr & Mrs J C Mann. *3m NW of Launceston. From Launceston B3254 turn W at St Stephens toward Egloskerry. Signed. Home-made teas.* **Adm £3, chd free (share to St Stephens Church 4 May, RNLI 1 June). Suns 4 May; 1 June (2-5).**
1-acre plantsman's garden. Elevated position with fine views. Trees and shrubs with interesting underplanting. Yr-round interest with climbers, herbaceous, alpines and troughs. Featured in 'Cornwall Today'.

  ✕ ⊕ ☕

Surprising haven in the centre of this county town . . .

26 INCE CASTLE

Saltash PL12 4RA. Lord and Lady Boyd. *3m SW of Saltash. From A38 at Stoketon Cross take turn signed Trematon, then Elmgate. No large coaches. Home-made teas.* **Adm £3.50, chd free. Suns 16 Mar; 13 Apr; 11 May (2-5).**
5-acre garden with camellias and magnolias, woodlands, borders, orchard, bulbs, shell house and lovely views of R Lynher. Featured in 'Sunday Times' and 'Country Living'.

  ♿ ☕

27 ◆ THE JAPANESE GARDEN & BONSAI NURSERY

St Mawgan TR8 4ET. Mr & Mrs Hore, 01637 860116, www.thebonsainursery.com. *6m E of Newquay. 1½ m from N coast. Signs from A3059 & B3276.* **Adm £3.50, chd £1.50, groups 10+ £3. Open daily (closed Xmas day to New Year's day) (10-6/earlier in winter). For NGS: Mons 26 May; 25 Aug (10-6).**
East meets West in unique Garden for All Seasons. Spectacular Japanese maples and azaleas, symbolic teahouse, koi pond, bamboo grove, stroll, woodland, zen and moss gardens. An oasis of tranquility. Entrance free to adjacent specialist Bonsai and Japanese garden nurseries. Featured on ITV West Great Little Escapes and in 'The English Garden' and 'Beautiful Britain' magazines. Gravel paths.

  ♿ ✕ ⊕

28 ◆ KEN CARO

Bicton, nr Liskeard PL14 5RF. Mr K R Willcock & Mrs Willcock, 01579 362446. *5m NE of Liskeard. From A390 to Callington turn off N at St Ive. Take Pensilva Rd, follow brown tourist signs, approx 1m off main rd.* **Adm £4.50, chd £2. Gps of 12+ £4. Daily 24 Feb to 30 Sept (10-5.30).**
5-acre connoisseur's garden. Panoramic views, full of unusual plants and shrubs with yr-round colour. Lily ponds, garden sculptures. Iris beds, shrub roses, hydrangeas, camellias, magnolias, good collection of hollies. Plenty of seating to watch the wild bird life. New picnic area. Dogs allowed in meadow and woodland walk. Partial wheelchair access, none to meadow/woodland.

  ♿ ⊕ ☕

29 KENNALL HOUSE

Ponsanooth TR3 7HJ. Mr & Mrs N Wilson-Holt, 01872 870557. *4m NW of Falmouth. A393 Falmouth to Redruth, L at Ponsanooth PO for 0.3m. Garden on L.* **Visitors welcome by appt March to October.**
6-acre garden in extended grounds in valley setting. Incl mixture of typical British species and exotics. Wide variety of trees, shrubs and herbaceous plants. Bisected by fast-flowing stream with ponds and walled garden.

30 KINGBERRY

Rhind Street, Bodmin PL31 2EL. Dr & Mrs M S Stead. *N side of town, 100yds uphill from Westbery Hotel. Limited parking on hill, otherwise car parks in town centre. Cream teas.* **Adm £3, chd free. Sun 24 Aug (2-6).**
Surprising haven in centre of this county town. ⅔ -acre formal town garden with abundantly planted herbaceous borders, original stone walls covered in climbers, ornamental pond, gravel terrace, conservatory filled with tender specimens and more informal orchard. Garden sculptures and unusual plants.

  ✕ ⊕ ☕

31 LADOCK HOUSE
Ladock TR2 4PL. Holborow family, 01726 882274. *7m NE of Truro. Just off B3275. Car park & entrance by church.* Cream teas in church. **Adm £3, chd free. Sun 4 May (2-5). Visitors also welcome by appt for groups of 10+.**
Georgian Old Rectory with 4 acres of lawns, rhododendrons, camellias and azaleas with many woodland glades, all planted during last 35 yrs. Bluebell walk.

32 ◆ LAMORRAN HOUSE
Upper Castle Road, St Mawes, Truro TR2 5BZ. Robert Dudley-Cooke, 01326 270800, www.lamorrangardens.co.uk. *A3078, R past garage at entrance to St Mawes. 3/4 m on L. 1/4 m from castle if using passenger ferry service.* **Adm £6, chd free, OAP £5. Weds, Fris, Apr to end Sept (10-5). For NGS: Sat 10 May (10-5).**
4-acre subtropical garden overlooking Falmouth bay. Designed by the owner in an Italianate/Cote d'Azur style. Extensive collection of Mediterranean and subtropical plants incl large collection of palms and tree ferns. Reflects both design and remarkable micro-climate. Beautiful collection of Japanese azaleas and tender rhododendrons. Gravel paths and steps.

5-acre wood where you can picnic . . .

33 ◆ LANHYDROCK
Bodmin PL30 5AD. The National Trust, 01208 265950, www.nationaltrust.org.uk. *2 1/2 m SE of Bodmin. 2 1/2 m on B3268. Stn: Bodmin Parkway 1 3/4 m.* **House and garden adm £9.90, chd £4.95, garden only adm £5.60, chd £2.80. Gardens open all yr (10 - 6). Please visit website or tel for house opening details. For NGS: Tue 6 May; Sat 19 July (10-5.30).**
Large formal garden laid out 1857. Good summer colour with herbaceous borders, shrub garden with fine specimens of rhododendrons and magnolias and lovely views. Partial wheelchair access, gravel paths and slopes to higher woodland garden.

34 LITTLE PARK FARM
Malpas TR1 1SX. Mr & Mrs W Roberts. *1 1/2 m S of Truro. A39/A390 roundabout at Truro Police Station, take exit to Malpas. Follow river on R, passing park and cricket ground, then 1st L up lane marked Park Farm. Little Park Farm 1st on R.* Home-made teas. **Adm £3, chd free (share to Cornwall Hospice Care). Sun 15 June (2-5).**
New garden created over last 6 yrs from farm land. Small formal area, newly-planted plum/apple orchard, large pond, lavender/santolina banks, vegetables, small wooded glade. Lovely S-facing views to river.

35 LONG HAY
Treligga, Delabole PL33 9EE. Bett & Mick Hartley. *10m N of Wadebridge. Take B3314 Pendoggett to Delabole Rd. Turn L at Westdowns from Pendoggett, R fom Delabole. Signed Treligga (N). Turn L after entering hamlet. Long Hay on L, after 30yds white gate. Parking past gate, turn L into farmyard.* Cream teas 1 June, Cornish pasties 21 June. **Adm £3, chd free (share to Merlin Project and Action for Disabled Development). Sun 1 June (2-5). Evening Opening wine, Sat 21 June (7-10).**
2/3 -acre abundant cottage garden with beautiful vistas of the N coast and sea. Herbaceous beds, shrubs, pond, greenhouse and lawns. Meadow overlooking sea with paths leading to copse, vegetable plots, orchard and greenhouse. Cornish coastal garden in beautiful but harsh environment.

36 NEW LOWER AMBLE GARDENS
Chapel Amble PL27 6EW. *3m N of Wadebridge. Take lane signed Middle Amble and Lower Amble opp Chapel Amble PO for 1/2 m, L by pond. Parking in field beyond farmhouse.* Home-made teas at Millpond Cottage. **Combined adm £5, chd free (share to Cancer Research UK). Sun 22 June (2-6).**
Lower Amble has become a hamlet from C18 origins as a mill farm powered by water from the stream, ponds and underground leats which are features of the area. We enjoy being at end of road, S-facing hillside above R Amble and Walmsley Bird Sanctuary. Paths wind through 5-acre wood where you can picnic and enjoy bird life.

NEW LOWER AMBLE COTTAGE
Mr & Mrs C Burr
Developing 1-acre garden of 6yrs with lawn areas, mixed beds, sculptures, small pond and young trees.

NEW MILLPOND COTTAGE GARDEN
Sheilagh Lees
Large young garden with emphasis on herbaceous plants, roses and hardy geraniums. Vegetable plot and orchard. Peaceful plot with wonderful views over countryside.

NEW WALMSLEY COTTAGE
Mr & Mrs Bell
Smallest garden of approx 1/2 acre. Front: gravel with bamboos, exotic plants and grasses. Rear: mainly shrubs and lawn.

37 ◆ MARSH VILLA GARDENS
St Andrew's Road, Par PL24 2LU. Judith Stephens, 01726 815920, www.marshvillagardens.com. *5m E of St Austell. Leave A390 at St Blazey T-lights, by church. 1st L, garden 600yds on L.* **Adm £4, chd free, disabled £3. Sun to Wed Apr to Oct (11-6). For NGS: Suns 15 June; 17 Aug (10-6).**
Approx 3-acre garden featuring large pond, streams, bog garden. Extensive herbaceous beds, mixed borders, woodland and marshland walks in former estuary. New features incl alpine bed and substantial rose and clematis pergola. Large fernery/bog garden under development. Featured in Western Morning News.

38 ◆ MOYCLARE
Lodge Hill, Liskeard PL14 4EH. Elizabeth & Philip Henslowe, 01579 343114, elizabethhenslowe@btinternet.com. *1/2 m S of Liskeard centre. Approx 300yds S of Liskeard railway stn on St Keyne-Duloe rd (B3254).* **Adm £3, chd free. Weekend & BH Mons, Apr, May, June (2-5). For NGS: Mon 5 May (2-5).**
Gardened by one family for over 80 yrs; mature trees, shrubs and plants (many unusual, many variegated). Once most televised Cornish garden. Now revived and rejuvenated and still a plantsman's delight, still full of

character. Camellia, Brachyglottis and Astrantia (all 'Moira Reid') and Cytisus 'Moyclare Pink' originated here.

 ♿ ✂

39 NANSAWSAN HOUSE
Ladock TR2 4PW. Michael & Maureen Cole, 01726 882392. *7m NE of Truro. On B3275, follow yellow signs. Use Falmouth Arms and Community Hall car parks.* Home-made teas. **Adm £3, chd free. Sun 27 Apr (2-5). Visitors also welcome by appt April, May only for groups of 10+.**
1½ -acre garden, once part of Victorian estate garden. From house, paths meander through rhododendrons, camellias, azaleas and perennial borders taking in secret corners, fishpond, greenhouse, summerhouse and gazebo with wider vistas. Unusual trees, shrubs and climbers. Family vegetable garden, soft fruits and ample seating around the garden. Gravel paths.
♿ ✂ ❀ ☕ ☎

40 NEW NORTHWOOD FARM WATER GARDENS
St Neot PL14 6QN. Mackenzie Bell, 01579 320030, www.northwoodgardens.co.uk. *2m NE of St Neot. From St Neot Church proceed up steep hill signed Bolventor & Northwood Water Gardens then follow signs.* Cream teas. **Adm £3, chd free. Mon 26 May; Sun 27 July (11-5). Visitors also welcome by appt, no coaches.**
Overlooking lovely river valley on S slopes of Bodmin Moor. AONB. 4-acre water garden. Bridges and pathways guide you through delightfully landscaped ponds featuring wildlife, streams, waterfalls and fountains. Idyllic lake and romantic island, giant gunnera, vibrant hydrangeas, tree ferns, phormiums, acers, water lilies, rhododendrons, pieris, secret walled herbaceous borders. Art studio, sculpture, art gallery.
✂ ❀ ☕ ☎

41 ◆ PENCARROW
Washaway, Bodmin PL30 3AG. Molesworth-St Aubyn family, 01208 841369, info@pencarrow.co.uk, www.pencarrow.co.uk. *4m NW of Bodmin. Signed off A389 & B3266.* **House and garden adm £8, chd £4, garden only adm £4, chd £1. Daily 1 Mar to 31 Oct (9.30-5.30), house 23**

Mar to 19 Oct (11-3). For NGS: Wed 9 Apr (9.30-5.30).
A surprise around every corner. Family-owned grade 2* listed garden. Find an Iron Age fort, Victorian rockery, Italian gardens, ice house, lakeside and woodland walks for dogs off leads! You can also visit the fine Georgian house with its superb collection of paintings, furniture, porcelain and some antique dolls. Featured on ITV Great Country Houses. Leaflets available from house entrance for those with mobility difficulties, explaining routes alternative to steps.
♿ ❀ ☕

Idyllic lake and romantic island . . .

42 ◆ PENJERRICK GARDEN
Budock, nr Falmouth TR11 5ED. Mrs Rachel Morin, 01872 870105, www.penjerrickgarden.co.uk. *3m SW of Falmouth. Between Budock-Mawnan Smith, opp. Penmorvah Manor Hotel. Coach parking by arrangement.* **Adm £2.50, chd £1.50. Mar to Sept, Sun, Wed, Fri (1.30-4.30). For NGS: Sun 20 Apr (1-4.30).**
15-acre subtropical garden, home to important rhododendron hybrids and the C19 Quaker Fox family. The upper garden with sea view contains rhododendrons, camellias, magnolias, bamboos, tree ferns and magnificent trees. Across a bridge a luxuriant valley features ponds in a wild primeval setting. Suitable for adventurous fit people wearing gumboots.

43 ◆ PINE LODGE GARDENS & NURSERY
Holmbush, St Austell PL25 3RQ. Mr & Mrs R H J Clemo, 01726 73500, www.pine-lodge.co.uk. *1m E of St Austell. On A390 between Holmbush & St Blazey at junction of A391.* **Adm £6.50, chd £3, concessions £6. Open daily (10-6, last entrance 5).**
30-acre estate comprises gardens within a garden. Some 6,000 plants, all labelled, have been thoughtfully laid out using original designs and colour combinations to provide maximum interest. Rhododendrons, magnolias, camellias, herbaceous borders with many rare and tender plants, marsh gardens, tranquil fish ponds, lake with black swans within the park, pinetum. Japanese garden and arboretum.

Holder of National Collection of Grevilleas. 3-acre winter garden. Featured in 'Cornwall Life' & 'Horticultural Weekly'.
♿ ✂ ❀ **NCCPG**

44 ◆ PINSLA GARDEN & NURSERY
Cardinham PL30 4AY. Mark & Claire Woodbine, 01208 821339, www.pinslagarden.net. *3½ m E of Bodmin. From A30 roundabout take A38 towards Plymouth, 1st L to Cardinham & Fletchers Bridge, 2m on R.* **Adm £2.50, chd free. Daily 1 Mar to 31 Oct (9-6). For NGS: Sats, Suns 17, 18 May; 21, 22 June (9-6).**
Romantic 1½ acres of inspirational planting and design surrounded by woodland. Herbaceous and shrub borders, jungle, ponds, cottage garden, orchard, alpines on scree; stone circle in meadow; tree tunnel. Paths lined with granite boulders and set with slate, stone and incised abstract patterns. Featured on BBC SW Spotlight and Garden News. Gravel paths.
♿ ❀ ☕

45 ◆ POPPY COTTAGE GARDEN
Ruan High Lanes TR2 5JR. Tina Pritchard & David Primmer, 01872 501411. *1m NW of Veryan. On the Roseland Peninsula, 4m from Tregony on A3078 rd to St Mawes.* **Adm £2.50, chd free. Tues, Weds, Thurs, Suns, March to Sept (2-5.30). For NGS: Sun 6 Apr (11-5).**
Inspirational plantsman's garden combining colour, form and texture, approx 1 acre, divided into many rooms. From established cottage garden, extra land acquired in 2003 enabled the creation of different gardens filled with many beautiful and unusual shrubs, trees, bulbs, herbaceous and exotics, all colour-themed. Wildlife pond with stream and bridge. Featured in Westcountry 'Glorious Gardens' and 'GGG'.
♿ ❀ ☕

PORTINGTON
See Devon.

46 ◆ POTAGER GARDEN
High Cross, Constantine TR11 5RE. Peter Skerrett & Dan Thomas, 01326 341258, www.potagergardennursery.co.uk. *7m SW of Falmouth. Towards Constantine. In High Cross turn L at grass triangle with white signpost to Port Navas. Garden 100yds on R.* **Adm £2.50, chd free, concessions**

£2. Open Suns only, Apr to Sept (11-5). For NGS: Sun 27 July (11-5). New organic garden emerging from old nursery near Helford Estuary. Garden provides relaxed environment with informal mix of herbaceous planting accentuated with vegetables and fruit. Home-made cooking in the Glasshouse Café, hammocks, games and sculpture make Potager a friendly and peaceful retreat. Featured in 'The Guardian' and on French/German TV.

&. ⊛ ☕

Pond with cascades and trickling fountain . . .

47 POUNDSTOCK GARDENS
Poundstock EX23 0AU. *5m S of Bude, off A39.* Lunches and light refreshments at Southfield. Cream teas at The Barn House. **Combined adm £4, chd free. Sun 30 Mar; Wed 6 Aug (11-5).**
Direction maps given to visitors.

THE BARN HOUSE
Penhalt. Tim & Sandy Dingle, 01288 361356, tdingle@toucansurf.com. *From A39 take Widemouth, Bude (coastal route). L at Widemouth Manor Hotel towards Millook for ¹/₂ m.* **Visitors also welcome by appt.**
Come and see what can be done in an exposed coastal situation. Begun in 1996. Herbaceous and shrub borders, pond and kitchen garden. Wildlife walk through 10 acres of field and scrub. Partial wheelchair access.

&. ⊛ ☕ ☎

SOUTHFIELD
Vicarage Lane. Mr P R & Mrs J A Marfleet, 01288 361233. *Off A39 at Bangor Xrds (chapel on corner). Turn into Vicarage Lane, signed Poundstock Church. Approx 200yds on L.* **Visitors also welcome by appt.**
3 acres of wildlife woodland and garden. Woodland walks with daffodils, rhododendrons and hydrangeas. Mainly broadleaf trees planted 1994. Garden with borders of mixed shrubs, trees and perennial plants giving yr-round interest. Kitchen garden.

Beautiful views. Many wild birds. Partial wheelchair access. Very steep grass paths in woodland.

&. ⊛ ☎

48 NEW PRIMROSE FARM
Skinners Bottom, Redruth TR16 5EA. Barbara & Peter Simmons, 01209 890350, babs@simmons26.freeserve.co.uk. *6m N of Truro. At Chiverton Cross roundabout on A30 take Blackwater turn. Down hill, R by Red Lion PH up North Hill, 1st L (mini Xrd), garden approx ¹/₂ m on L.* **Home-made teas. Adm £3, chd free. Sat 28 June (1-6). Visitors also welcome by appt.**
Rambling informal cottage-style garden with woodland glade. Mature trees and shrubs, herbaceous and mixed borders. Pond with cascades and trickling fountain. Patio area with exotic plants. Gravel path to pergola with scented climbers and summerhouse. A plantsman's garden. Featured on BBC2 Open Gardens.

&. 🏃 ☕ ☎

49 ◆ ROSELAND HOUSE
Chacewater TR4 8QB. Mr & Mrs Pridham, 01872 560451, www.roselandhouse.co.uk. *4m W of Truro. At Truro end of main st. Parking in village car park (100yds) or surrounding rds.* **Adm £3, chd free. Tues, Weds (1-6) Apr to Sept. For NGS: Sun 24, Mon 25 Aug (2-5).**
1-acre garden subdivided by walls and trellises hosting a wide range of climbers. Mixed borders of unusual plants, Victorian conservatory and greenhouse extend the gardening yr. Holders of National Collection of Clematis *viticella cvs.* Featured on Westcountry TV Georgeous Gardens. Some slopes.

&. ⊛ NCCPG ☕

50 ◆ ST MICHAEL'S MOUNT
Marazion TR17 0HT. James & Mary St Aubyn, 01736 710507, clare@manor-office.co.uk. *2¹/₂ m E of Penzance. ¹/₂ m from shore at Marazion by Causeway; otherwise by motor boat.* **Castle & garden £6.60, chd £3.30, garden only adm £3, chd £1. Gardens Mon-Fri, 1 May to 30 Jun; Thurs, Fris 1 Jul to 31 Oct. Castle Sun-Fri, 16 Mar to 2 Nov. For NGS: Wed 30 Apr (10.30-5.30).**
Flowering shrubs; rock plants,

spectacular castle; fine sea views. Steep climb to castle, uneven cobbled surfaces, sensible shoes advised.

🏃 ⊛ ☕

51 NEW SCORRIER HOUSE
Redruth TR16 5AU. Richard & Caroline Williams. *2¹/₂ m E of Redruth. From Truro A390, at 4th roundabout slip road A30 to Redruth for 2¹/₂ m, A3047 under railway bridge, L at mini roundabout to B3287 for ¹/₂ m, R on B3207 for 200yds, R by Lodge House. From Falmouth take A393 to Redruth for 7m then B3258, turn at 2nd lodge.* **Cream teas. Adm £3, chd free. Sun 20 Apr (3-6).**
Formal garden round old family house with herbaceous border, knot garden and conservatory. Walled garden filled with camellias, rhododendrons, magnolias and bluebells. All set in parkland with ha ha. Unfenced swimming pool.

☕

52 ◆ TREBAH
Mawnan Smith TR11 5JZ. Trebah Garden Trust, 01326 252200, www.trebah-garden.co.uk. *4m SW of Falmouth. Follow tourist signs from Hillhead roundabout on A39 approach to Falmouth or Treliever Cross roundabout on junction of A39-A394. Parking for coaches.* **Adm: 1 Mar to 31 Oct, £7, chd £2, concessions £6; 1Nov to 28 Feb, £3, chd £1, concessions £2.50. Daily all yr (10.30-5/dusk if earlier).**
26-acre S-facing ravine garden, planted in 1830s. Extensive collection rare/mature trees/shrubs incl glades; huge tree ferns 100yrs old, subtropical exotics. Hydrangea collection covers 2¹/₂ acres. Water garden, waterfalls, rock pool stocked with mature koi carp. Enchanted garden for plantsman/artist/family. Play area/trails for children. Use of private beach. Steep paths in places. 3 motorised buggies available, please book in advance.

&. ⊛ ☕

53 TREBARTHA
nr Launceston PL15 7PE. The Latham Family. *6m SW of Launceston. North Hill, SW of Launceston nr junction of B3254 & B3257.* **Cream teas. Adm £3, chd free. Suns 8 June; 21 Sept (2-5).**
Wooded area with lake surrounded by walks of flowering shrubs; woodland

trail through fine woods with cascades and waterfalls; American glade with fine trees. No coaches.

✿ ☕

54 NEW TREGONNING LODGE
Tregonning Road, Stithians TR3 7DA. Pat & Jeremy Thomas, 01209 861179. *4m NW of Falmouth. Stithians turning off A393 at Five Lanes Xrds ¾ m N of Ponsanooth. In village L at Xrds signed Trevales, garden 25yds.* Home-made teas. **Adm £3, chd free. Sun 13 July (1-5). Visitors also welcome by appt July/Aug only afternoons/eves for individuals/groups.**
New garden set on S-facing slope in 4 acres of woodland, shrubberies, beds and 2 natural ponds. 10yrs of planting have yielded a garden full of interest. Herbaceous borders and waterlilies are at their best in July and Aug. Partial wheelchair access, gravel paths, steps.
♿ ✿ ☕ ☎

55 TREGOOSE
Grampound TR2 4DB. Mr & Mrs Anthony O'Connor, www.tregoose.co.uk. *7m E of Truro, 1m W of Grampound. Off A390. Lane entrance is 100yds W of New Stables Xrds & ½ m E of Trewithen roundabout.* Cream teas. **Adm £3, chd free (share to Creed Church). Suns 27 Jan; 10, 24 Feb (1-4.30).**
2-acre garden. Woodland area with early spring shrubs underplanted with snowdrops, erythroniums, hellebores and small narcissus cultivars. Summer and autumn flowering areas incl walled garden overtopped by Acacia baileyana purpurea, scarlet blue and yellow border and potager full of herbs and cutting beds with arches covered with gourds, roses and honeysuckle.
✄ ✿ 🛏 ☕

56 ◆ TREGREHAN
Par PL24 2SJ. Mr T Hudson, 01726 814389, www.tregrehan.org. *1m W of St Blazey. Entrance on A390 opp Britannia Inn.* **Adm £4.50, chd free. Weds, Suns, Bank Hol Mons 15 Mar to 31 May (10.30-5); Weds only 4 June to 27 Aug (2-5). For NGS: Sun 6 Apr (10.30-5).**
Garden largely created since early C19. Woodland of 20 acres containing fine trees, award winning camellias raised by late owner and many

interesting plants forming a temperate rainforest. Show greenhouses built 1846, a feature containing softer species. Partial wheelchair access.
♿ ✄ ✿ 🛏 ☕

57 TREGULLOW
Scorrier TR16 5AY. Mr & Mrs James Williams. *2m E of Redruth. Leave A30 at Scorrier. Follow signs to St Day & Carharrack on B3298. 1m out of Scorrier turn R at Tolgullow Village sign. Go through white gates by lodge.* Cream teas. **Adm £3.50, chd £1. Mon 5 May (12.30-5).**
An idyllic Cornish spring garden a mere 3m from the Atlantic. Tregullow is blessed with unfolding vistas of intense colour as you explore your way around its 15 acres. First planted by the Williams family in C19, the gardens have been carefully restored and replanted since the 1970s. Mostly accessible to wheelchairs but 2 flights of granite steps need to be bypassed.
♿ ✿ ☕

Garden full of interest . . .

58 ◆ TRELISSICK
Feock TR3 6QL. The National Trust, 01872 862090, www.nationaltrust.org.uk. *4m S of Truro. Nr King Harry Ferry. On B3289.* **Adm £6.60, chd £3.30. Daily (10.30-5.30, last adm 5). For NGS: Sats 5 Apr; 19 July (10.30-5.30).**
Planted with tender shrubs; magnolias, camellias and rhododendrons with many named species characteristic of Cornish gardens. National Collection of Photinias and Azaras. Fine woodlands encircle the gardens through which a varied circular walk can be enjoyed. Superb view over Falmouth harbour. Georgian house, not open. Now accessible by foot ferry from Truro, Falmouth and St Mawes, Apr-Sept.
♿ ✄ ✿ NCCPG ☕

59 TRENARTH
High Cross, Constantine TR11 5JN. Mrs L M Nottingham, 01326 340444, lmnottingham@tiscali.co.uk. *6m SW of Falmouth. Nearest main rds A39-A394 Truro to Helston-Falmouth: follow signs for Constantine. At High Cross garage, 1½ m before Constantine, turn L signed Mawnan, then R after 30yds down dead end lane. Garden at end of lane.* **Visitors welcome by appt.**

4-acre garden surrounding C17 farmhouse in lovely pastoral setting - not a road in sight or sound. Yr-round interest. Emphasis on unusual plants, structure and form, with a hint of quirkiness - not all is what it seems! Courtyard, C18 garden walls, yew rooms, prize-winning vegetable garden, traditional potting shed, 'puddled' pond, orchard, green lane walk down to R Helford. Featured in 'The English Garden'.
☎

60 ◆ TRENGWAINTON
Madron TR20 8RZ. The National Trust, 01736 363148, www.nationaltrust.org.uk. *2m NW of Penzance. ½ m W of Heamoor. On Penzance-Morvah rd (B3312), ½ m off St Just rd (A3071).* **Adm £5.40, chd £2.70. Suns to Thurs and Good Fri, 10 Feb to 2 Nov (10.30-5). For NGS: Suns 23 Mar; 24 Aug (10.30-5).**
Sheltered garden with an abundance of exotic trees and shrubs. Picturesque stream running through valley and stunning views of Mounts Bay from terrace. Mysterious walled gardens, reputedly built to the dimensions of Noah's Ark. Early flowering camellias and rhododendrons. Free behind the scenes garden tour at 2pm on NGS days. Some gravel paths, steady incline.
♿ ✿ ☕

61 ◆ TRERICE
nr Newquay TR8 4PG. The National Trust, 01637 875404, www.nationaltrust.org.uk. *3m SE of Newquay. From Newquay via A392 & A3058; turn R at Kestle Mill (NT signs) or signed from A30 at Summercourt via A3058.* **House and garden adm £6.60, chd £3.30, concessions £5.60, garden only adm £2.30, chd £1.10, family/group concessions. Daily, house (11-5), garden (10.30-5). For NGS: Mon 28 Apr; Mon 18 Aug (11-5).**
Summer/autumn-flowering garden unusual in content and layout and for neutral alkaline soil varieties. Orchard planted with old varieties of fruit trees. Small museum traces history of lawn mower - 3rd largest in UK. Experimental Tudor garden developed in partnership with local primary school. Tour by Tamasin Batten, NGS Careership student and Gardener Warden-in-Charge, on NGS days. Kayling (Cornish skittles) available. No wheelchair access to Tudor garden (steep slope and steps). Alternative route to steps on front court.
♿ ✄ ✿ ☕

62 ◆ **TREVARNO GARDENS AND THE NATIONAL MUSEUM OF GARDENING**
Crowntown, Helston TR13 0RU. Messrs M Sagin & N Helsby, 01326 574274, www.trevarno.co.uk. *3m NW of Helston. Signed from Crowntown on B3303.* Museum and Garden adm £6.35, chd £2.10, concessions £5.50. Open daily except Xmas Day & Boxing Day (10.30-5).

Unforgettable gardening experience combining Victorian garden with fountain garden café, unique range of craft workshops and the National Museum of Gardening, Britain's largest and most comprehensive collection of antique tools, implements, memorabilia and ephemera. Vintage soap and nostalgic toy museum (small additional charge). Woodland adventure play area and estate walk. Extended 'Access for All' route now open.

63 **TREWAN HALL**
St Columb TR9 6DB. Mrs P M Hill. *6m E of Newquay. N of St Columb Major, off A39 to Wadebridge. 1st turning on L signed to St Eval & Talskiddy. Entrance 3/4 m on L in woodland.* Cream teas. **Adm £3, chd free.** Sun 11 May (2-5.30).

Set in 36 acres of fields and bluebell woodland, with gardens round the house. Mixed beds, roses and specimen trees. Driveway bordered by rhododendrons and hydrangeas. Lovely views over the Lanherne Valley. Trewan Hall (not open) built in 1633 is a fine centrepiece for garden. Children welcome. Small playground, large grass area for games. Gold David Bellamy Conservation Award.

64 ◆ **TREWITHEN**
Truro TR2 4DD. Mr & Mrs Michael Galsworthy, 01726 883647, www.trewithengardens.co.uk. *1/2 m E of Probus. Entrance on A390 Truro-St Austell rd. Signed.* **Adm £5. Mon to Sat, 1 Mar to 30 Sept; Suns Mar to May (10-4.30).**

Internationally renowned and historic garden of 30 acres laid out between 1912 and 1960 with much of original seed and plant material collected by Ward and Forrest. Famed for towering magnolias and rhododendrons and a very large collection of camellias. Flattish ground amidst original woodland park and magnificent landscaped lawn vistas.

65 ◆ **TREWOOFE HOUSE**
Lamorna TR19 6PA. Mrs H M Pigott, 01736 810269. *4m SW of Penzance. Take B3315 from Penzance via Newlyn towards Lamorna. At top of hill take sharp turn signed Trewoofe.* **Adm £3, chd free. Suns & Weds May, June; Suns July (2-5). Group visits welcome by prior arrangement. For NGS: Sat 5, Sun 6 July (11-5).**

2-acre garden at top of Lamorna Valley with ancient mill leat. Bog garden planted with a variety of primulas, many kinds of iris, astilbes and arums. Shrub and perennial beds planted for all-yr interest. Small fruit garden with espalier and cordon-trained apple and pear trees. Conservatory with semi-tender climbers and vine. Featured in 'Garden News'.

66 **TREWOOFE ORCHARD**
Lamorna TR19 6BW. Dick & Barbara Waterson, 01736 810214. *4m SW of*

Penzance. on B3315, Signed from Lamorna Cove turning. **Adm £2.50, chd free (share to RNLI). Most days, Feb to Oct (10-dusk). Please tel to confirm before travelling any distance.** Visitors also welcome by appt for groups, no coaches.

4-acre valley garden, secluded and tranquil. 2 acres of woodland; more formal planting around the house. Stunning waterfall, stream, still pond and rills. Spring bulbs, camellias, arums, hostas and new tree ferns. Plenty of seats and well-defined paths. Magical setting. Water everywhere to delight the senses. Full of butterflies, bird song and busy bees. Partial wheelchair access, some steps and steep slopes.

67 ◆ **TRIST HOUSE**
Veryan TR2 5QA. Mr & Mrs Graham Salmon, 01872 501422, www.tristhouse.co.uk. *6m SE of Truro. Centre of Veryan on Portloe rd just past Roseland stores. Disabled parking by house.* **Adm £3.50, chd 50p. Suns, Tues & Bank Hols (2-5.30), April to July and also by arrangement. For NGS: Sun 6 Apr (2-5.30).**

5 acres. Romantic, intimate garden in flower throughout spring and summer with lovely display of tulips, roses and herbaceous plants. Large rockeries built in the 1830s. Featured in 'Gardeners' World'. Partial wheelchair access to woodland/rockery areas.

WILDSIDE
See Devon.

Cornwall County Volunteers

County Organiser
William Croggon, Creed House , Creed, Grampound, Truro TR2 4SL, 01872 530372

County Treasurer
Nigel Rimmer, 11 Melvill Road, Falmouth TR11 4AS, 01326 313429

Leaflet Coordinator
Peter Stanley, Mazey Cottage, Tangies, Gunwalloe, Helston TR12 7PU, 01326 565868, stanley.m2@sky.com

Publicity
Hugh Tapper, Trethewey Barns, Ruan Lanihorne, Tregony, Truro TR2 5TH, 01872 530567, hugh@truro.tv

Assistant County Organisers
Ginnie Clotworthy, Trethew, Lanlivery, Bodmin PL30 5BZ, 01208 872612 giles.clotworthy@btopenworld.com
Lally Croggon, Creed House, Creed, Grampound, Truro TR2 4SL, 01872 530372
Caroline Latham, Stonaford Manor, North Hill, Launceston PL15 7PE, 01566 782970
Alison O'Connor, Tregoose, Grampound, Truro TR2 4DB, 01726 882460
Marion Stanley, Mazey Cottage, Tangies, Gunwalloe, Helston TR12 7PU, 01326 565868
Virginia Vyvyan-Robinson, Mellingey Mill House, St Issey, Wadebridge PL27 7QU, 01841 540511

CUMBRIA

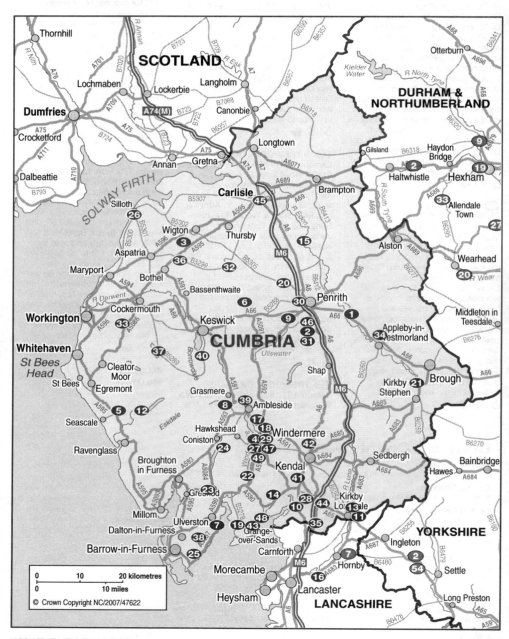

Opening Dates

March

FRIDAY 21
8 Copt Howe

SATURDAY 22
8 Copt Howe

SUNDAY 23
8 Copt Howe

MONDAY 24
8 Copt Howe

FRIDAY 28
8 Copt Howe

April

WEDNESDAY 2
8 Copt Howe

FRIDAY 4
8 Copt Howe

SUNDAY 6
44 Summerdale House

WEDNESDAY 9
8 Copt Howe

SATURDAY 12
8 Copt Howe

WEDNESDAY 16
8 Copt Howe

FRIDAY 18
8 Copt Howe

SUNDAY 20
8 Copt Howe

WEDNESDAY 23
8 Copt Howe

SUNDAY 27
9 Dalemain

WEDNESDAY 30
22 Lakeside Hotel

May

THURSDAY 1
8 Copt Howe

FRIDAY 2
6 Chapelside

SATURDAY 3
6 Chapelside
37 Rannerdale Cottage

SUNDAY 4
4 Brackenrigg Lodge
7 Conishead Priory
31 The Nook
37 Rannerdale Cottage
44 Summerdale House
47 Windy Hall

WEDNESDAY 7
8 Copt Howe

FRIDAY 9
8 Copt Howe

SATURDAY 10
1 Acorn Bank

SUNDAY 11
8 Copt Howe
10 Dallam Tower
26 Lilac Cottage Garden

WEDNESDAY 14
8 Copt Howe

FRIDAY 16
6 Chapelside

SATURDAY 17
5 Buckbarrow House
6 Chapelside
12 Galesyke
27 Lindeth Fell Country House Hotel
28 Lower Rowell Farm

SUNDAY 18
5 Buckbarrow House
11 Fell Yeat
12 Galesyke
28 Lower Rowell Farm
29 Matson Ground

TUESDAY 20
8 Copt Howe

WEDNESDAY 21
8 Copt Howe

SATURDAY 24
8 Copt Howe

SUNDAY 25
8 Copt Howe
14 Halecat
15 Hazel Cottage

WEDNESDAY 28
8 Copt Howe

FRIDAY 30
6 Chapelside
8 Copt Howe

SATURDAY 31
6 Chapelside

June

SUNDAY 1
8 Copt Howe
48 Yewbarrow House

FRIDAY 6
8 Copt Howe

SATURDAY 7
1 Acorn Bank

SUNDAY 8
2 Askham Hall
4 Brackenrigg Lodge
8 Copt Howe
20 Hutton-in-the-Forest

FRIDAY 9
8 Copt Howe

36 Quarry Hill House
47 Windy Hall

WEDNESDAY 11
8 Copt Howe
30 Newton Rigg Campus Gardens (Evening)

FRIDAY 13
6 Chapelside

SATURDAY 14
6 Chapelside

SUNDAY 15
3 Beech House
17 High Cross Lodge
44 Summerdale House
49 Yews

WEDNESDAY 18
8 Copt Howe

SATURDAY 21
8 Copt Howe
45 Tullie House

SUNDAY 22
14 Halecat
33 The Old Rectory
45 Tullie House

WEDNESDAY 25
8 Copt Howe
35 Pear Tree Cottage (Evening)

THURSDAY 26
39 Rydal Hall

FRIDAY 27
6 Chapelside
8 Copt Howe

SATURDAY 28
6 Chapelside

SUNDAY 29
16 Heywood House
42 Sprint Mill
46 Whitbysteads

July

TUESDAY 1
15 Hazel Cottage (Late afternoon & Evening)

WEDNESDAY 2
8 Copt Howe

FRIDAY 4
8 Copt Howe

SATURDAY 5
1 Acorn Bank

SUNDAY 6
25 Leece Village Gardens
48 Yewbarrow House

WEDNESDAY 9
8 Copt Howe
19 Holker Hall Gardens

FRIDAY 11
6 Chapelside
8 Copt Howe

SATURDAY 12
6 Chapelside
13 The Grange
34 Olde Oaks

SUNDAY 13
21 Kirkby Stephen Gardens
38 Redmayne Hall

FRIDAY 18
6 Chapelside

SATURDAY 19
6 Chapelside
41 Sizergh Castle

SUNDAY 20
14 Halecat
35 Pear Tree Cottage

THURSDAY 24
18 Holehird Gardens
39 Rydal Hall

SUNDAY 27
36 Quarry Hill House
42 Sprint Mill

August

SUNDAY 3
16 Heywood House
48 Yewbarrow House

WEDNESDAY 6
11 Fell Yeat (Evening)

SATURDAY 16
41 Sizergh Castle

SUNDAY 17
20 Hutton-in-the-Forest

SUNDAY 24
24 Lawson Park (Day & Evening)

THURSDAY 28
39 Rydal Hall

September

WEDNESDAY 3
22 Lakeside Hotel

SUNDAY 7
9 Dalemain
48 Yewbarrow House

WEDNESDAY 17
30 Newton Rigg Campus Gardens (Evening)

Gardens open to the public

1 Acorn Bank
7 Conishead Priory
8 Copt Howe
9 Dalemain
18 Holehird Gardens
19 Holker Hall Gardens

20 Hutton-in-the-Forest
39 Rydal Hall
41 Sizergh Castle
45 Tullie House

By appointment only

23 Langholme Mill
32 The Old Rectory
40 Scarthwaite
43 Stone Edge

Also open by appointment ☎

5 Buckbarrow House
6 Chapelside
12 Galesyke
16 Heywood House
22 Lakeside Hotel
24 Lawson Park
27 Lindeth Fell Country House Hotel
28 Lower Rowell Farm
31 The Nook
34 Olde Oaks
35 Pear Tree Cottage
36 Quarry Hill House
42 Sprint Mill
44 Summerdale House
47 Windy Hall
48 Yewbarrow House

The Gardens

1 ◆ ACORN BANK
Temple Sowerby CA10 1SP. The National Trust, 017683 61893, www.nationaltrust.org.uk. *6m E of Penrith. On A66; ½ m N of Temple Sowerby. Bus: Penrith-Appleby or Carlisle-Darlington; alight Culgaith Rd end.* Adm £3.80, chd £1.90. Wed to Sun Mar to Oct. For NGS: Sats 10 May; 7 June; 5 July (10-5).
Medium-sized walled garden; fine herb garden; orchard and mixed borders; wild garden with woodland/riverside walk leading to a partly restored watermill open to the public. Dogs on leads only in woodland walk.
♿ ✕ ⊗ ☕

Haphazard pruning and netted plants due to regular deer visitations . . .

2 ASKHAM HALL
Penrith CA10 2PF. Countess of Lonsdale. *5m S of Penrith. Turn off A6 for Lowther & Askham.* Home-made teas. Adm £3, chd free (share to Askham & Lowther Churches). Sun 8 June (2-5).
Askham Hall is a pele tower (not open), incorporating C14, C16 and early C18 elements in courtyard plan. Splendid formal outlines of garden with terraces of herbaceous borders and original topiary, probably from late C17. Herb garden and recently created meadow area with trees and pond. Kitchen garden, basically organic. Featured on Radio Cumbria.
✕ ⊗ ☕

3 BEECH HOUSE
Woodrow CA7 0AT. Mr & Mrs L B J McDonnell. *3m W of Wigton. On A595 take turning signed Waverton. At first xrds take turning signed Wigton. First house 250yds on L.* Home-made teas. Adm £3, chd free. Sun 15 June (2-5).
Approx ¾ acre of informal garden with lawns, mixed shrub/herbaceous borders, stream and ponds. Featured in 'Cumbria Life'.
♿ ✕ ⊗ ☕

4 BRACKENRIGG LODGE
Windy Hall Road, Bowness-on-Windermere LA23 3HY. Lynne Bush, www.brackenriggs.co.uk. *1m S of Bowness. Just off B5284 on Windy Hall Rd, opp Linthwaite House Hotel entrance.* Home-made teas at Windy Hall. Adm £3, chd free, Combined with **Windy Hall** adm £5. Suns 4 May; 8 June (10-5).
3 acres of wildlife garden run on organic lines with a combination of native and cultivated plants, shrubs and trees. Water features created from a diverted culvert giving streams, waterfall and pond. Woodland area, bog garden, wild flower meadows. Haphazard pruning and netted plants due to regular deer visitations. Stout footwear.
✕ 🛏 ☕

5 BUCKBARROW HOUSE
Denton Park Court, Gosforth CA20 1BN. John Maddison, 01946 725431, johnmaddgosf@aol.com. *13m S of Whitehaven. Turn off A595. Through centre of Gosforth Village. At 'Y' junction take L fork towards Wasdale. After 150yds turn L (before church) into Denton Park. Keep bearing R. House is last on R in Denton*

Park Court. Light refreshments & teas. **Adm £2.50, chd free.** Sat 17, Sun 18 May (11-5). **Also open Galesyke. Visitors also welcome by appt all year, groups max 10.**
Small densely-planted garden approx 23yds x 49yds. Numerous compartments incl wildlife pond, Japanese gravel garden, shrub area, cottage garden borders and natural stream. Decking area. Decorative stone front garden. Over 30 acers, mostly Japanese palmatum. A friend (I hope) described it as 'Delightfully wild'.

🌾 ⊗ ☕ ☎

6 CHAPELSIDE
Mungrisdale, Penrith CA11 0XR. Tricia & Robin Acland, 017687 79672. *12m W of Penrith. On A66 take unclassified rd N, signed Mungrisdale Village. House is far end of scattered village on L immed after tiny church on R. Use parish church room parking at foot of our short drive.* **Adm £2.50, chd free (share to Mungrisdale Parish Church).** Fris, Sats 2, 3, 16, 17, 30, 31 May; 13, 14, 27, 28 June; 11, 12, 18, 19 July (11-5). **Visitors also welcome by appt, teas for groups by arrangement.**
1 acre organic garden below fell, tiny stream, large pond. Extensive range of plants, many unusual, providing green texture and colour effects carefully or accidentally structured in a closely planted relaxed style. Always developing. Art constructions in and out, local stone used creatively. Fine views, so unkind winds. Featured in 'Gardens of the Lake District'.

🌾 ⊗ ☎

CLEARBECK HOUSE
See Lancashire, Merseyside & Greater Manchester.

7 ◆ CONISHEAD PRIORY
Ulverston, A5087 Coast Rd LA12 9QQ. Manjushri Kadampa Meditation Centre, 01229 584029, www.manjushri.org. *2m S of Ulverston on A5087 coast rd. 30 mins from M6 J36, follow A590 to Ulverston then L onto coastal rd. Car parking free.* **Adm £3, chd free.** Open weekends & Bank Hols Easter to end Oct (except festival times 17 May to 1 June; 19 July to 17 Aug incl). For NGS: Sun 4 May (2-5).
40 acres of gardens and woodland surrounding historic mansion. Temple garden an oasis of peace, restored greenhouse, lake and wildlife garden, arboretum, cottage gardens.

Woodland walks to Morecambe Bay. Free guided house tours with garden ticket. Gift shop and Tearoom.

♿ ⊗ ☕

On banks of River Irt with views of Wasdale Fells . . .

8 ◆ COPT HOWE
Chapel Stile, Great Langdale LA22 9JR. Professor R N Haszeldine, Open additional days Mar to July, tel 015394 37685 for recorded message. *5m W of Ambleside. On B4353, 1/4 m past Chapel Stile.* **Adm £3, chd free.** For NGS: Fri 21 to Mon 23, Fri 28 Mar; Weds 2 to 23, Fri 4, Sat 12, Fri 18, Sun 20 Apr; Thur 1, Weds 7 to 28, Thur 1, Fri 9, Sun 11, Tue 20, Sat 24, Sun 25, Fri 30 May; Sun 1, Fri 6, Sun 8, Weds 11 to 25, Sat 21, Fri 27 June; Weds, 2, 9, Fris 4, 11 July (12-5).
2-acre plantsman's mountain paradise garden. Superb views Langdale Pikes. Extensive collections of acers, camellias, azaleas, rhododendrons, oaks, beeches, rare shrubs, trees, unusual perennials; herbaceous and bulbous species; alpines, trough gardens; rare conifers; expedition plants from worldwide mountainous regions. Outstanding spring and autumn colour. Wildlife sanctuary, red squirrels, badgers, slow-worms, hotel for wild birds. Major new garden extensions. Featured in many papers, magazines, radio and TV programmes.

⊗

9 ◆ DALEMAIN
Penrith CA11 0HB. Mr & Mrs R B Hasell-McCosh, 017684 86450, www.dalemain.com. *3m SW of Penrith. On A592 Penrith to Ullswater, 3m from M6 J40.* **House and Garden adm £7.50, groups £5, Garden only adm £5, groups £4, chd free.** Suns - Thurs 3 Feb to 20 Mar (gdns 11-4), 23 Mar to 23 Oct (house 11.15-4). For NGS: Suns 27 Apr; 7 Sept (10.30-5).
Delightful 5-acre plantsman's gardens, set against the grandeur of the Lakeland Fells and parkland. Herbaceous borders; rose walk with

old-fashioned roses and named ancient apple trees; *Abies Cephalonica* fir; tulip tree and Tudor knot garden. Wild garden with blue Himalayan poppies. Woodland walks.

🌾 ⊗ ☕

10 DALLAM TOWER
Milnthorpe LA7 7AG. Mr & Mrs R T Villiers-Smith. *7m S of Kendal. 7m N of Carnforth. Nr junction of A6 & B5282. Stn: Arnside, 4m; Lancaster, 15m.* Cream teas. **Adm £3, chd free.** Sun 11 May (2-5).
Large garden; natural rock garden, water garden; wood walks, lawns, shrubs. C19 cast iron orangery.

☕

11 FELL YEAT
Casterton, nr Kirkby Lonsdale LA6 2JW. Mr & Mrs O S Benson. *1m E of Casterton Village. On the rd to Bull Pot. Leave A65 at Devils Bridge, follow A683 for 1m, take the R fork to High Casterton at golf course, straight across at two sets of Xrds, house on L, 1/4 m from no-through-rd sign.* Cream teas. **Adm £3, chd free.** Sun 18 May (1-5). **Evening Opening** £4, wine, Wed 6 Aug (6-9).
1-acre country garden with mixed planting, incl unusual trees, shrubs and some topiary. Small woodland garden, 2 small ponds which encourage dragonflies. An increasing number of species and varieties of hydrangea for later interest. National Collection of *Ligularia*. Some gravel paths, gentle slopes.

♿ 🌾 ⊗ NCCPG ☕

12 NEW GALESYKE
Wasdale CA20 1ET. Christine & Mike McKinley, 019467 26267, mckinley2112@sky.com. *From N follow signs to Nether Wasdale, through village take rd to The Lake & Wasdale Head. After approx 3/4 m Galesyke on R on sharp R-hand bend with wooden fence. From S turn R at Stanton Bridge, follow signs to Wasdale Head, Galesyke 2 1/2 m on R.* Light refreshments & teas. **Adm £2.50, chd free.** Sat 17, Sun 18 May (10.30-4.30). **Also open Buckbarrow House. Visitors also welcome by appt.**
Partially landscaped garden of several acres on banks of R Irt with views of Wasdale Fells, noted for its display of rhododendrons and azaleas.

☕ ☎

13 NEW THE GRANGE
Casterton LA6 2LD. Mrs T Sellers. *2m NE of Kirkby Lonsdale. Leave A65 at Devils Bridge and follow A683 for approx 2m. Entrance to The Grange is on L approx 100yds after The Grange Lodge.* Light refreshments & teas. **Adm £3, chd free. Sat 12 July (12-5).**
6½ -acre garden of which approx 4½ acres is woodland with meandering paths, informal pond and many interesting trees, shrubs and ferns. More formal garden around the house (not open) incl lawns, packed herbaceous borders, avenue of box balls and recently planted box, yew and lavender hedges.

14 HALECAT
Witherslack LA11 6RU. Mrs Michael Stanley. *10m SW of Kendal. From A590 turn into Witherslack following the Halecat brown signs. L in township at another brown sign & L again, signpost 'Cartmel Fell'; gates on L & Halecat Nursery. Map on Halecat website.* Light refreshments & teas at Nursery. **Adm £2, chd free. Suns 25 May; 22 June; 20 July (10-5).**
Medium-sized garden; mixed shrub and herbaceous borders, terrace, sunken garden; gazebo; daffodils and cherries in spring; wild flower meadow; beautiful view over Kent estuary to Arnside. Adjacent nursery. Steep slopes and gravel.

Perfumed white garden surrounds a delightful summerhouse . . .

15 HAZEL COTTAGE
Armathwaite CA4 9PG. Mr D Ryland & Mr J Thexton. *8m SE of Carlisle. Turn off A6 just S of High Hesket signed Armathwaite, after 2m house facing you at T-junction.* Cream teas. **Adm £3.50, chd free. Sun 25 May (12-5). Late Afternoon & Evening Opening £5, Tue 1 July (4-8).**
Developing flower arrangers and

plantsmans garden. Extending to approx 5 acres. Incls herbaceous borders, pergola, ponds and planting of disused railway siding providing home to wildlife. Many variegated and unusual plants. Varied areas, planted for all seasons, S-facing, some gentle slopes. Floral Art Demonstration (July). Featured in & on 'Cumbria Life, ITV Summer Gardens.

16 HEYWOOD HOUSE
Brookhouse LA2 9PW. Mike & Lorraine Cave, 01524 770977. *4m E of Lancaster. From J34 M6, follow A683 to Caton/Kirkby Lonsdale. At mini island turn R to Brookhouse. At Black Bull PH turn R, garden ¾ m on LH-side.* Home-made teas. **Adm £3, chd free. Suns 29 June; 3 Aug (11-5). Visitors also welcome by appt in June, groups 10+.**
Secluded 2-acre garden with many unusual trees and shrubs, sweeping lawns with beautiful herbaceous borders leading to large natural wildlife pond, gravel garden, pergolas with an abundance of roses and climbers, rockery, folly, woodland garden with natural stream. Under development. Garden railway train rides for adults and children.

17 HIGH CROSS LODGE
Bridge Lane, Troutbeck LA23 1LA. Mrs Linda Orchant. *2½ m N of Windermere. From Windermere, after Lakes School turn R into Bridge Lane off A591, next to YHA.* **Adm £3.50, chd free. Sun 15 June (11-4).**
Tropical-style garden designed by owner for all-yr interest. 1-acre gently sloping garden in a woodland setting with local slate terracing and cascading serpentine stream. Spectacular display of tree ferns, trachycarpus, cordylines and phormiums, many other non-hardy exotics. Collection of acers, ferns and pristine slug free hostas. New perfumed white garden surrounds a delightful summerhouse, new bog garden. Featured in 'GGG'.

18 ◆ HOLEHIRD GARDENS
Windermere LA23 1NP. Lakeland Horticultural Society, 015394 46008, www.holehirdgardens.org.uk. *2m N of Windermere. Off A592 Patterdale Rd.* Garden signed on R. **Adm £3, by donation, chd free. Open daily all yr. For NGS: Thur 24 July (10-5).**

The garden is run by volunteers with the aim of promoting knowledge of the cultivation of alpine and herbaceous plants, shrubs and trees, especially those suited to Lakeland conditions. One of the best labelled gardens in the UK. National Collections of *Astilbe, Hydrangea* and *Polystichum* (ferns). Set on the fellside with stunning views over Windermere the walled garden gives protection to mixed borders whilst alpine houses protect an always colourful array of tiny gems. Consistently voted among the top gardens in Britain and Europe. Visit our website. Featured in national & local press, specialist publications. Scientific Status for Hydrangea Collection.
NCCPG

19 ◆ HOLKER HALL GARDENS
Cark-in-Cartmel LA11 7PL. Lord & Lady Cavendish, 015395 53909, www.holker-hall.co.uk. *4m W of Grange-over-Sands. 12m W of M6 (J36) Follow brown 'tourist signs'.* **House and Garden adm £9.25, chd £5, concessions £8.50, Garden only adm £5.95, chd £3, concessions £5.25. Gardens 3 Feb to 23 Dec Sun to Fri. For hall see website. For NGS: Wed 9 July (10.30-5.30).**
A garden for all seasons within the Gulf Stream, benefiting plants from throughout the world incl exotic planting. Woodland garden with extensive collection of rhododendrons flowering Jan to late summer. National Collection of *Styracaceae*. Ancient oaks, magnolias, camellias and largest common lime in UK. Guided walks in garden 11.30am & 3pm starting from kiosk (donations to NGS).
NCCPG

20 ◆ HUTTON-IN-THE-FOREST
Penrith CA11 9TH. Lord Inglewood, 017684 84449, www.hutton-in-the-forest.co.uk. *6m NW of Penrith. On B5305, 3m from exit 41 of M6 towards Wigton.* **House and Garden adm £6, chd £3, Garden only adm £3.50, chd £1. Gardens Sun to Fri 20 Mar to 31 Oct 11-5. House Weds, Thurs, Suns, Bank Hol Mons Easter & May to Sept (tel for times). For NGS: Suns 8 June; 17 Aug (11-5).**
Magnificent grounds with C18 walled flower garden, terraces and lake. C19 low garden, specimen trees and topiary; woodland walk and dovecote. Medieval house with C17, C18 and C19 additions. Featured in 'Country Life'. Partial wheelchair access.

21 KIRKBY STEPHEN GARDENS
CA17 4PG. *2m N of Kirkby Stephen. North on A685 just N of Kirkby Stephen, turn L signed Gt Musgrave/Warcop (B6259) after approx 1m turn L as signed.* Teas at Winton Park. **Combined adm £4.50, chd free. Sun 13 July (11-5).**
A paired opening providing a contrast in style between creative use of space in a modest-sized town garden and large country garden.

WESTVIEW
Fletcher Hill. Reg & Irene Metcalfe. *Kirkby Stephen town centre, T-lights opp Pine Design*
Medium sized secret town-centre walled cottage-type garden with perennials, shrubs, large hosta bed (many varieties), central lawn, wildlife pond and adjoining prairie style nursery beds.

WINTON PARK
Mr Anthony Kilvington
2 acre country garden with many fine conifers, acers and rhododendrons, herbaceous borders, hostas, ferns, grasses and over 700 roses. Three formal ponds, plus secret wildlife pond with koi and other fish. Stunning views.

Wildlife incls deer, red squirrels, badgers, bats and slow worms . . .

22 LAKESIDE HOTEL
Lake Windermere, Newby Bridge LA12 8AT. Mr N R Talbot, 015395 30001, sales@lakesidehotel.co.uk. *1m N of Newby Bridge. On S shore of Lake Windermere. From A590 at Newby Bridge, cross the bridge which leads onto the Hawkshead rd. Follow this rd for 1m, hotel on the R. Complimentary parking available.* Light refreshments & teas. **Adm £3, chd free. Weds 30 Apr; 3 Sept (11-5). Visitors also welcome by appt.**
An award winning 4 star hotel on the

shores of Windermere, with exceptional gardens. Aromatherapy garden, scented pelargoniums collection, local heritage apple varieties. We welcome you to this idyllic Lakeland setting to meet the garden team, enjoy the gardens and the hospitality of Lakeside Hotel.

23 LANGHOLME MILL
Woodgate, Lowick Green LA12 8ES. Judith & Graham Sanderson, 01229 885215, info@langholmemill.co.uk. *7m NW of Ulverston. Take A5092 at Greenodd towards Broughton for 3¾ m on L ½ m after school.* **Adm £3, chd free (share to North West Air Ambulance). Visitors welcome by appt May to Sept.**
Approx 1 acre of woodland garden surrounding mill race stream with bridges, hosting well established rhododendrons, hostas and acers.

24 [NEW] LAWSON PARK
East of Lake Coniston. LA21 8AD. Grizedale Arts, 015394 41050, info@grizedale.org. *5m E of Coniston. From Coniston Village follow signs East of Lake/Brantwood, car park signed 1m after Brantwood car park. Please use free minibus (runs every 10 mins) from Machell's Coppice Forestry Commission car park. On foot 10 mins walk up footpath from car park.* Cream teas. **Adm £3.50, chd free (share to Grizedale Arts). Day & Early Evening Opening,** wine Sun 24 Aug (12-7). Visitors also welcome by appt July to Sept only, groups of between 10 - 20 (on site parking by prior arrangement).
Historic hill farm overlooking Coniston, which since 2001 has been restored to a working smallholding, productive and ornamental gardens, and artist's residency base. Approx 5 acres of reclaimed fellside in spectacular setting. Informal herbaceous, woodland, bog and wild gardens (incl wild flower meadow) and organic kitchen garden with apiary. Many experimental plantings and unusual seed-grown perennials and trees. Wildlife incls deer, red squirrels, badgers, bats and slow worms. Produce for sale. Contemporary Art Project on site.

25 LEECE VILLAGE GARDENS
LA12 0QP. *2m E of Barrow-in-Furness. 6m SW of Ulverston. J36 M6 onto A590 to Ulverston. A5087 coast rd to Barrow. Approx 8m turn R for Leece Village (signed, look for concrete sea wall on L). Village parking for gardens.* Light refreshments & teas. **Combined adm £3, chd free. Sun 6 July (11-5).**
Small village clustered around tarn. Maps given to all visitors. Featured in & on local press & radio.

BRIAR COTTAGE
June Pye
Small cottage garden in the countryside featuring wildlife pond and many herbaceous perennials. Adjacent to Downfield House and off-rd parking.

BRIAR HOUSE
Jeff Lowden
Informal garden with limestone rockery leading to interesting trees and young orchard, white garden; large flower meadow with maze and panoramic views across Low Furness and Morecambe Bay.

DOWNFIELD HOUSE
Mrs Alison Bolt
Approx ½ acre of mature garden containing an interesting collection of hardy geraniums and several varieties of buddleia. Trees, shrubs, wildlife pond and vegetables. Adjacent to Briar Cottage and parking.

[NEW] LANE END HOUSE
Mr & Mrs A Sharp
SW-facing garden with access steps. Terraces with cottage garden plants and herbaceous perennials. Small pond and alpine border, seating areas.

[NEW] 3 PEAR TREE COTTAGE
Jane & Rob Phizacklea
Traditional walled front garden with lawn and borders filled with herbaceous perennials and flowering shrubs. Stone steps lead to rear sloping garden. Long curved lawn, flowing cottage garden style borders and slate seating area.

RAISING HOUSE
Vivien & Neil Hudson
Plant lovers garden on SW slope. Developed (with still more to do) over last 5yrs with emphasis on

flowering plants, incl many unusual shrubs, grasses, herbaceous perennials and climbers. Alpine scree and troughs. Access by steps.

WINANDER
Mrs Enid Cockshott
1-acre, eco-friendly garden amid mature trees on an E-facing slope. Patio area with wildlife pond; large organic vegetable and fruit area. Alpines, mixed borders, quiet seating areas with views across Leece Tarn and out to Morecambe Bay.

WOOD GARTH
Harry & Rita Butcher
Sheltered village garden. Formal area with traditionally planted containers and herbaceous border. Trees and native flora to attract wildlife. Lawned area with differential mowing. Access by steps.

26 LILAC COTTAGE GARDEN
Blitterlees. CA7 4JJ. Lynn & Jeff Downham. *1m S of Silloth. On B5300 the Maryport to Silloth rd.* Home-made teas. **Adm £2.50, chd free.** Sun 11 May (11-4).
Approx 1-acre garden set in compartments in a coastal setting. Featuring raised and woodland gardens, herbaceous borders, large lawned areas and sandstone gazebo. Each garden has an individual theme, well stocked with plants, shrubs and trees providing colour and interest all-yr round.

27 LINDETH FELL COUNTRY HOUSE HOTEL
Lyth Valley Road, Bowness-on-Windermere LA23 3JP. Air Cdr & Mrs P A Kennedy, 015394 43286, www.lindethfell.co.uk. *1m S of Bowness. On A5074. From centre of Bowness opp St Martins church turn L, signed Kendal A5074. 200yds on L after Xrds at Ferry View.* Home-made teas. **Adm £3, chd free.** Sat 17 May (2-5). Visitors also welcome by appt May to Oct, short wheel base coaches only.
6 acres of lawns and landscaped grounds on the hills above Lake Windermere, designed by Mawson around 1909; conifers and specimen trees best in spring and early summer

with a colourful display of rhododendrons, azaleas and Japanese maples; grounds offer splendid views to Coniston mountains. Partial wheelchair access: To terrace in front of house looking over garden and view.

28 NEW LOWER ROWELL FARM
Milnthorpe LA7 7LU. John & Mavis Robinson, 015395 62270. *2m NE of Milnthorpe. Signed to Rowell off B6385. Garden ½ m up lane on L.* Home-made teas. **Adm £3, chd free.** Sat 17, Sun 18 May (1-5). Visitors also welcome by appt.
Approx ¾ -acre garden. Borders and beds with shrubs and interesting herbaceous perennials. Retro greenhouse and vegetable plots. Very peaceful with open views to Farleton Knott, Pennines and Lakeland hills.

29 MATSON GROUND
Windermere LA23 2NH. Matson Ground Estate Co Ltd. *⅔ m E of Bowness. From Kendal turn R off B5284 signed Heathwaite, 100yds after Windermere Golf Club. Garden on L after ⅓ m. From Bowness turn L onto B5284 from A5074. After ½ m turn L at Xrds. Garden on L ½ m along lane.* Home-made teas. **Adm £3, chd free.** Sun 18 May (2-5).
Stream flows through ornamental garden to large pond in the wild garden of spring bulbs, later wild flowers. Azaleas, rhododendrons, large mixed shrub/herbaceous borders, topiary work, white garden, spring/summer border. ½ -acre walled kitchen garden and greenhouses. 2-acre woodland.

30 NEWTON RIGG CAMPUS GARDENS
Newton Rigg, Penrith CA11 0AH. University of Cumbria, www.cumbria.ac.uk. *1m W of Penrith. 3m W from J40 & J41 off M6. ½ m off the B5288 W of Penrith.* **Adm £3, chd free. Evening Openings** Weds 11 June; 17 Sept (6.30-8.30). The gardens and campus grounds have much of horticultural interest incl herbaceous borders, ponds, organic garden with fruit cage and display of composting techniques, woodland walk, summer scented garden, 2

arboretums, tropical display house, annual meadows, pleached hornbeam walkway and extensive range of ornamental trees and shrubs. Guided tour of gardens will be lead by horticultural experts Con Maguire, Vera Turnball and Shelagh Todd. Featured in 'Cumbria Life'.

Very peaceful with open views to Farleton Knott, Pennines and Lakeland hills . . .

31 THE NOOK
Helton CA10 2QA. Brenda & Philip Freedman, pfreedman@helton.demon.co.uk. *6m S of Penrith. A6 S from Penrith. After Eamont Bridge turn R to Pooley Bridge. Fork L to Askham. Through Askham 1m to Helton. Follow signs.* Home-made teas. **Adm £3, chd free.** Sun 4 May (11-5). Visitors also welcome by appt.
Plantsman's hillside garden with long views down Lowther Valley. Mainly alpine plants many rare and unusual. Front, cottage garden, side garden has cordon, espalier and fan trained fruit trees, soft fruit and vegetables. Main garden with species rhododendrons, scree garden, troughs, conifers, herb garden and water feature. Steps into main garden, but can provide ramp.

33 THE OLD RECTORY
Caldbeck CA7 8DP. Mrs Anne Cartmell. *Caldbeck village centre, between shop & church over cattlegrid.* **Adm £3, chd free (share to Hospice at Home, Carlisle, N Lakeland).** Sun 22 June (11-4). Established garden surrounding Georgian house (not open). Mature trees and shrubs, formal and herbaceous area. Large walled vegetable garden.

32 THE OLD RECTORY
Dean, Workington CA14 4TH. Mr F
H & Mrs J S Wheeler, 01946 861840.
*5m SW of Cockermouth. Last house in
Dean on rd to Workington, on L
beyond church.* **Adm £2.50, chd free.**
**Visitors welcome by appt
throughout the year, individuals &
groups welcome.**
Over 1 acre. with interest throughout
the year from aconites and spring
bulbs to autumn colours. Informal
rooms with wide range of trees, shrubs
and herbaceous perennials, many
relatively rare and tender, various shrub
and climbing roses. Mixed shrubberies,
woodland and damp areas, scree
garden and rockeries. Featured in
'Gardens of the Lake District'.
✕ ☎

34 NEW OLDE OAKS
Croft Ends, Appleby CA16 6JW.
Chantal Knight, 017683 51304,
chantalknight@midwife.plus.co
m. *1½ m N of Appleby. Heading N
out of Appleby take rd to Long
Marton for 1m. 1st R, continue on
½ m, garden last on R.* Light
refreshments & teas. **Adm £3, chd
free. Sat 12 July (11-5).Visitors
also welcome by appt June to
Aug.**
Beautiful views of the Pennines
create a stunning backdrop for this
medium sized cottage-style
garden. Large herbaceous borders
are filled with interesting mixed
perennials and wildlife pond. A
wealth of summer bedding adorns
front of the property with stream
and pond containing koi carp.
Across the road is delightful 3-acre
mixed woodland walk. Dufton
Show - Best Garden.
✦ ✕ ✿ ☕ ☎

35 PEAR TREE COTTAGE
Dalton, Burton-in-Kendal LA6 1NN.
Linda & Alec Greening, 01524
781624,
www.peartreecottagecumbria.co.uk.
*4m W of Kirkby Lonsdale. 10m S of
Kendal. From village of Burton-in-
Kendal (A6070), follow Vicarage Lane
for 1m. Parking at farm, 50yds before
garden (signed).* Home-made teas.
Adm £3.00, chd free. Sun 20 July
(11-5). **Evening Opening £4.00,
wine, Wed 25 June (6-9).Visitors
also welcome by appt May to July
for groups of 15+.**
⅓ -acre cottage garden. A peaceful
and relaxing garden, harmonising with

its rural setting. Diverse planting areas,
including packed herbaceous borders,
rambling roses, wildlife pond and bog
garden, fernery and gravel garden.
Intensively planted, incl much to
interest the plantsman and general
garden visitor alike. Increasing
collections of ferns and hardy
geraniums. Newly-extended shade
planting. Featured in & on 'The
Lakeland Gardener', 'Gardens of the
Lake District', Border TV Summer
Gardens & Radio Cumbria.
✕ ✿ ☕ ☎

Beautiful views
of the Pennines
create a stunning
backdrop for this
medium sized
cottage-style
garden.

36 QUARRY HILL HOUSE
Mealsgate CA7 1AE. Mr & Mrs
Charles Woodhouse, 016973 71225,
charles.woodhouse@ukgateway.net.
*1m E of Mealsgate. Between
Boltongate & Mealsgate on B5299. ½
m W of Boltongate(8m SSW of
Wigton). At Mealsgate, on A595
Cockermouth to Carlisle rd, turn E onto
B5299 for Boltongate, Ireby &
Caldbeck. Approx 1m along rd,
entrance gates to Quarry Hill House on
L.* Home-made teas. **Adm £4, chd
free (share to Hospice at Home
Carlisle & N Lakeland).** Suns 8 June;
27 July (1.30-5.30).Visitors also
welcome by appt.
3 acre parkland setting country house
(not open) garden with good views.
Herbaceous borders, shrubs,
vegetable garden. 25 acre park incls
wild flower areas and extensively
planted arboretum with many
specimen trees, especially varieties of
sorbus with lovely woodland walks.
Regeneration projects since 2000 led
by groundsman Peter Whiles with
recent help from horticulturalist Louise
Stoddart, these incl recreation for
wildlife of former shooting ponds.
Featured in 'Cumberland News'.
✕ ✿ ☕ ☎

37 RANNERDALE COTTAGE
Buttermere CA13 9UY. The McElney
Family. *8m S of Cockermouth. 10m W
of Keswick. B5289 on Crummock
Water, in the Buttermere Valley.* Home-
made teas. **Adm £2.50, chd free. Sat
3, Sun 4 May (12-5).**
½ -acre cottage garden with beck and
woodland walk overlooking Crummock
Water, splendid mountain views.
Herbaceous, shrubs, roses, perennial
geraniums, tree peonies, pond with
fish.
✿ ☕

38 NEW REDMAYNE HALL
Little Urswick, Ulverston
LA12 0PL. Jennie Werry. *4m W of
Ulverston. A590 from Ulverston,
approx 2m to Little Urswick at
farthest end of village.* **Adm £2.50,
chd free. Sun 13 July (1-5).**
A very private private garden.
Mature shrubs, mixed beds, former
farmyard still evolving. Divided into
several area's. Peaceful country
setting.

39 NEW ◆ RYDAL HALL
Ambleside LA22 9LX. Diocese of
Carlisle, 01539 432050,
www.rydalhall.org. *2m N of
Ambleside. E from A591 at Rydal
signed Rydal Hall.* **Adm by
donation. Open daily. For NGS:
Thurs 26 June; 24 July; 28 Aug
(10-4).**
Formal Italianate gardens designed
by Thomas Mawson in 1911 set in
34 acres. The gardens have
recently been restored over a 2yr
period returning to their former
glory. Informal woodland garden,
leading to C17 viewing
station/summerhouse, fine
herbaceous planting, community
vegetable garden, orchard and
apiary. Partial wheelchair access.
✦ 🛏 ☕

40 SCARTHWAITE
Grange-in-Borrowdale, Keswick
CA12 5UQ. Mr & Mrs E C Hicks, By
written application only, please see
above. *5m S of Keswick. From
Keswick take B5289 to Grange. Cross
rd bridge, into village, house ¼ m on L.
Bridge NOT suitable for coaches but
mini buses may cross. (¼ m walk from
far side of bridge for coach parties).
The Keswick/Seatoller bus &
Stagecoach Honister Rambler bus
stop at Grange Bridge.* **Adm £2.50,**

chd free. Visitors welcome by appt on weekdays ONLY, not weekends or Bank Hols. Visitors welcome any season, weather permitting. Please keep children under strict control.
This 1/3 -acre garden gives the impression of woodland; focusing on naturalistic planting of ferns, hostas and bulbs, many varieties of hardy geraniums, clematis and other plants growing in the profusion of a cottage garden. The garden looks South into the Jaws of Borrowdale. The view is dominated by Castle Crag flanked either side by Kings Haw and Gate Crag with Glaramara and Great End in the background.
✕ ☎

Garden gives the impression of woodland; focusing on naturalistic planting of ferns, hostas and bulbs . . .

④ ◆ SIZERGH CASTLE
nr Kendal LA8 8AE. The National Trust, 015395 69813, www.nationaltrust.org.uk. 3m S of Kendal. Approach rd leaves A590 close to & S of A590/A591 interchange. Adm £4.25, chd £2.15. For opening details please see website or tel. For NGS: Sats 19 July; 16 Aug (11-5).
2/3 -acre limestone rock garden, largest owned by National Trust; collection of Japanese maples, dwarf conifers, hardy ferns, primulas, gentians, perennials and bulbs; water garden, aquatic plants; on castle walls shrubs and climbers, many half-hardy; south garden with specimen roses, lilies, shrubs and ground cover. Wild flower areas, herbaceous borders, crab apple orchard with spring bulbs, 'Dutch' garden. Terraced garden and lake; kitchen garden, vegetables, herbs, flowers; fruit orchard with spring bulbs. Guided walk by Head Gardener 3pm.
👷 ✕ ☕

㊷ SPRINT MILL
Burneside LA8 9AQ. Edward & Romola Acland, 01539 725168. 2m N of Kendal. From Burneside follow signs to Skelsmergh for 1/2 m then L to Sprint Mill. Light refreshments & teas. Adm £2.50, chd free. Suns 29 June; 27 July (11-5). Visitors also welcome by appt.
Unorthodox 5-acre organic garden (atypical NGS) combining the wild and natural alongside provision of owners' wood, fruit and vegetables. Riverside setting, hand-crafted seats, old water mill building to be explored. Large vegetable and soft fruit area, following no-dig and permaculture principles. Hand-tools prevail, scythe and fork rather than mower. Unconventional art and crafts display, green woodworking workshop, slide show of garden development.
✕ ☕ ☎

㊸ STONE EDGE
Jack Hill, Allithwaite LA11 7QB. Ian & Julie Chambers, 015395 33895. 2m W of Grange-over-Sands. On B5277. Jack Hill is on L just before Allithwaite Village. Parking available in The Pheasant Inn car park at bottom of Jack Hill approx 100 metres. Ltd parking for the not so fit near house. Home-made teas. Adm £3.50, chd free. Visitors welcome by appt all year.
A garden in harmony with nature; incl formal lavender garden; border with shrubs, climbers and perennials; herbs grown for use in the kitchen. Spectacular specimens form a Mediterranean garden; woodland garden meanders down to a pond. Steep slope in woodland garden. Pots abound. Fantasic views over Morecambe Bay. Garden room and new potting garden room. Featured in 'Cumbria Life'.
✕ ☕ ☎

㊹ SUMMERDALE HOUSE
Nook, nr Lupton LA6 1PE. David & Gail Sheals, 015395 67210, sheals@btinternet.com. 7m S of Kendal. 6m W of Kirkby Lonsdale. From J36 M6 take A65 to Kirkby Lonsdale, at Nook take R turn Farleton. Home-made soup & teas 6 Apr, home-made teas May/June. Adm £3.50, chd free. Suns 6 Apr; 4 May; 15 June (11-5). Visitors also welcome by appt Apr to Sept, groups of 10+.
1 1/2 -acre part-walled country garden restored and developed over last 10yrs by owners. Beautiful setting with fine

views across to Farleton Fell. Herbaceous borders, formal and informal ponds, woodland planting, old orchard and new meadow planting. Interesting range of herbaceous perennials, many of which are propagated by owners.
✕ ⊛ ☕ ☎

㊺ ◆ TULLIE HOUSE
Castle Street, Carlisle CA3 8TP. Carlisle City Council, 01228 618718, www.tulliehouse.co.uk. City Centre. Signed as Museum on brown signs, see website for map. Adm by donation. All year, except Christmas, Boxing & New Years day. For NGS: Sat 21 (10-5), Sun 22 June (11-5).
Beds in front of Jacobean house are planted to reflect C17. Mature Arbutus unedo and Cornus kousa grow alongside other recent planting incl Fatsia japonica variegata: Eucryphia glutinosa. Roman style planting incl fig, vines, myrtle, acanthus and variety of herbs. Music, plant stalls, environmental stands, childrens garden themed workshop, talks on areas of interest connected to the gardens. Green Flag Award.
👷 ⊛

㊻ WHITBYSTEADS
Askham CA10 2PG. Mr Thomas Lowther. 6m S of Penrith. Turn R at Eamont Bridge. Turn L at Y fork after railway bridge signed Askham. Turn R at Queen's Head up hill, ignore Dead End sign, garden 3/4 m from village. Cream teas. Adm £2.50, chd free (share to Lowther Parochial Church Council). Sun 29 June (2-5).
1-acre garden on several levels surrounding farmhouse (not open) on edge of fells, (850ft) high. Variety of shrub roses, unusual herbaceous plants and geraniums. Magnificent views over Eden Valley.
✕ 🛏 ☕

㊼ WINDY HALL
Crook Road, Windermere LA23 3JA. Diane & David Kinsman, 015394 46238, dhewitt-kinsman@googlemail.com. 1m S of Bowness-on-Windermere. On B5284 up Linthwaite House Hotel driveway. Home-made teas. Adm £3, chd free. Combined with Brackenrigg Lodge adm £5. Suns 4 May; 8 June (10-5). Visitors also welcome by appt.
4-acre owner designed and maintained garden. Woodland underplanted with species rhododendrons, camellias,

magnolias and hydrangeas; Japanese influenced quarry garden; alpine area with gunnera; wild flower meadow; kitchen, 'privy' and 'Best' gardens. Waterfowl garden with gunnera, many stewartias. Redesigned pond garden with plants raised from seed collected by David in China. NCCPG Collections of *Aruncus* and *Filipendula*; Naturalised moss gardens and paths in woodland, bluebells and foxgloves in abundance, wide variety of native birds, many nest in gardens. Black, multi-horned Hebridean sheep and lambs. Rare breeds of pheasants from China and Nepal, exotic ducks and geese. Featured in 'GGG' and 'The Impartial Reporter'.

🏹 ✸ NCCPG ☕ ☎

Naturalised moss gardens and paths in woodland, bluebells and foxgloves in abundance, wide variety of native birds . . .

48 YEWBARROW HOUSE
Hampsfell Road, Grange-over-Sands LA11 6BE. Jonathan & Margaret Denby, 015395 32469, www.yewbarrowhouse.co.uk. ¼ m *from town centre. Follow signs in centre of Grange. Turn R at HSBC Bank into Pig Lane, 1st L into Hampsfell Rd. Garden 200yds on L.* Cream teas. **Adm £3, chd free. Suns 1 June; 6 July; 3 Aug; 7 Sept (11-4). Visitors also welcome by appt, coaches permitted.**
New Mediterranean style garden on 4½ -acre elevated site with magnificent views over Morecambe Bay. The garden features a restored walled Victorian kitchen garden; Italianate terrace garden; exotic gravel garden; fern garden, Japanese Hot Spring pool. Dahlia trial beds and orangery. Featured in 'Country Life'.

✸ ☕ ☎

49 YEWS
Bowness-on-Windermere LA23 3JR. Sir Oliver & Lady Scott. *1m S of Bowness-on-Windermere. A5074. Middle Entrance Drive, 50yds.* Home-made teas. **Adm £3, chd free (share to Marie Curie & Macmillan Nurses).** Sun 15 June (2-5.30).
Medium-sized formal Edwardian garden; fine trees, ha-ha, herbaceous borders; greenhouse. Bog area being developed, bamboo, primula, hosta. Young yew maze and vegetable garden.

🏹 ✸ ☕

Cumbria County Volunteers

County Organisers
Alec & Linda Greening, Pear Tree Cottage, Dalton, Burton-in-Kendal, Carnforth LA6 1NN, 01524 781624, linda.greening@virgin.net

County Treasurer
Derek Farman, Mill House, Winster, Windermere, Cumbria LA23 3NW, 015394 44893, farman@f2s.com

Publicity
Tony Connor, 15 Morewood Drive, Burton-in-Kendal, Carnforth LA6 1NE, 01524 781119, tonconnor@aol.com

Assistant County Organisers
Diane Hewitt, Windy Hall, Crook Road, Windermere LA23 3JA, 015394 46238, dhewitt.kinsman@googlemail.com
South West John Maddison, Buckbarrow House, Denton Park Court, Gosforth, Seascale CA20 1BN, 019467 25431, JohnMaddGosf@aol.com
North Alannah Rylands, Crookdake Farm, Aspatria, Wigton CA7 3SH, 016973 20413, rylands@crookdake.com

DERBYSHIRE

Opening Dates

April

SUNDAY 6
60 Windward

SUNDAY 13
41 Meynell Langley Trials Garden

WEDNESDAY 16
4 Bluebell Arboretum
8 Cascades Gardens

SUNDAY 20
4 Bluebell Arboretum
10 10 Chestnut Way
30 37 High Street

TUESDAY 22
50 Renishaw Hall

May

SUNDAY 4
21 Dove Cottage
23 Eyam Hall
26 Gamesley Fold Cottage

MONDAY 5
6 The Burrows Gardens

SUNDAY 11
5 Broomfield Hall
12 Cloud Cottage
37 Locko Park
41 Meynell Langley Trials Garden
53 Southfield

SUNDAY 18
12 Cloud Cottage
25 Fir Croft
31 Highfield House
46 Parlour Barn

WEDNESDAY 21
4 Bluebell Arboretum
8 Cascades Gardens

SATURDAY 24
49 Quarryside

SUNDAY 25
4 Bluebell Arboretum
10 10 Chestnut Way
12 Cloud Cottage
21 Dove Cottage
26 Gamesley Fold Cottage
43 Monksway
49 Quarryside
61 Woodend Cottage

MONDAY 26
6 The Burrows Gardens
10 10 Chestnut Way

SATURDAY 31
2 334 Belper Road

June

SUNDAY 1
2 334 Belper Road

23 Eyam Hall
25 Fir Croft
36 Littleover Lane Allotments
43 Monksway
45 Park Hall

SUNDAY 8
26 Gamesley Fold Cottage
30 37 High Street
41 Meynell Langley Trials Garden
43 Monksway
48 Postern House
52 Shatton Hall Farm
60 Windward

SATURDAY 14
22 The Dower House

SUNDAY 15
1 Ashford Hall
9 Cashel
20 Dolly Barn
22 The Dower House
25 Fir Croft
58 24 Wheeldon Avenue
59 26 Wheeldon Avenue

WEDNESDAY 18
4 Bluebell Arboretum
8 Cascades Gardens

SUNDAY 22
1 Ashford Hall
4 Bluebell Arboretum
11 13 Chiltern Drive
24 Fanshawe Gate Hall
29 High Roost
33 Hillside

SUNDAY 29
21 Dove Cottage
24 Fanshawe Gate Hall
45 Park Hall

MONDAY 30
6 The Burrows Gardens

July

SATURDAY 5
57 Wharfedale

SUNDAY 6
13 Clovermead
16 8 Curzon Lane
24 Fanshawe Gate Hall
41 Meynell Langley Trials Garden
57 Wharfedale

SUNDAY 13
8 Cascades Gardens
16 8 Curzon Lane
24 Fanshawe Gate Hall
39 2 Manvers Street
46 Parlour Barn
48 Postern House
61 Woodend Cottage

MONDAY 14
6 The Burrows Gardens

TUESDAY 15
28 Hardwick Hall (Evening)

SATURDAY 19
7 Calke Abbey
28 Hardwick Hall
32 11 Highgrove Drive
51 Rosebank

SUNDAY 20
32 11 Highgrove Drive
40 Markham Villa
53 Southfield
58 24 Wheeldon Avenue

WEDNESDAY 23
4 Bluebell Arboretum

SATURDAY 26
14 The Cottage

SUNDAY 27
4 Bluebell Arboretum
13 Clovermead
14 The Cottage
20 Dolly Barn
21 Dove Cottage
52 Shatton Hall Farm

August

SATURDAY 2
47 19 Portland Street

SUNDAY 3
19 62A Denby Lane
38 9 Main Street
40 Markham Villa
47 19 Portland Street

TUESDAY 5
50 Renishaw Hall

WEDNESDAY 6
8 Cascades Gardens

SUNDAY 10
13 Clovermead
42 23 Mill Lane
56 7 Warren Drive
61 Woodend Cottage

SATURDAY 16
51 Rosebank

SUNDAY 17
41 Meynell Langley Trials Garden

WEDNESDAY 20
4 Bluebell Arboretum

THURSDAY 21
7 Calke Abbey

SUNDAY 24
4 Bluebell Arboretum
57 Wharfedale

MONDAY 25
6 The Burrows Gardens

55 Tissington Hall

September

FRIDAY 5
57 Wharfedale (Evening)

SUNDAY 7
36 Littleover Lane Allotments
60 Windward

MONDAY 8
6 The Burrows Gardens

SUNDAY 14
41 Meynell Langley Trials Garden

WEDNESDAY 24
4 Bluebell Arboretum

SUNDAY 28
4 Bluebell Arboretum

October

SUNDAY 12
41 Meynell Langley Trials Garden

WEDNESDAY 29
4 Bluebell Arboretum

November

SATURDAY 1
4 Bluebell Arboretum

Gardens open to the public

4 Bluebell Arboretum
6 The Burrows Gardens
7 Calke Abbey
8 Cascades Gardens
17 Dam Farm House
23 Eyam Hall
28 Hardwick Hall
35 Lea Gardens
41 Meynell Langley Trials Garden
48 Postern House
50 Renishaw Hall
55 Tissington Hall

By appointment only

3 Birchfield
15 Cuckoostone Cottage
18 Dam Stead
27 The Gardens at Dobholme Fishery
34 Horsleygate Hall
44 Otterbrook
54 Spindlewood
62 35 Wyver Lane

Also open by appointment ☎

1 Ashford Hall
2 334 Belper Road
9 Cashel
10 10 Chestnut Way
12 Cloud Cottage

13 Clovermead
14 The Cottage
16 8 Curzon Lane
18 Dam Stead
20 Dolly Barn
21 Dove Cottage
22 The Dower House
24 Fanshawe Gate Hall
26 Gamesley Fold Cottage
29 High Roost
31 Highfield House
33 Hillside
36 Littleover Lane Allotments
38 9 Main Street
39 2 Manvers Street
40 Markham Villa
43 Monksway
45 Park Hall
47 19 Portland Street
49 Quarryside
52 Shatton Hall Farm
56 7 Warren Drive
57 Wharfedale
58 24 Wheeldon Avenue
59 26 Wheeldon Avenue
60 Windward
61 Woodend Cottage

The Gardens

1 **ASHFORD HALL**
Ashford-in-the-Water, Bakewell DE45 1QA. Mr & Mrs Jasper Olivier, 01629 814798. *2m NW of Bakewell. On A6 turn onto A6020 towards Chesterfield, after 300yds turn R up drive immed after cricket field.* **Adm £3, chd free. Suns 15, 22 June (2-5). Visitors also welcome by appt for groups 12+, 14 Jun - 15 Jul only.** Large landscape garden with beautiful views beside R Wye. Magnificent old yew hedges, river walk, rose garden, orchard and walled kitchen garden.
⊛ ☕ ☎

BANCROFT FARM
See Staffordshire & part of West Midlands.

THE BEECHES
See Staffordshire & part of West Midlands.

2 **334 BELPER ROAD**
Stanley Common DE7 6FY. Gill & Colin Hancock, 0115 930 1061. *7m N of Derby. 3m W of Ilkeston. On A609, 3/4 m from Rose & Crown Xrds (A608). Please park in field up farm drive or Working Men's Club rear car park if wet.* Home-made teas. **Adm £2.50, chd free. Sat 31 May (2-5); Sun 1 June (12-5). Visitors also**

welcome by appt all yr-round.
Predominantly shrubs and perennials in a 3/4 -acre maturing garden with many seating areas. Large kitchen garden and greenhouses. Replanted pond area with bog plants, ferns and a renovated D.C.C workmans hut, now a summerhouse. 1/2 m walk around a 7yr old wood and 1/2 -acre lake. Highly recommended home-made cakes. Winner Erewash in Bloom 2007 'Best wildlife and environmental garden'.
🚻 🐾 ⊛ ☕ ☎

Dry garden with grasses and bamboos recently constructed . . .

3 **BIRCHFIELD**
Dukes Drive, Ashford in the Water, Bakewell DE45 1QQ. Brian Parker, 01629 813800, www.birchfieldgarden.com. *2m NW of Bakewell. On A6 to Buxton.* **Adm £2, chd free (share to Thornhill Memorial Trust). Visitors welcome by appt Apr - Sept.**
Beautifully situated terraced garden of approx 3/4 acre. Designed for yr-round colour, it contains wide variety of shrubs and perennials, bulbs and water gardens. Dry garden with grasses and bamboos recently constructed. Arboretum with wild flowers has been developed on a further 11/4 acres. Featured in 'Peak District Life'.
🐾 ☕ ☎

4 ◆ **BLUEBELL ARBORETUM**
Smisby LE65 2TA. Robert & Suzette Vernon, 01530 413700, sales@bluebellnursery.com. *1m N of Ashby-de-la-Zouch. Arboretum is clearly signed in Annwell Lane, 1/4 m S, through village of Smisby which is off B5006, between Ticknall & Ashby-de-la-Zouch.* **Adm £2.50, chd free. Open daily throughout yr (10.30-4.30) Closed Suns Nov-Feb, Easter Sun & 24 Dec to 1 Jan. For NGS: Wed 16, Sun 20 Apr; Wed 21, Sun 25 May; Wed 18, Sun 22 June; Wed 23, Sun 27 July; Wed 20, Sun 24 Aug; Wed 24, Sun 28 Sept; Wed 29 Oct; Sat 1 Nov (10.30-4.30).**
5-acre arboretum planted in last 16yrs

incl many specimens of rare trees and shrubs. Bring wellingtons in wet weather. Please be aware this is not a wood full of bluebells, despite the name. Adjacent specialist nursery. Featured in 'Gardens Illustrated' & autumn colour feature on BBC Gardeners World with Carol Klein. Ground difficult in wet weather.

&. ≈

BROOKSIDE COTTAGE
See Yorkshire.

5 **BROOMFIELD HALL**
Morley DE7 6DN. Derby College. *4m N of Derby. 6m S of Heanor On A608.* Light refreshments & teas. **Adm £2.50, chd free. Sun 11 May (11-4).** Landscaped garden of 25 acres. Shrubs, trees, rose collection, herbaceous borders; glasshouses; walled garden; garden tour guides. Themed gardens, plant centre. National Collection of old roses. Some parts of the garden are unsuitable for wheelchair access.

&. ≈ ⊛ **NCCPG** ☕

6 ◆ **THE BURROWS GARDENS**
Burrows Lane, Brailsford, Ashbourne DE6 3BU. Mr B C Dalton, 01335 360745, www.burrowsgardens.com. *5m SE of Ashbourne; 5m NW of Derby. From Ashbourne: A52 towards Derby 5m to Brailsford. Turn R after Rose & Crown PH, then 1st L. Continue 1/2 m, garden on R. From Derby: leave Derby on A52 towards Ashbourne, after Kirk Langley stay on A52 for 1 1/2 m. Turn L signed Dalbury. 1/2 m R at grass triangle, garden in front of you. Follow AA signs.* **Adm £3.50, chd free. Open every Sun 4 May to 14 Sept incl. Other times by appt. Coaches welcome. Group guided tours by Mr Dalton. For NGS: Mons 5, 26 May, 30 June ; 14 July; 25 Aug; 8 Sept (10.30-4.30).** Five acres of stunning garden set in beautiful countryside where the immaculate lawns show off the exotic rare plants and trees which mix with the old favourites in this fabulous garden. A vast variety of styles from the temple garden to a Cornish, Italian and English garden plus many more are gloriously designed and displayed. The owner is always on hand and delighted to discuss gardening matters with every visitor. Featured in 'English Garden' & '1000 Best Gardens in Britain & Ireland', 2007, magazines, local press and Radio Derby.

&. ≈ ⊛ ☕

7 ◆ **CALKE ABBEY**
Ticknall DE73 7LE. The National Trust, 01332 863822, www.nationaltrust.org.uk/calke. *10m S of Derby. On A514 at Ticknall between Swadlincote & Melbourne.* **House and garden adm £8.50, child £4.20, garden only adm £5.30, chd £2.70. March to October, Saturday to Wednesday. For NGS: Sat 19 July; Thur 21 Aug (11-5).** Extensive late C18 walled gardens. Flower garden with summer bedding and famous auricula theatre. Impressive collection of glasshouses and garden buildings. Vegetable garden growing heirloom varieties of fruit and vegetables, on sale to visitors. Aug 21 Sketching & Drawing in the garden, materials provided.

&. ≈ ⊛ ☕

Secret walled suburban garden packed with a myriad of plants . . .

8 ◆ **CASCADES GARDENS**
Clatterway, Bonsall DE4 2AH. Alan & Elizabeth Clements, 01629 822813, www.cascadesgardens.com. *5m SW of Matlock. From Cromford A6 T-lights turn towards Wirksworth. Turn R along Via Gellia, signed Buxton & Bonsall. After 1m turn R up hill towards Bonsall village. Cascades on R at top of hill.* Tea & coffee NGS days only. **Adm £3, chd free. Weds & Suns & B Hols 1 April to 30 Sept (10-5). For NGS: Weds 16 Apr; 21 May; 18 June; Sun 13 July; Wed 6 Aug (10-5).** Fascinating 4-acre garden in spectacular natural surroundings with woodland, high cliffs, stream, ponds, a ruined corn mill and old lead mine. Secluded areas provide peaceful views of the extensive collection of plants, shrubs and trees. The nursery has a wide range of unusual herbaceous perennial plants. Featured in 'The Derbyshire Magazine' June 2007. Gravel paths.

&. ⊛ 🛏 ☕

9 **CASHEL**
Kirk Ireton DE6 3JX. Anita & Jeremy Butt, 01335 370495. *2m S of Wirksworth. Turn off B5023 (Duffield-Wirksworth rd). Follow rd to Kirk Ireton, take sharp R turn at church corner. Follow lane for 200yds. Garden on RH-side. Parking on LH-side 80yds beyond house.* **Adm £3, chd free. Sun 15 June (2-5). Visitors also welcome by appt.** 3-acre garden situated on sloping site, featuring terraced ravine and several wood sculptures by local artists. Open views of surrounding countryside. Many interesting trees, shrubs and plants. New stone circle.

⊛ ☕ ☎ ☎

10 **10 CHESTNUT WAY**
Repton DE65 6FQ. Robert & Pauline Little, 01283 702267, rlittle@hotpop.com, www.littlegarden.org.uk. *6m S of Derby. From A38, S of Derby, follow signs to Willington, then Repton. In Repton turn R at roundabout. Chestnut Way is 1/4 m up hill, on L.* Home-made teas. **Adm £2.50, chd free. Sun 20 Apr; Sun 25, BH Mon 26 May (1-5). Visitors also welcome by appt for groups of 10+.** Meander through an acre of natural borders, spring bulbs, mature trees, and intimate woodland to a stunning butterfly bed and wild flower meadow. Behind the natural look, a pair of passionate, practical, organic gardeners gently manage the vast range of plants, incl hundreds of shrubs, herbaceous perennials and clematis. Enjoy.

&. ⊛ ☕ ☎

11 **NEW** **13 CHILTERN DRIVE**
West Hallam, Ilkeston DE7 6PA. Jacqueline & Keith Holness. *Approx 6m NE of Derby. 2m W of Ilkeston on A609. Take St Wilfred's Rd to West Hallam, 1st R Derbyshire Avenue, 3rd L is Chiltern Drive.* Home-made teas. **Adm £2.50, chd free. Sun 22 June (11-5).** Secret walled suburban garden packed with a myriad of plants, some rare and unusual. Summerhouse, two small ponds and fernery, together with seventy five acers and some well-hidden lizards! Garden on two levels separated by steps.

≈ ☕

54 & 59 CHURCH LANE
See Nottinghamshire.

12 CLOUD COTTAGE
**Simmondley SK13 6JN. Mr R G
Lomas, 01457 862033.** *1m SW of
Glossop. On High Lane between
Simmondley & Charlesworth. From
M67 take A57, turn R at Mottram (1st
T-lights) through Broadbottom &
Charlesworth. In Charlesworth up
Town Lane by the side of Grey Mare.
Cloud Cottage is ¹/₂ m on R. From
Glossop, A57 towards Manchester,
turn L at 2nd of two mini roundabouts
up Simmondley Lane, Cloud Cottage
is on L after passing Hare & Hounds.*
**Adm £3, chd free. Suns 11, 18, 25
May (2-5). Visitors also welcome by
appt during May.**
1¹/₄ -acre arboretum/rhododendron
garden. Altitude 750ft on side of hill in
Peak District National Park. Collections
of conifers, most over 40yrs old.
Species and hybrid rhododendron;
wide variety of shrubs; Japanese-
inspired garden with 3 ponds.
♿ ☎

13 CLOVERMEAD
**Commonpiece Lane, Findern, Derby
DE65 6AF. David & Rosemary
Noblet, 01283 702237.** *4m S of
Derby. From Findern village green, turn
R at church into Lower Green, R turn
into Commonpiece Lane, approx
500yds on R.* **Home-made teas. Adm
£2.50, chd free. Suns 6, 27 July; 10
Aug (2-5). Visitors also welcome by
appt.**
Cottage garden set in approx ³/₄ acre.
Garden rooms full of perennial flowers.
Honeysuckle, roses, jasmine and
sweet peas scent the air. Pergolas and
archways with clematis, fishponds and
bandstand with seating. Greenhouses,
vegetable plot and wildlife orchard.
✂ ⊛ ☕ ☎

7 COLLYGATE
See Nottinghamshire.

14 THE COTTAGE
**25 Plant Lane, Old Sawley, Long
Eaton NG10 3BJ. Ernie & Averil
Carver, 0115 9728659.** *2m SW of
Long Eaton. From Long Eaton green
take sign for town centre. Onto B6540
through to Old Sawley, take R at Nags
Head PH into Wiln Rd. 400yds take R
turn into Plant Lane at the Railway Inn.
Garden 200yds on R.* **Light
refreshments & home-made teas. Adm
£2, chd free (share to Canaan Trust
for the Homeless). Sat 26, Sun 27
July (2-5.30). Visitors also welcome**

by appt in July for groups 10+.
Cottage garden full of colour, steeped
in herbaceous borders. Annual plants
raised from the greenhouse. Number
of surprising features. Summerhouse in
a walled sheltered garden, providing a
charming environment. Finalist in Daily
Mail national garden competition 2007.
♿ ⊛ ☕ ☎

**15 NEW CUCKOOSTONE
COTTAGE**
**Chesterfield Road, Matlock
Moor, Matlock DE4 5LZ. Barrie &
Pauline Wild, 01629 582992,
pauline.wild@tesco.net.** *2¹/₂ m N
of Matlock on A632. Past Matlock
Golf Course look for Cuckoostone
Lane on L. Turn here & follow for ¹/₄
m. 1st cottage on bend.* **Adm £3,
chd free. Visitors welcome by
appt.**
Plantsman's ¹/₂ acre SW sloping
rural hillside garden at 850'
developed over last 5yrs. Large
collection of trees, shrubs and
perennials, many unusual. Colour-
themed borders, pond, bog garden
and conservatory make this a yr-
round garden but, perhaps, best in
spring and late summer.
✂ ☎

16 NEW 8 CURZON LANE
**Alvaston, nr Derby DE24 8QS.
Mrs Marian Gray, 01332 601596,
maz@cvnation.com.** *2m SE of
Derby city centre. From city centre
take A6 (London Rd) towards
Alvaston. Curzon Lane is on
LHside, approx ¹/₂ m before
Alvaston shops.* **Adm £2.50, chd
free. Suns 6, 13 July (1-6).
Visitors also welcome by appt
July only, no coaches.**
Mature garden with lawns, borders
packed full with perennials, shrubs
and small trees, tropical planting.
Ornamental and wildlife ponds, two
greenhouses, gravel area, large
patio with container planting.
✂ ⊛ ☕ ☎

17 ◆ DAM FARM HOUSE
**Yeldersley Lane, Ednaston
DE6 3BA. Mrs J M Player, 01335
360291.** *5m SE of Ashbourne. On
A52, opp Ednaston village turn, gate
on R 500yds.* **Adm £4, chd free. 1st
April to 31st October Mons, Tues &
Fris, or by appointment. Not open
Bank Holidays.**
3 acres incl a stunning young

arboretum, beautifully situated.
Contains mixed borders, scree.
Unusual plants have been collected.
From spring to autumn it is full of
colour with interesting rare trees and
plants, many of which are propagated
for sale in the nursery.
♿ ✂ ⊛

Cottage garden full of colour, steeped in herbaceous borders . . .

18 NEW DAM STEAD
**3 Crowhole, Barlow, Dronfield
S18 7TJ. Derek & Barbara
Saveall, 0114 2890802.** *3¹/₂ m
NW of Chesterfield. From A61
Sheffield/Derby take B6051 Barlow
at Chesterfield North. Through
Barlow, pass Tickled Trout PH on
L. Next R (unnamed rd). Last
house on R.* **Light refreshments.
Adm £2.50, chd free (share to
Weston Park Hospital Cancer
Appeal). Visitors welcome by
appt Apr to Oct, for groups 6+.**
³/₄ acre with stream, weir and dam
with an island. Long woodland
path, orchard, alpine
troughs/rockeries and mixed
planting. A natural wildlife garden
with large summerhouse with
seating inside and out.
✂ ☕ ☎

19 62A DENBY LANE
**Loscoe DE75 7RX. Mrs J
Charlesworth.** *12m NW of
Nottingham. Between Codnor &
Heanor, on A6007. Follow Denby sign.*
**Light refreshments & teas. Adm £2,
chd free. Sun 3 Aug (2-5).**
All-year round garden with hostas,
ferns, grasses, perennials, dahlias,
shrubs, conifers and vegetable plot.
Small pond with waterfall and stream.
Japanese features, pergola with
seating area and summer house. W.C.
✂ ⊛ ☕

20 NEW DOLLY BARN

Ash Lane, nr Etwall DE65 6HT. Glynis & Michael Smith, 01283 734002, dollybarn@ic24.net. *6m W of Derby. From A516 Etwall bypass turn into Ash Lane signed Sutton-on-the-Hill. After 1m take R turn at postbox. Dolly Barn 200yds on R. Light refreshments & teas.* **Adm £3, chd free. Suns 15 June; 27 July (1-5). Visitors also welcome by appt.**
Eclectic mix of contemporary, cottage and prairie styles in 2½ acre rural setting created from a cattle field. Walled garden (formerly cow yard) with 17m rill, 2 stainless steel water features and different planting styles from tropical to formal box hedging, with walkways. Large pond well stocked with fish and plants. Prairie and grass gardens. Large vegetable garden and greenhouse. Gravel drive, unfenced pond.

Eclectic mix of contemporary, cottage and prairie styles . . .

21 DOVE COTTAGE

Clifton, Ashbourne DE6 2JQ. Stephen & Anne Liverman, 01335 343545, astrantiamajor@hotmail.co.uk. *1½ m SW of Ashbourne. Enter Clifton village. Turn R at Xrds by church. Travel 100yds turn L, Dove Cottage 1st house on L. Always well signed on open days.* **Adm £3, chd free (share to Ashbourne British Heart Foundation). Suns 4, 25 May; 29 June; 27 July (1-5). Visitors also welcome by appt.**
¾ -acre garden by R Dove, extensively replanted winter 2003 - 2004.

Emphasis on establishing collections of hardy plants and shrubs incl alchemillas, alliums, berberis, geraniums, euphorbias, hostas, lilies, variegated and silver foliage plants inc astrantias. Plantsman's garden. Area growing new heucheras and other purple flowering plants and foliage. Woodland area planted with daffodils and shade loving plants. Featured on BBC East Midlands Today & in 'Derbyshire Magazine', 2007.

22 NEW THE DOWER HOUSE

Church Square, Melbourne DE73 8JH. Griselda Kerr, 01332 864756/07799883777, gmk@doho.fsnet.co.uk. *6m S of Derby. 5m W of exit 21A M1. Church Sq is at bottom of Church St in centre of Melbourne. Enter the square & turn R before church immed after war memorial. The Dower House is at west end of Norman church. Car parking limited. Park in & around the town & Church Square. Home-made teas.* **Adm £3, chd free. Sat 14, Sun 15 June (10-5). Visitors also welcome by appt Mar, Apr, Sept, groups 10+.**
Beautiful view of Melbourne Pool from balustraded terrace running length of 1821 house. Garden drops steeply by way of paths, steps and shrubbery to lawn with 70' herbaceous border. Rose tunnel, peaceful glade, young orchard, small area of woodland, hellebore bed, herb garden, small cottage garden with vegetables - all being developed since 2004. Next door to one of finest Norman churches in England. Wheelchair access limited to terrace level only.

EDITH TERRACE GARDENS
See Cheshire & Wirral.

23 ◆ EYAM HALL

Eyam S32 5QW. Mr & Mrs R H V Wright, 01433 631976, www.eyamhall.com. *6m N of Bakewell. Follow A623 through Stoney Middleton, turn R to Eyam, follow signs to Eyam Hall.* **House and garden adm £6.25, chd £4, concessions £5.75, garden only adm £2, chd £1. Easter week, Bank Hol Sun & Mon; Wed, Thur, Sun, 29 Jun - 31 Aug (12-4).**

For NGS: Suns 4 May; 1 June (12-5). C17 seat of the Wright family, the traditional walled garden has four distinct areas; the knot garden, the potager, the bowling green and the pleasure lawn with glorious rose walk and herbaceous border. A formal gravelled walk is edged with lavender and espaliered fruit trees and planted with exotic specimens. The restoration is ongoing and the garden continues to develop. Separate entrance for wheelchair users.

EYNORD
See Nottinghamshire.

24 FANSHAWE GATE HALL

Holmesfield S18 7WA. Mr & Mrs John Ramsden, 0114 2890391, www.fanshawegate.com. *2m W of Dronfield. Situated on the edge of the Peak National Park. Follow B6054 towards Owler Bar. 1st R turn after church signed Fanshawe Gate Lane. Light refreshments.* **Adm £2.50, chd free (share to Oesophageal Patients Assoc). Suns 22, 29 June; 6, 13 July (11-5). Visitors also welcome by appt June & July only, groups of 10+, small coaches.**
C13 seat of the Fanshawe family. Old-fashioned cottage-style garden. Many stone features, fine C16 dovecote. Upper walled garden with herbaceous, variegated and fern plantings, water features, topiary, terracing and lawns. Lower courtyard with knot garden and herb border. Restored terraced orchard representing a medieval tilt yard. Newly planted pleached hornbeam hedge. Featured in 'Reflections' and GGG 2008.

FELLEY PRIORY
See Nottinghamshire.

25 FIR CROFT

Froggatt Road, Calver S32 3ZD. Dr S B Furness, www.alpineplantcentre.co.uk. *4m N of Bakewell. At junction of B6001 with A625 (formerly B6054), adjacent to Power Garage.* **Adm by donation. Suns 18 May; 1, 15 June (2-5).**
Massive scree with many rarities. Plantsman's garden; rockeries; water garden and nursery; extensive collection (over 3000 varieties) of alpines; conifers; over 800 sempervivums, 500 saxifrages and 350 primulas. Tufa and scree beds.

Designed to encourage wildlife; planted in a wild, natural look . . .

26 GAMESLEY FOLD COTTAGE
Glossop SK13 6JJ. Mrs G Carr,
01457 867856,
www.gamesleyfold.co.uk. *2m W of
Glossop. Off A626 Glossop to Marple
rd, nr Charlesworth. Turn down lane
directly opp St Margaret's School.
White cottage at bottom.* Home-made
teas. **Adm £2, chd free.** Suns 4, 25
May; 8 June (1-4). **Visitors also
welcome by appt for groups during
May & June only. Coaches
permitted.**
Old-fashioned cottage garden. Spring
garden with herbaceous borders,
shrubs and rhododendrons, wild
flowers and herbs in profusion to
attract butterflies and wildlife. Good
selection of herbs and cottage garden
plants for sale. Many breeds of poultry
and fan-tailed doves.

GARDENERS COTTAGE
See Nottinghamshire.

**27 THE GARDENS AT
DOBHOLME FISHERY**
Main Road, Troway, nr Coal Aston
S21 5RR. Paul & Pauline Calvert,
01246 451337,
calvertpj@yahoo.co.uk. *3m NE of
Dronfield. Halfway along B6056,
Dronfield to Eckington rd, 2¹/₂ m from
each. Coming from Dronfield turn L at
Blackamoor Head Inn for Troway.
Follow signs in village.* **Adm £3.**
**Visitors welcome by appt for groups
of 15+.**
Situated in beautiful conservation area
of Moss Valley. Developed on sloping
site of approx 3 acres around fishing
ponds. Designed to encourage wildlife;
planted in a wild, natural look. Heavy
clay with many springs; stone quarried
from the site is widely used to pave the
pond sides. Sloping uneven terrain.
Potager vegetable garden and herb
garden.

GORENE
See Nottinghamshire.

GRAFTON COTTAGE
See Staffordshire & part of West
Midlands.

28 ♦ HARDWICK HALL
Doe Lea, Chesterfield S44 5QJ. The
National Trust, 01246 858400,
www.nationaltrust.org.uk. *8m SE of
Chesterfield. S of A617. Signed from
J29 M1.* **House and garden adm
£9.50, chd £4.75, garden only adm
£4.75, chd £2.30. 1 Mar to 2 Nov
Weds, Thurs, Sats, Suns (12-4.30).
Conservation tours, Wed to Sun
(11-12).** For NGS: **Evening
opening** £15, Tue 15 July (6-8). Sat
19 July (11-5.30).
Grass walks between yew and
hornbeam hedges; cedar trees; herb
garden; herbaceous and rose borders.
Finest example of Elizabethan house in
the country. £15 adm includes meet
the Head Gardener for a private tour of
Hardwick Gardens 15 Jul 6-8pm. Pre-
bookable on 01248 858400. Why not
enjoy a seasonal home-made meal
before the tour (pre-bookable) 5-6pm
£15pp.

29 HIGH ROOST
27 Storthmeadow Road,
Simmondley, Glossop SK13 6UZ.
Peter & Christina Harris, 01457
863888,
peter@pharris54.fsnet.co.uk. *³/₄ m
SW of Glossop. From M67 take A57,
turn R at Mottram (1st T-lights),
through Broadbottom and
Charlesworth. In Charlesworth turn R
up Town Lane by side of Grey Mare
PH, continue up High Lane, past Hare
& Hounds PH, Storthmeadow Rd is
2nd turn on L. From Glossop, A57
towards Manchester, L at 2nd mini
roundabout, up Simmondley Lane,
turn R into Storthmeadow Rd, nr top,
no 27 last house on L. On road parking
nearby, please take care not to block
drives.* Light refreshments & teas. **Adm
£2, chd free.** Sun 22 June (1-5).
**Visitors also welcome by appt,
visitors and groups welcome June -
Aug.**
Youngish suburban garden with
interesting layout on terraced slopes
with views over fields and hills.
Winding paths, archways and steps
explore different garden 'rooms'
packed with plants for yr-round interest
and colour, much of the planting

designed to attract wildlife.
Herbaceous borders give a blaze of
colour in summer. Tiered alpine bed,
vegetable garden, several small water
features. Statuary, pots, troughs and
planters. New for 2008 - arched
entrance to a secret corner. Craft stalls.
Winner 'Glossop in Bloom' (large
gardens) 2007.

30 37 HIGH STREET
Repton DE65 6GD. David & Jan
Roberts. *6m S of Derby. From A38,
A50 junction S of Derby follow signs to
Willington, then Repton. In Repton
continue past island and shops.
Garden is on LH-side.* Home-made
teas. **Adm £2.50, chd free.** Suns 20
Apr; 8 June (2-5.30).
1-acre garden for all seasons divided
by Repton Brook with formal and
wildlife ponds. Mixed borders of shrubs
and herbaceous perennials,
rhododendrons and woodland.
Grasses, bamboos and roses.
Container planting for spring and
summer colour and alpine troughs -
something for everyone. New water
feature for 2008. Wheelchair access to
top part of garden only.

31 HIGHFIELD HOUSE
Wingfield Road, Oakerthorpe,
Alfreton DE55 7AP. Paul & Ruth Peat
& Janet Costall, 01773 521342,
peatruth@aol.com. *Approx 1m from
Alfreton town centre on A615 Alfreton-
Matlock Rd. From Matlock: A615 to
Alfreton. Turn R into Alfreton Golf Club.
From Derby: A38 to Alfreton. A615 to
Matlock. After houses on L-hand side
of Wingfield Rd, turn L into Alfreton
Golf Club.* Home-made & cream teas.
Adm £2.50, chd free. Sun 18 May
(1-5). **Visitors also welcome by appt
last 2 weeks in May and all of June
only. Garden not accessible by
coach.**
Delightful family garden of ³/₄ of an
acre, laid out by current owners from
an abandoned vegetable garden and
field. Individual areas include a shady
garden, small area of woodland, tree
house, laburnum arch, orchard, lawns
and herbaceous borders. Pleasant
level walk to Derbyshire Wildlife Trust
Nature reserve, where there is a
pond and boardwalk and beautiful
spotted orchids. Delicious home-made
cakes. Garden on different levels;
steps, board walk and some gravel
areas.

32 11 HIGHGROVE DRIVE
Chellaston, Derby DE73 5XA. Ms
Sarah Bacon. *2m SE of city centre.
Leave Derby ring rd at Allenton (steel
footbridge) on rd to Melbourne via
Chellaston. 1m on R (A514). Leave
A50 at J3, head to Derby via
Chellaston. 1¹/₂ m on L (A514). Rd is
on hill top into 'new estate' on SE side
Derby. Limited street parking in cul-de-
sac. Disabled parking on drive.* Light
refreshments & teas. **Adm £2, chd
free. Sat 19 (2-6), Sun 20 July (11-5).**
Small suburban garden. Lawn, paved
areas, pond with waterfall, water
feature, Japanese corner,
Mediterranean yard, small patio with
topiary. Grape, kiwi, greenhouse and
garden shed in enclosed area. Pots,
hanging baskets, automatic watering,
lights and pond fountain. A big garden
in a small space.

 ♿ ✄ ☕

33 HILLSIDE
286 Handley Road, New
Whittington, Chesterfield S43 2ET.
E J Lee, 01246 454960. *3m N of
Chesterfield. From A6135, take B6052
through Eckington & Marsh Lane 3m.
Turn L at Xrds signed Whittington, then
1m. From Coal Aston (Sheffield), take
B6056 towards Chesterfield to give
way sign, then 1m. From Chesterfield,
take B6052.* Teas. **Adm £2, chd free.
Sun 22 June (2-5). Visitors also
welcome by appt all yr.**
¹/₃ -acre sloping site. Herbaceous
borders, rock garden, alpines, streams,
pools, bog gardens, asiatic primula
bed, and alpine house. Acers,
bamboos, collection of approx 150
varieties of ferns, eucalypts,
euphorbias, grasses, conifers,
Himalayan bed. 1500 plants
permanently labelled. Yr-round interest.
Featured in 'Reflections' May, 2007.

 ❀ ☕ ☎

34 HORSLEYGATE HALL
Horsleygate Lane, Holmesfield S18
7WD. Robert & Margaret Ford, 0114
289 0333. *6m NW of Chesterfield.
Follow B6051 from Owler Bar (A621)
towards Chesterfield; after 1m take 1st
L onto Horsleygate Lane. Drive in and
park near hall.* **Visitors welcome by
appt for groups April, May and early
June, individuals & small parties
welcome all year.**
2-acre plantsman's garden. Sloping
site incl woodland garden; hot sun
terrace; rockeries; pools; fern area;
jungle garden; mixed borders and
ornamental kitchen garden. An overall

theme of informality with walls,
terraces, paths and quirky statuary,
gazebo and breeze house thatched in
heather. Featured in GGG 2007.

 ❀ ☎

35 ◆ LEA GARDENS
Lea, Nr Matlock DE4 5GH. Mr & Mrs
J Tye, 01629 534380,
www.leagarden.co.uk. *5m SE of
Matlock. Lea. Off A6. Also off A615.*
**Adm £4, chd 50p, season ticket £7.
Daily 20 Mar to 30 June (10-5.30).**
Rare collection of rhododendrons,
azaleas, kalmias, alpines and conifers
in delightful woodland setting. Gardens
are sited on remains of medieval quarry
and cover about 4 acres. Specialised
plant nursery of rhododendrons and
azaleas on site. Teashop offering light
lunches and home-made cakes open
daily. Music Day Sun 15 June (12-5).

 ♿ ❀ ☕

**36 LITTLEOVER LANE
ALLOTMENTS**
19 Littleover Lane, Derby DE23 6JH.
Littleover Lane Allotments Assoc,
01332 770096,
davidkenyon@tinyworld.co.uk. *3m
SW of Derby. Off Derby ring rd A5111
into Stenson Rd. R into Littleover Lane.
Garden on L. On street parking opp
Foremark Ave.* Light refreshments &
teas. **Adm £3, chd free. Suns 1 June;
7 Sept (11-5). Visitors also welcome
by appt, evenings & weekends
March to Sept.**
Allotment site with plots cultivated in a
variety of styles. A Schools' Centre incl
greenhouses and walled garden and
museum collection of heritage
gardening equipment. A range of
heritage and unusual vegetable
varieties grown. Wildlife area now
open. Runners up in 2007 'Best Site' -
Allotments in Bloom. Paths stoned,
some slopes.

 ♿ ❀ ☕ ☎

37 LOCKO PARK
Spondon DE21 7BW. Mrs Lucy
Palmer. *6m NE of Derby. From A52
Borrowash bypass, 2m N via B6001,
turn to Spondon.* Home-made teas.
Adm £2, chd free. Sun 11 May (2-5).
Large garden; pleasure gardens; rose
gardens. House (not open) by Smith of
Warwick with Victorian additions.
Chapel (open) Charles II, with original
ceiling.

 ☕

LONG CLOSE
See Leicestershire & Rutland.

38 9 MAIN STREET
Horsley Woodhouse DE7 6AU.
Ms Alison Napier, 01332 881629,
ibhillib@btinternet.com. *3m SW of
Heanor. 6m N of Derby. Turn off A608
Derby to Heanor rd at Smalley,
towards Belper, (A609). Garden on
A609, 1m from Smalley turning.* Cream
teas. **Adm £2.50, chd free. Sun 3
Aug (2-5). Visitors also welcome by
appt.**
¹/₃ -acre hilltop garden overlooking
lovely farmland view. Terracing,
borders, lawns and pergola create
space for an informal layout with
planting for colour effect. Features incl
large wildlife pond with water lilies, bog
garden and small formal pool.
Emphasis on carefully selected
herbaceous perennials mixed with
shrubs and old-fashioned roses.
Wheelchair-adapted WC.

 ♿ ❀ ☕ ☎

> Emphasis on
> carefully selected
> herbaceous
> perennials mixed
> with shrubs and
> old-fashioned
> roses . . .

39 2 MANVERS STREET
Ripley DE5 3EQ. Mrs D Wood & Mr
D Hawkins, 01773 743962. *Ripley
Town centre to Derby rd turn L opp
Leisure Centre onto Heath Rd. 1st turn
R onto Meadow Rd, 1st L onto
Manvers St.* Light refreshments. **Adm
£2, chd free. Sun 13 July (2-6).
Visitors also welcome by appt, July
only.**
S-facing secluded colourful garden
with patio, lawn, mixed borders, incl
perennials, annuals and shrubs. Fish
pond, water features; pergola
supporting Virginia creeper and
clematis. Arbour with seating and
several summer hanging baskets and
planters. First Prize and Best Garden
overall Cup Winner 2007 Ripley Town
Council.

 ✄ ❀ ☕ ☎

40 MARKHAM VILLA
60 Alfreton Road, Newton
DE55 5TQ. Ann & Kevin Briggs,
01773 778982,
markhamvilla1@hotmail.com. *2m NE
of Alfreton. A38 N from Derby. Take
Alfreton/Matlock junction along A61.
Turn R following Blackwell signs. 1½ m
to Newton.* Home-made teas. **Adm
£3, chd free. Suns 20 July; 3 Aug**
(11-5). **Visitors also welcome by
appt for groups of 15+ July & Aug.**
Continually developing ⅔ acre plot with
a series of gardens, walkways and
seating to create areas for different
purposes and moods. Extensively
planted for all yr-round interest of
flower, foliage, colour and texture.
Fragrant parterre with chamomile lawn,
summerhouse, orchard, pond, wild
flower mound, greenhouses and well-
maintained productive vegetable plot.
A delightful surprise around every
corner.

41 ◆ MEYNELL LANGLEY
TRIALS GARDEN
Lodge Lane (off Flagshaw Lane),
Derby DE6 4NT. Robert & Karen
Walker, 01332 824358,
www.meynell-langley-
gardens.co.uk. *4m W of Derby, nr
Kedleston Hall. Head W out of Derby
on A52. At Kirk Langley turn R onto
Flagshaw Lane (signed to Kedleston
Hall) then R onto Lodge Lane. Follow
Meynell Langley Gdns sign for 1½ m.
From A38 follow signs for Kedleston
Hall (past first entrance).* Refreshments
on NGS days only. **Adm £2.50, chd
free. Open daily 13 April to 12 Oct.
For NGS: Suns 13 Apr; 11 May; 8
June; 6 July; 17 Aug; 14 Sept; 12
Oct** (10-5).
Formal ¾ -acre Victorian-style garden
established 15 yrs, displaying and
trialling new and existing varieties of
bedding plants, herbaceous perennials
and vegetable plants grown at the
adjacent nursery. Over 180 hanging
baskets and floral displays. 74 varieties
of apple, pear and other fruit. Summer
fruit tree pruning demonstrations 17
Aug. Featured in 'Derbyshire Life
Magazine', the 'Derbyshire Magazine'
and filmed for BBC East Midlands
Today, 2007.

42 23 MILL LANE
Condnor DE5 9QF. Mrs S Jackson.
*12m NW of Nottingham. 10m N of
Derby. Mill Lane situated opp Codnor
Market Place (Clock Tower) on A610. 2*

car parks nearby. Cream teas. **Adm
£1.50, chd free. Sun 10 Aug** (1-6).
Lawn, herbaceous borders, pond,
waterfall; clematis and Mediterranean
garden.

43 MONKSWAY
Summer Cross, Tideswell, nr Buxton
SK17 8HU. Mr & Mrs R Porter,
01298 871687,
www.monkswaygarden.co.uk. *9m
NE of Buxton. On the B6049. Turn up
Parke Rd, opp Nat West Bank, off
Queen St. Take L turn at top & then 1st
R onto Summer Cross. Monksway is
4th semi-detached house on L.
Limited parking.* **Adm £2, chd free.
Suns 25 May; 1, 8 June** (11-4).
**Visitors also welcome by appt for
groups of 10+.**
Gently sloping garden 1000ft above
sea level. Gravel/paved paths and
archways meander through well-
stocked beds and borders of
perennials, shrubs and climbers.
Garden planted for all-yr interest. An
aviary and water features complete the
scene.

**THE OLD RECTORY, CLIFTON
CAMPVILLE**
See Staffordshire & part of West
Midlands.

ONE HOUSE NURSERY
See Cheshire & Wirral.

44 OTTERBROOK
Alders Lane, Chinley, High Peak
SK23 6DP. Mary & Dennis Sharp,
01663 750335,
dennis.mary@ukgateway.net. *3m W
of Whaley Bridge. Otterbrook is
reached by 300yd walk up Alders Lane
on outskirts of village off Buxton Rd
(B6062) between Chinley & Chapel-en-
le-Frith. Parking is very limited at
house.* Light refreshments. **Adm
£2.50, chd free. Visitors welcome by
appt during June.**
Wander in this 1-acre garden between
colour-themed beds and borders,
along paths to focal points and views
of the surrounding hills. Trees, shrubs
and plants, many moisture-loving,
provide contrasting form and texture
and complement the ponds and bog
garden. Pergolas and structures
give cohesion. A small potager is
included.

THE PADDOCKS
See Nottinghamshire.

Varieties of apple, pear and other fruit . . .

45 PARK HALL
Walton Back Lane, Walton,
Chesterfield S42 7LT. Kim &
Margaret Staniforth, 01246 567412,
kim.staniforth@virgin.net. *2m SW of
Chesterfield. From Chesterfield take
A632 for Matlock. After start of 40mph
section take 1st R into Acorn Ridge
and then L into Walton Back Lane.
300yds on R, at end of high stone wall.
Park on field side of Walton Back Lane
only.* Home-made teas. **Adm £3, chd
50p (share to Bluebell Wood
Children's Hospice). Suns 1, 29 June**
(2-5.30). **Visitors also welcome by
appt for groups of 10+.**
2-acre plantsman's garden in a
beautiful setting surrounding C17
house, not open. Four main 'rooms' -
terraced garden, park area with forest
trees, croquet lawn and new
millennium garden now fully mature.
Within these are a woodland walk,
fernery, yew hedges and topiary, water
features, pergolas, arbours,
camellias, azaleas, hydrangeas, 150
roses, a circular pleached hedge, and
a small auricula theatre. Children's
Garden Trail & Prize.

46 NEW PARLOUR BARN
Brook Farm, Main Street, Milton
DE65 6EF. John & Lynne Clay.
*10m S of Derby. 10m NE of
Burton-on-Trent. From A38/A50
Toyota island, take B5008 to
Willington & Repton. Turn L into
Brook End at small roundabout in
Repton, signed to Milton. Follow up
into Milton where it takes sharp RH
turn. Parlour Barn is approx
200yds on L - park on Main St.*
**Adm £2, chd free. Suns 18 May;
13 July** (1-5).
A long mixed border with colourful
herbaceous perennials and shrubs
separates the garden from the
fields beyond. Two main lawns,
one with a pond to attract wildlife
and a small orchard area. Paths
lead round the garden and under
the clematis covered pergola with
fountain beneath. A still developing
modern garden planted by
enthusiasts.

47 19 PORTLAND STREET
Etwall DE65 6JF. Paul & Fran Harvey, 01283 734360. *6m W of Derby. In centre of Etwall Village, at Spread Eagle PH turn into Willington Rd then immed R into Portland St (behind PH car park).* Home-made teas. **Adm £2.50, chd free. Sat 2, Sun 3 Aug (11-5). Visitors also welcome by appt.**
Our tranquil garden is packed with plants for yr-round interest. This 1/3 acre has been developed since 1992 with significant changes every year. Many rare and unusual shrubs and perennials, fabulous colour and tremendous scent; pond, small stream; oriental garden; pergola; exhibition dahlias; collections incl picea, agapanthus and crocosmia, but no lawn. New planting in front garden in 2007.

🔲 🗡 ☕ ☎

48 ◆ POSTERN HOUSE
Turnditch DE56 2LX. Liz & Nick Ruby, 01773 550732, www.postern.co.uk. *3m W of Belper. Off A517 Belper to Ashbourne rd, entering Turnditch from Belper direction 50yds past bridge over river; turn L into unmarked lane (just before 30mph sign). 3rd house on R.* **Adm £2.50, chd free. Weds 18 Jun (6.30-9), Sun 29 Jun (2-5.30). For NGS: Suns 8 June: 13 July (2-5.30).**
1/3 -acre partially walled plant lover's garden in beautiful countryside. Small water features and pleasant seating areas encourage relaxation while enjoying large herbaceous borders and colourful shrubs. Climbers ramble over walls, trees and a large gazebo. Large hosta and hardy geranium collections, seasonal pots and baskets, additional fruit and vegetable areas make this a garden for everyone. Featured in 'Derbyshire Life & Countryside', 2007. Uneven paths, wheelchair access on lawns.

🔲 🟢 ☕

49 QUARRYSIDE
1 King Charles Court, Glossop SK13 8NJ. Sue & Ron Astles, 01457 857015. *1m S of Glossop town centre. From Glossop centre take A624 towards Hayfield & Chapel-en-le-Frith. About 3/4 m along turn L into Whitfield Ave. At top turn R into Hague St & 1st L into King Charles Court. Please park on Whitfield Ave, limited parking in close.* Home-made teas. **Adm £2, chd free (share to Stockport Canal Boat Trust). Sat 24, Sun 25 May. Visitors**

also welcome by appt June & July, groups 16 & under.
Small peaceful garden in quarry setting with exposed rock strata and interesting nooks and crannies on two terraces, with an emphasis on texture and colour. All yr-round natural planting with two water features to attract wildlife. Display of garden ceramics and sculptures by Gordon Cooke of Sale, many of which can be purchased. Featured in 'Amateur Gardening Magazine', July 2007; Winner 'Glossop in Bloom' (small garden) Sept 2007 and featured on BBC TV 'Open Gardens', Sept 2007.

🗡 🟢 ☕ ☎

Small peaceful garden in quarry setting with exposed rock strata . . .

50 ◆ RENISHAW HALL
Renishaw, nr Sheffield S21 3WB. Sir Reresby & Lady Sitwell, 01246 432310, www.renishaw-hall.co.uk. *4m W of Sheffield. From J30 M1 take A6135 towards Sheffield. Renishaw Hall is 3m from motorway.* **Adm £3, chd free. Thurs to Suns, BH Mons 20 Mar to 28 Sept (10.30-4.30). For NGS: Tues 22 Apr; 5 Aug (10.30-3.30).**
Home of Sir Reresby and Lady Sitwell. Romantic, formal 2 Italianate gardens divided into rooms by yew hedges. Bluebell woods, magnolias and rhododendrons in spring woodland gardens. Over a thousand roses in June with peonies and clematis. Deep herbaceous borders with collections of unusual plants. National Collection of Yuccas. Separate childrens garden with willow tunnel, maze and trails. Pastoral music to be played in garden (weather permitting). 10 min talk on the Sitwell Family (talk on the patio) (11.30 & 2.30). Featured in 'Sheffield Telegraph', 2007. Gravel & bark pathways.

🔲 🟢 NCCPG ☕

51 NEW ROSEBANK
303 Duffield Road, Allestree, Derby DE22 2DF. Patrick & Carol Smith. *2m N of Derby. Follow A6 from Derby towards Matlock. On crossing A38 island continue for 150 metres turning L into Gisborne Crescent then R into service rd.* Home-made teas. **Adm £2, chd free. Sats 19 July; 16 Aug (2-6).**
Interesting garden of variety on a gentle, upward sloping site. Access by steps and paths. Includes colourful borders with imaginative planting and a water feature in a natural setting. Small orchard and soft fruit garden, lawns, rockery, shrubs and trees. Wildlife friendly. Children welcomed.

☕

52 SHATTON HALL FARM
Bamford S33 0BG. Mr & Mrs J Kellie, 01433 620635, jk@shatton.co.uk, www.peakfarmholidays.co.uk. *3m W of Hathersage. Take A6187 from Hathersage, turn L to Shatton, after 2m (opp High Peak Garden Centre). After 1/2 m turn R through ford, drive 1/2 m & house is on L over cattle grids.* Home-made teas. **Adm £3, chd free. Suns 8 June; 27 July (1.30-5). Visitors also welcome by appt.**
Original walled garden of C16. Farmhouse now spills out to water gardens and sheltered slopes, planted informally and merging into the picturesque landscape. Among the great variety of unusual plants and shrubs, sculpture and willow features add interest to this maturing and still expanding garden. An increasing variety of live willow structures have been planted. Labelled walks in woodland and streamside. Featured in 'Reflection' Aug 2007.

🟢 🛏 ☕ ☎

53 NEW SOUTHFIELD
Bullbridge Hill, Fritchley, Belper DE56 2FL. Pete & Lot Clark. *4m N of Belper. Turn off A610 between Ripley & Ambergate under railway bridge & signed Bullbridge, Frichley, Crich. Proceed up hill towards Crich. In 1/2 m garden is on junction of Allen Lane (signed Fritchley) and Bullbridge Hill. Turn R into Allen Lane & park in village.* Home-made teas. **Adm £2.50, chd free. Suns 11 May; 20 July (1-5).**
1 1/2 acre all-yr round garden

surrounded by mature trees. Beds and borders of rhododendrons, flowering and foliage shrubs, mixed herbaceous plants and a rockery with small stream and pond ensure interest throughout the seasons. Raised beds, large terrace with bedding plants and Mediterranean garden complete the picture.

❀ ☕

54 SPINDLEWOOD
Strathallan Close, Darley Dale DE4 2HJ. Mr & Mrs J G Ball, 01629 735701. *3m N of Matlock, on A6. After The Grouse Inn, turn R up Whitworth Rd. Park on L by railings, on Whitworth Rd. Elderly/disabled may continue to private parking areas down the Close and within entrance to garden.* Teas/lunches by arrangement at local hall. **Adm £3, chd free. Visitors welcome by appt May, June, July & August. Coaches accommodated in Whitworth Road.**
A central stream cascades down a gentle slope and divides the ³/₄ -acre lawn. Pond is bridged alongside a bog garden. Herbaceous and shrubby beds extend around the whole area. Other sections incl herbs, wild area and semi-tropical plants in pots on large patio. A new section includes a tropical area in a sheltered nook. Find the prize gunnera that exceeds the dimensions quoted both in height and width. Slight slope between level grassed areas.

♿ ❀ ☕ ☎

STONEHILL QUARRY GARDEN
See Staffordshire & part of West Midlands.

TEVERSAL MANOR GARDENS
See Nottinghamshire.

55 ◆ TISSINGTON HALL
nr Ashbourne DE6 1RA. Sir Richard FitzHerbert, 01335 352200, www.tissington-hall.com. *4m N of Ashbourne. E of A515 on Ashbourne to Buxton rd.* **Adm £3.50, chd free. By appt for groups & societies. For NGS: Mon 25 Aug (1.30-4).**
Large garden; roses, herbaceous borders. Featured on BBC TV 'East Midlands Today', 2007.

♿ ✕ ❀ ☕

56 7 WARREN DRIVE
Linton DE12 6QP. Keith & Phyl Hutchinson, 01283 761088. *6m SE of Burton-on-Trent. Take A444 out of Burton for 5m. After Toons Warehouse*

on R, take 3rd exit at roundabout. Take 1st R & continue for 1m uphill past The Square & Compass PH on R. After 200yds turn L into Warren Drive. Home-made teas. **Adm £2, chd free. Sun 10 Aug (2-5.30). Visitors also welcome by appt for groups of 6+.**
This cottage-style garden on 2 levels, overlooking countryside is a plantperson's delight. Many unusual plants in an eclectic mix which fill colour-themed borders, pergolas, gazebo, stream, pond and pots galore. New perennials are continually sought and added. Quirky shapes, raised vegetable beds and a drought-tolerant front garden filled with hot colours, add further interest. Winding paths and various seating areas present new surprises. Featured in 'Garden News', 2007.

✕ ❀ ☕ ☎

Themed borders incl Mediterranean, late summer tropical . . .

57 WHARFEDALE
34 Broadway, Duffield, Belper DE56 4BU. Roger & Sue Roberts, 01332 841905, roberts34@btinternet.com. *4m N of Derby. Turn onto B5023 Wirksworth rd (Broadway) off A6 midway between Belper & Derby.* Home-made teas. **Adm £3, chd free. Sat 5, Sun 6 July; Sun 24 Aug (11-5) Evening Opening £4, wine, Fri 5 Sept (6.30-10). Visitors also welcome by appt, for groups of 15+ from 21 Apr to 10 Oct, evenings and weekends only.**
Plant enthusiasts' garden with over 800 varieties of choice and unusual shrubs, trees, perennials and bulbs. Themed borders incl Mediterranean, late summer tropical and single colour schemes. Cottage garden to front. 12yrs old with Italianate walled scented garden and woodland pond with raised walkway. Eclectic and unusual garden providing lots of ideas attracting international garden tours. New Japanese tea garden with stream and pavilion. Fully illuminated.

✕ ❀ ☕ ☎

58 NEW 24 WHEELDON AVENUE
Derby DE22 1HN. Laura Burnett, 01332 384893/342204 (Ian Griffiths). *1m N Derby city centre. Approached directly from Kedleston Rd or from A6, Duffield Rd via West Bank Ave. Limited on street parking. Good bus services on Kedleston Rd or Duffield Rd.* **Sun 15 June combined with 26 Wheeldon Ave £3.50. 20 July (2-4.30) £2, chd free. Visitors also welcome by appt for groups 6+.**
Small Victorian garden, with original walling supporting many shrubs and climbers with contrasting colour and texture. Circular lawn surrounded by herbaceous border with main colour scheme of blue, purple black, yellow and orange tones. This leads to a small area at rear of garden given to more natural planting to suit shade and natural habitat. This is a garden produced on a low income budget, with varied tones and textures throughout the planting. Hand-made cards & teddy bears for sale. 20% proceeds to 'Africat' charity.

♿ ❀ ☎

59 26 WHEELDON AVENUE
Derby DE22 1HN. Ian Griffiths, 01332 342204. *1m N of Derby. 1m from city centre & approached directly off the Kedleston Rd or from A6 Duffield Rd via West Bank Ave. Limited on-street parking.* **Combined opening with 24 Wheeldon Avenue adm £3.50. Sun 15 June (2-5). Visitors also welcome by appt June & July, groups of 6+. Adm £2, chd free.**
Tiny Victorian walled garden near to city centre. Lawn and herbaceous borders with old roses, lupins, delphiniums and foxgloves. Small terrace with topiary and herb garden. New water feature for 2008. Featured on BBC TV and 'Period Living' and 'Amateur Gardening' magazines.

♿ ❀ ☎

60 WINDWARD
62 Summer Lane, Wirksworth DE4 4EB. Audrey & Andrew Winkler, 01629 822681, www.grandmafrogsgarden.co.uk. *5m S of Matlock. ¹/₂ m from Wirksworth town centre off B5023 Wirksworth to Duffield rd. After approx 300yds, turn R at mini island onto Summer Lane. Windward is approx 500yds on R, rockery at roadside.*

Home-made teas. **Adm £3, chd free (share to Ruddington Framework Knitters Museum). Suns 6 Apr; 8 June; 7 Sept (11-5). Visitors also welcome by appt all year for groups of 15+.**
Lush, green garden of about 1 acre, wildlife-friendly and almost organic. Romantic ambiance with mature trees and shrubs and interesting nooks and crannies. Ponds, hostas, gravel garden, rockery, grasses, roses, rhododendrons, Leylandii crinkle-crankle hedge, woodland paths and bulbs, mixed borders and small meadow area. A garden for relaxation with several seating areas.

🍴 ☕ ☎

61 WOODEND COTTAGE
134 Main Street, Repton DE65 6FB. Wendy & Stephen Longden, 01283 703259. *6m S of Derby. From A38, S of Derby, follow signs to Willington, then Repton. In Repton, straight on at roundabout through village. Woodend Cottage is 1m on R before Woodend Children's Nursery.* Home-made teas. **Adm £2.50, chd free. Suns 25 May; 13 July; 10 Aug (1-5). Visitors also welcome by appt.**
Plant lover's garden with glorious views on sloping site. 2½ acres developed organically over last 6yrs for yr-round interest. On lower levels, hardy perennials, grasses, shrubs and shade-loving plants are arranged informally and connected via lawns, thyme bed, pond and pergolas. Grassed meadows beyond lead naturally into wildlife area, mixed woodland and fruit, vegetable and herb potager. Esp colourful in July and Aug. Featured in 'Country Living' magazine, 2007. Some gravel paths, steps and steep slopes.

🍴 ❀ ☕ ☎

62 35 WYVER LANE
Belper DE56 2UB. Jim & Brenda Stannering, 01773 824280. *8m N of Derby. Take A6 from Derby through Belper to T-lights at triangle. Turn L for A517 to Ashbourne, over river bridge, 1st R onto Wyver Lane. Parking in River Gardens, entrance on A6.* Teas available. **Entrance by donation. Visitors welcome by appt, groups** also welcome, April to July.
Cottage garden of approx 500sq yds on side of R Derwent opp Belper River Gardens. Full of hardy perennial plants with pergola, troughs, greenhouse, small pond.

❀ ☕ ☎

Derbyshire County Volunteers

County Organiser
Irene Dougan, Field Farm, Field Lane, Kirk Ireton, Ashbourne DE6 3JU, 01335 370958, dougan@lineone.net

County Treasurer
Graham Dougan, Field Farm, Field Lane, Kirk Ireton, Ashbourne DE6 3JU, 01335 370958, dougan@lineone.net

Publicity
Christine Morris, 9 Langdale Avenue, Ravenshead NG15 9EA, 01623 793827, christine@ravenshead.demon.co.uk

Leaflet Coordinator
Sarah Bacon, 11 Highgrove Drive, Chellaston, Derby DE73 5XA, 01332 690702, sarah@sarbac.wanadoo.co.uk

Assistant County Organisers
Ron & Sue Astles, Quarryside, 1 King Charles Court, Glossop SK13 8NJ, 01457 857015, sue.astles@ctaweb.co.uk
Gill & Colin Hancock, 334 Belper Road, Stanley Common, nr Ilkeston DE7 6FY, 01159 301061
Kate & Peter Spencer, The Riddings Farm, Kirk Ireton, Ashbourne DE6 3LB, 01335 370331

DEVON

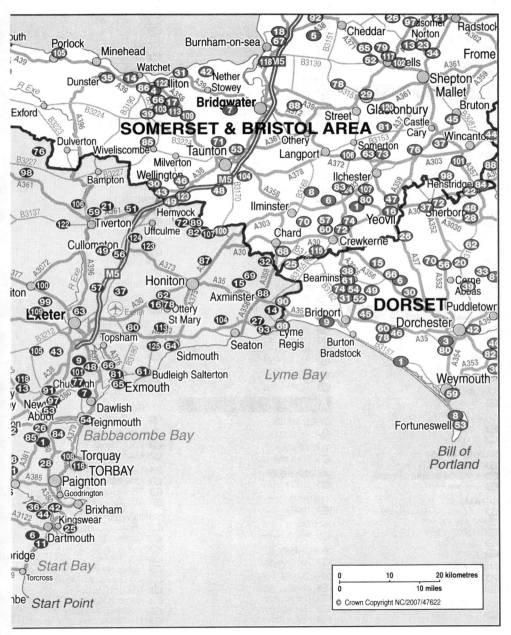

Opening Dates

January

SUNDAY 6
99 Sherwood

SUNDAY 13
99 Sherwood

SUNDAY 20
99 Sherwood

SUNDAY 27
99 Sherwood

February

SUNDAY 3
20 Cherubeer Gardens
63 Little Cumbre
99 Sherwood

SUNDAY 10
20 Cherubeer Gardens
63 Little Cumbre
99 Sherwood

SUNDAY 17
40 Glebe Cottage
63 Little Cumbre
99 Sherwood

SATURDAY 23
57 Killerton Garden

SUNDAY 24
63 Little Cumbre
99 Sherwood

March

DAILY 21 MARCH ONWARDS
24 Cliffe

SUNDAY 2
99 Sherwood
125 Yonder Hill

SATURDAY 8
72 Newton Farm

SUNDAY 9
72 Newton Farm
99 Sherwood

SATURDAY 15
19 Chapel Farm House
29 Coombe Sculpture Garden
72 Newton Farm

SUNDAY 16
29 Coombe Sculpture Garden
50 Higher Knowle
72 Newton Farm
99 Sherwood
125 Yonder Hill

FRIDAY 21
34 The Downes
125 Yonder Hill

SATURDAY 22
34 The Downes

72 Newton Farm

SUNDAY 23
33 Dippers
34 The Downes
50 Higher Knowle
56 Kia-Ora Farm & Gardens
65 Littleham House Cottage
72 Newton Farm
99 Sherwood
125 Yonder Hill

MONDAY 24
34 The Downes
50 Higher Knowle
56 Kia-Ora Farm & Gardens
125 Yonder Hill

TUESDAY 25
34 The Downes

WEDNESDAY 26
34 The Downes

THURSDAY 27
34 The Downes

FRIDAY 28
34 The Downes

SATURDAY 29
34 The Downes
42 Greenway Garden
123 Wood Barton

SUNDAY 30
34 The Downes
50 Higher Knowle
65 Littleham House Cottage
81 38 Phillipps Avenue
99 Sherwood
123 Wood Barton
125 Yonder Hill

MONDAY 31
34 The Downes

April

OPEN DAILY
24 Cliffe

TUESDAY 1
34 The Downes

WEDNESDAY 2
34 The Downes

THURSDAY 3
34 The Downes

FRIDAY 4
34 The Downes

SATURDAY 5
34 The Downes

SUNDAY 6
2 Alder
34 The Downes
46 Heathercombe
50 Higher Knowle

51 Holbrook Garden
56 Kia-Ora Farm & Gardens
71 Mothecombe House
91 Rock House Garden
99 Sherwood
105 Sowton Mill
125 Yonder Hill

MONDAY 7
34 The Downes

TUESDAY 8
34 The Downes

WEDNESDAY 9
34 The Downes

THURSDAY 10
34 The Downes

FRIDAY 11
34 The Downes

SATURDAY 12
34 The Downes

SUNDAY 13
9 Bickham House
34 The Downes
41 Gorwell House
50 Higher Knowle
81 38 Phillipps Avenue
99 Sherwood
109 Summers Place
125 Yonder Hill

MONDAY 14
34 The Downes

TUESDAY 15
9 Bickham House
34 The Downes
78 Otter Nurseries

WEDNESDAY 16
9 Bickham House
34 The Downes

THURSDAY 17
34 The Downes

FRIDAY 18
34 The Downes
68 Marwood Hill

SATURDAY 19
19 Chapel Farm House
34 The Downes
100 Shobrooke Park Gardens

SUNDAY 20
4 Andrew's Corner
18 Castle Hill
33 Dippers
34 The Downes
50 Higher Knowle
56 Kia-Ora Farm & Gardens
57 Killerton Garden
58 Kingston House
71 Mothecombe House
75 The Old Rectory

81 38 Phillipps Avenue
94 St Merryn
99 Sherwood
125 Yonder Hill

MONDAY 21
34 The Downes

TUESDAY 22
34 The Downes

WEDNESDAY 23
34 The Downes

THURSDAY 24
12 Bocombe Mill Cottage
34 The Downes

FRIDAY 25
34 The Downes

SATURDAY 26
34 The Downes
43 Haldon Grange
87 Pound Cottage

SUNDAY 27
21 Chevithorne Barton
25 Coleton Fishacre
34 The Downes
42 Greenway Garden
43 Haldon Grange
50 Higher Knowle
91 Rock House Garden
99 Sherwood
110 Taikoo
125 Yonder Hill

MONDAY 28
34 The Downes

TUESDAY 29
34 The Downes
78 Otter Nurseries

WEDNESDAY 30
34 The Downes

May

OPEN DAILY
24 Cliffe

THURSDAY 1
34 The Downes

FRIDAY 2
34 The Downes

SATURDAY 3
32 Dicot
34 The Downes
43 Haldon Grange
71 Mothecombe House
72 Newton Farm
82 Pikes Cottage
87 Pound Cottage
114 The Water Garden

SUNDAY 4
4 Andrew's Corner
8 Barleycott
32 Dicot
34 The Downes

43 Haldon Grange
47 Heddon Hall
50 Higher Knowle
51 Holbrook Garden
54 Jason's Garden
56 Kia-Ora Farm & Gardens
59 Knightshayes Court Garden
71 Mothecombe House
72 Newton Farm
73 North Boreston Farm
82 Pikes Cottage
98 Shapcott Barton Estate
99 Sherwood
114 The Water Garden
124 Woody Park
125 Yonder Hill

MONDAY 5
34 The Downes
43 Haldon Grange
50 Higher Knowle
51 Holbrook Garden
54 Jason's Garden
56 Kia-Ora Farm & Gardens
72 Newton Farm
73 North Boreston Farm
82 Pikes Cottage
114 The Water Garden
124 Woody Park
125 Yonder Hill

TUESDAY 6
34 The Downes

WEDNESDAY 7
34 The Downes
43 Haldon Grange
95 Saltram House

THURSDAY 8
34 The Downes

FRIDAY 9
34 The Downes

SATURDAY 10
19 Chapel Farm House
34 The Downes
74 The Old Glebe
114 The Water Garden
120 Wildside
122 Withleigh Farm
124 Woody Park

SUNDAY 11
6 Ash House Farm
9 Bickham House
22 The Cider House
34 The Downes
58 Kingston House
74 The Old Glebe
81 38 Phillipps Avenue
99 Sherwood
103 Southcombe Gardens
109 Summers Place
114 The Water Garden
118 Whitstone Farm
122 Withleigh Farm
124 Woody Park
125 Yonder Hill

MONDAY 12
34 The Downes

TUESDAY 13
9 Bickham House
34 The Downes
78 Otter Nurseries

WEDNESDAY 14
9 Bickham House
34 The Downes
43 Haldon Grange
85 Pleasant View

THURSDAY 15
4 Andrew's Corner (Evening)
34 The Downes

FRIDAY 16
34 The Downes
76 The Old Vicarage

SATURDAY 17
34 The Downes
74 The Old Glebe
76 The Old Vicarage
82 Pikes Cottage
100 Shobrooke Park Gardens
107 Springdale
114 The Water Garden

SUNDAY 18
2 Alder
18 Castle Hill
21 Chevithorne Barton
34 The Downes
37 Feebers Gardens
41 Gorwell House
46 Heathercombe
56 Kia-Ora Farm & Gardens
60 Langtrees
74 The Old Glebe
76 The Old Vicarage
82 Pikes Cottage
93 Rousdon Gardens
99 Sherwood
106 Spillifords Wildlife Garden
107 Springdale
114 The Water Garden
125 Yonder Hill

MONDAY 19
34 The Downes
107 Springdale

TUESDAY 20
34 The Downes

WEDNESDAY 21
34 The Downes
43 Haldon Grange

THURSDAY 22
34 The Downes

FRIDAY 23
34 The Downes

SATURDAY 24
34 The Downes
43 Haldon Grange
46 Heathercombe

70 Moretonhampstead Gardens
77 The Orangery
114 The Water Garden

SUNDAY 25
4 Andrew's Corner
10 Bideford East Gardens
34 The Downes
35 Durcombe Water
43 Haldon Grange
46 Heathercombe
51 Holbrook Garden
56 Kia-Ora Farm & Gardens
70 Moretonhampstead Gardens
71 Mothecombe House
77 The Orangery
91 Rock House Garden
94 St Merryn
99 Sherwood
103 Southcombe Gardens
110 Taikoo
114 The Water Garden
117 Westcott Barton
125 Yonder Hill

MONDAY 26
16 Cadhay
34 The Downes
35 Durcombe Water
51 Holbrook Garden
56 Kia-Ora Farm & Gardens
70 Moretonhampstead Gardens
103 Southcombe Gardens
114 The Water Garden
117 Westcott Barton
125 Yonder Hill

TUESDAY 27
34 The Downes

WEDNESDAY 28
34 The Downes

THURSDAY 29
12 Bocombe Mill Cottage
34 The Downes

FRIDAY 30
12 Bocombe Mill Cottage
34 The Downes

SATURDAY 31
12 Bocombe Mill Cottage
13 Bovey Tracey Gardens
34 The Downes
69 Membury Gardens
72 Newton Farm
102 South Tawton Gardens
104 Southleigh Gardens
114 The Water Garden

June

OPEN DAILY
24 Cliffe

SUNDAY 1
4 Andrew's Corner
13 Bovey Tracey Gardens
34 The Downes
41 Gorwell House

46 Heathercombe
69 Membury Gardens
72 Newton Farm
75 The Old Rectory
81 38 Phillipps Avenue
91 Rock House Garden
99 Sherwood
102 South Tawton Gardens
103 Southcombe Gardens
104 Southleigh Gardens
114 The Water Garden
116 4 Wellswood Heights
125 Yonder Hill

MONDAY 2
34 The Downes

SATURDAY 7
1 Abbotskerswell Gardens
72 Newton Farm
80 Owls Barn
88 Prospect House
100 Shobrooke Park Gardens
102 South Tawton Gardens

SUNDAY 8
1 Abbotskerswell Gardens
4 Andrew's Corner
6 Ash House Farm
9 Bickham House
20 Cherubeer Gardens
31 Dartington Hall Gardens
49 Higher Burnhaies
53 Ideford Gardens
56 Kia-Ora Farm & Gardens
71 Mothecombe House
72 Newton Farm
80 Owls Barn
81 38 Phillipps Avenue
85 Pleasant View
88 Prospect House
89 Regency House
98 Shapcott Barton Estate
99 Sherwood
102 South Tawton Gardens
103 Southcombe Gardens
125 Yonder Hill

TUESDAY 10
9 Bickham House

WEDNESDAY 11
9 Bickham House
85 Pleasant View

SATURDAY 14
27 Combpyne Manor
32 Dicot
82 Pikes Cottage
113 1 Tipton Lodge
115 Webbery Gardens

SUNDAY 15
8 Barleycott
27 Combpyne Manor
30 The Croft
32 Dicot
53 Ideford Gardens
60 Langtrees
82 Pikes Cottage

86 Portington
92 Rose Cottage
93 Rousdon Gardens
99 Sherwood
103 Southcombe Gardens
109 Summers Place
113 1 Tipton Lodge
115 Webbery Gardens
121 Winsford Walled Garden
125 Yonder Hill

WEDNESDAY 18
72 Newton Farm

FRIDAY 20
16 Cadhay

SATURDAY 21
14 Bramble Hayes
19 Chapel Farm House
23 Cleave House
26 Collepardo
29 Coombe Sculpture Garden
48 High Garden

SUNDAY 22
2 Alder
14 Bramble Hayes
23 Cleave House
26 Collepardo
29 Coombe Sculpture Garden
36 East Cornworthy Gardens
37 Feebers Gardens
48 High Garden
49 Higher Burnhaies
56 Kia-Ora Farm & Gardens
58 Kingston House
62 Little Ash Farm
64 Littlecourt Cottages
71 Mothecombe House
86 Portington
89 Regency House
91 Rock House Garden
92 Rose Cottage
99 Sherwood
112 Tanglewood
125 Yonder Hill

MONDAY 23
14 Bramble Hayes
26 Collepardo
36 East Cornworthy Gardens
64 Littlecourt Cottages

TUESDAY 24
26 Collepardo

WEDNESDAY 25
26 Collepardo
28 Compton Castle
72 Newton Farm

THURSDAY 26
12 Bocombe Mill Cottage
26 Collepardo

FRIDAY 27
12 Bocombe Mill Cottage
26 Colleparco
66 The Lookout
76 The Old Vicarage

SATURDAY 28
- 12 Bocombe Mill Cottage
- 22 The Cider House
- 23 Cleave House
- 26 Collepardo
- 72 Newton Farm
- 76 The Old Vicarage
- 101 South Kenwood
- 120 Wildside

SUNDAY 29
- 10 Bideford East Gardens
- 23 Cleave House
- 26 Collepardo
- 55 Kerscott House
- 66 The Lookout
- 72 Newton Farm
- 76 The Old Vicarage
- 79 Overbeck's
- 94 St Merryn
- 99 Sherwood
- 101 South Kenwood
- 106 Spillifords Wildlife Garden
- 125 Yonder Hill

July

OPEN DAILY
- 24 Cliffe

FRIDAY 4
- 27 Combpyne Manor
- 76 The Old Vicarage

SATURDAY 5
- 27 Combpyne Manor
- 72 Newton Farm
- 76 The Old Vicarage
- 107 Springdale

SUNDAY 6
- 8 Barleycott
- 27 Combpyne Manor
- 56 Kia-Ora Farm & Gardens
- 72 Newton Farm
- 75 The Old Rectory
- 76 The Old Vicarage
- 99 Sherwood
- 107 Springdale
- 125 Yonder Hill

MONDAY 7
- 107 Springdale

SATURDAY 12
- 48 High Garden
- 69 Membury Gardens
- 98 Shapcott Barton Estate

SUNDAY 13
- 9 Bickham House
- 48 High Garden
- 58 Kingston House (Evening)
- 69 Membury Gardens
- 96 School House
- 98 Shapcott Barton Estate
- 99 Sherwood
- 105 Sowton Mill
- 125 Yonder Hill

TUESDAY 15
- 9 Bickham House

WEDNESDAY 16
- 9 Bickham House
- 85 Pleasant View
- 98 Shapcott Barton Estate
- 111 Tamarisks

THURSDAY 17
- 111 Tamarisks

FRIDAY 18
- 16 Cadhay

SATURDAY 19
- 5 Arlington Court
- 17 Castle Drogo
- 19 Chapel Farm House
- 25 Coleton Fishacre
- 57 Killerton Garden
- 72 Newton Farm
- 79 Overbeck's
- 82 Pikes Cottage
- 95 Saltram House

SUNDAY 20
- 5 Arlington Court
- 30 The Croft
- 37 Feebers Gardens
- 41 Gorwell House
- 56 Kia-Ora Farm & Gardens
- 62 Little Ash Farm
- 72 Newton Farm
- 81 38 Phillipps Avenue
- 82 Pikes Cottage
- 85 Pleasant View
- 93 Rousdon Gardens
- 99 Sherwood
- 112 Tanglewood
- 121 Winsford Walled Garden
- 125 Yonder Hill

WEDNESDAY 23
- 98 Shapcott Barton Estate

THURSDAY 24
- 12 Bocombe Mill Cottage

FRIDAY 25
- 12 Bocombe Mill Cottage

SATURDAY 26
- 12 Bocombe Mill Cottage
- 32 Dicot
- 70 Moretonhampstead Gardens
- 98 Shapcott Barton Estate
- 110 Taikoo

SUNDAY 27
- 4 Andrew's Corner
- 32 Dicot
- 52 Hole Farm
- 64 Littlecourt Cottages
- 70 Moretonhampstead Gardens
- 91 Rock House Garden
- 98 Shapcott Barton Estate
- 99 Sherwood
- 118 Whitstone Farm
- 119 Wick Farm Gardens (Afternoon & Evening)

- 125 Yonder Hill

WEDNESDAY 30
- 47 Heddon Hall
- 72 Newton Farm

THURSDAY 31
- 98 Shapcott Barton Estate

August

OPEN DAILY
- 24 Cliffe

SATURDAY 2
- 72 Newton Farm
- 83 Pine Cottage
- 88 Prospect House
- 108 Squirrels

SUNDAY 3
- 56 Kia-Ora Farm & Gardens
- 72 Newton Farm
- 75 The Old Rectory
- 83 Pine Cottage
- 88 Prospect House
- 99 Sherwood
- 108 Squirrels
- 125 Yonder Hill

MONDAY 4
- 83 Pine Cottage

WEDNESDAY 6
- 51 Holbrook Garden
- 72 Newton Farm

THURSDAY 7
- 4 Andrew's Corner (Evening)

SATURDAY 9
- 14 Bramble Hayes
- 27 Combpyne Manor
- 62 Little Ash Farm
- 72 Newton Farm
- 98 Shapcott Barton Estate
- 108 Squirrels

SUNDAY 10
- 9 Bickham House
- 14 Bramble Hayes
- 27 Combpyne Manor
- 62 Little Ash Farm
- 72 Newton Farm
- 73 North Boreston Farm
- 81 38 Phillipps Avenue
- 98 Shapcott Barton Estate
- 99 Sherwood
- 121 Winsford Walled Garden
- 125 Yonder Hill

MONDAY 11
- 14 Bramble Hayes

TUESDAY 12
- 9 Bickham House

WEDNESDAY 13
- 9 Bickham House
- 72 Newton Farm

SATURDAY 16
- 19 Chapel Farm House

SUNDAY 17
- 30 The Croft
- 56 Kia-Ora Farm & Gardens
- 73 North Boreston Farm
- 93 Rousdon Gardens
- 99 Sherwood
- 125 Yonder Hill

WEDNESDAY 20
- 72 Newton Farm

SATURDAY 23
- 82 Pikes Cottage
- 97 Sedgewell Coach House Gardens

SUNDAY 24
- 3 32 Allenstyle Drive
- 10 Bideford East Gardens
- 37 Feebers Gardens
- 56 Kia-Ora Farm & Gardens
- 82 Pikes Cottage
- 97 Sedgewell Coach House Gardens
- 99 Sherwood
- 117 Westcott Barton
- 119 Wick Farm Gardens
- 125 Yonder Hill

MONDAY 25
- 3 32 Allenstyle Drive
- 56 Kia-Ora Farm & Gardens
- 82 Pikes Cottage
- 117 Westcott Barton
- 119 Wick Farm Gardens
- 125 Yonder Hill

THURSDAY 28
- 12 Bocombe Mill Cottage

SATURDAY 30
- 97 Sedgewell Coach House Gardens

SUNDAY 31
- 3 32 Allenstyle Drive
- 91 Rock House Garden
- 97 Sedgewell Coach House Gardens
- 99 Sherwood
- 116 4 Wellswood Heights
- 125 Yonder Hill

September

OPEN DAILY
- 24 Cliffe

FRIDAY 5
- 68 Marwood Hill

SUNDAY 7
- 3 32 Allenstyle Drive
- 22 The Cider House
- 41 Gorwell House
- 56 Kia-Ora Farm & Gardens
- 81 38 Phillipps Avenue
- 99 Sherwood
- 125 Yonder Hill

SATURDAY 13
- 72 Newton Farm

SUNDAY 14
- 3 32 Allenstyle Drive
- 8 Barleycott
- 59 Knightshayes Court Garden
- 60 Langtrees
- 72 Newton Farm
- 75 The Old Rectory
- 91 Rock House Garden
- 99 Sherwood
- 121 Winsford Walled Garden
- 125 Yonder Hill

TUESDAY 16
- 78 Otter Nurseries

WEDNESDAY 17
- 40 Glebe Cottage

FRIDAY 19
- 51 Holbrook Garden

SATURDAY 20
- 19 Chapel Farm House
- 51 Holbrook Garden
- 72 Newton Farm
- 120 Wildside

SUNDAY 21
- 72 Newton Farm
- 89 Regency House
- 93 Rousdon Gardens
- 99 Sherwood
- 125 Yonder Hill

SATURDAY 27
- 17 Castle Drogo
- 82 Pikes Cottage

SUNDAY 28
- 20 Cherubeer Gardens
- 82 Pikes Cottage
- 91 Rock House Garden
- 99 Sherwood
- 109 Summers Place
- 125 Yonder Hill

October

SUNDAY 5
- 41 Gorwell House
- 91 Rock House Garden
- 99 Sherwood
- 125 Yonder Hill

SUNDAY 12
- 99 Sherwood
- 125 Yonder Hill

SUNDAY 19
- 4 Andrew's Corner
- 99 Sherwood
- 125 Yonder Hill

SUNDAY 26
- 91 Rock House Garden
- 99 Sherwood
- 125 Yonder Hill

November

SUNDAY 2
- 99 Sherwood

SUNDAY 9
- 99 Sherwood

SUNDAY 16
- 99 Sherwood

SUNDAY 23
- 99 Sherwood

SUNDAY 30
- 99 Sherwood

December

SUNDAY 7
- 99 Sherwood

SUNDAY 14
- 57 Killerton Garden
- 99 Sherwood

SUNDAY 21
- 99 Sherwood

SUNDAY 28
- 99 Sherwood

January 2009

SUNDAY 4
- 99 Sherwood

SUNDAY 11
- 99 Sherwood

SUNDAY 18
- 99 Sherwood

SUNDAY 25
- 99 Sherwood

February 2009

SUNDAY 1
- 20 Cherubeer Gardens
- 63 Little Cumbre
- 99 Sherwood

SUNDAY 8
- 20 Cherubeer Gardens
- 63 Little Cumbre
- 99 Sherwood

SUNDAY 15
- 63 Little Cumbre
- 99 Sherwood

SUNDAY 22
- 63 Little Cumbre
- 99 Sherwood

Gardens open to the public

- 5 Arlington Court
- 11 Blackpool Gardens
- 15 Burrow Farm Gardens
- 17 Castle Drogo
- 18 Castle Hill
- 25 Coleton Fishacre
- 28 Compton Castle
- 31 Dartington Hall Gardens
- 38 The Garden House
- 40 Glebe Cottage
- 42 Greenway Garden

45 Hartland Abbey
47 Heddon Hall
51 Holbrook Garden
57 Killerton Garden
59 Knightshayes Court Garden
67 Lukesland
68 Marwood Hill
78 Otter Nurseries
79 Overbeck's
84 Plant World
90 RHS Garden Rosemoor
91 Rock House Garden
95 Saltram House
120 Wildside
121 Winsford Walled Garden

By appointment only

7 Ashcombe Road Gardens
39 The Gate House
44 Hamblyn's Coombe
61 Lee Ford

Also open by appointment ☎

2 Alder
3 32 Allenstyle Drive
4 Andrew's Corner
7 Apple Tree Cottage, Ashcombe Road Gardens
7 Arcadia, Ashcombe Road Gardens
8 Barleycott
9 Bickham House
12 Bocombe Mill Cottage
14 Bramble Hayes
19 Chapel Farm House
20 Higher Cherubeer, Cherubeer Gardens
22 The Cider House
23 Cleave House
30 The Croft
32 Dicot
34 The Downes
35 Durcombe Water
41 Gorwell House
43 Haldon Grange
46 Heathercombe
50 Higher Knowle
52 Hole Farm
53 Coombe Farm, Ideford Gardens
53 Well Cottage, Ideford Gardens
56 Kia-Ora Farm & Gardens
58 Kingston House
60 Langtrees
62 Little Ash Farm
63 Little Cumbre
65 Littleham House Cottage
69 Sixpenny Moon, Membury Gardens
70 Sutton Mead, Moretonhampstead Gardens
72 Newton Farm
73 North Boreston Farm
75 The Old Rectory
76 The Old Vicarage

82 Pikes Cottage
83 Pine Cottage
85 Pleasant View
87 Pound Cottage
88 Prospect House
89 Regency House
93 Green Lane Cottage, Rousdon Gardens
93 Hortus, Rousdon Gardens
94 St Merryn
96 School House
99 Sherwood
100 Shobrooke Park Gardens
103 Southcombe House, Southcombe Gardens
104 Popes Cottage, Southleigh Gardens
104 South Bank, Southleigh Gardens
105 Sowton Mill
106 Spillifords Wildlife Garden
110 Taikoo
111 Tamarisks
113 1 Tipton Lodge
115 Webbery Gardens
116 4 Wellswood Heights
117 Westcott Barton
118 Whitstone Farm
122 Withleigh Farm
123 Wood Barton
125 Yonder Hill

The Gardens

ABBOTSBURY GARDENS
See Dorset.

1 **NEW** **ABBOTSKERSWELL GARDENS**
TQ12 5PN. *2m SW of Newton Abbot town centre. Take A381 to Totnes, sharp L turn to village. Car parking at Fairfield or in village. Route maps available.* Cream teas at Church House, the oldest building in village. **Combined adm £4, chd free (share to Friends of St Marys). Sat 7, Sun 8 June (2-5).**
Abbotskerswell is an attractive and vibrant village of 800 homes clustered around C15 church, 2 PHs, village shop and PO. Centre of village has wealth of charming thatched cottages and other houses. Have fun finding your way around the maze of hidden pathways in village to gardens, map available. Plant sale at Fairfield.

NEW **1, 2 & 8 COURT FARM BARNS**
Wilton Way. Mike & Beryl Veale, Pat & Tony Parsons, Pat Mackness
3 tiny courtyard gardens in barn conversion next to church, showing a variety of creative ways to make the most of a small site.
 🚻 ✂

NEW **BRIAR COTTAGE**
1 Monk's Orchard. Peggy & David Munden
Informal, rambling cottage-style garden. Area around house set to vegetables, herbaceous, shrubs and rockery. Beyond is steep terraced slope with small coppice below. Many unusual and interesting plants abound - a plantsman's delight.
✂

NEW **COURT COTTAGE**
Mr & Mrs A R W Rooth. *50yds from PO, opp Vicarage Rd*
Delightful hidden walled garden. Pretty summerhouse for outdoor living, herbaceous borders with range of interesting plants incl asphodoline, agapanthus, clematis. Small pond, pergola and vegetable patch. When choosing new plants drought conditions are uppermost as most of garden is composed of shillet.
✂

NEW **FAIRFIELD**
Christine & Brian Mackness
$3/4$-acre walled garden, herbaceous borders with cottage overtones. Vegetable patch, pond with stepped rill. Recently-planted indigenous woodland plus arboretum of 70 species, set amongst winding grass pathways, total $1^1/4$ acre. Created to attract wildlife. Ramp over 4 steps available.
 🚻 ✂ ❀

NEW **1 LAKELAND**
Mary Brake & Alan Wheeler
Small cottage garden currently undergoing a makeover to incl mixed borders, raised vegetable beds and soft fruit area, greenhouse, container plants, small raised fish pond and wildlife pond under construction.
 🚻 ✂

Have fun finding your way around the maze of hidden pathways . . .

NEW 31 ODLEHILL GROVE
Christine Lewis
Small garden with good variety of shrubs, trees and flowers, incl roses and clematis.
&. ✗

NEW PLUMTREE COTTAGE
Slade Lane. Derek & Jenny Bellotti
2-acre cottage garden. Established wisteria, quince, nectarine and many shrubs. Pergola, seating areas, arched walkways, greenhouse, pond and terrace. Ditch being converted into stream with wildlife pond. A garden to be followed as it develops.
✗

2 ALDER
Lewdown EX20 4PJ. Bob & Anne Westlake, 01566 783909. *8m W of Okehampton, 8m E of Launceston. On old A30 (W Devon Drive).* Cream teas. **Adm £2.50, chd free.** Suns 6 Apr; 18 May; 22 June (2-6). **Visitors also welcome by appt.**
Large garden created over last 22yrs with shrubs and herbaceous areas and views over landscaped valley. Woodland walks with 4-acre lake in former quarry. Bluebell wood in spring. Rill and water feature. New 170metre lime avenue leading to new pond.
&. ✗ ⊗ ☕ ☎

3 32 ALLENSTYLE DRIVE
Yelland, Barnstaple EX31 3DZ. Steve & Dawn Morgan, 01271 861433, www.devonsubtropicalgarden.co.uk. *5m W of Barnstaple. Take B3233 towards Instow. Through Bickington & Fremington. L at Yelland sign into Allenstyle Rd. 1st R into Allenstyle Dr. Light blue bungalow.* Light refreshments & teas. **Adm £2.50, chd free.** Sun 24, Mon 25, Sun 31 Aug; Suns 7, 14 Sept (10.30-6). **Visitors also welcome by appt Aug & Sept only.**
Late-flowering incl large collection of rudbeckias and unusual tropical planting incl bananas (hardy, ornamental and edible), tropical and temperate passion flowers; hedychiums (ginger lilies) for colour and beautiful scent, paulownias, brugmansias and colochasias in our unconventionally evolving small garden.
✗ ⊗ ☕ ☎

Varied collection of sculptures, unusual planting schemes and farm animals . . .

4 ANDREW'S CORNER
Belstone EX20 1RD. Robin & Edwina Hill, 01837 840332, edwinarobin_hill@yahoo.co.uk. *3m E of Okehampton. Signed to Belstone. In village signed Skaigh. Parking restricted but cars may be left on nearby common.* Home-made teas. **Adm £2.50, chd free.** Suns 20 Apr; 4, 25 May; 1, 8 June; 27 July; 19 Oct (2.30-5.30). **Candlelit Evening Openings** £4, wine, Thurs 15 May; 7 Aug (7-10). **Visitors also welcome by appt.**
Well-established, wildlife-friendly, well-labelled plantsman's garden in stunning high moorland setting. Variety of garden habitats incl woodland areas, bog garden, pond; wide range of unusual trees, shrubs, herbaceous plants for yr-round effect incl alpines, rhododendrons, bulbs and maples; spectacular autumn colour. New organic kitchen garden, greenhouse and chickens. Wheelchair access difficult when wet.
&. ✗ ⊗ ☕ ☎

ANTONY
See Cornwall.

5 ◆ ARLINGTON COURT
Arlington, Barnstaple EX31 4LP. The National Trust, 01271 850296, www.nationaltrust.org.uk. *7m NE of Barnstaple. On A39. From E use A399.* **House and garden adm £7.80, chd £3.90, garden only adm £5.60, chd £2.80.** Suns to Fris, 16 Mar to 2 Nov (10.30-5). For NGS: Sat 19, Sun 20 July (10.30-5).
Rolling parkland and woods with lake. Rhododendrons and azaleas; fine specimen trees; small terraced Victorian garden with herbaceous borders and conservatory. Walled garden nearly restored, produce for sale. Regency house containing fascinating collections. Carriage collection in the stables, carriage rides.

19 July Guided walks with Head Gardener at 11 and 2; 20 July Green Garden Treasure Trail for children (11-3), 50p per chd. Gravel paths, some steep slopes.
&. ⊗ ☕

6 NEW ASH HOUSE FARM
Ash TQ6 0LR. Jane & Roger Davenport. *3m W of Dartmouth. From A3122 Halwell to Dartmouth rd R just before Sportsmans Arms. Follow yellow NGS signs for approx 2m. Parking on L, 300metres beyond Ash Tree Farm.* Cream teas. **Adm £4, chd free.** Suns 11 May; 8 June (2-5).
An interesting series of small gardens set within 10 acres of farmland. Formal garden areas around house mix with wild flower orchard centred about a stone circle. Walks lead to newly-planted arboretum and wetland bog area; reservoir, secluded decking area and copse. Varied collection of sculptures, unusual planting schemes and farm animals.
✗ ⊗ ☕

7 NEW ASHCOMBE ROAD GARDENS
nr Dawlish EX7 0QW. *2m NW of Dawlish. From Dawlish, follow Weech Rd to T-junction, R into Ashcombe Rd, gardens on L after 1½ m. Limited parking at each garden.* Teas. **Combined adm £3.50, chd free.** Visitors welcome by appt every Thursday from 29 May to 31 July.
Adjacent established gardens in Ashcombe Valley, both bordering the 'Dawlish Water'. Exploiting the microclimate of the valley floor. Both gardens encourage and support wildlife.
☕ ☎

NEW APPLE TREE COTTAGE
Mr & Mrs D Stephenson, 01626 895024, david@stephend.f9.co.uk. Visitors welcome by appt every Thursday from 29 May to 31 July.
SW-facing sloping site, abundantly planted. Herbaceous and mixed borders, ponds, bog garden, gazebo, decorative vegetable and fruit garden, greenhouse. Unfenced stream and pond.
⊗ ☎

NEW ARCADIA
Ric & Jo Gibson, 01626 862102. Visitors welcome by appt every Thursday from 29 May to 31 July.

1 acre packed full of interesting and unusual plants. Pond and bog garden, orange seaside garden, purple border, foliage garden, swings and 'Nessie'! Abundant fruit and vegetable garden. Herb bank. Unfenced pond and stream.

8 BARLEYCOTT
Blakewell EX31 4ES. Les & Barbara Shapland, 01271 375002, lb.shapland@onetel.net. *2m N of Barnstaple. ½ m past hospital off B3230 to Ilfracombe at Blakewell Fisheries. Follow signs to Barleycott.* Cream teas May, June, July, teas Sept. **Adm £2.50, chd free. Suns 4 May; 15 June; 6 July; 14 Sept (11-5). Visitors also welcome by appt.**
3-acre, S sloping garden started in 1989 set in beautiful countryside. Unusual trees, conifers and shrubs. Lavender walk, vegetable plot, orchard and pond. Lime tree avenue leading to folly and secret Japanese-style garden. Lower garden, rockpool, with large waterfall. Gravel paths, steep slopes.

9 BICKHAM HOUSE
Kenn EX6 7XL. John & Julia Tremlett, 01392 832671, jandjtremlett@hotmail.com. *6m S of Exeter. 1m off A38. Leave A38 at Kennford Services, follow signs to Kenn. 1st R in village, follow lane for ¾ m to end of no-through rd.* Cream teas. **Adm £3.50, chd free. Suns, Tues, Weds (2pm-5pm) 13, 15, 16 Apr; 11, 13, 14 May; 8, 10, 11 June; 13, 15, 16 July; 10, 12, 13 August. Visitors also welcome by appt.**
7 acres in secluded wooded valley; lawns, mature trees and shrubs, naturalised bulbs, mixed borders with unusual perennials, wild flower banks for butterflies. Edwardian conservatory, small formal parterre with lily pond; 1-acre walled kitchen garden with profusion of vegetables, fruit and flowers, palm tree avenue leading to Millennium summerhouse. Lakeside walk. Featured in 'GGG'.

10 NEW BIDEFORD EAST GARDENS
East Bideford EX39 4BW. *For Cherry Trees, from Bideford old bridge follow up hill past Royal Hotel on L. Follow signs to Pollyfield Centre to park. For Stone Farm follow signs to Alverdiscott Rd Industrial Estate, go straight across roundabout and follow Alverdiscott Rd for approx 1m.* Home-made teas at Stone Farm. **Combined adm £3.50, chd free. Suns 25 May; 29 June; 24 Aug (2-5).**

NEW CHERRY TREES WILDLIFE GARDEN
5 Sentry Corner, East The Water. Henry and Evelyn Butterfield
Small demonstration garden showing what can be done to bring wildlife into the town. Incl courtyard garden, summer cornfield, summer wildflower meadow, cottage garden border, woodland edge and ponds. Owners available for advice on wildlife gardening. Seeds for sale. Featured on BBC2 Open Gardens and in 'North Devon Journal'.

NEW STONE FARM
Alverdiscott Rd. Mr & Mrs Ray Auvray
1-acre garden in development in delightful rural setting. Vegetable garden with herbs and soft fruit, traditional orchard, white garden, striking herbaceous borders, bushes and trees. Woodland walk in bluebell woods. Some gravel paths but access to whole garden with some help.

11 ◆ BLACKPOOL GARDENS
Dartmouth TQ6 0RG. Sir Geoffrey Newman, 01803 770606, beach@blackpoolsands.co.uk. *3m SW of Dartmouth. From Dartmouth follow brown signs to Blackpool Sands on A379. Entrance to gardens via Blackpool Sands car park.* **Adm £2.50, chd free. Daily Apr to Sept (10-4).**
Tenderly restored C19 subtropical plantsman's garden with collection of mature and newly-planted tender and unusual trees, shrubs and carpet of spring flowers. Paths and steps lead gradually uphill to the Captain's seat

and spectacular coastal views. Recent plantings follow the S hemisphere theme with callistemons, pittosporums, acacias and buddlejas. Featured on BBC TV Countryfile.

> Mixed borders with unusual perennials, wild flower banks for butterflies . . .

12 BOCOMBE MILL COTTAGE
Bocombe EX39 5PH. Mr Chris Butler & Mr David Burrows, 01237 451293, www.bocombe.co.uk. *6m E of Clovelly, 9m SW of Bideford. From A39 just outside Horns Cross village, turn to Foxdown. At Xrds take lane signed Bocombe. At T-junction turn R. 100yds on R.* **Adm £3, chd £1. Thurs 24 Apr; Thurs, Fris, Sats 29, 30, 31 May; 26, 27, 28 June; 24, 25, 26 July; Thur 28 Aug (11-4). Visitors also welcome by appt May to Aug, groups of 10+.**
5 acres of gardens and wild meadow in small wooded valley, a wildlife haven. Many flower gardens, 3 newly-developed. Streams, bog gardens and small lakes. Kitchen garden, orchard, soft fruit garden, shrubbery. All grown organically. Goats on hillside. Plan and tree guide. Circular walk (boots or wellies needed) of just under 1m. Many steps, some steep slopes.

BOSCASTLE GARDENS
See Cornwall.

13 BOVEY TRACEY GARDENS
TQ13 9NA. *6m N of Newton Abbot. Gateway to Dartmoor. Take A382 to Bovey Tracey. Car parking available at Mary St, Station Rd, library car parks and at Whitstone.* Home-made teas at Hilary House. **Combined adm £3.50, chd free. Sat 31 May; Sun 1 June (2-6).**

DOWN PARK
Shewte Cross. Susan Macready. *1m from Fire Station roundabout on Manaton Rd. Parking available*
Well-maintained, colourful, mature garden. Great variety of rhododendrons, azaleas, camellias and unusual shrubs. Formal pond and alpine garden.
&. ✕

HILARY HOUSE
Ashburton Road. Alison & Stephen Arnold. *Past Brimley PO*
Mature garden presently undergoing a makeover. Incl modest kitchen garden, new orchard, herbaceous borders and natural woodland fronting onto small lake with pocket areas to enjoy different vistas at all times of day. Gravel paths, sloping lawn, unfenced lake.
&.

OLD WHITSTONE
Jinny & Richard Aldridge. *Park in Whitstone Quarry*
Come and see our old farmhouse garden undergoing renovation and enjoy the views to Haytor. Steps and gates divide herbaceous borders and small, steep wooded orchard. Visit also a meadow opposite with trees and ponds. Featured on ITV Gorgeous Gardens.
❀

PARKE VIEW
Fore Street. Peter & Judy Hall. *Next to The Old Cottage tea shop*
1-acre garden developed over 13 yrs, design largely dictated by old stone walls and outbuildings. Some unusual plants, wide selection of roses, shrubs and flowers. Some gravel paths.
&. ✕ ❀

NEW 15 STORRS CLOSE
Bob & Pauline Arnold. *From Crokers Meadow follow signs to Storrs Close or park in library car park, walk down Cromwell's Way to end, down steps to Bullen's Meadow, follow hedge to bottom garden entrance*
Small garden designed and built by present owners in past 4yrs. Very easily maintained with paving and chippings. Tiny but productive vegetable plot, raspberry canes, fruit trees, herb bed, colourful flower beds and

containers. Planted fish pond with water feature, attracting abundance of wild life. Stage decking overlooks garden.
✕

NEW WHITSTONE HOUSE
Laura Barclay. *Park in Whitstone Quarry at top of Whitstone Lane*
Mature garden with rhododendrons and azaleas. Glorious views of Dartmoor and Bovey valley. Woodland walk. Part of prize-winning vineyard also on view.

YONDER
Whitstone Lane, Moretonhampstead Rd. Mr & Mrs John Awcock
Mature cottage garden. Restoration in progress. Many varieties of acer and clematis. Interesting new plantings.
✕ ❀

Sensory garden with meandering paths . . . seaside/spiritual feel . . .

⑭ BRAMBLE HAYES
Yawl Hill Lane, Uplyme DT7 3RP. Martin & Celia Young, 01297 443084, martin@sittingspiritually.co.uk. *3m E of Axminster. From E A35, 100metres E of Devon sign, L into Red Lane, over 2 Xrds into Yawl Hill Lane, garden 0.8m on R. From W A35 through Raymonds Hill, R into Red Lane then as above. From Lyme Regis, B3165 through Uplyme/Yawl to Yawl Hill Lane.* Home-made teas. **Adm £3, chd free. Sats, Suns, Mons 21, 22, 23 June; 9, 10, 11 Aug (11-5). Visitors also welcome by appt.**
¹/₃ acre. Sensory garden with meandering paths. Seats for enjoying the vistas and plant combinations. Herbaceous perennials balance Feng Shui colour, texture and form. The seaside/spiritual feel within the garden and wooded backdrop provide perfect setting for sitting and contemplating. Wonderful lawn. Displays by local artist and swing seats made by garden owner. Featured on BBC2 Open Gardens.
☕ ☎

⑮ ◆ BURROW FARM GARDENS
Dalwood EX13 7ET. Mary & John Benger, 01404 831285, www.burrowfarmgardens.co.uk. *3¹/₂ m W of Axminster. From A35 turn N at Taunton Xrds then follow brown signs.* **Adm £4, chd 50p. Daily 1 Apr to 31 Oct (10-7).**
Secluded 10-acre garden of informal design with many unusual shrubs and herbaceous plants. Pergola walk with shrub roses. Woodland with rhododendrons and azaleas, ponds and large bog garden. Terraced courtyard featuring later flowering plants. Rill garden with water feature; traditional stone summerhouse and informal planting all with wonderful views. Partial wheelchair access.
&. ❀ ☕

⑯ CADHAY
Ottery St Mary EX11 1QT. Rupert Thistlethwayte. *1m NW of Ottery St Mary. On B3176.* **Adm £2, chd free. Mon 26 May; Fris 20 June; 18 July (2-4.30).**
Tranquil 2-acre garden in lovely setting between the Elizabethan Manor house (open) and ancient stew ponds. Carefully planned double herbaceous borders particularly colourful in summer. Small part-walled water garden, roses, lilies and clematis. Featured in 'Devon Life'.
&. ✕ ❀

⑰ ◆ CASTLE DROGO
Drewsteignton EX6 6PB. The National Trust, 01647 434135. *12m W of Exeter. 5m S of A30. Follow brown signs.* **House and Garden Adm £7.80, chd £3.90, Garden only Adm £5, chd £2.75. Apr to Oct (10.30-5.30). For NGS: Sats 19 July; 27 Sept (10.30-5.30).**
Medium-sized Grade II* listed garden with formal structures designed by George Dillistone during the late 1920s. These consist of formal rose beds, herbaceous borders and circular croquet lawn surrounded by mature yew hedges. Rhododendron garden overlooks spectacular views of Teign valley gorge and Dartmoor. 27 Sept - seed giveaway event.
&. ✕ ❀

⑱ ◆ CASTLE HILL
Filleigh EX32 0RQ. The Earl & Countess of Arran, 01598 760336 ext 1, office@castlehill-devon.com. *4m W of South Molton. From A361 Tiverton to Barnstaple leave at roundabout on B3226 signed Filleigh.*

Teas Suns/Bank Hols May to Aug; lunches and teas available for groups if ordered in advance. **Adm £4, chd free. Daily except Sats 21 Mar to 30 Sept (11-5). For NGS: Suns 20 Apr; 18 May (11-5).**
Palladian house in extensive C18 Grade I landscape park and garden. Arboretum and woodlands with camellias, rhododendrons, magnolias, azaleas and other shrubs and rare trees in abundance. Summer millenium garden designed by Xa Tollemache with topiary water sculpture by Giles Rayner. Many C18 follies and a 1730 castle on the hill with magnificent views to Exmoor, Dartmoor and Lundy Island. Featured in 'Country Life', 'Telegraph' and 'English Garden'.
☕

19 CHAPEL FARM HOUSE
Halwill Junction, Beaworthy EX21 5UF. Robin & Toshie Hull, 01409 221594. *12m NW of Okehampton. On A3079. At W end of village.* **Adm £2.50, chd free. Sats 15 Mar; 19 Apr; 10 May; 21 June; 19 July; 16 Aug; 20 Sept (11-5). Visitors also welcome by appt.**
Approx 1/2 -acre garden started in 1992 by present owners, landscaped with shrub borders, heathers, rhododendrons and azaleas. Alpine bed. Kitchen garden. 2 small greenhouses for mixed use. Small bonsai collection. 3 acres of mixed young woodland added in 1995 with wildlife and flowers.
♿ ✗ ❀ ☎

One of only two NCCPG oak collections situated in 12 hectares of parkland and comprising over 200 different species . . .

20 CHERUBEER GARDENS
Dolton EX19 8PP. *8m SE of Great Torrington. 2m E of Dolton. From A3124 turn S towards Stafford Moor Fisheries, take 1st R, gardens 500m on L. Light refreshments & teas at Higher Cherubeer.* **Combined adm £3 Feb 2008, £3.50 thereafter, chd free.** Suns 3, 10 Feb (1-5); 8 June; 28 Sept (2-6); 1, 8 Feb 2009 (1-5).
☕

CHERUBEER
Janet Brown
Cottage garden set around a C15 thatched house (not open). Garden divided into compartments with ponds, paths, and steps filled with colourful perennials and herbs set off by mature shrubs and trees.
✗

HIGHER CHERUBEER
Jo & Tom Hynes, 01805 804265, hynesjo@gmail.com. Visitors also welcome by appt.
1-acre country garden with gravelled courtyard, raised beds and alpine house, lawns, large herbaceous border, shady woodland beds, large kitchen garden, greenhouse, colourful collection of basketry willows. Winter opening for National Collection of hardy cyclamen, snowdrop varieties and hellebores. Featured on BBC2 Open Gardens. Partial wheelchair access if accompanied. Gravel paths, slopes and steps.
♿ ✗ ❀ **NCCPG** ☎

MIDDLE CHERUBEER
Heather Hynes
Colourful small garden. Three separate areas with bog garden, pond and massed herbaceous perennials interlinked with paths. Many cyclamen and snowdrop bank.
♿ ✗

21 CHEVITHORNE BARTON
Tiverton EX16 7QB. Michael & Arabella Heathcoat Amory. *3m NE of Tiverton. M5, J27, leave A361 by first exit after 300 yards, through Sampford Peverell and Halberton towards Tiverton. Immed past golf course, R then R at next T-junction. Over bridge, L through Craze Lowman, carry on through lanes to T-junction, R then 1st L. Home-made teas.* **Adm £3, chd free. Suns 27 Apr; 18 May (2-5.30).**
Terraced walled garden, summer

borders and romantic woodland of rare trees and shrubs. In spring, garden features large collection of magnolias, camellias, rhododendrons and azaleas. Also incl one of only two NCCPG oak collections situated in 12 hectares of parkland and comprising over 200 different species.
NCCPG ☕

CHIDEOCK MANOR
See Dorset.

22 THE CIDER HOUSE
Buckland Abbey, Yelverton PL20 6EZ. Mr & Mrs M J Stone, 01822 853285. *8m N of Plymouth. From A386 Plymouth to Tavistock rd, follow NT signs to Buckland Abbey. At Xrds before Abbey entrance turn N signed Buckland Monachorum. Drive 200yds on L, or short walk for visitors to Abbey. Lunch & cream teas 28 June, cream teas other days.* **Adm £3, chd free. Sun 11 May (2-6); Sat 28 June (11-5); Sun 7 Sept (2-6). Also open Wildside 28 June. Visitors also welcome by appt.**
3 acres in peaceful surroundings looking down to Tavy valley. Terrace gardens complement the medieval house (not open), herb garden, woodland and herbaceous borders, wild garden with rhododendrons, camellias and other shrubs. Former walled kitchen garden productively maintained to give abundance of fruit, vegetables and flowers.
✗ ❀ 🛏 ☕ ☎

23 CLEAVE HOUSE
Sticklepath EX20 2NL. Ann & Roger Bowden, 01837 840481, bowdens2@eclipse.co.uk, www.hostas-uk.com. *3 1/2 m E of Okehampton. On old A30 towards Exeter. Cleave House on L in village, on main rd just past R turn for Skaigh.* **Adm £2, chd free (share to NCCPG). Sats, Suns 21, 22, 28, 29 June (10.30-5). Visitors also welcome by appt.**
1/2 -acre garden with mixed planting for all season interest. National Collection of hostas with 1000 varieties. Some soft grass areas.
♿ ✗ ❀ **NCCPG** ☎

24 CLIFFE
Lee, Ilfracombe EX34 8LR. Dr & Mrs Humphreys. *3m W of Ilfracombe. Garden is past sea front at Lee, 150yds up coast rd, through wrought iron gates on L. Lee Bay car park 260yds (no parking on approach rd).*

Adm £2, chd free. Daily 21 Mar to 30 Sept incl (9-5).
Cliffside garden with spectacular coastal scenery. Mixture of planting incl shade and woodland. Camellias, daffodils and azaleas in spring. Always something to see. Mixed herbaceous borders. National collections of *Heuchera* and *Schizostylis*.

25 ◆ COLETON FISHACRE
nr Kingswear TQ6 0EQ. The National Trust, 01803 752466, www.nationaltrust.org.uk. *3m E of Dartmouth. Lower Ferry Rd. Follow brown signs. Lane leading to Coleton Fishacre is narrow and can be busy on fine days. Use of passing places and reversing may be necessary. Coach parties must book.* **House and garden adm £6.60, chd £3.30, garden only adm £6.10, chd £3.10. Weds to Suns 15 Mar to 2 Nov, Mons also 21 July to 31 Aug (10.30-5). For NGS: Sun 27 Apr; Sat 19 July (10.30-5).**
30-acre garden created by Rupert and Lady Dorothy D'Oyly Carte between 1925 and 1948. Re-established and developed by NT since 1983. Wide range of tender and uncommon trees and shrubs in spectacular coastal setting.

26 COLLEPARDO
3 Keyberry Park, Newton Abbot TQ12 1BZ. Betty & Don Frampton, www.sdmha.co.uk/frampton. *Take A380 for Newton Abbot. From Penn Inn roundabout follow sign for town centre. Take 1st L, 1st R, 2nd L.* Home-made teas. **Adm £2.50, chd free. Daily Sat 21 June to Sun 29 June (11-5).**
1/3-acre lawn-free garden laid out in series of interlinked colour-themed smaller areas. Incl 400 metres of meandering gravel pathways, circular rockery of 20 metres, herbaceous borders, pond, walkway, gazebo and over 1,500 different varieties of plants, shrubs and trees. Featured in 'Alan Titchmarsh Garden Calendar.'

27 COMBPYNE MANOR
EX13 8SX. Nicky & Donald Campbell. *4m W of Lyme Regis. From Rousdon (A3052) follow sign to Combpyne.* Cream teas. **Adm £2.50, chd free. Sat 14, Sun 15 Jun; Fri 4, Sat 5, Sun 6 Jul; Sat 9, Sun 10 Aug (11-5).**
3 1/2 acres of mature gardens geared to conservation and wildlife. Unusual

planting within medieval walls for yr-round interest. Large organic vegetable plot. 'Wild' garden with contoured paths managed to reduce fertility and create spectacular flower-rich slopes. Native woodland area. Wonderful views. Featured in 'Beautiful Britain' and 'Country Living'.

28 ◆ COMPTON CASTLE
Marldon, Paignton TQ3 1TA. The National Trust, 01803 843235, www.nationaltrust.org.uk. *3m W of Torquay. 1 1/2 m N of Marldon. From Newton Abbot - Totnes rd A381 turn L at Ipplepen Xrds & W off Torbay Ring Rd via Marldon.* **Adm £4, chd £2. Mons, Weds, Thurs, Apr to Oct (11-5). For NGS: Wed 25 June (11-5).**
Small formal courtyard gardens, rose garden, herb garden. Access to the usually private fruit and vegetable garden. Incl access to fortified Manor House with restored medieval great hall.

29 NEW COOMBE SCULPTURE GARDEN
Bradstone Coombe. PL19 0QS. Gary & Kay Vanstone. *9m W of Tavistock. On B3362 Tavistock to Launceston rd, garden signed.* Home-made teas Mar, light refreshments and teas June. **Adm £3, chd free (share to Childrens Hospice SW). Sats, Suns 15, 16 Mar (1-5). Adm £4, chd free 21, 22 June (11-5).**
2-acre S-sloping garden around C17 farmhouse in secluded wooded valley. Variety of garden habitats preserving ancient features with an emphasis on providing for wildlife. Planted with hellebores and bulbs incl magnolia campbellii to give interest in Mar. Unusual trees, shrubs and herbaceous plants for all-yr colour. Tamar valley fruit orchard, organic vegetable garden. Spring-fed streams, pools and mill pond. Some sculptures on view Mar, full exhibition June. Limited wheelchair access, steps but alternative access via slopes, some fairly steep.

COOMBEGATE COTTAGE
See Cornwall.

COTHAY MANOR GARDENS
See Somerset & Bristol Area.

30 THE CROFT
Yarnscombe EX31 3LW. Sam & Margaret Jewell, 01769 560535. *4m NE of Torrington, 8m S of Barnstaple. From A377, turn W opp Chapelton railway stn. After 3m drive on L at village sign. From B3232, 1/4 m N of Hunshaw TV mast Xrds, turn E for 2m. Parking in village hall car park nearby.* **Adm £3, chd free (share to N Devon Animal Ambulance). Suns 15 June; 20 July; 17 Aug (2-6). Visitors also welcome by appt.**
1-acre plantswoman's garden featuring exotic Japanese garden with tea house, koi carp pond and cascading stream, tropical garden with exotic shrubs and perennials. Herbaceous borders with unusual plants and shrubs. Bog garden with collection of irises, astilbes and moisture-loving plants, duck pond. New colour-coordinated beds for 2008. Featured in 'Devon Life'.

Habitats preserving ancient features with an emphasis on providing for wildlife . . .

31 ◆ DARTINGTON HALL GARDENS
Dartington TQ9 6EL. Dartington Hall Trust, 01803 862367, gardens@dartingtonhall.org.uk. *1 1/2 m NW of Totnes. From Totnes take A384, turn R at Dartington Parish Church. Proceed up hill for 1m. Hall & gardens on R. Car parking on L.* **Adm £3, chd free. For NGS: Sun 8 June (dawn to dusk).**
28-acre modern garden, created since 1925 around C14 medieval hall (not open). Courtyard and tournament ground. Dry landscape Japanese garden. Extensive wild flower meadows and mixed shrub and herbaceous border. Peter Randall-Page sculpture. Guided tour available at 2.30pm, £5, proceeds to NGS. Partial wheelchair access; please ask for advice or assistance.

32 DICOT
Chardstock EX13 7DF. Mr & Mrs F
Clarkson, 01460 220364,
www.dicot.co.uk. *5m N of Axminster.
Axminster to Chard A358 at Tytherleigh
to Chardstock. R at George Inn, L fork
to Hook, R to Burridge, 2nd house on
L.* Home-made teas. **Adm £2.50, chd
free. Sats, Suns 3, 4 May; 14, 15
June; 26, 27 July (2-5.30). Visitors
also welcome by appt.**
3-acre enthusiasts' garden; trees,
unusual shrubs and conifers, bog
orchids in June. Stream, mixed
borders, fish pool, Japanese garden,
and other surprises.

33 DIPPERS
Shaugh Prior PL7 5HA. Mr R J
Hubble & Mrs S M Tracey. *8m NE of
Plymouth. Garden 100yds down lane
opp church near top of village. Park in
village. No parking in lane but dropping
off point for disabled.* **Adm £2.50, chd
free. Suns 23 Mar; 20 Apr (1-5).**
³/₄ -acre eco-friendly plantsman's
garden containing around 2500
different plants. Emphasis on foliage
contrast and all-yr interest. Large
colour range of hellebores, extensive
collection of dwarf bulbs and alpines in
raised beds, troughs, tufa and alpine
house. Unusual trees and shrubs.
National Collection of dianthus species
(pinks).

NCCPG

34 THE DOWNES
Bideford EX39 5LB. Mr & Mrs R C
Stanley-Baker, 01805 622244. *3m
NW of Great Torrington. On A386
between Bideford & Torrington. Drive
leads off A386 4¹/₂ m from Bideford,
2¹/₂ m from Torrington. Do not go to
Monkleigh.* **Adm £3, chd free. Daily
Fri 21 Mar to Mon 2 June (12-5).
Visitors also welcome by appt.**
15 acres with landscaped lawns; fine
views overlooking fields and
woodlands in Torridge Valley; many
unusual trees and shrubs; small
arboretum; woodland walks, bluebells.

35 DURCOMBE WATER
Furzehill, Barbrook, Lynton
EX35 6LN. Pam & David Sydenham,
01598 753658. *3m S of Lynton. From
Barnstaple take A39 towards Lynton.
On entering Barbrook go past Total
garage (do not turn to Lynton) take the
next turn R (about 100yds). Follow this
single track rd for 2m, gates on L.*
Home-made teas. **Adm £3, chd free.**

**Sun 25, Mon 26 May (11-5). Visitors
also welcome by appt.**
Set in Exmoor National Park beside
open moorland with superb views,
delightfully secluded steeply-terraced
garden providing profusion of yr-round
colour. Includes conifers, heathers and
many old-fashioned annuals and
perennials. The garden offers peace
and tranquillity enhanced by spring-fed
streams and ponds, and waterfalls
dropping 40ft via 8 tiered ponds. Fruit
and vegetable garden. Many unusual
features. Large extension in progress
(2¹/₂ acres total garden) with ponds,
waterfalls, landscaping and small
woodland.

Peace and
tranquillity . . .
spring-fed
streams and
ponds,
waterfalls
dropping 40ft . . .

**36 NEW EAST
CORNWORTHY GARDENS**
TQ9 7HQ. *1m W of Dittisham.
B3122 from Dartmouth, turn at
Sportsmans Arms for Dittisham.
Keep L in village for E Cornworthy.*
Home-made teas at Brook.
**Combined adm £3.50, chd free.
Sun 22, Mon 23 June (2-5).**
East Cornworthy is a pretty hamlet
set in glorious countryside, 1m
from R Dart.

NEW BLACK NESS HOUSE
Tim & Lesley Taylor. *From
Dittisham, last house on R before
rd turns L and up hill*
Approx ¹/₂ acre with wonderful
views. Steps down to different
levels and areas. Walled gardens,
one Mediterranean themed with
agaves, olive trees, cypresses,
lavender and myrtle. Colour-
themed beds and borders, gravel
paths.

NEW BROOK
Peter & Bee Smyth. *From
Dittisham, 1st house on L on
bridge. From Cornworthy, last
house on R*
Particularly interesting mature
trees and shrubs. All yr flowering
such as embothrium, eucryphia,
drimys and large hoheria. Front
garden has splendid colourful
herbaceous beds each side of
path to front door. Large pond at
end of garden.

37 FEEBERS GARDENS
nr Broadclyst EX5 3DQ. *8m NE of
Exeter. From B3181 Exeter to Taunton
bear E at Dog Village to Whimple. After
1¹/₂ m fork L for Westwood.* Cream
teas. **Combined adm £3, chd free.
Suns 18 May; 22 June; 20 July; 24
Aug (2-6).**
3 cottage gardens in a Devon
hamlet.

1 FEEBERS COTTAGE
Mr & Mrs M J Squires
Evolving cottage garden of 1 acre
- a maze of pathways,
herbaceous, shrubs and trees. In
spring, 60 different snowdrops; in
autumn, colchicums and
cyclamen.

2 FEEBERS COTTAGE
Bob & Ena Williams
Colourful, formal garden, set
between 2 cottage gardens.
Delightful flower beds, small alpine
house and gravel area with variety
of potted shrubs and plants. Not a
weed to be seen.

3 FEEBERS COTTAGE
Richard & Karen Burrell
Contemporary cottage garden
with formal vegetable area,
established fruit trees, flower beds
and rose arbour. Some quirky
features incl BBQ house and a
mini petanque area within 'a
secret garden'. Numerous
places to sit and enjoy a cream
tea.

FERNHILL
See Somerset & Bristol Area.

FORDE ABBEY GARDENS
Chard. See Dorset.

A benign microclimate which allows many rare and tender plants to grow and thrive . . .

38 ◆ THE GARDEN HOUSE
Buckland Monachorum, Yelverton PL20 7LQ. The Fortescue Garden Trust, 01822 854769, www.thegardenhouse.org.uk. *10m N of Plymouth. Signed off A386 at Yelverton.* **Adm £5.50, chd £2, concessions £5. Open daily 23 Feb to 2 Nov (10.30-5).**
8 acres, incl romantic walled garden surrounding ruins of medieval vicarage. Other areas pioneering 'new naturalism' style, inspired by great natural landscapes. South African garden, quarry garden, cottage garden, acer glade. Stunning views and more than 6000 plant varieties. Famous for spring bulb meadow, rhododendrons, camellias, innovative planting and yr-round colour and interest. Limited wheelchair access, some steep slopes.
⬤ ✕ ⊗ ☕

39 THE GATE HOUSE
Lee EX34 8LR. Mr & Mrs D Booker, 01271 862409, booker@loveleebay.co.uk. *3m W of Ilfracombe. Park in village car park. Take lane alongside The Grampus public house. Garden is approx 30 metres past inn buildings.* **Adm by donation. Open most days throughout the yr but wise to check by phone/email. Visitors welcome by appt.**
2¼ acres, where no chemicals are used, only few minutes walk from the sea and dramatic coastal scenery. Peaceful streamside garden with range of habitats; bog garden, National Collection of Rodgersia, at their best June/July, woodland, herbaceous borders, patio gardens with semi-hardy 'exotics' and large vegetable garden. Local Arts & Crafts Exhibition and sale in Village Hall plus daily organ recitals in Village Church 1st 2 weeks Aug. Gravel paths.
⬤ ⊗ **NCCPG** ☎

40 ◆ GLEBE COTTAGE
Warkleigh EX37 9DH. Carol Klein, 01769 540554, www.glebecottageplants.co.uk. *5m SW of South Molton. On the road between Chittlehamholt and Chittlehampton - 1m from Chittlehamholt.* **Adm £3, chd free. Garden & nursery open Weds, Thurs, Fris (10-1, 2-5). For NGS: Sun 17 Feb; Wed 17 Sept (2-5).**
1-acre S-facing garden with variety of situations. In spring small woodland garden with stumpery, hellebores and pulmonarias is interesting. Terraced beds and 'brick' garden with many newly-planted areas, including hot summer and autumn flowers and foliage. Home of BBC Gardeners' World and Open Gardens presenter.
✕ ⊗

GOOSEHILL
See Somerset & Bristol Area.

41 GORWELL HOUSE
Barnstaple EX32 7JP. Dr J A Marston, 01271 323202, jamarston@lycos.co.uk. *1m E of Barnstaple centre on Bratton Fleming rd. Drive entrance between two lodges on L. Cream teas May to Sept.* **Adm £3, chd free. Suns 13 Apr; 18 May; 1 June; 20 July; 7 Sept; 5 Oct (2-6). Visitors also welcome by appt.**
Created mostly since 1979, this 4-acre garden overlooking the Taw estuary has a benign microclimate which allows many rare and tender plants to grow and thrive, both in the open and in the walled garden. Several strategically-placed follies complementing the enclosures and vistas within the garden. Some steep slopes.
⬤ ⊗ ☕ ☎

42 ◆ GREENWAY GARDEN
Galmpton nr Brixham TQ5 0ES. The National Trust, 01803 842382, www.nationaltrust.org.uk. *1½ m SE of Galmpton. A3022 towards Brixham. R turn signed Galmpton, follow brown signs for Greenway Quay. Entrance 1½ m on L. For ferry service from Dartmouth or Dittisham ring 01803 844010.* **Adm £6, chd £3, green transport users £5, chd £2.50. Wed to Sun incl, Mar to Oct (10.30-5). For NGS: Sat 29 Mar, Sun 27 Apr (10.30-5).**
Renowned for rare half-hardy plants underplanted with native wild flowers. Greenway has an atmosphere of wildness and timelessness, a true secret garden of peace and tranquillity with wonderful views of R Dart, associated with many fascinating characters.
⬤ ✕ ⊗ ☕

43 HALDON GRANGE
Dunchideock EX6 7YE. Ted Phythian, 01392 832349. *5m SW of Exeter. From A30 at Exeter pass through Ide village to Dunchideock 5m. In centre of village turn L to Lord Haldon Hotel, Haldon Grange just past hotel drive. From A38 (S) turn L on top of Haldon Hill follow Dunchideock signs, R at village centre (at thatched house) to Lord Haldon Hotel. Light refreshments & teas.* **Adm £3, chd free. Apr - Sat 26, Sun 27; May - Sat 3 to Mon 5, Weds 7, 14, 21, Sat 24, Sun 25 (1-5). Visitors also welcome by appt mid Apr to mid June.**
12-acre well-established garden with camellias, magnolias, azaleas and rhododendrons; rare and mature trees; small lake and ponds with river and water cascades as a feature.
✕ ⊗ ☕ ☎

44 HAMBLYN'S COOMBE
Dittisham TQ6 0HE. Bridget McCrum, 01803 722228, www.bridgetmccrum.com. *3m N of Dartmouth. From Red Lion Inn follow The Level until it forks & go straight up steep private rd and through 'River Farm' gate. Continue straight on to end of farm track as signed.* **Visitors welcome by appt all yr except July & Aug. No coaches.**
7-acre garden with stunning views across the river to Greenway House and sloping steeply to R Dart at bottom of garden. Extensive planting of trees and shrubs with unusual design features accompanying Bridget McCrum's stone carvings and bronzes. Wild flower meadow and woods. Good rhododendrons and camellias, ferns and bamboos, acers and hydrangeas. Exceptional autumn colour. Featured in 'Country Life' and 'English Garden'.
 ☎

HANGERIDGE FARMHOUSE
See Somerset & Bristol Area.

45 ◆ HARTLAND ABBEY
Hartland, nr Bideford EX39 6DT. Sir Hugh & Lady Stucley, 01884 860225, www.hartlandabbey.com. *15m W of Bideford, 15m N of Bude. Turn off A39 W of Clovelly Cross to Hartland. Abbey between Hartland & Hartland Quay.* **House and garden adm £9 (£6 Feb), chd £3 (free Feb), garden only adm £5 (£3 Feb), chd £1.50 (free Feb). Snowdrop Suns 10, 17 Feb (11-4); daily except Sats 21 Mar to 5 Oct (12-5).**
From snowdrop Suns (Feb), camellias and bulbs of spring to deep blue hydrangeas of late summer. Magical house and garden full of surprises. Bog garden and fernery designed by Jekyll, lost since 1914. C18 walled gardens and glasshouses thrive again growing tender and rare plants. Walk to the beach through carpets of bluebells in Apr. Peacocks, black sheep, donkeys. BBC Sense and Sensibility filmed here. Limited wheelchair access, steep paths and steps.

Informal, country feel with wild edges . . .

46 HEATHERCOMBE
Manaton TQ13 9XE. Claude & Margaret Pike Woodlands Trust, 01647 221222/01626 354404, www.heathercombe.com. *7m NW of Bovey Tracey. From Bovey Tracey take rd to Becky Falls and Manaton. Continue on same rd for 2m beyond village. At Heatree Cross follow sign straight ahead to Heathercombe. At top of hill continue straight ahead to Heathercombe. (From Widecombe take rd past Natsworthy). Cream teas.* **Adm £3, chd free. Sun 6 Apr (2-5.30); Sun 18, Sat 24, Sun 25 May; Sun 1 June (11-5.30). Visitors also welcome by appt.**

Tranquil wooded valley 1,000 feet up on Dartmoor provides setting for variety of developing garden areas extending over 30 acres, providing yr-round interest; woodland walks beside streams, ponds and lake amongst snowdrops, daffodils and bluebells; well-labelled 'parkland' plantings incl over 100 varieties of rhododendrons and 400 specimen trees, many providing autumn colour; medieval longhouse summer garden with varied rooms of herbaceous plantings; wild flower meadow in orchard of West Country fruit trees; sandy paths.

47 ◆ HEDDON HALL
Parracombe EX31 4QL. Mr & Mrs de Falbe, 01598 763541, info@heddonhallgardens.co.uk. *10m NE of Barnstaple. Follow A39 towards Lynton around Parracombe (avoiding village centre), then turn L down towards the village; entrance 200 yds on L.* **Adm £4, chd free. Suns Feb (11-4); Weds, Suns, May to July (10-5.30). For NGS: Sun 4 May; Wed 30 July (10-5.30).**
Stunning walled garden laid out by Penelope Hobhouse with clipped box and cordoned apple trees, herbaceous secret garden and natural rockery leading to a bog garden and 3 stew ponds. Very much a gardeners' garden, beautifully maintained, with many rare species, ferns, mature shrubs and trees all thriving in 4 acres of this sheltered Exmoor valley. 50% wheelchair access, some steep slopes/uneven paths.

48 NEW HIGH GARDEN
Chiverstone Lane, Kenton EX6 8NJ. Chris & Sharon Britton. *5m S of Exeter on A379 Dawlish Rd. Leaving Kenton towards Exeter, L into Chiverstone Lane, 50yds along lane. Entrance clearly marked. Home-made teas.* **Adm £2, chd free. Sat 21, Sun 22 June; Sat 12, Sun 13 July (2-6).**
Newly-planted garden adjoining plantsman's nursery (open), approx 5 acres. Mixed shrub/perennials, many unusual. 70metre double herbaceous border for all summer colour. Model fruit/vegetable garden. Tropical border.

HIGHCROFT GARDENS
See Cornwall.

49 NEW HIGHER BURNHAIES
Butterleigh, Cullompton EX15 1PG. Richard & Virginia Holmes. *3m W of Cullompton, 3m S of Tiverton. From Butterleigh, take rd to Silverton at T-junction. After 1/4 m, take unmarked L fork, continue to hamlet. Very narrow lanes. Cream teas.* **Adm £3, chd free. Suns 8, 22 June (2-6).**
2½-acre site started in 1997. Garden situated in the beautiful Burn Valley, surrounded by farmland. Plantsman's garden of herbaceous plantings with trees, shrubs and ponds. Informal, country feel with wild edges. Devon lane and wilderness walk. Vegetable garden. Uneven ground and steps, sometimes slippery. Guitar music, weather permitting.

50 HIGHER KNOWLE
Lustleigh TQ13 9SP. Mr & Mrs D R A Quicke, 01647 277275, quicke@connectfree.co.uk. *3m NW of Bovey Tracey. Take A382 towards Moretonhampstead. In 2½ m turn L for Lustleigh; in 1/4 m L then R; in 1/4 m steep drive L.* **Adm £2.50, chd free (share to Lustleigh Parish Church). Suns & Bank Hol Mons 16 Mar to 5 May incl (11-6). Visitors also welcome by appt.**
3-acre woodland garden surrounds romantic 1914 Lutyens-style house (not open) with spectacular views towards R Bovey and Dartmoor. Sheltered site provides excellent conditions for tender plants. Numerous well-rounded granite boulders add natural sculpture to old oak woodland, carpeted with primroses, bluebells and other wild flowers. Collections of camellias, magnolias, rhododendrons and other acid-loving shrubs thrive here and all are labelled. Wildlife pond with fountain adds interest to this lovely garden. Featured on BBC Spotlight. Slippery steep paths.

HIGHER TRUSCOTT
See Cornwall.

51 ◆ HOLBROOK GARDEN
Sampford Shrubs, Sampford Peverell EX16 7EN. Martin Hughes-Jones & Susan Proud, 01884 821164, www.holbrookgarden.com. *1m NW from M5 J27. From J27 follow brown signs to 'Minnows' camping site then continue 300 metres up Holbrook*

Hill (on Holcombe Rogus Rd). **Adm £3, chd free. Tues to Sats, Apr to Oct (9-5). For NGS: Sun 6 Apr; Suns, Mons 4, 5, 25, 26 May; Wed 6 Aug, Fri 19, Sat 20 Sept (10-4).**
2-acre S-facing garden with innovative plantings inspired by natural plant populations; vibrant Mediterranean colours; the garden continually evolves - many experimental plantings - wet garden, stone garden. Perfumes, songbirds and nests everywhere in spring and early summer. Fritillaries, pulmonarias April; crocosmia, National Collection of heleniums, late perennials Aug/Sept. Organic vegetable garden. Featured in 'Gardens Illustrated' and RHS 'The Garden'.
🌢 ⊛ **NCCPG**

52 HOLE FARM
nr Bickington TQ12 6PE. Rev Ian Graham-Orlebar, 01626 821298, ianorlebar@aol.com, www.holefarm.net. 5m NE of Ashburton. From A383 Ashburton to Newton Abbot rd, 3m NE of Ashburton signed Gale, Burne, Woodland. Follow signs to Farlacombe, after 2m, at top of hill, lane on R to Hole Farm. Homemade teas. **Adm £3, chd £1. Sun 27 July (2-5). Visitors also welcome by appt, no access for coaches.**
2½ -acre valley garden with woodland, wild garden, 2 ponds, 3 herbaceous borders, bog areas and wildlife plantation. Old farm and buildings, not open.
⅙ 🍵 ☎

HOOPER'S HOLDING
See Somerset & Bristol Area.

53 IDEFORD GARDENS
TQ12 3GS. 4m NNE of Newton Abbot. Between Ideford and Kingsteignton E off A380 (Newton Abbot to Exeter rd). Light refreshments & teas. **Combined adm £4, chd free (share to Ideford Millennium Green). Suns 8, 15 June (11-5).**
Both gardens are in small hamlets consisting of only a handful of houses, just 2m apart.
🍵

COOMBE FARM
Ideford Combe. Lyn and Nigel Edwards, 01626 351939, lynedwards44@hotmail.com. From Exeter S on A380, exit at Eagle Farm (signed B3195 Ideford Combe and Kingsteignton). 150yds L down 'no through rd', 1st on L. From S A380 exit at Eagle Farm (signed Kingsteignton

& Ideford Combe B3195). Follow signs to Ideford Combe. **Visitors also welcome by appt 1-15 June, special rates for groups of 10+, incl cream tea.**
Approx 1 acre, developed over past 9 yrs. Surrounded by mature trees and paddocks with views across valley. Divided into 7 distinct areas with a surprise around each corner. Herbaceous perennials, mixed beds, hedges and trees. Of special interest - many heavily-scented roses and productive kitchen garden.
🌢 ⊛ ☎

WELL COTTAGE
Olchard. **Joe & Wendy Taylor, 01626 852415.** S on A380, sharp L exit signed Olchard. Downhill, R opp postbox on pole, garden on L. N from Newton Abbot on A380, exit at Wapperwell. R under dual carriageway to T-junction. L then almost immed R into lane signed Olchard. ½ m, L opp post box, garden on L. **Visitors also welcome by appt.**
½ -acre of lawn/mixed borders on different levels. Beautifully planted with emphasis on creating a cottage garden.
🌢 ☎

INCE CASTLE
See Cornwall.

Stunning
clifftop garden
with 180°
panoramic
view of sea and
South Devon
coastline . . .

54 NEW JASON'S GARDEN
Eastcliff Walk, Teignmouth TQ14 8SZ. Jason's family. Teignmouth Seafront, L up hill past Teignmouth lido. **Adm £2, chd free. Sun 4, Mon 5 May (10-4).**
Stunning clifftop garden with 180° panoramic view of sea and S Devon coastline. Modern, stylish design with high quality landscaping and bold planting, creating areas of individuality within an harmonious whole. This tactile garden is accessible and of interest to all and its underlying ethos leaves a lasting impression. Seeing is believing. Garden is open for charity on other days with donations to NGS. Tel TIC 01626 215666. Featured on BBC2 Open Gardens.
⅙

KEN CARO
See Cornwall.

55 KERSCOTT HOUSE
Swimbridge EX32 0QA. Jessica & Peter Duncan, www.kerscottgarden.co.uk. 6m E of Barnstaple. On Barnstaple-Swimbridge-South Molton rd (not A361), 1m E of Swimbridge turn R at top of hill, immed fork L, 100yds on L, 1st gate past house. Cream teas. **Adm £2.50, chd free. Sun 29 June (2-6).**
6 acres surrounding C16 farmhouse (not open) in peaceful rural setting. Garden evolved from scratch since 1985, owner designed/maintained. Naturalistic site-generated planting flowing through vistas combining dry gravel, shady and boggy areas. Atmospheric and harmonious, with living willow constructions, woodland, ponds, wildlife meadow. Unusual plants, Mediterranean garden within roofless barn.
⅙ ⊛ 🍵

56 KIA-ORA FARM & GARDENS
Knowle Lane, Cullompton EX15 1PZ. Mrs M B Disney, 01884 32347, rosie@kiaorafarm.co.uk. 6m SE of Tiverton. J28 of M5. Straight through Cullompton town centre to roundabout, take 3rd exit into Swallow Way, follow rd through houses up to sharp R-hand bend. On bend turn L into Knowle Lane, garden beside Rugby Club. Cream teas. **Adm £2.50, chd free. Suns, Bank Hol Mons 23, 24 Mar; 6, 20 Apr; 4, 5, 18, 25, 26 May; 8,**

22 June; 6, 20 July; 3, 17, 24, 25 Aug; 7 Sept (2-6). Visitors also welcome by appt, coach access & parking, afternoon or evening, home-made cream teas, cakes & gateaux.

10 acres of extensively planted gardens and lakes. Charming, peaceful garden with lawns, large lakes, ponds, bog garden and various water features incl ducks and wildlife. Many areas with individual character, mature trees and shrubs, rhododendrons, azaleas, heathers, roses, herbaceous borders and rockeries. Several different features incl nursery avenue, wisteria walk, novelty crazy golf and many more! Surprises everywhere! Come and see what's new for 2008. Gravel entrance but mostly grass.

 ♿ ✝ ❊ ☕ ☎

57 ◆ KILLERTON GARDEN
Broadclyst EX5 3LE. The National Trust, 01392 881345, www.nationaltrust.org.uk. *8m N of Exeter. Take B3181 Exeter to Cullompton rd, after 7m fork left & follow NT signs.* **Please phone or visit website for opening times and adm prices.** For NGS: Sat 23 Feb (11-dusk); Sun 20 Apr; Sat 19 July (11-7); Sun 14 Dec (11-dusk).
20 acres of spectacular hillside gardens with naturalised bulbs, sweeping down to large open lawns. Delightful walks through fine collection of rare trees and shrubs; herbaceous borders.

 ♿ ✝ ❊

58 KINGSTON HOUSE
Staverton TQ9 6AR. Mr & Mrs M R Corfield, 01803 762235, www.kingston-estate.co.uk. *4m NE of Totnes. A384 Totnes to Buckfastleigh, from Staverton, 1m due N of Sea Trout Inn, follow signs to Kingston.* Cream teas. **Adm £3.50, chd 50p (share to Animals in Distress).** Suns 20 Apr; 11 May; 22 June (2-6). **Evening Opening** £5, wine, Sun 13 July (6-8). Visitors also welcome by appt, no coaches.
George II 1735 house Grade II (not open). Gardens restored in keeping with the period. Walled garden, rose garden, pleached limes and hornbeams, vegetable garden. Unusual formal garden with santolinas, lavender and camomile. Large formal parterre. 6000 tulips in bloom mid-May. Gravel paths.

 ♿ 🏠 ☕ ☎

59 ◆ KNIGHTSHAYES COURT GARDEN
Tiverton EX16 7RQ. The National Trust, 01884 254665, www.nationaltrust.org.uk. *2m N of Tiverton. Via A396 Tiverton to Bampton rd; turn E in Bolham, signed Knightshayes; entrance 1/2 m on L.* **House and garden adm £7.40, chd £3.70, garden only adm £5.90, chd £3. Daily 15 Mar to 2 Nov (11-5). House closed Fris.** For NGS: Suns 4 May; 14 Sept (11-5).
Large 'Garden in the Wood', 50 acres of landscaped gardens with pleasant walks and views over Exe valley. Choice collections of unusual plants, incl acers, birches, rhododendrons, azaleas, camellias, magnolias, roses, spring bulbs, alpines and herbaceous borders; formal gardens; walled kitchen garden.

 ♿ ✝ ❊

KNOWLE FARM
See Dorset.

---

60 NEW LANGTREES
10 Cott Lane, Croyde, Braunton EX33 1ND. Paul & Helena Petrides, 01271 890202, angelrest@lineone.net. *10m W of Barnstaple. From Barnstaple A361 to Braunton, L on B3231 to Croyde, past Croyde Bay Holidays on L. Cott Lane on R as rd narrows towards village centre. No parking in lane, park in village car park 200yds L by village hall.* Home-made teas. **Adm £3.50, chd free.** Suns 18 May; 15 June; 14 Sept (2-6). Visitors also welcome by appt.
1-acre plantsman's garden with eclectic selection of plants. Many S hemisphere shrubs and other tender species. Yr-round interest with landscaping and design features. Flowers all seasons from rhododendrons and magnolias in spring to salvias, cannas and ginger lilies in autumn. Interesting selection of trees.

 ✝ ❊ ☕ ☎

Golf putting course . . .

61 LEE FORD
Knowle, Budleigh Salterton EX9 7AJ. Mr & Mrs N Lindsay-Fynn, 01395 445894, crescent@leeford.co.uk. *31/2 m E of Exmouth.* Home-made teas for groups of 20+ by arrangement. **Adm £5, chd £3, groups of 20+ £4.** Visitors welcome by appt Mon to Thur (10-4) and other times by special arrangement.
Extensive, formal and woodland garden, largely developed in the 1950s, but recently much extended with mass displays of camellias, rhododendrons and azaleas, incl many rare varieties. Traditional walled garden filled with fruit and vegetables, herb garden, bog garden, rose garden, hydrangea collection, greenhouses. Ornamental conservatory and Adam pavilion.

 ♿ ☕ ☎

LIFT THE LATCH
See Somerset & Bristol Area.

62 LITTLE ASH FARM
Fenny Bridges, Honiton EX14 3BL. Sadie & Robert Reid, 01404 850271. *3m W of Honiton. Leave A30 at Iron Bridge from Honiton 1m, Patteson's Cross from Exeter 1/2 m, & follow NGS signs.* Home-made teas. **Adm £3, chd free.** Suns 22 June; 20 July; Sat 9, Sun 10 Aug (2-6). Visitors also welcome by appt, max 20 people.
Peaceful garden within 1 acre with adjoining farmland and extensive views. Immaculate lawns, new and established trees and shrubs. Three linked ponds and delightful rill through the garden. Fruit and new vegetable plot. Golf putting course. Furniture workshop and showroom. Entry across cobbled yard or gravel drive.

 ♿ ✝ 🏠 ☕ ☎

63 LITTLE CUMBRE
145 Pennsylvania Road, Exeter EX4 6DZ. Dr Margaret Lloyd, 01392 258315. *1m due N of city centre. From town centre take Longbrook St, continue N up hill approx 1m. Near top of hill.* **Adm £3, chd free.** Suns 3, 10, 17, 24 Feb 2008; Suns 1, 8, 15, 22 Feb 2009 (12-3.30). Visitors also welcome by appt Feb to June.
1-acre garden and woodland on S-facing slope with extensive views. Interesting areas of garden on different levels linked by grassy paths. Wonderful display of snowdrops, many

varieties, and colourful hellebores. Scented winter shrubs and camellias, spring bulbs. Featured in 'Devon Life'. Limited wheelchair access.

🚻 ✕ ⊕ ☎

64 LITTLECOURT COTTAGES
Seafield Road, Sidmouth EX10 8HF. Geoffrey Ward & Selwyn Kussman. *500yds N of Sidmouth seafront. From N take B3176 to Sidmouth seafront/Bedford Car Park. Take Station Rd, past Manor Rd and immed up Seafield Rd. Garden 100yds on R. Regret no parking at garden, car parks nearby. Home-made teas.* **Adm £3, chd free. Suns, Mons 22, 23 June; 27, 28 July (2-5.30).**
Oasis of calm in middle of Sidmouth. A series of rooms for the plantaholic. Courtyard gardens behind house; in front, main lawn and water feature. Rare and tender plants everywhere. Exceptional basket colour.

✕ ☕

This quirky garden has been planted for year-round interest . . .

65 LITTLEHAM HOUSE COTTAGE
11 Douglas Avenue, Exmouth EX8 2EY. Pat & Phil Attard, 01395 266750. *1/4 m from Exmouth seafront. Go E along seafront, turn L into Maer Rd by Fortes Kiosk, L again. Public car park on R. Short 250yd walk to garden. A little unrestricted parking in Douglas Ave. Home-made teas.* **Adm £2.50, chd free. Suns 23, 30 Mar (2-5.30). Visitors also welcome by appt.**
This secret garden is full of colour, foliage and flair. Winding paths lead you to horticultural surprises round every corner; spring bulbs, camellias and other treasures abound in this cottage garden. Organically-grown vegetables, herbs and a variety of fruit trees - something for everyone. Featured on BBC2 Open Gardens. Limited wheelchair access. Some very narrow gravel paths but main garden access mostly easy.

🚻 ⊕ ☕ ☎

66 NEW THE LOOKOUT
Sowden Lane, Lympstone EX8 5HE. Will & Jackie Michelmore. *9m SE of Exeter, 2m N of Exmouth. A376 to Exmouth. 1st R after Marine Camp signed Lower Lympstone, 1st R in village in The Strand, past Londis shop, village car park next L (please use as ltd parking). Follow rd out of village, 8min walk, R just before railway bridge, or stroll along beach from car park at low tide. New cycle park - unlimited bike parking. Light refreshments & teas.* **Adm £2.50, chd free. Fri 27 (2-5), Sun 29 June (2-6).**
2 wildlife-friendly acres on edge of Exe Estuary. Created from derelict site over last 5yrs by garden designer owner to harmonise with coast and countryside location and maximise on views. Flotsum and jetsum finds amongst naturalistic-style seaside planting. Walled garden, small jungly area, short circular walk through wild flower meadow to pond (unfenced), copse and river bank. Numerous places to stop and enjoy stunning views and sea air. Featured on BBC2 Open Gardens. Unsuitable for disabled, steep paths, gravel, steps.

✕ ⊕ ☕

67 ◆ LUKESLAND
Harford, Ivybridge PL21 0JF. Mrs R Howell & Mr & Mrs J Howell, 01752 691749/893390, www.lukesland.co.uk. *10m E of Plymouth. Turn off A38 at Ivybridge. 1 1/2 m N on Harford rd, E side of Erme valley.* **Adm £4, chd free, groups of 20+ £3.50. Suns, Weds & Bank Hols, 23 Mar to 15 June (2-6); Suns, Weds 12 Oct to 9 Nov (11-4). Also all Sats in May.**
24 acres of flowering shrubs, wild flowers and rare trees with pinetum in Dartmoor National Park. Beautiful setting of small valley around Addicombe Brook with lakes, numerous waterfalls and pools. Extensive and unusual collection of rhododendrons, a champion *Magnolia campbellii* and a huge *Davidia involucrata*. Superb spring and autumn colour. New Children's Trail for spring and autumn each yr. Other events advertised on website. Featured in local and National press and on BBC Spotlight; RHS award for rhododendrons and camellias.

68 ◆ MARWOOD HILL
Marwood EX31 4EB. Dr J A Snowdon, 01271 342528, www.marwoodhillgarden.co.uk. *4m N of Barnstaple. Signed from A361 & B3230. Outside Guineaford village, opp Marwood church. See website for map.* **Adm £4.50, chd free, £4 for groups. Gardens open Mar to Oct. For NGS: Fris 18 Apr; 5 Sept (9.30-5.30). Tea room and plant sales (11-5).**
20 acres with 3 small lakes. Extensive collection of camellias under glass and in open; daffodils, rhododendrons, rare flowering shrubs, rock and alpine scree; waterside planting; bog garden; many clematis; Australian native plants and many eucalyptus. National Collections of astilbe, *Iris ensata*, tulbaghia. Silver medal winner Devon County Show. Steep slopes, gravel paths.

🚻 ⊕ NCCPG ☕

MELPLASH COURT
See Dorset.

69 NEW MEMBURY GARDENS
Membury EX13 7AJ. *4m NW of Axminster.* **Combined adm £3.50, chd free. Sat 31 May; Sun 1 June; Sat 12, Sun 13 July (11-5).**
Two artistic gardens in pretty village, situated on edge of Blackdown Hills.

NEW CLEAVE HILL
Mr & Mrs A Pritchard. *From Membury Village, follow rd down valley. 1st R after Lea Hill B&B, last house on drive, approx 1m* Cottage-style garden, artistically planted to provide all-season structure, texture and colour. Designed around pretty thatched house and old stone barn. Wonderful views, attractive vegetable garden and orchard, wild flower meadow.

🚻

NEW SIXPENNY MOON
Lindsay & Ian Withycombe, 01404 881625. *In centre of village nr church. Park opp Village Hall. 2nd gate on R. Visitors also welcome by appt.*
Small walled garden, big on plants and naturally dividing into different areas. This quirky garden has been planted for yr-round interest with emphasis on foliage, colour and form, structural planting and sculpture.

⊕ ☎

Superb views of Taw Estuary . . .

⑦⓪ MORETONHAMPSTEAD GARDENS
TQ13 8PW. *12m W of Exeter & N of Newton Abbot. On E slopes of Dartmoor National Park. Parking at both gardens.* Cream teas. **Combined adm £3.50, chd free. Sat 24, Sun 25, Mon 26 May; Sat 26, Sun 27 July (2-6).**
Two complementary gardens of differing character in the geographical centre of Devon, close to the edge of Dartmoor. Superb walking country. Dogs on leads welcome.

MARDON
Graham & Mary Wilson. *From centre of village, head towards church, turn L into Lime St. Bottom of hill on R*
Spacious and well-maintained 4-acre garden surrounding Edwardian house (not open) in small Dartmoor coombe. Formal terraces leading from rose garden to large lawn with long herbaceous border and lower wildlife meadow bordering extensive rhododendron planting. Woodland walk along stream leading to fernery and pond with thatched boathouse, in richly-planted setting. Productive vegetable garden.

SUTTON MEAD
Edward & Miranda Allhusen, 01647 440296, miranda@allhusen.co.uk. *½ m N of village on A382. R at de-restriction sign.* **Visitors also welcome by appt.**
3½ -acre garden of contrasts on gently-sloping hillside. Woodland of mature and recent plantings, hornbeam tunnel and rill fed round pond. Potager vegetable garden with unusual concrete greenhouse. Granite walls mingling with imaginative planting of trees and shrubs. Croquet lawn, rhododendrons and azaleas. Spring-fed ponds with granite seat at water's edge. Bog garden and new orchard. Fine views of

Dartmoor from all corners of garden. Featured on ITV Gorgeous Gardens & BBC TV Open Gardens.

⑦① MOTHECOMBE HOUSE
Holbeton, nr Plymouth PL8 1LB. Mr & Mrs A Mildmay-White. *From A379 between Yealmpton & Modbury turn S for Holbeton. Continue 2m to Mothecombe.* Cream teas. **Adm £3.50, chd free (share to Devon Crimebeat). Suns 6, 20 Apr; Sat 3, Suns 4, 25 May; Suns 8, 22 June (2-5.30).**
Queen Anne house (not open) with Lutyens additions and terraces set in private estate hamlet. Walled pleasure gardens, borders and Lutyens courtyard. Orchard with spring bulbs, unusual shrubs and trees, camellia walk. Autumn garden, streams, bog garden and pond. Bluebell woods leading to private beach. Yr-round interest. Gravel paths, some slopes.

MOYCLARE
See Cornwall.

⑦② NEWTON FARM
Hemyock EX15 3QS. Mr & Mrs J F J M Ward, 01823 680410. *½ m S of Hemyock. On Old Dunkeswell Abbey Rd, from Wellington take Monument Hemyock Rd in centre of Hemyock, turn L by pump. From Honiton take Taunton rd top of hill L to Dunkeswell Cross aerodrome, turn R at first major Xrds, follow signs.* Home-made teas. **Adm £2.50, chd free. Sats, Suns, 8 Mar to 23 Mar; Sat 3 to Mon 5, Sat 31 May; Sats, Suns, Weds 1, 7, 8, 18, 25, 28, 29 June; Sats, Suns, 5, 6, 19, 20, Wed 30 July; Sats, Suns, Weds 2, 3, 6, 9, 10, 13, 20 Aug; Sats, Suns 13, 14, 20, 21 Sept. Weekends (10-5); Weds (2-5). Visitors also welcome by appt, coaches by appt.**
5 acres in Blackdown Hills with views over Culm Valley. S-facing garden: 8 large herbaceous borders, young maze, hornbeam walk, iris and hemerocallis garden. N garden: dwarf rhododendrons, dwarf conifers and pines. National Collections *Gentianas* and *Rhodohypoxis*, bog. Woodland garden, many rare and unusual trees. Planting and development continue. New 1½ acres open grown *Iris ensata* and hemerocallis for the visitor to walk through. Wild flower meadow approx 3 acres.

⑦③ NORTH BORESTON FARM
nr Morleigh TQ9 7LD. Rob & Jan Wagstaff, 01548 821320. *5m S of Totnes. From A381 Totnes to Kingsbridge rd, at Halwell take rd to Moreleigh. From edge of Moreleigh village, follow yellow NGS signs.* Home-made teas. **Adm £3, chd free. Sun 4, Mon 5 May; Suns 10, 17 Aug (2-5). Visitors also welcome by appt Apr to Sept.**
C17 farmhouse with steeply-sloping 3-acre garden of very different areas, plus 2-acre bluebell wood. Rhododendrons and camellias, over 100 varieties of each. Good range of hydrangeas. Herbaceous, fuchsias and acers. Large spring-fed ponds, stream. Collection of unusual crocosmias and hemerocallis. Bridge to exotic garden with palms, bamboos, bananas, tropical bulbs and many rare and unusual plants. Orchard. Unfenced ponds.

⑦④ THE OLD GLEBE
Eggesford EX18 7QU. Mr & Mrs Nigel Wright. *20m NW of Exeter. Turn S off A377 at Eggesford stn (halfway between Exeter & Barnstaple), cross railway & R Taw, drive straight uphill (signed Brushford) for ¾ m; turn R into bridleway.* Home-made teas. **Adm £2.50, chd £1 (share to Friends of Eggesford All Saints Trust). Sats, Suns 10, 11, 17, 18 May (2-5).**
7-acre garden of former Georgian rectory (not open) with mature trees and several lawns, courtyard, walled herbaceous borders, bog garden and small lake; emphasis on species and hybrid rhododendrons and azaleas, 750 varieties. Adjacent rhododendron nursery open by appt.

⑦⑤ THE OLD RECTORY
Ashford, Barnstaple EX31 4BY. Mrs Ann Burnham, 01271 377408, annburnham@btinternet.com. *3m W of Barnstaple. A361 to Braunton. At end of dual carriageway, R to Ashford. Approx 1m, follow rd round to L, 1st house on L.* Light refreshments & teas. **Adm £3, chd free. Suns 20 Apr; 1 June; 6 July; 3 Aug; 14 Sept (11-6). Visitors also welcome by appt.**
Recently-created garden of approx 1½ acres. Open, S-facing with superb views of Taw Estuary. Top garden has been redesigned with new and interesting planting. Lower garden, previously a paddock, now included in flower garden. Jazz band on some

dates. Featured in local press and on local TV. Steps to lower garden, also access via grass slope.

♿ ⊗ 🛏 ☕ ☎

THE OLD RECTORY, NETHERBURY
See Dorset.

76 THE OLD VICARAGE
West Anstey EX36 3PE. Tuck & Juliet Moss, 01398 341604. *9m E of South Molton. From South Molton 9m E on B3227 to Jubilee Inn. Sign to West Anstey. Turn L for 1/4 m then dog-leg L then R following signs. Through Yeomill to T-junction. R following sign. Garden 1st house on L.* Cream teas. Adm £2.50, chd free. Fri 16 to Sun 18 May; Fri 27 to Sun 29 June; Fri 4 to Sun 6 July (2-5.30). Visitors also welcome by appt.
Croquet lawn leads to multi-level garden overlooking three large ponds with winding paths, climbing roses and overviews. Brook with waterfall flows through garden past fascinating summerhouse built by owner. Benched deck overhangs first pond. Features rhododendrons, azaleas and primulas in spring and large collection of Japanese iris in summer. Featured in 'Exmoor' and on ITV Gorgeous Gardens.

☕ ☎

77 THE ORANGERY
Mamhead EX6 8HE. Sir Malcolm & Lady Field. *8m S of Exeter. From Exeter: A380, up steep hill, 1st L before bridge at top, L at end of slip road. From W: A380, L to Mamhead, 1st R in woods, over Xrds, down hill, 1st L at tiny Xrds. L down drive at black & white Dawlish Lodge.* Home-made teas. Adm £3.50, chd free. Sat 24, Sun 25 May (12-5).
Robert Adam C18 orangery (not open) surrounded by 7 acres of Capability Brown landscaping, incl original cedar trees. Garden being restored and redesigned with help of national designer Georgia Langton. Stunning views down to Exe Estuary. New planting of rhododendrons, camellias, azaleas and hydrangeas. Romantic hidden lake among trees. Ice house and steep woodland walks.

⊗ ☕

78 ◆ OTTER NURSERIES
Gosford Road, Ottery St Mary EX11 1LZ. Malcolm & Marilyn White, 01404 815815 ext 241, otter@otternurseries.co.uk. *Follow brown tourist signs on A30 Honiton to Exeter rd.* Adm £4 incl tea/coffee, chd free. For NGS: Tues 15, 29 Apr; 13 May; 16 Sept (10 onwards - please pre-book with Helen Wagstaffe).
Not a garden but a fascinating 'behind the scenes' tour of Devon's favourite garden centre. Owner Marilyn White guides you around nursery growing areas. Spring tours look at young plants raised to bring gardens to glorious summer colour. Autumn tour reveals the secrets of perfect poinsettias, colourful cyclamen, autumn and winter plants.

⚒ ⊗ ☕

79 ◆ OVERBECK'S
Sharpitor, Salcombe TQ8 8LW. The National Trust, 01548 842893, www.nationaltrust.org.uk. *1 1/2 m SW of Salcombe. Follow NT signs.* Adm £6, chd £3. For NGS: Sun 29 June; Sat 19 July (10-5).
7-acre exotic coastal garden, Grade II* listed, with rare plants and shrubs; spectacular views over Salcombe estuary. Garden tours at 1.30 with the Head Gardener.

⚒ ⊗ ☕

Children's quiz, playground, model village. Ample seating.

80 OWLS BARN
The Chestnuts, Aylesbeare EX5 2BY. Pauline & Ray Mulligan. *3m E of Exeter airport. A3052 Exeter to Sidmouth, turn L at Halfway Inn. 1/2 m, park in Village Way. Garden on R past school. From Ottery St Mary, go through West Hill, L onto B3180, R at Tipton X. At Aylesbeare, L through village, garden signed on L. Disabled parking only at The Chestnuts.* Home-made teas. Adm £2.50, chd free. Sat 7, Sun 8 June (2-5.30).
Peaceful 3/4 -acre village garden, a haven for wildlife. Small woodland, natural bog with pond, gravel areas and Mediterranean bed made on N-facing slope of heavy clay. Contrasting foliage with plenty of unusual perennials, grasses, billowing roses, clematis, fruit and vegetables. Imaginatively-designed with surprises round every corner. Featured on BBC2 Open Gardens. Gravel drive.

♿ ⚒ ⊗ ☕

81 38 PHILLIPPS AVENUE
Exmouth EX8 3HZ. Roger & Brenda Stuckey. *From Exeter, turn L just before 1st set of T-lights in Exmouth into Hulham Rd then 1st L into Phillipps Ave.* Adm £2, chd free. Suns 30 Mar; 13, 20 Apr; 11 May; 1, 8 June; 20 July; 10 Aug; 7 Sept (2-5).
Small highly-specialised suburban garden with extensive collection of alpine and rock garden plants in crevice gardens, scree beds, rock gardens, troughs and tufa bed. Many rare and unusual specimens. Small nursery attached to garden.

⊗

82 PIKES COTTAGE
Madford, Hemyock EX15 3QZ. Christine Carver, 01823 680345, bridget.carver@btinternet.com. *7m N of Honiton. Off A30 to Wolford Chapel & through Dunkeswell towards Hemyock, then follow signs from Gypsy Cross. Or 7m S of Wellington off M5 J26 to Hemyock, then follow signs. Turn in at gates opp Madford Farm & up rough farm track.* Cream teas. Adm £2.50, chd free. Sats, Suns, Bank Hol Mons 3, 4, 5, 17, 18 May; 14, 15 June; 19, 20 July; 23, 24, 25 Aug; 27, 28 Sept (2-6). Visitors also welcome by appt, no large coaches. Snowdrop visits from Feb 2009.
Set in 19 acres of bluebell woods (hilly access). 6 acres of cultivated garden incl herb garden, scree, prarie planting, sensory garden, rhododendrons and other shrubs. 1 1/2 -acre lawn slopes to large pond and bog garden. Wisteria tunnel, steps to snowdrops and arboretum. Children's quiz, playground, model village. Ample seating.

⊗ ☕ ☎

83 PINE COTTAGE
No 1 Fourways, Eggesford EX18 7QZ. Dick & Lorna Fulcher, 01769 580076, pcplants@supanet.com. *4m SW of Chulmleigh. Turn S off A377 at Eggesford stn (halfway between Exeter & Barnstaple). 1m uphill beside war memorial cross. Parking in field beside Tarka Trail.* Adm £2, chd free (share to connect). Sat 2, Sun 3, Mon 4 Aug (2-5). Visitors also welcome by appt.
Small plantsman's garden with a variety of hardy and tender perennials incl meconopsis, primulas, crocosmia and hedychiums etc. Many different plants propagated on site in nursery. National Collection of agapanthus, at their best in July and August.

⊗ **NCCPG** ☎

84 ◆ **PLANT WORLD**
St Marychurch Road, Newton Abbot
TQ12 4SE. Ray Brown, 01803
872939, www.plant-world-
seeds.com. *1½ m from Penn Inn
roundabout. Follow brown tourist signs
at the end of the A380 dual
carriageway from Exeter.* **Adm £3, chd
free. Please visit website for
opening dates and times.**
The 4 acres of landscape gardens with
fabulous views have been called
Devon's 'Little Outdoor Eden'.
Representing each of the five
continents, they offer an extensive
collection of rare and exotic plants from
around the world. Superb mature
cottage garden and Mediterranean
garden will delight the visitor. New
panoramic café with home-made food
and cakes. Wheelchair access to
nursery and shop only.

Over 150 species of rhododendrons plus camellias, azaleas . . .

85 **PLEASANT VIEW**
Newton Abbot TQ12 6DG. Mr & Mrs
B D Yeo, 01803 813388. *2m from
Newton Abbot. Two Mile Oak, nr
Denbury. On A381 to Totnes. R at Two
Mile Oak PH signed Denbury. ¾ m on
L.* **Adm £3.50, chd free. Wed 14
May; Sun 8, Wed 11 June; Wed 16,
Sun 20 July (11-5). Visitors also
welcome by appt for groups.**
5-acre plantsman's garden. Lawns
with island beds, 2 small ponds,
rockery. Many rare and unusual
shrubs. Large salvia collection. East
arboretum with huge collection of
specimen shrubs comprising many
genera, surrounded by wildflower
meadow. A haven for wildlife. Buddleia
avenue with 50 varieties. New West
arboretum with Mediterranean garden
around barn.

♿ ✕ ✿ ☎

86 **PORTINGTON**
nr Lamerton PL19 8QY. Mr & Mrs I A
Dingle. *3m NW of Tavistock. From
Tavistock B3362 to Launceston. ¼ m
beyond Blacksmiths Arms, Lamerton,
fork L (signed Chipshop). Over Xrds
(signed Horsebridge) first L then L
again (signed Portington). From
Launceston turn R at Carrs Garage
and R again (signed Horsebridge), then
as above. Home-made teas.* **Adm
£2.50, chd free (share to Plymouth
Samaritans). Suns 15, 22 June
(2-5.30).**
Garden in peaceful rural setting with
fine views over surrounding
countryside. Mixed planting with
shrubs and borders. Walk through
woodland and fields to small lake.

✿ ☕

87 **NEW POUND COTTAGE**
Beacon, Honiton EX14 4TT. John
& Naomi Lott, 07870 363171. *4m
E of Honiton. A30 from Honiton,
pass Little Chef, 1st L signed
Luppitt. Over bridge, 1.8m up hill,
1st R. Straight on at Pound Farm
(no through rd), garden on L.
Parking in field on R (limited parking
if wet). Home-made teas.* **Adm £3,
chd free. Sats 26 Apr; 3 May
(2-6). Visitors also welcome by
appt mid-Apr to mid-May, no
coaches please.**
1-acre hillside garden with
magnificent views, designed and
developed by owners over 22yrs.
Collection of over 150 species
rhododendrons plus camellias,
azaleas, pieris and many unusual
shrubs and trees, most of which
labelled. Bluebells, vegetable
garden and 1 acre across lane still
under development with orchard
and pond.

POUNDSTOCK GARDENS
See Cornwall.

THE BARN HOUSE
See Cornwall.

SOUTHFIELD
See Cornwall.

88 **PROSPECT HOUSE**
Lyme Road, Axminster EX13 5BH.
Peter Wadeley, 01297 631210,
wadeley@btinternet.com. *From
Axminster town centre (Trinity Square)
proceed uphill past George Hotel into
Lyme St & Lyme Rd. Garden approx ½
m up rd on R, just before petrol stn.*

Home-made teas. **Adm £3, chd free.
Sats, Suns 7, 8 June; 2, 3 Aug (1.30-
5.30). Visitors also welcome by
appt.**
1-acre plantsman's garden hidden
behind high stone walls and with Axe
valley views. Well-stocked borders with
rare shrubs and colourful perennials,
many reckoned to be borderline
tender. 200 varieties of salvia, some for
sale. A gem, not to be missed.

✕ ✿ ☕ ☎

89 **REGENCY HOUSE**
Hemyock EX15 3RQ. Mrs Jenny
Parsons, 01823 680238,
jenny.parsons@btinternet.com. *8m
N of Honiton. M5 J26. From Hemyock
take Dunkeswell-Honiton rd. Entrance
½ m on R from Catherine Wheel PH &
church. Disabled parking (only) at
house. Home-made teas.* **Adm £3.50,
chd free. Suns 8, 22 June; 21 Sept
(11-6). Visitors also welcome by
appt.**
5-acre plantsman's garden
approached across a private ford.
Many interesting and unusual trees and
shrubs. Visitors can try their hand at
identifying plants with the plant list.
Home-made teas or plenty of space to
eat your own picnic. Walled vegetable
and fruit garden, lake, ponds, bog
plantings and sweeping lawns. New
September date.

✿ 🛏 ☕ ☎

90 ◆ **RHS GARDEN ROSEMOOR**
Great Torrington EX38 8PH. The
Royal Horticultural Society, 01805
624067, www.rhs.org.uk/rosemoor.
*1m SE of Great Torrington. On A3124
to Exeter.* **Adm £6, chd £2, under 6
free. Every day except Christmas
Day. (10-5) Oct to Mar, (10-6) Apr to
Sept.**
65-acre plantsman's garden plus
woodlands; rhododendrons (species
and hybrids), ornamental trees and
shrubs, woodland garden, species and
old-fashioned roses, scree and raised
beds with alpine plants, arboretum.
2000 roses in 200 varieties, two
colour-theme gardens, herb garden,
potager, 220yds of herbaceous border,
large stream and bog garden, cottage
garden, foliage and fruit and vegetable
garden.

♿ ✕ ✿ ☕

91 ◆ **ROCK HOUSE GARDEN**
Station Hill, Chudleigh TQ13 0EE.
Mrs D B & B Boulton, 01626 852134,
www.therockgardens.co.uk. *8m SW
of Exeter. A38 Exeter to Plymouth*

signed Chudleigh. S edge of town.
Entrance at Rock Nursery. **Adm £3,
chd £1.50, concessions £1.50.** For
NGS: Suns 6, 27 Apr; 25 May; 1, 22
June; 27 July; 31 Aug; 14, 28 Sept;
5, 26 Oct (9-5).
Garden in ancient bishop's palace
quarry with massive limestone rock.
Delights for all seasons. Rare and
unusual trees and shrubs. Massed
bulbs in spring. Autumn brings one of
the finest displays of cyclamen. Cave
and ponds with koi and orfe. Walk with
spectacular views of Dartmoor and
access to Chudleigh rock, glen and
waterfall. 22 June display and advice
by S Devon Bonsai Group. Wheelchair
access to part of garden only, tea shop
and nursery.

Wooden staircase to pergola of antique carved pillars from Turkistan and dovecots for over 100 aviaried doves . . .

92 **NEW** **ROSE COTTAGE**
Crowden Road, Northlew
EX20 3ND. Irene & Ron Oldale.
*6m NW of Okehampton. Off A386
at Hilltown Cross to Northlew (6m).
In Northlew Square, NW corner,
take rd signed Highampton. Follow
signs. L after 400yds, garden ½ m.
Limited parking if wet.* Home-made
teas. **Adm £2.50, chd free.** Suns
15, 22 June (2-5.30).
2-acre naturalistic informal stroller's
garden of winding grass paths and
hidden views. Exuberantly-planted
mixed herbaceous borders;
attractive and productive kitchen
garden with vegetables, fruit, herbs
and flowers; mixed orchard with
crab apple walk; bog and water
garden; wild flower meadows;
young woodland copse, all
developed over last 10yrs.

93 **NEW** **ROUSDON
GARDENS**
Rousdon DT7 3XW. *3m E of
Seaton. On A3052 midway
between Seaton and Lyme Regis.
Look for roadside signs.* Home-
made teas at both gardens. **Adm
£3.50, chd free (share to
Himalayan Learning).** Suns 18
May; 15 June; 20 July; 17 Aug;
21 Sept (11-5).

NEW **GREEN LANE COTTAGE**
Green Lane. Toni & Helena
Williams-Pugh, 01297 443712,
helena@himalayanlearning.org.
*On the edge of Rousdon Village
just off A3052, 2m from Lyme
Regis.* Visitors also welcome by
appt May to July for groups of
10+.
Triple pond water feature, curving
lawns and flowerbeds crammed
with a succession of colour-
themed flowers. Small church
window set in tiny folly and
sunken walled patio. Wooden
staircase to pergola of antique
carved pillars from Turkistan and
dovecots for over 100 aviaried
doves. Featured on BBC2 Open
Gardens.

HORTUS
Shrubbery Bungalow, School
Lane. Marie-Elaine & Mark
Houghton, 01297 444019,
www.hortusnursery.com.
Visitors also welcome by appt.
¹/₃ acre planted in naturalistic
style. Gravel terrace with over
100 grasses, pebble beach with
seaside plants, colour-themed
borders, Mediterranean patio
with tender plants in pots and
Jurassic border. Adjacent
nursery. Tomato tasting Aug and
Sept.

94 **ST MERRYN**
Higher Park Road, Braunton
EX33 2LG. Dr W & Mrs Ros
Bradford, 01271 813805. *5m W of
Barnstaple. In centre of Braunton turn
R at T-lights round Nat West Bank. At
top of Heanton St turn L and immed R
into Lower Park Rd. Continue until you
see Tyspane Nursing Home on L then
turn L into unmarked lane & R at top.
Pink house 200yds on R. Parking
where available.* Home-made teas.
Adm £2.50, chd free. Suns 20 Apr;
25 May; 29 June (2-6). **Visitors also**

welcome by appt.
Very sheltered ³/₄ -acre, S-facing,
cottage garden with emphasis on
scent, colour and all-yr interest.
Thatched summerhouse leading
down to herbaceous borders; many
seating areas; winding paths
through lawns, shrubs and mature
trees. Fish ponds. New: Studio/
gallery, grassy knoll, gravel garden
and discreet resiting of greenhouse.
Exhibition of paintings and other art
work by owner.

95 ◆ **SALTRAM HOUSE**
Plympton PL7 1UH. The National
Trust, 01752 333500,
www.nationaltrust.org.uk. *3m E of
Plymouth. S of A38, 2m W of
Plympton.* **House and garden adm
£8.80, chd £4.40, garden only adm
£4.40, chd £2.20.** All yr, Sat to Thur.
Mar to Oct (11-4.30); Nov to Feb
(11-4). For NGS: Wed 7 May; Sat 19
July (11-4.30).
20 acres with fine specimen trees;
spring garden; rhododendrons and
azaleas. C18 orangery and octagonal
garden house. (George II mansion with
magnificent plasterwork and
decorations, incl 2 rooms designed by
Robert Adam). Good variety of
evergreens, incl many tender and
unusual shrubs, esp from the S
hemisphere. Long grass areas with
bulbs and wild flowers.

96 **SCHOOL HOUSE**
Little Torrington, Torrington
EX38 8PS. Mr & Mrs M Sampson,
01805 623445,
mjsampsonlt@btopenworld.com.
*2m S Torrington on A386. Village of
Little Torrington signed, follow signs to
village green, park here, walk 50yds
along bridle path to School House.*
Cream teas at Village Hall. **Adm £2.50,
chd free.** Sun 13 July (2-6). **Visitors
also welcome by appt June/July
only.**
²/₃ -acre informally planted cottage
garden. Wildlife pond with adjacent
'natural' planting under old apple tree.
2 ornamental pools. Arbour and
pergola with a variety of climbers.
Trees, shrubs, herbaceous and
annual planting with some colour-
themed areas. Small raised bed for
alpines.

97 NEW SEDGEWELL COACH HOUSE GARDENS
Olchard TQ12 3GU. Heather Jansch, www.heatherjansch.com. *4m N of Newton Abbot. 12m S of Exeter on A380, L for Olchard, straight ahead on private drive.* Adm £3, chd free. Sats, Suns 23, 24, 30, 31 Aug (10-5).
Heather Jansch, world-famous sculptor, brings innovative use of recycled materials to gardening. 14 acres unlike anything elsewhere incl stunning driftwood sculpture, wheelchair-friendly formal gardens, pools, herbaceous borders, medicinal herb gardens, woodland, fabulous views and timeless stream-bordered water meadow with exciting interactive kids' stuff. Come and picnic.
& ⚭ ✿

98 SHAPCOTT BARTON ESTATE
(East Knowstone Manor), East Knowstone, South Molton EX36 4EE. Anita Allen, 01398 341664. *13m NW of Tiverton. J27 M5 take Tiverton exit. 6½ m to roundabout, take exit South Molton 10m, on A361. Turn R signed Knowstone (picnic area). Leave A361 at this point, travel 1¼ m to Roachhill, through hamlet, turn L at Wiston Cross, entrance on L ¼ m.* Adm £3, chd £1 (share to Axehays Cats Protection). Suns 4 May; 8 June; Sat 12, Sun 13, Weds 16, 23, Sat 26, Sun 27, Thur 31 July; Sat 9, Sun 10 Aug (11-4.30).
Large garden of 200-acre estate around ancient historic manor house. Wildlife garden. Rare swallowtail butterflies seen in 2006. Restored old fish ponds, stream and woodland rich in birdlife. Unusual fruit orchard. Narcissi in May. June is even more floriferous before the flowering burst in July/Aug of National Plant Collections *Leucanthemum superbum* (shasta daisies) and buddleja davidii. Picnicers welcome. Featured in 'Gardens Illustrated'. Only limited wheelchair access.
✿ ⚭ NCCPG

99 SHERWOOD
Newton St Cyres, Exeter EX5 5BT. John & Prue Quicke, 01392 851216, www.quickes.co.uk. *2m SE of Crediton. Off A377 Exeter to Barnstaple rd, ¾ m Crediton side of Newton St Cyres, signed Sherwood, entrance to drive in 1¾ m.* Adm £3,

chd free (share to Newton St Cyres Parochial Church). Every Sun, 6 Jan 2008 to 22 Feb 2009 (2-5). Visitors also welcome by appt, large coaches must stop at bottom of drive, smaller coaches can turn at house.
15 acres, 2 steep wooded valleys. Wild flowers, especially daffodils; extensive collections of magnolias, camellias, rhododendrons, azaleas, berberis, heathers, maples, cotoneasters, buddleias, hydrangeas and late summer flowering perennials. Woodland garden with shade-loving perennials and epimediums. National Collections of magnolias, Knaphill azaleas and berberis. Featured in RHS 'Daily Telegraph'. Limited wheelchair access. Steep slopes, deep ponds.
& ⚭ NCCPG ☎

World-famous sculptor brings innovative use of recycled materials to gardening . . .

100 SHOBROOKE PARK GARDENS
Crediton EX17 1DG. Dr & Mrs J R Shelley, 01363 775153, garden@shobrookepark.com. *1m NE of Crediton. On A3072.* Cream teas. Adm £3, chd free. Sats 19 Apr; 17 May; 7 June (2-5). Visitors also welcome by appt April/May for groups of 15+.
15-acre woodland garden laid out in mid-C19 incl extensive Portland Stone terraces with views over 200-acre park with ponds. In process of being restored with extensive new planting amongst old rhododendrons incl reconstructed Victorian rose garden.
✿ ☕ ☎

101 SOUTH KENWOOD
Oxton, nr Kenton EX6 8EX. Sir John & Lady Jennings. *6m S of Exeter. From A380 (Exeter to Newton Abbot-Torquay rd) turn L signed Mamhead & Starcross. After 2m turn L for Oxton. Take next L for Oxton. In 1m turn L to South Kenwood. From coast rd turn R at Starcross into New Road. After ¼ m turn R for Mamhead. In 2m turn R for Oxton, then as above.* Home-made teas. Adm £2.50, chd free. Sat 28, Sun 29 June (2-5).
10-acre garden in wooded valley nestling under the Haldon hills. Streams running through, well-planted ponds, bog gardens and small lake with wildfowl. Colour-themed borders, lawns, terrace, pergola walk, rose garden and conservatory. Masses of interesting planting, shrubs and mature trees. Featured in 'English Garden' magazine.
⚭ ☕

102 SOUTH TAWTON GARDENS
EX20 2LP. *6m E of Okehampton. Park in village square, walk through churchyard.* Cream teas at Glebe House. Combined adm £4, chd free. Sats, Suns 31 May, 1, 7, 8 June (2-5.30).
Small village built around Parish Church. Historic church rooms recently restored open to public.
☕

BLACKHALL MANOR
Roger & Jacqueline Yeates
Small cottage garden around C16 thatched listed house (not open) on N edge of Dartmoor. Planted with trees, shrubs and herbaceous perennials to give interest throughout the year. Cobbled paths and pond. Exhibition of photographs and paintings by garden owner. Featured on BBC TV Countryfile.
✿ ⚭

GLEBE HOUSE
John & Welmoed Perrin. *Turning next to Seven Stars. Glebe House facing at end of rd*
Space with backdrop of hills, moor and meadow. A ha-ha conceals a young vineyard; mature trees frame two ponds and living arches. Rockeries support well stocked borders; an original courtyard creates a small orangerie.
✿ ⚭

103 SOUTHCOMBE GARDENS

Dartmoor, Widecombe-in-the-Moor TQ13 7TU. *6m W of Bovey Tracey. Take B3387 from Bovey Tracey. After village church take rd SW for 200yds then sharp R, signed Southcombe, up steep hill. After 200yds, pass C17 farmhouse & park on L. Alternatively park in public car park in village and walk. Teas at Southcombe Barn.* **Combined adm £3.50, chd free. Suns 11, 25, Mon 26 May; Suns 1, 8, 15 June (2-5).**
Village famous for its Fair, Uncle Tom Cobley and its C14 church - the 'Cathedral of the Moor'.

SOUTHCOMBE BARN
Amanda Sabin & Stephen Hobson
3-acre woodland garden with exotic and native trees between long lawn and rocky stream. Clearings blaze with wild flowers and survivor garden flowers. New meadow in recently-cleared area.

SOUTHCOMBE HOUSE
Widecombe-in-the-Moor. Dr & Mrs J R Seale, 01364 621365. Visitors also welcome by appt. 5 acres, SE-facing garden, arboretum and wild flower meadow with bulbs in spring and four orchid species (early purple, southern marsh, common spotted and greater butterfly). On steep slope at 900ft above sea level with fine views to nearby tors. Featured in RHS 'The Garden'.

Many nesting birds, including flycatchers and warblers; breeding butterflies; reptiles. Ponds and marsh areas . . .

104 SOUTHLEIGH GARDENS

EX24 6JB. *2m W of Colyton. Signs from Hangmans Cross on A3052 or from Hare & Hounds, Putt's Corner on Honiton-Sidmouth rd, then 2nd turning on L past Farway Wildlife Park, via 2m lane. Parking at village hall or considerably in rd below. Cream teas in Village Hall.* **Combined adm £3, chd free. Sat 31 May; Sun 1 June (2-5.30).**

POPES COTTAGE
Irene & Eric Daniels, 01404 871210. *Next to church.* **Visitors also welcome by appt May to Aug.**
2/3 -acre country garden blending into spectacular valley view. Mixed borders of shrubs, perennials and alpines, some unusual. Small fruit and vegetable section. Artificial stream through small ponds. Emphasis on wildlife.

SOUTH BANK
Jo Connor, 01404 871251. *Nr church.* **Visitors also welcome by appt May to Aug.**
1/2 acre. Mixed beds, pond, patio garden, orchard, small vegetable plot, shrubberies. Lovely views. Beautiful in spring/early summer. Pergola with swing seat overlooking pond.

105 SOWTON MILL

Dunsford EX6 7JN. A Cooke & S Newton, 01647 252347/252263, sonianewton@sowtonmill.eclipse.co.uk. *7m W of Exeter. From Dunsford take B3193 S for 1/2 m. Entrance straight ahead off sharp R bend by bridge. From A38 N along Teign valley for 8m. Sharp R after humpback bridge. Home-made teas.* **Adm £2.80, chd free (share to Cygnet Training Theatre). Suns 6 Apr; 13 July (2-6). Visitors also welcome by appt.**
4 acres laid out around former mill (not open), leat and river. Part woodland with multitudes of wild flowers in spring, ornamental trees and shrubs, mixed borders and scree. Yr-round interest.

106 SPILLIFORDS WILDLIFE GARDEN

Lower Washfield, Tiverton EX16 9PE. Dr Gavin Haig, 01884 252422, ghaig@fish.co.uk. *3m N of Tiverton. Take A396 Tiverton to Bampton rd, turn L over iron bridge signed Stoodleigh. Turn L again after crossing bridge marked Washfield, & L again on hill following Washfield sign. Bridge is approx 2m from link rd roundabout. Spillifords is 1st house on L after Hatswell - some 400 metres onwards. Parking in top field through double five barred gate (not suitable in damp conditions).* **Adm £3, chd free. Suns 18 May; 29 June (3-5.30). Visitors also welcome by appt.**
Specialist wildlife garden leading down to R Exe. Banks and islands of mixed wild flowers and herbs. Many nesting birds, including flycatchers and warblers; breeding butterflies; reptiles. Ponds and marsh areas. About 50 nestboxes. Annually 30 different butterflies - including rare Marsh Fritillary. Picnic areas. About 4 acres. Kingfisher, dipper and otter frequent visitors. Please telephone if weather in doubt. Wildlife Garden (Tiverton) winner. Some steep slopes.

107 SPRINGDALE

Smeatharpe, Honiton EX14 9RF. Graham & Ann Salmon. *8m N of Honiton. Park in field behind Village Hall, N end of Smeatharpe. Garden is through gate in hedge and down bridleway. Home-made teas.* **Adm £3.50, chd free (share to Blackdown Support Group). Sats, Suns, Mons 17, 18, 19 May; 5, 6, 7 July (2-6).**
On Devon/Somerset border, set in the magnificent Blackdown Hills, is a developing 2-acre plantsman's garden with adjoining 16 acres of SSSI. Extensive planting of choice trees, shrubs and perennials, waterside and alpine beds complemented by cacti and auricula collections. Damp, acid garden designed for plants, wildlife and people to enjoy. Featured in 'Somerset Life' and on ITV Gorgeous Gardens.

108 SQUIRRELS

98 Barton Road, Torquay TQ2 7NS. Graham & Carol Starkie. *From Newton Abbot take A380 to Torquay. After Focus DIY on L, turn L at T-lights up Old Woods Hill. 1st L into Barton Rd, bungalow 200yds on L. Teas.* **Adm £2.50, chd free. Sat 2, Sun 3, Sat 9 Aug (2-5).**
Plantsman's small town garden landscaped with small ponds and 7ft waterfall. Interlinked areas incl Japanese, Italianate, Tropical. Specialising in fruit incl peaches, figs, kiwi. Tender plants incl bananas, tree

fern, brugmansia, lantanas, oleanders, abutilons, bougainvilleas. Colourful pergolas and lawn area. Environmentally-friendly garden. Runner-up Super Class Torbay in Bloom. Featured in local press.

🏹 ✿ ☕

STOWLEYS
See Somerset & Bristol Area.

109 NEW SUMMERS PLACE
Little Bowlish, Whitestone EX4 2HS. Mr & Mrs Stafford Charles. *6m NW of Exeter. From M5, A30 towards Okehampton 1st exit, 1st exit on roundabout, 1m L onto B3212 and immediately R towards Crediton. 2m R towards Whitestone, follow signs. From Crediton, Fordton to Whitestone rd, follow signs, brief walk from car park.* Home-made teas. **Adm £3, chd free. Suns 13 Apr; 11 May; 15 June; 28 Sept (2-5).**
Sizeable woodland haven evolved from challenging steep north field and wooded valley. Stepped paths wander through sympathetic plantings plus less usual trees, shrubs and roses. Further enhanced by ruin, arbours, walkways, ponds (wild and fish), rills, rural views and strategic seats. New projects. Divided intimate areas surround house, many climbers and quirky features. Arabian horse stud open.

✿ ☕

110 TAIKOO
Belstone EX20 1QZ. Richard & Rosamund Bernays, 01837 840760, richard@bernays.net. *3m SE of Okehampton. Fork L at stocks in middle of village. 300yds on R. Park in field.* Cream teas. **Adm £3, chd free. Suns 27 Apr, 25 May; Sat 26 July (2-5). Visitors also welcome by appt.**
3-acre hillside moorland garden, restored over past 10yrs, recently extended to incl heathers and moorland plants. Interesting collections of rhododendrons, fuchsias, hydrangeas, magnolias, camellias, roses and other shrubs and trees. Herb garden and water features. Magnificent views over Dartmoor.

🏹 ☕ ☎

111 TAMARISKS
Inner Hope Cove, Kingsbridge TQ7 3HH. Barbara Anderson, 01548 561745, bba@talktalk.net. *6m SW of Kingsbridge. Turn off A381 at Malborough between Kingsbridge & Salcombe. 2m further, on entering Hope Cove, turn L at sign to Inner Hope. After 1/4 m, turn R into lane beneath Sun Bay Hotel. Tamarisks is next house. Park opp hotel or in lane (larger car park in Outer Hope, follow path leading to Inner Hope into lane).* Home-made teas. **Adm £2.50, chd free (share to Butterfly Conservation). Wed 16, Thur 17 July (11-6). Visitors also welcome by appt.**
Sloping 1/3 acre directly above sea with magnificent view. Garden is exciting with rustic steps, extensive stonework, ponds, rockeries, feature corners, patios, 'wild' terrace overlooking sea. Very colourful. Demonstrates what can flourish at seaside - notably hydrangeas, mallows, crocosmia, achillea, sea holly, convolvulus, lavender, sedum, roses, grasses, ferns, fruit trees. Bird and butterfly haven. Butterfly Conservation table with representatives and pamphlets. Featured on BBC TV Countryfile.

✿ ☕ ☎

112 NEW TANGLEWOOD
8 Perches Close, Membland, Newton Ferrers PL8 1HZ. Paul & Shirley Fleming. *12m E of Plymouth. From A379 between Yealmpton and Brixton at Kitley follow signs towards Newton Ferrers and Noss Mayo, L signed Bridgend. From Bridgend take rd inland signed Membland. At top of hill (1/2 m), Perches Close on R, garden at far end of cul-de-sac.* Home-made teas. **Adm £2.50, chd free. Suns 22 June; 20 July (2-6).**
9 yr-old 3/4 -acre plantsman's garden situated on SW facing valley site and backing onto woods. Many unusual trees, shrubs and herbaceous plants providing yr-round interest and colour. Secluded seating areas give varied aspects of the garden, which incl ponds with small stream and owners' ceramic sculptures.

☕

113 1 TIPTON LODGE
Tipton St John. EX10 0AW. Angela Avis & Robin Pickering, 01404 813371. *3m N of Sidmouth. From Exeter take A3052 towards Sidmouth. L on B3176 at Bowd Inn toward Ottery St Mary. After 1 1/2 m turn into Tipton St John. After village sign, 1 Tipton Lodge is the second driveway on R about 100yds before Golden Lion PH. Parking for disabled only, other parking in village.* Home-made teas. **Adm £2.50, chd free. Sat 14, Sun 15 June (11-5). Visitors also welcome by appt.**
3/4 acre designed to reflect mid-Victorian house. Formal grass walks between double herbaceous borders and avenue of white weeping roses. Old shrub roses, small woodland area incl tree ferns, potager-style vegetable garden. All organic. Exuberant romantic planting.

🏹 ✿ ☕ ☎

TREBARTHA
See Cornwall.

114 THE WATER GARDEN
Wembworthy EX18 7SG. Mr J M Smith. *10m NE of Okehampton. From A377 at Eggesford station follow signs to Wembworthy (2m W). From Winkleigh take Wembworthy to Eggesford rd (2m E). Turn at Xrd sign at Lymington Arms. Overflow car park at Lymington Arms (excellent lunches) 400yds to garden.* Home-made teas. **Adm £2.50, chd free. Sats, Suns, 3 to 31 May; Mons 5, 26 May; Sun 1 Jun (2-6).**
Naturalistic William Robinson-style 1-acre garden with 'wilderness' planting, incorporating exotics and native species around clay pond/swamp area with 60-metre board walk of distressed oak, allowing close inspection of plants and wildlife. Many other water features displayed among irises, ferns, trees, shrubs, clematis and unusual plants. Some hot, dry, stony slopes. Conservatory. Potager garden.

♿ 🏹 ✿ ☕

Divided intimate areas surround house, many climbers and quirky features . . .

WAYFORD MANOR
See Somerset & Bristol Area.

115 WEBBERY GARDENS
Alverdiscott EX39 4PS, 01271
858206, jayewdall@surfree.co.uk.
2½ m E of Bideford. Either from
Bideford (East the Water) along
Alverdiscott Rd, or from Barnstaple to
Torrington on B3232, take rd to
Bideford at Alverdiscott and pass
through Stoney Cross. Teas at Little
Webbery. **Combined adm £3.50, chd
free.** Sat 14, Sun 15 June (2-6).
Visitors also welcome by appt.

LITTLE WEBBERY
Mr & Mrs J A Yewdall
Approx 3 acres in valley setting
with pond, lake, mature trees and
2 ha-has. Walled kitchen garden
with yew and box hedging;
greenhouse; rose garden; trellises;
shrubs and climbing plants. 3
mature borders. Some gravel
paths.

LITTLE WEBBERY COTTAGE
Mr & Mrs J A Yewdall
Self-contained cottage garden
with wide selection of flowering
plants and shrubs incl pergolas
with roses, clematis and jasmine.

**116 NEW 4 WELLSWOOD
HEIGHTS**
Higher Erith Rd, Wellswood
TQ1 2NH. Mr & Mrs S W Tiller,
01803 296387, sue.tiller@
tiscali.co.uk. 1m from Torquay
town centre. From Torquay
harbourside towards Babbacombe,
Burlington Hotel on R. R after red
post box on R into Lincombe Hill
Rd then R at top, garden immed
on L. Home-made teas. **Adm £2,
chd free.** Suns 1 June; 31 Aug
(2-5). **Visitors also welcome by
appt Apr to Oct, max 10.**
Small exotic garden. Large variety
of exotics incl palms, tree ferns,
aloes and other unusual trees,
shrubs and succulents mainly from
S hemisphere. 25 steps to main
part of garden.

117 WESTCOTT BARTON
Marwood, Barnstaple EX31 4EF.
Howard Frank, 01271 812842,
www.westcottbarton.co.uk. 4m N of
Barnstaple. From Barnstaple 4m N to
Guineaford, continue N for 1m. Turn L,

signed Middle Marwood and Patsford,
2nd L at Westcott Barton sign. Cream
teas. **Adm £3, chd free.** Sun 25, Mon
26 May; Sun 24, Mon 25 Aug (2-6).
**Visitors also welcome by appt (no
large coaches).**
2-acre developing valley garden with
stream, bridge and several ponds.
Wide variety of planting:
rhododendrons, camellias, clematis,
hydrangeas, gunnera, rose garden.
Masses of interest. Garden surrounds
C12 farmhouse (not open) with
cobbled courtyard, range of
outbuildings and water wheel.

118 WHITSTONE FARM
Whitstone Lane, Bovey Tracey
TQ13 9NA. Katie & Alan Bunn,
01626 832258,
katie@whitstonefarm.co.uk. ½ m N
of Bovey Tracey. From A382 turn
toward hospital (signed opp golf range)
after ⅓ m turn L at swinging sign
'Private road leading to Whitstone'.
Follow lane uphill & bend to L.
Whitstone Farm on R at end of long
barn. Limited parking. **Adm £3, chd
free.** Suns 11 May; 27 July (2-5).
**Visitors also welcome by appt Apr
to Oct.**
Over 3 acres of steep hillside garden
with stunning views of Haytor and
Dartmoor. An aboretum planted 37yrs
ago of over 200 trees from all over the
world, incl magnolias, camellias, acers,
alders, betula and sorbus. Water
feature. Major new plantings of
rhododendron, cornus and eucryphias.

Large variety
of exotics
including
palms, tree
ferns, aloes
and other
unusual
trees . . .

**119 NEW WICK FARM
GARDENS**
Cookbury, Holsworthy
EX22 6NU. Martin & Jenny
Sexton. 3m E of Holsworthy. From
Holsworthy take Hatherleigh Rd for
2m, L at Anvil Corner, ¼ m then R
to Cookbury, garden 1½ m on L.
Light refreshments & teas. **Adm
£3.50, chd free.** **Afternoon &
Early Evening** Sun 27 July (2-8);
Sun 24, Mon 25 Aug (2-7).
1-acre garden, part arranged into
rooms with fernery, small
ornamental pond, borders and
garden statues. 2-acre garden
surrounding small lake with island.
Long border developed in 2006
with large variety of plants. All-yr
interest. Gravel paths, gentle
slopes.

120 ◆ WILDSIDE
Green Lane, Buckland Monachorum
PL20 7NP. Mr K & Mrs R Wiley,
01822 855755,
wildside.plants@virgin.net. ¼ m W of
Buckland Monachorum. Follow brown
signs to Garden House from A386.
Past Garden House, continue straight
on for 0.7m. Garden 300yds past
village on L. **Adm £3, chd free.**
**Garden and nursery open Thurs
only, 14 Feb to 30 Oct.** For NGS:
Sats 10 May; 28 June; 20 Sept
(10-5). Also open **The Cider House**
28 June.
Created from field since 2004 by ex
Head Gardener of The Garden House.
Wide range of habitats and different
plant varieties are grown in a
naturalistic style, giving displays of
colour throughout the season.
Featured in 'Country Living' and
'Devon Gardener'.

**121 ◆ WINSFORD WALLED
GARDEN**
Halwill Junction EX21 5XT. Aileen
Birks & Mike Gilmore, 01409
221477,
www.winsfordwalledgarden.com.
12m NW of Okehampton. On A3079
follow brown tourism signs from centre
of Halwill Junction. **Adm £4.50, chd
free.** Daily 1 May to 19 Oct (9-5, last
entry). For NGS: Suns 15 June; 20
July; 10 Aug; 14 Sept (9-5).
Walled summer flower garden since
1883. Latest evolution began 1999.
The achievement since will amaze and
inspire. Summer interest packed with
features past and present. Heading

towards 3000 varieties. Well-labelled. Original teak greenhouses, huge new alpine house. Highly informative exhibition. Guided tours. Featured in 'Devon Life'. Electric mobility vehicles.

& ▦ ☕

122 WITHLEIGH FARM
Withleigh Village, Tiverton EX16 8JG. T Matheson, 01884 253853. *3m W of Tiverton. On B3137, 10yds W of 1st small 30mph sign on L, entrance to drive by white gate.* Cream teas. **Adm £3, chd free (share to Arthritis Research & Cancer Research UK).** Sat 10, Sun 11 May (2-5). **Visitors also welcome by appt.** Peaceful undisturbed rural setting with valley garden, 24yrs in making; stream, pond and waterside plantings; bluebell walk under canopy of mature oak and beech; wild flower meadow, primroses and daffodils in spring; wild orchids in June. Dogs on leads please.

⊛ ☕ ☎

WOLVERHOLLOW
See Dorset.

123 WOOD BARTON
Kentisbeare EX15 2AT. Mr & Mrs Richard Horton, 01884 266285. *8m SE of Tiverton, 3m E of Cullompton. 3m from M5 J28. Take A373 Cullompton to Honiton rd. After 2m turn L signed Bradfield & Willand on Horn Rd for 1m, turn R at Xrds. Farm drive ¹/₂ m on L. Bull on sign.* Home-made teas. **Adm £3, chd free (share to Action Medical Research).** Sat 29, Sun 30 Mar (2-6). **Visitors also welcome by appt.**
2-acre arboretum planted 57yrs ago with species trees on S-facing slope. Magnolias, two davidia, azaleas, camellias, rhododendrons, acers;

several ponds and water feature. Autumn colour. Art exhibition will be on show in barn.

& ⊛ ☕ ☎

$^{3}/_{4}$-acre paradise started in 1992 . . . a garden with 'soul', must experience to appreciate . . .

124 WOODY PARK
Bradfield, Cullompton EX15 2RB. Colin & Enid Folds. *¹/₂ m E of Willand. M5 J28 towards Honiton. 1st L to Bradfield, follow signs. M5 J27 towards Wellington. R at 1st roundabout to Willand. Follow signs.* Cream teas by the lake. **Adm £3, chd free.** Sun 4, Mon 5, Sat 10, Sun 11 May (2-5).

35-acre water garden with landscaped lakes and ponds created by the owners from a maize field over last 15 yrs. Lakes and islands landscaped with trees, shrubs and marginals. Woodland with bluebells, large collection of hybrid rhododendrons and azaleas. Around house, lawns, beds and koi pond. Featured on BBC Open Gardens and ITV Gorgeous Gardens.

& ✕ ⊛ ☕

WRANGWAY GARDENS
See Somerset & Bristol Area.

125 YONDER HILL
Shepherds Lane, Colaton Raleigh EX10 0LP. Judy McKay & Eddie Stevenson, 01395 567075. *3m N of Budleigh Salterton. On B3178 between Newton Poppleford and Colaton Raleigh, take turning signed to Dotton, then immed R into small lane. ¹/₄ m, 1st house on R. Ample parking.* **Adm £2.50, chd £1.** Sun 2 Mar; every Sun 16 Mar to 26 Oct incl; Fri 21 Mar; Bank Hol Mons 24 Mar; 5, 26 May; 25 Aug (1-5). **Visitors also welcome by appt incl groups, weekdays (11-4). (Please tel at 10am to confirm).**
3¹/₄ -acre paradise started 1992. Unconventional planting. Shady walks, sunny glades, young woodland, ponds, herbaceous borders, orchard, vegetables, wildlife areas incl large wildlife pond made 2007. Several collections, many surprises. A garden with 'soul', must experience to appreciate. Tea/coffee and biscuits available, make it yourself as you like it. Picnics welcome. Featured in 'Devon Today'.

& ✕ ⊛ ☕ ☎

Devon County Volunteers

County Organisers and Central Devon area
Edward & Miranda Allhusen, Sutton Mead, Moretonhampstead TQ13 8PW, 01647 440296, miranda@allhusen.co.uk

County Treasurer
Julia Tremlett, Bickham House, Kenn, Nr Exeter EX6 7XL, 01392 832671, jandjtremlett@hotmail.com

Publicity
Alan Davis, Paddocks, Stafford Lane, Colyford EX24 6HQ, 01297 552472, alan.davis@theiet.org

County Organisers
North East Devon Dorothy Anderson, Ashley Coombe, Ashley, Tiverton EX16 5PA, 01884 259971, dorothyanderson@uku.co.uk
Torbay Jo Gibson, Arcadia, Ashcombe Road, Dawlish EX7 0QW, 01626 862102, hecate105@yahoo.co.uk
North Devon Jo Hynes, Higher Cherubeer, Dolton, Winkleigh EX19 8PP, 01805 804265, hynesjo@gmail.com
Exeter Margaret Lloyd, Little Cumbre, 145 Pennsylvania Road, Exeter EX4 6DZ, 01392 258315
South Devon Jo Smith, 2 Homefield Cottage, Sherford, Kingsbridge TQ7 2AT, 01548 531618, jofrancis5@btopenworld.com
South West Devon Michael & Sarah Stone, The Cider House, Buckland Abbey, Yelverton PL20 6EZ, 01822 853285, michael.stone@cider-house.co.uk
East Devon Peter Wadeley, Prospect House, Lyme Road, Axminster EX13 5BH, 01297 631210, wadeley@btinternet.com

DORSET

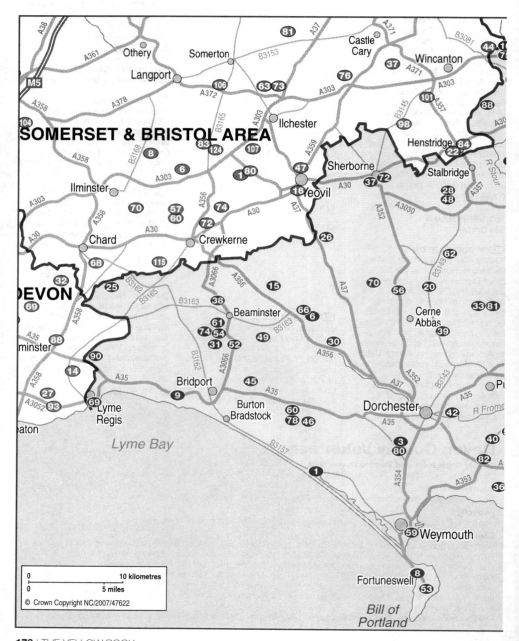

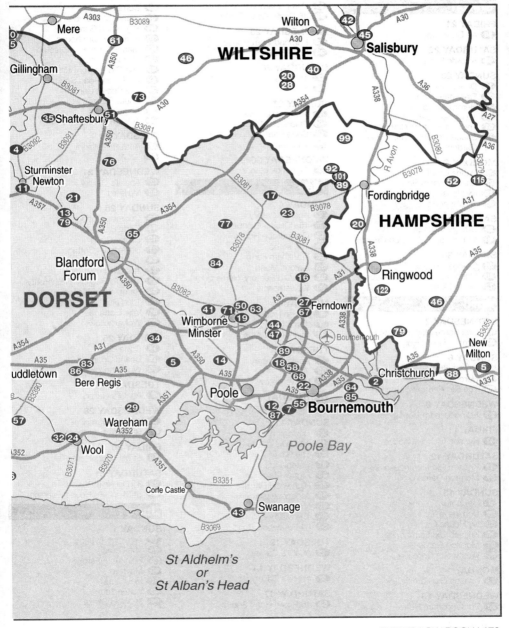

Opening Dates

February

SUNDAY 24
84 Welcome Thatch

March

FRIDAY 21
18 44 Daws Avenue

SATURDAY 22
45 Knowle Farm

SUNDAY 23
19 Deans Court
26 Frankham Farm
32 Herons Mead
55 10 Milner Road
61 The Old Rectory, Netherbury
75 Snape Cottage Plantsman's Garden

MONDAY 24
19 Deans Court
23 Edmondsham House
39 Ivy House Garden
55 10 Milner Road

SATURDAY 29
28 Grange Cottage
48 Manor Farm, Stourton Caundle

SUNDAY 30
28 Grange Cottage
48 Manor Farm, Stourton Caundle
73 Shute Farm

April

WEDNESDAY 2
17 Cranborne Manor Garden
23 Edmondsham House

SUNDAY 6
10 Chiffchaffs
32 Herons Mead
60 The Old Rectory, Litton Cheney

WEDNESDAY 9
23 Edmondsham House

FRIDAY 11
43 Knitson Old Farmhouse

SATURDAY 12
43 Knitson Old Farmhouse
57 Moreton Gardens

SUNDAY 13
5 Bexington
20 Domineys Yard
39 Ivy House Garden
43 Knitson Old Farmhouse
57 Moreton Gardens
85 Wentworth College

MONDAY 14
43 Knitson Old Farmhouse

WEDNESDAY 16
23 Edmondsham House

SATURDAY 19
22 35 Dunkeld Road

SUNDAY 20
6 Broomhill
66 Rampisham Manor
68 46 Roslin Road South

WEDNESDAY 23
23 Edmondsham House
38 Horn Park

SATURDAY 26
7 15a Cassel Avenue
45 Knowle Farm

SUNDAY 27
7 15a Cassel Avenue
9 Chideock Manor
14 Corfe Barn
27 The Glade

WEDNESDAY 30
9 Chideock Manor

May

SUNDAY 4
2 Analal's Gallery
7 15a Cassel Avenue
15 Corscombe House
24 The Ferns
26 Frankham Farm
32 Herons Mead
61 The Old Rectory, Netherbury
90 Wolverhollow

MONDAY 5
4 Beech House
7 15a Cassel Avenue
39 Ivy House Garden

TUESDAY 6
2 Analal's Gallery
59 'OLA'
90 Wolverhollow

WEDNESDAY 7
2 Analal's Gallery

SUNDAY 11
5 Bexington
18 44 Daws Avenue
27 The Glade
31 Hatchlands
33 Higher Melcombe
34 Highwood Garden
40 Japanese Gardens
50 Mayfield
54 The Mill House
64 54 Parkwood Road

TUESDAY 13
2 Analal's Gallery

WEDNESDAY 14
2 Analal's Gallery

SATURDAY 17
68 46 Roslin Road South

70 The Secret Garden

SUNDAY 18
8 Chesil Gallery & Chiswell Walled Garden
20 Domineys Yard
33 Higher Melcombe
34 Highwood Garden
36 Holworth Farmhouse
47 Manor Farm, Hampreston
52 Melplash Court
60 The Old Rectory, Litton Cheney
68 46 Roslin Road South
70 The Secret Garden
73 Shute Farm
74 Slape Manor
89 1692 Wimborne Road

TUESDAY 20
2 Analal's Gallery
59 'OLA'

WEDNESDAY 21
2 Analal's Gallery
50 Mayfield

SUNDAY 25
13 Coombe Cottage
14 Corfe Barn
19 Deans Court
21 Duckdown Cottage
24 The Ferns
27 The Glade
61 The Old Rectory, Netherbury
66 Rampisham Manor
79 Toad Hall
81 Vine Cottage
90 Wolverhollow

MONDAY 26
14 Corfe Barn
19 Deans Court
90 Wolverhollow

TUESDAY 27
2 Analal's Gallery

WEDNESDAY 28
2 Analal's Gallery
66 Rampisham Manor

FRIDAY 30
69 St Michael's House

SATURDAY 31
22 35 Dunkeld Road
69 St Michael's House (Evening)

June

SUNDAY 1
18 44 Daws Avenue
24 The Ferns
26 Frankham Farm
50 Mayfield
51 Mayo Farm
83 Watendlath
86 79 West Street

TUESDAY 3
59 'OLA'

WEDNESDAY 4
32 Herons Mead
51 Mayo Farm

SATURDAY 7
17 Cranborne Manor Garden
28 Grange Cottage (Evening)
41 Kingston Lacy
48 Manor Farm, Stourton Caundle (Evening)

SUNDAY 8
4 Beech House
5 Bexington
27 The Glade
28 Grange Cottage
36 Holworth Farmhouse
37 Honeycombe
39 Ivy House Garden
40 Japanese Gardens
41 Kingston Lacy
48 Manor Farm, Stourton Caundle
64 54 Parkwood Road
82 Warmwell House
89 1692 Wimborne Road

TUESDAY 10
60 The Old Rectory, Litton Cheney

WEDNESDAY 11
37 Honeycombe
77 Stanbridge Mill

SATURDAY 14
68 46 Roslin Road South
69 St Michael's House (Evening)

SUNDAY 15
3 Ashton Farm
8 Chesil Gallery & Chiswell Walled Garden
11 Coach House
29 Greenacres
30 Grovestall Farm
37 Honeycombe
68 46 Roslin Road South
69 St Michael's House
81 Vine Cottage

MONDAY 16
76 Springhead (Afternoon & Evening)

WEDNESDAY 18
3 Ashton Farm
32 Herons Mead
50 Mayfield
65 3 Priory Gardens

FRIDAY 20
45 Knowle Farm

SATURDAY 21
36 Holworth Farmhouse
63 Park Homer Drive Gardens

SUNDAY 22
31 Hatchlands
36 Holworth Farmhouse

63 Park Homer Drive Gardens
65 3 Priory Gardens
75 Snape Cottage Plantsman's Garden
78 Tithe Barn House
87 24a Western Avenue

WEDNESDAY 25
9 Chideock Manor
65 3 Priory Gardens

SUNDAY 29
8 Chesil Gallery & Chiswell Walled Garden
9 Chideock Manor
14 Corfe Barn
26 Frankham Farm
52 Melplash Court
58 4 Noel Road
65 3 Priory Gardens

July

TUESDAY 1
2 Analal's Gallery

WEDNESDAY 2
2 Analal's Gallery

SATURDAY 5
22 35 Dunkeld Road

SUNDAY 6
2 Analal's Gallery
6 Broomhill
24 The Ferns
36 Holworth Farmhouse
68 46 Roslin Road South
83 Watendlath
86 79 West Street
89 1692 Wimborne Road

TUESDAY 8
2 Analal's Gallery

WEDNESDAY 9
2 Analal's Gallery
38 Horn Park

SUNDAY 13
5 Bexington
8 Chesil Gallery & Chiswell Walled Garden
15 Corscombe House
35 Hilltop
47 Manor Farm, Hampreston
54 The Mill House
58 4 Noel Road
67 357 Ringwood Road

TUESDAY 15
2 Analal's Gallery

WEDNESDAY 16
2 Analal's Gallery

SATURDAY 19
41 Kingston Lacy

SUNDAY 20
21 Duckdown Cottage
29 Greenacres
35 Hilltop

76 Springhead (Evening)
82 Warmwell House

TUESDAY 22
2 Analal's Gallery

WEDNESDAY 23
2 Analal's Gallery

SATURDAY 26
19 Deans Court
71 The Secret Garden at Serles House (Evening)

SUNDAY 27
8 Chesil Gallery & Chiswell Walled Garden
16 Cottesmore Farm
19 Deans Court
35 Hilltop
36 Holworth Farmhouse
71 The Secret Garden at Serles House
87 24a Western Avenue

TUESDAY 29
2 Analal's Gallery

WEDNESDAY 30
2 Analal's Gallery
62 The Old Rectory, Pulham
67 357 Ringwood Road

August

SUNDAY 3
2 Analal's Gallery
8 Chesil Gallery & Chiswell Walled Garden
10 Chiffchaffs
16 Cottesmore Farm
35 Hilltop
62 The Old Rectory, Pulham

TUESDAY 5
2 Analal's Gallery

WEDNESDAY 6
2 Analal's Gallery

SUNDAY 10
5 Bexington
8 Chesil Gallery & Chiswell Walled Garden
20 Domineys Yard
35 Hilltop
67 357 Ringwood Road
71 The Secret Garden at Serles House

TUESDAY 12
2 Analal's Gallery

WEDNESDAY 13
2 Analal's Gallery

SUNDAY 17
29 Greenacres

TUESDAY 19
2 Analal's Gallery

WEDNESDAY 20
2 Analal's Gallery

6 Broomhill

SATURDAY 23
71 The Secret Garden at Serles House (Evening)

SUNDAY 24
13 Coombe Cottage
19 Deans Court
71 The Secret Garden at Serles House
79 Toad Hall

MONDAY 25
19 Deans Court
71 The Secret Garden at Serles House

TUESDAY 26
2 Analal's Gallery

WEDNESDAY 27
2 Analal's Gallery

September

SATURDAY 6
19 Deans Court
64 54 Parkwood Road (Evening)
71 The Secret Garden at Serles House (Evening)

SUNDAY 7
19 Deans Court
47 Manor Farm, Hampreston
71 The Secret Garden at Serles House

FRIDAY 12
43 Knitson Old Farmhouse

SATURDAY 13
43 Knitson Old Farmhouse

SUNDAY 14
5 Bexington
32 Herons Mead
43 Knitson Old Farmhouse
71 The Secret Garden at Serles House
85 Wentworth College

MONDAY 15
43 Knitson Old Farmhouse

SUNDAY 21
18 44 Daws Avenue

October

WEDNESDAY 8
23 Edmondsham House

WEDNESDAY 15
23 Edmondsham House

SUNDAY 19
20 Domineys Yard

WEDNESDAY 22
23 Edmondsham House

WEDNESDAY 29
23 Edmondsham House

December

SATURDAY 6
71 The Secret Garden at Serles House (Evening)

SUNDAY 7
64 54 Parkwood Road (Evening)

Gardens open to the public

1 Abbotsbury Gardens
10 Chiffchaffs
12 Compton Acres Gardens
17 Cranborne Manor Garden
23 Edmondsham House
25 Forde Abbey Gardens
35 Hilltop
36 Holworth Farmhouse
38 Horn Park
41 Kingston Lacy
42 Kingston Maurward Gardens
44 Knoll Gardens
49 Mapperton Gardens
56 Minterne
57 Moreton Gardens
72 Sherborne Castle
75 Snape Cottage Plantsman's Garden
76 Springhead
79 Toad Hall
80 Upwey Wishing Well

By appointment only

46 Langebride House
53 Mews Cottage
88 Weston House

Also open by appointment ☎

2 Analal's Gallery
5 Bexington
6 Broomhill
8 Chesil Gallery & Chiswell Walled Garden
11 Coach House
13 Coombe Cottage
20 Domineys Yard
27 The Glade
32 Herons Mead
33 Higher Melcombe
39 Ivy House Garden
40 Japanese Gardens
43 Knitson Old Farmhouse
45 Knowle Farm
47 Manor Farm, Hampreston
50 Mayfield
54 The Mill House
60 The Old Rectory, Litton Cheney
61 The Old Rectory, Netherbury
62 The Old Rectory, Pulham
66 Rampisham Manor
67 357 Ringwood Road
68 46 Roslin Road South

69 St Michael's House
71 The Secret Garden at Serles House
77 Stanbridge Mill
78 Tithe Barn House
87 24a Western Avenue
89 1692 Wimborne Road

The Gardens

1 ◆ ABBOTSBURY GARDENS
nr Weymouth DT3 4LA. Ilchester Estates, 01305 871412, www.abbotsbury-tourism.co.uk/gardens. *8m W of Weymouth. From B3157 Weymouth-Bridport, 200yds W of Abbotsbury village.* **Please phone for times/adm prices**
20 acres, started in 1760 and considerably extended in C19. Much recent replanting, very fine collection of rhododendrons, camellias, azaleas. Unique maritime micro-climate enables a flourishing Mediterranean bank and southern hemisphere garden to grow rare and tender plants. In summer there are palm trees, bananas, cannas; ponds and streamside plantings. Children's play area, sculpture trail, plant sales, shop, aviaries and Colonial tea-house.
♿ ⊛ ☕

2 NEW ANALAL'S GALLERY
25 Millhams Street. BH23 1DN. Anna & Lal Sims, 01202 567585. *Christchurch town centre. Park in Saxon Square PCP - exit to Millham St via alley at side of church.* **Adm £2.50, chd free. Suns 4 May, 6 July, 3 Aug; Tues, Weds, 6 May to 28 May; Tues, Weds 1 July to 27 Aug. Tues (10-1); Weds (10-4); Suns (12-4). Visitors also welcome by appt May, July, Aug.**
Unusual 100 yr-old cottage, home of two Royal Academy artists, and garden of varied artwork. Clematis-covered pencil gate arch leads to small Victorian walled garden filled with colour and scent of jasmine and honeysuckle. Sculptures and paintings hidden among the many colourful flowers and shrubs. 3 patio levels. A truly magical experience. Paintings and sculptures for sale - occasional art class in progress. The Ducking Stool Tea Rooms are nearby.
✂ ☎

APPLE COURT
See Hampshire.

❸ ASHTON FARM
**Martinstown DT2 9HA. James &
Jenny Shanahan.** *3m SW of
Dorchester. From A35 take A354
towards Weymouth, after ¾ m R to
Winterborne Monkton, through gated
rd for 1½ m. After sharp R-hand bend,
L into drive to car park.* Home-made
teas. **Adm £3, chd free. Sun 15, Wed
18 June (2-5.30).**
Nestling below Maiden Castle this
exuberant garden, surrounded by
meadow and woodland, is largely
informal with an emphasis on attracting
wildlife. Overflowing with old-fashioned
roses, flowering shrubs and
herbaceous borders, visitors are
enticed into the walled garden or led
along secret paths, some steep, onto
pastoral views. Exhibition of paintings.

✖ ❀ ☕

Enjoy being led
up the garden
path to discover
the surprises
that emerge . . .

❹ NEW BEECH HOUSE
**New Street, Marnhull DT10 1QA.
Linda & Peter Antell.** *2m NE of
Sturminster Newton. From A30
take B3092 signed Sturminster
Newton. In Marnhull, just past The
Crown PH, 2nd R beside church.
Garden ¼ m on R, just before
Xrds.* Home-made teas. **Adm £3,
chd free. Mon 5 May; Sun 8 June
(10-5).**
Approx 1acre of interesting
features and flowers. Enjoy being
led up the garden path to discover
the surprises that emerge in the
sequence of garden rooms behind
the house. Gravel entrance.

♿ ✖ ❀ ☕

❺ BEXINGTON
**Lime Kiln Road, Lytchett Matravers
BH16 6EL. Mr & Mrs Robin
Crumpler, 01202 622068.** *5m SW of
Wimborne Minster. Opp old school at
W end of village.* Cream teas. **Adm £2,
chd free (share to Alzheimers**

Disease Society (Poole branch)).
**Suns 13 Apr; 11 May; 8 June; 13
July; 10 Aug; 14 Sept (2-5.30).
Visitors also welcome by appt.**
Colourful garden of ½ acre maintained
by owners, with mixed borders of
many interesting and unusual plants,
shrubs and trees. Bog garden of
primulas, hostas etc. Rockery,
collection of grasses and ferns, with
walkways over bog area connecting
two lawns, making a garden of interest
from spring bulbs to autumn colour.

♿ ✖ ❀ ☕ ☎

BRAEMOOR
See Hampshire.

BRAMBLE HAYES
See Devon.

❻ BROOMHILL
**Rampisham DT2 0PU. Mr & Mrs D
Parry, 01935 83266.** *11m NW of
Dorchester. From Yeovil take A37
towards Dorchester, 7m turn R signed
Evershot. From Dorchester take A37 to
Yeovil, 4m turn L A356 signed
Crewkerne; at start of wireless masts R
to Rampisham. Follow signs.* Home-
made teas July & Aug. **Adm £3, chd
free. Sun 20 Apr; Sun 6 July; Wed 20
Aug (2-6). Also open Rampisham
Manor 20 April, combined adm £6.
Visitors also welcome by appt.**
Delightful 1-acre garden in lovely
peaceful setting, which incorporates a
disused farmyard and paddock. Pretty
trellised entrance leads to an
abundance of island beds and borders
planted with shrubs, roses and many
unusual and interesting herbaceous
plants, giving yr-round colour. Lawns
gently slope down to large wildlife
pond and bog garden. Mown paths
take you around pond to less formal
area of mixed trees and shrubs. New
late summer border.

♿ ✖ ❀ ☕ ☎

BUCKLAND STEAD
See Hampshire.

❼ 15A CASSEL AVENUE
**Westbourne BH13 6JD. John &
Jeannie Blay.** *2m W of Bournemouth.
From centre of Westbourne turn S into
Alumhurst Rd, take 8th turning on R
into Mountbatten Rd then 1st L into
Cassel Ave.* **Adm £2.50, chd free. Sat
26, Sun 27 Apr; Sun 4, Mon 5 May
(2-5).**
Unique Chine garden of ½ acre.
Wooded coastal site, steeply banked
and spanned by a bridge with 330
tonnes of Purbeck stone incorporated

in the original construction. 2 ponds,
formal lawn surrounded by clipped
hedge, Palladian rotunda and
sculptural pieces. Planting incl
subtropical species, ferns, mature
shrubs, azaleas, rhododendrons, pieris
and hydrangeas together with
numerous perennials. Due to steep
steps and uneven paths the garden is
unsuitable for the less mobile.

❀

CHERRY BOLBERRY FARM
See Somerset & Bristol Area.

**❽ CHESIL GALLERY &
CHISWELL WALLED GARDEN**
**Pebble Lane, Chiswell DT5 1AW.
Mrs Margaret Somerville, 01305
822738,
www.chiswellcommunity.org.** *3m N
of Portland Bill. S of Weymouth. Follow
signs to Portland; from Victoria Square
turn R into Chiswell & immed R into
Pebble Lane. Park in car park by
Bluefish Restaurant.* Cream teas in
Chiswell Walled Garden. **Adm £2.50,
chd free (share to Chiswell
Community Trust). Suns 18 May; 15,
29 June; 13, 27 July; 3, 10 Aug (1-5).
Visitors also welcome by appt.**
Small, delightful garden in lee of Chesil
Bank. 2 courtyard gardens provide
domestic adjunct to artists' studio. On
upper level flowering plants of coastal
regions have been naturalised.
Information on the flora of Chesil
Beach and the history of Chiswell is
available with entrance ticket at Chesil
Gallery. Both gardens, The Chesil
Gallery and The Chiswell Walled
Garden, a very successful community
project, grow plants which are tolerant
of extreme maritime situations. Partial
wheelchair access in Gallery, full
access in Walled Garden.

♿ ✖ ❀ ☕ ☎

❾ CHIDEOCK MANOR
**Chideock, nr Bridport DT6 6LF. Mr &
Mrs Howard Coates.** *2m W of
Bridport on A35. In centre of village
turn N at church. The Manor is ¼ m
along this rd on R.* Home-made teas.
**Adm £4, chd free. Sun 27, Wed 30
Apr; Wed 25, Sun 29 June (2-5).**
Large formal and informal gardens,
some in process of development. Bog
garden beside stream. Woodland and
lakeside walks. Walled vegetable
garden and orchard. Yew hedges and
many mature trees. Lime walk.
Herbaceous borders. Rose and
clematis arches. Fine views.

♿ ✖ ☕

10 ◆ CHIFFCHAFFS
Chaffeymoor, Bourton SP8 5BY. Mr & Mrs K R Potts, 01747 840841. *3m E of Wincanton. W end of Bourton. N of A303.* **Adm £3.50, chd free. Weds, Thurs, Mar to Sept incl; 1st & 3rd Suns Apr to June & Easter Sun. For NGS: Suns 6 Apr; 3 Aug (2-5).**
A garden for all seasons with many interesting plants, bulbs, shrubs, herbaceous border, shrub roses. Attractive walk to woodland garden with far-reaching views across Blackmore Vale.
✸ ❀

Luxuriant tropical planting; bananas, bamboos, gunneras and over 100 palms . . .

11 COACH HOUSE
Church Street, Sturminster Newton DT10 1DB. Ann & Hugh Hay, 01258 473139. *Bottom of Church St.* Home-made teas at Church Farm House (secluded tea garden opp Coach House). **Adm £2.50, chd free. Sun 15 June (2-5). Visitors also welcome by appt.**
Small town garden. Following 24 yrs at Sweetwell, Fiddleford, the Hays have made a new garden. 2½ yrs on, the former coach house and yard are transforming into a relaxed, informal garden with vista across river meadows. Partial wheelchair access.
♿ ☕ ☎

COMBPYNE MANOR
See Devon.

12 ◆ COMPTON ACRES GARDENS
164 Canford Cliffs Road. BH13 7ES. Bernard Merna, 01202 700778, events@comptonacres.co.uk, www.comptonacres.co.uk. *2m E of Poole.* Signed from Bournemouth & Poole. Wilts & Dorset Buses 150, 151. Yellow Bus 12 stops at entrance. **Adm £6.95, chd £3.95, concessions £6.45. Daily (not open Xmas Day/ Boxing Day), summer (9-6), winter (10-4).**
10 acres of themed gardens, rare and specie plants, spectacular views over Poole Harbour and Purbeck Hills.

Discover peace and tranquillity, and draw inspiration from the Japanese and Italian gardens. Enjoy the Heather Garden, the Wooded Valley and the Rock and Water garden with its large collection of Koi Carp.
♿ ✸ ❀ ☕

13 COOMBE COTTAGE
Shillingstone DT11 0SF. Mike & Jennie Adams, 01258 860220, mja@bryanston.co.uk. *5m NW of Blandford. On A357 next to PO Stores on main rd. Parking advised in Gunn Lane.* Teas at Toad Hall. **Adm £2.50, chd free. Suns 25 May; 24 Aug (2-6). Visitors also welcome by appt.**
⅓ -acre plantsman's mixed garden, delineated by walls, hedges and arbours, with a long season of herbaceous and woody perennials, climbers, bulbs and self-seeding annuals (many unusual and subtropical, combining flower-power with bold foliage), densely packed broad borders, pots and large plant house.
❀ ☎

14 CORFE BARN
Corfe Lodge Road, Broadstone BH18 9NQ. Mr & Mrs John McDavid. *1m W of Broadstone centre. From main roundabout in Broadstone, W along Clarendon Rd ¾ m, N into Roman Rd, after 50yds W into Corfe Lodge Rd.* Home-made teas. **Adm £2, chd free. Suns 27 Apr; 25 May, Mon 26 May; Sun 29 June (2-5).**
⅔ acre on three levels on site of C19 lavender farm. Informal country garden with much to interest both gardeners and flower arrangers. Parts of the original farm have been incorporated in the design. A particular feature of the garden is the use made of old walls. Exhibition of paintings by local artist.
✸ ❀ ☕

15 CORSCOMBE HOUSE
Corscombe DT2 0NU. Jim Bartos. *3½ m N of Beaminster. From Dorchester A356 to Crewkerne, take 1st turn to Corscombe, R signed Church. Or A37 Yeovil to Dorchester, turn W signed Sutton Bingham/ Halstock/ Corscombe. Straight past Fox Inn, up hill, L signed Church.* Cream teas 4 May only in Vicarage. **Adm £3.50, chd free. Suns 4 May; 13 July (2-5.30).**
Garden in grounds of former rectory with view of Church. Garden rooms with colour-themed cool and hot

borders, sunny and shady beds, parterre, reflecting pool, part-walled vegetable garden and orchard in meadow. New for 2008, secret garden in Persian style with central fountain, lemon trees in pots (July) and other Mediterranean planting. Featured in GGG.
❀ ☕

16 COTTESMORE FARM
Newmans Lane. BH22 0LW. Paul & Valerie Guppy. *1m N of West Moors. Off B3072 Bournemouth to Verwood rd.* Car parking in owner's field. Home-made teas. **Adm £3, chd free (share to Cats Protection). Suns 27 July; 3 Aug (2-4.30).**
Luxuriant tropical planting; bananas, bamboos, gunneras and over 100 palms. Many rare plants incl beds dedicated to Australian and S American species. Large herbaceous borders, grass beds and wild flower area. Fancy fowl and rare breed sheep making an acre of considerable interest.
♿ ✸ ☕

17 ◆ CRANBORNE MANOR GARDEN
Cranborne BH21 5PP. Viscount Cranborne, 01725 517248, www.cranborne.co.uk. *10m N of Wimborne on B3078.* **Adm £4, chd 50p, concessions £3.50. Weds Mar-Sept. For NGS: Wed 2 Apr; Sat 7 June (9-4).**
Beautiful and historic garden laid out in C17 by John Tradescant and enlarged in C20, featuring several gardens surrounded by walls and yew hedges: white garden, herb and mount gardens, water and wild garden. Many interesting plants, with fine trees and avenues.
♿ ✸ ❀ ☕

18 44 DAWS AVENUE
Wallisdown BH11 8SD. Carol & John Farrance. *3m W of Bournemouth. Going N from Wallisdown roundabout take 1st L into Canford Ave then 1st R into Daws Ave.* Home-made teas. **Adm £2, chd free. Fri 21 Mar; Suns 11 May; 1 June; 21 Sept (2-5).**
Small town garden offering yr-round interest with emphasis in spring on camellias and magnolias, underplanted with daphnes, hellebores, erythroniums and trilliums. Roses provide summer colour and in autumn rare hydrangeas, hibiscus and eucryphias are in bloom. Enjoy tea in the summerhouse where a view of the stream can be appreciated.
✸ ☕

⑲ DEANS COURT

Deans Court Lane, Wimborne Minster BH21 1EE. Sir Michael Hanham. *¼ m SE of Minster. Just off B3073 in centre of Wimborne. Entry from Deans Court Lane - continuation of High St at junction with East St & King St over pavement & past bollard. Free parking.* Home-made/cream teas in garden or house (down steps). **Adm £4, chd free, senior citizens £3. Suns, Mons 23, 24 Mar; 25, 26 May; Sat 26, Sun 27 July; Sun 24, Mon 25 Aug; Sat 6, Sun 7 Sept. Sats, Suns (2-6), Mons (10-6).**
13 acres on R Allen; partly wild, with historic specimen trees. House originally the Deanery to the Minster. Herb garden, rose garden. Long serpentine wall. The house will be open by prior written appointment. Organic kitchen garden. Gravel path.

 ♿ ✗ ✿ ☕

DICOT
See Devon.

Over 350 varieties of plants, many to encourage wildlife . . .

⑳ DOMINEYS YARD

Buckland Newton DT2 7BS. Mr & Mrs W Gueterbock, 01300 345295, www.domineys.com. *11m N of Dorchester, 11m S of Sherborne. 2m E A352 or take B3143. Take 'no through rd' between Church & Gaggle of Geese. Entrance 100metres on L. Park & picnic in arboretum on R, 10metres before garden entrance.* Home-made teas; soup lunch 19 Oct only. **Adm £3.50, chd free (share to Arthritis Research Campaign). Suns 13 Apr; 18 May; 10 Aug (2-6); 19 Oct (12-4). Visitors also welcome by appt.**
Attractive, all-seasons garden of 2½ acres, where change continues after 47 yrs. Small, separate, 13 yr-old arboretum full of interest - trees, shrubs and bulbs. Views and vistas, pots and patios, fruit and vegetables. A garden to enjoy every day come rain or shine. Each month brings highlights and variation and interest for all. Gravel drive, some grass paths.

 ♿ ✗ ✿ 🛏 ☕ ☎

㉑ NEW DUCKDOWN COTTAGE

Shaftesbury Road, Child Okeford DT11 8EQ. Richard & Sarah Mower. *6m N of Blandford. From Blandford take A350 N. Through Stourpaine village, ½ m turn L signed Child Okeford. On entering Child Okeford R at Memorial Cross signed Iwerne Minster. Garden ¾ m on L, parking 50yds past garden on R.* Home-made teas. **Adm £2.50, chd free (share to MS Society). Suns 25 May; 20 July (2-5). Also open Coombe Cottage and Toad Hall 25 May.**
Plantsman's garden on SW-facing slope overlooking open fields. Mixed cottage borders, formal areas and pretty meandering stream incorporating over 350 varieties of plants, many to encourage wildlife. Large Victorian planthouse, gravelled courtyard, raised deck terrace, kitchen garden and seating areas for quiet reflection.

 ✗ ☕

㉒ NEW 35 DUNKELD ROAD

Talbot Woods BH3 7EW. Helga Von Ow. *1m NW of Bournemouth. Off Glenferness Ave.* Home-made teas. **Adm £2.50, chd free. Sats 19 Apr; 31 May; 5 July (2-5).**
Plant enthusiast's garden with many different plants offering all-yr interest. Emphasis on shrubs and trees suitable for an urban garden, also many interesting flowers and grasses. Wildlife particularly encouraged. Owners keep bees.

 ♿ ✗ ✿ ☕

㉓ ◆ EDMONDSHAM HOUSE

Wimborne BH21 5RE. Mrs Julia Smith, 01725 517207. *9m NE of Wimborne. 9m W of Ringwood. Between Cranborne & Verwood. Edmondsham off B3081.* Home-made teas Weds in April & Oct only. **House and garden adm £5, chd £1, under 5 free, garden only adm £2.50, chd 50p, under 5 free. Suns, Weds, 2 Apr to 29 Oct (2-5), house also open Weds, Apr & Oct only & BH Mons. For NGS: Mon 24 Mar; Weds 2, 9, 16, 23 Apr; 8, 15, 22, 29 Oct (2-5).**
An historic 6-acre garden of C16 house. Interesting mature specimen trees and shrubs. Spring bulbs and blossom, autumn cyclamen. Early church, Victorian dairy and stable block, medieval grass cock pit. Walled

garden with vegetables, fruit and traditional herbaceous borders planted to sustain long period of interest. Managed organically. Gravel paths. No disabled toilet facilities.

 ♿ ✗ ✿ ☕

㉔ THE FERNS

East Burton, Wool BH20 6HE. John & Jill Redfern. *Approaching Wool from Wareham, turn R just before level crossing into East Burton Rd. Garden on R, just under a mile down this rd.* Home-made teas. **Adm £2, chd free. Suns 4, 25 May; 1 June; 6 July (2-5).**
Profusely planted with varied herbaceous borders and shrubs. Interesting use of hard landscaping. Fruit and vegetable garden leads to small woodland garden and stream and a scene from Dorset clay-mining history. 'A lovely, secret garden' (Dorset Life).

 ♿ ✿ ☕

㉕ ◆ FORDE ABBEY GARDENS

Chard TA20 4LU. Mr Mark Roper, www.fordeabbey.co.uk. *4m SE of Chard. Signed off A30 Chard-Crewkerne & A358 Chard-Axminster. Also from Broadwindsor.* **Please phone 01460 221290 for current times/adm prices. Gardens open daily throughout the yr (10 - last adm 4.30).**
30 acres, fine shrubs, magnificent specimen trees, ponds, herbaceous borders, rockery, bog garden containing superb collection of Asiatic primulas, Ionic temple, working kitchen garden supplying the restaurant. Centenary fountain, England's highest powered fountain. SW Tourism Small Visitor Attraction of the Year Gold Winner. Gravel paths, some steep slopes.

 ♿ ✿ ☕

FOREST LODGE
See Somerset & Bristol Area.

㉖ FRANKHAM FARM

Ryme Intrinseca DT9 6JT. Richard Earle. *3m S of Yeovil. A37 Yeovil-Dorchester; turn E; drive ¼ m on L.* Home-made teas. **Adm £2.50, chd free. Suns 23 Mar; 4 May; 1, 29 June (2-5).**
3½ -acre garden, begun in 1960s by the late Jo Earle for yr-round interest. Perennials and roses round house and stone farm buildings. Extensive wall plantings incl roses and clematis, herbaceous borders, productive vegetable and fruit garden. Many

unusual shrubs and trees, particularly hardwoods, shelter belts of trees forming woodland walks, underplanted with camellias, rhododendrons, hydrangeas and spring bulbs. Plenty to see from February onwards.

  ♿ ✕ ☕

GANTS MILL & GARDEN
See Somerset & Bristol Area.

㉗ THE GLADE
Woodland Walk, Ferndown BH22 9LP. Mary & Roger Angus, 01202 872789. *3/4 m NE of Ferndown centre. N off Wimborne Rd East, nr Tricketts Cross roundabout, Woodland Walk is a metalled but single carriageway lane with no parking bays; please park on main rd and access on foot (5 mins/330yds).* Home-made teas. **Adm £3, chd free.** Suns 27 Apr; 11, 25 May; 8 June (2-5.30). Visitors also welcome by appt for groups of 15+ Apr to June incl.

1*3/4* -acre landscaped garden in sylvan setting. Mature trees and shrubbery incl stewartia, taxodium, camellia, azalea, rhododendron, kalmia. Younger plantings incl prunus, malus, pieris, solanum, amalanchier, rambling roses. Woodland walks with wild anemones, primroses, bluebells. Stream and large wildlife pond with primulas, marginals and waterlilies. Bog garden, wet meadow, spring bulbs, herbaceous and mixed borders. 'Best Garden Open for Charity', Ferndown in Bloom.

  ✿ ☕ ☎

190 GOLDCROFT
See Somerset & Bristol Area.

㉘ NEW GRANGE COTTAGE
Golden Hill, Stourton Caundle DT10 2JP. Fleur Miles. *6m SE of Sherborne. Park at Manor Farm or The Trooper PH, walk up hill to thatched cottage on R.* Home-made teas at Manor Farm barn. **Adm £3.50, chd free.** Sat 29, Sun 30 Mar; Sun 8 June (2-5). **Evening Opening** Sat 7 June (6-8.30). Also open **Manor Farm.**
Come and discover the peace and tranquillity of a real cottage garden. Follow the meandering paths and find many flower borders, box and yew hedging, two ponds, topiary creatures and much more to delight you. Hellebores and spring bulbs a particular feature. Treasure trail for children.

  ✕ ☕

㉙ GREENACRES
Bere Road, Coldharbour, Wareham BH20 7PA. John & Pat Jacobs. *2*1/2 *m NW of Wareham. From roundabout adjacent to stn take Wareham-Bere Regis rd. House 1/2 m past Silent Woman Inn.* Home-made teas. **Adm £2.50, chd free.** Suns 15 June; 20 July; 17 Aug (2-6).

2/3 -acre plantswoman's garden nestling in Wareham Forest. Lawns punctuated by colourful island beds designed for summer interest. Unusual perennials, shrubs and specimen trees, incl a flowering-size liriodendron. Stone water feature with 2 small ponds connected by tumbling water. Stumpery with collection of ferns and grasses. Various breeds poultry.

  ♿ ✕ ✿ ☕

㉚ GROVESTALL FARM
Chilfrome DT2 0HA. Mr & Mrs David Orr. *10m NW of Dorchester. From Yeovil take A37 to Dorchester. 10*1/2 *m turn R into Maiden Newton, R at T-junction and 1st R to Chilfrome. From Dorchester take A37 to Yeovil. 7m turn L into Maiden Newton, then as above. Follow signs. Caution on narrow final lane.* Teas. **Adm £2.50, chd free.** Sun 15 June (2-6).

2-acre, 6-8 yr-old garden created around old farm buildings. Densely planted former rd, walled kitchen garden and 2 small, formal gardens linked by iris and lavender walk. The very rural setting includes a 6-acre 6 yr-old broadleaf wood with mown rides.

  ✕ ☕

㉛ HATCHLANDS
Netherbury DT6 5NA. Dr & Mrs John Freeman. *2m SW of Beaminster. Turn R off A3066 Beaminster to Bridport Rd, signed Netherbury. Car park at Xrds at bottom of hill. 200yds up bridle path.* Home-made teas June only. **Adm £3.50, chd free.** Suns 11 May; 22 June (2-6). Also open **The Mill House** 11 May, combined adm £5.
Country hillside garden within 3 acres. Tall yew and box hedges bordering rose gardens, herbaceous and fuchsia beds and many hardy geraniums beneath a long Georgian brick wall. Open sloping lawns and croquet court, spring-fed pond and mature broadleaf trees.

  ✿ ☕

HEDDON HALL
See Devon.

㉜ HERONS MEAD
East Burton Road, East Burton, Wool BH20 6HF. Ron & Angela Millington, 01929 463872. *6m W of Wareham on A352. Approaching Wool from Wareham, turn R just before level crossing into East Burton Rd. Herons Mead 3/4 m on L.* Home-made teas. **Adm £2.50, chd free.** Suns 23 Mar; 6 Apr; 4 May; Weds 4, 18 June; Sun 14 Sept (2-5). Visitors also welcome by appt for groups of 10+.

Long 1/2 -acre garden winding through plant-filled borders, island beds, tiny orchard, kitchen garden, exuberant cottage garden with old roses, finally circling a woodland garden. Spring bulbs, hellebores, epimediums, pulmonarias and foxgloves; grasses and a riot of late-summer colour. Very wildlife friendly. Cactus collection. Teas served around painted chattelhouse.

  ✿ ☕ ☎

Come and discover the peace and tranquillity of a real cottage garden . . .

㉝ HIGHER MELCOMBE
Melcombe Bingham DT2 7PB. Mr M C Woodhouse & Mrs L Morton, 01258 880251, lorel@lorelmorton.com. *11m NE of Dorchester. Puddletown exit on A35. Follow signs for Cheselbourne then Melcombe Bingham.* Home-made teas. **Adm £3.50, chd free.** Suns 11, 18 May (12-4). Visitors also welcome by appt.

Approached through a lime avenue up private rd, the 2-acre garden is set in quiet valley surrounded by downland. Traditional English garden around C16 manor house and chapel with herbaceous beds, roses and magnificent copper beech and wonderful woodland views.

  ☕ ☎

㉞ HIGHWOOD GARDEN
Charborough Park, Wareham BH20 7EW. H W Drax Esq, www.charborough.co.uk. *6m E of Bere Regis. Behind long wall on A31*

between Wimborne & Bere Regis. Enter park by Almer lodge if travelling from W, or Blandford or Lion Lodges if travelling from E. Follow signpost to Estate Office, then Highwood Garden. Home-made teas. **Adm £4, chd £2 (share to Morden PCC). Suns 11, 18 May (2.30-6).**
Large woodland garden with rhododendrons and azaleas.

35 ◆ HILLTOP
Woodville, Stour Provost SP8 5LY. Josse & Brian Emerson, 01747 838512, www.hilltopgarden.co.uk. *5m N of Sturminster Newton. On B3092 turn R at Stour Provost Xrds, signed Woodville. After 1¼ m thatched cottage on R.* **Adm £2, chd free. Every Thur June, July, Aug (2-6). For NGS: Suns 13, 20, 27 July; 3, 10 Aug (2-6).**
Well-established garden overflowing with a wealth of different and interesting perennials. Bold yet complementary plant combinations in curved and sweeping borders give a colourful and truly inspirational display. Relax, take a seat in this peaceful country garden and absorb the tranquillity of the Blackmore Vale. Nursery open Thurs, Mar-Sept. Featured in 'Period Living' and 'Country Gardener'.

36 ◆ HOLWORTH FARMHOUSE
Holworth, nr Owermoigne DT2 8NH. Anthony & Philippa Bush, 01305 852242, bushinarcadia@yahoo.co.uk. *7m E of Dorchester. 1m S of A352. Follow signs to Holworth. Through farmyard with duckpond on R. Ignore no access signs, 1st L.* **Adm £3.50, chd free. Weds 14 May to 27 Aug incl, groups by appointment. For NGS: Suns 18 May; 8 June; 6, 27 July; Sat, Sun 21, 22 June (2-6).**
Over past 27yrs this unique setting has been transformed into a garden with a range of styles and wide variety of features. Here you have the formal and informal, light and shade, running and still water, places to explore and places for peaceful contemplation. Planted with a wide range of mature and unusual trees, shrubs and perennials and surrounded by stunning views. We are also experimenting with hydroponics, with emphasis on water conservation. Featured in 'The English Garden'. Partial wheelchair access.

37 NEW HONEYCOMBE
13 Springfield Crescent, Sherborne DT9 6DN. Jean & Ted Gillingham. *From A352 (Horsecastle Lane), past Skippers PH, turn into Wynnes Rise then 1st L.* **Adm £2.50, chd free (share to St Margaret's Hospice, Yeovil). Sun 8, Wed 11, Sun 15 June (1.30-5).**
Many varieties of clematis scramble through trees, over arches and amongst a sumptuous display of roses, underplanted with a wide variety of herbaceous perennials in colour-themed borders.

38 ◆ HORN PARK
Tunnel Rd, Beaminster DT8 3HB. Mr & Mrs David Ashcroft, 01308 862212. *1½ m N of Beaminster. On A3066 from Beaminster, L before tunnel (see signs).* Teas by arrangement. **Adm £4, chd free. Tues to Thurs, Apr to Oct (9-5) by appt only, incl groups. For NGS: Weds 23 Apr; 9 July (2-5).**
Large garden with magnificent view to sea. Plantsman's garden, many rare plants and shrubs in terraced, herbaceous, rock and water gardens. Woodland garden and walks in bluebell woods. Good autumn colouring. Wild flower meadow with 164 varieties incl orchids. Partial wheelchair access.

Many varieties of clematis scramble through trees . . .

39 IVY HOUSE GARDEN
Piddletrenthide DT2 7QF. Bridget Bowen, 01300 348255, biddybowen@aol.com. *9m N of Dorchester. On B3143. In middle of Piddletrenthide village, opp PO/village stores near Piddle Inn.* Home-made teas. **Adm £3, chd free. Mon 24 Mar; Sun 13 Apr; Mon 5 May; Sun 8 June (2-5). Visitors also welcome by appt May/June, up to 20 people.**
Unusual and challenging ½ -acre plantsman's garden set on steep

hillside, with fine views. Themed areas and mixed borders, wildlife ponds, propagating garden, Mediterranean garden, greenhouses and polytunnel with nearby allotment. Daffodils, tulips, violets and hellebores in quantity for spring openings. Come prepared for steep terrain and a warm welcome. Wheelchair access to courtyard (and teas) only.

40 JAPANESE GARDENS
38 Bingham's Road, Crossways DT2 8BW. Mr & Mrs Geoffrey Northcote, 01305 854538. *6m E of Dorchester. Off Dick O th' Banks Rd, & the B3390. Parking in village.* **Adm £3, chd free. Suns 11 May; 8 June (1-5). Visitors also welcome by appt May to Sept, max 16 persons.**
Two unusual small gardens, designed by owner. Front garden features a green 'Turtle' island, pebble sea and contrasting yellow/blue borders. 'Sansui' and 'Moon Gate' mural paintings. Rear garden 26ft x 36ft symbolises 'River of Life' with 'Moon Waves' bridge, Torre gateway, railed paved terrace, hand-carved red granite features amid contrasting red/green foliage and flower forms. Design exhibition in garden room.

41 ◆ KINGSTON LACY
Wimborne Minster BH21 4EA. The National Trust, 01202 883402, kingstonlacy@nationaltrust.org.uk. *1½ m W of Wimborne Minster. On the Wimborne-Blandford rd B3082.* **House and garden adm £10, chd £5, garden only adm £5, chd £2.50. 15 Mar to 2 Nov incl, house closed Mons, Tues. Opening times vary according to season. Please phone or visit website for details. For NGS: Sat 7, Sun 8 June; Sat 19 July (10.30-6).**
43 acres of garden, 9 acres of lawn. Lime avenue, rhododendrons, azaleas and National Collection of convallarias. Parterre and sunken gardens planted with Edwardian schemes, spring and summer, incl tulips, hyacinths, begonias and heliotrope. Victorian fernery contains 35 varieties and National Collection of Anemone nemorosa. Rotunda planted with roses incl 'Bonica', 'Cardinal Hume', 'Nozomi' and 'Amber Queen'. Japanese garden restored to Henrietta Bankes' creation of 1910. Gravel paths and slopes.

42 ◆ KINGSTON MAURWARD GARDENS
Dorchester DT2 8PY. Kingston Maurward College, 01305 215003, www.kmc.ac.uk/gardens. *1m E of Dorchester. Off A35. Follow brown Tourist Information signs.* **Adm £5, chd £3, concessions £4.50. Open daily 4 Jan to 20 Dec (10-5.30 or dusk if earlier).**
National Collections of penstemons and salvias. Classic Georgian mansion (not open) set in 35 acres of gardens laid out in C18 and C20 with 5-acre lake. Terraces and gardens divided by hedges and stone balustrades. Stone features and interesting plants. Elizabethan walled garden laid out as demonstration. Nature and tree trails. Animal park. Partial wheelchair access. Gravel paths, steps and steep slopes.
♿ ✗ ⊛ NCCPG ☕

43 KNITSON OLD FARMHOUSE
Corfe Castle, nr Swanage BH20 5JB. Rachel & Mark Helfer, 01929 421681. *1m NW of Swanage. 3m E of Corfe Castle. Signed L off A351 Knitson. Ample parking in yard or in adjacent field.* Cream teas. **Adm £2.50, chd 50p. Daily Fri 11 to Mon 14 Apr; Fri 12 to Mon 15 Sept (1-5). Visitors also welcome by appt for individuals or small groups.**
Mature cottage garden. Herbaceous borders, rockeries, climbers, shrubs - 40 hostas. Large organic kitchen garden for self-sufficiency in fruit and vegetables incl kiwis! Many Roman and medieval Purbeck stone artefacts used in garden design, with ancient stone cottage and new moon-arch as backdrops. Some slopes and gravel paths in vegetable garden.
♿ ✗ ⊛ ☕ ☎

44 ◆ KNOLL GARDENS
Hampreston BH21 7ND. Mr Neil Lucas, 01202 873931, www.knollgardens.co.uk. *2¹/₂ m W of Ferndown. ETB brown signs from A31. Large car park.* **Adm £4.75, chd £3.25, concessions £4.25. Tues to Suns May to Nov incl (10-5). Other times on website.**
Exciting collection of grasses and perennials thrives within an informal setting of mature and unusual trees, shrubs and pools, creating a relaxed and intimate atmosphere. Mediterranean-style gravel garden, eye-catching Dragon Garden and Decennium border planted in the naturalistic style. Nationally acclaimed nursery specialising in grasses and perennials. National Collections of pennisetum, deciduous ceanothus and phygelius. Featured on BBC TV and in National Press, 'The English Garden', 'Gardens Illustrated' and 'Amateur Gardening' magazines.
♿ ✗ ⊛ NCCPG ☕

45 KNOWLE FARM
Uploders, nr Bridport DT6 4NS. Alison & John Halliday, 01308 485492, www.knowlefarmbandb.com. *1¹/₂ m E of Bridport. Leave A35 signed to Uploders about 2m E of Bridport. Turn back under A35 to reach Uploders. Turn L at T-junction (Crown Inn on L). Knowle Farm is 200yds on R, opp chapel. Careful roadside parking unless using Crown Inn (lunches served).* Home-made teas. **Adm £3, chd free. Sats 22 Mar; 26 Apr; Fri 20 June (1-6). Visitors also welcome by appt.**
1-acre informal valley garden on 3 levels with slopes and steps bordered by R Asker in conservation area. Tranquil setting with many restful seating areas. Wide variety of interesting and unusual plants. Extensive planting around old trees and mature shrubs. Bog garden, rose walk, small orchard meadow, riverside walk, kitchen garden, hens. Plantaholic's greenhouse. Partial wheelchair access, some steep grass slopes.
♿ ⊛ 🛏 ☕ ☎

46 LANGEBRIDE HOUSE
Long Bredy DT2 9HU. Mrs J Greener, 01308 482257. *8m W of Dorchester. S off A35, well signed. 1st gateway on L in village.* **Adm £3.50, chd free. Visitors welcome by appt Feb to July incl.**
Substantial old rectory garden with many designs for easier management. 200-yr-old beech trees, pleached limes, yew hedges, extensive collections of spring bulbs, herbaceous plants, flowering trees, shrubs and alpines. Some steep slopes.
♿ ✗ ☎

LIFT THE LATCH
See Somerset & Bristol Area.

THE LITTLE COTTAGE
See Hampshire.

MACPENNYS WOODLAND GARDEN & NURSERIES
See Hampshire.

MANOR FARM
See Somerset & Bristol Area.

47 MANOR FARM, HAMPRESTON
BH21 7LX. Guy & Anne Trehane, 01202 574223. *2¹/₂ m E of Wimborne, 2¹/₂ m W of Ferndown. From Canford Bottom roundabout on A31, take exit B3073 Ham Lane. ¹/₂ m turn R at Hampreston Xrds. House at bottom of village.* Home-made teas. **Adm £3, chd free. Suns 18 May; 13 July; 7 Sept (2-5). Visitors also welcome by appt.**
Traditional farmhouse garden designed and cared for by 3 generations of the Trehane family who have farmed here for over 90yrs. Garden now being restored and thoughtfully replanted with herbaceous borders and rose beds within box and yew hedges. Mature shrubbery, water and bog garden. Dorset hardy plant society autumn plant sale during Sept opening.
♿ ✗ ☕ ☕ ☎

48 NEW MANOR FARM, STOURTON CAUNDLE
Stourton Caundle DT10 2JW. Mr & Mrs O S L Simon. *6m E of Sherborne, 4 m W of Sturminster Newton. From Sherborne take A3030. At Bishops Caundle, L signed Stourton Caundle. After 1¹/₂ m, L opp Trooper Inn in middle of village.* Home-made teas. **Adm £4, chd free. Sat 29, Sun 30 Mar; Sun 8 June (2-5). Evening Opening wine, Sat 7 June (6-8.30). Also open Grange Cottage.**
C17 farmhouse and barns with walled garden in middle of village. Mature trees, shrubberies, herbaceous borders, lakes and vegetable garden. Lovingly created over last 40 yrs by current owners.
✗ ☕

Lovingly created over last 40 yrs by current owners . . .

49 ◆ MAPPERTON GARDENS
nr Beaminster DT8 3NR. The Earl &
Countess of Sandwich, 01308
862645, www.mapperton.com. *6m N
of Bridport. Off A35/A3066. 2m SE of
Beaminster off B3163.* **House and
garden adm £8.50, chd £4, garden
only adm £4.50, chd £2. Sun-Fri Mar
to Oct (11-5).**
Terraced valley gardens surrounding
Tudor/Jacobean manor house. On
upper levels, walled croquet lawn,
orangery and Italianate formal garden
with fountains, topiary, grottos, ponds
and herbaceous borders. Below, C17
summerhouse, fishponds, topiary and
borders. Lower garden with specimen
shrubs and rare trees, leading to
woodland and spring gardens.
Partial wheelchair access, upper levels
only.

50 NEW MAYFIELD
4 Walford Close, Wimborne
BH21 1PH. Mr & Mrs Terry
Wheeler, 01202 849838. *1/2 m N
of Wimborne. B3078 out of
Wimborne, R into Burts Hill, 1st L
into Walford Close.* Home-made
teas. **Adm £2, chd free. Sun 11,
Wed 21 May; Sun 1, Wed 18
June (2-5.30). Visitors also
welcome by appt May/June.**
Town garden of approx 1/4 acre.
Front: formal hard landscaping
planted with many drought-
resistant shrubs and perennials incl
cistus, halimiocistus, salvias and
sedum. Shady area has wide
variety of hostas. Back: contrasts
with winding beds separated
by grass paths and arches of
sweet pea and clematis. Ferns,
euphorbia beds, geraniums and
many other perennials. Pond and
greenhouse containing many
succulents.

51 MAYO FARM
Higher Blandford Road, Shaftesbury
SP7 0EF. Robin & Trish Porteous. *1/2
m E of Shaftesbury. On B3081
Shaftesbury to Blandford rd on
outskirts of Shaftesbury.* Home-
made/cream teas. **Adm £3, chd free.
Sun 1, Wed 4 June (2-6).**
2-acre garden, with walled areas,
ponds and herbaceous borders, which
has spectacular views of Melbury Hill
and the edge of the Blackmore Vale.

52 MELPLASH COURT
Melplash DT6 3UH. Mrs Timothy
Lewis. *4m N of Bridport. On A3066,
just N of Melplash. Turn W & enter
between main gates & long ave of
chestnut trees.* Home-made teas.
**Adm £4, chd free. Suns 18 May; 29
June (2-6).**
Gardens, originally designed by Lady
Diana Tiarks, continue to evolve and
consist of park planting, bog garden,
croquet lawn and adjacent borders.
Formal kitchen garden and herb
garden, ponds, streams and lake; new
borders and areas of interest are
added and opened up each yr.

Magnificent collection of camellias, magnolias and azaleas . . .

53 MEWS COTTAGE
34 Easton Street, Portland DT5 1BT.
Peter & Jill Pitman, 01305 820377,
penstemon@waitrose.com. *3m S of
Weymouth. Situated on top of the
Island, 50yds past Punchbowl Inn,
small lane on L. Park in main street &
follow signs.* Home-made teas by
arrangement. **Adm £1.50, chd free.
Visitors welcome by appt for groups
July/Aug/Oct to see 'work in
progress' nearing completion.**
Spring sees hellebores, snowdrops
and other bulbs. Summer, over 90
named agapanthus grow amongst
National Collection of penstemon.
Fernery with fossil collection. Autumn
colour is crowned by *Nerine bowdenii*,
plus pond with arum lilies and
herbaceous planting, all in 1/4 acre.
Reorganisation/reconstruction in
progress (to include better wheelchair
access).
NCCPG

54 THE MILL HOUSE
Crook Hill, Netherbury DT6 5LX.
Michael & Giustina Ryan, 01308
488267,
themillhouse@dial.pipex.com. *1m S
of Beaminster. Turn R off A3066
Beaminster to Bridport rd at signpost
to Netherbury. Car park at Xrds at
bottom of hill.* Home-made teas. **Adm
£3.50, chd free. Suns 11 May; 13
July (2-6). Also open 11 May
Hatchlands, joint adm £5. Visitors**

also welcome by appt for groups,
coaches permitted.
Several small gardens arranged round
the Mill, its stream and pond, incl
formal walled garden, terraced flower
garden, vegetable garden and mill
stream garden. Emphasis on scented
flowers, hardy geraniums, lilies, spring
bulbs, clematis and water irises.
Remaining 4 acres planted with a wide
variety of trees: magnolias, fruit trees,
acers, oaks, eucalyptus, birches,
liriodendrons, nothofagus, willows,
alders and conifers. Partial wheelchair
access.

55 10 MILNER ROAD
Westbourne BH4 8AD. Mr & Mrs
Colin Harding. *1 1/2 m W of
Bournemouth. E of Westbourne on
Poole Rd. S at T-lights into Clarendon
Rd. Cross over Westcliff Rd into
Westovercliff Dr. 1st R, then 1st L and
1st R into Milner Rd.* Home-made teas.
**Adm £3, chd free. Sun 23, Mon 24
Mar (11-6).**
Modern clifftop garden designed and
constructed by Colin Harding in 1986
in a natural style with key formal
accents incl many natural driftwood
sculptures. Wide range of fruit and
specimen trees encl by mature holly
and rhododendron hedges.
Magnificent collection of camellias,
magnolias and azaleas underplanted
with helebores and spring bulbs.

56 ◆ MINTERNE
Minterne Magna DT2 7AU. The Hon
Mr & Mrs Henry Digby, 01300
341370, www.minterne.co.uk. *2m N
of Cerne Abbas. On A352 Dorchester-
Sherborne rd.* **Adm £4, chd free.
Open daily Mar to Oct (10-6).**
Minterne valley, landscaped in C18,
home of the Churchill and Digby
families for 350yrs. Wild woodland
gardens are laid out in a horseshoe
below Minterne House, with over 1m
of walks, providing a new vista at each
turn. Rhododendrons and magnolias
tower over small lakes, streams, and
cascades. Maples and many rare trees
provide spectacular autumn colouring.

57 ◆ MORETON GARDENS
Moreton, nr Dorchester DT2 8RH.
The Penny Family, 01929 405084,
www.moretondorset.co.uk. *7m E of
Dorchester. 3m W of Wool. Signed
from B3390 & 1m E of Moreton stn.
Next to Lawrence of Arabia's grave in
village of Moreton.* **Adm £3.50, chd
free. Daily Mar to Oct (10-5); Weds**

to Suns, Nov/Dec (10-4); Sats, Suns Jan/Feb (10-4). For NGS: Sat 12, Sun 13 Apr (10-5).
A garden recreated in an old setting in the picturesque village of Moreton. 3½ acres of lawns, mixed borders, woodland, stream and ponds, bog garden, pergola; summerhouse and fountain. Spring flowers and much more. Enjoy a picnic in the garden.

MULBERRY HOUSE
See Hampshire.

58 4 NOEL ROAD
Wallisdown BH10 4DP. Lesley & Ivor Pond. *4m NE of Poole. From Wallisdown Xrds enter Kinson Rd. Take 5th rd on R, Kingsbere Ave. Noel Rd is first on R.* Home-made teas. **Adm £2, chd free. Suns 29 June; 13 July (2-5).**
Small garden, 100ft x 30ft, with big ideas. On sloping ground many Roman features incl water features and temple. Most planting is in containers. 'I also like a big element of surprise and you do not get more surprising than a Roman Temple at the end of a suburban garden' (Amateur Gardening magazine). Several new features. Camera is a must. Come and give us your opinion 'Is this garden over the top?'. Featured in 'Bournemouth Daily Echo' and on Solent Radio.

OAKDENE
See Hampshire.

59 'OLA'
47 Old Castle Road, Weymouth DT4 8QE. Jane Uff & Elaine Smith. *Rodwell, Weymouth. 1m from Weymouth centre. Follow signs to Portland. Off Buxton Rd, proceed to lower end of Old Castle Rd. Bungalow just past Sandsfoot Castle ruins/gardens. Easy access by foot off Rodwell Trail at Sandsfoot Castle.* Home-made teas. **Adm £2.50, chd free. Tues 6, 20 May; 3 June (2-5).**
Seaside garden with stunning views overlooking Portland Harbour. 1930s-designed garden, once part of Sandfoot Castle estate. Mixed herbaceous borders, shrubs and roses. Rockeries, fish pond, vegetables, orchard and '7 dwarfs' bank. Circular sunken stone walled area with box bushes and statuary. Lovingly restored from neglected overgrown 'jungle'.

60 THE OLD RECTORY, LITTON CHENEY
Dorchester DT2 9AH. Mr & Mrs Hugh Lindsay, 01308 482383, hughlindsay@waitrose.com. *9m W of Dorchester. 1m S of A35, 6m E of Bridport. Small village in the beautiful Bride Valley. Park in village and follow signs.* Home-made teas. **Adm £4, chd free. Suns 6 Apr; 18 May; Tue 10 June (2-5.30).** Feb opening for snowdrops (depending on season), please see website for details.
Visitors also welcome by appt.
Steep paths lead to 4 acres of natural woodland with many springs, streams and 2 small lakes; mostly native plants and many primulas. (Stout shoes recommended). Cloud-pruned boxes. Small walled garden, partly paved, formal layout with informal planting and prolific quince tree. Kitchen garden, orchard and wild flower lawn. Steep slopes (no wheelchair access), lakes, streams, slippery paths at times.

61 THE OLD RECTORY, NETHERBURY
DT6 5NB. Amanda & Simon Mehigan, 01308 488757. *2m SW of Beaminster. Turn off A3066 Beaminster/Bridport rd & go over river Brit, into centre of village & up hill. The Old Rectory is on L opp church.* Home-made teas. **Adm £3.50, chd free. Suns 23 Mar; 4, 25 May (2-6). Visitors also welcome by appt mid-May to mid-June only for groups of 10+.**
5-acre garden developed over last 13yrs surrounding C16 rectory (not open). Formal areas nr house with box-edged beds and topiary contrast with naturalistic planting elsewhere, especially in bog garden, which features large drifts of irises, bog primulas and arum lilies. Spring bulbs in orchard, vegetable garden, mature ginkgo. Featured in 'Bises' Japanese gardening magazine, starred entry in 'GGG'.

62 THE OLD RECTORY, PULHAM
DT2 7EA. Mr & Mrs N Elliott, 01258 817595, gilly.elliott@virgin.net. *13m N of Dorchester. 8m SE of Sherborne. On B3143 turn E at Xrds in Pulham. Signed Cannings Court.* Home-made teas. **Adm £4, chd free. Wed 30 July; Sun 3 Aug (2-6). Visitors also welcome by appt Mon-Fri only.**
4 acres of formal and informal gardens

surround C18 rectory (not open) with superb views. Yew hedges enclose circular herbaceous borders with late summer colour. Mature trees. Restored pond and waterfall. Exuberantly-planted terrace and purple and white terrace beds. Box parterres. Fernery. Pleached hornbeam circle. Ha-ha. Shrubbery and two 5-acre woods with mown rides. New bog garden.

35 OLD STATION GARDENS
See Somerset & Bristol Area.

Many Roman features including water features and temple . . .

63 PARK HOMER DRIVE GARDENS
Colehill BH21 2SR. *1m NE of Wimborne. From Canford Bottom roundabout where A31 meets B3073, exit N marked Colehill for 1m. Turn L into Park Homer Rd, leading to Park Homer Dr.* Cream teas. **Combined adm £4, chd free. Sat 21, Sun 22 June (11-5).**
4 very different gardens - 2 sloping and 2 level - showing a variety of plantings in a valley setting.

7 PARK HOMER DRIVE
Pauline Weaver
Steep woodland garden filled with shade-loving plants. Steps lead to a quiet sitting area. Unsuitable for the less mobile.

15 PARK HOMER DRIVE
Bill & Glenda Dunn
Suburban garden with small pond and waterfall, arches, rockery and gravel area. Planted extravagantly and colourfully. Partial wheelchair access.

18 PARK HOMER DRIVE
Carolyn & Alan Nash
Small, colourful garden. Densely-planted beds surround immaculate lawn and pond.

28 PARK HOMER DRIVE
Kay & Mike Jeffrey
After visit to gardens, come and relax at No. 28 for cream teas in attractive surroundings. Partial wheelchair access.
&

64 54 PARKWOOD ROAD
Bournemouth BH5 2BL. Mr & Mrs Andrew Rickett. *3m E of Bournemouth. Turn S off Christchurch Rd between Boscombe and Pokesdown Stn.* Home-made teas May/June. **Adm £2.50, chd free. Suns 11 May; 8 June (2-5). Evening Openings £3, wine, Sat 6 Sept (7.30-9.30); Sat 7 Dec (6-8).** Small town garden, approx 30ft x 120 ft, planted out by enthusiastic first time gardeners. Herbaceous perennials and shrubs with mature trees, small pond and lawn give the garden a natural, relaxed atmosphere. Contrasting areas of moisture, shade and dryness. Live music for evening openings, mulled wine Dec with Christmas music.
& ✕ ⊕ ☕

65 NEW 3 PRIORY GARDENS
Pimperne DT11 8XH. George & Karen Tapper. *Pimperne is 1m NE of Blandford Forum on A354 towards Salisbury. Please park sensibly in Church Rd and walk to garden. Parking for less able only in Priory Gardens.* Home-made teas. **Adm £2.50, chd free. Weds, Suns 18, 22, 25, 29 June (2-6).** See what can be achieved in a garden just 80ft x 50ft. Imaginatively-designed garden that belies its size and surprises at every turn. Not your normal back garden plot! Roses, clematis, hardy geraniums, hemerocallis, grasses and herbaceous planting create different areas. Formal and wildlife ponds.
✕ ⊕ ☕

PROSPECT HOUSE
See Devon.

66 RAMPISHAM MANOR
Rampisham DT2 0PT. Mr & Mrs Boileau, 01935 83612, harriet@cubbins.co.uk. *11m NW of Dorchester. From Yeovil take A37 towards Dorchester, 7m turn R signed Evershot. From Dorchester take A37 to Yeovil, 4m turn L A356 signed Crewkerne; at start of wireless masts R to Rampisham. Follow signs.* Cream teas. **Adm £4, chd free. Sun 20 Apr;**

Sun 25, Wed 28 May (2-5). Also open **Broomhill** 20 Apr, combined adm £6. Visitors are welcome by appt May, June, July.
So much to enjoy in 3-acre+ gardens set in glorious W Dorset landscape incl mown walks through conservation/wildlife area around lake. Carpets of spring bulbs, magnolias and blossom. Herbaceous and large iris bed. Plant sale May openings only.
✕ ☕ ☎

67 357 RINGWOOD ROAD
Ferndown BH22 9AE. Lyn & Malcolm Ovens, 01202 896071, www.mgovens.freeserve.co.uk. *¾ m S of Ferndown. On A348 towards Longham. Parking in Glenmoor Rd or other side rds. Avoid parking on main rd.* Home-made teas. **Adm £2, chd free. Sun 13, Wed 30 July; Sun 10 Aug. Suns (11-5), Wed (2-5). Visitors also welcome by appt late June to early Sept only.**
100ft x 30ft his and hers garden. Front in cottage style with a varied composition of perennials, lilies and 105 different clematis. Chosen to give a riot of colour into autumn. At rear, walk through a Moorish doorway into an exotic garden where brugmansia, cannas, oleander, banana etc come together in an eclectic design. Conservatory with bougainvillea. A garden that is loved and it shows. Owner's mosaics on display. Ferndown Common and Nature Reserve nearby.
✕ ⊕ ☕ ☎

68 46 ROSLIN ROAD SOUTH
Talbot Woods BH3 7EG. Mrs Penny Slade, 01202 510243. *1m NW of Bournemouth. W of N end of Glenferness Ave in Talbot Woods area of Bournemouth.* Home-made teas. **Adm £2.50, chd free. Sun 20 Apr; Sat 17, Sun 18 May; Sat 14, Sun 15 June; Sun 6 July (2-5). Visitors also welcome by appt Apr to Jul.**
Plantswoman's ⅓ -acre walled town garden planted with many unusual and rare plants. Sunken gravel garden with collection of grasses, surrounded by colourful mixed borders. Features incl many well planted containers, raised octagonal alpine bed, pergola leading to enclosed patio, cutting beds and fruit cage, greenhouses and frames. S-facing wall especially colourful for April and May openings.
& ✕ ⊕ ☕ ☎

ROUSDON GARDENS
See Devon.

69 ST MICHAEL'S HOUSE
Pound Street, Lyme Regis DT7 3HY. Penny Keiner Ross, 01297 442503, pennykeiner@rediffmail.com. *From town centre, proceed up Broad St, L into Pound St (A3052 to Exeter). 100yds on L. Street parking opp or in Holmbush car park further up on L.* Home-made teas. **Adm £3, chd free. Fri 30 May; Sun 15 June (2-6). Evening Opening £4, wine, Sats 31 May; 14 June (5-9). Visitors also welcome by appt.**
Formal enclosed town garden. Courtyard, planted 3 yrs ago on site of former hotel dining room, reflects owner's passion for India. Persian-style gazebo leads into jasmine and rose-scented garden with glimpses of Lyme Bay. 1st prize Lyme Regis in Bloom.
✕ ☕ ☎

Not your normal back garden plot! . . .

SANDLE COTTAGE
See Hampshire.

SANDLE COTTAGE
See Hampshire.

70 THE SECRET GARDEN
The Friary, Hilfield DT2 7BE. The Society of St Francis. *10m N of Dorchester. On A352. 1st L after village, 1st turning on R signed The Friary. From Yeovil turn off A37 signed Batcombe, 3rd turning on L.* Teas. **Adm £3, chd free. Sat 17, Sun 18 May (2-5).**
Small woodland garden begun in 1950s then neglected. Reclamation began in 1984. New plantings added in 1998-1999, bamboo in 2004, further plantings of rhododendrons and bamboo in 2006. Mature trees, rhododendrons, azaleas, magnolias, camellias (some camellias grown from seed collected in China), other choice shrubs with a stream on all sides crossed by bridges. Stout shoes recommended.
✕ ☕

71 THE SECRET GARDEN AT SERLES HOUSE
47 Victoria Road, Wimborne BH21 1EN. Ian Willis, 01202 880430. *Centre of Wimborne. On B3082 W of town, very near hospital, Westfield car*

park 300yds. Off-road parking close by. **Adm £2.50, chd free (share to Wimborne Civic Society). Sun 27 July; Suns 10, 24, Mon 25 Aug; Suns 7, 14 Sept. Evening Openings £3.50, wine, Sats 26 July (7-10); 23 Aug; 6 Sept (8-10); Sat 6 Dec (6-9). Visitors also welcome by appt.** Described by Alan Titchmarsh as one of the 10 best private gardens in Great Britain, this garden is for people of all ages. The plantings fit in with over 60 relics rescued from oblivion by Ian Willis. The Anglo-Indian conservatory, plant-pot man, tree-house and cannons from the Solent are highlights of this remarkable experience. Piano music during afternoon and evening openings. Special winter opening 6 Dec with Father Christmas, wine & mince pies. Featured in 'Dorset Life' and national press. Some shallow steps and gravel.

♿ ✕ ☎

72 ◆ **SHERBORNE CASTLE**
New Rd, Sherborne DT9 5NR. Mr J K Wingfield Digby, 01935 813182, www.sherbornecastle.com. *½ m E of Sherborne. On New Road B3145. Follow brown signs to 'Sherborne Castles' from A30 & A352.* **House and garden adm £9, chd free, senior citizens £8.50, garden only adm £4.50. Open daily except Mons and Fris, 22 Mar to 30 Oct (11-4.30).**
30+ acres. A Capability Brown garden with magnificent vistas across the surrounding landscape, incl lake and fine ruined castle. Herbaceous planting, notable trees, a mixture of ornamental planting and managed wilderness are all linked together with lawn and pathways providing colour and interest throughout the seasons. 'Dry Grounds Walk'. Gravel/grass paths and some steep slopes, please phone for further details.

♿ ☕

73 ◆ **SHUTE FARM**
Donhead St Mary SP7 9DG. Mr & Mrs J Douglas. *5m E of Shaftesbury. Take A350 towards Warminster from Shaftesbury. Turn R at 1st turning out of Shaftesbury, signed Wincombe & Donhead St Mary. At Donhead St Mary, turn R at T-junction. 1st house on L opp tel box.* Home-made teas. **Adm £3.50, chd free. Suns 30 Mar; 18 May (11-4).**
Cottage garden around thatched house. Plenty to see and explore, incl stream, pond, kitchen garden and wild flower garden. Neat and tidy garden by

house, getting wilder as it meets the fields. Alpacas, rare breed chickens, ducks and bees. Magnificent views over the Donheads.

✕ ⊛ ☕

74 ◆ **SLAPE MANOR**
Netherbury DT6 5LH. Mr & Mrs Antony Hichens. *1m S of Beaminster. Turn W off A3066 to village of Netherbury. House ⅓ m S of Netherbury on back rd to Bridport.* Home-made teas. **Adm £3, chd free (share to Marie Curie, Dorset). Sun 18 May (2-6).**
Manor with river valley garden, extensive lawns, streams and lake. Azaleas, magnolias, rhododendrons, large clump *Phyllostachys nigra* 'Boryana' and specimen trees. Lakeside walks. Slightly sloping lawns, some stone and gravel paths, unfenced water features.

♿ ⊛ ☕

River valley garden, lawns, streams and lake. Azaleas, magnolias, rhododendrons

75 ◆ **SNAPE COTTAGE PLANTSMAN'S GARDEN**
Chaffeymoor, Bourton, Gillingham SP8 5BZ. Ian & Angela Whinfield, 01747 840330 (evenings), www.snapestakes.com. *5m NW of Gillingham. At W end of Bourton, N of A303. Opp Chiffchaffs.* Home-made teas. **Adm £3, chd free. Last 2 Suns in each month Feb to Aug incl; every Thur May to Aug incl (10.30-5). Groups by prior arrangement. For NGS: Suns 23 Mar; 22 June (10.30-5).**
Country garden containing exceptional collection of hardy plants and bulbs, artistically arranged in informal cottage garden style, organically managed and clearly labelled. Main interests are plant history and nature conservation. Specialities incl snowdrops, hellebores, primula vulgaris cvrs, 'old' daffodils, pulmonarias, auriculas, dianthus, herbs, irises and geraniums. Wildlife pond, beautiful views, tranquil atmosphere. Featured on BBC Gardeners' World.

✕ ⊛ ☕

3 SOUTHDOWN
See Somerset & Bristol Area.

76 ◆ **SPRINGHEAD**
Mill St, Fontmell Magna SP7 0NU. The Springhead Trust, 01747 811206, www.springheadtrust.co.uk. *4m S of Shaftesbury. From Shaftesbury or Blandford take A350 to Fontmell Magna. In centre of village, turn E up Mill St, opp PH. Follow stream up twisty, narrow lane to Springhead on sharp bend. Large, white thatched house attached to mill.* **Adm £3.50, under 12s free. Mon 24 Mar, Sat 26, Sun 27 Apr (10-5). For NGS: Afternoon and Evening Opening, wine, Mon 16 June (2-9); Evening Opening, wine, Sun 20 July (6-9).**
Lakeside garden above mill. Icy spring water bubbles from beneath the chalk. Walks with prospects punctuated by peaceful resting places: noble trees, Venetian rotunda, terraced landscaping reflecting Iron Age Lynchets above. Bog garden, wild areas, themed planting of herbaceous beds, old roses and unusual shrubs. In good weather, evening light and reflections in lake very special. Guided tours. Wooden walkway, sloping sand and gravel path, grass areas difficult for wheelchairs in wet conditions.

♿ ✕ ⊛ ☕

77 **STANBRIDGE MILL**
nr Gussage All Saints BH21 5EP. Mr James Fairfax, 01258 841067. *7m N of Wimborne. On B3078 to Cranborne 150yds from Horton Inn on Shaftesbury rd.* Home-made teas. **Adm £4.50, chd free. Wed 11 June (10.30-5.30). Visitors also welcome by appt.**
Hidden garden created in 1990s around C18 water mill (not open) on R Allen. Series of linked formal gardens featuring herbaceous and iris borders, pleached limes, white walk and wisteria-clad pergola. 20-acre nature reserve with reed beds and established shelter belts. Grazing meadows with wild flowers and flock of Dorset Horn sheep.

♿ ✕ ⊛ ☕ ☎

78 **TITHE BARN HOUSE**
Chalk Pit Lane, Litton Cheney DT2 9AN. Letizia & Antony Longland, 01308 482219. *10m W of Dorchester. 1m S of A35. Small village in beautiful Bride Valley. Follow signs in centre of village. Park on verge.* Home-made teas. **Adm £3, chd free. Sun 22**

June (2-5.30). **Visitors also welcome by appt for groups of 10+.**
Just over an acre plus paddock. Wonderful views of almost the entire Bride Valley. Pergolas, lawns, mature trees, olives, shrubs, incl good roses, climbers and herbaceous plants, many pots, reflecting pool.

This diverse garden has something for everyone . . .

79 ◆ TOAD HALL
The Cross, Shillingstone DT11 0SP.
Elizabeth Arden & Norman Rogerson, 01258 861941, www.toadhalluk.co.uk. *5m NW of Blandford. On A357. Drive is opp Old Village Cross on highest point of village. Parking in village.* **Adm £3, chd 50p. Please phone or visit website for opening times. For NGS: Suns 25 May; 24 Aug (2-6). Also open Coombe Cottage both days, Duckdown Cottage 25 May.**
Plantsman's country garden still developing. 1 acre on S-facing slope with wonderful views. Several different styled areas and growing habitats. Gardens incl Italian, decking, water, rockery, vegetable and wild. A wonderful place just to sit and have tea. Easy access to decking overlooking garden.

80 ◆ UPWEY WISHING WELL
161 Church Street, Upwey DT3 5QE.
Pauline, John & Julia Waring, 01305 814470. *3m N of Weymouth. On B3159 & just off Dorchester to Weymouth rd (A354).* **Home-made lunches. Entrance through café, adm free, but donations welcomed for NGS charities. Open daily (10.30-5), closed 2 weeks over Christmas & New Year.**
A tranquil, well-stocked water garden. Large natural spring, which is the source of the R Wey, is known as the Wishing Well and is an ancient monument. A fine show of bog primulas in May/June. Huge gunneras and unusual foliage plants provide a unique and exotic setting.

81 VINE COTTAGE
Melcombe Bingham DT2 7PE.
Wendy & Robert Jackson. *11m NE of Dorchester. Melcombe Bingham is 5m N of Puddletown and 5m W of Milton Abbas. Vine Cottage is in centre of village and just ¼ m past Fox Inn.* **Home-made teas. Adm £2.50, chd free. Suns 25 May; 15 June (11-5).**
Compact, well-stocked cottage garden with a wealth of interesting and unusual perennials and numerous containers. Specific areas incl patios, pergola, arch trelliswork that host many roses and clematis, plus alpine-planted sink gardens. Emphasis on imaginative use of colour. Partial wheelchair access.

82 WARMWELL HOUSE
Warmwell DT2 8HQ. Mr & Mrs H J C Ross Skinner. *7m SE of Dorchester. Warmwell is signed off A352 between Dorchester & Wool. House is in centre of village. Entrance to car park through double gates ¼ m N on B3390.* **Home-made teas. Adm £3.50, chd free. Suns 8 June; 20 July (2-5).**
An old garden with a Jacobean house (not open) set on ancient site of Domesday building. The 1617 front with Dutch gabelling has informal gardens. Square Dutch garden and maze on hill behind house. Well grown topiary for sale. Slopes, possibly slippery on damp/wet days, suitable only for strong wheelchair attendant.

83 NEW WATENDLATH
7 North St, Bere Regis BH20 7LA. Peter & Carole Whittaker, 01929 471176, carole.whittaker7@btinternet.com. *13m W of Dorchester. From A35, A31 junction at Bere Regis. Enter village from the Wool rd, 1st R into north St, 200metres on R.* **Adm £3, chd free (share to Royal British Legion). Suns 1 June; 6 July (2-6). Groups welcome by appointment only. Also open 79 West Street.**
Wildlife-friendly garden of ⅓ acre, created by people who love flowering plants, colour and scent. Densely-packed with herbaceous borders, island beds, rose, vegetable and secret garden, pond, chickens and many containers. This diverse garden has something for everyone, particularly children, lots of interesting corners and a fine view.

WAYFORD MANOR
See Somerset & Bristol Area.

84 WELCOME THATCH
Witchampton BH21 5AR. Mrs Diana Guy. *3½ m N of Wimborne. B3078 L to Witchampton, through village past church & club to last but one house on R. Parking available in club car park, otherwise on road beyond the garden.* **Home-made teas. Adm £3, chd free. Sun 24 Feb (1-4.30).**
Large cottage garden in idyllic village setting. Traditional borders lushly planted with unusual plants for long season of interest. Interesting collection of hellebores, spring flowers and bulbs. Hanging baskets, containers, wildlife ponds and stream, productive greenhouse, dry garden, prairie-style borders, oriental garden and tropical border. Thatched summerhouse, garden room with tender plants. Ample seating, tranquil views. Hellebore specialist nursery in attendance Feb. Partial wheelchair access, some steps.

85 WENTWORTH COLLEGE
College Road, Boscombe, Bournemouth BH5 2DY. The Bursar. *3m E of Bournemouth. Turn N from Boscombe Overcliff Drive into Woodland Ave. Then 1st R into College Rd.* **Home-made teas. Adm £2.50, chd free. Suns 13 Apr; 14 Sept (2-4.30).**
Originally the seaside estate of Lord Portman, Wentworth Lodge was built in 1872. The main Victorian house has gradually been extended to accommodate the needs of Wentworth College. Formal gardens have been restored to reflect their origins. The grounds also incl woodland with mature specimen trees and rhododendrons in approx 3 acres.

86 NEW 79 WEST STREET
Bere Regis BH20 7HL. Mrs Laura Maunder. *10m E of Dorchester. From W follow signs from A35 and A31 to Bere Regis village centre. Turn into West St at bend by Royal Oak PH. Garden on R after PO, L opp garden to car park. From Dorchester take Bere Regis exit off A31. R at end of slip rd. Follow rd into village, garden on L, R opp garden to car park.* **Home-made teas (at Royal British Legion Club if inclement). Adm £2.50, chd free (share to Royal**

British Legion). Suns 1 June; 6 July (2-6). Also open **Watendlath.**
Steeply-sloping terraced garden. Climb steps through beds of succulents and Mediterranean-style planting to patio with ponds and grape vines, then a few more steps to summerhouse and view over village. Garden created from chalk bank 3 yrs ago - an unexpected delight. Children must be supervised on terraces.

87 **24A WESTERN AVENUE**
Branksome Park, Poole BH13 7AN. Mr & Mrs Peter Jackson, 01202 708388, peter@branpark.wanadoo.co.uk. *3m W of Bournemouth.* $1/2$ *m inland from Branksome Chine beach. From S end Wessex Way (A338) take The Avenue. At T-lights turn R into Western Rd. At church turn R into Western Ave.* Home-made teas. **Adm £3, chd free. Suns 22 June; 27 July (2-6). Visitors also welcome by appt mid-June to end of July for groups of 10+.**
'This secluded and magical 1-acre garden captures the spirit of warmer climes and begs for repeated visits' ('Gardening Which'); 'A dream of tropical planting... like coming into a different world' ('Amateur Gardening'). June sees the rose garden at its best whilst herbaceous beds shine in July. Italian courtyard, wall and woodland gardens, topiary and driftwood sculptures.

88 **WESTON HOUSE**
Weston St, Buckhorn Weston SP8 5HG. Mr & Mrs E A W Bullock, 01963 371005. *4m W of Gillingham, 3m SE of Wincanton. From A30 turn N to Kington Magna, continue towards Buckhorn Weston & after railway bridge take L turn towards Wincanton. 2nd on L is Weston House.* Home-made teas by arrangement. **Adm £3, chd free. Visitors welcome by appt Apr to Sept, individuals and groups.**
$1^{1}/_{2}$ -acre garden. Old walls host climbers, clematis and roses. Approx 90 rose varieties throughout garden. Mixed borders of colourful perennials, shrubs and bulbs lead to woodland area of shade-loving plants and orchard incl tough perennials and ornamental grasses. Attractive lawns lead to wild flower areas, wildlife pond and hayfields with views of Blackmore Vale.

WHITE BARN
See Hampshire.

89 **NEW** **1692 WIMBORNE ROAD**
Bear Cross BH11 9AL. Sue & Mike Cleall, 01202 573440. *5m NW of Bournemouth. On A341, 200yds E of Bear Cross roundabout.* Home-made teas. **Adm £2.50, chd free. Suns 18 May; 8 June; 6 July (2-5). Visitors also welcome by appt.**
Suburban garden 120ft x 50ft. Spring colour provided by rhododendrons, azaleas and acers underplanted with hellebores,

trilliums and woodland plants. For the summer, pergola with roses and climbers, hydrangeas and herbaceous borders. Man-made stream with waterfall runs through lawned area with primulas, ferns and gunnera. Wildlife pond.

Climb steps through beds of succulents and Mediterranean-style planting . . .

90 **WOLVERHOLLOW**
Elsdons Lane, Monkton Wyld DT6 6DA. Mr & Mrs D Wiscombe. *4m N of Lyme Regis. 4m NW of Charmouth. Monkton Wyld is signed from A35 approx 4m NW of Charmouth off dual carriageway. Wolverhollow is next to the church.* Home-made teas. **Adm £3, chd free. Sun 4, Tue 6, Sun 25, Mon 26 May (11-5).**
Over 1 acre of informal garden. Lawns, with unusual summerhouse, lead past borders and rockeries to shady valley with babbling brook. Numerous paths pass wide variety of colourful and uncommon plants. An area, once field, sympathetically extends the garden with streamside planting and meadow. Must be seen.

Dorset County Volunteers

County Organiser
Harriet Boileau, Rampisham Manor, Dorchester DT2 0PT, 01935 83612 harriet@cubbins.co.uk

County Treasurer
Michael Gallagher, 6 West Street, Chickerell, Weymouth DT3 4DY, 01305 772557, michael.gallagher1@virgin.net

Publicity
Howard Ffitch, Brook House, Purse Caundle, Sherborne DT9 5DY, 01963 250120, h.ffitch@btinternet.com

Events
Carol Lindsay, The Old Rectory, Litton Cheney, Dorchester DT2 9AH, 01308 482383, hughlindsay@waitrose.com

Assistant County Organisers
North Caroline Renner, Croft Farm, Fontmell Magna, Shaftesbury SP7 0NR, 01747 811140, jamesrenner@talktalk.net
North East Trish Neale, Lawn House, Slough Lane, Horton, Wimborne BH21 7JL, 01202 820531, trishneale1@yahoo.co.uk
Central Wendy Jackson, Vine Cottage, Melcombe Bingham, Dorchester DT2 7PE, 01258 880720, wendyjacks@fsmail.net
West Central Lindy Ball, Catsley House, Catsley Lane, Corscombe, Dorchester DT2 0NR, 01935 891922, lindy@catsleyhouse.co.uk
South Philippa & Anthony Bush, Holworth Farmhouse, Holworth, Dorchester DT2 8NH, 01305 852242, bushinarcadia@yahoo.co.uk
South West Christine Corson, Stoke Knapp Cottage, Norway Lane, Stoke Abbott, Beaminster DT8 3JZ, 01308 868203
East Dorset, Bournemouth & Poole Penny Slade, 46 Roslin Road South, Bournemouth BH3 7EG, 01202 510243
Ferndown Mary Angus, The Glade, Woodland Walk, Ferndown BH22 9LP, 01202 872789, mary@gladestock.co.uk

Mark your diary with these special events in 2008

EXPLORE SECRET GARDENS DURING CHELSEA WEEK

Tue 20 May, Wed 21 May, Thur 22 May, Fri 23 May
Full day tours: £78 per person, 10% discount for groups
Advance Booking required, telephone 01932 864532 or
email pennysnellflowers@btinternet.com

Specially selected private gardens in London, Surrey and Berkshire. The tour price includes transport and lunch with wine at a popular restaurant or pub.

FROGMORE – A ROYAL GARDEN (BERKSHIRE)

Tue 3 June 10am - 5.30pm (last adm 4pm)
Garden adm £4, chd free. Advance booking recommended telephone 01483 211535 or email orders@ngs.org.uk

A unique opportunity to explore 30 acres of landscaped garden, rich in history and beauty.

FLAXBOURNE FARM – FUN AND SURPRISES (BEDFORDSHIRE)

Sun 8 June 10am - 5pm Adm £5, chd free
No booking required, come along on the day!

Bring the whole family and enjoy a plant fair and garden party and have fun in this beautiful and entertaining garden of 2 acres.

WISLEY RHS GARDEN – MUSIC IN THE GARDEN (SURREY)

Tue 19 August 6 - 9pm
Adm (incl RHS members) £7, chd under 15 free

A special opening of this famous garden, exclusively for the NGS. Enjoy music and entertainment as you explore a range of different gardens.

For further information visit www.ngs.org.uk or telephone 01483 211535

DURHAM & NORTHUMBERLAND

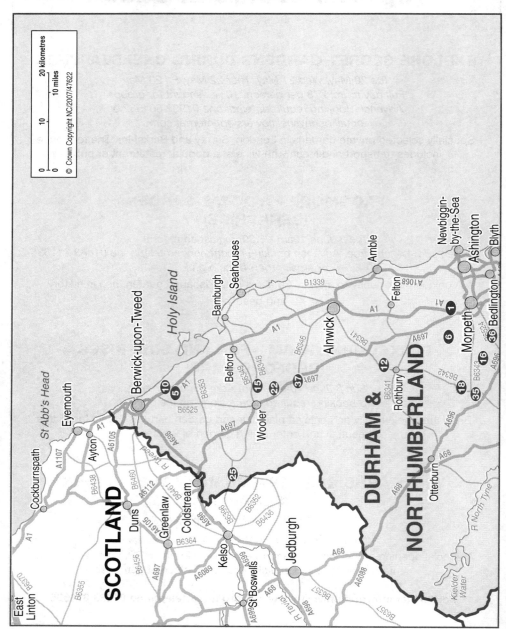

20 kilometres

10 miles

10

0

0

© Crown Copyright NC/2007/47622

Newbiggin-by-the-Sea

Ashington

Blyth

Amble

Felton

A1068

Bedlington

1

Morpeth

36

6

A697

Seahouses

Bamburgh

B1339

Alnwick

A1

B6341

16

12

Holy Island

B6346

Rothbury

B6342

18

35

A696

Belford

B6346

B6342

B6343

Berwick-upon-Tweed

10

A1

B6353

15

22

37 A697

5

St Abb's Head

B6525

Wooler

A697

Otterburn

A68

R North Tyne

Eyemouth

A1

A6105

DURHAM & NORTHUMBERLAND

Cockburnspath

A1107

Ayton

B6438

B6460

25

A698

B6352

Kielder Water

East Linton

B6370

A1

Duns

A6105

Greenlaw

B6364

Coldstream

B6461

B6350

B6436

Jedburgh

A68

A696

SCOTLAND

B6456

A697

Kelso

A6089

B6397

St Boswells

A68

A699

B6357

A698

B6357

B6355

A68

A6088

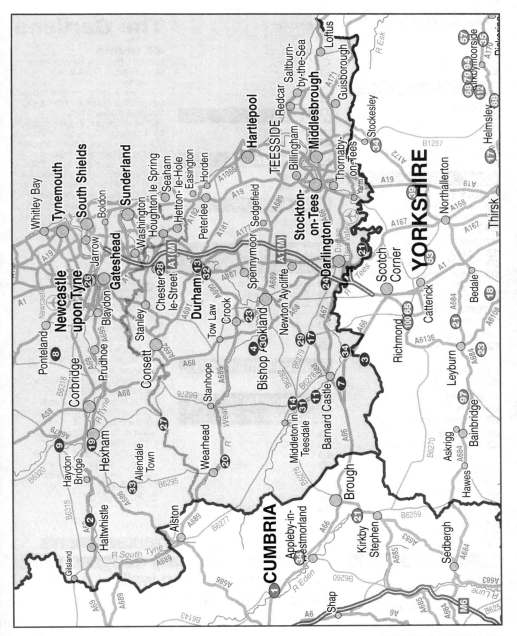

Opening Dates

March

SUNDAY 30
- 26 Moorbank Botanic Garden

April

SATURDAY 19
- 6 Bide-a-Wee Cottage

SUNDAY 20
- 35 Wallington

May

SUNDAY 11
- 3 Barningham Park
- 9 Chesters Walled Garden

SUNDAY 18
- 22 Lilburn Tower
- 26 Moorbank Botanic Garden

June

SUNDAY 1
- 27 Newbiggin House
- 33 Thornley House
- 37 Wooperton Hall

SUNDAY 8
- 1 Ashfield
- 13 Crook Hall & Gardens
- 19 Hexham Community Walled Garden
- 28 25 Park Road South

SATURDAY 14
- 21 Hurworth Gardens

SUNDAY 15
- 15 Fowberry Mains Farmhouse

THURSDAY 19
- 18 Herterton House

SUNDAY 22
- 25 Mindrum
- 31 Romaldkirk Gardens

WEDNESDAY 25
- 26 Moorbank Botanic Garden (Evening)

SUNDAY 29
- 2 The Barn
- 4 Bedburn Hall
- 5 Berryburn
- 10 Cheswick House
- 17 Gorst Hall
- 20 High Hill Top
- 24 Low Walworth Hall

July

SUNDAY 6
- 11 Cotherstone Village Gardens
- 34 Thorpe Gardens
- 36 Whalton Manor Gardens

SUNDAY 13
- 8 Cheeseburn Grange
- 14 Eggleston Village Gardens
- 16 Garden Cottage
- 32 St Margaret's Allotments

THURSDAY 17
- 18 Herterton House

SATURDAY 19
- 12 Cragside
- 35 Wallington

SUNDAY 27
- 7 Browside

August

THURSDAY 7
- 18 Herterton House

September

SUNDAY 28
- 30 Ravensford Farm

November

SUNDAY 2
- 26 Moorbank Botanic Garden

Gardens open to the public

- 6 Bide-a-Wee Cottage
- 9 Chesters Walled Garden
- 12 Cragside
- 13 Crook Hall & Gardens
- 18 Herterton House
- 29 Raby Castle
- 35 Wallington

By appointment only

- 23 10 Low Row

Also open by appointment ☎

- 2 The Barn
- 5 Berryburn
- 16 Garden Cottage
- 19 Hexham Community Walled Garden
- 20 High Hill Top
- 22 Lilburn Tower
- 24 Low Walworth Hall

- 26 Moorbank Botanic Garden
- 28 25 Park Road South
- 30 Ravensford Farm

The Gardens

1 ASHFIELD
Hebron NE61 3LA. Barry & Rona McWilliam. *3m N of Morpeth. 1½ m E of Heighley Gate. 1m off A1 on C130. S side of Hebron. Car park is through field gate.* Cream teas. **Adm £3, chd free. Sun 8 June (12-5).**
Plantsmans garden, largely grown from seed. Set within 5 acres are collections of sorbus, betula and malus, beautiful hedging and remarkable alpines in full bloom from around the world. The long lawns are bounded by herbaceous and shrub borders which contrast with the tranquil woodland set with meandering grass paths and varied under planting. Home-made teas worth making journey for. Featured in 'The English Garden' 'Morpeth Herald'. Finalist in Morpeth in Bloom.
&. ⊛ ☕

2 NEW THE BARN
Henshaw NE47 7EN. Mrs Pauline Ellis & Mr John Rutherford, 01434 344453. *14m W of Hexham. On A69, into village, 1st L following rd round.* Home-made teas. **Adm £2.50, chd free. Sun 29 June (2-5). Visitors also welcome by appt.**
Newly-established plantswoman's garden innovationally designed with local stone retaining walls incorporating attractive rill, small pond and rockery. Locally made willow arches and screens. Old roses, variety of clematis, grasses and succulents. Small vegetable garden. Entire garden is wildlife friendly. Home-grown vegetables for sale. Some gravel paths.
&. ✕ ⊛ ☕ ☎

Newly-established plantswoman's garden innovationally designed with local stone retaining walls incorporating attractive rill . . .

3 BARNINGHAM PARK
nr Barnard Castle. Sir Anthony Milbank. *9m W of Scotch Corner. Turn S off A66 at Greta Bridge or A66 Motel via Newsham*. Lunches & home-made teas in Barningham Village Hall. **Adm £3, chd free (share to St Michael & All Angels Church, Barningham). Sun 11 May (1-5).**
Woodland walks, trees and rock garden on steep slope with ponds and waterfalls. Shrub and perennial borders. House (not open) built 1650. Limited wheelchair access, steep slopes and gravel drive.
&. ⊗

4 BEDBURN HALL
Hamsterley DL13 3NN. I G Bonas. *9m NW of Bishop Auckland. From A68 at Witton-le-Wear, turn off W to Hamsterley; turn N from Hamsterley to Bedburn, 1m. From Wolsingham on B6293 turn SE for 3m*. Home-made teas. **Adm £3, chd free. Sun 29 June (2-6).**
Medium-sized S-facing terraced garden with large conservatory and greenhouse, lake, streams, woodland, lawns. Fuchsia collection and lavender bed, herbaceous border, fruit cage and rose garden. Gardener on hand to advise. Gravel paths, some slopes.
&. ☀ ⊗ ☕

5 BERRYBURN
Ancroft TD15 2TF. Mr & Mrs W J Rogers-Coltman, 01289 387332. *6m S of Berwick-upon-Tweed. Turn off A1 to Ancroft Mill. 2nd turning on R after 1m*. Home-made teas. **Adm £3, chd free (share to Ancroft Memorial Hall). Sun 29 June (12-5).** Visitors also welcome by appt.
The Berry Burn winds through 6 acres of lawns, mixed borders and woodland walks with a varied collection of coniferous trees. Child friendly. Gravel drive.
&. ⊗ ☕ ☎

6 ◆ BIDE-A-WEE COTTAGE
Stanton, Morpeth NE65 8PR. Mr M Robson, 01670 772238, www.bideawee.co.uk. *7m NNW of Morpeth. Turn L off A192 out of Morpeth at Fairmoor. Stanton is 6m along this rd*. **Adm £2.50, chd free. Weds & Sats 26 Apr to 30 Aug 1.30-5. For NGS: Sat 19 Apr (1.30-4).**
Unique secret garden created over the last 26yrs out of a small sandstone quarry, it features rock and water. Unusual perennials are woven within a matrix of ferns, trees and shrubs. The

garden contains the National Collection of centaurea, and many other plants seldom seen.
&. ☀ ⊗ NCCPG

7 BROWSIDE
Boldron, Barnard Castle DL12 9RQ. Mr & Mrs R D Kearton. *3m S of Barnard Castle. On A66 3m W of Greta Bridge, turn R to Boldron, then proceed ½ m, entrance opp junction. From Barnard Castle take A67 to Bowes, after 2m turn L to Boldron*. Home-made teas. **Adm £2.50, chd free. Sun 27 July (1-5.30).**
1¼ acres with unusual water features and large collection of conifers, wide range of plants and imaginative stone objects.
&. ⊗ ☕

8 NEW CHEESEBURN GRANGE
Stamfordham NE18 0PT. Mr & Mrs S Riddell. *8m W of Newcastle upon Tyne. From A1 take B6324 through Westerhope, Stamfordham. Cheeseburn is 1.8m beyond Plough Inn on R. From Stamfordham Village take signs to Newcastle, after approx 1m take 1st R signed Newcastle. 1st entrance on L*. Home-made teas. **Adm £3, chd free. Sun 13 July (2-5.30).**
Peaceful oasis just 8m from Newcastle, this garden of approx 7 acres has been developed by present owners in last 15yrs. Extensive lawns with flowering cherries and bulbs in spring surround the Dobson designed house (not open) and chapel (open). Mature trees and parkland views, roses, mixed borders and parterre. Vegetable area, fruit trees and greenhouse in Victorian walled garden. Woodland walk with many varieties of birds.
☕

9 ◆ CHESTERS WALLED GARDEN
Chollerford NE46 4BQ. Mrs S White, 01434 681483, www.chesterswalledgarden.co.uk. *6m N of Hexham. Off the B6318. ½ m W of Chollerford*. **Adm £3, chd under 10 free. Daily mid Mar to end Oct, by appt in winter. For NGS: Sun 11 May (10-5).**
Delightful 2-acre walled garden, planted in relaxed style; wild flowers mingle with unusual perennials and extensive collection of herbs. Three

National Collections; marjoram, sanguisorba and thyme, grown on famous Thyme Bank. Roman garden; knot garden, ponds and vegetables. Organically run, the walled garden is a haven for wildlife incl red squirrels. Featured in 'Country Living'.
&. ☀ ⊗ NCCPG

10 NEW CHESWICK HOUSE
Cheswick TD15 2RL. Mr & Mrs P Bennett. *4m S of Berwick upon Tweed. Turn E from A1 signed Goswick/Cheswick*. Home-made teas. **Adm £3, chd free (share to Ancroft Memorial Hall). Sun 29 June (12-5).**
Large garden incl woodland with specimen trees, croquet lawn, formal walled garden and woodland walk. The garden is undergoing a restoration programme begun in 2002 which incl converted curling rink with pond and raised beds. Gravel paths.
&. ⊗ ☕

Peaceful
oasis
just 8m
from
Newcastle . . .

11 COTHERSTONE VILLAGE GARDENS
DL12 9PQ. *4m NW of Barnard Castle. On B6277 Middleton-in-Teesdale rd*. Home-made teas. **Adm £3, chd free. Sun 6 July (11-5).**
Picturesque Teesdale village at the confluence of rivers Tees and Balder. Over 13 country gardens open, showing a wide range of plants, bird watchers and artists' plot. Art Exhibition. Village tree walk, play and painting area for children. Special Gardeners Lunch available at Red Lion, booking advisable 01833 650236. Partial wheelchair access, some gravel paths and steep slopes.
&. ⊗ ☕

⑫ ◆ CRAGSIDE

Rothbury NE65 7PX. The National Trust, 01669 620333, www.nationaltrust.org.uk. *13m SW of Alnwick. (B6341); 15m NW of Morpeth (A697).* **Adm £7, chd £3. For opening details please tel or see website. For NGS: Sat 19 July (10.30-5).**

Formal garden in the 'High Victorian' style created by the 1st Lord Armstrong. Fully restored Italian terrace, orchard house, carpet bedding, dahlia walk and fernery. 3½ acres of rock garden with its restored cascades. Extensive grounds of over 1000 acres famous for rhododendrons and beautiful lakes.

Artistically and lovingly created colourful 1-acre garden . . .

⑬ ◆ CROOK HALL & GARDENS

Sidegate, Durham City DH1 5SZ. Maggie Bell, 0191 384 8028, www.crookhallgardens.co.uk. *Crook Hall is short walk from Durham's Market Place. Follow the tourist info signs. Parking available at entrance.* **House and Garden adm £5.50, chd £4.50, concessions £5. Easter 21 - 24 Mar; daily 6 Apr to 28 Sept (except Fris & Sats). For NGS: Sun 8 June (11-5).**

Described in Country Life as having 'history, romance and beauty'. Intriguing medieval manor house surrounded by 4 acres of fine gardens. Visitors can enjoy magnificent cathedral views from the 2 walled gardens. Other garden 'rooms' incl the silver and white garden, orchard, moat, pool and maze. Featured in and on various publications and BBC/TV. Limited wheelchair access.

⑭ NEW EGGLESTON VILLAGE GARDENS

DL12 0AH. Dr G Herbert. *6m NW of Barnard Castle. Take B6278 from Barnard Castle NW, or from Stanhope S on B6278.* Refreshments available locally. **Adm £3.50, chd free (share to Eggleston Village Hall). Sun 13 July (1.30-5.30).**

6-8 gardens of various sizes individually designed to accommodate the unusual topography of this picturesque village in the N Pennines area of outstanding natural beauty. Despite hostile conditions many gardens contain unusual plants against a backdrop of stunning views of Teesdale. National Collection of Jovibarba. Limited wheelchair access.

NCCPG

⑮ NEW FOWBERRY MAINS FARMHOUSE

Wooler NE71 6EN. Mr & Mrs A F McEwen. *2m W of Chatton, 3m E of Wooler. Signed between Wooler & Chatton on B6348.* Home-made teas. **Adm £3, chd free (share to Wansbeck Wishbone Fund). Sun 15 June (2-6).**

Artistically and lovingly created colourful 1-acre garden, developed and planted since 1999, still evolving. Relaxed country style featuring informal beds with hardy perennials, roses and shrubs, well stocked mixed herbaceous borders. Newly designed gravel beds with grasses and drought tolerant plants. Productive vegetable garden. Small wild area being developed.

⑯ GARDEN COTTAGE

Bolam Hall, Bolam, Morpeth NE61 3UA. Mr & Mrs J A Russell, 01661 881660, heather@bolamhall.demon.co.uk. *8m N of Ponteland. Turn R off A696 at Belsay for Bolam Lake. Take next 2 R turns. Field access nr Bolam Church.* **Adm £3.50, chd free. Sun 13 July (2-6). Visitors also welcome by appt.**

Colourful and creative garden (over 1 acre) in lovely setting with good structure and imaginative planting. Artistic use of colour, texture and sculpture. Interesting gravel areas and new contemplation garden with easy maintenance planting. Meadow

garden, with stunning views to Simonside. Always something new. Overall winner Best Garden Competiton, Morpeth Borough Council. Gravel paths.

⑰ NEW GORST HALL

12 South Green, Staindrop DL2 3LD. Major & Mrs William Trotter. *11m W of Darlington, 5m E of Barnard Castle. Central Staindrop, pink house opp Spar shop.* Cream teas. **Adm £3, chd free. Sun 29 June (2-5).**

1-acre Queen Anne walled village garden. Well stocked herbacous borders. 2 rose beds, shrubs, vegetable and soft fruit garden.

⑱ ◆ HERTERTON HOUSE

Hartington NE61 4BN. Mr Frank Lawley, 01670 774278. *12m W of Morpeth. 23m NW of Newcastle. 2m N of Cambo on the B6342 signed to Hartington. Brown signs.* **Adm £3, chd free. Mons, Weds, Fris, Sats & Suns 1 Apr to 30 Sept. For NGS: Thurs 19 June; 17 July; 7 Aug (1.30-5.30).**

1 acre of formal garden in stone walls around C16 farmhouse (not open). Incl small topiary garden, physic garden, flower garden, fancy garden, gazebo and nursery garden. Featured in 'The Northumbrian'.

⑲ HEXHAM COMMUNITY WALLED GARDEN

Whetstone Bridge Road. NE46 3JB. Queen Elizabeth High School, 07930 969756 (Emma Thompson), 01434 607350 (Keda Norman). *½ m W of Hexham. From Hexham bus stn drive in a westerly direction. When you reach 3 way T-lights - Fox PH on R, turn L up Allendale Rd, after layby on L, take 2nd R turn up lane. Car park will be signed.* Light refreshments & teas. **Adm £2.50, chd free. Sun 8 June (11-5). Visitors also welcome by appt.**

¼ -acre walled garden developed by young people and community groups. Cottage garden style incl ponds, vegetables, fruit and herbaceous planting. Victorian greenhouse. Willow tunnels. Gold Winner - Nothumberland in Bloom. Partial wheelchair access, gravel paths.

20 **NEW** **HIGH HILL TOP**
St John's Chapel DL13 1RJ. Mr & Mrs I Hedley, 01388 537952. *7m W of Stanhope. On A689. Turn L into Harthope Rd after Co-op shop in St John's Chapel. Up hill for ½ m past the Animal Hotel. Garden is next house on L.* Home-made teas. **Adm £2.50, chd free. Sun 29 June (10-4). Visitors also welcome by appt, no coaches.** See what can be achieved in an exposed garden at 1200ft. Mixed planting incls wonderful collection of sorbus, hostas, ferns, eucalyptus and candelabra primulas. Magnificent backdrop of North Pennines. Featured on Tyne Tees TV.

🏃 ⊗ ☕ ☎

21 **HURWORTH GARDENS**
Hurworth-on-Tees DL2 2AA. *2m SE of Darlington. Off A167 Darlington to Northallerton rd.* Home-made teas. **Combined adm £4, chd free. Sat 14 June (2-5).** 6 varied village gardens incl 2 new ones with spectacular views over R Tees. Courtyard garden with hot and shady areas. 3 individual medium size cottage gardens. Inspiring peonies, roses, delphiniums and clematis. Some steep slopes.

♿ ⊗ ☕

22 **LILBURN TOWER**
Alnwick NE66 4PQ. Mr & Mrs D Davidson, 01668 217291, davidson309@btinternet.com. *3m S of Wooler. On A697.* Home-made teas. **Adm £3, chd free. Sun 18 May (2-6). Visitors also welcome by appt May-Sept.** 10 acres of walled and formal gardens incl conservatory and large glasshouse. Approx 30 acres of woodland with walks and pond garden. Rhododendrons and azaleas. Also ruins of Pele Tower, and C12 church. Limited wheelchair, gravel paths.

♿ ⊗ ☕ ☎

23 **10 LOW ROW**
North Bitchburn, Crook DL15 8AJ. Mrs Ann Pickering, 01388 766345. *3m NW of Bishop Auckland. A689 N to Howden Le Wear, R up the bank before petrol stn. 1st R in village at 30mph sign.* **Visitors welcome by appt all year (not Tues).** Quirky original garden with 90% grown from seeds and cuttings. Extensive views over the Wear valley. An amazing garden created without commercially bought plants or expense. Totally organic and environmentally friendly. A haven for wildlife. Featured on TV North East News.

🏃 ☎

24 **LOW WALWORTH HALL**
Darlington DL2 2NA. Mr & Mrs Worrall, 01325 468004/07718908345, vanessaworrall@hotmail.com. *3½ m NW of Darlington. On B6279 Staindrop rd (½ m drive).* Home-made teas. **Adm £3.50, chd free. Sun 29 June (2-5). Visitors also welcome by appt.** Old walled garden; herbaceous borders, shrubs, roses; formal and wildlife ponds. Japanese and Zen gardens. Millennium fantasy garden and secret garden. Fruit and vegetable gardens. Tree walk. African theme garden. New for 2008 wildlife lake area. Featured on TV Hidden Gardens. Some gravel paths.

♿ ⊗ ☕ ☎

25 **MINDRUM**
nr Cornhill on Tweed & Yetholm TD12 4QN. Hon P J & Mrs Fairfax. *6m SW of Coldstream, 9m NW of Wooler. 4m N of Yetholm. 5m from Cornhill on Tweed on B6352.* Home-made teas. **Adm £3, chd free. Sun 22 June (2-6).** Old-fashioned roses; rock and water garden; shrub borders. Wonderful views along Bowmont Valley. Approx 3 acres. Or more if you like to wander by river. Limited wheelchair access, gravel and steep paths.

♿ ⊗ ☕

26 **MOORBANK BOTANIC GARDEN**
Claremont Road, Newcastle upon Tyne NE1 7RU. University of Newcastle, 01434 602403, hightreesgarden@btinternet.com. *¾ m from Newcastle Haymarket. W end of Claremont Rd, just E of Cat & Dog shelter. Shared entrance with Town Moor Superintendents Farm (blue gate). 12 mins walk up Claremont Rd from Exhibition Park entrance roundabout. No parking in garden.* **Adm £2.50, chd free (share to Friends of Moorbank Garden). Suns 30 Mar; 18 May (2-5); Evening Opening** wine, Wed 25 June (6-9); Sun 2 Nov (1-4). Visitors also welcome by appt, for groups of 10+.** 3 acre university botanic garden with collections of rare conifers, rhododendrons, sorbus, pond, perennials, herb garden, meadow. Extensive plantings under glass with tropical plants, succulants, insectivorous plants. Many original collections, originally from Kilbryde Gardens, Corbridge. Outside plantings maintained with volunteer help. Guided walks around garden, sales of plants, trees and plant pots. Grass and slopes.

♿ 🏃 ⊗ ☕ ☎

See what can be achieved in an exposed garden at 1200ft . . .

27 **NEW** **NEWBIGGIN HOUSE**
Blanchland DH8 9UD. Mrs A Scott-Harden. *12m S of Hexham. From Blanchland village take Stanhope Rd. ½ m along narrow rd follow yellow signs up tarmac drive into car park.* **Adm £3, chd free. Sun 1 June (2-6).** 5-acre landscaped garden at 1000ft, started in 1996 and is maturing beautifully. Old-fashioned herbaceous border, shrubs, roses, bog and wild garden incl wild rose walk. Magnificent collection of unusual trees and shrubs. Wonderful cream teas in The Monk Tearooms, Blanchland. Featured in 'Country Life'. Partial wheelchair access.

♿ 🏃 ☕

28 **25 PARK ROAD SOUTH**
Chester le Street DH3 3LS. Mrs A Middleton, 0191 388 3225. *4m N of Durham. A167 N towards Chester le Street. L at roundabout (Durham Rd) to town centre. 1st R for parking and rear access to garden only. S from A1 - 3rd roundabout then R as above.* Home-made teas (dependent on weather). **Adm £2.50, chd free (share to St Cuthbert's Hospice, Durham). Sun 8 June (1-4). Visitors also welcome by appt. May to Aug, groups of 10+.** Plantswoman's garden with all-yr round interest, colour, texture and foliage. Unusual perennials, grasses, shrubs and container planting. Cool courtyard garden using foliage only. Small front gravel garden.

🏃 ⊗ ☕ ☎

29 ◆ RABY CASTLE
Staindrop DL2 3AH. Lord Barnard,
01833 660202,
www.rabycastle.com. *12m NW of
Darlington, 1m N of Staindrop. On
A688 8m NE of Barnard Castle.* **House
and Garden adm £9, chd £4,
concessions £8, Garden only adm
£5, chd under 12 free, 12-15 £3,
concessions £4. Easter Sat to Mon,
Bank Hols Sats; Sun to Wed May,
June & Sept; daily except Sats July,
Aug (gdn 11-5.30, castle 12.30-5).**
C18 walled gardens set within the
grounds of Raby Castle. Designers
such as Thomas White and James
Paine have worked to establish the
gardens, which now extend to 5 acres,
display herbaceous borders, old yew
hedges, formal rose gardens and
informal heather and conifer gardens.

Pergolas and walls, festooned with rambling roses and clematis . . .

30 RAVENSFORD FARM
Hamsterley DL13 3NH. Mr & Mrs J
Peacock, 01388 488305,
peacock@ravensford.eclipse.co.uk.
*7m W of Bishop Auckland. From A68
at Witton-le-Wear turn off W to
Hamsterley. Go through village & turn L
just before tennis courts.* Home-made
teas under cover. **Adm £3, chd 50p.
Sun 28 Sept (2.30-5).** Visitors also
welcome by appt.
A first-ever opportunity to see this 20yr
old country garden of varied areas and
moods in its autumn glory. Many
flowers chosen for late colour, also
ornamental fruits and berries. Featured
in 'Darlington & Stockton Times' &
'Northern Echo'. Wheelchair access
only with assistance.

31 ROMALDKIRK GARDENS
DL12 9DZ. *6m NW of Barnard Castle.
On B6277, 2m S of Eggleston.* Cream
teas. **Adm £3, chd free.** Sun 22 June
(2-5.30).
Group of 10 gardens of great variety:
some cottage gardens, one with pond
and grotto. Clustered round village
green in historic village.

**32 NEW ST MARGARET'S
ALLOTMENTS**
Margery Lane, Durham
DH1 4QG. Diocese of Durham.
*From A1 take A690 to city
centre/Crook. Straight ahead at T-
lights after passing 4 roundabouts.
Pedestrians walk up Sutton St from
big roundabout at viaduct.
Allotments L in Margery Lane.*
Home-made teas in church hall, 5
mins walk (access by car available).
Adm £2.50, chd free. Sun 13 July
(2-5.30).
5 acres of 82 allotments against
the spectacular backdrop of
Durham Cathedral. This site has
been cultivated since the middle
ages, and was saved from
development 20yrs ago, allowing a
number of enthusiastic gardeners
to develop their plots which display
a great variety of fruit, vegetables
and flowers. History of site. Winner
Britain in Bloom, Neighbourhood
Award of Merit.

33 THORNLEY HOUSE
Allendale, Northum NE47 9NH. Ms
Eileen Finn, 01434 683255,
www.thornleyhouse.co.uk. *1m W of
Allendale. From Allendale town, down
hill from Hare & Hound to 5th rd
junction, 1m Thornley House is big
house in field in front.* Home-made
teas. **Adm £3, chd free (share to
Brook Charity for Working Animals).**
Sun 1 June (2-5).
Unusual 1-acre garden consisting of
woodland, stream, pond, vegetable
and fruit garden, rose avenue and
mixed planting. A feline theme is
evident throughout this child-friendly
garden. Seek and find quiz is
available for family fun. Maine Coon
cats and ornamental animals enhance
this garden. Featured in 'Hexham
Courant'.

34 THORPE GARDENS
DL12 9TU. *5m SE of Barnard Castle.
9m from Scotch Corner W on A66.
Turn R at Peel House Farm Shop
signed Wycliffe and Whorlton, 1m from
A66.* Home-made teas. **Adm £3, chd
free.** Sun 6 July (2-5).
Charming hamlet, 3 cottage gardens,
one approx 1/4-acre with some unusual
plants. Incl Thorpe Hall, a large
interesting garden in the course of
development by a professional
designer. Wood Carving
Demonstration.

35 ◆ WALLINGTON
Cambo NE61 4AR. The National
Trust, 01670 774389,
www.nationaltrust.org.uk. *12m W of
Morpeth. From N B6343; from S via
A696 from Newcastle, 6m W of Belsay,
B6342 to Cambo.* **House and Garden
adm £9.25, chd £4.65, Garden only
adm £6.40, chd £3.20. Garden daily
Apr - Sept 10-7, Oct 10-6, Nov - Mar
10-4. For NGS: Sun 20 Apr; Sat 19
July (10-7).**
Walled, terraced garden with fine
herbaceous and mixed borders;
Edwardian conservatory; 100 acres
woodland and lakes. National
Collection of sambucus. House dates
from 1688 but altered, interior greatly
changed c1740; exceptional rococo
plasterwork by Francini brothers. Plant
Sale for NGS.

**36 NEW WHALTON MANOR
GARDENS**
Whalton NE61 3UT. Mr & Mrs T
R P S Norton,
www.whaltonmanor.co.uk. *5m W
of Morpeth.* Teas. **Adm £3.50, chd
free.** Sun 6 July (2-5).
The historic Whalton Manor, altered
by Sir Edwin Lutyens in 1908, is
surrounded by 3 acres of
magnificent walled gardens,
designed by Lutyens with the help
of Gertrude Jekyll. The gardens
have been developed by the
Norton family since the 1920s and
incls extensive herbaceous
borders, 30yd peony border, rose
garden, listed summerhouses,
pergolas and walls, festooned with
rambling roses and clematis. Some
stone steps.

Seek and find quiz is available for family fun. Maine Coon cats and ornamental animals enhance this garden . . .

37 **WOOPERTON HALL**
nr Wooler NE66 4XS. Mr & Mrs Robert Fleming. *6m S of Wooler. Signed off the A697, 3m N of Powburn.* Home-made teas. **Adm £3, chd free. Sun 1 June (1.30-5.30).** 5-acre garden in the foothills of Cheviots, restored since 1996. Set on E-facing slope with wonderful views it features colour-themed terraces, mixed borders, rhododendrons and azaleas in a woodland setting with naturalised bulbs. Productive fruit and vegetable garden, greenhouse and wild bog garden adjacent to farm pond.

Durham & Northumberland County Volunteers

County Organiser
Shanah Smailes, The Stables, Chapman's Court, Catterick Village, North Yorkshire DL10 7UE, 01748 812887, shanah@smailes.go-plus.net

County Treasurers
Northumberland Anne & David Kinniment, Sike View, Kirkwhelpington NE19 2SA, 01830 540393
Durham Shanah Smailes, The Stables, Chapman's Court, Catterick Village, North Yorkshire DL10 7UE. 01748 812887, shanah@smailes.go-plus.net

Publicity
Susie White, Chesters Walled Garden, Chollerford, Hexham NE46 4BQ Tel 01434 681483, susie@chesterswalledgarden.fsnet.co.uk

Assistant County Organisers
Elizabeth Carrick, Green House, Stone Man Lane, Gayles, nr Richmond, North Yorkshire DL11 7JB, 01833 621199
Patricia Fleming, Wooperton Hall, Alnwick NE66 4XS 01668 217009

ESSEX

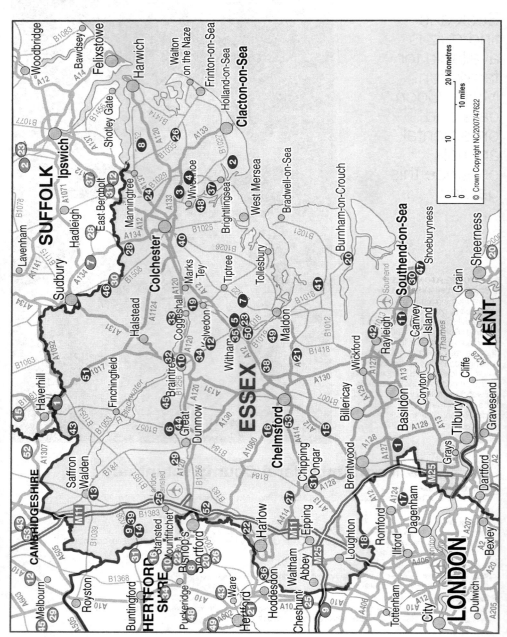

Opening Dates

March
SUNDAY 9
53 Writtle College

MONDAY 24
5 Braxted Place

SUNDAY 30
24 Green Island

April
THURSDAY 3
1 Barnards Farm

FRIDAY 4
23 Glen Chantry

THURSDAY 10
1 Barnards Farm

SATURDAY 12
48 Tudor Roost

SUNDAY 13
47 South Shoebury Hall
48 Tudor Roost

THURSDAY 17
1 Barnards Farm
16 Dragons

SATURDAY 19
48 Tudor Roost

SUNDAY 20
5 Braxted Place
27 Hobbans Farm
48 Tudor Roost

THURSDAY 24
1 Barnards Farm

FRIDAY 25
50 Wickham Place Farm

SATURDAY 26
44 St Helens

SUNDAY 27
49 Ulting Wick

May
THURSDAY 1
1 Barnards Farm

FRIDAY 2
19 Feeringbury Manor
23 Glen Chantry
50 Wickham Place Farm

SATURDAY 3
25 Haditha

SUNDAY 4
5 Braxted Place
6 19 Brookfields
25 Haditha
27 Hobbans Farm
48 Tudor Roost

MONDAY 5
5 Braxted Place
48 Tudor Roost

WEDNESDAY 7
45 Saling Hall

THURSDAY 8
1 Barnards Farm

FRIDAY 9
19 Feeringbury Manor
50 Wickham Place Farm

SATURDAY 10
2 Barnfield

SUNDAY 11
2 Barnfield
13 90 Debden Road

WEDNESDAY 14
13 90 Debden Road
45 Saling Hall

THURSDAY 15
1 Barnards Farm
16 Dragons

FRIDAY 16
19 Feeringbury Manor
35 4 Millbridge Road
50 Wickham Place Farm

SATURDAY 17
51 Willow Cottage

SUNDAY 18
7 Casa Mia
13 90 Debden Road
27 Hobbans Farm
51 Willow Cottage

WEDNESDAY 21
13 90 Debden Road
45 Saling Hall

THURSDAY 22
1 Barnards Farm

FRIDAY 23
19 Feeringbury Manor
50 Wickham Place Farm

SUNDAY 25
5 Braxted Place
8 Chippins
36 The Mount

MONDAY 26
5 Braxted Place
29 Little Easton Gardens

WEDNESDAY 28
45 Saling Hall

THURSDAY 29
1 Barnards Farm

FRIDAY 30
19 Feeringbury Manor
50 Wickham Place Farm

SATURDAY 31
26 Hannams Hall

June
SUNDAY 1
12 Cressing Temple
15 23 Docklands Avenue
21 Furzelea
26 Hannams Hall
27 Hobbans Farm
37 Moverons
38 The Old Rectory
42 Orchard Cottage
43 Parsonage House

WEDNESDAY 4
45 Saling Hall

THURSDAY 5
1 Barnards Farm

FRIDAY 6
19 Feeringbury Manor
23 Glen Chantry
35 4 Millbridge Road
37 Moverons
50 Wickham Place Farm

SATURDAY 7
44 St Helens

SUNDAY 8
39 The Old Vicarage

TUESDAY 10
34 60 Mill Lane

WEDNESDAY 11
20 4 Fernlea Road
41 One Brook Hall Cottages
45 Saling Hall

THURSDAY 12
1 Barnards Farm

FRIDAY 13
19 Feeringbury Manor
37 Moverons
50 Wickham Place Farm

SUNDAY 15
9 Clavering Gardens
11 Court View
17 Edelweiss
27 Hobbans Farm
32 Lyons Hall

TUESDAY 17
48 Tudor Roost

WEDNESDAY 18
45 Saling Hall
48 Tudor Roost

THURSDAY 19
1 Barnards Farm
16 Dragons

FRIDAY 20
19 Feeringbury Manor

37 Moverons
50 Wickham Place Farm

SUNDAY 22
15 23 Docklands Avenue
36 The Mount

WEDNESDAY 25
45 Saling Hall

THURSDAY 26
1 Barnards Farm

FRIDAY 27
19 Feeringbury Manor
35 4 Millbridge Road
37 Moverons
50 Wickham Place Farm

SATURDAY 28
10 352 Coggeshall Road

SUNDAY 29
1 Barnards Farm
8 Chippins
10 352 Coggeshall Road
27 Hobbans Farm
32 Lyons Hall

July

WEDNESDAY 2
45 Saling Hall

THURSDAY 3
1 Barnards Farm

FRIDAY 4
19 Feeringbury Manor
23 Glen Chantry
35 4 Millbridge Road
37 Moverons
50 Wickham Place Farm

SUNDAY 6
6 19 Brookfields
31 Little Myles

TUESDAY 8
34 60 Mill Lane

WEDNESDAY 9
45 Saling Hall

THURSDAY 10
1 Barnards Farm

FRIDAY 11
19 Feeringbury Manor
37 Moverons
50 Wickham Place Farm

SUNDAY 13
24 Green Island
27 Hobbans Farm
53 Writtle College

WEDNESDAY 16
45 Saling Hall

THURSDAY 17
1 Barnards Farm
16 Dragons

FRIDAY 18
19 Feeringbury Manor

37 Moverons
50 Wickham Place Farm

SATURDAY 19
2 Barnfield

SUNDAY 20
2 Barnfield
7 Casa Mia
11 Court View
42 Orchard Cottage
47 South Shoebury Hall

WEDNESDAY 23
45 Saling Hall

THURSDAY 24
1 Barnards Farm

FRIDAY 25
19 Feeringbury Manor
37 Moverons
50 Wickham Place Farm

SATURDAY 26
48 Tudor Roost

SUNDAY 27
17 Edelweiss
48 Tudor Roost

WEDNESDAY 30
45 Saling Hall

THURSDAY 31
1 Barnards Farm

August

FRIDAY 1
23 Glen Chantry

TUESDAY 5
34 60 Mill Lane

WEDNESDAY 6
36 The Mount

THURSDAY 7
1 Barnards Farm

SATURDAY 9
2 Barnfield (Afternoon & Early Evening)
30 Little Foxes
48 Tudor Roost

SUNDAY 10
30 Little Foxes
48 Tudor Roost

THURSDAY 14
1 Barnards Farm

SATURDAY 16
11 Court View

SUNDAY 17
11 Court View
18 Fairwinds

THURSDAY 21
16 Dragons

SUNDAY 24
14 Deers
17 Edelweiss

36 The Mount
48 Tudor Roost

MONDAY 25
17 Edelweiss
48 Tudor Roost

SUNDAY 31
27 Hobbans Farm

September

FRIDAY 5
19 Feeringbury Manor
50 Wickham Place Farm

SATURDAY 6
44 St Helens

SUNDAY 7
1 Barnards Farm
6 19 Brookfields
37 Moverons
43 Parsonage House

WEDNESDAY 10
13 90 Debden Road

FRIDAY 12
19 Feeringbury Manor
50 Wickham Place Farm

SATURDAY 13
11 Court View

SUNDAY 14
11 Court View
13 90 Debden Road
27 Hobbans Farm

WEDNESDAY 17
13 90 Debden Road
20 4 Fernlea Road
41 One Brook Hall Cottages

THURSDAY 18
16 Dragons

FRIDAY 19
19 Feeringbury Manor
50 Wickham Place Farm

FRIDAY 26
19 Feeringbury Manor
50 Wickham Place Farm

October

SUNDAY 12
4 The Bishops House

November

SUNDAY 9
24 Green Island

February 2009

SUNDAY 8
24 Green Island

Gardens open to the public

3 Beth Chatto Gardens
12 Cressing Temple

- 22 The Gibberd Garden
- 23 Glen Chantry
- 24 Green Island
- 33 Marks Hall Gardens & Arboretum

By appointment only

- 28 Horkesley Hall
- 40 Olivers
- 46 Shrubs Farm
- 52 Woolards Ash

Also open by appointment ☎

- 1 Barnards Farm
- 2 Barnfield
- 5 Braxted Place
- 8 Chippins
- 10 352 Coggeshall Road
- 13 90 Debden Road
- 16 Dragons
- 17 Edelweiss
- 19 Feeringbury Manor
- 20 4 Fernlea Road
- 27 Hobbans Farm
- 35 4 Millbridge Road
- 36 The Mount
- 37 Moverons
- 41 One Brook Hall Cottages
- 42 Orchard Cottage
- 44 St Helens
- 45 Saling Hall
- 47 South Shoebury Hall
- 48 Tudor Roost
- 49 Ulting Wick
- 50 Wickham Place Farm

The Gardens

1 BARNARDS FARM

Brentwood Road, West Horndon CM13 3LX. Bernard & Sylvia Holmes & The Christabella Charitable Trust, 01277 811262, sylvia@barnardsfarm.eu, www.barnardsfarm.eu. *5m S of Brentwood. On A128, 1½ m S of A127. Halfway House flyover. From the junction continue on A128 under the railway bridge. Garden on R just past bridge.* Teas (Suns), Light lunches (Thurs). **Adm £5, chd free (share to St Francis Church, West Horndon). Thurs 3 Apr to 14 Aug (11-4.30); Suns 29 June; 7 Sept (2-5.30). Visitors also welcome by appt, groups of 30+, school or special needs 10+.**
A sculpture collection, incl works by Frink, Gormley and Thomas Heatherwick in 17 hectares of garden, woodland and ponds. Panoramic views from rose-covered belvedere, Japanese, vegetable and bog gardens. Home to the National Collection of malus. Grass runway, aviators welcome (PPO). On Sundays you can also visit the 1920s bicycle shop and motor museum. Tours by golf buggy available for less able people. Light music in the garden and guided tours of the sculptures 3pm (Suns). Thomas Heatherwick's Hairy Sitooterie frequently featured in design magazines. Wheelchair accessible WC.
& ☒ ☸ NCCPG ☕ ☎

2 BARNFIELD

35 Point Clear Road, St Osyth CO16 8EP. Christine & Paul Harman, 01255 820215, wifeykins@hotmail.com. *4m W of Clacton on Sea. W of Xrds in village, towards Point Clear, across the dam approx 300yds up hill on L.* Light refreshments & cream teas. **Adm £2, chd free. Sats, Suns 10, 11 May; 19, 20 July (11-5). Afternoon and Early Evening Opening** wine, Sat 9 Aug (12-7). **Visitors also welcome by appt anytime.**
Over 1½ acres. Collection of native and specimen trees, black poplar, gingko, katsura, dwarf Chinese elm, sweet gum, honey locust. Southern hemisphere area has collection of eucalyptus and rare Wollemi pine. Ornamental pond with water feature, natural pond with bog garden, dry and alpine gardens, 2 greenhouses containing cacti and succulents, fern garden. Plenty of seats to rest. Working model railway layout, also new this year, garden model railway. 'Summer Concert' special event (Aug). Leigh Mummers and Musical Entertainers. Local pottery and plants for sale at all openings. Gravel path, gradual slope by pond.
& ☒ ☸ ☕ ☎

3 ◆ BETH CHATTO GARDENS

Elmstead Market CO7 7DB. Mrs Beth Chatto, 01206 822007, www.bethchatto.co.uk. *¼ m E of Elmstead Market. On A133 Colchester to Clacton Rd in village of Elmstead Market.* **Adm £4.50, under 14 chd free. Mons to Sats, Mar to Oct (9-5); Mons to Fris Nov to Feb (9-4). Closed Suns.**
6 acres of attractively landscaped garden with many unusual plants, shown in wide range of conditions from hot and dry to water garden. Famous gravel garden and woodland garden. Disabled wc and parking.

Featured in 'Gardens Illustrated', 'Gardeners World' Hampton Court special programme.
& ☒ ☸ ☕

4 NEW THE BISHOPS HOUSE

Rectory Road, Frating, Colchester CO7 7HQ. Mr & Mrs Christopher Pertwee. *2m E of Elmstead Market. From Elmstead Market going towards Clacton/Frinton, take 1st turning R (Church Rd). House 1m on R.* **Adm £3.50, chd £1. Sun 12 Oct (2-5).**
Stunning 4-acre garden originally designed by Peter Coates. Formal gardens with mixed borders bursting with colour and interest, inspired by Hidcote and Christopher Lloyd. Mown paths meander through trees to the immaculate lawns. Superb early autumn colour from a wide variety of unusual plants.
&

Mown paths meander through trees to the immaculate lawns . . .

5 BRAXTED PLACE

Kelvedon Road, Little Braxted CM8 3LD. Mr & Mrs J Booker, 01621 891502. *2m S of Witham. J22 A12 follow signs to Little Braxted along narrow winding lane past mill & church. 1m on, the lane joins Kelvedon Rd. Straight on for 400yds keep L at village green. House ahead with Green Man PH on R. Turn L into small parking area opp chapel.* Home-made teas. **Adm £2.50, chd free. Mons, Suns 24 Mar; 20 Apr; 4, 5, 25, 26 May (11-5). Visitors also welcome by appt.**
Mature organic garden of approx 1 acre surrounding Georgian former rectory (not open), with attached Victorian chapel (open with garden). Walled kitchen and herb garden, conservatory, gravel garden. Informal lawns, borders, wild areas and mature trees give a romantic feel especially in spring.
☒ ☸ ☕ ☎

6 NEW **19 BROOKFIELDS**
Stebbing CM6 3SA. Trevor &
Diane Vaughan. *3m NE of Great
Dunmow. Leave Gt Dunmow on
B1057, at Bran End turn R to
Stebbing Village, then 1st R into
Brookfields.* **Adm £2.50, chd free
(share to Helen Rollason Heal
Cancer Charity). Suns 4 May; 6
July; 7 Sept (12-5).**
0.6 acre tranquil site leading down
to Stebbing Brook and overlooking
an ancient meadow and farmland
to the rear. The garden features
mixed borders, limestone rock
garden, gravel area, vegetable
beds, small woodland area with
several mature trees and new
plantings. Unusually large pergola
festooned with climbing roses,
clematis, jasmine and morning
glory.
⚒ ✿ ☕

Tranquil site
leading down to
Stebbing Brook
and overlooking
an ancient
meadow and
farmland to the
rear . . .

7 **CASA MIA**
Rookery Lane, Great Totham,
Maldon CM9 8DF. Ted & Linda
Walker. *2m S of Tiptree. Situated in Gt
Totham N, Rookery Lane is off B1022
Maldon to Colchester rd.* **Adm £2.50,
chd free. Suns 18 May; 20 July (1-5).**
Surprising garden with plant collections
of roses, hemerocallis, clematis,
rhododendrons and, in spring, many
bulbs. In the distance a wooded glen
with stream, waterside plants and
amazing swathe of intensely blue
hydrangeas. Ponds with koi carp and
small waterfall.
⚒

8 **CHIPPINS**
Heath Road, Bradfield CO11 2UZ.
Kit & Ceri Leese, 01255 870730,
ceri.leese1@tiscali.co.uk. *3m E of
Manningtree. On B1352, take main rd*
through village. Bungalow is directly
opp primary school. *Home-made teas.*
**Adm £2.50, chd free. Suns 25 May;
29 June (11-5). Visitors also
welcome by appt, May to July only.**
Plantaholics' paradise packed with
interest all yr. Mixed borders with
decorative trees, shrubs and
perennials. 30ft stream and ponds,
densely planted with hostas, tree ferns
and some tropical marginals. Irises,
tree peony and alliums in spring.
Explosion of colour in summer with
unusual hemerocallis and abundance
of tubs and hanging baskets.
⚒ ✿ ☕ ☎

9 **CLAVERING GARDENS**
Saffron Walden CB11 4PX. *7m N of
Bishop's Stortford. On B1038. Turn W
off B1383 at Newport.* Home-made
teas at Piercewebbs. **Combined adm
£4, chd free. Sun 15 June (2-5).**
Popular village with many C16 & C17
timber-framed dwellings, beautiful C14
church, village green with thatched
cricket pavilion and pitch. New moon
gate at Deers.
☕

APRIL COTTAGE
CB11 4SJ. Mr & Mrs Harris
Charming thatched cottage with
small, very colourful garden
packed with many unusual plants,
old fashioned roses, bog garden
and raised pond, to be discovered
down winding paths.
✿

DEERS
Mr & Mrs S H Cooke
(See separate entry).
PIERCEWEBBS
Mr & Mrs B R William-Powlett
Old walled garden, shrubs, lawns,
ha-ha, yew with topiary and stilt
hedges, pond and trellised rose
garden. Extensive views.
⚒

10 **352 COGGESHALL ROAD**
Braintree CM7 9EH. Sau Lin Goss,
01376 329753,
richiegoss@btinternet.com. *15m W
of Colchester. 10m N of Chelmsford.
From M11 J8 take A120 Colchester.
Follow A120 to Braintree roundabout
(McDonalds). 1st exit into Cressing Rd
follow to T-lights. R into Coggeshall Rd.
500yds on R opp bus company.* Tea &
selection of fresh home-made cakes
£1.75. **Adm £2.50, chd free. Sat 28,
Sun 29 June (1.30-5). Visitors also
welcome by appt June to Sept.**
Sau Lin arrived from Hong Kong to
become enthralled with English
gardening. 'This is my little heaven',
she says of her garden which has
various themed areas, perennials,
roses and many other plants.
Japanese style mixed border garden,
fruit trees and shrubs. Various seating
and relaxing areas, fish pond with
many plants and wildlife.
Mediterranean style patio area, with old
established grape vine, passion flowers
and numerous pot plants of varying
sizes. Featured in 'Essex Life', 'Essex
Chronicle' & 'Braintree & Witham
Times'.
✿ ☕ ☎

11 NEW **COURT VIEW**
276 Manchester Drive, Leigh-on-
Sea SS9 3ES. Ray Spencer. *4m
W of Southend, off Kingswood
Chase. From A127 London: Under
A129 (Rayleigh) to next T-lights. R
to Leigh-on-Sea, at T-lights turn R.
At roundabout (Old Vienna
Restaurant) straight on to dual
carriageway. 3rd turning on R into
Kingswood Chase. Straight over
Bonchurch Ave, L to Manchester
Drive. From A13: 3rd rd W from
Somerfield (supermarket) turn N
into Kingswood Chase, R into
Manchester Drive.* Home-made
teas. **Adm £3, chd free (share to
HARP). Suns 15 June; 20 July;
Sats, Suns 16, 17 Aug; 13, 14
Sept (2-6).**
Front providing scent, colour
throughout the yr. Rear densely
planted with exotic species.
Colourful patio with insectivorous
plants; shady, scented arbour,
intimate dining area, sculptural
butterfly bench overlooking pond
fed by a winding stream. Hidden
beyond bamboo is a deck with
vibrant pots of colour, meditative
Buddha, vines and vegetables.
⚒ ✿ ☕

12 ◆ **CRESSING TEMPLE**
Witham Road, Cressing CM77 8PD.
Essex County Council, 01376
584903,
www.cressingtemple.org.uk. *3m S of
Braintree. Midway between Braintree &
Witham on B1018. Follow brown
tourist signs.* **Adm £3.50, chd/
concessions £2.50. Daily (not Sat) 1
March to 31 Oct 10-5, Mon to Fri 1
Nov to 28 Feb 10-4. For NGS: Sun 1
June (10-5).**
Tudor themed walled garden in tranquil
setting, featuring reconstructed
Elizabethan knot garden, forecourt,
nosegay garden, medicinal border and

fountain centrepiece. Inspired by 'A Midsummer Night's Dream', only plants, trees and foliage available to the Tudor gardener are found here. Guided tours are available on request. Recently-planted Cullen garden is lawn with curving borders enclosed by herbaceous plants and shrubs. Two 800 yr-old timber framed barns built by the Knights Templar form a beautiful backdrop to the walled garden. Visitors can wander the 7 acres of this ancient moated site.

⑬ NEW 90 DEBDEN ROAD

Saffron Walden CB11 4AL. Helen Riches, 01799 500426, frontdoorflora@ntlworld.com. *1/2 m from centre of Saffron Walden. From town centre head S on High St (B184), follow rd slightly to R past war memorial, take Debden Rd (B1052). No.90 on R just past the water tower. Park in rd or town car park, 10-15min walk (uphill).* Teas (Suns only). **Adm £3, chd free. Suns, Weds 11, 14, 18, 21 May; 10, 14, 17 Sept (10-5). Visitors also welcome by appt weekdays only.**

Beautiful, atmospheric town garden 200ft x 42ft, designed and maintained by Helen Riches, garden designer. It is full of planting and design solutions featuring evergreen structural planting, imaginative use of seasonal perennials, grasses, paths and pots that lead the eye. This tranquil space is full of surprise with interesting garden buildings and artefacts. Sculpture is occasionally on show during garden openings. Featured in 'Gardeners' World'.

⑭ DEERS

Clavering CB11 4PX. Mr & Mrs S H Cooke. *7m N of Bishop's Stortford. On B1038. Turn W off B1383 (old A11) at Newport.* Home-made teas. **Adm £3.50, chd free. Sun 24 Aug (2-5). Open with Clavering Gardens Sun 15 June.**

9 acres. Judged by visitors to be a very romantic garden. Shrub and herbaceous borders; 3 ponds with water lilies; old roses in formal garden; pool garden; walled vegetable garden; moon gate; field and woodland walks. Plenty of seats to enjoy the tranquillity of the garden.

⑮ 23 DOCKLANDS AVENUE

Ingatestone CM4 9DS. Paul & Doreen Crowder. *6m SW of Chelmsford. Take A414 to Margaretting, then B1002 to Ingatestone (6m). Docklands Ave 1st L at village sign (opp playing field).* Home-made teas. **Adm £2.50, chd free. Suns 1, 22 June (11-5).**

True plant enthusiast's mature 1-acre garden, full of surprises. Gravelled area of poppies, eremurus and iris; copse of tree ferns and cardiocrinum, underplanted with Paris, arisaema and hosta, 'pale and interesting' border, pond with iris and primula, huge delphiniums, 100+ clematis, orchid house and much more.

⑯ DRAGONS

Boyton Cross, Chelmsford CM1 4LS. Mrs Margot Grice, 01245 248651, mandmdragons@tiscali.co.uk. *5m W of Chelmsford. On A1060. 1/2 m west of The Hare PH.* **Adm £2.50, chd free. Thurs 17 Apr; 15 May; 19 June; 17 July; 21 Aug; 18 Sept (10-5). Visitors also welcome by appt.**

Plantsman's garden of 2/3 acre. Front garden, mature dwarf conifers and grasses, 2 ponds, patios, scree garden and colour-themed borders. Summerhouse overlooking stream and farmland. Planted for yr round interest, over 100 clematis.

⑰ EDELWEISS

20 Hartland Road, Hornchurch RM12 4AD. Joan H Hogg & Pat F Lowery, 01708 454610. *6m SW of Brentwood. From Romford E along the A124 past Tesco on L, turn R into Albany Rd opp church on corner of Park Lane on the L. Go to the bottom of Albany Rd, humps all the way, turn L at the end into Hartland Rd.* Cream teas. **Adm £2, chd free. Suns 15 June; 27 July; 24, Mon 25 Aug (3-6). Visitors also welcome by appt June & July.**

Small town garden 200ft x 25ft. Laid out to maximise small narrow plot and featuring many containers, baskets, seasonal bedding and mixed borders. Narrow access and steps not suitable for push-chairs or wheelchairs. Vegetable plot, dovecote and tiny prize-winning front garden. 'Secret Garden' with Pets' Remembrance Corner. Prize-winner Best Front Garden', Havering in Bloom'.

⑱ NEW FAIRWINDS

Chapel Lane, Chigwell Row IG7 6JJ. David & Sue Coates. *2m SE of Chigwell. Tube: 10 mins walk up hill from Grange Hill. Turn R at exit. Car: nr M25 J26 & North Circular. Signed Chigwell. Turning off Lambourne Rd. Park opp Chapel Lane in Lodge Close car park.* Light refreshments & teas. **Adm £3, chd free. Sun 17 Aug (2-5).**

Country garden in the suburbs (200ft x 40ft). Approach by private rd to gravelled front garden. Side entrance leads to open area with large mixed borders. Path leads past children's 'fire pit' and ornamental greenhouse to decked area by the pool, woodland and children's flower beds. Look out for dragons! Rustic fence separates wildlife pond and vegetable plot. Paths uneven in places so assistance advised.

This tranquil space is full of surprise with interesting garden buildings and artefacts . . .

⑲ FEERINGBURY MANOR

Coggeshall Road, Feering CO5 9RB. Mr & Mrs Giles Coode-Adams, 01376 561946, sonia@coode-adams.demon.co.uk. *12m SW of Colchester. Between Coggeshall & Feering on Coggeshall Rd, 1m from Feering.* **Adm £4, chd free (share to Firstsite). Fris, 2 May to 25 July; 5 Sept to 26 Sept (8-4). Visitors also welcome by appt.**

Flower beds and arboretum expand with a huge range of plants, many very unusual. We have gone wild in the pursuit of continual colour.The ex-rose bed, now pink and purple, is newly backed by a fantastic sculptured steel trellis, 50 metres long, by Ben Coode-Adams. Some steep slopes.

⑳ 4 FERNLEA ROAD

Burnham-on-Crouch CM0 8EJ. Frances & Andrew Franklin, franklins@f2s.com, www.franklins.f2s.com. *Take B1010 to Burnham-on-Crouch. Cross the railway bridge then take 4th turn on R, Hillside Rd. Fernlea Rd 2nd L, no.4 nr end of cul de sac on L.* Teas at Brook Hall Cottages. **Adm £2.50, chd free. Combined with Brook Hall Cottages adm £4. Weds 11 June; 17 Sept (2-6).** Visitors also welcome by appt June & July only.
Small Mediterranean style garden on edge of riverside park. The planting, which is informal and exuberant, features several unusual varieties. Several seating areas, large covered pergola, mosaics, sculptures, water features and loads of pots - also a number of innovative solutions for dealing with drought. Featured on BBC Essex.
&. ☕ ☎

㉑ NEW FURZELEA

Bicknacre Road, Danbury CM3 4JR. Avril & Roger Cole-Jones. *4m E of Chelmsford, 4m W of Maldon. A414 to Danbury. In village centre (Eves Corner) turn S into Mayes Lane. Take R past Cricketers PH, then L onto Bicknacre Rd. Parking in NT car park. Garden on R.* Home-made teas. **Adm £3, chd free. Sun 1 June (2-6).**
Country garden for scent and colour, approx 2/3 acre. Mixed planting of trees, shrubs, climbers, bulbs, grasses and perennials - many scented roses. Informal planting carefully colour themed, woven between formal topiary, meandering to a thatched summerhouse on the lower circular lawn, past pond and white garden.
🏃 ☕

㉒ ◆ THE GIBBERD GARDEN

Marsh Lane, Harlow CM17 0NA. The Gibberd Garden Trust, 01279 442112, www.thegibberdgarden. co.uk. *3m E of Harlow. Marsh Lane is a narrow turning off B183 (to Hatfield Heath), approx 2m E of junction with A414. Look for 'Gibberd Garden' brown signs on A414 & on R opp garden entrance on B183.* **Adm £4, chd free, concessions £2.50. Sats, Suns, Weds, Bank Hols Mar to Sept 2-6.**
7-acre C20 garden designed by Sir

Frederick Gibberd, on side of small valley. Terraces, wild garden, landscaped vistas, pools and streams, 'Roman Temple', moated log 'castle', gazebo, tree house and large collection of modern sculpture. Limited wheelchair access.
&. ☕

㉓ ◆ GLEN CHANTRY

Ishams Chase, Wickham Bishops CM8 3LG. Mr & Mrs W G Staines, 01621 891342, www.glenchantry. demon.co.uk. *1½ m SE of Witham. Take Maldon Rd, 1st L to Wickham Bishops. Cross narrow bridge over R Blackwater. Turn immed L up Ishams Chase by side of Blue Mills.* **Adm £3.50, chd 50p. Fris, Sats 4 Apr to 30 Aug. For NGS: Fris 4 Apr; 2 May; 6 June; 4 July; 1 Aug (10-4).**
3-acre garden, emphasis on mixed borders, unusual perennials and shrub roses. Limestone rock gardens, ponds, formal specialist white garden, foliage beds with grasses and hostas. Famous adjacent specialist perennial nursery.
🏃 ❀ ☕

Frogs paradise – they spawn in the stream and spend the remainder of the year contemplating in adjacent ponds . . .

㉔ ◆ GREEN ISLAND

Park Road, Ardleigh CO7 7SP. Fiona Edmond, 01206 230455, www.greenislandgardens.co.uk. *3m NE of Colchester. From Ardleigh village centre, take B1029 towards Great Bromley. Park Rd is 2nd on R after level Xing. Garden is last on L.* **Adm £3, chd £1, groups of 20+ £2.50 per head. Suns, Weds, Thurs, Bank Hol Mons, 1 March to 12 Oct, 1st 2 Suns Nov & Feb. For NGS: Suns 30 Mar; 13 July; 9 Nov (10-5) 2009 Sun 8 Feb.**
Professionally designed by Fiona Edmond, beautifully situated in 19

acres of woodland. Huge variety of unusual plants with lots of interest all yr with emphasis on scent and autumn colour. Stunning mixed borders, water garden, woodland walks, seaside garden, tree house, gravel garden and Japanese garden. Garden design exhibition, photographic display. Large area of woodland redevelopment. Snowdrops and bluebells not to be missed.
&. 🏃 ❀ ☕

㉕ NEW HADITHA

New Road, Elsenham CM22 6HA. Barbara & Dennis Haslam. *4m NE of Bishop's Stortford. From Elsenham Rail Stn go W 100yds (New Rd, 2nd house on L). By kind permission of the owner free parking available in stn car park on E side of stn. Please display NGS leaflet.* Home-made teas. **Adm £2.50, chd free. Sat 3, Sun 4 May (10-4).**
Welcome to our spring garden with its splendid magnolia and abundance of well established rhododendrons, azaleas and camellias, plus a diverse variety of spring flowers, many unusual tropical plants and features. Frogs paradise - they spawn in the stream and spend the remainder of the year contemplating in adjacent ponds. A surprisingly peaceful village garden. Woodturning demonstration, art exhibition and plant stall. Very shallow steps on paths.
&. ❀ ☕

㉖ HANNAMS HALL

Thorpe Road, Tendring CO16 9AR. Mr & Mrs W Gibbon. *10m E of Colchester. From A120 take B1035 at Horsley Cross, through Tendring Village (approx 3m) pass Cherry Tree PH on R, after 1/3 m over small bridge 1st house L.* **Adm £3, chd free. Sat 31 May; Sun 1 June (2-6).**
C17 house (not open) set in 6 acres of formal and informal gardens and grounds with extensive views over open countryside. Herbaceous borders and shrubberies, many interesting trees. Lawns and mown walks through wild grass and flower meadows, woodland walks, ponds and stream. Walled vegetable potager and orchard.
&. 🏃 ❀ ☕

24 HILLS ROAD
See London.

27 HOBBANS FARM

Bobbingworth, Ongar CM5 0LZ. **John & Ann Webster, 01277 890245.** *10m W of Chelmsford. N of A414 between Ongar Four Wantz roundabout & N Weald 'Talbot' roundabout, turn R past Blake Hall Gardens. 1st farm entrance on R after St Germain's Church.* Home-made teas. **Adm £3, chd free.** Suns 20 Apr; 4, 18 May; 1, 15, 29 June; 13 July; 31 Aug; 14 Sept (2-5). **Visitors also welcome by appt.**

Romantic, tranquil gardens. Herbaceous treasures, shrubs and old roses. Honeysuckle, roses and clematis clamber over trees, walls and arches. Crab apples underplanted with narcissi, unusual trees. Walk through meadows past willow and young birch to wild garden, wood and pond with bridge to ancient oak. Teas in pot yard. May - blossom, bulbs, birds, bees. June - riot of roses, peonies, aquilegia, geraniums. July - clambering clematis. Sept - mellow fruitfulness, rich colours, hazy daisies, windflower, sedums and bees.

28 HORKESLEY HALL

Little Horkesley, Colchester CO6 4DB. **Mr & Mrs Johnny Eddis, 01206 271371, pollyeddis@ hotmail.com.** *3m N of Colchester. W of A134. Access is via church car park.* **Adm £4, chd free. Visitors welcome by appt,** any size group, teas by arrangement.

7-8 acres of romantic garden surrounding classical house (not open) with appeal for all ages. Stream feeds 2 lakes, many wonderful trees some very rare. The largest ginkgo tree outside Kew. Walled garden, pear avenue, acer walk, fruit, cut flowers and vegetables, blossom, bulbs, rhododendrons, herbaceous, autumn colour and many spring bulbs and blossom. Rare hens and black swans. Featured in 'The English Garden'. Gravel paths and slopes.

29 LITTLE EASTON GARDENS

CM6 2HZ. *½ m N of Great Dunmow. 1st turning L, on the B184 to Thaxted.* Home-made teas in Elmbridge Mill. **Combined adm £3.50, chd free (share to Little Easton Church, RC Church Dunmow).** Mon 26 May (2-5).

Small village with lovely church and lakes.

CHURCH LODGE

Vivienne Crossland
A fun garden. Infused with vibrance and peace which will both surprise and delight! Many quirky corners and interesting features - look for the surprising stag.

ELMBRIDGE MILL

Dr & Mrs Grahame Swan
Mill house (not open) with mill stream one side flowing under the house, R Chelmer on other. Approx 1 acre of trees, flowers and shrubs; roses climbing through orchard trees; walk up to mill pool with the addition of a new bridge across the mill race. Romantic garden full of interesting plants.

30 LITTLE FOXES

Marcus Gardens, Thorpe Bay SS1 3LF. **Mrs Dorothy Goode.** *2½ m E of Southend. From Thorpe Bay stn (S-side) proceed E, take 4th on R into Marcus Ave then 2nd L into Marcus Gdns.* **Adm £2.50, chd 50p.** Sat 9, Sun 10 Aug (2-5).

This award-winning garden, close to the sea, has been described as an oasis of foliage and flowers. Secluded by trees, the ⅓ acre features island beds and long borders set in lawns and planted with an interesting variety of colourful hardy perennials, grasses, flowering shrubs and beautiful foliage. Many planted containers. Colour-themed areas and pretty water feature. Collection of special hostas. Tranquil garden for plant lovers. Seaside walks and views close by. Featured in & on 'Essex Style Magazine', BBC Essex Radio.

31 LITTLE MYLES

Ongar Road, Stondon Massey CM15 0LD. **Judy & Adrian Cowan.** *1½ m SE of Chipping Ongar. Turn off A128 at Stag PH, Marden Ash, (Ongar) towards Stondon Massey. Over bridge, 1st house on R after S bend. (400yds the Ongar side of Stondon Massey Church).* Home-made teas. **Adm £3.50, chd £1.** Sun 6 July (11-4).

Romantic garden surrounded by wild flowers and grasses, set in 3 acres. Full borders, hidden features, meandering paths, pond, hornbeam pergola and stream. Herb garden, full of nectar-rich and scented herbs, used for handmade herbal cosmetics. Asian

garden with pots, statues and bamboo, ornamental vegetable plot, woven willow Gothic window feature.

32 NEW LYONS HALL

Braintree CM7 9SH. **Lord & Lady Dixon-Smith.** *Signed R off A131 to Sudbury, 2m from junction with A120 Braintree bypass.* Home-made teas. **Adm £3, chd free (share to Essex Friends of the YMCA).** Suns 15, 29 June (2.30-5).

Tranquil lakeside garden with lawns, shrubs and roses. Delightful yew and box edged parterre planted with lavender, euonymous and eleagnus. The Reverend Thomas Hooker, famed Puritan lecturer, lived at historic Lyons Hall (not open) and sailed for America on 'The Lyon' in 1632. Partial wheelchair access.

Delightful yew and box edged parterre planted with lavender, euonymous and eleagnus . . .

33 ◆ MARKS HALL GARDENS & ARBORETUM

Coggeshall CO6 1TG. **Thomas Phillips Price Trust, 01376 563796, www.markshall.org.uk.** *1½ m N of Coggeshall. Follow brown & white tourism signs from A120 Coggeshall by pass.* **Adm £3.20, chd £1.** Tues to Sun Apr to Oct (10.30-5), Fri to Sun Nov to Mar 10.30 - dusk.

The walled garden at Marks Hall is a unique blend of traditional long borders within C17 walls and 5 contemporary gardens. These combine inventive landscaping, grass sculpture and stunningly colourful mass plantings. On the opp lake bank is a millennium walk designed for winter shape, scent and colour surrounded by over 100 acres of arboretum, incl species from all continents. Featured in 'Gardens Illustrated' & 'House & Garden'.

34 NEW **60 MILL LANE**
Cressing CM77 8HW. Pauline & Arthur Childs. *2m S of Braintree. 15m W of Colchester, 5m N of Witham. From M11 J8 take A120 Colchester, follow A120 to Braintree roundabout, then take B1018 to Witham approx ³/₄ m (Tye Green), turn R into Mill Lane 400yds on L. House facing towards you on green.* Home-made teas. **Adm £2, chd free. Tues 10 June; 8 July; 5 Aug (11-5).**
Small village estate garden which is a plantaholic's paradise. Very colourful, with 2 water features. Patio with pots and hanging baskets. Lover of penstemons and fuchsias. Many hostas, ferns and some unusual plants.
🎏 ⊛ ☕

Architectural foliage, bamboos and bananas all jostle for position . . .

35 NEW **4 MILLBRIDGE ROAD**
Witham CM8 1HB. Sebastian & Andrew, 01376 503112. *A12 N exit 21 Witham, follow rd to 1st set T-lights, turn L. At T-junction turn R then 1st L Guithavon Rd, 1st L Millbridge St. A12 S exit 22 Witham, follow rd to 2nd set of T-lights turn R, at mini roundabout turn L then 1st R Guithavon Valley, double mini roundabout turn R Guithavon Rd, 1st R Millbridge Rd. Witham train stn 10 min walk.* **Adm £2.50, chd free. Fris16 May; 6, 27 June; 4 July (10-4.30). Visitors also welcome by appt.**
Surprising small town garden 129ft x 29ft. Designed into themed areas, laid out to maximise space. Wander through Mediterranean style, British theme into oasis of tranquillity. Mixed borders, perennials, architectural foliage, bamboos and bananas all jostle for position. Large fish pond and hidden features, several seating areas to sit and contemplate.
🎏 🎏 ☎

36 NEW **THE MOUNT**
Epping Road, Roydon CM19 5HT. David & Liz Davison, 077112 31555, davidandlizzy@aol.com. *2m W of Harlow in Roydon Village. W from Harlow on B181 Roydon Rd, enter Roydon Village. Pass the High St, garden approx 500yds on R. Look for a board & yellow balloons on green light bollards.* Light refreshments & teas, wine. **Adm £3.50, chd free. Suns 25 May; 22 June; Wed 6, Sun 24 Aug (11-5). Visitors also welcome by appt, groups of 10+, access for small coaches.**
The Mount is a family garden designed to accommodate our 5 retrievers. Set in 8 acres. 3 acres of formal garden and 5 acres of newly planted woodland. Meadow with wide walkways winding through the trees. Designed as 8 separate areas, the formal gardens offer a wide variety of plants and shrubs with a superb G Gauge Model Railway, great for children. For disabled we can offer free use of golf buggy. Free loan of scooters and w/chairs by appt.
♿ 🎏 ☕ ☎

37 **MOVERONS**
Brightlingsea CO7 0SB. Lesley Orrock, 01206 305498, lesley@moverons.com. *7m SE of Colchester. B1027. Turn R in Thorrington onto B1029 signed Brightlingsea. At old church turn R signed Moverons Farm, follow lane & garden signs for approx 1m.* Home-made teas (Suns only). **Adm £3, chd free. Sun 1 June; Fris 6 June to 25 July; Sun 7 Sept (11-5). Visitors also welcome by appt, groups of 10+, coaches welcome.**
Maturing 4¹/₂ -acre garden designed by owner. Wide variety of planting incl walled garden, bog and poolside, hot colours, drought beds and range of mixed beds for sun and shade filled with shrubs and perennials. 2 large ponds with landscaped vistas, mature trees and stunning estuary views.
🎏 ⊛ ☕ ☎

38 **THE OLD RECTORY**
Boreham CM3 3EP. Sir Jeffery & Lady Bowman. *4m NE of Chelmsford. Take B1137 Boreham Village, turn into Church Rd at Red Lion PH. ¹/₂ m along on R opp church.* Home-made teas. **Adm £2.50, chd free (share to Farleigh Hospice). Sun 1 June (2-5).**

2¹/₂ acre garden surrounding C15 house (not open). Ponds, stream, with bridges and primulas, small meadow and wood with interesting trees and shrubs, herbaceous borders and vegetable garden. Constantly being improved.
♿ 🎏 ⊛ ☕

39 NEW **THE OLD VICARAGE**
Church End, Rickling CB11 3YL. Mr & Mrs C Firmin. *5m N of Stansted Mountfitchet. B1383 towards Newport. Turn L to Rickling Green through village towards church (1¹/₂ m). Garden on rd to Wicken & Newport.* Home-made teas. **Adm £3.50, chd free. Sun 8 June (2-5).**
Early Victorian vicarage (not open) surrounded by 1¹/₂ acres of mature gardens. Old wall and well-established hedges provide shelter and excellent backdrop to large closely planted borders, filled with a mixture of shrubs, herbaceous plants and old roses. Wild area, pond, formal rose garden and small walled vegetable garden. Gravel driveway and paths.
♿ 🎏 ⊛ ☕

40 **OLIVERS**
Olivers Lane, Colchester CO2 0HJ. Mr & Mrs D Edwards, 01206 330575, gay.edwards@virgin.net. *3m SW of Colchester. Between B1022 & B1026. From zoo continue 1m towards Colchester. Turn R at roundabout (Cunobelin Way) & R into Olivers Lane. From Colchester via Maldon Rd turn L at roundabout, R into Olivers Lane.* Light refreshments & teas (for paries of 15+). **Adm £4, chd free. Visitors welcome by appt any time of year, any number. Parking for 2 coaches. Tour of garden and refreshments included for parties of 15+.**
Peaceful wooded garden overlooking Roman river valley. Dramatic bedding, yew backed borders closely planted with wide variety of plants. Refreshments on terrace of C18 redbrick house (not open) overlooking lakes, lawns and meadow. Woodland with fine trees, underplanted with shrubs and carpeted with a mass of spring bulbs and bluebells.
♿ 🎏 ☕ ☎

41 NEW ONE BROOK HALL COTTAGES
Steeple Road, Latchingdon
CM3 6LB. John & Corinne
Layton, corinne@arrow250.
fsnet.co.uk. *1m from Latchingdon
Church. From Maldon drive
through Latchingdon to mini
roundabout at church taking exit
towards Steeple & Bradwell.
Approx 1m turn R at bungalow
onto gravel drive.* Home-made
teas. **Adm £2.50, chd free.
Combined with 4 Fernlea Road
adm £4. Weds 11 June, 17 Sept
(2-6). Visitors also welcome by
appt June & Sept, groups of 10+.**
Organic ¹/₂ -acre garden on 3
levels. Mixed informal borders
planted to suit different conditions
and encourage wildlife. Natural
pond with bog area, formal lawn
with pleached limes and box
hedges, decked area overlooking
farmland. Narrow paths and steep
steps - not suitable for children and
people with walking difficulties.

42 ORCHARD COTTAGE
219 Hockley Road, Rayleigh
SS6 8BH. Heather & Harry
Brickwood, 01268 743838. *1m NE
from town centre. Leave A127 at
Rayleigh and take B1013 to Hockley.
Garden opp the white & blue sign for
Hockley. Park opp on grass.* Home-
made teas. **Adm £2.50, chd free.
Suns 1 June; 20 July (11-5). Visitors
also welcome by appt May to Aug.**
The ³/₄ acre-garden has been
enhanced by the rebuilding of the
stream and ponds. The herbaceous
borders surrounding the stream have
been enlarged. For the June opening
the main feature will be the aquilegias,
100s; of them, these will be backed up
by roses, lilies and numerous other
herbaceous perennials. The July
features will be hemerocallis, more
lilies, agapanthus plus colour themed
beds. There is a pond, stream and
many flowering shrubs. Featured on
BBC Essex. Gravel/lawn paths.

43 PARSONAGE HOUSE
Helions Bumpstead CB9 7AD. The
Hon & Mrs Nigel Turner. *3m S of
Haverhill. 8m NE of Saffron Walden.
From Xrds in village centre turn up
Church Hill, follow rd for 1m. Park in
field opp.* Home-made teas. **Adm
£3.50, chd free. Suns 1 June; 7 Sept
(2-5).**

C15 house (not open) surrounded by 3
acres of formal gardens with mixed
borders, topiary, pond, potager and
greenhouse. Further 3-acre wild flower
meadow with rare trees and further 3
acres of newly-planted orchard of old
East Anglian apple varieties. Featured
in 'The English Garden'.

44 ST HELENS
High Street, Stebbing CM6 3SE.
Stephen & Joan Bazlinton, 01371
856495, revbaz@care4free.net. *3m E
of Great Dunmow. Leave Gt Dunmow
on B1256. Take 1st L to Stebbing, at
T-junction turn L into High St, garden
2nd house on R.* Home-made teas.
**Adm £2.50, chd free (share to
Dentaid). Sats 26 Apr; 7 June; 6
Sept (10-4). Visitors also welcome
by appt.**
1-acre garden, created out of a damp
bat willow plantation from 1987.
Sloping S-wards with springs flowing
into a hidden pond crossed by 'Monet'
bridge. Mature hedges create vistas of
surprise as gentle paths weave
through shrubs and plants blending to
achieve peace and purpose in this rural
idyll. Featured in & on local press &
radio.

45 SALING HALL
Great Saling, Braintree CM7 5DT. Mr
& Mrs Hugh Johnson. *6m NW of
Braintree. Turn N off B1256 (old A120)
between Gt Dunmow & Braintree
signed Great Saling & the Bardfields.
Saling Hall is at end of village on L.*
**Adm £3, chd free (share to St
James's Church, Gt Saling). Weds 7
May to 30 July (2-5). Visitors also
welcome by appt, groups,
weekdays only, by written
application, see above.**
12-acre garden of many moods
created since 1960s, around a C17
House (not open). Old walled flower
gardens; landscape with many rare
trees and shrubs; moat, ponds, groves
and glades. Temple of Pisces. Hugh
Johnson has published his gardening
diary monthly since 1975, as
'Tradescant' and now in 'Gardens
Illustrated'.

46 SHRUBS FARM
Lamarsh CO8 5EA. Mr & Mrs Robert
Erith, 01787 227520,
bob@shrubsfarm.co.uk,
www.shrubsfarm.co.uk. *1¹/₄ m from
Bures. On rd to Lamarsh, the drive is
signed to Shrubs Farm.* Home-made
teas by arrangement. **Adm £4, chd
free. Visitors welcome by appt all yr,
but Apr to Oct preferred. Guided
tours for individuals, small or large
parties welcome. Ample parking for
cars and coaches.**
2 acres of mature and developing
gardens with shrub borders, lawns,
roses and trees. For walkers there are
50 acres of parkland and meadow with
wild flower paths and woodland trails.
Dogs on leads in this area. Much new
hedgerow and tree planting incl over
50 species of oak has taken place over
the past 25yrs. Superb 10m views to N
and E over the Stour valley. Ancient
coppice and pollard trees in the woods
incl the largest goat (pussy) willow
(*Salix caprea*) in England. Rare Bee
orchid variety *bicolour* was found in
June 2005; with 27 plants it is the
largest colony yet discovered in the
British Isles. Display of Bronze age
burial urns (circa 1000 BC). Wollemi
pine. Large traditional C18 Essex barn
suitable for talks, displays and
refreshments. Featured in 'Essex Life'
& local press.

For walkers
there are 50
acres of
parkland and
meadow with
wild flower
paths and
woodland
trails . . .

47 NEW SOUTH SHOEBURY HALL
Church Road, Shoeburyness
SS3 9DN. Mr & Mrs M Dedman,
01702 299044. *4m E of Southend-
on-Sea. Enter Southend on A127
to Eastern Ave A1159 signed
Shoebury. R at roundabout to join
A13. Proceed S to Ness Rd. R into
Church Rd. Garden on L 50
metres.* Home-made teas. **Adm
£3, chd free. Suns 13 Apr; 20
July (2-5). Visitors also welcome
by appt.**
Delightful, 1-acre walled garden
close to sea. An established
garden surrounding Grade 2 listed
house (not open) and bee round
house. Unusual trees and shrubs.
Many spring bulbs and outstanding
agapanthus varieties in late July.
Rose borders, dry garden areas,
Mediterranean and Southern
Hemisphere plants plus 30yr old
geraniums.

48 TUDOR ROOST
18 Frere Way, Fingringhoe CO5 7BP.
Chris & Linda Pegden, 01206
729831,
christopher.pegden@virgin.net. *5m
S of Colchester. In centre of village by
Whalebone PH. Follow sign to Ballast
Quay, after 1/2 m turn R into Brook Hall
Rd, then 1st L into Frere Way.* Home-
made teas. **Adm £2.50, chd free.
Sats, Suns 12, 13, 19, 20 Apr; 4 May;
Mon 5 May; Tue, Wed 17, 18 June;
Sats, Suns 26, 27 July; 9, 10, 24
Aug; Mon 25 Aug (2-5.30). Visitors
also welcome by appt. Evening
visits also welcome.**
An unexpected hidden colourful 1/4 -
acre garden. Well manicured grassy
paths wind round island beds and
ponds. Densely planted subtropical
area with architectural and exotic
plants - cannas, bananas, palms,
agapanthus, agaves and tree ferns
surround a colourful gazebo. Garden
planted to provide yr-round colour and
encourage wildlife. Many peaceful
seating areas. Within 1m of local
Nature reserve. Featured on BBC Look
East.

49 ULTING WICK
Maldon CM9 6QX. Mr & Mrs B
Burrough, 01245 380216,
philippa.burrough@btinternet.com.
*3m NW of Maldon. Take turning to
Ulting (Ulting Lane) off B1019 at
Langford, after 2.2m at T-junction,*

garden is opp. Home-made teas. **Adm
£3, chd free. Sun 27 Apr (2-5).
Visitors also welcome by appt,
groups of 15+. Parking space for 2
coaches.**
4-acre garden set around C16
farmhouse and barns (C17 barn open)
still undergoing major changes with
emphasis on colour. Herbaceous
borders, spring, striking pink, white
and cutting gardens provide yr-round
interest. Natural pond and stream
bordered by mature willows and beds
containing moisture and shade loving
plants. Vegetable garden with Victorian
style glasshouse, 3-acre woodland
planted in 2004. Walk to peaceful All
Saints Ulting Church by R Chelmer,
signed from garden. Church will be
open for talk on its history.

**WALTHAM FOREST REGISTER
OFFICE, E17**
See London.

Rose borders, dry garden areas, Mediterranean and Southern Hemisphere plants plus 30yr old geraniums . . .

50 WICKHAM PLACE FARM
Station Road, Wickham Bishops
CM8 3JB. Mrs J Wilson, 01621
891282, enquiries@
wickhamplacefarm.co.uk,
www.wickhamplacefarm.co.uk.
*2 1/2 m SE of Witham. Take B1018 from
Witham to Maldon. After going under
A12 take 3rd L (Station Rd). 1st house
on L.* Home-made teas. **Adm £3, chd
free** (share to Farleigh Hospice). **Fris
25 Apr to 25 July; 5 Sept to 26 Sept
(11-4). Visitors also welcome by
appt, groups and coaches 10+,
anytime.**

2-acre walled garden with huge
climbers and roses filled by shrubs,
perennials and bulbs. Renowned for
stunning wisterias in May/June, one
over 250ft long. 12 acres of mixed
woodland, superb in Sept, incl rabbit-
resistant plants and bulbs, features
lovely walks. Yr-round colour; knot
garden. Featured in 'The Garden',
'Daily Express' & 'East Anglian Daily
Times'.

51 NEW WILLOW COTTAGE
4 Stambourne Road, Great
Yeldham CO9 4RA. Mr & Mrs R
Templeman. *1m from Gt Yeldham
Church. From Braintree N on
A1017. Follow sign to Gosfield &
on to Gt Yeldham. Pass church,
1st L Stambourne Rd, entrance
400yds on R.* Cream teas. **Adm
£2.50, chd free. Sat 17, Sun 18
May (2-5).**
Pretty cottage garden set in 3/4 acre
adjacent to farmland. Mixed
borders full of plants and shrubs
that attract birds, bees and
butterflies.

52 WOOLARDS ASH
Hatfield Broad Oak CM22 7JY. Mr &
Mrs Michael Herbert, 01279 718284,
mleqh@woolardsash.fsnet.co.uk.
*5m SE of Bishop's Stortford. From
Hatfield Broad Oak follow B183 N
(towards Takeley). After 3/4 m take 1st R
(signed to Taverners Green &
Broomshawbury), then 2nd R to
Woolards Ash. From Takeley, B183 S
(towards Hatfield Broad Oak). After
3/4 m 1st L (signed Canfield & High
Roding), then 2nd L to Woolards Ash.*
Teas & wine. **Adm £5, chd free.
Visitors welcome by appt May to
July only (10-7), groups of 10+,
coaches permitted.**
Peacocks, guinea fowl and bantams
roam this beautiful 3-acre garden,
divided into 5 areas by beech and yew
hedges, all set in a pastoral landscape.
The main area has 2 large subtly
planted borders of old roses, shrubs,
herbaceous plants and ha-ha with
distant views. The walled pool garden
provides a tranquil setting for mature
borders with further shrub borders,
mature trees and wild areas planted
with bulbs and old roses, small
vegetable garden. Featured in 'Essex
Life' magazine.

Mixed borders full of plants and shrubs that attract birds, bees and butterflies . . .

53 WRITTLE COLLEGE
Writtle CM1 3RR, www.writtle.ac.uk.
4m W of Chelmsford. On A414, nr Writtle village, clearly signed. **Adm £3.50, chd free, concessions £2. Suns 9 Mar; 13 July (10-4).**
Approx 15 acres; informal lawns with naturalised bulbs in spring and wild flowers in summer, large tree collection, mixed shrub and herbaceous borders, heathers and alpines. Landscaped gardens designed and built by students including 'Centenary' garden and sub tropical 'Hot 'n' Spicy' garden. Development of new 13-acre parkland area. Orchard meadows, recently started on the site of an old apple orchard. Landscaped glasshouses and wide range of seasonal bedding displays. Horticultural information from Writtle College tutors.

Essex County Volunteers

County Organiser
Susan Copeland, Wickets, Langley Upper Green, Saffron Walden CB11 4RY, 01799 550553, susan.copeland2@btinternet.com

County Treasurer
Neil Holdaway, Woodpeckers, Mangapp Chase, Burnham-on-Crouch CM0 8QQ, 01621 782137, lindaholdaway@btinternet.com

Publicity
Arliss Porter, 16 Anglesea Road, Wivenhoe, Colchester CO7 9JR, 01206 828227, aporter211@yahoo.co.uk

Assistant County Organisers
Derek Bracey, Park Farm, Chatham Hall Lane, Great Waltham, Chelmsford CM3 1BZ, 01245 360871
Doug Copeland, Wickets, Langley Upper Green, Saffron Walden, Essex CB11 4RY, 01799 550553, susan.copeland2@btinternet.com
Jill Cowley, Park Farm, Chatham Hall Lane, Great Waltham CM3 1BZ, 01245 360 871
Linda Holdaway, Woodpeckers, Mangapp Chase, Burnham-on-Crouch CM0 8QQ, 01621 782137, lindaholdaway@btinternet.com

GLOUCESTERSHIRE

North & Central

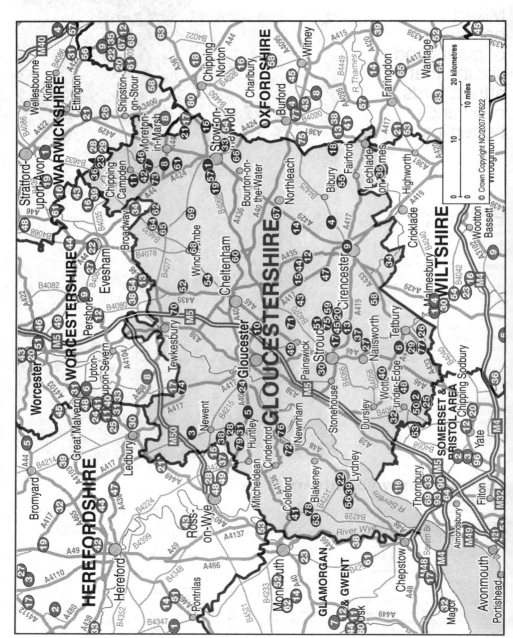

Opening Dates

January
SUNDAY 27
28 Home Farm

February
TUESDAY 5
70 Tinpenny Farm

WEDNESDAY 6
70 Tinpenny Farm

THURSDAY 7
70 Tinpenny Farm

SUNDAY 10
28 Home Farm
71 Trench Hill

MONDAY 11
47 The Old Rectory, Duntisbourne Rous

TUESDAY 12
70 Tinpenny Farm

WEDNESDAY 13
70 Tinpenny Farm

THURSDAY 14
70 Tinpenny Farm

SUNDAY 17
71 Trench Hill

TUESDAY 19
70 Tinpenny Farm

WEDNESDAY 20
70 Tinpenny Farm

THURSDAY 21
70 Tinpenny Farm

SUNDAY 24
35 Kempsford Manor

TUESDAY 26
70 Tinpenny Farm

WEDNESDAY 27
70 Tinpenny Farm

THURSDAY 28
70 Tinpenny Farm

March
SUNDAY 2
22 Green Cottage
35 Kempsford Manor

TUESDAY 4
70 Tinpenny Farm

WEDNESDAY 5
70 Tinpenny Farm

THURSDAY 6
70 Tinpenny Farm

SUNDAY 9
22 Green Cottage
35 Kempsford Manor

MONDAY 10
47 The Old Rectory, Duntisbourne Rous

TUESDAY 11
70 Tinpenny Farm

WEDNESDAY 12
70 Tinpenny Farm

THURSDAY 13
70 Tinpenny Farm

SUNDAY 16
22 Green Cottage
28 Home Farm
35 Kempsford Manor
52 Pear Tree Cottage

TUESDAY 18
70 Tinpenny Farm

WEDNESDAY 19
70 Tinpenny Farm

THURSDAY 20
70 Tinpenny Farm

FRIDAY 21
42 Mill Dene Garden

SUNDAY 23
6 Beverston Castle
37 Lammas Park
71 Trench Hill

MONDAY 24
3 Baldwins
6 Beverston Castle
42 Mill Dene Garden
71 Trench Hill

TUESDAY 25
70 Tinpenny Farm

WEDNESDAY 26
70 Tinpenny Farm

THURSDAY 27
70 Tinpenny Farm

SUNDAY 30
43 Misarden Park

April
TUESDAY 1
70 Tinpenny Farm

WEDNESDAY 2
70 Tinpenny Farm

THURSDAY 3
70 Tinpenny Farm

SUNDAY 6
24 Highnam Court
28 Home Farm
42 Mill Dene Garden
63 South Lodge

TUESDAY 8
70 Tinpenny Farm

WEDNESDAY 9
70 Tinpenny Farm

THURSDAY 10
70 Tinpenny Farm

SUNDAY 13
1 Abbotswood
35 Kempsford Manor
46 The Old Chequer

TUESDAY 15
70 Tinpenny Farm

WEDNESDAY 16
39 Lydney Park Spring Garden
70 Tinpenny Farm

THURSDAY 17
70 Tinpenny Farm

SUNDAY 20
41 Meadow Cottage
52 Pear Tree Cottage
58 Rodmarton Manor
65 Stanway Fountain & Water Garden
66 Stone House

MONDAY 21
36 Kiftsgate Court
47 The Old Rectory, Duntisbourne Rous

TUESDAY 22
70 Tinpenny Farm

WEDNESDAY 23
70 Tinpenny Farm

THURSDAY 24
70 Tinpenny Farm

SUNDAY 27
3 Baldwins
28 Home Farm
35 Kempsford Manor

TUESDAY 29
70 Tinpenny Farm

WEDNESDAY 30
70 Tinpenny Farm

May
THURSDAY 1
70 Tinpenny Farm

SUNDAY 4
14 Chedworth Gardens
17 Eastcombe, Bussage and Brownshill Gardens
22 Green Cottage
24 Highnam Court
30 Humphreys End House
56 Ramblers
63 South Lodge
79 Willow Lodge

MONDAY 5
- (17) Eastcombe, Bussage and Brownshill Gardens
- (79) Willow Lodge

TUESDAY 6
- (70) Tinpenny Farm

WEDNESDAY 7
- (70) Tinpenny Farm

THURSDAY 8
- (4) Barnsley House
- (70) Tinpenny Farm

SUNDAY 11
- (12) Cerney House Gardens
- (21) Grange Farm
- (22) Green Cottage
- (54) Pigeon House
- (73) Upton Wold

MONDAY 12
- (47) The Old Rectory, Duntisbourne Rous

TUESDAY 13
- (39) Lydney Park Spring Garden
- (70) Tinpenny Farm

WEDNESDAY 14
- (70) Tinpenny Farm

THURSDAY 15
- (70) Tinpenny Farm

SUNDAY 18
- (18) Eastleach House
- (22) Green Cottage
- (41) Meadow Cottage
- (52) Pear Tree Cottage
- (65) Stanway Fountain & Water Garden
- (67) Stowell Park
- (74) Vine Farm

TUESDAY 20
- (70) Tinpenny Farm

WEDNESDAY 21
- (70) Tinpenny Farm

THURSDAY 22
- (70) Tinpenny Farm

SATURDAY 24
- (29) Hookshouse Pottery

SUNDAY 25
- (22) Green Cottage
- (29) Hookshouse Pottery
- (34) Kemble Mill
- (35) Kempsford Manor
- (48) Ozleworth Park
- (77) Westonbirt School Gardens
- (79) Willow Lodge

MONDAY 26
- (3) Baldwins
- (29) Hookshouse Pottery
- (35) Kempsford Manor
- (38) Lower Farm House
- (77) Westonbirt School Gardens
- (79) Willow Lodge

TUESDAY 27
- (29) Hookshouse Pottery
- (70) Tinpenny Farm

WEDNESDAY 28
- (19) Eyford Gardens
- (29) Hookshouse Pottery
- (70) Tinpenny Farm

THURSDAY 29
- (8) Bourton House Garden
- (29) Hookshouse Pottery
- (70) Tinpenny Farm

FRIDAY 30
- (29) Hookshouse Pottery

SATURDAY 31
- (29) Hookshouse Pottery

June

SUNDAY 1
- (11) Campden House
- (22) Green Cottage
- (24) Highnam Court
- (27) Holcombe Glen Cottage
- (29) Hookshouse Pottery
- (54) Pigeon House
- (78) The White House

TUESDAY 3
- (70) Tinpenny Farm
- (72) Upper Merton House (prebook)

WEDNESDAY 4
- (20) France Lynch
- (22) Green Cottage
- (70) Tinpenny Farm
- (71) Trench Hill
- (72) Upper Merton House (prebook)

THURSDAY 5
- (70) Tinpenny Farm
- (72) Upper Merton House (prebook)

FRIDAY 6
- (26) Hodges Barn

SATURDAY 7
- (5) Berrys Place Farm
- (30) Humphreys End House
- (45) The Old Chapel

SUNDAY 8
- (5) Berrys Place Farm
- (7) Blockley Gardens
- (22) Green Cottage
- (25) Hillesley House
- (26) Hodges Barn
- (32) Hunts Court
- (37) Lammas Park
- (45) The Old Chapel
- (46) The Old Chequer
- (56) Ramblers
- (60) Sandywell Gardens
- (74) Vine Farm

MONDAY 9
- (26) Hodges Barn
- (45) The Old Chapel

TUESDAY 10
- (45) The Old Chapel
- (70) Tinpenny Farm

WEDNESDAY 11
- (16) Daylesford House
- (22) Green Cottage
- (45) The Old Chapel
- (57) Rockcliffe
- (70) Tinpenny Farm
- (71) Trench Hill

THURSDAY 12
- (4) Barnsley House
- (45) The Old Chapel
- (70) Tinpenny Farm

FRIDAY 13
- (45) The Old Chapel

SATURDAY 14
- (15) Cotswold Farm
- (45) The Old Chapel

SUNDAY 15
- (15) Cotswold Farm
- (22) Green Cottage
- (32) Hunts Court
- (45) The Old Chapel
- (52) Pear Tree Cottage
- (64) Stanton Gardens

MONDAY 16
- (3) Baldwins
- (45) The Old Chapel
- (47) The Old Rectory, Duntisbourne Rous

TUESDAY 17
- (21) Grange Farm
- (45) The Old Chapel
- (70) Tinpenny Farm

WEDNESDAY 18
- (22) Green Cottage
- (45) The Old Chapel
- (57) Rockcliffe
- (70) Tinpenny Farm
- (71) Trench Hill

THURSDAY 19
- (45) The Old Chapel
- (70) Tinpenny Farm

FRIDAY 20
- (45) The Old Chapel

SATURDAY 21
- (13) Chalford Gardens
- (45) The Old Chapel

SUNDAY 22
- (9) 25 Bowling Green Road
- (13) Chalford Gardens
- (22) Green Cottage
- (43) Misarden Park
- (45) The Old Chapel
- (51) Paulmead
- (55) Quenington Gardens
- (60) Sandywell Gardens
- (63) South Lodge
- (67) Stowell Park

75 Wells Cottage

MONDAY 23
9 25 Bowling Green Road

TUESDAY 24
70 Tinpenny Farm

WEDNESDAY 25
19 Eyford Gardens
57 Rockcliffe
62 Snowshill Manor
70 Tinpenny Farm
71 Trench Hill

THURSDAY 26
8 Bourton House Garden
70 Tinpenny Farm

SUNDAY 29
3 Baldwins
9 25 Bowling Green Road
33 Icomb Place
44 Moor Wood
59 Rookwoods

MONDAY 30
9 25 Bowling Green Road

July

TUESDAY 1
70 Tinpenny Farm
72 Upper Merton House (prebook)

WEDNESDAY 2
70 Tinpenny Farm
72 Upper Merton House (prebook)

THURSDAY 3
70 Tinpenny Farm
72 Upper Merton House (prebook)

FRIDAY 4
29 Hookshouse Pottery (Evening)

SATURDAY 5
5 Berrys Place Farm
29 Hookshouse Pottery

SUNDAY 6
5 Berrys Place Farm
9 25 Bowling Green Road
10 Brockworth Court
24 Highnam Court
61 Sezincote
69 Temple Guiting Manor

MONDAY 7
9 25 Bowling Green Road

TUESDAY 8
70 Tinpenny Farm

WEDNESDAY 9
70 Tinpenny Farm

THURSDAY 10
70 Tinpenny Farm

SUNDAY 13
9 25 Bowling Green Road
41 Meadow Cottage

MONDAY 14
9 25 Bowling Green Road

TUESDAY 15
70 Tinpenny Farm

WEDNESDAY 16
70 Tinpenny Farm

THURSDAY 17
70 Tinpenny Farm

SATURDAY 19
23 Hidcote Manor Garden

SUNDAY 20
9 25 Bowling Green Road
71 Trench Hill

MONDAY 21
9 25 Bowling Green Road
47 The Old Rectory, Duntisbourne Rous

TUESDAY 22
70 Tinpenny Farm

WEDNESDAY 23
70 Tinpenny Farm

THURSDAY 24
30 Humphreys End House (Evening)
70 Tinpenny Farm

SUNDAY 27
40 The Matara Garden

TUESDAY 29
70 Tinpenny Farm

WEDNESDAY 30
70 Tinpenny Farm

THURSDAY 31
8 Bourton House Garden
70 Tinpenny Farm

August

SUNDAY 3
24 Highnam Court

TUESDAY 5
70 Tinpenny Farm
72 Upper Merton House (prebook)

WEDNESDAY 6
70 Tinpenny Farm
72 Upper Merton House (prebook)

THURSDAY 7
53 Pemberley Lodge (Day & Evening)
70 Tinpenny Farm
72 Upper Merton House (prebook)

SUNDAY 10
7 Blockley Gardens
35 Kempsford Manor
79 Willow Lodge

MONDAY 11
36 Kiftsgate Court
79 Willow Lodge

TUESDAY 12
70 Tinpenny Farm

WEDNESDAY 13
70 Tinpenny Farm

THURSDAY 14
70 Tinpenny Farm

SUNDAY 17
35 Kempsford Manor

TUESDAY 19
70 Tinpenny Farm

WEDNESDAY 20
70 Tinpenny Farm

THURSDAY 21
4 Barnsley House
70 Tinpenny Farm

SUNDAY 24
35 Kempsford Manor
41 Meadow Cottage
71 Trench Hill

MONDAY 25
35 Kempsford Manor

TUESDAY 26
70 Tinpenny Farm

WEDNESDAY 27
70 Tinpenny Farm

THURSDAY 28
8 Bourton House Garden
53 Pemberley Lodge (Day & Evening)
70 Tinpenny Farm

SUNDAY 31
10 Brockworth Court
78 The White House

September

TUESDAY 2
70 Tinpenny Farm

WEDNESDAY 3
70 Tinpenny Farm

THURSDAY 4
70 Tinpenny Farm

FRIDAY 5
42 Mill Dene Garden (Evening)

SATURDAY 6
50 Park Farm

SUNDAY 7
24 Highnam Court
32 Hunts Court
71 Trench Hill

TUESDAY 9
70 Tinpenny Farm

WEDNESDAY 10
70 Tinpenny Farm

THURSDAY 11
70 Tinpenny Farm

SUNDAY 14
32 Hunts Court
35 Kempsford Manor
76 Westbury Court Garden

MONDAY 15
47 The Old Rectory, Duntisbourne Rous

TUESDAY 16
70 Tinpenny Farm

WEDNESDAY 17
70 Tinpenny Farm

THURSDAY 18
70 Tinpenny Farm

TUESDAY 23
70 Tinpenny Farm

WEDNESDAY 24
70 Tinpenny Farm

THURSDAY 25
8 Bourton House Garden
70 Tinpenny Farm

SUNDAY 28
40 The Matara Garden

TUESDAY 30
70 Tinpenny Farm

October
WEDNESDAY 1
70 Tinpenny Farm

THURSDAY 2
70 Tinpenny Farm

FRIDAY 3
42 Mill Dene Garden (Evening)

SUNDAY 5
68 Sudeley Castle Gardens & Exhibitions

TUESDAY 7
70 Tinpenny Farm

WEDNESDAY 8
70 Tinpenny Farm

THURSDAY 9
70 Tinpenny Farm

TUESDAY 14
70 Tinpenny Farm

WEDNESDAY 15
70 Tinpenny Farm

THURSDAY 16
70 Tinpenny Farm

TUESDAY 21
70 Tinpenny Farm

WEDNESDAY 22
70 Tinpenny Farm

THURSDAY 23
70 Tinpenny Farm

TUESDAY 28
70 Tinpenny Farm

WEDNESDAY 29
70 Tinpenny Farm

THURSDAY 30
8 Bourton House Garden

70 Tinpenny Farm

February 2009
SUNDAY 8
71 Trench Hill

SUNDAY 15
71 Trench Hill

Gardens open to the public
8 Bourton House Garden
12 Cerney House Gardens
18 Eastleach House
23 Hidcote Manor Garden
32 Hunts Court
35 Kempsford Manor
36 Kiftsgate Court
39 Lydney Park Spring Garden
40 The Matara Garden
42 Mill Dene Garden
43 Misarden Park
49 Painswick Rococo Garden
58 Rodmarton Manor
61 Sezincote
62 Snowshill Manor
65 Stanway Fountain & Water Garden
66 Stone House
68 Sudeley Castle Gardens & Exhibitions
76 Westbury Court Garden
77 Westonbirt School Gardens

By appointment only
2 Alderley Grange
31 Huntley Manor
72 Upper Merton House

Also open by appointment ☎
3 Baldwins
4 Barnsley House
9 25 Bowling Green Road
7 Colebrook House, Blockley Gardens
15 Cotswold Farm

21 Grange Farm
25 Hillesley House
28 Home Farm

29 Hookshouse Pottery
30 Humphreys End House
37 Lammas Park
41 Meadow Cottage
44 Moor Wood
46 The Old Chequer
47 The Old Rectory, Duntisbourne Rous
55 The Old Rectory, Quenington Gardens
50 Park Farm
52 Pear Tree Cottage
53 Pemberley Lodge
54 Pigeon House
60 Barn House Sandywell Gardens
60 Garden Cottage, Sandywell Gardens
70 Tinpenny Farm
71 Trench Hill
73 Upton Wold
78 The White House
79 Willow Lodge

The Gardens

1 ABBOTSWOOD
Stow-on-the-Wold GL54 1EN. Mr R Scully. *1m W of Stow-on-the-Wold. On B4068 nr Lower Swell or B4077 nr Upper Swell.* Home-made teas. **Adm £4, chd free.** Sun 13 Apr (1.30-6). Massed plantings of spring bulbs, heathers, flowering shrubs and rhododendrons in dramatic, landscaped hillside stream gardens; fine herbaceous planting in elegant formal gardens with lily pond, terraced lawn and fountain created by Sir Edwin Lutyens.
& ☕

2 ALDERLEY GRANGE
Alderley GL12 7QT. Mr Guy & the Hon Mrs Acloque, 01453 842161. *2m S of Wotton-under-Edge. Turn NW off A46 Bath to Stroud rd, at Dunkirk.* **Adm £3, chd free.** Visitors welcome by appt **June only.**
Walled garden with fine trees, roses; herb gardens and aromatic plants.
& ✄ ☎

ASTHALL MANOR
See Oxfordshire.

3 BALDWINS
Birches Lane, nr Newent GL18 1DN. Mrs Sue Clive, 01531 821640/020 7834 8233. *1½ m N of Newent. Off B4215, half-way between Newent & Dymock, signed Botloes Green & Pool Hill. Baldwins, formerly The Bungalow, is first on L on edge of Three Choirs Vineyard.* Home-made teas other days.

Fine herbaceous planting in elegant formal gardens . . .

Tea only 24 Mar. **Adm £2.50, chd free (share to Downs Syndrome Assoc). Mon 24 Mar; Sun 27 Apr; Mon 26 May; Mon 16, Sun 29 June (1.30-5). Visitors also welcome by appt May & June.**
With the Malvern Hills and Three Choirs Vineyard as a backdrop this 1/2 -acre garden takes an individual and naturalistic approach. Herbaceous, cottage and wild flowers, hard and soft fruits, unusual custom-built water and architectural features and terraced vegetable beds are brought together with artistic intent.

4 BARNSLEY HOUSE
nr Cirencester GL7 5EE. Mr Tim Haigh & Mr Rupert Pendered, 01285 740000, reception@barnsleyhouse.com. *4m NE of Cirencester. On B4425.* Light refreshments & teas available at The Village Pub. **Adm £5, chd £2.50. Thurs 8 May; 12 June; 21 Aug (11-5). Visitors also welcome by appt.**
Mature family garden, created by the late Rosemary Verey, with interesting collection of shrubs and trees; ground cover; herbaceous borders; pond garden; laburnum walk; knot and herb gardens; potager; C18 summerhouses. C17 house (not open). Garden open to the public on only five days during the year.

5 BERRYS PLACE FARM
Churcham GL2 8AS. Anne Thomas. *6m W of Gloucester. A40 towards Ross. Turning R into Bulley Lane at Birdwood.* Home-made & cream teas. **Adm £3, chd free (share to The Forge). Sat 7, Sun 8 June; Sat 5, Sun 6 July (11-6).**
Country garden, approx 1 acre, surrounded by farmland and old orcharding. Lawns and mixed herbaceous borders with some old roses. Formal kitchen garden and new rose arbour leading to lake and summerhouse with a variety of water lilies and carp. All shared with peacocks and ducks.

6 BEVERSTON CASTLE
nr Tetbury GL8 8TU. Mrs A L Rook. *2m W of Tetbury. On A4135 rd to Dursley between Tetbury & Calcot Xrds.* Home-made teas. **Adm £3.50, chd free under 14 free, concessions £2.50 (OAP). Sun 23, Mon 24 Mar (2.30-5).**

Overlooked by romantic C12-C17 castle ruin (not open), overflowingly planted paved terrace leads from C18 house (not open) across moat to sloping lawn with spring bulbs in abundance, and full herbaceous and shrub borders. Large walled kitchen garden and greenhouses, orchids. Wheelchair access dependent on weather.

Popular Cotswold hillside village with great variety of high quality gardens . . .

7 BLOCKLEY GARDENS
GL56 9DB. *3m NW of Moreton-in-Marsh. Take A44 either from Moreton or Broadway and follow signs to Blockley.* Home-made teas at Box Cottage 8 June; The Manor House 10 August. **Combined adm £6, 8 June, £5, 10 Aug, chd free. Suns 8 June; 10 Aug (2-6).**
Popular Cotswold hillside village with great variety of high quality gardens; some walking necessary and some gardens not safe for small children. Bus provided 8 June and 10 Aug.

BOX COTTAGE
Patricia Milligan-Baldwin. Not open Sun 10 Aug.
Terraced garden with a range of garden rooms, bordering Blockley Brook. Teas served in garden in June opening.

NEW COLEBROOK HOUSE
Lower Street. , 0771 2528539, claire.baron1@btinternet.com. Not open Sun 10 Aug. Visitors also welcome by appt.
Three acres of garden where two streams converge. On different levels and divided into discrete areas with some formal structure (box, yew etc) with selection of unusual trees, lawns, herbaceous borders and a wild area. Unfenced water, steps and slopes.

3 THE DELL
Ms E Powell. Not open Sun 10 Aug.
Very small garden situated on the side of Blockley Brook. Restricted entry.

4 THE DELL
Viola & Bernard Stubbs. Not open Sun 10 Aug.
Fairly small garden, sloping down to Blockley Brook.

GRANGE COTTAGE
Mill Lane. Alison & Guy Heitmann, www.garden-designer.biz
Mature terraced gardens, with interest from May to Oct. Mixture of traditional and contemporary, from lush perennial plantings to cool green spaces.

HOLLYROSE HOUSE
3 The Clementines. Mr & Mrs Peter Saunders. Not open Sun 10 Aug.
Small terraced garden.

THE MANOR HOUSE
George & Zoe Thompson. *Next to church*
Top garden with lawn, roses, lavender and pergola. Lower garden beneath listed wall terraced with borders, box hedging and lawn leading to brook. Separate vegetable and herb garden with espaliered and cordoned fruits.

MILL DENE GARDEN
School Lane. Mr & Mrs B S Dare, info@milldenegarden.co.uk. *From A44 follow brown signs from Bourton on the Hill* (See separate entry). We close at 5pm. Featured in 'The English Garden' Mar 2007; 'Le Monde' July 2007. Partial wheelchair access. Gravel paths, slopes. Children must be accompanied at all times - dangerous water.

THE OLD CHEQUER
Mr & Mrs Linley. Not open Sun 10 Aug.
(See separate entry).

PEAR TREES
Mrs J Beckwith
Entrance at rear. Long narrow garden with dry shade-tolerant planting leading to open sunny lawn surrounded by mixed beds of roses, clematis and herbaceous plants.

PORCH HOUSE
Mr & Mrs C Johnson. Not open Sun 10 Aug.
Centrally located village garden with countryside views. Pear tree walk, knot garden and mixed borders.

NEW SHEAFHOUSE COTTAGE
Mrs Jennifer Lidsey. Not open Sun 8 June.
Small cottage garden. Pond and rural views at rear. Gravelled frontage.

4 THE CLEMENTINES
Kathy Illingworth. Not open Sun 10 Aug.
Hillside garden on several levels with views over Cotswold countryside. Features a range of herbaceous perennials and shrubs, pond and stream, deck, lawned area and meadow with wild flowers.

8 ◆ BOURTON HOUSE GARDEN
Bourton-on-the-Hill GL56 9AE. Mr & Mrs R Paice, 01386 700754, www.bourtonhouse.com. *2m W of Moreton-in-Marsh.* On A44. **Adm £5.50, chd free, concessions £5. Weds to Fris 28 May to 31 Aug; Thurs & Fris, Sept to end Oct; Bank Hols Sun, Mon end May & end Aug (10-5).** For NGS: Thurs 29 May; 26 June; 31 Aug; 28 Aug (10-7); Thurs 25 Sept; 30 Oct (10-5).
Surrounding a delightful C18 Cotswold manor house (not open) and C16 tithe barn, this exciting 3-acre garden positively fizzes with ideas. Featuring flamboyant borders, imaginative topiary, profusions of herbaceous borders and exotic plants and, not least, a myriad of magically planted pots; a plantsman's paradise. Featured on BBC TV 'Gardeners World' 2007. Some gravel paths; 70% wheelchair access.

9 25 BOWLING GREEN ROAD
Cirencester GL7 2HD. Fr John & Susan Beck, 01285 653778, sjb@beck-hems.org.uk. *On NW edge of Cirencester.* Take A435 to Spitalgate/Whiteway T-lights, turn into The Whiteway, then 1st L into Bowling Green Rd to No 25 on R of rd bend. Please respect neighbours' driveways, no pavement parking. **Adm £2.50, chd free.** Suns 22, 29, Mons 23, 30 June; Suns, Mons 6, 7, 13, 14, 20, 21 July. Suns (2-5); Mons (11-4). **Visitors also welcome by appt mid June to end July, groups welcome.**
Mount an expedition to meander amidst pergolas, pots, pools and paths and muse on myriads (400+) of delightful, daring and different daylilies, (incl Rosy Rhinos and Blushing Jellyfish), vying for space with countless curvaceous clematis, romantic roses, graceful grasses, friendly frogs, hopeful hostas, priceless perennials and sylph-like lawns. Featured in 'The English Garden', July 2007; BBC2 'Gardeners' World', 2007.

Romantic walled garden filled with old-fashioned roses . . .

10 BROCKWORTH COURT
Brockworth GL3 4QU. Mr & Mrs Tim Wiltshire. *6m E of Gloucester; 6m W of Cheltenham.* From A46 Stroud/Cheltenham off A417 turn into Mill Lane. At T-junction turn R, L, R. Garden next to St George's Church - Court Rd. Home-made teas. **Adm £3.50, chd free.** Suns 6 July; 31 Aug (2-5).
Small manor house (not open) which once belonged to Llanthony Priory and the Guise family. Restored C13 tithe barn (open). Garden approx 1½ acres, has recently undergone much restoration work. Dew pond with Monet bridge, carp and water lilies. Many unusual plants and mostly of farmhouse style. Interesting former monastic kitchen garden, organic. Craft demonstration. Craft sales. Vintage tractors. Featured in 'Gloucester Citizen', July 2007. Some gravel paths.

11 CAMPDEN HOUSE
Chipping Campden GL55 6UP. The Hon Philip & Mrs Smith. *½ m SW of Chipping Campden.* Entrance on Chipping Campden to Weston Subedge rd, approx ¼ m SW of Campden, 1¼ m drive. Home-made teas. **Adm £3.50, chd free.** Sun 1 June (2-6).
2 acres featuring mixed borders of plant and colour interest around house and C17 tithe barn (neither open). Set in fine parkland in hidden valley with lakes and ponds. Woodland walk, vegetable garden. Gravel paths.

12 ◆ CERNEY HOUSE GARDENS
North Cerney GL7 7BX. Sir Michael & Lady Angus, 01285 831300, barbara@cerneygardens.com. *4m NW of Cirencester.* On A435 Cheltenham rd. Turn L opp Bathurst Arms, past church up hill, pillared gates on R. **Adm £4, chd £1. Tues, Weds, Fris, Suns, Easter to end July (10-5).** For NGS: Sun 11 May (12-5).
Romantic walled garden filled with old-fashioned roses and herbaceous borders. Working kitchen garden, scented garden, well-labelled herb garden, Who's Who beds and genera borders. Spring bulbs in abundance all around the wooded grounds. Bothy pottery. Gravel paths and some inclines.

13 CHALFORD GARDENS
Chalford Vale GL6 8PN. *4m E of Stroud; 9m from Cirencester.* On A419 to Cirencester. Gardens are high above Chalford Vale & reached on foot by steep climb from car park on main rd or from High St. **Combined adm £4, chd free.** Sat 21, Sun 22 June (12-5).
Hillside village with many quaint lanes, S-facing. Studio exhibition at Old Chapel, featuring garden, plant and landscape studies.

MARLE HILL HOUSE
Mike & Leslie Doyle-Davidson
1-acre Victorian woodland garden, containing a number of interlinked secret, formal and natural areas on steep terraced hillside with ponds, folly, nut tunnel, moongate and ship treehouse.

THE OLD CHAPEL
Marle Hill. F J & F Owen
(See separate entry).

THANET HOUSE
High Street. Jennifer & Roger Tann. *On Chalford Vale High St nr PO*
Streamside multi-level garden with Italian flavour; a ruin, pond, packhorse bridge and (former) textile industry connections.

Family day out. Wildlife trail, quiz, pond dipping . . .

CHASTLETON GARDENS
See Oxfordshire.

⑭ CHEDWORTH GARDENS
GL54 4AN. 7m NE of Cirencester. Off Fosseway, A429 between Stow-on-the-Wold (12m) & Cirencester. Car parking in field above York House only (signposted). **Combined adm £5, chd free (share to St Andrew's Church, Chedworth). Sun 4 May (11-6).**
Varied collection of two country house and three cottage gardens, nestling in the lower Chedworth Valley with tributary of R Coln running below. Stunning views. Featuring unusual water features, pretty terraces, black and white border, country remedy herb bed, potager, wild flower orchards and hints from a Chelsea winning garden. Teas available (& toilet facilities) Cotswold Farm Fayre, Fields Rd, Chedworth, (Chedworth Farm Shop).
☕

COBBLERS COTTAGE
Lower Chedworth. C Powell & A Shah
Classic Cotswold cottage garden with terraces and lovely valley views. Spring bulbs, herbaceous borders using traditional cottage planting, interesting herb bed, planted with varieties of old country remedies. Backdrop of original cobbler's workshop.
✗

DENFURLONG HOUSE
Lower Chedworth. Christopher & Juliet Stainforth
With far reaching views over the valley this series of walled gardens has been created around C16 farmhouse (not open), and includes many roses. Mature and varied terraces and borders.
✗

KEENS COTTAGE
Lower Chedworth. Sue & Steve Bradbury, www.bradburydesigns.co.uk
Tranquil cottage garden, restored by its garden designer owner/Chelsea medal winner. Featuring topiary, black and white border and archway walk, dividing traditional garden from orchard with spring flowering bulbs. Working pump and fernery.
✗ ✿

NEW THE OXBYRE
Lower Chedworth. Mike & Caroline Burgess
Cottage garden with views across valley. Wisteria pergola, water features incl waterfall from pumphouse. Rose and herbaceous borders. Herb and fruit gardens. Wild area with beech hedge and early bulb maze. Garden art.
✗

NEW YORK HOUSE
Lower Chedworth. Mrs C Singer & Dr J McCarron
Spring garden surrounding pretty Georgian house (not open) with wonderful valley views. Stone walls and hedges divide into lawned areas, gravel garden, wild flower gardens, terrace, woodland area and orchard. Potager with glasshouse.
✗

CONDERTON MANOR
See Worcestershire.

⑮ COTSWOLD FARM
nr Duntisbourne Abbots, Cirencester GL7 7JS. **Mrs Mark Birchall, 01285 821857.** *5m NW of Cirencester. Off the old A417. From Cirencester turn L signed Duntisbourne Abbots Services, then immed R & R again into underpass. Private drive straight ahead. From Gloucester turn L signed Duntisbourne Abbots Services. Pass services; private drive on L.* Home-made teas. **Adm £4, chd free (share to A Rocha). Sat 14, Sun 15 June (11-5). Visitors also welcome by appt.**
Cotswold garden in lovely position overlooking quiet valley on different levels with terrace designed by Norman Jewson in 1938; shrubs and trees, mixed borders, snowdrops, alpine border, shrub roses and newly replanted 'bog garden'. Croquet and toys for children on lawn. Walled

kitchen garden. Family day out. Wildlife trail, quiz, pond dipping, bring picnic. Orchids, 100s wild flower species, Roman snails etc. Glos Wildlife Trust and other groups involved.
✿ ☕ ☎ ☎

⑯ DAYLESFORD HOUSE
Daylesford GL56 0YG. Sir Anthony & Lady Bamford. *5m W of Chipping Norton. Off A436. Between Stow-on-the-Wold & Chipping Norton.* Light refreshments & teas at Daylesford Farm Shop. **Adm £4, chd free. Wed 11 June (2-5).**
Magnificent C18 landscape grounds created 1790 for Warren Hastings, greatly restored and enhanced by present owners. Lakeside and woodland walks within natural wild flower meadows. Large walled garden planted formally, centred around orchid, peach and working glasshouses. Trellised rose garden. Collection of citrus within period orangery. Secret Garden with pavilion and formal pools. Very large garden with substantial distances to be walked. Uneven gravel paths.
♿ ✗ ☕

⑰ EASTCOMBE, BUSSAGE AND BROWNSHILL GARDENS
GL6 8DD. 3m E of Stroud. 2m N of A419 Stroud to Cirencester rd on turning signed to Bisley & Eastcombe. Home-made teas at Eastcombe Village Hall. **Combined adm £4, chd free (share to Cotswold Care Hospice, Cobalt Unit Appeal & Victim Support Glos). Sun 4, Mon 5 May (2-6).**
A group of gardens, large and small, set in a picturesque hilltop location. Some approachable only by foot. (Exhibitions may be on view in village hall). Please park considerately in villages.
☕

NEW 22 BRACELANDS
Eastcombe. Mrs O M Turner
Large ex-council house garden with borders, pond and large vegetable garden. Access to end of garden and return by same route.
♿ ✿

NEW BYWAYS
6 Velhurst Drive, Brownshill. Joy Elias
Level garden with lawn, water feature, small courtyard. Raised beds, mature trees and shrubs. Gravel drive.

NEW THE GLEN
Brownshill. Caren Cook.
Through lane by allotments, 2nd L (not Beech Lane)
Spiritual and tranquil garden; a place to retreat and for family interaction.
 ♿ ✄

HAMPTON VIEW
The Ridge, Bussage. Geraldine & Mike Carter
Extensively planted garden offers opportunities to relax. Archway from path invites you up steps to raised lawn with fresh water pond and private sitting area. Path leads through fruit tree pergola to summerhouse and greenhouse.

NEW 1 HIDCOTE CLOSE
Eastcombe. Mr & Mrs J Southall
An evolving small back garden to encompass recent re-design, with circular lawn, raised beds and patio. Structural planting with emphasis on leaf shape and textures, perennials, with seasonal additions.
✄

NEW 12 HIDCOTE CLOSE
Eastcombe. Mr & Mrs K Walker
Estate garden with pond feature, deck areas, greenhouse, pergola and arbour, raised vegetable beds and well-stocked with shrubs.
♿

NEW HIGHLANDS
Dr Crouch's Road, Eastcombe. Helen Wallis
Small cottage-style, plantlover's garden.
✄

MOUNT PLEASANT COTTAGE
Wells Road, Eastcombe. Mr & Mrs R Peyton
$1/2$ acre garden on two levels. Upper garden formal with herbaceous borders and enclosed vegetable garden. Lower garden has sloping lawns with pond edging onto woodland.

NEW SILVERTREES
Manor Farm Lane, Eastcombe. Mr & Mrs Adcock
Garden consists mainly of mixed borders. Hexagonal pond, two lawned areas with a selection of trees and a dry shingle area with a mixture of acers, grasses and rockery plants.
♿

1 THE LAURELS
The Street, Eastcombe. Andrew & Ruth Fraser
Terraced garden on several levels joined by flights of steps with herbaceous borders, shrubs, small pond and terraced vegetable garden, largely reconstructed by present owners.
✄

VATCH RISE
Eastcombe. Peggy Abbott
Well-stocked garden with wide variety of bulbs, colour co-ordinated herbaceous borders and small vegetable garden. Outstanding views of Toadsmoor Valley.
♿ ☂

WOODLANDS HOUSE
Cowswell Lane, Bussage. Amy Cleary
Small sloping garden with steps leading down to sunken area. Also small Japanese garden and deck with views over Toadsmoor Valley. Vegetable and soft fruit section.
✄

WOODVIEW
Wells Road, Eastcombe. Julian & Eileen Horn-Smith
Recently terraced and replanted with pretty views over the Toadsmoor Valley. Covering a hillside, this garden is unsuitable for those with walking difficulties.

Walled and rill gardens, with modern herbaceous borders . . .

18 ♦ EASTLEACH HOUSE
Eastleach Martin GL7 3NW. Mrs David Richards,
www.eastleachhouse.com. *5m NE of Fairford. From Fairford on A417, signed to Eastleach on L. 4m to village, turn R down hill towards bridge. Entrance to garden by church gates. No access for coaches - drop visitors at gate and park outside village, or off A361 bet Burford & Lechlade.* Teas in village hall. **Adm £5, chd under 16 free. 13, 20, 27 June; 11, 25, July (2-5) Groups by arrangement.** For NGS: **Sun 18 May (2-5).**
Large traditional all-yr-round garden. Wooded hilltop position with long views S and W. New parkland, lime avenue and arboretum. Wild flower walk, wildlife pond, lawns, walled and rill gardens, with modern herbaceous borders, yew and box hedges, iris and paeony borders, lily ponds, formal herb, topiary and knot gardens. Rambling roses into trees. Featured in 'Country Homes & Interiors', May 2007; British Country Gardens Calendar 2007 by Clive Nichols; 'English Garden' magazine, Aug 2007. Gravel paths and some steep slopes.
♿ ✄ ☂ ☕

19 EYFORD GARDENS
Upper Slaughter GL54 2JN. *3m W of Stow on the Wold. On the B4068 (formerly A436), between Lower Swell & Naunton.* Home-made teas 28 May at Eyford House; 25 June Teas at Rockcliffe garden. **Combined adm £5, chd £1. Wed 28 May (11.30-4); Wed 25 June (2-5).**
2 gardens near to each other, just outside village.
☕

EYFORD HOUSE
Mrs C A Heber Percy. *Stone Lodge on R, with white iron gates & cattle grid*
$1^1/2$ -acre sloping N garden, ornamental shrubs and trees. Laid out originally by Graham Stuart Thomas, 1976. West garden and terrace, red border, walled kitchen garden, two lakes with pleasant walks and views (boots needed). Holy well.

EYFORD KNOLL
Mrs S Prest. *At Xrds turn R for Cotswold Farm Park, entrance 400yds on R*
Cottage garden, with C18 fountain from Faringdon House, gardens redesigned 9yrs ago by Lady Aird.

Outstanding herbaceous borders and unusual plant species . . .

20 FRANCE LYNCH
nr Stroud GL6 8LP. *5m E of Stroud. Turn off A419 at Chalford signed Chalford Hill. Follow signs to France Lynch..* Home-made teas at Orchard Cottage. **Combined adm £4.50, chd free. Wed 4 June (2-6).**
Hillside village of old cottages and pretty lanes, with views across valley.

THE ANCHORAGE
Brantwood Road. Simon & Carol Smith
Small landscaped garden with gravel paths, pond and mixed borders of herbaceous perennials.

CREEDS COTTAGE
Sturmyes Road. Mrs Janet Gaskell
Garden mainly on one level laid out to lawn, herbaceous plants and shrubs with two specimen trees. Interesting hard landscaping with dry stone walls.

DUNDRY LODGE
Lynch Road. David & Stella Martin
Approx 1/2 -acre walled garden evolved over past 35yrs, planned for structure and form with colour. Terraced vegetable garden and 2 greenhouses aimed to produce yr-round crops. Featured on BBC TV 'Open Gardens' 2007.

LILAC COTTAGE
Sturmyes Road. Mr & Mrs Malcolm Heath
Small cottage garden. Roses, clematis, phlox, day lilies. Tiny vegetable patch.

LITTLE OAKS
Coppice Hill. Mr & Mrs David Calvert
E-facing sloping garden with mixed curved borders to complement the undulating countryside. Some steep steps.

ORCHARD COTTAGE
Lynch Road. Charles & Pat Willey

Large cottage garden with mixed flower borders incl old roses. Lawns, woodland, small meadow and vegetable and fruit areas. Gravel paths & slopes.

NEW WOODLANDS HOUSE
GL6 8LJ. Pete Woodley & Hilary Burgess
Large split-level garden with mixed, herbaceous borders, herb garden and small ponds. Lower section has spring-fed large pond feeding smaller ponds down hill. Features include willow walk, fernery, standing stones, specimen trees and wild areas. Gently sloping paths; lower section grass only.

FROGS NEST
See Worcestershire.

GADFIELD ELM HOUSE
See Worcestershire.

21 GRANGE FARM
Evenlode, nr Moreton-in-Marsh GL56 0NT. Lady Aird, 01608 650607, meaird@aol.com. *3m N of Stow-on-the-Wold. E of A429 Fosseway & 1 1/2 m from Broadwell.* Light refreshments & home-made teas. **Adm £3, chd free. Sun 11 May; Tue 17 June (10.30-5). Visitors also welcome by appt May, June, July only. Coaches permitted.**
From the rose covered house, past the lawn and herbaceous borders to the water garden and ancient apple trees spreading over spring bulbs in May this garden is full of yr-round interest. Vegetable garden, sunken garden and yew circle and shady tranquil places to sit.

22 GREEN COTTAGE
Lydney GL15 6BS. Mr & Mrs F Baber. *1/4 m SW of Lydney. Approaching Lydney from Gloucester, keep to A48 through Lydney. Leaving Lydney turn R into narrow lane at de-limit sign. Garden 1st R. Shady parking.* Home-made teas (Suns May & June only). **Adm £2.50, accompanied chd free. Suns 2, 9, 16 Mar (1-4); Suns, 4, 11, 18, 25 May; Suns, 1, 8, 15, 22 June; Weds, 4, 11, 18 June (2-5).**
1 1/2 -acre country garden planted for seasonal interest and wildlife. Mature trees, stream, duckpond and bog garden. Developing woodland area

planted with ferns, hellebores, daphnes and other shade lovers. Cottage garden. Wide range of herbaceous peonies, incl National Collection of rare Victorian and Edwardian lactiflora cultivars (best in June), early peonies May. NOT suitable for wheelchairs at March openings due to location of hellebores.

HELLENS
See Herefordshire.

23 ◆ HIDCOTE MANOR GARDEN
Hidcote Bartrim, Chipping Campden, nr Mickleton GL55 6LR. The National Trust, 01386 438333, www.nationaltrust.org.uk. *4m NE of Chipping Campden. Off B4081, close to the village of Mickleton.* **Adm £8.50, chd £4.25.** Phone or see website for other opening times. **For NGS: Sat 19 July (10-5).**
One of England's great gardens, 10 1/2 -acre 'Arts and Crafts' masterpiece created by Major Lawrence Johnston. Series of outdoor rooms, each with a different character and separated by walls and hedges of many different species. Many rare trees and shrubs, outstanding herbaceous borders and unusual plant species from all over the world. Wheelchair access to one third of garden.

HIGH GLANAU MANOR
See Glamorgan.

24 HIGHNAM COURT
Highnam GL2 8DP. Roger Head. *2m W of Gloucester. Leave Gloucester on A40 towards Ross on Wye. DO NOT take Newent turning, but proceed to next big Highnam roundabout. Take R exit for Highnam Court entrance directly off roundabout.* Light refreshments & home-made teas. **Adm £4, chd free (share to Highnam Church). Suns 6 Apr; 4 May; 1 June; 6 July; 3 Aug; 7 Sept (11-5).**
40 acres of Victorian landscaped gardens surrounding magnificent Grade I house (not open), set out by the artist Thomas Gambier Parry. Lakes, shrubberies and listed Pulhamite water gardens with grottos and fernery. Exciting ornamental lakes, and woodland areas. New extensive 1-acre rose garden and many new features incl wood carvings. Gravel paths and steps. No disabled toilets.

25 HILLESLEY HOUSE
Hillesley, nr Wotton-under-Edge GL12 7RD. Fiona & Jeremy Walsh, 01454 323852/07971 854260 Stewart (Head Gardener), haggis@info.com. *3m from Wotton-under-Edge. On rd to Hawkesbury Upton & A46 from Wotton-under-Edge.* Light refreshments & teas. **Adm £3, chd free. Sun 8 June (2-6). Visitors also welcome by appt. Please call or email.**
Extensive revamping and planting of 4 acres of walled, secret and open garden, plus vegetable garden and arboretum. Unusual topiary. Rose beds and borders. Plenty of exciting ideas are being continued this yr and new shrub borders created for 2008. Featured in 'Daily Telegraph' weekend section by Mary Keen, 2007.

✿ ☕ ☎

26 HODGES BARN
Shipton Moyne GL8 8PR. Mrs C N Hornby. *3m S of Tetbury. On Malmesbury side of village.* **Adm £5, chd free. Fri 6, Sun 8, Mon 9 June (2-6).**
Very unusual C15 dovecote converted into family home (not open). Cotswold stone walls act as host to climbing and rambling roses, clematis, vines, hydrangeas, and together with yew, rose and tapestry hedges create formality around house. Mixed shrub and herbaceous borders, shrub roses; water garden; woodland garden planted with cherries, magnolias and spring bulbs. Also open for NGS, adjoining garden of Hodges Farmhouse by kind permission of Mrs Clive Lamb.

&

27 HOLCOMBE GLEN COTTAGE
Minchinhampton GL6 9AJ. Christine & Terry Sharpe. *1m E of Nailsworth. From Nailsworth take Avening Rd B4014. Turn L at Weighbridge Inn. Turn L 100yds into Holcombe Glen. 1st house on L. From Minchinhampton 1¼ m via Well Hill or New Rd.* Light refreshments & teas. **Adm £3, chd free (share to Cotswold Care Hospice). Sun 1 June (11-5).**
3 acres incl springs and ponds. Small waterfalls feed river and stream, giving bog and meadow areas full of wildlife and wild flowers. Above these, terraced walled garden for vegetables and herbaceous plants.

✿ ☕

Woodland walk with giant redwoods; exotic waterfowl and peacocks roam the grounds . . .

28 HOME FARM
Huntley GL19 3HQ. Mrs T Freeman, 01452 830209. *4m S of Newent. On B4216 ½ m off A40 in Huntley travelling towards Newent.* **Adm £2.50, chd free. Suns 27 Jan; 10 Feb; 16 Mar; 6, 27 Apr (2-5). Visitors also welcome by appt, coaches only by appoint.**
Set in elevated position with exceptional views. 1m walk through woods and fields to show carpets of spring flowers. Enclosed garden with fern border, sundial and heather bed. White and mixed shrub borders. Stout footwear advisable in winter.

☎

29 HOOKSHOUSE POTTERY
Hookshouse Lane, Tetbury GL8 8TZ. Lise & Christopher White, 01666 880297, hookshouse@hotmail.co.uk. *2½ m WSW of Tetbury. From Tetbury take A4135 towards Dursley, then take 2nd L signed Leighterton. Hookshouse pottery is 1½ m on R.* Home-made & cream teas. **Adm £2.50, chd free. Daily Sat 24 May to Sun 1 June; Sat 5 July (11-6). Evening Opening Fri 4 July, wine & garden games £3.50, child 50p. Visitors also welcome by appt, coaches permitted, groups of 10+.**
Interesting layout with alternation of open perspectives and intimate corners. Borders, shrubs, woodland glade, water garden with flowform cascades, vegetable garden with raised beds, orchard. Handthrown pots made on premises, sculptural pieces, garden games. Run on organic principles. Water treatment ponds for house waste. Pottery showroom incl stoneware garden pots (all dates). Art & craft exhibition incl garden sculptures 24 May to 1 June only. BBC2 'Open Gardens' Sept 2007, & local press. Two unfenced ponds, some gravel.

& ✿ ☕ ☎

30 HUMPHREYS END HOUSE
Randwick, nr Stroud GL6 6EW. Pat & Jim Hutton, 01453 765401, pathutton1@gps-footpaths.co.uk. *2m NW of Stroud. M5 J13, follow signs to Cashes Green & Randwick. At Townsend, turn R. Parking, look for signs.* Cream teas. **Adm £2.50, chd free. Sun 4 May; Sat 7 June (2-6). Evening Opening £3.50, wine, Thur 24 July (6-9). Visitors also welcome by appt.**
Different areas of contrasting mood and interesting planting surrounding listed C16 farmhouse (not open). A wildlife friendly garden. New pond area, old roses, grasses and organic vegetables.

✗ ✿ ☕ ☎

31 HUNTLEY MANOR
Huntley GL19 3HQ. Prof Tim Congdon & Mrs Dorianne Congdon. *4m S of Newent. Newent Lane. On B4216 ½ m off A40 in Huntley travelling towards Newent.* **Adm £5, chd free. Visitors welcome by appt apply in writing to Mrs D Congdon, Huntley Manor, Huntley, Glos GL19 3HQ.**
Park-like grounds surround the gothic 'French Ch,teau' style house (open by arrangement) built in 1862 by S S Teulon. Informal beds of mature shrubbery and rare specimen trees (tulip tree reputed to be tallest in the country after Kew), intersperse with sweeping lawns down to lake. Woodland walk with giant redwoods; exotic waterfowl and peacocks roam the grounds. Excellent for club outings, picnics and AGMs. Informal garden concerts available by harpist Venetia Congdon.

& ✗ ☎

32 ◆ **HUNTS COURT**
**North Nibley GL11 6DZ. Mr & Mrs T
K Marshall, 01453 547440.** *2m NW of
Wotton-under-Edge. From Wotton
B4060 Dursley rd turn R in North
Nibley at Black Horse; fork L after* $1/4$ *m.*
Home-made teas NGS. **Adm £3.50,
chd free. Tues to Sats all yr (9-12.30
& 1.45-5) except Good Fri & Aug.**
For NGS: Suns, 8, 15, June; 7, 14
Sept (2-6).
A plant lover's garden with unusual
shrubs, 450 varieties old roses, large
collection of penstemons and hardy
geraniums in peaceful $2^1/2$ -acre
garden set against tree-clad hills and
Tyndale monument. Recently planted
mini-arboretum. House (not open)
possible birthplace of William Tyndale.
Picnic area.
& ✕ ✿ ☕

33 **ICOMB PLACE**
**Icomb, nr Stow-on-the-Wold
GL54 1JD. T L F Royle.** *2m S of
Stow. After 2m on A424 Burford Rd
turn L to Icomb village.* Cream teas.
**Adm £5, chd £2 (share to Deus
Laudamus Trust). Sun 29 June (2-6).**
Gardens were laid down in first
decade of C20 and consist of ponds,
water garden and arboretum with a
potager added by the present owners.
One of the first gardens opened under
the NGS. Unfenced water & steep
paths.
& ✕ ☕

ILMINGTON MANOR
**See Warwickshire & part of West
Midlands.**

34 **KEMBLE MILL**
**nr Somerford Keynes, Cirencester
GL7 6ED. Vittoria & Simon Thornley,
www.kemblemill.com.** *5m S of
Cirencester. From A419 (Cotswold
Water Park exit), go W towards Ashton
Keynes. Follow spine rd for 2m. Go
over Xrds & after 1.5m turn R on lane
signposted Old Mill Farm. 1st house on
R.* Cream teas & wine. **Adm £3, chd
free. Sun 25 May (2-5).**
C16 watermill (house not open) on
banks of infant Thames. Formal, walled
garden with rose arches and pond.
Kitchen and fruit garden; plantation of
mixed trees; cottage garden; island
garden bordered by mill race with
apple orchard and woodland walk. 8
acre field with donkeys and chickens.
Playground. Unfenced water; rabbit
holes in field.
✕ ✿ ☕

35 ◆ **KEMPSFORD MANOR**
**High Street, Kempsford GL7 4EQ.
Mrs Z I Williamson, 01285 810131,
www.kempsfordmanor.co.uk.** *3m S
of Fairford. Take A419 from Cirencester
or Swindon. Kempsford is signed 10m
(approx) from each. The Manor is in
the centre of village.* **Adm £3, chd
free. By appt for groups, Feb-Oct:
garden & house open £6, lunch £7,
tea & talk £4.** For NGS: Suns 24 Feb;
2, 9, 16 Mar; 13, 27 Apr; Sun 25,
Mon 26 May; Suns 10, 17, 24, Mon
25 Aug; Sun 14 Sept (2-5).
Early spring garden with variety of
bulbs incl snowdrop walk along old
canal. Peaceful, expansive summer
garden for relaxation, adjacent to
cricket field, croquet and outdoor
games for children. Occasional plant
sales; frequently classical or jazz
music; games and quizzes for children.
Featured in 'Glos Echo', 2007.
& ✕ ⊨ ☕

KENCOT GARDENS
See Oxfordshire.

Island garden
bordered by
mill race . . .

36 ◆ **KIFTSGATE COURT**
**nr Chipping Campden GL55 6LN. Mr
& Mrs J G Chambers, 01386 438777,
www.kiftsgate.co.uk.** *4m NE of
Chipping Campden. Adjacent to
Hidcote National Trust Garden. 1m E of
B4632 & B4081.* **Adm £6, chd £2.
Open 23 Mar-29 Sept 2008. Daily
except Thur & Fri May, June & July
(12-6); Sun, Mon, Wed, Apr, Aug &
Sept (2-6).** For NGS: Mons 21 Apr;
11 Aug (2-6).
Magnificent situation and views; many
unusual plants and shrubs; tree
peonies, hydrangeas, abutilons,
species and old-fashioned roses, incl
largest rose in England, *Rosa filipes*
'Kiftsgate'. Steep slopes & steps.
✕ ✿ ☕

KINGSTONE COTTAGES
See Herefordshire.

37 ◆ **LAMMAS PARK**
**Cuckoo Row, Minchinhampton
GL6 9HA. Mr P Grover, 01453
886471.** *4m SE of Stroud. From
Market Sq down High St for 100yds,
turn R at Xrds. After 300yds turn L,
Lammas Park 100yds on L.* Light
refreshments & teas. **Adm £3, chd
free. Suns 23 Mar; 8 June (12-5).
Visitors also welcome by appt Mar
to Sept.**
$2^1/2$ acres around Cotswold 'Arts and
Crafts' style house (not open).
Herbaceous borders, pleached lime
allée, wild garden, alpines, restored
C17 'hanging gardens' with tunnel.
Superb views.
& ☕ ☎

THE LONG BARN
See Herefordshire.

38 **LOWER FARM HOUSE**
**Cliffords Mesne GL18 1JT. Gareth &
Sarah Williams.** *2m S of Newent.
From Newent follow signs to Cliffords
Mesne & Birds of Prey Centre (1$1/2$ m).
Approx* $1/2$ *m beyond 'centre', turn L at
Xrds. Signed Kents Green. Garden
150yds down hill on bend. Car park
(limited if wet).* Home-made teas. **Adm
£3, chd free. Mon 26 May (2-6).**
2-acre garden, incl woodland, stream
and large natural lily pond with rockery
and bog garden. Herbaceous borders,
pergola walk, terrace with ornamental
fishpond, kitchen and herb garden;
many interesting and unusual trees and
shrubs.
& ✿ ☕

39 ◆ **LYDNEY PARK SPRING
GARDEN**
**Lydney GL15 6BU. The Viscount
Bledisloe, 01594 842844/842922,
mrjames@phonecoop.coop.** $1/2$ *m
SW of Lydney. On A48 Gloucester to
Chepstow rd between Lydney &
Aylburton. Drive is directly off A48.*
**Adm £4, chd 50p. 23 Mar-8 June,
Suns, Weds & some other days.**
For NGS: Wed 16 Apr; Tue 13 May
(10-5).
Spring garden in 8-acre woodland
valley with lakes, profusion of
rhododendrons, azaleas and other
flowering shrubs. Formal garden;
magnolias and daffodils (April). Picnics
in deer park which has fine trees.
Important Roman Temple site and
museum. Teas in family dining room
(otherwise house not open)l.
✿ ☕

40 ◆ THE MATARA GARDEN
Kingscote GL8 8YA. Herons Mead
Ltd, 01453 861050,
www.matara.co.uk. *5¹/₂ m NW of
Tetbury. On A4135 towards Dursley. At
the Hunters Hall Inn turn R into
Kingscote village. Enter Park at 1st
gate on R.* Teas. **Adm £4, chd free,
concessions £2.50. Tues & Thurs 1
May to 30 Sept (2-5). For NGS: Suns
27 July; 28 Sept (1-5).**
A unique meditative garden alive with
inspiration from around the world.
Labyrinths, medicine wheel, ponds,
sculptures and walled ornamental herb
garden. We are developing an Eastern
woodland walk and wild flower
meadow. Matara is a spiritual garden
dedicated to the full expression of the
human spirit. All set within a 28-acre
parkland.

41 MEADOW COTTAGE
59 Coalway Road, Coalway, nr
Coleford GL16 7HL. Mrs Pamela
Buckland, 01594 833444. *1m SE of
Coleford. From Coleford take Lydney &
Chepstow Rd at T-lights in town. Turn
L after police stn, signed Coalway &
Parkend. Garden on L ¹/₂ m up hill opp
layby.* Home-made teas. **Adm £2.50,
chd free. Suns 20 Apr; 18 May; 13
July; 24 Aug (2-6). Visitors also
welcome by appt April to Sept,
individuals & groups.**
¹/₃ -acre cottage garden, a plantaholic
craftworker's creation with shrubs,
perennials, spring bulbs in colourful
borders and interlinking garden rooms.
Lawned area. Gravel paths leading to
small pond with waterfall and bog
garden. Vegetable garden in raised
beds. Gravel garden with grasses,
bamboos and pots and containers in
abundance.

42 ◆ MILL DENE GARDEN
School Lane, Blockley GL56 9HU.
Mr & Mrs B S Dare, 01386 700457,
www.milldenegarden.co.uk. *3m NW
of Moreton-in-Marsh. From A44, follow
brown signs from Bourton-on-the-Hill,
to Blockley. 1¹/₃ m down hill turn L
behind village gates. Parking for 8 cars.
Coaches by appoint.* Sept & Oct
evenings, wine. **Adm £5, chd £1,
concessions £4.50. Tues to Fris 18
Mar to 31 Oct (10-5). Last entry
4pm. Closed 20-25 Jul incl. For
NGS: Fri 21 Mar (10-5), Mon 24 Mar;
Sun 6 Apr (2-5). Evening Opening
£7, wine, Fri 5 Sept (7-9); Fri 3 Oct
(6.30-9).**

This garden surrounds a Cotswold
stone water-mill, set in a tiny steep
sided valley. It seems to have evolved
naturally in English 'country garden'
style. A millpond, stream, grotto,
potager and trompe l'oeil all contribute
to the owner's design for surprise,
concealment, scent, colour and, above
all, fun. New - 'scratch & sniff' herb
garden with rills. Mar & Apr - bulbs &
blossom; Sept & Oct - new lighting in
the garden, enjoy with a glass of wine;
all yr garden hunt for children under 13.
Featured in 'The English Garden', Mar
2007; 'Birmingham Post', Apr 2007;
'Le Monde', July 2007. Partial
wheelchair access; gravel paths &
slopes. Children must be accompanied
at all times because of mill pond.

Aboretum with spring bulbs en masse . . .

43 ◆ MISARDEN PARK
Miserden GL6 7JA. Major M T N H
Wills, 01285 821303,
www.misardenpark.co.uk. *6m NW of
Cirencester. Follow signs off A417 or
B4070 from Stroud.* **Adm £4, chd
free. Tues, Weds,Thurs (9.30-4.30).
For NGS: Suns 30 Mar; 22 June
(2-6).**
Essentially formal, dating from C17,
magnificent position overlooking the
Golden Valley. Walled garden with long
newly planted mixed borders, yew
walk leading to a lower lawn with rill
and summerhouse. Aboretum with
spring bulbs en masse. Climbing roses
and rose walk linking parterre. Silver
and grey border, blue border and
scented border. New blue/gold
walkway below house.

44 MOOR WOOD
Woodmancote GL7 7EB. Mr & Mrs
Henry Robinson, 01285 831397,
henry@moorwood.fslife.co.uk. *3¹/₂ m
NW of Cirencester. Turn L off A435 to
Cheltenham at North Cerney, signed
Woodmancote 1¹/₄ m; entrance in
village on L beside lodge with white*

gates. **Adm £3, chd free. Sun 29
June (2-6). Visitors also welcome by
appt.**
2 acres of shrub, orchard and wild
flower gardens in isolated valley
setting. Holder of the National
Collection of rambler roses.

NCCPG

THE NURTONS
See Glamorgan.

45 THE OLD CHAPEL
Marle Hill, Chalford Vale GL6 8PN. F
J & F Owen. *4m E of Stroud. On A419
to Cirencester. Above Chalford Vale,
steep climb from car park on main rd,
up Marle Hill.* **Adm £3, chd free. Daily
Sat 7 June to Sun 22 June (10-5).
Also opening with Chalford
Gardens 21, 22 June (12-5).**
1-acre Victorian chapel garden on
precipitous hillside. A tiered tapestry of
herbaceous borders, formal potager,
small orchard, pond and
summerhouse, old roses. Gothic
pergola and rose tunnel, all laid out on
terraced S-facing Marle Cliff.

46 THE OLD CHEQUER
Draycott, nr Blockley GL56 9LB. Mr
& Mrs H Linley, 01386 700647. *2m
NE of Moreton-in-Marsh. Nr Blockley.*
Home-made teas. **Adm £2.50, chd
free. £6 with Blockley Gardens 8
June. Sun 13 Apr (12-4.30); Sun 8
June (2-6). Visitors also welcome by
appt, Apr to June.**
A natural garden, created by owner,
set in 2 acres of old orchard with
original ridge and furrow. Emphasis on
spring planting but still maintaining yr-
round interest. Kitchen garden/soft
fruit, herbaceous and shrubs in island
beds. Croquet lawn, unusual plants,
alpines and dry gravel borders.

THE OLD CORN MILL
See Herefordshire.

**47 THE OLD RECTORY,
DUNTISBOURNE ROUS**
Duntisbourne Rous GL7 7AP.
Charles & Mary Keen,
mary@keengardener.com. *4m NW of
Cirencester. From Daglingworth NW of
Cirencester take rd to the
Duntisbournes; or from A417 from
Gloucester take Duntisbourne Leer
turning.* **Adm £3.50, chd free. Mon 11
Feb; Mon 10 Mar (11-4); Mon 21
Apr; Mon 12 May (11-5); Mon 16
June; Mon 21 July; Mon 15 Sept
(11-6). Visitors also welcome by
appt for groups 10+. Written or**

email appt **The Old Rectory,
Duntisbourne Rous GL7 7AP.**
Garden in an exceptional setting made
by designer and writer Mary Keen.
Subject of many articles and Telegraph
column. Designed for atmosphere, but
collections of Galanthus, Hellebores,
Auriculas and half hardies - especially
Dahlias - are all features in their
season. Plants for sale occasionally.
Beautiful early church, schoolroom with
DIY tea & coffee where you can read
about the garden.

OVERBURY COURT
ee Worcestershire.

48 OZLEWORTH PARK
**Wotton-under-Edge GL12 7QA. Mr
& Mrs M J C Stone.** *5m S of Dursley.
Approach from A4135 Tetbury to
Dursley rd. At junction with B4058,
turn S on single track lane signed
Ozleworth. Follow signs for approx 2m
until reaching gates with eagles on
gateposts. Follow signs down drive.*
Adm £4, chd free. Sun 25 May (2-5).
Renovated over past 12yrs. Approx 10
acres with rose garden, Victorian bath
house, lily ponds, small lake; also
glasshouses, orchard and vegetable
area. Waterfall area not accessible.

**49 ◆ PAINSWICK ROCOCO
GARDEN**
**Painswick GL6 6TH. Painswick
Rococo Garden Trust, 01452
813204, www.rococogarden.org.uk.**
*¼ m N of Painswick. ½ m outside
village on B4073.* **Adm £5.50, chd
£2.75, concessions £4.50. Daily 10
Jan to 31 Oct (11-5).**
Unique C18 garden from the brief
Rococo period, combining
contemporary buildings, vistas, ponds,
kitchen garden and winding woodland
walks. Anniversary maze.

50 PARK FARM
**Alderley GL12 7QT. Mr & Mrs A J V
Shepherd, 01453 842123.** *1½ m S of
Wotton-under-Edge. Just before
village.* Home-made teas. **Adm £3,
chd free. Sat 6 Sept (2-6). Visitors
also welcome by appt.**
The lake with its waterside plants and
large koi carp is the pivotal attraction in
a scenically designed 2½ -acre
garden. Maturing herbaceous borders,
young trees and rose garden. Sunken
garden.

51 PAULMEAD
**Bisley GL6 7AG. Judy & Philip
Howard.** *5m E of Stroud. On S edge
of Bisley at head of Toadsmoor Valley
on top of Cotswolds. Garden & car
park well signed in Bisley village.
Disabled can be dropped off at garden
prior to parking car.* **Adm £3, chd free.
Combined with Wells Cottage £4.
Sun 22 June (2-6).**
Approx 1-acre landscaped garden
constructed in stages over last 18yrs.
Terraced in three main levels: natural
stream garden; formal herbaceous and
shrub borders; yew and beech
hedges; formal vegetable garden;
lawns; summerhouse with exterior
wooden decking by pond and
thatched roof over well head. New
unusual tree house.

an informal
peaceful
feel . . .

52 PEAR TREE COTTAGE
**58 Malleson Road, Gotherington
GL52 9EX. Mr & Mrs E Manders-
Trett, 01242 674592.** *4m N of
Cheltenham. From A435 turn R into
Gotherington 1m after end of Bishop's
Cleeve bypass. Garden is on L approx
100yds past Shutter Inn.* **Adm £3, chd
free. Suns 16 Mar; 20 Apr; 18 May;
15 June (2-5). Visitors also welcome
by appt.**
Mainly informal country garden approx
½ -acre with pond and gravel garden,
grasses and herbaceous borders,
trees and shrubs surrounding lawns.
Wild garden and orchard lead to
greenhouses, herb and vegetable
gardens. Spring bulbs and early
summer perennials and shrubs
particularly colourful.

53 PEMBERLEY LODGE
**Churchend Lane, Old Charfield
GL12 8LJ. Rob & Yvette
Andrewartha, 01454 260885.** *3½ m
SW of Wotton-under-Edge. Off B4058
from Wotton-under Edge through
Charfield Village. At top of Charfield
Hill, turn L. 2m from M5 J14, at Xrds
on B4509 go straight across into

Churchend Lane. Light refreshments.
**Adm £4, chd free. Late afternoon &
Evening Opening** wine, Thurs 7, 28
Aug (4-8). **Visitors also welcome by
appt.**
Small private garden designed and
planted in 2002 by Lesley Rosser.
Densely planted for all-yr-round
interest, maturing well. Incorporates
trees, shrubs, perennials, grasses,
water, gravel and hard landscaping to
give an informal peaceful feel. New roof
garden added in 2006.

54 PIGEON HOUSE
**Southam Lane, Southam GL52 3NY.
Mrs DeeTaylor, 01242 529342,
dee.taylor@zen.co.uk.** *3m NE of
Cheltenham. Off B4632 toward
Winchcombe. Parking available
adjacent to Southam Tithe Barn.* **Adm
£3, chd free. Suns 11 May; 1 June
(2-5). Visitors also welcome by appt.**
2-acre garden surrounding Cotswold
stone manor (not open) of medieval
origin. Small lake with island and
separate water garden with linked
pools featuring water margin and bog
plants. Extensive lawns on several
levels; wide range of flowering shrubs
and borders designed to create a
multitude of vistas; woodland area with
shade-loving plants and many spring
bulbs.

55 QUENINGTON GARDENS
nr Fairford GL7 5BW. *8m NE of
Cirencester.* Home-made teas at The
Old Rectory. **Combined adm £4, chd
free. Sun 22 June (2-5.30).**
A rarely visited Coln Valley village
delighting its infrequent visitors with
C12 Norman church and C17 stone
cottages (not open). An opportunity to
discover the horticultural treasures
behind those Cotswold stone walls
and visit 4 very different but charming
gardens incorporating everything from
the exotic and the organic to the
simple cottage garden; a range of
vistas from riverside to seclusion.

BANK VIEW
Mrs J A Moulden
Terraced garden with wonderful
views over the R Coln.

**THE OLD RECTORY,
QUENINGTON**
**Mr & Mrs D Abel Smith, 01285
750358,
lucy@realityandbeyond.co.uk,
freshairart.org. Visitors also**

welcome by appt.
On the banks of the mill race and the R Coln, this is an organic garden of variety. Mature trees and new plantings, large vegetable garden, herbaceous, shade, pool and bog gardens. Featured in GGG 2007, County Life, Home & Garden & local press, all 2007.

POOL HAY
Mrs E A Morris
Small beautiful riverside garden - old-fashioned roses a feature.

YEW TREE COTTAGES
Mr J Lindon
Quintessential cottage garden.

56 RAMBLERS
Lower Common, Aylburton, nr Lydney GL15 6DS. Jane & Leslie Hale. *1¹/₂ m W of Lydney. Off A48 Gloucester to Chepstow Rd. From Lydney through Aylburton, out of de-limit turn R signed Aylburton Common, ³/₄ m along lane.* Home-made teas. **Adm £3, chd free. Suns 4 May; 8 June (2-6).**
Peaceful medium-sized country garden with informal cottage planting, herbaceous borders and small pond looking through hedge 'windows' onto wild flower meadow. Front woodland garden with shade-loving plants and topiary. Large productive vegetable garden. Recently planted apple orchard. Featured in 'The Independent' magazine, May 2007, & 'The English Garden', June, 2007.

Well structured garden with herbaceous borders to colour themes . . .

57 ROCKCLIFFE
nr Lower Swell GL54 2JW. Mr & Mrs Simon Keswick. *2m SW of Stow-on-the-Wold. On B4068. From Stow-on-the-Wold to Cheltenham go through Lower Swell. Climb hill staying on B4068. Converted barn on L. Round*

corner & start dropping down hill. Rockcliffe halfway down on R. *Home-made teas.* **Adm £4.50, chd free (share to Kates Home Carers). Weds 11, 18, 25 June (10-5).**
Large traditional English garden 7 acres incl pink, white and blue gardens, herbaceous border, rose terrace; walled kitchen garden and orchard; greenhouses and new stone dovecot with pathway of topiary birds leading up through orchard to it.

58 ◆ RODMARTON MANOR
Cirencester GL7 6PF. Mr & Mrs Simon Biddulph. *5m NE of Tetbury. Off A433. Between Cirencester & Tetbury.* **House and garden adm £7, chd £3.50, garden only adm £4, chd £1. Weds & Sats May to Sept (2-5). For NGS: Sun 20 Apr (2-5).**
The 8-acre garden of this fine 'Arts and Crafts' house is a series of outdoor rooms each with its own distinctive character. Leisure garden, winter garden, troughery, topiary, hedges, lawns, rockery, containers, wild garden, kitchen garden, magnificent herbaceous borders. Snowdrop collection. House NOT OPEN on NGS day.

59 ROOKWOODS
Waterlane, nr Bisley GL6 7PN. Mr & Mrs Des Althorp. *5m E of Stroud. Between Sapperton & Bisley. Turn down No Through Rd in Waterlane then follow signs.* Home-made teas. **Adm £3, chd free. Sun 29 June (2-6).**
3-acre, well structured garden with herbaceous borders to colour themes. Pleached whitebeam around pool area. Wide variety of old-fashioned and modern climbing and shrub roses (mostly labelled), water gardens and outstanding views.

60 SANDYWELL GARDENS
nr Whittington, Cheltenham GL54 4HF. *5m E of Cheltenham. On A40 between Whittington & Andoversford.* Home-made teas at Barn House. **Combined adm £4, chd free. Suns 8, 22 June (11-5).**
Two vibrant, plant-packed, complementary walled gardens, totalling 3 acres and featuring areas both traditional and contemporary. Mature trees, varied borders, secret corners, lawns, water features, walkways, avenues and vistas.

BARN HOUSE
Shirley & Gordon Sills, 01242 820606, shirley.sills@tesco.net. Visitors also welcome by appt June & July only, groups 10+. Coaches permitted.
Plantaholic designer's own 2¹/₂ -acre walled garden. Maintained by owners. Exuberantly planted for form, scent and colour. Herbaceous, roses, climbers, shrubs, trees, lawns, hedges, structures, formal water features. Spring-fed stream and pond. Constantly evolving.

GARDEN COTTAGE
Charles Fogg & Gilly Bogdiukiewicz, 01242 820606, shirley.sills@tesco.net. Visitors also welcome by appt.
Peaceful, ¹/₂ -acre, cottage garden with four interconnecting walled areas, of different character and separate levels, incl; borders, lawns, gravel areas and patios. Also stone, marble and wooden features, urns, tubs, baskets and greenhouse.

61 ◆ SEZINCOTE
nr Moreton-in-Marsh GL56 9AW. Mr & Mrs D Peake, 01386 700444, www.sezincote.co.uk. *3m SW of Moreton-in-Marsh. From Moreton-in-Marsh turn W along A44 towards Evesham; after 1¹/₂ m (just before Bourton-on-the-Hill) take turn L, by stone lodge with white gate.* **Adm £5, chd £1.50. House, Thurs, Fris, BH Mons, May to Sept (2.30-6). Garden, Thurs, Fris & BH Mons (2-6) except Jan. For NGS: Sun 6 July (2-6).**
Exotic oriental water garden by Repton and Daniell with lake, pools and meandering stream, banked with massed perennials. Large semi-circular orangery, formal Indian garden, fountain, temple and unusual trees of vast size in lawn and wooded park setting. House in Indian manner designed by Samuel Pepys Cockerell. Gravel paths & steep slopes.

62 ◆ SNOWSHILL MANOR
nr Broadway WR12 7JU. The National Trust, 01386 852410, snowshillmanor@nationaltrust.org.uk. *2¹/₂ m S of Broadway. Off A44 bypass into Broadway village.* **House and garden adm £8.10, chd £4.10, garden only adm £4.40, chd £2.20. Wed to Sun. Apr to Oct. For NGS:**

Wed 25 June (11-5.30).
An Arts & Crafts inspired terraced garden in which organic and natural methods only are used. Highlights incl tranquil ponds, old roses, old-fashioned flowers and herbaceous borders rich in plants of special interest. Working kitchen garden.

✗ ✿

63 SOUTH LODGE
Church Road, Clearwell, Coleford GL16 8LG. Andrew & Jane MacBean. *2m S of Coleford. Off B4228. Follow signs to Clearwell. Garden on L of castle driveway. Park at Castle Farm.* Home-made teas. Teas in village hall 4 May. **Adm £2.50, chd free (share to Assoc of Children's Palliative Care).** Suns 6 Apr (2-5); 4 May (12-4); 22 June (11-5).
Set in the peaceful, rural village of Clearwell, this 2-acre, organic garden is on a sloping site which used to be a part of the grounds of Clearwell Castle. A developing garden which includes large area of trees and shrubs, with some unusual specimens; good selection of fruit trees; wild flower meadow and wildlife pond; colourful borders; vegetable garden and small formal pond. Sun 4 May, Church Flower Festival. Featured in Glos Citizen, 2007.

✗ ✿ ☕

64 STANTON GARDENS
nr Broadway WR12 7NE. Mr K J Ryland. *3m SW of Broadway. Off B4632, between Broadway (3m) & Winchcombe (6m).* Home-made teas. **Adm £4.50, chd free.** Sun 15 June (2-6).
One of the most picturesque and unspoilt C17 Cotswold villages with many gardens to explore (24 open in 2007) ranging from charming cottage to large formal gardens which should appeal to visitors of all tastes. More formal gardens have wheelchair access while the Burlams Hall has disabled facilities.

♿ ✿ ☕

65 ◆ STANWAY FOUNTAIN & WATER GARDEN
nr Winchcombe GL54 5PQ. Lord Neidpath, 01386 584469, www.stanwayfountain.co.uk. *9m NE of Cheltenham. 1m E of B4632 Cheltenham to Broadway rd or B4077 Toddington to Stow-on-the-Wold rd.* House and garden adm £6, chd £1.50, concessions £4.50, garden only adm £4, chd £1, concessions

£3. Tues & Thurs, June, July, Aug (2-5). For NGS: Suns 20 Apr; 18 May (2-5).
20 acres of planted landscape in early C18 formal setting. Recent restoration of canal, upper pond and 165ft high fountain have re-created one of the most interesting baroque water gardens in Britain. Striking C16 manor with gatehouse, tithe barn and church. Britain's highest fountain, the world's highest gravity fountain.

☕

66 ◆ STONE HOUSE
Wyck Rissington GL54 2PN. Mr & Mrs Andrew Lukas, 01451 810337, www.stonehousegarden.co.uk. *3m S of Stow-on-the-Wold. Off A429 between Bourton-on-the-Water & Stow-on-the-Wold. Last house in village behind high bank on R.* Refreshments in village hall. **Adm £4, chd free.** For NGS: Sun 20 Apr (2-6).
2 acres full of unusual bulbs, shrubs and herbaceous plants. Crab apple walk, rose borders, herb and water garden, meadow walk. Plantswoman's garden with yr-round interest. Plant Sales: 7 Mar; Hellebores (10-1), 18 Apr; Primula Auricula, woodland plants & bulbs (10-1), 26 May; Rare Plant Sale (10-2), 16 Sept; Autumn plant sale (10-3). Please contact for further info.

♿ ✗ ✿ ☕

67 STOWELL PARK
Northleach GL54 3LE. The Lord & Lady Vestey, 01285 720610 Neil, Head Gardener. *8m NE of Cirencester. Off Fosseway A429 2m SW of Northleach.* Home-made teas. **Adm £4, chd free (share to church 18 May; British Legion 22 June).** Suns 18 May; 22 June (2-5).
Magnificent lawned terraces with stunning views over Coln Valley. Fine collection of old-fashioned roses and herbaceous plants, with pleached lime approach to C14 house (not open). Two large walled gardens containing vegetables, fruit, cut flowers and range of greenhouses. Long rose pergola and wide, plant-filled borders divided into colour sections. Plant Sale - 18 May onlyl.

✗ ☕ ☎

68 ◆ SUDELEY CASTLE GARDENS & EXHIBITIONS
Winchcombe GL54 5JD. Lord & Lady Ashcombe & Henry & Mollie Dent Brocklehurst, 01242 602308, www.sudeleycastle.co.uk. *8m NE of*

Cheltenham. On B4632 (A46) or 10m from J9 M5. Bus service operates bet Winchcombe & Cheltenham or Broadway. **House & gardens adm £7.20, chd £4.20, concessions £6.20. Exhibition & gardens Mon to Sun, 15 Mar to 26 Oct (10.30-5).** For NGS: Sun 5 Oct (10-30-5).
Magnificent gardens work themselves seamlessly around castle buildings. Individual gardens incl Queen's Garden with old-fashioned roses, annuals and herbs; examples of fine topiary incl Tudor Knot Garden; exotic plantings in the Secret Garden and autumn colour throughout gardens. A fine collection of rare and colourful pheasants create added interest. Featured in The Times, Garden magazine, Kew magazine & BBC Gardeners' World, 2007. Limited wheelchair access; gravel paths.

♿ ✗ ✿ ☕

> ## Wild flower meadow and wildlife pond . . .

69 TEMPLE GUITING MANOR
Temple Guiting, nr Stow on the Wold GL54 5RP. Mr S Collins. *7m from Stow on the Wold. From Stow on the Wold take B4077 towards Tewkesbury. On descending hill bear L to village (signed) ½ m. Garden in centre of village on R.* **Adm £3, chd free.** Sun 6 July (2-6).
Newly designed formal contemporary gardens to Grade I listed historic manor house (not open) in Windrush Valley. Designed by Jinny Blom, gold medal winner Chelsea Flower Show 2007.

✗ ✿ ☕

70 TINPENNY FARM
Fiddington, nr Tewkesbury
GL20 7BJ. E S Horton, 01684
292668. *2½ m SE of Tewkesbury.
From M5 J9 take A46 exit towards
Evesham. Just after T-lights turn R to
Fiddington. After 1½ m turn R to
Walton Cardiff. Entrance 1st on R.*
**Adm £2.50, chd free. Tues, Weds,
Thurs, 5 Feb to 30 Oct (9-1). Visitors
also welcome by appt.**
Amazing collection of plants incl
hellebores, iris, hemerocallis, hostas.
Do not expect a weed-free zone! But
to see what can be achieved with a
wind-swept site on impenetrable clay,
please do visit.

♿ ✖ ⦿ ☎

71 TRENCH HILL
Sheepscombe GL6 6TZ. Celia &
Dave Hargrave, 01452 814306,
celia.hargrave@btconnect.com. *1½
m E of Painswick. On A46 to
Cheltenham after Painswick, turn R to
Sheepscombe. Approx 1½ m (before
reaching village) turn L by telegraph
poles, Trench Hill at top of lane.* Home-
made teas. **Adm £2.50, chd free.
Suns 10, 17 Feb (11-4); Sun 23, Mon
24 Mar (11-6); Weds, 4, 11, 18, 25
June (2-6); Suns 20 July; 24 Aug; 7
Sept (11-6); Suns 8, 15 Feb 2009
(11-4). Visitors also welcome by
appt.**
Approx 3 acres set in small woodland
with panoramic views. Variety of
herbaceous and mixed borders, rose
garden, extensive vegetable plots, wild
flower areas, plantings of spring bulbs
with thousands of snowdrops and
hellebores, woodland walk, 2 small
ponds, waterfall and larger
conservation pond. Interesting wooden
sculptures. Run on organic principles.

♿ ✖ ⦿ ☕ ☎

72 UPPER MERTON HOUSE
High Street, Newnham-on-Severn
GL14 1AD. Roger Grounds & Diana
Grenfell, 01594 517146,
diana@uppermerton.co.uk. *Halfway
bet Chepstow & Gloucester on A48.
On service rd parallel to High St bet
library & Dean Rd.* **Adm £2.50.
Visitors welcome by appt Tues,
Weds, Thurs 3, 4, 5, June; 1, 2, 3,
July; 5, 6, 7, Aug (2-5).**
Small, recently created, formal but
exuberantly planted, town garden.
Collection of hostas, daylilies,
ornamental grasses, ferns, palms and
many unusual plants displayed to
benefit from different levels, incl stone
steps, courtyards and terrace. National

Collection of miniature hosta.
Refreshments available at The Lower
George, High St. Featured in 'Glos
Echo', Aug 2007.

✖ NCCPG ☎

> Small, recently
> created, formal
> but exuberantly
> planted, town
> garden . . .

73 UPTON WOLD
nr Moreton-in-Marsh GL56 9TR. Mr
& Mrs I R S Bond, 01386 700667,
admin@northwickestate.co.uk. *3½
m W of Moreton-in-Marsh. On A44 1m
past A424 junction at Troopers Lodge
Garage.* **Adm £5, chd free. Sun 11
May (10-6). Visitors also welcome by
appt May to July.**
Ever-developing and changing garden,
architecturally and imaginatively laid
out around C17 house (not open) with
commanding views. Yew hedges;
herbaceous walk; some unusual plants
and trees; vegetables; pond and
woodland gardens. National Collection
of Juglans.

✖ ⦿ NCCPG ☎

74 VINE FARM
Malvern Road, Staunton GL19 3NZ.
Alex & Jane Morton. *7m NE of
Newent. Staunton ½ way between
Ledbury & Gloucester on A417. In
village, from mini roundabout, take
B4208 to Malvern. Approx ½ m on L is
Vine Farm.* Home-made teas. **Adm
£2.50, chd free. Suns 18 May; 8
June (2-6).**
Developing garden. Herbaceous
borders, roses, honeysuckles and
clematis. Also large productive
vegetable garden with pergola. Mature
trees surround the property of several
acres, and the aim is a peaceful blend
of countryside and garden. Newly
planted vineyard/cherry orchard. This is
a wildlife country garden.

✖ ☕

75 WELLS COTTAGE
Wells Road, Bisley GL6 7AG. Mr &
Mrs Michael Flint. *5m E of Stroud.
Garden & car park well signed in Bisley
village. Garden lies on S edge of village
at head of Toadsmoor Valley, above
A419.* **Adm £3, chd free. Combined
with Paulmead £4. Sun 22 June
(2-6).**
Just under an acre. Terraced on
several levels with beautiful views over
valley. Much informal planting of trees
and shrubs to give colour and texture.
Lawns and herbaceous borders.
Collection of grasses. Formal pond
area. Rambling roses on rope pergola.
Vegetable garden with raised beds.

🛌

**76 ◆ WESTBURY COURT
GARDEN**
Westbury-on-Severn GL14 1PD. The
National Trust, 01452 760461,
www.nationaltrust.org.uk. *9m SW of
Gloucester. On A48.* **Adm £4.50, chd
£2.25. For NGS: Sun 14 Sept (10-5).**
Formal Dutch-style water garden,
earliest remaining in England; canals,
summerhouse, over 100 species of
plants grown in England, and recreated
vegetable plots, growing crops all from
before 1700. Fine hard gravel, flat
garden.

♿ ✖

WESTON MEWS
See Herefordshire.

**77 ◆ WESTONBIRT SCHOOL
GARDENS**
Westonbirt GL8 8QG. Westonbirt
School, 01666 881338,
doyle@westonbirt.gloucs.sch.uk. *3m
SW of Tetbury. Opp Westonbirt
Arboretum, on the A433 (follow brown
tourist information signs).* **Adm £3.50,
chd £2. 25 Mar to 13 April; 10 July to
31 Aug; Thur to Sun (11-4) ; 25 Oct
to 2 Nov, every day. For NGS: Sun
25, Mon 26 May (2-4).**
22 acres. Former private garden of
Robert Holford, founder of Westonbirt
Arboretum. Formal Victorian gardens
incl walled Italian garden, terraced
pleasure garden, rustic walks, lake,
statuary and grotto. Rare, exotic trees
and shrubs. Beautiful views of
Westonbirt House, now Westonbirt
School, not open. Gravel paths &
steep slopes.

♿ ☕

WHITCOMBE HOUSE
See Worcestershire.

78 NEW THE WHITE HOUSE

Clearwell, nr Coleford GL16 8JR. Allan & Jean Smith, 01594 832090. *1m S of Coleford. From B4228 (Coleford to Chepstow rd) take tourist sign route to Clearwell Caves. The White House is 1st house past the caves by 30mph sign into village.* Home-made teas. **Adm £2.50, chd free. Suns 1 June; 31 Aug (2-6). Visitors also welcome by appt from Apr to Sept during the week, groups 12 or less.** ½ acre of tranquility. Large pond and shady area with trees and shrubs overlooking the expansive lawn and long banked perennial border in hues of pinks, mauves and blues. Soft fruit border and tiered salad/vegetable plot. Climbers, containers and courtyard with hot beds. A shady pergola and a secret garden too. Art Exhibition. Some gravel paths.

 ♿ ☕ ☎

WHITEHILL FARM
See Oxfordshire.

79 WILLOW LODGE

nr Longhope GL17 0RA. John & Sheila Wood, 01452 831211, wood@willowgardens.fsnet.co.uk, www.willowgardens.fsnet.co.uk. *10m W of Gloucester, 6m E of Ross-on-Wye. On A40 between Huntley & Lea.* Home-made teas. **Adm £3, chd free. Sun 4, Mon 5, Sun 25, Mon 26 May; Sun 10, Mon 11 Aug (1-5). Visitors also welcome by appt Apr to Aug, coaches permitted.** Plantsmans garden with unusual and rare plants, herbaceous borders, shrubs and alpine garden. Many woodland plants incl trilliums, erythroniums, hellebores etc. Large bog garden with marginals and Asiatic primulas. Fish pond and stream. Exceptional arboretum containing approx 400 different trees and shrubs, from all over the temperate world. Areas of wild flowers in 4-acre grounds. Plants labelled.

♿ ✂ ❀ ☕ ☎

WOODPECKERS
See Warwickshire & part of West Midlands.

Long banked perennial border in hues of pinks, mauves and blues . . .

Gloucestershire County Volunteers

County Organiser
Norman Jeffery, 28 Shrivenham Road, Highworth, Swindon SN6 7BZ, 01793 762805, normjeffery28@aol.com

County Treasurer
Graham Baber, 11 Corinium Gate, Cirencester GL7 2PX, 01285 650961, grayanjen@onetel.com

Leaflet Coordinator
John Sidwell, Lavender Down, Cheltenham Road, Painswick, Stroud GL6 6SJ, 01452 814244, john@johnsidwell.plus.com

Assistant County Organisers
Barbara Adams, Warners Court, Charfield, Wotton under Edge GL12 8TG, 01454 261078, adams@waitrose.com
Pamela Buckland, Meadow Cottage, 59 Coalway Road, Coalway, Coleford GL16 7HL, 01594 833444
Trish Jeffery, 28 Shrivenham Road, Highworth, Swindon SN6 7BZ, 01793 762805
Tony Marlow, Greenedge, 32 Dr Browns Road, Minchinhampton GL6 9BT, 01453 883531
Stella Martin, Dundry Lodge, France Lynch, Stroud GL6 8LP, 01453 883419, martin@franlyn.fsnet.co.uk
Anne Palmer, 10 Vineyard Street, Winchcombe GL54 5LP, 01242 603761
Shirley Sills, Barn House, Sandywell Park, Whittington, Cheltenham GL54 4HF, 01242 820606, shirley.sills@tesco.net

HAMPSHIRE

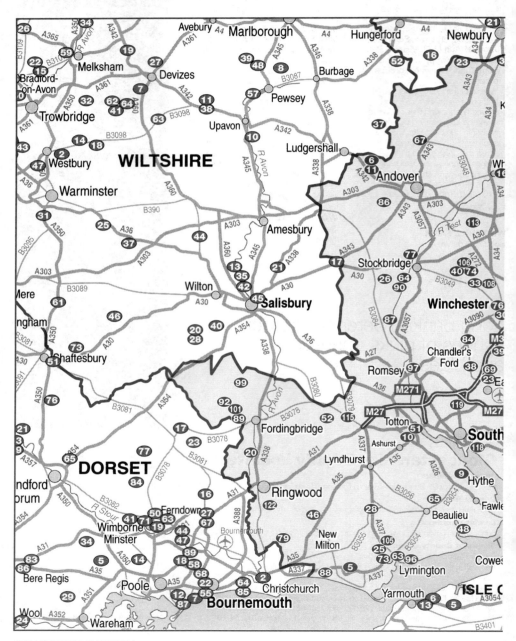

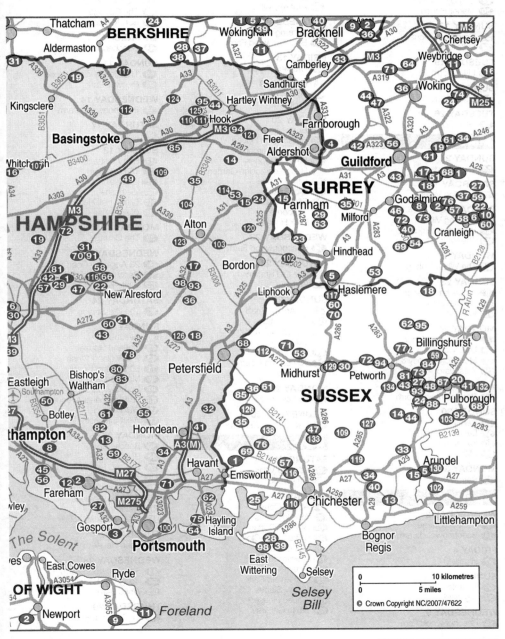

Opening Dates

February

SATURDAY 9
22 Brandy Mount House
80 Manor House

SUNDAY 17
21 Bramdean House
74 Little Court

TUESDAY 19
74 Little Court

SUNDAY 24
74 Little Court

TUESDAY 26
74 Little Court

March

SUNDAY 2
56 Heathlands

SATURDAY 15
9 Atheling Villas

SUNDAY 16
9 Atheling Villas
21 Bramdean House
123 The White Cottage

MONDAY 17
123 The White Cottage

SUNDAY 23
6 Appleshaw Manor
46 Durmast House
119 Westward

MONDAY 24
6 Appleshaw Manor
74 Little Court
87 Mottisfont Abbey & Garden
119 Westward

WEDNESDAY 26
14 Beechenwood Farm

SUNDAY 30
16 Bere Mill
47 East Lane
50 Flintstones
85 Mittens

MONDAY 31
16 Bere Mill

April

WEDNESDAY 2
1 Abbey Cottage
14 Beechenwood Farm

FRIDAY 4
57 Highfield

SUNDAY 6
56 Heathlands
57 Highfield

WEDNESDAY 9
14 Beechenwood Farm

SUNDAY 13
99 St Christopher's

TUESDAY 15
9 Atheling Villas

WEDNESDAY 16
9 Atheling Villas
14 Beechenwood Farm

FRIDAY 18
40 Crawley Gardens

SATURDAY 19
60 Hinton Ampner
103 'Selborne'

SUNDAY 20
21 Bramdean House
24 Broadhatch House
40 Crawley Gardens
60 Hinton Ampner
64 Houghton Lodge Garden
76 Litton Lodge
94 Old Thatch
99 St Christopher's
103 'Selborne'
116 Weir House

WEDNESDAY 23
14 Beechenwood Farm

SATURDAY 26
93 The Old Station
114 Walbury

SUNDAY 27
2 80 Abbey Road
17 Berry Cottage
63 Hordle Walhampton School
69 53 Ladywood
71 60 Lealand Road
114 Walbury

MONDAY 28
69 53 Ladywood

WEDNESDAY 30
14 Beechenwood Farm

May

SATURDAY 3
9 Atheling Villas
75 Littlewood

SUNDAY 4
1 Abbey Cottage
9 Atheling Villas
18 Bluebell Cottage
23 6 Breamore Close
38 The Cottage
75 Littlewood
96 Pylewell Park
98 Rotherfield Park
102 Sandy Slopes
113 Wades House
124 White Gables

MONDAY 5
1 Abbey Cottage
18 Bluebell Cottage
23 6 Breamore Close
38 The Cottage
102 Sandy Slopes

WEDNESDAY 7
14 Beechenwood Farm

SUNDAY 11
65 The House in the Wood
96 Pylewell Park

WEDNESDAY 14
14 Beechenwood Farm

SATURDAY 17
103 'Selborne'

SUNDAY 18
17 Berry Cottage
38 The Cottage
61 Holywell
103 'Selborne'
110 Tylney Hall Hotel
116 Weir House

MONDAY 19
38 The Cottage

WEDNESDAY 21
4 23 Anglesey Road
14 Beechenwood Farm
122 White Barn

SATURDAY 24
93 The Old Station

SUNDAY 25
13 Beechcroft
29 Chilland House
45 7 Downland Close
71 60 Lealand Road
86 Monxton Gardens
97 Romsey Gardens
100 28 St Ronan's Avenue
115 Waldrons
117 West Silchester Hall

MONDAY 26
13 Beechcroft
16 Bere Mill
29 Chilland House
45 7 Downland Close
86 Monxton Gardens
97 Romsey Gardens
115 Waldrons
117 West Silchester Hall

TUESDAY 27
43 Dean House

WEDNESDAY 28
14 Beechenwood Farm
64 Houghton Lodge Garden
122 White Barn

THURSDAY 29
28 21 Chestnut Road

FRIDAY 30
28 21 Chestnut Road (Day & Evening)
74 Little Court

SATURDAY 31
53 Froyle Gardens

June

SUNDAY 1
23 6 Breamore Close
41 Crookley Pool
50 Flintstones
53 Froyle Gardens
70 Lake House
74 Little Court
82 Meon Orchard
110 Tylney Hall Hotel

MONDAY 2
23 6 Breamore Close
50 Flintstones

TUESDAY 3
70 Lake House
112 The Vyne

WEDNESDAY 4
7 Appletree House
14 Beechenwood Farm
25 Buckland Stead
122 White Barn

FRIDAY 6
57 Highfield

SATURDAY 7
10 Barhi, 27 Reynolds Dale
15 Bentley Village Gardens
51 The Fountains
107 Timaru

SUNDAY 8
10 Barhi, 27 Reynolds Dale
11 Barncroft Gardens
15 Bentley Village Gardens
19 Borough Farm
37 Conholt Park
42 Cygnet House
51 The Fountains
57 Highfield
81 Martyr Worthy Gardens
83 Meonstoke Gardens
107 Timaru

MONDAY 9
1 Abbey Cottage
11 Barncroft Gardens
42 Cygnet House

TUESDAY 10
19 Borough Farm
50 Flintstones (Evening)

WEDNESDAY 11
14 Beechenwood Farm
122 White Barn

FRIDAY 13
32 Clibdens
83 Meonstoke Gardens (Evening)
103 'Selborne' (Day & Evening)

SATURDAY 14
28 21 Chestnut Road
60 Hinton Ampner
103 'Selborne'

SUNDAY 15
21 Bramdean House
28 21 Chestnut Road
31 Church Close
32 Clibdens
39 Cranbury Park
49 Farleigh House
72 Linden Barn
77 Longstock Park Water Garden
89 Oakdene
90 The Old Rectory, Houghton
103 'Selborne'

MONDAY 16
31 Church Close
90 The Old Rectory, Houghton

TUESDAY 17
9 Atheling Villas

WEDNESDAY 18
9 Atheling Villas
25 Buckland Stead
43 Dean House
73 The Little Cottage
122 White Barn

FRIDAY 20
20 Braemoor

SATURDAY 21
8 Appletrees

SUNDAY 22
8 Appletrees
17 Berry Cottage
20 Braemoor
37 Conholt Park
44 Dipley Mill
45 7 Downland Close
69 53 Ladywood
71 60 Lealand Road
80 Manor House
88 Mulberry House
89 Oakdene
116 Weir House
126 Wrens Farm

MONDAY 23
45 7 Downland Close
69 53 Ladywood

WEDNESDAY 25
64 Houghton Lodge Garden
122 White Barn

THURSDAY 26
40 Crawley Gardens

SATURDAY 28
27 2 Carisbrooke Road
114 Walbury

SUNDAY 29
12 19 Barnwood Road
27 2 Carisbrooke Road
40 Crawley Gardens

46 Durmast House
88 Mulberry House
89 Oakdene
111 Tylney House
114 Walbury
124 White Gables
126 Wrens Farm

July

WEDNESDAY 2
25 Buckland Stead
122 White Barn

FRIDAY 4
20 Braemoor
35 The Coach House (Evening)

SATURDAY 5
87 Mottisfont Abbey & Garden
118 26 & 29 Weston Allotments

SUNDAY 6
17 Berry Cottage
20 Braemoor
35 The Coach House
43 Dean House
92 The Old Ship
110 Tylney Hall Hotel
117 West Silchester Hall
118 26 & 29 Weston Allotments
121 Whispers
125 1 Wogsbarne Cottages

WEDNESDAY 9
7 Appletree House
92 The Old Ship
122 White Barn

FRIDAY 11
2 80 Abbey Road (Evening)

SUNDAY 13
61 Holywell
95 The Priors Farm
101 Sandle Cottage

WEDNESDAY 16
25 Buckland Stead
73 The Little Cottage
122 White Barn

THURSDAY 17
26 The Buildings
106 Tanglefoot

SATURDAY 19
60 Hinton Ampner
112 The Vyne

SUNDAY 20
17 Berry Cottage
21 Bramdean House
26 The Buildings
45 7 Downland Close
62 The Homestead
100 28 St Ronan's Avenue
104 Shalden Park House
106 Tanglefoot
108 Treeside

MONDAY 21
45 7 Downland Close
108 Treeside

TUESDAY 22
108 Treeside

WEDNESDAY 23
43 Dean House
122 White Barn

FRIDAY 25
12 19 Barnwood Road (Evening)
20 Braemoor

SATURDAY 26
93 The Old Station

SUNDAY 27
20 Braemoor
66 The Hyde
82 Meon Orchard
87 Mottisfont Abbey & Garden
101 Sandle Cottage

TUESDAY 29
66 The Hyde

WEDNESDAY 30
122 White Barn

August

FRIDAY 1
30 Christchurch Road Gardens (Evening)

SATURDAY 2
54 Garden Cottage
100 28 St Ronan's Avenue (Evening)
103 'Selborne'

SUNDAY 3
30 Christchurch Road Gardens
43 Dean House
54 Garden Cottage
58 Hill House
84 Merdon Manor
101 Sandle Cottage
103 'Selborne'
123 The White Cottage

MONDAY 4
103 'Selborne'
123 The White Cottage

TUESDAY 5
58 Hill House

WEDNESDAY 6
25 Buckland Stead
73 The Little Cottage

THURSDAY 7
91 The Old Rectory, Swarraton

SATURDAY 9
119 Westward

SUNDAY 10
17 Berry Cottage
21 Bramdean House
91 The Old Rectory, Swarraton
119 Westward

SATURDAY 16
120 Wheatley House

SUNDAY 17
66 The Hyde
117 West Silchester Hall
120 Wheatley House

TUESDAY 19
66 The Hyde

WEDNESDAY 20
25 Buckland Stead

THURSDAY 21
26 The Buildings

FRIDAY 22
20 Braemoor

SUNDAY 24
1 Abbey Cottage
20 Braemoor
26 The Buildings
52 Fritham Lodge
56 Heathlands

MONDAY 25
1 Abbey Cottage
55 Hambledon House

SUNDAY 31
85 Mittens
94 Old Thatch
113 Wades House

September

MONDAY 1
113 Wades House

WEDNESDAY 3
73 The Little Cottage

SUNDAY 7
17 Berry Cottage
49 Farleigh House
67 Ibthorpe Tower
74 Little Court
82 Meon Orchard

WEDNESDAY 10
67 Ibthorpe Tower

SUNDAY 14
21 Bramdean House
35 The Coach House
59 2 Hillside Cottages
98 Rotherfield Park
116 Weir House

WEDNESDAY 17
7 Appletree House

THURSDAY 18
26 The Buildings

SATURDAY 20
60 Hinton Ampner

SUNDAY 21
24 Broadhatch House
26 The Buildings
60 Hinton Ampner

WEDNESDAY 24
4 23 Anglesey Road

February 2009

SUNDAY 15
21 Bramdean House

SUNDAY 22
74 Little Court

MONDAY 23
74 Little Court

TUESDAY 24
74 Little Court

Gardens open to the public

3 Alverstoke Crescent Garden
5 Apple Court
21 Bramdean House
48 Exbury Gardens & Steam Railway
60 Hinton Ampner
64 Houghton Lodge Garden
79 Macpennys Woodland Garden & Nurseries
87 Mottisfont Abbey & Garden
105 Spinners
112 The Vyne

By appointment only

33 The Clock House
34 Closewood House
36 Colemore House Gardens
68 Kimpton House
78 Longthatch
109 Tunworth Old Rectory

Also open by appointment

2 80 Abbey Road
4 23 Anglesey Road
7 Appletree House
9 Atheling Villas
10 Barhi, 27 Reynolds Dale
12 19 Barnwood Road
13 Beechcroft
14 Beechenwood Farm
15 Avenue Cottage, Bentley Village Gardens
16 Bere Mill
17 Berry Cottage
19 Borough Farm
20 Braemoor
24 Broadhatch House
25 Buckland Stead
31 Church Close
32 Clibdens
35 The Coach House
38 The Cottage
41 Crookley Pool
42 Cygnet House
45 7 Downland Close
46 Durmast House
50 Flintstones

51 The Fountains
52 Fritham Lodge
53 2 Colthouse Lane, Froyle Gardens
55 Hambledon House
57 Highfield
59 2 Hillside Cottages
62 The Homestead
65 The House in the Wood
66 The Hyde
69 53 Ladywood
70 Lake House
71 60 Lealand Road
72 Linden Barn
73 The Little Cottage
74 Little Court
82 Meon Orchard
84 Merdon Manor
85 Mittens
88 Mulberry House
89 Oakdene
92 The Old Ship
97 4 Mill Lane, Romsey Gardens
98 Rotherfield Park
99 St Christopher's
100 28 St Ronan's Avenue
101 Sandle Cottage
102 Sandy Slopes
103 'Selborne'
106 Tanglefoot
113 Wades House
114 Walbury
116 Weir House
117 West Silchester Hall
118 26 & 29 Weston Allotments
119 Westward
120 Wheatley House
122 White Barn
123 The White Cottage
126 Wrens Farm

A small garden with big ideas. Bold foliage plants, trees and shrubs jostle for space . . .

The Gardens

1 ABBEY COTTAGE
Itchen Abbas SO21 1BN. Patrick Daniell, www.abbeycottage.net. *2¹/₂ m W of Alresford. On B3047 between Kingworthy and Alresford, ¹/₂ m E of the Trout Inn at Itchen Abbas.* Home-made teas. **Adm £3, chd free. Wed 2 Apr; Suns, Mons 4, 5 May; 9 June; 24, 25 Aug (12-5). Also open 9 June Cygnet House.**
This organic garden, on alkaline soil, is a fine garden by any standards. Inside the C18 walls of an old kitchen garden there are enclosures, on different levels, which together create an inspirational garden. The adjoining meadow contains specimen trees, an orchard, spring bulbs, summer wild flowers and a plantation of native trees.

  ♿ ☓ ✿ ☕

2 80 ABBEY ROAD
Fareham PO15 5HW. Brian & Vivienne Garford, 01329 843939, vgarford@aol.com. *1m W of Fareham. From M27 J9 take A27 E towards Fareham for approx 2 miles. At top of hill (past Titchfield gyratory) turn L at T-lights into Highland Rd. Turn 4th R into Blackbrook Rd. Abbey Rd 4th turning on L.* Home-made teas. **Adm £2.50, chd free. Sun 27 Apr (11-5). Evening Opening £3.50, wine, Fri 11 July (6-9). Visitors also welcome by appt.**
Small garden with extensive collection of herbs and unusual plants of botanical and historical interest, many of which are for sale. Formal box edging provides structure for the more relaxed planting. Interesting use of containers, and other ideas for small gardens. Two small ponds and tiny meadow area attract wide range of butterflies and other wildlife. Garden trails for children. Living willow seat, trained grapevine. Featured on BBC Breakfast TV to launch the celebrations for the NGS's 80th birthday.

  ☓ ✿ ☕ ☎

3 ◆ ALVERSTOKE CRESCENT GARDEN
Crescent Road, Gosport PO12 2DH. Gosport Borough Council, 02392 586403. *1m S of Gosport. From A32 & Gosport follow signs for Stokes Bay. Continue alongside bay to small roundabout, turn L into Anglesey Rd. Crescent Garden signed 50yds on R.* **Adm by donation. Open daily all yr.**
Restored Regency ornamental garden, designed to enhance fine Crescent (Owen, 1826). Trees, walks and flowers lovingly maintained by community/Council partnership. Garden's considerable local historic interest now highlighted by impressive restoration and creative planting of adjacent St Mark's churchyard. Worth seeing together - heritage, history and horticulture: a fascinating package. Winner Green Flag Award (Civic Trust) and Green Heritage Site Award (both 2007/8) in conjunction with St Mark's churchyard. Gravel paths, limited wheelchair access to churchyard.

  ♿

4 23 ANGLESEY ROAD
Aldershot GU12 4RF. Adrian & Elizabeth Whiteley, 01252 677623. *On E edge of Aldershot. From A331 take A323 towards Aldershot. Keep in R-hand lane, turn R at T-lights into North Lane, then immed L into Lower Newport Rd. Round bend turn immed R into Newport Rd, 1st R into Wilson Rd. Round L-hand bend turn immed R into Roberts Rd, Anglesey Rd 1st on L. Please park considerately in local rds.* **Adm £2, chd free. Weds 21 May; 24 Sept (2-6). Visitors also welcome by appt.**
A small garden with big ideas. Bold foliage plants, trees and shrubs jostle for space with perennials, annuals and bulbs grown for ever-changing colour. Hollies, ferns and bamboos provide an evergreen backdrop in dramatic triangular beds, a greenhouse protects exotics and a pond harbours frogs, dragonflies and newts.

  ☓ ✿ ☕ ☎

5 ◆ APPLE COURT
Hordle Lane, Hordle, Lymington SO41 0HU. Charles & Angela Meads, 01590 642130, www.applecourt.com. *4m W of Lymington. From A337 between Lymington & New Milton, turn into Hordle Lane at Royal Oak at Downton Xrds.* **Adm £3, chd free. Fris, Sats, Suns & Bank Hol Mons 7 Mar to 31 Oct (10-5).**
1¹/₂ -acre formally designed and exuberantly planted sheltered walled garden. Theatrical white garden, extensive ornamental grass plantings, subtropical borders. 70 metre hosta walk. International display gardens of day lilies, fern walk, Japanese-style garden with koi pond. Featured on Solent Radio and in 'Hampshire Country Gardener' & 'Hampshire Life'.

  ♿ ☓ ✿ 🛏 ☕

6 APPLESHAW MANOR
nr Andover SP11 9BH. **Mr & Mrs
Patrick Walker.** 5m NW of Andover.
Take A342 Andover to Marlborough rd.
Turn to Appleshaw 1m W of Weyhill.
Fork L at playing field, on R after 1/2 m,
nr church. Disabled parking by house.
Home-made teas. **Adm £3, chd free
(share to St Peter in the Wood
Church).** Sun 23, Mon 24 Mar (2-5).
7-acre walled mature gardens, incl
wide lawns, wood garden, arboretum,
kitchen garden and pond. Carpets of
spring bulbs and notable yew and
beech hedges.
&. ⊛ ☕

7 APPLETREE HOUSE
Station Road, Soberton SO32 3QU.
Mrs J Dover, 01489 877333. 10m N
of Fareham. A32 N to Droxford, at Xrds
turn R B2150. Turn R under bridge into
Station Rd, garden 1m. Parking in lay-
by 300yds or in rd. Light lunches &
teas. **Adm £2.50, chd free.** Weds 4
June; 9 July; 17 Sept (12-3.30).
**Visitors also welcome by appt, small
groups/individuals welcome.**
This small and closely planted country
garden has over 55 varieties of
clematis and 45 of roses growing over,
under and in between numerous
shrubs, some unusual as well as over
obleisks and arches. Perennials and
grasses fill the gaps. Paths meander,
seating areas give lovely vistas accross
the garden. Featured on Radio Solent
and Meridian TV.
✵ ⊛ ☕ ☎

8 APPLETREES
267 Botley Rd, Burridge SO31 1BS.
Kath & Ray Butcher. From A27 take
A3051 Park Gate to Botley, on L after
1 1/2 m. From Botley take A3051,
Appletrees is 2m on R. **Adm £3, chd
free.** Sat 21, Sun 22 June (2-5).
Flower arrangers' 1/3 -acre garden
densely planted with perennials, good
foliage. Large patio with sinks and
containers. Many winding paths with
seats, small pond and waterfall.
✵

9 ATHELING VILLAS
16 Atheling Road, Hythe,
Southampton SO45 6BR. **Mary &
Peter York, 02380 849349,
athelingvillas@mac.com.** 7m E of
Lyndhurst. Leave M27 J2, follow A326
signed Hythe and Fawley. Go across all
roundabouts until Dibden roundabout
(1/2 m after Marchwood Priory
Hospital). Turn L towards Hythe. After
Shell garage, Atheling Road is 2nd L.

Home-made teas. **Adm £2.50, chd
free (share to Hythe2000).** Sat 15,
Sun 16 Mar; Tue 15, Wed 16 Apr;
Sat 3, Sun 4 May; Tue 17, Wed 18
June (2-5). **Visitors also welcome by
appt, groups of 10+.**
'Winding paths, archways,
shrubberies, dry weather planting,
shady nooks, and sunny flower beds.
A garden for all seasons, with surprises
around every corner' (Waterside
Herald). 1/3 acre with wide range of less
usual trees and shrubs. Species bulbs;
trained fruit on original garden wall;
teas in gardener's cottage. Self-guide
leaflet.
✵ ⊛ ☕ ☎

10 BARHI, 27 REYNOLDS DALE
Ashurst, Southampton SO40 7PS.
**Ms F Barnes, 02380 860046,
fbarnes@barhi.net.** 6m W of
Southampton. From M27, J2 take
A326 to Fawley. At 4th roundabout L
into Cocklydown Lane. At mini
roundabout L into Ibbotson Way. 1st L
into Reynolds Dale and follow signs.
Home-made teas. **Adm £2.50, chd
free.** Sat 7, Sun 8 June (2-5). **Also
open nearby The Fountains.
Visitors also welcome by appt.**
Compact 6yr-old 'modern cottage'
garden shared with 3 lively Springer
Spaniels, designed around a
chambered nautilus spiral. No lawn, so
lots of space for plants. The dense
planting, meandering paths, secluded
pergola, rasied formal pond and feature
patio have led visitors to describe the
garden as 'Tardis-like'. Our dogs will be
in the garden on open days.
&. ☕ ☎

11 BARNCROFT GARDENS
Appleshaw SP11 9BU. 5m NW of
Andover. Take A342 Andover to
Marlborough rd. Turn to Appleshaw
1m W of Weyhill. After 1/2 m park on R
in field. Home-made teas at Haleakala.
Combined adm £4, chd free. Sun 8,
Mon 9 June (2-5.30).
Small pretty village, population approx
500. Lovely church, pub and village
green.
☕

HALEAKALA
Jenny & Roger Bateman
Half-acre 7yr-old shrub and
herbaceous garden, designed by
owners for yr-round colour and
interest. Winding paths, large
pond and rockery, summerhouse,
gravel garden, secret sitting
places, unusual plants.
✵

THE JAYS
Judith & Alec Clarke
1/2 -acre garden redesigned and
restored in past 7yrs. Various fruit
and flowering trees, mixed
borders, rockeries, fish pond and
bog garden. This garden is
specially designed to attract
wildlife.
✵ ⊛

Shady nooks,
and sunny
flower beds.
A garden for
all seasons,
with surprises
around every
corner . . .

12 19 BARNWOOD ROAD
Fareham PO15 5LA. **Jill & Michael
Hill, thegarden19@btinternet.com.**
1m W of Fareham. From M27 J9 take
A27 towards Fareham. At top of hill
past Titchfield Mill PH turn L at T-lights
into Highlands Rd. Take 4th turning R
into Blackbrook Rd, Meadow Bank 4th
turning on R. Barnwood Rd is off
Meadow Bank. Home-made teas.
Adm £2.50, chd free. Sun 29 June
(11-5). **Evening Opening £3.50,
wine & light refreshments, Fri 25
July (6-10). Visitors also welcome by
appt. Please email or apply in
writing.**
Step through the gate to an
enchanting garden designed for peace
with an abundance of floral colour and
delightful features. Greek-style
courtyard leads to natural pond with
bridge and bog garden,
complemented by a thatched
summerhouse and jetty, designed and
built by owners. Secret pathways,
mosaic seating area and hexagonal
greenhouse.
✵ ⊛ ☕ ☎

13 **NEW** **BEECHCROFT**
Hundred Acres Road, Wickham, Fareham PO17 6HY. Maggie & David Smith, 01329 835122, david.smith@physics.org. *5m N of Fareham, 1¹/₂ m E of Wickham. From A32 at Wickham take B2177 E. Turn 1st L after 1¹/₂ m into Hundred Acres Rd, Beechcroft approx ¹/₄ m on R over brow of hill.* Home-made teas. **Adm £2.50, chd free. Sun 25, Mon 26 May (11-5). Visitors also welcome by appt.**
Challenging 1-acre plot developed over the last 5yrs. Main garden has generous borders with wide variety of trees, shrubs and perennials, 2 wildlife ponds and greenhouse. Steeply-sloping wild flower bank with fruit trees and coppiced willows descends to natural pond and bog garden and rises to orchard and large fruit/vegetable cage. Steep slopes, limited disabled access.
&. ❀ ☕ ☎

14 **BEECHENWOOD FARM**
Odiham RG29 1JA. Mr & Mrs M Heber-Percy, 01256 702300, beechenwood@totalise.co.uk. *5m SE of Hook. Turn S into King St from Odiham High St. Turn L after cricket ground for Hillside. Take 2nd turn R after 1¹/₂ m, modern house ¹/₂ m.* Home-made teas. **Adm £3, chd free. Every Wed 26 Mar to 11 June (2-5). Visitors also welcome by appt Apr to June only, no coaches.**
2-acre garden of many parts; woodland garden with spring bulbs, walled herb garden, rose garden, pergola, containers, orchard and rock garden with grasses and ferns. Belvedere with spectacular views. 8-acre copse of native species (planted 1992) with grassed rides and paths. Gravel drive.
&. ❀ ☕ ☎

15 **BENTLEY VILLAGE GARDENS**
GU10 5JA. *4m NE of Alton off A31 (Bentley bypass). Turn off A31 into village. At Xrds, Main Road, three gardens at E end of village, one at W end. Follow signs.* Home-made teas at Tila. **Combined adm £4, chd free. Sat 7, Sun 8 June (2-5.30).**
Four gardens, each very different, in Bentley village. Maps given to all visitors. Art work at Avenue Cottage, plants for sale at The Kilns.
☕

AVENUE COTTAGE
David & Rosie Darrah, 01420 23225. *At Main Rd turn E, ¹/₂ m on R.* **Visitors also welcome by appt.**
Pretty, partly-walled cottage garden, formal herb garden and potager. Art studio. Featured in 'Country Living' feature: Inspiration for Small Gardens. Gravel path.
&. ✗ ❀ ☎

BAY TREE COTTAGE
Andrew & Mary Thomson. *At Main Rd turn E, approx ¹/₄ m on R. Opp playing field*
Cottage garden of approx ¹/₄ acre. Curving lawn leads past shrubbery, herbaceous, vegetable and soft fruit areas. Small pond with visiting newts.
&. ✗

THE KILNS
Mascha & Richard Tyrrell. *L at Xrds, 200yds on R is lane marked Bentley Garden Farm. Last house down lane on R*
Garden reclaimed from a concrete wasteland. Unusual plants in mixed herbaceous borders; courtyard and lawns.
✗ ❀

NEW **TILA**
John & Lizzie Jackson. *At Main Rd, turn E, approx ¹/₄ m on L*
Garden in wooded setting. Lawned area surrounded by mixed borders with herbaceous and shrub roses. Vegetable and soft fruit areas and greenhouse. Gravel paths.
&. ✗ ❀

16 **BERE MILL**
London Road, Whitchurch RG28 7NH. Rupert & Elizabeth Nabarro, rnabarro@aol.com. *9m E of Andover, 12m N of Winchester. In centre of Whitchurch, take London Rd at roundabout. Up hill 1m, turn R 50yds beyond The Gables on R. Drop-off point for disabled at garden.* **Adm £4, chd free (share to The Smile Train). Sun 30, Mon 31 Mar; Mon 26 May (2-6). Visitors also welcome by appt throughout year, Fris and eves preferred, £5 per person.**
Garden created since 1993 around the 1712 mill (not open) where Portals first made bank notepaper. Set by the R Test and carrier streams, a large lozenge-shaped site, loosely fashioned on a Japanese stroll garden.

Herbaceous and Mediterranean beds; replanted walled orchard and vegetable garden; wisteria garden and lake with Japanese tea-house. Extensively planted with bulbs; irises a speciality. Sculpture. Belted Galloway cattle, black Welsh mountain sheep and lambs. Featured in 'Country Homes & Interiors', 'Hampshire Chronicle' & 'Hampshire Country Magazine'. Unfenced and unguarded rivers and streams.
&. ❀ ☕ ☎

Wild flower bank with fruit trees and coppiced willows descends to natural pond . . .

17 **BERRY COTTAGE**
Church Road, Farringdon, nr Alton GU34 3EG. Mrs P Watts, 01420 588318. *3m S of Alton off A32. Turn L at Xrds, Ist L into Church Rd. Follow rd past Masseys Folley, 2nd house on R opp church.* Cream teas. **Adm £2.50, chd free. Suns 27 Apr; 18 May; 22 June; 6, 20 July; 10 Aug; 7 Sept (2.30-6). Visitors also welcome by appt in June & July.**
Small organic cottage garden with all-yr interest. Spring bulbs, roses, clematis and herbaceous borders. Pond and bog garden. Shrubbery and small kitchen garden. Featured as Reader's Garden in 'Amateur Gardening'.
☕ ☎

18 **BLUEBELL COTTAGE**
Broadway, Froxfield, Petersfield GU32 1DT. Mr & Mrs T Clarke. *3¹/₂ m NW of Petersfield. Between top of Stoner Hill & Froxfield Green, or take sign to Froxfield off A272 opp Bordean House & follow yellow signs.* **Adm £2.50, chd free. Sun 4, Mon 5 May (2-6).**
One-acre, owner-maintained garden incl a small bluebell wood, mature trees, lawns, mixed borders, arbour overlooking the pond, summerhouse, bridge over dry ditch, conservatory, kitchen garden with raised beds, fruit garden and greenhouse. Featured in 'Period Living'.
✗

Plants that thrive with no watering on thin chalk soil address the challenge of climate change . . .

Traditional 6-acre garden on chalk, famous for mirror-image herbaceous borders. Carpets of bulbs, especially snowdrops, in the spring. Very many unusual plants incl collection of old-fashioned sweet peas. 1-acre kitchen garden featuring prizewinning vegetables, fruit and flowers. Group visits by arrangement, not weekends, £4.50 per person. Featured the the 'FT' as one of the 5 best gardens to visit this summer.

  ♿ ⚲ ❀ ⊕ ☕

㉒ BRANDY MOUNT HOUSE
Alresford SO24 9EG. Caryl & Michael Baron, www.brandymount.co.uk. *nr Alresford centre. From centre, 1st R in East St before Sun Lane. Please leave cars in Broad St or stn car park.* Home-made teas. **Adm £3, chd free. Sat 9 Feb (11-4).**
1-acre, informal plantsman's garden. Spring bulbs, hellebores, species geraniums. National Collections of snowdrops and daphnes. European primulas, expanding collection of dwarf narcissi, herbaceous and woodland plants. New raised bed to display early spring bulbs. Limited wheelchair access: no unsupervised wheelchairs or mobility cars allowed.

  ♿ ❀ **NCCPG** ☕

㉓ 6 BREAMORE CLOSE
Eastleigh SO50 4QB. Mr & Mrs R Trenchard. *1m N of Eastleigh. M3 J12, follow signs to Eastleigh. Turn R at roundabout into Woodside Ave, then 1st L into Broadlands Ave (park here). Breamore Close 3rd on L.* Home-made teas. **Adm £2.50, chd free. Suns, Mons 4, 5 May; 1, 2 June (1-5.30).**
Delightful ½ -acre plant lover's garden designed with coloured foliage and unusual plants, giving a pleasing tapestry effect of texture and colour. Many different hostas displayed in pots. The peaceful garden is laid out in distinctive planting themes with many seating areas to sit and contemplate. Over 60 clematis scramble up fences, through roses and over a pergola which displays a magnificent wisteria (flowers 3ft-4ft long) in late spring.

  ♿ ⚲ ❀ ☕

㉔ BROADHATCH HOUSE
Bentley, Farnham GU10 5JJ. Bruce & Lizzie Powell, 01420 23185, lizzie.powell@btconnect.com. *4m NE of Alton. Turn off A31 (Bentley bypass), R through village up School*

Lane. R to Perrylands, after 300yds drive on R. Home-made teas. **Adm £3, chd free. Suns 20 Apr; 21 Sept (2-5.30). Visitors also welcome by appt in June & July.**
3½ acres with yew hedges separating different gardens. Formal pools and large borders, climber-covered walls, and potager. Very wide range of interesting and rare plants. Gravel paths in some areas.

  ♿ ⚲ ❀ ⊕ ☕ ☎

㉕ BUCKLAND STEAD
Sway Road, nr Lymington SO41 8NN. Valerie & John Woolcott, 01590 673465, valwoolcott@ukonline.co.uk. *1m N of Lymington town centre. Off A337. Pass Toll House Inn, 1st L into Sway Rd. After 300yds, at sharp R-hand bend, turn L into Buckland Granaries entrance. Follow signs to garden.* **Adm £2.50, chd free. Weds 4, 18 June; 2, 16 July; 6, 20 Aug (2-5). Also open The Little Cottage** 18 June, 16 July, 6 Aug. **Visitors also welcome by appt.**
Two gardens in one: 'His and Hers'. Tranquil ¼ acre designed and maintained by owners. His: formal rose garden with lavender edging filling the air with fragrance. Shady walk through 'neutral zone' to Hers: less formal with colour themes using herbaceous perennials and grasses. Winding paths, archways, pergola and water features.

  ♿ ⚲ ❀ ☕ ☎

㉖ NEW THE BUILDINGS
Broughton, Stockbridge SO20 8BH. Dick & Gillian Pugh. *3m W of Stockbridge. NGS yellow signs 2m W of Stockbridge off A30, or 6m N of Romsey off B3084.* Light refreshments. **Adm £3, chd free (share to Friends of St Mary's Broughton with St James' Bossington). Thurs, Suns 17, 20 July; 21, 24 Aug; 18, 21 Sept (2-6).**
In the old cattle yard of this converted downland farmstead, a circular dry garden flourishes. Plants that thrive with no watering on thin chalk soil address the challenge of climate change. An adjoining area features an exuberant pergola. Dramatic grasses, many viticella clematis and rare pelargoniums are specialities. Far-reaching views.

  ♿ ⚲ ❀ ☕

㉙ NEW BOROUGH FARM
SO21 3AA. Mr & Mrs J Dockray, 01962 774026, gilldockray@waitrose.com. *Nr Winchester. On Stoke Charity road out of Micheldever village.* Home-made teas. **Adm £3, chd free. Sun 8 (2-5), Tue 10 June (11-5). Visitors also welcome by appt.**
Traditional farmhouse country garden and old farm buildings. Manicured lawns with shrub borders and trees; old walled garden planted with an abundance of colourful perennials, peonies, poppies and grasses.

  ☕ ☎

㉚ BRAEMOOR
Bleak Hill, Harbridge, Fordingbridge BH24 3PX. Tracy & John Netherway & Judy Spratt, 01425 652983, jnetherway@btinternet.com. *2½ m S of Fordingbridge. Turn off A338 at Ibsley. Go through Harbridge village to T-junction at top of hill, turn R for ¼ m.* Cream teas. **Adm £2.50, chd free. Fris, Suns 20, 22 June; 4, 6, 25, 27 July; 22, 24 Aug (2-5.30). Visitors also welcome by appt.**
¾ -acre garden of mixed cottage-style herbaceous borders overflowing with colourful planting, roses and unusual plants. Realistic stream and pond. New beach style area. Two greenhouses with collections of cacti and carnivorous plants. Vegetables, fruit and wild flower beds. Small adjacent nursery.

  ⚲ ❀ ☕ ☎

㉑ ◆ BRAMDEAN HOUSE
Bramdean SO24 0JU. Mr & Mrs H Wakefield, 01962 771214. *4m S of Alresford. In centre of village on A272.* **Adm £3.50, chd free. For NGS: Suns 17 Feb; 16 Mar; 20 Apr; 15 June; 20 July; 10 Aug; 14 Sept (2-5). Sun 15 Feb 2009.**

27 2 CARISBROOKE ROAD
Gosport PO13 0HQ. Chris & Norma Matthews. *3m S of Fareham. Exit M27 J11 signed Fareham Central. Follow A32, Gosport. Take fork at Newgate Lane signed Lee-on-Solent. At 3rd roundabout 1st exit B3334 signed Rowner. L at T-lights, 1st house on R.* Home-made teas. **Adm £3, chd free. Sat 28, Sun 29 June (10-4).** 1/3 -acre cottage-style garden developed by owners over 17yrs. Shrubs, herbaceous perennials, gravel and alpine gardens give yr-round interest. Raised organic kitchen garden. Interesting colourful baskets and containers with plants propagated by owners. Wildlife area and garden, birds enthusiastically encouraged. Fishpond and miniature wildlife pond.

28 21 CHESTNUT ROAD
Brockenhurst SO42 7RF. Iain & Mary Hayter. *4m S of Lyndhurst. S on A337 to Brockenhurst, take R fork B3055, Grigg Lane, opp Careys Manor Hotel. Garden 500yds from junction via 2nd L Chestnut Rd and 2nd L again for no 21. Parking limited; please use village car park nearby.* Home-made teas. **Adm £3, chd free. Thur 29 May (11-5); Fri 30 May, Day (11-5, £3) & Evening Opening (6-9, £3.50),** wine. **Sat 14 June (11-5), Sun 15 June (2-6).**
From pastels to hots, this colourful garden has sunny and shady areas and a secret kitchen and wild flower garden which mix with formal and casual areas. American irises, roses and climbers adorn a circular pergola. Raised deck over a wildlife pond accompany further water features in this 1/3 -acre garden. Photographic exhibition of American irises. Featured in 'Woman's Weekly'.

29 CHILLAND HOUSE
Martyr Worthy SO21 1EB. Mr & Mrs Andrew Impey. *7m NE of Winchester. On B3047 between Martyr Worthy & Itchen Abbas, signed Chilland.* **Adm £3, chd free. Sun 25, Mon 26 May (2-5).**
4 acres with stream overlooking R Itchen and watermeadows, woods and farmland beyond. Large collection of mature shrubs planned for yr-round colour effects. Many fine trees and shrubs incl huge plane and ancient mulberry, nutwalk, spring bulbs, clematis, herbaceous borders and flowering shrubs.

30 NEW CHRISTCHURCH ROAD GARDENS
Winchester SO23 9SR. *Leave centre of Winchester by Southgate St, 1st R into St James Lane, 3rd L into Christchurch Rd.* Home-made teas. **Combined adm £5, chd free. Evening Opening,** wine, **Fri 1 Aug (6-8). Sun 3 Aug (2-6).** Spacious town gardens in central Winchester.

NEW CARLTON LODGE
13 Christchurch Road. The Louden family
A variety of groundcover perennials, with all-yr interest. Compatible with busy family and dogs. Specimen hoheria, koelreuteria and Irish yew.

NEW 12 CHRISTCHURCH ROAD
Mrs Penny Patton
Exuberant planting in town garden. Drive has slate-edged rill bordered by climbers. Small front garden designed to be viewed from bedrooms.

31 CHURCH CLOSE
Northington SO24 9TH. Mr & Mrs Swithinbank, 01962 733623, sharon.swithinbank@googlemail.com. *4m N of Alresford. Follow B3046 N from Alresford to Northington. From Basingstoke or Winchester take A33, turning at dual carriageway to Northington. Park in church car park.* Home-made teas. **Adm £2.50, chd free. Sun 15, Mon 16 June (11-5).** Also open 15 June **Linden Barn.** Visitors also welcome by appt.
Hidden away below the church you will find a pretty cottage garden with views across the Candover valley. You are drawn into the garden through borders planted with different colour themes. A gap in the mature yew hedge beckons you to explore the lower garden with its unexpected circular potager and wild flowers.

32 CLIBDENS
Chalton PO8 0BG. Michael & Jacqueline Budden, 02392 592172. *6m S of Petersfield. Turn L off A3 N at Horndean then directly R over motorway to Chalton. Clibdens is 1st turning on L in village, directly before Chalton village sign.* Home-made teas and wine. **Adm £3.50, chd free. Fri**

13, Sun 15 June (11-5.30). **Visitors also welcome by appt May & June.** 1-acre walled garden surrounded by farmland with fine views to Windmill Hill. Chalk garden with 4 rooms of lawn, shrubs and herbaceous plants. Terrace with stone pots of agapanthus, box, lavender and yew topiary. Gravel garden, stump garden and wildlife pond. Rose garden with oak posts and rope arches. All beautifully gardened and maintained. Reopening for NGS after 3 years.

Hidden away below the church you will find a pretty cottage garden with views across the Candover valley . . .

33 THE CLOCK HOUSE
nr Sparsholt, Winchester SO21 2LX. Mr & Mrs Robert Harman, 01962 776461, rozzieharman@freeuk.com. *3 1/2 m W of Winchester. Off B3049 between Winchester & Stockbridge (3 1/2 m & 6 1/2 m). Watch for staggered sign with bend on B3049, then turn N up farm lane opp hoardings for Sparsholt College. After 300yds turn L & go to end. Avoid signs to Sparsholt College. Parking in field.* Home-made teas. **Adm £3, chd free. Visitors welcome by appt May to Aug, groups of 20+ welcome.**
2 acres incl large walled garden with traditional herbaceous borders and climbing roses. Wisteria and laburnum arch. Mature specimen trees. Pond and extensive views. Large greenhouse, well stocked.

34 CLOSEWOOD HOUSE
Newlands Lane, Denmead PO7 6TP.
Mrs P Clowes, 02392 264213. *1m W of Waterlooville. Take Closewood Rd to W of B2150 between Waterlooville & Denmead. Turn L at T-junction after 1/2 m. Signs to car park after 330yds.* **Adm £3.50. Visitors welcome by appt May to 15th July.**
4 1/2 acres. Collection of scented roses incl large climbers and shrubs with good vistas between sections. 200 different specimen trees and grass walk. Box parterre, fishpond and large abstract sculpture. Picnics welcome by stream.

35 THE COACH HOUSE
South Warnborough RG29 1RR.
John & Sarah Taylor, 01256 862782, johntaylormw@hotmail.com. *5m N of Alton on B3349. In the middle of village opp village shop/post office. Car parking in lay-by opp.* Home-made teas Suns only. **Adm £2.50, chd free. Suns 6 July; 14 Sept (2-6). Evening Opening** £4, wine, Fri 4 July (5-9). **Visitors also welcome by appt June, July & Sept only, groups of 10+.**
3/4 acre of semi-walled garden almost entirely given over to plantings of perennials and grasses in a naturalistic and informal style. Gravel planting and deep generous beds with an emphasis on height and proximity to plants. Featured on BBC TV Gardeners' World and in 'Period Living'.

36 COLEMORE HOUSE GARDENS
Colemore, Alton GU34 3RX. Mr & Mrs Simon de Zoete, 01420 588202, simondezoete@gmail.com. *5m S of Alton. Take turning to Colemore (Shell Lane) off A32, just S of E Tisted.* **Adm £3, chd free. Visitors welcome by appt, groups of 20+.**
Situated in beautiful unspoilt country, 2 1/2 acres with wide variety of unusual plants. Yew and box hedges, mixed herbaceous and shrub borders, yellow and blue garden, rose walk and excellent lawns. Garden is being constantly developed and incl spectacular water rill, swimming pool garden and the creation of a wild flower, tree and shrub area. Many different roses, salvias, penstemons and tender plants and bulbs.

37 CONHOLT PARK
Hungerford Lane, nr Chute SP11 9HA. Professor Caroline Tisdall. *7m N of Andover. Turn N off A342 Andover to Devizes rd at Weyhill Church. Go 5m N through Clanville & Tangley Bottom. Turn L at Conholt 1/2 m on R, just off Chute causeway. A343 to Hurstbourne Tarrant, turn to and go through Vernham Dean, next turn L signed Conholt.* Home-made teas. **Adm £3.50, chd free. Suns 8, 22 June (2-5).**
10 acres surrounding Regency house (not open), rose, 'Calor', Shakespeare, winter and secret gardens. Restored 1 1/2 -acre walled garden with potager, berry wall, rare fruit orchard, white border, mahonia, hardy geraniums and allium collections. All completely organic. Romantic Edwardian Ladies' Walk and possibly longest maze in Britain. Ornate copper rose fountain. On farm unusual animals incl bison, wild boar and a shire horse.

Mature woodland garden bejewelled with luminous camellias . . .

38 THE COTTAGE
16 Lakewood Road, Chandler's Ford SO53 1ES. Hugh & Barbara Sykes, 02380 254521. *2m NW of Eastleigh. Leave M3 at J12, follow signs to Chandler's Ford. At King Rufus on Winchester Rd, turn R into Merdon Ave, then 3rd rd on L.* Home-made teas. **Adm £2.50, chd free. Suns, Mons 4, 5, 18, 19 May (2-6). Visitors also welcome by appt in Apr & May.**
3/4 acre. Azaleas, bog garden, camellias, dogwoods, erythroniums, free-range bantams, greenhouse grapes, honey from our bees, irises, jasmines, kitchen garden, landscaping began in 1950, maintained by owners, new planting, osmunda, ponds, quiz for children, rhododendrons, smilacina, trilliums, unusual plants, viscum, wildlife areas, eXuberant foliage, yr-round interest, zantedeschia. Described in 'Hampshire Life' as 'a mature woodland garden bejewelled with luminous camellias'.

39 CRANBURY PARK
Otterbourne SO21 2HL. Mr & Mrs Chamberlayne-Macdonald. *3m NW of Eastleigh. Main entrance on old A33 between Winchester and Southampton, by bus stop at top of Otterbourne Hill. Entrances also in Hocombe Rd, Chandler's Ford and next to church in Otterbourne.* Home-made teas. **Adm £5, chd free (share to St Matthew's Church, Otterbourne). Sun 15 June (2-6).**
Extensive pleasure grounds laid out in late C18 and early C19 by Papworth; fountains, rose garden, specimen trees and pinetum, lakeside walk and fern walk. Family carriages and collection of prams will be on view, also photos of King George VI, Eisenhower and Montgomery reviewing Canadian troops at Cranbury before D-Day. Make this your Fathers' Day outing.

40 CRAWLEY GARDENS
nr Winchester SO21 2PU. *5m NW of Winchester. Off A272 or A3049 Winchester to Stockbridge rd. Parking at top of village nr church or in Littleton Rd.* Home-made teas at Village Hall, or Little Court, weather permitting. **Combined adm: April £4, June £5, chd free. Fri 18, Sun 20 Apr; Thur 26, Sun 29 June (2-5.30).**
Exceptionally pretty small village with thatched houses, C14 church and village pond. Many other good front gardens visible from the road.

BARN COTTAGE
Mr & Mrs K Wren. Not open April dates.
3/4 -acre landscaped garden surrounds a converted barn. To the front, an informal area of coppiced birch, small trees and shrubs incl a magnificent rose 'Cerise Bouquet', all surrounded by clipped hedging. To the rear, painted trellising divides a courtyard garden into 3 areas where viticella clematis, roses and jasmine scramble and bee-loving plants abound.

NEW BAY TREE HOUSE
Julia & Charles Whiteaway. Not open April dates.
Contemporary garden created during the last 5yrs. Features incl a rill, pleached lime square, large borders, potager and fruit trees with wild flowers. Development ongoing. Gravel drive and path.

NEW COB HOUSE
SO21 2PZ. Mr & Mrs R A Bayford. Not open June dates.
Flowering trees, long sweeping border with shrubs. Stunning views, to the church and across open countryside. Gravel drive and paths.
♿ ✂

LITTLE COURT
Prof & Mrs A R Elkington
(See separate entry).
♿ ✂ ☘

PAIGE COTTAGE
Mr & Mrs T W Parker. Not open June dates.
1 acre of traditional English country garden incl grass tennis court (not open) and walled Italian-style swimming pool (not open); spring garden with large variety of bulbs and wild flowers.
♿ ✂

TANGLEFOOT
Mr & Mrs F J Fratter. Not open April dates.
(See separate entry).
♿ ✂ ☘

41 CROOKLEY POOL
Blendworth Lane, Horndean PO8 0NB. Mr & Mrs Simon Privett, 02392 592662. *5m S of Petersfield. 2m E of Waterlooville, off A3. From Horndean village go up Blendworth Lane between bakery and hairdresser. Entrance 200yds before church on L with white railings, behind Gales Brewery.* Home-made teas. **Adm £4, chd free.** Sun 1 June (2-5). Visitors also welcome by appt.
English country garden built around a Victorian swimming pool. Large greenhouse, overflowing borders full of colour. Wisteria-covered pergolas and walls, orchard, herb garden, walled kitchen garden. Organic. Free range bantams & other animals. Flower paintings on view.
♿ ✂ ☘ ☕ ☎

42 CYGNET HOUSE
Martyr Worthy SO21 1DZ. Mr & Mrs Shane Chichester, 01962 779315. *5m E of Winchester. On B3047, 1st house on R after war memorial.* Home-made teas. **Adm £2.50, chd free.** Sun 8 June (2-6), Mon 9 June (10.30-5). Opening with **Martyr Worthy Gardens** 8 June. Also open 9 June **Abbey Cottage.** Visitors also welcome by appt.
Attractively laid out terraced garden, with stunning views over the Itchen Valley, developed by the owners since 1980. Large number of old-fashioned roses, many repeat flowering. Interesting shrubs and climbers and wide range of perennials incl many that do well in the shady, wooded area. Emphasis on colour, good structure and design, ensuring there is something to see throughout the year. Gravel paths. Unfenced swimming pool.
♿ ☘ ☕ ☎

43 DEAN HOUSE
Kilmeston SO24 0NL. Mr P H R Gwyn, www.deanhousegardens.co.uk. *5m S of Alresford. Via village of Cheriton or off A272 signed at Cheriton Xrds.* Cream teas. **Adm £3, chd free.** Tue 27 May; Wed 18 June; Sun 6, Wed 23 July; Sun 3 Aug (Tues, Weds 10-4, Suns 12-5).
The 9 acres has been described as 'a well-kept secret hidden beside the elegant facade of its Georgian centrepiece' with mixed and herbaceous borders, symmetrical rose garden, pond garden, working walled garden and glasshouses, sweeping lawns, York stone and gravel pathways and many young and mature trees and hedges. Wheelchair access to main part of garden, many gravel paths.
♿ ☘ ☕

44 DIPLEY MILL
Dipley RG27 8JP. Mr J P McMonigall. *2m NE of Hook. Turn E off B3349 at Mattingley (1½ m N of Hook) signed Hartley Wintney, West Green and Dipley. Dipley Mill ½ m on L just over bridge.* Home-made teas. **Adm £3, chd free (share to St Michael's Hospice).** Sun 22 June (2-5).
Mentioned in Domesday Book, Mill House (not open) sits on an island site beside the R Whitewater in remarkably picturesque setting. Large garden where herbaceous borders surround millpond. Tree ferns, fuchsia garden, pleached hornbeams, roses, hothouse with subtropical plants. Wild flower meadow.
✂ ☕

45 NEW 7 DOWNLAND CLOSE
Locks Heath, nr Fareham SO31 6WB. Roy Dorland, 01489 571788, roydorland@hotmail.co.uk. *3m W of Fareham. Leave M27 J9 (Whitely). Follow A27 on Southampton Rd to Park Gate. L into Locks Rd, 3rd R into Meadow Ave, 2nd L into Downland Close.* Home-made teas. **Adm £2.50, regret not suitable for small children.** Suns, Mons 25, 26 May; 22, 23 June; 20, 21 July (11-5). Visitors also welcome by appt, June to Aug, groups of 10+ only.
Visit this beautiful and inspirational 45ft x 45ft plantsman's garden, packed with ideas for the 'modest-sized' plot. Many varieties of hardy geraniums, hostas, heucheras, shrubs, ferns and other unusual perennials, weaving a tapestry of harmonious colour. Attractive water feature, plenty of seating areas and charming summerhouse. Gold Medal and Overall Plantsman's Winner, Fareham in Bloom.
✂ ☘ ☕

46 DURMAST HOUSE
Burley BH24 4AT. Mr & Mrs P E G Daubeney, 01425 403527, philip@daubeney.co.uk. *5m SE of Ringwood. Off Burley to Lyndhurst rd, nr White Buck Hotel.* Cream teas. **Adm £3, chd free (share to Delhi Commonwealth Womens' Assn Clinic).** Suns 23 Mar; 29 June (2-5). Visitors also welcome by appt.
2008 is the centennial of the planting of the Gertrude Jekyll garden which is in the process of being restored from the original plans. Formal rose garden edged with Munstead lavender, 130 yr-old Monterey pine, rare Pinus armandii from Kew and Victorian rockery. Lutyens-style summerhouse on original site, restored azalea walk and Jekyll herbaceous borders. Listed in Hampshire Register of Historic Gardens. Featured on Gardeners' World.
♿ ☘ ☕ ☎

2008 is the centennial of the planting of the Gertrude Jekyll garden which is in the process of being restored . . .

Plantswoman's garden designed for continual interest with vegetable plot, wildlife ponds and chickens. 'Cottage garden meets the Good Life'. Visits from hedgehogs, newts, frogs and the occasional grass snake. . . .

47 EAST LANE

Ovington SO24 0RA. Sir Peter & Lady Ramsbotham. *1m W of Alresford, off A31. From A31, Winchester to Alresford, immed after roundabout 1m W of Alresford, small sign to Ovington. Turn sharp L up incline, down small country rd to Ovington. East Lane is only house on L, 500yds down hill towards Bush Inn.* Home-made teas. **Adm £3.50, chd free. Sun 30 Mar** (2-5.30).
Charming 5-acre woodland garden. Large lawn leading up to white gazebo and arboretum with fine views. Collection of mature shrubs interspersed with an acre of spring bulbs. Herbaceous borders. Walled rose garden. Large terraced water garden overlooking water meadows with stream flowing through.
❀ ☕

48 ◆ EXBURY GARDENS & STEAM RAILWAY

Southampton SO45 1AZ. Edmund de Rothschild, 02380 891203, www.exbury.co.uk. *16m S of Southampton. 4m Beaulieu. Exbury 20mins M27 J2.* **Adm £7.50, chd £1.50, concessions £7. Open daily 8 Mar to 9 Nov** (10-5.30).
Created by Lionel de Rothschild in the 1920s, the gardens are a stunning vision of his inspiration offering 200 acres of natural beauty and horticultural variety. Woodland garden with world-famous displays of rhododendrons, azaleas, camellias and magnolias. Rock garden, exotic garden, herbaceous gardens, ponds, cascades, river walk and seasonal trails. Steam railway (wheelchair accessible) and Summer Lane Garden are popular favourites.
♿ ❀ ☕

49 FARLEIGH HOUSE

Farleigh Wallop, nr Basingstoke RG25 2HT. The Earl & Countess of Portsmouth. *3m SE of Basingstoke. Off B3046 Basingstoke to Preston Candover rd.* Cream teas. **Adm £3.50, chd free. Suns 15 June; 7 Sept** (2-5).
Contemporary garden of great tranquillity designed by Georgia Langton, surrounded by wonderful views. 3-acre walled garden in three sections: ornamental potager, formal rose garden and wild rose garden. Greenhouse full of exotics, serpentine yew walk, contemplative pond garden and lake with planting for wildlife. Approx 10 acres and 1 hour to walk around.
♿ ☕

50 FLINTSTONES

Sciviers Lane, Durley SO32 2AG. June & Bill Butler, 01489 860880. *5m E of Eastleigh. From M3 J11 follow signs for Marwell Zoo. From B2177 turn R opp Woodman PH. From M27 J7 follow signs for Fair Oak then Durley, turn L at Robin Hood PH.* Teas Apr, home-made teas June. **Adm £2.50, chd free** (share to Camphill Village Trust & Durley Church). **Sun 30 Mar** (2-5); **Sun 1, Mon 2 June** (2-6). **Evening Opening** £4, wine, **Tue 10 June** (6.30-8.30). **Visitors also welcome by appt in Apr, May & June only, for 30 max, no coaches.**
³/₄ acre designed and developed entirely by owners. Plantswoman's garden densely planted on clay, with many unusual and interesting plants, providing a pleasing tapestry effect of texture and colour, for all-yr interest. Wheelchair mobility difficult if very wet.
♿ ⚡ ❀ ☕ ☎

51 THE FOUNTAINS

34 Frampton Way, Totton SO40 9AE. Mrs J Abel, 02380 865939. *5m W of Southampton. M271 J3 onto A35 Totton bypass for lm to roundabout. Circle roundabout and return up A35. Immed L into Rushington Ave, then follow signs.* Home-made teas. **Adm £2.50, chd free. Sat 7, Sun 8 June** (2-5). **Also open nearby Barhi, 27 Reynolds Dale. Visitors also welcome by appt.**
Unusually shaped ¼ -acre garden bordered by hedges and filled with a variety of fruit trees, soft fruit cordons and espaliers. Trellis covered in rambling roses and clematis. Plantswoman's garden designed for continual interest with vegetable plot, wildlife ponds and chickens. 'Cottage garden meets the Good Life'. Visits from hedgehogs, newts, frogs and the occasional grass snake.
❀ ☕ ☎

52 FRITHAM LODGE

Fritham SO43 7HH. Mr & Mrs Christopher Powell, 02380 812650, chris.powell@ddblondon.com. *6m N of Lyndhurst. 3m NW of M27 J1 Cadnam. Follow signs to Fritham.* Cream teas. **Adm £3, chd free. Sun 24 Aug** (2-5). **Visitors also welcome by appt.**
Set in heart of New Forest in 18 acres; with 1-acre old walled garden round Grade II listed C17 house (not open) originally one of Charles II hunting lodges. Parterre of old roses, potager with wide variety of vegetables, herbs and fruit trees, pergola, herbaceous and blue and white mixed borders, ponds, walk across hay meadows to woodland and stream, with ponies, donkeys, rare breed Poitou donkeys and rare breed hens.
♿ ❀ ☕ ☎

53 FROYLE GARDENS

GU34 4LJ. *5m NE of Alton. Access to Lower Froyle from A31 between Alton & Farnham, at Bentley. Follow signs from Lower Froyle to Upper Froyle.* Home-made teas at Lower Froyle Village Hall. **Combined adm £5, chd free. Sat 31 May; Sun 1 June** (2-6). 'The Village of Saints'. Maps given to all visitors. Display of C16 & C17 vestments in Froyle Church.
☕

BRAMLINS

Lower Froyle. Mrs A Blunt
Informally planted to harmonise with surrounding countryside and to provide variety of material for

nationally-known flower arranger. Wild flowers in small orchard. Conservatory with unusual plants. Gravel drive.

&♿ ⊛

BROCAS FARM
Lower Froyle. Mr & Mrs J Dundas
Grade II listed house (not open) covered in roses, wisteria and clematis. 2 acres of well-established mature gardens divided by yew and beech hedges. Herbaceous borders, interesting small arboretum, orchard and charming box hedged kitchen garden.

&♿ ✂

NEW 2 COLTHOUSE LANE
West End Farm, Upper Froyle. Susan & Tony Goodsell, 01420 525272. Visitors also welcome by appt in June & July.
Cottage garden full of colour. Vegetables, fruit, greenhouses and several interesting features. Chickens and vintage tractors.

&♿ ✂ ☎

THE COTTAGE
Lower Froyle. Mr & Mrs Carr
Not only plants, but a collection of animals frequently associated with a true cottage garden.

✂ ⊛

THE OLD SCHOOL
Upper Froyle. Nigel & Linda Bulpitt
Mature and revamped garden, mainly perennials with climbing roses and shrubs. Small wild area making a foil between garden and countryside.

&♿ ✂

WALBURY
Lower Froyle. Ernie & Brenda Milam
(See separate entry).

&♿ ⊛

WARREN COTTAGE
Lower Froyle. Mrs A A Robertson
Garden surrounds C18 cottage (not open). Many interesting plants and lovely views.

✂ ⊛

54 GARDEN COTTAGE
3 St Helens Road, Hayling Island PO11 0BT. Mr & Mrs Norman Vaughan. *6m S of Havant. From Beachlands on seafront, turn R, then 3rd on R into Staunton Ave, then 1st L.*

Parking in drive. Police dispensation for rd parking. Light refreshments & teas. **Adm £2.50, chd free. Sat 2, Sun 3 Aug (11-5).**
Highly maintained residential garden on $1/3$ acre. Ongoing refurbishment to reduce labour-intensive maintenance, but retaining main features of interesting trees, shrubs and roses, set off by fine lawn, thatched summerhouse, large planting of dahlias and David Austin shrub roses, water feature with koi. Photographic exhibition of urban landscapes.

&♿ ✂ ⊛ ☕

55 HAMBLEDON HOUSE
Hambledon PO7 4RU. Capt & Mrs David Hart Dyke, 02392 632380. *8m SW of Petersfield, 5m NW of Waterlooville. In village centre.* Home-made teas. **Adm £3, chd free. Mon 25 Aug (2-5). Visitors also welcome by appt Apr to Sept for groups.**
2 acres partly walled plantsman's garden for all seasons. Large borders filled with wide variety of unusual shrubs and imaginative plant combinations. Large collection of salvias, hardy geraniums and ornamental grasses. Hidden, secluded areas reveal surprise views of garden and village rooftops. Featured in 'Period Living'.

✂ ⊛ ☕ ☎

Secluded areas reveal surprise views of garden . . .

56 HEATHLANDS
47 Locks Road, Locks Heath, nr Fareham SO31 6NS. Dr & Mrs John Burwell. *5m W of Fareham. From M27 J9, go W on A27 towards Southampton. After 1m in Parkgate (just after pelican crossing) turn L into Locks Rd. No. 47 is 1m down on R.* Home-made teas. **Adm £3, chd free. Suns 2 Mar; 6 Apr; 24 Aug (2-5.30).**
1-acre plantsman's garden designed and developed by owner since 1967. Yr-round interest against background of evergreens and mature trees. Spring bulbs, rhododendrons, paulownias, cyclamen, ferns and many unusual

plants. Topiary peacock, small herbaceous border, scree and secret garden. National Collection of Japanese anemones. Starred garden in 'GGG'.

&♿ ⊛ NCCPG ☕

57 HIGHFIELD
Malthouse Close, Easton SO21 1ES. Mr & Mrs Geoff Dee, 01962 779426. *3m E of Winchester. From B3047 (Winchester to Alresford) take turn signed Easton. Pass Cricketers Inn on L, and immed turn R up hill. In 200yds turn R into Malthouse Close, Highfield at end.* **Adm £2.50, chd free. Fri 4, Sun 6 Apr; Fri 6, Sun 8 June (2-5). Visitors also welcome by appt Apr to July.**
This $1/2$ -acre garden started in 1967 when a local farmer rotavated it for us. Now we have a pond, many herbaceous borders, vegetable garden, terrace and conservatory, together yielding colour most of the year. In 2003 a further $1/2$ acre of the adjoining field was acquired giving a feling of space. No steep steps, slopes are gentle with plenty of seats.

&♿ ⊛ ☎

58 HILL HOUSE
Old Alresford SO24 9DY. Mrs W F Richardson. *1m W of Alresford. From Alresford 1m along B3046 towards Basingstoke, then R by church.* Home-made teas. **Adm £2.50, chd free. Sun 3, Tue 5 Aug (1.30-5).**
2 acres with large old-fashioned herbaceous border, established in 1938, and shrub beds set around large lawn; large kitchen garden. Dried flowers. Dexter cows and bantams.

&♿ ⊛ ☕

59 2 HILLSIDE COTTAGES
Trampers Lane, North Boarhunt PO17 6DA. John & Lynsey Pink, 01329 832786. *5m N of Fareham. 3m E of Wickham. From A32 at Wickham take B2177 E. Trampers Lane 2nd on L (approx 2m). Hillside Cottages approx $1/2$ m on L.* Home-made teas. **Adm £2.50, chd free. Sun 14 Sept (2-6). Visitors also welcome by appt.**
An acre of plantsman's garden with sweeping mixed borders. Island bed annually planted with exotic plants and salvias dominates the view from the house. Holders of the National Collection of salvia spp which are planted throughout the garden along with many unusual shrubs and herbaceous plants.

&♿ ⊛ NCCPG ☕ ☎

60 ◆ **HINTON AMPNER**
Alresford SO24 0LA. The National Trust, 01962 771305, www.nationaltrust.org.uk. 3½ m S of Alresford. S on A272 Petersfield to Winchester rd. House & garden adm £6.80, chd £3.40. Garden only £5.90, chd £2.95. Mid Mar to end Oct. Days & times vary according to season; please phone or see website for details. For NGS: Sats, Suns 19, 20 Apr; 14 June; 19 July; 20, 21 Sept (11-5).
12 acres; C20 shrub garden designed by Ralph Dutton. Strong architectural elements using yew and box topiary; spectacular views. Bold effects using simple plants, restrained and dramatic bedding. Orchard with spring wild flowers and bulbs within formal box hedges; magnolia and philadelphus walks. Dell garden made from chalk pit. Shrub rose border dating from 1950s. Walled garden now restored.
& ✗ ☕

Garden created by the owner to reflect her flower arranging passion for colour and texture . . .

61 **HOLYWELL**
Swanmore SO32 2QE. Earl & Countess of Clarendon. 12m SE of Winchester. On A32 S of Droxford between Droxford and Wickham. Light refreshments & home-made teas. Adm £4, chd free. Suns 18 May; 13 July (2-6).
Large garden in rural woodland and lakeside setting. Colourful organic kitchen garden, greenhouse, borders, roses, trees and shrubs. Pergola walk. Mature woodland garden with many acid-loving specimens.
& ✗ ✾ ☕

62 **THE HOMESTEAD**
Northney Road, Hayling Island PO11 0NF. Stan & Mary Pike, 02392 464888. 3m S of Havant. From A27 Havant/Hayling Island roundabout, travel S over Langstone Bridge & turn

immed L into Northney Rd. 1st house on R after Langstone Hotel. Home-made teas. Adm £2.50, chd free. Sun 20 July (1-5). Visitors also welcome by appt.
1-acre garden developed and maintained by owners. Features incl pleached lime walk, pergola, arbour and ponds. Lawn surrounded by herbaceous beds and shrub borders with additional alpine beds and interesting trees. Small walled garden contains trained fruit trees, formal herb garden and vegetables.
& ✾ ☕ ☎

63 **HORDLE WALHAMPTON SCHOOL**
Beaulieu Road, Lymington SO41 5ZG. Hordle Walhampton School Trust Ltd. 1m E of Lymington. From Lymington follow signs to Beaulieu (B3054) for 1m & turn R into main entrance at 1st school sign 200yds after reaching top of hill. Adm £3.50, chd free (share to St John's Church). Sun 27 Apr (2-6).
97-acre grounds of C18/19 manor (not open). Landscape: naturalistic derived from styles of: early C18 formal, English and late C18 picturesque (influenced by Capability Brown); early C19 picturesque/Gothic; late C19/early C20 Italianate revival (influence of Peto); early C20 Arts and Crafts (Mawson's designs). Features: lakes, canal, mount, banana house, shell grotto, vistas and views of IOW. Guided tours. Gravel paths, lakes and ponds, grassy slopes.
& ✗ ☕

64 ◆ **HOUGHTON LODGE GARDEN**
nr Stockbridge SO20 6LQ. Captain M W Busk, 01264 810502, www.houghtonlodge.co.uk. 1½ m S of Stockbridge. From A30 on minor rd towards Houghton village. Adm £5, chd free. Daily Mar to Oct 10-5, Weds by appt (except NGS days). For NGS: Sun 20 Apr; Weds 28 May; 25 June (10-5).
Tranquil setting of spacious lawns and fine trees frames an enchanting C18 Cottage Orné overlooking the unspoilt beauty of R Test, fringed with wild flowers. Mown meadow walks. Traditional kitchen garden. Formal and informal planting. New displays of spring bulbs, greenhouses with orchids. Children's quiz and drawing materials. Snorting topiary 'dragon'. Lots of seats and 2 alpacas.
& ☕

65 **THE HOUSE IN THE WOOD**
Beaulieu SO42 7YN. Victoria Roberts, 01590 612089, mail@beaulieufinearts.co.uk. 8m NE of Lymington. Leaving the entrance to Beaulieu motor museum on R (B3056) take the next R turn signed Ipley Cross. Take 2nd gravel drive on RH-bend, approx ½ m. Cream teas. Adm £3.50, chd free. Sun 11 May (2-6). Visitors also welcome by appt, groups of 10+.
Charming woodland garden set in 12 acres specialising in rhododendrons and azaleas. Large lawn, views and walk down to a lake at the bottom. The area was used during the war to train the Special Operations Executive.
✾ ☕ ☎

66 **THE HYDE**
Old Alresford SO24 9DH. Sue Alexander, 01962 732043. 1m W of Alresford. From Alresford 1m along B3046 towards Basingstoke. House in centre of village, opp village green. Home-made teas. Adm £3, chd free. Suns, Tues 27, 29 July; 17, 19 Aug (1.30-5). Visitors also welcome by appt in Aug, coaches permitted.
Tucked away behind an old field hedge, a delightful ¾ -acre garden created by the owner to attract wildlife and reflect her flower arranging passion for colour and texture. Flowing borders contain an abundant mixture of perennials, half-hardies, annuals, grasses and shrubs. Interesting planting for shady areas. Featured in BBC The Gardener's Year. Short gravel drive at entrance.
& ✗ ✾ ☕ ☎

67 **IBTHORPE TOWER**
Windmill Hill, Hurtsbourne Tarrant SP11 0DQ. Mr & Mrs P Gregory. 5m N of Andover. Off A343 at top of Hurstbourne Hill, signed The Chutes and Tangley. 1st turning on R. Home-made teas. Adm £3, chd free. Sun 7, Wed 10 Sept (11-5).
3½ acres of garden planted in contemporary style, focusing on colour and texture, in tranquil spot, elevated and with glorious views. Large wildlife pond, woodland garden, potager and long banks and large borders planted with hardy perennials in imaginative drifts.
✾ ☕

KENT HOUSE
See Sussex.

68 KIMPTON HOUSE
Lower Durford Wood, nr Petersfield GU31 5AS. Mr & Mrs Christopher Napier, 01730 892151. *1½ m NE of Petersfield. B2070 N of Petersfield towards Rake. Pass A272 junction to Midhurst. ½ m further on turn R into white gates marked 'Durford Wood, Lower Wood only'. Kimpton House ½ m on R.* **Adm £3. Visitors welcome by appt in July & Aug only for groups of 10+. No coaches.**
10 acres of gardens with panoramic views of S Downs. Large traditional herbaceous and shrub borders with topiary in a formal setting. Contemporary tropical garden where temperatures regularly reach 110°F. Formal French garden of pleaching and topiary. Herb garden. Woodland areas. Water features and wild flower butterfly meadow.

69 53 LADYWOOD
Eastleigh SO50 4RW. Mr & Mrs D Ward, 023 8061 5389, sueatladywood@btinternet.com. *1m N of Eastleigh. Leave M3 J12. Follow signs to Eastleigh. Turn R at roundabout into Woodside Ave, then 2nd R into Bosville. Ladywood 5th on R. Park in Bosville.* **Cream teas Suns only. Adm £3, chd free. Suns (11-5), Mons (2-5) 27, 28 Apr; 22, 23 June. Visitors also welcome by appt Apr to July for groups of 10+.**
45ft x 45ft with dozens of ideas for small gardens. Over 1800 different plants labelled. Trellis fences provide vertical space for many clematis and unusual climbers to wander. Many special interest foliage plants from pulmonarias in spring, through brunneras, heucheras and miniature hostas to a wonderful display of phlox paniculata and grasses in July. All carefully designed to create peace and harmony in a delightful town garden.

70 LAKE HOUSE
Northington SO24 9TG. Lord Ashburton, 01962 734256, or apply in writing. *4m N of Alresford. Off B3046. Follow English Heritage signs to The Grange, then directions.* **Home-made teas. Adm £4, chd free. Sun 1, Tue 3 June (12.30-5). Visitors also welcome by appt, coaches permitted, groups of 10+ preferred.**
2 large lakes in Candover Valley set off by mature woodland with waterfalls, abundant bird life, long landscaped vistas and folly. 1½-acre walled garden, mixed borders, long herbaceous border, rose pergola leading to moon gate. Formal kitchen garden, flowering pots, conservatory and greenhouses. Picnicking by lakes.

71 60 LEALAND ROAD
Drayton, Portsmouth PO6 1LZ. Mr F G Jacob, 02392 370030, jacob60lea@tiscali.co.uk. *2m E of Cosham. Old A27 (Havant Rd) between Cosham & Bedhampton.* **Home-made teas. Adm £2.50, chd free. Suns 27 Apr; 25 May; 22 June (1-5). Visitors also welcome by appt.**
Prizewinning garden with a difference, created by the owner since 1969. Plants from around the world incl palms, yuccas, echiums and cannas. Designed for maximum effect with lily ponds and rockery. Incl collection of bamboos and grasses, also cacti and other exotics in greenhouse.

72 NEW LINDEN BARN
Church Barns, Church Bank Road, East Stratton SO21 3XA. Terry & Vanessa Winters, 01962 774778, terry.winters@skyline.co.uk. *8m N of Winchester. 1m off A33 Basingstoke to Winchester rd, signed to East Stratton. Opp village church.* **Home-made teas in the church opp the garden. Adm £3, chd free. Sun 15 June (11-5). Also open Church Close. Visitors also welcome by appt May, June & July weekends only, £4 per person.**
⅓-acre garden created from old farmyard in 2001. Flowing herbaceous planting contained within topiary hedging with emphasis on structure and colour combinations. Gravel and paved paths, seating areas and many interesting vistas. Planting scheme creates drifts of colours using classic cottage garden plants alongside contemporary species. Specimen trees create woodland escape against backdrop of village church. Finalist in Daily Mail National Garden Competition 2007. Featured in '25 Beautiful Gardens', 'Daily Mail', 'House Beautiful' and foreign press.

73 THE LITTLE COTTAGE
Southampton Road (A337), Lymington SO41 9GZ. Peter & Lyn Prior, 01590 679395, web.mac.com/peternimrod. *1m N of Lymington town centre. On A337 opp Toll House Inn.* **Adm £2.50. Weds 18 June; 16 July; 6 Aug (2-5); 3 Sept (11-1 & 2-5). Also open Buckland Stead (not 3 Sept). Visitors also welcome by appt 18 June to 24 Sept only.**
Garden of unique and artistic design using unusual and interesting plants arranged to form pictures with arches, arbours and urns in secret rooms. Each room is hidden from the next and contrasts sharply in style and colour to stimulate, calm, excite or amaze, incl an outrageous black and white garden. Regret unsuitable for children. Occasional steps.

Planting scheme creates drifts of colours using classic cottage garden plants . . .

74 LITTLE COURT
Crawley, nr Winchester SO21 2PU. Prof & Mrs A R Elkington, 01962 776365, elkslc@tiscali.co.uk. *5m NW of Winchester. Off A272 or B3049, in Crawley village; 300yds from either village pond or church.* **Home-made teas (Suns & Bank Hol only) at Village Hall or Little Court, weather permitting. Adm £3.50, chd free. Suns, Tues 17, 19, 24, 26 Feb (2-5); Easter Mon 24 Mar; Fri 30 May; Sun 1 June; Sun 7 Sept (2-5.30). Sun 22, Mon 23, Tue 24 Feb 2009. Opening with Crawley Gardens Fri 18, Sun 20 Apr; Thur 26, Sun 29 June. Visitors also welcome by appt.**
Carpets of crocuses, then cowslips in the labyrinth. Large collection of perennials in harmonious colours, and climbers on ancient walls. This sheltered garden is in 7 parts, each with seating. Tree house with spectacular view appeals to all ages. Fine lawns, topiary, bantams and newts, fun for children. Traditional kitchen garden.

75 LITTLEWOOD
West Lane, Hayling Island PO11 0JW. Mr & Mrs Steven Schrier. *3m S of Havant. From A27 Havant/Hayling Island junction, travel S for 2m, turn R into West Lane and continue 1m. House set back from rd in wood. Disabled should drive to very top of drive.* Home-made teas. **Adm £3, chd free. Sat 3, Sun 4 May (11-5).**
2½ -acre woodland garden surrounded by fields and near sea, protected from sea winds by multi-barrier hedge. Rhododendrons, azaleas, camellias and many other shrubs. Woodland walk to full size tree house. Features incl pond, bog garden, house plants, summerhouse and many places to sit outside and under cover. Dogs on leads and picnickers welcome.
♿ ⊛ ☕

76 NEW LITTON LODGE
Clifton Road, Winchester SO22 5BP. Dr & Mrs J Theaker. *After passing city Westgate, cross railway bridge and take 2nd rd on R up hill, signed Clifton Rd.* Home-made teas. **Adm £3, chd free (share to Winchester Night Shelter). Sun 20 Apr (2-5).**
With fine views over the city, the ½ -acre, flint walled garden forms a microclime. Uncommon and exotic species of shrubs, spring bulbs and perennials create attractive colour-themed borders. Also of interest in this 'garden of all seasons' are the sedum thatch, rain harvester, working glasshouse, woodland and herb gardens.
♿ ☠ ⊛ ☕

77 LONGSTOCK PARK WATER GARDEN
nr Stockbridge SO20 6JF. Leckford Estate Ltd, part of John Lewis Partnership, www.longstockpark.co.uk. *4m S of Andover. From A30 turn N on to A3057; follow signs to Longstock.* Home-made teas at Longstock Park Nursery. **Adm £5, chd £1 (prices may alter). Sun 15 June (2-5).**
Famous water garden with extensive collection of aquatic and bog plants set in 7 acres of woodland with rhododendrons and azaleas. A walk through park leads to National Collections of *Buddleia* and *Clematis viticella*; arboretum, herbaceous border.
♿ ☠ ⊛ ☕

78 LONGTHATCH
Lippen Lane, Warnford SO32 3LE. Peter & Vera Short, 01730 829285. *12m N of Fareham. On A32, turn R from N or L from S at George & Falcon PH. After 100yds turn R at T-junction, continue for ¼ m; thatched C17 house on R.* **Adm £3, chd free. Visitors welcome by appt.**
3½ acres, plantsman's garden on R Meon. Rare trees and shrubs. Fine lawns, herbaceous borders, island beds and bog gardens. Spring-fed ponds, woodland area with hellebores, primulas and shade-loving plants. Bantams. Wheelchair access to lawn areas only.
♿ ☠ ⊛ ☎

LOWDER MILL
See Sussex.

2 different but complementary gardens ¼ mile apart, joined by lovely walk along Pilgrims Way through Itchen valley . . .

79 ◆ MACPENNYS WOODLAND GARDEN & NURSERIES
Burley Road, Bransgore, Christchurch BH23 8DB. Mr & Mrs T M Lowndes, 01425 672348, www.macpennys.co.uk. *6m S of Ringwood, 5m NE of Christchurch. Midway between Christchurch & Burley. From A35, at Xrds by The Crown Bransgore turn R & proceed ¼ m. From A31 (towards Bournemouth) L at Picket Post, signed Burley, then R at Burley Cross. Garden on L after 2m.* **Adm by donation. Daily 10 Jan to 24 Dec (10-5).**
12 acres; 4-acre gravel pit converted into woodland garden; many unusual plants. Large Gold awarded at New Forest & Hampshire County Show & Sir James Scott Cup for Best in Class.
⊛

MALT HOUSE
See Sussex.

80 MANOR HOUSE
Church Lane, Exton SO32 3NU. Mrs Charles Blackmore. *Off A32 just N of Corhampton. Next to Church.* Home-made teas 9 Feb, wine & light refreshments 22 June. **Adm £3, chd free. Sat 9 Feb (2-4); Sun 22 June (12-3).**
Step into an enchanting mature walled garden with splendid views. Woodland walk, masses of spring bulbs and plants. Garden rooms with large herbaceous borders, designed for peace and tranquillity, with an abundance of colours, old roses, clematis and many delightful features. Kitchen garden, box and pond areas. Featured in 'Country Homes & Interiors'.
☠ ⊛ ☕

81 MARTYR WORTHY GARDENS
SO21 1DZ. *5m E of Winchester. On B3047.* Home-made teas at Village Hall. **Adm £2.50 each garden, chd free. Sun 8 June (2-6).**
2 different but complementary gardens ¼ m apart, joined by lovely walk along Pilgrims Way through Itchen Valley. Plenty of parking at both.
☕

CYGNET HOUSE
Mr & Mrs Shane Chichester
See separate entry.
♿ ⊛

THE MANOR HOUSE
Charles & Isobel Pinder
Large garden, roses, mixed borders, lawns, shrubs and fine trees, next to C12 church and footbridge over R Itchen. Gravel drive and paths.
♿

MEADOW HOUSE
See Berkshire.

82 MEON ORCHARD
Kingsmead, N of Wickham PO17 5AU. Doug & Linda Smith, 01329 833253, doug.smith@btinternet.com. *5m N of Fareham. From Wickham take A32 N for 1½ m. Turn L at Roebuck Inn. Continue ½ m.* **Adm £3, chd free. Suns 1 June; 27 July; 7 Sept (2-6). Visitors also welcome by appt, groups welcome.**
1½ -acre garden designed and constructed by current owners. An exceptional range of rare, unusual and

architectural plants incl National Collections of Eucalyptus, Podocarpaceae & Araliaceae. Much use made of dramatic foliage plants from around the world, both hardy and tender, big bananas, huge taros, tree ferns, cannas, hedychiums and palms. Streams and ponds, combined with an extensive range of planters, complete the display. Owners available to answer questions. Plant sale of the exotic and rare Sun 7 Sept.

&. ⊛ NCCPG ☕ ☎

83 MEONSTOKE GARDENS
SO32 3NF. *12m SE of Winchester. Just off A32 between Corhampton & Droxford. Parking in field on R in Rectory Lane, opp Barton House.* Cream teas. **Combined adm £4, chd free. Sun 8 June (2-6). Evening Opening £5, wine, Fri 13 June (5-8).** Small pretty village on Meon River with village pub and beautiful C13 church.
☕

BARTON HOUSE
Rectory Lane. Peter Neill & Alison Munro
4-acre village garden on chalk adjoining church. Traditional flint and cob walled garden with peonies, roses, herbaceous plants; arched gateway (with horse teeth paving) leading to large outer garden with mature trees, extensive lawns, orchard, vegetable garden, pond, grass court, putting green and bunker. Wooden bridge over Winterbourne to churchyard.
&. ⋇ ⊛

THE OLD STORE
High Street. Ian & Jane McCormick
1/3 -acre cottage garden on chalk, with views of Corhampton Down. Terraced and designed in the last 10yrs by owners to make max use of sloping garden. Planted with 85 roses, over 50 varieties, mainly English shrub, climbers and old-fashioned. Compact vegetable garden using raised beds. Trees, shrubs, herbaceous and herbs.
⋇ ⊛

84 MERDON MANOR
Hursley SO21 2JJ. Mr & Mrs J C Smith, 01962 775215/281, vronk@bluebottle.com. *5m SW of Winchester. From A3090 Winchester to Romsey rd, turn R at Standon to Slackstead; proceed 1 1/2 m.* Home-made teas. **Adm £3, chd free. Sun 3 Aug (2-6). Visitors also welcome by**

appt, any number at any time by arrangement.
5 acres with panoramic views; herbaceous border, water lilies, large wisteria; selection of roses; fruit-bearing lemon trees and small secret walled water garden. Ha-ha and black Hebridean (St Kilda) sheep.
&. ⋇ ⊛ ☕ ☎

85 MITTENS
Mapledurwell RG25 2LG. Mr & Mrs David Hooper, 01256 321838. *3 1/2 m E of Basingstoke. Off A30 at Hatch, signed Mapledurwell. Over M3 bridge take 2nd R, Frog Lane, to Xrds at pond. 300yds up rd to Tunworth. No dedicated disabled parking.* Home-made teas. **Adm £3, chd free. Suns 30 Mar; 31 Aug (2-5). Visitors also welcome by appt.**
1 1/2 acres. Created from farmland in conservation area; spring bulbs, children's garden with rill and ivy house, secret garden with pool, pergola, nut arch, purple border, 2 major borders of red and yellow with colour from dahlias, cannas, gladioli and roses and hedges forming rooms. Gravel drive.
&. ⋇ ⊛ ☕ ☎

86 MONXTON GARDENS
SP11 8AS. *3m W of Andover. Between A303 & A343; parking in field on L in Chalkpit Lane.* Cream teas at village hall. **Combined adm £4, chd free. Sun 25, Mon 26 May (2-5.30).**
☕

HUTCHENS COTTAGE
Mr & Mrs R A Crick
3/4 -acre cottage garden with interesting scented plants: old roses, clematis, shrubs incl daphnes, mature trees, small orchard; mixed thyme patch and kitchen garden with developed compost and leaf mould systems.
&. ⋇ ⊛

WHITE GABLES
Mr & Mrs D Eaglesham
Cottage-style garden of 1/3 acre, leading down to Pill Hill Brook. Interesting trees, incl a young giant redwood, and shrubs, old roses and herbaceous plants.
&. ⋇ ⊛

87 ◆ MOTTISFONT ABBEY & GARDEN
Romsey SO51 0LP. The National Trust, 01794 340757, www.nationaltrust.org.uk. *4 1/2 m NW of Romsey. From A3057 Romsey to Stockbridge turn W at sign to*

Mottisfont. 6 wheelchairs & battery car service available at garden. **Adm £7.50, chd £3.80. Opening days & times vary according to season; please phone or see website for details. For NGS: Mon 24 Mar; Sat 5, Sun 27 July (11-5).**
Built C12 as Augustinian priory, now house of some note. 30-acre landscaped garden incl spring or 'font', from which house derives its name, magnificent ancient trees and walled gardens with National Collection of over 300 varieties of old roses. Tranquil walks in grounds, along the R Test and in the glorious countryside of the estate. Guided walks with Head Gardener on 5 July at 11.30 and 2.30.
&. ⋇ ⊛ NCCPG ☕

> Dramatic foliage plants from around the world, both hardy and tender, big bananas, huge taros . . .

88 MULBERRY HOUSE
7 Moorland Avenue, Barton-on-Sea, New Milton BH25 7DB. Rosemary & John Owen, 01425 612066, rojowen@btinternet.com. *6m W of Lymington. From the A337 (S of New Milton), going W, take L turn into Barton Court Ave and 4th R into Moorland Ave.* Home-made teas. **Adm £2.50, chd free (share to Oakhaven Hospice). Suns 22, 29 June (2-5). Visitors also welcome by appt.**
Pretty family garden of 1/4 acre with old-fashioned and modern roses; a scramble of clematis; traditional fruit trees incl medlar, mulberry and quince, plus hazel and cob nuts; good selection of hardy geraniums, and herb and vegetable areas. Late summer colour with a number of viticella clematis, salvias and penstemons. Relaxed, organic garden with much native planting to attract insect and bird life. Mason bee nests. Some narrow paths.
&. ⋇ ⊛ ☕ ☎

89 OAKDENE
Sandleheath, Fordingbridge
SP6 1TD. Shirley & Chris Stanford,
01425 652133, christopher.stanford
@homecall.co.uk. 1½ m W of
Fordingbridge. Adjacent to St
Aldhelm's Church. Cream teas. **Adm
£3, chd free. Suns 15, 22, 29 June
(2-5.30). Visitors also welcome by
appt.**
Think of a picture postcard country
garden with its croquet lawn, rose
garden and herbaceous borders; think
of lavender, clipped box and the scent
of 400 roses, an orchard with hens
foraging under apple, pear and plum
trees and with resident white doves
murmuring by a children's village shop.
Add a mature walled kitchen garden
with an abundance of vegetables, soft
fruits and flowers for cutting, then enter
a tea garden to enjoy in Joe Swift's
words 'the best tea in Hampshire'. This
is Oakdene, a joy for everyone.

OLD PINES HOUSE
See Berkshire.

90 NEW THE OLD RECTORY, HOUGHTON
**Church Lane, Houghton,
Stockbridge SO20 6LJ. Mr & Mrs
Richard Priestley.** 2m S of
Stockbridge. From Stockbridge
take minor rd S signed to
Houghton (2m). Turn R by war
memorial (opp Boot Inn) into
Church Lane. Garden 200yds on R
before church. Home-made teas.
**Adm £3, chd free. Sun 15 (2-6),
Mon 16 June (12-4).**
Fine views of the church and Test
Valley from this 4-acre village
garden. Traditional flint and cob
walled garden with prolific old-
fashioned roses. Mixed
herbaceous borders, rockery, herb
potager with pond, yew and thuja
hedges, rolling lawns. Teas in the
attractive yellow and blue pool
garden. Gravel paths.

91 NEW THE OLD RECTORY, SWARRATON
SO24 9TQ. Pam & Peter
Davidson. 4m N of Alresford.
Follow B3046 N from Alesford to
Swarraton, or from A33 turn at
dual carriageway to Northington,
then R at T-junction. Home-made
teas. **Adm £3, chd free. Thur 7
(11-5), Sun 10 Aug (2-6).**
Interesting, well designed 2-acre
garden with 13 acres of fields and
woodland. Courtyard garden with
topiary alongside thatched barn.
Subtle combinations of perennials
and unusual annuals, raised in
Victorian-style greenhouse,
cascade down terraced beds with
flint walls. Long traditional border.
Vegetable corner. Woodland walk
with old beeches. Alpacas.
Unfenced ponds.

92 NEW THE OLD SHIP
**Sandleheath, Fordingbridge
SP6 1PY. Mr & Mrs Marwood
Yeatman, 01425 656310,
anya@ayaltd.com.** 2m W of
Fordingbridge. From
Fordingbridge, 200yds past
Sandleheath Xrds, on L. Home-
made teas. **Adm £3, chd free.
Sun 6, Wed 9 July (2-7). Visitors
also welcome by appt.**
Modern English 2-acre garden,
carefully crafted, flowing and
informal with wild and controlled
areas. Richly-coloured borders of
contrasting textures featuring
alliums, euphorbias, salvias,
grasses etc. Gravel garden,
vegetable garden, meadow with
heritage fruit trees, circular pond
with great crested newts, managed
woodland and hazel coppice and
puggy mill. Chestnut structures,
ornamental willow and osier bed.

93 NEW THE OLD STATION
**Station Road, East Tisted
GU34 3QU. Susy Smith & Alex
Evans.** 4m S of Alton. At East
Tisted turn off A32 signed Hawkley,
Selborne and Priors Dean. Pass
church and village shops. Turn R
by pond. Home-made teas. **Adm
£3, chd free (share to Garden
Organic). Sats 26 Apr; 24 May;
26 July (2-6).**
Half-acre organic garden designed
around old railway buildings,
platforms, bridge and track with
carriage. Formal front garden with
box hedging and pleached limes,
looser planting in gravel behind. Lily
pond. Small orchard with wildlife
pond and bantams. Sunset
viewing deck. Kitchen garden with
glasshouse. Auricula collection.
Auriculas for sale.

94 NEW OLD THATCH
**Sprats Hatch Lane, Winchfield,
Hook RG27 8DD. Jill Ede.** 3m W
of Fleet. From A287 Odiham to
Farnham rd turn N to
Dogmersfield. L by Queens Head
PH and L opp Barley Mow PH.
From Winchfield stn car park turn R
towards Dogmersfield and after
1.3m R opp Barley Mow. Follow
signs for parking and disabled
access. Home-made teas. **Adm
£3, chd free. Suns 20 Apr; 31
Aug (2-5).**
Evolving smallholding alongside the
Basingstoke Canal (unfenced). A
succession of spring bulbs, a
profusion of wild flowers,
perennials and home-grown
annuals pollinated by our own bees
and fertilised by the donkeys, who
await your visit.

95 THE PRIORS FARM
**Reading Road, Mattingley
RG27 8JU. Mr & Mrs Miles Hudson.**
1½ m N of Hook. On B3349 Reading
Rd. Parking on green just N of Leather
Bottle PH. Entrance by gate on green
parking area. Light refreshments &
teas. **Adm £3, chd free. Sun 13 July
(2-5).**
3½-acre mixed border garden, rose
garden and orchard area with cedar
and other trees. Bog garden area and
swimming pool area. C15 granary and
goatery. Herb bed. Statuary.

Profusion of wild flowers, perennials
and home-grown annuals pollinated
by our own bees and fertilised by the
donkeys, who await your visit . . .

THE PRIORY
See Berkshire.

96 PYLEWELL PARK
Lymington SO41 5SJ. Lord
Teynham. *2m E of Lymington. Beyond
IOW car ferry.* **Adm £3, chd free.
Suns 4, 11 May (2-5).**
Very large garden of botanical
interest, dating from 1900. Fine trees,
flowering shrubs, rhododendrons,
with walk beside the lakes and
seashore.

97 ROMSEY GARDENS
SO51 8EU. *All within walking distance
of Romsey Abbey, clearly signed. Car
parking by King John's Garden.* Home-
made teas at King John's Garden.
**Combined adm £4, chd free. Sun
25, Mon 26 May (11-5.30).**
Small attractive market town with
notable Norman C12 Abbey, backdrop
to 4 Mill Lane. No hills and all shops
within walking distance.

KING JOHN'S GARDEN
Church Street. Friends of King
John's Garden & Test Valley
Borough
Listed C13 house (not open).
Historic garden planted with
material available up to 1700.
Award-winning Victorian garden
and North Courtyard with water
features. Some gravel paths.

THE LAKE HOUSE
64 Mill Lane. David & Lorraine
Henley. *At bottom of Mill Lane*
4½ acres, part garden, part
meadow, part lake. Wonderful
views from all aspects. Tranquillity
just 5 mins from Romsey town
centre.

4 MILL LANE
Miss J Flindall, 01794 513926.
Visitors also welcome by appt,
garden clubs and artists
welcome, up to 20 people.
Small, long, floriferous town
garden. S-facing. Backdrop
Romsey Abbey; original sculpture
and attractive hard landscaping.

98 ROTHERFIELD PARK
East Tisted, Alton GU34 3QE. Sir
James & Lady Scott, 01420 588207.
4m S of Alton on A32. **Adm £2.50,
chd free. Suns 4 May; 14 Sept (2-5).**
Visitors also welcome by appt in
May & Sept only.

Take some ancient ingredients: ice
house, ha-ha, lime avenue; add a
walled garden, fruit and vegetables,
trees and hedges; set this 12-acre plot
in an early C19 park (picnic here from
noon) with views to coin clichés about.
Mix in a bluebell wood in May and
apple-picking in September.
Reasonable wheelchair access.

99 ST CHRISTOPHER'S
Whitsbury, Fordingbridge SP6 3PZ.
Christine Southey & David Mussell,
01725 518404. *3½ m NW of
Fordingbridge. In village centre,
200yds down from Cartwheel PH.*
Cream teas & home-made cakes in
village hall. **Adm £2.50, chd free.
Suns 13, 20 Apr (1-6). Visitors also
welcome by appt May to July for
individuals and groups.**
Tranquil ³/₄ -acre long, sloping garden
with superb views. Alpines in S-facing
scree bed with unusual bulbs, incl
dwarf iris, tulips and narcissi, and
alpine troughs. In spring, wild banks of
bluebells and primroses, fern bed with
erythronium, hellebores and anemone
blanda. Many spring shrubs incl
mimosa. Pond and bog gardens full of
primula, a conservatory with many
unusual plants. In summer, 25ft
rambling roses, beds of delphiniums,
perennial geraniums, eremurus and
many herbaceous treasures. Fruit and
vegetable garden and several secret
seating areas. Breathtaking local
bluebell walks on public footpaths
adjacent to garden, map provided.
Featured in 'Hampshire Life'.

In spring, wild
banks of
bluebells and
primroses,
fern bed with
erythronium,
hellebores
and anemone
blanda . . .

100 28 ST RONAN'S AVENUE
Southsea PO4 0QE. Mr I Craig,
02392 787331,
ian.craig93@ntlworld.com,
www.28stronansavenue.com.
*Turn into St Ronan's Rd from Albert Rd
at junction opp Trinity Methodist
Church. St Ronan's Ave is a cul-de-
sac off St Ronan's Rd. Alternatively,
follow signs to seafront and then follow
yellow NGS signs from canoe lake and
Eastern Parade. Park at Craneswater
School.* Home-made teas. **Adm £2,
chd free (share to Craneswater
School). Suns 25 May; 20 July (2-6).
Evening Opening £3.50, wine, Sat
2 Aug (5-8). Visitors also welcome
by appt.**
Town garden 145ft x 25ft. Contains
many architectural and tender plants
including king protea, hedychium,
bananas, wild flower area, bog garden
and dry garden. Recycled items have
been used to create sculptures.
Featured in 'Hampshire Life' &
'Amateur Gardening'.

SANDHILL FARM HOUSE
See Sussex.

101 SANDLE COTTAGE
Sandleheath, Fordingbridge
SP6 1PY. Peter & Yo Beech, 01425
654638, peter@sandlecottage.com,
www.sandlecottage.com. *2m W of
Fordingbridge. Turn R at Sandleheath
Xrds. Entrance 50yds on L. Ample field
parking.* Home-made teas. **Adm £3,
chd free (share to Fordingbridge
URC). Suns 13, 27 July; 3 Aug (1.30-
5.30). Visitors also welcome by appt
in July only for groups,of 20+,
coaches welcome.**
3-acre garden designed and
maintained by the owners with displays
of dahlias (best on 27 July and 3 Aug),
annuals, sweet peas (best on 13 July)
and exotics. Features incl traditional
walled kitchen garden with many
varieties of vegetables; pretty sunken
garden; formal lawn with sharp edges;
3 greenhouses; lake with cascading
waterfall; circular summerhouse in
own cottage garden, a display of
fuchsias and woodland walk. Featured
in 'Kitchen Garden' & 'Wiltshire
Society'.

SANDLEFORD PLACE
See Berkshire.

102 SANDY SLOPES

Honeysuckle Lane, Headley Down GU35 8EH. Mr & Mrs R Thornton, 01428 717604. *6m S of Farnham. From A3 take B3002 through Grayshot, on to Headley Down. Turn L at mini roundabout by garage, down hill to 2nd turning L, bungalow 3rd drive on R. From Headley village take B3002 towards Grayshot, after S bend on to sharp L bend up hill to Honeysuckle Lane on R. Parking very limited.* Home-made teas. **Adm £2.50, chd £1. Sun 4, Mon 5 May (2-6). Visitors also welcome by appt.**
Sloping and partly terraced plantsman's and garden lecturer's garden with many special features incl woodland with rhododendrons, camellias, meconopsis, primulas and other seasonal plants. Stream and pool, herbaceous mixed shrub borders. Rock gardens. Many trees and unusual plants within about ¼ acre. Not suitable for those with walking difficulties; steep slopes and steps.

✕ ✿ ☕ ☎

103 'SELBORNE'

Caker Lane, East Worldham, Alton GU34 3AE. Brian & Mary Jones, 01420 83389, mary.trigwell-jones@virgin.net. *2m SE of Alton. On B3004 at Alton end of East Worldham opp The Three Horseshoes PH (please note, NOT in the village of Selborne). Parking signed.* Home-made teas. **Adm £2.50, chd free (share to St Mary's Church May & June, Tafara Mission Zimbabwe Aug). Sats, Suns: 19, 20 Apr; 17, 18 May (2-5); Fri 13 (also Evening Opening, see below), Sat 14, Sun 15 June (2-6); Sat 2, Sun 3, Mon 4 Aug (2-6). Evening Opening, £3.50, wine, Fri 13 June (6-8). Visitors also welcome by appt May to early Aug, individuals and groups welcome.**
½ -acre mature garden with old established orchard of named varieties. Meandering paths provide changing vistas across farmland. Mixed borders feature a large collection of hardy geraniums and other herbaceous plants and shrubs designed for yr-round effect. Shrubbery, soft fruit garden with greenhouse feature, metal and stone sculptures, containers, summerhouses. Listen to birdsong as you enjoy tea in the orchard's dappled shade, or in the conservatory. Book stall. Sandpit and garden quizzes for children. Some narrow paths may be slippery when wet.

♿ ✿ ☕ ☎

104 SHALDEN PARK HOUSE

The Avenue, Shalden GU34 4DS. Michael D C C Campbell. *4½ m NW of Alton. B3349 from Alton or J5 M3. Turn W at Golden Pot PH marked Herriard, Lasham, Shalden. Entrance ¼ m on L.* Light refreshments & home-made teas. **Adm £3, chd free (share to Red Cross, Hampshire). Sun 20 July (2-5).**
4-acre garden surrounded by woodland, redesigned in 2005/6 by Georgia Langton. Extensive views. Herbaceous borders. Walled kitchen garden and glasshouses. Early stage arboretum. Early picnics welcome.

♿ ☕

Listen to birdsong as you enjoy tea in the orchard's dappled shade . . .

105 ♦ SPINNERS

Spinners, School Lane, Boldre SO41 5QE. Peter Chappell, 01590 673347. *1½ m N of Lymington. Signed off A337 Brockenhurst to Lymington rd (do not follow sign to Boldre Church).* **Adm £3, chd under 6 free. Tues to Sats, 1 Apr to 13 Sept (10-5).**
Azaleas, rhododendrons, hydrangeas, maples and other rare shrubs interplanted with huge range of plants and woodland bulbs, especially erythroniums and trilliums. Plantings of Teller lace-cap hydrangeas and a range of the newer magnolias. Arboretum of magnolias and cornus open for the first time, on request. Free wheelchair entry to part of garden.

✕ ✿

SWALLOWFIELD HORTICULTURAL SOCIETY
See Berkshire.

106 TANGLEFOOT

Crawley, nr Winchester SO21 2QB. Mr & Mrs F J Fratter, 01962 776243, fred@tanglefoot-house.demon.co.uk. *5m NW of Winchester. Private lane beside entrance to Crawley Court (Arqiva). Drop-off & disabled parking only at house, parking in field 50m.* Cold drinks. **Adm £2.50, chd free. Thur 17, Sun 20 July (2-5.30). Opening with Crawley Gardens Thur 26, Sun 29 June. Visitors also welcome by appt, summer only.**
Approx ½ acre on chalk, designed and developed by owners, with mature shrubs and a wide variety of herbaceous plants, incl British natives. Features incl colour-themed herbaceous and mixed borders, raised lily pond, herb wheel and wild flower area. Magnificent Victorian boundary wall protects trained top fruit and compact productive kitchen garden and greenhouse.

♿ ✕ ✿ ☎

THRIVE'S TRUNKWELL GARDEN PROJECT
See Berkshire.

107 NEW TIMARU

24 Southington, Overton RG25 3DD. Celia & Ian Lamb. *12m W of Basingstoke. On B3400 London rd. 11m E of Andover through Whitchurch on B3400 London rd.* Home-made teas. **Adm £2.50, chd free. Sat 7 June (11-5), Sun 8 June (2-5).**
⅓ -acre colourful and curvaceous cottage garden created from nothing. Lots of creative and contrasting areas with imaginative planting schemes. Artistic features incl stained glass mosaic garden, art and metal work made by owners. Raised pond, bog area, gravel garden, wild flower area and unusual chickens.

✕ ✿ ☕

108 NEW TREESIDE

New Road, Littleton SO22 6QR. Mr & Mrs Alan Lyne. *2m NW of Winchester. Between B3049 and B3420 (A272) off Main Rd, Littleton, near and on same side as the Running Horse. Park on grass verge in New Rd.* Home-made teas. **Adm £2.50, chd free. Sun 20, Mon 21, Tue 22 July (1-5).**
⅓ acre, 6 seating areas for different times of the day. 2 unusual water features. Original raised beds for vegetables. Fruit cage, divided greenhouse and cold frames. Split ponds, young wild flower area with increasing plant and insect species. Mainly shrubs with flowers highlighting key areas. Quiz for children. Short gravel drive.

♿ ✕ ☕

109 TUNWORTH OLD RECTORY
Tunworth, nr Basingstoke
RG25 2NB. The Hon Mrs Julian
Berry, 01256 471436. *4m SE of
Basingstoke. Turn S off A30 at sign to
Tunworth.* Home-made teas. **Adm £3,
chd free. Visitors welcome by appt
Apr to end Sept, teas by
arrangement. Picnickers welcome.**
Laid out with yew hedges, enclosing
different aspects. Double mixed
border; ruby wedding garden;
pleached hornbeam walk; lime
avenue; ornamental pond;
interesting trees incl beech-lined
walk to church. Decorative pots.
Walks in park, woodland walk. On
request, the gardener will take
wheelchair users round the garden in
golf buggy.
♿ ⚅ ☕ ☎

110 TYLNEY HALL HOTEL
Ridge Lane, Rotherwick RG27 9AZ.
The Manager, www.tylneyhall.com.
*3m NW of Hook. From M3 J5 via A287
& Newnham, M4 J11 via B3349 &
Rotherwick.* Cream teas. **Adm £3, chd
free. Suns 18 May; 1 June; 6 July
(10-5).**
Large garden of 66 acres with
extensive woodlands and fine vistas
being restored with new planting. Fine
avenues of wellingtonias;
rhododendrons and azaleas; Italian
garden; lakes, large water and rock
garden, dry stone walls originally
designed with assistance of Gertrude
Jekyll.
⚅ ☕

111 TYLNEY HOUSE
Ridge Lane, Rotherwick, Hook
RG27 9AT. Mr & Mrs A E M Barlow.
*Approx 3/4 m S of Rotherwick village.
Opp Tylney Hall Hotel.* Home-made
teas. **Adm £3, chd free. Sun 29 June
(2-5.30).**
Tylney House (not open), Arts and
Crafts design after the style of Voysey,
once part of Tylney Estate. English
country garden of approx 1 acre
features large central lawn;
established well-stocked herbaceous
borders with many specialist plants.
Rose pergola, cornus, conifers and
large shrubbery. Unusual dovecote in
paddock.
♿ ⚅ ☕

UPPARK
See Sussex.

112 ◆ THE VYNE
Sherborne St John RG24 9HL. The
National Trust, 01256 883858,
www.nationaltrust.org.uk. *4m N of
Basingstoke. Between Sherborne St
John & Bramley. From A340 turn E at
NT signs.* **Garden adm £5.50, chd
£2.25. Opening dates and times
vary according to season. Please
phone or visit for details. For NGS:
Tue 3 June Special NGS Event:
Exclusive tour of formal garden
with Garden Steward, with
Cream Tea £6.50 bookable in
advance only, limited numbers
(3.15-5); Sat 19 July (11-5).**
13 acres with extensive lawns, lake,
fine trees, herbaceous border and
Edwardian-style summerhouse garden.
Extensive woodland and parkland
walks.
♿ ⚅ ☕

113 WADES HOUSE
Barton Stacey SO21 3RJ. Mr & Mrs
A Briscoe, 01962 760516,
jenny.roo@btinternet.com. *Midway
between A303 & A30 nr Andover.
Approached from S entrance to village.*
Home-made teas. **Adm £3, chd free.
Suns 4 May; 31 Aug; Mon 1 Sept
(2.30-5.30). Visitors also welcome by
appt.**
2 acres on shallow chalky soil of formal
herbaceous borders, rose garden of
old-fashioned roses and pergola,
landscaping, orchard, woodland walk
and kitchen garden. Spectacular
seasonal planting in tubs.
Greenhouses and enviable lawns.
♿ ⚅ 🍽 ☕ ☎

114 WALBURY
Lower Froyle, Alton GU34 4LJ. Ernie
& Brenda Milam, 01420 22216,
walbury@uwclub.net. *5m NE of
Alton. Access to Lower Froyle from
A31 between Alton and Farnham at
Bentley. Walbury nr village hall where
parking available.* Home-made teas.
**Adm £2.50, chd free. Sats, Suns 26,
27 Apr; 28, 29 June (2-6). Opening
with Froyle Gardens 31 May, 1
June. Visitors also welcome by appt
Apr to July.**
Cottage garden atmosphere with small
pond. Lower area is a small, formal,
colour-themed garden, informally
planted with many unusual plants.
Many spring bulbs and new alpine
house. Featured in 'The English
Garden'.
♿ ⚅ ☕ ☎

115 WALDRONS
Brook SO43 7HE. Major & Mrs J
Robinson. *4m N of Lyndhurst. On
B3079 1m W from J1 M27. 1st house
L past Green Dragon PH & directly opp
Bell PH.* Home-made teas. **Adm
£2.50, chd free. Sun 25, Mon 26 May
(2-5).**
Secluded 1-acre garden on the edge
of the New Forest containing shrubs,
herbaceous and rose beds, and a
raised gravel garden. A variety of
cottage plants cover the arbour, trellis
and arches. Small kitchen and herb
garden with Victorian-style
greenhouse. Conservatory open for
teas and ample seating in the garden
to relax and enjoy the atmosphere and
views.
♿ ⚑ ☕

> Contemporary
> vegetable and
> cut flower garden
> incorporating
> many different
> crops, surprising
> uses for
> scaffolding . . .

116 WEIR HOUSE
Abbotstone Road, Alresford
SO24 9DG. Mr & Mrs G Hollingbery,
01962 735549, gmeh@mac.com. *1/2
m N of Alresford. From Alresford down
Broad St (B3046) past Globe PH. Take
1st L, signed Abbotstone. Park in
signed field.* Light refreshments & teas
(not 15 Apr or 16 Sept). **Adm £3, chd
free. Suns 20 Apr; 18 May; 22 June;
14 Sept (2-5). Visitors also welcome
by appt for groups of 10+.**
Spectacular riverside garden.
Contemporary vegetable and cut
flower garden incorporating many
different crops, surprising uses for
scaffolding and painters' ladders and
sculpture by Mark Merer. Children can
use the playground at their own risk.
Featured on BBC TV Gardeners'
World. Garden mostly accessible but
some small obstacles for wheelchair
users. Much open water, children must
be supervised at all times.
♿ ⚅ ☕ ☎

Pond now filled and replaced with pebble area and fountain for display of sun-loving plants . . .

⑰ WEST SILCHESTER HALL
Silchester RG7 2LX. Mrs Jenny Jowett, 0118 970 0278. *7m N of Basingstoke. 7m S of Reading, off A340 (signed from centre of village).* Home-made teas. **Adm £3, chd free. Sun 25, Mon 26 May; Suns 6 July; 17 Aug (2-5.30). Visitors also welcome by appt Apr to end Aug, for groups of 6+ only, coaches permitted.**
1¹/₂ acres, plantsman artist's garden with interest over a long period. Good herbaceous borders, rose and shrub borders, rhododendrons and many acid-loving plants. Pond and bog garden, kitchen garden, interesting display of half hardies. Studio open with exhibition of botanical and landscape paintings, cards and prints by owners.

⑱ 26 & 29 WESTON ALLOTMENTS
Newtown Road, Woolston SO19 9HX. Mrs Belinda Hayes, 07759 321229. *3m E of Southampton City Centre. Leave M27 J8, follow signs for Hamble-le-Rice. At Windhover roundabout, take 2nd exit past Tesco into Hamble Lane B3397. R into Portsmouth Rd, 1m L at 2nd mini roundabout into Upper Weston Lane, 2nd L into Newtown Rd. Allotments opp phone box. Disabled parking only at allotments, other parking on public rd.* Home-made teas. **Adm £2.50, chd free. Sat 5, Sun 6 July (2-5). Visitors also welcome by appt, July only, groups of 10+.**
Allotments packed with salad crops, vegetables, fruit and flowers for floral art, greenhouse and scarecrow. Come and get tips to get you started.

⑲ WESTWARD
11 Ridgemount Avenue, Bassett, Southampton SO16 7FP. Jan & Russ Smith, 02380 767112, russjsmith@btinternet.com. *3m N of Southampton city centre. From end of M3 J14 continue down A33 to 2nd roundabout and head back to M3. Ridgemount Ave 2nd on L.* Teas Mar, home-made teas Aug. **Adm £3, chd free. Sun 23, Mon 24 Mar; Sat 9, Sun 10 Aug (2-5). Visitors also welcome by appt.**
Very colourful ¹/₄ -acre garden with diverse selection of planting. Early spring: many bulbs, hellebores and irises. Summer: lilies, fuchsias, heucheras and acers. Many baskets and containers full of summer colour. Hosta border, vegetable garden, summerhouse, clear pond with koi and goldfish. Waterfall and wildlife pond. Large collection of cacti and succulents. Gold Award winner Southampton in Bloom.

⑳ WHEATLEY HOUSE
between Binsted and Kingsley GU35 9PA. Mr & Mrs Michael Adlington, 01420 23113, mikeadlington36@tiscali.co.uk. *4m E of Alton, 5m SW of Farnham. From Alton follow signs to Holybourne & Binsted. At end of Binsted turn R signed Wheatley. ³/₄ m down lane on L. From Farnham/Bordon on A325 take turn signed Binsted at Buckshorn Oak. 1¹/₂ m turn L signed Wheatley.* Home-made teas. **Adm £3, chd free. Sat 16, Sun 17 Aug (1.30-5.30). Visitors also welcome by appt, groups of 10+, coaches permitted.**
Magnificent setting with panoramic views over fields and forests. Sweeping mixed borders, shrubberies and grasses. 1¹/₂ acres, designed by artist-owner. The colours are spectacular. New 'white & black' border. Craft stalls in old barn, also paintings, mainly of gardens and flowers.

㉑ WHISPERS
Chatter Alley, Dogmersfield RG27 8SS. Mr & Mrs John Selfe. *3m W of Fleet. Turn N to Dogmersfield off A287 Odiham to Farnham rd. Turn L by Queen's Head PH.* Home-made teas. **Adm £3, chd free. Sun 6 July (12-5).**
Two-acre garden of wide sweeping lawns interspersed with large floating borders of vibrant colour, texture and form for all-yr display. Wide variety of plants and trees incl many from the S hemisphere. Spectacular waterfall cascading over large slabs of rock magically disappears below terrace. Environmental issues tackled head on with infectious enthusiasm. Mulching master class given. Other features incl gazebo, bamboo tea house, rockstone seat, kitchen garden and greenhouse.

㉒ WHITE BARN
Woodend Road, Crow Hill, Ringwood BH24 3DG. Marilyn & Barrie Knight, 01425 473527, bandmknight@btinternet.com. *2m SE of Ringwood. From Ringwood take B3347 towards Winkton & Sopley. After 1m turn L immed after petrol stn into Moortown Lane, proceed 1m, Woodend Rd, a gravel rd on L by pillar box.* Light refreshments. **Adm £3, chd free. Every Wed 21 May to 30 July (10.30-5). Visitors also welcome by appt for individuals and groups.**
Beautiful ³/₄ -acre cottage style garden. Visitors comment: 'we went to a garden and we are in heaven'; 'our first visit to an NGS garden, hope it's the first of many'; 'a view at every turn'; 'alive with birds and butterflies'; 'fascinating array of unusual and harmonised planting'.

㉓ THE WHITE COTTAGE
35 Wellhouse Road, Beech, Alton GU34 4AQ. Mr & Mrs P Conyers, 01420 89355. *2m N of Alton. Leave Alton on Basingstoke Rd A339. After approx 1m turn L to Medstead & Beech. Wellhouse Rd is 2nd on R. Parking at village hall at bottom of rd, limited parking at house.* **Adm £2.50, chd free. Suns, Mons 16, 17 Mar; 3, 4 Aug (2-5). Visitors also welcome by appt.**
1-acre chalk garden with wide range of shrubs and plants; colourful herbaceous borders and large collection of hellebores and bulbs. Greenhouses, conservatory with exotics and scree bed. Pond now filled and replaced with pebble area and fountain for display of sun-loving plants. Steep drive but access by car. Grass paths.

True cottage garden with flowers, vegetables, ornamental pond and alpine garden . . .

124 WHITE GABLES
Breach Lane, Sherfield-on-Loddon
RG27 0EU. Terry & Brian
Raisborough. *5m N of Basingstoke.
From Basingstoke follow A33 towards
Reading for approx 5m. Breach Lane is
unmade lane immed before Sherfield-
on-Loddon roundabout on R. Limited
parking for disabled by house. Main
parking in 2 free signed car parks in
main village. Short walk to garden.*
Light refreshments 4 May, home-made
teas 29 June. **Adm £3, chd free.**
Suns 4 May; 29 June (1-5).
Plantaholic's paradise of 1/3 acre
created by owner since 1997.
Interesting themed areas containing
massed planting of tropical plants,
unusual shrubs, perennials and roses.
Oriental border with arbour, raised
banana bed, gravel garden with 3
small ponds, conifer bed, tropical
border, numerous tender plants in pots

on patio. Raised vegetable garden,
cottage garden planting with rose,
jasmine and honeysuckle arches.
Spring bulbs, camellias and
rhododendrons in pots.
🏃 ⊛ ☕

WILDHAM
See Sussex.

125 1 WOGSBARNE COTTAGES
Rotherwick RG27 9BL. Mr R & Miss
S Whistler. *2 1/2 m N of Hook. M3 J5,
M4 J11, A30 or A33 via B3349.*
Home-made teas. **Adm £2.50, chd
free.** Sun 6 July (2-5.30).
True cottage garden with flowers,
vegetables, ornamental pond and
alpine garden. Small vintage
motorcycle display (weather
permitting). Some gravel paths.
♿ 🏃 ⊛ ☕

126 WRENS FARM
Lower Bordean GU32 1ER. Major &
Mrs R A Wilson, 01730 263983. *4m
W of Petersfield, 3m E of W Meon Hut.
From A3 take A272 towards
Winchester. After 3m turn R at small
Xrds with bicycle symbol on sign, then
immed R again.* Home-made teas &
wine. **Adm £2.50, chd free.** Suns 22,
29 June (2-6). Visitors also welcome
by appt.
Plantsman's garden in former farmyard
setting. Mixed and herbaceous
borders. Gravel beds focus on plants
for hot, dry conditions. Mediterranean-
type terrace with vine-covered pergola
and sun-loving plants. Wine tasting
available.
♿ 🏃 ⊛ ☕ ☎

Hampshire County Volunteers

County Organiser
and Central West area Patricia Elkington, Little Court, Crawley, Winchester, Hampshire SO21 2PU, 01962 776365,
elkslc@tiscali.co.uk

County Treasurer
Fred Fratter, Tanglefoot, Crawley, Winchester, Hampshire SO21 2QB, 01962 776243, fred@tanglefoot-house.demon.co.uk

Assistant County Organisers
Central-East Jane Chichester, Cygnet House, Martyr Worthy, Winchester SO21 1DZ, 01962 779315,
janechichester@hotmail.co.uk
North East Rosie & David Darrah, Avenue Cottage, Main Road, Bentley, Farnham, Surrey GU10 5JA, 01420 23225,
dtdarrah@msn.com
East Sally Macpherson, Stedham House, Droxford, Southampton SO32 3PB, 01489 877006, sally@macp.clara.co.uk
North Cynthia Oldale, Yew Tree Cottage, School Lane, Bentley, nr Farnham GU10 5JP, 01420 520438
North-West Carol Pratt, Field House, Monxton, Andover, Hampshire SP11 8AS, 01264 710305, carolacap@yahoo.co.uk
West Christopher Stanford, Oakdene, Sandleheath, Fordingbridge, Hampshire SP6 1TD, 01425 652133,
christopher.stanford@homecall.co.uk
South Barbara Sykes, The Cottage, 16 Lakewood Road, Chandlers Ford, Hampshire SO53 1ES, 02380 254521,
barandhugh@aol.com
South-West Sybil Warner, Birch Wood House, New Forest, Cadnam, Southampton, Hampshire SO40 2NR, 02380 813400,
sybilwarnerhome@aol.com

HEREFORDSHIRE

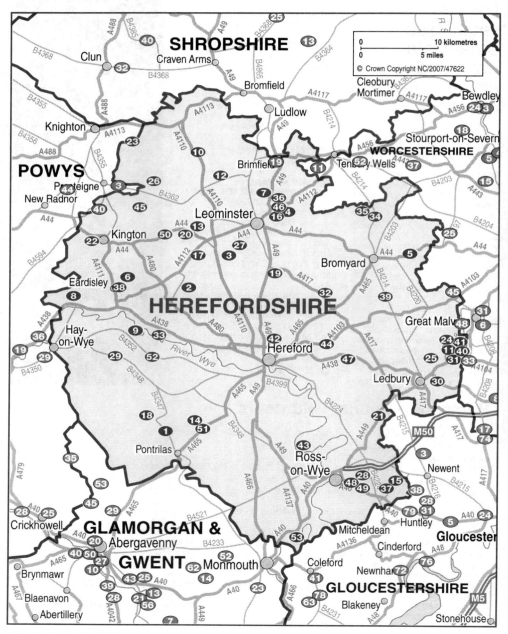

Opening Dates

February

THURSDAY 7
27 Ivy Croft

THURSDAY 14
27 Ivy Croft

THURSDAY 21
27 Ivy Croft

SUNDAY 24
14 Galanthus Gallery Gardens

THURSDAY 28
27 Ivy Croft

March

SUNDAY 9
51 Whitfield

SATURDAY 15
34 Moors Meadow

FRIDAY 21
37 The Old Corn Mill

MONDAY 24
37 The Old Corn Mill

SUNDAY 30
32 Lower Hope

April

SATURDAY 5
47 Tarrington Court

SUNDAY 6
9 Brobury House Gardens

FRIDAY 11
46 Stockton Bury Gardens Ltd

SATURDAY 12
25 Hope End House

SUNDAY 13
25 Hope End House

MONDAY 14
25 Hope End House

TUESDAY 15
25 Hope End House

WEDNESDAY 16
25 Hope End House

THURSDAY 17
25 Hope End House

FRIDAY 18
25 Hope End House

SATURDAY 19
25 Hope End House
34 Moors Meadow
37 The Old Corn Mill

SUNDAY 20
25 Hope End House
37 The Old Corn Mill
40 Perrycroft

50 Westonbury Mill Water Garden

MONDAY 21
25 Hope End House

TUESDAY 22
25 Hope End House

WEDNESDAY 23
25 Hope End House

THURSDAY 24
25 Hope End House

FRIDAY 25
25 Hope End House

SATURDAY 26
25 Hope End House

SUNDAY 27
3 Aulden Farm
11 Caves Folly Nursery
25 Hope End House
27 Ivy Croft
31 Longacre

MONDAY 28
25 Hope End House

TUESDAY 29
25 Hope End House

WEDNESDAY 30
25 Hope End House

May

THURSDAY 1
25 Hope End House

FRIDAY 2
25 Hope End House

SATURDAY 3
25 Hope End House
33 Monnington Court (Evening)

SUNDAY 4
8 Brilley Court
25 Hope End House
33 Monnington Court (Evening)
39 The Orchards

MONDAY 5
25 Hope End House
28 Kingstone Cottages
33 Monnington Court (Evening)
37 The Old Corn Mill

TUESDAY 6
25 Hope End House
28 Kingstone Cottages

WEDNESDAY 7
7 Berrington Hall
25 Hope End House
28 Kingstone Cottages

THURSDAY 8
25 Hope End House
28 Kingstone Cottages

FRIDAY 9
25 Hope End House
28 Kingstone Cottages

SATURDAY 10
6 Batch Cottage
25 Hope End House
28 Kingstone Cottages

SUNDAY 11
6 Batch Cottage
17 The Great House
25 Hope End House
28 Kingstone Cottages
51 Whitfield

MONDAY 12
25 Hope End House
28 Kingstone Cottages

TUESDAY 13
18 The Griggs
25 Hope End House
28 Kingstone Cottages

WEDNESDAY 14
25 Hope End House
28 Kingstone Cottages
30 The Long Barn

THURSDAY 15
25 Hope End House
28 Kingstone Cottages
30 The Long Barn

FRIDAY 16
25 Hope End House
28 Kingstone Cottages
30 The Long Barn

SATURDAY 17
25 Hope End House
28 Kingstone Cottages
30 The Long Barn
34 Moors Meadow

SUNDAY 18
2 Arrow Cottage Garden
20 Hardwick House
28 Kingstone Cottages
30 The Long Barn
32 Lower Hope

MONDAY 19
28 Kingstone Cottages
30 The Long Barn

TUESDAY 20
18 The Griggs
28 Kingstone Cottages
30 The Long Barn

WEDNESDAY 21
28 Kingstone Cottages
30 The Long Barn

THURSDAY 22
28 Kingstone Cottages
30 The Long Barn

FRIDAY 23
28 Kingstone Cottages

30 The Long Barn

SATURDAY 24
23 Hill House Farm
28 Kingstone Cottages
30 The Long Barn

SUNDAY 25
3 Aulden Farm
11 Caves Folly Nursery
23 Hill House Farm
27 Ivy Croft
28 Kingstone Cottages
30 The Long Barn
31 Longacre
48 Weston Hall

MONDAY 26
28 Kingstone Cottages
30 The Long Barn
37 The Old Corn Mill

TUESDAY 27
18 The Griggs
28 Kingstone Cottages
30 The Long Barn

WEDNESDAY 28
28 Kingstone Cottages
30 The Long Barn

THURSDAY 29
28 Kingstone Cottages
30 The Long Barn

FRIDAY 30
28 Kingstone Cottages
30 The Long Barn

SATURDAY 31
18 The Griggs
28 Kingstone Cottages
30 The Long Barn

June

SUNDAY 1
13 Eardisland Gardens
28 Kingstone Cottages
30 The Long Barn

MONDAY 2
28 Kingstone Cottages
30 The Long Barn

TUESDAY 3
18 The Griggs
28 Kingstone Cottages
30 The Long Barn

WEDNESDAY 4
28 Kingstone Cottages
30 The Long Barn

THURSDAY 5
28 Kingstone Cottages
30 The Long Barn

FRIDAY 6
28 Kingstone Cottages
30 The Long Barn

SATURDAY 7
6 Batch Cottage

28 Kingstone Cottages
30 The Long Barn

SUNDAY 8
5 The Bannut
6 Batch Cottage
10 Bury Court (known as Wrinkly Bottom)
28 Kingstone Cottages
30 The Long Barn

MONDAY 9
28 Kingstone Cottages
30 The Long Barn

TUESDAY 10
18 The Griggs
28 Kingstone Cottages
30 The Long Barn

WEDNESDAY 11
28 Kingstone Cottages
30 The Long Barn

THURSDAY 12
28 Kingstone Cottages
30 The Long Barn

FRIDAY 13
12 Croft Castle
28 Kingstone Cottages
30 The Long Barn

SATURDAY 14
28 Kingstone Cottages
30 The Long Barn

SUNDAY 15
28 Kingstone Cottages
30 The Long Barn
39 The Orchards

MONDAY 16
28 Kingstone Cottages
30 The Long Barn

TUESDAY 17
18 The Griggs
28 Kingstone Cottages
30 The Long Barn

WEDNESDAY 18
28 Kingstone Cottages
30 The Long Barn

THURSDAY 19
28 Kingstone Cottages
30 The Long Barn

FRIDAY 20
21 Hellens
28 Kingstone Cottages
30 The Long Barn

SATURDAY 21
21 Hellens (Afternoon & Evening)
28 Kingstone Cottages
30 The Long Barn
34 Moors Meadow
43 Shieldbrook

SUNDAY 22
4 Bachefield House
8 Brilley Court

14 Galanthus Gallery Gardens
28 Kingstone Cottages
30 The Long Barn
35 Netherwood Manor
43 Shieldbrook

MONDAY 23
28 Kingstone Cottages
30 The Long Barn

TUESDAY 24
18 The Griggs
28 Kingstone Cottages
30 The Long Barn

WEDNESDAY 25
28 Kingstone Cottages
30 The Long Barn

THURSDAY 26
28 Kingstone Cottages
30 The Long Barn

FRIDAY 27
28 Kingstone Cottages
30 The Long Barn

SATURDAY 28
18 The Griggs
28 Kingstone Cottages
30 The Long Barn

SUNDAY 29
3 Aulden Farm
11 Caves Folly Nursery
27 Ivy Croft
28 Kingstone Cottages
30 The Long Barn
31 Longacre

MONDAY 30
28 Kingstone Cottages
30 The Long Barn

July

TUESDAY 1
18 The Griggs
28 Kingstone Cottages
30 The Long Barn

WEDNESDAY 2
28 Kingstone Cottages
30 The Long Barn

THURSDAY 3
28 Kingstone Cottages
30 The Long Barn

FRIDAY 4
28 Kingstone Cottages
30 The Long Barn

SATURDAY 5
30 The Long Barn

SUNDAY 6
30 The Long Barn
32 Lower Hope
40 Perrycroft

MONDAY 7
30 The Long Barn

TUESDAY 8
- **18** The Griggs
- **30** The Long Barn

WEDNESDAY 9
- **30** The Long Barn

THURSDAY 10
- **30** The Long Barn

FRIDAY 11
- **30** The Long Barn

SATURDAY 12
- **30** The Long Barn

SUNDAY 13
- **5** The Bannut
- **30** The Long Barn
- **53** Woodview

MONDAY 14
- **30** The Long Barn

TUESDAY 15
- **18** The Griggs
- **30** The Long Barn

WEDNESDAY 16
- **30** The Long Barn

THURSDAY 17
- **30** The Long Barn

FRIDAY 18
- **30** The Long Barn

SATURDAY 19
- **30** The Long Barn

SUNDAY 20
- **14** Galanthus Gallery Gardens
- **30** The Long Barn
- **53** Woodview

MONDAY 21
- **30** The Long Barn

TUESDAY 22
- **18** The Griggs
- **30** The Long Barn

WEDNESDAY 23
- **30** The Long Barn

THURSDAY 24
- **30** The Long Barn

FRIDAY 25
- **30** The Long Barn

SATURDAY 26
- **30** The Long Barn
- **34** Moors Meadow

SUNDAY 27
- **30** The Long Barn
- **38** The Old Quarry
- **52** The Wiggly Garden

MONDAY 28
- **30** The Long Barn

TUESDAY 29
- **18** The Griggs
- **30** The Long Barn

WEDNESDAY 30
- **30** The Long Barn

THURSDAY 31
- **30** The Long Barn

August

FRIDAY 1
- **30** The Long Barn

SATURDAY 2
- **30** The Long Barn

SUNDAY 3
- **9** Brobury House Gardens
- **11** Caves Folly Nursery
- **30** The Long Barn
- **31** Longacre
- **38** The Old Quarry

MONDAY 4
- **30** The Long Barn

TUESDAY 5
- **30** The Long Barn

WEDNESDAY 6
- **19** Hampton Court
- **30** The Long Barn

THURSDAY 7
- **30** The Long Barn

FRIDAY 8
- **30** The Long Barn

SATURDAY 9
- **15** Gorsley Gardens
- **30** The Long Barn

SUNDAY 10
- **4** Bachefield House
- **15** Gorsley Gardens
- **30** The Long Barn
- **41** The Picton Garden

MONDAY 11
- **30** The Long Barn

TUESDAY 12
- **30** The Long Barn

WEDNESDAY 13
- **30** The Long Barn

THURSDAY 14
- **30** The Long Barn

FRIDAY 15
- **30** The Long Barn
- **39** The Orchards (Evening)

SATURDAY 16
- **22** Hergest Croft Gardens
- **30** The Long Barn

SUNDAY 17
- **5** The Bannut
- **30** The Long Barn

MONDAY 18
- **30** The Long Barn

TUESDAY 19
- **30** The Long Barn

WEDNESDAY 20
- **30** The Long Barn

THURSDAY 21
- **30** The Long Barn

FRIDAY 22
- **30** The Long Barn

SATURDAY 23
- **30** The Long Barn

SUNDAY 24
- **3** Aulden Farm
- **23** Hill House Farm
- **27** Ivy Croft
- **30** The Long Barn
- **41** The Picton Garden

MONDAY 25
- **23** Hill House Farm
- **30** The Long Barn

TUESDAY 26
- **30** The Long Barn

WEDNESDAY 27
- **30** The Long Barn

THURSDAY 28
- **30** The Long Barn

FRIDAY 29
- **30** The Long Barn

SATURDAY 30
- **30** The Long Barn
- **34** Moors Meadow

SUNDAY 31
- **30** The Long Barn
- **50** Westonbury Mill Water Garden

September

MONDAY 1
- **30** The Long Barn

TUESDAY 2
- **30** The Long Barn

WEDNESDAY 3
- **30** The Long Barn

THURSDAY 4
- **30** The Long Barn

FRIDAY 5
- **30** The Long Barn

SUNDAY 7
- **39** The Orchards

SATURDAY 13
- **41** The Picton Garden
- **47** Tarrington Court

SATURDAY 20
- **22** Hergest Croft Gardens

SUNDAY 21
- **27** Ivy Croft

SUNDAY 28
- **20** Hardwick House

MONDAY 29
- **41** The Picton Garden

October

SUNDAY 5
32 Lower Hope

THURSDAY 9
41 The Picton Garden

SUNDAY 12
40 Perrycroft

SATURDAY 18
41 The Picton Garden

SUNDAY 19
31 Longacre

February 2009

THURSDAY 5
27 Ivy Croft

THURSDAY 12
27 Ivy Croft

THURSDAY 26
27 Ivy Croft

Gardens open to the public

1 Abbey Dore Court Garden
2 Arrow Cottage Garden
3 Aulden Farm
5 The Bannut
7 Berrington Hall
9 Brobury House Gardens
12 Croft Castle
14 Galanthus Gallery Gardens
19 Hampton Court
21 Hellens
22 Hergest Croft Gardens
27 Ivy Croft
34 Moors Meadow
41 The Picton Garden
45 Staunton Park
46 Stockton Bury Gardens Ltd
50 Westonbury Mill Water Garden
52 The Wiggly Garden

By appointment only

16 Grantsfield
24 The Hollies
26 Ivy Cottage
29 Little Llanavon
33 Monnington Court
36 Old Chapel House
38 The Old Quarry
42 The Rambles
44 Shucknall Court
49 Weston Mews

Also open by appointment ☎

6 Batch Cottage
8 Brilley Court
11 Caves Folly Nursery
17 The Great House

18 The Griggs
23 Hill House Farm
25 Hope End House
28 Kingstone Cottages
31 Longacre
37 The Old Corn Mill
39 The Orchards
43 Shieldbrook
47 Tarrington Court
48 Weston Hall

The Gardens

1 ◆ ABBEY DORE COURT GARDEN
Abbey Dore HR2 0AD. Mrs Charis Ward, 01981 240419, www.abbeydorecourt.co.uk. *11m SW of Hereford. From A465 midway Hereford-Abergavenny turn W, signed Abbey Dore, then 2½ m.* **Adm £3.50, chd 50p. Visitors to the garden most days, essential to tel first, teas by arrangement.**
Peaceful 6-acre garden comprising 6 widely differing areas. A field, now a garden, with trees, shrubs, borders and gazebo. The long purple, gold and silver borders leading to the riverside walk and wild garden. A bridge across the R Dore into the meadow with interesting trees. Cottage type garden round the house and walled garden with formal arches, paths and borders, all full of interesting shrubs and herbaceous perennials, especially hellebores, peonies, astrantia and clematis.
&♿ ✖ ⊛

Charming traditional ²/₃ -acre cottage garden on hill slope, designed for yr-round interest . . .

2 ◆ ARROW COTTAGE GARDEN
Ledgemoor, nr Weobley HR4 8RN. David & Janet Martin, 01344 622181, www.arrowcottagegarden.co.uk. *8m SE of Kington. From Weobley take unclassified rd direction Wormsley (Kings Pyon-Canon Pyon), after 1m,* turn L signed Ledgemoor. 2nd R (no through rd). 1st house on L. Park in field before the cottage. **Adm £3.85, chd £1. Fris to Suns 1 May to 31 Aug. For NGS: Sun 18 May (11-4).**
Set amidst an idyllic landscape in rural countryside, this romantic 2-acre garden combines formal design, follies, water features and topiary with exuberant and imaginative planting. The 23 separate rooms each stand alone, whilst combining to make a truly fascinating, cohesive garden. Show of work by local painters. Featured in Dream Gardens; 100 Inspirational Gardens'.
✖ ⊛ ⊨ ☕

3 ◆ AULDEN FARM
Aulden, Leominster HR6 0JT. Alun & Jill Whitehead, 01568 720129, www.auldenfarm.co.uk. *4m SW of Leominster. From Leominster take Ivington/Upper Hill Rd. ³/₄ m after Ivington Church, turn R (signed Aulden), garden 1m on R. From A4110 signed Ivington, take 2nd R (approx ³/₄ m), garden ³/₄ m on L.* Teas at Ivy Croft (NGS days only). **Adm £2.50, chd free. Tues & Thurs Apr to Aug, Thurs Mar & Sept (10-5). For NGS: Suns 27 Apr; 25 May; 29 June; 24 Aug (2-5.30). Also open Ivy Croft.**
Informally planted country garden and nursery surrounding old farmhouse. 3 acres planted with wildlife in mind. Numerous iris incl ditch containing ensatas, sibiricas by natural pond. Hemerocallis with grasses and kniphofias for added zing. Emphasis on structure and form with a hint of quirkiness. Garden started from scratch in 1997, feels mature but still evolving. Home-made ice-cream NGS days only.
✖ ⊛ ☕

4 BACHEFIELD HOUSE
Kimbolton HR6 0EP. Jim & Rowena Gale. *3m E of Leominster. Take A4112 off A49 (signed Leysters), after 10yds 1st R (signed Stretford/Hamnish). 1st L to Grantsfield over Xrds (signed Bache), continue for approx 1m garden on R past rd to Gorsty Hill.* Home-made teas. **Adm £3, chd free. Suns 22 June; 10 Aug (2-5.30).**
Charming traditional ²/₃ -acre cottage garden on hill slope, designed for yr-round interest. Pond, summerhouse with fine views, mixed borders, emphasis on old roses, hemerocallis, hardy geraniums, cyclamens and range of unusual plants. Collection of old-fashioned pinks.
✖ ⊛ ☕

BALDWINS
See Gloucestershire North & Central.

5 ◆ THE BANNUT
Bringsty WR6 5TA. Daphne & Maurice Everett, 01885 482206, www.bannut.co.uk. *2½ m E of Bromyard. On A44 Worcester Rd, ½ m E of entrance to National Trust, Brockhampton.* **Adm £3.50, chd £1.50. Weds, Sats, Suns & Bank Hols 21 Mar to 28 Sept.** For NGS: Suns 8 June; 13 July; 17 Aug (12.30-5).
Approx 3 acres of formal and informal gardens, with much to enjoy throughout the seasons and lovely views to the Malvern Hills. Manicured hedges divide colourful garden rooms, which incl a yellow and white garden, romantic arbour garden, secret garden and unusual knot garden. Spectacular heather gardens, woodland garden, many unusual and interesting trees and shrubs. Featured in and on Yearbook of the Heather Society, BBC Radio Hereford & Worcester.
& ⊛ ☕

6 BATCH COTTAGE
Almeley HR3 6PT. Jeremy & Elizabeth Russell, 01544 327469. *16m NW of Hereford. 2m off A438-A4111 to Kington, turn R at Eardisley.* Home-made teas. **Adm £3, chd free. Sats, Suns 10, 11 May; 7, 8 June (2-5.30).** Visitors also welcome by appt.
Established conservation-oriented garden of some 2½ acres with streams and large pond, set in a natural valley, surrounded by woodland and orchard. Over 360 labelled trees and shrubs, mixed borders, fern and bog beds, wild flower bank, stumpery, woodland walk and wooden sculptures. (Steep slope (optional), unfenced pond).
& ✕ ⊛ ☕ ☎

7 ◆ BERRINGTON HALL
Leominster HR6 0DW. The National Trust, 01568 615721, www.nationaltrust.org.uk. *3m N of Leominster. On A49, signed. Buses: Midland Red (W) 92, 292 alight Luston 2m.* **House and Garden adm £6.50, chd £3.25, Garden only adm £4.80, chd £2.40. Sats to Weds 17 Mar to 2 Nov.** For NGS: Wed 7 May (11-5).
Extensive views over Capability Brown park; formal garden; wall plants, unusual trees, camellia collection, herbaceous plants, wisteria. Woodland walk, rhododendrons, walled garden with historic apple collection.

Costumed tours of servants quarters. Featured in local press.
& ✕ ⊛ ☕

THE BINDERY
Presteigne. See Powys.

BIRTSMORTON COURT
See Worcestershire.

Set in rolling countryside, commanding magnificent views in NW Herefordshire . . .

8 BRILLEY COURT
Whitney-on-Wye HR3 6JF. Mr & Mrs David Bulmer, 01497 831467. *6m NE of Hay-on-Wye. 5m SW of Kington. 1½ m off A438 Hereford to Brecon rd signed to Brilley.* Cream teas. **Adm £3, under 12 chd free. Suns 4 May; 22 June (2-5.30).** Visitors also welcome by appt groups of 10+, coaches permitted.
3-acre garden, walled, ornamental kitchen garden. Spring tulip collection, summer rose and herbaceous borders. 7-acre wild valley stream garden. Limited wheelchair access.
& ✕ ☕ ☎

9 ◆ BROBURY HOUSE GARDENS
Brobury by Bredwardine HR3 6BS. Keith & Pru Cartwright, 01981 500229, www.broburyhouse.co.uk. *10m W of Hereford. S off A438 signed Bredwardine & Brobury. Garden 1m L before bridge.* Teas NGS days only. **Adm £3, chd £1. Open daily all yr 10-5 or dusk if earlier.** For NGS: Suns 6 Apr; 3 Aug (11-5).
5 acres of gardens, set on the banks of an exquisitely beautiful section of the R Wye, offer the visitor a delightful combination of Victorian terraces with mature specimen trees, inspiring water features, architectural planting and woodland areas. Redesign and development is ongoing. Bring a picnic, your paint brushes, binoculars and linger awhile. Wheelchair users, strong able-bodied assistant advisable.
& 🛏 ☕

10 NEW BURY COURT (KNOWN AS WRINKLY BOTTOM)
Wigmore HR6 9US. *10m N of Leominster. ½ m off A4110 at E end of Wigmore Village, on rd to Ludlow.* Home-made teas. **Combined adm £4, chd free. Sun 8 June (2-5.30).**
3 small gardens, created on the site of former farmyard. Set in rolling countryside, commanding magnificent views in NW Herefordshire, close to Ludlow and Welsh borders. Wigmore, with its own castle ruins and Norman Church, enjoys views of Croft Ambrey, Gatley Bringewood and Wigmore Rolls.
☕

NEW THE BARN HOUSE
John & Joan Markland
2 small gardens on 2 sides of barn. Rickyard wall makes a good area for a variety of plants incl roses and climbers. Small beds made after stones unearthed when making gardens from builder's rubble over 8yrs.
✕

NEW CROFT VIEW
Ivan & Cathy Jones
Small garden with beautiful views. Herbaceous and evergreen shrub borders, pond, bog garden, gravelled areas, patio, pergola with climbers, raised beds with companion planting, greenhouse, arbour, paved seating and sun areas, lawns. Specimen trees, fruit area and watering system.
✕

NEW STONY OAK
Vic & Gill Harnett
Small well drained garden built on stone, much of which has been used within the garden. Deep borders incl shrubs, perennials, iris, roses and climbers. Grasses are prominent by small stream, pond and bog garden.
✕

11 CAVES FOLLY NURSERY
Evendine Lane, Colwall WR13 6DY. Wil Leaper & Bridget Evans, 01684 540631, www.cavesfolly.com. *1¼ m NE of Ledbury. B4218. Between Malvern & Ledbury. Evendine Lane, off Colwall Green. Car parking at Caves Folly.* Home-made teas. **Combined with Longacre adm £3.50, chd free. Suns 27 Apr; 25 May; 29 June; 3**

Aug (2-5). **Visitors also welcome by appt June to Sept, groups of 10+, coaches permitted.**
Organic nursery established 22 yrs specialising in alpines, herbaceous perennials and grasses, some unusual. All plants grown peat-free and organically. Herbaceous borders, solar powered water features and display gardens. Meadow walk with pond, ducks and 'willow dome'. Grass and gravel paths.

Exceptionally pretty black and white village on the River Arrow . . .

⑫ ◆ CROFT CASTLE
Leominster HR6 9PW. The National Trust, 01568 780246, croftcastle@nationaltrust.org.uk. *5m NW of Leominster. On B4362 (off B4361, Leominster to Ludlow rd).* **Adm £4, chd £2. Weds to Suns 19 Mar to 31 Oct. For NGS: Fri 13 June (11-5).**
Large garden; borders; walled garden; landscaped park and walks in Fishpool Valley; fine old avenues.
👤 🐾 ⊛ ☕

⑬ NEW EARDISLAND GARDENS
HR6 9BW. *5m W of Leominster. From Leominster take A44 towards Rhayder, then R on B4529 Eardisland. Follow parking signs in village.* **Combined adm £3.50, chd free. Sun 1 June (11-5).**
Exceptionally pretty black and white village on the R Arrow. Teas & lunches in the village.

NEW ANGLERS REST
St Mary's Walk. Alan & Val Holloway. *From car park with Cross Inn on R walk towards church, house directly in front*
Planted over 9yrs this small new garden has evolved for the owners' pleasure. Pea gravel paths lead round the circular lawn, passing heather and perennial beds. Vegetable patch hides behind trellis wall.
🐾

NEW BRIDGEND
Peter Glenn. *From Leominster turn R at bridge over R Arrow. From Pembridge cross bridge over RArrow turn L. NB No parking*
Small, approx ⅕ -acre cottage garden thickly planted with old style roses and some perennials. Shady bed near house with cowslips and other primulas.
🐾

NEW GLAN ARROW
Christopher & Lotty James. *5m W of Leominster on B4529. Cross bridge & immediately turn sharp L up driveway*
4-acre English riverside garden with herbaceous borders, roses, bog garden leading to small lake, wild flower meadow and potager.
🐾

⑭ ◆ GALANTHUS GALLERY GARDENS
Wormbridge HR2 9DH. Mr & Mrs D Kellett, 01981 570506, www.galanthusgallery.com. *8m SW of Hereford. On the A465 towards Abergavenny. Galanthus Gallery signed immed off rd in centre of Wormbridge.* **Adm £3, chd free. Open daily, except Wed (gallery & garden). For NGS: Suns 24 Feb; 22 June; 20 July (10-4.30).**
2½ -acre garden with wonderful views to the Black Mountains, next to contemporary art gallery. Walled garden with magnolia, acers and herbaceous borders, leading to sloped garden with rill. Thousands of snowdrops in drifts are a particular feature in early spring. Duck pond, magnificent copper beeches and swamp cypresses. (Cafe with sunny courtyard provides home-made light lunches, teas and irresistible cakes (closed Weds).
⊛ ☕

⑮ NEW GORSLEY GARDENS
Gorsely, Kilcot & Aston Crews GL18 1PG. *From M50 J3 towards Newent B4221. At Roadmaker PH turn R and at T-junction turn L. ½ m to Xrds, straight on ½ m take next R (Darnells Lane) to Lilley Hall. From Newent, take B4221 through Gorsley past Roadmaker PH and take next L. Follow directions as above. 5m E of Ross-on-Wye. A40 Ross to Gloucester. From A40 at Lea take B4222 (T-lights) signed*

Newent and at top of hill (1m) turn L to Linton, follow rd round to R to Hill View House. **Combined adm £5, chd free. Sat 9, Sun 10 Aug (12-5).**
Three gardens of widely differing styles and content situated in or near the village of Gorsley. Lunches & teas at local PHs.

NEW COVER POINT
Chris & Anne Tormey.
½-acre of informal gardens incl large raised pool and sitting area, mixed borders planted for colour, scent and all-yr interest. Shade areas, pergolas, patios, vegetables and soft fruit, fruit trees. Gentle sloping lawns, may be slippery when wet.
👤 🐾

NEW HIGH VIEW HOUSE
Aston Crews. Mr & Mrs Martin Bradney
2-acre informal garden with woodland walk, shrubberies and productive vegetable plot with extensive views of the Malverns and May Hill.
🐾

NEW LILLEY HALL
Nick & Nicky Jones
New 4-acre organic garden being created in an old orchard. Recently planted formal quincunx orchard, kitchen garden, pleached lime walk, shrub and perennial beds plus trees, climbers, grasses and a bit of tropical. Access only on grass, some parts quite steep.
👤 🐾

⑯ GRANTSFIELD
nr Kimbolton, Leominster HR6 0ET. Colonel & Mrs J G T Polley, 01568 613338. *3m NE of Leominster. A49 N from Leominster, A4112 turn R & follow signs. No parking for coaches - drop & collect visitors in village; (minibus acceptable). A44 W to Leominster. Turn R at Drum Xrds (notice up).* Home-made teas. **Adm £3, chd free. Visitors welcome by appt Apr to end Sept, anytime, but please tel before coming. Teas on request.**
Contrasting styles in gardens of old stone farmhouse; wide variety of unusual plants, trees and shrubs, old roses, climbers, herbaceous borders, superb views. 1½ -acre orchard and kitchen garden with flowering and specimen trees and shrubs. Spring bulbs.
👤 🐾 ⊛ ☕ ☎

⑰ THE GREAT HOUSE
Dilwyn HR4 8HX. Tom & Jane Hawksley, 01544 318007, www.thegreathousedilwyn.co.uk. *7m W of Leominster. A44 from Leominster joining A4112 (signed Brecon). Turn L into Dilwyn village. House on RH-side opp village green.* Home-made teas. **Adm £3, chd free. Sun 11 May (2-5). Visitors also welcome by appt.**
1½ -acre all-yr garden, designed and created by owners over the last 10yrs. Spring bulbs, traditional rose gardens, yew and beech hedging, raised knot garden, decorative stone and brickwork. 40ft reflecting pool and pleached hornbeams lining the drive all add interest to this country garden which is fronted by wonderful C18 wrought iron gates. Plant nurseries. Featured on Radio Hereford & Worcester. Gravel paths and slopes.
& ✖ ❀ ⊫ ☕ ☎

⑱ THE GRIGGS
Newton St Margarets HR2 0QY. John & Bridget Biggs, 01981 510629, www.artaura.co.uk/thegriggs. *14m SW of Hereford. Take B4348 to Vowchurch, turn L, signed Michaelchurch Escley, continue for 2½ m, then follow NGS signs. Signs will be posted locally for those approaching from Longtown & Ewyas Harold.* Home-made teas. **Adm £3.50, chd free (share to Community Action, Nepal). Every Tues 13 May to 29 July; Sats 31 May; 28 June (2-6). Visitors also welcome by appt.**
Located in a remote scenic setting between the Golden Valley and the Black Mountains, a floriferous country garden of 1½ acres, managed organically and incl extensive mixed borders, wild flower meadows, wildlife pond and large productive kitchen garden. A garden to lose oneself in. Some gravel paths.
& ✖ ☕ ☎

⑲ ◆ HAMPTON COURT
Hope-under-Dinmore HR6 0PN, 01568 797777, www.hamptoncourt.org.uk. *5m S of Leominster. On A417, 500yds from junction with A49.* **Adm £5, chd £3, concessions £4.50. Tues to Thurs, weekends & Bank Hols Apr to 28 Oct. For NGS: Wed 6 Aug (11-5).**
Exciting mix of new and old gardens within the grounds of C15 castle. Work started to rebuild gardens in 1996. Newly restored formal walled garden,

herbaceous borders, Dutch garden, sunken garden with waterfall and thatched hermitage and organic kitchen garden.
& ✖ ❀ ☕

⑳ NEW HARDWICK HOUSE
Pembridge, Leominster HR6 9HE. Mr & Mrs D J Collins. *6m E of Leominster. Between Eardisland & Pembridge. Take A44 from Leominster, 1m before Pembridge, turn up lane signed Bearwood & Hardwick. Drive entrance 250yds up lane, over cattlegrid between stone pillars.* **Adm £3.50, chd free. Suns 18 May (11-6); 28 Sept (11-5).**
Large garden with extensive lawns, colourful shrubberies and ornamental trees. Fine views over unspoilt countryside. Ponds with collection of waterfowl. Teas available locally.
& ✖

Sloping paths to Oak Pool 200ft below house . . .

㉑ ◆ HELLENS
Much Marcle HR8 2LY. PMMCT, 01531 660504. *6m from Ross-on-Wye. 4m SW of Ledbury, off A449.* **Adm £2.50, chd free. For NGS: Fri 20 June (2-5). Afternoon & Evening Opening** (wine 6-7.30), **Sat 21 June (2-7.30).**
In the grounds of Hellens Manor House, the gardens are being gently redeveloped to reflect the C17 ambience of the house. Incl a rare octagonal dovecot. 2 knot gardens and yew labyrinth, lawns, herb and kitchen gardens; short woodlands and pond walk. Longer walk to Hall Wood, site of SSI.
& ❀ ☕

㉒ ◆ HERGEST CROFT GARDENS
Kington HR5 3EG. Mr W L Banks, 01544 230160, www.hergest.co.uk. *½ m W of Kington. ½ m off A44 on Welsh side of Kington. Turn L at Rhayader end of bypass; then 1st R; gardens ¼ m on L.* **Adm £5.50, chd free. Weekends in Mar; daily 21 Mar**

to 2 Nov. For NGS: Sat 16 Aug; Sat 20 Sept (12-5.30).
4 gardens for all seasons, from spring bulbs to spectacular autumn colour, incl spring and summer borders, roses, brilliant azaleas and old-fashioned kitchen garden growing unusual vegetables. Brightly coloured rhododendrons 30ft high grow in Park Wood. Over 60 champion trees in one of the finest collections of trees and shrubs in the British Isles. Some areas not accessible to wheelchairs.
& ❀ NCCPG ☕

㉓ NEW HILL HOUSE FARM
Knighton LD7 1NA. Simon & Caroline Gourlay, 01547 528542, simon@maryvalefarms.co.uk. *4m SE of Knighton. S of A4113 via Knighton (Llanshay Lane, 3m) or Bucknell (Reeves Lane, 3m).* Home-made teas. **Adm £3, chd free. Sat 24, Suns 25 May; 24, Mon 25 Aug (2-6). Visitors also welcome by appt, June - Aug individuals and small groups.**
S-facing 5-acre hillside garden developed over past 40yrs with magnificent views over unspoilt countryside. Herbaceous area amongst magnificent mature oak trees, extensive lawns and paths surrounded by roses, shrubs and specimen trees. Sloping paths to Oak Pool 200ft below house. Transport available from bottom of garden if needed.
✖ ☕ ☎

㉔ NEW THE HOLLIES
Old Church Road, Colwall WR13 6EZ. Margaret & Graham White, 01684 540931. *3m SW of Malvern. Take B4218 past Old Court Nursery, Picton, turn R into Church Rd. Hollies 250yds on R.* Home-made teas. **Adm £3, chd free. Visitors welcome by appt Feb to Oct, individuals & groups, plants and teas sometimes available.**
Hardy planter's ½ -acre garden developed over the last 12yrs from a plot containing mature trees but little else. Continually evolving beds containing a wide mixture of shrubs, bulbs and perennials planted to provide interest throughout the yr. A gently sloping site with views toward the Malvern Hills.
☎

25 HOPE END HOUSE
Raycombe Lane, Hope End
HR8 1JQ. Mrs P J Maiden, 01531
635890,
sharonmaiden@btinternet.com,
www.hopeendhouse.com. *2m NE of
Ledbury. From Ledbury, take
Bromyard rd N. 1/3 m from stn turn R
signed Wellington Heath & Hope End,
uphill for 11/2 m to T-junction, turn R.
Continue for 1/2 m. Turn into Raycombe
Lane, entrance from this lane on R.
Signed after 1m. Parking in woodland
& lane.* Home-made teas. **Adm £2.50,
chd free.** (Woodland only) daily Sat
12 Apr to Sat 17 May; (woodland &
garden) Sat 12, Thur 17, Sat 26 Apr;
Mon 5, Thurs 8, 15 May (10-4).
**Visitors also welcome by appt clubs
etc Thurs, May to July. Please call to
arrange.**
Woodland walk through 30 acres
parkland (not garden), Oyster Hill
originally laid out in the early C19. 6-
acre bluebell walk through Cockshute,
steep slopes in woodland. Perfect for
picnics.
🛏 ☎

26 IVY COTTAGE
Kinsham LD8 2HN. Jane & Richard
Barton, 01544 267154,
richard@barton3.freeserve.co.uk.
*12m NW of Leominster. From
Mortimers Cross take B4362 towards
Presteigne. Turn R at Combe towards
Lingen for 1m. Easy parking.* **Adm £3,
chd free. Visitors welcome by appt
May to Sept, groups welcome.**
Cottage garden developed over 16yrs.
Mixed borders planted for colour, scent
and all-yr interest. Shrub roses,
clematis and wide range of perennials,
some unusual, incl many hardy
geraniums, astrantias and campanulas.
Shade areas, pergolas, vegetable
garden and fruit trees in 1/2 -acre
setting.
🗡 ✿ ☎

27 ◆ IVY CROFT
Ivington Green, Leominster
HR6 0JN. Sue & Roger Norman,
01568 720344, rogerandsue@
ivycroft.freeserve.co.uk,
www.ivycroft.freeserve.co.uk. *3m
SW of Leominster. From Leominster
take Ryelands Rd to Ivington. Turn R at
church, garden 3/4 m on R. From
A4110 signed Ivington, garden 13/4 m
on L.* **Adm £2.50, chd free. Every
Thurs Apr - Sept 9-4. For NGS:
Thurs 7, 14, 21, 28 Feb (9-4); Sun 21
Sept (2-5.30). Also open Aulden
Farm Suns 27 Apr; 25 May; 29**

June; 24 Aug (2-5.30) 2009 Thurs 5,
12, 19, 26 Feb.
Garden created since 1997 surrounds
C17 cottage in 4 acres of rich
grassland. Plant lovers' garden
designed for all-yr interest. Raised
beds, mixed borders, trees, alpines,
troughs, formal vegetable garden
framed by trained fruit trees; collections
of ferns, willows and snowdrops.
🗡 ✿

6-acre bluebell walk through Cockshute . . .

28 KINGSTONE COTTAGES
Weston under Penyard, nr Ross-on-
Wye HR9 7PH. Mr & Mrs M Hughes,
01989 565267,
www.hoohouse.plus.com. *2m E of
Ross-on-Wye. A40 Ross to
Gloucester, turn off at Weston Cross
PH to Linton, then 2nd L to Rudhall.*
Adm £2, chd free. Daily Mon 5 May
to Fri 4 July (10-5). **Visitors also
welcome by appt.**
Informal 11/2 -acre cottage garden
containing National Collection of old
pinks and carnations and other
unusual plants. Terraced beds, ponds,
grotto, summerhouse, lovely views.
Separate parterre garden containing
the collection. Much of the garden
replanted and being extended into new
areas. Featured in various press
articles & on BBC Gardeners' World.
🗡 ✿ NCCPG ☎

29 LITTLE LLANAVON
Dorstone HR3 6AT. John & Jenny
Chippindale, 01981 550984,
john.chippindale@virgin.net. *2m W
of Peterchurch. In the Golden Valley,
15m W of Hereford on B4348, 1/2 m
towards Peterchurch from Dorstone.*
**Adm £2.50, chd free. Visitors
welcome by appt May - Sept.
Parties welcome..**
1/2 -acre S-facing cottage-style walled
garden in lovely rural location.
Meandering paths among shrubs in
shady spring garden. Hot gravel area
and herbaceous borders closely
planted with select perennials and
grasses, many unusual. Good late
colour. Featured in 'Ideal Home' &
'Homes & Gardens'.
♿ 🗡 ☎

LLANTHONY AND DISTRICT GARDENS
See Gwent.

LLOWES COURT
See Powys.

30 THE LONG BARN
Eastnor HR8 1EL. Fay & Roger
Oates. *2m E of Ledbury. On A438
Ledbury to Tewkesbury rd. From
Ledbury take Malvern rd & turn R after
11/4 m towards Eastnor-Tewkesbury.
Roger Oates Studio 3/4 m along rd, on
LH-side. Situated behind the design
studio of Roger Oates Design Co.
Parking in car park.* **Adm Donation
(share to The Gloucester MS
Information Therapy Centre). Daily
Weds to Fris 14 May to Fri 5 Sept;
(10-5).**
Garden with strong design structure in
an idyllic setting of Eastnor parkland.
Dense and natural planting of mixed
perennials and herbaceous plants
selected for the owners pleasure with
texture and fragrance paramount. The
Garden is an enclosed 1/3 -acre, set
within a 3-acre orchard.
🗡

31 LONGACRE
Evendine Lane, Colwall Green
WR13 6DT. Mr D M Pudsey, 01684
540377, davidpudsey@onetel.com.
*3m S of Malvern. Off Colwall Green.
Off B4218.* Car parking at Caves Folly
Nursery. Home-made teas at Caves
Folly (not Oct). **Adm £2, chd free,
combined Caves Folly £3.50, chd
free. Combined Suns 27 Apr; 25
May; 29 June; 3 Aug (2-5) Longacre
only Sun 19 Oct (2-5). Visitors also
welcome by appt.**
3-acre garden-cum-arboretum
developed since 1970. Island beds of
trees and shrubs, some underplanted
with bulbs and herbaceous perennials,
present a sequence of contrasting
pictures and views through the
seasons. There are no 'rooms' - rather
long vistas lead the eye and feet, while
the feeling of spaciousness is
enhanced by glimpses caught
between trunks and through gaps in
the planting. Over 50 types of conifer
provide the background to maples,
rhododendrons, azaleas, dogwoods,
eucryphias etc.
♿ 🗡 ☕ ☎

32 LOWER HOPE
Ullingswick HR1 3JF. Mr & Mrs Clive
Richards. *5m S of Bromyard. From
Hereford take A465 N to Bromyard.
After 6m turn L at Burley Gate on A417*

signed Leominster. Approx 2m take 3rd turning on R signed Lower Hope & Pencombe, 1/2 m on LH-side. Tea & cake. **Adm £3, chd £1. Suns 30 Mar; 18 May; 6 July; 5 Oct (2-5).**
5-acre garden facing S and W. Herbaceous borders, rose walks and gardens, laburnum tunnel, Mediterranean garden, bog gardens. Lime tree walk, lake landscaped with wild flowers; streams, ponds. Conservatories and large glasshouse with exotic species orchids, bougainvilleas. Prizewinning herd of pedigree Hereford cattle, flock of pedigree Suffolk sheep.

Medieval dovecote, with parkland backdrop . . .

MAESLLWCH CASTLE
See Glasbury-on-Wye.

㉝ MONNINGTON COURT
Monnington-on-Wye, Hereford HR4 7NL. Mr & Mrs Bulmer, 01981 500044, www.monnington-morgans.co.uk. *9m W of Hereford. S off A438. Monnington-on-Wye. Lane to village & Monnington Court.* Home-made teas, BBQ, lunch, supper. **House and Garden £6, chd £3.50, Garden only £5, chd £3 (share to Monnington Court). Daily Sat 3 May to Mon 5 May (10-7).** Visitors welcome by appt.
25 acres, lake, river, cider press, sculpture garden (Mrs Bulmer is sculptor Angela Conner). Famous mile-long avenue of pines and yews, favourite of Sir John Betjeman and in Kilvert's Diary. Foundation Farm of British Morgan Horse, living replicas of statues in Trafalgar Square. C13 Moot Hall, C15 and C17 house. Horse display daily 4pm.

㉞ ◆ MOORS MEADOW
Collington HR7 4LZ. Ros Bissell, 01885 410318, www.moorsmeadow.co.uk. *4m N of Bromyard. On B4214 turn L up lane, over two cattle grids turn R.* **Adm £4, chd £1. Fris to Tues Mar to end Sept.** For NGS: **Sats 15 Mar; 19 Apr; 17 May; 21 June; 26 July; 30 Aug (11-5).**
Enchanting unique organic 7-acre

heaven overlooking the beautiful Kyre valley and brimming with trees, shrubs, flowers, ferns, grasses and bulbs from around the world. Comprising several gardens ingeniously created within one garden incl intriguing features and sculptures, potager and pools, myriad wildlife, eccentric plantswomen, nursery. Artist blacksmith on some days.

㉟ NEW NETHERWOOD MANOR
Tenbury Wells WR15 8RT. Lord & Lady Clifton. *5m N of Bromyard. 1/2 way between Bromyard & Tenbury Wells on B4214. Signed from rd in Stoke Bliss.* Home-made teas. **Adm £4, chd free (share to Thornbury Church). Sun 22 June (2-5).**
Well established garden centred on medieval dovecote, with parkland backdrop. Several distinct areas, each with own interest, incl walled garden with herbaceous borders, 'wilderness' garden, gravel garden and ponds (unfenced). Other areas in development, wide variety of unusual shrubs and trees.

㊱ OLD CHAPEL HOUSE
Kimbolton, Leominster HR6 0HF. Stephen & Penny Usher & Audrey Brown, 01568 611688, pennyusher@totalise.co.uk. *2m NE of Leominster. A49 N from Leominster. A4112 into Kimbolton. Garden on R at bottom of hill. From Tenbury Wells S A4112 6m Kimbolton. Park in village hall car park 5mins walk, please follow signs. Disabled parking at garden.* **Visitors welcome by appt.**
S-facing 1-acre garden with mill stream and mill race developed into a wildlife garden. Potager and cutting garden for flower arranger. Formal box parterre with old roses and lavender walk. Croquet lawn with gazebo and herbaceous borders.. This garden was devastated by the floods in July 2007; new and interesting developments following substantial re-instatement.. Gravel paths.

㊲ THE OLD CORN MILL
Aston Crews HR9 7LW. Mrs Jill Hunter, 01989 750059. *5m E of Ross-on-Wye. A40 Ross to Gloucester. Turn L at T-lights at Lea Xrds onto B4222 signed Newent. Garden 1/2 m on L. Parking for disabled down drive.*

Home-made teas. **Adm £2.50, chd free. Fri 21, Mon 24 Mar; Sat 19, Sun 20 Apr; Mons 5, 26 May (11-5).** Visitors also welcome by appt all yr for individuals & small groups, coaches permitted, photographers & artists most welcome.
Interesting valley garden surrounding award-winning mill conversion densely planted. Best in Spring but yr-round interest. Ponds, streams, meadows and native trees support a variety of wildlife. Picnics welcome. Featured 'GGG'.

㊳ THE OLD QUARRY
Almeley Road, Eardisley HR3 6PR. John & Anne Davis, 01544 327264, old.quarry@virgin.net. *16m NW of Hereford. 3/4 m off A438-A4111 to Kington, turn R at Eardisley.* Home-made teas. **Adm £3, chd free (share to Acorns Childrens Hospice). Suns 27 July; 3 Aug (2-5).** Visitors welcome by appt.
Gently-sloping garden of 21/2 acres, laid out in the 1930s now being renovated and developed for yr-round interest, previously open in spring. Terraces and old quarry gardens with rhododendrons and mature trees, parterre, vegetable garden and herbaceous beds. Far-reaching views of Black Mountains and Hay Bluff.

㊴ THE ORCHARDS
Golden Valley, Bishops Frome, nr Bromyard WR6 5BN. Mr & Mrs Robert Humphries, 01885 490273, theorchards.humphries@btinternet. com. *14m E of Hereford. A4103 turn L at bottom of Fromes Hill, through village of Bishops Frome on B4214. Turn R immed after de-regulation signs along narrow track for 250yds. Park in field by garden.* Home-made teas. **Adm £2.50, chd free. Suns 4 May; 15 June; 7 Sept (2-6). Evening Opening £6 incl Ploughmans supper (ticket only), Fri 15 Aug (6.30-9.30).** Visitors also welcome by appt.
1-acre garden designed in areas on various levels. 15 water features incl Japanese water garden and tea house, Mediterranean area, rose garden with rill, also aviary. Large rose, clematis, fuchsia and dahlia collections. Seating areas on all levels. New projects every yr.

PEN-Y-MAES
See Powys.

40 NEW PERRYCROFT
Jubilee Drive, Upper Colwall
WR13 6DN. Gillian & Mark
Archer. *Between Malvern &
Ledbury. From A449 Malvern to
Ledbury rd, take B4232 at British
Camp (Jubilee Drive). Garden 1m
on L. Park in Gardiners Quarry car
park on R (pay & display), short
walk to garden.* Adm £3, chd free.
Suns 20 Apr; 6 July; 12 Oct
(10-4).
10-acre garden and woodland on
upper slopes of Malvern Hills with
magnificent views. Arts and Crafts
house (not open), garden partly
designed by CFA Voysey. Ongoing
restoration, walled garden, yew
hedges, spring bulbs, natural wild
flower meadows, ponds
(unfenced), bog garden, gravel and
grass walks. Some steep and
uneven paths.
🍴 ☕

41 ◆ THE PICTON GARDEN
Old Court Nurseries, Colwall
WR13 6QE. Mr & Mrs Paul Picton,
01684 540416,
www.autumnasters.co.uk. *3m W of
Malvern. On B4218 (Walwyn Rd) N of
Colwall Stone. Turn off A449 from
Ledbury or Malvern.* Adm £3.50, chd
free. Weds to Suns in Aug, daily
Mon 1 Sept to Sun 12 Oct, Sat 18,
Sun 19 Oct. For NGS: Suns 10, 24
Aug; Sat 13, Mon 29 Sept; Thur 9,
Sat 18 Oct (1-5).
$1\frac{1}{2}$ acres W of Malvern Hills. A myriad
of late summer perennials in Aug. In
Sept and Oct huge, colourful borders
display The National Collection of
Michaelmas daisies; backed by
autumn colouring trees and shrubs.
Many unusual plants to be seen, incl
bamboos, ferns and acers. Featured in
'Daily Telegraph', 'Dream Gardens' &
'The English Garden'.
🍴 ⊛ NCCPG

42 NEW THE RAMBLES
Shelwick, Hereford HR1 3AL.
Shirley & Joe Fleming, 01432
357056, joe.eff@virgin.net. *E of
Hereford at A4103/A465
roundabout take Sutton St
Nicholas/Bodenham rd, after 1m
under railway bridge turn L signed
Shelwick, under another bridge.
The Rambles is behind 1st house
on L.* Adm £2.50, chd free.
Visitors welcome by appt, May
to Sept, garden clubs welcome.
Plantaholics $\frac{1}{3}$-acre garden
packed with a wide range of

interesting plants, colour themed
borders, large covered shade area,
and water feature. Many pots with
tender plants.
🚻 🍴 ☎

THE ROCK HOUSE
See Powys.

Garden and woodland on upper slopes of Malvern Hills . . .

43 SHIELDBROOK
Kings Caple HR1 4UB. Sue & Oliver
Sharp, 01432 840670. *7m S of
Hereford. Take A49 from Hereford or
Ross. Take 1st rd signed to Hoarwithy
(there are 3). Go past New Harp PH on
R, then next R over R Wye. Up the hill
take 2nd R into Kings Caple, down hill
over Xrds then Shieldbrook $\frac{1}{2}$ m on L.*
Home-made teas. Adm £3, chd free.
Sat 21, Sun 22 June (2-5). Visitors
also welcome by appt May-Oct.
Coaches up to 50.
1-acre country garden planted for yr-
round interest featuring grasses,
shrubs and perennials. Rose garden
and orchard, healing garden with pond
and rockery. Sculpture garden of local
sculptor's work is of special interest,
many on display. Stream runs through
the garden and there are many secret
corners. Garden managed organically.
Featured in 'Hereford Times'. Some
gravel.
🚻 🍴 ☕

44 SHUCKNALL COURT
Hereford HR1 4BH. Mr & Mrs Henry
Moore, 01432 850230,
cessa.moore@btconnect.com. *5m E
of Hereford. On A4103, signed
(southerly) Weston Beggard.* Adm £3,
chd free. Visitors welcome by appt 1
May-30 June.
Tree peonies in May. Large collection of
species, old-fashioned and shrub roses.
Mixed borders in old walled farmhouse
garden. Wild garden, small stream
garden, vegetables and fruit. Featured in
'Hereford Times'. Gravel path.
🚻 🍴 ⊛ ☕ ☎

SHUTTIFIELD COTTAGE
See Worcestershire.

45 ◆ STAUNTON PARK
Staunton-on-Arrow HR6 9LE. Susan
Fode, 01544 388556,
stauntonpark@btinternet.com,
www.stauntonpark.co.uk. *3m N of
Pembridge. From Pembridge (on A44)
take rd signed Presteigne, Shobdon.
After 3m look out for red phone box on
R. Staunton Park is 150yds on L. Do
not go to Staunton-on-Arrow.* Home-
made teas. Adm £3, chd free. Daily
Thurs 15 May to Thur 11 Sept (11-5).
10-acre garden and grounds incl drive
with stately wellingtonias, rose garden,
separate kitchen garden, herbaceous
borders and Victorian rock garden,
lake and lakeside walk with views.
Specimen trees incl mature monkey
puzzle, gigantic liriodendron, Davidia
involucrata, *Ginkgo bilobas* and several
ancient oak.
🚻 🍴 ⊛ ☕

**46 ◆ STOCKTON BURY
GARDENS LTD**
Kimbolton HR6 0HB. Raymond G
Treasure Esq, 01568 613432. *2m NE
of Leominster. On A49 turn R onto
A4112 Kimbolton rd. Gardens 300yds
on R.* Adm £4.50, chd free. Wed -
Sun & Bank Hols 2 April - 28 Sept.
For NGS: Fri 11 Apr (12-5).
Superb, sheltered 4-acre garden with a
very long growing season giving colour
and interest all yr. Extensive collection
of plants, many rare and unusual set
amongst medieval buildings, a real
kitchen garden. Pigeon house; tithe
barn; grotto; cider press; pools; ruined
chapel and rill, all surrounded by
unspoilt countryside. Unsuitable for
children. (This is no ordinary garden).
Restaurant (lunches & teas).
🚻 🍴 ⊛ ☕

**47 NEW TARRINGTON
COURT**
Tarrington HR1 4EX. Mr & Mrs K
C Jago, 01432 262827,
catherine@cirenenergy.com,
www.simplesite.com/
tarringtoncourt. *7m W of Ledbury,
7m E of Hereford. Tarrington Village
on A438. Follow signs from
Tarrington Arms. Park as directed.
Only disabled parking at house.*
Home-made teas in cider barn.
Adm £5, chd free (Share to St
Michaels Hospice). Sats 5 Apr;
13 Sept (12-5). Visitors also
welcome by appt, all-yr, talks &
workshops also available.
Coaches permitted.
C16 timber framed farmhouse (not
open), set in 5-acre mature garden

planted for all-yr interest. Many newly designed and planted features incl magnificent tulip display, Italian herbaceous, Mediterranean, cutting, hot, courtyard, Gothic rose and kitchen gardens. Arboretum, turf mounds, orangery, woodland, orchard and vineyard. Garden full of unusual statuary and design features. Talks in Apr on spring bulbs and in Sept on small-scale vine planting for wine production. Slight slope in places.

♿ ✂ ✿ ☕ ☎

TAWRYN
See Powys.

THE WALLED GARDEN
See Powys.

48 WESTON HALL
Weston-under-Penyard HR9 7NS. Mr P & Miss L Aldrich-Blake, 01989 562597. *1m E of Ross-on-Wye. On A40 towards Gloucester. Parking in field with entrance off lane 1/4 m before house.* **Adm £4, chd free. Sun 25 May (2-6). Visitors also welcome by appt for groups.**
6 acres surrounding Elizabethan house (not open). Large walled garden with herbaceous borders, vegetables and fruit, overlooked by Millennium folly. Lawns with both mature and recently planted trees, shrubs with many unusual varieties. Ornamental ponds and small lake. Traditional country house garden, but evolving after 4 generations in the family.

♿ ✂ ✿ ☕

49 WESTON MEWS
Weston-under-Penyard HR9 7NZ. Ann Rothwell & John Hercock, 01989 563823. *2m E of Ross-on-Wye. Going towards Gloucester on A40, continue approx 100yds past the*

Weston Cross PH and turn R into grey brick-paved courtyard. **Adm £3, chd free (share to St Michael's Hospice). Visitors welcome by appt June - Aug. Refreshments available.**
Walled ex-kitchen garden divided by yew and box hedges. Traditional in style and planting with large herbaceous beds and borders at different levels. Broad range of plants incl roses. Enclosed garden with sundial. Large vine house.

♿ ✂ ☕ ☎

50 ◆ WESTONBURY MILL WATER GARDEN
Pembridge HR6 9HZ. Mr & Mrs Richard Pim, 01544 388650, www.westonburymillwatergardens.com. *8m W of Leominster. On A44 1 1/2 m W of village of Pembridge, L into signed drive.* **Adm £3.50, chd £1. Daily Easter to 30 Sept. For NGS: Suns 20 Apr; 31 Aug (11-5).**
2-acre water mill garden situated amid fields and orchards. Colourful waterside plantings of bog and moisture-loving plants around a tangle of streams and ponds, together with a natural bog garden in the area of the Old Mill pond. Unusual water features incl stone tower with water wheel.

♿ ✿ ☕

51 WHITFIELD
Wormbridge HR2 9BA. Mr & Mrs Edward Clive, 01981 570202, tboyd@globalnet.co.uk. *8m SW of Hereford. On A465 Hereford to Abergavenny rd.* Home-made teas. **Adm £3.50, chd free. Suns 9 Mar; 11 May (2-5).**
Parkland, wild flowers, ponds, walled garden, many flowering magnolias (species and hybrids), 1780 ginkgo tree, 1 1/2 m woodland walk with 1851 redwood grove. Picnic parties welcome.

✿ ☕

52 ◆ THE WIGGLY GARDEN
Wiggly Wigglers, Blakemere HR2 9PX. Duchy of Cornwall, 01981 500391, www.wigglywigglers.co.uk. *9m W of Hereford. On B4352, halfway between Hereford and Hay-on-Wye.* **Adm £3, chd £1. For NGS: Sun 27 July (2-5).**
The Wiggly Garden: Bringing nature home: Our walled garden is an oasis for wildlife, full of wild flowers, perennials, trees and hedges to attract wildlife. This year we will be having a series of short informal talks on bees, bugs, worms, composting and a lot more. For children, pond dipping, nature trails. Farmer Phil's Tractor Safari prebook by email pwg@lowerblakemere.co.uk. Featured on BBC Hereford & Worcester.

♿ ✿ ☕

53 NEW WOODVIEW
Great Doward, Whitchurch HR9 6DZ. Janet & Clive Townsend. *6m SW of Ross-on-Wye, 4m NE of Monmouth. A40 Ross/Monmouth. At Whitchurch follow signs to Symonds Yat West. Then signs to Dowards Park Campsite. Take uneven forest track, 1st L, garden 2nd on L.* Light refreshments & teas. **Adm £3, chd free. Suns 13, 20 July (2-5).**
Formal and informal gardens approx 2 acres in woodland setting. Herbaceous borders, hosta collection, mature trees, shrubs and seasonal bedding. Gently sloping lawns. Statuary and found sculpture, local limestone, rockwork and pools. Woodland garden, wild flower meadow and indiginous orchids.

♿ ☕

Herefordshire County Volunteers

County Organiser
Mrs R Verity, The Mill, Eyton, Leominster HR6 OAD, 01568 615200, crowards@tiscali.co.uk

County Treasurer
Mr Michael Robins, Newsholme, 77 Bridge Street, Ledbury HR8 2AN, 01531 632232

Publicity
Mrs Sue Evans, The Nest, Moreton, Eye, nr Leominster HR6 0DP, 01568 614501, sue@thenest99.freeserve.co.uk

Leaflet Coordinator & Distributor
Mrs Debra Tritton, Swinmore House, Munsley, Ledbury HR8 3SJ, 01531 670336, debra.T2@ukonline.co.uk

Assistant County Organisers
Lady Curtis, South Parade House, Ledbury, Herefordshire HR8 2HB
Dr J A F Evans, 7 St Margaret's Road, Hereford HR1 1TS, 01432 273000, antliz@talktalk.net
Mrs Nicola Harper, Kymmin Cottage, Hopley's Green, Almeley, Hereford HR3 6QX, 01544 340680
Mrs Gill Mullin, The White House, Lea, Ross-on-Wye HR9 7LQ, 01989 750593, gill@longorchard.plus.com
Mr Graham Spencer, 4 Nightingale Way, Hereford HR1 2NQ, 01432 267744, gramy.spencer@virgin.net

HERTFORDSHIRE

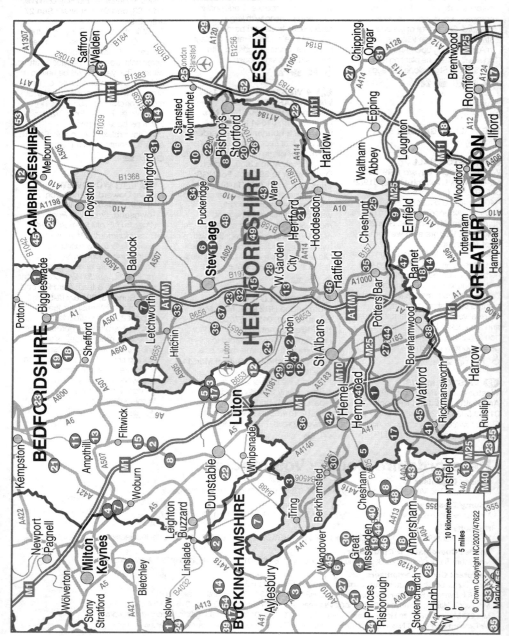

Opening Dates

March

SATURDAY 1
9 Capel Manor Gardens

SUNDAY 2
9 Capel Manor Gardens

SUNDAY 30
31 Pelham House

April

SUNDAY 6
39 St Paul's Walden Bury

SUNDAY 13
38 St Mary's Croft

SUNDAY 20
2 Amwell Cottage

SUNDAY 27
29 20 Park Avenue South

May

SUNDAY 4
30 Patchwork
31 Pelham House
36 Ragged Hall

FRIDAY 9
44 The Walled Garden (Evening)

SUNDAY 11
1 The Abbots House
21 Jenningsbury
38 St Mary's Croft

SUNDAY 18
10 Cockhamsted
19 High Elms Gardens
25 Marina Gardens
47 West Lodge Park

SUNDAY 25
17 Great Sarratt Hall
35 Queenswood School
48 The White House

MONDAY 26
35 Queenswood School

FRIDAY 30
15 The End House (Late Afternoon & Evening)

June

SUNDAY 1
8 Bromley Hall
15 The End House

THURSDAY 5
41 Stresa (Evening)

SUNDAY 8
16 Furneux Pelham Gardens
32 Plummers Farm
43 Thundridge Hill House

FRIDAY 13
44 The Walled Garden (Evening)

SUNDAY 15
3 Ashridge
18 13 Greenhill Park
40 Serge Hill Gardens
49 Woodhall Park

WEDNESDAY 18
28 106 Orchard Road

SUNDAY 22
14 207 East Barnet Road
24 Mackerye End Gardens
28 106 Orchard Road

SUNDAY 29
6 Benington Lordship
29 20 Park Avenue South
45 Waterdell House

July

WEDNESDAY 2
37 Rustling End Cottage

FRIDAY 4
37 Rustling End Cottage (Late Afternoon & Evening)

SATURDAY 5
11 Croft Cottage

SUNDAY 6
4 2 Barlings Road
11 Croft Cottage
12 38 The Deerings
26 Moor Place
37 Rustling End Cottage

FRIDAY 11
44 The Walled Garden (Evening)

SATURDAY 12
34 The Pump House

SUNDAY 13
5 The Barn
34 The Pump House

FRIDAY 18
46 West Garden at Hatfield House

SUNDAY 20
13 35 Digswell Road
22 Kennel Farm

SATURDAY 26
42 9 Tannsfield Drive

SUNDAY 27
33 The Priory
41 Stresa

August

SUNDAY 3
42 9 Tannsfield Drive

FRIDAY 15
7 44 Broadwater Avenue (Evening)

SUNDAY 17
7 44 Broadwater Avenue

SUNDAY 24
1 The Abbots House

September

SUNDAY 7
27 45 Oakridge Avenue
30 Patchwork

FRIDAY 12
44 The Walled Garden (Evening)

October

SATURDAY 4
9 Capel Manor Gardens

SUNDAY 5
9 Capel Manor Gardens

SUNDAY 19
47 West Lodge Park

Gardens open to the public

6 Benington Lordship
9 Capel Manor Gardens
20 Hopleys
23 Knebworth House Gardens
39 St Paul's Walden Bury
44 The Walled Garden
46 West Garden at Hatfield House

Also open by appointment ☎

1 The Abbots House
8 Bromley Hall
11 Croft Cottage
13 35 Digswell Road
14 207 East Barnet Road
28 106 Orchard Road
30 Patchwork
31 Pelham House
37 Rustling End Cottage
38 St Mary's Croft
41 Stresa
42 9 Tannsfield Drive
43 Thundridge Hill House
45 Waterdell House
47 West Lodge Park
48 The White House

Large orchard of mature apples, plums and pear laid out with paths . . .

The Gardens

1 THE ABBOTS HOUSE
10 High Street, Abbots Langley
WD5 0AR. Peter & Sue Tomson,
01923 264946,
peter.tomson@btinternet.com. *5m
NW of Watford. Exit J20 on M25. Take
A4251 signed Kings Langley. R at 1st
roundabout (Home Park Industrial
Estate). R at T-junction. Follow rd,
under railway bridge and the yellow
signs will become apparent. Free
parking in village car park.* Home-made
teas. **Adm £3.50, chd free (share to
Friends of St Lawrence Church).
Suns 11 May; 24 Aug (2-5). Visitors
also welcome by appt.**
1¾ -acre garden with interesting trees,
shrubs, mixed borders, sunken
garden, pond, wild flower meadow,
conservatory. Exotic garden. A garden
of 'rooms' with different styles and
moods. Many half-hardy plants. Plants
propagated from the garden. Some
gravel paths.

2 NEW AMWELL COTTAGE
Amwell Lane, Wheathampstead
AL4 8EA. Colin & Kate Birss. *½ m
S of Wheathampstead. From St
Helens Church, Wheathampstead
turn up Brewhouse Hill. At top L
fork (Amwell Lane), 300yds down
lane, park in field opp.* Home-made
cream teas. **Adm £3, chd free.
Sun 20 Apr (2-5).**
Well established garden of approx
2½ acres and C17 cottage (not
open). Large orchard of mature
apples, plums and pear laid out
with paths. Stone seats with views,
many daffodils, yew hedges, roses
and woodland pond. Access from
main gravel drive to grass paths.

3 ASHRIDGE
Berkhamsted HP4 1NS. Ashridge
(Bonar Law Memorial Trust),
www.ashridge.org.uk. *3m N of
Berkhamsted. A4251, 1m S of Little
Gaddesden.* Cream teas. **Adm £3.50,
chd /concessions £2. Sun 15 June
(2-6).**
The gardens at Ashridge cover 190
acres and form part of the Grade II*
Registered Landscape of Ashridge
Park. Based on designs by Humphry
Repton in 1813 which were modified
by Jeffry Wyatville, the gardens are
made up of a number of small
gardens, as well as a large lawn area

leading to avenues of trees affording
views out to the old parkland. House
not open. Paths lead to many features
within the formal gardens, areas of
parkland not accessible to
wheelchairs.

> Grassy paths
> lead round
> packed island
> beds. 2 'secret'
> gardens with
> seating for quiet
> contemplation . . .

4 NEW 2 BARLINGS ROAD
Harpenden AL5 2AN. Liz & Jim
Machin. *1m S of Harpenden. Take
A1081 S from Harpenden, after 1m
turn R into Beesonend Lane, bear R
into Burywick to T-junction, turn R into
Barlings rd.* **Adm £2.50, chd free. Sun
6 July (2-5). Also open 38 The
Deerings.**
90ft x 90ft secluded plantsman's
garden. Trees, shrubs and unusual
perennials provide yr round structure
and interest. Grassy paths lead round
packed island beds. 2 'secret' gardens
with seating for quiet contemplation.
Formal pond and unusual water
feature complete the picture.

5 THE BARN
Stoney Lane, Bovingdon HP3 0LY.
Richard Daynes & Lorraine Donnelly.
*3m SW of Hemel Hempstead. At lower
end of Bovingdon High St turn into
Church St, Bull PH on corner, car park
60yds on L, short walk to garden.*
Home-made teas. **Adm £3, chd free
(share to St Lawrence Church). Sun
13 July (2-6).**
Medium-sized garden around
converted agricultural building in 16
acres. Garden divided into rooms;
roses along with clematis,
honeysuckle, topiary, water features
and woodland. Wild flower meadow
and pond along with small orchard.

6 ◆ BENINGTON LORDSHIP
nr Stevenage SG2 7BS. Mr & Mrs R
R A Bott, 01438 869668,
www.beningtonlordship.co.uk. *5m E
of Stevenage. In Benington Village,
signs off A602. Next to church.* **Adm
£4, chd under 12yrs free, 12-16yrs
£2. For opening details, please tel or
see website. For NGS: Sun 29 June
(12-6).**
7-acre garden incl historic buildings,
kitchen garden, lakes, roses.
Spectacular herbaceous borders,
unspoilt panoramic views. Benington
Floral Festival.

7 44 BROADWATER AVENUE
Letchworth Garden City SG6 3HJ.
Karen & Ian Smith. *½ m SW
Letchworth town centre. A1(M) J9
signed Letchworth. Straight on at 1st
three roundabouts, 4th roundabout
take 4th exit then R into Broadwater
Ave.* Home-made teas. **Adm £2.50,
chd free. Evening Opening** wine,
Fri 15 Aug (6-9), Sun 17 Aug (1-5).
Town garden in the Letchworth Garden
City conservation area that
successfully combines a family garden
with a plantswoman's garden. Out of
the ordinary, unusual herbaceous
plants and shrubs. Rare pelargoniums
in pots. Attractive front garden
designed for yr-round interest.

8 BROMLEY HALL
Standon, Ware SG11 1NY. Julian &
Edwina Robarts, 01279 842422,
edwina.robarts@btinternet.com. *6m
W of Bishop's Stortford. On Standon
to Much Hadham rd.* **Adm £4, chd
free. Sun 1 June (2-5.30). Visitors
also welcome by appt for groups of
10+.**
Mature 4½ -acre garden surrounding
C16 farmhouse (not open). It is both
an architectural and a plantsman's
garden with an immaculate kitchen garden.
Good use has been made of walls and
hedges to shelter borders filled with a
mixture of shrubs, foliage plants and
unusual perennials. Mown paths
through rough grass reveal glimpses of
countryside beyond. Petanque court.
Access over gravel.

9 ◆ CAPEL MANOR GARDENS
Bullsmoor Lane, Enfield, Middlesex
EN1 4RQ. Capel Manor Charitable
Corporation,
www.capelmanorgardens.co.uk. *2m
from Cheshunt. 3 mins from junction*

M25/A10. **Adm £6, chd £3, concessions £5. For other dates please tel or see website. For NGS: Sats, Suns 1, 2 Mar; 4, 5 Oct (10-6).** 30 acres of historical and modern theme gardens, Japanese garden, large Italian style maze, rock and water features. Walled garden with rose collection and woodland walks. Also trial gardens run by 'Gardening Which?' together with small model gardens, incl new front gardens designed to inspire and provide ideas. National Collection of Sarcococca. Chrysanthemum Show (Oct).

  ⬡ **NCCPG** ☕

CLAVERING GARDENS
See Essex.

⑩ COCKHAMSTED
Braughing SG11 2NT. **David & Jan Marques.** *7m N of Ware. W of Bishops Stortford. 2m E of village towards Braughing Friars. 1st turn L in Friars Rd.* Home-made teas. **Adm £3.50, chd free. Sun 18 May (2-6).** Lovely country garden surrounded by open fields. 2 acres of informal planting. Alliums, grasses, tree paeonies, early roses. Island surrounded by C14 moat. Remote and romantic with extensive views.

  ⬡ ☕

Rose and
clematis
shaded
arbour with
view over
fields. Small
Japanese
maple garden
with
pool and
seats . . .

⑪ NEW CROFT COTTAGE
9 Church Green, Benington SG2 7LH. **Richard Arnold-Roberts & Julie Haire,** 01438 869688, **richard@richardar.plus.com.** *4m E of Stevenage. M1 J7. A602 Hertford, L at 6th roundabout, down short hill to mini roundabout, straight across (Broadwater Lane). Through Aston to Xrds (1½ m). Straight across. Cottage on R after 1½ m opp church.* **Adm £3, chd free. Sat 5, Sun 6 July (11-5). Visitors also welcome by appt.** C16 cottage (not open) with small but extensively planted garden divided by hedges and tall shrubs into several different areas. The garden's impact is achieved mainly by the use of varigated and colourful-leafed shrubs and perennials. Small mixed border devoted to shades of blue, pink and white. Small pool with gold fish, water feature and seat. Rose and clematis shaded arbour with view over fields. Small Japanese maple garden with pool and seats. Further 2 seater bench with view across main garden to C13 church. Gravel paths.

  ☎

⑫ NEW 38 THE DEERINGS
Harpenden AL5 2PE. **Christine & David Viollet.** *1m S of Harpenden. Turn W off A1081 between St Albans & Harpenden at Beesonend Lane, bear R, L at 1st T-junction, R at 2nd T-junction 300 yds on R.* **Adm £2.50, chd free. Sun 6 July (2-5). Also open 2 Barlings Road.** ½-acre garden with many shrubs and mixed borders, sunken garden with ornamental pond, and natural pond. 2 greenhouses and 4 vegetable beds. A garden of different 'rooms', some formal, some informal.

  ✚

⑬ 35 DIGSWELL ROAD
Welwyn Garden City AL8 7PB. **Adrian & Clare de Baat,** 01707 324074, **adrian.debaat@ntlworld.com.** *½ m N of Welwyn Garden City centre. From the Campus roundabout in centre of City take N exit just past public library into Digswell Rd. Over the White Bridge, 200yds on L.* Home-made

teas. **Adm £3, chd free. Sun 20 July (2-5.30). Visitors also welcome by appt June to Sept.** Large mature trees and hedges surround town garden of approx ⅓ acre. Wide Oudolf-inspired naturalistic herbaceous borders with perennial and ornamental grasses surround lawn. Beyond, grass paths link island beds and contemporary style planting gradually gives way to the exotic, leading finally to small jungle garden with unusual less hardy plants. Featured on BBC Open Gardens. Grass paths, gentle slopes.

  ✚ ⬡ ☕ ☎

⑭ 207 EAST BARNET ROAD
New Barnet EN4 8QS. **Margaret Chadwick,** 020 8440 0377, **magg1ee@hotmail.com.** *M25 J24 then A111 to Cockfosters. Underground stations High Barnet or Cockfosters. On bus route 184, 307 & 326.* Home-made teas. **Adm £2, chd free. Sun 22 June (2-5). Visitors also welcome by appt.** Delightful example of minute courtyard garden 25ft x 30ft. High fences are covered with clematis, honeysuckle and passion flowers, roses and vines scramble over an arch above a seat. Small pond with goldfish and water plants. Many interesting and unusual plants, mainly in pots. Featured in 'Garden News'.

  ✚ ⬡ ☕ ☎

⑮ THE END HOUSE
15 Hangmans Lane, Welwyn AL6 0TJ. **Sarah Marsh.** *2m NE of Welwyn. A1 J6 over 2 roundabouts turn R at next roundabout onto B197 for approx 1½ m towards Knebworth. Turn L into Cannonfield Rd after 1m car park on L. Short woodland walk to garden. Disabled parking only at garden.* Home-made teas. **Adm £3, chd free (share to The United Bristol Hospitals). Late Afternoon & Evening Opening** wine, Fri 30 May (4-9), Sun 1 June (12-6). Plantswoman's peaceful ½-acre woodland garden which incls jungle walk, tropical planting, bog and dell garden, pond and various water features. Archway to secret garden. Designer bantams and Moroccan treehouse. Interesting and inspirational. Featured on BBC2 Open Gardens.

  ✚ ⬡ ☕

FURNEUX PELHAM GARDENS

SG9 0LD. *5m SE of Buntingford. From A10 at Puckeridge take B1368. Turn R through Braughing village. Approx 3m, turn L Furneux Pelham. From A120 Little Hadham, take Albury rd. Approx 3m, turn L Furneux Pelham. Car parking in field by Hall Gardens.* Cream teas at Furneux Pelham Hall. **Combined adm £5, chd free. Sun 8 June (2-6).**

☕

FURNEAUX PELHAM HALL
SG9 0LB. Mr & Mrs A Brunner
Lovely C16 hall (not open), once lived in by Lord Monteagle of Guy Fawkes fame. Walled herbaceous garden; lake with ornamental waterfowl, islands and bridges. Peaceful water and bog gardens. Vegetable garden and greenhouses.
& ⚓ ❀

THE OLD VICARAGE
SG9 0LD. Mr & Mrs J Lockhart.
In centre of village adjoining historic C13 church
An interesting vicarage garden containing ancient sycamores, yews and later specimen trees; shrub and herbaceous borders; water feature and woodland walk.
& ⚓ ❀

⑰ GREAT SARRATT HALL
Sarratt, Rickmansworth WD3 4PD. Mr H M Neal. *5m N of Rickmansworth. From Watford N via A41 (or M1 J5) to Kings Langley; left (W) to Sarratt; garden is 1st on R after village sign.* Home-made cream teas. **Adm £4, chd free (share to The Courtauld Institute of Art). Sun 25 May (2-6).**
4 acres. Herbaceous and mixed shrub borders; pond, moisture-loving plants and trees; walled kitchen garden; rhododendrons, magnolias, camellias; new planting of specialist conifers and rare trees.
& ⚓ ❀ ☕

⑱ 13 GREENHILL PARK
Barnet EN5 1HQ. Sally & Andy Fry. *1m S of High Barnet. ½ m S of High Barnet tube stn. Take 1st L after Odeon Cinema, Weaver PH on corner.* Buses: 34, 234, 263, 326, 84. Home-made teas. **Adm £2.50, chd free. Sun 15 June (2-5).**
An oasis in suburbia. Approx ¼ -acre. Entrance via living willow and clematis arbour. Colourful herbaceous borders,

wildlife pond, summer house, mature trees, shady fern garden. Series of rustic arches link main garden to path through wildlife-friendly secret garden, incorporating tree fern collection, acers, stumpery and architectural plants.
⚓ ❀ ☕

⑲ HIGH ELMS GARDENS
Harpenden AL5 2JU. *On B487 Redbourn Lane off A1081 St Albans to Harpenden Rd.* Home-made teas at The Spinney. **Combined adm £5, chd free. Sun 18 May (2-6).**
☕

9 HIGH ELMS
Pat & Bill Gordon
⅓ -acre garden begun 10yrs ago. Mature trees to front and side underplanted with shrubs and spring bulbs. Sheltered scree garden for plants needing some protection. Patio garden, pergola, raised beds, rockery, lawns and sundial.

THE SPINNEY
Tina & Michael Belderbos
A changing and developing ½ -acre garden for yr-round interest.
& ❀

Wild flower meadow designed by Julie Toll, moat, ponds and borders created to attract wildlife . . .

⑳ ◆ HOPLEYS
High Street, Much Hadham SG10 6BU. Mr Aubrey Barker, 01279 842509, www.hopleys.co.uk. *5m W of Bishop's Stortford. On B1004. M11 (J8) 7m or A10 (Puckeridge) 5m via A120. 50yds N of Bull PH in centre of Much Hadham.* **Donations. Open every Mon, Wed to Sat (9-5), Sun Mar to Oct (2-5).**
4 acres of constantly developing garden; trees, shrubs, herbaceous and grasses; island beds with mixed planting in parkland setting; pond.
& ⚓ ❀ ☕

THE HYDE WALLED GARDEN
See Bedfordshire.

㉑ JENNINGSBURY
Hertford Heath SG13 7NS. Barry & Gail Fox. *1m SE of Hertford. From A414 between A10 & Hertford take B1197 to Hertford Heath & Hoddesdon (Foxholes roundabout, Lancaster Mercedes Garage). ½ m on RH-side at post & rail fence.* Home-made teas. **Adm £3.50, chd free. Sun 11 May (2-5.30).**
Approx 3 acres of wild flower meadow designed by Julie Toll; moat, ponds and borders created to attract wildlife. Approx 1 acre formal, mixed planting surrounds C17 farmhouse (not open).
& ⚓ ❀ ☕

㉒ KENNEL FARM
Albury End, Little Hadham, Ware SG11 2HS. Mr & Mrs Oliver Weaver. *4m W of Bishops Stortford. From A10 take A120 signed Bishops Stortford, 3m turn L to Albury School/Albury End. 1st house on L. From M11 follow A120 1st R after Little Hadham T-lights.* Home-made teas. **Adm £3.50, chd free. Sun 20 July (2-5.30).**
Tranquil 2-acre garden surrounding Tudor farmhouse (not open). Mixed borders of shrubs and herbaceous. 8 acre mature park, woodland and nut grove. Bowtop gipsy caravan.
& ⚓ ☕

㉓ ◆ KNEBWORTH HOUSE GARDENS
Knebworth SG3 6PY. The Hon Henry Lytton Cobbold, 01438 812661, www.knebworthhouse.com. *28m N of London. Direct access from A1(M) J7 at Stevenage. Stn & bus stop: Stevenage 3m.* **Park adm £7.50, family ticket (4) £26. For opening details, please tel or see website.**
Historic home of Bulwer Lytton, Victorian novelist and statesman. Knebworth's magnificent gardens were laid out by Lutyens in 1910. Lutyens' pollarded lime avenues, Gertrude Jekyll's herb garden, the newly restored maze, yew hedges, roses and herbaceous borders are key features of the formal gardens with peaceful woodland walks beyond. Gold garden, green garden, brick garden, walled vegetable and herb garden.
& ⚓ ☕

24 MACKERYE END GARDENS
Harpenden AL5 5DR. *1m E of Harpenden. A1 J4, follow signs Wheathampstead then Luton. Gardens on R. M1 J10 follow Lower Luton Rd (B653) to Cherry Tree Restaurant. Turn L follow signs to Mackerye End.* Teas. **Combined adm £5, chd free. Sun 22 June (2-5).**
Small hamlet between Batford and Porters End.

EIGHTACRE
Mr & Mrs S Cutmore
2-acre garden incl shrub and herbaceous beds, wildlife pond, raised vegetable beds, greenhouse and orchards.

HOLLYBUSH COTTAGE
Mr & Mrs Prosser
Well established cottage garden around this listed house (not open).

MACKERYE END FARM
Mr & Mrs A Clark
3-acre garden in grounds of restored, listed C16 farmhouse (not open) with extensive new mixed borders, yew hedge and large pond, rose garden and fountain. Rear borders lead to old mulberry tree, small arboretum, laurels, orchard with various fruit trees and well-house.

MACKERYE END HOUSE
Mr & Mrs G Penn
1550 Grade 1 manor house (not open) set in 11 acres of gardens and park. Front garden set in framework of formal yew hedges with long border and fine C17 tulip tree. Victorian walled garden now divided into smaller sections; path maze; cutting garden; quiet garden. W garden enclosed by pergola walk of old English roses and vines.

Tranquil country garden, crammed full of late summer colour . . .

25 NEW MARINA GARDENS
Cheshunt EN8 9QZ. *1m N M25 J25 - take A10 N, R at 1st T-lights into College Rd, 2nd L then 2nd L again.* Home-made teas at 11 Marina Gardens. **Combined adm £2.50, chd free. Sun 18 May (12-5).**

NEW 11 MARINA GARDENS
Sandra & Anthony Tonge
Colourful town garden filled with trees, shrubs and perennials. Planting planned for yr round interest with little maintenance or watering. Divided into 'rooms' to create enjoyment from different aspects around the garden.

NEW 11A MARINA GARDENS
Mavis Mold
Small town garden completely redesigned 4yrs ago around established shrubs, seasonal perennials and herbaceous planting make this an attractive and very enjoyable garden.

26 MOOR PLACE
Much Hadham SG10 6AA. **Mr & Mrs B M Norman.** *5m W of Bishop's Stortford. Entrance either at war memorial or at Hadham Cross.* Home-made teas. **Adm £4, chd free. Sun 6 July (2-5.30).**
2 C18 walled gardens. Herbaceous borders. Large area of shrubbery, lawns, hedges and trees. 2 ponds. Approx 10 acres.

27 NEW 45 OAKRIDGE AVENUE
Radlett WD7 8EW. **Leonora & Edgar Vaughan.** *1m N of central Radlett. Off A5183, Watling St. From S, through Radlett Village last turning on L.* Cream teas. **Adm £3, chd free. Sun 7 Sept (2-6).**
Tranquil country garden, crammed full of late summer colour. Wide range of choice planting. Small pond, vegetable patch and soft fruit. Unusual plants for sale. Shingle.

28 106 ORCHARD ROAD
Tewin AL6 0LZ. **Linda Adams,** 01438 798147, alannio@btinternet.com, www.tewinvillage.co.uk. *3m N of Welwyn Garden City. Take B1000 between Hertford & Welwyn Garden City signed Tewin. In village stay on L past the Rose & Crown PH on to Upper Green Road towards Burnham Green. Pass Plume of Feathers PH. Tewin Orchard 200yds on L. Park in field opp.* Home-made teas. **Adm £3.50, chd free. Wed 18 (10.30-1), Sun 22 June (2-6). Visitors also welcome by appt, May to Sept, incl groups of 10+.**
Spacious garden behind listed modern movement house (not open). Elements of 1935 garden - lawns, lily pond, topiary, maze, colourful beds and borders. Productive fruit and vegetable cage. Orchard part of the Hertfordshire Millennium orchard. Unusual trees and shrubs. Peaceful country setting and beautiful views. Front garden features rabbit-resistant plants.

29 20 PARK AVENUE SOUTH
Harpenden AL5 2EA. **Miss Isobel M Leek.** *6m N of St Albans. Off A1081 turn W by The Cock Inn & War Memorial up Rothamsted Ave Hill; 3rd on L.* **Adm £3, chd free. Suns 27 Apr; 29 June (2-5).**
Topiary animals and quirky features enhance a profusion of small trees, grasses and perennials. Tulips, gold and brown leaved shrubs, primulas and pulmonarias delight in spring. Yr-round interest from perennials, colourful vegetables in small raised beds, experimental, drought-combating, gravel gardens. Pond and bog garden. Greenhouse, conservatory, aviary. Many seats.

30 PATCHWORK
22 Hall Park Gate, Berkhamsted HP4 2NJ. **Jean & Peter Block,** 01442 864731. *3m W of Hemel Hempstead. Entering E side of Berkhamsted on A4251, turn L 200yds after 40mph sign.* Light refreshments & teas. **Adm £2.50, chd free. Suns 4 May; 7 Sept (2-5). Visitors also welcome by appt, March to Oct.**
1/4 -acre garden with lots of yr-round colour, interest and perfume; a riot of colour on opening days. Sloping site with background of colourful trees, rockeries, two small ponds, patios, shrubs and trees, spring bulbs, herbaceous border, roses, bedding, fuchsias, sweet peas, dahlias, patio pots and tubs galore and hanging baskets.

31 PELHAM HOUSE
Brent Pelham SG9 0HH. Mr & Mrs D K Haselgrove, 01279 777473. *8 m NW of Bishops Stortford. On B1038 E side of village.* Home-made teas. **Adm £3.50, chd free. Suns 30 Mar; 4 May (2-5). Visitors also welcome by appt.** 3½ -acre informal garden on alkaline clay started by present owner in 1986. Plenty of interest to the plantsman. Wide variety of trees and shrubs especially birches and oaks. Bulb frames, raised beds with alpines and acid-loving plants and small formal area with ponds. Many daffodils and tulips.

Lavender walk, double herbaceous border and fine collection of old cedars . . .

32 PLUMMERS FARM
nr Welwyn AL6 9UE. Mrs Helena Hodgins. *1m N of Welwyn. On B656 turn R signed Rabley Heath & Potters Heath follow lane for 1m. Turn L into Sally Deards Lane, Plummers Farm on R approx ¼ m.* **Adm £3, chd free. Sun 8 June (2-6).** Large country garden, beautifully maintained with open sunny borders, planted in the contemporary style, aromatic garden, large mixed borders. Oak pergola planted with wisteria and late flowering clematis. Small wild flower meadow establishing. Featured in 'The English Garden'.

33 THE PRIORY
Little Wymondley SG4 7HD. John & Ann Hope. *1m W of Stevenage. Travelling N A1(M) J8, 2nd exit to Little Wymondley, then 1st R Priory Lane. Garden approx ½ m on R.* Light refreshments & cream teas. **Adm £3.50, chd free. Sun 27 July (11-5).** C16 priory (not open) surrounded by newly planted 2 acre garden within the confines of the moat, part of which remains filled. 4 acres parkland with

many interesting new trees. Teas in magnificent tythe barn overlooking moat and bog garden. Formal kitchen garden. Colourful borders filled with half hardy annuals and herbaceous plants.

34 NEW THE PUMP HOUSE
Coles Park, Westmill SG9 9LT. Lord & Lady Carter of Coles. *3m S of Buntingford. Off A10, leave Westmill heading for Dane End & follow rd for approx 1m. Farm on L, then drive in front of lodge through gate posts for Coles Park.* Cream teas. **Adm £4, chd free. Sat 12, Sun 13 July (12-6).** Part of the landscaped park and pleasure gardens for Coles Park (now demolished). The gardens incl lavender walk, double herbaceous border and fine collection of old cedars. Extensive lawns and splendid views over parkland.

35 QUEENSWOOD SCHOOL
Shepherds Way, Brookmans Park, Hatfield AL9 6NS. *3m N of Potters Bar. From S: M25 J24 signed Potters Bar. In ½ m at lights turn R onto A1000 signed Hatfield. In 2m turn R onto B157. School is ½ m on R. From N: A1000 from Hatfield. In 5m turn L onto B157.* Light refreshments & teas. **Adm £3, chd £1.50. Sun 25, Mon 26 May (11-5.30).** 120 acres of informal gardens and woodlands. Rhododendrons, fine specimen trees, shrubs and herbaceous borders. Glasshouses. Fine views to Chiltern Hills. Picnic area. Some gravel paths.

36 RAGGED HALL
Gaddesden Row, nr Hemel Hempstead HP2 6HJ. Mr & Mrs Anthony Vincent. *4m N of Hemel Hempstead. Take A4146 to Water End. Turn R up hill for 2m, turn R at T-junction. House is 3rd L past Chequers PH.* Home-made teas. **Adm £3.50, chd free. Sun 4 May (2-5.30).** Garden of 1½ acres. Lovely spring garden. Mixed borders. Some unusual plants. Pond garden and cutting garden. Potager with vegetables and flowers. Tulips in May.

RECTORY FARM HOUSE
See Cambridgeshire.

37 RUSTLING END COTTAGE
Rustling End, nr Codicote SG4 8TD. Julie & Tim Wise, 01438 821509, juliewise@f2s.com, www.rustlingend.com. *1m N of Codicote. From B656 turn L into '3 Houses Lane' then R to Rustling End. House is 2nd on L.* **Adm £3.50, chd free. Wed 2, Sun 6 July (12-5), Late Afternoon & Evening Opening wine, Fri 4 July (4-9). Visitors also welcome by appt, groups of 10+.** Attractive C18 cottage (not open) surrounded by fields and woodland. ½ -acre plantswoman's garden, continually evolving. Walk through the meadow to a cottage garden with contemporary planting incl a sunny gravel terrace with drought tolerant planting. N-facing shady borders, topiary, wildlife pond with bog planting, late flowering deep perennial borders and small kitchen garden. Featured in 'Country Living'.

38 ST MARY'S CROFT
Fortune Lane, Elstree WD6 3RY. Hilde & Lionel Wainstein, 020 8953 3022, hildewainstein@hotmail.co.uk. *2m SW of Borehamwood. Off A411 Barnet Lane. Leave M25 at J23, then take A1 London. R at first roundabout, L at next roundabout into Barnet Lane, Fortune Lane is on L in Elstree Village. Careful parking on Barnet Lane and in Fortune Lane.* Light refreshments & teas. **Adm £3.50, chd free (share to Herts & Beds NCCPG). Suns 13 Apr; 11 May (2-6). Visitors also welcome by appt.** 1-acre designer/plantswoman's garden. Grass, shrub and perennial plantings, wild flower meadow, large wildlife pond, bog garden, herbs, rock garden, delightful spring woodland, summerhouse. National collection of Akebias flowering April. Continuing interest throughout the season. Wide range of unusual plants for sale, most propagated from garden. Access over shingle.

39 ◆ ST PAUL'S WALDEN BURY
Hitchin SG4 8BP. Simon & Caroline Bowes Lyon, 01438 871218, spw@boweslyon.demon.co.uk. *5m S of Hitchin. On B651; ½ m N of Whitwell.* **Adm £3.50, chd 50p, concessions £2. Suns 27 April; 18 May. For NGS: Sun 6 Apr (2-7).** Formal woodland garden, covering 60 acres, laid out 1730. Grade 1 listed. Long rides lined with clipped beech

hedges lead to temples, statues, lake, ponds, and outdoor theatre. Seasonal displays of snowdrops, daffodils, irises, magnolias, rhododendrons, woodland paeonies and lilies. Wild flower areas. Childhood home of the late Queen Mother. Featured in 'Telegraph'.

40 **SERGE HILL GARDENS**
WD5 0RY. $1/2$ m E of Bedmond. Turn into Serge Hill Lane by white tin church. Turn R after 200yds to stay on Serge Hill Lane. Home-made teas at Serge Hill. **Combined adm £6, chd free (share to Herts Garden Trust).** Sun 15 June (2-5).

THE BARN
Tom Stuart-Smith & family
2 contrasting areas, enclosed courtyard, recently redesigned with paved area and above ground tanks of water, more open area laid out within a formal framework comprising wide range of herbaceous perennials and shrubs tolerant of generally dry conditions. Area of naturalistic planting, 5-acre wild flower meadow.

SERGE HILL
Sir Murray & Lady Stuart-Smith
Regency house (not open) in parkland setting with fine kitchen garden of $1/2$ acre, large greenhouse with vegetables. Range of unusual wall plants, mixed border, 100yds long.

41 **STRESA**
126 The Drive, Rickmansworth WD3 4DP. Roger & Patt Trigg, 01923 774293, patt.trigg@tiscali.co.uk. 1m NW of Rickmansworth. From M25 J18 take A404 towards Rickmansworth for 200yds, turn R into The Clump, then 1st L into The Drive. From Rickmansworth take A404 toward Amersham for approx $1/3$ m, L into Valley Road, 1st L into The Drive. Home-made teas. **Adm £2.75, chd free. Evening Opening £4, wine, Thur 5 June (6.30-9.30); Sun 27 July (2-6). Visitors also welcome by appt June - mid Sept, groups of 10-25. Coffee & teas available by prior arrangement.**
Approx $1/2$ -acre plantsman's garden. The front garden is a sunny part-gravel area of alpines, Mediterranean plants, borderline-hardiness plants, dogwoods and collection of grasses. Small

woodland area leads to rear garden which features continually evolving borders of perennials and shrubs incl hostas, heucheras, euphorbias, rhododendrons and other shade-loving plants. Astilbes and phlox highlight the summer display; conservatory features sub-tropical plants. (Plant-identifying map and list is available for visitors). Large plant sale (July).

SUMMERLAWN
See London.

42 **NEW** **9 TANNSFIELD DRIVE**
Hemel Hempstead HP2 5LG. Peter & Gaynor Barrett, 01442 393508, tterrabjp@ntlworld.com. 1m NE of Hemel Hempstead town centre. Approx 2m W of J8 on M1 take A414 straight over 3 roundabouts. 1st R Leverstock Green Rd into High St Green, L at Ellingham Rd. R at Orchard Close, L at Tannsmore Close leading to Tannsfield Drive. **Adm £2.50, chd free.** Sat 26 July; Sun 3 Aug (11-5). **Visitors also welcome by appt, Apr to July only, £3 per person.**
A truly interesting small town garden. 50ft x 25ft garden has been imaginatively laid out and creatively planted. Wide variety of grass, ferns, clematis. Fuchsia and ornamental trees feature in densely planted flower beds which incl shade and gravel planting, mini orchard and water features.

43 **THUNDRIDGE HILL HOUSE**
Cold Christmas Lane, Ware SG12 0UF. Mr & Mrs Christopher Melluish, 01920 462500, c.melluish@btopenworld.com. 2m NE of Ware. $3/4$ m from The Sow & Pigs PH off the A10 down Cold Christmas Lane, crossing new bypass. Cream teas. **Adm £3.50, chd free.** Sun 8 June (2-6). **Visitors also welcome by appt, anytime.**
Well-established garden of approx $2^1/2$ acres; good variety of plants, shrubs and roses, attractive hedges. Fast developing 'yellow only' bed is a feature. Several delightful places to sit. Wonderful views in and out of the garden with fine views down to the Rib Valley. 'A most popular garden to visit', Plant stall.

44 **NEW** ◆ **THE WALLED GARDEN**
Radlett Lane, Shenley WD7 9DW. Shenley Park, 01923 852629, www.shenleypark.co.uk. 5m S of St Albans. 2m S of M25 J22, 1m E of Radlett on Radlett to Shenley rd. At the edge of Shenley Village. **Adm £3, chd free. For opening details, please tel or see website. For NGS: Evening Openings Fris 9 May; 13 June; 11 July (6-9); 12 Sept (6-8.30).**
2 acre C16 walled garden. Uniquely designed ornamental garden with terracing on 3 levels, and amphitheatre. Mature planting, ancient fruit trees, interesting features. Fine views over adjacent countryside. 3 working Victorian greenhouses with plants sales.

3 working Victorian greenhouses with plant sales . . .

45 **WATERDELL HOUSE**
Little Green Lane, Croxley Green WD3 3JH. Mr & Mrs Peter Ward, 01923 772775. $1^1/2$ m NE of Rickmansworth. M25, J18, direction Rickmansworth to join A412 towards Watford. From A412 turn L signed Sarratt, along Croxley Green, fork R past Coach & Horses, cross Baldwins Lane into Little Green Lane, then L at top. Home-made teas. **Adm £5, chd free.** Sun 29 June (2-5.30). **Visitors also welcome by appt.**
$1^1/2$ -acre walled garden systematically developed over more than 50yrs by present owner/gardener: mature and young trees, topiary holly hedge, herbaceous borders, modern island beds of shrubs, old-fashioned roses, grasses and pond gardens.

46 ◆ WEST GARDEN AT HATFIELD HOUSE

AL9 5NQ. The Marquess of Salisbury, 01707 287093, www.hatfield-house.co.uk. *Opp Hatfield Stn, 21m N of London, M25 J23. 7m A1(M) J4 signed off A414 & A1000.* **Garden and Park only adm £5.50, chd £4. Easter to end Sept. For NGS: Fri 18 July (11-5.30).** Dating from C17, the garden at Hatfield House has evolved into a gardeners' paradise. Enjoy the peaceful west garden's scented garden and fountains. View the famous knot garden adjoining the Tudor Old Palace. Delightful formal gardens planted for yr round colour and interest. Featured in & on TV, national & regional press.

 ♿ ⚡ ☕

47 WEST LODGE PARK

Cockfosters Road, Hadley Wood EN4 0PY. Beales Hotels, 020 8216 3904, headoffice@bealeshotels.com. *2m S of Potters Bar. On A111. J24 from M25 signed Cockfosters.* Light refreshments & teas. **Adm £3, chd free. Suns 18 May (2-5); 19 Oct (1-4). Visitors also welcome by appt.** 10-acre Beale Arboretum consists of over 700 varieties of trees and shrubs, incl National Collection of Hornbeam cultivars, with a good selection of conifers, oaks, maples and mountain ash. A network of paths has been laid out, and most specimens are labelled. 2 rare Wollemi pines. Limited access by gravel paths.

 ♿ ⚡ ⊗ NCCPG ⊨ ☕ ☎

48 THE WHITE HOUSE

Munden Road, Dane End, Ware SG12 0LP. Jonathan & Sally Pool, 01920 438733, jonathanpool@waitrose.com. *5m N of Hertford. Off A602 turn N to Dane End. 2m W of Watton at Stone.* Cream teas. **Adm £3.50, chd free. Sun 25 May (2.30-5).** Visitors also welcome by appt May, June & Sept only. 24yr-old 1½-acre country garden, designed by owner surrounding 1830s Dower House (not open) to incl vegetables, orchard, hedges, shrubs and herbaceous plants. Featured on BBC2 Open Gardens.

 ♿ ⚡ ⊗ ☕ ☎

Fine views down to Rib Valley . . .

WIMPOLE HALL

See Cambridgeshire.

49 WOODHALL PARK

Watton-at-Stone SG14 3NF. Mr & Mrs Ralph Abel Smith, www.woodhallestate.co.uk. *4m N of Hertford. 6m S of Stevenage, 4m NW of Ware. Main lodge entrance to Woodhall Park is on A119, Hertford to Stevenage, between villages of Stapleford & Watton-at-Stone.* Home-made teas. **Adm £4, chd free. Sun 15 June (12-5.30).** Mature 4-acre garden created out of surrounding parkland in 1957 when C18 stable block was converted (not open). Special features: courtyard, climbing and shrub roses, herbaceous and mixed borders, kitchen garden and areas to sit with unspoilt views. Grassland park full of mature trees incl ancient oak and hornbeam, traversed by river and lake. Visitors welcome to walk and picnic in the park. Featured in 'Hertfordshire Mercury'. Gravel paths.

 ♿ ⚡ ⊗ ☕

Hertfordshire County Volunteers

County Organiser
Edwina Robarts, Bromley Hall, Standon, Ware SG11 1NY, 01279 842422, edwina.robarts@btinternet.com

County Treasurer
Virginia Newton, South Barn, Kettle Green, Much Hadham SG10 6AE, 01279 843232, vnewton@southbarn.net

Assistant County Organisers
Michael Belderbos, 6 High Elms, Hatching Green, Harpenden AL5 2JU, 01582 712612
Marigold Harvey, Upwick Hall, Little Hadham, Ware SG11 2JY, 01279 771769, marigold@upwick.com
Gail Fox, Jenningsbury, London Road, Hertford SG13 7NS, 01992 583978, foxgail@fox06.wanadoo.co.uk
Rösli Lancaster, Manor Cottage, Aspenden, Buntingford SG9 9PB, 01763 271171
Jan Marques, Cockhamsted, Braughing, Ware SG11 2NT, 01279 771312, cockhamsted@freeuk.com
Sarah Marsh, 15 Hangmans Lane, Welwyn AL6 0TJ, 01438 714956, sarahkmarsh@hotmail.co.uk
Christopher Melluish, Thundridge Hill House, Cold Christmas Lane, Ware SG12 0UF, 01920 462500, c.melluish@btinternet.com
Karen Smith, 44 Broadwater Avenue, Letchworth Garden City SG6 3HJ, 01426 673133, 1.smith@laingorouke.com
Julie Wise, Rustling End Cottage, Rustling End, Nr Codicote SG4 8TD, 01438 821509, juliewise@f2s.com

ngs

**gardens open
for charity**

Old gardener (Gaywood
Farm, Pulborough) learns
new tricks! Started from
scratch but framed by old
forest trees and with glimpses
of the Downs . . .

Westacre, Sussex

ISLE OF WIGHT

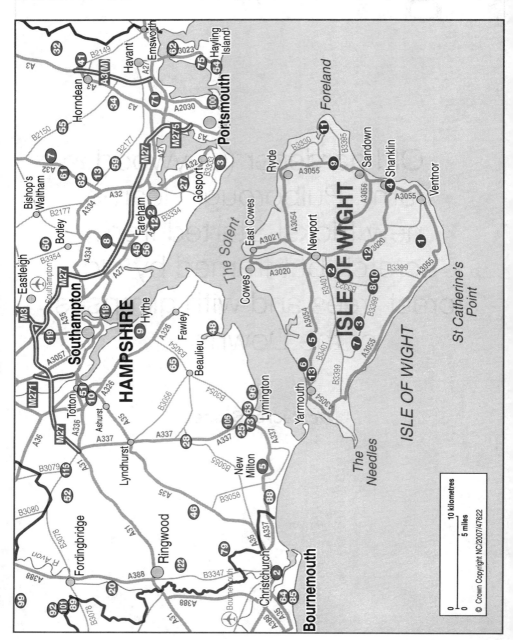

Opening Dates

March
SUNDAY 23
⑧ Northcourt Gardens

April
THURSDAY 17
⑪ Pitt House

May
SUNDAY 18
② Badminton

June
SUNDAY 8
④ Chine House
⑨ Nunwell House

SUNDAY 15
⑩ The Old Rectory

SATURDAY 21
⑫ Rookley Manor

SUNDAY 22
⑫ Rookley Manor

THURSDAY 26
⑪ Pitt House

SUNDAY 29
③ Brighstone Village Gardens

July
TUESDAY 1
⑦ Mottistone Manor Garden

SATURDAY 5
① Ashknowle House

SUNDAY 6
① Ashknowle House

SUNDAY 13
⑬ Thorley Manor

THURSDAY 31
⑪ Pitt House

August
SUNDAY 17
⑤ Crab Cottage

THURSDAY 28
⑪ Pitt House

September
SUNDAY 7
④ Chine House

SUNDAY 28
⑧ Northcourt Gardens

Gardens open to the public
⑦ Mottistone Manor Garden
⑨ Nunwell House

By appointment only
⑥ Highwood

Also open by appointment ☎
⑤ Crab Cottage
⑪ Pitt House

The Gardens

① ASHKNOWLE HOUSE
Whitwell PO38 2PP. Mr & Mrs K Fradgley. *4m W of Ventnor. From Ventnor rd turn for Ashknowle Lane next to Old Rectory. Lane is unmade. Car parking in village but field parking available, except when wet.* **Adm £3, chd free.** Sat 5, Sun 6 July (1-4).
A variety of features to explore in the grounds of this Victorian house. Mature and young woodlands, borders, wildlife pond and other water features. The well-maintained kitchen garden is highly productive and boasts a wide range of fruit and vegetables grown in cages, tunnels, glasshouses and raised beds. Children's woodland trail.
🏹 ⊛ ☕

Cream teas in the Music Room accompanied by a pianist . . .

② BADMINTON
Clatterford Shute, Carisbrooke PO30 1PD. Mr & Mrs G S Montrose. *1½ m SW of Newport. Free parking in Carisbrooke Castle car park. Public footpath to Millers Lane in corner of car park leads down to garden, approx 200yds. Parking for disabled can be arranged; please telephone prior to opening.* Home-made teas. **Adm £3, chd free.** Sun 18 May (2-5).
One-acre garden on sheltered S- and W-facing site with good vistas. Planted for all-yr interest with many different shrubs, trees and perennials to give variety, structure and colour. Natural stream and pond being developed alongside kitchen garden.
⊛ ☕

③ BRIGHSTONE VILLAGE GARDENS
PO30 4BP. *7m from both Newport and Freshwater. B3399 from Newport or turn off Military Rd at Grange Farm, signed to Brighstone.* Home-made teas at the Brighstone Scout Hut. **Combined adm £4, chd free.** Sun 29 June (12-5).
Attractive large village with interesting C12 church. Tickets available at both village shops, The Elms and Yultide. Village map given to visitors. Picnic in some gardens.
☕

THE ELMS
David & Alison Harding
An attempt to grow everything in a small garden: vegetables, fruit, flowers, topiary and greenhouse.
♿ 🏹

GREENS BUTT
Margaret Ratcliffe
One woman's garden - developed over 20 yrs from a wilderness of weeds.
🏹

KIPLINGS
David & Margaret Williamson
Gently sloping small garden planted for all-yr interest, with mixed borders, pond, rockery, vegetable patch and unusual double-skinned greenhouse.
♿ 🏹

MILLER'S COTTAGE
Jean Renouf
Difficult sloping site on builder's spoil and clay planted in tiers with shrubs, grasses and perennials for easy maintenance.
🏹

THE OLD RECTORY
Rectory Lane. John & Jillo Waddington-Ball
Atmospheric old rectory garden under sensitive ongoing restoration.
♿ 🏹

NEW 6 ST MARY'S COURT
Sheila Francis
Small colourful back garden newly planted this year with shrubs, trees, herbaceous perennials and annuals. Also vegetables in raised beds. Front garden designed with gravel, rocks, pebbles and drought-resistant plants and grasses.
🏹

NEW 3 ST MARY'S COURT
Inge Bailey
Small 5yr-old garden on 2 levels. All-yr interest with a touch of the seaside.

NEW ST MARY'S HOUSE
Ken & Evelyn Taylor
Mature remnant of once-famous Brighstone Tea Gardens, with shrubs for sun and dry shade.

NEW TEAPOTS
9 St Mary's Court. June Thompson
Pretty, restful and productive cottage-style garden with its mix of flowers with vegetables, fruit bushes and trees.

WAYTES COURT FARM
Broad Lane. Lyn & John Wannop
Farmhouse garden established many yrs ago, recently developed to incl pond, fruit cage, vegetables and rose arches.

NEW 2 WILBERFORCE ROAD
Sue Crook
Small village garden with interesting features, recently developed.

YULTIDE
Joan & Rob Snow
Home of the Brighstone bean! The Good Life garden.

❺ CRAB COTTAGE
Mill Road, Shalfleet PO30 4NE. Mr & Mrs Peter Scott, 01983 531319, mencia@btinternet.com. *3½ m E of Yarmouth. Turn past New Inn into Mill Rd. Please park before going through NT gates. Entrance is first on L, less than 5 mins walk.* Home-made teas. **Adm £2.50, chd free. Sun 17 Aug (11-5). Visitors also welcome by appt.**
Lovely views over Newtown Creek and Solent. 1¼ acres of gravelly soil exposed to the Westerlies. Walled garden with herbaceous borders leading to terraced sunken garden with ornamental pond and pavilion planted with exotics, tender shrubs and herbaceous perennials. Mixed rose borders. Croquet lawn leading to grass path through wild flower meadow and flowering shrubs to waterlily pond and woodland walk. Gravel paths.

❻ HIGHWOOD
Cranmore PO41 0XS. Mr & Mrs Cooper, 01983 760550. *2m E of Yarmouth on A3054. 2m from Yarmouth, turning on LH-side, opp bus shelter, unmade rd.* **Adm £2.50, chd free. Visitors welcome by appt all yr, please phone first.**
We welcome visitors all yr to our unforgiving clay garden (boots necessary in inclement weather!). Approx 2½ acres of garden on a 10-acre S-facing slope, incl pond, borders of shrubs and perennials and oak copse full of interesting 'woodlanders'.

❹ CHINE HOUSE
Chine Avenue, Shanklin Old Village PO37 6AQ. Sue & Geoff Heald. *In centre of village opp Vernon Meadow car park. White Georgian house.* **Adm £3, chd free. Suns 8 June; 7 Sept (2-5).**
Traditional front garden and tropical rear garden, with many rare and unusual plants. A number of water features incl rill and pond with waterfalls. Bridge and Victorian gazebo, ¾ acre.

❼ ◆ MOTTISTONE MANOR GARDEN
Mottistone PO30 4ED. The National Trust, 01983 714302, www.nationaltrust.org.uk. *8m SW Newport on B3399 between Brighstone & Brook.* **Adm £3.70, chd £1.90, family £9.30. Opening days and times vary according to season. Phone or see website for details. For NGS: Tue 1 July (11-5.30).**
Magical garden planted to allow for climate change, with mirrored

herbaceous borders, formal rose garden, kitchen garden, wild flower banks and unusual trees. The garden surrounds an Elizabethan manor house in a sheltered valley. All plantings organically maintained. Free children's trails.

❽ NORTHCOURT GARDENS
Shorwell PO30 3JG. Mrs C D Harrison, Mr & Mrs J Harrison. *4m SW of Newport. On entering Shorwell from Carisbrooke, entrance on R, immed after rustic footbridge.* Cream teas in the Music Room accompanied by a pianist. **Adm £3, chd 50p on Easter Sun for Easter Egg Hunt, Sept free. Suns 23 Mar; 28 Sept (1.30-5).**
15-acre garden surrounding Jacobean Manor House incl bathhouse, walled kitchen garden, stream, terraces, magnolias and camellias. Subtropical planting incl many salvias. Easter Egg Hunt at 3pm on Easter Sun.

❾ ◆ NUNWELL HOUSE
Coach Lane, Brading PO36 0JQ. Colonel & Mrs J A Aylmer, 1983 407240. *3m S of Ryde. Signed off A3055 in Brading into Coach Lane.* **House & garden adm: couple £9, individual £5, concessions £4. Garden only £2.50, chd (under 10) £1. Sun 25, Mon 26 May. 30 June to 3 Sept, Mons to Weds 1-5. For NGS: Sun 8 June (1-5).**
5-acres of beautifully set formal and shrub gardens with *Cornus kousa* and old-fashioned shrub roses prominent. Exceptional Solent views from the terraces. Small arboretum laid out by Vernon Russell Smith and walled garden with herbaceous borders. House (not open) developed over 5 centuries and full of architectural interest.

❿ THE OLD RECTORY
Kingston Road, Kingston, Ventnor PO38 2JZ. Derek & Louise Ness. *8m S of Newport. On entering Shorwell from Carisbrooke, take L turn at mini roundabout towards Chale (B3399). Follow rd until you see Kingston sign, house 2nd on L after this. Park in adjacent field.* Home-made teas. **Adm £3, chd free. Sun 15 June (2-5).**
Country garden with formal structure developing, containing rambling planting incl a growing collection of old

Mature remnant of once-famous Brighstone Tea Gardens, with shrubs for sun and dry shade . . .

and English roses. Also of interest are the ornamental walled kitchen garden and recently-planted orchard.

❀ ☕

⑪ PITT HOUSE

Love Lane, Bembridge PO35 5NF. Mr L J Martin, 01983 872243, lj_martin99@hotmail.com. *Enter Bembridge village, pass Co-op Stores & take 1st L into Love Lane. Continue down lane (5 min walk) as far as bend; Pitt House is on L. Enter tall wrought iron gates. By car enter Ducie Ave 1st L before Co-op. Pitt House at bottom on R. Parking in Ducie Ave.* Light refreshments & home-made teas. **Adm £2.50, chd free. Thurs 17 Apr; 26 June; 31 July; 28 Aug (1-5). Visitors also welcome by appt.**
Approx 4 acres with varied aspects and beautiful sea views. A number of sculptures dotted around garden; also Victorian greenhouse, mini waterfall and 4 ponds. Summer bedding display and hanging baskets. Gravel paths, accessible grass areas.

♿ ✂ ☕ ☎

⑫ NEW ROOKLEY MANOR

Niton Road, Rookley PO38 3NR. Mr M Eastwood & Mr M von Brasch. *Enter Niton Rd from Rookley village. Manor is 8th house on R.* Home-made teas. **Adm £2.50, chd free. Sat 21, Sun 22 June (10-5).**
Beautiful, mature 1-acre garden surrounding a Georgian manor house (not open). Stunning views of the Downs. Features incl ancient trees, palms, exotics, dry garden, pond, unusual flowers and shrubs. Emphasis is on wildlife and plant compositions. Garden has been developed to require no extra watering or chemicals. Art exhibition of Island artist Marius von Brasch.

✂ ❀ ☕

Delightful informal gardens of over 3 acres surrounding Manor House . . . The long-neglected water garden has been fully restored. Charming walled garden for tea . . .

⑬ THORLEY MANOR

Yarmouth PO41 0SJ. Mr & Mrs Anthony Blest. *1m E of Yarmouth. From Bouldnor take Wilmingham Lane. House ½ m on L.* Home-made teas. **Adm £2.50, chd free. Sun 13 July (2.30-5).**
Delightful informal gardens of over 3 acres surrounding Manor House (not open). The long-neglected water garden has been fully restored. Charming walled garden for tea. Eccentric head gardener.

✂ ❀ ☕

KENT

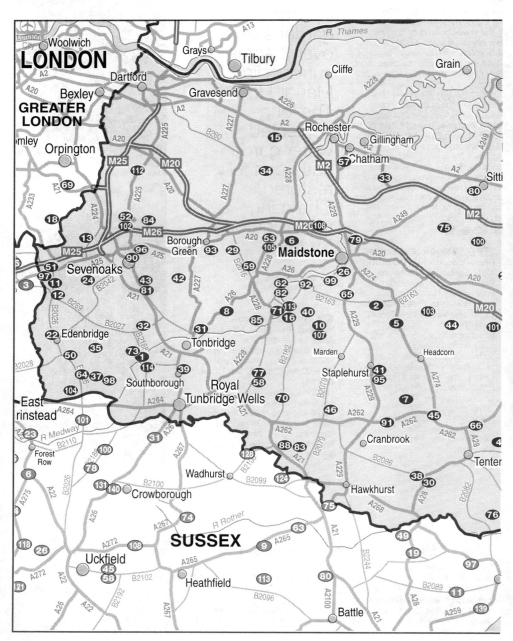

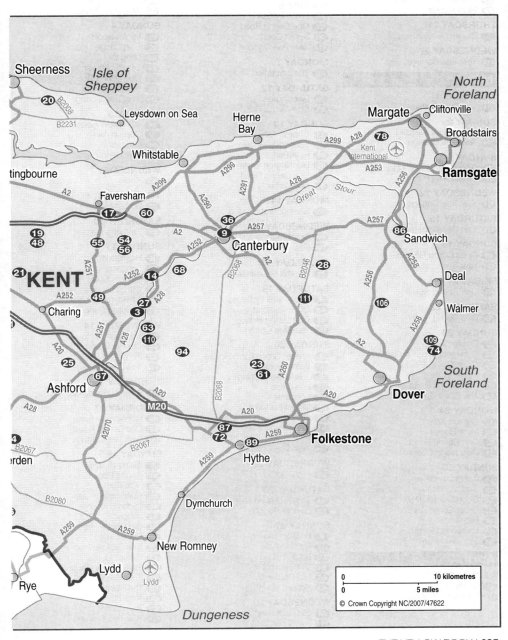

Sheerness
Isle of Sheppey
20
B2006
B2231
Leysdown on Sea
Herne Bay
Margate
Cliftonville
North Foreland
Broadstairs
78
Kent International
Ramsgate
Whitstable
A299
A299
A28
A253
A256
...tingbourne
A2
Faversham
17
60
A299
A290
A291
A28
Great
Stour
A257
36
9
Canterbury
A257
86
Sandwich
19
48
55
54
56
A2
A252
B2068
28
A256
A258
Deal
21
KENT
A251
A252
14
68
B2068
111
106
Walmer
49
A252
27
3
A28
B2046
A2
A258
109
74
Charing
63
110
94
23
61
A260
South Foreland
25
A20
67
Ashford
A20
M20
B2068
A20
A20
Dover
A28
A2070
B2067
87
72
89
A259
Folkestone
...erden
B2067
Hythe
B2080
A259
A259
Dymchurch
A259
New Romney
Lydd
Lydd
Rye
Dungeness

0		10 kilometres
0		5 miles

© Crown Copyright NC/2007/47622

Opening Dates

February

SUNDAY 17
- 57 190 Maidstone Road
- 59 Mere House

THURSDAY 21
- 8 Broadview Gardens

WEDNESDAY 27
- 114 Yew Tree Cottage

March

SATURDAY 1
- 114 Yew Tree Cottage

SUNDAY 2
- 29 Great Comp Garden
- 114 Yew Tree Cottage

SUNDAY 9
- 28 Goodnestone Park Gardens
- 29 Great Comp Garden

WEDNESDAY 12
- 114 Yew Tree Cottage

SATURDAY 15
- 114 Yew Tree Cottage

SUNDAY 16
- 29 Great Comp Garden
- 114 Yew Tree Cottage

FRIDAY 21
- 67 One Dering Road

SATURDAY 22
- 67 One Dering Road

SUNDAY 23
- 17 Copton Ash
- 25 Godinton House & Gardens
- 29 Great Comp Garden
- 59 Mere House
- 67 One Dering Road
- 74 The Pines Garden

MONDAY 24
- 17 Copton Ash
- 59 Mere House
- 67 One Dering Road
- 71 Parsonage Oasts

SUNDAY 30
- 15 Cobham Hall
- 25 Godinton House & Gardens
- 27 Godmersham Park
- 29 Great Comp Garden
- 36 Highlands
- 49 Laurenden Forstal
- 98 Stonewall Park

April

WEDNESDAY 2
- 43 Knole
- 114 Yew Tree Cottage

SATURDAY 5
- 67 One Dering Road
- 114 Yew Tree Cottage

SUNDAY 6
- 56 Luton House
- 67 One Dering Road
- 95 Spilsill Court
- 114 Yew Tree Cottage

MONDAY 7
- 86 The Salutation

SATURDAY 12
- 39 Honnington Farm
- 67 One Dering Road

SUNDAY 13
- 17 Copton Ash
- 22 Edenbridge House
- 38 Hole Park
- 39 Honnington Farm
- 67 One Dering Road
- 89 Sea Close

MONDAY 14
- 91 Sissinghurst Garden

WEDNESDAY 16
- 30 Great Maytham Hall
- 114 Yew Tree Cottage

THURSDAY 17
- 81 Riverhill House Gardens

SATURDAY 19
- 7 1 Brickwall Cottages
- 64 Old Buckhurst
- 67 One Dering Road
- 114 Yew Tree Cottage

SUNDAY 20
- 2 Amber Green Farm House
- 4 Boldshaves
- 7 1 Brickwall Cottages
- 32 Hall Place
- 54 Longacre
- 60 Mount Ephraim
- 64 Old Buckhurst
- 67 One Dering Road
- 85 St Michael's Gardens
- 114 Yew Tree Cottage

WEDNESDAY 23
- 64 Old Buckhurst

SATURDAY 26
- 64 Old Buckhurst
- 83 Rogers Rough

SUNDAY 27
- 6 Bradbourne House and Gardens
- 17 Copton Ash
- 56 Luton House
- 64 Old Buckhurst
- 65 Old Orchard
- 83 Rogers Rough

WEDNESDAY 30
- 64 Old Buckhurst
- 114 Yew Tree Cottage

May

SATURDAY 3
- 67 One Dering Road
- 114 Yew Tree Cottage

SUNDAY 4
- 21 Eagleswood
- 22 Edenbridge House
- 54 Longacre
- 64 Old Buckhurst
- 67 One Dering Road
- 98 Stonewall Park
- 114 Yew Tree Cottage

MONDAY 5
- 16 Congelow House
- 17 Copton Ash
- 54 Longacre
- 67 One Dering Road

WEDNESDAY 7
- 43 Knole

THURSDAY 8
- 30 Great Maytham Hall

SATURDAY 10
- 24 Emmetts Garden

SUNDAY 11
- 36 Highlands
- 54 Longacre
- 61 Mounts Court Farmhouse
- 64 Old Buckhurst
- 79 11 Raymer Road
- 87 Sandling Park

WEDNESDAY 14
- 22 Edenbridge House
- 64 Old Buckhurst
- 73 Penshurst Place
- 114 Yew Tree Cottage

THURSDAY 15
- 81 Riverhill House Gardens

SATURDAY 17
- 39 Honnington Farm
- 67 One Dering Road
- 114 Yew Tree Cottage

SUNDAY 18
- 3 Bilting House
- 11 Charts Edge
- 38 Hole Park
- 39 Honnington Farm
- 46 Ladham House
- 54 Longacre
- 64 Old Buckhurst
- 65 Old Orchard
- 67 One Dering Road
- 77 Puxted House
- 85 St Michael's Gardens
- 92 Smiths Hall
- 96 The Spinney
- 100 Torry Hill
- 101 Tram Hatch
- 114 Yew Tree Cottage

WEDNESDAY 21
- **58** Marle Place
- **82** Rock Farm

FRIDAY 23
- **45** Kypp Cottage

SATURDAY 24
- **7** 1 Brickwall Cottages
- **45** Kypp Cottage
- **67** One Dering Road
- **82** Rock Farm
- **83** Rogers Rough

SUNDAY 25
- **4** Boldshaves
- **7** 1 Brickwall Cottages
- **19** Doddington Place
- **32** Hall Place
- **45** Kypp Cottage
- **54** Longacre
- **63** Olantigh
- **67** One Dering Road
- **74** The Pines Garden
- **83** Rogers Rough

MONDAY 26
- **17** Copton Ash
- **45** Kypp Cottage
- **54** Longacre
- **64** Old Buckhurst
- **67** One Dering Road
- **83** Rogers Rough

FRIDAY 30
- **41** Iden Croft Herb Gardens
- **45** Kypp Cottage

SATURDAY 31
- **41** Iden Croft Herb Gardens
- **45** Kypp Cottage
- **108** Wickham Lodge

June

SUNDAY 1
- **18** Cottage Farm
- **20** 53 Drake Avenue
- **34** Haydown
- **45** Kypp Cottage
- **64** Old Buckhurst
- **93** Sotts Hole Cottage
- **105** West Malling Gardens

MONDAY 2
- **91** Sissinghurst Garden

TUESDAY 3
- **45** Kypp Cottage

WEDNESDAY 4
- **43** Knole
- **45** Kypp Cottage
- **64** Old Buckhurst
- **114** Yew Tree Cottage

THURSDAY 5
- **45** Kypp Cottage
- **76** Primrose Cottage

FRIDAY 6
- **45** Kypp Cottage
- **76** Primrose Cottage

SATURDAY 7
- **9** Canterbury Cathedral Gardens
- **45** Kypp Cottage
- **51** Little Gables
- **67** One Dering Road
- **76** Primrose Cottage
- **114** Yew Tree Cottage

SUNDAY 8
- **9** Canterbury Cathedral Gardens
- **10** Chainhurst Cottage Gardens
- **18** Cottage Farm
- **22** Edenbridge House
- **45** Kypp Cottage
- **48** Larch Cottage
- **51** Little Gables
- **57** 190 Maidstone Road
- **62** Nettlestead Place
- **67** One Dering Road
- **76** Primrose Cottage
- **84** St Clere
- **100** Torry Hill
- **103** Ulcombe Place
- **114** Yew Tree Cottage

TUESDAY 10
- **45** Kypp Cottage

WEDNESDAY 11
- **10** Chainhurst Cottage Gardens (Evening)
- **30** Great Maytham Hall
- **45** Kypp Cottage

THURSDAY 12
- **45** Kypp Cottage
- **64** Old Buckhurst

FRIDAY 13
- **18** Cottage Farm (Evening)
- **45** Kypp Cottage

SATURDAY 14
- **45** Kypp Cottage
- **67** One Dering Road
- **83** Rogers Rough

SUNDAY 15
- **11** Charts Edge
- **13** Chevening
- **18** Cottage Farm
- **40** Hunton Gardens
- **45** Kypp Cottage
- **49** Laurenden Forstal
- **53** Little Went
- **67** One Dering Road
- **77** Puxted House
- **79** 11 Raymer Road
- **83** Rogers Rough
- **101** Tram Hatch

TUESDAY 17
- **45** Kypp Cottage

WEDNESDAY 18
- **22** Edenbridge House (Evening)
- **45** Kypp Cottage
- **58** Marle Place

82 Rock Farm
104 Upper Pryors (Day & Evening)
114 Yew Tree Cottage

THURSDAY 19
- **42** Ightham Mote
- **45** Kypp Cottage

FRIDAY 20
- **45** Kypp Cottage

SATURDAY 21
- **23** Elham Gardens
- **44** Knowle Hill Farm (Evening)
- **45** Kypp Cottage
- **67** One Dering Road
- **70** Orchard End
- **82** Rock Farm
- **114** Yew Tree Cottage

SUNDAY 22
- **2** Amber Green Farm House
- **3** Bilting House
- **5** Boyton Court
- **18** Cottage Farm
- **21** Eagleswood
- **33** 25 Hanover Drive
- **36** Highlands
- **38** Hole Park
- **45** Kypp Cottage
- **64** Old Buckhurst
- **67** One Dering Road
- **68** The Orangery
- **70** Orchard End
- **78** Quex Gardens
- **85** St Michael's Gardens
- **109** Windy Ridge
- **110** Withersdane Hall
- **114** Yew Tree Cottage

TUESDAY 24
- **45** Kypp Cottage

WEDNESDAY 25
- **45** Kypp Cottage
- **82** Rock Farm

THURSDAY 26
- **45** Kypp Cottage

FRIDAY 27
- **45** Kypp Cottage

SATURDAY 28
- **41** Iden Croft Herb Gardens
- **45** Kypp Cottage
- **82** Rock Farm
- **111** Womenswold Gardens

SUNDAY 29
- **4** Boldshaves
- **18** Cottage Farm
- **31** 115 Hadlow Road
- **41** Iden Croft Herb Gardens
- **45** Kypp Cottage
- **64** Old Buckhurst
- **90** Sevenoaks Allotments
- **92** Smiths Hall
- **95** Spilsill Court
- **111** Womenswold Gardens

July

WEDNESDAY 2
- 12 Chartwell
- 43 Knole
- 82 Rock Farm
- 114 Yew Tree Cottage

SATURDAY 5
- 67 One Dering Road
- 82 Rock Farm
- 114 Yew Tree Cottage

SUNDAY 6
- 67 One Dering Road
- 112 The World Garden at Lullingstone Castle
- 114 Yew Tree Cottage

TUESDAY 8
- 97 Squerryes Court

WEDNESDAY 9
- 58 Marle Place
- 82 Rock Farm

THURSDAY 10
- 55 Lords

SATURDAY 12
- 67 One Dering Road
- 82 Rock Farm

SUNDAY 13
- 15 Cobham Hall
- 55 Lords
- 64 Old Buckhurst
- 67 One Dering Road
- 101 Tram Hatch
- 113 Yalding Gardens

WEDNESDAY 16
- 58 Marle Place
- 64 Old Buckhurst
- 114 Yew Tree Cottage

SATURDAY 19
- 26 The Godlands
- 88 Scotney Castle
- 114 Yew Tree Cottage

SUNDAY 20
- 11 Charts Edge
- 19 Doddington Place
- 20 53 Drake Avenue
- 27 Godmersham Park
- 36 Highlands
- 37 Hoath House
- 48 Larch Cottage
- 64 Old Buckhurst
- 69 Orchard Cottage
- 80 Riddles Road Allotments
- 89 Sea Close
- 100 Torry Hill
- 114 Yew Tree Cottage

WEDNESDAY 23
- 58 Marle Place
- 78 Quex Gardens (Evening)

THURSDAY 24
- 86 The Salutation

SATURDAY 26
- 26 The Godlands
- 47 212 Langley Way
- 51 Little Gables
- 67 One Dering Road
- 70 Orchard End

SUNDAY 27
- 31 115 Hadlow Road
- 47 212 Langley Way
- 51 Little Gables
- 61 Mounts Court Farmhouse
- 64 Old Buckhurst
- 67 One Dering Road
- 68 The Orangery
- 70 Orchard End
- 93 Sotts Hole Cottage
- 109 Windy Ridge
- 110 Withersdane Hall

WEDNESDAY 30
- 64 Old Buckhurst
- 114 Yew Tree Cottage

August

FRIDAY 1
- 45 Kypp Cottage

SATURDAY 2
- 45 Kypp Cottage
- 64 Old Buckhurst
- 114 Yew Tree Cottage

SUNDAY 3
- 45 Kypp Cottage
- 50 Leydens
- 64 Old Buckhurst
- 114 Yew Tree Cottage

WEDNESDAY 6
- 43 Knole

FRIDAY 8
- 45 Kypp Cottage

SATURDAY 9
- 45 Kypp Cottage
- 67 One Dering Road

SUNDAY 10
- 45 Kypp Cottage
- 67 One Dering Road

MONDAY 11
- 91 Sissinghurst Garden

WEDNESDAY 13
- 114 Yew Tree Cottage

FRIDAY 15
- 45 Kypp Cottage

SATURDAY 16
- 45 Kypp Cottage
- 67 One Dering Road
- 114 Yew Tree Cottage

SUNDAY 17
- 45 Kypp Cottage
- 49 Laurenden Forstal
- 67 One Dering Road
- 106 West Studdal Farm
- 114 Yew Tree Cottage

FRIDAY 22
- 45 Kypp Cottage

SATURDAY 23
- 14 Chilham Castle
- 45 Kypp Cottage
- 67 One Dering Road

SUNDAY 24
- 31 115 Hadlow Road
- 37 Hoath House
- 45 Kypp Cottage
- 54 Longacre
- 67 One Dering Road

MONDAY 25
- 45 Kypp Cottage
- 54 Longacre
- 67 One Dering Road

TUESDAY 26
- 45 Kypp Cottage

WEDNESDAY 27
- 45 Kypp Cottage

THURSDAY 28
- 45 Kypp Cottage

FRIDAY 29
- 45 Kypp Cottage

SATURDAY 30
- 45 Kypp Cottage

SUNDAY 31
- 45 Kypp Cottage

September

TUESDAY 2
- 97 Squerryes Court

WEDNESDAY 3
- 22 Edenbridge House
- 64 Old Buckhurst
- 78 Quex Gardens (Evening)
- 114 Yew Tree Cottage

SATURDAY 6
- 64 Old Buckhurst
- 108 Wickham Lodge
- 114 Yew Tree Cottage

SUNDAY 7
- 8 Broadview Gardens
- 64 Old Buckhurst
- 114 Yew Tree Cottage

WEDNESDAY 10
- 64 Old Buckhurst

SATURDAY 13
- 64 Old Buckhurst
- 70 Orchard End

SUNDAY 14
- 22 Edenbridge House
- 28 Goodnestone Park Gardens
- 62 Nettlestead Place
- 64 Old Buckhurst
- 70 Orchard End
- 78 Quex Gardens
- 93 Sotts Hole Cottage
- 109 Windy Ridge

The Gardens

1 ABBOTSMERRY BARN
Salmans Lane, Penshurst TN11 8DJ.
Margaret & Keith Wallis, 01892 870900, abbotsmerry@aol.com, www.abbotsmerry.co.uk. *5m W of Tonbridge. Off B2176 in direction Leigh: 200yds N of Penshurst turn L, 1m down lane with speed ramps.* **Adm £4, chd free. Visitors welcome by appt at most times, incl groups. Please phone out of gardening hours.**
Garden developed over 24yrs on a 7½-acre undulating S-facing slope to take advantage of existing features and differing planting conditions. Herbaceous plants and roses are complemented by bulbs, shrubs and trees to provide a cheerful variety of flowers and foliage.

2 NEW AMBER GREEN FARM HOUSE
Amber Lane, Chart Sutton ME17 3SF. Cathryn Draper. *3½ m S of Maidstone. M20 J8 Leeds Castle. From A20 take B2163 to Xrds, straight over towards Chart Sutton. L at Chart Corner then R onto Amber Lane. Follow lane, NGS signs on R.* Home-made teas. **Adm £3, chd free. Suns 20 Apr; 22 June (12-5).**
Last opened in 1993, enchanting 1-acre cottage garden with new and old plantings (a garden is never finished!). Natural wildlife ponds accompany mature and less common trees incl swamp cypresses, Indian bean tree and platt of Kentish cobs. Mass of spring-flowering bulbs and hellebores followed by many old varieties of roses, clematis and summer-flowering perennials. Featured on BBC TV Open Gardens.

A garden is never finished . . . !

ARDEN LODGE
See Surrey.

BATEMAN'S
See Sussex.

❸ BILTING HOUSE
nr Ashford TN25 4HA. Mr John Erle-Drax. *5m NE of Ashford. A28, 9m from Canterbury. Wye 1¹⁄₂ m.* Home-made teas. **Adm £3.50, chd free. Suns 18 May; 22 June (2-6).**
6-acre garden with ha-ha set in beautiful part of Stour Valley. Wide variety of rhododendrons, azaleas and ornamental shrubs. Woodland walk with spring bulbs. Mature arboretum with new planting of specimen trees. Rose garden and herbaceous borders. Conservatory.

  ♿ ✕ ✿ ☕

❹ BOLDSHAVES
Woodchurch, nr Ashford TN26 3RA. Mr & Mrs Peregrine Massey, 01233 860302, masseypd@hotmail.co.uk. *Between Woodchurch & High Halden. From A28 towards Ashford, turn R at village green in High Halden. 2nd R, Redbrook St, towards Woodchurch, before R on unmarked lane. After ¹⁄₂ m R through brick entrance. Ignore oast house on L, follow signs to car park.* Cream teas. **Adm £4, chd free (share to Kent Minds). Suns 20 Apr; 25 May; 29 June (2-6). Visitors also welcome by appt last Sun of month (not Apr, May, June) for groups of 8+, minibuses but no coaches please.**
7-acre garden with a number of new features being developed. Partly terraced, S-facing, with ornamental trees and shrubs, walled garden, herbaceous borders, bluebell walks, woodland and ponds. Grass paths.

  ♿ ✕ ✿ ☕ ☎

❺ BOYTON COURT
Sutton Valence ME17 3BY. Richard & Patricia Stileman, 01622 844065, richstileman@aol.com. *5m SE of Maidstone. ¹⁄₂ m E of centre of Sutton Valence, turn R at 1st Xrds on rd from Sutton Valence to E Sutton, Boyton Court 200yds on L.* Light refreshments & home-made teas. **Adm £3.50, chd free. Sun 22 June (11-5). Visitors also welcome by appt, groups of 10+.**
3-acre garden on S edge of greensand ridge affording spectacular views over the Weald. Garden falls in series of slopes and terraces through which water from a natural spring has been harnessed to create ponds and other

water features. Large mixed borders and several intimate areas featuring yew, box, Austin roses, irises, lavender, perennial geraniums, sedums etc.

  ✕ ▭ ☕ ☎

❻ BRADBOURNE HOUSE AND GARDENS
East Malling ME19 6DZ. East Malling Trust for Horticultural Research, www.bradbournehouse.org.uk. *4m NW of Maidstone. Entrance is E of New Rd, which runs from Larkfield on A20 S to E Malling.* Home-made teas. **Adm £3.50, chd free. Sun 27 Apr (2-5).**
The Hatton Fruit Garden consists of demonstration fruit gardens of particular interest to amateurs, in walled former kitchen garden and incl intensive forms of apples and pears. Members of staff will be available for questions. Interactive scientific exhibits, tree walk, plant and produce sales. Children's quiz, musical entertainment and viewing of Bradbourne House also provided. Featured in 'Kent Messenger' and on BBC Radio Kent.

  ♿ ✕ ✿ ☕

Rhododendrons, azaleas and ornamental shrubs . . . woodland walk with spring bulbs . . .

❼ 1 BRICKWALL COTTAGES
Frittenden TN17 2DH. Mrs Sue Martin, 01580 852425. *6m NW of Tenterden. E of A229 between Cranbrook & Staplehurst & W of A274 between Biddenden & Headcorn. Park in village & walk along footpath opp school.* Home-made teas. **Adm £2, chd free. Sats, Suns 19, 20 Apr; 24, 25 May (2-5.30). Visitors also welcome by appt.**
Small cottage garden in centre of village which incl borders full of unusual hardy perennials. The new pergola and pond are becoming established with interesting plants. Massed bulbs for spring and some slightly tender climbers on the pergola. The National

Collection of geums should be looking good on both open weekends. Shade areas with woodland plants.

  ♿ ✿ NCCPG ☕ ☎

❽ ◆ BROADVIEW GARDENS
Hadlow College, Hadlow TN11 0AL. Hadlow College, www.hadlow.ac.uk. *4m NE of Tonbridge. On A26 9m SW of Maidstone.* **Adm £2.50, chd free. Gardens open all yr 10-4. For NGS: Thur 21 Feb; Sun 7 Sept (10-4).**
8 acres of ornamental planting in attractive landscape setting; 100 meter double long border, island beds with mixed plantings, lakes and water gardens; series of demonstration gardens incl Italian, oriental and cottage gardens. National Collections of *Anemone japonica* and hellebores.

  ♿ ✕ ✿ NCCPG ☕

❾ CANTERBURY CATHEDRAL GARDENS
CT1 2EP, www.canterbury-cathedral.org. *Canterbury Cathedral Precincts. Enter Precincts by main Christchurch gate. No access for cars: please use park & ride and public car parks. Gardens will be signed within Precincts.* Light refreshments & teas. **Combined Cathedral and NGS gardens ticket £10, concessions £8.50. Precinct pass holders £4. Sat 7 June (11-5.30), Sun 8 June (2-5.30).**
Five Canonical gardens all set against the magnificent backdrop of Canterbury Cathedral, plus the Medicinal Herb Garden, Water Tower Garden, Memorial Garden and Campanile Mound.

  ▭ ☕

ARCHDEACONRY 29 THE PRECINCTS
The Archdeacon, Sheila Watson
³⁄₄ -acre medieval walled garden incl the historic mulberry tree in the former Cellarer's Hall. The garden is under renovation, mixing architectural planting with the more traditional elements of the former design and introducing new varieties and approaches to planting. Gravel paths and uneven surfaces.

  ♿ ✕

THE DEANERY
The Dean
Large garden of over 1 acre with small orchard and 'wild' area, lawns, herbaceous border and vegetable garden.

  ♿ ✕

15 THE PRECINCTS
Canon & Mrs E Condry
Large walled garden bounded on one side by the City Wall. Large herbaceous bank. A little more formal, in keeping with the historical house. Gravel paths.

19 THE PRECINCTS
Canon Irvine
Small enclosed garden with a view dominated by the Cathedral.

22 THE PRECINCTS
Canon Clare Edwards
Front garden planted to attract birds and insects. Back garden a very small walled 'secret' garden. Gravel paths.

10 CHAINHURST COTTAGE GARDENS
Chainhurst, Marden TN12 9SU. *6m S of Maidstone, 3m N of Marden. From Marden proceed along Pattenden Lane; at T-junction turn L, follow signs to Chainhurst. In Chainhurst take 2nd turning on L. From Maidstone take A229. At Stile Bridge Inn fork R, then 1st R until NGS signs appear.* Home-made teas. **Combined adm £4, chd free. Sun 8 June (2-6). Evening Opening, £4.50, wine, Wed 11 June (6-9).** Rural hamlet surrounded by arable farmland.

1 CHAINHURST COTTAGES
Audrey & John Beeching
Informal cottage garden, gravel area with mixed grasses and water feature alongside a blue and yellow border. Meadow with hedge of native species. Summerhouse, paved terrace, lily pond, vegetable and cutting garden. Wheelchair access to all but vegetable garden.

3 CHAINHURST COTTAGES
Heather & Richard Scott
Cottage garden of more formal design with clipped box hedging and Mediterranean planting. Double herbaceous borders with burgundy and silver plants. Greenhouse, vegetable beds and pergola leading to lower gravelled area with vine-covered wall. Featured in 'Homes & Gardens'.

Double herbaceous borders with burgundy and silver plants . . .

11 ◆ CHARTS EDGE
Westerham TN16 1PL. Mr & Mrs J Bigwood, 07833 385169, pignmix@blueyonder.co.uk, www.chartsedgegardens.co.uk. *1/2 m S of Westerham, 4m N of Edenbridge. On B2026 towards Chartwell.* **Adm £3.50, chd free. Suns & Fris mid Apr to mid Sept. For NGS: Suns 18 May; 15 June; 20 July (2-5).**
7-acre hillside garden being restored by present owners; large collection of rhododendrons, azaleas and magnolias; specimen trees and newly-planted mixed borders; many rare plants; majority of plants labelled; Victorian folly; walled fruit garden; rock garden. Water gardens and cascade. Rainbow borders and rill. Fine views over N Downs. Featured in 'Kent Life'. Partial wheelchair access.

12 ◆ CHARTWELL
Mapleton Road, nr Westerham TN16 1PS. The National Trust, 01732 868381, www.nationaltrust.org.uk. *4m N of Edenbridge. 2m S of Westerham. Fork L off B2026 after 1½ m.* **House & garden £11.20, chd £5.60. Garden only £5.60, chd £2.80. Weds to Suns 15 Mar to 29 June & 3 Sept to 2 Nov. Tues to Suns 1 July to 31 Aug (11-5). For NGS: Wed 2 July (11-5).**
12-acre informal gardens on hillside with glorious views over Weald of Kent. Water garden and lakes together with red-brick wall built by Sir Winston Churchill, former owner of Chartwell. Avenue of golden roses given by Sir Winston's children on his golden wedding anniversary runs down the centre of a productive kitchen garden.

13 CHEVENING
nr Sevenoaks TN14 6HG. The Board of Trustees of the Chevening Estate. *4m NW of Sevenoaks. Turn N off A25 at Sundridge T-lights on to B2211; at Chevening Xrds 1½ m turn L.* Home-

made teas. **Adm £3.50, chd £1. Sun 15 June (2-5).**
27 acres with lawns and woodland garden, lake, maze, formal rides, parterre. Gravel paths, unfenced lake.

14 ◆ CHILHAM CASTLE
Chilham CT4 8DB. Mr & Mrs Wheeler, 01227 733100, www.chilham-castle.co.uk. *6m SW of Canterbury. Follow signs for car park and gardens entrance from A252, 1/2 m from Chilham village towards Charing, signed on L. Village Hall/Chilham Park. Car park & entrance at top of hill.* **Adm £4, chd under 5 free, concessions £3. Open second Tuesday of month, May to Sept (10-3). For NGS: Sats 23 Aug; 18 Oct (2-5.30).**
Garden surrounding Jacobean mansion (not open) leads onto C17 terraces with herbaceous borders comprehensively restored and designed by Lady Mary Keen and Pip Morrison. Topiary frames the magnificent views with lake walk below. Extensive kitchen and cutting garden beyond spring bulb filled Quiet Garden. Established trees and ha-ha lead onto park.

15 ◆ COBHAM HALL
Cobham DA12 3BL. Mr N G Powell (Bursar), 01474 825925, www.cobhamhall.com. *5m N of Rochester. 8m E of M25 J2. Take A2 to exit signed Cobham, Shorne, Higham. Driveway entrance within 100m on S side of A2.* **House & garden £4.50, chd £3.50. Garden only £2.50, chd free. Suns & Weds 19 Mar to 9 Apr, 9 July to 31 Aug, also Good Fri & Easter/Aug Bank Hol Mons. Evening Garden Stroll Thur 7 Aug (7-9.30, £5). For NGS: Suns 30 Mar; 13 July (2-5).**
Beautiful Elizabethan mansion in 142 acres, landscaped by Humphry Repton at end C18. Herbaceous borders, formal parterres, C17 and C18 garden walls, yew hedges, lime avenue. Parkland with veteran trees (cedars, oaks, planes, ginkgos, chestnuts, walnuts, cherries) with naturalised daffodils, snowdrops, crocus and bluebells. Garden follies' restoration completed 2007, wooded areas cleared for return to woodland glades and parkland vistas. Limited wheelchair access; video available for disabled, please phone ahead.

COLUMCILLE
See London.

16 CONGELOW HOUSE
Benover Road, Yalding ME18 6EU.
Mrs M B Cooper & Miss C Murr. *6m SW of Maidstone. 1/4 m S of Yalding on B2162, on R-hand side.* Home-made teas. **Adm £2, chd free. Mon 5 May (2-5.30).**
4-acre garden created from an orchard in 1973; backbone of interesting ornamental trees planted about 1850, with a variety of recent plantings. Pleasure gardens incl daffodils, rhododendrons, irises, roses and shrub roses. Walled kitchen garden.

17 COPTON ASH
105 Ashford Road, Faversham ME13 8XW. Drs Tim & Gillian Ingram, 01795 535919. *1/2 m S of Faversham. On A251 Faversham to Ashford rd, opp E-bound J6 with M2.* Home-made teas. **Adm £2.50, chd free. Sun 23, Mon 24 Mar (12-5); Suns 13, 27 Apr; Mons 5, 26 May (2-5.30).** Visitors also welcome by appt.
Garden grown out of a love and fascination with plants from an early age. Contains very wide collection incl many rarities and newly introduced species raised from wild seed. Special interest in woodland flowers, snowdrops and hellebores of spring. Wide range of drought-tolerant plants. Raised beds with choice alpines and bulbs.

18 COTTAGE FARM
Cacketts Lane, Cudham TN14 7QG.
Phil & Karen Baxter, 01959 532506. *5m NW of Sevenoaks, 4m SW of Orpington. Sign for Cudham from Green-Street-Green roundabout on A21. 3m into village, turn L past garage. 2nd block cottages on R. Entrance through working farmyard.* Home-made teas. **Adm £4, chd free** (share to Harris HospisCare). **Suns 1, 8, 15, 22, 29 June (1.30-6), (Sun 15 June followed by BBQ, extra £4). Evening Opening £6, cheese & wine, Fri 13 June (7-9.30).** Visitors also welcome by appt in June only.
Cottage garden. No lawns! Intimate and individual style. Approx 1 acre. Self-sufficient vegetable and fruit gardens, with raised beds growing vegetables for exhibition. Tropical garden, cut flower garden, fernery, greenhouses with tender and tropical fruits and flowers; rose-covered pergolas and wildlife ponds. Created and maintained by owner. BBQ following 15 June opening. Many gravel and bark paths, wheelchair user will need strong pusher.

Mature intimate piece of paradise . . .

19 ♦ DODDINGTON PLACE
nr Sittingbourne ME9 0BB. Mr & Mrs Richard Oldfield, 01795 886101, www.doddingtonplacegardens.co.uk. *6m SE of Sittingbourne. From A20 turn N opp Lenham or from A2 turn S at Teynham or Ospringe (Faversham), all 4m.* **Adm £4, chd £1. Suns & Bank Hol Mons Easter to end Sept (2-5). For NGS: Suns 25 May; 20 July; 21 Sept (2-5).**
10-acre garden, landscaped with wide views; trees and clipped yew hedges; woodland garden with azaleas and rhododendrons; Edwardian rock garden recently renovated (not wheelchair accessible); formal garden with mixed borders. Gothic folly.

20 NEW 53 DRAKE AVENUE
Minster on Sea, Sheerness ME12 3SA. Mrs Jeannette Harrison, 01795 873432, jeannette@harrison3000.fsnet.co.uk. *A249 Sheppey Crossing, R at roundabout B2231 Minster, 3rd L Scocles Rd, 2nd L Drake Ave.* **Adm £3, chd free. Suns 1 June; 20 July (11-5).** Visitors also welcome by appt May to Aug for groups of under 25.
Mature intimate piece of paradise. BBC Gardener of the Year 2005 finalist and award-winning garden. Meander through this small but well-stocked garden. Butterfly and wildlife haven. Herbaceous perennials reach for the sky. A garden for all seasons. Art for sale.

21 NEW EAGLESWOOD
Slade Road, Warren Street, Lenham, Maidstone ME17 2EG. Mike & Edith Darvill. *Going E on A20 nr Lenham, L into Hubbards Hill for approx 1m then 2nd L into Slade rd. Garden 150yds on R.* Light refreshments. **Adm £3.50, chd free** (share to Demelza House Children's Hospice). **Suns 4 May; 22 June; 12 Oct (11-5).**
1 1/2 -acre plantsman's garden situated high on N Downs, developed over the past 20 yrs. Wide range of trees and shrubs (many unusual), herbaceous material and woodland plants grown to give yr-round interest. Grass paths may be slippery when wet.

22 ♦ EDENBRIDGE HOUSE
Edenbridge TN8 6SJ. Mrs M T Lloyd, 01732 862122, dg.loyd@btinternet.com. *1 1/2 m N of Edenbridge. Nr Marlpit Hill, on B2026.* Teas on NGS days. **Adm £3.50, chd free. Tues, Weds & Thurs, Apr to Sept (2-5). For NGS: Suns, Weds: 13 Apr; 4, 14 May; 8 June; 3, 14 Sept (Suns 2-6, Weds 1-5). Evening Opening, £4.50, wine, 18 June (6-9). Also open 18 June (1-9) Upper Pryors.**
House part C16 (not open). 5-acre garden laid out in 1930s as a series of rooms, with herbaceous and mixed borders, old-fashioned and shrub roses, alpines, ornamental trees and shrubs, water and gravel gardens, orchard and wildlife pond, kitchen garden and greenhouses; many unusual plants. Group visits by arrangement.

23 ELHAM GARDENS
CT4 6TU. *10m S of Canterbury, 6m N of Hythe. Enter Elham from Lyminge off A20 or Barham off A2. Car parking on the Green and in village square, maps provided at car park and village shop.* Special NGS ploughmans lunches at Kings Arms £5 (12-2.30). Home-made teas. **Combined adm £4, chd free. Sat 21 June (2-6).**
Situated in the heart of the idyllic Elham Valley, an old market village with a beautiful church and surrounding countryside. 8-10 very different gardens: traditional cottage gardens, fun and leisure gardens and scenic gardens with fine views over the village.

24 ◆ **EMMETTS GARDEN**
Ide Hill TN14 6AY. The National Trust, 01732 868381, www.nationaltrust.org.uk. *5m SW of Sevenoaks. 1¹/₂ m S of A25 on Sundridge-Ide Hill Rd. 1¹/₂ m N of Ide Hill off B2042.* **Adm £5.90, chd £1.50. Tues to Suns 15 Mar to 1 Jun. Weds to Suns 4 June to 29 June. Weds, Sats & Suns 2 July to 2 Nov (11-5). For NGS: Sat 10 May (11-5 last adm 4.15).**
5-acre hillside garden, with the highest tree top in Kent, noted for its fine collection of rare trees and flowering shrubs. The garden is particularly fine in spring, while a rose garden, rock garden and extensive planting of acers for autumn colour extend the interest throughout the season.
&. ⊛ ☕

FELBRIDGE COPSE
See Surrey.

FELBRIDGE COURTYARD
See Surrey.

Famous for having inspired Frances Hodgson Burnett to write 'The Secret Garden' . . .

25 ◆ **GODINTON HOUSE & GARDENS**
Godinton Lane, Ashford TN23 3BP. Godinton House Preservation Trust, 01233 632652, www.godinton-house-gardens.co.uk. *1¹/₂ m W of Ashford. M20 J9 to Ashford. Take A20 towards Charing and Lenham, then follow brown tourist signs.* **House & garden £7, chd under 16 free. Garden only £4, chd under 16 free. Gardens Thurs to Mons 21 Mar to 27 Oct. House Fris to Suns 21 Mar to 5 Oct. For NGS: Easter Sun 23 Mar, Sun 30 Mar (2-5.30).**

Formal area designed c1900 by Reginald Blomfield. Famous for its vast yew hedge, cut to reflect the distinctive gables, topiary, formal and informal ponds. In spring the wild garden is a mass of daffodils with fritillaries and other spring flowers. Walled garden contains the Delphinium Society's border, greenhouse and cutting garden. The intimate Italian garden has Mediterranean-style planting. Rose garden. Wonderful setting for the Jacobean house. Sun 23 Mar, Easter Event with children's entertainment, games and crafts.
&. ✗ ⊛ ☕

26 **NEW** **THE GODLANDS**
Straw Mill Hill, Tovil, Maidstone ME15 6XB. The Kent Fire & Rescue Service, 01662 692121, www.kent.fire-uk.org. *1m S of Maidstone. From Maidstone town centre follow signs to Tovil, turn L after Woodbridge Drive up Straw Mill Hill, towards Kent Fire HQ (2nd on L).* Home-made teas. **Adm £3, chd free (share to Dandelion Trust for Children). Sats 19, 26 July (1-5). Visitors also welcome by appt, last weekend in month, May, June & Aug. Groups of 15+, coaches permitted, no refreshments.**
3 acres of grounds laid out in the 1890s around an Arts & Crafts style house (not open). Substantial replanting and work over the last 3yrs. Mature specimen trees and shrubs. Terrace, rockery and woodland paths with rock features. An office with unusual appeal. Woodland paths not wheelchair-accessible.
&. ☕ ☎

27 **GODMERSHAM PARK**
Godmersham CT4 7DT. Mr John B Sunley. *5m NE of Ashford. Off A28, midway between Canterbury & Ashford.* Home-made teas. **Adm £4, chd free. Suns 30 Mar (1-5); Sun 20 July, with Flower Festival (11-6).**
Associations with Jane Austen. Early Georgian mansion (not open) in beautiful downland setting, 24 acres of formal and landscaped gardens, topiary, rose beds, herbaceous borders and superb daffodils in restored wilderness. Flower Festival on 20 July with lunches & teas.
⊛ ☕

28 ◆ **GOODNESTONE PARK GARDENS**
Wingham CT3 1PL. Margaret, Lady FitzWalter, 01304 840107, www.goodnestoneparkgardens.co.uk. *6m SE of Canterbury. Village lies S of B2046 from A2 to Wingham. Brown tourist signs off B2046.* **Adm £4.50, chd (6-16) £1, concessions £4. 17 Feb to 9 Mar: Suns only. 12 Mar to 31 May: closed Mons & Tues. 3 June to 3 Oct: closed Mons & Sats. For NGS: Suns 9 Mar; 14 Sept (12-5).**
10-12 acres; good trees; woodland garden, snowdrops, spring bulbs, walled garden with old-fashioned roses. Connections with Jane Austen who stayed here. 2 arboretums planted 1984 and 2001, gravel garden established 2003. Picnics allowed.
&. ✗ ⊛ ☕

29 ◆ **GREAT COMP GARDEN**
Comp Lane, Platt, nr Borough Green TN15 8QS. Great Comp Charitable Trust, 01732 886154, www.greatcomp.co.uk. *7m E of Sevenoaks. A20 at Wrotham Heath, take Seven Mile Lane, B2016; at 1st Xrds turn R; garden on L ¹/₂ m.* **Adm £4.50, chd £1. Daily 1 Apr to 31 Oct (11-5). For NGS: Suns 2, 9, 16, 23, 30 Mar; Sun 2 Nov (11-5).**
Skilfully designed 7-acre garden of exceptional beauty. Spacious setting of well-maintained lawns and paths lead visitors through plantsman's collection of trees, shrubs, heathers and herbaceous plants. Good autumn colour. Early C17 house (not open). Magnolias, hellebores and snowflakes are great feature in spring. A great variety of perennials in summer incl salvias, dahlias and crocosmias.
&. ✗ ⊛ ☕

30 **GREAT MAYTHAM HALL**
Maytham Road, Rolvenden TN17 4NE. The Sunley Group. *3m from Tenterden. Maytham Rd off A28 at Rolvenden Church, ¹/₂ m from village on R.* **Adm £4, chd free. Wed 16 Apr Thur 8 May; Wed 11 June (1.30-5).**
Lutyens-designed gardens famous for having inspired Frances Hodgson Burnett to write 'The Secret Garden' (pre-Lutyens). Parkland, woodland with bluebells. Walled garden with herbaceous beds and rose pergola. Pond garden with mixed shrubbery and herbaceous borders. Interesting specimen trees. Large lawned area with far-reaching views. Paths slippery when wet.
✗

31 115 HADLOW ROAD
Tonbridge TN9 1QE. Mr & Mrs Richard Esdale, 01732 353738. *1½ m N of Tonbridge stn. Take A26 from N end of High St signed Maidstone, house 1m on L in service rd.* **Adm £3, chd free. Suns 29 June; 27 July; 24 Aug (2-6). Visitors also welcome by appt.**
⅓ -acre unusual terraced garden with large collection of modern roses, island herbaceous border, many clematis, hardy fuchsias, heathers, grasses, hostas, phormiums, and ferns, shrub borders, alpines, annuals, kitchen garden and pond; well labelled.

✗ ☕ ☎

32 HALL PLACE
Leigh TN11 8HH. The Lady Hollenden. *4m W of Tonbridge. From A21 Sevenoaks to Tonbridge, B245 to Hildenborough, then R onto B2027 through Leigh & on R.* Home-made teas. **Adm £5, chd £2. Suns 20 Apr; 25 May (2-6).**
Large outstanding garden with 11-acre lake, lakeside walk crossing over picturesque bridges. Many rare and interesting trees and shrubs. Rolls-Royce Enthusiasts' Club 25 May.

♿ ☕

33 NEW 25 HANOVER DRIVE
Wigmore, Gillingham ME8 0RF. Joan & Fred Jepson. *3m S of Gillingham. From M2 J4 A278, 1st roundabout 3rd exit to Wigmore. R at roundabout into Wigmore Rd, L at roundabout into Bredhurst Rd, 3rd R into Georgian Way, 1st L Hanover Drive.* Home-made teas. **Adm £3, chd free (share to St Matthew's Church). Sun 22 June (2-5).**
Developed and maintained by owners for 34yrs believing the garden to be an extension of the house. Enter through a small courtyard leading to the main garden. Lawn, trees, ponds and herbaceous mixed borders. 3 small secret gardens and plenty of seating to enjoy this secluded garden.

♿ ✗ ✿ ☕

34 HAYDOWN
Great Buckland, Luddesdown DA13 0XF. Dr & Mrs I D Edeleanu, 01474 814329. *6m W of Rochester. 4m S of A2. Take turning for Cobham, at war memorial straight ahead down hill, under railway bridge to T-junction.*

Turn R, after 200yds take L fork, follow narrow lane for 1½ m. Entrance on L. Teas & wine. Seating areas suitable for own picnics. **Adm £4, chd free (share to Rotary Club of Northfleet). Sun 1 June (11-5). Visitors also welcome by appt May to Aug, no coaches.**
9-acre garden on North Downs created over the past 35yrs. Formerly scrubland, it now incl woodland of indigenous and unusual trees, orchard, ponds, vineyard (wine available) and meadowland with many varieties of wild orchids. Haven for wildlife, incl badgers. Conducted garden tours. Featured on BBC Radio Kent.

✿ ☕ ☎

Enjoy home-made teas in this enchanting garden with stunning views over rural Kent . . .

35 ◆ HEVER CASTLE & GARDENS
nr Edenbridge TN8 7NG. Broadland Properties Ltd, 01732 865224, www.hevercastle.co.uk. *3m SE of Edenbridge. Between Sevenoaks & East Grinstead off B2026. Signed from J5 & J6 of M25, A21, A264.* **House & garden £11.50, chd £6.30, Senior £9.70. Garden only £9.30, chd £6, Senior £7.90. Family ticket available. Opening days and times vary according to season; please phone or visit website for details.**
Romantic double moated castle, the childhood home of Anne Boleyn, set in 30 acres of formal and natural landscape. Topiary, Tudor herb garden, magnificent Italian gardens with classical statuary, sculpture and fountains. 35-acre lake, yew and water mazes. Walled rose garden with over 3000 roses, 110 metre-long herbaceous border. New for 2008: walks around the lake. Partial wheelchair access.

♿ ✗ ✿ ☕

36 HIGHLANDS
Hackington Close, St Stephen's, Canterbury CT2 7BB. Dr & Mrs B T Grayson. *1m N of Canterbury. At the foot of St Stephen's Hill, 200yds N of Archbishops School, on rd to Tyler Hill & Chestfield. Car parking on St Stephen's Hill Rd or Downs Rd, opp Hackington Close or nearby side sts.* Home-made teas. **Adm: Mar & May £3; June & July £3.50, chd free. Suns 30 Mar; 11 May (2-5). Suns 22 June; 20 July (11-5).**
2-acre peaceful garden, set in S-facing bowl, with sweeps of narcissus in spring and island beds of herbaceous perennials, roses, azaleas, acers, hydrangeas, hebes and other shrubs. Many conifer and broad-leafed trees, incl plantation of ornamental trees. Two ponds, small alpine bed and hanging gardens feature.

♿ ✗ ☕

37 NEW HOATH HOUSE
Chiddingstone Hoath, Edenbridge TN8 7DB. Mr & Mrs Mervyn Streatfeild. *4m SE of Edenbridge via B2026. At Queens Arms PH turn E to Markbeech. Approx 1m E of Markbeech.* Home-made teas. **Adm £3.50, chd free (share to St Mary's Church). Suns 20 July; 24 Aug (2-5.30). Also open 20 July Old Buckhurst.**
Mediaeval and Tudor family house (not open) surrounded by both mature and unusual young trees, gravel garden in former stable yard, knot garden, shaded garden, herbaceous borders, yew hedges, raised beds, productive vegetable garden. Enjoy home-made teas in this enchanting garden with stunning views over rural Kent. Featured on BBC TV Open Gardens and in 'Wealden Times'.

✿ 🛏 ☕

38 ◆ HOLE PARK
Rolvenden, Cranbrook TN17 4JB. Mr & Mrs E G Barham, 01580 241344, www.holepark.com. *4m SW of Tenterden. Midway between Rolvenden & Benenden on B2086.* **Adm £5, chd 50p. Weds & Thurs Easter to end Oct, Suns & Bank Hols Mons Easter to end June, Suns in Oct; For NGS: Suns 13 Apr; 18 May; 22 June; 12 Oct (2-6).**
First opened in 1927. 15-acre garden surrounded by parkland with beautiful views, yew hedges, large lawns and specimen trees. Walled gardens, pools

and mixed borders combine with bulbs, rhododendrons and azaleas. Massed bluebells in woodland walk, standard wisterias, orchids in flower meadow and glorious autumn colours make this a garden for all seasons.

♿ ✗ ✿ ☕

39 HONNINGTON FARM
Vauxhall Lane, Southborough, Tunbridge Wells TN4 0XD. Mrs Ann Tyler, 07780 800790, sianburgess@gmail.com. *Between Tonbridge and Tunbridge Wells, E of A26 signed Honnington Equestrian Centre*. Light refreshments & cream teas. **Adm £3.50, chd free. Sats, Suns 12, 13 Apr; 17, 18 May (10-4.30). Visitors also welcome by appt Apr to Sept for groups of 5+.**
6-acre garden, its heavy clay soil enriched yearly and producing a wide range of habitats, incl water and bog gardens, primrose and bluebell walks. Wildlife promotion a priority. Natural swimming pool in wild flower meadow. New gravel garden under development. Rose and clematis walkways, rockery, lakes and water features. Large herbaceous beds, some with New Zealand influence. Wonderful views. Picnic area with small playground. Resident sculptor exhibiting.

✗ ✿ ☕ ☎

40 HUNTON GARDENS
ME15 0QT. *6m S of Maidstone. Via B2163 turn S down Hunton Hill and West St. Or via Yalding into Vicarage Rd. Gardens and car parks signed.* Home-made teas at Elphicks Farmhouse & 3 New Cottages. **Combined adm £4, chd free. Sun 15 June (11-5).**
Small spread-out village with quiet lanes and church.

☕

2 BISHOPS OAST
Ken & Christine McSweeney
³/₄ -acre garden, developed over the last 8yrs, with pleached hornbeam, cloud-pruned box hedge, ornamental vegetable garden, orchard, herbaceous borders and woodland edge garden. Gravelled areas.

♿

ELPHICKS FARMHOUSE
James Redman
Set in a working farm with orchards. Owners have further developed an existing garden that dates back more than 200yrs.

Approx 1 acre with established trees, shrubs hedging, water features and vegetable garden.

♿

HILLSIDE
Barn Hill. Sylvia & Gary Thomas
2-acre garden on S-facing slope with superb views over the Weald. Semi-formal area bounded on one side by C19 wall; kitchen garden, pond and old apple orchard.

♿

3 NEW COTTAGES
Barn Hill. David & Sue Heaton
¹/₄ -acre garden with southerly aspect. Formal rose garden, kitchen garden, old roses, herbaceous borders; informal and formal pond areas and cutting garden.

✗

SOUTHOVER
Grove Lane. David & Anke Way
1¹/₂ -acre enthusiasts' garden with many different features from formal to informal and naturalistic. Positive wildlife management. Wide range of plants incl many new and unusual perennials. Strong on internal and external vistas. 3rd Gold Award for Wildlife Gardening. Partial wheelchair access.

♿

41 ◆ IDEN CROFT HERB GARDENS
Frittenden Road, Staplehurst TN12 0DH. Mr Philip Haynes, 01580 891432, www.herbs-uk.com. *9m S of Maidstone. Brown tourist signs on A229 just S of Staplehurst.* **Adm £4, chd free, concessions £3. Mons to Sats (9-5), Suns & Bank Hols (11-5). For NGS: Fri 30, Sat 31 May; Sat 28, Sun 29 June (11-5).**
Created over the past 34yrs. Threaded with winding paths, which lead to Tudor walled garden. Unique atmosphere, with massed rosemary, wall plants and herbaceous borders. Themed gardens incl culinary, medicinal, pot-pourri and sensory. National Plant Collections of mentha, nepeta and origanum and large collections of lavenders and thyme.

♿ ✿ NCCPG ☕

42 ◆ IGHTHAM MOTE
Ivy Hatch TN15 0NT. The National Trust, 01732 810378, www.nationaltrust.org.uk. *6m E of Sevenoaks. Off A25, 2¹/₂ m S of Ightham. Buses from rail stns Sevenoaks or Borough Green to Ivy*

Hatch, ¹/₂ m walk to Ightham Mote. **Adm £9.85, chd £4.95. 15 Mar to 2 Nov Thur to Sun. For NGS: Thur 19 June (10-5, last adm 4.30).**
14-acre garden and moated medieval manor c1320, first opened for NGS in 1927. North lake and woodland gardens, ornamental pond and cascade created in early C19. Orchard, enclosed, memorial, vegetable and cutting gardens all contribute to the fames sense of tranquillity. New for 2008: guided walks around South lake. Free guided tours; garden team on hand giving advice.

♿ ✗ ✿ ☕

43 ◆ KNOLE
Sevenoaks TN15 0RP. The Lord Sackville & The National Trust, 01732 462100, www.nationaltrust.org.uk. *¹/₂ m SE of Sevenoaks, well signed. Stn: Sevenoaks.* **Adm £2, chd £1. Mid-Mar to end Oct: opening days and times vary according to season; please phone or visit website for details. For NGS: Weds 2 Apr; 7 May; 4 June; 2 July; 6 Aug (11-4).**
Pleasance, deer park, landscape garden and herb garden. The garden commands the most beautiful view of the house and visitors can witness the changing seasons in the garden from early srping to late autumn.

♿ ✗ ☕

Natural swimming pool in wild flower meadow . . .

44 KNOWLE HILL FARM
Ulcombe ME17 1ES. The Hon Andrew & Mrs Cairns, 01622 850240, elizabeth.cairns@btinternet.com. *7m SE of Maidstone. From M20 J8 follow A20 towards Lenham for approx 2m. Turn R to Ulcombe. After 1¹/₂ m, 1st L, ¹/₂ m 2nd R Windmill Hill. Past Pepper Box PH, ¹/₂ m 1st L. R at T-junction.* Home-made teas, Sun only. **Adm £4, chd free (share to All Saints Church). Evening Opening, wine, Sat 21 June (5-8). Sun 21 Sept (2-6). Visitors also welcome by appt May to Sept, groups welcome.**

1½ -acre garden created over last 22yrs on S-facing slope of North Downs with spectacular views. Mixed borders contain Mediterranean and tender plants, roses and grasses. Pool and rill enclosed within small walled garden planted mainly with white flowers. Easy-care planting around entrance. New layout and planting incl mini vegetable and herb garden.

&. ⊛ ☕ ☎

45 KYPP COTTAGE
Woolpack Corner, Biddenden TN27 8BU. Mrs Zena Grant, 01580 291480. *5m N of Tenterden. 1m S of Biddenden on A262 at junction with Benenden Rd.* Home-made teas. Adm £2.50, chd free (share to All Saints Church, Biddenden). Fri, Sat, Sun, Mon 23, 24, 25, 26 May; Fri 30, Sat 31 May. All June **not Mons**. Every Fri, Sat & Sun in Aug also Mon 25 Aug to Thur 28 Aug incl (Mons to Sats 11-5, Suns 2-5). Visitors also welcome by appt in June & Aug only for groups of 10+.
Not for the tidy minded! ½ -acre romantic foliage enfolding garden where shrubs, 200 different roses, mainly scented, and 60 clematis ramble and entwine. Thick tapestry of ground cover, predominantly geraniums, ferns and shade lovers in semi-woodland. Summerhouse. Garden created from builder's yard, planted and maintained by owner. Small collection hydrangeas and Eucryphia Nymansay. Featured in 'Gardens Illustrated'.

⋉ ☕ ☎

46 LADHAM HOUSE
Goudhurst TN17 1DB. Mr Guy Johnson. *8m E of Tunbridge Wells. On NE of village, off A262. Through village towards Cranbrook, turn L at The Chequers PH. 2nd R into Ladham Rd, main gates approx 500yds on L.* Home-made teas. Adm £3.50, chd 50p. Sun 18 May (2-5).
10 acres with rolling lawns, fine specimen trees, rhododendrons, camellias, azaleas, shrubs and magnolias. Arboretum. Spectacular twin mixed borders; ha-ha; fountain and bog gardens. Fine view. Edwardian rockery reopened but inaccessible to wheelchairs.

&. ⋉ ☕

47 NEW 212 LANGLEY WAY
West Wickham BR4 0DU. Fleur Wood, fleur.wood@ntlworld.com. *1½ m SW of Bromley. At junction of A232 (Croydon to Orpington rd) with the B265 T-lights, turn N into Baston Road. At mini roundabout junction with B251 turn L into Pickhurst Lane. Follow rd to Pickhurst PH, then 1st L into Langley Way.* Light refreshments & teas. Adm £3, chd free (share to National Hospital Development Foundation). Sat 26, Sun 27 July (11-5.30). Visitors also welcome by appt for groups of 10+, Mar to Sept.
Not your average suburban back garden! Enter through old oak door under brick arch into cool white courtyard garden. In contrast, fiery Mediterranean terrace with marble fountain and fish, and pergola with vines. Natural cottage garden, a tree house in jungle garden, vegetable area with raised beds, greenhouses, fruit trees and chickens. Everything grown organically with emphasis on wildlife. Narrow paths, rear of garden not wheelchair accessible.

&. ⋉ ⊛ ☕ ☎

Not your average suburban back garden . . . !

48 LARCH COTTAGE
Seed Road, nr Doddington ME9 0NN. Tony & Lesley Bellew, www.larchcottagegarden.co.uk. *2½ m S of Doddington, 9m S of Sittingbourne. From A2 nr Ospringe to Newnham turn L by church, 2½ m S along Seed Rd. From A20 nr Lenham proceed to Warren St. At Harrow turn N, follow signs for Newnham along Slade Rd, approx 1½ m. From Doddington village follow signs up Hopes Hill (opp butcher).* Home-made teas. Adm £3, chd free. Suns 8 June; 20 July (11-5).
3-acre garden on N Downs. Contrasting areas incl knot garden, woodland and rhododendrons, colour-themed mixed borders, ponds and secret garden. Watercolour/pastel demonstrations and art display by Susan Amos. Featured in 'Kent Messenger'.

&. ⋉ ⊛ ☕

49 LAURENDEN FORSTAL
Blind Lane, Challock TN25 4AU. Mrs M Cottrell. *6m N of Ashford. Close to junction of A251 & A252, access from both. All parking in field off village hall car park behind house.* Home-made teas. Adm £3, chd £2. Suns 30 Mar; 15 June; 17 Aug (2-6).
2-acre garden with woodland and rhododendrons, around part C14 house (not open). Rose walk and extensive yew hedging framing lawns and borders. Partly walled rose garden overlooking large wildlife pond; courtyard white garden. Vegetable garden with raised beds, living willow shelter with earth seat overlooking pond. Crested newts in the pond, newt spotting whenever possible.

&. ⊛ ☕

50 LEYDENS
Edenbridge TN8 5NH. Mr Roger Platts. *1m S of Edenbridge. On B2026 towards Hartfield (use Nursery entrance & car park).* Adm £3.50, chd free. Sun 3 Aug (12-5). **Also open Old Buckhurst**.
Private garden of garden designer, nursery owner and author who created the NGS Garden at Chelsea in 2002, winning Gold and Best in Show. Garden at Leydens started in 1999/2000 and under constant development, featuring a wide range of shrubs and perennials. Plenty of planting ideas, several water features, plants clearly labelled and fact sheet available. Wild flower meadow and adjacent nursery, display and propagation beds. New area of garden for 2008.

&. ⋉ ⊛ ☕

51 NEW LITTLE GABLES
Holcombe Close, Westerham TN16 1HA. Peter & Elizabeth James. *Centre of Westerham. Off E side of London Rd A233, 200yds from The Green.* Home-made teas. Adm £2.50, chd free. Sats, Suns: 7, 8 June; 26, 27 July (2-6).
¾ -acre garden extensively planted with a wide range of trees, shrubs, perennials etc, incl many unusual ones. Collection of climbing and bush roses and clematis. Large pond with fish, water lilies and bog garden. Fruit and vegetable garden. Large greenhouse.

⋉ ☕

52 LITTLE OAST
High Street, Otford TN14 5PH. Mrs Pam Hadrill, 01959 523637. *3m N of Sevenoaks. At W end of village, just past Horns PH, turn R into private drive. (Please park in public car park opp Bull PH or in Catholic Church car park 80yds past Little Oast).* Home-made teas. **Adm £3, chd free. Visitors welcome by appt, groups of up to 25.**
$\frac{1}{2}$ -acre garden with patios, pots, a pond and 3 summerhouses, and lots of seats in secluded corners for enjoying their tea. Regretfully, owing to old age, the owner has had to give up her usual opening in Sept, but small groups are still very welcome by appt.
⊗ ☕ ☎

53 LITTLE WENT
106 High Street, West Malling ME19 6NE. Anne Baring, 01732 843388. *5m W of Maidstone. In middle of West Malling car park; entry through gates marked.* Home-made teas. **Adm £3, chd under 12 free. Sun 15 June (12-6). Visitors also welcome by appt, groups of 10+.**
Long narrow secret garden, fish ponds, aviary with lovebirds, conservatory, gravel garden and parterre. Exhibition and sale of paintings by Anne Baring. Featured in 'Amateur Gardening'.
& ✗ ⊗ ☕ ☎

54 LONGACRE
Selling ME13 9SE. Dr & Mrs G Thomas, 01227 752254, graham@longacre64.freeserve.co.uk. *5m SE of Faversham. From A2 (M2) or A251 follow signs for Selling, passing White Lion on L. 2nd R & immed L, continue for $\frac{1}{4}$ m. From A252 at Chilham, take turning signed Selling at Badgers Hill Garden Centre. L at 2nd Xrds, next R, L & then R.* Home-made teas. **Adm £3, chd free. Sun 20 Apr; Suns 4, 11, 18, 25 May, Bank Hol Mons 5, 25 May; Sun 24, Mon 25 Aug (2-5). Visitors also welcome by appt, no coaches.**
Plantsman's garden with wide variety of interesting plants, gravel garden and raised vegetable beds. We aim to have colour and interest throughout spring and summer using bulbs, annuals and many containers with cannas, eucomis, *Arundo donax*, etc. Conservatory displays range of tender plants.
✗ ⊗ ☕ ☎

We aim to have colour and interest throughout spring and summer . . .

55 LORDS
Sheldwich, Faversham ME13 0NJ. Jane Wade. *4m S of Faversham. From A2 or M2 take A251. $\frac{1}{2}$ m S of Sheldwich church find entrance lane on R side adjacent to wood.* **Adm £3, chd free. Thur 10, Sun 13 July (2-5.30).**
C18 walled garden with organic vegetables, Mediterranean herb terrace, rose walk and flowery mead under fruit trees. Old specimen trees incl 100ft tulip tree, yew hedges, lawns, cherry orchard, ponds and woodland walk.
✗

56 LUTON HOUSE
Selling ME13 9RQ. Sir John & Lady Swire. *4m SE of Faversham. From A2 (M2) or A251 make for White Lion, entrance 30yds E on same side of rd.* **Adm £3, chd free. Suns 6, 27 Apr (2-6). Visitors also welcome by appt in early summer for small groups. Please apply in writing.**
6 acres; C19 landscaped garden; ornamental ponds; trees underplanted with azaleas, camellias, woodland plants. Hellebores, spring bulbs, magnolias, cherries, daphnes, halesias, maples, Judas trees and cyclamen.
✗ ☎

57 190 MAIDSTONE ROAD
Chatham ME4 6EW. Dr M K Douglas, 01634 842216. *1m S of Chatham on A230.* Home-made teas (not 17 Feb). **Adm £2, chd free. Suns 17 Feb; 8 June (2-5). Visitors also welcome by appt.**
Informal $\frac{1}{4}$ -acre garden; herbaceous borders on either side of former tennis court; scree garden and pool; many snowdrops and other spring bulbs. Doll's house ($\frac{1}{12}$ scale model of house) may also be viewed.
✗ ⊗ ☕ ☎

58 ◆ MARLE PLACE
Brenchley TN12 7HS. Mr & Mrs Gerald Williams, 01892 722304, www.marleplace.co.uk. *8m SE of Tonbridge. From A21 Kippings Cross roundabout take B2160 to Matfield, R to Brenchley, then follow brown tourist signs. From A21 Forstal Farm roundabout take B2162 Horsmonden rd and follow signs.* **Adm £4.50, chd £1, concessions £4. Fris to Mons 21 Mar to 6 Oct. For NGS: Weds 21 May; 18 June; Weds 9 16, 23 July; Wed 24 Sept (10-6).**
Victorian gazebo, plantsman's shrub borders, walled scented garden, Edwardian rockery, herbaceous borders, bog and kitchen gardens. Woodland walks, mosaic terrace, artists' studios and gallery with contemporary art. Autumn colour. Restored Victorian 40ft greenhouse with orchid collection. C17 listed house (not open). Collection of interesting chickens. Special exhibition of NGS art and Participation Landart for July openings.
& ✗ ⊗ ☕

59 MERE HOUSE
Mereworth ME18 5NB. Mr & Mrs Andrew Wells, www.mere-house.co.uk. *7m E of Tonbridge. From A26 turn N on to B2016 & then into Mereworth village. $3\frac{1}{2}$ m S of M20/M26 J, take A20, then B2016 to Mereworth.* Home-made teas. **Adm £3, chd free. Sun 17 Feb (11.30-3.30); Sun 23, Mon 24 Mar; Sun 12 Oct (2-5).**
6-acre garden with C18 lake. Daffodils, lawns, herbaceous borders, ornamental shrubs and trees with foliage contrast and striking autumn colour. Woodland walk and major tree planting and landscaping. New park walk. Featured in 'Kent Life'.
& ⊗ ☕

MERRIMENTS GARDENS
See Sussex.

60 ◆ MOUNT EPHRAIM
Hernhill, Faversham ME13 9TX. Mrs M N Dawes, Mr & Mrs E S Dawes, 01227 751496, www.mountephraimgardens.co.uk. *3m E of Faversham. From end of M2, then A299 take slip rd 1st L to Hernhill, signed to gardens.* **Adm £4.50, chd £2.50. 13 Apr to end Sept, Weds, Thurs, Sats, Suns (1-5) & Bank Hols (11-5). For NGS: Suns 20 Apr; 28 Sept (1-5).**

Herbaceous border; topiary; daffodils and rhododendrons; rose terraces leading to small lake. Rock garden with pools; water garden; young arboretum. Rose garden with arches and pergola planted to celebrate the millennium. Magnificent trees. Superb views over fruit farms to Swale estuary. New grass maze. Limited wheelchair access, steep slopes & steps.

61 MOUNTS COURT FARMHOUSE

Acrise, nr Folkestone CT18 8LQ. Graham & Geraldine Fish, 01303 840598, graham.s.fish@btinternet.com. *6m NW of Folkestone. From A260 Folkestone to Canterbury rd, turn L at Swingfield (Densole) opp Black Horse Inn, 1½ m towards Elham & Lyminge, on N side.* Home-made teas. **Adm £3, chd free. Suns 11 May; 27 July (2-5). Visitors also welcome by appt, coaches permitted.**

1½ acres surrounded by open farmland; variety of trees, shrubs, grasses and herbaceous plants; pond and bog garden. 20,000 gallon rainwater reservoir waters garden and keeps pond topped up; compost heats to 170° for fast turnover.

62 NETTLESTEAD PLACE

Nettlestead ME18 5HA. Mr & Mrs Roy Tucker, www.nettlesteadplace.co.uk. *6m W/SW of Maidstone. Turn S off A26 onto B2015 then 1m on L, next to Nettlestead Church.* Home-made teas. **Adm £5, chd free. Suns 8 June; 14 Sept (2-5.30).**

C13 manor house in 10-acre plantsman's garden. Large formal rose garden. Large herbaceous garden of island beds with rose and clematis walkway leading to garden of China roses. Fine collection of trees and shrubs; sunken pond garden, terraces, bamboos, glen garden, acer lawn. Young pinetum adjacent to garden. Sculptures. Wonderful open country views. Church adjacent to garden with fine early C15 windows. Starred garden in 'GGG'. Gravel paths. Sunken pond garden not wheelchair accessible at water level.

63 OLANTIGH

Olantigh Road, Wye TN25 5EW. Mr & Mrs J R H Loudon. *10m SW of Canterbury, 6m NE of Ashford. Turn off A28 to Wye. 1m from Wye on Olantigh rd towards Godmersham.* **Adm £3, chd free. Sun 25 May (2-5).**

Edwardian garden in beautiful 20-acre setting; wide variety of trees; river garden; rockery; shrubbery; herbaceous border; extensive lawns; tree sculpture and woodland walks. Sorry, no teas, but please feel free to bring your own.

64 ◆ OLD BUCKHURST

Markbeech, nr Edenbridge TN8 5PH. Mr & Mrs J Gladstone, 01342 850825, www.oldbuckhurst.co.uk. *4m SE of Edenbridge. B2026, at Queens Arms PH turn E to Markbeech. In approx 1½ m, 1st house on R after leaving Markbeech.* **Adm £3, chd free. Thur, Fri Sat 24, 25, 26 July. For NGS: Sats, Suns, Weds 19, 20, 23, 26, 27, 30 Apr; Suns 4, 11, Wed 14, Sun 18, Mon 26 May; Sun 1, Wed 4, Thur 12, Suns 22, 29 June; Suns, Weds 13, 16, 20, 27, 30 July; Sat 2, Sun 3 Aug; Weds, Sats, Suns 3, 6, 7, 10, 13, 14 Sept (11-5). Also open 20 July Hoath House.**

1-acre partly-walled cottage garden around C15 listed farmhouse with catslip roof (not open). Shrubs, clematis, climbing and shrub roses, anemones, astilbes, campanulas, eryngiums, day lilies in May, July/Aug, hardy geraniums, grasses, iris, jasmine, lilies, peonies, poppies, penstemons, wisteria, fruit and vegetables. Yr-round interest using structure, texture, scent and colour. WC. Groups welcome by arrangement. Featured on UK Style TV.

65 OLD ORCHARD

56 Valley Drive, Loose, Maidstone ME15 9TL. Mike & Hazel Brett, 01622 746941, mandh.brett@tiscali.co.uk. *2½ m S of Maidstone. From Maidstone A229, turn R towards Loose village and park on hill. At top of hill take footpath to Valley Drive. On-site parking for disabled, please phone for directions.* Home-made teas. **Adm £2.50, chd free (share to Talking Newspapers and Magazines). Suns 27 Apr; 18 May (2-6). Visitors also welcome by appt.**

Plantlovers' S-facing acre garden adjoining Loose Valley Conservation

Area. Meandering grass paths around informal island beds containing many unusual trees, shrubs and perennials. Extensive rockeries, screes and troughs. Predominantly a spring garden with alpines and bulbs in the sunnier sites and trilliums and erythroniums etc in the shady parts. Small arboretum for foliage form and colour.

66 OLD PLACE FARM

High Halden TN26 3JG. Mr & Mrs Jeffrey Eker, 01233 850202. *10m SW of Ashford. From A28, centre of village, take Woodchurch Rd (opp Chequers PH) for ½ m.* Home-made teas by prior arrangement. **Adm £4, chd free. Groups & guided tours £5. Visitors welcome by appt, individuals & groups.**

4-acre garden, mainly designed by Anthony du Gard Pasley, surrounding period farmhouse (not open) and buildings, with paved herb garden and parterres, small lake, ponds, lawns, mixed borders, cutting garden and potager, old shrub roses, foliage plants and specimen trees. 2 bridges leading to woodland and fields. New woodland topiary garden, a whimsical creation. Tulips a special feature. Starred garden in 'GGG'.

> New woodland topiary garden, a whimsical creation . . .

67 ONE DERING ROAD

Ashford TN24 8DB TN24 8DB. Mrs Claire de Sousa Barry, 07979 816104, nazgulnota-bene@ntlworld.com. *Town centre. Just off Hythe Rd nr Henwood roundabout. Short walk from pay and display car park located just past fire stn in Henwood Rd. Please do not park in Dering Rd.* Fairtrade tea, coffee & delicious home-made cakes on all dates. **Adm £3, regret children not admitted. Easter weekend, Fri 21 to Mon 24 Mar incl; Sats, Suns: Apr (not 26,27); May (not 10, 11); June (not 28, 29); July (not 19, 20); Aug (not 30, 31). Bank Hol Mons 5, 26 May; 25 Aug (2-5). Visitors also** welcome by appt May to Aug, for groups of 10+, no coaches. Private visits for disabled. Teas by arrangement.

Plantsperson's romantic town garden with optimum use of space. Successional planting for yr-round interest. Pittosporum, robinia, crinodendron, cardiocrinum. Cascading roses, clematis, jasmine, honeysuckle, delphiniums, arisaemas, trilliums, uvularias, camellias and rhododendrons. A host of other unusual plants. Visitors say: 'inspiring, exceptional, really lovely. Surprises round every corner, I'll be back!'. Featured on BBC TV Secret Gardens, on Radio Kent and in 'Kent Life'. Please note: no WC.

🌂 ⊗ ☕ ♨

68 THE ORANGERY

Mystole CT4 7DB. Rex Stickland & Anne Prasse. *5m SW of Canterbury. Turn off A28 through Shalmsford Street. After 1¹/₂ m at Xrds turn R down hill. Keep straight on, ignoring rds on L (Pennypot Lane) & R. Ignore drive on L signed 'Mystole House only' & at sharp bend in 600yds turn L into private drive signed Mystole Farm.* Home-made teas. **Adm £3, chd free. Suns 22 June; 27 July (1-7).**

1¹/₂ -acre gardens around C18 orangery, now a house (not open). Front gardens, established well-stocked herbaceous border and large walled garden with a wide variety of shrubs and mixed borders. Splendid views from terraces over ha-ha and paddocks to the lovely Chartham Downs. Water features and very interesting collection of modern sculptures set in natural surroundings.

♿ ☕

69 ORCHARD COTTAGE

3 Woodlands Road, Bickley, Bromley BR1 2AD. Mrs J M Wall. *1¹/₂ m E of Bromley. About 400yds from the A222. From Bickley Park Rd turn into Pines Rd, then 1st R into Woodlands Rd, No 3 is 1st house on L.* Home-made teas. **Adm £2.50, chd free (share to Diabetes UK). Sun 20 July (2-5).**

Attractive, colourful and varied ¹/₃ -acre garden, compartmentalised and themed, with many interesting and unusual herbaceous plants and shrubs. Incl areas of scree beds, troughs and pots with alpines and other specialist plants. Unusual plants & local honey for sale.

♿ 🌂 ⊗ ☕

70 ORCHARD END

Cock Lane, Spelmonden Road, Horsmonden TN12 8EQ. Mr & Mrs Hugh Nye, 01892 723118. *8m E of Tunbridge Wells. From A21 going S turn L at roundabout towards Horsmonden on B2162. After 2m turn R into Spelmonden Rd, ¹/₂ m to top of hill, R into Cock Lane. Garden 50yds on R.* Light refreshments & teas. **Adm £3, chd free. Sats, Suns 21, 22 June; 26, 27 July; 13, 14 Sept (11-5.30). Visitors also welcome by appt.**

Classically English garden on 1¹/₂ -acre sloping site, landscaped 12yrs ago by owners' garden designer son. Divided into rooms with linking vistas. Incl hot borders, cottage and white gardens, exotics with pergola, raised summerhouse overlooking lawns and drive planting. Formal fish pond with bog garden. Ornamental vegetable and fruit areas. Wildlife orchard. Display of pictures by local artists.

🌂 ⊗ ☕ ☎

71 PARSONAGE OASTS

Hampstead Lane, Yalding ME18 6HG. Edward & Jennifer Raikes. *6m SW of Maidstone. On B2162 between Yalding village & stn, turn off at Anchor PH over canal bridge, continue 100yds up lane. House and car park on L.* Home-made teas. **Adm £2, chd free. Easter Mon 24 Mar (2-5.30). Visitors also welcome by appt. Please apply in writing.**

³/₄ -acre riverside garden with walls, shrubs, daffodils, spectacular magnolia. Display of Raku pottery by Nichola Hanman. Unfenced river bank. Gravel paths and a few shallow steps.

♿ 🌂 ☕ ☎

72 PEDLINGE COURT

Pedlinge, Saltwood CT21 4JJ. Mr & Mrs J P Scrivens, 01303 269959. *¹/₂ m W of Hythe. Top of hill, on A261 from Hythe up hill signed M20 & Ashford opp sign 'Pedlinge'. From Newingreen 1m opp sign 'Hythe twinned with....'.* **Adm £3 (share to Cats Protection). Visitors welcome by appt mid May to mid July, for small groups.**

1¹/₂ -acre garden with a profusion of interesting plants around C14 farmhouse (not open), birthplace of the orchid foxglove 'Saltwood Summer'. Wide variety of cottage garden plants, ferns, old shrub roses, medicinal and culinary herbs with a backdrop of trees and shrubs incl topiary.

🌂 ⊗ ☎

73 ◆ PENSHURST PLACE

Penshurst TN11 8DG. Viscount De L'Isle, 01892 870307, www.penshurstplace.com. *6m NW of Tunbridge Wells. SW of Tonbridge on B2176, signed from A26 N of Tunbridge Wells.* **House & garden £8.50, chd £5.50. Garden only £7, chd £5. Weekends from 1 Mar, daily from 21 Mar to 2 Nov, gardens 10.30-6, house 12-4. For NGS: Wed 14 May.**

10 acres of garden dating back to C14; garden divided into series of rooms by over a mile of clipped yew hedge; profusion of spring bulbs; herbaceous borders; formal rose garden; famous peony border. Woodland trail. All-yr interest. Toy museum.

♿ 🌂 ☕

Birthplace of the orchid foxglove 'Saltwood Summer' . . .

74 ◆ THE PINES GARDEN

St Margaret's Bay CT15 6DZ. St Margaret's Bay Trust, 01304 851737, www.baytrust.org.uk. *4¹/₂ m NE of Dover. Approach village of St Margaret's-at-Cliffe off A258 Dover/Deal rd. Continue through village centre & down Bay Hill. Signed just before beach.* **Adm £3, chd 50p, concessions £2.50. Garden open all yr (10-5), not Christmas Day. Phone or see website for museum & tearoom information. For NGS: Suns 23 Mar; 25 May; 28 Sept (10-5).**

Adjacent to cliff walks and beach, this mature garden offers a mixture of open undulating parkland, trees, shrubs and secluded areas. Lake, waterfall, grass labyrinth, roundhouse shelter, famous Oscar Nemon statue of Winston Churchill. Chalk-constructed conference centre with grass-covered roof. Garden open all yr (10-5), not Christmas Day. For Museum and Tearoom information please phone or visit website. Access for disabled, ample seating, picnics.

♿

Minarette fruit trees underplanted with wild flowers . . .

75 PLACKETTS HOLE
Bicknor, nr Sittingbourne ME9 8BA. Mr & Mrs D P Wainman, 01622 884258, aj@aj-wainman.demon. co.uk. *5m S of Sittingbourne. W of B2163. Bicknor is signed from Hollingbourne Hill & from A249 at Stockbury Valley. Placketts Hole is midway between Bicknor & Deans Hill.* **Adm £3. Visitors welcome by appt May, June & July only, for groups of 10+, regret no coaches owing to single track road.**
3-acre garden in Kent Downs AONB created round C16 house with Georgian additions (not open). Formal herb garden, rose garden, informal pond, small walled kitchen garden. In May and June early-flowering wild hybrid and Scottish roses are at their best with a large variety of shrubs, specimen trees, early clematis and irises. In July many old fashioned roses follow, with later-flowering clematis, perennials and hostas. Some gravel paths and short steep slopes.

76 PRIMROSE COTTAGE
Rose Hill, Wittersham, Tenterden TN30 7HE. Jenny & Michael Clarke, 01797 270820, j.m.g.clarke@btinternet.com. *6m S of Tenterden. Signed off B2082 1m E of centre of Wittersham at highest point of Isle of Oxney. Sorry, no teas, but you are welcome to picnic in our field.* **Adm £2.50, chd free. Thur 5 June to Sun 8 June incl (2-5). Visitors also welcome by appt in June & July for groups of 8+.**
Joyful jumble of cottage garden plants, many unusual. Rose pergola walk, well and water feature. Vegetable garden in blocks for easy maintenance. Spectacular views to N Downs. A peaceful garden maintained by owners.

77 PUXTED HOUSE
Brenchley Road, Brenchley TN12 7PB. Mr P J Oliver-Smith, pjospux@aol.com. *6m SE of Tonbridge. From A21, 1m S of Pembury turn N onto B2160, turn R at Xrds in Matfield signed Brenchley. ¼ m from Xrds stop at 30mph sign at village entrance.* Cream teas 18 May only, no teas in June. **Adm £3, chd free. Suns 18 May; 15 June (2-6). Visitors also welcome by appt.**
1½ acres, planted with scented and coloured foliage shrubs selected to ensure yr-long changing effects. Meandering gravel paths lead from the alpine garden via herbaceous borders and croquet lawn with its thyme terrace to formal rose garden and thereafter swing amongst oriental woodland plants and bamboos about a lily pond. Large glasshouse protects many Australasian shrubs and cacti.
& ✗ ❀ 👟 ☎

78 ◆ QUEX GARDENS
Quex Park, Birchington CT7 0BH. Quex Museum Trust, 01843 842168, www.quexmuseum.org. *3m W of Margate. 10m NE of Canterbury. A28 towards Margate, then rd to Acol to Quex Park. Follow signs for Quex Museum, Quex Park.* **House & garden £7, chd/concessions £6. Garden £2, chd/concessions £1.50. Mid Mar to end Oct, Suns to Thurs (11-5); Nov to mid Mar Suns only 1-3.30. For NGS: Sun 22 June (11-5). Evening Openings Weds 23 July; 3 Sept (6-9). Sun 14 Sept (11-5).**
15 acres of woodland and gardens with fine specimen trees unusual on Thanet, spring bulbs, wisteria, shrub borders, old figs and mulberries, herbaceous borders. Victorian walled garden with cucumber house, long glasshouses, cactus house, fruiting trees. Peacocks, dovecote, woodland walk, wildlife pond, children's maze, croquet lawn, picnic grove, lawns and fountains.
& ✗ ❀ 👟

79 NEW 11 RAYMER ROAD
Penenden Heath, Maidstone ME14 2JQ. Mrs Barbara Badham. *From M20 J6 at Running Horse roundabout take Penenden Heath exit along Sandling Lane. At T-lights turn into Downsview Rd and follow signs.* Home-made teas. **Adm £3, chd free. Suns 11 May; 15 June (11-5).**
Compact garden with lovely views of North Downs. Divided into different areas containing wide range of plants, shrubs, fruit and vegetables for yr-round interest. Large strawberry tree, new apple arch, wisteria, magnolias, azaleas, tulips, roses, hardy geraniums, peonies and foxgloves. Minarette fruit trees underplanted with wild flowers. Raised vegetable beds, small pond.
✗ ❀ ☕

80 RIDDLES ROAD ALLOTMENTS
Sittingbourne ME10 1LF. Sittingbourne Allotment and Gardeners' Society. *½ m S of Sittingbourne. At A2/A249 junction turn E off roundabout towards Sittingbourne. After approx 1m turn R into Borden Lane, just after Coniston Hotel. Riddles Rd 2nd L after approx ½ m.* Light refreshments. **Adm £2.50, chd free. Sun 20 July (11-4).**
This is a standard allotment site with a multitude of plots of various sizes. A number of plots will be demonstrated showing a variety of horticultural techniques for growing fruit, vegetables and some flowers. Featured in 'Kent Messenger', 'East Kent Gazette' & 'Sittingbourne Extra'.
✗ ❀ 👟

81 ◆ RIVERHILL HOUSE GARDENS
Sevenoaks TN15 0RR. The Rogers Family, 01732 458802, jane@riverhillgardens. *2m S of Sevenoaks on A225.* **Adm £3.50, chd 50p. Suns & Bank Hol weekends, Easter to 22 June. For NGS: Thurs 17 Apr; 15 May (11-5).**
Mature hillside garden with extensive views; specimen trees, sheltered terraces with roses and rare shrubs; bluebell wood with rhododendrons and azaleas; picnics allowed. Unsuitable for wheelchairs but users may have free access to the tea terrace - on the level and with views across the garden.
✗ ❀ ☕

82 ROCK FARM
Gibbs Hill, Nettlestead ME18 5HT. Mrs S E Corfe, 01622 812244. *6m W of Maidstone. Turn S off A26 onto B2015, then 1m S of Wateringbury turn R up Gibbs Hill.* **Adm £4, chd free (share to St Mary the Virgin). Weds, Sats: 21, 24 May; 18, 21, 25, 28 June; 2, 5, 9, 12 July (11-5). Visitors also welcome by appt.**

2-acre garden set around old Kentish farmhouse (not open) in beautiful setting; created with emphasis on all-yr interest and ease of maintenance. Plantsman's collection of shrubs, trees and perennials for alkaline soil; extensive herbaceous border, vegetable area, bog garden and plantings around two large natural ponds. Featured in 'Kent Life'.

✕ ▨ ☎

83 ROGERS ROUGH
Chicks Lane, Kilndown TN17 2RP. Richard & Hilary Bird, 01892 890554, richardbird@rogersrough.demon.co. uk. *10m SE of Tonbridge. From A21 2m S of Lamberhurst turn E into Kilndown; take 1st R down Chicks Lane until rd divides.* Home-made teas. **Adm £3, chd free. Sat, Sun 26, 27 Apr; Sat, Sun, Mon 24, 25, 26 May; Sat, Sun 14, 15 June (11-5.30). Visitors also welcome by appt May, June & July.**
Garden writer's 1^1/$_2$ -acre garden, divided into many smaller gardens containing herbaceous borders, rock gardens, shrubs, small wood and pond. Very wide range of plants, incl some unusual ones. Extensive views. Widespread press coverage

&. ✕ ✿ ☕ ☎

84 ST CLERE
Kemsing TN15 6NL. Mr & Mrs Ronnie Norman. *6m NE of Sevenoaks. Take A25 from Sevenoaks toward Maidstone; 1m past Seal turn L signed Heaverham & Kemsing. In Heaverham take rd to R signed Wrotham & W Kingsdown; in 75yds straight ahead marked private rd; 1st L & follow rd to house.* Home-made teas. **Adm £3.50, chd 50p (share to St Mary's Church). Sun 8 June (2-5.30).**
4-acre garden, full of interest. Formal terraces surrounding C17 mansion (not open), with beautiful views of the Kent countryside. Herbaceous and shrub borders, productive kitchen and herb gardens, lawns and rare trees.

✕ ☕

85 ST MICHAEL'S GARDENS
East Peckham TN12 5NH. *5m NE of Tonbridge, 5m SW of Maidstone. On A26 at Mereworth roundabout take S exit (A228 Paddock Wood). After 1^1/$_2$ m turn L into Roydon Hall Rd. Gardens ^{1}/$_2$ m up hill on L. From Paddock Wood A228 towards West Malling. 1m after roundabout with Wheelbarrow turn R into Roydon Hall Rd.* Home-made teas. **Combined**

adm £3.50, chd free (share to Roydon Church). Suns 20 Apr; 18 May; 22 June (2-5).
Victorian house, cottage garden and cottage yard.

☕

CUCKOO COTTAGE
Mr Gavin Walter & Mrs Emma Walter
Born from a desire to add life and colour to a derelict and shady yard, a slate scree base is used with pots and containers.

&. ✿

ST MICHAEL'S COTTAGE
Mr Peter & Mrs Pauline Fox
Garden designed so it cannot be seen all at once. Traditional cottage garden with collection of lavenders, hostas, clematis, shrubs, ferns, heathers and wildlife area.

✿

ST MICHAEL'S HOUSE
Brig & Mrs W Magan
Grey stone old vicarage with yew topiary hedges surrounding flower beds planned in coordinated colours. Lovely display of tulips followed by splendid irises, then a mass of roses from red-hot to old soft colours. Wonderful views from the meadow.

&. ✿

86 NEW ◆ THE SALUTATION
Knightrider Street, Sandwich CT13 9EW. Mr & Mrs Dominic Parker, 01304 619919, www.the-salutation.com. *In the heart of Sandwich. Turn L at Bell Hotel and into Quayside car park. Entrance on far R-hand corner of car park.* **Adm £4.50, chd £3, family £14. 21 Mar to 31 Oct, Mon to Sat (10-6). 1 Nov to Easter 2009, Mon to Fri (10-4). Closed 12 Dec 08 to 12 Jan 09. For NGS: Mon 7 Apr; Thur 24 July; Sat 11 Oct (10-4.30).**
3^1/$_2$ acres of ornamental and formal gardens by Sir Edwin Lutyens and Gertrude Jekyll in 1911 surrounding Grade I listed house. Designated historic park and garden. Lake, white, yellow, spring, woodland, rose, kitchen, vegetable and herbaceous gardens. Designed to provide yr-round changing colour. Previously unseen for nearly 25 yrs. TV and radio coverage of official opening by Monty Don.

&. ✕ ✿ ▨ ☕

Lovely display of tulips followed by splendid irises . . .

87 SANDLING PARK
Hythe CT21 4HN. The Hardy Family. *1^1/$_2$ m NW of Hythe. Entrance off A20 only. From M20 J11 turn E onto A20. Entrance ^{1}/$_4$ m.* Home-made teas. **Adm £4, chd free (share to Saltwood Church). Sun 11 May (10-5).**
25-acre woodland garden with an extensive collection of trees and shrubs with rhododendrons, azaleas, magnolias and other interesting plants that also relish acid soil.

✕ ☕

88 ◆ SCOTNEY CASTLE
Lamberhurst TN3 8JN. The National Trust, www.nationaltrust.org.uk. *6m SE of Tunbridge Wells. On A21 London-Hastings, brown tourist signs. Bus: (Mon to Sat) Tunbridge Wells-Wadhurst, alight Lamberhurst Green.* **House & garden £8.80, chd £4.40. Garden only £6.60, chd £3.30. Opening dates & times vary according to season. Please visit website for details. For NGS: Sat 19 July (11-4.30).**
Picturesque landscape garden, created by the Hussey family in the 1840s surrounding moated C14 Castle. Picnic area in car park.

&. ✕ ✿

89 SEA CLOSE
Cannongate Road, Hythe CT21 5PX. Major & Mrs R H Blizard, 01303 266093. *^{1}/$_2$ m from Hythe towards Folkestone (A259), on L. Signed.* Light refreshments. **Adm £3, chd free (share to Royal Signals Benevolent Fund). Suns 13 Apr; 20 July (2-5). Visitors also welcome by appt at any time. Clubs, societies, groups of 10+ incl guided tour, teas £1 extra. Multiple visits to study seasonal changes: 2@£5; 4@£10; 6@£12.50.**
Connoisseurs garden on steep hillside overlooking Channel. Equitable climate, TLC, knowledge of site, allows many unusual and tender plants incl *Sophora, Crinodendron patagu, Lespedeza, Fascicularia* and many more growing in the open. Planting combinations achieve monthly changing scenario.

✕ ✿ ☕ ☎

Gardeners cite
healthy produce,
exercise and
relaxation in a
beautiful open
space as
reasons to rent
a plot . . .

90 SEVENOAKS ALLOTMENTS
**Allotment Lane, off Quaker Hall
Lane, Sevenoaks TN13 3TX.
Sevenoaks Allotment Holders Assn,
www.sevenoaksallotments.co.uk.**
*Quaker Hall Lane is off A225, St John's
Hill. Site directly behind St John's
Church.* **Home-made teas. Adm £3,
chd free (share to Spring House
Family Support Centre). Sun 29
June (10-5).**
The Association self-manages 11¹/₂
acres of productive allotment gardens
situated in the heart of the town. A
wide cross-section of allotment owners
grow a massive variety of flowers, fruit
and vegetables using a number of
different techniques. Gardeners cite
healthy produce, exercise and
relaxation in a beautiful open space as
reasons to rent a plot. Featured on
Radio Kent and in Sevenoaks Festival
brochure 2008.
&. ⊛ ☕

91 ◆ SISSINGHURST GARDEN
**Sissinghurst TN172AB. The National
Trust, 01580 710700,
www.nationaltrust.org.uk.** *16m E of
Tunbridge Wells. On A262 1m E of
village. Bus: Arriva Maidstone to
Hastings, alight Sissinghurst 1¹/₄ m.
Direct bus Tue, Fri & Sun. Stn:
Staplehurst. Ring for details.* **Adm £9,
chd £4.40. 15 Mar to 2 Nov: Mons,
Tues, Fris (11-6.30); Sats, Suns,
Bank Hols (10-6.30). For NGS: Mons
14 Apr; 2 June; 11 Aug; 6 Oct (11-
6.30).**
Garden created by the late Vita
Sackville-West and Sir Harold
Nicolson. Spring garden, herb garden,
cottage garden, white garden, rose
garden. Tudor building and tower,
partly open to public. Moat. Exhibition

on history of the garden and property
in the oast buildings. 14 Apr Farmers'
Market & Plant Fair (11-4).
&. ✕ ⊛ ☕

92 NEW SMITHS HALL
**Lower Road, West Farleigh
ME15 0PE. Mr S Norman.** *3m W
of Maidstone. A26 towards
Tonbridge, turn L into Teston Lane
B2163. At T-junction turn R onto
Lower Rd B2010. Opp Tickled
Trout PH.* **Home-made teas. Adm
£4, chd free (share to The
Dandelion Trust). Suns 18 May;
29 June (1-5).**
3-acre formal and informal garden.
Bluebell woodland walk leading to
newly-designed 9-acre parkland,
incl native woodland, wild flower
meadow, and American tree
species. Garden surrounds Queen
Anne house (not open). Long
formal herbaceous borders,
rose garden, rose walk, sunken
water garden, peony border and
walled garden.
&. ☕

93 SOTTS HOLE COTTAGE
**Crouch Lane, Borough Green
TN15 8QL. Mr & Mrs Jim Vinson.** *7m
E of Sevenoaks. Crouch Lane runs SE
from A25 between Esso garage &
Black Horse PH, garden at bottom of
2nd hill, approx ³/₄ m.* **Home-made
teas. Adm £3, chd free (share to
Heart of Kent Hospice). Suns 1
June; 27 July; 14 Sept (11-6).**
6 acres of landscaped cottage
garden relying entirely on the threat of
visitors to motivate the owners to
maintain it. We look forward to seeing
you.
✕ ☕

94 SOUTH HILL FARM
**Hastingleigh TN25 5HL. Sir Charles
Jessel, 01233 750325,
sircjj@btinternet.com.** *4¹/₂ m E of
Ashford. Turn off A28 to Wye, go
through village & ascend Wye Downs.
In 2m turn R at Xrds marked
Brabourne & South Hill, then 1st L. Or
from Stone St (B2068) turn W opp
Stelling Minnis, follow signs to
Hastingleigh. Continue towards Wye &
turn L at Xrds marked Brabourne &
South Hill, then 1st L.* **Adm £3.50 incl
tea & biscuits, chd free. Visitors
welcome by appt June & July only,
groups of 8+, coaches permitted.**

2 acres high up on N Downs, C17/18
house (not open). Old walls, ha-ha,
formal water garden; old and new
roses, unusual shrubs, perennials and
foliage plants.
&. ✕ ☕ ☎

95 SPILSILL COURT
**Frittenden Road, Staplehurst
TN12 0DJ. Mrs Doonie Marshall.** *8m
S of Maidstone. To Staplehurst on
A229 (Maidstone to Hastings). From S
enter village, turn R immed after
garage on R & just before 30mph sign,
into Frittenden Rd; garden ¹/₂ m on L.
From N go through village to 40mph
sign, immed turn L into Frittenden Rd.*
**April tea/coffee & biscuits all day. June
tea/coffee 11-1, cream teas 2.30-4.30.
Adm £2, chd 50p. Sun 6 Apr; Sun 29
June (11-5).**
Approx 4 acres of garden, orchard
and paddock; series of gardens incl
blue, white and silver; roses; lawns;
shrubs, trees and ponds. Small private
chapel. Jacob sheep and unusual
poultry.
&. ✕ ⊛ ☕

96 THE SPINNEY
**38 Wildernesse Mount, Sevenoaks
TN13 3QS. Patricia McAlister, 01732
461434.** *1¹/₂ m N of Sevenoaks. 3m
from M25 J5, follow A25 towards
Maidstone to Seal Hollow Rd. Turn R
at T-lights; 400yds, turn R at Hillingdon
Avenue & 1st L into Wildernesse
Mount. Proceed to turning circle
(¹/₄ m). No 38 on L.* **Light refreshments
& teas. Adm £3, chd free,
concessions £2.50. Sun 18 May
(12-5). Visitors also welcome by
appt.**
Garden set in ²/₃ acre surrounding
house (not open). Mainly spring garden
- camellias, magnolias,
rhododendrons, azaleas and pieris.
Good collection of trees - rowans
(hybrids), liriodendron (variegated),
eucalyptus, cercidiphyllum, robinia,
birch, amelanchier, various acers, pine,
Atlantic cedar, various conifers.
Interesting water feature.
Lawns/garden on 3 levels incl terrace
garden.
✕ ☕ ☎

97 ◆ SQUERRYES COURT
**Westerham TN16 1SJ. Mrs John
Warde, 01959 562345,
www.squerryes.co.uk.** *¹/₂ m W of
Westerham. Signed from A25.* **House
& garden £6.50, chd £3.50,
concessions £6. Garden only £4,
chd £2, concessions £3.50. Weds,
Suns & Bank Hol Mons, 2 Apr to 28**

Sept. House not open NGS days.
For NGS: Tues 8 July; 2 Sept (11.30-5, last entry 4.30).
15 acres of well-documented historic garden, C18 landscape. Part of the formal garden has been restored by the family using C18 plan. Lake, spring bulbs, azaleas, herbaceous borders, C18 dovecote, cenotaph commemorating Gen Wolfe; woodland walks.

98 STONEWALL PARK
Chiddingstone Hoath, nr Edenbridge TN8 7DG. Mr & Mrs Valentine Fleming. *4m SE of Edenbridge. Via B2026. Halfway between Markbeech & Penshurst.* Home-made teas. **Adm £4, chd free (share to Sarah Matheson Trust & St Mary's Church). Suns 30 Mar; 4 May (1.30-5).**
Romantic woodland garden in historic setting featuring species rhododendrons, magnolias, azaleas, a range of interesting trees and shrubs, wandering paths and lakes. Parkland with cricket ground, Victorian walled garden with herbaceous borders and vegetable garden backed by 100 yr-old espalier pear trees. Sea of wild daffodils in March.

99 TIMBERS
Dean Street, East Farleigh, nr Maidstone ME15 0HS. Mrs Sue Robinson, 01622 729568, sue@suerobinson.wanadoo.co.uk. *2m S of Maidstone. From Maidstone take B2010 to East Farleigh. Opp The Bull turn into Vicarage Lane, then L into Forge Lane and L into Dean St. Garden 50yds on R, park through gates in front of house.* Home-made teas. **Adm £3, chd free. Visitors welcome by appt Apr to July, & Sept, for groups of 8+, coaches permitted.**
5-acre garden, well stocked with unusual hardy plants, annuals and shrubs designed with flower arranger's eye. Formal areas comprising parterre, pergola, herbaceous, vegetables, fruit, lawns and mature specimen trees surrounded by 100yr-old Kentish cobnut plat, wild flower meadow and woodland. Featured in 'Kent Life' and on BBC Radio Kent.

TITSEY PLACE GARDENS
See Surrey.

Well stocked with unusual hardy plants, annuals and shrubs designed with a flower arranger's eye . . .

100 TORRY HILL
Frinsted/Milstead ME9 0SP. The Lord & Lady Kingsdown, 01795 830258, lady.kingsdown@btinternet.com. *5m S of Sittingbourne. From M20 J8 take A20 (Lenham). At roundabout by Ramada Inn turn L Hollingbourne (B2163). Turn R at Xrds at top of hill (Wormshill). Thereafter Wormshill-Frinsted-Doddington (not suitable for coaches), then Torry Hill & NGS signs. From M2 J5 take A249 towards Maidstone, first L and L again (Bredgar-Milstead), then Torry Hill and NGS signs.* Home-made teas. **Adm £3, chd free (share to St Dunstan's Church). Suns 18 May; 8 June; 20 July (2-5). Visitors also welcome by appt, groups up to 30 accepted.**
8 acres; large lawns, specimen trees, flowering cherries, rhododendrons, azaleas and naturalised daffodils; walled gardens with lawns, shrubs, herbaceous borders, rose garden incl shrub roses, wild flower areas and vegetables. Extensive views to Medway and Thames estuaries. No wheelchair access to rose garden but can be viewed from pathway.

101 TRAM HATCH
Charing Heath TN27 0BN. Mrs P Scrivens, 01233 713373. *10m NW of Ashford. A20 turn towards Charing railway stn. Continue on Pluckley Rd over motorway, 1st R signed Barnfield to end. Turn L, follow lane past Barnfield, Tram Hatch on L.* Home-made teas. **Adm £3.50, chd free. Suns 18 May; 15 June; 13 July (1.30-5). Visitors also welcome by appt, groups of 15+, coaches permitted.**

C14 manor house with tithe barn (not open) set in 3 acres of formal garden with the Great River Stour edging its boundary. Vegetable and fruit garden, orchard, rose garden, bog garden and 2 large ponds, one with ornamental wildfowl. Large variety of plants and trees.

102 TROUTBECK
Otford TN14 5PH. Dr & Mrs Huw Alban Davies, 01959 525439, box@river-garden.co.uk. *3m N of Sevenoaks. At W end of village.* **Adm £3, chd free. Visitors welcome by appt June, July & Sept only, for groups.**
3-acre garden surrounded by branches of R Darent. Developed over 17yrs combining the informal landscape of the river, a central pond and small wild meadow with structural planting using box and yew. Knots and topiary shapes are displayed. Topiary demonstration for groups by arrangement. Featured in 'Daily Telegraph'.

103 NEW ULCOMBE PLACE
Ulcombe Hill, nr Maidstone ME17 1DN. Gina & Dale Jennings, 01622 842019, gina.jennings@btopenworld.com. *7m SE of Maidstone. 3m N of Headcorn, through village, turn L in church car park.* Home-made teas. **Adm £4, chd free (share to Help for Heroes). Sun 8 June (2-6). Visitors also welcome by appt.**
3 acres of informal gardens around C13 house (not open). Walled garden, herbaceous borders, wide variety of interesting trees (over 50) and shrubs. Views across The Weald to Hastings.

104 UPPER PRYORS
Butterwell Hill, Cowden TN8 7HB. Mr & Mrs S G Smith. *4½ m SE of Edenbridge. From B2026 Edenbridge-Hartfield, turn R at Cowden Xrds & take 1st drive on R.* Home-made teas. **Adm £3.50, chd free. Day £3.50 (1-6) & Evening Opening £4.50, wine, Wed 18 June (6-9). Also open 6-9 Edenbridge House.**
10 acres of country garden surrounding C16 house with herbaceous colour, magnificent lawns, water gardens and wooded/field areas.

105 NEW WEST MALLING GARDENS

ME19 6NE. *Tickets, map and list of gardens available from Brome House, 148 High St (next to St Mary's Church) or from Went House, Swan St. Parking available in town car park or station car park. Follow the yellow signs.* Home-made teas at Brome House. **Adm £5, chd free. Sun 1 June** (12-5.30).
West Malling is an attractive small market town with some fine buildings. Most of the gardens are within walking distance of the High Street. Some wheelchair access; information available from Brome House or phone 01732 521268.
  ♿ ☕

106 WEST STUDDAL FARM

West Studdal, nr Dover CT15 5BJ. Mr Peter Lumsden. *4m SW of Deal. 6m N of Dover halfway between Eastry & Whitfield. Take A256 from A2. At 1st roundabout turn S signed Studdal. At top of hill turn R, entrance ¼ m by yellow cottage.* Home-made teas. **Adm £2.50, chd free. Sun 17 Aug** (2-5.30).
Medium-sized garden around old farmhouse (not open) set by itself in small valley; herbaceous borders, roses and fine lawns protected by old walls and beech hedges.
  ♿ ❀ ☕

107 WHITEHURST

Chainhurst TN12 9SU. John & Lyn Mercy, 01622 820616. *6m S of Maidstone, 3m N of Marden. From Marden stn turn R into Pattenden Lane & under railway bridge; at T-junction turn L; at next fork bear R to Chainhurst, then 2nd turning on L.* Home-made teas. **Adm £4, chd £1. Sun 28 Sept to Wed 1 Oct incl** (2-5). **Visitors also welcome by appt.**
1½ acres of romantic, rather wild garden with many delightful and unexpected features. Victorian spiral staircase leads to a treetop walk; water tumbles down stone steps to a rill and on to several ponds; tunnels of yew and dogwood; walled rose garden; courtyards and lawns. Exhibition of root dwellings.
  ♿ ✂ ☕ ☎

108 NEW WICKHAM LODGE

The Quay, High Street, Aylesford ME20 7AY. Cherith & Richard Bourne, www.wickhamlodge.co.uk. *3m NW of Maidstone. Off High St on riverbank, turning into The Quay by Chequers PH. Park in village car park.* Light refreshments & cream teas. **Adm £3.50, chd free (share to St Peter & St Paul Church). Sats 31 May; 6 Sept** (11-4).
Every corner of this walled and terraced ½ -acre plot has been used to create 14 inspirational small gardens that could be picked up and recreated anywhere. Journey from productive kitchen gardens to formal Tudor, from Japanese to funky banana foliage. Endless surprises are here in abundance.
  ❀ 🛏 ☕

> Every corner of this walled and terraced plot has been used to create 14 inspirational small gardens that could be picked up and recreated anywhere . . .

109 WINDY RIDGE

Victory Road, St Margarets-at-Cliffe CT15 6HF. Mr & Mrs D Ryder, 01304 853225, www.gardenplants-nursery.co.uk. *4½ m NE of Dover. From Duke of York roundabout on A2 N of Dover follow A258 signed Deal. Take 3rd rd on R (Station Rd), then 3rd rd on L (Collingwood Rd). Continue onto unmade track & follow signs (approx ½ m). Telephone for map.* Light refreshments & home-made teas. **Adm £2.50, chd free. Suns 22 June; 27 July; 14 Sept** (2-6).
Plantsman's garden on top of chalk hill, with extensive views over open country and sea. Island beds of shrubs and perennials (many rare). Large collection of penstemon and salvia. Wildlife pond. Gravel seating area and viewpoint. Additional ⅔ -acre extension to garden incl shrub and kniphofia border. Small specialist nursery.
  ❀ ☕

110 WITHERSDANE HALL

Wye TN25 5AH. Imperial College Wye Campus. *3m NE of Ashford. A28 take fork signed Wye. Bus from Ashford to Canterbury via Wye. Pass Imperial College Wye Campus & continue up Scotton St.* **Adm £3, chd 50p. Suns 22 June; 27 July** (2-5).
Large country garden, part laid out in 1950s on formal lines within the old walled kitchen garden, recently redesigned. Culinary herb garden, pool garden, herbaceous borders, rose garden and wild flower garden. Many unusual trees and shrubs incl toothache tree, *Zanthoxylum americanum*, and *Photinia beauverdiana*. Much of planting labelled. Slope to allow easier access.
  ♿ ✂

111 WOMENSWOLD GARDENS

CT4 6HE. *6m S of Canterbury. Midway between Canterbury & Dover, E of A2, take B2046 signed Wingham at Barham Crossover. After about ¼ m turn R at Armada Beacon, following signs for gardens and car parking.* Home-made teas. **Adm £3.50, chd free. Sat 28, Sun 29 June** (2-6).
Several colourful and very different gardens in picturesque C18 hamlet, situated mostly around C13 church. These incl 1-acre plantsman's garden with many interesting features and cottage garden with selection of climbing and shrub roses and large collection of over 100 kniphofias and hemerocallis.
  ♿ ❀ ☕

112 ◆ THE WORLD GARDEN AT LULLINGSTONE CASTLE

Eynsford DA4 0JA. Guy Hart Dyke, 01322 862114, www.lullingstonecastle.co.uk. *1m from Eynsford. M25 J3, signs to Brands Hatch then Eynsford. In Eynsford turn R at church over ford bridge. Follow lane under viaduct, with Lullingstone Roman Villa on R, to private rd sign, follow signs for World Garden via Gatehouse.* **Adm £6, chd £3, concessions £5.50. April to Sept, Fris & Sats 12-5, Suns & Bank Hol Mons** (2-6). **For NGS: Sun 6 July** (2-6).

Interactive world map of plants laid out as a map of the world within a walled garden. The oceans are your pathways as you navigate the world in 1 acre. You can stroll around Mt Everest, sip water from an Asian waterfall, see Ayers Rock and walk alongside the Andes whilst reading intrepid tales of plant hunters. Discover the origins of plants - you'll be amazed where they come from! Featured on BBC TV.

⑬ YALDING GARDENS
ME18 6HX. *6m SW of Maidstone on B2010. A few parking spaces for disabled at Court Lodge.* Teas at Court Lodge. **Combined adm £3, chd free. Sun 13 July (2-5.30).**
Two contrasting gardens, 200yds apart, in the centre of a pretty village.

THE COURT LODGE
High Street. Jonathan & Joy Virden. *In centre of village* Medium-sized garden round 300 yr-old farmhouse (not open). 2 contrasting vegetable areas, fruit trees, newly-replanted herbaceous border. Large greenhouse.

NEW MANNA OAST
Oast Court. Richard & Barbara Huckerby. *1st L off Kenward Rd (after turning off High St)* Small garden completely redesigned in 2005 in conjunction with house extension. New lawns, semi-mature trees and

herbaceous borders with attractive hard landscaping. Very interesting for those considering a garden design project.

⑭ YEW TREE COTTAGE
Penshurst TN11 8AD. Mrs Pam Tuppen, 01892 870689. *4m SW of Tonbridge. From A26 Tonbridge to Tunbridge Wells, join B2176 Bidborough to Penshurst rd. 2m W of Bidborough, 1m before Penshurst. Utterly unsuitable for coaches. Please phone if needing advice for directions.* Light refreshments. **Adm £2, chd free. Wed 27 Feb, then Weds, Sats & Suns, first & third week of each month, Mar to Sept incl (11-5). Please see diary section for exact dates. Visitors also welcome by appt.**

Small, romantic, hillside cottage garden with steep entrance. Lots of seats and secret corners, full of unusual plants - hellebores, spring bulbs, old roses, many special perennials. Small pond; something to see in all seasons. Created and maintained by owner. Please visit throughout long opening period to ease pressure on small garden. Featured in 'Kent Life'.

Very interesting for those considering a garden design project . . .

Kent County Volunteers

County Organiser
Felicity Ward, Hookwood House, Shipbourne TN11 9RJ, 01732 810525, hookwood1@yahoo.co.uk

County Treasurer
Stephen Moir, Little Worge Barn, Willingford Lane, Brightling, E Sussex TN32 5HN, 01424 838136, moirconsult@btinternet.com

Publicity
Claire Tennant-Scull, Wellington House, Oaks Road, Tenterden, Kent TN30 6RD, 01580 766694, claire@wellingon-house.co.uk

Radio
Jane Streatfeild, Hoath House, Chiddingstone Hoath, Edenbridge, Kent TN8 7DB, 01342 850362, jane@hoath-house.freeserve.co.uk

Leaflet distribution
Susan Moir, Little Worge Barn, Willingford Lane, Brightling, E Sussex TN32 5HN, 01424 838136, moirconsult@btinternet.com

Assistant County Organisers
Marylyn Bacon, Ramsden Farm, Stone-cum-Ebony, Tenterden, Kent TN30 7JB, 01797 270300, streakybacon@kent.uk.net
Clare Barham, Hole Park, Rolvenden, Cranbrook TN17 4JB, 01580 241386, clarebarham@holepark.com
Virginia Latham, Stowting Hill House, Ashford TN25 6BE, 01303 862881, vjlatham@hotmail.com
Caroline Loder-Symonds, Denne Hill Farm, Womenswold, Canterbury CT4 6HD, 01227 831203, cloder_symonds@hotmail.com
Ingrid Morgan Hitchcock, 6 Brookhurst Gardens, Southborough, Tunbridge Wells TN4 0NA, 01892 528341, ingrid@morganhitchcock.co.uk
Elspeth Napier, 53 High Street, East Malling, Kent ME19 6AJ, 01732 522146, elspeth@cherryvilla.demon.co.uk

LANCASHIRE

Merseyside, Greater Manchester & surrounding areas

Opening Dates

February

SUNDAY 17
28 Weeping Ash

SUNDAY 24
28 Weeping Ash

April

SUNDAY 20
28 Weeping Ash

May

SATURDAY 3
26 The Stones & Roses Garden

SUNDAY 4
22 The Ridges

SATURDAY 10
26 The Stones & Roses Garden

SUNDAY 18
4 Bretherton Gardens
10 Crosby Hall

SUNDAY 25
7 Clearbeck House

SATURDAY 31
19 Montford Cottage

June

SUNDAY 1
1 480 Aigburth Road
19 Montford Cottage

SATURDAY 7
2 Barrow Nook Gardens
9 Crabtree Lane Gardens

SUNDAY 8
2 Barrow Nook Gardens
9 Crabtree Lane Gardens
18 Mill Barn & Primrose Cottage

SUNDAY 15
6 Casa Lago

SUNDAY 22
7 Clearbeck House
11 Cypress House
13 Foxbury
18 Mill Barn & Primrose Cottage
27 Tudor House

SATURDAY 28
12 Dutton Hall

SUNDAY 29
3 Birkdale Village Gardens
7 Clearbeck House
12 Dutton Hall
16 Hesketh Bank Village Gardens
24 Sefton Park Gardens
30 Wroxham Gardens

July

SUNDAY 6
23 14 Saxon Road

SATURDAY 12
25 Southlands
26 The Stones & Roses Garden

SUNDAY 13
4 Bretherton Gardens
25 Southlands
26 The Stones & Roses Garden

SATURDAY 19
5 Brookfield

SUNDAY 20
5 Brookfield
28 Weeping Ash

SUNDAY 27
13 Foxbury
15 Hawthornes Nursery Garden

August

SUNDAY 10
4 Bretherton Gardens
17 Huntingdon Hall

SUNDAY 24
14 Greenacre
21 142 Ribchester Road
22 The Ridges

MONDAY 25
14 Greenacre
21 142 Ribchester Road

FRIDAY 29
20 The Old Zoo Garden

SUNDAY 31
20 The Old Zoo Garden

September

SUNDAY 7
6 Casa Lago

SATURDAY 13
26 The Stones & Roses Garden

SATURDAY 20
26 The Stones & Roses Garden

SUNDAY 21
28 Weeping Ash

February 2009

SUNDAY 15
28 Weeping Ash

SUNDAY 22
28 Weeping Ash

Gardens open to the public

8 Cobble Hey Farm & Gardens
22 The Ridges

By appointment only

29 Willow House

Also open by appointment ☎

4 Hazel Cottage, Bretherton Gardens
4 Magnolia Cottage, Bretherton Gardens
5 Brookfield
9 79 Crabtree Lane, Crabtree Lane Gardens
9 81 Crabtree Lane, Crabtree Lane Gardens
16 31 Becconsall Lane, Hesketh Bank Village Gardens
16 11 Douglas Avenue, Hesketh Bank Village Gardens
16 Wedgwood, Hesketh Bank Village Gardens
11 Cypress House
14 Greenacre
15 Hawthornes Nursery Garden
16 74 Chapel Road, Hesketh Bank Village Gardens
18 Mill Barn & Primrose Cottage
20 The Old Zoo Garden
23 14 Saxon Road
25 Southlands
26 The Stones & Roses Garden

The Gardens

1 480 AIGBURTH ROAD
Liverpool L19 3QE. Mrs Bridget Spiegl. *4m S of Liverpool town centre. On main rd (A561) between city & Runcorn bridge. Just past Liverpool Cricket Club, on LH-side of rd going towards the city.* **Adm £1.50, chd free (share to Mpala Mobile Clinic). Sun 1 June (2-5).**
Plantswoman's small town garden. Mixed herbaceous and shrubs. Some interesting and unusual plants.
✗ ❀

Neighbouring gardens of very different styles within a short walking distance . . .

② NEW BARROW NOOK GARDENS

Bickerstaffe L39 0ET. *5m SW of Ormskirk. From M58, J3 to Southport (A570) to T-lights at Stanley Gate PH, turn L into Liverpool Rd, then 1st L into Church Rd, then Hall Lane, approx 1m into Barrow Nook Lane.* Cream teas. **Combined adm £3, chd free. Sat 7, Sun 8 June (1-5).**
Barrow Nook Gardens are 3 neighbouring gardens of very different styles within a short walking distance, set in rural surroundings.

NEW BARROW NOOK FARM
Cynthia & Keith Moakes
1/2 acre country garden overlooking fields with mature trees, shrubs, roses and many old favourite perennials, wildlife pond and bog garden. Pergola leads to orchard with soft and stoned fruit. Homemade jams for sale.

NEW 18 BARROW NOOK LANE
Paul & Sheila Davies
Small diverse garden, rockery, water feature, herbs, island beds, herbaceous borders, pergola, fruit trees and raised vegetable beds. Garden started from scratch 12yrs ago and still being developed. Gravel paths.

NEW 26 BARROW NOOK LANE
Gary Jones
Low maintenance garden for people with limited time and budget who appreciate outdoor living, dining and relaxing. Garden incls pathways, ponds, water features, BBQ area, pergola, lawns and other works in progress.

③ NEW BIRKDALE VILLAGE GARDENS

PR8 2AX,
www.birkdalevillagegardens.co.uk. *1m S of Southport. Off A565 Southport to Liverpool rd. 4th on L after roundabout, opp St James Church. By train short walk from Birkdale Stn, exit L for Saxon Rd & R for Liverpool Rd.* Home-made teas at 14 Saxon Road.
Combined adm £4, chd free (share to Queenscourt Hospice). Sun 29 June (10.30-5.30).
Three gardens, 2 opp each other and 1 within easy walking distance through Victorian village of Birkdale. Maps available at each location or on line.

NEW 55 LIVERPOOL ROAD
PR8 4BD. Anne & Bob France. *Short walk from Birkdale Stn through village shops on A5267*
Approaching through front seaside garden with grasses and rocks, into small courtyard area with clematis and perennial border into main garden area. Patio, pergola, shady areas, informal planting, fruit trees and mature shrubs. Gravel paths.

NEW 14 SAXON ROAD
Margaret & Geoff Fletcher. Also open Sun 6 July.
(see separate entry).

NEW 19 SAXON ROAD
Marie O'Neill & Linus Birtles
Victorian house (not open). Mature gardens and trees, lawn, herbaceous borders and shrubs. Newly created period style walled garden, orangery, fruit, flower and vegetable beds planted for the first time this year by 'L' plate gardeners. Gravel path.

④ BRETHERTON GARDENS

PR26 9AN. *8m SW of Preston. Between Southport & Preston, from A59, take B5247 towards Chorley for 1m. Gardens off North Rd (B5248) & South Rd (B5247).* Home-made teas. **Combined adm £3 (May), £4 (July), £3.50 (Aug), chd free.** Suns 18 May; 13 July; 10 Aug (12-5).
Contrasting gardens in this attractive, spacious village with a conservation area at its heart. Maps available at each garden.

BRIAR COTTAGE
187 South Road. PR26 9AJ. Gary & Simone Connor. Not open 18 May, 10 Aug.
Small S-facing walled garden adjacent to a Grade 2 listed long barn. The garden features well stocked herbaceous and shrub borders, raised beds; gravelled walkway through rose, honeysuckle and clematis covered pergola, summerhouse and entertainment area. Featured on BBC Radio Lancs. Gravel paths.

HAZEL COTTAGE
6 South View, Bamfords Fold. John & Kris Jolley, 01772 600896. Visitors also welcome by appt.
Plant and wildlife lovers' garden developed from Victorian subsistence plot. Series of themed spaces delights the senses and the intellect. Courtyard ponds, mixed borders, kitchen garden, Yorkshire and Lancashire beds, meadow and orchard.

◆ HAZELWOOD
North Road. Jacqueline Iddon & Thompson Dagnall, 01772 601433, www.jacquelineiddonhardyplants.co.uk. Adm £2.50, chd free. Weds 7 May to 13 Aug 1-5.
1 1/2 acre garden and hardy plant nursery, originally orchard, now has gravel garden with silver and variegated foliage plants, shrubs, herbaceous borders and large stream-fed pond with woodland walk. Sculpture and Victorian fern house. Newly completed oak-framed, brick summerhouse. Winner Large Gold & Challenge Trophy - Southport Flower Show.

Orangery, fruit, flower and vegetable beds planted for the first time this year by 'L' plate gardeners . . .

MAGNOLIA COTTAGE
South Road. Mikki Boston, 01772 600895. Not open 18 May. Visitors also welcome by appt July to Aug.
Small shady garden architecturally designed creating 3 rooms each with their own individual features; shade-loving plants, mostly green and white, give the garden an air of peace and tranquillity. Featured in 'Beautiful Britain Magazine'.
 ♿ ✖ ☎

5 BROOKFIELD
11 Irlam Road, Flixton M41 6JR. Bob & Beryl Wheeler, 0161 748 6985, rcpwheeler@aol.com. *2¹/₂ m SW of Urmston. From J10 on M60 go S through 2 roundabouts to T-lights, turn R into Moorside Rd. At next roundabout take 2nd rd signed Lymm, after next T-lights take 5th rd on R Irlam Rd.* Home-made teas. **Adm £2.50, chd free. Sat 19, Sun 20 July (2-5). Visitors also welcome by appt, groups of 10+, coaches permitted.**
¹/₃ -acre town garden on triangular plot divided into sections with several pathways. Herbaceous beds and borders with mature trees and shrubs planned for yr-round effect; rockery, pond and water feature; shade areas; patio with troughs and containers. Greenhouse.
✖ ⚛ ☕ ☎

6 NEW CASA LAGO
1 Woodlands Park, Whalley BB7 9UG. *Carole Ann Cronshaw & Stephen Powers. 2¹/₂ m S of Clitheroe. Leave M6 J31, take A59 towards Clitheroe. 9m take 2nd exit at roundabout for Whalley. After 2m reach village, straight on at mini roundabout, turn 1st R Woodlands Drive, 1st L Woodlands Park. Garden 25yds on L. Parking available in village car parks (300yds) or nearby.* **Adm £2.50, chd free. Suns 15 June; 7 Sept (1-5).**
This small garden is tightly packed with interest. Within its limited space. 2 fish ponds, tree ferns, acers, bamboos, grasses, bananas and succulents. Interesting features incl black limestone wall, the owner makes distinctive garden furniture and ornaments from naturally felled Ribble Valley trees. Teeming with ideas to inspire.
✖ ⚛ ☕

Rapunzel's tower, temple, turf maze, walk-through pyramid . . .

7 CLEARBECK HOUSE
Mewith Lane, Higher Tatham LA2 8PJ. Peter & Bronwen Osborne. *13m NE of Lancaster. Signed from Wray (M6 J34, A683, B6480) & Low Bentham.* Home-made teas. **Adm £2.50, chd free. Suns 25 May; 22, 29 June (11-5).**
'A surprise round every corner' is the most common response as visitors encounter fountains, streams, ponds, sculptures, boathouses and follies: (Rapunzel's tower, temple, turf maze, walk-through pyramid). 2-acre wildlife lake attracts many species of insects and birds. Planting incl herbaceous borders, grasses, bog plants and many roses. Featured in 'GGG' & 'WI Life'. Partial wheelchair access.
♿ ⚛ ☕

8 ◆ COBBLE HEY FARM & GARDENS
Claughton-on-Brock PR3 0QN. Mr & Mrs D Miller, 01995 602643, www.cobblehey.co.uk. *4m S of Garstang. Leave M6 at J32 or 33. Take brown sign from A6 nr Bilsborough. Claughton is 2m E, up Butt Hill Lane, 2nd farm rd on L.* **Adm £3, chd £1.50, concessions £2.50. Open Thurs to Mons Feb 1 to 24 Dec 10.30-4.30.**
2-acre hillside garden on working farm. Mature beds of hardy herbaceous perennials; over 200 species of phlox, primulas and hellebores; natural streams with stone banks. Woodland and colour-themed garden, prairie and potterage under development. Featured in 'Lancashire Life', Prize winner Lancashire & Blackpool TB.
♿ ✖ ⚛ ☕

9 CRABTREE LANE GARDENS
Burscough L40 0RW, 01704 893239. *3m NE of Ormskirk. Follow A59 Preston - Liverpool rd to Burscough. From N before 1st bridge turn R into Redcat Lane - brown sign Martin Mere. From S pass through village over 2nd bridge, then L into Redcat Lane, after ³/₄ m turn L into Crabtree Lane. Gardens by level Xing.* Home-made teas at 79 Crabtree Lane. **Combined**

adm £3, chd free. Sat 7, Sun 8 June (1-5).
Featured in 'Lancashire Life'.
☕

79 CRABTREE LANE
Sandra & Peter Curl, 01704 893713. Visitors also welcome by appt.
¹/₂ acre comprising different areas. Patio with hostas and grasses; herbaceous area surrounded by beech hedge, island beds with conifers and shrubs. Rose garden and 2 ponds; pergola for relaxing surrounded by climbers and wisteria.
♿ ✖ ⚛ ☎

81 CRABTREE LANE
Prue & Barry Cooper, 01704 893239. Visitors also welcome by appt.
Medium sized garden with 6ft wall, pond, water features, old fashioned rockery, vine covered pergola, trompe l'oeils. Central gazebo with climbers and other plants. Beds containing some shrubs, but mostly herbaceous plants. Arches with clematis and roses.
✖ ☎

10 CROSBY HALL
Back Lane, Little Crosby, Liverpool L23 4UA. Mark Blundell. *8m N of Liverpool. From church in Little Crosby take Back Lane. Entrance ¹/₄ m on R.* Light refreshments & teas. **Adm £3, chd free (share to Crosby Hall Educational Trust). Sun 18 May (2-5).**
4-acre garden, originally designed by John Webb circa 1815, set in parkland of 120-acre estate. Many fine trees, rhododendrons and azaleas. Special features in this developing garden incl Victorian stone archway, decorative walled garden, espalier pears and wisteria, new orchard and Zen garden. Gravel paths throughout.
♿ ✖ ⚛ ☕

11 CYPRESS HOUSE
Higher Lane, Dalton, nr Wigan WN8 7RP. David & Coleta Houghton, 01257 463822, www.cypresshousegarden.com. *5m E of Ormskirk. M6 J27. Follow A5209 in direction of Ormskirk. Proceed to 1st mini-roundabout E of Newburgh, turn L onto Higher Lane. Garden 1m on R.* Home-made teas. **Combined with Tudor House adm £4, chd free. Sun 22 June (1-6). Visitors also welcome by appt.**

¾ -acre garden, exposed and overlooking the West Lancashire plain. Mixed informal plantings which incl shrubs and trees, conifers, acers, hostas, heucheras, herbaceous and grasses. Many rare and unusual plants. Large rockery and water feature. Alpine and vine house. ¼ -acre young arboretum with rare and unusual trees.

✄ ✿ ☕ ☎

12 NEW DUTTON HALL
Gallows Lane, Ribchester PR3 3XX. Mr & Mrs A H Penny. *2m NE of Ribchester. Signed from B6243 & B6245.* Cream teas. **Adm £3.50, chd free. Sat 28, Sun 29 June (1-5).**
A fine collection of old-fashioned roses in a developing garden with extensive views over Ribble Valley. More formal garden at front within attractive setting of C17 house (not open). Orangery with interesting range of conservatory plants.

✄ ✿ ☕

13 NEW FOXBURY
47 Westbourne Road, Birkdale PR8 2HY. Pam & Richard James. *2m S of Southport. Off A565 Southport to Liverpool rd. Turn R at 2nd T-lights after roundabout, turn L at end, house on L.* Home-made teas. **Adm £2, chd free. Suns 22 June; 27 July (10.30-5.30).**
½ acre suburban garden just inland from dunes and famous golf course of Birkdale, very low lying. Mature pine shelters, water feature, mixed beds and newly planted trees are interspersed through a well maintained lawn. Mature shrubs and hedges shelter this developing garden from off-shore winds, giving a peaceful atmosphere.

✄ ✿ ☕

14 GREENACRE
157 Ribchester Road, Clayton-le-Dale BB1 9EE. Dorothy & Andrew Richards, 01254 249694. *3½ m N of Blackburn. Leave M6 J31. Take A59 towards Clitheroe. In 7m at T-lights turn R towards Blackburn along B6245. Garden ½ m on RH-side. Park nearby or at Salesbury Memorial Hall, 500yds on RH-side. Disabled parking nearby.* **Combined with 142 Ribchester Road adm £3.50, chd free (share to Vitalise). Sun 24, Mon 25 Aug (1.30-5).** Visitors also

welcome by appt May, July to early Sept, groups of 14 to 25.
Peaceful 1-acre garden on edge of Ribble Valley. Broad sweep of lawn with mixed beds, colour phased throughout the yr. Late summer wow factor with dahlias, begonias, perennials. Emphasis on colour, shapes, textures and contrasts, raised deck for viewing. Visitor information by flowerbeds. Original sculpture in woodland setting. A continually evolving garden. Featured in 'Lancashire Evening Telegraph' & 'Clitheroe Advertiser'.

♿ ✄ ✿ ☕ ☎

Suburban garden just inland from dunes and famous golf course of Birkdale . . .

15 HAWTHORNES NURSERY GARDEN
Marsh Road, Hesketh Bank PR4 6XT. Mr & Mrs R Hodson, 01772 812379, richardhaw@talktalk.net, www.hawthornesnursery.co.uk. *10m SW of Preston. From Preston take A59 towards Liverpool. Turn R at T-lights for Tarleton. Through Tarleton Village into Hesketh Bank. Large car park at Station Rd/Shore Rd. WC.* Home-made teas. **Adm £2.50, chd free. Sun 27 July (1-5). Visitors also welcome by appt June to Sept, coaches permitted.**
1-acre plant lover's garden. Intensively planted borders and beds with 150 old-fashioned shrub and climbing roses, over 200 clematis. (Rare and unusual herbaceous and viticella clematis. National Collection of viticellas). Interplanted with dramatic collection of hardy geraniums, phlox, aconitums, lythrums and heleniums for later colour. Adjoining nursery. Featured in 'GGG'.

♿ ✿ **NCCPG** ☕ ☎

16 HESKETH BANK VILLAGE GARDENS
PR4 6RQ. *10m SW of Preston. From Preston take A59 towards Liverpool, then turn R at T-lights for Tarleton village. Straight through Tarleton to Hesketh Bank.* Teas. **Combined adm £3.50, chd free. Sun 29 June (11-5).**
Free vintage bus between gardens. Maps available at each garden.

☕

31 BECCONSALL LANE
Mr & Mrs J Baxter, 01772 813018. Visitors also welcome by appt.
Cottage-style garden with pond, white and green beds and semi-woodland walk. Organic garden. Hot bed.

♿ ✄ ✿ ☎

74 CHAPEL ROAD
Mr & Mrs T Iddon, 01772 813172. Visitors also welcome by appt June & July only.
Compact colourful garden. Wide variety of plants. Pond, arbour and gazebo.

✄ ✿ ☎

11 DOUGLAS AVENUE
Mr & Mrs J Cook, 01772 813727. Visitors also welcome by appt May & June.
Large established garden with lawns, mature trees, topiary, box wheel, mixed herbaceous borders and naturalised areas, with pond. Wheelchair access to certain areas.

♿ ✄ ✿ ☎

155 STATION ROAD
Mr & Mrs G Hale
Large garden with lawns; cottage-style herbaceous borders. Summerhouse and pond.

♿ ✄

WEDGWOOD
Shore Road. Mr & Mrs D Watson, 01772 816509, heskethbank@aol.com. Visitors also welcome by appt, June & July only.
An old garden which is being developed into diverse planting areas. These incl gravel, woodland, herbaceous, formal pond, lawns, large glasshouse, orchard with meadow and colour-themed parterre rainbow-garden.

♿ ✄ ✿ ☎

⑰ HUNTINGDON HALL
Huntingdon Hall Lane, Dutton
PR3 2ZT. Mr & Mrs J E Ashcroft. *6m
NE of Preston. Leave M6 J31. Take
A59 towards Clitheroe, turn L at 1st T-
lights to Ribchester along B6245. After
bridge over R Ribble take next R up
Gallows Lane. T-junction turn L. Next R
into Huntingdon Hall Lane.* Home-
made teas & wine. **Adm £2.50, chd
free. Sun 10 Aug (11-5).**
C17 house (not open) in glorious
countryside. Garden features incl:
formal layout with pleached limes,
developing herbaceous beds,
woodland walk, terraced pond, many
unusual plants.

&♿ ✖ ⊛ ☕

⑱ MILL BARN & PRIMROSE COTTAGE
Goosefoot Close, Samlesbury
PR5 0SS. Chris Mortimer & Susan
Childs, 01254 853300,
chris@millbarn.net. *6m E of Preston.
From M6 J31 2½ m on A59/A677
B/burn. Turn S. Nabs Head Lane, then
Goosefoot Lane.* Cream teas. **Adm £3,
chd free. Suns 8, 22 June (12-5).
Visitors also welcome by appt May
to July only.**
Tranquil terraced garden along the
banks of R Darwen. A garden to
stimulate the imagination, ranging from
the semi-formal to the bucolic.
Primrose Bank (adjacent garden), is a
relaxed garden sensitively controlled.
Garden ceramics from our studio on
sale (20% proceeds to NGS).

&♿ � ☕ ☎

⑲ MONTFORD COTTAGE
Cuckstool Lane, Fence, nr Burnley
BB12 9NZ. Craig Bullock & Tony
Morris, www.montford.p3online.net.
*4m N of Burnley. From J13 M65, take
A6068 (signs for Fence) & in 2m turn L
onto B6248 (signs for Brierfield).
Proceed down hill for ½ m (past Forest
PH). Entrance to garden on L, with
limited car park further down hill.*
Cream teas. **Adm £3, chd 50p. Sat 31
May; Sun 1 June (2-6).**
Well established 1-acre walled
garden, with recent projects
synthesizing with mature plantings to
enhance this plantsman's collection,
artist/photographer/floral designer
having created a garden with
individual identity. Many seats and
shelters provide the opportunity
to relax and soak up the
atmosphere.

&♿ ⊛ ☕

⑳ THE OLD ZOO GARDEN
Cherry Drive, Brockhall Village
BB6 8AY. Gerald & Linda Hitman,
01254 244811. *5m N Blackburn.
Leave M6 J31, take A59 Clitheroe
approx 10m. Follow signs for Old
Langho & Brockhall Village. Just prior
to Blackburn roundabout (junction
A666) follow signs to The Old Zoo.
Partial access for wheelchairs & prams.*
Light refreshments & teas. **Adm £5,
chd free. Fri 29, Sun 31 Aug (11-4).
Visitors also welcome by appt.**
Guided tours of garden and use of
leisure facilities of The Avenue Hotel
are availabe to parties 20+. For
details www.theavenuehotel.co.uk.
15 acres. The Old Zoo garden is
constructed with pleasure in mind; it
encloses figurative sculpture, 16
varieties of Lancashire apples, water
courses, unusual planting and very
unusual earth workings. The size and
speed with which The Old Zoo has
been constructed has made it one of
the North's premier gardens, with its
acclaim growing by the week.

☕ ☎

㉑ 🆕 142 RIBCHESTER ROAD
Clayton-le-Dale BB1 9EE. Susan
& David Brown. *3½ m N of
Blackburn. Exit M6 J31, take A59
towards Clitheroe. In 7m at T-lights
turn R towards Blackburn on
B6245. Garden ½ m on L. Park
nearby or at Salesbury Memorial
Hall, 500yds on R. Disabled
parking nearby.* **Combined with
Greenacre adm £3.50, chd free.
Sun 24, Mon 25 Aug (1.30-5).**
¾ acre incl a developing tree
collection, colourful herbaceous
beds, still pond, shrubbery
encouraging wildlife, beautiful
views over Pendle Hill and Ribble
Valley.

&♿ ✖ ☕

㉒ ◆ THE RIDGES
Weavers Brow, Cowling Road,
Limbrick PR6 9EB. Mr & Mrs J M
Barlow, 01257 279981,
www.bedbreakfast-gardenvisit.com.
*2m SE of Chorley. J27 M6 or J8 M61
approaching Chorley on A6, follow
signs for Chorley, then signs for
Cowling & Rivington. From A6 S turn R
at 1st roundabout, R at Morrison's. Up
Brooke St, take Cowling Brow, approx
¼ m garden on RH-side.* **Adm £2.50,
chd free. Bank Hols Suns, Mons
May, Aug 11-5; Weds in June, July

(11-7). For NGS: Suns 4 May; 24 Aug
(11-5).**
3 acres. Incl old walled kitchen garden,
cottage-style; herbaceous borders;
natural garden with stream, ponds.
Laburnum arch leads to large formal
lawn, surrounded by natural woodland.
Shrub borders and trees with
contrasting foliage. Walled area planted
with scented roses and herbs. Paved
area with dovecote. Wall feature with
Italian influence. New woodland walk
and wild flower garden.

&♿ ⊛ 📖 ☕

Shrubbery
encouraging
wildlife,
beautiful
views over
Pendle Hill
and Ribble
Valley . . .

㉓ 14 SAXON ROAD
Birkdale PR8 2AX. Margaret & Geoff
Fletcher, 01704 567742. *1m S of
Southport. Off A565 Southport to
Liverpool rd. 4th rd on L after
roundabout opp St James Church.*
Home-made teas. **Adm £2.50, chd
free (share to Queenscourt
Hospice). Sun 6 July (10.30-4.30).
Also open with Birkdale Village
Gardens 29 June. Visitors also
welcome by appt, groups 10+.**
¼-acre walled garden transformed
over 12yrs from rectangular lawn with
long borders to an exciting mix of
secret areas, informal beds and water
features, accessed by winding bank
and gravel paths. New for 2008
redesigned front garden.

&♿ ✖ ⊛ ☕ ☎

24 NEW **SEFTON PARK GARDENS**

Liverpool L8 3SA. *3m S of Liverpool city centre. From end of M62 take A5058 Queens Drive ring rd through Allerton to Sefton Park and follow Palm House signs. Park roadside in Sefton Park.* Light refreshments & teas in Palm House. **Combined adm £4, chd free. Sun 29 June (12-5).**
Two large city gardens and nearly 100 allotments open to celebrate Liverpool's Capital of Culture year 2008. Rare and unusual plants for sale, musical entertainment and refreshments in the restored Victorian Sefton Park Palm House. Private gardens and allotments never previously opened to the public. Traditional music from 'Mostly Madrigals', floral display by NAFAS.

NEW **PARKMOUNT**
38 Ullet Road. Jeremy Nicholls
Developing garden with mixed borders, woodland paths, moroccan patio, some surprises and many rare plants in one of Liverpool's old merchant houses overlooking Sefton Park.

NEW **SEFTON PARK ALLOTMENTS**
Greenbank Drive. Sefton Park Allotments Society. *Next door to Sefton Park cricket club*
Nearly 100 individually tended fruit and vegetable plots with a wide variety of produce. The site incls many interesting community facilities, a plot adapted for disabled gardeners. Try our potato taste challenge. The site has featured in national TV and film productions - see the 'Bread' shed where Li-low Lil held her trysts on plot 89.

NEW **VICE CHANCELLOR'S GARDEN**
12 Sefton Park Road. University of Liverpool, Vice -Chancellor Prof J Drummond Bone & Mrs Vivian Bone, Gardener Mr Brian Farrington
Collection of old shrub roses, formal terrace, grape vine, shrub borders and large weeping ash. Gravel paths.
&

25 **SOUTHLANDS**
12 Sandy Lane, Stretford M32 9DA. Maureen Sawyer & Duncan Watmough, 0161 283 9425, moe@southlands12.com, www.southlands12.com. *3m S of Manchester. Sandy Lane (B5213) is situated off A5181 (A56) ¼ m from M60 J7.* Home-made teas. **Adm £3, chd free (share to Christie Hospital NHS Trust). Sat 12, Sun 13 July (1-6). Visitors also welcome by appt June to end of Aug. Guided tour for groups of 10+.**
Artist's ¼ -acre town garden making full use of structures and living screens to create a number of intimate gardens each with its own theme incl courtyard, Mediterranean, ornamental, woodland and organic kitchen gardens with large glasshouse. Many exotics and unusual herbaceous perennials, 2 ponds and water feature. Moss garden. Live jazz twice daily (weather permitting). Art exhibition. Featured in & on 'All Things Bright & Beautiful', BBC Radio Manchester.

See the 'Bread' shed where Li-low Lil held her trysts on plot 89 . . .

26 **THE STONES & ROSES GARDEN**
White Coppice Farm, White Coppice PR6 9DF. Raymond & Linda Smith, 01257 277633, stonesandroses@btinternet.com, www.stonesandroses.org. *3m NE of Chorley. J8 M61. A674 to Blackburn. 3rd R to Heapey & White Coppice. Parking next to garden.* Teas (May, Sept), Cream teas (July). **Adm £2.50, chd free. Sats 3, 10 May; Sat 12, Sun 13 July; Sats 13, 20 Sept (2-5). Visitors also welcome by appt, groups of 10+.**
Still developing 3-acre garden where the cows used to live. Sunken garden, 500 roses, fountains, waterfalls, stonework, rockery, herbaceous,

stumpery. Colour themed planting, fruit tree walk down to dewpond with jetty. Hundreds of bulbs and wallflowers for May opening. Featured on BBC Northwest. Gravel paths.

27 NEW **TUDOR HOUSE**
Higher Lane, Dalton, nr Wigan WN8 7RP. Steve & Dorothy Anders. *5m E of Ormskirk. M6 J27 follow A5209 direction of Ormskirk, at 1st mini roundabout E of Newburgh turn L into Higher Lane, garden 1.2m on L.* Home-made teas. **Combined with Cypress House adm £4, chd free. Sun 22 June (1-6).**
Set in 1½ acres with panoramic views stretching to the Fylde coast this garden has many interesting features incl a bridge over dry stone bed, rockery and many grasses. Small folly with clematis and grape vine. Many unusual shrubs amongst interesting landscape.

28 **WEEPING ASH**
Bents Garden Centre, Warrington Road, Glazebury WA3 5NS. John Bent, 01942 266300, www.bents.co.uk. *15m W of Manchester. Located next to Bents Garden Centre, just off the East Lancs rd A580 at Greyhound roundabout nr Leigh. Follow brown 'Garden Centre' signs.* Light refreshments & teas at Bents Garden Centre next to garden. **Adm £2, chd free. Suns 17, 24 Feb; 20 Apr; 20 July; 21 Sept (11-4.30). 2009 Suns 15, 22 Feb.**
Created by retired nurseryman and photographer John Bent, Weeping Ash is a garden of all-yr interest. Broad sweeps of colour lend elegance to the initial view of the sweeping garden,

where herbaceous perennials over spill their boundaries and offer a riot of vivid colours. Curving lawns are framed with an eclectic mix of foliage, flowers and form to create simply stunning visual sensations.

♿ ✂ ☕

29 WILLOW HOUSE
106 Higher Walton Road, Walton-le-Dale PR5 4HR. Sue & Michael Coupe, 01772 257042, francescoupe@hotmail.com. *3m SW of Preston. Exit 29 M6. M65 exit 1, M61 exit Bamber Bridge/Chorley. Bungalow on A675 (nr to Inside Out Restaurant).* **Adm £2, chd 50p (share to RPH Renal Unit).** **Visitors** welcome by appt.
Approx ⅓ acre, overlooking fields to ancient woodland. Herbaceous borders, small box parterre. Pond with koi; rockery and summerhouse. Grasses and alpine troughs. Thyme path. Many unusual ideas. Featured in 'Amateur Gardening'. Gravel paths, some steps.

♿ ✂ ❀ ☎

30 WROXHAM GARDENS
Davyhulme M41 5TE. *1m SW of Urmston. From J10 on M60 follow Urmston signs, to 2nd roundabout, take 3rd exit and immediate 1st R into Davyhulme Rd. Gardens short walk behind St Mary's Church.* Home-made teas at 1 Wroxham Avenue.
Combined adm £2.50, chd free. Sun 29 June (1-5).
Six suburban gardens in various styles and size, packed with interesting plants and ideas for smaller garden. Family friendly gardens, pottery making, crepe making and childrens quiz.

☕

12 BOWERS AVENUE
Mel & Phil Gibbs. *Access via 10 Wroxham Avenue*
Small town garden, with many cottage style plants, incl roses and clematis, pots, shrubs and patio for all-round interest.

✂ ❀

1 WROXHAM AVENUE
Liz & Emile Auld
Town garden with shaped lawn; borders with shrubs and perennials; patio area. Raised decking area wtih hosta borders and passiflora arch. Pebble water feature, minature pond and small vegetable/herb area.

♿ ✂ ❀

2 WROXHAM AVENUE
Margaret & Bren Kinnucane
Town garden with raised edge beds containing mature shrubs and herbaceous perennials; wildlife pond with seating area and raised patio with troughs, containers and water feature.

❀

9 WROXHAM AVENUE
Jonathan & Katrina Myers
Triangular SE-facing formal garden comprising stone patio, an irregularly-shaped lawn, shrubs, conifers and heather. To the E corner there is a terracotta pot water feature, whilst in the opp corner a traditional two-tier fountain. Slightly raised area bordered by grasses and phormium.

♿ ✂ ❀

10 WROXHAM AVENUE
Petra Dorman
Plants growing in higgledy piggledy fashion. No colour

scheme, self seeding and spreading plants prevail. Astrantia, helleborus, linaria, thalictrum, hesperis and companula. Pottery exhibition.

♿ ✂ ❀

11 WROXHAM AVENUE
Alan Slack
Unusual triangular-shaped plot with lots going on. Decking; patio areas; pergola with climbers; vegetable plot, herb garden; alpine sinks; pond with waterfall; rockery; lawn area. Well-stocked mature borders, much 'architectural'. Conservatory; greenhouse; shed and kennel.

♿ ❀

Lancashire, Merseyside, Greater Manchester & surrounding areas County Volunteers

County Organisers
Ray & Brenda Doldon, 2 Gorse Way, Formby, Merseyside L37 1PB, 01704 834253, ray@doldon.plus.com

County Treasurer
Ray Doldon, 2 Gorse Way, Formby, Merseyside L37 1PB, 01704 834253, ray@doldon.plus.com

Publicity
Christine Ruth, 15 Princes Park Mansions, Croxteth Road, Liverpool L8 3SA, 0151 727 4877, caruthchris@aol.com

Assistant County Organisers
Margaret & Geoff Fletcher, 14 Saxon Road, Birkdale, Southport, Merseyside PR8 2AX, 01704 567742, geoffwfletcher@hotmail.co.uk
Dorothy & Andrew Richards, Greenacre, 157 Ribchester Rd, Clayton-Le-Dale, Blackburn BB1 9EE, 01254 249694, andrewfrichards@talk21.com

LEICESTERSHIRE & RUTLAND

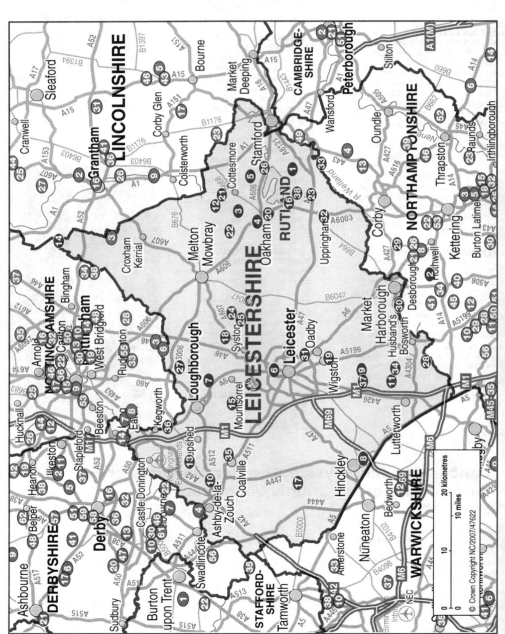

Opening Dates

March

SUNDAY 2
- ⑭ The Homestead
- ⑱ 1700 Melton Road

SUNDAY 16
- ⑤ Barnsdale Gardens

SUNDAY 23
- ㉔ Parkside

April

SUNDAY 6
- ⑮ Long Close

SUNDAY 27
- ㉑ The Old Hall

May

SUNDAY 4
- ④ Barleythorpe Gardens
- ⑥ Belgrave Hall Museum & Gardens
- ㉔ Parkside
- ㉕ Pine House

MONDAY 5
- ㉔ Parkside
- ㉕ Pine House

SUNDAY 11
- ⑯ Manton Gardens
- ㊱ Whatton Gardens

WEDNESDAY 14
- ㉚ Thorpe Lubenham Hall

SATURDAY 17
- ⑮ Long Close (Evening)

SUNDAY 18
- ⑪ Gilmorton Gardens
- ⑲ Mill House
- ㉒ The Old Vicarage
- ㉟ Warren Hills Cottage

WEDNESDAY 21
- ⑪ Gilmorton Gardens (Day & Evening)

SUNDAY 25
- ㉜ Uppingham Gardens

June

SUNDAY 1
- ⑩ The Dairy
- ㉖ Prebendal House
- ㉞ Walton Gardens

WEDNESDAY 4
- ② Arthingworth Gardens
- ㉙ Stoke Albany House
- ㉞ Walton Gardens

SUNDAY 8
- ③ Ashwell Gardens

WEDNESDAY 11
- ② Arthingworth Gardens

- ㉙ Stoke Albany House

SATURDAY 14
- ⑮ Long Close (Evening)

SUNDAY 15
- ⑪ Gilmorton Gardens
- ㉘ South Kilworth Gardens
- ㊳ Wing Gardens

WEDNESDAY 18
- ② Arthingworth Gardens
- ㉙ Stoke Albany House
- ㉝ Wakerley Manor (Evening)

SUNDAY 22
- ⑦ Beveridge Street Gardens
- ⑨ Coldor
- ㉓ The Park House
- ㉗ Ridgewold Farm

WEDNESDAY 25
- ② Arthingworth Gardens
- ㉘ South Kilworth Gardens (Day & Evening)
- ㉙ Stoke Albany House

July

WEDNESDAY 2
- ② Arthingworth Gardens
- ㉙ Stoke Albany House

SATURDAY 5
- ⑩ The Dairy (Evening)

SUNDAY 6
- ㊱ Whatton Gardens

WEDNESDAY 9
- ② Arthingworth Gardens
- ㉙ Stoke Albany House

SUNDAY 13
- ① Acre End
- ⑬ Hill Park Farm

WEDNESDAY 16
- ② Arthingworth Gardens
- ㉙ Stoke Albany House

SUNDAY 20
- ⑫ Hill House
- ⑲ Mill House
- ㉟ Warren Hills Cottage

WEDNESDAY 23
- ② Arthingworth Gardens
- ㉙ Stoke Albany House

SUNDAY 27
- ⑰ Market Bosworth Gardens
- ㉛ University of Leicester 'Harold Martin' Botanic Garden
- ㊲ Willoughby Gardens

August

SUNDAY 3
- ⑨ Coldor

SUNDAY 24
- ⑳ Mirwood

September

SUNDAY 7
- ⑫ Hill House

SUNDAY 14
- ⑥ Belgrave Hall Museum & Gardens

October

SUNDAY 5
- ⑱ 1700 Melton Road

SUNDAY 26
- ⑤ Barnsdale Gardens

Gardens open to the public

- ⑤ Barnsdale Gardens
- ⑱ 1700 Melton Road
- ㊱ Whatton Gardens
- ㊾ Wingwell

By appointment only

- ⑧ Burbage Gardens
- ⑧ 6 Denis Road, Burbage Gardens
- ⑧ 13 Hall Road, Burbage Gardens
- ⑧ 18 Hall Road, Burbage Gardens
- ⑧ 7 Hall Road, Burbage Gardens

Also open by appointment ☎

- ① Acre End
- ② Arthingworth Manor Garden, Arthingworth Gardens
- ② Bosworth House, Arthingworth Gardens
- ⑥ Belgrave Hall Museum & Gardens
- ⑨ Coldor
- ⑩ The Dairy
- ⑪ 'Al Manzel', Gilmorton Gardens
- ⑪ Ulverscroft Close, Gilmorton Gardens
- ㊲ Farmway, Willoughby Gardens
- ⑭ The Homestead
- ⑮ Long Close
- ⑰ Rainbow Cottage, Market Bosworth Gardens
- ⑲ Mill House
- ⑳ Mirwood
- ㉑ The Old Hall
- ㉒ The Old Vicarage
- ㉘ Croft Acre, South Kilworth Gardens
- ㉘ Oak Tree House, South Kilworth Gardens
- ㉞ Orchards, Walton Gardens
- ㉕ Pine House
- ㉙ Stoke Albany House
- ㉟ Warren Hills Cottage

The Gardens

❶ ACRE END
The Jetties, North Luffenham
LE15 8JX. Jim & Mima Bolton,
01780 720906, mmkb@mac.com.
*7m SE of Oakham. Via Manton & Edith
Weston, 7m SW of Stamford via
Ketton. 2m off A47 through Morcott
village.* Light refreshments & teas at
North Luffenham Community Centre.
**Adm £3.50, chd free. Sun 13 July
(11-5). Visitors also welcome by
appt mid Jun to mid Aug, groups
welcome.**
1-acre garden, imaginatively designed
and intensively planted, incl knot
garden, oriental courtyard garden,
mixed borders, circular lawn with island
beds, herb and scented garden.
Working fruit and vegetable garden,
long herbaceous border and woodland
garden. Many unusual trees, shrubs,
herbaceous perennials and tender
exotics in containers. All organically
managed to encourage wildlife. Studio
Art Exhibition (share to NGS).
Challenging Quiz. Wildlife wood
carvings. Featured on BBCTV East
Midlands Today, Aug 2007. Mainly
grass paths & lawns, some gravel.
& ✖ ✿ ☕ ☎

Working fruit and vegetable garden . . .

❷ NEW ARTHINGWORTH GARDENS
LE16 8JT. *6m S of Market
Harborough. From Market
Harborough via A508, at 4m L to
Arthingworth. From N'pton on
A508 turn R just after Kelmarsh at
bottom of hill. Follow to village,
keep church on L, farm on R,
parking opp at office.* Teas in village
hall. **Combined adm £3, chd free.
Weds, 4 June to 23 July; (2-5).**
☕

ARTHINGWORTH MANOR GARDEN
Braybrooke Road,
Arthingworth, Market
Harborough. W L S Guinness,
01858 525431,
jkirby@overmans.co.uk. Visitors
also welcome by appt June/
July only.
White garden; delphiniums,
herbaceous and mixed borders;
vegetables and fruit. 3-acre
arboretum. Gravel paths, steep
slopes, some steps.
& ☎

NEW BOSWORTH HOUSE
Arthingworth LE16 8LA. Mrs C
E Irving-Swift, 01858 525202,
irvingswift@btinternet.com.
Visitors also welcome by appt
June/July.
1½ acre of lawns, herbaceous
borders, little orchard, small
spinney, vegetable patch. A few
magnificent old trees and rose
bed. Panoramic views.
✖ ☎

❸ ASHWELL GARDENS
LE15 7LW. *3m N of Oakham. Via
B668 towards Cottesmore, turn L for
Ashwell.* Light refreshments & teas.
**Combined adm £3, chd free (share
to Ashwell Church). Sun 8 June
(11.45-6).**
☕

ASHWELL COTTAGE
Church Close. Mr & Mrs I
Menzies-Gow
Village garden of approx ¾ acre
surrounding a thatched cottage.
Informal lawns and flower beds
are boundaried by mature trees
and shrubs. Gravel paths.
&

ASHWELL HOUSE
Mr & Mrs S D Pettifer
Over 20yrs of opening this 1½ -
acre walled vicarage garden,
1812. Against background of
ancient trees; front lawns are
bordered by interesting shrubs
and plants with classical summer
pavilion. The formal swimming
pool garden leads to traditional
planting of vegetables and fruit.
& ✿

❹ BARLEYTHORPE GARDENS
LE15 7EQ. *1m from Oakham on
A6006 towards Melton Mowbray. Car
park in Pasture Lane 1st turn L in
Barleythorpe by phone box. Please*

park in field on L not on lane. Home-
made teas. **Combined adm £3, chd
free (share to East Midlands
Accident Care Service). Sun 4 May
(2-5).**
☕

BARLEYTHORPE HOUSE
8 Manor Lane. Mr R Turner &
Mrs J Turner
Flowering shrubs, large weeping
trees, small lake and woodland
walk.
&

DAIRY COTTAGE
Pasture Lane. Mr & Mrs W
Smith
Cottage-style garden at rear with
interesting shrubs and spring
bulbs. Paved/walled garden to
front (with pond) and lime hedge.
Separate semi-formal orchard.
Gravel access to main garden.
& ✿

❺ ◆ BARNSDALE GARDENS
The Avenue, Exton, nr Oakham
LE15 8AH. Nick & Sue Hamilton,
01572 813200,
www.barnsdalegardens.co.uk. *3m E
of Oakham. Turn off A606 at Barnsdale
Lodge Hotel then 1m on L.* **Adm £6,
chd £2, concessions £5. For NGS:
Suns 16 Mar; 26 Oct (9-5).**
8 acres of individual gardens used by
the late Geoff Hamilton for BBC TV
'Gardeners' World'. Wide variety of
ideas and garden designs for all-yr
interest. Enjoyed by gardeners and
non-gardeners alike. Featured on
BBC2 'Gardeners' World', June &
Sept, 2007.
& ✖ ✿ ☕

BAXTER FARM
See Nottinghamshire.

❻ BELGRAVE HALL MUSEUM & GARDENS
Church Road off Thurcaston Road,
Belgrave, Leicester LE4 5PE.
Leicester City Council, 0116 2666
590, www.leicester.gov.uk/museums
- for other open dates. *1½ m N of
Leicester. From A6/A563 junction at
Redhill roundabout take A6030
Loughborough Rd towards city, signed
Outdoor Pursuits Centre. Turn R at 1st
T-lights and L at Talbot PH.* Home-
made teas. **Adm £2, chd free. Suns
May; 14 Sept (1-4.30). Visitors also
welcome by appt.**
Historic Grade II listed garden. House
and walled garden date from 1709.
Includes formal garden, herbaceous
garden, rose walks, Victorian

evergreen garden, rock and water garden, botanic beds, herb border, woodland garden. Alpine, temperate and tropical glasshouses with wide collection of plants incl banana and citrus.

❼ BEVERIDGE STREET GARDENS

Barrow upon Soar LE12 8PL. *2m S of Loughborough.* Home-made teas at 4 Beveridge St. **Combined adm £2, chd free. Sun 22 June (11-4).**
An old Leicestershire village with pleasant walks along banks of River Soar.

APRICOT COTTAGE
11 Beveridge Street. Jane Atkinson. *Follow signs to village centre, High St, then 1st R to church, 1st R*
Small garden of intrigue and serenity with architectural plants, lights and water.

THE OLD WALLED GARDEN
49 Beveridge Street. Roger & Jo Chappell
Very old walled garden with mainly cottage-style herbaceous plants in a variety of settings incl lawns and borders, ponds, hot and shady areas, rockery and herb garden. Many plants take advantage of the walls incl clematis, climbing roses, vines and fruit trees.

BLUEBELL ARBORETUM
See Derbyshire.

❽ BURBAGE GARDENS
LE10 2LR. *1m S of Hinckley. From M69 J1, take B4109 signed Hinckley. 1st L after 2nd roundabout into Sketchley Manor Estate then 1st R, 1st L. All gardens within walking distance.* **Adm £2, chd free. Visitors welcome by appt.**
A pleasant West Leicestershire village. Individual appointments for each garden. More than one garden may be available. Please phone for details.

6 DENIS ROAD
Mr & Mrs D A Dawkins, 01455 230509. *Sketchley Manor Est.* **Visitors welcome by appt Feb to June, please ring.**
Small garden designed to appear much larger with wide range of plants incl hardy geraniums, ferns, hostas, foliage plants, species

clematis, hellebores and spring bulbs. Alpines in sinks. Large collection of snowdrops.

7 HALL ROAD
Don & Mary Baker, 01455 635616. *Sketchley Manor Est.* **Visitors welcome by appt Feb to June, please phone.**
Medium-sized garden; mixed borders; foliage plants; good mixture of shrubs. Hellebores and spring bulbs, collection of snowdrops. Hostas, hardy geraniums and unusual perennials; pond. Late summer colour.

13 HALL ROAD
Mr & Mrs G A & A J Kierton, 01455 632416. *Sketchley Manor Est.* **Visitors welcome by appt May to end Aug.**
Decorative medium-sized flower garden, incoporating pool and waterfall, herbaceous borders, central lawn, scree garden, 2 patios, pergola, summer house; greenhouse and small fountain. Abundance of summer colour.

18 HALL ROAD
Mrs M A Clamp, 01455 230509. *Sketchley Manor Est.* **Visitors welcome by appt May to end Aug, groups 10+.**
Small garden, newly redesigned incl herbaceous borders. Shrubs. Pergola and gravel area.

CHESTNUT COTTAGE
See Nottinghamshire.

Very old walled garden with mainly cottage-style herbaceous plants . . .

❾ NEW COLDOR
4 Arnesby Lane, Peatling Magna, Leicester LE8 5UN. Colin & Doreen Shepherd, 01162 478407. *9m S of Leicester. 2m W of Arnesby on A5199. Arnesby Lane is opp Cock Inn, Peatling Magna. Garden is on private drive 100yds from Cock Inn. Parking on Main St.* Home-made teas. **Adm £2, chd free (share to All Saints Church, Peatling Magna). Suns 22 June; 3 Aug (11-5). Visitors also welcome by appt May to Sept.**
$1/4$ acre garden with immaculate lawns, mixed herbaceous and shrub borders. Small pond and water feature. Patio with many plants in containers. Garden nursery, quality plants for sale.

THE COTTAGE
See Derbyshire.

❿ THE DAIRY
Moor Lane, Coleorton LE67 8FQ. Mr & Mrs J B Moseley, 01530 834539. *2m E of Ashby De La Zouch. Moor Lane is off A512 200yds W of Peggs Green roundabout.* Home-made teas & light refreshments. **Adm £2.50, chd free. Sun 1 June (1.30-5). Evening Opening £4, chd free, wine, Sat 5 July (6-9). Visitors also welcome by appt May, June & July only, groups of 10+, coaches permitted.**
Approx $1/2$-acre of mature trees, shrubs and herbaceous borders containing many unusual and architectural plants. Herb garden, fragrant roses, pergola, Japanese garden and dry area with grasses and agaves. The separate 'rooms' of the garden create surprises around every corner. Summer flowering plants create a riot of colour in June and July.

THE DOWER HOUSE
See Derbyshire.

⓫ GILMORTON GARDENS
Nr Lutterworth LE17 5LY. *12m S of Leicester. 4m from J20 of M1. Proceed through Lutterworth town centre. Turn R at police stn. Follow signs to Gilmorton. From Leicester follow A426 towards Lutterworth. At Dunton Bassett turn L signed to Gilmorton. Also A5199 Leicester/Northampton Rd via*

Bruntingthorpe signed Gilmorton. Light refreshments & teas in village hall. **Combined adm £3, chd free.** Sun 18 May; Sun 15 June (11-6). **Day & Evening Opening** £3, Wed 21 May (2-8). Sun 15 June combined with **South Kilworth Gardens** optional combined adm £5 to cover all gardens open in both villages. Gilmorton, Saxon origin, listed in Domesday survey. Examples of mud walled, thatched cottages (1500s), a motte (1100s), and brick cottages dating from 1710. Church (will be open), of Norman origin, was extensively rebuilt in 1860. Notable are its reredos and fine examples of Kempe stain glass windows.

'AL MANZEL'
Main Street. David & Janet Grundy, 01455 556586. *Nr Crown PH end of Main St opp Porlock Drive.* **Visitors also welcome by appt end of May, June, July, Aug. Individuals & groups welcome, coaches permitted.**
Average-size plant lovers' garden constructed from an old walled farmyard, with many interesting plants, structures and features. Ponds and running water, rockery, gravel garden, greenhouse, formal garden. Extensive use of small trees, clematis and plants in pots.

MOATFIELD
Church Lane. Mr & Mrs R P Morgan. **Not open Sun 15 June.**
Garden around barn conversion next to church started in 1995. Lawns, climbers, roses, unusual shrubs, flower borders and raised beds for acid loving plants in original walled farmyard area. Field with large natural pond, collection of trees; rowans, birches, hollies etc, and old moat area. Open views of countryside.

ULVERSCROFT CLOSE
Ashby Road. Mr & Mrs M J Maddock, 01455 553226, michael.maddock@care4free. net, www.maddock-garden.co.uk. **Visitors also welcome by appt May, June, July, Aug. Individuals & groups welcome, coaches permitted.**
$1/2$ -acre garden on two levels. Upper level features conservatory, courtyard, tree-lined paved walkway. Lower level has pond,

bog garden and stream situated in colourful herbaceous and shrub borders hosting over 120 clematis. Formal kitchen garden.

⑫ HILL HOUSE
18 Teigh Road, Market Overton LE15 7PW. Brian & Judith Taylor. *6m N of Oakham. Beyond Cottesmore, 5m from A1 via Thistleton, 10m E from Melton Mowbray via Wymondham.* Home-made teas. **Adm £2, chd free. Suns 20 July; 7 Sept (11-5).**
Owner-maintained plant enthusiasts' garden consisting mainly of mixed beds designed to provide colour and interest from mid-June to the end of Sept. The emphasis is on architectural plants and unusual hardy and tender perennials. Ornamental pond.

Wonderful views over Charnwood Forest . . .

⑬ HILL PARK FARM
Dodgeford Lane, Belton, Loughborough LE12 9TE. John & Jean Adkin. *6m W of Loughborough. Dodgeford Lane off B5324 bet Belton & Osgathorpe.* Home-made teas. **Adm £2.50, chd free. Sun 13 July (11-5).**
Medium-sized garden to a working farm with wonderful views over Charnwood Forest. Herbaceous borders, rock garden; many planted stone troughs and new pergola with clematis and roses.

HOLYWELL HALL
See Lincolnshire.

⑭ THE HOMESTEAD
Normanton-by-Bottesford NG13 0EP. John & Shirley Palmer, 01949 842745. *8m W of Grantham. From A52. In Bottesford turn N, signed Normanton; last house on R before disused airfield. From A1, in Long Bennington follow signs S to Normanton, 1st house on L.* Home-made teas. **Adm £1.50, chd free. Sun 2 Mar (1-5). Visitors also welcome by appt.**

$3/4$ -acre informal plant lover's garden. Vegetable garden, small orchard, woodland area, many hellebores, snowdrops and single peonies and salvias. Collections of hostas and sempervivums. National Collection of heliotropes.

⑮ LONG CLOSE
Main St, Woodhouse Eaves LE12 8RZ. John & Pene Oakland, 01509 890376. *4m S of Loughborough. Nr M1 J23. From A6, W in Quorn. Tickets on day of visit from Gift Shop opp. If shop closed tickets at garden.* **Adm £4, chd 50p. Daily Tues to Sats & Bank Hol weekends Mar to July; Sept & Oct (9.30-5.30). Sun 6 Apr (1-5)** with home-made teas. **Evening Openings: Sat 17 May,** £5, wine, (6-8). Sat 14 June, Songs in the Garden. Coalville & District Male Voice Choir. £8, wine & nibbles (7-9). Also group visits by appointment, catering by arrangement.
5-acres spring bulbs, rhododendrons, azaleas, camellias, magnolias, many rare shrubs, mature trees, lily ponds; terraced lawns, herbaceous borders, potager in walled kitchen garden, penstemon collection, wild flower meadow walk. New contemplation quiet area. Winter, spring, summer and autumn colour, a garden for all seasons. Plants for sale.

THE MALTINGS
See Northamptonshire.

MANOR FARM HOUSE
See Nottinghamshire.

⑯ MANTON GARDENS
LE15 8SR. *3m N of Uppingham. 3m S Oakham. Manton is on S shore of Rutland Water $1/4$ m off A6003. Please park carefully in village.* Home-made teas in village hall. **Combined adm £3, chd free. Sun 11 May (2-6).**
Small village with many stone houses and an interesting church, at western end south shore of Rutland Water.

FRYERS COTTAGE
Priory Road. LE15 8ST. Martin & Patricia Lawrence
$3/4$ -acre developing garden with views of Rutland Water. Shrubs, roses, mixed herbaceous, gravel and small ornamental vegetable and fruit garden.

HALL COTTAGE
St Mary's Road. Mike & Mary Stenson
Walled country cottage garden with a random mix of planting, incl roses, shrubs and perennials. Emphasis on shape, colour and texture. Small 'secret' areas, informal pond with waterfall.

HOLLYTOP HOUSE
48 Lyndon Road. Brian & Janett Barwick. *Lyndon Rd on E-side of Manton 20 metres before mini roundabout. Turn down gravel drive (parking available for disabled)*
2½ -acre garden consisting of trees and shrubs, walled cloister-like private garden with water features, pots and flower beds.

MANTON GRANGE
1 Lyndon Road. Mr & Mrs Mark Taylor
2½ -acre garden with interesting trees, shrubs and herbaceous borders. Kitchen garden. Rose garden. Water features; lime tree walk and pergola walk with many clematis.

MANTON LODGE FARM
LE15 8SS. Mrs A G Burnaby-Atkins,
www.mantonlodge.co.uk
Stone country house (not open) nestled into hillside, with wonderful views from the sloping gardens. Shrubs, roses, mixed planting and newly planted pond area.

Sheltered small garden for all seasons . . .

❶❼ MARKET BOSWORTH GARDENS
CV13 0JS. *13m W of Leicester; 8m N of Hinckley. 1m off A447 Coalville to Hinckley Rd, 3m off A444. Burton to Nuneaton Rd. Leave M42 at A444 exit, then 10m to Market Bosworth.* Teas at 13 Spinney Hill. **Combined adm £4, chd free (share to Bosworth in Bloom). Sun 27 July (1-6).** East Midlands in Bloom Gold Award winners 2004, 2005 and 2006. Tickets and gardens map available at Market Place. Additional gardens may be open on the day.

GLEBE FARM HOUSE
13 Station Road. Mr Peter Ellis & Ms Ginny Broad
An informal courtyard garden.

HARLEYS COURT
120 Station Road. Marilyn & Chris Hooker
Flower and vegetable garden with fruit trees, pond and greenhouse. Examples of small space vegetable gardening. Gravel path to vegetable garden.

❲NEW❳ HOME FARM COTTAGE
23 Barton Road. Mrs Anne Kitching & Mr R Kitching
Japanese garden, woodland, pond, patio and hot tub areas. Herbaceous borders and bog garden are all incorporated in ³/₄ acre.

4 LANCASTER AVENUE
Mr Peter Bailiss
Garden with pond and bamboo summerhouse.

MICHAELMAS HOUSE
4 Main Street. Tim & Lorraine Richardson
A small walled, town house garden with sculpture.

❲NEW❳ RAINBOW COTTAGE
Shenton Lane. Mrs Sandra Callis, 01455 291519, 4countieselec@btconnect.com.
Visitors also welcome by appt any dates weekends; appointments for weekdays. Cottage garden with small lawned areas. Lots of pots and hanging baskets. Huge variety of plants from foxgloves, lupins, Canterbury Bells and lilies. Wild and cultivated roses.

15 SHENTON LANE
Mr & Mrs B Claybrook
Informal pond and water feature. Water lily and fish pond. Vegetable garden.

❲NEW❳ 4 SPINNEY HILL
Ms Liz Penny
Sheltered small garden for all seasons. On gentle slope, three levels connected by steps. Informal mixed planting. Patio, pots, pond, seating areas and ever shrinking lawn.

13 SPINNEY HILL
Mrs J Buckell
Woodland edge garden. Vegetable plot. Mixed borders, pond, cool greenhouse. Home-made jams and cakes for sale. Cream teas and refreshments.

93 STATION ROAD
Mr J Scott
Medium-sized traditional garden.

❶❽ ♦ 1700 MELTON ROAD
Rearsby LE7 4YR. Mrs Hazel Kaye. *6m NE of Leicester. On A607.* **Adm £2, chd free. Tues to Sat, (10-5); Sun (10-12) Mar to Oct inc.** For NGS: Suns 2 Mar; 5 Oct (2-5). In March hellebores, early flowering shrubs and daffodils feature; in October Michaelmas daisies, colchicum and shrubs with colourful berries and foliage. 1½ acres with wide range of interesting plants. National Collection of *Tradescantia* (Andersoniana Group). Grass paths.

❶❾ MILL HOUSE
118 Welford Road, Wigston, Leicester LE18 3SN. Mr & Mrs P Measures, 01162 885409. *4m S of Leicester. 1m S of Wigston, on main old A50.* Light refreshments & teas. **Adm £1.60, chd free.** Suns 18 May; 20 July (11-5). **Visitors also welcome by appt.**
Walled town garden; large amount of plant variety. Unusual and interesting design features.

❷⓿ MIRWOOD
69a Brooke Road, Oakham LE15 6HG. Kevin & Kate O'Brien, 01572 755535. *200yds from town centre. Turn into Mill St at roundabout opp library at X-roads/T-lights. Parking available in Brooke Rd car park (free on Sun). Garden 200yds on RH-side.* Cream teas. **Adm £3, chd free.** Sun 24 Aug (1-6). **Visitors also welcome by appt.**

3/4 -acre garden containing large collection of rare and unusual shrubs and trees. Seasonal formal beds, recently built folly, vegetable garden, yr-round interest particularly with spring bulbs.

  ♿ ✺ ☕ ☎

NEWBRAY HOUSE
See Nottinghamshire.

21 THE OLD HALL
Main Street, Market Overton LE15 7PL. Mr & Mrs Timothy Hart, 01572 767145, stefa@hambleton.co.uk. 6m N of Oakham. Beyond Cottesmore; 5m from A1 via Thistleton. 10m E from Melton Mowbray via Wymondham. Light refreshments & home-made teas (in village hall if wet). Adm £3, chd free. Sun 27 Apr (2-6). Visitors also welcome by appt £4 entry.
Garden is set on a southerly ridge overlooking Catmose Vale. Garden now on four levels with stone walls and yew hedges dividing the garden up in to enclosed areas with herbaceous borders, shrubs, and young and mature trees. In 2006 the lower part of garden was planted with new shrubs to create a walk with mown paths. There are plans to tackle the ponds at the bottom of the garden and to design a small vegetable garden adjacent to the swimming pool. Gravel paths & steep slopes.

  ♿ ⚯ ✺ ☕ ☎

THE OLD RECTORY, CLIFTON CAMPVILLE
See Staffordshire & part of West Midlands.

22 THE OLD VICARAGE
Whissendine LE15 7HG. Prof P N & Dr S H Furness, 01664 474549, shfdesign@pathology.plus.com, www.pathology.plus.com/garden/. 5m N of Oakham. Whissendine village is signed from A606 between Melton Mowbray & Oakham. Head for church - very visible tower. The Old Vicarage is adjacent, higher up the hill. Main entrance is on opp side, 1st L on Station Rd; alternative entrance from churchyard. Maps available on http://www.pathology.plus.com/Garden/. Home-made teas at the church. Adm £2, chd free. Sun 18 May (1-5.30). Visitors also welcome by appt.
For 2008 we will have created a new walled area with olive trees, fountain, tiered beds and tender plants backed by a small gothic orangery. In the rest

of the 0.7 acre garden is a terrace with topiary, 'white walk', herbaceous borders and wisteria tunnel leading to an orchard with naturalised bulbs. Plant stall & art exhibition. Gravel drive, some steps.

  ♿ ⚯ ✺ ☕ ☎

23 THE PARK HOUSE
Glaston Park, Spring Lane, Glaston LE15 9BW. Sheila & Stuart Makings. 6m S of Oakham on A47. 2m E of A6003 Uppingham roundabout travelling on A47 towards Peterborough. Teas. Adm £2.50, chd free. Sun 22 June (2-6).
4 acres approx of historic parkland, formerly part of grounds of Glaston Hall. Informal walks incl extensive lime arbour. Serpentine yew hedge, mature trees, medieval ha-ha and fish ponds. Herbaceous borders, traditional rose garden. Rural views, wildlife friendly. Ornamental wildfowl. Gravel paths, sloping grounds. Unfenced water, children welcome but must be supervised at all times.

  ♿ ⚯ ☕

Herb and potager garden and wisteria archway to Victorian vinery . . .

24 PARKSIDE
6 Park Hill, Gaddesby LE7 4WH. Mr & Mrs D Wyrko. 8m NE of Leicester. From A607 Rearsby bypass turn off for Gaddesby. L at Cheney Arms. Garden 400yds on R. Adm £3, chd free. £4 combined with Pine House, Gaddesby, 4, 5 May. Sun 23 Mar; Sun 4, Mon 5 May (11-5).
1 1/4 -acre garden and woodland in process of re-development from original planting. Mature trees and shrubs, together with informal mixed borders, planted to encourage wildlife and provide a family friendly environment. Newly created vegetable and fruit area together with garden pond. Many spring bulbs and hellebores in a woodland setting. Flower Festival at St Luke's, Gaddesby on 3, 4, 5 May.

  ✺ ⚯ ☕

PIECEMEAL
See Nottinghamshire.

25 PINE HOUSE
Gaddesby LE7 4XE. Mr & Mrs T Milward, 01664 840213. 8m NE of Leicester. From A607, turn off for Gaddesby. Home-made teas. Adm £4, chd under 10 free. Sun 4, Mon 5 May (11-5). Combined with Parkside, 6 Park Hill, Gaddesby. Visitors also welcome by appt coaches permitted and groups of 10 +; Apr to Sept.
2-acre garden with fine mature trees, woodland walk, and water garden. Herb and potager garden and wisteria archway to Victorian vinery. Pleached lime trees, mixed borders with rare and unusual plants and rock garden; new gravel garden and terracotta pot garden. Interesting topiary hedges and box trees. Flower Festival at St Luke's, Gaddesby.

  ✺ ⚯ ☕ ☎

26 PREBENDAL HOUSE
Empingham LE15 8PS. Mr & Mrs J Partridge. 5m E of Oakham. 5m W of Stamford. On A606. Home-made teas. Adm £3, chd free. Sun 1 June (2-5). House (not open) built in 1688; summer palace for the Bishop of Lincoln. 4-acre garden incl herbaceous borders, water garden, topiary and kitchen gardens. Featured in local press & radio, 2007.

  ⚯ ☕

27 NEW RIDGEWOLD FARM
Burton Lane, Wymeswold, Loughborough LE12 6UN. Robert & Ann Waterfall. 5m SE of Loughborough. Off Burton Lane between A6006 & B676. Cream teas. Adm £2, chd free. Sun 22 June (11-5).
1 1/2 acre garden formed over last seven years featuring a rill and bog garden. Herbaceous border, shrub borders, rose garden, orchard and kitchen garden. Newly planted arboretum and traditional woodland.

  ☕

28 SOUTH KILWORTH GARDENS
Nr Lutterworth LE17 6DX. 15m S of Leicester. From M1 J20, take A4304 towards Market Harborough. At Walcote turn R, signed South Kilworth. Home-made teas at Croft Acre. Combined adm £3, chd free. Sun 15

June (11-6). **Day & Evening Opening** £3, (2-5) £4, (6-9) wine, Wed 25 June. **Combined with Gilmorton Gardens Sun 15 June. Optional combined adm £5 to cover all gardens.**
Small village tucked away in SW corner of Leicestershire, with excellent views over Avon valley and Hemplow hills.

CROFT ACRE
The Belt, South Kilworth. Colin & Verena Olle, 01858 575791, colin.olle@tiscali.co.uk. *At White Hart PH take rd signed North Kilworth. The Belt is a bridleway 250yds on R. Parking on North Rd.* **Visitors also welcome by appt June to mid July.**
1-acre garden, herbaceous borders, island beds, wide selection of shrubs and perennials. Rose and wisteria pergolas. Ponds and small stream. Rose garden with water feature. Vegetable garden. New Yin Yang land sculpture. Summerhouse and garden room seating areas.

OAK TREE HOUSE
North Road, South Kilworth. Pam & Martin Shave. *From centre of village take rd to N Kilworth. 300yds down North Rd on RH-side (just after bridleway, The Belt).* **Visitors also welcome by appt contact Croft Acre.**
Newly created garden of ²/₃ acre. Formal layout with greenhouse, ornamental vegetable plot, pond and herbaceous borders. Patio with numerous pots and hanging baskets. Arched pergola with roses and clematis, leading to gravel patio. Access to pond & greenhouse via steps.

29 STOKE ALBANY HOUSE
Stoke Albany LE16 8PT. Mr & Mrs A M Vinton, 01858 535227. *4m E of Market Harborough. Via A427 to Corby; turn to Stoke Albany; R at the White Horse (B669); garden ½ m on L.* **Adm £3.50, chd free (share to Marie Curie Cancer Care). Weds, 4 June to 23 July; (2-4.30). Visitors also welcome by appt June to July, Tues & Weds for groups only.**
4-acre country-house garden; fine trees and shrubs with wide herbaceous borders and sweeping striped lawn. Good display of bulbs in spring, roses June and July. Walled grey garden; nepeta walk arched with roses, parterre with box and roses. Mediterranean garden. Heated greenhouse, potager with topiary, water feature garden and sculptures.

30 NEW THORPE LUBENHAM HALL
Lubenham LE16 9TR. Sir Bruce & Lady MacPhail. *2m W of Market Harborough. From Market Harborough take 3rd L off main rd, down Rushes Lane, past church on L, under old railway bridge and straight on up private drive.* **Adm £3, chd free (share to Leics Air Ambulance). Wed 14 May (9-4).**
15 acres of formal and informal garden surrounded by parkland and arable. Many mature trees. Traditional herbaceous borders and various water features. Large wild flower meadow and ha ha wall. Rose and lavender beds circling large pond. Walled pool garden with raised beds. Ancient moat area along driveway. Gravel paths & some steep slopes.

31 UNIVERSITY OF LEICESTER 'HAROLD MARTIN' BOTANIC GARDEN
'The Knoll', Glebe Road, Oadby LE2 2NA. University of Leicester. *1½ m SE of Leicester. On outskirts of city opp race course.* **Adm £2, chd free. Sun 27 July (11-4).**
16-acre garden incl grounds of Beaumont Hall, The Knoll, Southmeade and Hastings House. Wide variety of ornamental features and glasshouses laid out for educational purposes incl National Collections of aubrieta, Lawson cypress, hardy fuchsia and skimmia.

Rose and lavender beds circling large pond . . .

32 UPPINGHAM GARDENS
LE15 9TT. *It is suggested that visitors start at Westlands on the Leicester Rd 1km W of Uppingham town centre. Then drive to the centre where parking is available in and around the Market Sq and where refreshments are available in the Church Hall. From here all other gardens can be reached on foot. Gower Lodge 400m W of Market Sq along High Street West and L past Uppingham School to Spring Back Way. Meadowsweet Lodge and The Orchard in Station Rd can be reached through churchyard or from Gower Lodge down Spring Back Way and over Kettering Rd.* Light refreshments & teas in church hall, Market Square. **Combined adm £3.50, chd free.** Sun 25 May (11-5).
Historic stone-built market town with school and many antique shops.

GOWER LODGE
Dr C R & Mrs E L Jones. *From Market Sq in centre of Uppingham W along High St past Uppingham School. Take 1st L down Spring Back Way*
1-acre S-facing sloping garden. Sandstone overlying clay with spring at interface and small stream with damp fringe and wild flower areas. Upper garden mainly flowers with meconopsis and primulas, herbaceous borders and some interesting trees. Kitchen garden on lower slope. Steps and some steep slopes.

MEADOWSWEET LODGE
South View. The Hon Mrs Wright
Sloping garden containing a variety of roses, herbaceous plants, spring bulbs, shrubs and many young trees. Gravel drive, sloping lawns.

THE ORCHARD
Doug & Margaret Stacey. *From Uppingham Market Square take London Rd S. After 100yds turn L into South View. At junction bear R into Station Rd, then almost immed R into private drive descending to The Orchard*
½ -acre S-facing garden slopes down below sheltered terrace to small stream. Mature trees frame outlook across valley. Small orchard, vegetable garden and an interesting variety of trees, shrubs, bulbs and herbaceous perennials.

WESTLANDS
68 Leicester Road. Peter & Maxine Ind. *1/2 m from centre of Uppingham - nr Shepherds Way. 1st house on RH-side after fields* 2/3 *-acre irregular shaped garden packed with herbaceous plants, climbers, flowering shrubs and trees. Many unusual varieties. Wildlife friendly.*

33 WAKERLEY MANOR
Wakerley, nr Uppingham LE15 8PA. Mr A D A W Forbes. *5m E of Uppingham. R off A47 Uppingham to Peterborough rd through Barrowden, or from A43 Stamford to Corby rd between Duddington & Bulwick.* **Evening Opening £3, chd free (Share to St Mary the Virgin Church, South Luffenham), wine, Wed 18 June (5-8.30).**
4 acres lawns, shrubs, herbaceous; kitchen garden; 3 greenhouses.

34 WALTON GARDENS
LE17 5RP. *4m NE of Lutterworth. M1 exit 20 and, via Lutterworth follow signs for Kimcote and Walton, or from Leicester take A5199. After Shearsby turn R signed Bruntingthorpe. Follow signs.* Home-made teas at Orchards. **Combined adm £3, chd free.** Sun 1, Wed 4 June (11-5).
Small village in South Leicestershire. Village maps given to all visitors.

THE MEADOWS
Mowsley Lane. Mr & Mrs Falkner
Plantsman's garden, with emphasis on wildlife friendly flowers. Two ponds, conservatory with unusual plants and many plants in containers. A collection of unusual plants, shrubs and roses developing every year.

THE OLD HALL
Hall Lane, Walton. Mr & Mrs Field
1 1/2 -acre garden with interesting trees and large natural pond. Play area for children.

ORCHARDS
Hall Lane. Mr & Mrs G Cousins, 01455 556958, orchards @cousins88.fsnet.co.uk. Visitors also welcome by appt June to Aug.
1 1/4 -acre green leaf garden with colour from flowers not foliage.

Extensive use of grasses. Views of the countryside. 'Quite unlike any other garden' (RHS Garden Finder).

SANDYLAND
Hall Lane. Martin & Linda Goddard
Gently sloping cottage garden with attractive rural views. Herbaceous plants, shrubs, containers, terraced garden, pond and kitchen garden.

7 WARREN DRIVE
See Derbyshire.

Colour and interest changing through the season from spring to autumn . . .

35 WARREN HILLS COTTAGE
Warren Hills Road, Coalville LE67 4UX. Mr Graham Waters, 01530 812350, warrenhills@tinyworld.co.uk, www.warrenhills.co.uk. *5m NW of Leicester. Approx 4m NW of M1 J22 on B587 Copt Oak to Whitwick Rd, between Bulls Head and Forest Rock PH.* Cream teas. **Adm £2, chd 50p.** Suns 18 May; 20 July (12-5). **Visitors also welcome by appt for groups of 10+, May to Aug, evenings or weekends.**
Established 2-acre cottage-style garden filled with hardy and unusual perennials incl display area for National Collection of astrantias. Features incl large well-stocked pond, stream, raised beds, pergola and alpine area. Colour and interest changing through the season from spring to autumn. Gold Medal Winner, Shrewsbury Flower Show, 2007; Silver Medal

Winner, Hampton Court, 2007. Some gravel areas & slopes.

36 ◆ WHATTON GARDENS
nr Loughborough LE12 5BG. Lord & Lady Crawshaw, 01509 842225, whattho@tiscali.co.uk. *4m NE of Loughborough. On A6 between Hathern & Kegworth; 2 1/2 m SE of J24 on M1.* Refreshments on NGS days. **Adm £3, chd free. Suns to Fris, Mar to Oct incl (11-4). Coaches & groups welcome. Refreshments by arrangement.** For NGS: Suns 11 May; 6 July (11-5).
Dating from the 1800, 15 acres of varied nooks and crannies, from formal rose garden, arboretum with many fine trees, large traditional herbaceous borders, ponds, many shrubs. Large variety of spring bulbs. Described by many visitors as one of East Midlands unknown treasures. Featured on 'East Midlands Today', Aug 2007.

37 NEW WILLOUGHBY GARDENS
LE8 6UD. *9m S of Leicester. From Leicester take A426. Turn L at T-lights at Dunton Bassett Xrds. Follow signs to Willoughby. From M1 J20 take A426 through Lutterworth. Turn R at Dunton Bassett Xrds.* Cream teas at village hall. **Combined adm £2.50, chd free (share to Red Cross).** Sun 27 July (2-5).
Old village in S Leicestershire with a variety of architecture. Church with its Norman tower will be open. Village map and historical leaflet is available.

NEW FARMWAY
Church Farm Lane. Miss E V Spencer, 0116 2478321, eileenfarmway9@msn.com. *Nr General Elliott PH.* **Visitors also welcome by appt July/Aug, max 20. Evening visits also welcome.**
W-facing, 1/4 acre garden with views across Leicestershire. Mature plant lover's garden, closely planted with a wide variety of shrubs, herbaceous plants, roses and clematis. Two ponds, vegetable area, herb garden and extensive collection of containers. Featured on cover of 'Garden Answers' magazine, Feb 2007.

NEW **THE OLD CHAPEL**
Main Street. Mona & Tony Wright. *Next to phone box*
Small, secluded garden on different levels at the rear of a former primitive Methodist chapel. The continuously evolving garden has a pond, shrubs and borders containing some unusual specimen plants.

Evolving garden with emphasis on bold use of plants . . .

38 **WING GARDENS**
nr Oakham LE15 8SE. *2m S of Rutland Water. Off A6003 between Oakham & Uppingham.* Home-made teas at village hall. **Combined adm £3.50, chd free, concessions £2.50. Sun 15 June (2-6).**
Pretty stone village with medieval church and turf maze. C17 country inn.

TOWNSEND HOUSE
David & Jeffy Wood. *Opp village hall*
Cottage garden with mixed borders, roses and clematis. Walled gravel garden with swimming pool, vegetable garden.

◆ **WINGWELL**
5 Top Street. John & Rose Dejardin, 01572 737727, www.artdejardin.co.uk. *2m S of Rutland Water off A6003 bet Oakham & Uppingham. Signed to 'Sculpture Garden' on main st of village.* **Open Wed to Sun, 18 May to 7 Sept (10-5).**
Evolving garden with emphasis on bold use of plants, particularly herbaceous, and interesting use of stone and paving with water. Open throughout the summer for an exhibition in the garden and grounds of contemporary sculpture, in a range of media, by notable artists. Details on website. Article in 'Craft Arts International', Mar 2007. Partial wheelchair access.

Leicestershire & Rutland County Volunteers

County Organiser Leicestershire
John Oakland, Long Close, Woodhouse Eaves, Loughborough LE12 8RZ, 01509 890376

County Treasurer Leicestershire
Martin Shave, Oak Tree House, North Road, South Kilworth
Lutterworth, LE17 6DU, 01455 556633, martinshave@kilworthaccountancy.co.uk

Publicity Leicestershire
Jacqui Fowler, 37 Barrow Road, Quorn, Loughborough LE12 8DH, 07958 490631, jacqui.fowler@btopenworld.com

Assistant County Organisers Leicestershire
Colin Olle, Croft Acre, The Belt, South Kilworth, Lutterworth LE17 6DX, 01858 575791, colin.olle@tiscali.co.uk
Sue Milward, Pine House, Gaddesby LE7 4XE, 01664 840213

County Organiser Rutland
Jennifer Wood, Townsend House, Morcott Road, Wing, Nr Oakham LE15 8SA, 01572 737465, rdavidwood@easynet.co.uk

County Treasurer Rutland
David Wood, Townsend House, Morcott Road, Wing, nr Oakham LE15 8SA, 01572 737465, rdavidwood@easynet.co.uk

Publicity Rutland
Michael Peck, Parsons Orchard, Post Office Lane, Lyndon, Nr Oakham LE15 8TX, 01572 737248

Assistant County Organiser Rutland
Rose Dejardin, 5 Top Street, Wing, Nr Oakham LE15 8SE, 01572 737557

LINCOLNSHIRE

© Crown Copyright NC/2007/47622

Opening Dates

February

SATURDAY 9
26 Little Ponton Hall

SUNDAY 10
26 Little Ponton Hall

SATURDAY 23
5 21 Chapel Street

SUNDAY 24
5 21 Chapel Street

March

SUNDAY 16
8 Doddington Hall Gardens

FRIDAY 21
9 Easton Walled Gardens

MONDAY 24
5 21 Chapel Street

April

SUNDAY 6
22 Holly Tree Farm

SUNDAY 20
17 Grimsthorpe Castle
49 Woodlands

WEDNESDAY 23
22 Holly Tree Farm

THURSDAY 24
22 Holly Tree Farm

SATURDAY 26
2 Belton House

SUNDAY 27
11 Fen View
15 Goltho House
33 The Old Rectory

May

THURSDAY 1
3 Belvoir Castle

SATURDAY 3
3 Belvoir Castle

SUNDAY 4
3 Belvoir Castle

MONDAY 5
3 Belvoir Castle

TUESDAY 6
3 Belvoir Castle

WEDNESDAY 7
3 Belvoir Castle

THURSDAY 8
3 Belvoir Castle

SATURDAY 10
3 Belvoir Castle

SUNDAY 11
3 Belvoir Castle

MONDAY 12
3 Belvoir Castle

TUESDAY 13
3 Belvoir Castle

WEDNESDAY 14
3 Belvoir Castle

THURSDAY 15
3 Belvoir Castle

SATURDAY 17
3 Belvoir Castle

SUNDAY 18
3 Belvoir Castle
46 10 Wendover Close
49 Woodlands

MONDAY 19
3 Belvoir Castle

TUESDAY 20
3 Belvoir Castle

WEDNESDAY 21
3 Belvoir Castle

THURSDAY 22
3 Belvoir Castle

SATURDAY 24
3 Belvoir Castle

SUNDAY 25
3 Belvoir Castle
11 Fen View
33 The Old Rectory
40 2 School House

MONDAY 26
3 Belvoir Castle

TUESDAY 27
3 Belvoir Castle

WEDNESDAY 28
3 Belvoir Castle
22 Holly Tree Farm

THURSDAY 29
3 Belvoir Castle
22 Holly Tree Farm

SATURDAY 31
3 Belvoir Castle
43 Walters Cottage

June

SUNDAY 1
29 Marigold Cottage
43 Walters Cottage

SUNDAY 8
12 Fishtoft Drove Gardens
24 Kexby House
30 Martin Gardens

WEDNESDAY 11
8 Doddington Hall Gardens

THURSDAY 12
31 The Moat

SUNDAY 15
1 Alkborough and Burton Stather Gardens
13 Frog Hall Cottage
16 Grantham House
25 Les Allées
42 Station House
48 Whinlatter

THURSDAY 19
17 Grimsthorpe Castle

FRIDAY 20
36 The Orchards (Evening)

SATURDAY 21
38 68 Pennygate

SUNDAY 22
6 The Coach House
22 Holly Tree Farm
28 Manor House
36 The Orchards
38 68 Pennygate
41 South Lodge

WEDNESDAY 25
22 Holly Tree Farm

THURSDAY 26
22 Holly Tree Farm

FRIDAY 27
23 Holywell Hall

SUNDAY 29
18 Guanock House
42 Station House

July

SUNDAY 6
27 The Long House

WEDNESDAY 9
45 68 Watts Lane

THURSDAY 10
14 The Garden House
47 West Barn

SUNDAY 13
7 Cobwebs
15 Goltho House
34 The Old Vicarage
35 Old White House
39 73 Saxilby Road
40 2 School House
42 Station House

SATURDAY 26
2 Belton House
38 68 Pennygate

SUNDAY 27
38 68 Pennygate

42 Station House
49 Woodlands

WEDNESDAY 30
22 Holly Tree Farm

THURSDAY 31
22 Holly Tree Farm

August

THURSDAY 7
14 The Garden House
47 West Barn

SUNDAY 10
19 Gunby Hall
21 Harrington Hall
45 68 Watts Lane

SATURDAY 16
7 Cobwebs

SUNDAY 17
32 Old Quarry Lodge

MONDAY 25
16 Grantham House

September

THURSDAY 4
5 21 Chapel Street

SATURDAY 6
20 Hall Farm

SUNDAY 7
20 Hall Farm

SATURDAY 13
4 56 Burringham Road

SUNDAY 14
4 56 Burringham Road

SATURDAY 27
2 Belton House

SUNDAY 28
49 Woodlands

October

SUNDAY 5
5 21 Chapel Street
39 73 Saxilby Road

February 2009

SATURDAY 21
5 21 Chapel Street

SUNDAY 22
5 21 Chapel Street

Gardens open to the public

2 Belton House
3 Belvoir Castle
8 Doddington Hall Gardens
9 Easton Walled Gardens
14 The Garden House
16 Grantham House

17 Grimsthorpe Castle
19 Gunby Hall
20 Hall Farm

By appointment only

10 15 Elmhirst Road
37 Overbeck
44 Washdyke Farm

Also open by appointment ☎

4 56 Burringham Road
5 21 Chapel Street
18 Guanock House
22 Holly Tree Farm
23 Holywell Hall
24 Kexby House
29 Marigold Cottage
31 The Moat
32 Old Quarry Lodge
33 The Old Rectory
34 The Old Vicarage
38 68 Pennygate
40 2 School House
45 68 Watts Lane
49 Woodlands

The Gardens

1 NEW **ALKBOROUGH AND BURTON STATHER GARDENS**
DN15 9JW. *9m N of Scunthorpe. 12m W of Humber Bridge. Follow brown signs from A1077 for Julian's Bower.* Home-made teas at Alkborough Chapel. **Combined adm £3, chd free. Sun 15 June (1-6).**
Attractive villages, both within conservation areas. Alkborough is noted for the turf maze, known as Julian's Bower. Situated on the escarpment, it overlooks the confluence of the Humber, Trent and Ouse. Fine church and chapel. Burton Stather is 3m S of Alkborough and 1m from Normanby Park.

NEW **CHARNWOOD**
Front Street, Alkborough. Dave & Pam Batty
An imaginative garden created out of a former stackyard. Lawned area with attractive trees and shrubs, leading through a stepped archway to a productive fruit and vegetable area. Many varieties of flowering plants.

NEW **2 CHURCH SIDE**
Alkborough. Mrs Carole Vessey
Pretty garden with variety of

perennials, scree bedding and numerous different containers. Spectacular panoramic views over the confluence of the rivers Humber, Trent and Ouse. Limited wheelchair access, sloping garden.
&

NEW **HOLLY COTTAGE**
5 Normanby Road, Burton upon Stather. Ms Patricia Brown. *3m S of Alkborough. Take Walcott Rd through to Tee Lane. Turn R into Burton Stather village & follow rd (B1430) to end of High St. Garden entrance via path bet 36 High St & 7 Normanby Rd*
Small cottage garden with colourful informal planting in raised borders enclosing 150yr old end cottage with original outbuildings. Wildlife pond area with ferns and grasses. Raised lawn with herbaceous border. Seating areas. Owner knows every plant.
✂

NEW **RAVENDALE**
Front Street, Alkborough. Avis & John Ablott
Fruit and flowers intermingle in true cottage style. Paved secluded areas, with container planting. Walk through pergola to grassed area, leading to island beds and wildlife pond, finally reaching organic vegetable plot. Limited access to walled courtyard.
& ✿

Spectacular panoramic views over the confluence of the rivers Humber, Trent and Ouse . . .

ASKHAM GARDENS
See Nottinghamshire.

THE BEECHES
See Nottinghamshire.

② ◆ BELTON HOUSE
Grantham NG32 2LS. The National Trust, 01476 566116, angelamarshell@nationaltrust.org.uk. *3m NE of Grantham. On A607 Grantham to Lincoln rd. Easily reached & signed from A1 (Grantham N junction).* **House and garden adm £9.50, chd £5.50, garden only adm £7.50, chd £4.50. Open daily Wed to Sun Mar to end Oct. For NGS: Sats 26 Apr; 26 July; 27 Sept (11-5.30).** Belton House gardens include formal Italian and Dutch areas with informal gardens that are an inspiration to all gardeners. These 35 acres to the north of the house are a popular attraction in their own right. Five main areas each have their own unique planting scheme. Orangery by Sir Jeffrey Wyatville. Gravel paths, some steps.

�& ☆ ⊕ ☕

③ ◆ BELVOIR CASTLE
Grantham NG32 4DQ. The Duke & Duchess of Rutland, 01476 871002, www.belvoircastle.com. *9m from Grantham. Follow brown heritage signs for Belvoir Castle on A52, A1, A607.* **House and garden adm £12, concessions £10, chd £6, garden only adm £6, chd £2, concessions £5. Open every day except Fris 20 Mar to 30 Sept. For NGS: Mons, Tues, Weds, Thurs, 1 May to 29 May; Sats, Suns, 3 May to 31 May; (11-4); Sats (11-3).** English Heritage Grade 2 garden. Secluded in steep woodland 1/2 m from castle. A haven of tranquillity created around original moss house. Magical hillside setting in natural amphitheatre with fresh water springs. Many mature specimen trees and shrubs ensure all-yr colour. Rhododendrons, azaleas, naturalised daffodils, primroses and bluebells. Tallest bird cherry (90ft) and yew tree (93ft) in British Isles. Flat shoes essential. Rose garden with sculpture exhibition. Some steep paths.

�& ☆ ☕

④ 56 BURRINGHAM ROAD
Ashby, Scunthorpe DN17 2DE. Mr & Mrs Foster, 01724 334480, kevin56foster@yahoo.co.uk. *1/2 m S of Scunthorpe, in district of Ashby. Approaching Scunthorpe A159 from S turn L on B1450 (Burringham Rd).*

Garden 200yds on L. Park in Monks Rd. Parking also outside garden, no restrictions but busy road. Light refreshments & teas. **Adm £2, chd free (share to Lindsey Lodge Hospice, Scunthorpe). Sat 13, Sun 14 Sept (10-5). Visitors also welcome by appt any dates weekend or evenings. July to Sept. Please give 7 days notice.** 1/3 -acre plantsman's garden full of rare and exotic treasures, featuring plants from all regions of the world. Species include cactus, succulents, gingers, cannas, dahlias, echiums, unusual salvias, various bananas, proteas, leucodendrons, restios, grasses and several varieties of tree ferns. September is the best month to see garden in its full maturity. Large koi and wildlife pond. Free seed collecting. 'Lincolnshire Life' photo shoot Sept 2007.

�& ☆ ⊕ ☕ ☎

⑤ 21 CHAPEL STREET
Hacconby, Bourne PE10 0UL. Cliff & Joan Curtis, 01778 570314. *3m N of Bourne. A15, turn E at Xrds into Hacconby.* Home-made teas. **Adm £2, chd free. Sat 23, Sun 24 Feb; Mon 24 Mar (11-5); Thur 4 Sept (2-6); Sun 5 Oct (11-5); Sat 21, Sun 22 Feb 2009 (11-5). Visitors also welcome by appt anytime.** Cottage garden overflowing with plants for yr-round interest; special interest alpines, bulbs, herbaceous. Early opening for hellebores and snowdrop collection. Asters for late opening.

☆ ⊕ ☕ ☎

⑥ NEW THE COACH HOUSE
1A Hereward Street. LN1 3EW. Jo & Ken Slone. *Central Lincoln. Coming off the A46 N circular take B1226 to Newport. 150yds from Radio Lincs turn into Rasen Lane, then take1st R into Hereward St.* Home-made teas & wine. **Adm £2.50, chd free. Sun 22 June (11-5).** Small courtyard garden behind Victorian town house, 5mins walk from historic quarter of Lincoln. Brimming with unusual plants, climbers and sculpture. Many plants grown in containers for versatility, complemented by summer bedding. No on site parking. Use Bail area car parks or roads in vicinity. Tiny gravel area.

�& ☆ ⊕ 🛏 ☕

⑦ NEW COBWEBS
Moor Road, North Owersby, Market Rasen LN8 3PR. Ms Pauline Gass. *41/2 m N of Market Rasen. Turn off A46 at North Owersby sign. Garden 200yds on R.* **Adm £2.50, chd free. Sun 13 July; Sat 16 Aug (12-5).** Mature cottage garden extending to two thirds of an acre amid open countryside. Many large herbaceous borders crammed with unusual and colourful perennials and grasses. Steps leading to patio and pergola clothed in clematis and wisteria. Wildlife pond. Nursery offering many of the plants grown in the garden.

�& ☆ ⊕ ☕

Pergola clothed in clematis and wisteria . . .

⑧ ◆ DODDINGTON HALL GARDENS
Lincoln LN6 4RU. Claire & James Birch, 01522 694308, www.doddingtonhall.com. *5m W of Lincoln. Signed clearly from A46 Lincoln bypass & A57, 3m.* Lunches at Doddington Farm Shop from 12noon. Booking advisable 01522 688581. **House and garden adm £6, chd £3, garden only adm £4, chd £2. Suns and Easter Mon 17 Feb-end April (1-5). Weds, Suns & BH Mons May-Sept incl (12-5). House opens 1pm. For NGS: Sun 16 Mar (1-5); Wed 11 June (12-5).** 5 acres of romantic walled and wild gardens. Pageant of naturalised spring bulbs and scented shrubs from Feb to May. Spectacular iris display late May/early June in box-edged parterres of West Garden. Sumptuous herbaceous borders throughout summer; extraordinary ancient chestnut trees; turf maze; temple of the winds. Newly resurrected walled Kitchen Garden opened Apr 2007. Very much a family-owned and run garden. 'BBC Gardeners' World' & 'Country Life' June 2007, local press & radio. Variety of surfaces; gravel, grass. Can get muddy. Electric buggy available for free hire, booking advisable. Sensory tours of house & gardens for visually impaired visitors.

�& ☆ ☕

9 ◆ EASTON WALLED GARDENS

Easton NG33 5AP. Sir Fred & Lady Cholmeley, 01476 530063, www.eastonwalledgardens.co.uk. *7m S of Grantham. 1m off A1 N of Colsterworth roundabout. Follow village signposts via B6403.* **Adm £4.50, chd 50p. Open regularly Feb-Dec. Please phone or visit website. For NGS: Fri 21 Mar (11-4).**
12 acres of forgotten gardens undergoing extensive renovation. Set in parkland with dramatic views. C16 garden with Victorian embellishments. Italianate terraces; yew tunnel; snowdrops and cut flower garden. David Austin roses, iris, daffodil and sweet pea collections. Please wear sensible shoes suitable for country walking. Open Good Friday. Daffodil collection in full bloom. Featured in 'Country Life' June 2007 & BBC July 2007. For wheelchair & disabled access please see website.

   ⚒ ❀ ☕

10 15 ELMHIRST ROAD

Horncastle LN9 5AT. Sylvia Ravenhall, 01507 526014, john.ravenhall@btinternet.com. *From A158 Lincoln Rd turn into Accommodation Rd, go to end, turn L into Elmhirst Rd. No 15 approx 80yds on L.* Light refreshments. **Adm £2, chd free. Visitors welcome by appt 25 May-27 July. Individuals or groups. Coaches welcome.**
Plantswoman's long and narrow town garden with beds and borders of mainly herbaceous plants combined with climbers, shrubs and small trees. Variety of hostas are grown in containers and in the ground. Winding paths with shallow steps give varied access to all areas. Featured in 'Amateur Gardening', Sept 2007.

⚒ ❀ ☕ ☎

11 NEW FEN VIEW

Fen Lane, East Keal PE23 4AY. Mr & Mrs Geoffrey Wheatley. *2m SW of Spilsby. Park at The Old Rectory, path to Fen View.* Catering at The Old Rectory. **Combined adm with The Old Rectory, East Keal £3.50, chd free.** Suns 27 Apr (2-5); 25 May (11-5).
Sloping secluded 1/2 acre garden re-developed by owners over last 4yrs to reflect their interest in gardening for wildlife. Designed around a number of different themed areas, ponds, vistas, sculptures and plenty of seating.

12 FISHTOFT DROVE GARDENS

Frithville, Boston PE22 7ES. *3m N of Boston, 1m S of Frithville. Unclassified rd. On W side of the West Fen Drain.* Home-made teas at Holly House. **Combined adm £2.50, chd free (share to Pilgrim Heart & Lung Fund). Sun 8 June (12-5).**

☕

BARLEY END COTTAGE
Andy & Yvonne Mathieson. *100yds W of Holly House*
1/5-acre traditional cottage garden, very informal. Relaxed mixture of borders, shrubs, vegetables, natural areas, with some quirky features.

❀

HOLLY HOUSE
Sally & David Grant
Approx 1-acre informal mixed borders, scree beds, old sinks with alpines and steps leading down to large pond with cascade and stream. Small woodland area. Quiet garden with water feature. Extra 2 1/2 acres devoted to wildlife with dewpond. Featured in 'Amateur Gardening', May 2007.

⚒ ❀ ❀ ☕

13 NEW FROG HALL COTTAGE

New York LN4 4XH. Kathy Wright. *B1192 2m S of New York Xrds. 3 1/2 m N of Langrick Bridge.* **Adm £2, chd free. Sun 15 June (11-5).**
3/4 acre garden. Patio with many unusual plants, stream, courtyard-style patio, large gravelled area with raised beds and an arbour, again planted for interest. Lawned area with large island beds, unfenced pond. Classic-style garden planted with roses, shrubs and perennials.

❀ ❀

Magical garden rooms full of roses and herbaceous plants . . .

14 ◆ THE GARDEN HOUSE

Saxby, Lincoln LN8 2DQ. Chris Neave & Jonathan Cartwright, 01673 878820, www.thegardenhousesaxby.com. *8m N of Lincoln; 2 1/4 m E of A15.* **Adm £3, chd free. Fri, Sat, Sun 1 Apr to 30 Sept (10-5) & Bank Hols. Saxby snowdrops mid to end of Feb. For NGS: Thurs 10 July; 7 Aug (10-5). Open with West Barn.**
7 acre landscaped garden packed with interest. Yew hedging and walls enclose magical garden rooms full of roses and herbaceous plants. Long terrace, Dutch, pergola and obelisk gardens link to a lavender walk. Large natural damp garden. Dry garden leading onto hillside planted with rarer trees overlooking a large reflective pond. Native woodland areas, prairie and wild flower meadow planted with massed bulbs. Wonderful views. Adjacent to C18 classical church. Gravel paths, steep slopes.

   ⚒ ❀ ❀

15 GOLTHO HOUSE

Goltho LN8 5NF. Mr & Mrs S Hollingworth, www.golthogardens.com. *10m E of Lincoln. On A158, 1m before Wragby. Garden on LH-side (not in Goltho Village).* Home-made teas. **Adm £3, chd free. Suns 27 Apr; 13 July (10-4).**
4 1/2-acre garden started in 1998 but looking established with long grass walk flanked by abundantly planted herbaceous borders forming a focal point. Paths and walkway span out to other features incl nut walk, prairie border, wild flower meadow, rose garden and large pond area.

❀ ❀ ☕

16 ◆ GRANTHAM HOUSE

Castlegate, Grantham NG31 6SS. Earl of Leitrim & Mr A Kerr, 01476 564705, grantham.house@homecall.co.uk. *In Grantham. Entrance in Castlegate opp St Wulfram's Church.* **Adm £4, chd £2. First Sun of each month Apr to Nov (2-5). For NGS: Sun 15 June; Mon 25 Aug (2-5).**
Nestled behind imposing stone walls, the secret gardens of this historic house seem a world away from the bustling town that adjoins them. Set on 7 acres and currently under restoration, the expansive lawns, woodland walk, orchard, walled garden and vegetable and herb gardens are among its many inspirational features. All paths are shallow gravel.

   ⚒ ❀ ❀ ☕

17 ◆ GRIMSTHORPE CASTLE
Bourne PE10 0LY. Grimsthorpe &
Drummond Castle Trust, 01778
591205, www.grimsthorpe.co.uk. *3m
NW of Bourne. 8m E of A1 on A151
from Colsterworth junction.* **Castle &
garden adm £9, concessions £8,
chd £3.50, garden only adm £4, chd
£2, concessions £3.50. Suns &
Thurs Apr & May. Suns to Thurs
June to Sept (11-6). For NGS: Sun
20 Apr; Thur 19 June (11-6).**
15 acres of formal and woodland
gardens incl bulbs and wild flowers.
Formal gardens encompass fine
topiary, roses, herbaceous borders and
unusual ornamental kitchen garden.
Gravel paths.
🚻 ✕ ☕

18 GUANOCK HOUSE
Guanock Gate, Sutton St Edmund
PE12 0LW. Mr & Mrs Michael
Coleman, 07799463437 (Gardener,
Robin Parker). *16m SE of Spalding.
From village church turn R, cross rd,
then L Guanockgate. Garden at end of
rd, RH-side.* Home-made teas. **Adm
£3, chd free. Sun 29 June (2-5.30).
Visitors also welcome by appt Mon-
Fri, May-Sept.**
Former home of garden designer Arne
Maynard. 5 acres. Herbaceous border,
knot garden, rose garden and lime
walk. Orchard, walled kitchen garden,
Italian garden. Guanock House is a
C16 manor house built in the flat fens
of S Lincs.
🚻 ✕ ☕ ☎

Spinney
with native
wild flowers . . .

19 ◆ GUNBY HALL
Spilsby PE23 5SS. The National
Trust, 07870 758876,
www.gunbyhall.ic24.net. *2½ m NW
of Burgh-le-Marsh. 7m NW of
Skegness. On A158. Signed off Gunby
roundabout.* **Adm £4, chd £2, family
£10. Gardens open Weds & Thurs 2
Apr to end Sept. For NGS: Sun 10
Aug (11-5).**
7 acres of formal and walled gardens;
old roses, herbaceous borders; herb
garden; kitchen garden with fruit trees
and vegetables. Greenhouses, carp
pond and sweeping lawns. Tennyson's
'Haunt of Ancient Peace'. House built
by Sir William Massingberd 1700.
Featured on local radio. Gravel paths
but wheelchairs allowed on lawns.
🚻 ⊗ ☕

20 ◆ HALL FARM
Harpswell, Gainsborough
DN21 5UU. Pam & Mark Tatam,
01427 668412, www.hall-farm.co.uk.
*7m E of Gainsborough. On A631. 1½
m W of Caenby Corner.* **Adm £3, chd
free. For NGS: Sat 6, Sun 7 Sept
(10-5).**
1½ -acre garden with mixed borders of
trees, shrubs, old roses and unusual
perennials. Sunken garden, pond,
courtyard garden, walled gravel garden
and orchard. Short walk to old moat
and woodland. Free seed collecting in
garden Sept 6 & 7. Free seed
collection. Featured in 'English
Garden', July 2007; 'Country Homes &
Interiors', Aug 2007.
🚻 ✕ ⊗ ☕

21 HARRINGTON HALL
Harrington, Spilsby PE23 4NH. Mr &
Mrs David Price,
www.harringtonhallgardens.co.uk.
*6m NW of Spilsby. Turn off A158
(Lincoln-Skegness) at
Hagworthingham, 2m to Harrington.*
Home-made teas. **Adm £2.50, chd
free. Sun 10 Aug (2-5).**
Approx 6-acre Tudor and C18 walled
gardens, incl 3 walled gardens;
herbaceous borders, croquet lawn
leading to viewing terrace, Tennyson's
High Hall Garden in 'Maud'. Organic
kitchen garden, shrub borders, roses
and wildlife pond. Local radio coverage.
🚻 ✕ ⊗ ☕

22 HOLLY TREE FARM
Hallgate, Sutton St Edmund
PE12 0LN. Mr & Mrs C Pate, 01945
700773. *18m SE of Spalding. 16m
from Peterborough, 8m from Wisbech.
In village facing S take R into Chapel*

*Rd. Next L onto Hallgate, farm 1st on
R.* Cream teas. **Adm £2, chd free.
Sun 6, Wed 23, Thur 24 Apr; Wed
28, Thur 29 May; (11-4); Sun 22 June
(2-6), Wed 25, Thur 26 June; Wed
30, Thur 31 July (11-4). Visitors also
welcome by appt coaches and
groups 10+ any day for NGS.**
3-acre family garden, perennial beds
full of cultivated and native plants for
wildlife. Vegetables, fruit, scree, all in
cottage garden-style; white beds,
chickens. Spinney with native wild
flowers. Organic. Dew pond for wildlife.
Featured in 'Garden Answers' 2006.
🚻 ✕ ⊗ ☕ ☎

HOLMES VILLA
See Nottinghamshire.

23 HOLYWELL HALL
Holywell PE9 4DT. Mr & Mrs R
Gillespie, 01780 410665. *8m N of
Stamford. From A1 signed Clipsham.
Through Clipsham then turn R to
Holywell. Entrance to Hall 2m on L.*
Light refreshments & teas. **Adm £3.50,
chd 50p. Fri 27 June (2-6). Visitors
also welcome by appt.**
The beautiful gardens at Holywell are
among the most handsome and
historically interesting in S Lincolnshire.
Nestled in a vale they are laid out on a
broad S-facing slope overlooking C18
lake. Numerous water features, walled
vegetable garden, stunning
herbaceous borders, chapel, fishing
temple and orangery. Wild flower
meadow. New colourful flower garden
created by Head Gardener Brian
Oldman in 2007.
☕ ☎

THE HOMESTEAD
See Leicestershire & Rutland.

24 KEXBY HOUSE
Gainsborough DN21 5NE. Herbert &
Jenny Whitton, 01427 788759. *12m
NNW of Lincoln. 6m E of
Gainsborough. On B1241, outskirts of
Kexby village.* Light refreshments &
teas. **Adm £4, chd free. Sun 8 June
(11-5). Visitors also welcome by
appt.**
Approx 5 acres of gardens which have
evolved over last 100yrs. Long
herbaceous borders, unusual plants,
wildlife pond and bog garden, scree
gardens and all-white border, wild
flower area. New perennial prairie-style
meadow. Most of garden accessible
except for scree beds.
🚻 ⊗ ☕ ☎

25 LES ALLÉES

12 Frieston Road, Caythorpe NG32 3BX. Alan & Marylyn Mason. *8m N of Grantham. From Grantham A607 towards Lincoln. L turn to Caythorpe village, immed L again into Frieston Rd. No 12 300yds ahead.* **Adm £3, chd free. Sun 15 June (2-6).** A plantsman's garden created by Alan Mason, TV gardener and garden designer. Ornamental potager, woodland walk, specimen trees and shrubs, Italian avenue of cypresses. Pond; large mixed borders; tree house; subtropical border. A garden of different styles and atmospheres which link seamlessly. Avenues and allées lead round the garden.
♿ ✂ ☕

A garden
of different
styles and
atmospheres
which link
seamlessly . . .

26 LITTLE PONTON HALL

Grantham NG33 5BS. Mr & Mrs Alastair McCorquodale. *2m S of Grantham. 1/2 m E of A1 at S end of Grantham bypass.* Light refreshments. **Adm £3.50, chd free. Sat 9, Sun 10 Feb (11-4).**
3 to 4-acre garden. Spacious lawns with cedar tree over 200yrs old. Many varieties of old shrub roses and clematis; borders and young trees. Stream, spring blossom and hellebores; bulbs and river walk with massed snowdrops and aconites. Formal walled kitchen garden and listed dovecote. Victorian greenhouses with many plants from exotic locations. Local village church open. Special car park for disabled visitors. Good access on all hard paths (not suitable on grass). Disabled WC.
♿ ✂ ☕

27 NEW THE LONG HOUSE

Gelston NG32 2AE. Dr Lisanne Radice. *5m N of Grantham. 16m S of Lincoln. Between Hough-on-the-Hill & Marston.* Home-made teas. **Adm £2.50, chd free (share to All Saints Church, Hough-on-the-Hill). Sun 6 July (2.30-5).**
2 acre garden with extensive views over the Vale of Belvoir. There are roses in abundance, a knot garden, an informal arrangement of borders and a newly designed pond to encourage wildlife. Small woodland garden has just been added. Book stall.
✂ ⚅ ☕

28 NEW MANOR HOUSE

Walcott LN4 3SN. Tina & Simon Grantham. *2m N of Billinghay on B1189. Next to Manor Farm on High St.* **Adm £2.50, chd 50p. Sun 22 June (2-5).**
Plant collectors garden in 3/4 of an acre, various rooms incl a walled garden, wild area with natural pond, alpine area, shrub and herbaceous borders. Parking in a courtyard surrounded by converted farm buildings at Manor Farm next door.
♿ ✂ ⚅ ☕

29 MARIGOLD COTTAGE

Hotchin Road, Sutton-on-Sea LN12 2JA. Stephanie Lee, 01507 442151, http://uk.geocities.com/ marigoldlee@btinternet.com/. *From High St facing sea, turn R at Corner House Café, along Furlong's Rd past playing fields, round bend, into Hotchin Rd. Garden 2nd on L.* **Adm £2, chd free. Sun 1 June (11-4). Visitors also welcome by appt.**
1/2 -acre seaside garden containing a large variety of unusual hardy perennials. Paths, pergolas, arches and secret trails make the garden magical. Features incl Japanese bed, slate dry water feature, planting schemes to excite the palette and Oriental courtyard with wheelchair friendly raised beds. Featured in GGG 2008; Gertrude Yates Challenge Cup, Sutton-on-Sea Horticultural Society best large garden, 2007.
♿ ⚅ ☕ ☎

30 MARTIN GARDENS

LN4 3QY. *15m SE of Lincoln. On B1191. 4m W of Woodhall Spa. Martin Gardens on main rd. Parking on roadside. Blankney Barff garden* signed off B1189. Home-made teas at Holmdale House. **Combined adm £2, chd 50p (share to MARTIN 'LIVES'). Sun 8 June (11-5).**
☕

HOLMDALE HOUSE
High Street. Ian Warden & Stewart MacKenzie
1-acre plantsman's garden started March 2000, surrounding Victorian farmhouse and barns (not open). Informal mixed borders planted to reflect owners' interest in unusual hardy plants, especially good foliage and variegated leaf forms. Collection of hostas, large pond, courtyard gardens and nursery. Newly acquired 1/2 acre under development with white garden, pickery, grasses bed and woodland area.
✂ ⚅

LABOURERS COTTAGE
Blankney Barff. Mrs Linda Brighty. *Signed off B1189 between Metheringham & Martin* 1850s cottage in approx 3 acres. 2 ponds, bog garden, borders and beds of mixed plantings, hedged rose garden, various trees, vegetable and fruit garden. Over past 10 yrs we have changed a meadow into a wildlife-friendly garden. Garden currently undergoing further exciting developments.
✂ ⚅

MILL HILL HOUSE
See Nottinghamshire.

31 THE MOAT

Newton, Sleaford NG34 0ED. Mr & Mrs Mike Barnes, 01529 497462. *Off A52 halfway between Grantham & Sleaford. In Newton village, opp church. Please park sensibly in village.* Home-made teas. **Adm £3, chd free. Thur 12 June (2-5). Visitors also welcome by appt groups 10+.**
2 1/2 -acre country garden, formerly a farmyard, now 6yrs old. Island mixed beds, natural pond, courtyard garden with topiary and many interesting trees and plants.
✂ ☕ ☎

32 OLD QUARRY LODGE

15 Barnetby Lane, Elsham, nr Brigg DN20 0RB. Mel & Tina Welton, 01652 680309. *6m S of Humber Bridge. Leave M180 at J5. Drive past 'Little Chef' into Elsham village. Old Quarry Lodge is 1st house on R on*

entering village. Home-made teas. **Adm £2.50, chd free. Sun 17 Aug (10.30-5). Visitors also welcome by appt groups 10+, clubs etc. June, July, Aug.**
Approx 1/2 -acre sloping garden with formal and informal features. Abundant borders and island beds with architectural focal points, Mediterranean influence in parts. Highly imaginative garden with exciting mixture of the flamboyant and the quintessentially 'English'. Featured in 'Lincs Journal' Aug 2007; 'Amateur Gardening' Oct 2007. Gravel drive.

33 THE OLD RECTORY
East Keal PE23 4AT. Mrs Ruth Ward, 01790 752477. *2m SW of Spilsby. Off A16. Turn into Church Lane by PO.* Light refreshments & home-made teas. **Combined adm with Fen View £3.50, chd free. Sun 27 Apr (2-5); Sun 25 May (11-5). Visitors also welcome by appt for individuals and groups; teas by arrangement.**
Beautifully situated, with fine views, rambling cottage garden on different levels falling naturally into separate areas, with changing effects and atmosphere. Steps, paths and vistas to lead you on, with seats well placed for appreciating special views and plant combinations or relaxing and enjoying the peace. New dry border. Featured in 'Hortus' no 82 summer 2007.

34 THE OLD VICARAGE
Low Road, Holbeach Hurn PE12 8JN. Mrs Liz Dixon-Spain, 01406 424148. *2m NE of Holbeach. Turn off A17 N to Holbeach Hurn, past post box in middle of village, 1st turn R into Low Rd. Old Vicarage on R approx 400yds.* Home-made teas. **Combined adm with The Old White House, Holbeach Hurn £4, chd free. Sun 13 July (12-5). Visitors also welcome by appt.**
2 acres of gardens with mature trees, old grass tennis court and croquet lawns surrounded by borders of shrubs, roses, herbaceous; informal areas incl pond and bog garden, wild flowers, grasses and bulbs, shrub roses and herb garden in old paddock area. Environmentally maintained and fun for kids too.

35 OLD WHITE HOUSE
Holbeach Hurn PE12 8JP. Mr & Mrs A Worth. *2m N of Holbeach. Turn off A17 N to Holbeach Hurn, follow signs to village, go straight through, turn R after Rose & Crown at Baileys Lane.* Home-made teas. **Combined adm with The Old Vicarage, Holbeach Hurn £4, chd free. Sun 13 July (12-5).**
1½ acres of mature garden, featuring herbaceous borders, roses, patterned garden, herb garden and wild garden with small pond. Walled kitchen garden.

36 NEW THE ORCHARDS
Old Somerby, nr Grantham NG33 4AG. Mrs P Dean. *3m E of Grantham. In School Lane, Old Somerby.* Light refreshments & wine, Fri 20 June at The Orchards; Teas at South Lodge, Sun 22 June. **Adm £2.50, chd 50p. Sun 22 June (2-5). Evening Opening £3, chd 50p, wine, Fri 20 June (5-9).**
Yew trees dominate this 1 acre village garden created from scratch in last 10yrs on site of old farm steddings. Mixed borders, pond, bog garden, fruit and vegetable area. Large lawn for sporting grandchildren. Wine tasting by The Wine & Glass Co; Smoked food from Black Mountains Smokery; Exhibition of paintings by wildlife artist Ben Hoskyns. Some gravel.

37 NEW OVERBECK
46 Main Street, Scothern LN2 2UW. John & Joyce Good, 01673 862200, john.good4@btinternet.com. *4m E of Lincoln. Scothern is signed from A46 at Dunholme & A158 at Sudbrooke. Overbeck is at E end of Main St.* **Adm £2, chd free. Visitors welcome by appt May to Sept. Individuals, groups and/or coaches.**
Approx 1/2 acre garden in quiet village. Long herbaceous borders and colour-themed island beds with some unusual perennials. Hosta border, gravel bed with grasses, fernery, trees, numerous shrubs and climbers and a prolific vegetable and fruit area. Two thirds of garden suitable for wheelchairs. Ground rises steeply to veg & fruit.

38 68 PENNYGATE
Spalding PE11 1NN. Mr & Mrs Carroll, 01775 767554. *1m W of Spalding. Take A151 towards Bourne. Turn R onto Park Rd immediately after rail crossings. Then 1st L onto Pennygate. No 68 on L.* Home-made teas. **Adm £2, chd free. Sat 21, Sun 22 June; Sat 26, Sun 27 July (10-4). Visitors also welcome by appt.**
A plantswoman's garden, island beds and border planted with a wide range of flowering perennials and shrubs, large pond with rocky and bog garden.

ROSELEA
See Nottinghamshire.

39 73 SAXILBY ROAD
Sturton by Stow LN1 2AA. Charles & Tricia Elliott, 01427 788517. *9m NW of Lincoln. On B1241. Halfway between Lincoln & Gainsborough.* **Adm £2.50, chd free. Garden/nursery open Mar-Oct. Please phone first. NGS collecting box. Suns 13 July (1-5); 5 Oct (11-5).**
Extensively cultivated plot planted in a relaxed cottage garden style and mainly devoted to a wide selection of summer and autumn flowering perennials and late season grasses. Shrub borders with some unusual shrubs and small trees chosen to give early interest in leaf colour and shape and to produce good autumn colour. Large display of tender fuchsias. Small hardy plant nursery. 13 July only - Art Exhibition by garden owners.

> **Beautifully situated, with fine views, rambling cottage garden on different levels . . .**

40 2 SCHOOL HOUSE
Stixwould, nr Woodhall Spa LN10 5HP. Andrew & Sheila Sankey, 01526 352453. *1½ m N of Woodhall Spa. From roundabout in Woodhall Spa, take rd to Bardney past Petwood Hotel. Follow rd for 1½ m and at sharp*

RH bend turn off L into Stixwould. Garden is on main rd opp red phone box. **Adm £2, chd free. Suns 25 May; 13 July (2-5). Visitors also welcome by appt.**

¼ -acre garden, redesigned in Oct 1994 by owners in cottage garden style, to incl front garden with unusual perennials and shrubs, herb garden, and small turf maze.

✟ ⦿ ☕ ☎

Lots of plant and shrub variety with 'quirky' accessories . . .

41 NEW SOUTH LODGE
Ropsley NG33 4AS. Nicholas Turner. *4m E of Grantham. From Grantham take Ropsley turn off A52. Proceed along Long Lane. Garden 1m on R.* **Teas. Adm £3, chd 50p. Sun 22 June (2-5).**
The garden at South Lodge is built around four large ponds. Mixed borders, specimen trees and shrubs flank the perimeter, whilst four walk through, mounded borders add height to the central area. Around the house are formal borders of roses and topiary. Garden contains over fifty different species of roses.

♿ ✟ ⦿ ☕

SQUIRREL LODGE
See Nottinghamshire.

42 NEW STATION HOUSE
Station Road, Potterhanworth, Lincoln LN4 2DX. Carol & Alan Harvey. *6m S of Lincoln. B1178 immed on L under railway bridge before reaching Potterhanworth village.* **Adm £2, chd free. Suns 15, 29 June; Suns 13, 27 July (1-5).**
Old Station Master's house in ¼ acre gardens. Very informal style with mixed borders, lawns and two ponds with particular emphasis on wildlife. Lots of plant and shrub variety with 'quirky' accessories. Garden owners keen ornithologists. One path not suitable for wheelchairs.

43 NEW WALTERS COTTAGE
6 Hall Road, Hacconby, nr Bourne PE10 0UY. Ivan & Sadie Hall. *3m N of Bourne A15. Turn E at Xrds to Hacconby. Turn R at Hare & Hounds PH.* **Home-made teas. Adm £2, chd free. Sat 31 May; Sun 1 June (11-5).**
Country cottage garden of over ¼ of an acre developed over the past 5yrs. Various themed areas. Walled garden with hornbeam allée, topiary and rill. Woodland area with wildlife pond and plants. Sunken garden. Long herbaceous borders, lawns and collection of hostas. Garden is well-stocked with many interesting and rare plants with added features.

✟ ⦿ ☕

44 WASHDYKE FARM
Lincoln Road, Fulbeck NG32 3HY. Anna Greenhalgh, 01400 272880, gary.greenhalgh@treasuretransport. co.uk. *10m N of Grantham; 15m S of Lincoln. On A607 in dip opp Washdyke Lane.* **Cream teas. Adm £2.50, chd free. Visitors welcome by appt from 19 May to 31 July. Coach parties & small groups welcome.**
Approx 2 acres with meandering paths leading to interesting features and contrasting moods. Lawns with cottage-style mixed borders; attractive waterside planting alongside stream; wildlife pond and woodland walk with mature trees.

✟ ☕ ☎

45 68 WATTS LANE
Louth LN11 9DG. Mr & Mrs R Grasham, 01507 601004/07977 318145. *½ m S of Louth town centre. Watts Lane off B1200 Louth to Mablethorpe rd. Turn by pedestrian lights and Londis shop/post office.* **Home-made teas. Adm £2, chd free (share to Louth and District Hospice).** Wed 9 July (11-6); Sun 10 Aug (1-6). **Visitors also welcome by appt July & Aug, coaches permitted.**
Blank canvas of ⅕ acre. Developed over 12yrs into lush, colourful, tropical to traditional plant packed haven. A whole new world on entering from street. Generous borders, raised tropical island, long hot tropical border, ponds, water features, summerhouse, conservatory with grapevine, cutting garden and secluded seating along garden's journey.

♿ ✟ ⦿ ☕ ☎

56 WELL CREEK ROAD
See Norfolk.

46 10 WENDOVER CLOSE
Rippingale PE10 0TQ. Chris & Tim Bladon. *5½ m N of Bourne. Rippingale is signed on the A15. On entering village at the Rippengale / Kirby Underwood Xrd, Wendover Close is 1st turning on L. Garden at end of the close.* **Home-made teas. Adm £2, chd free. Sun 18 May (11-5).**
Peaceful village garden of approx ½ an acre containing usual and unusual herbaceous plants, shrubs and trees of general and specialist interest in a secluded situation. Shingle drive of 30 metres access to garden.

♿ ✟ ⦿ ☕

47 WEST BARN
Saxby, Lincoln LN8 2DQ. Mrs E Neave. *8m N of Lincoln; 2¼ m E of A15.* **Combined adm with The Garden House £3, chd free. Thurs 10 July; 7 Aug (10-5).**
Formal walled courtyard garden with loggia, box hedging, shrub roses, climbers and herbaceous planting. Water feature and pots with seasonal planting.

✟

48 NEW WHINLATTER
Hundle House Lane, New York, Lincoln LN4 4YW. Mrs Joanna Feready. *8m N of Boston. B1192 ¾ m S of New York. At 30mph limit Xrds turn L opp school.* **Home-made teas. Adm £2, chd free (share to Alzheimers Society, Boston). Sun 15 June (11-5).**
Approx ½ acre, started in 1991 which has gently evolved. Borders and island beds planted with usual and unusual specimens. Wooded areas, water feature, mostly paved paths to give wheelchair accessibility. Also 3 acre meadow walk with abundance of wildlife, not suitable for wheelchairs. Sensible footwear recommended. Ramps into room for tea; appropriate WC.

♿ ✟ ☕

49 WOODLANDS
Peppin Lane, Fotherby, Louth LN11 0UW. Ann & Bob Armstrong, 01507 603586. *2m N of Louth. On A16. Leave bypass (A16) signed Fotherby. Woodlands is situated nr far end of Peppin Lane, a no through rd,*

running E from village centre. No parking at garden. Please park on RH verge opp allotments and walk (approx 250yds) to garden. Home-made teas. **Adm £2, chd free. Suns 20 Apr; 18 May; 27 July; 28 Sept (11-5). Visitors also welcome by appt.**

Mature woodland garden being further developed by the present owners. Packed with rare and unusual perennials, shrubs, ferns and climbers. Meandering paths lead to surprises around every corner. In contrast, the planting nearer the house takes advantage of the more open aspect but is equally interesting. Award winning professional artist's studio/gallery open to visitors. Plant nursery featured in RHS Plantfinder. Featured in 'Garden News' May 2007.

Meandering paths lead to surprises around every corner . . .

Lincolnshire County Volunteers

County Organiser
Susie Dean, The Orchards, Old Somerby, Grantham NG33 4AG, 01476 565456

County Treasurer
Peter Sandberg, Croft House, Ulceby DN39 6SW, 01469 588330, peterhsandberg@hotmail.com

Publicity
Erica McGarrigle, Corner House Farm, Little Humby, Grantham NG33 4HW, 01476 585909, colinmcgarrigle@tiscali.co.uk

Leaflet Coordinator
Lucy Dawes, The Grange, Bulby, Bourne PE10 0RU, 01778 591220

Assistant County Organisers
Ursula Cholmeley, The Dower House, Easton, Grantham NG33 5AP, 01476 530063, eastonwalledgardens.co.uk
Sally Grant, Holly House, Fishtoft Drove, Boston PE22 7ES, 01205 750486
Lizzie Milligan-Manby, Wykeham Hall Farm, East Wykeham, Ludford, Market Rasen LN8 6AU, 01507 313286,
  lizzie@milliganmanby.plus.com
Margaret Sandberg, Croft House, Ulceby DN39 6SW, 01469 588330, peterhsandberg@hotmail.com

LONDON

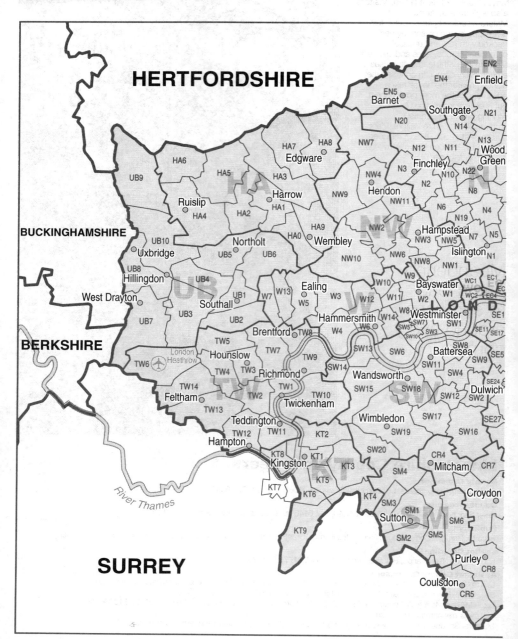

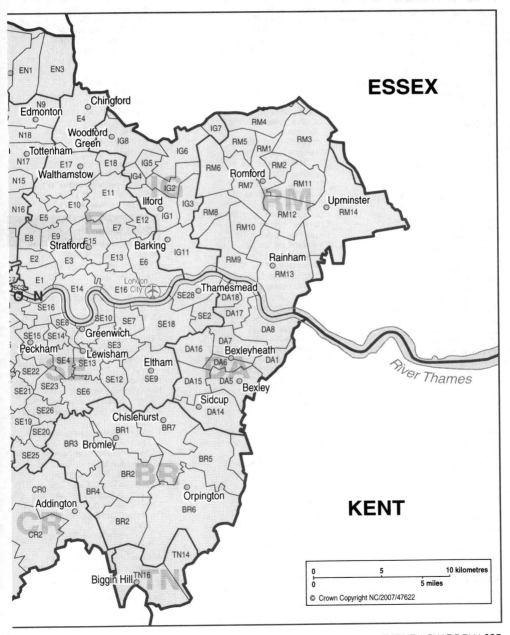

ESSEX

KENT

River Thames

London gardens listed by postcode

Inner London postcodes

Lower Clapton Gardens E5
42 Latimer Road E7
Albion Square & London Fields E8
24 Middleton Road E8
12 Bushberry Road E9
17 Daintry Way E9
47 Maynard Road E17
Waltham Forest Register Office E17
Amwell Gardens Group EC1
Charterhouse EC1

N, NW

37 Alwyne Road N1
De Beauvoir Gardens N1
Islington Gardens N1
Malvern Terrace Gardens N1
66 Abbots Gardens N2
The Bungalow N2
East Finchley Cottage Gardens N2
15 Lytton Close N2
2 Stanley Road N2
44 Cholmeley Crescent N6
51 Cholmeley Crescent N6
7 The Grove N6
2 Millfield Place N6
3 The Park N6
Southwood Lodge N6
1a Hungerford Road N7
62 Hungerford Road N7
90 St George's Avenue N7
5 New Road N8
5 Cecil Road N10
15 Dukes Avenue N10
46 Dukes Avenue N10
6 Methuen Park N10
5 St Regis Close N10
27 Wood Vale N10
33 Wood Vale N10
Golf Course Allotments N11
71 Fallowcourt Avenue N12
15 Norcott Road N16
13 Queen Elizabeth's Walk N16
39 Arundel Gardens N21
Railway Cottages N22
70 Gloucester Crescent NW1
The Holme NW1
Regents College's Garden NW1
Royal College of Physicians Garden NW1
64 Blenheim Gardens NW2
10 Hoveden Road NW2
72 Tanfield Avenue NW2
208 Walm Lane, The Garden Flat NW2
180 Adelaide Road NW3
17 Belsize Lane NW3
15a Buckland Crescent NW3
6 Emerald House NW3
Fenton House NW3

Frognal Gardens NW3
Little House A NW3
37a Redington Road, Garden Flat NW3
27 Blenheim Road NW8
116 Hamilton Terrace NW8
170 Doyle Gardens NW10
Asmuns Hill Gardens NW11
113 Corringham Road NW11
157 Hampstead Way NW11
5 Hillcrest Avenue NW11
94 Oakwood Road NW11
5 Wildwood Rise NW11
86 Willifield Way NW11
89 Willifield Way NW11
91 Willifield Way NW11

S, SE, SW

Downings Road Mooring Barge Gardens SE1
Lambeth Palace SE1
Museum of Garden History SE1
35 Camberwell Grove SE5
34 Grove Park SE5
Roots and Shoots SE11
41 Southbrook Road SE12
28 Granville Park SE13
Centre for Wildlife Gardening SE15
Choumert Square SE15
5 Lyndhurst Square SE15
71 Central Hill SE19
13 Gipsy Hill SE19
9 Howard Road SE20
26 Stodart Road SE20
142 Court Lane SE21
Dulwich Gardens SE21
14 Frank Dixon Way SE21
Mulberry House SE21
North House SE21
167 Rosendale Road SE21
66A East Dulwich Road SE22
33 Mundania Road SE22
174 Peckham Rye SE22
22 Scutari Road SE22
Tewkesbury Lodge Garden Group SE23
82 Wood Vale SE23
5 Burbage Road SE24
20 Rollscourt Avenue SE24
South London Botanical Institute SE24
14 Radlet Avenue SE26
18 Sydenham Hill SE26
27 Thorpewood Avenue SE26
Ardlui Gardens SE27
24 Chestnut Road SE27
Eccleston Square SW1
38 Killieser Avenue SW2
Chelsea Physic Garden SW3
17 Crescent Lane SW4
7 Sibella Road SW4
18 Sibella Road SW4
The Hurlingham Club SW6
Natural History Museum Wildlife Garden SW7
225a Brixton Road SW9
28 Old Devonshire Road SW12

2 Western Lane SW12
Barnes Gardens SW13
11 Woodlands Road SW13
96 East Sheen Avenue SW14
33 Balmuir Gardens SW15
31 Roedean Crescent SW15
66 Woodbourne Avenue SW16
19 Montana Road SW17
28 Multon Road SW18
101 Pitt Crescent SW19
Southside House SW19
13 Cambridge Road SW20

W

Mill Hill Road Gardens W3
Stone (Zen) Garden W3
Chiswick Mall W4
23 Woodville Road W5
All Seasons W5
Edwardes Square W8
57 St Quintin Avenue W10
29 Addison Avenue W11
12 Lansdowne Road W11
8 Lansdowne Walk W11
Stanley Crescent Garden W11
49a Loftus Road W12
27 St James Avenue W13

Outer London postcodes

Harcourt House, Bromley BR1
36 Downs Hill, Bromley BR3
Columcille, Chislehurst BR7
Wellwood, Chislehurst BR7
Elm Tree Cottage, South Croydon CR2
Myddelton House Gardens, Enfield EN2
7 Byng Road, High Barnet EN5
Barnet Gardens, Barnet EN5
54 Ferndown, Northwood Hills HA6
Summerlawn, Moor Park HA6
Hornbeams, Stanmore HA7
24 Hills Road, Buckhurst Hill IG9
4 Stradbroke Grove, Buckhurst Hill IG9
The Watergardens, Kingston upon Thames KT2
Badgers Retreat, New Malden KT3
52A Berrylands Road, Surbiton KT5
Little Lodge, Thames Ditton KT7
10 Arnison Road, East Molesey KT8
340 Walton Road, West Molesey KT8
239a Hook Road, Chessington KT9
Pembridge Cottage, Twickenham TW1
7 St George's Road, Twickenham TW1
Whitton CRC, Whitton TW2
Osterley Park and House, Isleworth TW7
Kew Gardens Station Group TW9
Kew Green Gardens TW9
38 Leyborne Park, Kew TW9
95 North Road, Kew TW9

Richmond Riverside TW9
Short Lots Allotments, Kew TW9
Ham House and Garden, Richmond
TW10
Ormeley Lodge, Richmond TW10
Petersham House, Petersham TW10
Rosebank, Petersham TW10
St Michael's Convent, Richmond
TW10
18 Cranmer Road, Hampton Hill
TW12
Holly Cottage, Hampton TW12
Hope Villa, Hampton TW12
Tudor Road Gardens, Hampton
TW12

Opening Dates

February

SUNDAY 24
Myddelton House Gardens

March

SUNDAY 23
Chelsea Physic Garden, SW3

SUNDAY 30
167 Rosendale Road, SE21
72 Tanfield Avenue, NW2

April

SUNDAY 6
Edwardes Square, W8
7 The Grove, N6

SUNDAY 13
8 Lansdowne Walk, W11

SUNDAY 20
Natural History Museum Wildlife
Garden, SW7
Osterley Park and House
3 The Park, N6

SATURDAY 26
The Holme, NW1

SUNDAY 27
5 Burbage Road, SE24
36 Downs Hill
The Holme, NW1
Malvern Terrace Gardens, N1
Mulberry House, SE21
Myddelton House Gardens
5 St Regis Close, N10
7 Sibella Road, SW4
18 Sibella Road, SW4
Southside House, SW19
Stanley Crescent Garden, W11

WEDNESDAY 30
7 Sibella Road, SW4 (Evening)
18 Sibella Road, SW4 (Evening)

May

SUNDAY 4
38 Leyborne Park
Southwood Lodge, N6
18 Sydenham Hill, SE26

MONDAY 5
38 Leyborne Park
Waltham Forest Register Office, E17

SATURDAY 10
Lambeth Palace, SE1
Museum of Garden History, SE1

SUNDAY 11
66 Abbots Gardens, N2
18 Cranmer Road
Eccleston Square, SW1
Elm Tree Cottage
14 Frank Dixon Way, SE21
70 Gloucester Crescent, NW1
2 Millfield Place, N6
94 Oakwood Road, NW11
Southside House, SW19
Summerlawn
2 Western Lane, SW12
91 Willifield Way, NW11

WEDNESDAY 14
12 Lansdowne Road, W11

THURSDAY 15
Fenton House, NW3 (Evening)

SATURDAY 17
Regents College's Garden, NW1
Stone (Zen) Garden, W3
Tudor Road Gardens

SUNDAY 18
39 Arundel Gardens, N21
Centre for Wildlife Gardening, SE15
15 Dukes Avenue, N10
46 Dukes Avenue, N10
East Finchley Cottage Gardens, N2
Kew Green Gardens
Little House A, NW3
33 Mundania Road, SE22
Petersham House
Rosebank
22 Scutari Road, SE22
2 Stanley Road, N2
Stone (Zen) Garden, W3
Tudor Road Gardens
The Watergardens
33 Wood Vale, N10
11 Woodlands Road, SW13

SATURDAY 24
Tewkesbury Lodge Garden Group,
SE23 (Evening)

SUNDAY 25
39 Arundel Gardens, N21
33 Balmuir Gardens, SW15
Chiswick Mall, W4
Little Lodge
Myddelton House Gardens
14 Radlet Avenue, SE26

Tewkesbury Lodge Garden Group,
SE23

SATURDAY 31
35 Camberwell Grove, SE5 (Evening)
The Hurlingham Club, SW6

June

SUNDAY 1
37 Alwyne Road, N1
Ardlui Gardens, SE27
24 Chestnut Road, SE27
170 Doyle Gardens, NW10
66A East Dulwich Road, SE22
71 Fallowcourt Avenue, N12
Islington Gardens, N1
Lower Clapton Gardens, E5
6 Methuen Park, N10
101 Pitt Crescent, SW19
167 Rosendale Road, SE21
7 St George's Road

WEDNESDAY 4
Little Lodge (Day & Evening)
Whitton CRC

THURSDAY 5
Fenton House, NW3 (Evening)

FRIDAY 6
Wellwood (Evening)

SATURDAY 7
34 Grove Park, SE5
Richmond Riverside (Evening)
Roots and Shoots, SE11

SUNDAY 8
Barnes Gardens, SW13
44 Cholmeley Crescent, N6
Choumert Square, SE15
142 Court Lane, SE21
17 Crescent Lane, SW4
Elm Tree Cottage
70 Gloucester Crescent, NW1
7 The Grove, N6
Holly Cottage
239a Hook Road
Hope Villa
9 Howard Road, SE20
1a Hungerford Road, N7
62 Hungerford Road, N7
Kew Gardens Station Group
5 Lyndhurst Square, SE15
15 Norcott Road, N16
North House, SE21
174 Peckham Rye, SE22
20 Rollscourt Avenue, SE24
Roots and Shoots, SE11
90 St George's Avenue, N7
41 Southbrook Road, SE12
26 Stodart Road, SE20
89 Willifield Way, NW11

WEDNESDAY 11
239a Hook Road (Evening)

FRIDAY 13
28 Granville Park, SE13 (Evening)

SATURDAY 14
Little House A, NW3
27 Thorpewood Avenue, SE26
(Evening)

SUNDAY 15
Albion Square & London Fields, E8
De Beauvoir Gardens, N1
Dulwich Gardens, SE21
Holly Cottage
10 Hoveden Road, NW2
Little House A, NW3
28 Old Devonshire Road, SW12
Pembridge Cottage
27 Thorpewood Avenue, SE26
208 Walm Lane, The Garden Flat,
    NW2
2 Western Lane, SW12

TUESDAY 17
Charterhouse, EC1 (Evening)

WEDNESDAY 18
5 Burbage Road, SE24 (Evening)
2 Millfield Place, N6 (Evening)
28 Old Devonshire Road, SW12
    (Evening)

SATURDAY 21
St Michael's Convent

SUNDAY 22
64 Blenheim Gardens, NW2
15a Buckland Crescent, NW3
12 Bushberry Road, E9
113 Corringham Road, NW11
17 Daintry Way, E9
Frognal Gardens, NW3
116 Hamilton Terrace, NW8
5 Hillcrest Avenue, NW11
Ormeley Lodge
Pembridge Cottage
South London Botanical Institute,
    SE24
340 Walton Road (Evening)

WEDNESDAY 25
5 Hillcrest Avenue, NW11 (Evening)

SATURDAY 28
27 Wood Vale, N10

SUNDAY 29
Amwell Gardens Group, EC1
Asmuns Hill Gardens, NW11
Badgers Retreat
5 Cecil Road, N10
9 Howard Road, SE20
15 Lytton Close, N2
19 Montana Road, SW17
5 St Regis Close, N10
5 Wildwood Rise, NW11
27 Wood Vale, N10
66 Woodbourne Avenue,
    SW16

July

WEDNESDAY 2
Badgers Retreat (Evening)
Roots and Shoots, SE11 (Evening)

FRIDAY 4
6 Methuen Park, N10 (Evening)

SATURDAY 5
Ham House and Garden
7 St George's Road (Evening)

SUNDAY 6
36 Downs Hill
66A East Dulwich Road, SE22
Harcourt House
Natural History Museum Wildlife
    Garden, SW7
Railway Cottages, N22
22 Scutari Road, SE22
82 Wood Vale, SE23

WEDNESDAY 9
49a Loftus Road, W12 (Evening)

SUNDAY 13
52A Berrylands Road
71 Central Hill, SE19
Elm Tree Cottage
70 Gloucester Crescent, NW1
24 Hills Road
Mill Hill Road Gardens, W3
Old Palace Lane Allotments
Royal College of Physicians Garden,
    NW1
57 St Quintin Avenue, W10
Short Lots Allotments

WEDNESDAY 16
86 Willifield Way, NW11 (Evening)

SUNDAY 20
180 Adelaide Road, NW3
All Seasons, W5
Barnet Gardens
The Bungalow, N2
18 Cranmer Road (Evening)
116 Hamilton Terrace, NW8 (Evening)
157 Hampstead Way, NW11
47 Maynard Road, E17
95 North Road (Day & Evening)
37a Redington Road, Garden Flat,
    NW3
31 Roedean Crescent, SW15
2 Western Lane, SW12
86 Willifield Way, NW11

THURSDAY 24
27 Blenheim Road, NW8 (Evening)

SATURDAY 26
The Holme, NW1
42 Latimer Road, E7

SUNDAY 27
29 Addison Avenue, W11
10 Arnison Road
27 Blenheim Road, NW8
Downings Road Mooring Barge
    Gardens, SE1
The Holme, NW1
42 Latimer Road, E7
47 Maynard Road, E17
57 St Quintin Avenue, W10
5 St Regis Close, N10

August

SATURDAY 2
225a Brixton Road, SW9
13 Gipsy Hill, SE19

SUNDAY 3
180 Adelaide Road, NW3
10 Arnison Road
170 Doyle Gardens, NW10

SUNDAY 10
66A East Dulwich Road, SE22
96 East Sheen Avenue, SW14
Elm Tree Cottage
70 Gloucester Crescent, NW1
Summerlawn

WEDNESDAY 13
208 Walm Lane, The Garden Flat,
    NW2 (Evening)

SUNDAY 17
Columcille
27 St James Avenue, W13

SUNDAY 31
13 Cambridge Road, SW20
Golf Course Allotments, N11
19 Montana Road, SW17
28 Multon Road, SW18
13 Queen Elizabeth's Walk, N16
23 Woodville Road, W5

September

SATURDAY 6
Regents College's Garden, NW1

SUNDAY 7
66 Abbots Gardens, N2
17 Belsize Lane, NW3
7 Byng Road
24 Chestnut Road, SE27
    (Evening)
66A East Dulwich Road, SE22
    (Evening)
54 Ferndown
8 Lansdowne Walk, W11
2 Stanley Road, N2

SATURDAY 13
Stone (Zen) Garden, W3

SUNDAY 14
70 Gloucester Crescent, NW1
6 Methuen Park, N10
Stone (Zen) Garden, W3

FRIDAY 19
Petersham House

SUNDAY 21
72 Tanfield Avenue, NW2

October

FRIDAY 3
36 Downs Hill

SUNDAY 19
The Watergardens

February 2009

SUNDAY 22
Myddelton House Gardens

Gardens open to the public

Chelsea Physic Garden, SW3
Fenton House, NW3
Ham House and Garden
Museum of Garden History, SE1
Myddelton House Gardens
Natural History Museum Wildlife
Garden, SW7
Osterley Park and House
Roots and Shoots, SE11

By appointment only

51 Cholmeley Crescent, N6
6 Emerald House, NW3
Hornbeams
38 Killieser Avenue, SW2
24 Middleton Road, E8
5 New Road, N8
4 Stradbroke Grove

Also open by Appointment ☎

180 Adelaide Road, NW3
17 Belsize Lane, NW3
225a Brixton Road, SW9
5 Burbage Road, SE24
35 Camberwell Grove, SE5
5 Cecil Road, N10
13 College Cross, Islington Gardens,
N1
Columcille
18 Cranmer Road
158 Culford Road, De Beauvoir
Gardens, N1
17 Daintry Way, E9
Dorset Road, Railway Cottages,
N22
36 Downs Hill
170 Doyle Gardens, NW10
66A East Dulwich Road, SE22
Elm Tree Cottage
54 Ferndown
70 Gloucester Crescent, NW1
7 The Grove, N6
116 Hamilton Terrace, NW8
Harcourt House
5 Hillcrest Avenue, NW11
239a Hook Road
9 Howard Road, SE20
62 Hungerford Road, N7
The Hurlingham Club, SW6
8 Lansdowne Walk, W11
46 Lavender Grove, Albion Square &
London Fields, E8
Little Lodge
Mapledene Road, Albion Square &
London Fields, E8

47 Maynard Road, E17
6 Methuen Park, N10
2 Millfield Place, N6
65 Mill Hill Road, Mill Hill Road
Gardens, W3
19 Montana Road, SW17
24 Myddleton Square, Amwell
Gardens Group, EC1
21 Northchurch Terrace, De Beauvoir
Gardens, N1
94 Oakwood Road, NW11
28 Old Devonshire Road, SW12
3 The Park, N6
Pembridge Cottage
101 Pitt Crescent, SW19
167 Rosendale Road, SE21
58 Rushmore Road, Lower Clapton
Gardens, E5
7 St George's Road
57 St Quintin Avenue, W10
5 St Regis Close, N10
22 Scutari Road, SE22
7 Sibella Road, SW4
18 Sibella Road, SW4
Southwood Lodge, N6
2 Stanley Road, N2
Summerlawn
18 Sydenham Hill, SE26
72 Tanfield Avenue, NW2
45 Tudor Road, Tudor Road
Gardens
Waltham Forest Register Office, E17
2 Western Lane, SW12
33 Wood Vale, N10
82 Wood Vale, SE23
23 Woodville Road, W5

The Gardens

NEW 66 ABBOTS GARDENS, N2
East Finchley N2 0JH. *Stephen & Ruth Kersley. Buses: 102, 143, 234, 263 stop at Abbots Gdns. Tube: East Finchley, 6 mins walk leaving from rear stn entrance along the Causeway (pedestrian) to East End Rd, 2nd L into Abbots Gdns.* **Adm £2.50, chd free. Suns 11 May; 7 Sept (2-5.30).** Designed for tranquillity and all-yr interest, this 3yr old S-facing garden 20m x 10m uses plant form, colour, texture and a strong underlying asymmetrical geometry, to create a calming yet dramatic environment with grasses, herbaceous perennials, ornamental shrubs and trees, water features and discreet vegetable plot. Circular N-facing front garden. Stephen studied garden design at Capel Manor.

A calming yet dramatic environment . . .

29 ADDISON AVENUE, W11
W11 4QS. **David & Shirley Nicholson.** *No entry for cars from Holland Park Ave, approach via Norland Square & Queensdale Rd. Tube: Holland Park. Buses: 94, 148, 295.* **Adm £2, chd free. Sun 27 July (2-6). Also open 57 St Quintin Ave.** Garden designed to be at its peak in July and August. Unusual wall shrubs, itea, schizophragma, clerodendrum, surround beds of colourful perennials, phlox, monarda, agastache, eupatorium. A pear tree dominates the central lawn and a giant *Euonymus japonicus*, 150yrs old, amazes all who see it.

180 ADELAIDE ROAD, NW3
Swiss Cottage NW3 3PA. **Simone Rothman,** simonerothman@ukonline.co.uk. *Tube: Swiss Cottage, 100yds. Buses: 13, 46, 82, 113 on Finchley Rd; 31 & C11 on Adelaide Rd. 50yds from Marriott Hotel, Winchester Rd.* Light refreshments & teas. **Adm £2, chd free. Suns 20 July; 3 Aug (3-5). Visitors also welcome by appt.** Small 25ft x 30ft S-facing walled garden with profuse and colourful climbers and shrubs. Numerous densely-planted containers on gravel with roses, herbaceous perennials, annuals and box. Front garden with lawn and shrubs.

ALBION SQUARE & LONDON FIELDS, E8
E8 4ES. *2m N of Liverpool St stn (mainline & tube). 1m S of Dalston/Kingsland stn (mainline). Buses: 67, 149, 242, 243, alight Downham Rd. By car approach from Queenbridge Rd northbound, turning L into Albion Drive leading to Albion Square.* Home-made teas. **Combined adm £5, chd free. Sun 15 June (2-5.30).**

15 ALBION DRIVE
Izi Glover & Michael Croton
Much-used 100ft family garden with defensive box hedging, trained fruit trees, meadow area,

pond, secluded seating area and silver birch glade. Tree house tucked away. Native plants combine with foxglove tree in front garden.

12 ALBION SQUARE
Michael & Sarah Parry
Surprisingly spacious garden with a Victorian Gothic church backdrop. Trees and shrubs allow unfolding areas of interest incl established borders, sunny herb garden and willow arbour.

NEW 46 LAVENDER GROVE
Richard Sharp, 020 7683 9671, sharpr1966@lycos.co.uk. Visitors also welcome by appt max 10 people.
Small garden behind terraced Victorian house packed with fruit trees, vine fruit and perennial flowers. Bulbs bloom in spring, followed by dahlias and echinacea in mid-summer.

NEW 55 LAVENDER GROVE
Matthew & Charlotte-Anne Griffiths
Formal walled garden, 60 ft x 18 ft, created 7 yrs ago. Box-edged rose garden and rambler-covered arbour lead to small white garden and S-facing terrace. Pretty, country garden planting (roses, clematis, nepeta, iris, geraniums) and box topiary. Mini parterre in front garden with standard ramblers, lavender and box.

NEW 53 MAPLEDENE ROAD
Tigger Cullinan, 020 7249 3754. Visitors also welcome by appt June to Aug, small groups only.
90ft x 15ft N-facing back garden, divided in 3, crammed full by plantaholic. Roses, clematis, and other climbers clamber together. Colour-coordinated areas.

ALL SEASONS, W5
97 Grange Road, Ealing W5 3PH. Dr Benjamin & Mrs Maria Royappa.
Tube: walking distance Ealing Broadway. Light refreshments & teas. **Adm £2, chd free.** Sun 20 July (1-6). Garden designed and planted by owners since moving in 2003. Features incl ponds, pergolas, Japanese gardens, tropical house for orchids and exotics, aviaries, recycled features,

composting and rain water harvesting, orchard, kiwi, grape vines, architectural and unusual plants, collections incl ferns, bamboos, conifers and cacti. WC.

37 ALWYNE ROAD, N1
N1 2HW. Mr & Mrs J Lambert.
Buses: 38, 56, 73, 341 on Essex Rd; 4, 19, 30, 43 on Upper St, alight at Town Hall; 271 on Canonbury Rd, A1. Tube: Highbury & Islington. Home-made teas. **Adm £2.50, chd free (share to Rose Bowl Youth Club). Sun 1 June (2-6).**
The New River curves around the garden, the trees and sky are big, you could be in the country. Clipped box, holly and yew keep things in order - pots reclaim space for colour. Hidden formal garden; old-fashioned roses along the river. Shelter if it rains. Plants for sale are carefully chosen for all seasons: astrantia and agapanthus for summer; cyclamen, liriope and aconites for autumn; iris for winter, and more. Wheelchairs possible only with own assistant for 3 entrance steps.

NEW AMWELL GARDENS GROUP, EC1
South Islington EC1R 1YE. *Tube: Angel, 10 mins walk. Buses: 19, 38 Rosebery Ave; 30, 73 Pentonville Rd.* **Combined adm £5 or £2 each garden, chd free. Sun 29 June (2-5.30).**
Contrasting group of gardens in the historic Amwell Street area, all within a few mins walk of each other.

NEW 7 LLOYD SQUARE
Lloyd Square Garden Committee
The pedimented facades to the houses around the square provide the backdrop to this secluded London square. Recently much work has gone into restoring the paths and arbour and replanting the borders.

NEW 24 MYDDELTON SQUARE
Professor Diana Leonard, d.leonard@ioe.ac.uk. Visitors also welcome by appt.
Small roof-top garden on a Regency terrace house, overlooking a square and with views to St Paul's, the Post Office Tower and Sadler's Wells. 65

steps from pavement to roof garden.

NEW 27 MYDDELTON SQUARE
Sally & Rob Hull
Small landscaped courtyard with lush cottage garden planting and pond. A surprising oasis packed with clematis and unusual perennials.

NEW NEW RIVER HEAD
Myddelton Passage. New River Head EC1 Residents. *The Nautilus Building*
Gardens surrounding the historic New River Head, where the 400yr-old New River brought fresh water to London. Roses, stylish herbaceous and shrub borders, a fountain and a pergola with wisteria, jasmine, honeysuckle and clematis.

Two gardens separated by a few metres, but so different in scale and style . . .

NEW ARDLUI GARDENS, SE27
West Norwood SE27 9HL.
Mainline stns: West Norwood, Tulse Hill or West Dulwich. Buses: 2, 68, 196, 322, 468 to W Norwood High St, then 5 mins walk. Street parking available. Home-made teas at 45 Idmiston Rd. **Combined adm £4, chd free. Sun 1 June (2-5). Also open 24 Chestnut Rd, 66A East Dulwich Rd & 167 Rosendale Rd.**
Two London gardens separated by a few metres, but so different in scale and style.

NEW 45 IDMISTON ROAD
David Aitman & Marianne Atherton
Tranquil 100ft S-facing garden on 2 levels: upper level parterre with architectural plants, patio roses, alliums, lavender, clematis; lower level with ancient apple trees on

beds of geraniums, shady beds of thalictrum, eryngium and brunnera. All approached through a wisteria- and laburnum-clad pergola.

NEW 37 TOWTON ROAD
Josie Slade. *Access to garden via garage on Ardlui Road*
Delightful small back garden, 20ft x 20ft, newly planted in 2006. Decking and pergola with climbing roses and akebia. Beautiful rambling rose. Flower beds packed with an abundance of perennials and semi-hardy plants. Central circle, gravel, stepping stones, millstone pond, colourful baskets, potted hosta collection. A city garden to relax in.

NEW 10 ARNISON ROAD
10 Arnison Road, East Molesey KT8 9JJ. David Clarke. *1/2 m from Hampton Court. Towards East Molesey via Bridge Rd, Arnsion Rd 3rd on R.* Light refreshments & teas. **Adm £2.50, chd free. Suns 27 July; 3 Aug (1-6).**
Medium-sized garden with natural planting designed to attract wildlife and insects. Large collection of fragrant lilies. Restful koi pond with waterfall, to sit and contemplate and possibly feed the fish.

39 ARUNDEL GARDENS, N21
Winchmore Hill N21 3AG. Julie Floyd. *Mainline stn: Winchmore Hill, then approx 7 mins walk. Turn along Hoppers Rd, Arundel Gardens 3rd on L. Tube/bus: Southgate tube, then W9 Hoppa bus along Hoppers Rd.* Home-made teas. **Adm £2, chd free. Suns 18, 25 May (2-6).**
100ft x 30ft town garden planted in informal cottage style with unusual shrubs, climbers and herbaceous plants. Over 30 clematis incl National Collection of Clematis alpina; arbour, water features and conservatory with a collection of cacti and succulents.
NCCPG

NEW ASMUNS HILL GARDENS, NW11
Hampstead Garden Suburb NW11 6ES. *Close to Finchley Rd & N Circular. Tube: Golders Green then bus H2 to Willifield Green or buses 82, 102, 460 to Temple Fortune, then 2 mins walk along*

Hampstead Way, Asmuns Hill 2nd on L. Home-made teas.
Combined adm £4.50, chd free. Sun 29 June (2-6). Also open 15 Lytton Close & 5 Wildwood Rise.
Two very different Arts and Crafts gardens in the Artisan's Quarter of Hampstead Garden Suburb.

NEW 25 ASMUNS HILL
Ms Lorraine Wilder
Densely planted beds brimming with colour and texture, mature trees and York stone terrace enhance this historic Arts and Crafts house. A grassy track leads past a vegetable parterre to a secret orchard at the end of this 1/2 -acre country garden.

NEW 4 ASMUNS HILL
Peter & Yvonne Oliver
Cottage garden with many clematis and other climbers both front and back. Pond, patio, herbaceous bed, shade area. Many succulents, acers and other plants in pots and containers. Sculptures and objets trouvés.

Large collection of fragrant lilies. Restful koi pond with waterfall, to sit and contemplate and possibly feed the fish . . .

BADGERS RETREAT
39 Motspur Park, New Malden KT3 6PS. Peter Barham & Jenny McCarter. *3m N Kingston town centre. Buses: 213 from Kingston or Sutton; K9 from Epsom. 7-10 mins walk Motspur Park railway stn. By car: A3 to New Malden roundabout, L to Worcester Park, 3rd turning on L.* Home-made teas. **Adm £3, chd free (share to Wildlife Aid). Sun 29 June (2-6). Evening Opening £3.50,**

wine, Wed 2 July (6-9).
Garden designed by owner with Japanese theme featuring a waterfall, wildlife and fish ponds and wide variety of planting incl tree ferns, palms, banana, acers and bamboos. Various seating areas and water features. Secluded decking with pergola, pots, scented plants and summerhouse. All in 90ft x 40ft.

33 BALMUIR GARDENS, SW15
Putney SW15 6NG. Mrs Gay Wilson. *5 mins walk from Putney mainline stn. Off the Upper Richmond Rd on corner with Howards Lane. Buses: 337, 430.* **Adm £2.50, chd 50p. Sun 25 May (2-6).**
Designer's garden with secluded tiny mixed borders backed by stained beams, slate and pebble mosaics, formal pond with waterfall through moose antlers and still water lily pond. Plenty of planting for shade. Passionate plantswoman who tries out different colour combinations. All crammed into 80ft x 38ft at widest, only 16ft at narrowest.

BARNES GARDENS, SW13
SW13 0JB. **Adm £2 each garden, chd free. Sun 8 June (2-6).**

8 QUEEN'S RIDE
H H Sir Frank & Lady White. *Mainline: Barnes, R down Rocks Lane, then L Queen's Ride. Bus: 22 to Putney Hospital. Disabled parking in drive*
Country-style, informal large garden on a tree-lined corner site facing Barnes Common. Croquet lawn surrounded by a variety of mixed borders. Rose beds and History of the Rose garden. Garden quiz.

2 ST MARY'S GROVE
Tim & Hilary Steele. *5 mins walk across Common from Barnes stn. Private rd, free parking*
Contemporary walled urban family garden divided into a decked area with raised herb bed and pergola, pool area with lavender border, lawn with border of maples, birches and grasses, and, to the rear of the garden, a children's play area separated by olive trees and bamboo. Featured in 'Evening Standard' magazine' & 'Homes & Gardens'.

12 WESTMORELAND ROAD

Mrs Norman Moore. *Buses: 33, 72, 209, 283, 419 to the Red Lion from Hammersmith*
Raised stone terrace planted with choisya, wisteria, jasmine and decorative herbs. Two lower lawns, densely planted borders and pretty gazebo with solanum, golden hop, roses and clematis. Circular lawn with mulberry tree, hydrangeas, ferns and hostas.

BARNET GARDENS

EN5 1EJ. *Tube: Midway between High Barnet and Totteridge & Whetstone stns, 20 mins walk. Buses: 34, 234, 263, 326, alight at junction of Great North Rd, Cherry Hill and Lynsdown Ave.* Home-made teas & wine. **Combined adm £3.50, chd free (share to North London Hospice). Sun 20 July (1-5.30).**

10 CHERRY HILL

Graham & Jean Shaddick
Modern, colourful front garden of terraced house. Back garden 60ft x 18ft immaculately maintained and planted for maximum colour impact.

45 GREAT NORTH ROAD

Ron & Miriam Raymond
80ft x 80ft cottage-style front garden. Wide variety of unusual plants. Rear garden consists of tiered beds, a small pond and features an extensive variety of well-planted tubs and specialist begonias. Interesting collections of origanums and ferns. 'Name that Plant' competition and children's treasure trail. 2nd prize London Borough of Barnet Best Front Garden.

NEW 17 BELSIZE LANE, NW3

Hampstead NW3 5AD. Maureen Michaelson & Ivan Fiser, 020 7435 0510, mm@maureenmichaelson.com. *Tube: Belsize Park, 5 mins or Finchley Rd 15 mins. Mainline stn: Hampstead Heath 10 mins. Buses: C11, 168 & 268 stop opp Royal Free Hospital off corner of Belsize Lane, 13, 46, 82 & 113 all 10 mins.* **Adm £2.50, chd free. Sun 7 Sept (2-6). Visitors also welcome by appt all yr, coaches permitted.** Newly-created garden (autumn 2006) rapidly establishing, with backdrop of mature trees. Irregularly shaped plot gradually reveals design of different moods and all-yr colour and texture. Pergolas with many climbers; small pond; unusual plants; container planting. Curved beds for dry, shady, woodland planting. Sculptural installations and work of contemporary artists, incl stunning ceramic pots. Access for wheelchair 69cm.

Small, deep pond (protected by pots) with unusually friendly frogs . . .

52A BERRYLANDS ROAD

Surbiton KT5 8PD. Dr Tim & Mrs Julia Leunig. *A3 to Tolworth; A240 (dir Kingston) for approx 1m, then R into Berrylands Rd (after Fire Stn). 52A is on R after Xrds.* Home-made teas. **Adm £2.50, chd free. Sun 13 July (2.30-5.30).**
Professionally designed and planted T-shaped garden. Lawn and patio surrounded by lavender, cistus, albizia, tetrapanex, abutilon, roses and ginger. Natural wooded area under copper beech arranged around pond, stream and waterfall with eucalyptus, bamboo, tree fern, gunnera etc.

64 BLENHEIM GARDENS, NW2

NW2 4NT. Claudia Kerner. *5 mins walk from Willesden Green tube. Buses: 260, 266, 460 to corner of Walm Lane & Anson Rd.* **Adm £2.50, chd free. Sun 22 June (2-5).**
Mixed shrubs, roses, climbers and perennials informally planted to give a lush and dense effect. Garden is organically maintained. Pergola area with wildlife pond. Small, shady hideaway. Courtyard with statue and containers. Recent changes incl more grasses to achieve a natural, soft appearance and patio pots with long-lasting displays of acers, palm trees and bamboos.

NEW 27 BLENHEIM ROAD, NW8

NW8 0LX. Jan Morgan. *Tube: St John's Wood 7/8mins walk. Buses: 13, 113 stop at Marlborough Place off Finchley Rd, or 139, 189 request stop for Blenheim Rd on Abbey Rd. (Free parking at open times).* Home-made teas. **Adm £3, chd free. Sun 27 July (3-5.30). Evening Opening £4, chd free, Pimm's, Thur 24 July (6.30-8.30).**
Stylish front garden with profusion of topiary and fragrant seasonally changed flowers. Winner of many awards. Back garden is a series of garden 'rooms' defined by beds crammed with climbers, perennials, cottage garden annuals and occasional fruit and vegetables. Small, deep pond (protected by pots) with unusually friendly frogs. Winner Marylebone in Bloom.

NEW 225A BRIXTON ROAD, SW9

SW9 6LW. Deborah Nagan & Michael Johnson, 020 7735 8250, www.naganjohnson.co.uk. *Tube: Oval or Brixton. Buses: 3, 59, 133, 159. Brixton Rd is the A23; 225a is on E side, next to Mostyn Rd.* Home-made teas, wine & light refreshments. **Adm £3, chd free. Sat 2 Aug (3-8). Visitors also welcome by appt Aug to Sept only, max 6 people. 1 week's notice required.**
New garden to complement modern extension. Basement level with pool and upper level of metal raised beds. Mixed vegetable, fruit and perennial planting in 'rusty' colour palette. A modern urban oasis. Children must be supervised around pond and steps.

15A BUCKLAND CRESCENT, NW3

NW3 5DH. Lady Barbirolli. *Tube: Swiss Cottage. Buses: 46, 113 (6 mins) or 268 (request stop nearby).* **Adm £2.50, chd free. Sun 22 June (2.30-5.30).**
1/3 -acre; well-kept and interesting collection of shrubs and plants, incl a small bamboo bed, in well-designed garden, personally designed and maintained at all times.

THE BUNGALOW, N2
15 Elm Gardens. N2 0TF. Paul Harrington & Patsy Joseph. *Tube: E Finchley, then East End Rd for ³/₄ m, R into Church Lane, 1st L Elm Gardens. Bus: 143 to Five Bells PH, then 2 mins walk; 263 to E Finchley Library, then 5 mins walk up Church Lane.* **Adm £2.50, chd free. Sun 20 July (2-6).** Mediterranean cottage-style front garden crammed with tender exotics: aloes, beschorneria, manettia, melaleucas and a 12ft high tetrapanax. Side garden an array of ferns under a canopy of climbing trachelospermum and mandevilla. Leafy rear garden. Thalia dealbata which flowered in 2005 takes centre stage in a small pond, also home for 2 terrapins.
✖ ☕

5 BURBAGE ROAD, SE24
SE24 9HJ. Crawford & Rosemary Lindsay, 020 7274 5610, www.rosemarylindsay.com. *Nr junction with Half Moon Lane. Herne Hill mainline stn, 5 mins walk. Buses: 3, 37, 40, 68, 196, 468.* Home-made teas. **Adm £2.50, chd free. Sun 27 Apr (2-5). Evening Opening** £3, wine, Wed 18 June (6-8.30). **Also open 27 Apr Mulberry House. Visitors also welcome by appt.** Garden of member of The Society of Botanical Artists. 150ft x 40ft with large and varied range of plants. Herb garden, herbaceous borders for sun and shade, climbing plants, pots, terraces, lawns. Newly planted gravel areas to reduce watering.
✖ ❀ ☕ ☎

NEW 12 BUSHBERRY ROAD, E9
Bushberry Vale E9 5SX. Molly St Hilaire. *Mainline stn: Homerton, then 5 mins walk. Buses: 26, 30, 388 and S2, alight Hackney Wick.* Home-made teas. **Adm £1.50, chd free. Sun 22 June (2-5). Also open 17 Daintry Way.** Petite courtyard garden with water feature. Rambling roses, jasmine, vine and clematis cover the overarching pergola. 2nd prizewinner Hackney In Bloom, Best Container Garden.
❀ ☕

7 BYNG ROAD
High Barnet EN5 4NW. Mr & Mrs Julian Bishop, 020 8440 2042. Home-made teas. **Adm £2.50, chd free (share to Barnet Hospital**

Special Care Baby Unit). **Sun 7 Sept (2-5).** Plantaholic heaven, packed with unusual flowers, incl many salvias, rudbeckias and crocosmias. Organic garden divided into different sections - bright 'hot' coloured area and more subdued planting through an arch. Tropical border. Experimental Piet Oudolf-inspired front garden with knautias, persicarias, helianthus and contrasting yellows. Many pots full of pampered treasures.
✖ ❀ ☕

> ## Hidden away at end of unmade track lies this ¹/₂-acre 'secret garden', formerly a Victorian nursery . . .

35 CAMBERWELL GROVE, SE5
SE5 8JA. Lynette Hemmant & Juri Gabriel, 020 7703 6186, jurigabriel@compuserve.com. *From Camberwell Green go down Camberwell Church St. Turn R into Camberwell Grove.* **Adm £3.50, chd free (share to St Giles Church Restoration Fund). Evening Opening,** wine, Sat 31 May (5-8.30). **Visitors also welcome by appt May 15 to end June, groups of 10+, coaches permitted.** 120ft x 20ft garden with backdrop of St Giles Church. Evolved over 22yrs into country-style garden brimming with colour and overflowing with pots. In June spectacular roses swamp the artist's studio and festoon an old iron staircase. Featured in 'Time Out'.
✖ ☎

13 CAMBRIDGE ROAD, SW20
SW20 0SQ. Mike & Gail Werkmeister. *1m Wimbledon town centre. Mainline stn: Raynes Park, 5 mins walk. Tube: Wimbledon. Buses: 57, 131, 152, 163, 200. Close to Coombe Lane (A238) junction of A3.* Home-made teas. **Adm £2.50, chd free (share to NCT). Sun 31 Aug (12-6).**

Garden designer's secluded garden of approx ¹/₆ acre. Stone terrace with formal pond leading to lawn, gravel paths and mixed borders abundantly planted with trees, shrubs and herbaceous plants for yr-round interest. Features incl unusual plants, yew hedges, ancient mulberry and strawberry trees and conservatory with prolific grapevine.
✖ ❀ ☕

CAPEL MANOR GARDENS
See Hertfordshire.

5 CECIL ROAD, N10
Muswell Hill N10 2BU. Ben Loftus, 020 8883 6695. *Just off Alexandra Park Rd between Muswell Hill & N Circular Rd, off Roseberry Rd.* **Adm £2.50, chd free. Sun 29 June (2-5). Also open 5 St Regis Close. Visitors also welcome by appt.** Garden designer's sloping garden with unusual small trees, shrubs and perennials. Garden office with green roof of bulbs etc.
✖ ☎

71 CENTRAL HILL, SE19
SE19 1BS. Sue Williams. *Stns: Gipsy Hill & Crystal Palace. On Central Hill, midway between Harold Rd & Rockmount Rd, is narrow, unmade road. Proceed to bottom of this and garden is through cast iron gates. No parking in lane.* Home-made teas. **Adm £3, chd free. Sun 13 July (2-5).** Hidden away at end of unmade track lies this ¹/₂-acre 'secret garden'. Formerly a Victorian nursery, the garden is now an eclectic mix of large traditional herbaceous beds and structural Mediterranean planting. Wildlife pond, 2 formal ponds and numerous objects of C19 architectural salvage provide further interest.
✖ ☕

CENTRE FOR WILDLIFE GARDENING, SE15
28 Marsden Road, Peckham SE15 4EE. The London Wildlife Trust, 020 7252 9186, www.wildlondon.org.uk. *Stn: East Dulwich, 10 mins walk. Behind Goose Green, between Ondine & Oglander Rds.* Light refreshments & teas. **Adm £2, chd free (share to London Wildlife Trust). Open Tues, Weds, Thurs & Suns 10.30-4.30, closed 2 weeks Christmas. For NGS: Sun 18 May (12.30-4.30).** Inspirational community wildlife garden. Hedges, ponds and meadows complement beds brimming with

herbs, cottage garden plants and wild flowers. Yr-round interest. Organic vegetable beds, wild flower nursery and tree scheme, beehives. Visitor Centre with wildlife gardening displays and advice, workshops and children's craft activities. Picnic and family areas. Groups of up to 20 during opening times by appt. Green Pennant Award.

CHARTERHOUSE, EC1
Charterhouse Square EC1M 6AN. *Buses: 4, 55. Tube: Barbican. Turn L out of stn L into Carthusian St & into square. Entrance through car park.* **Evening Opening £5, wine, Tue 17 June (6-9).** Enclosed courtyard gardens within the grounds of the historic Charterhouse, which dates back to 1347. 'English Country Garden' style featuring roses, ancient mulberry trees and small pond. Various garden herbs found here are still used in the kitchen today. Buildings not open. Meet the gardener who will answer questions. Gravel paths.

◆ CHELSEA PHYSIC GARDEN, SW3
66 Royal Hospital Road. SW3 4HS. Chelsea Physic Garden self-funding charity, 020 7352 5646, www.chelseaphysicgarden.co.uk. *Bus: 239. Tube: Sloane Square (10 mins). Parking Battersea Park (charged). Entrance in Swan Walk (except wheelchairs).* **Adm £7, chd/concessions £4. 1st & 2nd weekends in Feb (11-4); 19 Mar to 31 Oct, Weds, Thurs, Fris (12-5), Suns & Bank Hol Mons (12-6). For NGS: Sun 23 Mar (12-6).** Oldest Botanic Garden in London. 3¾ acres; medicinal and herb garden, perfumery border; family order beds; historical walk, glasshouses. Cool fernery and Robert Fortune's tank pond. Guided and audio tours.

24 CHESTNUT ROAD, SE27
West Norwood SE27 9LF. Paul Brewer & Anne Rogerson. *Stns: West Norwood or Tulse Hill. Buses: 2, 68, 196, 322, 432, 468. Off S end of Norwood Rd, nr W Norwood Cemetery.* **Home-made teas. Adm £1.50, chd free, concessions £1 (share to Sound Minds). Sun 1 June (2-5). Evening Opening £3, wine, Sun 7 Sept (6-8.30). Also open 1 June Ardlui Gardens, 66A East Dulwich Rd & 167 Rosendale Rd.**

Well-stocked front garden. Compact rear garden with patios, decking, pond and unusual gazebo in recycled wood. Lush planting with gunnera, vintage ferns, bamboos and banana. Lots of pots. Penguin.

CHEVENING
See Kent.

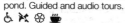

Wire-work pergola reveals wild garden with ancient apple trees, climbing roses and beehive . . .

CHISWICK MALL, W4
W6 9TN. *Tube: Stamford Brook. Buses: 27, 190, 267 & 391 to Young's Corner from Hammersmith through St Peter's Sq under A4 to river. By car A4 westbound turn off at Eyot Gdns S, then R into Chiswick Mall.* **Home-made teas. Adm £2 each garden, chd free. Sun 25 May (2-6).** Riverside community near Chiswick Eyot.

EYOT COTTAGE
Mrs Peter Trumper
Two interconnecting gardens, both with beautiful river frontage. One an old walled garden with many unusual white plants and shrubs, the other an upper terrace garden laid out by owners with imaginative use of old stones and pavers.

16 EYOT GARDENS, W6
Ms Dianne Farris
Small town garden. Front garden planted to complement Victorian house. Back garden shows what

can be done with a small space, by using the walls for yr-round interest. Terrace, fountain and garden art.

LINGARD HOUSE
Rachel Austin
Walled garden divided into brick courtyard and terrace with huge acacia tree; formal lawn with miniature pond and water-spout and unusual herbaceous planting. Wire-work pergola reveals wild garden with ancient apple trees, climbing roses and beehive.

SWAN HOUSE
Mr & Mrs George Nissen
Informal walled garden. Herbaceous border, fruit trees, small vegetable garden. Tiny greenhouse. Small wild flower area. 2 ponds and a rill.

NEW 44 CHOLMELEY CRESCENT, N6
N6 5HA. Mrs Patrizia Gutierrez, 07850 756784, yulia@gardenshrink.com. *Tube: Highgate. Buses: 43, 134.* **Home-made teas. Adm £2.50, chd free. Sun 8 June (2-6.30). Visitors also welcome by appt.** Contemporary family garden designed by Chelsea medal winner, Yulia Badian. Hardwood decking extends the living space. A boardwalk through 3 arches leads to summerhouse with green roof. Gabion baskets planted and filled with slate form an unusual retaining wall. Immaculate lawn. Low maintenance planting gives yr-round colour and scent.

51 CHOLMELEY CRESCENT, N6
Highgate N6 5EX. Ernst Sondheimer, 020 8340 6607, ernst@sondheimer.fsnet.co.uk. *Between Highgate Hill & Archway Rd, off Cholmeley Park. Tube: Highgate.* **Adm £2, chd free. Visitors welcome by appt.** Approx ⅙-acre garden with many alpines in screes, peat beds, tufa, troughs and greenhouse; shrubs, rhododendrons, camellias, magnolias, pieris, ceanothus etc. Clematis, bog plants, roses, primulas, tree ferns. Water features. Garden on steep slope with many steps and narrow paths.

CHOUMERT SQUARE, SE15
SE15 4RE. **The Residents.** *Via wrought iron gates off Choumert Grove. Peckham Rye mainline stn is visible from the gates, & buses galore (12, 36, 37, 63, 78, 171, 312, 345) less than 10 mins walk. Free car park 2 mins.* Light refreshments, teas & wine. **Adm £2.50, chd 50p, concessions £1.50 (share to St Christopher's Hospice).** Sun 8 June (1-6). **Also open 5 Lyndhurst Square.**
About 46 mini gardens with maxi-planting in a Shangri-la situation that the media has described as a 'Floral Canyon', which leads to small communal 'secret garden'. Art, craft and home-made produce stalls and live music. Delicious refreshments. Gardens and village Fête in one!. Winner Best Community Garden Southwark in Bloom. Featured in 'The Guardian'.
  🚫 ✕ ⊕ ☕

COLUMCILLE
9 Norlands Crescent, Chislehurst BR7 5RN. **Nancy & Jim Pratt, 020 8467 9383, nancyandjim@btinternet.com.** *Off A222 turn into Cricket Ground Rd, then 1st R into Norlands Cres. approx ½ m from Chislehurst BR stn. Buses: 162 or 269, Bank House stop.* Home-made teas. **Adm £3, chd free.** Sun 17 Aug (2-5). **Visitors also welcome by appt June to Sept.**
Small garden featuring Japanese sanctuary, influenced by Zen tradition, incl water feature, lanterns, traditional Japanese plants and garden shed transformed into a tea house. Also cottage garden section with colourful display of roses, lupins, peonies and delphiniums, especially in June; dahlias and day lilies Aug and Sept.
  🚫 ✕ ⊕ ☕ ☎

NEW 113 CORRINGHAM ROAD, NW11
Hampstead Garden Suburb NW11 7DL. **Veronica Clein.** *Tube: Golders Green, then 10mins walk. Entrance to courtyard between 101 & 117 Corringham Rd (Hampstead Way end).* Home-made teas. **Adm £2.50, chd free.**
Sun 22 June (2-6).
Garden designer and plantswoman's garden created since 2005 behind a house in a listed Arts and Crafts courtyard. The formal garden is profusely planted with perennials, unusual annuals and shrubs, with an emphasis on painterly colour

combinations. Small woodland garden, atmospheric sculptured figure, potager, greenhouse and lavishly planted containers. Prizewinner Hampstead Garden Suburb Hort Soc 'Suburb in Bloom' Best Garden competition 2007.
  🚫 ✕ ⊕ ☕

COTTAGE FARM
See Kent.

142 COURT LANE, SE21
Dulwich SE21 7EB. **Jeremy & Jackie Prescott.** *Nr Court Lane entrance to Dulwich Park, ½ m from Dulwich Village (N Dulwich mainline stn & P4 bus). Also buses 40, 176, 185.* Light refreshments & teas. **Adm £3, chd free (share to St Christopher's Hospice).** Sun 8 June (2-6) **with live guitar music. Also open North House & 174 Peckham Rye.**
½ -acre garden at former home of Anne Shelton (the Forces' Favourite), backing on to Dulwich Park. 'Country' garden planted from 1994 featuring roses, mixed borders, fruit trees and vegetable garden, all on a circular theme. New sundial.
  🚫 ✕ ☕

Planting is intended to be robust enough to cope with the attentions of a small dog . . .

18 CRANMER ROAD
Hampton Hill TW12 1DW. **Bernard Wigginton, 020 8979 4596.** *Between A312 (Uxbridge Rd) & A313 (Park Rd). Bus: 285 from Kingston stops at end of rd. Stn: Fulwell 15 mins walk.* **Adm £2.50, chd free.** Sun 11 May (2-5). **Evening Opening £3.50, wine, Sun 20 July (5-8). Visitors also welcome by appt May to July only.**
Medium-sized garden with herbaceous and mixed borders. WW2 air raid shelter transformed as rockery and water garden with azaleas, helianthemums and foliage plants. Dahlia bed, containers with seasonal planting and small wild flower meadow. Wheelchair access to main lawn only.
  🚫 ✕ ☎

NEW 17 CRESCENT LANE, SW4
SW4 9PT. **Sue Sumner.** *Near junction of Abbeville Rd and Crescent Lane. nb NOT in one-way part of Crescent Lane.* Home-made teas. **Adm £2, chd free.** Sun 8 June (3-6).
Long garden, opening into a square lawn, surrounded by roses, shrubs and trees with a pond, backed by a yew hedge. The design is unusual and the planting predominantly focuses on blue and white and is intended to be robust enough to cope with the attentions of a small dog.
  ✕ ☕

NEW 17 DAINTRY WAY, E9
E9 5JJ. **Mr Ebrahim Sali, 07931 767993, h2osali@yahoo.co.uk, www.thelawns.org/sali.** *Silverlink: Hackney Wick, then 5 mins walk. By car, from Eastway (A12) turn L into Osborn Rd (opp Hackney Baths Community Centre), then immed R into Daintry Way. Parking available.* **Adm £1.50, chd free.** Sun 22 June (2-5). **Also open 12 Bushberry Rd. Visitors also welcome by appt June to Aug.**
Invaluable garden to visit for planting ideas in a small space. Front 15ft x 4ft, rear 20ft x 6ft, incl seating area and tiny 'work area' for potting on. Container and hanging basket planting incl herbaceous plants, climbers and shrubs. A mimosa, banana and palm trees provide height. Plant list available. Demonstration of plant cuttings and seed sowing on request. Winner Best Container Garden Hackney in Bloom.
  🚫 ✕ ⊕ ☎

DE BEAUVOIR GARDENS, N1
N1 4LH. *Tubes: Highbury & Islington then buses 30 or 277 from St Paul's Rd; or Angel tube then 38 or 73 bus, alight at stop after Essex Rd stn. Cars via Southgate Rd, park in Northchurch Rd or via Kingsland & Downham Rd.* **Combined adm £3.50, or £2 each garden.** Sun 15 June (2-6).
2 mature gardens in a leafy enclave of period houses.
☕

  158 CULFORD ROAD
Gillian Blachford, 020 7254 3780, gmblachford@btopenworld.com. Visitors also welcome by appt, June only.
Small town garden, long and

narrow, with a romantic feel. Winding path and herbaceous borders, incl shrubs, small trees and perennials. Many unusual plants.

21 NORTHCHURCH TERRACE

Ms Nancy Korman, 020 7249 4919, n.korman@lse.ac.uk. **Visitors also welcome by appt June only, up to 8 at one time.** Walled town garden (30ft x 75ft) with formal feel. Deep herbaceous borders, pond, fruit trees, pergola, patio pots and herb beds. Entrance down 4 steps.

NEW DOWNINGS ROAD MOORING BARGE GARDENS, SE1

31 Mill Street. SE1 2AX. Mr Nicholas Lacey. *Close to Tower Bridge & Design Museum. Mill St off Jamaica Rd, between London Bridge & Bermondsey stns, Tower Hill also nearby. Buses: 47, 188, 381, RV1.* **Adm £3, chd free. Sun 27 July (2-5).** Series of 7 floating barge gardens connected by walkways and bridges. Gardens have an eclectic range of plants for yr-round seasonal interest. Marine environment: suitable shoes and care needed. Not suitable for small children. Featured in RHS 'The Garden'. Cover photograph for 'Time Out' waterways supplement. Highly Commended Southwark in Bloom competition.

36 DOWNS HILL

Beckenham BR3 5HB. Marc & Janet Berlin, 020 8650 9377. *3m W of Bromley. 2 mins from Ravensbourne mainline stn nr top of Foxgrove Rd.* **Adm £2, chd free. Suns 27 Apr; 6 July; Fri 3 Oct (2-5). Also open 6 July Harcourt House. Visitors also welcome by appt.** Long 2/3 -acre E-facing, award-winning, garden sloping steeply away from house. Ponds, water courses and sheltered patio area with many tender unusual plants and hundreds of pots. Wooded area, dense planting of trees, shrubs and flowers. Raised beds, paths and patio areas. Alpine house, bulbs in pots. Display of auriculas in April.

170 DOYLE GARDENS, NW10

Kensal Rise/Willesden NW10 3SU. James Duncan Mattoon, 020 8961 6243. *Tube: Kensal Green, up College Rd, L into Liddell Gdns which becomes Doyle Gdns.* Home-made teas. **Adm £2.50, chd free. Suns 1 June; 3 Aug (2-7). Visitors also welcome by appt.** Professional plantsman's private fantasy garden with an impossibly tropical theme: musa, trachycarpus, yucca, puya, plumbago, grasses. Garden 95% organic and incl many native and introduced wild flowers to help create a natural effect and promote wildlife. Frog and newt pond, log piles and over 350 plant species, living with slugs and snails! Featured on BBC2 Open Gardens.

15 DUKES AVENUE, N10

N10 2PS. Vivienne Parry. *Short walk from main Muswell Hill roundabout. Buses: 43, 134, alight Muswell Hill Broadway or 7 from Finsbury Park. Tube: Highgate, then bus 43 or 134.* Home-made teas. **Adm £2.50, chd free. Sun 18 May (2-5). Also open 46 Dukes Ave & 33 Wood Vale.** Mediterranean-style gravel front garden in silver, lilacs, pinks and blues. Small lawned back garden with wide variety of plants, many unusual. Large plant sale including rarer salvias and other plants for dry, sunny sites.

46 DUKES AVENUE, N10

Muswell Hill N10 2PU. Judith Glover, www.judithglover.com. *Short walk from main Muswell Hill roundabout. Tube: Highgate then bus 43 or 134 to Muswell Hill Broadway or bus 7 from Finsbury Park.* **Adm £2.50, chd free. Sun 18 May (2-5). Also open 15 Dukes Ave & 33 Wood Vale.** Designer and botanical illustrator's country-style garden described as being 'just on the right side of controlled chaos'. Organic, curvy beds with foxgloves, aquilegias, irises and valerian anchored with clipped evergreens. Topiary, grasses and driftwood throne from medal-winning garden designed for Chelsea Flower Show. Featured in 'Ideal Home' magazine & '25 Beautiful Gardens'. Steep steps, not suitable for small children or the infirm.

DULWICH GARDENS, SE21

SE21 7BJ. *Mainline: London Bridge to N Dulwich & from Victoria to W Dulwich then 10-15 mins walk. Tube: Brixton then P4 bus passes both gardens. Street parking.* Home-made teas. **Combined adm £4.50, chd free (share to Macmillan, Local Branch). Sun 15 June (2-5). Also open 27 Thorpewood Ave.** 2 Georgian houses with large gardens, 2 mins walk from Dulwich Picture Gallery and Dulwich Park.

103 DULWICH VILLAGE

Mr & Mrs N Annesley About 1/2 -acre 'country garden in London'. Long herbaceous border, spacious lawn, ornamental pond, roses and many and varied other plants, plus fruit and vegetable garden.

105 DULWICH VILLAGE

Mr & Mrs A Rutherford. About 1/2 acre, mostly herbaceous with lawns and lots of old-fashioned roses. Shrubbery, ornamental pond, water garden. Very pretty garden with many unusual plants.

> Series of 7 floating barge gardens connected by walkways and bridges . . . suitable shoes and care needed . . .

66A EAST DULWICH ROAD, SE22

East Dulwich. SE22 9AT. Kevin Wilson, 020 8693 3458. *Basement flat overlooking Goose Green, opp Dulwich swimming baths. Walking distance East Dulwich mainline stn. Buses: 37, 176, 185.* **Adm £2.50, chd £1 (share to Goose Green School). Suns 1 June; 6 July; 10 Aug (12-6). Evening Opening £3.50, wine, Sun 7 Sept (4-9). Visitors also welcome by appt, parties of 10+.**

Exciting Secret Garden, 135ft long, full of delights with a very special atmosphere. Lush planting, with owner's own sculpture throughout. A perfect spot for contemplation.

NEW EAST FINCHLEY COTTAGE GARDENS, N2

N2 8JJ. *Tube: East Finchley 12 mins walk. Bus: 263 to library, turn L into Church Lane, R into Trinity Rd. Car: turn into Trinity Rd from Long Lane, off Church Lane.* **Combined adm £3, chd free. Sun 18 May (2-5.30).**
Three very different cottage gardens.

NEW 399 LONG LANE
Jonathan Maitland
Tiny front and back gardens created from scratch in the last 18 months. Selection of evergreen shrubs form backdrop to curved raised beds and collection of pots. Small pond. Places to sit in this yr-round intimate refuge.

NEW 20 TRINITY ROAD
Jane Meir
Densely planted small town garden belonging to student of horticulture. Inherited harsh hard landscaping fast disappearing to create exuberant and varied planting space. Some areas still evolving and used as 'test' areas.

NEW 22 TRINITY ROAD
J Maitland
Densely planted courtyard of vivid contrasts. Cottage garden plants mingle happily with elegant ferns and grasses. A majestic black bamboo towers over pots of dainty annuals. Neatly clipped box accentuates sprawling climbers. Giant trachycarpus palm falls over a feathery tamarix. Sturdy fig tree guards a small pond. Completely organic garden.

NEW 96 EAST SHEEN AVENUE, SW14
SW14 8AU. **Alex Clarke.** *Buses: 33, 367 along Upper Richmond Rd, alight end of East Sheen Ave.* **Adm £3, chd free. Sun 10 Aug (2-5).**
70ft x 30ft garden, recently redesigned to incl an innovative stream water feature. Plantaholic's collection of tender and unusual plants providing yr-round interest and vibrant colour, shape and texture. Shed with green roof. At end of garden are hidden, established and very well maintained allotments, also open.

ECCLESTON SQUARE, SW1
SW1V 1NP. **Roger Phillips & the Residents.** *Off Belgrave Rd nr Victoria stn, parking allowed on Suns.* Home-made teas. **Adm £3, chd £1.50. Sun 11 May (2-5).**
Planned by Cubitt in 1828, the 3-acre square is subdivided into mini-gardens with camellias, iris, ferns and containers. Dramatic collection of tender climbing roses and 20 different forms of tree peonies. National Collection of ceanothus incl more than 70 species and cultivars.
NCCPG

EDWARDES SQUARE, W8
W8 6HL. **Edwardes Square Garden Committee.** *Tube: Kensington High St & Earls Court. Buses: 9, 10, 27, 28, 31, 49 & 74 to Odeon Cinema. Entrance in South Edwardes Square.* Home-made teas. **Adm £3.50, chd free. Sun 6 Apr (12-5).**
One of London's prettiest secluded garden squares. 3½ acres laid out differently from other squares, with serpentine paths by Agostino Agliothe, Italian artist and decorator who lived at no.15 from 1814-1820, and a beautiful Grecian temple which is traditionally the home of the gardener. Romantic rose tunnel winds through the middle of the garden. Good displays of bulbs and blossom.

ELM TREE COTTAGE
85 Croham Road, South Croydon CR2 7HJ. **Wendy Witherick & Michael Wilkinson,** 020 8681 8622. *2m S of Croydon. Off B275 from Croydon, off A2022 from Selsdon, bus 64.* **Adm £2.50. Suns 11 May; 8 June; 13 July; 10 Aug (1-5). Visitors also welcome by appt May to Aug for groups of 6+, no coaches.**
Cottage garden transformed into an oasis of sharp gardening. Agaves, grasses, yuccas, olives, kniphofia, iris, alliums, phormiums, phlomis, figs. Topiary boxwood, taxus and much more. Designed to be drought-tolerant/low maintenance. Not suitable for those unsteady on their feet and beware spikes of 50 varieties of agave! Regret no children.

6 EMERALD HOUSE, NW3
1c King Henry's Road, Primrose Hill NW3 3QP. **Dr Catherine Horwood Barwise,** 020 7483 2601, cbarwise@gmail.com, www.emerald-house.co.uk. *Tube: Chalk Farm, 5 mins walk. Buses: 31, 168, 393 or C11, 274, 24, 27 (10 mins).* **Adm £3, chd free. Visitors welcome by appt July & Aug for groups of 5-15.**
Stunning S-facing L-shaped roof terrace garden stuffed with unusual shrubs, tender perennials, clematis and succulents, chosen to cope with extreme weather conditions. Raised trays and tubs of alpines surround water feature topped with wind-swept hanging baskets of echeverias and sempervivums. Species pelargoniums and exotic aeoniums compete with breathtaking views across London.

71 FALLOWCOURT AVENUE, N12
Finchley N12 0BE. **Yasuko & John O'Gorman.** *7 mins walk from West Finchley stn, between Ballards Lane & Finchley High Rd. Buses: 82, 125, 263 & 460 to Finchley Memorial Hospital.* Home-made teas & light refreshments. **Adm £2, chd free. Sun 1 June (2-5.30).**
Well maintained 120ft x 30ft S-facing plot. Densely planted garden of trees, shrubs and perennials, at its first peak in May/June. Sunlit borders and shaded area with an intimate patio at rear, not immediately visible from the house. Many Japanese varieties: tree peonies, maples, magnolias, cherry blossoms, azaleas, hydrangeas, hostas and irises.

Densely planted courtyard of vivid contrasts. . . .

◆ FENTON HOUSE, NW3

Hampstead Grove. NW3 6RT. *The National Trust*, 020 7435 3471, **www.nationaltrust.org.uk.** *300yds from Hampstead tube. Entrances: top of Holly Hill & Hampstead Grove.* For NGS: **Evening Openings** £3.50, chd £1.50, wine, Thurs 15 May; 5 June (6.30-8.30).

Timeless 1½ -acre walled garden, laid out on three levels, containing imaginative plantings concealed by yew hedges. The herbaceous borders give yr-round interest while the brick-paved sunken rose garden provides a sheltered hollow of scent and colour. The formal lawn area contrasts with the rustic charm of the kitchen garden and orchard. Vine house. In spring, good borders and underplanted orchard.

54 FERNDOWN

Northwood Hills HA6 1PH. David & Ros Bryson, 020 8866 3792. *Tube: Northwood Hills 5 mins walk. R out of stn, R down Briarwood Drive then 1st R.* **Adm £3, chd free.** Sun 7 Sept (10-5). **Visitors also welcome by appt.**
Unusual collection of exotics, cacti and Australasian plants. Palm trees, tree ferns and bananas set in an original design. Elevated deck overlooks the garden underplanted with rare ferns and aroids.

14 FRANK DIXON WAY, SE21

SE21 7ET. Frank & Angie Dunn. *Stn: W Dulwich. From Dulwich Village pass Dulwich Gallery on R, Frank Dixon Way (private rd) 500metres on L.* Home-made teas. **Adm £3, chd free.** Sun 11 May (2-5).
Large family garden surrounded by mature trees, low maintenance shrub borders and annual plantings. Lawns. Sit-on railway around the garden for children's rides.

FROGNAL GARDENS, NW3

Hampstead NW3 6UY. *Tube: Hampstead. Buses: 46, 268 to Hampstead High St. Frognal Gardens 2nd R off Church Row from Heath St.* Home-made teas. **Combined adm £3, chd 50p.** Sun 22 June (2-5).
Two neighbouring gardens divided by path lined with trellises of cascading roses and clematis, underplanted with carpets of flowers.

5 FROGNAL GARDENS

Ruth & Brian Levy
Long narrow structured garden romantically planted with soft colours and profusion of unusual climbers and cottage perennials.

5A FROGNAL GARDENS

Ian & Barbara Jackson
Small, beautifully landscaped garden with lawn, colourful flower beds and containers. A garden to enjoy and relax in.

NEW 13 GIPSY HILL, SE19

Crystal Palace SE19. Jon & Eils Digby-Rogers. *Stn: Gipsy Hill. Bus: 322 from Clapham Junction via Herne Hill goes up Gipsy Hill, Crystal Palace buses within walking distance.* **Adm £3, chd free.** Sat 2 Aug (2-5.30).
Secluded town garden, 17m x 17m, protected by high brick wall and steep shrub-covered bank. York stone terraced areas with many coloured glazed and terracotta pots. Wide variety of different shrubs, climbers and perennials for yr-round colour. Wisteria-covered oak-framed pergola, summerhouse, large blown glass and copper fountain, all providing outside rooms for the home.

70 GLOUCESTER CRESCENT, NW1

NW1 7EG. Lucy Gent & Malcolm Turner, 020 7485 6906, **l.gent@tiscali.co.uk.** *Camden Town. Bus: any passing through Camden Town. Tube: Camden Town 2 mins, Mornington Crescent 10 mins. Limited metered parking in Oval Rd.* **Adm £2.50, chd free.** Suns 11 May; 8 June; 13 July; 10 Aug; 14 Sept (2-5.30). **Visitors also welcome by appt.**
An unexpected oasis 1 min from Camden Lock, 1840s end-of-terrace house (not open) once lived in by Mrs Charles Dickens. Challenging spaces and shade constraints countered by rich and versatile planting, small trees and large shrubs creating spaces for layers of smaller plants and tender perennials. All-yr interest with a climax of colour in August. Pretty front garden next door.

GOLF COURSE ALLOTMENTS, N11

Winton Avenue N11 2AR. GCAA/Haringey, **http://www.gcaa.pwp.blueyonder.co .uk.** *Tube: Bounds Green approx 1km. Buses: 102, 184, 299 to Sunshine Garden Centre, Durnsford Rd. Then Bidwell Gardens (on foot through park) to Winton Ave. Gate opp junction with Blake Rd.* Light refreshments & teas. **Adm £2.50, chd free (share to GCAA).** Sun 31 Aug (1-4).
Large, long-established allotment with over 200 plots maintained by culturally diverse community growing a wide variety of flowers, fruit and vegetables - some working towards organic cultivation. Picturesque corners and charming sheds. Exhibits and sale of produce and bric-a-brac. Caution needed on rough paths.

28 GRANVILLE PARK, SE13

SE13 7EA. Joanna Herald. *Parking available on street, Suns & eves. 10 mins walk up hill (N) towards Blackheath from Lewisham mainline & DLR stns.* **Adm £3.50, chd free.** **Evening Opening**, wine, Fri 13 June (6-9).
Garden designer's family garden in three sections. Pool garden, mixed herbaceous and shrub planting with bulbs around circular lawns, gravel garden and sunken terrace with pots. 100ft x 35ft.

Challenging spaces and shade constraints countered by rich and versatile planting . . .

NEW 34 GROVE PARK, SE5
Camberwell SE5 8LG.
Christopher & Philippa
Matthews. 1/2 m S of Camberwell.
Stn: Peckham Rye, 10mins walk.
Buses: all to Camberwell Green.
Access to Grove Park by car either
from Chadwick Rd or top of
Camberwell Grove (closed further
down). Home-made teas. Adm
£2.50, chd free. Sat 7 June (2-
5.30).
120ft x 40ft garden started in
2006, designed for yr-round
flowers. Large colour-themed beds
with abundant perennials, old
English roses, alliums, echiums,
cardoons and climbers. Secret
wood at end of garden (limited
access). Packed 100ft S-facing
front garden, best described as
organised chaos.

7 THE GROVE, N6
Highgate Village. N6 6JU. Mr
Thomas Lyttelton, 07713 638161.
The Grove is between Highgate West
Hill & Hampstead Lane. Tube:
Archway or Highgate Village. Buses: 143,
210, 271 to Highgate Village from
Archway, 214 from Camden Town.
Home-made teas. Adm £2.50, chd
free (share to North London
Hospice). Suns 6 Apr; 8 June
(2-5.30). Visitors also welcome by
appt.
1/2 acre designed for max all-yr
interest with its variety of conifers
and other trees, ground cover, water
garden, vistas, 19 paths, surprises.
Exceptional camellias in April.
Wheelchair access to main lawn
only; many very narrow paths.

◆ HAM HOUSE AND GARDEN
Ham, Richmond TW10 7RS. The
National Trust, 020 8940 1950,
www.nationaltrust.org.uk. Mid-way
between Richmond & Kingston. W of
A307 on Surrey bank of R Thames.
Follow National Trust signs. House &
garden £9, chd £5, family £23.
Garden only £3, chd £2, family £8.
Opening days & times vary
according to season; please phone
or visit website for details. For NGS:
Sat 5 July (11-6).
The beautiful C17 gardens incl Cherry
Garden, featuring lavender parterres
flanked by hornbeam arbours; S
terrace with clipped yew cones,
hibiscus and pomegranate trees; eight
grass plats; maze-like wilderness; C17

orangery with working kitchen garden
and licensed café and terrace. Garden
Tours.

116 HAMILTON TERRACE, NW8
NW8 9UT. Mr & Mrs I B Kathuria,
020 7625 6909,
gkathuria@hotmail.co.uk. Tubes:
Maida Vale, 5 mins walk, St John's
Wood, 10 mins walk. Buses: 16, 98
from Marble Arch to Cricklewood.
Home-made teas. Adm £2.50, chd
50p (share to St Mark's Church
Repair Appeal). Sun 22 June (2-6).
Evening Opening £4, chd free,
wine, Sun 20 July (5-9). Visitors also
welcome by appt.
Lush front garden full of dramatic
foliage with a water feature and tree
ferns. Large back garden of different
levels with Yorkshire stone paving,
many large terracotta pots and
containers, water feature and lawn.
Wide variety of perennials and
flowering shrubs, many unusual, and
subtropical plants, succulents, acers,
ferns, hebes, climbers, roses, fuchsias
and prizewinning hostas. Packed with
colour and rich foliage of varied texture.
Prizewinner Hampstead Horticultural
Society; featured in 'GGG'.

> ## Winding pathways, fern garden, Hercules secret garden . . .

157 HAMPSTEAD WAY, NW11
Hampstead Garden Suburb
NW11 7YA. Richard & Carol Kemp.
Tube: Golders Green, then H2 bus to
Hampstead Way. Adm £2.50, chd
free. Sun 20 July (2-5.30). Also open
86 Willifield Way.
Charming, 100ft split-level SW-facing
cottage garden containing a wealth of
colourful and informally planted hardy
perennials and succulents, against a
backdrop of interesting shrubs.
Designed for all-yr interest. Take care,
steps slippery when wet.

NEW HARCOURT HOUSE
Grasmere Road, Bromley
BR1 4BB. Freda Davis, 07958
534074, fredagdavis@aol.com.
11/2 m W of Bromley. WD buses
208, 227 to junction of Highland
Rd. Adm £2, chd free. Sun 6 July
(2-5). Also open 36 Downs Rd,
Beckenham. Visitors also
welcome by appt June to Sept,
coaches permitted or groups of
10+.
Colourful Victorian garden wrapped
around large Victorian house.
Winding pathways, fern garden,
Hercules secret garden, water
features, many statues, unusual
objects incl French antique
lampposts placed among planted
areas. Dozens of pots, many
hanging baskets, large
conservatory in the Victorian style.
Winner Bromley in Bloom Premier
Back Garden.

5 HILLCREST AVENUE, NW11
NW11 0EP. Mrs R M Rees, 020 8455
0419, Ruthmrees@aol.com. Hillcrest
Ave is off Bridge Lane. Buses: 82, 102,
460 to Temple Fortune. Tube: Golders
Green or Finchley Central. Walk down
Bridge Lane. Home-made teas. Adm
£2, chd free (share to Alzheimers
Society, Barnet). Sun 22 June (2-6).
Evening Opening £3, wine, Wed 25
June (5-9). Visitors also welcome by
appt.
Small labour-saving colourful garden
with many interesting features; rockery,
fish pond, conservatory, tree ferns,
secluded patio. Urban jungle front
garden with drought-resistant plants,
traditional back garden. Chairlift
available from decking to main
garden.

24 HILLS ROAD
Buckhurst Hill IG9 5RS. Sue
Hargreaves. Situated between
Epping and Woodford. 5m from
M25 J26, off A104 Epping New Rd.
Mainline: Chingford or Buckhurst Hill.
Home-made teas & renowned wheat-
free cakes. Adm £1.50, chd 50p.
Sun 13 July (2-6).
Herbalist's organic garden
designed by artist. Narrow Victorian
garden featuring elements of
potager using traditional and
contemporary materials and planting.
Many unusual features and details.
Five distinctive areas linked together:
shady sunken terrace, herb garden,

raised sleeper herbaceous beds, vegetable and trained fruit trees. Front garden imaginatively redesigned.

HOLLY COTTAGE
40 Station Road, Hampton TW12 2DA. Marianne Cartwright. *3m W of Kingston. Buses: 68 & 267 to Hampton Church. From river end 5 mins walk. Buses: 111 & 216 pass the house. Alight police stn 100yds. Hampton mainline stn 5 mins.* Home-made teas. **Adm £2, chd free. Suns 8, 15 June (2-6).**
Long front garden planted for winter and spring interest leads on to enchanting paved cottage garden (30ft x 25ft). Densely planted, it contains many roses, clematis and hardy geraniums. Pergola, planted in shades of blue and white, links the two gardens. Ferns, pool, home grown mistletoe on old apple tree.

THE HOLME, NW1
Inner Circle, Regents Park. NW1 4NT. Lessee of The Crown Commission. *Opp Open Air Theatre. Tube: Regents Park or Baker St, over York bridge then L at Inner Circle.* **Adm £3.50, chd free. Sats, Suns 26, 27 Apr; 26, 27 July (2.30-5.30).**
4-acre garden filled with interesting and unusual plants. Sweeping lakeside lawns intersected by islands of herbaceous beds. Extensive rock garden with waterfall, stream and pool. Formal flower garden with unusual annual and half hardy plants, sunken lawn, fountain pool and arbour. Teas available in nearby rose garden. Gravel paths.

239A HOOK ROAD
Chessington KT9 1EQ. Mr & Mrs D St Romaine, 020 8397 3761, derek@gardenphotolibrary.com. *4m S of Kingston. A3 from London, turn L at Hook underpass onto A243 Hook Rd. Garden approx 300yds on L. Parking opp in park. Buses: K4, 71, 465 from Kingston & Surbiton to North Star PH.* **Adm £2.50, chd £1. Sun 8 June (2-6). Evening Opening, £3.50, wine, Wed 11 June (6-9). Visitors also welcome by appt.**
Garden photographer's garden. 1/4 -acre garden divided into two. Flower garden contains a good mix of herbaceous plants, shrubs, climbers

and topiary. Also gravel garden, rose tunnel and pond. Potager, divided by paths into small beds, has many vegetables, soft fruit, fruit trees and herbs all planted with flowers.

Long front garden planted for winter and spring interest leads on to enchanting paved cottage garden . . .

NEW HOPE VILLA
74 High Street, Hampton TW12 2SW. Mrs Elizabeth Joy Lawrence. *100yds from river to Hampton High St. Buses: 111 from Kingston, 216 from Richmond, R68 from Twickenham.* Home-made teas. **Adm £2, chd free. Sun 8 June (2-5.30).**
SW-facing rear cottage garden (50ft x 25ft), densely planted, with small water feature and pergola. Seating areas and many interesting pots. Colour combination of pink and blue with roses and clematis.

HORNBEAMS
Priory Drive, Stanmore HA7 3HN. Dr & Mrs R B Stalbow, 020 8954 2218. *5m SE of Watford. Tube: Stanmore. Priory Drive private rd off Stanmore Hill (A4140 Stanmore-Bushey Heath Rd).* **Adm £3, chd free. Visitors welcome by appt.**
Yr-round garden with creative landscaping designed by owner. In winter incl viburnums, witch hazels, snowdrops; spring, species tulips; summer, colourful containers and ornamental potager; autumn, Muscat grape shading conservatory, cyclamen and schizostylus. All these and much more.

10 HOVEDEN ROAD, NW2
NW2 3XD. Ian Brownhill & Michael Hirschl. *Tube: Kilburn or Willesden Green. Buses: 16, 32, 189, 226, 245, 260, 266 & 316 to Cricklewood Broadway, then consult A-Z.* **Adm £2.50, chd £1.50. Sun 15 June (2-6). Also open 208 Walm Lane.**
70ft x 25ft award-winning urban garden. Stylish deck with pergola and fish pond leads into attractive circular paved area surrounded by box hedging and deeply planted borders. Shade area at the end of the garden features gazebo. No access for wheelchairs or prams.

9 HOWARD ROAD, SE20
Penge SE20 8HQ. Marc Carlton & Nigel Lees, 020 8659 5674, www.foxleas.com. *1m from Beckenham or Crystal Palace. 6 mins walk from Penge East, Anerley & Kent House stns, and Ave Road Tramlink stop. Buses 75, 157, 176, 194, 197, 227, 249, 342, 354, 356, and 358.* **Adm £2.50, chd free (share to St Christopher's Hospice). Suns 8, 29 June (2-5). Also open 8 June 26 Stodart Rd. Visitors also welcome by appt 1 Apr to 31 July.**
40ft x 120ft suburban garden. Organic and wildlife friendly, designed to incorporate many native species, but without sacrificing aesthetic standards. Wetland areas, nectar border and wild bee house. Information sheets available about many aspects of gardening for wildlife. Featured in 'Permaculture' magazine.

1A HUNGERFORD ROAD, N7
N7 9LA. David Matzdorf. *Tube: Caledonian Rd, 6 mins walk. Buses: 29 & 253 to Hillmarton Rd stop in Camden Rd; 17, 91 & 259 to last stop in Hillmarton Rd; 10 to York Way at Market Rd & 274 to junction of Market Rd & Caledonian Rd.* **Adm £2, chd/concessions £1 (share to Terrence Higgins Trust). Sun 8 June (12-6). Also open 62 Hungerford Rd & 90 St George's Ave.**
Unique eco-house with walled, lush front garden planted in modern-exotic style. Floriferous 'green roof' resembling scree slope. Front garden densely planted with palms, acacia, ginger lilies, brugmansias, bananas, euphorbias and yuccas. The 'green roof' is planted with agaves, aloes, cacti, bromeliads, alpines, sedums, mesembryanthemums, bulbs, grasses

and aromatic herbs - access via ladder only to part of roof (for safety reasons, can be seen from below). Garden and roof each 50ft x 18ft.

62 HUNGERFORD ROAD, N7
N7 9LP. John Gilbert & Lynne Berry, 020 7609 7223, john@john-gilbert.co.uk. *Directions as 1a Hungerford Rd.* **Adm £2, chd free. Sun 8 June (2-6). Also open 1a Hungerford Rd & 90 St George's Ave. Visitors also welcome by appt.**
Densely planted mature town garden at rear of Victorian terrace house which has been designed to maximise space for planting and create several different sitting areas, views and moods. Arranged in a series of paved rooms with a good range of perennials, shrubs and trees. Professional garden designer's own garden.

THE HURLINGHAM CLUB, SW6
Ranelagh Gardens. SW6 3PR, ellen.wells@hurlinghamclub.org.uk. *Main gate at E end of Ranelagh Gardens. Tube: Putney Bridge (110yds).* Light refreshments, teas & wine. **Adm £5, chd free. Sat 31 May (11-4), optional guided tour at 2. Visitors also welcome by appt for groups.**
40-acre 'country-house' garden with lawns mainly laid to bowls, croquet and tennis, surrounded by shrubberies, herbaceous borders and formal bedding. Several mature trees of interest. 2-acre lake with water fowl. River walk.

ISLINGTON GARDENS, N1
N1 1BE. *Tube: Kings Cross or Angel. Buses: 17, 91, 259 to Caledonian Rd.* Home-made teas at 36 Thornhill Square. **Combined adm £6 or £2 each garden, chd free. Sun 1 June (2-6).**
Walk through Islington's Georgian streets and squares to these contrasting gardens.

8 COLLEGE CROSS
Anne Weyman & Chris Bulford
Walled town garden, 70ft x 20ft, with over 400 different plants incl many unusual shrubs and herbaceous plants; varied collections of hostas and hardy geraniums; walls covered with climbers. Plant list available.

13 COLLEGE CROSS
Diana & Stephen Yakeley, diana@yakeley.com. **Visitors also welcome by appt.**
Black slate bench and cantilevered glass balustrade provide contemporary design interest in this peaceful green oasis. Paved areas for dining surrounded by architectural plants chosen for form and texture are enlivened by white flowers incl several different types of lily. Good examples of plants that work in London shade for all-yr interest. Winner London Garden Society award for best small back garden 2007.

44 HEMINGFORD ROAD
Dr Peter Willis
Surprisingly lush, country-style garden in the city with interesting trees, shrubs, perennials, lawns and pond in a very small space. Matured over 29 yrs in symbiosis with honey fungus.

36 THORNHILL SQUARE
Anna & Christopher McKane
Old roses, hardy geraniums, clematis and alliums give a country garden atmosphere in curved beds in this 120ft long garden. Bonsai collection displayed on the patio. Many unusual plants propagated for sale.

KEW GARDENS STATION GROUP
Kew TW9 4DA. Home-made teas at 355 Sandycombe Road. **Combined adm £4, £2.50 each garden, chd free. Sun 8 June (2-6).**
Two gardens nr Kew Gardens Station.

355 SANDYCOMBE ROAD
Kew. Henry Gentle & Sally Woodward Gentle. *200m S of Kew Gardens Stn. Garden entrance between house nos. 351 & 353.* **(share to REACT).**
Unexpectedly large urban garden on two levels. Terracing with wooden sleepers, bricks and decking provide distinct areas of interest incl lavenders, olives, grasses, euphorbias and other plants for sandy soils and shady areas. A garden for adults and children alike.

31 WEST PARK ROAD
Anna Anderson. *By Kew Gardens Stn, on E side of railway line*
Modern botanical garden with an oriental twist. Emphasis on foliage and an eclectic mix of plants, reflecting pool and rotating willow screens which provide varying views or privacy. Dry bed, shady beds, mature trees and a private paved dining area with dappled light and shade.

A garden for adults and children alike . . .

KEW GREEN GARDENS
TW9 3AH. *NW side of Kew Green. Tube: Kew Gardens. Mainline stn: Kew Bridge. Buses: 65, 391. Entrance via towpath.* **Combined adm £5, chd free. Sun 18 May (2-6).**
Four long gardens behind adjacent C18 houses on the Green; close to Royal Botanic Gardens.

65 KEW GREEN
Giles & Angela Dixon
Long, narrow garden divided into four separate mini-gardens, with a large summerhouse. Organic.

69 KEW GREEN
Mr & Mrs John Godfrey
Mature English garden, profusely planted. Formal garden and terrace nr house, wilder further down. Nuttery, meadow planting. Interesting shrubs and plants.

71 KEW GREEN
Mr & Mrs Jan Pethick
Large and informal London garden, laid out around tall, old trees; traditional border, irises and shaded borders within woodland. Well-established shrubs in crowded planting.

73 KEW GREEN
Donald & Libby Insall
The garden wanders from the main lawn and border by house, through woodland and surprises by arriving at a modern planting of espaliered miniature fruit trees.

38 KILLIESER AVENUE, SW2

SW2 4NT. Mrs Winkle Haworth, 020 8671 4196, **winklehaworth@hotmail.com.** *Mainline stn: Streatham Hill, 5 mins walk. Buses: 133, 137, 159 to Telford Ave. Killieser Ave 2nd turning L off Telford Ave.* **Adm £3.50.** Visitors welcome by appt, **coaches permitted.**

Densely-planted, romantic, 90ft x 28ft garden divided into four distinct areas. Unusual perennial plants and shrubs provide the backbone. Miniature cascade, wall fountain, Gothic seating arbour and gravel garden with drought-tolerant plants. Rose-filled parterre provides a formal element and stunning tulip display in spring. Featured in 'House Beautiful'.

LAMBETH PALACE, SE1

SE1 7JU. The Church Commissioners, **www.archbishopofcanterbury.org.** *Mainline stn & tube: Waterloo. Tube: Westminster, Lambeth North & Vauxhall, all about 10 mins walk. Buses: 3, C10, 76, 77, 77a, 344. Entry to garden on Lambeth Palace Rd (not at gatehouse).* Home-made teas. **Adm £3, chd free. Sat 10 May (2-5.30).** Also open **Museum of Garden History.**

Lambeth Palace garden is one of the oldest and largest private gardens in London. Site occupied by Archbishops of Canterbury since end C12. Formal courtyards with historic white fig (originally planted 1555). Parkland-style garden with mature trees, woodland and native planting, pond, hornbeam allée. Also formal rose terrace, summer gravel border, chapel garden and beehives. Gravel paths, but level. Ramp to rose terrace.

12 LANSDOWNE ROAD, W11

W11 3LW. The Lady Amabel Lindsay. *Turn N off Holland Park Ave nr Holland Park stn or W off Ladbroke Grove halfway along. Buses: 12, 88, GL 711, 715. Bus stop & tube: Holland Park, 4 mins.* **Adm £3, chd free. Wed 14 May (2-6).**

Medium-sized fairly wild garden; borders, climbing roses, shrubs; mulberry tree 200yrs old.

NEW 8 LANSDOWNE WALK, W11

W11 3LN. Nerissa Guest, 020 7229 3661, **nmguest@waitrose.com.** *Tube: Holland Park, then 2 mins walk N. Buses: 94, 148.* Home-made teas. **Adm £2.50, chd free. Suns 13 Apr; 7 Sept (2-6).** **Visitors also welcome by appt.**

Medium-sized garden with all-yr interest peaking with specialist collection of camellias in spring and choice salvias in late summer/early autumn. Emphasis on foliage, texture and scent with unusual and eclectic mix of exotic, herbaceous and grasses entwined with many clematis. Containers incl *Pseudopanax ferox, Metrosideros excelsa, Woodwardia radicans* and *echiums*. Access by steep steps.

NEW 42 LATIMER ROAD, E7

Forest Gate E7 0LQ. Janet Daniels. *8 mins walk from Forest Gate or Wanstead Park stn. From Forest Gate cross to Sebert Rd, then 3rd rd on L.* Light refreshments & teas. **Adm £2.50, chd free. Sat 26, Sun 27 July (11-5.30).**

Plantaholic's terraced house garden, with every planting opportunity maximised through a colourful abundance of baskets, climbers, shrubs and fruit trees. Raised koi carp pond. 4 steps down to secret garden with exuberant mixed borders, wildlife pond with gunnera and small green oasis lawn with arbour.

38 LEYBORNE PARK

Kew TW9 3HA. Ann & Alan Sandall. *2m N of Richmond. 5 mins walk from Kew Gardens stn. Buses: 391 to Kew Gdn Stn, 65 to Kew Gdns, Victoria Gate.* **Adm £2, chd free. Sun 4, Mon 5 May (2-5).**

Long narrow garden maturing with its owners. Some trendy bits: blue shed, finds from skips, bananas. Then the urge to do that bit less: extended terrace, pots, statuesque shrubs, collection of peonies. A plantaholic trying to simplify - without success.

LITTLE HOUSE A, NW3

16A Maresfield Gardens, Hampstead NW3 5SU. Linda & Stephen Williams. *5 mins walk Swiss Cottage or Finchley Rd tube. Off Fitzjohn's Ave and 2 doors away from Freud Museum (signed).* Light refreshments & teas. **Adm £3, chd free.** Sun 18 May; Sat 14, Sun 15 June (2-6).

1920s Arts & Crafts house (not open) built by Danish artist Arild Rosenkrantz. Award-winning front and rear garden set out formally with water features, stream and sculpture. Unusual shrubs and perennials, many rare, incl *Paeonia rockii* and *Dicksonia fibrosa*. Wide collections of hellebores, hostas, toad lilies, acers, clematis and astrantia.

LITTLE LODGE

Watts Road, Thames Ditton KT7 0BX. Mr & Mrs P Hickman, 020 8339 0931. *2m SW of Kingston. Mainline stn Thames Ditton 5 mins. A3 from London; after Hook underpass turn L to Esher; at Scilly Isles turn R towards Kingston; after 2nd railway bridge turn L to Thames Ditton village; house opp library after Giggs Hill Green.* Home-made teas. **Adm £2.50, chd free (share to Cancer Research UK).** Sun 25 May (11.30-5.30); Wed 4 June (2.30-6) £2.50 & **Evening Opening** (6-8.30) £3.50, wine. **Visitors also welcome by appt.**

Partly walled informal flower garden filled with shrubs and herbaceous plants that create an atmosphere of peace. Small secret garden; terracotta pots; stone troughs and sinks; roses; clematis; topiary; very productive parterre vegetable garden.

NEW 49A LOFTUS ROAD, W12

W12 7EH. Emma Plunket, **www.plunketgardens.com.** *Tube: walk from Shepherds Bush. Free street parking.* **Evening Opening** £3.50, chd free, wine, Wed 9 July (6-9).

Garden designer's inspiring 60ft walled garden. Richly planted with architectural topiary, drifts of perennials, herb tapestry and camomile lawn. Fruit and raised vegetable bed; shared orchard beyond with magnificent trees. Open and peaceful with swifts and evening fragrance. Garden plan, plant list and advice. Featured on BBC 2 Open Gardens. Access via steps.

LOWER CLAPTON GARDENS, E5
E5 0RL. *Tubes: Bethnal Green, then bus 106, 254, or Manor House, then bus 253, 254, alight Lower Clapton Rd. By car: leave Lower Clapton Rd by Millfields or Atherden Rd, R into Rushmore Rd and follow signs.* Home-made teas at 58 Rushmore Rd.
Combined adm £5, chd free. Sun 1 June (2-6).
Lower Clapton is an area of Victorian villas on a river terrace stretching down to the R Lea. A varied group of gardens each reflecting their owner's taste and providing tranquillity in an otherwise hectic area of E London.

8 ALMACK ROAD
Mr Philip Lightowlers
Long walled garden in 2 rooms: the first has a yellow and blue theme, with lawn, shrubs and water feature; the second a sunny garden with brick paths, tropical foliage, succulents and a secluded seating area.

NEW 99 POWERSCROFT ROAD
Rose Greenwood
Small town garden on 3 levels featuring a decked balcony, running water over rock and a thatched gazebo. Beds contain classic herbaceous perennials with some unusual shrubs.

58 RUSHMORE ROAD
Annie Moloney, 07989 803196, anniemoloney58@yahoo.co.uk. *If driving, entry to Rushmore Rd via Atherden or Millfields Rd only.* **Visitors also welcome by appt.**
Garden on two levels: lower level 2m x 3m, lots of pots and wall fountain; upper level 3m x 4m reached by spiral staircase. Many subtropical plants, tree fern, oleander and many climbers. ☎

5 LYNDHURST SQUARE, SE15
Peckham Rye SE15 5AR. Martin Lawlor & Paul Ward. *Stn: Peckham Rye (reduced service on Suns), 5 mins walk NW. Buses: 36 from Oval tube or 171 from Waterloo. Free parking in Lyndhurst Square.* Home-made teas.
Adm £3, chd free (share to Terrence Higgins Trust). Sun 8 June (2-5). Also open Choumert Square.
90ft x 50ft secret garden in the heart of London offering a mix of traditional and unusual herbaceous plants and shrubs. The design combines Italianate

and Gothic themes and offers a secluded green vista.

NEW 15 LYTTON CLOSE, N2
Hampstead Garden Suburb N2 0RH. Edwin & Toni Fine. *Tube: Golders Green, then H2 bus to corner of Linden Lea and Lytton Close.* Light refreshments & teas.
Adm £3, chd free. Sun 29 June (2-6). Also open Asmuns Hill Gardens & 5 Wildwood Rise.
Stunning formal garden, 120ft x 60ft, planted for yr-round interest with emphasis on texture and contrasting forms. Wide terrace with integral fishpond and fernery overlooks 60ft herbaceous border guarded by windsock seagulls set in impeccable lawns and leading to children's garden with playhouse and giant sunflowers. Pots of over 50 ornamental grasses line the eastern border, the whole surrounded by mature trees.

Children's garden with playhouse and giant sunflowers. Herbaceous border guarded by windsock seagulls. . .

MALVERN TERRACE GARDENS, N1
N1 1HR. *Approach from S via Pentonville Rd into Penton St, then into Barnsbury Rd. From N via Thornhill Rd opp Albion PH. Tube: Angel, Highbury & Islington. Buses: 19, 30 to Upper St, Town Hall.* Home-made teas. **Adm £3, chd free. Sun 27 Apr (2-5.30).**
Group of unique 1830s London terrace houses built on the site of Thomas Oldfield's dairy and cricket field. Cottage-style gardens in cobbled cul-de-sac. Music and plant stall.

47 MAYNARD ROAD, E17
Walthamstow E17 9JE. Don Mapp, 020 8520 1565, don.mapp@gmail.com. *10 mins walk from Walthamstow (central stn). Bus to Tesco on Lea Bridge Rd then walk through Barclay Path or bus W12 to Addison Rd. Turn R to Beulah Path.*
Adm £2, chd free. Suns 20, 27 July (11-6). Visitors also welcome by appt.
Plant collector's paradise. An eclectic mix of exotic plants in a 40ft x 16ft space, entered via a densely planted front garden.

6 METHUEN PARK, N10
Muswell Hill N10 2JS. Yulia Badian, 07850 756784, yulia@gardenshrink.com. *Tube: Highgate, then bus 43, 134 to Muswell Hill Broadway, 3rd on L off Dukes Ave or Finsbury Park tube then W7 bus.* Home-made teas. **Adm £2.50, chd free. Suns 1 June; 14 Sept (1-6.30). Evening Opening £5, wine, Fri 4 July (6-11). Visitors also welcome by appt.**
Contemporary family garden designed by Chelsea medal winner. Hardwood decking extends the living space. Across the formal pond the beach grows into a path. An arch doubles as a swing. Flowing curves and unique planting create an enchanting peaceful space. Tree house provides hours of entertainment. Sonic installation designed by Yulia Badian with soundtrack by Andres Bosshart.

24 MIDDLETON ROAD, E8
E8 4BS. Ann Jameson, 020 7421 3696, annjam@globalnet.co.uk. *2m N of Liverpool St stn (mainline & tube). 1m S of Dalston/Kingsland stn (mainline). Buses: 67, 149, 242, 243, alight Middleton Rd. By car approach from Queenbridge Rd northbound, turning L into Albion Drive leading to Albion Square. Middleton Rd runs parallel to Albion Drive on N side of Square.* **Visitors welcome by appt 11 Apr to 10 Sept (not Thurs), no group larger than fitting into private car.**
Walled garden. Lawn surrounded by beds with mixed planting; fruit trees incl medlar and mulberry. Actinidia spreading to the rooftop on S and E walls of the house, producing kiwi fruit Dec to Apr.

NEW **MILL HILL ROAD GARDENS, W3**
Acton W3 8JE. *Tube: Acton Town, turn R, Mill Hill Rd 3rd on R.* Home-made teas. **Combined adm £6, chd free (share to Chicken Shed).** Sun 13 July (2-6).

41 MILL HILL ROAD
Acton W3 8JE. **Marcia Hurst**
120ft x 40ft garden. Hot gravel garden with unusual plants. Lawn with herbaceous border and lavender hedge. Raised terrace with topiary. Owner compulsive plantaholic.

NEW **65 MILL HILL ROAD**
Ms Anna Dargavel, 020 8992 1723. **Visitors also welcome by appt weekends only.**
Typically long narrow London garden, paved, with borders and planted with fruit trees and shrubs. My garden is wildlife-friendly with ponds and flowers to which bees and other insects are attracted. Frogs and dragonflies abound.

NEW **REDWING**
69 Mill Hill Road. **Mr & Mrs M Temple**
Secluded, contemplative wildlife-friendly garden containing an abundance of young and mature trees, deep pond, wild flower mound, sculpture, herbaceous and herb beds. The garden meanders from a brick patio, it is lush and colourful. 120ft x 19ft.

2 MILLFIELD PLACE, N6
N6 6JP, 020 8348 6487. *Off Highgate West Hill, E side of Hampstead Heath. Buses: C2, C11 or 214 to Parliament Hill Fields.* Home-made teas (Sun only). **Adm £2.50, family ticket £5.** Sun 11 May (2-6). **Evening Opening** £3.50, wine, Wed 18 June (5.30-9). **Visitors also welcome by appt, please tel Mr & Mrs Peter & June Lloyd.**
1½ -acre spring and summer garden with camellias, rhododendrons, many flowering shrubs and unusual plants. Spring bulbs, herbaceous borders, small orchard, spacious lawns. Wheelchair assistance available.

19 MONTANA ROAD, SW17
Tooting Bec SW17 8SN. **Nigel Buckie, 020 8682 9300, www.objectarchitecture.co.uk.** *Tube: Tooting Bec.* Home-made teas. **Adm £2, chd free.** Suns 29 June; 31 Aug (1.30-5.30). **Also open Sun 31 Aug 28 Multon Rd. Visitors also welcome by appt.**
Architect's jungle! A dense planting of exotics with 5m high bananas and palms, interestingly underplanted with ginger, ferns, agaves and other tender plants. A flowering canopy of abutilon and gunnera grows next to the rill water feature and one of 3 seating areas. Featured in 'The Guardian' & garden style guide 'The Work'.

Hot gravel garden with unusual plants . . .

MULBERRY HOUSE, SE21
37a Alleyn Park, Dulwich SE21 8AT. **Mr & Mrs A Bingham.** *1m S of Dulwich Village. Off A205 (S Circular Rd) by Dulwich College playing fields. Continue under railway bridge bearing L. Garden opp Dulwich College Prep School.* Home-made teas. **Adm £2.50, chd free.** Sun 27 Apr (2-5). **Also open 5 Burbage Rd.**
Large family garden surrounded by mature trees. Planting scheme by Iris Lynch commenced 2004, development ongoing. Formal terrace with pond and semi-formal planting. Steps to lawn and herbaceous borders. Pond with wildlife. Parterre with mulberry, bay, apple and plum trees, vines and roses. Front garden redesigned in 2006. Garden sculpture by Kate Semple from Somerset and local artist Margret Gottschalk.

28 MULTON ROAD, SW18
SW18 3LH. **Victoria & Craig Orr, www.victoriasbackyard.co.uk.** *Mainline: 10mins walk from Earlsfield or Wandsworth Common. Bus: 219 & 319 along Trinity Rd.* Home-made teas. **Adm £2, chd free.** Sun 31 Aug (2-6). **Also open 19 Montana Rd.**
70ft x 40ft subtropical suburban oasis, designed to defy the depredations of global warming, garden pests and kids without recourse to carbon emissions, chemicals or cranial damage. Contemporary in concept, but not minimalist, planting incl phormium,

loquat, fig, cordyline, canna, tree fern, astelia, yucca and grasses. Spectacular golden-stemmed bamboo in front garden. Innovative features incl Arundo donax (Spanish reed) as screen for trampoline. Lots of seating, and goldfish pond. Featured in 'The Independent'.

NEW **33 MUNDANIA ROAD, SE22**
SE22 0NH. **Dr Helen Penn.** *For directions see 22 Scutari Rd. Mundania Rd intersects Scutari Rd.* **Adm £2.50, chd free.** Sun 18 May (2-6). **Also open 22 Scutari Rd.**
Plantswoman's mature garden, last open in 1992, now overgrown and shared with goldfinches. Wildlife pond, fruit trees - apricot, fig, mulberry, quince and pears. Back garden 40ft x 120ft, front 40ft x17ft. Some garden features date back to original Victorian owners.

◆ **MUSEUM OF GARDEN HISTORY, SE1**
Lambeth Palace Road. SE1 7LB, 020 7401 8865, **www.museumgardenhistory.org.** *Tube: Lambeth North, Vauxhall, Waterloo. Bus: 507 Red Arrow from Victoria or Waterloo mainline & tube stns (C10 only on Sundays); alight Lambeth Palace.* **Adm £3, chd free, concessions £2.50 (share to Museum of Garden History). Tues to Suns, not 2 week Christmas period. For NGS: Sat 10 May (10.30-5). Also open Lambeth Palace.**
Reproduction C17 knot garden with period plants, topiary and box hedging. Wild garden in front of graveyard area; drought planting at front entrance. Historic tools, information displays, changing exhibitions, shop and café housed in former church of St-Mary-at-Lambeth.

◆ **MYDDELTON HOUSE GARDENS**
Bulls Cross, Enfield EN2 9HG. **Lee Valley Regional Park Authority, 01992 717711, www.leevalleypark.org.uk.** *2m N of Enfield. J25 (A10) off M25 S towards Enfield. 1st T-lights R into Bullsmoor Lane, L at end along Bulls Cross.* Light refreshments & teas on NGS days. **Adm £2.60, chd under 5 free, concessions £2 (prices may alter).**

Mon to Fri, Apr to Sept (10-4.30), Oct to Mar (10-3); Suns & Bank Hol Mons Easter to end Oct (12-4). For NGS: Suns 24 Feb; 27 Apr; 25 May (12-4). Sun 22 Feb 2009.

4 acres of gardens created by E A Bowles. Gardens feature diverse and unusual plants incl National Collection of award-winning bearded irises. Large pond with terrace, conservatory and interesting historical artefacts. A garden for all seasons.

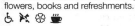

◆ **NATURAL HISTORY MUSEUM WILDLIFE GARDEN, SW7**
Cromwell Road. SW7 5BD, 020 7942 5011, www.nhm.ac.uk/wildlife-garden. *Tube: South Kensington, 5 mins walk.* **Adm £2, chd free. Daily 1 Apr to 31 Oct 12-5. For NGS: Suns 20 Apr; 6 July (2-5).**
Set in the Museum grounds, the Wildlife Garden has provided a lush and tranquil habitat in the heart of London since 1995. It reveals a varied range of British lowland habitats, incl deciduous woodland, meadow and ponds. With over 2000 plant and animal species, it beautifully demonstrates the potential for wildlife conservation in the inner city. Meet the scientists and browse stalls selling wild flowers, books and refreshments.

5 NEW ROAD, N8
Crouch End N8 8TA. The Misses S & M West, 020 8340 8149. *Bus: W7 Muswell Hill to Finsbury Park or W5, alight Wolsey Rd. New Rd is cul-de-sac. Some parking rear of Health Centre, better parking Middle Lane or Park Rd.* **Donations welcome. Visitors welcome by appt.**
Traditional country garden 60ft x 24ft in heart of Crouch End, evolved over 50yrs. Small prizewinning front garden adjoins colourful conservatory leading to back garden planted for yr-round interest. Many unusual and borderline tender plants - abutilons, streptocarpus, achimenes, crinum. Fruit trees, ornamental shrubs and trees, small pond, lawn and productive greenhouse create a delightful experience of cherished nostalgia.

15 NORCOTT ROAD, N16
N16 7BJ. Amanda & John Welch. *Buses: 67, 73, 76, 149, 243. Clapton & Rectory Rd mainline stns. One way system: by car approach from Brooke Rd which crosses Norcott Rd, garden*

in S half. Home-made teas. **Adm £2, chd free. Sun 8 June (2-6).**
Largish (for Hackney) walled back garden developed by present owners over 28yrs, with pond, long-established fruit trees, abundantly planted with a great variety of herbaceous plants, especially perennial geraniums and campanulas, day lilies, flag and other irises. This year opening 3 weeks later for a more blousy look.

NORTH HOUSE, SE21
93 Dulwich Village. SE21 7BJ. Vivian Bazalgette & Katharine St John-Brooks. *Dulwich Village next to Oddbins, 8 mins straight walk from N Dulwich stn or 10 mins from W Dulwich stn via Belair Park. Bus P4.* Light refreshments & teas. **Adm £2.50, chd free (share to Dulwich Helpline). Sun 8 June (2-6). Also open 142 Court Lane & 174 Peckham Rye.**
$2/3$ -acre mature garden with lawns, trees, climbing roses and flowerbeds, unusual shape, pleasant borrowed landscape. Gravel at front of property.

95 NORTH ROAD
Kew TW9 4HQ. Michael le Fleming & Colin Chenery. *50yds S of Kew Gardens stn on its E down-line side. Exit in North Rd.* Home-made teas. **Adm £2, chd free. Day & Evening Opening wine, Sun 20 July (2-7).**
This old-fashioned garden is designed to disguise its basic plot and to conceal nearby buildings. It winds through mixed planting and foliage contrasts with summer hot spots of reds and golds, but has hidden corners of peace and shade. A stone terrace, pond, conservatory, pots and urns complete our picture of a grand garden trying to get out! Bric-a-brac stall.

94 OAKWOOD ROAD, NW11
Hampstead Garden Suburb NW11 6RN. Michael Franklin, 07836 541383, mikefrank@onetel.com. *Tube: Golders Green. Bus: H2 to Northway.* Home-made teas. **Adm £2.50, chd free. Sun 11 May (2-5.30). Also open 91 Willifield Way. Visitors also welcome by appt.**
Large garden divided into 2 rooms by box hedging and an arch. Lawns, woodland with apple and pear blossom, old wisteria, tree peonies, beds filled with colour and foliage.

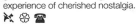

28 OLD DEVONSHIRE ROAD, SW12
SW12 9RB. Georgina Ivor, 020 8673 7179, georgina@giamanagement.com. *Tube and mainline: Balham, 5 mins walk.* Cream teas. **Adm £2, chd free (share to Trinity Hospice). Sun 15 June (2-5.30). Evening Opening £3, Pimm's & Prosecco, Wed 18 June (6-8.30). Also open 15 June 2 Western Lane. Visitors also welcome by appt.**
Drought-tolerant plants thrive in the sun-drenched front garden. A pear tree dominates the secluded 45ft x 20ft rear garden, with curving lawn surrounded by planting for yr-round interest. A eucalyptus tree, Rosa 'Rambling Rector' and strawberry tree (Arbutus unedo) add height, while a balustraded wooden balcony creates another level for herbs and tender climbers. Featured in 'Essential Local'.

Secret garden in the heart of Richmond . . .

NEW OLD PALACE LANE ALLOTMENTS
Old Palace Lane, Richmond TW1 1PG. Old Palace Lane Allotment Group. *Next to White Swan PH, through gate in wall. Mainline and tube: Richmond. Parking on meters in lane or round Richmond Green, or in Old Deer Park car park, entrance on A316 Twickenham Rd.* Light refreshments. **Adm £3, chd free. Sun 13 July (2-5).**
Secret garden in the heart of Richmond. 33 allotments on the site of Old Richmond Palace, squeezed between an ancient wall and a railway viaduct midway between Richmond Green and the river.

ORCHARD COTTAGE
See Kent.

ORMELEY LODGE
Ham Gate Avenue, Richmond
TW10 5HB. Lady Annabel
Goldsmith. *From Richmond Park, exit
at Ham Gate into Ham Gate Ave. 1st
house on R. From Richmond, A307;
after 1½ m, past New Inn on R, at T-
lights turn L into Ham Gate Ave.* **Adm
£3, chd £1.** Sun 22 June (3-6).
Large walled garden in delightful rural
setting on Ham Common. Wide
herbaceous borders and box hedges.
Walk through to orchard with wild
flowers. Vegetable garden, knot
garden, aviary. Trellised tennis court
with roses and climbers.

◆ **OSTERLEY PARK AND HOUSE**
Jersey Road, Isleworth TW7 4RB.
The National Trust, 020 8232 5050,
www.nationaltrust.org.uk. *4m N of
Richmond. Tube: Osterley, turn L on
leaving station, ½ m walk. Access via
Thornbury Rd on N side of A4 between
Gillette Corner & Osterley tube station.
Follow brown tourist signs. Car Park
£3.50.* **House & garden £8, chd £4.
Garden only £3.50, chd £1.75.** Wed
to Sun 12 Mar-2 Nov (house 1-4.30,
garden 11-5). For NGS: Sun 20 Apr
(11-5).
Rare C18 garden created by the Child
family, owners of Osterley Park House,
in 1770s and 1780s. The garden is
currently being restored to its former
glory following recent research incl the
discovery in America of documents
showing lists of plants to be purchased
for the garden in 1788. Highlights incl
the Robert Adam designed Garden
House and Mrs Child's Flower
Garden. Introductory talks, meet the
gardeners.

3 THE PARK, N6
N6 4EU. Mr & Mrs G Schrager, 020
8348 3314,
bunty1@blueyonder.co.uk. *Off
Southwood Lane. 3 mins from
Highgate tube, up Southwood Lane.
The Park is 1st on R. Buses: 43, 134,
143, 263.* Home-made teas. **Adm
£2.50, chd free (share to St Mary's
Hospital Kidney Patients Assn).** Sun
20 Apr (2-5). Visitors also welcome
by appt at any time.
Large garden with pond and frogs, fruit
trees and eclectic planting. Interesting
plants for sale. Treasure hunt for
children.

174 PECKHAM RYE, SE22
SE22 9QA. Mr & Mrs Ian Bland. *Stn:
Peckham Rye. Overlooks Peckham
Rye Common from Dulwich side.
Reached by alley to side of house.*
**Adm £2.50, chd free (share to St
Christopher's Hospice).** Sun 8 June
(2.30-5.30). Also open **142 Court
Lane & North House.**
100ft x 30ft rear garden originally
designed by Judith Sharpe. Easy-care
and child-friendly, the garden is
frequently changed but always displays
a wide variety of contrasting foliage
and yr-round interest. Best in early
June when pink and purple flowers
predominate, especially in woodland
and semi-shade borders.

Unusual plants from China, Australia and Mexico . . .

PEMBRIDGE COTTAGE
10 Strawberry Hill Road,
Twickenham TW1 4PT. Ian & Lydia
Sidaway, 020 8287 8993. *1m from
Twickenham town centre. Close to
Strawberry Hill mainline stn.* Light
refreshments, teas & wine. **Adm £2.50,
chd free.** Suns 15, 22 June (2-6).
Visitors also welcome by appt.
140ft x 20ft constantly evolving artist's
garden with studio building. Divided
into several brick, gravel and wooden
seating areas. Strong evergreen shrub
structure providing yr-round interest.
Many thin Italian cypress, maples,
trimmed and shaped box, lonicera,
lavender, santolina, laurels and
viburnum. Euphorbias, bamboo, herbs,
ferns and gunnera. A packed garden
influenced by Mediterranean,
Japanese and N European styles.
Featured in 'The Independant', &
'Garden Illustrated', BBC Gardeners
World.

PENSHURST PLACE
See Kent.

PETERSHAM HOUSE
Petersham TW10 7AA. Francesco &
Gael Boglione. *Stn: Richmond, then
65 bus to Dysart PH. Entry to garden
off Petersham Rd, through nursery.*

Light refreshments & teas at adjoining
nursery. **Adm £3, chd free.** Sun 18
May (9-5); Fri 19 Sept (11-5). **Also
open Rosebank.**
Broad lawn with large topiary,
generously planted double borders.
Productive vegetable garden with
chickens. Extensive press coverage of
Petersham Nurseries.

101 PITT CRESCENT, SW19
SW19 8HR. Karen Grosch, 020 8893
3660,
info@whettonandgrosch.co.uk. *Tube:
Wimbledon Park 10 mins walk.
Bus: 156 along Durnsford Rd. Limited
parking in Pitt Crescent.* Home-made
teas. **Adm £2, chd free.** Sun 1 June
(2-6). Visitors also welcome by appt
in June only.
Small terraced town garden of 100ft x
25ft, cleverly planted with shrubs and
ornamental trees on different levels.
Soft colours of grey, green and
variegated plants. Pebbled patio leads
up to vine-covered pergola, in turn
leading to enclosed fruit and vegetable
garden edged with roses and clematis,
with apple and plum arbour,
greenhouse, formal raised beds.
Featured in RHS 'The Garden' &
'GGG' and on BBC TV. Wheelchair
access to bottom terrace only, steps to
upper terraces.

**13 QUEEN ELIZABETH'S WALK,
N16**
N16 5UZ. Lucy Sommers. *From
Manor House tube go S down Green
Lanes, then 2nd left off Lordship Park.*
Light refreshments. **Adm £2.50, chd
free.** Sun 31 Aug (2.30-6).
Plantsperson's 30m x 7m garden for all
seasons with emphasis on foliage,
textures and unusual plants from
China, Australia and Mexico in both
sunny and shady areas. Interest for
children without encroaching on the
plants or design, and with fairly minimal
maintenance. Overhead rainwater
irrigation system. Drought tolerant
plants, succulents, bromeliads,
leonotis. Quirky front garden leaf
sculpture fence.

14 RADLET AVENUE, SE26
SE26 4BZ. Chester Marsh. *Stn:
Forest Hill. At end of cul-de-sac off
Thorpewood Ave. Easy parking.*
Home-made teas. **Adm £3, chd free.**
Sun 25 May (2-5). Also open
**Tewkesbury Lodge Garden
Group.**

Unusual and evolving garden on several levels with semi-tropical plants and rare trees providing an overhead canopy and evoking a feeling of the Caribbean. Open spaces with drought-resistant plants and water features. Steep paths lead to surprise views. A very different garden for this part of London. Steep and narrow paths not suitable for very young children or pushchairs.

RAILWAY COTTAGES, N22
Alexandra Palace N22 7SN. *Tube: Wood Green, 10 mins walk. Stn: Alexandra Palace, 3 mins. Buses: W3, 184, 3 mins. Free parking in Bridge Rd, Buckingham Rd, Palace Gates Rd, Station Rd.* Home-made teas at 2 Dorset Road. **Combined adm £3.50, chd free. Sun 6 July (2-5.30).** Front gardens of a row of railway cottages and 2 railway cottage back gardens.

15 BRIDGE ROAD
Sherry Zeffert
Magical transformation from railway cottage backyard to plant lover's secluded courtyard garden. Circular island bed surrounded by gravel paths and densely planted borders. Profusion of perennials, over 40 climbers and large collection of species clematis. Raised terrace packed with specimen camellias, bamboos, grasses, ferns, evergreen irises and figs. Plant list available. Inspirational use of limited space. Steep steps, unsuitable for small children or elderly.

2 DORSET ROAD
Jane Stevens, janestevens_london@yahoo.co.uk. Visitors also welcome by appt June & July, small groups only.
Tranquil country-style back garden full of interest. Topiary and clipped box contrasts with climbing roses, jasmine and honeysuckle. Long mixed hedge and pond. Mulberry, quince, fig and apple trees. Mixed borders with shrubs, herbaceous and annuals chosen for scent and colour. Containers and pots provide all-yr interest and colour.

14 DORSET ROAD
Cathy Brogan
Front garden of railway cottage

with mixed planting, herbs, flowers and aromatic shrubs. Emphasis on sustainability and organic methods.

22 DORSET ROAD
Mike & Noreen Ainger
Small but interesting front garden incl jasmine, flax, fig, fuchsia, vines and climbing rose.

NEW 37A REDINGTON ROAD, GARDEN FLAT, NW3
Hampstead NW3 7QY. Dianne Supperstone. Entrance on Oakhill Ave. *Close to Finchley Rd & Hampstead Village. Tube: Hampstead or Finchley Rd. Buses: 46, 268 Hampstead High St and 13, 82, 113 along Finchley Rd to Frognal.* **Adm £2.50, chd free. Sun 20 July (1-8).**
A garden to make you smile. Ferns, banana plants, cannas, gingers and agapanthus mingle comfortably with traditional cottage plants. Lively cool and hot borders burst with herbaceous perennials, grasses, clematis, sweet peas, and dahlias which in turn are punctuated with ceramics and sculptures. Further interesting stories created on side paths.

A garden to make you smile . . .

REGENTS COLLEGE'S GARDEN, NW1
Inner Circle, Regents Park. NW1 4NS. *Located at the junction of York Bridge & the Inner Circle. Baker St tube 5 mins walk. Buses: 13, 18, 27, 30, 74, 82, 113, 139, 159, 274. Enter main gate or garden gate adjacent to footbridge at Clarence Gate.* **Adm £3, chd £1. Sats 17 May; 6 Sept (12-5).**
Occupying 11 acres in the heart of Regents Park, the grounds beyond the college buildings comprise the 'Secret Garden' (formerly the Botany Garden), subtropical rockery with 'folly building', thought to be an old ice house, Moroccan tea garden, extensive lawns and borders full of unusual plantings.

RICHMOND RIVERSIDE
Friars Lane, Richmond TW9 1NR. *Tube & mainline stn: Richmond, then 5 mins walk via Richmond Green to Friars Lane towards river, just beyond car park.* **Combined adm £4, chd free. Evening Opening**, wine, Sat 7 June (6-8).
Two small secret artists' studio gardens.

1 ST HELENA TERRACE
Christina Gascoigne
Walled secret garden with water.

3 ST HELENA TERRACE
Raphael & Marillyn Maklouf
Profusion of plants, pots and imaginative water design. Roses and climbing plants in abundance. Original use of limited space.

133 31 ROEDEAN CRESCENT, SW15
SW15 5JX. Francine Watson Coleman. *Roedean Crescent lies just outside Roehampton Gate of Richmond Park.* **Adm £2.50, chd 50p. Sun 20 July (2-6).**
Spacious organic, wildlife-friendly formal garden. Interesting and beautiful fruit, vegetables and herbs are planted amongst choice shrubs and perennials in the established hot and cool borders in the newly remodelled areas. The dedicated kitchen garden has trained fruit, raised beds, compost bins, greenhouse and nursery. Pots of lemon, limes, figs, olives, grapes and herbs add a touch of the exotic.

NEW 20 ROLLSCOURT AVENUE, SE24
Herne Hill SE24 0EA. Ms Clare Checkland. *Stns: North Dulwich or Herne Hill, then less than 10 mins walk. Buses: 68 to end of road or 3, 37, 196, 322 to Herne Hill stn.* Cream teas. **Adm £2, chd free. Sun 8 June (2-5). Also open South London Botanical Institute.**
Woodland garden, 90ft x 15ft, divided up with circular lawns and meandering paths with clever use of willow panels and open fencing to create an illusion of width. Ornamental trees incl Prunus maakii, multi-stemmed Betula albosinensis and magnolia are underplanted with ferns, euphorbia and Thalictrum aquifolium. *Small vegetable /herb garden, scuptural bench and formal circular pool with fish pond.*

The plants are labelled and arranged by continent . . .

◆ **ROOTS AND SHOOTS, SE11**
Walnut Tree Walk. SE11 6DN.
Trustees of Roots and Shoots, 020
7587 1131,
www.rootsandshoots.org.uk. *Tube:
Lambeth North. Buses: 3, 59, 159. Just
off Kennington Rd, 5 mins from
Imperial War Museum. No car parking
on site. Pedestrian entrance through
small open space on Fitzalan St.* Adm
£2, chd free. Mon to Fri (10-4) all yr,
not Bank Hols. For NGS: Sat 7, Sun
8 June (11-4). **Evening Opening**
Wed 2 July (6.30-8.30).
1/2 -acre wildlife garden run by
innovative charity providing training and
garden advice. Summer meadow,
observation beehives, 2 large ponds,
hot borders, Mediterranean mound,
old roses and echiums. Learning
centre with photovoltaic roof, solar
heating, rainwater catchment, three
planted roofs, one brown roof. Study
room for wildlife garden. Displays, nest
box cameras, observation beehives
and beekeeping demonstrations.
Exhibitions of work by local children
and artists. Children's activities Sun 8
June. Limited wheelchair access.
♿ 🏹 ✿ 🐝 ☕

ROSEBANK
Petersham TW10 7AG. Mr & Mrs
Ball. *Stn: Richmond, then bus 65 to
Dysart PH. House next to entrance to
nursery or via alleyway off River Lane.*
Adm £3, chd free. Sun 18 May (11-
5). Also open **Petersham House**.
Traditional Victorian walled garden,
newly designed. Raised herbaceous
borders, pond, unusual shrubs,
hornbeam aerial hedge in progress and
clipped box.
🏹

167 ROSENDALE ROAD, SE21
West Dulwich SE21 8LW. Mr & Mrs
A Pizzoferro, 020 8766 7846. *At
junction of Rosendale & Lovelace Rds.
Stns: Tulse Hill, West Dulwich.* Home-
made teas. Adm £2, chd free (share

to London Children's Flower
Society). Sun 30 Mar (2-5); Sun 1
June (2-6). Also open 1 June **Ardlui
Group & 24 Chestnut Rd.** Visitors
also welcome by appt.
Back garden 100ft long with stream
(which runs naturally in winter), through
small woodland area. Bog garden and
wildlife pond bordered by timber deck.
Central shingle and cobble circle
surrounded by generous mixed
borders. Collections of hostas, acers
and pittosporums in pots in alleyway.
Front garden has a hotter colour theme
with range of euphorbias. Featured in
'House Beautiful'.
🏹 ✿ ☕ ☎

**ROYAL COLLEGE OF
PHYSICIANS GARDEN, NW1**
11 St Andrew's Place, Outer Circle,
by SE corner of Regents Park
NW1 4LE. Royal College of
Physicians of London,
www.rcplondon.ac.uk/garden. *Tube:
Great Portland St, turn L along
Marylebone Rd for 100yds, R to Outer
Circle, 150yds on R.* Light
refreshments & teas. Adm £3, chd
free. Sun 13 July (10-5).
Garden replanted between 2005 and
2007 to display plants used in
conventional and herbal medicines
around the world and in past centuries,
and plants with historical links to
physicians associated with the College.
The plants are labelled and arranged
by continent. Guided tours highlighting
current and ancient medicinal uses of
plants. Featured on BBC London
News and in 'Herbs' magazine,
'Historic Gardens' & 'Ham & High'.
♿ ☕

**NEW 90 ST GEORGE'S
AVENUE, N7**
Tufnell Park N7 0AH. Ms J
Chamberlain & Mr R Hamilton.
*Tube:Tufnell Park, then bus 4 to
Tufnell Park Rd, alight Dalmeny Rd.*
Adm £2, chd free. Sun 8 June
(2-6). Also open **1A & 62
Hungerford Rd.**
Long rear garden created 8yrs ago
with trees and shrubs providing
structure and yr-round interest, incl
acers, Pittosporum *tobira*, Choisya
ternata and cordyline. The front
garden has won many certificates
of merit and contains mostly
drought-tolerant, silver-leaved
Mediterranean plants.
🏹

7 ST GEORGE'S ROAD
St Margaret's, Twickenham
TW1 1QS. Mr & Mrs R Raworth, 020
8892 3713,
jenny@jraworth.freeserve.co.uk,
www.raworthgarden.com. *11/2 m SW
of Richmond. Off A316 between
Twickenham Bridge & St Margaret's
roundabout.* Home-made teas. Adm
£3, chd 50p. Sun 1 June (11-5).
Evening Opening £4, wine, Sat 5
July (6-8). Visitors also welcome by
appt May & June for groups of 10+.
Exuberant displays of old English roses
and vigorous climbers with unusual
herbaceous perennials. Massed
scented crambe cordifolia. Pond with
bridge converted into child-safe lush
bog garden. Large N-facing luxuriant
conservatory with rare plants and
climbers. Pelargoniums a speciality.
Sunken garden and knot garden.
Featured in 'The English Garden' &
'GGG'.
🏹 ✿ ☕ ☎

27 ST JAMES AVENUE, W13
Ealing W13 9DL. Andrew & Julie
Brixey-Williams. *7m from Central
London. Uxbridge Rd (A206) to West
Ealing; Leeland Terrace leads to St
James Ave.* Light refreshments & teas.
Adm £3, chd free. Sun 17 Aug
(2-5.30).
Designed by Jason Payne, our garden
takes advantage of London's particular
microclimate to create an evocation of
far-away landscapes. Sheltered by
groves of bamboo, bananas and
palms, and divided by a full-width
butterfly-shaped pond, the garden
features many Antipodean and Asian
rarities, incl spectacular Tetrapanax *rex
papyrifera*.
🏹 ☕

ST MICHAEL'S CONVENT
56 Ham Common, Richmond
TW10 7JH. Community of the
Sisters of the Church. *2m S of
Richmond. From Richmond or
Kingston, A307, turn onto the common
at the Xrds nr New Inn, 100yds on the
R adjacent to Martingales Close.
Mainline trains to Richmond &
Kingston also tube to Richmond, then
bus 65 from either to Ham Common.*
Adm £3, chd free (share to Church
Extension Assn). Sat 21 June (11-4).
4-acre organic garden comprises
walled vegetable garden, orchards,
vine house, ancient mulberry tree,
extensive borders, meditation and
Bible gardens.
🏹 ✿ ☕

57 ST QUINTIN AVENUE, W10
W10 6NZ. Mr H Groffman, 020 8969
8292. *1m from Ladbroke Grove or
White City tube. Buses: 7, 70 from
Ladbroke Grove stn; 220 from White
City, all to North Pole Rd.* Light
refreshments & teas. **Adm £2.80, chd
free. Suns 13, 27 July (2-6.30). Also
open 27 July 29 Addison Ave.
Visitors also welcome by appt.**
30ft x 40ft walled garden; wide
selection of plant material incl
evergreen and deciduous shrubs for
foliage effects. Patio area mainly
furnished with bedding material, colour
themed, incl topical carpet bedding
display. Special features and focal
points throughout. Exhibition and
bedding display to celebrate family
centenary, 1908, the birth year of Mr
Groffman's parents. Prizewinner
Kensington Gardeners' Club, London
Gardens Society & London in Bloom.
Steps from house to patio, assistance
available.

5 ST REGIS CLOSE, N10
Alexandra Park Road. N10 2DE. Ms
S Bennett & Mr E Hyde, 020 8883
8540. *2nd L in Alexandra Park Rd from
Colney Hatch Lane. Tube: Bounds
Green or E Finchley then bus 102 or
299. Alight at St Andrew's Church on
Windermere Rd. Bus: 43 or 134 to
Alexandra Park Rd.* Home-made teas.
**Adm £2.50, chd free. Suns 27 Apr;
29 June; 27 July (2-7). Also open 29
June 5 Cecil Rd. Visitors also
welcome by appt.**
Unique artists' garden renowned for
colourful architectural features created
on site, incl Baroque temple, pagodas,
turquoise raku-tiled mirrored oriental
enclosure concealing plant nursery.
American Gothic garden shed
alongside compost heap enclosure
with medieval pretensions. Maureen
Lipman's favourite garden - humour
and trompe-l'oeil combine with wildlife-
friendly carp ponds, waterfalls, lawns,
abundant borders and imaginative
container planting to create an
inspirational restoring experience.
Open ceramics studio. Featured on ITV
News to publicise the 80th birthday of
the NGS with Charlie Dimmock.

22 SCUTARI ROAD, SE22
East Dulwich SE22 0NN. Sue
Hillwood-Harris & David Hardy, 020
8693 3710,
david.hardy04@btinternet.com. *S
side of Peckham Rye Park. B238
Peckham Rye/Forest Hill Rd, turn into
Colyton Rd (opp Herne Tavern). 3rd on
R. Bus: 63. Stn: East Dulwich.* Home-
made teas. **Adm £2.50, chd free.
Suns 18 May; 6 July (2-6). Also open
18 May 33 Mundania Rd. Visitors
also welcome by appt.**
Our pretty new garden, created from
really boring scratch 4yrs ago, is still
work in progress, but now has
cottagey area, water, trees and lots of
attractive shrubs. Plus palatially-
housed chickens (eggs on sale for
NGS funds, subject to the whim of the
hens). Tea and cakes of memorable
standard. Featured on BBC2 Open
Gardens.

SHORT LOTS ALLOTMENTS
Watcombe Cottages, Kew
TW9 3BD. Short Lots Users' Group.
*NE side of Kew Green. Mainline: Kew
Bridge. Tube: Kew Gardens. Buses:
65, 391. Entrance from Watcombe
Cottages off Kew Green by Kew pond,
or from towpath.* Home-made teas at
St Anne's Church, Kew Green. **Adm
£2.50, chd free. Sun 13 July (2-5).**
Long-established, tree-fringed
allotment site of 50 plots of different
shapes and sizes, tucked away
between Bushwood Rd and riverbank.
Wide variety of fruit, flowers and
vegetables. Many varieties of dahlia
and other garden plants for sale. Partial
wheelchair access, main path only.

7 SIBELLA ROAD, SW4
SW4 6JA. Mrs Jane Landon, 020
7622 5724. *From Clapham High Rd,
take Gauden Rd. 2nd R into Bromfelde
Rd, Sibella Rd on L. From Wandsworth
Rd, take Albion Ave, continue over
Larkhall Rise into Sibella Rd. Tube:
Clapham North less than 10 mins walk.*
Light refreshments & wine. **Adm
£2.50, chd free. Sun 27 Apr (3-7),
Evening Opening £3.50, Wed 30
Apr (6-8). Also open 18 Sibella Rd.
Visitors also welcome by appt Apr
to June, groups of 4+.**
Long NW-facing garden with
contrasting areas and country feel.
Central specimen maple tree
surrounded by lawn and mixed
herbaceous borders. Shady areas nr
house with woodland planting, tiarellas,
pulmonaria, tulips and other spring
bulbs. Far beds with new planting
designed to overcome some of the
problems of heat and drought.
Featured in 'Red' magazine.

> Small walled
> garden where
> the formal
> layout is
> softened by
> colour-themed
> planting . . .

18 SIBELLA ROAD, SW4
SW4 6HX. Judith & Michael Strong,
020 7622 6159,
jmistrong@btinternet.com.
Directions, see 7 Sibella Rd. **Adm
£2.50, chd free. Sun 27 Apr (3-6).
Evening Opening £3.50, wine, Wed
30 Apr (6-8). Also open 7 Sibella
Rd. Visitors also welcome by appt
Apr to June, groups of 4+.**
Small walled garden where the formal
layout is softened by colour-themed
planting. Mediterranean-inspired patio
and miniature woodland area under old
bramley. The tiny octagonal lawn is
surrounded by deep herbaceous beds
with lilac and cloud-pruned ceanothus
adding height. Different varieties of
dicentras, hostas, ferns, foxgloves and
white alliums frame the terrace, roses
and clematis (over 25 varieties) climb
the walls and festoon the trees. In
spring bulbs and flowering shrubs
combine with colourful emerging
foliage, and in early summer the roses
take centre stage. Featured in 'Evening
Standard'.

**SOUTH LONDON BOTANICAL
INSTITUTE, SE24**
323 Norwood Road. SE24 9AQ,
www.slbi.org.uk. *Mainline stn: Tulse
Hill. Buses: 68, 196, 322 & 468 stop at
junction of Norwood & Romola Rds.*
Home-made teas. **Adm £2, chd free
(share to South London Botanical
Institute). Sun 22 June (2-5). Also
open 26 Rollscourt Ave.**
London's smallest botanic garden,
formally laid out with paved paths.
Densely planted with over 500 labelled
species and many rare and interesting
plants of worldwide origin incl
medicinal, carnivorous, British plants
and ferns.

41 SOUTHBROOK ROAD, SE12
Blackheath SE12 8LJ. Barbara & Marek Polanski. *Off Sth Circular at Burnt Ash Rd. Mainline stns: Lee & Hither Green, both 10 mins walk.* Home-made teas. **Adm £2.50, chd free. Sun 8 June** (2-5.30).
Large suburban garden in rural setting. Formal paving and pond to the rear divided from the main garden by a parterre with climbing roses and arbours. Large lawn with deep herbaceous borders. Sunny terrace close to house.

Completely wheelchair-friendly without aesthetic compromise . . .

SOUTHSIDE HOUSE, SW19
3-4 Woodhayes Road, Wimbledon Common SW19 4RJ. Pennington Mellor Munthe Charity Trust, www.southsidehouse.com. *1m W of Wimbledon Village. House at junction of Cannizaro, Southside and Woodhayes Rds.* Home-made teas. **Adm £2.50 (garden only), chd free. Suns 27 Apr; 11 May** (11-5).
Romantic country garden extending to almost 2 acres. Mature trees and hedges and a long informal canal form the structure of this unique and amusing garden. 2 grottos, 2 temples, pet cemetery, young orchard and wild flower meadow. Many of the smaller plantings are being gradually renovated. Lovely swathes of bluebells and small fernery. House open for guided tours Sats, Suns, Weds, from Easter Sat to 28 Sept. Closed Wimbledon tennis fortnight.

SOUTHWOOD LODGE, N6
33 Kingsley Place. N6 5EA. Mr & Mrs C Whittington, 020 8348 2785, suewhittington@hotmail.co.uk. *Tube: Highgate, 4 mins walk Highgate Village. Off Southwood Lane. Buses: 143, 210, 214, 271.* Home-made teas. **Adm £2.50, chd free. Sun 4 May** (2-5.30). **Visitors also welcome by appt Apr to July.**

Secret garden hidden behind C18 house (not open), laid out last century on steeply sloping site, now densely planted with wide variety of shrubs, climbers and perennials. Ponds, waterfall, frogs and newts. Many unusual plants are grown and propagated for sale. Toffee hunt for children.

STANLEY CRESCENT GARDEN, W11
Notting Hill W11 2NA. The Trustees. *Tube: Holland Park. Entrance in Kensington Park Gardens, adjacent to 1 Stanley Crescent.* **Adm £3, chd free. Sun 27 Apr** (2-5), wine.
2½-acre communal garden in Notting Hill, part of the Ladbroke Estate, much of which was designed and built by Thomas Allom in the 1850s. Regarded by many as one of the least altered squares in the area, it has been described as a plantsman's garden.

[NEW] 2 STANLEY ROAD, N2
East Finchley N2 0NB. Tudor & Hilary Spencer, 020 8883 7301, tudorspencer@hotmail.com. *Tube: East Finchley, then 10 mins walk. Bus: 143, or any bus to High Rd, then 5 mins walk.* Home-made teas. **Adm £2, chd free. Suns 18 May; 7 Sept** (2-5.30). **Visitors also welcome by appt.**
Recently transformed front and rear garden of Edwardian semi, with formal 'heron-proof' pond. central circle and viewing platform. Densely planted to create 8 distinct areas incorporating colourful vegetable plot, alpine bed, ferns and tree fern, bamboos and perennials. Boundaries softened with varied climbers for scent and foliage. Designed to be completely wheelchair-friendly without aesthetic compromise in hard landscape or planting. A garden for yr-round enjoyment.

26 STODART ROAD, SE20
Anerley SE20 8ET. Les Miller & Elizabeth Queen. Home-made teas. **Adm £2.50, chd free. Sun 8 June** (2-5). **Also open 9 Howard Road.**
Small sloping town garden on different levels. Mature shrubs and trees provide green oasis. Rose arches, clematis, honeysuckle and tiny pond. Shady

area with ferns, hellebores and symphytum. A cottage garden in an urban environment.

STONE (ZEN) GARDEN, W3
55 Carbery Avenue, Acton W3 9AB. Three Wheels Buddhist Centre, www.threewheels.org.uk. *5 mins walk. Tube: Acton Town 5 mins walk, 200yds off A406.* Home-made teas. **Adm £2, chd free. Sats, Suns 17, 18 May; 13, 14 Sept** (2-6).
Pure Japanese Zen garden (so no flowers) with twelve large and small rocks of various colours and textures set in islands of moss and surrounded by a sea of grey granite gravel raked in a stylised wave pattern. Garden surrounded by trees and bushes outside a cob wall. Oak-framed wattle and daub shelter with Norfolk reed thatched roof. Japanese Tea Ceremony demonstrations.

4 STRADBROKE GROVE
Buckhurst Hill IG9 5PD. Mr & Mrs Brighten, 020 8505 2716, carol@cbrighten.fsnet.co.uk. *Between Epping & Woodford, 5m from M25 J26. Tube: Buckhurst Hill, turn R cross rd to Stradbroke Grove.* **Adm £2.** Visitors welcome by appt, **June only, coaches permitted.**
Secluded garden, designed to enhance its sloping aspect. Steps wind downwards to thickly planted pergola, leading to rose-screened vegetable and fruit garden. Central gravelled area with an unusual mix of grasses, shells, pots and succulents.

SUMMERLAWN
29 Astons Road, Moor Park, Northwood HA6 2LB. Frankie & Leslie Lipton, leslie@leslielipton.co.uk. Light refreshments & cream teas. **Adm £3, chd free. Suns 11 May; 10 Aug** (2-6). **Visitors also welcome by appt for groups of 10+, no large coaches.**
Approx ¾ acre laid out in 3 rooms: herbaceous, formal and orchard, each with water feature. House and garden set within Conservation Area with fine views. Paths leading to 6 terraces with seating areas, gazebo and summerhouse. Wildlife-friendly garden for all seasons. Guide dogs allowed. Jazz band. Featured on BBC TV Open Gardens. Unprotected ponds.

NEW 18 SYDENHAM HILL, SE26
SE26 6SR. Mrs Margaret Thomas Tetlow & Mr Geoffrey Tetlow, 020 8778 0218. *Stn: Sydenham Hill. Buses: any to Crystal Palace, 363 along Sydenham Hill.* Home-made teas. **Adm £3, chd free. Sun 4 May** (2-6). Visitors also welcome by appt.
Mature woodland garden belonging to old Georgian farmhouse, being the first recorded house built on Sydenham Hill. Walkway through 22 different species of trees opening to large lawn bordered by mature shrubs and perennial flower beds. Well and old pump.

NEW 72 TANFIELD AVENUE, NW2
NW2 7RT. Mr Orod Ohanians, 07887 853090, oohanians@yahoo.co.uk. *Tube: Neasden, then short walk.* Light refreshments & teas. **Adm £2, chd free. Suns 30 Mar; 21 Sept** (11-4). Visitors also welcome by appt for groups of any size under 20 people.
Garden designed to be a 'mini botanical garden', packed with many exotic plants from China, New Zealand, Australia, Chile, central America, Middle East, Mediterranean, S Africa and Britain. Plants carefully chosen to survive, with a bit of care, in the British climate and complemented by rocks, pond, waterfall and bog garden. Exhibition of unique pottery suitable for garden use.

Plants carefully chosen to survive, with a bit of care, in the British climate . . .

TEWKESBURY LODGE GARDEN GROUP, SE23
Forest Hill SE23 3DE. *Off S Circular (A205) behind Horniman Museum & Gardens. Stn: Forest Hill, 10 mins walk. Buses: 176, 185, 312, P4.* Home-made teas at 53 Ringmore Rise. **Combined adm £4, chd free (share to Marsha Phoenix Trust & St Christopher's Hospice). Sun 25 May** (2-6). **Evening Opening** £5, wine, Sat 24 May (6-9). **Also open 14 Radlet Ave.**
A group of very different gardens with spectacular views.

THE COACH HOUSE
3 The Hermitage. Pat Rae
Sculptor's mature courtyard and roof garden, crammed full of unusual plants and sculptures. Water features, wildlife interest, vegetables and decorative plants in containers large and small, many of which have been fired in the artist's kiln and are for sale.

27 HORNIMAN DRIVE
Rose Agnew
Small, low maintenance, N-facing front garden with shrubs creating tapestry of green. Evolving back garden with emphasis on colour harmony using perennials, roses and shrubs. Vegetable areas, greenhouse, views over S London and N Downs.

53 RINGMORE RISE
Valerie Ward
Corner plot with spectacular views over London. Front garden inspired by Beth Chatto's dry garden, with stunning borders in soft mauves, yellows and white. Rear garden on three levels. Themed beds, some shaded, others sunny. Large pond; patio with pergola. Sloping garden with some steps.

30 WESTWOOD PARK
Jackie McLaren
Garden designer's sloping creation, herb garden, water features, winding paths with modern elements, unusual plant combinations. Unusual pots and hanging baskets link patio and garden. Featured in 'The English Garden', 'Gardeners' World' magazine, 'Homes & Gardens', 'House Beautiful' & 'Evening

Standard'. Steep slopes, regret no pushchairs.

27 THORPEWOOD AVENUE, SE26
Sydenham. SE26 4BU. Barbara & Gioni Nella. *1/2 m from Forest Hill Stn. Just off the S Circular (A205) turning up Sydenham Hill nr Horniman Gardens or Dartmouth Rd from Forest Hill stn. Buses: 122, 176, 312 to Thorpewood Ave.* Home-made teas. **Adm £3, chd free (share to NSPCC). Sun 15 June** (2-5.30). **Evening Opening** £3.50, wine, Sat 14 June (6-9).
Mature tree-bordered 1/2 -acre garden on gently sloping site. Mixed borders with lots of interesting shrubs and perennials. Formal vegetable plot and gravel slope growing Mediterranean and alpine plants, pond and varied sitting areas. Small 'Jungle' growing bamboos, bananas and tree ferns.

TUDOR ROAD GARDENS
Hampton TW12 2NG. *3m W of Kingston. Bus: R70 from Twickenham & Richmond to Tudor Ave, Hampton. Buses: 111, 216 to Hampton mainline stn. Tudor Rd 7 mins walk.* Home-made teas. **Combined adm £5, chd free. Sat 17, Sun 18 May** (2-7). Three neighbouring gardens in leafy W London suburb. Tickets from 45 Tudor Rd only. Small art exhibition and interesting workshop at no. 45 and hobbies studio at no. 88.

45 TUDOR ROAD
Rita & Colin Armfield, 020 8941 3315, ritacolin@tudor45.plus.com. Visitors also welcome by appt 19-23 May only, for groups of 10+.
Surprising W-facing garden (140ft x 25ft). Chinese side entrance gate - wall mural painted by artist/owner. Raised terrace with seating and many planted pots, citrus, fig, palms etc. Spring shrubs and trees divide the garden into rooms. York stone path gently curves past pond and waterfall, greenhouse and herbaceous planting through to bamboos, ferns and raised woodland area. Tasteful, artistic features throughout the garden. Featured in 'Amateur Gardening' and shortlisted in Daily Mail National Garden Competition 2007.

84 TUDOR ROAD
Ian & Lynda Clark
Tranquil, urban garden of 130ft, offering privacy and greenery. Stocked with mature shrubs and trees including well-established Japanese maple tree. Water feature flows over smooth pebbles and slate and a pergola offers a secluded and shaded seating area. At the end of the garden is a decked area surrounded by semi-tropical planting.

88 TUDOR ROAD
Alexandra & Barrington Skinner
Pretty 130ft x 20ft garden at rear of Edwardian semi-detached villa. Old climbing Noisette rose covered arbour, weeping cherry tree and fish pond. Lawns surrounded by mixed plantings. Small vegetable patch with selected produce. Plenty of seating for those tranquil summer evenings. Natural areas to encourage wildlife.

208 WALM LANE, THE GARDEN FLAT, NW2
NW2 3BP. Miranda & Chris Mason, www.thegardennw2.co.uk. *Tube: Kilburn. Garden at junction of Exeter Rd & Walm Lane. Buses: 16, 32, 189, 226, 245, 260, 266, 316 to Cricklewood Broadway, then consult A-Z. Home-made teas.* **Adm £2.50, chd free. Sun 15 June (2-7). Evening Opening with music £3.50, wine, Wed 13 Aug (5-9). Also open 15 June 10 Hoveden Road.**
Large S-facing oasis of green with big sky. Meandering lawn with island beds, fishpond with fountain, curved and deeply planted borders of perennials and flowering shrubs. Shaded mini woodland area of tall trees underplanted with rhododendrons, ferns and hostas with winding path from oriental-inspired summerhouse to secluded circular seating area.

WALTHAM FOREST REGISTER OFFICE, E17
106 Grove Road, Walthamstow E17 9BY. Garden Curator, Teresa Farnham, 07761 476651, farnhamz@yahoo.co.uk. *On corner of Grove Rd & Fraser Rd. Bus to Lea Bridge Rd, Bakers Arms & 5 mins walk up Fraser Rd. Home-made teas.* **Adm £1, chd free. Mon 5 May (11-4). Visitors also welcome by appt.**

Front and rear gardens of former Victorian vicarage in Walthamstow, created using cuttings as well as plants from seed to survive drought and shallow soil, and plants that look after themselves until they are pruned! Walkway, planted with roses and passion flowers, leads to honeysuckle and clematis arbour. Mixed borders, oak and Judas tree. Good to visit for low maintenance ideas for yr-round cover. Chemical-free. Hedgehogs, frogs and many bird species. Quiet area for contemplation with wild and native flowers. Book & plant sale, free gardening advice.

> Walkway, planted with roses and passion flowers, leads to honeysuckle and clematis arbour . . . quiet area for contemplation . . .

340 WALTON ROAD
West Molesey KT8 2JD. Anita Newman & Garry Wilson. *1½ m W of Hampton Court. Mainline stn: Hampton Court. Buses: 216, 411 alight Lord Hotham PH, ½ min walk.* **Evening Opening £3, wine, Sun 22 June (6-9).**
Long, narrow SW-facing garden (25m x 5m) featuring Mediterranean patio with pergola, water feature, variety of climbers and containers, creating intimate dining areas, leading down onto lawned garden cleverly designed to maximise space. Incl covered seating area, shrubs, trees, climbers, fig tree, lavenders and arum lilies, all forming calm green oasis.

THE WATERGARDENS
Warren Road, Kingston-upon-Thames KT2 7LF. The Residents' Association. *1m E of Kingston. From Kingston take A308 (Kingston Hill) towards London; after about ½ m turn R into Warren Rd.* **Adm £3, chd £1. Suns 18 May; 19 Oct (2-4.30).**
Japanese landscaped garden originally part of Coombe Wood Nursery, approx 9 acres with water cascade features. Some steep slopes and steps.

NEW WELLWOOD
Watts Lane, Chislehurst BR7 5PJ. Jennifer & Mark Taylor. *Nr Chislehurst cricket ground and golf club. Approx 300yds from mini roundabout at junction of Bromley Rd and Watts Lane.* **Adm £3.50. Evening Opening, wine, Fri 6 June (6-8.30).**
Comparatively young garden, designed and planted by Joanna Herald in 2005. A wide terrace links a decked pool surround and an adjacent lawned area. Planting largely Mediterranean with olive trees and silver foliage, bulbs and a pebbled area with pots.

2 WESTERN LANE, SW12
SW12 8JS. Mrs Anne Birnhak, annebirnhak@castlebalham.fsnet. co.uk. *Tube: Clapham South or Balham. Wandsworth Common mainline stn. Please park in Nightingale Lane.* **Adm £2. Suns 11 May; 15 June; 20 July (3-4.30). Also open 15 June only 28 Old Devonshire Rd.** Visitors also welcome by appt. Groups of 20+ by appt only, coaches permitted.
Enchanting patio garden, 28ft x 22ft, crammed with 2000 different plants. Walkways offer views of the spectacular clematis collection (250 varieties). Stunning wooden pergola, thundering waterfall, metal parasols and containers stacked in tiers. Anne's insatiable appetite for collecting rare plants gives visitors the opportunity to enjoy a constantly changing display. Featured in 'Wandsworth Borough News', 'Essential Local' and 'Brightside'. No access for wheelchairs, prams or bicycles.

WHITTON CRC

1 Britannia Lane, off Constance Road, Whitton TW2 7JX. London Borough of Richmond. *3m W of Richmond. Mainline stn: Whitton. Bus: H22 alight at Whitton stn. No parking in Britannia Lane. Free parking in Constance Rd & surrounding streets.* Light refreshments & teas. **Adm £2, chd free. Wed 4 June (11-3).**
Narrow 180ft organic garden maintained by staff and people with learning disabilities whose day centre occupies the remainder of the site. The cottage-style planting has produced a mass of colour and scent with a lavender and fuchsia bed, mixed borders, butterfly garden, wildlife pond and raised bed of shrubs and roses. Leaf cutter bees. Winner Richmond in Bloom (Best Environmental Garden).

NEW 5 WILDWOOD RISE, NW11

Hampstead Garden Suburb NW11 6TA. Ms Judy Green. *Tube: Golders Green, then H2 bus to Wildwood Rd. Off Wildwood Rd, last house on L.* Home-made teas. **Adm £2.50, chd free. Sun 29 June (2-6). Also open Asmuns Hill Gardens & 15 Lytton Close.**
Stunningly beautiful garden close to Hampstead Heath. Architectural planting with some interesting clipped trees, especially the 'cloud' bay tree. Good selection of unusual and decorative shrubs and perennials throughout the yr.

86 WILLIFIELD WAY, NW11

Hampstead Garden Suburb NW11 6YJ. Diane Berger. *Tube: Golders Green, then H2 bus to Willifield Way.* Home-made teas. **Adm £2.50, chd free. Sun 20 July (2-5.30). Evening Opening £4, wine, Wed 16 July (6-9). Also open 20 July only 157 Hampstead Way.**
Mature trees and hedges frame this 120ft x 50ft award-winning cottage garden, a plantsman's delight, densely planted with interesting perennials, trees and shrubs. Features incl pergola walk draped in roses and clematis leading to secret, shady decked patio; herbaceous and hot borders and terraced pond area. Winner Best Garden, Hampstead Garden Suburb Horticultural Society.

NEW 89 WILLIFIELD WAY, NW11

Hampstead Garden Suburb NW11 6YH. Mr & Mrs Pulvernis. *Off Finchley Rd, nr N Circular. Tube: Golders Green then bus H2 to Willifield Green or 82, 102, 460 to Temple Fortune.* **Adm £2.50, chd free. Sun 8 June (2-6).**
Romantic cottage garden with a pergola draped in old roses and clematis and a gazebo entwined with roses and jasmine. Mature trees, shrubs and borders create an intimate haven of tranquillity.

NEW 91 WILLIFIELD WAY, NW11

Hampstead Garden Suburb NW11 6YH. Ms Karen Grant. *Off Finchley Rd, nr N Circular. Tube: Golders Green. Buses: H2 to Willifield Green or 82, 102, 460 to Temple Fortune.* Home-made teas. **Adm £2.50, chd free. Sun 11 May (2-5). Also open 94 Oakwood Road.**
Windows and doors are framed by topiaried pyracantha. Re-creation of an Elizabethan knot garden with 4 box-edged beds densely planted for yr-round interest. Dovecote, mosaic floor, sink troughs with alpines and succulents.

27 WOOD VALE, N10

N10 3DJ. Mr & Mrs A W Dallman. *Muswell Hill 1m. A1 to Woodman PH; signed Muswell Hill. From Highgate tube, take Muswell Hill Rd, sharp R into Wood Lane leading to Wood Vale.* Home-made teas. **Adm £2.50, chd 50p, under 5 free. Sat, Sun 28, 29 June (1.30-6).**
³/₄-acre garden, 300ft long, abounding with surprises. Herbaceous borders, shrubbery, pond and a new feature every yr. Once inside you would think you were in the countryside. Seating for over 90 people, with shady areas and delicious home-made teas. Every effort is made to make our visitors welcome.

33 WOOD VALE, N10

N10 3DJ. Mona Abboud, 020 8883 4955. *Tube: Highgate, 10 mins walk. Buses: W3, W7 to top of Park Rd.* Light refreshments & teas. **Adm £2, chd free. Sun 18 May (2-6). Also open 15 & 46 Dukes Ave. Visitors also welcome by appt.**
Very long garden entered via steep but safe staircase. Unusual Mediterranean shrubs with emphasis on shapes, textures and foliage colour. Garden on two levels, first more formal with a centrepiece fountain, second meandering. Featured in 'Ham & High Broadway'.

82 WOOD VALE, SE23

SE23 3ED. Nigel & Linda Fisher, fisher.nigel@googlemail.com, www.woodvalegarden.blogspot.com. *Off S Circular Rd. Mainline stn: Forest Hill. Buses: 176, 185, 363 & P13. Ample street parking.* Home-made teas. **Adm £3, chd free (share to Southwark MIND). Sun 6 July (2-5). Also open 66A East Dulwich Rd. Visitors also welcome by appt.**
Large 90ft x 180ft contemporary garden designed by Christopher Bradley-Hole. A jigsaw of perennial and grass bays with a range of views offering yr-round interest for plantsmen, designers and children. Starred garden in 'GGG'.

66 WOODBOURNE AVENUE, SW16

SW16 1UT. Brian Palmer & Keith Simmonds. *Enter from Garrads Rd by Tooting Bec Common (by car only).* Home-made teas. **Adm £2, chd 50p. Sun 29 June (1-6).**
Garden designer's garden, constantly evolving. Cottage-style front garden 40ft x 60ft containing roses and herbaceous plants with a subtropical twist with bananas and palms. Rear garden approx 40ft x 80ft with recently added features, shrubs, trees and gazebo, creating a tranquil oasis in an urban setting. 13th yr of opening in 2008.

Big leaves, giant grasses, ferns, meat-eaters and spiky things all come together evoking a strange and faraway land . . .

11 WOODLANDS ROAD, SW13

SW13 0JZ. Victor & Lesley West.
Take Vine Rd off Upper Richmond Rd to find Woodlands Rd 2nd L. Cream teas. **Adm £2, chd 50p. Sun 18 May (12-6).**
Higgledy piggledy planting of trees, shrubs and perennials hides a softly structured garden design. Gentle colour schemes planted for low maintenance throughout the seasons with special emphasis on attracting birds, bees and pondlife, all of which makes for a relaxed town space.

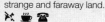 23 WOODVILLE ROAD, W5

Ealing W5 2SE. John & Julia Argyropoulos, 020 8997 4841, john@argyropoulos.vispa.com, www.cooltropicalplants.com.
Tube/mainline: Ealing Broadway, then approx 200m N. Easy unrestricted parking in nearby rds. Home-made teas. **Adm £3, chd free. Sun 31 Aug (2-7). Visitors also welcome by appt in Aug & Sept only.**
120ft walled garden featuring a mixture of stunning tender and hardy exotics. These magnificent beauties cloak the garden which encompasses 3 levels and 2 ponds. Big leaves, giant grasses, ferns, meat-eaters and spiky things all come together evoking a strange and faraway land.

THE WORLD GARDEN AT LULLINGSTONE CASTLE

See Kent.

Lodon County Volunteers

County Organiser
Penny Snell, Moleshill House, The Fairmile, Cobham, Surrey KT11 1BG, 01932 864532, pennysnellflowers@btinternet.com

County Treasurer & London Tours
Richard Raworth, 7 St George's Road, St Margaret's, Twickenham TW1 1QS, 07831 476088, raworth.r@blueyonder.co.uk

Assistant County Organisers
NW London Susan Bennett & Earl Hyde, 5 St Regis Close, Alexandra Park Road, Muswell Hill, London N10 2DE, 020 8883 8540
SW London Joey Clover, 13 Fullerton Road, London SW18 1BU, 020 8870 8740, joeyclover@dsl.pipex.com
Hampstead Anne Crawley, 116 Willifield Way, London NW11 6YG, 020 8455 7618, annecrawley@waitrose.com
SE London Gillian Davies, 32 Chestnut Road, London SE27 9LF, 020 8670 8916, cag.davies@btinternet.com
E London Teresa & Stuart Farnham, 17 Greenstone Mews, London E11 2RS, 020 8530 6729, farnhamz@yahoo.co.uk
Hackney Izi Glover, 15 Albion Drive, London E8 4LX, 020 7683 0104, glover@gayhurst.hackney.sch.uk
SE & Outer London Winkle Haworth, 38 Killieser Avenue, London SW2 4NT, 020 8671 4196, winklehaworth@hotmail.com
Islington Anna McKane, 36 Thornhill Square, London N1 1BE, 020 7609 7811, a.r.mckane@city.ac.uk
Outer W London Anita Newman, 340 Walton Road, West Molesey, Surrey KT8 2JD, 020 8941 1170
W London, Barnes & Chiswick Jenny Raworth, 7 St George's Road, St Margaret's, Twickenham TW1 1QS, 020 8892 3713, jenny@jraworth.freeserve.co.uk
Highgate, St John's Wood & Holland Park Sue Whittington, Southwood Lodge, 33 Kingsley Place, London N6 5EA, 020 8348 2785, suewhittington@hotmail.co.uk

Mark your diary with these special events in 2008

EXPLORE SECRET GARDENS DURING CHELSEA WEEK

Tue 20 May, Wed 21 May, Thur 22 May, Fri 23 May
Full day tours: £78 per person, 10% discount for groups
Advance Booking required, telephone 01932 864532 or
email pennysnellflowers@btinternet.com

Specially selected private gardens in London, Surrey and Berkshire. The tour price includes transport and lunch with wine at a popular restaurant or pub.

FROGMORE – A ROYAL GARDEN (BERKSHIRE)

Tue 3 June 10am - 5.30pm (last adm 4pm)
Garden adm £4, chd free. Advance booking recommended telephone 01483 211535 or email orders@ngs.org.uk

A unique opportunity to explore 30 acres of landscaped garden, rich in history and beauty.

FLAXBOURNE FARM – FUN AND SURPRISES (BEDFORDSHIRE)

Sun 8 June 10am - 5pm Adm £5, chd free
No booking required, come along on the day!

Bring the whole family and enjoy a plant fair and garden party and have fun in this beautiful and entertaining garden of 2 acres.

WISLEY RHS GARDEN – MUSIC IN THE GARDEN (SURREY)

Tue 19 August 6 - 9pm
Adm (incl RHS members) £7, chd under 15 free

A special opening of this famous garden, exclusively for the NGS. Enjoy music and entertainment as you explore a range of different gardens.

For further information visit www.ngs.org.uk or telephone 01483 211535

NORFOLK

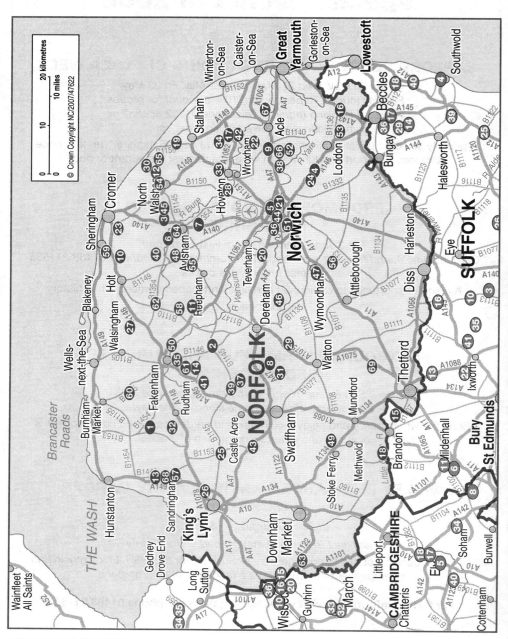

Opening Dates

February

SUNDAY 10
- 1 Bagthorpe Hall
- 39 Lexham Hall

March

SUNDAY 23
- 69 Wretham Lodge

MONDAY 24
- 69 Wretham Lodge

SUNDAY 30
- 9 Burlingham Gardens

April

SUNDAY 6
- 15 Desert World Gardens
- 25 Gayton Hall

SATURDAY 12
- 19 East Ruston Old Vicarage

SUNDAY 13
- 45 The Old Cottage

SUNDAY 27
- 8 Bradenham Hall
- 13 Croft House
- 60 Sly's Farm

May

SUNDAY 4
- 16 Devils End
- 26 Grasmere
- 40 Mannington Hall
- 62 Stody Lodge

MONDAY 5
- 26 Grasmere
- 30 Hill Cottage
- 65 Witton Hall

WEDNESDAY 7
- 33 Hoveton Hall Gardens

SUNDAY 11
- 51 The Plantation Garden
- 52 Plovers Hill
- 54 Rivermount
- 60 Sly's Farm

SUNDAY 18
- 34 How Hill Farm
- 39 Lexham Hall
- 62 Stody Lodge

SATURDAY 24
- 67 Woodlands Farm

SUNDAY 25
- 14 Derwen
- 18 East Lode
- 59 Sheringham Park
- 61 'Sol'
- 62 Stody Lodge
- 67 Woodlands Farm

MONDAY 26
- 10 Chestnut Farm
- 14 Derwen
- 45 The Old Cottage
- 53 Raveningham Hall
- 61 'Sol'
- 62 Stody Lodge

FRIDAY 30
- 22 Fairhaven Woodland & Water Garden (Evening)

June

SUNDAY 1
- 7 Bolwick Hall
- 42 The Mowle
- 62 Stody Lodge

SUNDAY 8
- 17 The Dutch House
- 43 Narborough Hall
- 59 Sheringham Park

SATURDAY 14
- 63 56 Well Creek Road

SUNDAY 15
- 3 Beck House
- 30 Hill Cottage
- 41 Manor House Farm
- 47 Old Sun House
- 49 Oxburgh Hall Garden & Estate
- 56 Sallowfield Cottage
- 63 56 Well Creek Road

SATURDAY 21
- 37 Kempstone Manor Farm

SUNDAY 22
- 5 Bishop's House
- 31 Holme Hale Hall
- 43 Narborough Hall
- 69 Wretham Lodge

SUNDAY 29
- 28 Heggatt Hall
- 44 North Lodge

July

SUNDAY 6
- 4 Bergh Apton Manor
- 15 Desert World Gardens
- 29 High House Gardens
- 32 Houghton Hall Walled Garden
- 45 The Old Cottage
- 46 The Old Rectory

FRIDAY 11
- 50 Pensthorpe Nature Reserve & Gardens (Evening)

SUNDAY 13
- 35 6 Jarvis Drive
- 64 West Lodge

SATURDAY 19
- 6 Blickling Hall
- 23 Felbrigg Hall

SUNDAY 20
- 49 Oxburgh Hall Garden & Estate
- 3 Beck House
- 33 Hoveton Hall Gardens
- 52 Plovers Hill
- 66 Woodland View
- 68 Woodwynd

SUNDAY 27
- 8 Bradenham Hall
- 24 The Garden in an Orchard

August

SUNDAY 3
- 45 The Old Cottage

SUNDAY 10
- 52 Plovers Hill
- 58 Severals Grange
- 66 Woodland View

SUNDAY 17
- 21 The Exotic Garden
- 36 Jungle Garden

SUNDAY 24
- 26 Grasmere
- 55 Salle Park

MONDAY 25
- 26 Grasmere

September

SUNDAY 7
- 20 Easton Lodge
- 48 Oulton Hall
- 51 The Plantation Garden

SATURDAY 13
- 67 Woodlands Farm

SUNDAY 14
- 2 Beck Farm
- 43 Narborough Hall
- 67 Woodlands Farm

SATURDAY 20
- 24 The Garden in an Orchard

SUNDAY 21
- 24 The Garden in an Orchard
- 29 High House Gardens

SUNDAY 28
- 8 Bradenham Hall
- 40 Mannington Hall

October

SATURDAY 4
- 19 East Ruston Old Vicarage

Gardens open to the public

- 6 Blickling Hall
- 8 Bradenham Hall
- 19 East Ruston Old Vicarage
- 21 The Exotic Garden

22 Fairhaven Woodland & Water Garden
23 Felbrigg Hall
32 Houghton Hall Walled Garden
33 Hoveton Hall Gardens
40 Mannington Hall
49 Oxburgh Hall Garden & Estate
50 Pensthorpe Nature Reserve & Gardens
51 The Plantation Garden
53 Raveningham Hall
57 Sandringham Gardens
58 Severals Grange
59 Sheringham Park
62 Stody Lodge

By appointment only

11 Church House Garden
12 The Cottage
27 Hawthorn House
38 Lake House

Also open by appointment ☎

3 Beck House
7 Bolwick Hall
9 Burlingham Gardens
10 Chestnut Farm
15 Desert World Gardens
17 The Dutch House
18 East Lode
24 The Garden in an Orchard
25 Gayton Hall
30 Hill Cottage
31 Holme Hale Hall
39 Lexham Hall
42 The Mowle
43 Narborough Hall
45 The Old Cottage
48 Oulton Hall
52 Plovers Hill
63 56 Well Creek Road
65 Witton Hall
66 Woodland View
68 Woodwynd

The Gardens

1 BAGTHORPE HALL
Bagthorpe PE31 6QY. Mr & Mrs D Morton. 3¹/₂ m N of East Rudham, off A148. At King's Lynn take A148 to Fakenham. At East Rudham (approx 12m) turn L by Cat & Fiddle PH. 3¹/₂ m into hamlet of Bagthorpe. Farm buildings on L, wood on R, white gates set back at top. Home-made teas & soup. **Adm £3, chd free. Sun 10 Feb (11-4).**
Snowdrops carpeting woodland walk, snowdrop walk. Decoupage plant pots for sale.
✕ ⊗ ⊨ ☕

2 NEW BECK FARM
The Green, Brisley NR20 5LL. Bridget Diggens. *6m SW of Fakenham. Situated S of Brisley Green off B1145. Turn down farm track opp pill box on N Elmham side of Brisley.* Home-made teas at Brisley Hall. **Adm £4, chd free. Sun 14 Sept (12-4).**
1-acre garden developed over 18yrs by garden designer/owner, to incl formal hedging and topiary, bog and water planting, herbacous border, mixed shrub and rose borders. Of special interest, 14 mophead holm oaks dividing garden.
♿ ✕ ⊗ ☕

3 BECK HOUSE
Bridge Road, Colby, nr Aylsham NR11 7EA. Hazel & Tony Blackburn, 01263 733167. *14m N of Norwich. Take B1145 from N Walsham to Aylsham, after 3¹/₂ m turn R into Bridge Rd opp Banningham Bridge Old Garage, next to school (Colby).* Home-made teas. **Adm £3, chd free. Suns 15 June; 20 July (11-5). Visitors also welcome by appt.**
1¹/₂ acres, packed borders of unusual perennials, shrubs and trees, large natural pond and paths through wild areas with lovely views across the river. S-facing front garden with drought-loving plants; sit and enjoy the tranquil views on the many seats provided. Featured in 'Amateur Gardening'. Parents be aware dangers for children: pond and river unfenced, gravel drive.
♿ ✕ ⊗ ☕ ☎

4 BERGH APTON MANOR
Threadneedle Street, Bergh Apton NR15 1BL. Kip & Alison Bertram. *8m SW of Norwich. Take A146 (Beccles Rd) from Norwich. Exactly 5m from Southern bypass see Fina signpost pointing down Mill Rd to Bergh Apton. Take this turning, ¹/₂ m on Xrds turn L. Garden ¹/₂ m on L.* Home-made teas. **Adm £3.50, chd free. Sun 6 July (2-5).**
Established walled garden as part of Georgian Manor House (not open). Recently designed by Tomothy Carless, this beautiful garden is planted for colour throughout the yr with formal edged borders and beds, pond, summerhouse, thyme lawn and terrace with vistas across 60 acres of wooded parkland which can be walked.
♿ ✕ ☕

Sit and enjoy the tranquil views on the many seats provided . . .

5 BISHOP'S HOUSE
Bishopgate, Norwich NR3 1SB. The Bishop of Norwich. *City centre. Entrance opp Law Courts on Bishopgate on N side of Cathedral (not through The Close). Through Archway on R. Public car parking nearby. No parking at Bishop's House.* Home-made teas. **Adm £2.50, chd free. Sun 22 June (2-5).**
4-acre walled garden dating back to C12. Extensive lawns with specimen trees. Borders with many rare and unsual shrubs. Spectacular herbaceous borders flanked by yew hedges. Rose beds, meadow labyrinth, kitchen garden, woodland walk and long border with hostas. New bamboo walk. Popular plant sales area. Gravel paths.
♿ ✕ ⊗ ☕

6 ◆ BLICKLING HALL
Aylsham NR11 6NF. The National Trust, 01263 738030, www.nationaltrust.org.uk. *15m N of Norwich. 1¹/₂ m NW of Aylsham on N side of B1354.* **House and Garden £9.10, chd £4.50, Garden only £6, chd £3. Weds to Suns & BH Mons 15 Mar to 2 Nov. For NGS: Sat 19 July (10.15-5.15).**
Large garden, orangery, crescent lake, azaleas, rhododendrons, herbaceous borders. Historic Jacobean house. 80yds of new double border planted in 2006, in the style of Norah Lindsay. Special opening of kitchen garden.
♿ ✕ ⊗ ☕

7 BOLWICK HALL
Marsham NR10 5PU. Mr & Mrs G C Fisher, 01263 732131, www.bolwick.com. *¹/₂ m S of Aylsham. On A140 towards Aylsham, take 1st R past Plough PH at Marsham, then next R onto private rd to front of Hall.* Home-made teas. **Adm**

£3, chd free. Sun 1 June (1-5).
Visitors also welcome by appt.
Landscaped gardens and park, attributed to Humphry Repton, surrounding late Georgian hall (not open) and stable block. Collection of mature trees, woodland walks around stream and mill pond, as well as more recently planted borders and working vegetable garden. Partial wheelchair access, gravel paths.

⑧ ◆ **BRADENHAM HALL**
Bradenham IP25 7QP. Chris & Panda Allhusen, 01362 687243/687279, www.bradenhamhall.co.uk. *6m E of Swaffham. 5m W of East Dereham off A47. Turn S signed Wendling & Longham. 1m turn S signed Bradenham, 2m.* **Garden only adm £4, chd free. 2nd & 4th Suns Apr to Sept.** For NGS: Suns 27 Apr; 27 July; 28 Sept (2-5.30).
A garden for all seasons. Flower gardens, formally designed and richly planted, formal rose gardens, paved garden, unusual climbers, herbaceous and shrub borders, traditional kitchen gardens with 2 glasshouses. Arboretum of over 800 different trees, all labelled. Massed daffodils in spring. A delight and an education.

⑨ **BURLINGHAM GARDENS**
31 Main Road, North Burlingham NR13 4TA. Ms Linda Laxton, 01603 716615, linda@wildflowers.co.uk. *7m E of Norwich. Off A47 signed North Burlingham, onto slip rd, near far end on L into grounds of British Wild Flower Plants.* Home-made teas. **Adm £3, chd free. Sun 30 Mar (10-4). Visitors also welcome by appt.**
The National Collection of Forsythia. 70 species and varieties, the majority in flower, incl dwarf, semi dwarf and larger varieties, over 300 planted in a walk and beds in lovely surroundings. Wild flower nursery (open), incl preview of plants grown for a garden at this years, Chelsea Flower Show. The grounds are being developed with wildlife in mind, using native species and installing wildlife friendly production systems and bird boxes complete with web-cams, for blue tits, robins, swallows and woodpeckers. Other nurseries will be selling specialist plants; holistic health practitioner to make your visit to our open day special.

Springtime brings a riot of colour, continuing through to autumn . . .

⑩ **CHESTNUT FARM**
West Beckham NR25 6NX. Mr & Mrs John McNeil Wilson, 01263 822241, john@mcneil-wilson.freeserve.co.uk. *2½ m S of Sheringham. Mid-way between Holt & Cromer. 1m S off the A148 at the Sheringham Park entrance. Sign post indicates 'By Rd to W Beckham'. Chestnut Farm located behind the village sign. Lots of free parking, WC.* Light refreshments & teas. **Adm £3, chd free. Mon 26 May (11-5). Visitors also welcome by appt March to Sept, open for groups, coaches permitted.**
3-acre garden, incl herbaceous border, woodland walk, traditional kitchen garden, pond and small aboretum. Plant collection built up over 40yrs by keen gardener and plant enthusiast, which incl many rare and unusual trees and shrubs surrounding C16 farmhouse (not open). The garden continues to grow and incl many new features. Visiting nurseries and will incl artists work in response to the garden.

⑪ NEW **CHURCH HOUSE GARDEN**
Hindolveston Road, Foulsham NR20 5RX. Mrs K Losco-Bradley, 01362 683583. *Take R by water tower off A1067 between Bintree & Fakenham. Keep straight on into Foulsham. Blue painted house just before church on R.* **Visitors welcome by appt June to Aug only, small parties.**
Small garden; plantsman's delight. Interesting and unusual plants - mostly flowering shrubs and small ornamental trees, accumulated by owner over more than 30yrs. Garden totally accessible by wheelchair.

⑫ **THE COTTAGE**
Hennesseys Loke, Edingthorpe Green NR28 9SS. Tim & Mary Richardson, 01692 402738, tmprichardson@hotmail.com. *2½ m NE of North Walsham. Off B1150 halfway between Bacton and North Walsham, turn L at village sign and follow signs to car park and cottage.* **Visitors welcome by appt June & July only for groups 10+, Evening openings wine & canapes.**
½ -acre garden with 4 ponds, bog areas, densely planted with reeds, bamboos and gunneras. Roses, clematis and shrubs all jostle for space giving the garden a lush and relaxed atmosphere. A haven for wildlife and all creatures are respected. No chemicals for over 30yrs within the garden. 3 summerhouses provide tranquil and restive settings.

⑬ **CROFT HOUSE**
111 Manor Road, Dersingham PE31 6YW. Walter & Jane Blaney. *8m NE of King's Lynn. Take A149 N from King's Lynn then B1440 into Dersingham. At T-lights turn R into Chapel Rd. In ½ m bear R into Manor Rd. Croft House opp church car park. Park in adjacent rds & church hall car park.* Cream teas in adjacent church hall. **Adm £3, chd free. Sun 27 Apr (2-5).**
An evolving garden designed with hidden areas of special interest. Paths meander through shrubberies, mature woodlands and around ponds, leading to formal gardens and orchard. Patios around the house incl formal pond, gravel mosaic and statuary. Springtime brings a riot of colour, continuing through to autumn.

⑭ NEW **DERWEN**
Whissonsett Road, Colkirk NR21 7NL. Alan & Maureen Piggott. *2m S of Fakenham. Between B1146 & A1065 (Colkirk not signed from A1065), follow NGS signs.* Home-made teas. **Combined with 'Sol' adm £3, chd free. Sun 25 (2-5), Mon 26 May (11-4).**
Herbaceous borders, shrubs, fruit trees, ponds, gravel garden, vegetable plots, unusual plants and shrubs, lawned areas. 2 greenhouses, chickens. Gravel driveway, some narrow paths.

15 DESERT WORLD GARDENS
Santon Downham IP27 0TU. Mr & Mrs Barry Gayton, 01842 765861. *4m N of Thetford. On B1107 Brandon 2m.* Light refreshments & teas. **Adm £3, chd free. Suns 6 Apr; 6 July (10-5). Visitors also welcome by appt.**
1¼ acres plantsman's garden, specialising in tropical and arid plants, hardy succulents - sempervivums, hanging gardens of babylon (plectranthus). Main garden - bamboos, herbaceous primula theatre, spring/summer bulbs, particularly lilies. View from roof garden. Radio Norfolk gardener. Glasshouses cacti/succulents 12500, viewing by appt only on a different day. Plant identification and expert advice.

In spring, masses of primroses and bluebells . . .

16 DEVILS END
Church Lane, Haddiscoe NR14 6PB. Peter Manthorpe. *7m SW of Gt Yarmouth. Nr junction of A143 & B1136. Park in Haddiscoe Church car park, accessed from B1136. Short walk to garden.* Home-made teas in church. **Adm £3.50, chd free. Sun 4 May (12-6).**
Romantic, 1-acre enthusiasts garden laid out on S-facing slope with some steep steps. Contains parterre, topiary, woodland walks, pond, potager and colour-themed borders. Many interesting plants.

17 THE DUTCH HOUSE
Ludham NR29 5NS. Mrs Peter Seymour, 01692 678225. *5m W of Wroxham. B1062 Wroxham to Ludham 7m. Turn R by Ludham village church into Staithe Rd. Garden ¼ m from village.* Home-made teas. **Adm £3, chd free. Sun 8 June (2-5).**

Visitors also welcome by appt June only, groups 10+, coaches wellome.
Long, narrow garden of approx 2½ acres leading through marsh and wood to Womack Water. Designed and planted originally by the painter Edward Seago and recently replanted by the present owner. Access to Womack Water limited due to steep bridge and uneven paths. Further re-planting in hand. Wheelchair access possible but difficult, terrace, cobbles and steps.

18 NEW EAST LODE
Nursery Lane, Hockwold-cum-Wilton IP26 4ND. Patricia & Keith Mansey, 01842 827096. *2m from Brandon. In Main St, Hockwold, turn down Church Lane, bear L at iron seat, then 1st house on R.* Light refreshments & teas. **Adm £3, chd free. Sun 25 May (11-5). Visitors also welcome by appt incl groups.**
Cottage garden of ½ acre, filled with colour throughout the yr by keen gardener/plantswoman. Many hellebores in spring, roses and clematis in summer, silver and evergreens for autumn and winter, tremendous underplanting of bulbs, plus wide range of unusual plants. Small pond, greenhouse, scree beds and conservatory. A haven for bees and butterflies. Small nursery. Member of Cottage Garden Society.

19 ◆ EAST RUSTON OLD VICARAGE
East Ruston NR12 9HN. Alan Gray & Graham Robeson, 01692 650432, www.eastrustonoldvicarage.co.uk. *3m N of Stalham. Turn off A149 onto B1159 signed Bacton, Happisburgh. After 2m turn R 200yds N of East Ruston Church (ignore sign to East Ruston).* **Adm £5, chd £1. Weds, Fris, Sats, Suns & Bank Hol Mons 21 Mar to 25 Oct. For NGS: Sats 12 Apr; 4 Oct (2-5.30).**
20-acre exotic coastal garden incl traditional borders, exotic garden, desert wash, sunk garden, topiary, water features, walled and Mediterranean gardens. Many rare and unusual plants, stunning plant combinations, wild flower meadows, old-fashioned cornfield, vegetable and cutting gardens.

20 EASTON LODGE
Lodge Road, Easton NR9 5EL. Mr & Mrs M Rampton. *6m W of Norwich. Cross the new southern Norwich bypass at the Easton roundabout & take the Ringland Rd.* Home-made teas. **Adm £3.50. Sun 7 Sept (2-5).**
Late Georgian house with Jacobean centre portion (not open). Large garden, in magnificent setting above river, surrounded by fine trees. Walks amongst interesting flower meadow and lake. Wheelchair access limited.

ELY GARDENS II
See Cambridgeshire.

21 ◆ THE EXOTIC GARDEN
126 Thorpe Road, Thorpe, Norwich NR1 1UL. Mr Will Giles, 01603 623167, www.exoticgarden.com. *Off A47. New entrance & car park via side entrance of Alan Boswell Insurance 126 Thorpe Rd next to DEFRA. Approx ½ m from Thorpe railway stn.* **Adm £4, chd free. Suns 15 June to 26 Oct. For NGS: Sun 17 Aug (1-5). Also open Jungle Garden.**
Exotic city garden covering approx 1 acre on a S-facing hillside incl new ½ -acre garden. In high summer the garden is a riot of colour among towering architectural plants such as cannas, bananas, aroids, palms etc giving the garden a truly subtropical feel, especially with its use of houseplants as bedding. New xerophytic garden (desert garden). Author of The Encyclopedia of Exotic Plants for Temperate Gardens.

22 NEW ◆ FAIRHAVEN WOODLAND & WATER GARDEN
School Road, South Walsham NR13 6DZ. Louise Rout, 01603 270449, www.fairhavengarden.com. *9m E of Norwich. At School Rd. Signed on A47 at B1140 junction,.* **Advance ticket £10, chd £8, on gate £12, chd £10 (incls hog roast & entertainment). Open every day except Christmas Day, summer 10-5, winter 10-4. For NGS: Evening Opening wine, Fri 30 May (6.30 for 7-9).**
130 acres of ancient woodland and water garden with private Broad. Excellent bird watching from boat. In spring, masses of primroses and bluebells, with azaleas and rhododendrons in several areas.

several areas. Candelabra primulas and unusual plants grow near the waterways. In summer, a variety of wild flowers. Special Evening Opening featuring the UK's finest collection of naturalised candelabra primulas with hog roast and entertainment. Scooter available to hire.

 ♿ ⚘ ☕

㉓ ◆ FELBRIGG HALL
Cromer NR11 8PR. The National Trust, 01263 837444, www.nationaltrust.org.uk. $2^{1}/_{2}$ m SW of Cromer. S of A148; main entrance from B1436. House and Garden £7.90, chd £3.70, Garden only £3.70, chd £1.60. For NGS: Sat 19 July (11-5).
Large pleasure gardens; mainly lawns and shrubs; orangery with camellias; large walled garden restored and restocked as fruit, vegetable, herb and flower garden; vine house; dovecote; dahlias; National Collection of *Colchicum*; wooded parks. 1 electric and 2 manual wheelchairs available.

♿ ✖ ⚘ NCCPG ☕

㉔ THE GARDEN IN AN ORCHARD
Mill Road, Bergh Apton NR15 1BQ. Mr & Mrs R W Boardman, 01508 480322. 6m SE of Norwich. Off A146 at Hellington Corner signed to Bergh Apton. Down Mill Rd 300yds. Adm £3, chd free. Sun 27 July; Sat 20, Sun 21 Sept (11-6). Visitors also welcome by appt.
$3^{1}/_{2}$ -acre garden created by the owners set in old orchard. Many rare plants set out in an informal pattern of wandering paths. $^{1}/_{2}$ acre of wild flower meadows, many bamboos, species roses and Michaelmas daisies. 9 species of eucalyptus. A plantsman's garden. Garden sculpture. Exhibition of botanical embroidery. Grass paths may be difficult when wet.

♿ ⚘ ☕ ☎

㉕ GAYTON HALL
Gayton PE32 1PL. The Earl & Countess of Romney, 01553 636259. 6m E of King's Lynn. On B1145; R on B1153. R down Back St 1st entrance on L. Home-made teas. Adm £3.50, chd free. Sun 6 Apr (1-5). Visitors also welcome by appt.
20-acre water garden, with over 2m of paths. Lawns, woodland, lakes, streams and bridges. Many unusual trees and shrubs. Spring bulbs and autumn colour. Traditional and

waterside borders. Primulas, astilbes, hostas, lysichitums, gunneras and many more. Gravel paths.

♿ ⚘ ☎

㉖ NEW GRASMERE
57 Ullswater Avenue, South Wootton PE30 3NJ. Steve & Elsa Carden. 4 NE of King's Lynn. On A149 King's Lynn by-pass follow signs Hunstanton/Sandringham until reaching Knights Hill Hotel, turn L towards N & S Wootton/ docks. After $^{1}/_{2}$ m turn L into Sandy Lane, rd bears L and becomes Ullswater Ave at T-junction, turn L garden on R by metal gates. Adm £3, chd free. Suns, Mons 4, 5 May; 24, 25 Aug (11-5).
0.2-acre garden generously planted plantspersons organic garden, with many acid loving plants incl camellias, acers and azaleas, unusual shrubs and plants for almost yr-round scent/structure. Lots of under-planting, grasses and phormiums. Tender plants and hidden rooms create an 'Aladdin's Cave' garden. Agave and succulant collection. Tearooms available 5mins drive away.

✖

Tender plants and hidden rooms create an 'Aladdin's Cave' garden.

㉗ HAWTHORN HOUSE
Moorgate Road, Hindringham NR21 0PT. Bryony Jacklin, 01328 878441, bryony.jacklin@btinternet.com. 18m SW of Cromer. Between Fakenham and Holt, off A148. Take Hindringham Rd at Crawfish PH. Continue 2m to village, past church, 2nd R. Adm £3, chd free. Visitors welcome by appt May to July, individuals & groups. Teas by arrangement.
Large 3-acre garden featuring herbaceous borders, island beds, pond and bog, gravel and herb gardens, willow work, traditional kitchen garden, orchard, butterfly garden and wild beds. Highly Commended in the 'Daily Mail' Garden of the Year Award. Gravel paths around house.

♿ ✖ ⚘ ☕ ☎

㉘ HEGGATT HALL
Horstead NR12 7AY. Mr & Mrs Richard Gurney. 6m N of Norwich. Take B1150 North Walsham rd out of Norwich go for N 6m. R at small Xrds signed Heggatt Hall. Turn L at T-junction house 400yds on L. Home-made teas. Adm £3.50, chd free. Sun 29 June (11.30-5).
Elizabethan house (not open) set in large gardens surrounded by parkland with ancient chestnut trees. Herbaceous border, sunken garden. Walled knot/rose garden leading into kitchen garden with wisteria walk and further flower beds.

✖ ☕

㉙ HIGH HOUSE GARDENS
Blackmoor Row, Shipdham IP25 7PU. Mr & Mrs F Nickerson. 6m SW of Dereham. Take the airfield or Cranworth Rd off A1075 in Shipdham. Blackmoor Row is signed. Home-made teas. Adm £3, chd free. Suns 6 July; 21 Sept (2-5.30).
Plantsman's garden with colour-themed herbaceous borders with extensive range of perennials. Box-edged rose and shrub borders. Woodland garden, pond and bog area. Newly planted orchard and vegetable garden. Wildlife area. Glasshouses.

♿ ✖ ⚘ ☕

㉚ HILL COTTAGE
School Road, Edingthorpe NR28 9SY. Shirley Gilbert, 01692 403519, shirley@flandershouse. demon.co.uk. 3m NE of North Walsham. Off B1150 halfway between North Walsham and Bacton, leave main rd at Edingthorpe Green and continue straight towards Paston for $^{3}/_{4}$ m. Cottage on L at top of hill. Parking in adjacent field. Home-made teas. Adm £3, chd free. Mon 5 May; Sun 15 June (11-5). Also open Witton Hall 5 May. Visitors also welcome by appt.
Cottage garden, approx $^{1}/_{4}$ acre, surrounding former farm workers' cottages. Organically cultivated and densely planted with both traditional and unusual varieties of drought resistant climbers, shrubs, perennial and annuals. Fruit, vegetable and herb gardens, greenhouse and pond. A real butterfly and wildlife paradise. Small nursery. Member of Norfolk Cottage Garden Society.

♿ ✖ ⚘ ☕ ☎

HOLLY TREE FARM
See Lincolnshire.

31 HOLME HALE HALL

Holme Hale IP25 7ED. Mr & Mrs Simon Broke, 01760 440328, broke@freenet.co.uk. *6m E of Swaffham, 8m W Dereham. Exit A47 King's Lynn/Norwich rd at Necton Garden Centre. Continue through Necton village and Holme Hale village approx 1½ m. At T-junction turn L, Hall gates on L immed after Low Common Rd.* Home-made teas. **Adm £4, chd free. Sun 22 June (2-6). Visitors also welcome by appt.**
Contemporary walled kitchen garden and front garden designed and planted in 2000 by Chelsea award winner Arne Maynard. The garden incorporates herbaceous, trained fruit, vegetables and traditional lean-to greenhouse. The garden is noted for its spring display, incl 3500 late spring tulips and its mid-summer and autumn flowering. Featured in 'House & Garden'. Partial wheelchair access.

32 ◆ HOUGHTON HALL WALLED GARDEN

Houghton PE31 6UE. The Marquess of Cholmondeley, 01485 528569, www.houghtonhall.com. *11m W of Fakenham. Signed from A148 approx halfway between King's Lynn and Fakenham.* **House and Garden £8, chd £3, family £20, Garden only £5, chd £2, family £15. Weds, Thurs, Suns & Bank Hol Mons Easter Sun to 28 Sept.** For NGS: Sun 6 July (11-5.30).
5-acre walled garden, divided by clipped yew hedges into 'garden rooms'. Stunning 120yd double herbaceous border, full of colour all summer. Orchid greenhouse, rustic temple. Rose parterre with old and new roses, sunken fountain and statues. Mixed kitchen garden. Wisteria pergola, pleached limes, spring and summer bulbs. Croquet lawn. New contemporary sculpture in the park. Permanent pieces by Richard Long, James Turrell, (Houghton Skyspace) Stephen Cox and Sol LeWitt.

33 ◆ HOVETON HALL GARDENS

nr Wroxham NR12 8RJ. Mr & Mrs Andrew Buxton, 01603 782798, www.hovetonhallgardens.co.uk. *8m N of Norwich. 1m N of Wroxham Bridge. Off A1151 Stalham Rd - follow brown tourist signs.* **Adm £5, chd 5-14yrs £2, wheelchairs & carers £2.50. Easter Sun & Bank Hol Mon,**

Sun 30 Mar to Sept, Weds, Thurs, Fris, Suns, BH Mon up to 14 Sept (10.30-5). For NGS: Wed 7 May; Sun 20 July (10.30-5).
15-acre gardens and grounds featuring daffodils, azaleas, rhododendrons and hydrangeas in woodland. Mature walled herbaceous garden, and redesigned walled kitchen garden. Water plants and lakeside walk. Woodland and gravel paths. Early C19 house (not open).

Family garden, to live in and enjoy, not just to look at . . .

34 HOW HILL FARM

Ludham NR29 5PG. Mr P D S Boardman. *2m W of Ludham. On A1062; then follow signs to How Hill. Farm garden S of How Hill.* **Adm £3, chd free. Sun 18 May (1-5).**
2 pretty gardens around house, 3rd started 1968 leading to 3-acre Broad dug 1978 with views over R Ant and Turf Fen Mill. About 10 acres incl Broad, 4 ponds, site of old Broad with 5ft Tussock sedges, about an acre of indigenous ferns under oak and alder. Paths through rare conifers, rhododendrons, azaleas, ornamental trees, shrubs, bamboos and herbaceous plants. Collection of holly species and varieties. Some sloping and soft paths.

35 NEW 6 JARVIS DRIVE

Colkirk NR21 7NG. Geoff Clark & Jenny Filby. *2m S of Fakenham. From Fakenham take B1145 towards Dereham. Through Pudding Norton then 1st R (signed Byway to Colkirk). Follow lane into village, Jarvis Drive is opp The Crown PH. Drop-off & pick-up only in Jarvis Drive (narrow cul-de-sac). Please park in surrounding rds or The Crown PH (Sunday lunch bookable).* Home-made teas. **Adm £3, chd free. Sun 13 July (1-5).**

A heaven for plants lovers! Over 300 varieties of shrubs and perennials create spectacular borders bursting with colour. Large vegetable and fruit garden, wild flower areas and many other features provide interest to all visitors. Full planting plans available and owners happy to advise. Gravel front drive.

36 NEW JUNGLE GARDEN

Tollhouse Road, Norwich NR5 8QF. Jon Kelf. *2m W of Norwich. Off A1074 Dereham Rd nr the ring rd, on LH-side travelling away from the city just past Kwik Fit & Gatehouse PH. Limited off street parking available.* Teas at The Exotic Garden. **Adm £2, chd free. Sun 17 Aug (1-5). Also open The Exotic Garden.**
Small town garden approx 26ft x 60ft with 5 levels of decking surrounded by dense, lush exotic planting, incl palms, bamboos, bananas, gingers, cannas and more.

37 NEW KEMPSTONE MANOR FARM

Litcham, King's Lynn PE32 2LG. Mr & Mrs N Bertram. *From Litcham take rd to Dunham, garden approx 1m along rd. From A47 turn off at Little Dunham and drive approx 3m, towards Litcham follow NGS signs, house on R.* Cold drinks & cakes. **Adm £3, chd free. Sat 21 June (12-5).**
The garden was in a delapidated state when we brought the property in 1992. Since then we have created several separate areas surrounding the house (not open). 2 meadows of wild flowers and grass paths, orchard, vegetable patch and greenhouse, plus a woodland walk which will be ongoing for the next few years. It is a family garden, to live in and enjoy, not just to look at. Partial wheelchair access, gravel and grass paths.

38 LAKE HOUSE

Postwick Lane, Brundall NR13 5LU. Mr & Mrs Garry Muter, 01603 712933. *5m E of Norwich. On A47; take Brundall turn at roundabout. Turn R into Postwick Lane at T-junction.*

Visitors welcome by appt **Feb to Nov, coaches permitted.**
2 acres of water gardens set among magnificent trees in steep cleft in river escarpment. Informal flower beds with interesting plants; naturalist's paradise; unsuitable for young children or the infirm. Stout shoes advisable. Beautiful lake - shore restoration. Featured on BBC TV The Flying Gardener.

✿ ☎

39 LEXHAM HALL
nr Litcham PE32 2QJ. Mr & Mrs Neil Foster, 01328 701288, neilfoster@lexhamestate.co.uk. *2m W of Litcham. 6m N of Swaffham off B1145.* Light refreshments & teas (Feb), Home-made teas (May). **Adm £4, chd free. Suns 10 Feb (11-4); 18 May (11-5). Visitors also welcome by appt May to July, min 20+, coaches welcome, £7pp incl tea/coffee & biscuits/cake.**
Fine C17/C18 Hall (not open). Parkland with lake and river walks. Formal garden with terraces, yew hedges, roses and mixed borders. Traditional kitchen garden with crinkle crankle wall. Extensive collection of scented, winter flowering shrubs, and woods, carpeted with snowdrops. 3-acre woodland garden with azaleas, rhododendrons, camellias, spring bulbs, and fine trees. Dogs on leads welcome Feb only. Featured in 'Gardens Illustrated'.

& ✕ ✿ ☕ ☎

40 ◆ MANNINGTON HALL
nr Saxthorpe/Corpusty NR11 7BB. The Lord & Lady Walpole, 01263 584175, www.manningtongardens.co.uk. *18m NW of Norwich. 2m N of Saxthorpe via B1149 towards Holt. At Saxthorpe/Corpusty follow sign posts to Mannington.* **Adm £5, chd free, concessions £4. Suns May to Sept (12-5), Weds, Thurs, Fris June to Aug (11-5). For NGS: Suns 4 May; 28 Sept (12-5).**
20 acres feature shrubs, lake, trees and roses. History of the Rose display and period gardens. Borders. Sensory garden. Extensive countryside walks and trails. Moated manor house and Saxon church with C19 follies. Wild flowers and birds.

& ✕ ✿ ☕

41 MANOR HOUSE FARM
Wellingham PE32 2TH. Robin & Elisabeth Ellis, www.manor-house-farm.co.uk. *7m from Fakenham, 8m*

from Swaffham, 1/2 m off A1065 N of Weasenham. Garden is beside the church. Home-made teas. **Adm £3.50, chd free. Sun 15 June (2-6).**
Charming 4-acre garden surrounds an attractive farmhouse. Many interesting features. Formal quadrants with obelisks. 'Hot Spot' with grasses and gravel. small arboretum with specimen trees, pleached lime walk, vegetable parterre and rose tunnel. Unusual 'Taj' garden with old-fashioned roses, tree peonies, lilies and pond. Small herd of Formosan Sika deer.

✕ ▭ ☕

42 THE MOWLE
Staithe Road, Ludham NR29 5NP. Mrs N N Green, 01692 678213, ann@mowlegreen.fsnet.co.uk. *5 W of Wroxham. B1062 Wroxham to Ludham 7m. Turn R by Ludham village church into Staithe Rd. Garden 1/4 m from village.* Home-made teas. **Adm £3.50, chd free. Sun 1 June (12.30-5). Visitors also welcome by appt anytime, please call first.**
Approx 2 1/2 acres running down to marshes. The garden incl several varieties of catalpa. Japanese garden and enlarged wildlife pond with bog garden. A special border for gunnera with a view to holding a National Collection. Possibly a sculpture demonstration.

& ✕ ✿ ☕ ☎

43 NEW NARBOROUGH HALL
Narborough PE32 1TE. Dr Joanne Merrison, 01760 339923, www.narborough-hall.co.uk. *5m NW of Swaffham. Off A47 signed Narborough, hall entrance signed from village.* Home-made teas. **Adm £3.50, chd free. Suns 8, 22 June; 14 Sept (11-5). Visitors also welcome by appt June to Sept, for groups of 10+, coaches permitted.**
Gently evolving garden in romantic setting. Beautiful C18 parkland. C16 & C17 hall (not open). Restored organic walled kitchen garden with fruit tasting. Chocolate and plum herbaceous borders, wild flower planting, blue garden, topiary, dragons and old roses. Delicious cake at 'The Perfect Spot'. Fruit tasting and herbal tea tasting (strawberries June, apples and pumpkins in Sept). Some gravel paths.

& ✿ ☕ ☎

Delicious cake at 'The Perfect Spot' . . .

44 NEW NORTH LODGE
NR2 3TN. Bruce Bentley & Peter Wilson. *1 1/2 m W of Norwich City Centre. In Bowthorpe Rd off Dereham Rd, turn after 150 metres N through cemetery gates (opp end of Bond St) to North Lodge. Parking restricted, can park outside gates. FirstBus services 16, 19, 20, 21, 22 and Connect service 5 stop at Dereham Rd - Bowthorpe Rd junction.* **Adm £2.50, chd free. Sun 29 June (11-5).**
Town garden 0.1 acre to Victorian Gothic Cemetery Lodge (not open), created from barren, challenging triangular plot over past 10yrs. Strong structure and attention to internal vista incl Gothic conservatory, formal pond, pergola, and classical-style summerhouse. Predominantly herbaceous planting. Adjacent associated historic parkland cemetery also worth a visit.

✕ ☕

45 THE OLD COTTAGE
Colby Corner, nr Aylsham NR11 7EB. Judith & Stuart Clarke, 01263 734574, www.enchantinggardens.co.uk. *14m N of Norwich. Take B1145 from Aylsham to N Walsham. After 3 1/2 m turn L opp Banningham Bridge Inn Garage onto Bridge Rd. Pass Colby school on R & continue straight, following Colby Corner sign. Garden on the L, parking by the poly tunnel.* Light refreshments & teas. **Adm £4, chd free (share to Arthritis Research Campaign). Sun 13 Apr (11-5); Mon 26 May (2-6); Suns 6 July (11-5); 3 Aug (2-6). Visitors also welcome by appt, group visits welcome Apr to Sept.**
Come and enjoy this garden at anytime of the year, always full of colour and interest. Plants seen in the garden settling on sale from Enchanting Plants Nursery on site. Featured in 'Garden News', 'Womans Weekly' and various local press.

& ✕ ✿ ▭ ☕ ☎

46 NEW THE OLD RECTORY

Stone Lane, Brandon Parva NR9 4DL. Mr & Mrs S Guest. *9m W of Norwich. Leave Norwich on B1108 towards Watton, turn R at sign for Barnham Broom. L at T-junction, stay on rd approx 3m until L turn to Yaxham. L at Xrds, house on R. Limited parking.* Home-made teas. **Adm £3.50, chd free. Sun 6 July (11-4).**

4-acre, mature, predominantly shrub garden planted by previous owner. Walkways with pergolas covered with climbing plants lead to large lawn surrounded by boldly planted borders. This leads to an area of woodland with grass paths and pond. Walled garden and further lawns complete the garden.

47 OLD SUN HOUSE

Damgate, Wymondham NR18 0BH. Leonie Woolhouse. *At T-lights on B1172 at edge of Wymondham turn to town centre. Immed turn L, follow main st, 50 metres past market cross, turn L into car park. From top of car park down Chandlers Hill turn R then L into Damgate.* Home-made teas. **Adm £3, chd free. Sun 15 June (11-5). Also open Sallowfield Cottage.**

Plantsperson's and artist's garden, approx 1 1/3 acres, borders, mature trees, river frontage, old roses, bog garden, fruit trees, wild flower meadow, new mini arboretum. Hens, shrubs, ferns, interesting out-buildings. Colour and interest at all times of yr. Owner's artwork for sale. Gravel drive, lawn and woodchip paths.

48 OULTON HALL

Oulton, Aylsham NR11 6NU. Clare & Bolton Agnew. *4m W of Aylsham. From Aylsham take B1354. After 4m Turn L for Oulton Chapel, Hall 1/2 m on R. From B1149 (Norwich/Holt rd) take B1354, next R, Hall 1/2 m on R.* Home-made teas. **Adm £4, chd free. Sun 7 Sept (12-5). Visitors also welcome by appt, by written application, May to Sept for groups 10+.**

C18 manor house (not open) and clocktower set in 6-acre garden with lake and woodland walks. Chelsea designer's own garden - herbaceous, Italian, bog, wild, verdant, sunken and parterre gardens. All flowing from one to another but connected by vistas. Developed over 15yrs with emphasis on structure, height and texture.

Gothic fountain, newly re-built Gothic alcove, restored rustic bridge and summerhouse . . .

49 ◆ OXBURGH HALL GARDEN & ESTATE

Oxborough PE33 9PS. The National Trust, 01366 328258, www.nationaltrust.org.uk. *7m SW of Swaffham. At Oxborough on Stoke Ferry rd.* **House and Garden Adm £7.10, chd £3.70, Garden only Adm £3.70, chd £2.10. Sats to Weds 25 Mar to 27 Sept 11-5.30; 30 Sept to 29 Oct 11.4.30. For NGS: Sun 15 June; Sat 19 July (11-5).**

Hall and moat surrounded by lawns, fine trees, colourful borders; charming parterre garden of French design. Orchard and vegetable garden. Woodland walks. A garden steward is on duty on open days to lead 4 free tours throughout the day. Gravel paths.

50 ◆ PENSTHORPE NATURE RESERVE & GARDENS

Fakenham NR21 0LN. Bill & Deb Jordan, 01328 851465, www.pensthorpe.com. *1m E of Fakenham. On A1067 to Norwich.* **Daily Jan-Mar (10-4), Apr-Dec (10-5). For NGS: Evening opening Adm £4, chd £1.50, concessions £3, Fri 11 July (4.30-7.30).**

Pensthorpe appeals to everyone who loves nature, wildlife and the outdoors. As well as its beautiful lakes and nature trails it has magnificent gardens designed by the Chelsea Flower Show award winners - the spectacular Millennium garden by Piet Oudolf, and New Wave garden by Julie Toll.

51 ◆ THE PLANTATION GARDEN

4 Earlham Road, Norwich NR4 7NH. Plantation Garden Preservation Trust, 01603 621868, www.plantationgarden.co.uk. *Nr St John's R C Cathedral. Parking available at Black Horse PH Earlham Rd.* Teas Suns end Apr to end Sept. **Adm £3, chd free. Daily (9-6 or dusk if earlier). For NGS: Suns 11 May; 7 Sept (2-5).**

3-acre Victorian town garden created 1856-97 in former medieval chalk quarry. Undergoing restoration by volunteers. Remarkable architectural features incl 60ft Italianate terrace, unique 30ft Gothic fountain, newly re-built Gothic alcove, restored rustic bridge and summerhouse. Surrounded by mature trees. Beautifully tranquil atmosphere.

52 PLOVERS HILL

Buckenham Road, Strumpshaw NR13 4NL. Jim & Jan Saunt, 01603 714587, jamessaunt@hotmail.com. *9m E of Norwich. Off A47 at Brundall continuing through to Strumpshaw village. Turn R 300yds past PO, then R at T-junction. Plovers Hill is 1st on R up the hill.* Home-made teas. **Adm £3, chd free (share to How Hill Educational Trust). Sun 11 May (11-5); Combined with Woodland View £4.50, Suns 20 July; 10 Aug (11-5). Visitors also welcome by appt.**

1-acre garden of contrasts, small C18 house (not open) with RIBA award winning orangery. Formal lawn hedged with yew and lesser species, huge mulberry, gingko, liquidambar and Japanese bitter orange, herbaceous borders with a range of varied plants and spring bulbs. Kitchen garden with orchard and soft fruits. Garden sculpture. UEA & SCVA Garden Greats, Nature and the Arts online exhibition. Some shallow steps.

53 ◆ RAVENINGHAM HALL

Raveningham NR14 6NS. Sir Nicholas Bacon, www.raveningham.com. *14m SE of Norwich. 4m from Beccles off B1136.* **Adm £4, chd free, concessions £3. Mon-Fri, Easter to Aug Bank Hol (11-4); Bank Hols Suns, Mons (2-5). For NGS: Mon 26 May (2-5).**

Traditional country house garden with an interesting collection of herbaceous plants and shrubs. Restored Victorian conservatory and walled kitchen garden. Newly planted arboretum, lake and herb garden. Contemporary sculpture.

♿ ✿

54 RIVERMOUNT
Hall Lane, Knapton NR28 9SW. Mrs E Purdy. *2m NE North Walsham. B1150 through North Walsham towards Bacton. 2nd turning on L after Blue Bell PH & pond. Ample parking.* **Adm £3, chd free. Sun 11 May (2-5).**
Traditional style garden. Brick terrace, sloping lawn to woodland garden. Herbaceous borders enclosed by climbing rose trellis. Paved kitchen garden with herb garden and old-fashioned rose beds. Many unusual and species plants and bulbs. Orchard and wild flower meadow walk. Not brilliant for wheelchairs but manageable with assistance. Gravel paths and narrow brick paths.

♿ ✕ ✿ ☕

55 SALLE PARK
Salle, Norwich NR10 4SF. Sir John White. *1m N of Reepham. Off B1145, between Cawston & Reepham.* Home-made teas. **Adm £3.50, chd free (share to Salle Parish/Professional Gardeners Guild Trust). Sun 24 Aug (12-5).**
Very varied estate gardens consisting of delightful, fully productive Victorian kitchen garden with original vine houses, double herbaceous borders, display glasshouse, ice house, orchard and wild flowers. Formal Georgian pleasure gardens with yew topiary, rose gardens, lawns, specimen trees and exotically planted orangery. Featured in local press and interview on Radio Norfolk. Gravel and bark paths, gentle slopes.

♿ ✿ ☕

Hidden
rooms and
pathways . . .

56 NEW SALLOWFIELD COTTAGE
Wattlefield Road, Wymondham NR18 9PA. Caroline Musker, www.sallowfieldcottage.co.uk. *2m S of Wymondham. Leave A11 signed Wymondham & Spooner Row. Turn R for Spooner Row, into village straight over Xrds at Boars PH. At T-junction take L, after 1½ m, grey barrels on L. Disabled parking near the house.* Home-made teas. **Adm £3, chd free. Sun 15 June (11-5). Also open Old Sun House.**
1-acre garden with large pond, clematis, old roses and herbaceous plants among the walnut trees. Some gravel paths, but mostly grass.

♿ ✕ ⛺ ☕

57 ◆ SANDRINGHAM GARDENS
Sandringham PE35 6EN. Her Majesty The Queen, 01553 612908, www.sandringhamestate.co.uk. *6m NW of King's Lynn. By gracious permission, the House, Museum & Gardens at Sandringham will be open.* **House and Garden £9, concessions £7, chd £5, Garden only £6, chd £3.50, concessions £5. Daily 22 Mar to 25 July, 3 Aug to 26 Oct (garden 10.30-5) (house 11-4.45).**
60 acres of formal gardens, woodland and lakes, with rare plants and trees. Donations are given from the Estate to various charities. Gravel paths.

♿ ✕ ✿ ☕

58 ◆ SEVERALS GRANGE
Holt Road, Wood Norton NR20 5BL. Jane Lister, 01362 684206, www.hoecroft.co.uk. *8m S of Holt, 6m E of Fakenham. 2m N of Guist on LH-side of B1110. Guist is situated 5m SE of Fakenham on A1067 Norwich rd.* **Adm £2.50, chd free. Thurs to Suns 1 Apr to mid Oct (Donations to NGS) 10-4. For NGS: Sun 10 Aug (2-5).**
This 17yr-old garden has evolved from a bare field and is a perfect example of how colour, shape and form can be created by the use of foliage plants, from large shrubs to small alpines. Movement and lightness is achieved by interspersing these plants with a wide range of ornamental grasses, which are at their best in late summer. Featured on Radio Norfolk.

♿ ✿ ☕

59 ◆ SHERINGHAM PARK
Upper Sheringham NR26 8TL. The National Trust, 01263 820550, www.nationaltrust.org.uk. *2m SW of Sheringham. Access for cars off A148 Cromer to Holt Rd, 5m W of Cromer, 6m E of Holt, signs in Sheringham town.* **Adm £4 per car, coaches free (must book). Daily (dawn til dusk), refreshment kiosk (11-5). For NGS: Suns 25 May; 8 June (dawn til dusk).**
50 acres of species rhododendron, azalea and magnolia. Also numerous specimen trees incl handkerchief tree. Viewing towers, waymarked walks, sea and parkland views. Special walkway and WCs for disabled.

♿ ✿ ☕

60 NEW SLY'S FARM
NR21 9JQ. Mr & Mrs J Finch. *Between North & South Creake. From Fakenham take B1355 off King's Lynn rd (A148) towards Burnham Market. After South Creak Farm 1st on L. If you reach the church you have gone too far.* Coffee & home-made teas. **Adm £2.50, chd free. Suns 27 Apr; 11 May (11-4).**
Walled 1-acre matured garden, established by my mother, Peggy Schlman. Hidden rooms and pathways revealing wide variety of texture, colour and diversity of plants. Created for all seasons, with flowering trees and bulbs glorious in spring.

✿ ☕

61 NEW 'SOL'
Whissonsett Road, Colkirk NR21 7NJ. Rod & Marjorie Diaper. *2m S of Fakenham. Between B1146 & A1065 Colkirk not signed on A1065. Follow NGS signs.* Home-made teas. **Combined with Derwen adm £3, chd free. Sun 25 (2-5), Mon 26 May (11-4).**
Large front garden set to lawns and various flower beds, patio area, greenhouse and summerhouse. Some narrow paths.

♿ ✕ ✿ ☕

62 ◆ STODY LODGE
Melton Constable NR24 2ER. Mrs Ian MacNicol, 01263 860572, www.stodyestate.co.uk. *16m NW of Norwich, 3m S of Holt. Off B1354. Signed from Melton Constable on Holt Rd.* **Adm £4.50, chd under 12 free.**

For NGS: Suns 4, 18, 25, Mon 26 May; Sun 1 June (2-5).
Spectacular gardens having one of the largest concentrations of rhododendrons and azaleas in East Anglia with both Japanese water gardens and formal garden. Stunning walks and vistas are enhanced by a large variety of mature trees, magnolias, acers and cedars. Daffodils in early May give way to carpets of bluebells. Featured in local press & on Radio Norfolk.

&. ⊕ ☕

63 NEW 56 WELL CREEK ROAD
Outwell PE14 8SA. Tim Meakin & Nick Bergamaschi, 01945 774064. *6m W of Downham Market. 2m W of Nordelph on A1122. Take bridge on L immed after 'Middle Level Main Drain' sign, 3rd house, approx 100metres from bridge.* **Adm £3.50, chd free.** Sat 14, Sun 15 June (11-5). **Visitors also welcome by appt max of 25, no coaches.**
Well stocked plantsman's garden of ¾ acre. Planted with emphasis on form and foliage with wide use of salvaged natural materials for structural interest. Many unusual plants, and particular use made of collections of grasses, hebes, hederas and heucheras. Island beds, shaded areas, gravel garden, ponds and vegetable garden.

✕ ⊕ ☕ ☎

64 WEST LODGE
Aylsham NR11 6HB. Mr & Mrs Jonathan Hirst. *¼ m NW of Aylsham. Off B1354 Blickling Rd out of Aylsham, turn R down Rawlinsons Lane, garden on L.* **Adm £3, chd free.** Sun 13 July (2-5).
9-acre garden with lawns, splendid mature trees, rose garden, well-stocked herbaceous borders, ornamental pond, magnificent C19 walled kitchen garden (maintained as such). Georgian house (not open) and outbuildings incl a well-stocked toolshed (open) and greenhouses.

&. ⊕ ☕

WHITE HOUSE FARM
See Suffolk.

65 WITTON HALL
nr North Walsham NR28 9UF. Sally Owles, 01692 650239. *3½ m from North Walsham. Off B1150 halfway between North Walsham & Bacton. Take R fork to Bacton Woods picnic area, driveway 200yds on L.* Light refreshments & home-teas. **Adm £3, chd free.** Mon 5 May (11-5). **Also open Hill Cottage. Visitors also welcome by appt May only.**
A natural woodland garden. Walk past the handkerchief tree and wander through carpets of English bluebells, rhododendrons and azaleas. Stunning views over farmland to the sea. Wheelchair access difficult through woodland paths.

&. ✕ ⊕ ☕ ☎

66 NEW WOODLAND VIEW
2 Woodland View, Norwich Road, Strumpshaw NR13 4NW. Mike & Gillian Page, 01603 712410, skyview@clara.co.uk. *8m E of Norwich. A47 at Brundall carry on through Brundall St toward Strumpshaw Garden on R 200yds after Strumpshaw Church at rear of Pages Garage.* Teas at Plovers Hill. **Adm £3, chd free, Combined with Plovers Hill £4.50.** Suns 20 July; 10 Aug (11-5). **Visitors also welcome by appt July & Aug.**
3-acre conservation area comprising woodland walk and formal garden with large pond. Woodland planted in 1993 with pond and borders commenced in 2004. Dragonflies, butterflies, birds and wildlife abound. Broadlands District Council Conservation award winning area. Photographic display of wildlife/seasonal pictures from the garden. Radio Norfolk Garden Award Winner. Separate wheelchair access, grass paths, some slopes and small gravel area.

&. ✕ ☕ ☎

67 WOODLANDS FARM
Stokesby, Gt Yarmouth NR29 3DX. Vivienne Fabb. *2m E of Acle. From Norwich A47 to Acle, A1064 to Caister, 1st R after bridge over river to Stokesby. Turn L into Filby Rd just past Bungalow Stores, 1st L after the end of 30mph limit. From Gt Yarmouth A1064 via Caister, L to Stokesby & Runham then as above.* Light refreshments & teas. **Adm £3, chd free.** Sats, Suns 24, 25 May; 13, 14 Sept (11-5).
Large mature garden with trees, interesting shrubs and herbaceous plants. Good spring and autumn colour. Vegetable garden and woodland walk. Gravel paths.

&. ✕ ⊕ ⊨ ☕

68 WOODWYND
6 Dodds Hill Road, Dersingham PE31 6LW. Mr & Mrs D H Dingle, 01485 541218. *8m NE of King's Lynn. ¾ m N of Sandringham House. Take B1440 from Sandringham & continue into Dersingham. Turn R into Dodds Hill Rd just past the Feathers Hotel.* Light refreshments & teas. **Adm £3.50, chd free (share to Tapping House Hospice).** Sun 20 July (11.30-5). **Visitors also welcome by appt, July only.**
Unique holly topiary, gravel garden, S-facing terrace features contemporary

Planted with emphasis on form and foliage with wide use of salvaged natural materials for structural interest . . .

design garden room. Sweeping lawns, island beds, and borders. Steps and pathways wind through dell to meandering brook. Fine mature trees create dappled canopy above informal naturalistic planting of lush vegetation. Encompassed by Sandringham's Royal Woodland. Fresh filled rolls and delicious home-made cakes. Steep slopes in dell.

Dragonflies, butterflies, birds and wildlife abound . . .

69 WRETHAM LODGE
East Wretham IP24 1RL. Mr Gordon Alexander. *6m NE of Thetford. A11 E from Thetford, L up A1075, L by village sign, R at Xrds then bear L.* Teas in Church. **Adm £3, chd free.** Sun 23, Mon 24 Mar; (11-5); Sun 22 June (2-5).
In spring masses of species tulips, hellebores, fritillaries, daffodils and narcissi; bluebell walk. In June hundreds of old roses. Walled garden, with fruit and interesting vegetable plots. Mixed borders and fine old trees. Double herbaceous borders. Wild flower meadows.

Norfolk County Volunteers

County Organisers
Fiona Black, The Old Rectory, Ridlington, North Walsham NR28 9NZ, 01692 650247, blacks7@email.com
Anthea Foster, Lexham Hall, King's Lynn PE32 2QJ, 01328 701341, antheafoster@lexhamestate.co.uk

County Treasurer
Neil Foster, Lexham Hall, King's Lynn PE32 2QJ, 01328 701288, neilfoster@lexhamestate.co.uk

Publicity
Annette Bowler, 260 Aylsham Road, Norwich NR3 2RG, 01603 301110, annette.bowler@ntlworld.com

Assistant County Organisers
Panda Allhusen, Bradenham Hall, Bradenham, Thetford IP25 7QP, 01362 687243/687279, panda@bradenhamhall.co.uk
Stephanie Powell, Creake House, Wells Road, North Creake, Fakenham NR21 9LG, 01328 730113, stephaniepowell@creake.com
Jim & Jan Saunt, Plovers Hill, Buckenham Road, Strumpshaw NR13 4NL, 01603 714587, jamessaunt@hotmail.com

NORTHAMPTONSHIRE

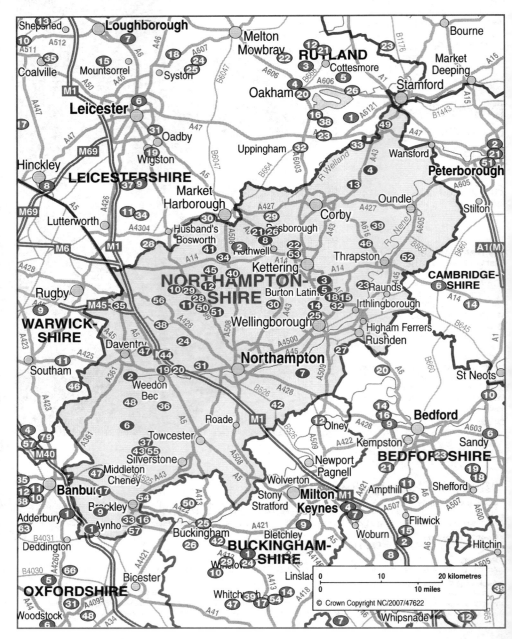

Opening Dates

February

SUNDAY 17
③ Beech House
㉗ Greywalls

SUNDAY 24
⑭ Dolphins
㊿ Rosemount

March

SUNDAY 16
㊻ The Old Rectory, Sudborough

SATURDAY 22
㊶ The Maltings

SUNDAY 23
㊶ The Maltings

MONDAY 24
㉓ Great Addington Manor
㊶ The Maltings

SUNDAY 30
㊵ Maidwell Hall

April

SUNDAY 13
⑳ Flore Spring Gardens

SATURDAY 19
㉙ Guilsborough Spring Gardens

SUNDAY 20
㉙ Guilsborough Spring Gardens
㉞ Kelmarsh Hall

SUNDAY 27
(51) Spratton Gardens

May

SUNDAY 4
⑯ Evenley Wood Garden
㉔ Great Brington Gardens
㉖ Greenway

MONDAY 5
⑯ Evenley Wood Garden
㊶ The Maltings

TUESDAY 6
⑪ Coton Manor Garden

SATURDAY 17
㉘ Guilsborough & Hollowell May Gardens

SUNDAY 18
⑬ Deene Park
㉘ Guilsborough & Hollowell May Gardens
(55) Turweston Gardens

SUNDAY 25
⑯ Evenley Wood Garden
㊲ Lois Weedon House
㊸ Old Barn
㊹ The Old Rectory, Brockhall

MONDAY 26
⑯ Evenley Wood Garden

June

SUNDAY 1
⑰ Farthinghoe Gardens
㊱ Litchborough Gardens
㊼ Park House
㊽ Preston Capes Gardens

THURSDAY 5
㉖ Greenway (Evening)

SUNDAY 8
② Badby and Newnham Gardens
⑱ Finedon Gardens
㉟ Kilsby Gardens
㊺ The Old Rectory, Haselbech
(53) Top Lodge

THURSDAY 12
㉜ 67-69 High Street (Evening)

SATURDAY 14
㊶ The Maltings
㊻ The Old Rectory, Sudborough
(52) Titchmarsh House

SUNDAY 15
⑭ Dolphins
㉕ Great Harrowden Lodge
㊳ Long Buckby Gardens
㊴ Lyveden New Bield
㊶ The Maltings

THURSDAY 19
㉜ 67-69 High Street (Evening)

SATURDAY 21
⑲ Flore Gardens

SUNDAY 22
⑧ Cedar Farm
⑲ Flore Gardens
㉒ Glendon Hall
㉛ Harpole Gardens
㊾ Rosebriar

SATURDAY 28
㊷ The Menagerie

SUNDAY 29
① Aynho Gdns
⑨ Charlton Gardens
㉖ Greenway (Afternoon & Evening)
㉞ Kelmarsh Hall
(55) Weedon Lois Gardens

July

THURSDAY 3
⑮ Driftwood (Evening)

SUNDAY 6
⑮ Driftwood
㉚ Hannington Gardens
(56) West Haddon Gardens

THURSDAY 10
㉖ Greenway (Evening)

SATURDAY 12
⑤ Burton Latimer Gardens

SUNDAY 13
⑤ Burton Latimer Gardens

SATURDAY 19
⑥ Canons Ashby House
㊴ Lyveden New Bield

SUNDAY 20
④ Bulwick Gardens
⑦ Castle Ashby House

SUNDAY 27
⑫ Cottesbrooke Hall Gardens
㉑ Froggery Cottage

August

SUNDAY 24
㊹ The Old Rectory, Brockhall

September

SATURDAY 6
⑥ Canons Ashby House

SUNDAY 7
⑬ Deene Park
㉖ Greenway

SUNDAY 14
⑩ Coton Lodge
㊻ The Old Rectory, Sudborough

February 2009

SUNDAY 15
⑭ Dolphins

SUNDAY 22
㉗ Greywalls

Gardens open to the public

⑥ Canons Ashby House
⑦ Castle Ashby House
⑪ Coton Manor Garden
⑫ Cottesbrooke Hall Gardens
⑬ Deene Park
⑯ Evenley Wood Garden
㉞ Kelmarsh Hall
㊴ Lyveden New Bield
㊷ The Menagerie
㊻ The Old Rectory, Sudborough

By appointment only

㉝ Hill Grounds
(57) Woodchippings

Also open by appointment ☎

③ Beech House
㊳ 45 Brington Road, Long Buckby Gardens
⑧ Cedar Farm

- **48** City Cottage, Preston Capes Gardens
- **15** Driftwood
- **28** Dripwell House, Guilsborough & Hollowell May Gardens
- **21** Froggery Cottage
- **22** Glendon Hall
- **28** Gower House, Guilsborough & Hollowell May Gardens
- **27** Greywalls
- **32** 67-69 High Street
- **41** The Maltings
- **38** Mill House, Long Buckby Gardens
- **51** Mulberry Cottage, Spratton Gardens
- **19** The Old Bakery, Flore Gardens
- **43** Old Barn
- **37** Old Barn, Lois Weedon House
- **44** The Old Rectory, Brockhall
- **24** The Old Rectory, Great Brington Gardens
- **45** The Old Rectory, Haselbech
- **5** 36 Station Road, Burton Latimer Gardens
- **5** 58 Station Road, Burton Latimer Gardens
- **48** Old West Farm, Preston Capes Gardens
- **49** Rosebriar
- **50** Rosemount
- **52** Titchmarsh House
- **53** Top Lodge
- **48** Village Farm, Preston Capes Gardens

The Gardens

1 AYNHO GDNS
Banbury OX17 3BG. *6m SE of Banbury on B4100.* Home-made teas at village hall. **Combined adm £4, chd free. Sun 29 June (2-5.30).**
A charming stone built village with gardens of varying sizes.
☕

ALMS COTTAGES
19 & 20 Bowmans Lea. Ms J Wade (19) & Mr J Russell (20).
Entrance is at side of cul-de-sac
Interesting and clever division of 2 small cottage gardens with different styles, keeping their individuality without fences or walls.

AYNHO PARK
Mr James Perkins
13 acres of parkland surround the house (not open). Sweeping lawns contrast with woodland left in its natural state to provide a rich habitat for wildlife. Seasonal flower beds, herbaceous borders,

graceful groupings of trees and limewalk. Fully restored icehouse.
✗

6 BLACKSMITHS HILL
Roger & Winifred Wilkes
Mature country garden, large shrub beds, herbaceous borders, roses, 2 espaliered pears, lavender and a small herb bed with box border.

10 THE BUTTS
Mr & Mrs K McClellan
Mature garden with varied and interesting shrubs, trees, beds and small pond.

CATTON HOUSE
Mrs C H Harmer
Well-established small walled garden with mature trees, various shrubs and specialising in roses and clematis, sunken walled rose garden.

FRIAR'S WELL
Mr & Mrs T R Sermon
3-acre garden on top of hill with magnificent views, divided into sections with mixed hedges and stone wall, pleached limes and hornbeams, unusual shrubs and roses.

NEW THE GRAMMAR HOUSE
Dr & Mrs C J Hodges
1⅓-acre garden, newly landscaped. Some gravel paths & slopes.
&. ✗

NEW ROSE COTTAGE
6 Banbury Road. Mr & Mrs D Watkins
1-acre garden featuring formal area with rose garden and herbaceous border, S-facing terrace with grape vine, large pond and several fruit and nut trees.

16 ROUNDTOWN
Miss A Bazin
Old-fashioned cottage garden with inner walled section, herbaceous borders, pond, roses, shrubs and fruit trees.

Keeping their individuality without fences or walls . . .

2 BADBY AND NEWNHAM GARDENS
Daventry NN11 3AR. *3m S of Daventry. E side of A361.* Home-made teas at St Mary's Church. **Combined adm £3.50, chd free. Sun 8 June (12-5).**
Maps provided for visitors.
☕

HILLTOP
Church Street. David & Mercy Messenger
Constantly evolving 3-acre cottage-style, with mature trees and shrubs to focus, and separate areas. Lovely views, dense planting, spring bulbs. Largely organic. Garden room and newly extended vegetable beds. Copper cascade water feature. A wild flower meadow in the making. Current challenge - fern and birch tree shady dell.
❀

NEW THE LILACS
School Lane. Matthew and Ruth Moser
Medium sized walled cottage garden partly terraced, lawn, mixed borders, vegetables and orchard with spring bulbs under the trees. 14 steps to main garden.

THE MILL
Charles & Susan Rose. *House on the River Nene on Preston Capes Lane*
Extensive mixed garden with gravel garden and large borders, designed and planted by James Alexander-Sinclair. Woodland walk with a mixture of traditional and contemporary planting. To be featured in 'Country Living'.
✗

SHAKESPEARES COTTAGE
Sarah & Jocelyn Hartland-Swann
Small garden surrounding C18 thatched cottage, reclaimed by present owners after some years of neglect. Raised stone beds, sloping lawn to rear, mixed borders. Flagstone, terracotta and gravelled seating areas with colourful pots.

THE OLD HOUSE
Dr & Mrs M MacGregor.
Opposite Badby Church
A medium-sized enclosed garden with fine views over Badby woods. Secluded courtyard, mostly stone-raised beds, densely

planted with many traditional herbaceous plants and roses.

TRIFIDIA
Church Hill. Dr & Mrs C M Cripps
Medium-sized country garden with internal yew and beech hedges enclosing mixed borders. Some interesting plants, clipped yews, shady border, pond, vegetable garden and conservatory.

③ BEECH HOUSE
73 Church Street, Burton Latimer NN15 5LU. Mr & Mrs Nicholas Loake, 01536 723593, gloake@mac.com. *4m S of Kettering. From High St turn into Church St by War Memorial, Beech House on L 100yds past church.* Home-made teas. **Adm £2.50, chd free. Sun 17 Feb (10-4). Visitors also welcome by appt.**
Semi-formal garden with winter/spring interest. Clipped box and yew hedging frame borders containing over 150 cultivars of snowdrops plus hellebores etc. Featured in 'The English Garden'.

④ BULWICK GARDENS
Corby NN17 3DZ. *10m SW of Stamford. 1/2 m off A43.* Home-made teas. **Combined adm £3, chd free. Sun 20 July (2-5).**
Unspoilt Northamptonshire stone conservation village. Interesting C14 church and PH.

BULWICK HALL
Mr & Mrs G T G Conant
Formal terraced 8-acre walled garden leading to river and island. Double herbaceous borders, holly walk ending at attractive C17 wrought iron gates. C19 orangery and C17 arcade, large kitchen garden, fine mature trees, topiary, peacocks. (House not open).

19 CHURCH LANE
David Haines
Small cottage garden with fruit trees and vegetables, courtyard and water features.

THE SHAMBLES
12 Main Street. Roger Glithero
Herbaceous plants, many containers, vegetable garden with fruit and original village well, lawns, hedges and stone walls.

Through arch to wildlife pond, leading to lawn with colourful borders . . .

⑤ BURTON LATIMER GARDENS
NN15 5NX. *3m S of Kettering. Approached from A14, A509 & A6. Parking by kind permission of Sunseeker Windows 72-84 Station Road.* Home-made teas at 58 Station Road & 14 Bridle Road. **Combined adm £2, chd free (share to Air Ambulance). Sat, Sun 12 & 13 July (1.30-5).**

14 BRIDLE ROAD
Mr & Mrs John Hollis
Long shrub border to side of bungalow, through arch to wildlife pond, leading to lawn with colourful borders, vegetable plot with fruit trees and bushes to rear.

36 STATION ROAD
John & Pat Freeman, 01536 723693, patricia.freeman1@tesco.net. **Visitors also welcome by appt, 26 June -21 July.**
Picket fenced cottage style garden with a variety of shrubs and plants, patios, pergolas and water features, benefiting from a lovely back drop of mature trees beyond old stone wall.

58 STATION ROAD
Bill & Daphne Frum, 01536 722455, bcfrum@googlemail.com. **Visitors also welcome by appt, 26 June -21 Jul, max 20.**
100ft town garden specialising in clematis in more than 75 different situations, many in containers. Areas of special interest with hostas, grasses, ferns, fuchsias, and lilies. Fruit and vegetables in raised beds.

⑥ ◆ CANONS ASHBY HOUSE
Daventry NN11 3SD. The National Trust, 01327 861344, chris.smith@national trust.org.uk. *12m NE of Banbury, 9m S of Daventry. On unclassified rd between B4525 and A5. Follow NT signs.* **House and Garden adm £7.50, chd £3.75, Garden only adm £2.75, chd £1.50. For NGS: Sats 19 July; 6 Sept (11-5) House (1-4.30).**
Formal gardens of London and Wise style enclosed by walls. Gate piers from 1710, fine topiary, axial arrangement of paths and terraces, wild flowers, old varieties of fruit trees, herb border, newly planted gardens. Phase 1 of a 5yr plan to restore gardens to designs of 1880-1900. New beds with bedding schemes. Home of the Dryden family since C16, Manor House 1550. Ramp access to garden on request. Gravel paths. Wheelchairs to borrow.

⑦ ◆ CASTLE ASHBY HOUSE
Northampton NN7 1LQ. Earl Compton, 01604 696187. *6m E of Northampton. 1 1/2 m N of A428; turn off between Denton & Yardley Hastings.* **Adm £5, chd £4, under 10 free, concessions £4. Apr-Sept (10-5.30), Oct & Mar (10-4.30). For NGS: Sun 20 July (1-5).**
25 acres within a 10,000acre estate of both formal and informal gardens, incl Italian gardens with orangery and arboretum with lakes, all dating back to the 1860s. Tea rooms, plant centre and gift shop. Gravel paths.

⑧ CEDAR FARM
Copelands Road, Desborough NN14 2QD. Mr & Mrs R Tuffen, 01536 763992, thetuffenfamily@aol.com. *6m N of Kettering, 5m S of Market Harborough, from A6. Signed from centre of Desborough.* Home-made teas. **Adm £3, chd free. Sun 22 June (2-6). Visitors also welcome by appt.**
2-acre garden with a further 8 acres. Secret garden with roses and clematis. Avenue of mature limes. Large colour planted borders filled with unusual plants and shrubs. Large mirror pond, wildlife ponds, vegetables. Massed snowdrops and spring bulbs, wonderful autumn colour, small arboretum. Featured in 'The English Garden' and 'Homes and Antiques'.

9 CHARLTON GARDENS
Banbury OX17 3DR. *7m SE of Banbury, 5m W of Brackley. From B4100 turn off N at Aynho, or from A422 turn off S at Farthinghoe.* Home-made teas. **Combined adm £4, chd free. Sun 29 June (2-6).**
Well preserved stone village, lunch at pub.

THE COTTAGE
Lady Juliet Townsend
Flowering shrubs, raised cottage garden, lawns, woodland walk, stream and lakes.

HOLLY HOUSE
Miss Alice Townsend
Walled garden with beautiful views. Kitchen garden. C18 house, not open. Some shallow steps in garden.

HOME FARM HOUSE
Mrs N Grove-White
Paved courtyard with tubs, containers and climbers. Walled garden with roses and clematis, herbaceous border and fruit garden.

NEW WALNUT HOUSE
Sir Paul & Lady Hayter
Large garden behind C17 farmhouse. Colour themed borders, separate enclosures with beech and yew hedges. Orchard with wild flowers, old fashioned vegetable garden. Wilderness (in C18 sense), archery lawn. Created since 1992.

100 CHURCH GREEN ROAD
See Buckinghamshire.

10 COTON LODGE
Guilsborough NN6 8QE. Peter Hicks & Joanne de Nobriga, 01604 740215, jo@cotonlodge.co.uk. *10m NW of Northampton, 10m E of Rugby. 1m W of Guilsborough on West Haddon Rd on L.* Teas. **Adm £3.50, chd free. Sun 14 Sept (12-5).**
Mature 2-acre garden with panoramic views over beautiful unspoilt countryside. Intimate enclosed areas are complemented by an informal woodland stream and pond giving interest throughout the seasons.

11 ◆ COTON MANOR GARDEN
Guilsborough NN6 8RQ. Mr & Mrs Ian Pasley-Tyler, 01604 740219, pasleytyler@cotonmanor.co.uk. *10m N of Northampton, 11m SE of Rugby. From A428 & A5199 follow tourist signs.* **Adm £5, chd £2, concessions £4.50. Tues to Sats, 21 Mar-27 Sept. Suns in April & May. BH weekends. For NGS: Tue 6 May (12-5.30).**
10-acre garden set in peaceful countryside with old yew and holly hedges, extensive herbaceous borders containing many unusual plants, rose, water, herb and woodland gardens, famous bluebell wood, wild flower meadow. Adjacent specialist nursery with over 1000 plant varieties propagated from the garden. Slopes, some gravel & narrow paths.

12 ◆ COTTESBROOKE HALL GARDENS
Cottesbrooke NN6 8PF. Mr & Mrs A R Macdonald-Buchanan, 01604 505808, www.cottesbrookehall.co.uk. *10m N of Northampton. Signed from J1 on A14.* **House and Garden adm £8, chd £3.50, concessions, £6.50, Garden only adm £5.50, chd £2.50, concessions £4.50. Weds & Thurs, May, June; Thurs, July to Sept. For NGS: Sun 27 July (2-5.30).**
Award winning gardens of great variety incl fine old cedars, specimen trees, water and wild gardens and recently designed herbaceous borders. Unusual plants home grown. Contact admin for disabled access.

Intimate enclosed areas are complemented by an informal woodland stream and pond . . .

COWPER & NEWTON MUSEUM GARDENS
See Buckinghamshire.

13 ◆ DEENE PARK
Corby NN17 3EW. Mr E Brudenell & The Hon Mrs Brudenell, 01780 450278, admin@deenepark.com. *5m N of Corby. On A43 Stamford-Kettering rd.* **Adm £4, chd £1.50, concessions £3. Suns & Bank Hols; Jun - Aug. For NGS: Suns 18 May; 7 Sept (2-5).**
Interesting garden set in beautiful parkland. Large parterre with topiary designed by David Hicks echoing the C16 decoration on the porch stonework, long mixed borders, old-fashioned roses, tudor court and white garden. Large lake and waterside walks with rare mature trees in natural garden.

14 DOLPHINS
Great Harrowden NN9 5AB. Mr & Mrs R C Handley. *2m N of Wellingborough. 5m S of Kettering on A509.* Light refreshments & teas. **Adm £2 Feb, £3 June combined with Great Harrowden Lodge, chd free. Suns 24 Feb (10-4); 15 June (12-5); 15 Feb 2009 (10-4).**
2-acre country garden surrounding old stone house (not open). Many old roses grown among interesting trees, shrubs and wide range of hardy perennials. Irises and peonies a special favourite, early opening for snowdrops and hellebores. Very free draining with beech hedges and firm gravel paths. Featured in 'Garden News'.

15 DRIFTWOOD
11b Thrapston Road, Finedon NN9 5DG. Bill & Elaine Gardiner, 01933 680708. *3m NE of Wellingborough. A14 junction11, W to Finedon. 3rd house on R as you enter. A510 3m E of Wellingborough, cross A6, ¼ m on L next to factory.* Light refreshments & cream teas. **Adm £3.00, chd free. Thurs 3 July (6-9) Evening Opening £3.00, wine; Sun 6 July (2-6). Visitors also welcome by appt 20 Jun-3 July.**
½ -acre garden featuring small lake with island. Well stocked with fish, various water birds, wildlife and aquatic plants, surrounded by lawns, flower beds, shrubs and pergolas. Craft demonstration - woodturning. Free use of electric wheelchair at users own risk.

16 ◆ **EVENLEY WOOD GARDEN**
Brackley NN13 5SH. Timothy
Whiteley, 01280 844938,
www.evenleywoodgarden.co.uk.
¾ m S of Brackley. A43, turn L to
Evenley straight through village
towards Mixbury, 1st turning L. **Adm
£5, chd £1. See website or phone
for details. For NGS: Suns, Mons; 4,
5, 25, 26 May (2-6).**
Woodland garden spread over a 60-
acre mature wood. Acid and alkaline
soils, magnolias, rhododendrons,
azaleas, malus, quercus, acers,
euonymus collection and many other
species. Spectacular display of spring
bulbs, lilies and snowdrops.

17 **FARTHINGHOE GARDENS**
NN13 5NZ. 3m NW of Brackley. A422
between Brackley and Banbury.
Home-made teas at The Old Rectory.
**Combined adm £3, chd free. Sun 1
June (2-6).**

THE OLD RECTORY
Mr & Mrs David Montagu-Smith
1½ acres. Mixed borders, rose
circle, beech hedged paeony
garden. Fine views over
surrounding countryside.

**THE OLD RECTORY STABLE
HOUSE**
Simon Cox
Developing 1-acre garden,
borders, 2 small courtyards,
½ -acre walled garden comprising
pool garden, lawn and water
feature. Numerous small individual
gardens and greenhouse.
&

WINDY RIDGE
Mr & Mrs M Phipps
Approx ⅓ acre, planted entirely by
present owners. Pergolas, patio
area, rockery, borders, vegetable
plot and mature trees.
Greenhouses and recently
constructed summer house.
⊛

18 **FINEDON GARDENS**
NN9 5JN. 2m NE of Wellingborough.
6m SE Kettering, A6/A510 junction.
Teas at 67- 69 High St. **Combined
adm £3, chd free. Sun 8 June (2-6).**

67-69 HIGH STREET
Mary & Stuart Hendry
(See separate entry).
& ✗ ⊛

INDEGARDEN
24 Albert Road. Ray & Honor
Parbery
Approx 50ft - walk through
pergola with climbers, colourful
mixed border of annuals and
perennials, pots and containers,
miniature house in the garden,
patio.

4 IRTHLINGBOROUGH ROAD
Jenny & Roger Martin
Small front garden with cottage
style planting and enclosed rear
garden with raised beds, raised
fish pond and containers.
✗

7 WALKERS WAY
Mrs D Humphrey
Small recently-established garden
with gravel areas, decking,
containers and pond.

NEW WELLS COTTAGE
11 Thrapston Rd. John & Gillian
Ellson
⅕ -acre cottage garden with
lawns and mixed borders, gravel
and paved seating areas with
planters and water features.
Pergola, rose arches, summer
house and tree house. Mixed
vegetable plot, soft fruit and apple
trees. Limited wheelchair access.
& ✗

Gravel and paved seating areas with planters . . .

19 **FLORE GARDENS**
NN7 4LQ. 7m W of Northampton. 5m
E of Daventry. On A45. Lunches &
home-made teas in Church & Chapel
School Room. **Combined adm £3.50,
chd free (share to All Saints Church).**
Sat 21, Sun 22 June (11-6).
Part of the established (45th) Village
Flower and Garden Festival. Maps
provided at official car park.

24 BLISS LANE
John & Sally Miller
Small cottage garden filled with
flowers, fruit, herbs and
vegetables. Victorian-style
greenhouse and dry garden.

BLISS LANE NURSERY
Geoff & Chris Littlewood
Informal garden and nursery
opening out to a larger garden
with views overlooking the Nene
Valley, closely packed perennial
plants in wide borders with small
trees and shrub roses.

NEW BERTHA PATCH
17 Collins Hill. Claire Ryan
Family garden with central lawn
and 3 principal perennial areas
and a woodland area. Raised
vegetable patch.
& ✗

THE CROFT
John & Dorothy Boast
⅓ -acre cottage garden planted
for yr-round interest. Deciduous
trees and shrubs, perennials, 2
lawns, vegetable patch and plenty
of seats. Help provided with gravel
paths.
&

THE GARDEN HOUSE
Edward & Penny Aubrey-
Fletcher
Former walled kitchen garden
replanted when the new house
was built in the 90's. Approx
½ -acre of formal design with
informal planting that changes as
the garden matures. Gravel paths.
&

THE OLD BAKERY
John Amos & Karl Jones, 01327
349080. **Visitors also welcome
by appt June & July, groups 10+.**
5yr-old garden arranged over
different levels. Divided into
smaller rooms with terraces and a
small lawn. Many unusual plants
for full sun and shade. Formal and
informal planting. C19 pergola
with 'Empresses of India' theme.
Small vegetable garden.

31 SPRING LANE
Margaret Clarke
A small garden, still evolving. Front
planted for dry conditions,
herbaceous beds, shrubs and
some vegetables in containers at
the back.
✗

33 SPRING LANE
Rosemary Boyd
Small garden with herbaceous
flower beds, fruit trees and a
vegetable and herb area.

STONE COTTAGE
John & Pat Davis
Medium-sized informal cottage garden with pond, patios, fruit and vegetables.

17 THE CRESCENT
Lindsey Butler & Edward Atkinson
30m long with shrub and perennial borders, patios, seating areas and summer house.

20 FLORE SPRING GARDENS
NN7 4LQ. *7m W of Northampton. 5m E of Daventry on A45.* Home-made teas. **Combined adm £3, chd free.** Sun 13 Apr (2-6).
Map provided at the official car park, signed.

NEW 38 HIGH STREET
Mrs J M Harrison
1/2 acre lawn, borders, trees, shrubs and beautiful views. Slope to lawn.

BLISS LANE NURSERY
Chris & Geoff Littlewood
Spring colours consisting of acer phoenix, hellebores, anemones and bluebells, with drifts of daffodils and tulips in the borders. Views over Nene valley.

3 MEADOW FARM CLOSE
Eric & Jackie Ingram
Woodland garden with spring planting around the house.

4 MEADOW FARM CLOSE
Bob & Lynne Richards
Petite, pretty and peaceful.

NEW OAKLANDS
Martin & Rose Wray
Medium sized garden planted with spring bulbs and shrubs under a canopy of mature oak trees.

Maturing bluebells and primroses in three small copses . . .

21 FROGGERY COTTAGE
85 Breakleys Road, Desborough NN14 2PT. Mr John Lee, 01536 760002, johnlee@froggerycottage85. fsnet.co.uk. *6m N of Kettering. 5m S of Market Harborough. Signed off A6 & A14.* Lunches & home-made teas. **Adm £2, chd free.** Sun 27 July (11.30-6). **Visitors also welcome by appt, Jul & Aug, groups 10+.**
3/4 -acre plantsman's garden full of rare and unusual plants. National Collection of 435 varieties of penstemons incl dwarfs and species. Artefacts on display incl old ploughs and garden implements. Workshops during day - penstemons from seeds to winter care.

GILMORTON GARDENS
See Leicestershire & Rutland.

22 GLENDON HALL
Kettering NN14 1QE. Rosie Bose, Tracey Bottomley, Gary Proctor, Jim & Sally Scott, Rosie Bose on 01536 711732. *1 1/2 m E of Rothwell. A6003 to Corby (J7 on A14) W of Kettering, turn L onto Glendon Rd, signed Rothwell, Desborough, Rushton. Entrance 1 1/2 m on L.* Home-made teas. **Adm £2.50, chd free.** Sun 22 June (2-6). **Visitors also welcome by appt.**
Mature specimen trees, topiary, box hedges, herbaceous borders stocked with many unusual plants, large walled kitchen gardens with restored glass house. Some gravel.

23 GREAT ADDINGTON MANOR
Great Addington NN14 4BH. Mr & Mrs G E Groome. *7m SE of Kettering. Junction 11, A510 exit off A14 signed Finedon & Wellingborough. Turn 2nd L to the Addingtons.* Home-made teas. **Adm £3, chd 5+ £1.** Mon 24 Mar (2-5).
4 1/2 -acre manor gardens with terrace, lawns, mature trees, mulberry, yew hedges, pond and spinney, spring daffodils. Gravel paths, steps & slopes.

24 GREAT BRINGTON GARDENS
NN7 4JJ. *7m NW of Northampton. Off A428 Rugby Rd. 1st L turn past main gates of Althorp.* Coffee & home-made lunches at Reading Room. Teas at Church. **Combined adm £3.50, chd free.** Sun 4 May (11-5).
Tickets (maps and programmes) at

Church, Reading Room and free car park. 7 gardens of great variety signed in village. Small attractive stone and thatch village with Spencer and Washington connections and C12 church. Village history exhibition & plant stalls.

BEARD'S COTTAGE
Captain Bill Bellamy
1/2 -acre of lawns, shrubs and herbaceous borders. Large orchard with maturing bluebells and primroses in three small copses.

8 BEDFORD COTTAGES
Anne & Bob Billingsby
Long sloping N-facing garden with outstanding views. Designed, created and maintained by the owners. Many shrubs and herbaceous plants for all-yr interest.

BRINGTON LODGE
Peter & Jenny Cooch
3/4 -acre, partly walled, beautiful mature garden overlooking the Althorpe Estate.

THE OLD RECTORY
Mr & Mrs R Thomas, 01604 770727, jewelbrington@hotmail.com. Visitors also welcome by appt April-Sept.
3-acre garden with mature trees, yew hedging, formal rose garden, vegetable garden, flower borders and 1/3 acre orchard, secret garden. Gravel paths but all level.

RIDGWAY HOUSE
Mr & Mrs R Steedman
1 1/2 -acres, a blend of more formal areas, inc 2 rose gardens and orchard, and less formal herbaceous borders, many spring flowering shrubs and bulbs. Gravel drive.

ROSE COTTAGE
David Green & Elaine MacKenzie
Small cottage garden continues to evolve with the acquisition of the 'new' garden next door. Shady woodland area and pond garden. Work in progress includes a patio/dining area, water features and a small sensory garden.

THE STABLES
Mr & Mrs A George
Small cottage garden containing shrubs, herbaceous plants and climbers. Compact and unusual shape with water feature and summer house.

25 GREAT HARROWDEN LODGE
The Slips. NN9 5AE. Mrs J & Mr A J Green. *2m N of Wellingborough. 5m S of Kettering on A509. Situated 3/4 m from Great Harrowden Church on lane to Finedon.* **Adm £3, chd free.** Sun 15 June (12-5). **Combined with Dolphins.**
1 1/4 -acre garden on a dry exposed site. Wide variety of herbaceous plants in long borders and island beds. Herb garden.

26 GREENWAY
Pipewell Road, Desborough NN14 2SN. Robert Bass. *6m NW of Kettering, 5m SE of Market Harborough. On B576. 150 metres E of Pipewell Rd railway bridge and Travis Perkins builders' yard.* Home-made teas 4-May, 29-Jun, 7-Sept. **Adm £2, £5 on 29-Jun, chd free.** Suns 4 May; 7 Sept (2-6). **Evening Openings** wine, Thurs 5, 10 July (6-9). **Afternoon and Evening Opening** Sun 29th June (2-9).
Constantly evolving arboretum style garden set in 1/3 acre with over 50 acers (Japanese maple cultivars) in containers and open planting. Many garden structures, water features, statuary and containers to provide year round interest. Recent additions incl gothic folly with fernery and a viewing platform. Covered seating areas for contemplation. 29 Jun - Painting in the Garden.

27 GREYWALLS
Farndish NN29 7HJ. Mrs P M Anderson, 01933 353495, patricia@greywalls.tradaweb.net. *2 1/2 m SE of Wellingborough. A609 from Wellingborough, B570 to Irchester, turn to Farndish by cenotaph. House adjacent to church.* Light refreshments & teas. **Adm £3, chd free (share to St Katherine's Church).** Sun 17 Feb (12-4); 22 Feb 2009. **Visitors also welcome by appt in Feb, incl coaches.**
2-acre mature garden surrounding old vicarage (not open). Over 100 varieties of snowdrops, drifts of hardy cyclamen

and hellebores. Alpine house and raised alpine beds. Water features and natural ponds with views over open countryside. Special hens and Bantams - eggs for sale. Partial wheelchair access.

Woodland with wild flowers, paddocks and a wonderful view, enhanced by llamas, mares and foals . . .

28 GUILSBOROUGH & HOLLOWELL MAY GARDENS
NN6 8PY. *10m NW Northampton, 5m S of junction 1 on A14. Between A5199 and A428.* Cream teas. **Combined adm £4 May, chd free.**
Sat 17, Sun 18 May (1-5).
3 plantsman's gardens with azaleas, shrubs, woodland, alpines and many rare and unusual plants. 2 small hilltop village gardens and a large garden down a terraced N-facing slope. Wild flowers, vegetable gardens and orchards. Ponds, a bog garden and use of natural springs featured.

DRIPWELL HOUSE
Mr J W Langfield & Dr C Moss, 01604 740755, cattimoss@aol.com. Visitors also welcome by appt in May & June, combined with Gower House.
3-acre mature garden. Many fine trees and shrubs on partly terraced slope. Rock garden, herbaceous borders, herb, wild flower and vegetable gardens, soft fruit and apple orchard. Unusual shrubs, rhododendrons and azaleas in woodland garden.

GOWER HOUSE
Peter & Ann Moss, 01604 740755. Visitors also welcome by appt in May & June, combined with Dripwell House.
Small garden evolving since 1991 on part of Dripwell vegetable garden. Plantsman's garden with herbaceous, alpine, climbing plants and shrubs.

ROSEMOUNT
Mr & Mrs J Leatherland
See separate entry.

29 GUILSBOROUGH SPRING GARDENS
NN6 8PT. *10m NW of Northampton. 10m E of Rugby. Between A5199 & A428. Parking for Guilsborough Gardens in field at Guilsborough House.* **Combined adm £4, chd free.**
Sat 19, Sun 20 Apr (1-5).
Village set in beautiful rolling countryside. 6 gardens of different styles and sizes, most with wonderful views and plenty of room to sit and relax. Maps provided. Lunches & teas in village.

FOUR ACRES
Mark & Gay Webster
2-acre garden planted for yr-round interest. Long gravel drive.

NEW THE GATE HOUSE
Mr & Mrs M W Edwards
Small multi-level encl cottage garden with pond. Well stocked borders with flowers, shrubs, vegetables, fruit and trees. Some steps, but help available.

GUILSBOROUGH HOUSE
Mr & Mrs John McCall
Country garden, terraces, lawns and hedges and mature trees with emphasis on texture and form. Plenty of room and shade for picnic in field - improved access.

NEW OAK DENE
Mr & Mrs A Darker
Small cottage garden with a selection of greenery and added colour all year round. A flower arranger's dream. Gravel drive.

THE OLD HOUSE
Richard & Libby Seaton Evans
1-acre of lawns, herbaceous borders, spring flowers and walled kitchen garden. Additional woodland with wild flowers, paddocks and a wonderful view, enhanced by llamas, mares and foals. Access difficult in some areas.

THE OLD VICARAGE
John & Christine Benbow
1 1/2 -acre garden revitalised over the past five years. Colourful herbaceous borders with spring

bulbs, especially tulips. Woodland areas, small pond, new walled vegetable garden leading down to orchard in meadow.

♿ ⚘

③⓪ HANNINGTON GARDENS
Hannington Village NN6 9HH. *5m S of Kettering. On A43 Hannington is signed at Xrds opposite garage.* Home-made teas at Village Hall. **Combined adm £3, chd free. Sun 6 July (11-5).**
Small village combining Grade II listed stone dwellings with modern homes. Historically and architecturally interesting C13 church - unique nave with central pillars - associated with the Gilbertine monasteries of Norman times and with 2 bishops.
☕

BROOKMEAD
6 Orchard Close. Mr & Mrs A Shardlow. *Orchard Close is 1st R on entering village*
Established medium-sized garden featuring lawns, shrubs and herbaceous borders. Climbers, seating areas and small water feature. Open countryside views.
♿ ⚘ ✿

NEW GREEN WING
Main Street. Mr & Mrs C J Hicks
Established garden with open countryside views. Lawns, trees, shrubs and herbaceous borders.
♿ ⚘

KARMIRA
Bridle Road. Mr & Mrs P Gyselynck. *From A43 Bridle Rd is 1st L*
Medium-sized garden of lawns, shrubs and herbaceous borders. Mature trees, patio and seating areas. Pot plants, pergola walk, dovecote and fish pond.

③① HARPOLE GARDENS
NN7 4BX. *4m W Northampton. On A45 towards Weedon. Turn R at The Turnpike Hotel into Harpole.* Home-made teas at The Close. **Combined adm £3, chd free. Sun 22 June (12-6).**
Village maps given to all visitors.
☕

THE CLOSE
Michael Orton-Jones
Old-fashioned English country garden with large lawns, herbaceous borders and mature trees. Stone house (not open).
♿ ✿

74 LARKHALL LANE
Mr & Mrs J Leahy
Medium-sized informal garden with a wide variety of plants, shrubs, some mature trees, climbers, alpines, grasses, small pond and a variety of pots. 1 step from patio, 1 path unsuitable, others paved.
♿ ✿

19 MANOR CLOSE
Mr & Mrs E Kemshed
40yds x 10yds flower arranger's garden on an estate, cultivated by present owners since 1975.

17 MANOR CLOSE
Mr & Mrs I Wilkinson
Small, well stocked garden with lawns, gravel areas, pond and mixed borders.
♿

MILLERS
Mr & Mrs M Still
Old stone farmhouse (not open) with 1 acre of lawns and mixed borders, mainly shrubs, some mature trees, good views overlooking the farm and strawberry field.

Pleasantly rural with good ridge and furrow fields around . . .

③② 67-69 HIGH STREET
Finedon NN9 5JN. Mary & Stuart Hendry, 01933 680414. *6m SE Kettering, junction A6 & A510.* **Adm £2.50, chd free. Evening Openings** wine, Thurs 12, 19 June (5-9). Visitors also welcome by appt Feb to Sept, incl groups.
Constantly evolving, 1/3-acre rear garden of C17 cottage (not open). Mixed borders, obelisks and containers, kitchen garden and herb bed. Rope border, spring garden, snow drops and hellebores, late summer borders. Also open with Finedon Gardens. Featured in 'The Kitchen Garden'.
♿ ⚘ ✿ ☎

③③ HILL GROUNDS
Evenley NN13 5RZ. Mr & Mrs C F Cropley, 01280 703224, bob@cropley.freeserve.co.uk. *1m S of Brackley. On A43, turn L into Evenley. R off Church Lane.* **Adm £4 inc tea or coffee, chd free. Visitors welcome by appt.**
Plantsman's garden of 2 acres, surrounded by C19 200yd yew hedge. Planted for yr-round interest. Bulbs, terrace, rose pergola, double herbaceous borders. Many rare and less hardy plants grown. Millennium 'arborette'. Cuttings & seedlings as they come.
♿ ⚘ ✿ ☕ ☎

③④ ◆ KELMARSH HALL
Northampton NN6 9LY. The Kelmarsh Trust, 01604 686543, www.kelmarsh.com. *5m S of Market Harborough. On A508, 1/2 m N of junction with A14. Entrance at Xrds in Kelmarsh Village.* **Adm £4, chd £3.50, concessions £2.50, Garden only. Easter Sun-28 Sept, Suns, Tues, Weds, Thurs. For NGS: Suns 20 Apr; 29 June (2-5).**
1730 Palladian house by James Gibbs. C18 landscape with lake, woods and triangular walled garden. C20 garden by Nancy Lancaster. Spring bulbs, rose gardens, scented garden, herbaceous borders planted by Norah Lindsay, woodland walks, cut flower borders and vegetables. Croome Court Furniture Collection open in house on 20 Apr. Featured in 'The Garden Journal'. Gravel paths.
♿ ✿ ☕

③⑤ KILSBY GARDENS
CV23 8XP. *5m SE of Rugby. 6m N of Daventry on A361. On A428 turn R on B4038 through village.* Home-made teas at and in aid of Kilsby Village Hall. **Combined adm £3, chd free. Sun 8 June (1-5).**
Compact village with interesting mix of old and new houses, 2 pubs, village school and historic church. Pleasantly rural with good ridge and furrow fields around. Embroidery exhibition in Kilsby Room.
☕

NEW 30 RUGBY ROAD
Mr T L Wright
Small garden divided to create rooms. Mature trees, shrubs, climbers, ponds.

NEW 8 INDEPENDENT STREET
Mr & Mrs A Malins
Garden on split levels. Mature

hedges and trees, herbaceous borders, lawn, climbing roses, vegetables and fruit, greenhouse.

THE LIMES
3 Main Road. Mr & Mrs H Grainger
Roses, mixed borders. Variety of shrubs and mature trees.

MOATHOUSE FARM
Mrs C Walker
Small country garden on different levels. Small pond and courtyard.

PYTCHLEY HOUSE
Mr & Mrs T F Clay
Garden downsized to 1/2 -acre and being developed and re-shaped. 2 ponds, one a C19 reservoir discovered while creating a new herbaceous bed. Linked lawns with island beds. Vegetables in deep beds, fruit trees and soft fruit.

5 THE LAWNS
Mr C Smedley
Small, partially secluded garden split into 2 distinct areas incl vegetables and fruit. Shows what can be done with limited space on a modern housing development.

36 LITCHBOROUGH GARDENS
NN12 8JF. *10m SW of Northampton, nr Towcester. Please use car park nr village green. Maps provided.* Home-made teas at village hall. **Combined adm £3.50, chd free (share to St Martins Church). Sun 1 June (2-6).**
A small attractive ironstone village with conservation area, listed buildings and C13 church.

ABBOTS LEA
M Cronin
Lawn with surrounding flower beds.

BRUYERE COURT
Mr R M Billington
3 acres of landscaped garden. Lawns, 2 ornamental lakes with rock streams and fountain, shrubs, rhododendrons, azaleas and herbaceous borders, old-fashioned roses, ornamental trees and conifers.

THE HALL
Mr & Mrs A R Heygate
Large garden with open views of parkland, laid to lawns and borders with clipped hedges. Extensive woodland area has large numbers of specimen trees and shrubs. Walks wind through this area and around the lakes. No access to woodland glade, gravel paths elsewhere.

2 KILN LANE
Anna Steiner
Flag like sculptures capturing natural elements of the garden, wind, shadows and movement. A green garden with oak tree and willows.

4 KILN LANE
Mr & Mrs Morling
300yr-old cottage (not open) with modern cottage garden. Developed over 10yrs following levelling, terracing and hard landscaping incl the construction of 2 ponds, retaining existing trees and shrubs.

ORCHARD HOUSE
Mr & Mrs B Smith
Landscape architects' country garden surrounding listed building (not open) designed for low maintenance. Orchard, pools, conservatory and working pump.

TIVY FARM
Mr & Mrs J Pulford
Lawn sloping down to large wildlife pond surrounded by beautiful trees. Patio with lovely pots and containers.

51 TOWCESTER ROAD
Mr Norman Drinkwater
Small council house garden featuring lawns, shrubs, rockery and productive vegetable garden.

Haven of peace and harmony, home to unusual wildlife . . .

37 LOIS WEEDON HOUSE
NN12 8PJ. **Sir John & Lady Greenaway.** *7m W of Towcester. On the eastern edge of village. Last entrance on R going E towards Wappenham.* Cream teas. **Combined with The Old Barn Adm £3, chd free (share to St Loys School). Sun 25 May (2-6).**
Large garden with terraces and fine views, lawns, pergola, water garden, mature yew hedges, pond. Some slopes.

38 LONG BUCKBY GARDENS
NN6 7RE. *8m NW of Northampton, midway between A428 & A5. 6 gardens in village close to Square, WC and parking. Mill House at junction of A428 and Ravensthorpe Rd, 1m distant.* Home-made teas at 45 Brington Road. **Combined adm £3, chd free. Sun 15 June (1-6).**

23 BERRYFIELD
Mr & Mrs C M Robins
Lawns, gravel bed with pots, pond, patios, stone feature, flower beds, greenhouse. Ornamental garden on a slope.

45 BRINGTON ROAD
Derick & Sandra Cooper, 01327 843762. Visitors also welcome by appt.
1/3 -acre organic village garden designed to create haven of peace and harmony, home to unusual wildlife. Features incl rose walk, 4 varied water features, Victorian-style greenhouse and summerhouse surrounded by box-edged raised vegetable plots. All constructed from reclaimed materials.

36 HIGH STACK
Mike & Jenny Pollard
Patio area, lawn, paths, various flowerbeds and shrubs.

7 HIGH STACK
Tiny & Sheila
Cottage garden on 2 levels, established over 6 yrs. Mixed borders, vegetables and fruit, pond, patio and seating area. Gravelled front garden with perennial planting.

MILL HOUSE
Long Lane. Ken and Gill
Pawson, 01604 770103,
gill@gpplanning.co.uk. Visitors
also welcome by appt in June.
Over 1 acre in open countryside.
Large vegetable plot with some
old and rare varieties. Owner is
Heritage Seed Library Guardian.
Orchard, pergola, pond, grasses,
hot garden, borders and shady
areas. Foundations of East
Haddon Windmill.

TORESTIN
10 Lime Ave. June Ford
$1/3$ -acre mature garden divided
into 3 separate areas
incorporating water features,
rockeries and pergolas. Interesting
perennials, clematis and roses.

LONG CLOSE
See Leicestershire & Rutland.

Planted terrace
area overlooking
lawn, ha-ha
and magnificent
trees . . .

39 ◆ LYVEDEN NEW BIELD
Oundle PE8 5AT. The National Trust,
01832 205358,
lyveden@nationaltrust.org.uk. *5m
SW of Oundle, 3m NE of Brigstock.
Signed off A247 & A6116.* **Adm £4,
chd free. Wed to Sun, Apr-Nov. Daily
Aug. For NGS: Sun 15 June; Sat 19
July (10.30-5).**
One of England's oldest garden
landscapes, abandoned in 1605 after
family involvement in the Gunpowder
Plot, Lyveden still retains original
terraces, prospect mounts, canals and
the impressive garden lodge built to
symbolise the Tresham's catholic faith.
Recently replanted 5-acre orchard of
pre-C17 tree varieties. Garden tours,
12 & 2pm.

40 MAIDWELL HALL
Maidwell NN6 9JG. Maidwell Hall
School. *6m S of Market Harborough.
Take A508 N from Northampton,
entrance via main drive on S edge of
village.* **Adm £3, chd £3. Sun 30 Mar
(2-5).**

45 acres of lawns, playing fields,
woodland, daffodils, spring bulbs,
mature rose garden, lake and
arboretum.

41 THE MALTINGS
10 The Green, Clipston LE16 9RS.
Mr & Mrs Hamish Connell, 01858
525336,
j.connell118@btinternet.com. *4m S
of Market Harborough, 9m W of
Kettering. From A14 take junction 2,
A508 N. After 2m turn L for Clipston. 2
houses away from Old Red Lion.*
Cream teas. **Adm £3, chd free. Sat
22, Sun 23, Mar (1-6), Mons 24 Mar;
5 May (11-6); Sat 14 Jun (1-6), Sun
15 June (11-6). Visitors also
welcome by appt, groups of 10+.
Meals at village PH.**
$3/4$ acre sloping plantsman's garden
designed for all year interest by the
present owner over the last 10 years.
Many unusual plants, shrubs, old and
new trees. Over 50 different clematis,
wild garden walk, spring bulb area,
over 20 different species roses, 2
ponds connected by a stream, bog
garden, many different fruits and
vegetables. Home made cake stall.
Featured in Local Press. Older people
may need a stick and some help.

42 ◆ THE MENAGERIE
Newport Pagnell Road, Horton
NN7 2BX. Mr A Myers, 01604
870710. *6m S of Northampton. 1m S
of Horton. On B526, turn E at lay-by,
across field.* **Adm £5, chd £1.50,
concessions £4. For NGS: Sat 28
June (2-6).**
Newly developed gardens set around
C18 folly, with 2 delightful thatched
arbours. Recently completed large
formal walled garden with fountain,
used for vegetables, fruit and cutting
flowers. Recently extended exotic bog
garden and native wetland area. Also
rose garden, shrubberies, herbaceous
borders and wild flower areas.

MIDDLETON CHENEY GARDENS
See Oxfordshire.

43 OLD BARN
Weedon Lois NN12 8PL. Mr & Mrs
John Gregory, 01327 860577,
irisgregory@tiscali.co.uk. *7m N of
Brackley.* In the centre of the village
adjacent to the parish church.
**Combined with Lois Weedon
House Adm £3, chd free (share to**

St Loys School). **Sun 25 May (2-6).
Visitors also welcome by appt.**
Garden has matured over the last
25yrs and reflects the owner's
enthusiasm for hardy plants, inc
collections of campanula, euphorbia,
geraniums and violas supported by
clematis and roses.

**44 THE OLD RECTORY,
BROCKHALL**
NN7 4JY. Mrs J Quarmby, 01327
340280,
jane.quarmby@tqtraining.co.uk. *2m
E of Weedon towards Flore. In village,
as you enter from Flore, opp church.*
Home-made teas. **Adm £3, chd free.
Suns 25 May; 24 Aug (2-5.30).
Visitors also welcome by appt.**
$4^1/2$ -acres being restored by the
owners. Large sweeping lawns, very
colourful flower cutting gardens, newly
created shady planting area, $1/2$ -acre
working kitchen garden, arboretum,
pool garden and herbaceous borders.
Gravel, & mown grass paths.

**45 THE OLD RECTORY,
HASELBECH**
Cottesbrook Road. NN6 9LJ. Mr &
Mrs P C Flory, 01604 686432. *12m N
of Northampton. L turn off A508 just S
of A14 junction, 2m to village. A14
junction 2, take A508 towards
Northampton. 1st R to Haselbech.*
Home-made teas. **Adm £3.50, chd
free (share to St Michaels Church).
Sun 8 June (2-6). Visitors also
welcome by appt, incl coaches.**
1-acre garden set in 9 acres, incl tree
plantations, with glorious unspoilt
views, surrounding Georgian rectory
(not open). Old walled garden,
herbaceous borders, rose garden with
clipped box hedge, yew and beech
hedges. Small potager vegetable
garden and interesting bog garden.
Lovely planted terrace area overlooking
lawn, ha-ha and magnificent trees.
Overlooking farmland and totally
unspoilt views. Featured in 'The English
Garden'. One steep slope, some gravel
paths.

**46 ◆ THE OLD RECTORY,
SUDBOROUGH**
NN14 3BX. Mr & Mrs A Huntington,
01832 733247,
info@oldrectorygardens.co.uk. *8m
NE of Kettering. Exit 12 off A14. Village
just off A6116 between Thrapston &
Brigstock.* **Adm £4, £5 14 Jun, chd**

free. **Tues, Apr–Sept.** For NGS: Sun 16 Mar; Sat 14 June **Special Open Day** in conjunction with Marie Curie; Sun 14 Sept (2-6).
Classic 3-acre country garden with extensive herbaceous borders of unusual plants. Magnolias and cornus in spring, containers of bulbs and large plantings of tulips, early rare hellebores. Formal rose circle and box edged potager designed by Rosemary Verey, woodland walk and pond alongside Harpers Brook. Rare plants throughout summer. Some gravel paths.

47 PARK HOUSE
Norton NN11 5ND. **Mr & Mrs J H Wareing Russell.** *3¹/₂ m N of Weedon. From A5 take 2nd Norton/Daventry turn L. Entrance L before village.* Home-made teas. **Adm £3, chd free.** Sun 1 June (2-5).
5-acres, lawns leading down to lakes. Wonderful trees and shrubs incl many unusual species, herbaceous borders, heather beds, azaleas, roses and ¹/₄ m lakeside walk.

48 PRESTON CAPES GARDENS
NN11 3TF. *6m SW of Daventry. 13m NE of Banbury. 3m N of Canons Ashby.* Lunches & home-made teas. **Combined adm £4, chd free.** Sun 1 June (12-5).
Unspoilt rural village in the Northamptonshire uplands. Local sandstone houses and cottages, Norman Church. Village maps for all visitors.

CITY COTTAGE
Mr & Mrs Gavin Cowen, 01327 361603. Visitors also welcome by appt.
Mature garden in the middle of attractive village. Walled herbaceous border, rose beds, flowering shrubs and wisteria.

LADYCROFT
Mervyn & Sophia Maddison
Contemporary garden, planted since 2005 for yr-round interest, on exposed site with fine views. Gravel drive.

LANGDALE HOUSE
Michael & Penny Eves
1-acre country garden with far-reaching views re-designed by the owners since 1993. Foliage plants

for sun and shade, maturing herbaceous border, semi-formal wildlife pond planted with mainly native species and Mediterranean gravel bed.

NORTH FARM
Mr & Mrs Tim Coleridge
Rural farmhouse garden maintained by owners. Outstanding view towards Fawsley and High Wood.

OLD WEST FARM
Mr & Mrs Gerard Hoare, 01327 361263, claire.hoare@virgin.net. *³/₄ m E of Preston Capes.* **Visitors also welcome by appt.**
Rural 2-acre garden. Borders of interesting and unusual plants, roses and shrubs. Woodland area underplanted with shrubs. Exposed site with shelter planting, maintained by the owners without help, so designed for easy upkeep. Small vegetable garden.

VILLAGE FARM
Trevor & Julia Clarke, 01327 361819. **Visitors also welcome by appt.**
Large garden on steeply sloping site. Interesting trees and shrubs, 3 large wildlife ponds and wonderful views over unspoilt countryside.

WEST ORCHARD FARM HOUSE
Mr & Mrs Nick Price
1-acre informal garden with outstanding views. Renovated completely by Caroline Price and replanted with shrubs and herbaceous plants.

49 ROSEBRIAR
83 Main Road, Collyweston PE9 3PQ. Jenny Harrison, 01780 444389. *On A43 3¹/₂ m SW of Stamford. 3 doors from pub.* **Adm £3, chd free** (share to Hearing Dogs). Sun 22 June (11-6). **Visitors also welcome by appt.**
The garden, which is on quite a steep slope, contains a variety of areas with alpine and grass beds, water feature with stream and bog garden, surrounded by herbaceous and shrub borders lavishly planted with exciting combinations, linked by gravel paths and patios.

Exposed site with shelter planting . . . designed for easy upkeep . . .

50 ROSEMOUNT
Church Hill, Hollowell NN6 8RR. Mr & Mrs Leatherland, 01604 740354. *10m NW of Northampton, 5m S junction 1 A14. Between A5199 and A428.* **Adm £2, chd free.** Sun 24 Feb (11-4). **Visitors also welcome by appt, Feb to Aug, groups 10+.**
¹/₂ -acre plantsman's garden. Unusual plants and shrubs, alpine garden, fish pond, small collections of clematis, camellias and abutilons. Snowdrops, hellebores and spring bulbs. Unusual varieties for sale. Also open with Guilsborough and Hollowell May Gardens.

SOUTH KILWORTH GARDENS
See Leicestershire & Rutland.

CROFT ACRE
See Leicestershire & Rutland.

51 SPRATTON GARDENS
NN6 8HL. *6¹/₂ m NNW of Northampton. From Northampton on A5199 turn L at Holdenby Rd for Spratton Grange Farm, after ¹/₂ m turn L up long drive. For other gardens turn R at Brixworth Rd. Car park signed.* Refreshments & teas at St Andrews Church. **Combined adm £4, chd free.** Sun 27 Apr (11-5).
Attractive village with many C17 ironstone houses and C12 church. Tickets and maps at gardens.

THE GRANARY
Stephanie Bamford & Mark Wilkinson
Semi-formal courtyard garden with circular pond, walled rear garden with circular lawn, mixed shrub and flower borders, archways through to small orchard.

11 HIGH STREET
Philip & Frances Roseblade
Small and compact, making full use of a difficult shape. Neat hedging and topiary.

MULBERRY COTTAGE
Mr & Mrs M Heaton, 01604 846032. Visitors also welcome by appt, April to July, groups 10+, £2.50 ea.
1/2 -acre part cottage-style. Feature mulberry tree, lawns, herbaceous, rose and shrub borders, shady planting and water features.

NORTHBANK HOUSE
Mr & Mrs J Knight
1/3 -acre part walled cottage garden with herbaceous and shrub borders, roses, vegetables and lawns.

SPRATTON GRANGE FARM
Dennis & Christine Yardy
2-acre garden in an elevated position with superb country views, courtyard, parterre and large walled area with mature borders. A naturally fed pond with bog garden leading to a small spinney. Steep slopes in pond area.

THE STABLES
Mr & Mrs A Woods
3/4 -acre garden planted for plant lovers. Large range of plants grown in a variety of settings, gravel garden, pergola, ponds, stream and rockery, shrub and herbaceous borders, vegetable garden. Some gravel paths.

WALTHAM COTTAGE
Norma & Allan Simons
Small cottage garden that has evolved over the years - some interesting features.

STOKE ALBANY HOUSE
See Leicestershire & Rutland.

STOWE LANDSCAPE GARDENS
See Buckinghamshire.

THORPE LUBENHAM HALL
See Leicestershire & Rutland.

52 TITCHMARSH HOUSE
Chapel Street. NN14 3DA. Sir Ewan & Lady Harper, 01832 732439, jenny.harper@church-schools.com.
2m N of Thrapston. 6m S of Oundle. Exit A14 at A605 junction, Titchmarsh signed as turning to E. Light refreshments & teas at village fete. **Adm £3, chd free. Sat 14 June (12-5). Visitors also welcome by appt April to 14 June only.**
4 1/2 -acres extended and laid out since 1972. Cherries, magnolias, herbaceous, irises, shrub roses, range of unusual shrubs, walled borders and ornamental vegetable garden.

53 TOP LODGE
Violet Lane, Glendon NN16 1QL. Glenn & Anne Burley, 01536 511784.
3m NW of Kettering. Take A6003 to Corby, off roundabout W of Kettering turn L onto Glendon Rd, signed at T-lights, approx 2m L into Violet Lane. Cream teas. **Adm £2.50, chd free. Sun 8 June (2-5.30). Visitors also welcome by appt.**
1 1/2 -acre garden surrounding main house (not open) set in countryside. Many structural features enhanced by large collection of climbers, herbaceous plants and shrubs separating defined areas, incl water garden with pond, stream, waterfalls and woodland area. Mediterranean and secluded garden.

54 TURWESTON GARDENS
Brackley NN13 5JY. *A43 from M40 J10. On Brackley bypass turn R on A422 towards Buckingham, 1/2 m turn L sign Turweston.* Cream teas at Versions Farm. **Combined adm £3.50, chd free. Sun 18 May (2-5.30).** Charming stone built village near the head of the Great Ouse River.

THE OLD SCHOOL HOUSE
Mr & Mrs Hugh Carey
Small cottage garden with clipped box hedges surrounding herbaceous borders.

TURWESTON MILL
Mr & Mrs Harry Leventis
5-acre beautifully designed garden making full use of the mill stream with water garden waterfall and wildlife ponds. Lawns with lovely trees and herbaceous borders.

VERSIONS FARM
Mrs E T Smyth-Osbourne
3-acre plantsman's garden, wide-range of unusual plants, shrubs and trees. Old stone walls, terraces, old-fashioned rose garden, pond. Conservatory. Part of the garden has been re-designed. Mostly wheelchair access.

WALTON GARDENS
See Leicestershire & Rutland.

55 WEEDON LOIS GARDENS
NN12 8PL. *7m N of Brackley. 8m W of Towcester. In centre of village, close to Parish Church.* Light refreshments & homemade teas. **Combined adm £4, chd free (share to St Loys School). Sun 29 June (2-6).**

HOME CLOSE
Clyde Burbidge
2-acre garden established over last 9 yrs. Informal cottage garden surrounding stone barn conversion. Meadow, ponds and small spinney, vegetable garden, new herbaceous borders. Gravel paths, some steps.

OLD BARN
Mr & Mrs John Gregory, 01327 860577. Visitors also welcome by appt.
Over the past 25yrs this garden has matured and reflects the owner's enthusiasm for hardy plants, inc collections of campanula, euphorbia, geranium and violas. A fine display of clematis and roses.

STABLE COTTAGE
Mr & Mrs Medlicott-Walker
Pretty courtyard garden with informal planting of trees, herbaceous plants and vegetables.

Wildlife and wild flower garden inhabited by frogs, toads, hedgehogs, grass snakes and more . . .

56 WEST HADDON GARDENS

NN6 7AY. *10m NW of Northampton. Off A428 between Rugby & Northampton, 4m E of M1 J18. Village now bypassed.* Home-made teas at West Cottage. **Combined adm £3.50, chd free. Sun 6 July (2-6).**
A traditional village, predominantly brick but some local stone and thatch, plus modern housing estates. A few shops, PHs with restaurants and a well preserved church and chapel. Tickets and maps at all gardens, 3 of which are large and 5 small.

NEW 2 PARNELL CLOSE
Jane & Brian Cartlidge
$1/5$ acre 5 yr old garden in modern development with cottage style borders, shrubs, vegetables, fruit trees, greenhouse and lawn. A 400-yr old protected hedge runs along one boundary.

CLOVER COTTAGE
Helen & Stephen Chown
Walled cottage garden with terraces, cobbles, gravel, pots and decking. Very sunny sheltered space with a lovely lemon tree, orange bush and bougainvillea.

THE CROWN COURTYARD
Mark Byrom
Public House courtyard with C16 outbuildings decorated with hanging baskets, containers and cascading flora.

LIME HOUSE
Lesley & David Roberts
$1/2$ -acre walled garden with rockeries, herbaceous borders, walk-through shrubbery, rose beds, croquet lawn.

Summerhouse, patio with greenhouse and a variety of garden statues and ornaments.

RIVENDELL
Mr & Mrs E Maclean
Medium-sized family garden with lawns, mixed borders and pond.

TOWNLEY BARN
Kate & Richard Tilt
1-acre organic garden with wild flower meadow, kitchen garden, stream, waterfall, pond, shrubs, flowers and peaceful inner courtyard. Beautiful views over meadow. Gravel drive.

WESLYAN COTTAGE
Arnie & Gillean Stensones
Small densely planted walled garden on various levels where lush plants and climbers jostle for space. Summer house smothered with clematis.

WEST COTTAGE & 45 WEST END
Geoff & Rosemary Sage
1-acre of mixed borders, lawns, ponds, lawn tennis court, kitchen

garden and greenhouses with straw bale cultivation. Wildlife and wild flower garden inhabited by frogs, toads, hedgehogs, grass snakes, great crested newts, woodpeckers, spotted flycatchers and more.

WILLOUGHBY GARDENS
See Leicestershire & Rutland.

57 WOODCHIPPINGS
Juniper Hill NN13 5RH. Richard Bashford & Valerie Bexley, 01869 810170. *3m S of Brackley. Off A43. 3m N J10 M40, S of Croughton roundabout take L turn, $1/2$ m to Juniper Hill.* **Adm £3, chd free.**
Visitors welcome by appt individuals & groups, Feb to 31 July.
$1/3$ -acre plantsman's garden surrounding stone cottage. Densely and abundantly planted for colour and scent. Snowdrops, hellebores and woodland garden in spring. Vibrant perennials in hot borders in summer. Planting especially for insects. Narrow paths may be unsuitable for infirm or very young. Small nursery. Featured in 'Period Living' & 'Country Life'.

Northamptonshire County Volunteers

County Organiser
Annabel Smyth-Osbourne Versions Farm, Turweston, Brackley NN13 5JY, 01280 702412, annabelso@aol.com

County Treasurer
Michael Heaton, Mulberry Cottage, Yew Tree Lane, Spratton NN6 8HL, 01604 846032, ngs@mimomul.co.uk

Publicity
Ingram Lloyd, The Old Forge, Sulgrave, Banbury OX17 2RP, 01295 760678, ingramlloyd@dial.pipex.com

Assistant County Organisers
David Abbott, Wroxton Lodge, Church Hill, Finedon, Wellingborough NN9 5NR, 01933 680363, d_j_abbott@btinternet.com
Ruth Dashwood, Farthinghoe Lodge, Farthinghoe, Brackley NN13 5NX, 01295 710377, rmdashwood@aol.com
Philippa Henmann, The Old Vicarage, Broad Lane, Evenley, Brackley NN13 5SF, 01280 702409, philippaheumann@andreas-heumann.com
Gay Webster, Four Acres, The Green, Guilsborough NN6 8PT, 01604 740 203, egwebster16@hotmail.com

NOTTINGHAMSHIRE

Opening Dates

February

SUNDAY 10
4 The Beeches

SUNDAY 24
4 The Beeches

March

SUNDAY 30
49 Roselea

April

SUNDAY 13
21 Felley Priory
52 Teversal Manor Gardens

SUNDAY 20
1 Ashdene

WEDNESDAY 23
55 The White House

SUNDAY 27
1 Ashdene
4 The Beeches
24 Gardeners Cottage
41 The Old Vicarage

May

SUNDAY 4
15 Darby House
53 University of Nottingham Gardens

MONDAY 5
12 7 Collygate
26 Gorene
37 Mill Hill House

WEDNESDAY 7
55 The White House

SUNDAY 11
23 The Garden House
27 Gringley Gardens
51 Squirrel Lodge

SATURDAY 17
9 4 Clare Valley

SUNDAY 18
1 Ashdene
5 Bishops Manor
16 Dumbleside
32 61 Lambley Lane
40 Norwell Nurseries
41 The Old Vicarage

WEDNESDAY 21
50 125 Shelford Road
55 The White House

SUNDAY 25
45 Papplewick Hall

MONDAY 26
31 Holmes Villa
47 Piecemeal

WEDNESDAY 28
55 The White House

June

SUNDAY 1
33 17 Main Street
48 Redland House

SUNDAY 8
3 Baxter Farm
6 Chestnut Cottage
7 54 Church Lane
8 59 Church Lane
23 The Garden House
43 Oxton Gardens
54 Wellow Village Gardens

WEDNESDAY 11
55 The White House

SUNDAY 15
20 Eynord
34 Manor Farm House
38 Newbray House
52 Teversal Manor Gardens

WEDNESDAY 18
28 Hall Farm Cottage (Evening)

SATURDAY 21
9 4 Clare Valley

SUNDAY 22
2 Askham Gardens
12 7 Collygate

WEDNESDAY 25
14 Cropwell Court (Day & Evening)

SUNDAY 29
35 Meadowside
39 Norwell Gardens
42 Orchard House

July

WEDNESDAY 2
39 Norwell Gardens (Evening)

SUNDAY 6
13 Cornerstones
46 48 Penarth Gardens
49 Roselea
56 Woodside Cottage

WEDNESDAY 9
13 Cornerstones (Evening)

SUNDAY 13
17 Elm House
18 The Elms
22 Fuchsia View
25 16 Glensford Gardens
36 Melrose
44 20 The Paddocks
47 Piecemeal

WEDNESDAY 16
44 20 The Paddocks (Evening)
50 125 Shelford Road (Evening)

THURSDAY 17
22 Fuchsia View (Evening)

SATURDAY 19
11 Clumber Park Walled Kitchen Garden

SUNDAY 27
10 Clarence House
26 Gorene

THURSDAY 31
22 Fuchsia View (Evening)

August

SUNDAY 3
22 Fuchsia View
42 Orchard House
47 Piecemeal
56 Woodside Cottage

SUNDAY 10
13 Cornerstones
19 Elms Farm

SUNDAY 17
53 University of Nottingham Gardens

SUNDAY 24
41 The Old Vicarage (Evening)
51 Squirrel Lodge

September

SUNDAY 7
4 The Beeches
41 The Old Vicarage

SUNDAY 14
50 125 Shelford Road

SATURDAY 20
11 Clumber Park Walled Kitchen Garden

SUNDAY 21
52 Teversal Manor Gardens

SUNDAY 28
30 Holme Pierrepont Hall

Drifts of grasses and plants mingle in a soft and naturalistic form . . .

Gardens open to the public

- **11** Clumber Park Walled Kitchen Garden
- **21** Felley Priory
- **29** Hodsock Priory Gardens
- **30** Holme Pierrepont Hall
- **40** Norwell Nurseries
- **52** Teversal Manor Gardens

Also open by appointment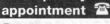

- **3** Baxter Farm
- **4** The Beeches
- **7** 54 Church Lane
- **8** 59 Church Lane
- **12** 7 Collygate
- **13** Cornerstones
- **15** Darby House
- **16** Dumbleside
- **18** The Elms
- **22** Fuchsia View
- **23** The Garden House
- **26** Gorene
- **31** Holmes Villa
- **37** Mill Hill House
- **41** The Old Vicarage
- **42** Orchard House
- **44** 20 The Paddocks
- **47** Piecemeal
- **48** Redland House
- **49** Roselea
- **50** 125 Shelford Road
- **55** The White House
- **56** Woodside Cottage

The Gardens

1 ASHDENE
Radley Road, Halam NG22 8AH. Glenys & David Herbert. *1m W of Southwell. From B6386 in Halam village 300yds past church.* Home-made teas. **Adm £3, chd free.** Suns 20, 27 Apr; 18 May (1-5.30).
Many mature trees incl magnificent walnut (200yrs), paulownia (50yrs) and mulberry. Japanese-style garden incl mature spiral yew. Species and scented rose and woodland gardens. Many clematis, hebes.

2 ASKHAM GARDENS
Markham Moor NG22 0RP. *6m S of Retford. On A638, in Rockley village turn E to Askham.* Home-made teas at Manor Lodge. **Combined adm £3.50, chd free (share to St Nicholas' Church, Askham).** Sun 22 June (2-6).
A variety of pleasant English village

gardens with a flower festival in church.

DOVECOTE COTTAGE
Town Street. Mrs C L Slack
Traditional English cottage garden incl roses on the wall.

NEW FERN LEA
Top Street. Mr & Mrs B Cooley
Small ornamental garden with lawns and borders at different levels.

MANOR LODGE
Town Street. Mr & Mrs K Bloom
Large garden with spreading lawns, gazebo and summerhouses.

NURSERY HOUSE
Top Street. Mr & Mrs D Bird, photos.davidbird.eu
Secluded and very private garden, with every plant meticulously labelled; waterfall and well-stocked pond. Deep gravel at front.

THORN LEA COTTAGE
Church Lane. Mr & Mrs M Hunter-Wyatt, 01777 839256. Visitors also welcome by appt.
Small English cottage garden near church, complete with chickens. New pond and new raised beds.

3 BAXTER FARM
Willoughby on the Wolds LE12 6SY. Peter & Pru Tatham, 01509 880975, tatham@onetel.com. *10m S of Nottingham, 12m N of Leicester. About ¼ m off A46 at E end of Main St.* Home-made teas. **Combined adm £3 with Chestnut Cottage, chd free.** Sun 8 June (1-5). **Visitors also welcome by appt.**
Old farmhouse and barns. 1-acre garden planted last 25yrs. Conservatory, old cattle drinking pond now planted, herbaceous borders, informal plantings of old roses, hardy geraniums, salvias and many climbers. Pergola, Chinese garden, beech and yew hedged walks. Kitchen garden.

4 THE BEECHES
The Avenue, Milton, Tuxford, Newark NG22 0PW. Margaret & Jim Swindin, 01777 870828. *1m S A1 Markham Moor. Exit A1 at Markham Moor roundabout, take Walesby sign*

into village (1m). Soup & roll (Feb) Home-made teas Apr & Sept. **Adm £3, £2.50 Feb, chd free.** Suns 10, 24 Feb (11-4); Suns 27 Apr; 7 Sept (2-5.30). **Visitors also welcome by appt** Feb, Apr, June, July, Aug.
1-acre all seasons garden well stocked with colourful, desirable plants incl over 160 varieties of snowdrops, and spring bulbs. Herbaceous areas incl over 50 different clematis and a wild flower meadow. Tunnel and raised beds with organically grown fruit and vegetables. Many autumn species and grasses are at their best in our Sept opening. Newcastle Mausoleum (adjacent) open to view in Apr & Sept. Featured on Radio Nottingham, Radio Hallam, Trax FM & in 'Nottingham Guardian' & 'Newark Advertiser' 2007.

Herbaceous borders, informal plantings of old roses . . .

5 BISHOPS MANOR
Bishops Drive, Southwell NG25 0JR. The Rt Reverend George Cassidy, Bishop of Southwell. *Centre of Southwell, end of Bishops Dr on S side of Minster.* **Adm £3.50, chd free.** Sun 18 May (2-5).
House built into part of old medieval palace of the Archbishops of York. Ruins form delightful enclosed garden, lawns and 4-seasons tree garden in unusual setting. Large garden with Edwardian layout, includes herb knot garden and other features.

6 CHESTNUT COTTAGE
Main Street, Willoughby-on-the-Wolds LE12 6SY. Dr Olivia Williams. *10m S of Nottingham; 12m N of Leicester. About ¼ m off A46 at W end of Main St.* Cold drinks. **Combined adm £3 with Baxter Farm, chd free.** Sun 8 June (1-5).
One of the owner's artistic outlets! This small S-facing garden was re-landscaped by the owner in 1999, with a wildlife pond, decking, summerhouse, water feature and container plants. Many interesting and unusual plants.

7 **NEW** **54 CHURCH LANE**
**Thrumpton NG11 0AW. Carol &
Mike Staves, 0115 983 0720.** *7m
SW of Nottingham. Thrumpton is
off A453 between Nottingham &
J24 of M1. From Nottingham 1st R
signed Thrumpton approx 2m after
Crusader PH in Clifton. In 1/2 m R
No 54 is 1/2 m on RH-side. From
M1 approx 3m along A453 turn L
just after power station. 1st R then
L in 1/2 m. No 54 is 1/2 m on R.*
Home-made teas. **Combined
adm with 59 Church Lane
£2.50, chd free. Sun 8 June (2-6).
Visitors also welcome by appt.**
Herbaceous borders overflowing
with shrubs, perennials and many
different types of roses wandering
through trees, fences and shrubs.
Larger front garden is tiered on two
levels and has patio area at front.
Back garden has beautiful views
stretching for miles, with two
further patio areas, plus water
feature.
&. ✕ ☕ ☎

8 **59 CHURCH LANE**
**Thrumpton, Nottingham NG11 0AW.
Valerie & John Collins, 0115 983
0533.** *7m SW of Nottingham.
Thrumpton is off A453 between
Nottingham and J24 of M1. From
Nottingham, 1st R signed Thrumpton
approx 2m after Crusader PH in
Clifton. In 1/2 m R. No 59 is 1/2 m on
LH-side. From M1 approx 3m along
A453 turn L just after power stn. 1st R,
then L in 1/2 m. No 59 is 1/2 m on L.*
Home-made teas. **Combined adm
£2.50 with 54 Church Lane, chd
free. Sun 8 June (2-6). Visitors also
welcome by appt.**
Two different styles of garden here.
Drifts of grasses and plants mingle in a
soft and naturalistic form creating an
unusual gravel front garden with pond
and waterfall. Overflowing with
herbaceous perennials, shrubs and
trees, the back garden is artistically
arranged with an eye for colour and
form. Small wild flower patch and
woodland with a rural landscape
beyond complete this 'garden with a
view'.
&. ✕ ☕ ☎

9 **4 CLARE VALLEY**
**The Park, Nottingham NG7 1BU.
Gudrun Sowerby.** *Enter the Park
either via Castle entrance (pass gate
house on L then take 1st R turn into
Park Valley. Follow rd round LH-bend
and Clare Valley is ahead). Or via Derby
Rd entrance (pass through gates and
take 2nd rd on L down steep hill to one
way system. Turn L to pass bowling
and tennis clubs and Clare Valley is
next L turn).* **Adm £2, chd free. Sats
17 May; 21 June (3-6).**
This heavily shaded garden
demonstrates what will grow, and
indeed what can be achieved under a
tall tree canopy. Colour and impact of
informed planting will delight all those
who view it from the high rear terrace,
and then descend down the steps into
it. Relax after the bustle of a shopping
trip in a haven of tranquillity 5 mins
away from the city centre.
✕

10 **NEW** **CLARENCE HOUSE**
**Cropwell Road, Radcliffe on
Trent NG12 2JG. Pam & Greg
Stevens.** *1m S of A52/A46
junction (Saxondale roundabout).
From A52 Radcliffe on Trent follow
signs to Cropwell Butler. From A46
follow signs to Radcliffe on Trent
down Cropwell Rd.* Light
refreshments & teas. **Adm £2.50,
chd free. Sun 27 July (1-6).**
S-facing 1/2 acre garden of curves
and circles. Wander along the
meandering paths, cross the grass
river bridge, sit a while in the shady
garden or the secluded arbour.
Relax on the sunny terrace or the
raised deck and view the colourful
borders of shrubs, perennials and
annuals.
✕ ☕

Wander along the meandering paths . . .

11 **◆ CLUMBER PARK WALLED
KITCHEN GARDEN**
**Clumber Park, Worksop S80 3AZ.
The National Trust, 01909 476592,
www.nationaltrust.org.uk.** *4m S of
Worksop. From main car park follow
directions to the Walled Kitchen
Garden. Turn L up Cedar Ave to
wrought iron gates.* **Adm £2.50, chd
free. See website for other opening
times. For NGS: Sats 19 July; 20
Sept (10-6).**
Beautiful 4-acre walled kitchen garden,
growing unusual and varied varieties of
vegetables, fruit trees, herbs and
ornamentals, incl the magnificent
recently extended 400ft long double
herbaceous borders. 450ft long
glasshouse (the longest owned by the
National Trust), with grape vines,
peaches, nectarines and figs. Museum
of gardening tools. Featured in
'Gardening Which' & 'Kitchen Garden'
magazines & local TV & press, 2007.
Gravel paths & slopes. Self drive
mobility scooters available free of
charge, pre-booking advisable 01909
544911.
&.

COBWEBS
See Lincolnshire.

12 **7 COLLYGATE**
**Swingate, Kimberley NG16 2PJ.
Doreen Fahey & John Arkinstall,
0115 919 2690.** *6m W of Nottingham.
From M1 J26 take A610 towards
Nottingham. L at next island on B600
into Kimberley. At Sainsbury's mini
island take L. L at top. Park on this rd
in 500yds. Collygate on R.* Home-
made teas. **Adm £2.50, chd free
(share to Oasis Breast Cancer
Trust). Mon 5 May; Sun 22 June
(1-5). Visitors also welcome by appt
May to Sept.**
Delightful garden created by serious
plant addicts tucked away at the end
of a short narrow lane in Swingate. It
greets you with an impact of
unexpected colour and delights you
with the variety and sensitivity of the
planting. A peaceful backwater in an
urban setting.
&. ✕ ❀ ☕ ☎

7 COLLYGATE
See Nottinghamshire.

13 **CORNERSTONES**
**15 Lamcote Gardens, Radcliffe-on-
Trent, Nottingham NG12 2BS. Judith
& Jeff Coombes, 0115 845 8055,
judith.coombes@ntlworld.com.** *4m E
of Nottingham. From A52 take
Radcliffe exit at the RSPCA junction,
then 2nd L just before hairpin bend.*
Home-made teas. **Adm £3, chd free.
Suns 6 July; 10 Aug (2-6). Evening
Opening £4, wine, Wed 9 July (6-9).
Visitors also welcome by appt July
& Aug for groups 10+.**
Plant lover's garden, approaching 1/2 an
acre. Flowing herbaceous borders,
containing rare and unusual plants,
provide a wealth of colour and interest,
whilst an abundance of produce is

grown in the unique vegetable/fruit garden. Bananas, palms, fernery, fish pond, summerhouse, greenhouse and areas for relaxation. Featured in 'Nottingham Evening Post', 2007. Some barked paths & unfenced ponds.

THE COTTAGE
See Derbyshire.

14 CROPWELL COURT
Cropwell Road, Cropwell Butler NG12 2LZ. Mr & Mrs M Rowen. *1m S of A52/A46 junction (Saxondale roundabout). A46/Cropwell Rd junction follow signs to Radcliffe-on-Trent. At Radcliffe-on-Trent A52/Cropwell Rd junction follow signs to Cropwell Butler. On A46 not in village.* Home-made teas or wine & light refreshments. **Adm £5 (to include tea & home-made cake or glass of wine & canapés,) chd free. Late afternoon & Evening Opening** Wed 25 June (4-9).
Large garden with mature herbaceous borders and sunken box garden. Walled kitchen and herb garden with greenhouse. New area started in 2006, work still ongoing. Re-furbished Victorian greenhouse. Well-manicured lawns. Parkland with mature trees and small wild flower area. Garden for all seasons. Reed beds. No smoking.

15 DARBY HOUSE
10 The Grove, Southey Street, Nottingham NG7 4BQ. Jed Brignal, 07960 065042. *¾ m NE of city centre take A610, turn R into Forest Rd, first L into Southey St.* **Adm £2, chd free. Sun 4 May (2-5). Visitors also welcome by appt.**
Unusual city garden designed and developed by artist owner is a tranquil oasis in unlikely location. Victorian walled garden with ponds, waterfall, gazebos and a fairy-tale shady area surrounded by mature trees. House (1849) and garden provide temporary home and sanctuary for actors, writers, dancers and other creative visitors. Rare plant nursery stalls. Ceramics, jewellery & bespoke lamps for sale.

DODDINGTON HALL GARDENS
See Lincolnshire.

THE DOWER HOUSE
See Derbyshire.

16 DUMBLESIDE
17 Bridle Road, Burton Joyce NG14 5FT. Mr & Mrs P Bates, 0115 931 3725. *5m NE of Nottingham. In Burton Joyce turn off A612, Nottingham to Southwell Rd into Lambley Lane. Bridle Rd is an impassable looking rd to the R off Lambley Lane. Car parking easiest BEYOND garden.* **Combined adm £3.50, chd free with 61 Lambley Lane. Sun 18 May (2-6). Visitors also welcome by appt coaches or groups.**
2 acres of varied habitat. Natural spring and stream planted with primulas, fritillaries and fine specimen shrubs. A small meadow is being developed with large variety of bulbs and wild flowers planted and seeded into grass. 60yd mixed border. Ferns are an important feature in spring, cyclamen in Aug and Sept and through the winter.

Unusual city garden designed and developed by artist owner is a tranquil oasis . . .

17 ELM HOUSE
5 Mapperley Hall Drive, Mapperley Park, Nottingham NG3 5EP. Malcolm Bescoby & Michael Blood. *1m N of Nottingham city centre. On R off A60 to Mansfield.* **Combined adm £2.50, chd free with Melrose House, 3 Mapperley Hall Drive. Sun 13 July (1-5).**
Small town garden on two levels. Intensively planted with tropical and herbaceous specimens to complement the architectural features which include summerhouse, pond and statues. Two gardens are connected by an ornamental cast iron gate. Flights of steps in and out of gardens.

18 THE ELMS
Main Street, North Leverton DN22 0AR. Tim & Tracy Ward, 01427 881164, Tracy@wardt2.fsnet.co.uk. *5m E of Retford, 6m SW of Gainsborough. From Retford town centre take the rd to Leverton for 5m, into North Leverton with Habblesthorpe.* Teas. **Adm £2.50, chd free. Sun 13 July (2-6). Visitors also welcome by appt.**
This small garden is very different, creating an extension to the living space. Inspiration comes from tropical countries, giving a Mediterranean feel. Palms and bananas, along with other exotics, create drama, and yet make a statement true to many gardens, that of peace and calm. North Leverton Windmill (English Heritage) is located just outside village & open to public.

19 NEW ELMS FARM
Bassingfield, Nottingham NG12 2LG. Philip & Jane Parker. *2m SE of Trent Bridge, Nottingham. Off A52 Lings Bar Rd to Tollerton, Bassingfield 1st L.* **Adm £2.50, chd free. Sun 10 Aug (2-6).**
Garden developed in the last fifteen years, approx 2 acres. Unusual trees, shrubs and herbaceous plants in island beds and borders. Large pond and stream. Plenty of seating areas. Annual bed display.

20 NEW EYNORD
Church Hill, Sutton-in-Ashfield NG17 1EW. Peter & Judy Ford. *3m E of J28 M1. From M1 A38 into Sutton town centre. Garden opp public swimming baths. A60 from Nottingham, Ravenshead A6014 to Sutton town centre.* Light refreshments & teas. **Adm £2.50, chd free (share to Rotary International). Sun 15 June (12-5).**
Classic 1930s town house with its one third of an acre, recently restored garden, displaying well-stocked borders surrounding immaculate lawns. Countless tender specimens in pots, a decked-over air-raid shelter, leading to a clematis pergola with adjacent fruit garden. Peaceful garden hidden away in a busy town centre.

21 ◆ FELLEY PRIORY
Underwood NG16 5FJ. The Hon Mrs
Chaworth Musters, 01773 810230.
*8m SW of Mansfield. Off A608 ¹/₂ m W
M1 J27.* **Adm £3, chd free. Tues,
Weds & Fris (9-12.30), every 2nd &
4th Wed (9-4); every 3rd Sun (11-4).
For NGS: Sun 13 Apr (11-4).**
Garden for all seasons with yew
hedges and topiary, snowdrops,
hellebores, orchard of daffodils,
herbaceous borders and old-fashioned
rose garden. There are pergolas, a
medieval garden, a small arboretum
and borders filled with unusual trees,
shrubs, plants and bulbs. The grass-
edged pond is planted with primulas,
bamboo, iris, roses and eucomis.
Small specialised plant fair, approx 4-6
stalls.

22 FUCHSIA VIEW
9 Winster Avenue, off Cromford
Avenue, Carlton NG4 3RW. Mr & Mrs
J Thorp, 0115 911 5734. *4m N of
Nottingham. Follow the Carlton Rd into
Carlton. Turn L at Tesco past police
stn. Over the mini island pass the
cemetery up Cavendish Rd. R into
Cromford Ave. 1st L into Winster Ave.*
Home-made & cream teas. **Adm £2,
chd free. Suns 13 July; 3 Aug (11-5).
Evening Opening £3.50, wine, Thur
17, 31 July (6-9). Visitors also
welcome by appt.**
The abundance of colour in this garden
is achieved by 120 varieties of fuchsias
incl many standards, penstemons,
roses and perennials. 5 patio areas
give a panoramic view over Carlton
while enjoying a strawberry scone or
home-made cake. In the evening enjoy
the chef's canapés with a glass of
wine.

**23 NEW THE GARDEN
HOUSE**
86 Chatsworth Drive, Mansfield
NG18 4QX. Mrs V A Jelley, 01623
627887. *1m S of Mansfield.
Approaching Mansfield on A60
from Nottingham, with West Notts
College in view turn R into Old
Newark Rd/Litchfield Lane. On L-
hand bend turn R into Chatsworth
Drive.* Home-made teas. **Adm
£2.50, chd free. Suns 11 May; 8
June (1-5). Visitors also welcome
by appt, no coaches.**
Plantaholic's organically maintained
terraced garden of approx 1000sq
yds. All-yr round interest. Lawn on
two levels. Rill, stream, pond.

Magnolias, camellias,
rhododendrons, tree paeonies. In
excess of 100 newly planted
clematis for winter, spring, summer
and autumn colour. Some steps.

24 GARDENERS COTTAGE
Rectory Lane, Kirkby in Ashfield
NG17 8PZ. Martin & Chris Brown.
*1m W of Kirkby. From the A38, take
the B6018 towards Kirkby in Ashfield.
Straight across mini island. Rectory
Lane (no parking) is at the side of St
Wilfrid's Church, on Church St.* Home-
made teas. **Adm £3, chd free. Sun 27
Apr (1-5).**
An exciting garden full of special
plants, imaginative features and new
developments (the latest, a Tuscan-
style terrace) which will not disappoint
even the most discerning visitor, or one
who is looking for inspiration. Please
note only one opening in 2008. Steps,
steep slopes & gravel areas.

Garden is planted and cared for with wildlife in mind . . .

25 16 GLENSFORD GARDENS
Nottingham NG5 5BG. Don & Vicky
Butt. *5m N of Nottingham city centre.
From N or city, approach on A611
(Nottingham-Hucknall). Opposite
Bulwell golf course turn into Bestwood
Park Dr West at T-lights. 1st L
Brownlow Dr. Glensford Gardens is 4th
R. Park on Brownlow Dr please.* **Adm
£3, chd free. Sun 13 July (11-5).**
Garden packed with surprises,
colourful containers, hanging baskets
and fish pond with its own stream and
waterfalls. There's something for
everyone incl palm trees, cordylines
and bananas! Featured in magazines
and on BBC TV and described by
Tommy Walsh of 'Groundforce' as
'paradise'. Highly praised by John
Stirland and Martin Fish BBC TV
garden presenters.

26 GORENE
20 Kirby Road, Beauvale Estate,
Newthorpe NG16 3PZ. Gordon &
Irene Middleton, 01773 788407. *5m
NE of Nottingham. From M1 J26 take
A610 (Eastwood & Kimberley bypass)
exit Langley Mill (not Eastwood). At
island turn R to Eastwood to 1st set
of T-lights. Keep L down Mansfield
Rd, turn R at bollards (Greenhills
Rd).Turn R at the 7th rd - Kirby Rd.*
**Adm £2, chd free. Mon 5 May; Sun
27 July (1-5). Visitors also welcome
by appt.**
This year the garden 'Gorene' is
celebrating its 40th year. A warm
welcome awaits you at this small, but
intensely packed garden where the
teas and cakes have become
legendary! This garden proves just how
much can be achieved in a small
space, with water features, secret
garden and exotic aviary.

27 GRINGLEY GARDENS
Gringley-on-the-Hill, Doncaster
DN10 4QX. *On A631 between Bawtry
& Gainsborough. Approach Gringley
on A631. From dual carriageway
bypass there is clear signage into
village. Parking is on streets of village.*
**Combined adm £2.50, chd free
(share to St Peter's Church,
Gringley-on-the-Hill). Sun 11 May
(1.30-5).**
Tranquil village on the northern tip of
Nottinghamshire. Picturesque old
cottage properties coupled with
tasteful new development.

HONEYSUCKLE COTTAGE
Hunters Drive. Miss J Towler
This old garden is tucked away in
a corner of the village and has a
real cosy feel to it. It has been
carefully crafted around old sheds,
ancient walls and paving, and has
sympathetic planting giving great
charm.

YEW TREE COTTAGE
Middle Bridge Road. Sue
Tallents
Peaceful 1¹/₄ -acre garden still
undergoing restoration. New areas
include a pond, vegetable and
herbaceous beds, shrub and
woodland borders. Areas of old
orchard remain and garden is
planted and cared for with wildlife
in mind. Unfenced pond. Slippery
slope if wet.

28 HALL FARM COTTAGE
Hall Lane, Kinoulton NG12 3EF. Mrs Bel Grundy. *8m SE of West Bridgford. Kinoulton is off A46 just N of intersection with A606. Into village to T-junction with PH on L. Turn L & immed R on to Hall Lane. Pass PO. Cottage is at very end of lane on L.* **Adm £2.50, chd free (share to Macmillan Cancer Support). Evening Opening Wed 18 June (6.30-8.30).**
Plantaholic's small cottage garden. A masterclass in the positioning and management of plants which have to move if they don't behave! Extensive collection of home-grown bonsai demonstrates attention to detail and the quality of 'plants for sale' ensures that Bel has no escape from her addiction.
✗ ✿

HARDWICK HALL
See Derbyshire.

29 ◆ HODSOCK PRIORY GARDENS
Blyth, Worksop S81 0TY. Sir Andrew & Lady Buchanan & Mr George Buchanan (Hodsock Priory Trust), 01909 591204,
www.snowdrops.co.uk. *2m from A1(M) at Blyth. 4m N of Worksop off B6045, Blyth-Worksop rd approx 2m from A1. Well signed.* **Adm £4.50, chd £1. Daily 1 Feb to 2 Mar (10-4).**
5-acre private garden on historic Domesday site. Sensational winter garden plus snowdrop wood. Many fragrant winter flowering shrubs, trees, hellebores and bulbs. Some gravel. Wood NOT suitable for wheelchairs if wet. Magnificent new pavilion. Toilets & shop now inside. Some gravel.
& ✗ ✿ ☕

30 ◆ HOLME PIERREPONT HALL
Holme Pierrepont, Nottingham NG12 2LD. Mr & Mrs Robin Brackenbury, 0115 933 2371, www.holmepierreponthall.com. *5m E of Nottingham. From Nottingham A52 E-bound, follow signs for National Watersports Centre. Continue 1m past main entrance. House on LH-side next to church. Park outside church.* **House and garden adm £5, chd £1.50, garden only adm £3, chd £1. Mons, Tues, Weds Feb to 19 Mar; 2nd Suns Feb, Mar, Apr. For NGS: Sun 28 Sept (2-5).**
In the courtyard the romantic summer planting gives way to the fiery tones of autumn from dahlias and crocosmias.

The sharpness of the newly clipped yews in the East Garden, contrasts with the more relaxed feel of the new autumn border with grasses and late flowering perennials in shades of purple and gold.
&

31 HOLMES VILLA
Holmes Lane, Walkeringham, nr Gainsborough DN10 4JP. Peter & Sheila Clark, 01427 890233, clarkshaulage@aol.com. *4m NW of Gainsborough. A620 from Retford or A631 from Bawtry/Gainsborough & A161 to Walkeringham then towards Misterton. Follow yellow signs for last mile. Home-made teas.* **Adm £2, chd free. Mon 26 May (1-5). Visitors also welcome by appt.**
1¾ -acre plantsman's interesting and inspirational garden; surprises around every corner with places to sit and ponder; gazebos; arbours; ponds; hosta garden; unusual perennials and shrubs for flower arranging. Plant stalls. Driftwood for sale. Featured in 'Yorkshire Post' 2007.
& ✗ ✿ ☕ ☎

Sensational winter garden plus snowdrop wood . . .

THE HOMESTEAD
See Leicestershire & Rutland.

KEXBY HOUSE
See Lincolnshire.

32 61 LAMBLEY LANE
Burton Joyce NG14 5BG. Mr & Mrs R B Powell. *6m N of Nottingham. In Burton Joyce turn off A612 Nottingham to Southwell Rd into Lambley Lane.* **Combined adm with Dumbleside £3.50, chd free. Sun 18 May (2-6).**
Approx ¾ -acre of spring flowering shrubs, plants and bulbs. Mixed borders, greenhouse and terrace, cacti, vegetable garden. Colourful display of azaleas and camellias. Unusual plants for sale. Steep drive to entrance.
✿

LONG CLOSE
See Leicestershire & Rutland.

33 NEW 17 MAIN STREET
Keyworth NG12 5AA. Graham & Pippa Tinsley. *7m S of Nottingham. Follow signs to Keyworth from A60 or A606 and head for the church. Garden about 50yds past the Co-op on L. Some parking on Main St. Car parking at village hall and public car parks.* **Adm £3, chd free. Sun 1 June (1-5).**
The old gardens and paddock behind the farmhouse have been developed over thirty years to give a peaceful haven near the centre of a busy village. Full of unexpected views and hidden places. Nicely maturing trees incl cedars and chestnuts. Yew hedges, ponds, secret rose garden and a turf mound. Access to garden via gravel yard & path. Some steps & slopes.
& ✗

34 MANOR FARM HOUSE
Plungar Road, Granby NG13 9PX. Brenda & Philip Straw. *14m E of Nottingham. 2m off A52 signed Granby. Next to church. Teas at Newbray House.* **Combined adm £3.50 with Newbray House, chd free (share to Sight Savers Int). Sun 15 June (2-6).**
⅓ -acre garden surrounding grade II listed C18 farmhouse. Cottage garden style planting with climbing roses, hardy geraniums, delphiniums, white garden, yellow corner, daisy steps and mixed borders. Church wall, brick outbuildings and old walnut tree provide perfect backdrop for this plant enthusiasts' garden.
& ✗

35 MEADOWSIDE
Main Street, Epperstone NG14 6AD. John & Barbara Phillips. *8m NE of Nottingham, 5m SW of Southwell. Epperstone lies off the A6097 between Lowdham & Oxton. Meadowside is opp Cross Keys PH on Main St. Home-made teas.* **Adm £2.50, chd free. Sun 29 June (12.30-5).**
Well-established front and larger than average rear garden that enjoys an extensive open outlook over fields, stocked with plant collections, shrubs and trees. It has been meticulously worked over many years to achieve a garden full of colour and impact that without doubt will give pleasure to the visitor. No toilet facilities. Sloping lawn.
& ✗ ✿ ☕

36 MELROSE

3 Mapperley Hall Drive, Mapperley Park, Nottingham NG3 5EP. Sir Joseph & Lady Pope. *1m N of Nottingham city centre. On R off A60 to Mansfield.* Home-made teas. **Combined adm with Elm House, 5 Mapperley Hall Drive** £2.50, chd free. Sun 13 July (1-5).

This town garden set on two levels has evolved gradually and is complementary to Elm House, which is connected by an ornamental iron gate. Strong Japanese influence with the use of stone lanterns and a stream that gurgles prettily over rocks and shingle. Acers, camellias and hostas add a light touch to this peaceful garden.

Benefits from undulating landscape incorporating design, texture, colour . . .

37 MILL HILL HOUSE

Elston Lane, East Stoke NG23 5QJ. Mr & Mrs R J Gregory, 01636 525460, millhill@talk21.com. *5m S of Newark. Elston Lane. On A46 turn to Elston. Garden 1/2 m on R. Entrance via car park (signed).* **Adm** £2, chd free. Mon 5 May (11-5). **Visitors also welcome by appt May/June, coaches permitted.**

1/2 -acre country garden close to site of Battle of East Stoke (1487). Closely planted with many unusual hardy/half hardy plants providing yr-round interest and tranquil atmosphere. This established and mature country garden has enjoyed some new planting. Wildlife is encouraged. National Collection of Berberis.

⊛ NCCPG ☎

38 NEWBRAY HOUSE

Church Street, Granby NG13 9PU. Shirley & Stan Taylor. *14m E of Nottingham. 2m off A52 signed Granby.* **Combined adm with Manor Farm House** £3.50, chd free (share to Sight Savers International). Sun 15 June (2-6).

With views towards Belvoir Castle, this 2-acre garden has been developed to complement the attractive Victorian house. Strong structure is overlaid by imaginative planting. Many unusual plants are found in large herbaceous beds full of colour and interest over a long season. Ponds, gravel, herb and vegetable areas. Scented roses and wisteria climb pergolas and walls. Picnics in the orchard.

39 NORWELL GARDENS

NG23 6JX. *6m N of Newark. Off A1 at Cromwell turning.* Home-made teas in village hall, wine at Norwell Nurseries. **Combined adm** £3, chd free. Sun 29 June (2-5). **Evening Opening** £3.50, wine, Wed 2 July (6.30-9).

Beautiful 'hidden away' village with parish church of St Lawrence having notable C15 clerestory and views over water meadows. The gardens are an eclectic mix of design and planting, providing inspiration for all. Church will focus on the windows with explanations of their history and content. Flowers will reflect this theme. There will be extensive heritage and children's trails around the village.

BLACK HORSE FARM
Main Street. Mr & Mrs Craig Bown
Extensive country garden, with many features and a great variety of planting and landscaping.

CHERRY TREE HOUSE
5 Foxhall Close. Mr & Mrs S Wyatt
New garden with many innovative features. Formal box front garden with decorative mulches. Decking, water features, lush plantings with architectural screens and colourful schemes.

NORWELL NURSERIES
Woodhouse Road. Andrew & Helen Ward (See separate entry).

SOUTHVIEW COTTAGE
Main Street. Mr & Mrs Les Corbett
Richly planted cottage garden with mature trees, mixed borders. Imaginatively planted gravel garden. Pond and wildlife, natural plantings.

40 ◆ NORWELL NURSERIES

Woodhouse Road, Norwell NG23 6JX. Andrew & Helen Ward, 01636 636337, norwellnurseries.co.uk. *6m N of Newark. Turn off A1 at Cromwell turning.* **Adm** £2, chd free. Daily (10-5) except Sats & Tues from 1 Mar to 20 Oct. Closed Aug. **For NGS:** Sun 18 May (2-5).

A treasure trove of over 2000 different, beautiful, rare and unusual plants set out in 3/4 -acre plantsman's garden incl woodland with orchids and meconopsis, specimen grasses. Large alpine and scree area, bell garden with penstemons and dierama, and new pond with bog gardens. Extensive herbaceous borders, hot beds and sumptuous colour-themed beds. Featured in 'Nottinghamshire Today', Feb 2007 and about to feature in 'Garden News'. GGG & Gardeners' Favourite Nurseries, 2007.

41 THE OLD VICARAGE

Halam Hill, Halam Village NG22 8AX. Mrs Beverley Perks, 01636 812181, perks.family@talk21.com. *1m W of Southwell. On approach to Halam village down hill on LH-side or from A614 through Farnsfield & Edingley villages over Xrds in Halam, last house on RH-side.* Home-made teas. **Adm** £3, chd free. Suns 27 Apr (1-5); 18 May (1-5.30); 7 Sept (1-5). **Evening Opening** £3.50, wine, Sun 24 Aug (5-8). **Visitors also welcome by appt in June. Groups/garden clubs of 20+.**

Plantsman's garden of 2 acres surrounded by woodland and fields, begun 12yrs ago from nothing. Benefits from undulating landscape incorporating design, texture, colour, unusual plants and trees. Peaceful roams, nooks, crannies, borrowed views of hills and farmland. A children's haven. Just lovely and very welcoming. Delicious cakes to add to enjoyment. Mainly lawned access, slopes but help/assistance available to all garden.

42 ORCHARD HOUSE

High Oakham Road, Mansfield NG18 5AJ. Mr & Mrs Michael Bull, 01623 623884. *S side of Mansfield. High Oakham Rd joins the A60-Nottingham Rd at junction with Forest Rd and Waverley Rd, leading to Atkin Lane at the western end.* Home-made teas. **Adm** £2.50, chd free. Suns 29 June; 3 Aug (1-5). **Visitors also** welcome by appt from 15 June to 10 Aug. Groups 5-25.

This mature garden is one of Mansfield's treasures in a quiet and secluded area. Diverse colourful planting of shrubs, herbaceous borders and specimen trees. Clever use of water, statuary and other unique features enhance this garden, providing interest for discerning gardeners throughout the summer.

43 NEW OXTON GARDENS

NG25 0SS. *4m SW of Southwell. From B6386 turn into Oxton village (Blind Lane).* Home-made teas. **Combined adm £4, chd free.** Sun 8 June (1.30-5).

NEW CROWS NEST COTTAGE

Forest Road. Joan Arnold & Tom Heinersdorff. *From B6386 turn R into Oxton village (Blind Lane). At T-junction turn R into Forest Rd. Garden is approx 200yds on R*

A bird-friendly, colourful mature garden wrapped round the cottage. Incredibly, the large wildlife ponds, streams and waterfalls are only 2 yrs old! Enjoy clematis, peonies, fuchsia and some unusual shrubs and plants. Unfenced ponds, deep water.

HOME FARM COTTAGE

Blind Lane, Oxton. Pauline & Brian Hansler. *From B6386 turn into Oxton village (Blind Lane). Home Farm Cottage is on L opp Green Dragon PH, immed before T-junction*

Each corner of this magical cottage garden offers a new and exciting experience. At every turn, from the hidden alpine garden, through the imaginative stumpery and woodland grotto to the selection of unusual plants, it reveals a horticultural heaven. Gravel paths & steps.

OAKWOOD COTTAGE

Forest Road, Oxton. Tracey & Paul Akehurst. *From B6386 turn into Oxton village (Blind Lane). At T-junction turn R onto Forest Rd. Oakwood Cottage is immed on RH-side up a gravel drive (no parking)*

Both a wind tunnel, and a frost pocket, this secluded cottage

garden proves that a small space should never limit the imagination. Abundant planting and clever use of recycled materials provides continual interest throughout the year.

NEW ROMAN WAY

Blind Lane. Corby & Lewie Lewington. *From B6386 turn into Oxton village (Blind Lane). Roman Way is on R next to Green Dragon PH, immed before T-junction*

With a mixture of paved, lawned and planted areas, this unusual small corner plot has been lovingly developed over the last few years; its tranquility provides the perfect antidote to busy living.

44 20 THE PADDOCKS

Nuthall NG16 1DR. Mr & Mrs Bowness-Saunders, 0115 938 4590. *5m NW of Nottingham. From M1 J26, A610 towards Nottingham. At 1st roundabout take B600 towards Kimberley. Paddocks is 2nd rd on L after Three Ponds PH. Parking in cul-de-sac restricted, please park on main rd or on L as you enter The Paddocks.* Home-made teas. **Adm £3, chd free.** Sun 13 July (1-5). **Evening Opening** £3.50, wine, Wed 16 July (6-9). **Visitors also welcome by appt.**

Fun garden shared with children and dogs which unlike oil and water do mix in this unusual combination of interesting gardens. Many inspirational ideas incl beach, well, living willow structures, ponds, mature trees, herbaceous borders and vegetables. Mainly organic encouraging a variety of wildlife. A gardener's playground not to be missed (200 x 80ft).

45 PAPPLEWICK HALL

Papplewick NG15 8FE. Mr & Mrs J R Godwin-Austen, www.papplewickhall.co.uk. *7m N of Nottingham. N end of Papplewick village on B683, off the A60. Parking at Hall.* Home-made teas. **Adm £3, chd free (share to St James's Church).** Sun 25 May (2-5).

This mature 8-acre established garden, mostly shaded woodland, abounds with rhododendrons, hostas, ferns, and spring bulbs. A programme of re-planting ornamental trees and shrubs is being carried out.

46 48 PENARTH GARDENS

Sherwood Vale, Nottingham NG5 4EG. Josie & Geoff Goodlud. *Approx 2½ m N of Nottingham city centre off B684 (Woodborough Rd). From city, turn L into Woodthorpe Rd, after Millennium Garage, L again (Penarth Rise). L again to Penarth Gardens (No 48).* Home-made teas. **Adm £2.50, chd free.** Sun 6 July (1-5).

One of Nottingham city's hidden gems is to be found in the unlikely setting of a small back garden in Sherwood Vale, but it will please and surprise both by its planting and bold design. Its setting is amongst dense housing packed into the old Nottingham brickworks quarry, the overgrown face of which is steadily being transformed into an extension to a densely packed garden. Featured in 'Nottinghamshire Today' Oct 2007.

A bird-friendly, colourful mature garden wrapped round the cottage . . .

47 NEW PIECEMEAL

123 Main Street, Sutton Bonington, Loughborough LE12 5PE. Mary Thomas, 01509 672056, admet123@btinternet.com. *2m SE of Kegworth (M1 J24). 6m NE of Loughborough. Almost opp St Michael's Church.* **Adm £2.50, chd free.** Mon 26 May (1-6); Suns 13 July; 3 Aug (1-5). **Visitors also welcome by appt June to Aug inclusive. Max 10 per visit.**

Plant enthusiast's garden in tiny, sheltered courtyard enabling extensive collection of interesting shrubs, perennials and climbers to thrive in over 200 containers. Many unusual and not fully hardy, and a number from the southern hemisphere (list available). Busy herbaceous borders. Fern-filled well. Water feature. Conservatory overflowing with tender specimens.

48 REDLAND HOUSE

Main Street, Cropwell Butler NG12 3AB. Shelagh Barnes, 0115 933 3082. *Cropwell Butler lies to the E of Nottingham, off A52, signposted to village. Cross A46 after 1 1/2 m. 1/2 m on, find garden on R.* Home-made teas. **Adm £3, chd free. Sun 1 June (2-6). Visitors also welcome by appt June/July only. Groups 10+.**
A chance for a garden visitor to see a larger than average garden under development and overgrown Leylandii hedges, unwanted shrubs and ivy grubbed out and soil enriched. Knowledgeable and enthusiastic planting under a flower arranger's eye is underway. This is a garden to watch! In a couple of years it will be stunning, but if you miss it now you will be unable fully to appreciate it then. Gravel paths, paved and grass slopes.
⌖ ✕ ✿ ☕ ☎

49 ROSELEA

40 Newark Road, Coddington NG24 2QF. Bruce & Marian Richmond, 01636 676737, richmonds@roselea47.fsnet.co.uk. *1 1/2 m E of Newark. Leave A1 signed Coddington, 100yds from junction S; 300yds from junction N.* Light refreshments & home-made teas. **Adm £2, chd free. Suns 30 Mar; 6 July (11-5). Visitors also welcome by appt.**
Picturesque plantsman's garden. Mixed borders, shrubs, roses, clematis and geraniums. Many unusual plants. Hostas and ferns in pots. Small alpine area. Pergolas covered with climbers. Compost area. Places to sit and ponder. Come and enjoy home-made cakes and light lunches.
⌖ ✕ ✿ ☕ ☎

73 SAXILBY ROAD
See Lincolnshire.

50 125 SHELFORD ROAD

Radcliffe on Trent NG12 1AZ. John & Elaine Walker, 0115 911 9867. *4m E of Nottingham. From A52 follow signs to Radcliffe. In village centre take turning for Shelford (by Co-op). Approx 3/4 m on LH-side.* Teas. **Adm £2.50, chd free. Wed 21 May (2-5); Sun 14 Sept (2-5.30). Evening Opening £3.50, wine, Wed 16 July (6-9). Visitors also welcome by appt for groups of 10+.**
Just under 1/2 an acre designed for overall effect of colour, texture and movement, incorporating many unusual varieties especially hardy

perennials and grasses. Front garden is formal in layout with packed borders incl hot and cool colour-themed beds and prairie-style borders planted for late summer colour. Back is based on flowing curves with informal planting and incl gazebo, pond, bog garden and jungle area with turf dragon. 'A stunning garden', Monty Don. 'Back garden is truly spectacular', Prof David Stevens. Hand-crafted garden mirrors and artwork for sale. Featured in 'Nottinghamshire Today', July 2007; 'Amateur Gardening' Mar 2007; 'English Garden' Nov 2007.
✕ ✿ ☕ ☎

51 SQUIRREL LODGE

2 Goosemoor Lane, Retford DN22 7JA. Peter & Joan Whitehead. *1m S of Retford. Travelling S out of Retford on A638, last R turn before railway bridge.* Home-made teas. **Adm £2.50, chd free. Suns 11 May; 24 Aug (2-5).**
The garden visitor will be well rewarded for journeying a little further north in the county by a garden that has been skilfully crafted into a corner plot. Some is in deep shade, but the colour and vibrance of this garden will both delight and please, just as much as will the welcome and the teas. Featured on Lincolnshire Radio and in 'Gardening News'.
⌖ ✿ ☕

52 ◆ TEVERSAL MANOR GARDENS

Buttery Lane, Teversal Old Village, Nr Sutton in Ashfield NG17 3JN. Mrs Janet Marples, 01623 554569, www.teversalmanor.co.uk. *4m NW of Mansfield. From M1 J28: take A38 towards Mansfield. After 3m turn L onto A6014 Skegby. After 2m turn R at mini island for Teversal. Turn R at Carnarvon Arms for Teversal Village. R into Buttery Lane. Manor on R after 2 sharp bends. From M1 J29: take A6175 for Clay Cross. Turn off 1st L for Stanley. 1m after Stanley just before Carnarvon Arms turn L for Teversal Village. Then as above.* **Adm £4.50, chd £2.50, concesssions £3.50. Thurs, Fris, Sats (10-5.30). Suns & BHols (11-5). For NGS: Suns 13 Apr; 15 June; 21 Sept (11-5).**
Teversal Manor featured as Wragby Hall in D H Lawrence's 'Lady Chatterley's Lover'. It is one of the East Midlands' oldest gardens and was developed on a grand scale. Neglected for many decades, it is now being brought back to life. The terrraced site is now being gardened in

a different, but interesting style in its magnificent setting. The exciting redevelopment of the garden is an ongoing project that is being undertaken with great enthusiasm. Featured in 'Nottinghamshire Star' awards, 2007; BBC Radio Nottingham & East Midlands Today, 2007. Approx 60 per cent wheelchair access.
⌖ ✕ ✿ ☕

> **Walled garden will be alive with vibrant exotic plantings . . .**

53 UNIVERSITY OF NOTTINGHAM GARDENS

University Park, Nottingham NG7 2RD. Ian Cooke, www.nottingham.ac.uk/estate/ friends. *1 1/2 m W of Nottingham city centre. We suggest visitors arrive at the north entrance which is on the A52 adjacent to the QMC roundabout. The event is based at the Millennium Garden which is on University Park and well signed within the campus. No buses within campus on Sunday.* Light refreshments & teas not for NGS. **Adm £2.50, chd free. Suns 4 May; 17 Aug (2-5).**
University Park has many beautiful gardens incl the award-winning Millennium Garden with its dazzling flower garden, timed fountains and turf maze. Visitors in late spring will see extensive plantings of bulbs throughout the park incl in our Jekyll Garden. During summer the walled garden will be alive with vibrant exotic plantings. In total 300 acres of landscape and gardens. Green Flag Award 2007/2008.
⌖ ☕

54 WELLOW VILLAGE GARDENS

NG22 0EB. *12m NW of Newark. Wellow is on the A616 between Ollerton & Newark & can also be reached from the A614 via Rufford Mill turning. Car parking in various* *locations around village. Two fields on Potter Lane. No parking on Potter Lane please. No coaches please.* Light refreshments & teas in Memorial Hall, disabled access & toilets. **Combined adm £4.50, chd free (share to Wellow Memorial Hall). Sun 8 June (11-5).**

Wellow, formerly Wellah, from the number of wells in the village, has a large open green and a famous maypole. Not so well known is the Gorge Dyke, which surrounds the village and can still be seen in some places. Now come and see some Wellow gardens. Various artists will be demonstrating and selling garden sculptures and installations. Craft demonstrations.

THE OLD VICARAGE
Potter Lane. John & Tricia Hawley
Extensive hard landscaping complements this plant-filled garden. Well-placed walls and hedges sub-divide it into themed areas, where plants and shrubs have been allowed to intertwine to create visual impact.

4 POTTER LANE
Anne & Fred Allsop
Created over more than 20 yrs, this series of gardens has a section of the Wellow Dyke at the top and has a well-tended vegetable garden. Shade garden at side and colourful pleasure garden in centre. Relaxing terrace adjoins the house. Original well is still in place in front garden.

TITHE BARN
Potter Lane. Andrew & Carrie Young
The grass-lined approach to this garden sets the tone to the wide sweeps of lawn and generous terrace. The mature planting of shrubs and weeping trees enhance this pretty barn conversion on the edge of the Wellow Dyke.

55 THE WHITE HOUSE
Nicker Hill, Keyworth NG12 5EA.
Tony & Gillian Hill, 0115 937 2049. *8m SE of Nottingham. From A606 at Stanton-on-the-Wolds turn into Browns Lane beside petrol station. Follow rd 1½ m into Stanton Lane becoming Nicker Hill.* Teas. **Adm £2, chd free. Weds 23 Apr; 7, 21, 28 May;11 June (2-5). Visitors also welcome by appt groups 10+. Coaches permitted.**

¾ -acre re-designed garden with seats and views. New pergola, newly hedged secret garden. Full, relaxed, varied planting incl roses, agapanthus, poppies. Front garden now gravelled with mounded beds; rare trees, plants, scents. All-yr interest. Still madly propagating unusual subjects for large plant stall. We've only 'retired', not thrown in the trowel.

56 NEW WOODSIDE COTTAGE
Hucknall Road, Newstead Village NG15 0BD. Ivan & Jean Kirby, 0115 963 1137. *2m N of Hucknall. From Hucknall take A611 towards Mansfield/M1. Turn R T-lights signed Newstead Village. Cottage 200m on L. From Mansfield/M1 J27 proceed towards Hucknall. Turn L at T-lights signed Newstead Village. Cottage 200m on L. Off road parking 250m. Drop off point. No on road parking.* Home-made teas. **Adm £2.50, chd free (share to Oasis Breast Cancer Trust). Suns 6 July; 3 Aug (1-5). Visitors also welcome by appt.**

Country garden of ½ an acre set against a woodland backdrop. Lawns with borders of coloured foliage, conifers and shrubs interlaced with herbaceous plants. Climbing roses and clematis-clad pergola. Gravel planting. Paths with dry stone walls lead to rock garden, with converted well and millstone water features. Silver birch spinney and specimen trees together with wood and stone ornaments make up a developing garden. Featured on BBC Radio Nottingham, 2007. Gravel paths.

Nottinghamshire County Volunteers

County Organiser
Irene Dougan, Field Farm, Field Lane, Kirk Ireton, Ashbourne DE6 3JU, 01335 370958, dougan@lineone.net

County Treasurer
Michael Bull, Orchard House, High Oakham Road, Mansfield, NG18 5AJ, 01623 623884, mabull@tiscali.co.uk

Assistant County Organisers
Anne Bull, Orchard House, High Oakham Road, Mansfield NG18 5AJ, 01623 623884. mabull@tiscali.co.uk
Georgina Denison, 27 Campden Hill Road, London W8 7DX, 020 7937 0557. campden27@aol.com
Ann Henstock, 4 Lytham Drive, Edwalton, Nottingham NG12 4DQ, 0115 9235679, Annhenstock@aol.com
Beverley Perks, The Old Vicarage, Halam Hill, Halam NG22 8AX, 01636 812181, perks.family@talk21.com
Dulce Threlfall, Gringley Hall, Gringley on the Hill, Doncaster DN10 4QT, dulce@gringleyhall.fsnet

ngs gardens open
for charity

Half-acre organic garden
designed around old
railway buildings,
platforms, bridge and
track with carriage . . .

The Old Station, Hampshire

OXFORDSHIRE

Opening Dates

February

SUNDAY 17
73 Waterperry Gardens

SUNDAY 24
58 Ramsden House

March

SUNDAY 9
69 Trinity College

SUNDAY 16
14 Buckland Lakes
39 Kingston Bagpuize House

MONDAY 24
9 Brook Cottage
38 Kencot Gardens

SUNDAY 30
43 Lingermans
72 Wadham College

April

TUESDAY 1
65 Stansfield

SUNDAY 6
3 Ashbrook House
22 Epwell Mill
44 Magdalen College
53 The Old Rectory, Coleshill
59 St Hilda's College

SUNDAY 13
81 Wolfson College

SUNDAY 20
42 Lime Close
60 St Hugh's College
73 Waterperry Gardens

SATURDAY 26
24 Far Field

SUNDAY 27
78 Wick Hall & Nurseries
79 Wildwood

May

SATURDAY 3
26 Garsington Manor

SUNDAY 4
1 Adderbury Gardens
11 Broughton Grange
40 Lady Margaret Hall

MONDAY 5
51 Nuffield Place

TUESDAY 6
65 Stansfield

WEDNESDAY 7
83 Woolstone Mill House

SATURDAY 10
82 Wood Croft

SUNDAY 11
32 Hollyhocks
48 Monks Head

WEDNESDAY 14
83 Woolstone Mill House

SATURDAY 17
28 Greys Court
30 Hearns House

SUNDAY 18
20 Church Farm Field
22 Epwell Mill
29 Headington Gardens
30 Hearns House
33 Holywell Manor
66 Steeple Aston Gardens
74 Wayside

WEDNESDAY 21
83 Woolstone Mill House

SUNDAY 25
5 Barton Abbey

MONDAY 26
64 Sparsholt Manor

WEDNESDAY 28
83 Woolstone Mill House

SATURDAY 31
31 Hill Court

June

SUNDAY 1
6 Blenheim Palace
11 Broughton Grange
13 Broughton Poggs & Filkins Gardens
23 Evelegh's
31 Hill Court
42 Lime Close
75 Westwell Manor

MONDAY 2
32 Hollyhocks (Evening)
48 Monks Head (Evening)

TUESDAY 3
65 Stansfield

WEDNESDAY 4
83 Woolstone Mill House

SUNDAY 8
8 Brize Norton Gardens
32 Hollyhocks
41 Langford Gardens
48 Monks Head

WEDNESDAY 11
83 Woolstone Mill House

SUNDAY 15
2 All Saints Convent & St Johns Home
36 Iffley Gardens
45 Manor Farm

47 Middleton Cheney Gardens
49 North Moreton Gardens
50 North Oxford Gardens
61 Sibford Gower Gardens
71 Upper Chalford Farm
76 Wheatley Gardens

WEDNESDAY 18
83 Woolstone Mill House

SUNDAY 22
7 Blewbury Gardens
12 Broughton Grounds Farm
16 Charlbury Gardens
27 Greenfield Farm
37 Keble College
77 Whitehill Farm

WEDNESDAY 25
83 Woolstone Mill House

FRIDAY 27
4 Asthall Manor (Evening)

SUNDAY 29
71 Upper Chalford Farm

July

TUESDAY 1
65 Stansfield

WEDNESDAY 2
83 Woolstone Mill House

THURSDAY 3
70 University of Oxford Botanic Garden (Evening)

SUNDAY 6
11 Broughton Grange
62 Somerville College
83 Woolstone Mill House

WEDNESDAY 9
83 Woolstone Mill House

SUNDAY 13
1 Adderbury Gardens
17 Chastleton Gardens
72 Wadham College

WEDNESDAY 16
83 Woolstone Mill House

SATURDAY 19
19 Christ Church Masters', Pocock and Cathedral Gardens
46 Merton College Fellows' Garden

SUNDAY 20
15 Chalkhouse Green Farm

TUESDAY 22
30 Hearns House (Evening)

WEDNESDAY 23
83 Woolstone Mill House

SATURDAY 26
24 Far Field

SUNDAY 27
⑩ Broughton Castle
㉞ Home Close
(69) Trinity College

WEDNESDAY 30
(83) Woolstone Mill House

August

SUNDAY 3
(55) 12 Park Terrace
(56) Pots 'n Rocks

TUESDAY 5
(65) Stansfield

WEDNESDAY 6
(83) Woolstone Mill House

WEDNESDAY 13
(83) Woolstone Mill House

WEDNESDAY 20
(83) Woolstone Mill House

SUNDAY 24
㉚ Hearns House

MONDAY 25
⑨ Brook Cottage
㉚ Hearns House
(51) Nuffield Place

WEDNESDAY 27
(83) Woolstone Mill House

SUNDAY 31
(57) Radcot House

September

TUESDAY 2
(65) Stansfield

WEDNESDAY 3
(83) Woolstone Mill House

SUNDAY 7
③ Ashbrook House
⑳ Church Farm Field
㉒ Epwell Mill
㊴ Kingston Bagpuize House
(53) The Old Rectory, Coleshill

WEDNESDAY 10
(83) Woolstone Mill House

WEDNESDAY 17
(83) Woolstone Mill House

SUNDAY 21
㉖ Garsington Manor
(57) Radcot House
(73) Waterperry Gardens

WEDNESDAY 24
(83) Woolstone Mill House

Gardens open to the public

⑥ Blenheim Palace
⑨ Brook Cottage
⑩ Broughton Castle
㉘ Greys Court
㊴ Kingston Bagpuize House
㊹ Magdalen College
(51) Nuffield Place
(70) University of Oxford Botanic Garden
(73) Waterperry Gardens
(99) Chastleton House

By appointment only

⑱ Chivel Farm
㉑ Clock House
㉕ The Filberts
㉟ Home Farm
(54) The Old Vicarage, Bledington
(63) South Newington House
(67) Swalcliffe Lea House
(68) Tadmarton Manor
(80) Willow Tree Cottage

Also open by appointment ☎

① Fairfield, Adderbury Gardens
① Placketts, Adderbury Gardens
⑮ Chalkhouse Green Farm
⑯ Heathfield, Charlbury Gardens
⑳ Church Farm Field
㉗ Greenfield Farm
㉙ 10 Kennett Road, Headington Gardens
㉙ 40 Osler Road, Headington Gardens
㉚ Hearns House
㉞ Home Close
㊱ 71 Church Way, Iffley Gardens
㊱ The Thatched Cottage, Iffley Gardens
㊷ Lime Close
㊽ Monks Head
㊿ 9 Rawlinson Road, North Oxford Gardens
(52) Old Church House
(57) Radcot House
(59) St Hilda's College
(60) St Hugh's College
(65) Stansfield
(71) Upper Chalford Farm
(74) Wayside
(76) The Manor House, Wheatley Gardens
(77) Whitehill Farm
(83) Woolstone Mill House

Tapestry of beautiful plants and a patchwork of colour . . .

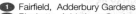

The Gardens

① ADDERBURY GARDENS

OX17 3LS. *3m S of Banbury. J10 M40, onto A43 signed Northampton, then A4260 to Adderbury, or A4260 S from Banbury.* Home-made teas at The Institute. **Combined adm £5 (4 May) £4 (13 July), chd free (share to Katharine House Hospice). Sun 4 May; Sun 13 July (2-6).**
Attractive Hornton stone village with a fine church. Village maps given to all visitors.

BERRY HILL HOUSE

Berry Hill Road. Mr & Mrs J P Pollard. *Off A4260 signed Milton, Bloxham, W Adderbury.* **Not open 13 July.**
2 acres; mature trees and lawns with countryside views; features separate garden areas linked together informally in a tranquil setting; many unusual plant varieties; kitchen garden and orchard.

CROSSHILL HOUSE

Manor Road. Mr & Mrs Gurth Hoyer Millar. Not open 13 July.
Georgian house (not open) surrounded by 4-acre classic Victorian walled gardens.

FAIRFIELD

Cross Hill Road. Mr & Mrs Mike Adams, 01295 810109. Not open 4 May. Visitors also welcome by appt.
This exquisite, tiny, paved garden is a tapestry of beautiful plants and a patchwork of colour, interwoven with a selection of unusual and interesting clematis and climbers.

HOLLY BANK

Berry Hill Road. Malcolm & Erica Brown. Not open 4 May.
Interesting re-development of one third of an acre garden with island beds which include a variety of trees, shrubs, bulbs and herbaceous plants. Limited wheelchair access. Main lower part of garden is accessible but upper terrace access has quite steep steps.

HOME FARM HOUSE
Manor Road. Mr & Mrs J V Harper. Not open 13 July.
2 acres; lawns, mature trees and shrubs, landscaped paddock, carp pond and flower borders.
&

PLACKETTS
High Street. Dr D White. *Nr Church.* **Visitors also welcome by appt jointly with Fairfield.**
Queen Anne cottage (not open); 0.2-acre walled garden, sheltered gravel courtyard. Main garden exposed and sunny with views. Many tulips, euphorbias, primulas, anemones. Numerous clematis, roses and lilies.
✕ ☎

② ALL SAINTS CONVENT & ST JOHNS HOME
St Mary's Road, East Oxford OX4 1RU. Society of All Saints Sisters of the Poor. *1m E of Oxford. Bus 1 or 5 from Queen St along Cowley Rd. Alight at Manzil Way, cross Cowley Rd, 1st turn R into Leopold St, then 1st L into St Mary's Rd and 1st gateway on L.* **Adm £2.50, chd free (share to St John's Home). Sun 15 June (2-5).**
Approx 2-acre garden with lawns, mature trees, shrubberies, mixed herbaceous and shrub borders. Vegetable garden; secluded quiet garden and wild flower meadow. Comper Chapel open. Common spotted orchids in the wild flower meadow. Unfenced pond & uneven path.
& ✕

③ ASHBROOK HOUSE
Blewbury OX11 9QA. Mr & Mrs S A Barrett. *4m SE of Didcot. Turn off A417 in Blewbury into Westbrook St. 1st house on R.* **Adm £3, chd free. Suns 6 Apr; 7 Sept (2-6).**
3½ -acre chalk garden with small lake, stream, spring bulbs and herbaceous borders. New glasshouse and bog garden.
& ❀ ☕

④ ASTHALL MANOR
Asthall, nr Burford OX18 4HW. Rosanna Taylor. *3m E of Burford. At roundabout between Witney & Burford on A40, take turning to Minster Lovell. Turn immed L (signed to Asthall). At bottom of hill, follow avenue of trees and look for car park signs.* **Adm £6, chd free. Evening Opening** wine, Fri 27 June (6-9).

6 acres of garden surround this C17 manor house (not open) once home to the Mitford family and overlooking the R Windrush. Sloping parterres and formal lawns, woodland lake, wild flower meadows, grass mound, banks of wild roses and borders spilling over gravel paths. This year's opening includes adm to On Form - an exhibition of sculpture in stone. Featured in GGG 2007 & 2008.
✕ ❀

Secluded quiet garden and wild flower meadow . . .

⑤ BARTON ABBEY
Steeple Barton OX25 4QS. Mr & Mrs P Fleming. *8m E of Chipping Norton. On B4030, ½ m from junction of A4260 & B4030.* Home-made teas. **Adm £4, chd free. Sun 25 May (2-5).**
15-acre garden with views from house (not open) across sweeping lawns and picturesque lake. Walled garden with colourful herbaceous borders, separated by established yew hedges and espalier fruit, contrasts with more informal woodland garden paths with vistas of specimen trees and meadows. Working glasshouses and fine display of fruit and vegetables.
& ❀ ☕

BARTON HOUSE
See Warwickshire & part of West Midlands.

⑥ ◆ BLENHEIM PALACE
Woodstock OX20 1PX. His Grace the Duke of Marlborough, 01993 810530, www.blenheimpalace.com. *8m N of Oxford. Bus: 20 Oxford-Chipping Norton, alight Woodstock.* **Adm £4, chd £2, concessions £3.**
For NGS: Sun 1 June (10-6).
Blenheim Gardens, originally laid out by Henry Wise, include the formal Water Terraces and Italian Garden by Achille Duchêne, Rose Garden, Arboretum, and Cascade. The Secret Garden, opened in 2004, offers a stunning garden paradise for all seasons. Blenheim Lake, created by 'Capability' Brown and spanned by Vanburgh's Grand Bridge, is the focal point of over

2,000 acres of landscaped parkland. The Pleasure Gardens complex includes the Herb and Lavender Garden and Butterfly House. Other activities incl the Marlborough Maze, putting greens, adventure play area, giant chess and draughts. Some gravel paths & slopes.
& ✕ ☕

⑦ BLEWBURY GARDENS
OX11 9QB. *4m SE of Didcot. On A417. Follow yellow signs for car parks.* Light refreshments & home-made teas. **Combined adm £4, chd free. Sun 22 June (2-6).**
4 gardens in a charming downland village. Continuing to welcome visitors having featured in 'Rachel's Flower Hour' Gardeners' World Special. Plants for sale in various locations.
☕

NEW ABNERS
Joyce Gilbert
The view from the gate draws you into this natural cottage garden. Joyce (age 85) is President of the Village Produce Association and has stocked many Blewbury gardens over the years.
✕ ❀

GREEN BUSHES
Phil Rogers
A garden created by Rhon (died 2007), a true plant lover, developed around a C16 cottage (not open). Large range of plants grown in a variety of settings; colour-themed borders, ponds and poolside planting, alpine troughs, ferns, pleached limes and roses.
✕

HALL BARN
Malcolm & Deirdre Cochrane
Garden and paddocks extend to 4 acres with traditional herbaceous borders and a kitchen garden. Special features include a quality croquet lawn, C16 dovecote, a thatched cob wall and clear chalk streams.
& ✕

STOCKS
Norma & Richard Bird
Around this early cruck-constructed thatched cottage (not open), a densely planted collection of lime-tolerant herbaceous perennials offers tiers of colour throughout the year.
& ✕ ❀

Cottage garden with country feel . . .

8 BRIZE NORTON GARDENS
OX18 3NN. *3m SW of Witney. Brize Norton village, S of A40, or on Burford Rd.* Home-made teas. **Combined adm £3.50, chd free (share to Brize Norton Church & Brownies). Sun 8 June (1-6).**
Pretty village. Church open with Flower Festival. Teas by WI in Elderbank Hall. Large recreation ground for picnics. Ice creams and plants available for NGS.

BARNSTABLE HOUSE
Manor Road. Mr & Mrs P Butcher
C17 converted Cotswold stone barn (not open) with Mediterranean-style patio and planting. Courtyard garden with lawn surrounded by tightly packed borders against a backdrop of lime trees.

10 CHICHESTER PLACE
David & Claire Harrison. *Follow signs to rear of terrace*
Small easily maintained garden stuffed with plants. Gravel path, narrow path. People who like to hold an arm due to mobility problems may knock at front door.

17 CHICHESTER PLACE
Mr & Mrs Howard
Family garden with decking and barbeque areas, borders and water feature. Seating area and conservatory.

CHURCH FARM HOUSE
Philip & Mary Holmes
A garden designed with seating areas at different levels and viewpoints and including herb garden, rockery, water features, mixed borders, pergola, gazebo, greenhouse and pool enclosure with bougainvillea and oleanders.

NEW CLUMBER
Elm Grove. Mr & Mrs S Hawkins
Good-sized rear garden with large hosta bed, long pergola surrounded by many varieties of flowering plants. Front garden with large willow tree and numerous areas of charm.

16 DAUBIGNY MEAD
Bob & Margaret Watts
Garden is loosely based on room system, divided into various sections. Contains many shrubs. Water feature. Stream runs the length of garden. Back lawn is home to two guinea pigs. Small step.

NEW 2 ELM GROVE
Mr & Mrs Brian De'ath
Garden of medium size, front, side and rear areas. Patio, front and rear ponds with stream. Pergola with mixed climbers, borders with mixed herbaceous plants and shrubs, variety of ornamental trees and large lawned areas.

GAYLYN
Burford Road. Mike & Benita Wallace
1/3 of an acre garden, with mature trees, herbaceous borders, roses and lawns.

GRANGE FARM
Burford Road. Mr & Mrs Mark Artus
Family garden in lovely rural peaceful setting with C14 dovecote in back field as well as new vegetable garden, children's play area, fruit trees and wild flower areas.

LINGERMANS
Burford Road. Mrs E Dobson. *Follow signs for Foxbury Farm; their land is adjacent OS map 163. Approx 2m from village* (See separate entry). Teas, home-made cakes. WC.

MIJESHE
Elm Grove. Mr & Mrs M Harper
Established garden with many areas of interest incl herbaceous borders, patios, pond and many features.

4 MOAT CLOSE
John & Andrea Moss
Family garden with mixed borders and two small ponds.

PAINSWICK HOUSE
Carterton Road. Mr & Mrs T Gush
Approx 3/4 -acre mature garden; old apple trees; herb garden; vegetable garden, new pond area, herbaceous borders.

SCHOOL GARDEN
Station Road. Brize Norton Primary School
Flowers; vegetables; beautiful pond area; sound garden, willow dome and quiet area. All created and maintained with the help of the school children.

STONE COTTAGE
Station Road. Mr & Mrs K Humphris
Cottage garden with country feel. Patio area, wisteria and pear tree surrounded by pots, pergola, raised beds and perennial borders. One border contains a good selection of hostas and ferns. Another is full of delphiniums.

NEW UPPER HADDON BARN
114 Station Road. Mrs June Geraghty
Fairly large garden with variety of mature shrubs and trees, plus flowers - many roses. Fish pond and other features.

9 ◆ BROOK COTTAGE
Well Lane, Alkerton OX15 6NL. Mrs David Hodges, 01295 670303 or 670590, www.brookcottagegarden.co.uk. *6m NW of Banbury. 1/2 m off A422.* Follow signs in village. DIY tea, coffee, biscuits daily; other refreshments for groups by appt. **Adm £5, chd free, concessions £4. 24 Mar to 31 Oct, every Mon to Fri (9-6). For NGS: Mons 24 Mar; 25 Aug (9-6).**
4-acre hillside garden formed since 1964. Wide variety of trees, shrubs and perennials in areas of differing character. Water gardens; gravel garden; colour coordinated borders. Over 200 shrub and climbing roses. Many clematis; interesting throughout season.

10 ◆ BROUGHTON CASTLE
nr Banbury OX15 5EB. The Lord Saye & Sele, 01295 276070, www.broughtoncastle.com. *2 1/2 m SW of Banbury. On Shipston-on-Stour rd (B4035).* **House and garden adm**

£6.50, concession £5.50, chd £2.50, garden only adm £3, chd £1, concessions £2. Weds & Suns 1 May to 15 Sept; also Thurs in July & Aug; Bank Hol Mons (2-5). For NGS: Sun 27 July (2-5).

1 acre; shrubs, herbaceous borders, walled garden, roses, climbers seen against background of C14-C16 castle surrounded by moat in open parkland. House also open, extra charge.

⑪ BROUGHTON GRANGE
Wykham Lane, Broughton
OX15 5DS. *1/4 m out of village. From Banbury take the B4035 to village of Broughton. At the Seye & Sele Arms PH turn L up Wykham Lane (one way). Follow rd out of village along lane for 1/4 m. Entrance on R.* **Adm £5, chd free.**
Suns 4 May; 1 June; 6 July (9-5).
An impressive 25 acres of gardens and light woodland in an attractive Oxfordshire setting. The centrepiece is a large terraced walled garden created by Tom Stuart-Smith in 2001. Vision has been used to blend the gardens into the countryside. Good early displays of bulbs followed by outstanding herbaceous planting in summer. Formal and informal areas combine to make this a special site incl newly laid arboretum with many ongoing projects.

⑫ BROUGHTON GROUNDS FARM
North Newington OX15 6AW. Mr & Mrs Andrew Taylor. *3m from Banbury. 3m off B4035 through North Newington. Leave Banbury on Shipston Rd, B4035. Turn R to N Newington, follow rd signed Shutford. On L 3/4 m signed B & B.* Home-made teas. **Adm £2.50, chd free.** Sun 22 June (2-5).
One of the few farms to achieve recognition under the 'High Level Stewardship Scheme'. You will see rare wild flowers, grasses and wildlife in an area set in an 18 acre meadow. Also includes an old mill race and views of the deserted (1914) village of Hazelford. An area 'species rich'.

⑬ BROUGHTON POGGS & FILKINS GARDENS
GL7 3JH. *3m N of Lechlade. 5m S of Burford.* Home-made teas in Filkins village hall. **Combined adm £3.50, chd free.** Sun 1 June (2-5.30).
Two beautiful Cotswold stone villages. Finalist, Calor Village of the Year competition 2007. Gardens of widely varied scale and character. Village maps will be available. Communally-run village shop (ices etc). Swinford Museum of Cotswold tools and artefacts. Woollen weavers.

BROUGHTON HALL
Broughton Poggs. Karen & Ian Jobling
Formal walled garden, together with less formal grounds; ha-ha and views out to Thames valley; medieval carp pond; Roman well. Gravel paths.

BROUGHTON POGGS MILL
Charles Payne & Avril Inglis. *On B4477 as it crosses Broadwell Brook, between Filkins & Broughton Poggs*
Contemporary garden, with newly-formed linked 'rooms' in a traditional Cotswold watermill setting, dramatically combining local materials with modern planting. Fast-running unfenced water.

FILKINS FARMHOUSE
Filkins. Chris & Barbara Bristow
Traditional walled farmhouse garden. Lawns, borders, rose trellis, orchard. Gravel paths.

NEW FILKINS HALL
Filkins Hall Residents
Never previously open to public. House (not open) rebuilt 1912. Grand landscape setting now under rejuvenation: lawns, ha-ha, venerable trees, shrubs, herbaceous borders, wall shrubs; parkland pasture beyond. Gravel drive & paths.

LITTLE PEACOCKS
Filkins. Colvin & Moggridge
Garden made by Brenda Colvin 1956 onwards, very strong structure from walls and colours and textures of foliage.

NEW THE MILLER'S COTTAGE
Luke Bailey
Small garden yet with several character areas; eccentric plan form defined by beech hedge; lawn, miniature flowery borders, shrubs, small trees. An object lesson in what can be done with a smaller garden.

NO 1 COACH HOUSE
Filkins. Mrs Elizabeth Gidman
Small, intensive, semi-formal walled garden of many elements: terrace, pool, pergola, seats, form and texture of plants, grey plants.

PIP COTTAGE
Filkins. G B Woodin
Village house garden - formal in front; lawn, hedges and a view at the back.

NEW POGGS COTTAGE
Broughton Poggs. Phil & Helen Dunmall
A young reworking of an older garden: patio, lawn, island beds, mature shrubs, raised organic vegetable beds, soft fruit. Gravel driveway, 1 shallow step up to patio.

ST PETER'S HOUSE
Filkins. John Cambridge Esq
Large garden of lawns and trees, herbaceous borders, rose garden (2005), sunken paved garden with pool.

⑭ BUCKLAND LAKES
nr Faringdon SN7 8QR. The Wellesley family. *3m NE of Faringdon. Signed to Buckland off A420, lane between two churches.* Home-made teas. **Adm £3, chd free (share to Richard Wellesley Memorial Transport).** Sun 16 Mar (2-5).
Six acres of parkland surround the lakeside walk, designed by Richard Woods; fine trees; daffodils; shrubs. Norman church adjoins garden. C18 icehouse; thatched boathouse; exedra and temple. Fairly steep slope down to lakes.

Good early displays of bulbs followed by outstanding herbaceous planting . . .

15 CHALKHOUSE GREEN FARM
nr Kidmore End RG4 9AL. Mr & Mrs
J Hall, 01189 723631. *2m N of
Reading, 5m SW of Henley-on-
Thames. Situated between A4074 &
B481. From Kidmore End take
Chalkhouse Green Rd. Follow yellow
signs.* Home-made teas. **Adm £3, chd
free.** Sun 20 July (2-6). Visitors also
welcome by appt at any time.
1-acre garden and open traditional
farmstead. Herbaceous borders, herb
garden, shrubs, old-fashioned roses,
trees incl medlar, quince and
mulberries, walled ornamental kitchen
garden. Rare breed farm animals incl
an ancient breed of British White cattle,
sheep, Suffolk punch horse, donkeys,
Berkshire pigs, piglets, goats,
chickens, ducks and turkeys. Vintage
farm machinery displays. Farm trail and
donkey rides, vintage tractor trailer
rides. Swimming in covered pool, plant
stall. Ancient orchard, vintage farm
implements demonstration, rare breed
information & display, Suffolk horse
plaiting demonstration.

16 CHARLBURY GARDENS
OX7 3PP. *6m SE of Chipping Norton.*
Light refreshments & teas at Charlbury
Memorial Hall. **Combined adm £4,
chd free.** Sun 22 June (2-6).
Large Cotswold village on B4022
Witney-Enstone rd.

GOTHIC HOUSE
Mr & Mrs Andrew Lawson. *In
Church St, nr Bell Hotel*
¹/₃-acre walled garden, designed
for sculpture display and colour
association. New area of planted
squares replaces lawn. False
perspective, pleached lime walk,
trellis, terracotta containers.
Gravel paths.

HEATHFIELD
**Browns Lane. Helen & Trevor
Jones,** 01608 810644,
trevor.jones@ophiopogon.com.
*In Browns Lane between
Spendlove car park & The Bull.*
Visitors also welcome by appt.
¹/₂-acre walled garden. Mixed
borders, with a variety of
interesting plants, have been
created over the last nine years,
by the owners, around newly
designed landscape features and
existing trees. Some gravel paths.

LYDBROOK
Crawborough. **Aija &
Christopher Hastings.** *Close to
centre of Charlbury on a road
from the Playing Close*
A typical long 1930's garden that
has been divided into a number of
rooms including patios, lawns and
a small pond. Planting includes
some exotic species such as tree
ferns, bananas and bamboos.
Featured in 'Evening Standard' -
Homes & Property, July 2007.

THE PRIORY GARDEN
Church Lane, Charlbury. **Dr D El
Kabir & Colleagues.** *White gate
off St Mary's church yard*
1 acre of formal terraced topiary
gardens with Italianate features.
Foliage colour schemes, shrubs,
parterres with fragrant plants, old
roses, water features, sculpture
and inscriptions aim to produce a
poetic, wistful atmosphere.
Arboretum of over 3 acres borders
the R Evenlode and incl wildlife
garden and pond. Share to
Wytham Hall Ltd. Gravel paths.

Old-fashioned
roses, trees
including medlar,
quince and
mulberries . . .

17 CHASTLETON GARDENS
GL56 0SZ. *4m NW of Chipping
Norton. 3m SE of Moreton-in-Marsh
on A44.* Light refreshments & cream
teas at Chastleton Glebe. **Combined
adm £5, chd free.** Sun 13 July (2-6).
3 very different gardens: Prue Leith's 5
acre garden with views, lake, Cotswold
terraces (one red), rose tunnel, woods,
vegetable and flower parterres; Glebe
Cottage (Pearse's) plantsman's
gardener's cottage with pond and
alpines, baskets and pots; and
Chastleton House, Jacobean manor
house with topiary and parkland.

CHASTLETON GLEBE
Prue Leith
5 acres, old trees, terraces (one all
red); small lake, island; Chinese-
style bridge, pagoda; formal
vegetable garden; views; rose

tunnel. Vegetable and flower
parterres. Gravel paths & grass
areas dependent on weather.

◆ CHASTLETON HOUSE
The National Trust. *From A436
off A44. Car park 270yds from
garden*
3-acre garden with a typical
Elizabethan/Jacobean layout, ring
of fascinating topiary at its heart.
At Chastleton House (not open)
the rules of modern croquet were
codified in 1866. Croquet lawn
survives.

1 GLEBE COTTAGE
Mr & Mrs Ray Pearse
Plantsman's garden comprising
intensely planted island beds,
herbaceous borders, alpine
garden, pond, many clematis,
baskets and pots.

18 CHIVEL FARM
Heythrop OX7 5TR. Mr & Mrs J D
Sword, 01608 683227,
rosalind.sword@btinternet.com. *4m
E of Chipping Norton. Off A361 or A44.*
Adm £3. Visitors welcome by appt.
Beautifully designed country garden,
with extensive views, designed for
continuous interest. Colour-schemed
borders with many unusual trees,
shrubs and herbaceous plants. Small
formal white garden. Conservatory.

**19 CHRIST CHURCH
MASTERS', POCOCK AND
CATHEDRAL GARDENS**
St Aldate's, Oxford OX1 1DP. *Enter
from St Aldate's into War Memorial
Gardens, into Christ Church Meadow,
then turn L into Masters' garden gate.*
**Adm £2.50 (share to Cancer
Research UK).** Sat 19 July (2-5).
**Combined with Merton College
adm £3.50.**
The Masters' Garden created in 1926
features colourful herbaceous and
shrub borders. Venture through into
Pocock Garden, pass by the oriental
plane, planted in 1636, and shade-
loving plant border. Then enter into the
Cathedral Garden, where the Alice in
Wonderland stories took their
inspiration. Gravel paths.

20 CHURCH FARM FIELD
Church Lane, Epwell OX15 6LD. Mr
V D & Mrs D V D Castle, 01295
788473. *7¹/₂ m W of Banbury on N*

side of Epwell. **Adm £2, chd free. Suns 18 May; 7 Sept (2-6). Also open Epwell Mill 18 May & 7 Sept. Visitors also welcome by appt.** Woods; arboretum with wild flowers (planting started 1992); over 150 different trees and shrubs in 4½ acres. Paths cut through trees for access to various parts. Can be slippery at times.

21 CLOCK HOUSE
Coleshill SN6 7PT. Denny Wickham & Peter Fox, 01793 762476. *3½ m SW of Faringdon. On B4019.* **Adm £2.50, chd free. Visitors welcome by appt.**
Rambling garden on hilltop overlooking NT parkland and Vale of the White Horse. On the site of Coleshill House, burnt down in 1952, the floor plan has been laid out as a garden with lavender and box 'walls' and gravel 'rooms' full of self-sown butterfly-attracting flowers. Exuberant, not too tidy, garden with unusual plants; walled garden; greenhouse; vegetables.

DAYLESFORD HOUSE
See Gloucestershire North & Central.

22 EPWELL MILL
nr Banbury OX15 6HG. Mrs William Graham & Mrs David Long. *7m W of Banbury. Between Shutford & Epwell.* **Home-made teas. Adm £2, chd free. Suns 6 Apr; 18 May; 7 Sept (2-6). Also open Church Farm, Epwell 18 May & 7 Sept.**
Medium-sized peaceful garden, interestingly landscaped in open country, based around former watermill with terraced pools. Spring bulbs in April, azaleas in May and early autumn colour in September. White double border.

23 EVELEGH'S
High Street, Long Wittenham OX14 4QH. Dr & Mrs C S Ogg. *3m NE of Didcot. Take A415 from Abingdon to Clifton Hampden, turn R at T-lights. Cross river to Long Wittenham. Drive into village - Evelegh's is next to The Plough on RH-side.* **Home-made teas by WI in village hall. Adm £3, chd free. Sun 1 June (2-6).**
¾ -acre garden leading through areas of different characters to River Thames. Well stocked with many unusual shrubs, bulbs and perennials, incl collections of old bush roses,

delphiniums, tree and herbaceous peonies, irises and clematis. Art exhibition and sale.

24 NEW FAR FIELD
Bayswater Road, Headington OX3 9RZ. Mrs J Cunningham. *3m NE of Oxford. At Headington roundabout take sign to crematorium. Go past crematorium last house on LH side.* **Home-made teas. Adm £3, chd free, concessions £2.50. Sats 26 Apr; 26 July (2-6).**
Two wildlife meadows within a large natural garden: the spring meadow is a carpet of cowslips and in summer there is an extensive variety of wild flowers. The garden is shaped by a variety of trees, shrubs and a collection of species buddleia with a well-stocked herbaceous border and 2 Kiftsgate roses. Uneven surface on lawn.

The spring meadow is a carpet of cowslips . . .

25 THE FILBERTS
North Moreton OX11 9AT. Mr & Mrs S Prescott & Mrs Gladys Kirkman, 01235 815353, janetmprescott@aol.com. *3m SE of Didcot. Off A4130 (Didcot-Wallingford rd).* **Home-made teas. Adm £3.50, chd free. Visitors welcome by appt in June & July for groups.**
1-acre garden featuring island beds planted for shade, architectural foliage and drought tolerance. Colourful mixed borders with many unusual plants, over 120 varieties of clematis and more than 50 of penstemon; lily and fish ponds; vegetable garden; sweet peas; rose beds in parterre form and an orchard. Gravel paths, some narrow.

26 GARSINGTON MANOR
28 Southend, Garsington, nr Oxford OX44 9DH. Mrs R Ingrams. *3m SE of Oxford. N of B480. 1½ m S of Wheatley.* **Home-made teas. Adm £4, chd free. Sat 3 May; Sun 21 Sept (2-5).**
C17 Manor house of architectural, literary and musical interest (not open). Early monastic fish ponds, water garden, dovecote c1700. Lake and flower parterre, Italianate terrace and loggia and Italian statues laid out by Philip and Lady Ottoline Morrell c1915-1923. Celebrated literary gatherings up to 1928, and summer opera festival since 1990. Gravel paths, steps, steep slopes.

27 GREENFIELD FARM
Christmas Common, nr Watlington OX49 5HG. Andrew & Jane Ingram, 01491 612434. *4m from J5 of M40, 7m from Henley. J5 M40; A40 towards Oxford for ½ m; turn L signed Christmas Common. ¾ m past Fox & Hounds. Turn L at 'Tree Barn' sign.* **Light refreshments & teas. Adm £3, chd free (share to Farm Wildlife Advisory Group). Sun 22 June (2-5). Visitors also welcome by appt May, June, Aug & Sept. Evenings preferred.**
10-acre wild flower meadow, surrounded by woodland, established 12 yrs ago under the Countryside Stewardship Scheme. Traditional Chiltern chalkland meadow in beautiful peaceful setting with 80 species of perennial wild flowers and grasses (incl Chiltern gentian, pyramidal greater-spotted bee orchids). ½ m walk from parking area. Opportunity to return via typical Chiltern beechwood.

28 ◆ GREYS COURT
Rotherfield Greys, Henley-on-Thames RG9 4PG. The National Trust, 01491 628529, greyscourt@nationaltrust.org.uk. *2m W of Henley-on-Thames. Signed from Nettlebed taking B481. Direct route from Henley-on-Thames town centre (unsigned for NT): follow signs to Badgemore Golf Club towards Rotherfield Greys, about 3m out of Henley.* **Adm £4, chd £2. Tues to Sats 22 Mar to 27 Sept (12-5). Last adm 4.30pm. For NGS: Sat 17 May (12-5).**
8 acres amongst which are the ruined walls and buildings of original fortified manor. Rose, cherry, wisteria and white

gardens; lawns; kitchen garden; ice house; Archbishop's maze. Tudor house (not open) with C18 alterations on site of original C13 house fortified by Lord Grey in C14. Donkey wheel and tower. A band plays during the afternoon. Tours of garden on the day. Gravel paths throughout garden. Gentle slopes. Cobbles in places.

 ♿ ✝ ☕

29 HEADINGTON GARDENS
Old Headington, Oxford OX3 9BT. *2m E from centre of Oxford. After T-lights, centre of Headington, towards Oxford, 2nd turn on R into Osler Rd. Gardens at end of rd in Old Headington. 2 gardens in Kennett Rd opp Osler Rd across London Rd.* Teas at Ruskin College. **Combined adm £3.50, chd free (share to Ruskin College Walled Garden). Sun 18 May (2-6).**
Attractive village of Saxon origin hidden within the bounds of Oxford.

☕

NEW 10 KENNETT ROAD
Linda Clover, 01865 765881, linda.clover@lmm.ox.ac.uk. *Leave Osler Rd by turning L into London Rd, Kennett Rd 1st R.* **Visitors also welcome by appt.**
Delightful small (20'x90') densely-planted suburban oasis in central Headington with 3 distinct areas created for yr-round interest. Includes mixed shrub and herbaceous planting, succulents and cactus, secluded fernery and small, unfenced wildlife pond. Current holder of Oxford in Bloom - Best Kept Large Back Garden & Best New Entry.

✝ ☎

NEW 39 KENNETT ROAD
Stephanie Jenkins, www.headington.org.uk/private/garden. *Leave Osler Rd, L into London Rd, Kennett Rd 1st R*
Traditional laundress-length (150') garden behind 1920s semi in heart of Headington. Cottage-style garden includes shrubs, perennials, bamboos, an ancient apple tree and is brought to life with 6 exotic hens to keep children amused.

✝

THE COACH HOUSE
The Croft, Headington. Mr & Mrs David Rowe. *After T-lights in centre of Headington, 2nd turn on R towards Oxford into Osler Rd. R again off Osler Rd*

Two linked gardens of differing character: one laid to lawn with formal hedges, flower beds and small woodland area; the other a sunny courtyard with ponds on two levels, a gravel garden and sculpture. Some gravel paths.

 ♿

40 OSLER ROAD
Oxford. Mr & Mrs N Coote, 01865 767680, nicholas@coote100.freeserve.co.uk. *2m E from centre of Oxford. Off London Rd, 3/4 m inside ring rd. After T-lights in centre of Headington towards Oxford, 2nd turn on R, Osler Rd.* **Visitors also welcome by appt.**
Spacious 32yr-old town garden 2/3 acre with mature specimens of exotics. Passion for design and planting, use of decorative pots, mosaic paths, whitewashed walls, shutters: Mediterranean fantasy in a cold climate.

✝ ☎

35 ST ANDREWS ROAD
Old Headington. Mrs Alison Soskice. *Opp end of Osler Rd* Charming 1/4 -acre garden with trees, shrubs and herbaceous plants. Gravel drive, but wheelchair access nr entrance to reduce travel over gravel.

♿

STOKE COTTAGE
Stoke Place. Steve & Jane Cowls. *End of Osler Rd to St Andrew's Rd to Stoke Place*
Mature trees and old stone walls provide a framework for a linked series of paths and flower beds containing many contrasting shrubs and plants which give an atmosphere of seclusion.

♿ ✝

30 HEARNS HOUSE
Gallows Tree Common RG4 9DE. John & Joan Pumfrey, 0118 972 2848. *5m N of Reading, 5m W of Henley. From A4074 turn E at The Fox, Cane End.* Home-made teas. **Adm £3, chd free. Sat 17, Sun 18 May; Sun 24, Mon 25 Aug (10-12 & 2-5). Evening Opening £7.50, Tue 22 July (6.30-9.30). Visitors also welcome by appt.**
2-acre garden in woodland setting provides design and planting ideas for small as well as larger gardens. Good foliage and single colour areas with totally drought-tolerant paved courtyard, water features and shady

walks. Black spiral garden. Wide variety of hardy plants incl many new varieties, chosen and propagated for yr-round interest in the garden and in the nursery. Jazz evening Tues 22 July with picnic tables bookable. Studio open with exhibition of artworks on 18 May. NCCPG collection of Brunnera & Omphalodes, visits by appointment.

♿ ❊ NCCPG ☕ ☎

Terraces including silver, pink and blue plantings . . .

31 HILL COURT
Tackley OX5 3AQ. Mr & Mrs Andrew C Peake. *9m N of Oxford. Turn off A4260 at Sturdy's Castle.* Home-made teas. **Adm £2.50, chd free. Sat 31 May; Sun 1 June (2-6).**
Walled garden of 2 acres with yew cones at top of terrace as a design feature by Russell Page in the 1960s. Terraces incl silver, pink and blue plantings, white garden, herbaceous borders, shrubberies, orangery. Many rare and unusual plants. Entry incl History Trail with unique geometric fish ponds (1620), C17 stables, pigeon house, C18 lakes, ice house (not suitable for wheelchairs). Gravel paths, steep slopes, paving.

♿ ✝ ❊ ☕

32 NEW HOLLYHOCKS
North Street, Islip, nr Kidlington OX5 2SQ. Avril Hughes. *3m NE of Kidlington. From A34 - exit Bletchingdon/Islip. B4027 direction Islip, turn L into North St.* Teas at Monkshead. **Adm £2.50, chd free. Combined adm with Monkshead, Bletchingdon £4. Suns 11 May; 8 June (2-5). Evening Opening Mon 2 June (6-8).**
Small Edwardian plantaholic's garden brimming with yr-round interest. Divided into areas with herbaceous borders, roses, clematis, shade and woodland planting as well as lots of pots around the house.

✝

33 HOLYWELL MANOR
Manor Road, Oxford OX1 3 UH. Balliol College Graduate Centre. *1m E of Carfax. In town centre. Corner of Manor Rd & St Cross Rd off Longwall.* Light refreshments & teas. **Adm £2, chd free. Sun 18 May (2-5).**
Garden of approx 1 acre, not normally open to the public. Imaginatively laid out 50yrs ago around horse chestnut to give formal and informal areas. Mature gingko avenue, spinney with spring flowers and bulbs. Basketry demonstration (subject to confirmation). Unfenced pond.

34 HOME CLOSE
Southend, Garsington OX44 9DH. Ms M Waud & Dr P Giangrande, 01865 361394. *3m SE of Oxford. Southend. N of B480. Opp Garsington Manor.* Home-made teas. **Adm £3, chd free. Sun 27 July (2-6). Visitors also welcome by appt 1 Apr to 30 Sept.**
2-acre garden with listed house (not open) and granary. Trees, shrubs and perennials planted for all-yr effect. Terraces, walls and hedges divide the garden into ten distinct areas to reflect a Mediterranean interest.

35 HOME FARM
Balscote OX15 6JP. Mr Godfrey Royle, 01295 738194. *5m W of Banbury. 1/2 m off A422.* Light refreshments & teas. **Adm £3, chd free. Visitors welcome by appt.**
C17 house and barn (not open), -1/2 -acre plant lover's peaceful garden giving yr-round interest with unusual plants, coloured foliage, flowering shrubs, bulbs and perennials created by garden owners over 20yrs in an informal way. Two lawns give a feeling of spaciousness and a small terrace has views of surrounding countryside. Featured in GGG 2008.

36 IFFLEY GARDENS
Iffley Village OX4 4EJ. *2m S of Oxford. Within Oxford's ring rd, off A4158 from Magdalen Bridge to Littlemore roundabout.* Map provided at each garden. **Combined adm £4, chd free. Sun 15 June (2-6).**
Secluded old village with renowned Norman church, featured on cover of Pevsner's Oxon guide. Short footpath from Mill Lane leads to scenic Iffley Lock and Sandford to Oxford towpath.

6 ABBERBURY AVENUE
Philippa Scoones
Established 1-acre family garden with mature borders, shrubs, terrace, formal vegetable garden, water garden and wild flower area. Many features of the original 1930s layout remain. Unusual and interesting plants throughout.

15 ABBERBURY ROAD
Allen & Boglarka Hill
Variety of beds planted over the last 10yrs in different styles featuring many shrubs, climbers, and perennials.

65 CHURCH WAY
Mrs J Woodfill
Small English cottage garden with a few Californian plants.

71 CHURCH WAY
Mr & Mrs Harrison, 01865 718224. Visitors also welcome by appt.
Small garden, professionally designed. Mixed planting of small trees, shrubs, herbaceous plants. View of river valley across to Boars Hill.

122 CHURCH WAY
Sir John & Lady Elliott
Small secluded cottage style garden with trees, shrubs, roses and herbaceous plants behind listed house (not open) with view of church tower.

THE THATCHED COTTAGE
2 Mill Lane. Mr & Mrs Bones, 01865 711453, chrisbones01@yahoo.co.uk. *Mill Lane.* **Visitors also welcome by appt.**
Delightful 3/4 -acre garden tucked behind C16 village house (not open). Range of specimen trees and plants in terracing; water features, formal gardens and water meadow with Thames frontage.

37 NEW KEBLE COLLEGE
Parks Road. OX1 3PG. Keble College, www.keble.ox.ac.uk/about/gardens. *Central Oxford. On Parks Rd. S of University Parks & opp*

University Museum. Home-made teas (3-5). **Adm £3, chd free. Sun 22 June (2-6).**
Dramatic lawned quads (4 1/2 acres) with recently completed, flowery, modern planting by Sarah Ewbank. Warden's private garden, in the style of Russell Page, is open. The college chapel, containing the 'Light of the World' painting and the college hall (Oxford's longest!) are both open to visitors. No wheelchair access to Warden's garden; one small garden pebbled but both gardens can be viewed from suitable vantage points.

> Six plots containing vegetables, fruit and flowers, with emphasis on organic gardening . . .

KEMPSFORD MANOR
See Gloucestershire North & Central.

38 KENCOT GARDENS
nr Lechlade GL7 3QT. *5m NE of Lechlade. E of A361 between Burford & Lechlade.* Home-made teas in village hall. **Combined adm £3, chd free. Mon 24 Mar (2-6).**
Charming Cotswold village with interesting Norman church.

THE ALLOTMENTS
Amelia Carter Trust
Six plots containing vegetables, fruit and flowers, with emphasis on organic gardening.

DE ROUGEMONT
Mr & Mrs D Portergill
1/2 -acre garden with mature trees, shrubs and container plants, soft fruits, apples, pears, spring bulbs and flowers, vegetables, beds for perennials, fuchsias, conifers and heathers, herb garden with box hedging, well, greenhouse with vines. Gravel drive, help available.

IVY NOOK
Mr W Gasson & Mrs G Cox
Cottage garden with rockeries, shrubs and mixed borders providing yr-round colour. Well-stocked pond with waterfall. 150yr-old apple tree.

KENCOT HOUSE
Mr & Mrs Andrew Patrick
Well-established 2-acre garden, lovingly designed for a peaceful atmosphere. Interesting trees (incl gingko) and shrubs. Quantities of various daffodils and other spring bulbs, roses: over 50 different clematis. Interesting carved C13 archway adds to the attractions.
✕

MANOR FARM
Mr & Mrs J R Fyson
2-acre garden. Naturalised daffodils, fritillaries, wood anemones in mature orchards, incl quince, medlar and mulberry; pleached limewalk, pergola with rambling gallica roses. Pair of resident geese, 2 alpacas and small flock of bantams patrol the paddock. C17 listed house, not open.
🦽 ✕ ❀

39 ◆ KINGSTON BAGPUIZE HOUSE
nr Abingdon OX13 5AX. Mrs Francis Grant, 01865 820259, www. kingstonbagpuizehouse.org.uk. *5m W of Abingdon. In Kingston Bagpuize just off A415, 1/4 m S of A415/A420.* **House and garden adm: adult £5, concessions £4.50, chd £2.50, garden only adm £3, chd free. Open many days throughout the year. Please phone or visit website for details. For NGS: Suns 16 Mar; 7 Sept (2-5.30).**
Notable collection of unusual trees, incl magnolias, shrubs, perennials and bulbs, incl snowdrops, providing yr-round interest and colour. Large mixed borders, interesting summer flowering trees and shrubs. Some gravel paths, majority of garden accessible by wheelchair. Disabled WC. Steps into tearoom, but also outside area with tables & chairs.
🦽 ✕ ❀ ☕

40 LADY MARGARET HALL
Norham Gardens, Oxford OX2 6QA. **Principal & Fellows of Lady Margaret Hall.** *1m N of Carfax. From Banbury Rd, R at T-lights into Norham Gdns.* **Adm £2.50, chd free. Sun 4 May (2-5).**
A chance to see this wonderful college garden in spring. Late tulips, huge wisterias and many interesting trees plus sunken garden with new armillary (celestial) sundial.
✕ ❀

41 LANGFORD GARDENS
nr Lechlade GL7 3LF. *E of A361 Burford-Lechlade; W of A409 Burford-Faringdon.* Teas. **Combined adm £4, chd free. Sun 8 June (2-6).**
Mixture of cottage and formal gardens in old limestone village which makes a feature of roses. Saxon church, known for Saxon carvings (Langford Rood), decorated with flowers. Large car park.
☕

BAKERY COTTAGE
Mr & Mrs R Robinson
Walled garden with flower beds and lawn. Mixed cottage garden planting with roses.

THE BARN
Lechlade Road. **Mr & Mrs D E Range**
Set in an old farmyard this Cotswold walled garden features the original animal feeding troughs. A mixed cottage garden with roses.

BAY TREE COTTAGE
Mr & Mrs R Parsons
Informal cottage garden with mixed herbaceous and shrub borders.

BRIDGEWATER HOUSE
Mr & Mrs T R Redston
Old farmhouse with barn in yard and large garden behind. Mixed borders, vegetable patch, fruit cage, old apple trees.

2 CHURCH LANE
Chris Donlan & Mandy Wood
Small cottage garden.

5 CHURCH LANE
Mr D Carden
Garden laid out in 3 sections divided by a yew hedge and dry stone walls. Cottage-style garden, enclosed semi-formal pond and lawn.

2 COOKS FARM COTTAGES
Mr & Mrs R Hicks
After 3 yrs development, the garden is bright and relaxing with herbaceous borders, lawn, rockery and many climbers. A small waterfall trickles into large koi pond which runs into a planted stream and smaller pond.

CORKSCREW COTTAGE
Fiona Gilbert & Garry Maguire
Christopher Lloyd says a garden is more than just a collection of plants but he obviously hasn't visited this one.

COTSWOLD BUNGALOW
Mr & Mrs J Dudley
S-facing plot of approx 1/3 of an acre originally laid out in the early 1950s. Well-established vegetable plot, herbaceous borders, fruit trees and shrubs remain, together with a more recent pergola, decked area and greenhouses.
🦽

26 THE ELMS
Mr R Stacey
Cottage garden.

FAIRCROFT
Filkins Road. **Mr & Mrs Swain**
Walled Cotswold cottage garden set in just under 3/4 of an acre. Working kitchen garden, old courtyard with fountain, two wildlife ponds and full of old-fashioned charm.

KEMPS YARD
Mr & Mrs R Kemp
Established in spring 2003, this is an informal courtyard garden with raised cottage beds, lots of roses and a pond.

LIME TREE COTTAGE
Diane & Michael Schultz
1/2 -acre cottage garden, featuring old roses, herbaceous borders and kitchen garden.

LOCKEY HOUSE
Ian & Susan Dunstall
Well-established, much loved garden. Contains a good collection of old-fashioned roses and clematis. Some gravel and single steps though we try to make it fully accessible.

Mixture of cottage and formal gardens in old limestone village which makes a feature of roses . . .

LOWER FARM HOUSE
Mr & Mrs Templeman
Large walled semi-formal garden with shrubs, roses and herbaceous borders.

NEW MILLFIELD HOUSE
Filkins Road. Mr & Mrs J Spence
This pretty little garden is like a secret room with its archway of white wisteria, hydrangeas, roses and pots of geraniums. The perfect place to relax whilst the sun goes down.

MOSS COTTAGE
Mr & Mrs Guy Charrison
Small cottage garden.

THE OLD BAKERY
Mr & Mrs C Smith
New garden redesigned for low maintenance with water feature and no grass.

THE OLD SCHOOL
David Freeman Esq
Small formal garden designed in 1973 by Sir Hardy Amies KCVO. His collection of old roses incl Rosa de Rescht, Ferdinand Pichard and Rosa Mundi.

THE OLD VICARAGE
Mr & Mrs A Radcliffe
Traditional Cotswold garden with mixed flower beds of roses, herbaceous plants and shrubs. Fish pond with large koi carp. Garden enclosed by stone walling.

NEW PEMBER HOUSE
The Lane. Mr & Mrs J Potter
There are several aspects to the gardens ranging from a formal knot garden, wildlife pond, mature flower beds and informal woodland areas. Overall the gardens have a wonderful feeling of peace and tranquility.

NEW RECTORY FARM
Church Lane. Mr & Mrs R Kirby
Large mature walled garden with trees and shrubs. Vegetable garden. Very peaceful setting.

ROSEFERN COTTAGE
Mr & Mrs J Lowden
Pretty cottage garden overflowing with roses, herbaceous plants, flowering shrubs and ferns. Small but beautiful.

STONECROFT
David & Christine Apperley
Very pretty traditional cottage garden with a pond and water feature, also a vegetable plot.

NEW 1 THE ELMS
Mr & Mrs A Tinson
Recently modernised garden with several small beds filled with colourful flowers and roses. Brightly filled containers of fuchsias and geraniums. Delightful dahlias in late summer. Pond and waterfall for the wildlife of newts and frogs.

THREEWAYS
Mrs M Wilson
Garden created from old farmyard in 1960s in five sections. Cotswold barn and old cowsheds, fish pond and vegetable patch.

Secret room with its archway of white wisteria, hydrangeas, roses and pots of geraniums . . .

42 LIME CLOSE
35 Henleys Lane, Drayton, Abingdon OX14 4HU. M C de Laubarede, mail@mclgardendesign.com. *2m S of Abingdon. Henleys Lane is off main rd through Drayton.* **Adm £3.50, chd free (share to CLIC Sargent).** Suns 20 Apr; 1 June (2-5.30). **Visitors also welcome by appt in writing or email for groups 10+.**
3-acre mature plantsman's garden with rare trees, shrubs, perennials and bulbs. Mixed borders, raised beds, pergola, unusual topiary and shade borders. Herb garden designed by Rosemary Verey. Listed C16 house (not open). New cottage garden designed by owner, a professional garden designer, focusing on colour combinations and an iris garden with over 100 varieties of tall bearded irises.
  ⚙ ☕ ☎

43 LINGERMANS
Burford Road, Brize Norton OX18 3NZ. Mrs E Dobson. *3m SW of Witney; 3m SE of Burford. Turn off A40 1m W of roundabout at end of Witney bypass, signed Brize Norton. Lingermans ¾ m on L. From Brize Norton take Burford Road 1½ m on R.* Home-made teas. **Adm £3, chd free.** Sun 30 Mar (2-5).

Masses of spring bulbs - snowdrops, aconites, different daffodils, narcissi, hellebores, flowering spring shrubs, trees. All in 1 acre garden with lawns, mature trees, herbaceous borders, sunken dry gravel with pergola, scented border, wildlife areas with frog pond, secret garden, vegetable and fruit areas.
  ♿ ☕

44 ◆ MAGDALEN COLLEGE
Oxford OX1 4AU. Magdalen College, 01865 276000, www.magd.ox.ac.uk. *Entrance in High St.* **Adm £3, chd £2, concessions £2. See website for other opening times.** For NGS: Sun 6 Apr (1-6).
60 acres incl deer park, college lawns, numerous trees 150-200yrs old, notable herbaceous and shrub plantings; Magdalen meadow, where purple and white snake's-head fritillaries can be found, is surrounded by Addison's Walk, a tree-lined circuit by the R Cherwell developed since the late C18. An ancient herd of 60 deer is located in the grounds.
  ♿ ✗ ☕

45 MANOR FARM
Minster Lovell OX29 0RR. Lady Parker, 01993 775728. *1½ m W of Witney. Off B4047 rd between Witney/Burford. Follow sign opp White Hart down to R Windrush, 100yds over bridge turn R at Old Swan & up village street. Manor Farm is last house on R before continuing to Crawley. Parking: enter at end of 1st field towards Crawley if approaching from village. Drive back across field to enter close to garden. No parking in village.* Home-made teas. **Adm £3, chd free.** Sun 15 June (2-5).
6-acre garden of C15 farmhouse (not open) with open access to adjoining Minster Lovell Hall ruins. Old shrub and climbing roses, fish ponds, herbaceous and lawns. Old barns within garden area. Grasses area.
  ♿ ⚙ ☕

THE MANOR HOUSE, HAMBLEDEN
See Buckinghamshire.

46 MERTON COLLEGE FELLOWS' GARDEN
Oxford OX1 4JD. Warden & Fellows. *Merton St, parallel to High St.* **Adm £2.50, chd free.** Sat 19 July (2-5). **Combined adm £3.50 with Christ Church** Sat 19 July.
Ancient mulberry said to have

associations with James I; specimen trees incl Sorbus and Malus vars; long mixed border; recently established herbaceous bed; view of Christ Church meadow.

&. ✕

47 MIDDLETON CHENEY GARDENS
OX17 2NP. *3m E of Banbury. From M40 J11 follow A422, signed Middleton Cheney. Map available at all gardens.* Home-made teas at Peartree House. **Combined adm £4, chd free.** Sun 15 June (1-6).
Large village with a diversity of gardens. Late C13 church with Pre-Raphaelite stained glass and William Morris ceiling open 1-6 with gardens.
☕

CHURCH COTTAGE
12 Church Lane. David & Sue Thompson. *Back garden off High Street*
Entry to private back garden through rear garden of 8 Church Lane. Typical English cottage garden-style with 'Mediterranean' influences. Public front garden by church path, yellow and white themed borders.
&. ✕

8 CHURCH LANE
Mr & Mrs Style. *Gate entrance next to 37 High Street*
Cottage garden in the process of being renovated since 2005. Mixed borders, vegetable and fruit area, pergola.
&.

NEW CALM RETREAT
8 Stanwell Lea. Clive & Kate Chamberlain
Large low maintenance garden with many interesting features.
✕ ✿

15 CHURCH LANE
Dr Jill Meara. *Entrance in narrow lane to L of church spire*
A series of open spaces incl cottage garden, vegetable patch, orchard area and field ending in a stream.
✿

5 LONGBURGES
Mr & Mrs D Vale. *Access is via a good footpath at rear of garden*
Small SW-facing garden on three levels with patios, ponds, lawn and planting. Collection of acers predominate with herbaceous,

mixed and spring borders. Small container grown fruit and herb patio.
✿

38 MIDWAY
Margaret & David Finch. *Take High St. First R into Bull Baulk. L into Midway*
Small front garden. Back garden with mixed borders and shrubs. Water feature with pond and waterfall and other interesting features.
✕ ✿

PEARTREE HOUSE
Roger & Barbara Charlesworth. *Glovers Lane is 200yds N of All Saints Church*
Approx 1/3 -acre cottage garden with extensive water feature.
✕

2 QUEEN STREET
Lynn Baldwin. *At roundabout take 1st exit. Queen St is 1st L after 30 mph sign*
Small front and back garden. Informal and densely planted.
✕

14 QUEEN STREET
Brian & Kathy Goodey
Mature cottage garden that has evolved through family use. Rooms in a rectangle where there is always room for an extra plant.
✕ ✿

27 STANWELL LEA
Frank & Jane Duty. *B4525 Northampton. Xrds R into village. Take L Stanwell Drive, L Stanwell Lea*
Cottage garden with surprises, Water feature and penstemon collection.
&. ✿

48 MONKS HEAD
Weston Road, Bletchingdon OX5 3DH. Sue Bedwell, 01869 350155. *Approx 4m N of Kidlington. From A34 take B4027 to Bletchingdon, turn R at Xrds into Weston Rd.* Home-made teas. **Adm £2.50, chd free. Combined with Hollyhocks, Islip £4.** Sun 11 May; Sun 8 June (2-5). **Evening Opening** Mon 2 June (6-8). Visitors also welcome by appt all yr. £2 groups 10+; £3 groups of under 10.
Plantaholics' garden for all-yr interest. Bulb frame and alpine area, greenhouse.
✕ ✿ ☕ ☎

A line of mature fig trees against a brick wall . . .

49 NEW NORTH MORETON GARDENS
OX11 9AT. Mrs E Haycock. *3m SE of Didcot. Off A4130 (Didcot-Wallingford Rd). Follow signs for car park.* Home-made teas in C17 barn. **Combined adm £4, chd free (share to All Saints' Church).** Sun 15 June (2-6).
Charming small village with many listed buildings. Gardens vary in size and style. Interesting Grade 1 medieval church with photographic exhibition.
☕

NEW ALDERS FARM HOUSE
Long Wittenham Road. Mrs Caroline Delves
This garden is a mixture of contemporary with traditional layout and planting. Garden features a pergola and a line of mature fig trees against a brick wall.
✕

THE FILBERTS
High Street. Mr & Mrs Prescott & Mrs Gladys Kirkman
(See separate entry).
&. ✕ ✿

NEW LITTLE ORCHARD
Long Wittenham Road. Patrick & Mary Greene
Long interesting garden with mixed orchard. Rear garden in three sections planted with a mixture of shrubs, roses and perennials with feature fish pond and waterfall. Wheelchair access via sloping gravel at rear entrance.
&. ✕

NEW PECKWATER
High Street. Mr & Mrs R Haycock
1/2 acre garden planted to enhance the view and as a structure for shrubs and herbaceous planting.
&. ✕

NEW STAPLETON'S CHANTRY
Long Wittenham Road. Dr & Mrs M A Parker
2 acre traditional country house garden, herbaceous borders, vegetable garden, unfenced pond, lawns, mature trees. Many unusual and interesting plants and shrubs, roses, clematis, paeonies, euphorbia. Gravel driveway, some steps.

  🚻 ✕ 🛏

50 NEW NORTH OXFORD GARDENS
OX2 6UE. *3/4 m N of Oxford centre. Within Oxford ring rd 1/4 m S of Summertown bet Banbury Rd A4165 & Woodstock Rd A44. Map provided at each garden.* **Adm £3.50, chd free.** Sun 15 June (2-6).
Three very different superbly designed town gardens in North Oxford.

NEW 14 FARNDON ROAD
Mrs Judith Lane. *3/4 m N of Oxford city centre. Off Woodstock Rd*
Professionally designed long narrow town garden with visual impact. Formal layout divided into 'rooms' by yew hedges. Restrained planting and colour scheme - box, bay, ivies, roses, peonies. Designed for privacy. Has featured in 'The Sunday Times' & 'The English Garden'.

✕

NEW 16 LINTON ROAD
Sophie & Nick Bowers. *Off Banbury Rd midway between Oxford city centre & Summertown shops*
Large, walled, S-facing, contemporary town garden. Sub-divided by yew hedges to provide areas for herbaceous planting, lawn, dry areas, vegetables, water features and play areas for children. Superbly designed and created in 2000 with a brief for low maintenance.

✕

9 RAWLINSON ROAD
Oxford. Rani Lall, 01865 559614. *3/4 m N of Oxford Centre. Rawlinson Rd runs between Banbury & Woodstock Rds midway between Oxford City Centre & Summertown shops.* **Visitors also welcome by appt.**

Small town garden with structured disarray of roses. Terrace of stone inlaid with brick and enclosed by Chinese fretwork balustrade, chunky brick and oak pergola covered with roses, wisteria and clematis; potted topiary. Until autumn, garden delightfully replete with aconites, lobelias, phloxes, daisies and meandering clematis. Featured in gardening section Saturday 'Guardian' June 2007.

🚻 ✕ ☎

51 NEW ◆ NUFFIELD PLACE
Huntercombe, Henley-on-Thames RG9 5RX. Nuffield College, Oxford, 01491 641224, www.nuffield-place.com. *Halfway bet Wallingford & Henley-on-Thames, just off A4130. Turn opp Crown Inn.* **Adm £4, chd free. Regular open days house & garden in summer - see website. For NGS: Mons 5 May; 25 Aug (2-5).**
4 acres, laid out during and just after the 1st World War. Mature specimen trees, yew hedges, pergola, pond, herbaceous borders and rockery. Hidden pathways. Plant sale. Display of old garden tools. 5 May only, walk through glorious adjoining bluebell wood.

✕ ✿ ☕

Chunky brick and oak pergola covered with roses, wisteria and clematis . . .

52 OLD CHURCH HOUSE
Priory Road, Wantage OX12 9DD. Dr & Mrs Dick Squires, 01235 762785. *Situated next to Parish Church nr Wantage market square.* Light refreshments & teas at Vale & Downland Centre, Church Street. **Adm £2, chd free. Daily Apr to Oct (10.30-4.30). Visitors also welcome by appt.**
Unusual town garden running down to the Letcombe Brook. Much interest with different levels, follies, water, mature trees and many special plants.

🚻 ✕ ☕ ☎

53 THE OLD RECTORY, COLESHILL
SN6 7PR. Sir George & Lady Martin. *3m SW of Faringdon. Coleshill (NT village) is on B4019.* Home-made teas. **Adm £2, chd free.** Suns 6 Apr; 7 Sept (2-5).
Medium-sized garden; lawns and informal shrub beds; wide variety shrubs, incl old-fashioned roses, 50yr-old standard wisteria. Distant views of Berkshire and Wiltshire Downs. House (not open) dates from late C14.

🚻 ☕

THE OLD RECTORY FARNBOROUGH
See Berkshire.

54 THE OLD VICARAGE, BLEDINGTON
Main Street, Bledington, Chipping Norton OX7 6UX. Sue & Tony Windsor, 01608 658525, tony.windsor@tiscali.co.uk. *6m SW of Chipping Norton. 4m SE of Stow-on-the-Wold. On the main st, B4450, through Bledington. NOT next to church.* **Adm £3, chd free.** Visitors welcome by appt.
1 1/2 -acre garden attached to late Georgian (1843) vicarage (not open). Rose garden with over 350 David Austin roses, borders of hardy perennials, small pond and paddock with shrubs and beds. Garden situated on sloping ground, all accessible but quite hard work.

🚻 ✿ ☎

55 NEW 12 PARK TERRACE
Thame OX9 3HZ. Maggie & Colin Sear. *1/2 m E of Thame centre. From centre of Thame follow signs for Chinnor (B4445). At junction with Postcombe Rd (B4012) Park Terrace is on R (opp Shell garage). Garden at end on R. Coming from centre of Thame park on Station Approach, L off B4012, signposted to Postcombe.* Teas at 18 Willow Rd. **Adm £2.50, chd free. Combined opening with Pots 'n Rocks,18 Willow Road £3.50.** Sun 3 Aug (2-6).
Small quiet oasis at end of cul-de-sac. Husband's fine gravel and grass garden at front. Back garden designed and created by keen plantswoman. Shrubs and plants chosen for foliage and long flowering period to provide interest and variety throughout the year. Attractive water feature.

56 NEW POTS 'N ROCKS
18 Willow Road, Thame
OX9 3BE. Mrs K M Pease. $^1/_4$ m
N of Thame centre. M40 J 7/8.
Signs to Thame. Park in public car
park opp entrance to Waitrose. Up
Lashlake Rd nearly opp Waitrose -
Willow Rd. 2nd on R - down end of
rd on R. Light refreshments & teas.
**Adm £2.50, chd free (share to
Children with Leukaemia).
Combined adm with 12 Park
Terrace £3.50.** Sun 3 Aug (1-5).
Quirky and unique small garden
with an amazing range of plants in
pots and hanging baskets - tender
tropical to bonsai. For children and
keen observers there are
numerous hidden animals and
features to be found and counted
as well as a small 9 hole putting
green. Very child friendly.

Waves of snowdrops through 2 acre Victorian garden . . .

57 RADCOT HOUSE
Clanfield OX18 2SX. Robin & Jeanne
Stainer, 01367 810231,
rstainer@radcothouse. $1^1/_4$ m S of
Clanfield. On A4095 bet Witney &
Faringdon, 200yds N of Radcot bridge.
Adm £4, chd free. Suns 31 Aug; 21
Sept (2-6). Visitors also welcome by
appt.
Started in 2000, with many new
developments over the last two years.
Dramatic planting nearer the house,
shady areas, formal pond, wood, fruit
and vegetable cages. Convenient
seating at key points enables relaxed
observation and reflection. Extensive
use of grasses and unusual perennials.
No plant labels. Featured on BBC
Oxford, 2007. Unfenced ponds.

58 NEW RAMSDEN HOUSE
Akeman Street, Ramsden
OX7 3AX. Laura Sednaoui. Off
B4022 midway Charlbury/Witney.
Middle of Ramsden, adjacent to
church. Home-made teas. **Adm
£3, chd free.** Sun 24 Feb (2-5).

Waves of snowdrops through 2
acre Victorian garden, originally
planted 1862. Many mature trees
and shrubs. Present owner now
restoring Victorian wild garden.
Snowdrop sale.

59 ST HILDA'S COLLEGE
Cowley Place, Oxford OX4 1DY. St
Hilda's College, 01865 276808,
gerri.cane@st-hildas.ox.ac.uk. $^1/_2$ m
E of Oxford/Carfax centre. Approx
15mins walk E of city centre. Cross
Magdalen Bridge & turn R at
roundabout into Cowley Place. College
lodge at end on R, or park in public car
park at St Clements. **Adm £3, chd
free.** Sun 6 Apr (2-6). Visitors also
welcome by appt.
Approx 5 acres laid to lawns with
mature trees and flower beds with
flood plain meadow containing
interesting wild flowers; walk by River
Cherwell. Some gravel paths. No
access to flood plain meadow for
wheelchairs.

60 ST HUGH'S COLLEGE
St Margaret's Road, Oxford
OX2 6LE, 01865 274998. 1m N of city
centre. Corner of St Margaret's Rd &
Banbury Rd. Cream teas. **Adm £3.50,
chd free.** Sun 20 Apr (2.30-5).
Visitors also welcome by appt.
Springtime garden, well planted with a
variety of flowering bulbs, fine trees,
shrub borders and herbaceous
plantings in a 14 acre site with plenty
of interest throughout the yr in a
relaxed and informal setting.

61 SIBFORD GOWER GARDENS
OX15 5RX. 7m W of Banbury. Nr the
Warwickshire border, S of B4035, in
centre of village nr Wykham Arms PH.
Home-made teas at Temple Mill
(garden not open for NGS). **Combined
adm £3, chd free.** Sun 15 June (2-6).
Small village with charming thatched
houses and cottage gardens.   .

BUTTSLADE HOUSE
Temple Mill Road (also known
as Colony Road). Mrs Diana
Thompson
7-yr-old garden designed by
previous owner. Areas of formal
and informal planting. $^1/_3$ of an
acre packed with plants. Roses a
speciality.

CARTER'S YARD
Sue & Malcolm Bannister. Use
entrance up steps next to
Wykham Arms
Newly designed cottage garden,
small vegetable area with
espaliered apples and pears,
exciting new planting round
house.

GOWERS CLOSE
Judith Hitching & John Marshall
Garden writer's cottage garden,
tucked behind a wisteria clad
thatched house (not open). Box
parterre, herb garden, clipped yew
hedges, rose smothered pergola
and bosky borders in purples and
pinks, small kitchen garden.

THE MANOR HOUSE
Temple Mill Road. Michael
Donovan & Alison Jenkins
Combination of well established
garden and charming extensive
patio area provides romantic
setting for rambling thatched
Manor House (not open).

62 SOMERVILLE COLLEGE
Woodstock Road, Oxford OX2 6HD.
Somerville College. $^1/_2$ m E of Carfax
Tower. Enter from the Woodstock Rd,
S of the Radcliffe Infirmary. **Adm
£2.50, chd free (share to Friends of
Oxford Botanic Garden).** Sun 6 July
(2-6).
Approx 2 acres, robust college garden
planted for yr-round interest. Formal
bedding, colour-themed and vibrant
old-fashioned mixed herbaceous
borders.

63 SOUTH NEWINGTON HOUSE
Barford Road, South Newington
OX15 4JW. Mr & Mrs John Ainley,
01295 721207,
rojoainley@btinternet.com. 6m SW
of Banbury. South Newington is
between Banbury and Chipping
Norton, on A361; take lane signed The
Barfords, 200yds on L. Light
refreshments & home-made teas. **Adm
£3, chd free.** Visitors welcome by
appt. Open all yr. Coaches
welcome. No group too small.
C17 yeomans hall house (not open) set
in 5 acres paddocks and garden. A
charming garden, created for yr-round
interest. Tumbling rambling roses,
softly coloured herbaceous borders.
Ponds, organic fruit and vegetables.

Walled garden has been re-designed to place more emphasis on the parterre and box topiary.

64 SPARSHOLT MANOR
nr Wantage OX12 9PT. Sir Adrian & Lady Judith Swire. *3¹/₂ m W of Wantage. Off B4507 Ashbury Rd.* Teas in village hall. **Adm £2, chd free. Mon 26 May (2-6).**
Lakes and wildfowl; ancient boxwood, wilderness and summer borders. Wheelchair access around house and its immediate surroundings.

65 STANSFIELD
49 High Street, Stanford-in-the-Vale SN7 8NQ. Mr & Mrs David Keeble, 01367 710340. *3¹/₂ m SE of Faringdon. Park in street.* Home-made teas. **Adm £3, chd free. Tues 1 Apr; 6 May; 3 June; 1 July; 5 Aug; 2 Sept (10-4). Visitors also welcome by appt.**
1¹/₄ -acre plantsman's garden on alkaline soil. Wide variety of unusual trees, shrubs and hardy plants. Scree, damp and kitchen gardens, copse underplanted with woodlanders as well as flower arrangers' and drought resistant plants. Guided tours if wished.

66 STEEPLE ASTON GARDENS
OX25 4SP. *14m N of Oxford, 9m S of Banbury. ¹/₂ m E of A4260.* Home-made teas in village hall. **Combined adm £4.50, chd free. Sun 18 May (1-6).**
Beautiful stone village bordering Cherwell valley; interesting church and winding lanes with a variety of charming stone houses and cottages. Map available at all gardens. Lunches & Plant Fair at school (11.30-4.30).

ACACIA COTTAGE
Jane & David Stewart. *Southside - limited parking possible*
Approx ¹/₂ -acre garden within high stone walls. Herbaceous border, newly paved area around Edwardian summerhouse and old stone barns. Box edged parterre with white planting in a courtyard setting.

NEW CANTERBURY HOUSE
Peter & Harriet Higgins. *Park at village hall*
Much of this 1 hectare garden has been redesigned and replanted by the garden designer John Hill. It contains a large walled garden, lovely herbaceous borders and a pond. Separate shrub border and large vegetable garden. Gravel paths.

KRALINGEN
Fenway. Mr & Mrs Roderick Nicholson. *Possible to park on Fenway, with care. Large car park at Steeple Aston Village Hall*
2-acre informal garden created over many yrs by present owners. Many varieties of interesting trees and shrubs and mixed borders lead down to the tranquil woodland/water/bog garden, with candelabra primulas, bluebells, golden saxifrage, fernery etc. Slope is hard work for wheelchairs.

THE LONGBYRE
Mr Vaughan Billings. *Park at village hall*
Hornton stone house (not open) in ¹/₄ acre. Garden constructed in old orchard. Water feature, mixed perennials, shrubs, tubs on different levels.

PAYNE'S HILL HOUSE
Paynes Hill. Tim & Caroline Edwards. *Park at village hall*
Established walled garden with intensively planted, colour-themed borders. The large garden then opens out to a lavender bank, and a David Austin modern shrub rose garden. Also some vegetables, informal bog garden, and groups of decorative native trees.

PRIMROSE COTTAGE
North Side. Richard & Daphne Preston. *Parking in North Side is limited, park at village hall*
Former walled kitchen garden of approx 1 acre on southerly elevation. Shrubs, herbaceous borders, ponds, glasshouses and large vegetable plot. Many features designed and constructed by the owners. Garden offering interest throughout the yr.

NEW TOUCHWOOD
No 2 Nizewell Head. Gary Norris. *Heyford Road*
Small cottage garden with ponds on 2 levels. Truly astonishing array of plants and colour crammed into this small space, with view to lovely countryside beyond.

NEW THE WHITE HOUSE
Fir Lane. Mr & Mrs Neil Everett. *Park at village hall*
Professionally landscaped 3 acre garden with pleached lime hedges, semi-mature trees, stunning borders, raised vegetable beds, old orchard and wonderful views to countryside and William Kent's eyecatcher folly.

WICKHAMS
Paynes Hill. Caroline Owen-Lloyd. *Park at village hall*
Partially terraced small cottage garden with mature fruit trees and herbaceous borders. The garden also features vegetable and cut flower patches.

> With candelabra primulas, bluebells, golden saxifrage, fernery etc . . .

67 SWALCLIFFE LEA HOUSE
Swalcliffe Lea OX15 6ET. Jeffrey & Christine Demmar, 01295 788278. *6m W of Banbury. Off the B4035. At Lower Tadmarton, turn (as posted) to Swalcliffe Lea & Shutford. Turn L, single track road. Bear R at fork, 250yds to entrance, take 1st drive on L.* **Adm £2.50, chd free. Visitors welcome by appt.**
Mature terraced garden with densely planted mixed borders; pergola, herb garden, vegetable garden and orchard. Two informal ponds. Stream and small woodland. Range of specimen trees, many varieties of clematis and other herbaceous plants. Some slopes and uneven steps. 2 unfenced ponds.

Delightful old farmhouse garden brimming with old-fashioned roses . . .

68 TADMARTON MANOR
Upper Tadmarton OX15 5TD. Mr & Mrs R K Asser, 01295 780212. *5m SW of Banbury. On B4035.* **Adm £2.50, chd free. Visitors welcome by appt.**
Old-established 2½ -acre garden; beautiful views of unspoilt countryside; great variety of perennial plants and shrubs; tunnel arbour; C15 barn and C18 dovecote. Agapanthus bed (Aug); bank of autumn cyclamen; stilted hornbeam hedge. Wildlife pond. Tree sculptures.
  🚻 ⊕ ☎

69 TRINITY COLLEGE
Oxford OX1 3BH. Dr C R Prior, Garden Master. *Central Oxford. Entrance in Broad St.* Cream teas 9 Mar; Home-made teas 27 July. **Adm £2, chd free, concessions £1.50. Suns 9 Mar; 27 July (2-5).**
Historic main College Gardens with specimen trees incl aged forked catalpa, spring bulbs, fine long herbaceous border and handsome garden quad originally designed by Wren. President's Garden surrounded by high old stone walls, mixed borders of herbaceous, shrubs and statuary. Fellows' Garden: small walled terrace, herbaceous borders; water feature formed by Jacobean stone heraldic beasts. Award-winning lavender garden and walk-through rose arbour.
  🚻 ⊕ ☕

TURWESTON MILL
See Northamptonshire.

VERSIONS FARM
See Northamptonshire.

TYTHROP PARK
See Buckinghamshire.

70 ◆ UNIVERSITY OF OXFORD BOTANIC GARDEN
Rose Lane, Oxford OX1 4AZ. University of Oxford, 01865 286690, www.botanic-garden.ox.ac.uk. *1m S of Oxford city centre. Bottom of High Street in central Oxford, on the banks of the R Cherwell by Magdalen Bridge & opp Magdalen College Tower.* **See website for other opening times.** For NGS: **Evening Opening** £3, chd free, concessions £2.50, Thur 3 July (6-8).
The Botanic Garden contains more species of plants per acre than anywhere else on earth. These plants are grown in 7 glasshouses, water and rock gardens, large herbaceous border, walled garden and every available space. In total there are 6,700 different plants to see. National Collection of Euphorbia. Gravel paths. Wheelchair access to WC.
  🚻 ⊕ NCCPG

71 UPPER CHALFORD FARM
between Sydenham & Postcombe OX39 4NH. Mr & Mrs Paul Rooksby, 01844 351320. *4½ m SE of Thame. M40 J6, then A40. At Postcombe turn R signed Chalford (turn L if on A40 from Oxford direction). After 1 mile on LH-side at 1st telegraph pole. (House is ½ -way Sydenham to Postcombe).* Clotted cream teas. **Adm £3, chd free. Suns 15, 29 June (2-5.30). Visitors also welcome by appt minimum 10. Also evening visits, wine.**
Delightful old farmhouse garden brimming with old-fashioned roses, perennials, shrubs, unusual trees and splendid old pine. Sundial garden, conservatory with plumbagoes and vine. Spring garden overlooking natural pond flowing into stream banked by wild flowers leading to natural woodland reserve. Peaceful places to sit. Paddock with donkeys and chicks. Setting for 'Midsomer Murders' 2007.
  🚻 ⊕ ☕ ☎

72 WADHAM COLLEGE
Oxford OX1 3PN. The Warden & Fellows. *Central Oxford. Parks Road.* **Adm £2.50, chd free (share to Sobell House Hospice). Suns 30 Mar (2-5); 13 July (2-6).**
5 acres, best known for trees, spring bulbs and mixed borders. In Fellows' main garden, fine ginkgo and *Magnolia acuminata*; bamboo plantation; in Back Quadrangle very large *Tilia tomentosa* 'Petiolaris'; in Mallam Court white scented garden est 1994; in

Warden's garden an ancient tulip tree; in Fellows' private garden, Civil War embankment with period fruit tree cultivars, recently established shrubbery with unusual trees and ground cover amongst older plantings.
  🚻

73 ◆ WATERPERRY GARDENS
Wheatley OX33 1JZ. Mrs P Maxwell, Secretary, 01844 339254, www.waterperrygardens.co.uk. *9m E of Oxford. M40 J8 from London (turn off Oxford-Wheatley, first L to Wheatley, follow brown rose symbol). J8a from Birmingham (turn R Oxford-Wheatley over A40, first R Wheatley, follow brown rose symbol. We are 2½ m N of Wheatley.* **Adm £4.95, chd £3.30, concessions Feb £3; other dates £3.95. Adult Feb £3, child £3. Open every day except bet Xmas & New Year. See website for details.** For NGS: Suns 17 Feb (10-4.30); 20 Apr; 21 Sept (10-5).
The gardens at Waterperry are quite simply an inspiration. 8 acres of landscaped gardens include a rose and formal knot garden, water lily canal, riverside walk and one of the finest purely herbaceous borders in the country. There's also a quality plant centre, teashop, art gallery, museum and Saxon church. National Collection of Saxifraga. 17 Feb, Snowdrop Weekend (10-4.30). 21 Sept, Michaelmas Daisy Weekend celebrations (10-4.30). Featured on 'BBC Gardeners' World', Apr 2007, BBC Radio Oxford & ITV Thames Valley, 2007. Access to riverside walk maybe limited if very wet.
  🚻 ⊕ NCCPG ☕

74 WAYSIDE
82 Banbury Road, Kidlington OX5 2BX. Margaret & Alistair Urquhart, 01865 460180. *5m N of Oxford. On the RH-side of A4260 travelling N through Kidlington.* **Adm £2.50, chd free. Sun 18 May (1-6). Visitors also welcome by appt May to July only.**
¼ -acre garden with wide variety of plants and mature trees; mixed borders with hardy geraniums, clematis and bulbs. Conservatory, greenhouse and fern house with tender plants. Woodland garden with unusual species of tree ferns and extensive collection of hardy ferns; drought resistant planting in gravel garden.
🚻 ⊕ ☕ ☎

75 WESTWELL MANOR
nr Burford OX18 4JT. Mr & Mrs
T H Gibson. *2m SW of Burford.
From A40 Burford-Cheltenham, turn L
1/2 m after Burford roundabout on
narrow rd signed Westwell. Unspoilt
hamlet with delightful church.* **Adm
£4, chd free (share to St Mary's
Church, Westwell).** Sun 1 June
(2-6.30).
6 acres surrounding old Cotswold
manor house (not open), knot garden,
potager, shrub roses, herbaceous
borders, topiary, earth works,
moonlight garden, rills and water
garden. Some unprotected water.
Some surfaces slippery in wet weather,
stone and wood.
✄ ✿

76 WHEATLEY GARDENS
Wheatley OX33 1XX. *5m E of Oxford.
Leave A40 at Wheatley, turn into High
St. Gardens at W end of High St.
Cream teas at The Manor House.*
Combined adm £3.50, chd free. Sun
15 June (2-6).
Three adjoining gardens in the historic
coaching village of Wheatley. Access
from the High St, the original Oxford
to London Rd, before it climbs onto
the Shotover plain. Youth music
making.
☕

BREACH HOUSE GARDEN
Liz Parry. *Entrance via The Manor
House*
1-acre garden with coppiced
hazel wood. Main established area
with extensive shrubs and
perennials, also a more
contemporary reflective space
with a wild pond.
✄

THE MANOR HOUSE
High Street, Wheatley. Mr & Mrs
Edward Hess, 01865 875022.
Visitors also welcome by appt.
1 1/2 -acre garden of Elizabethan
manor house (not open). Formal
box walk; herb garden, cottage
garden with rose arches and a
shrubbery with old roses. A
romantic oasis in this busy village.
Some gravel paths, two shallow
steps, assistance given.
♿ ✄ ☎

THE STUDIO
S & A Buckingham. *Access via
The Manor house*
Cottage-style walled garden
developed from previous farm
yard. Herbaceous borders,

climbing roses and clematis,
shrubs, vegetable plot and fruit
trees. Gravel drive & shallow step
between Manor House & Studio.

**WHICHFORD & ASCOTT
GARDENS**
See Warwickshire & part of West
Midlands.

Moonlight
garden, rills
and water
garden . . .

77 WHITEHILL FARM
Widford nr Burford OX18 4DT. Mr &
Mrs Paul Youngson, 01993 823218.
*1m E of Burford. From A40 take turn
signed Widford. Follow signs to
Whitehill Farm Nursery.* Home-made
teas. **Adm £2.50, chd free.** Sun 22
June (2-6). **Visitors also welcome by
appt.**
2 acres of hillside gardens and
woodland with spectacular views
overlooking Burford and Windrush
valley. Informal plantsman's garden
being continuously developed in
various areas. Herbaceous and shrub
borders, pond and bog area, old-
fashioned roses, ground cover,
ornamental grasses, bamboos and
hardy geraniums.
✿ ☕ ☎

WHITEWALLS
See Buckinghamshire.

78 WICK HALL & NURSERIES
Audlett Drive, Radley OX14 3NF. Mr
& Mrs P Drysdale. *2m NE of
Abingdon. Between Abingdon &
Radley on Audlett Drive.* Home-made
teas & cream teas. **Adm £2.50, chd
50p.** Sun 27 Apr (2-5).
Approx 10 acres lawns and wild
garden; topiary; pond garden;
rockeries; walled garden enclosing
knot garden; young arboretum. Early
C18 house (not open), barn and
greenhouses, large display of old
horticultural and agricultural tools.
♿ ✄ ✿ ☕

79 WILDWOOD
Farnborough OX17 1EL. Mr & Mrs M
Hart. *5m N of Banbury, 8m S of
Southam. On A423 at Oxon/Warwicks
border. Next to Farnborough Garden
Centre.* Home-made teas. **Adm £2,
chd free.** Sun 27 Apr (2-6).
Delightful 1/2 -acre garden in the
country set amongst mature trees and
shrubs providing a haven for wildlife.
Garden is stocked with many unusual
plants and shrubs and also contains
interesting rustic garden features,
many of which are made by the owner.
✄ ✿ ☕

80 WILLOW TREE COTTAGE
Chapel Lane, Salford, Chipping
Norton OX7 5YN. Mr & Mrs J
Shapley, 01608 642478,
john.shapley@virgin.net. **Adm £2.50,
chd free.** Visitors welcome by appt
April to Sept incl.
Small walled twin gardens with shrub
and herbaceous borders, many
clematis; one garden created from old
farmyard with large alpine garden.
Small grass beds. Plantsman's garden
with many interesting plants.
♿ ✄ ✿ ☎

81 WOLFSON COLLEGE
Oxford OX2 6UD. President &
Fellows of Wolfson College,
www.wolfson.ox.ac.uk. *3/4 m N of
Oxford city centre. Turn R off Banbury
Rd to end of Linton Rd.* Home-made
teas & light refreshments. **Adm £2.50,
chd free.** Sun 13 Apr (2-6).
A splendid modern garden of 9 acres
by R Cherwell developed in recent yrs
with comprehensive plant collection
tolerant of alkaline soils, grown in
interesting and varied habitats around
a framework of fine mature trees. Plant
sale money to college charity - AMREF.
✿ ☕

82 WOOD CROFT
Boars Hill OX1 5DH. St Cross
College. *2m S of Oxford. From ring rd
follow signs to Wootton & Boars Hill.
From junction at top Hinksey Hill,
house 1st on L.* Light refreshments.
**Adm £2, chd free (share to Royal
Marsden Hospital Charity).** Sat 10
May (2-5).
1 1/2 acres designed and planted by the
late Prof G E Blackman FRS.
Rhododendrons, camellias, azaleas,
many varieties primula in woodland
and surrounding natural pond; fine
trees. Woodlands paths & large
ponds.
✿ ☕

1¹/₂ -acre garden in pretty hidden village . . .

WOODCHIPPINGS
See Northamptonshire.

WOOLLEY PARK
ee Berkshire.

83 WOOLSTONE MILL HOUSE
Woolstone, nr Faringdon SN7 7QL.
Mr & Mrs Anthony Spink, 01367
820219. *7m W of Wantage. 7m S of
Faringdon. Woolstone is a small village
off B4507 below Uffington White Horse
Hill.* Home-made & cream teas. **Adm
£3, chd free. Weds 7 May to 24
Sept; (2-5); Sun 6 July (2-6). Visitors
also welcome by appt.**
1¹/₂ -acre garden in pretty hidden
village. Stream runs through garden.
Large mixed herbaceous and shrub
circular border bounded by yew
hedges. Topiary. Medlars and old-
fashioned roses. Bog garden and new
tree house with spectacular views to
White Horse and Dragon Hill. Kitchen
garden. C18 mill house and barn, not
open.

 **gardens open for charity**

Newly-built Huf house sits in the middle of this woodland haven and around the house find contemporary, innovative planting . . .

Fulvens Hanger, Surrey

SHROPSHIRE

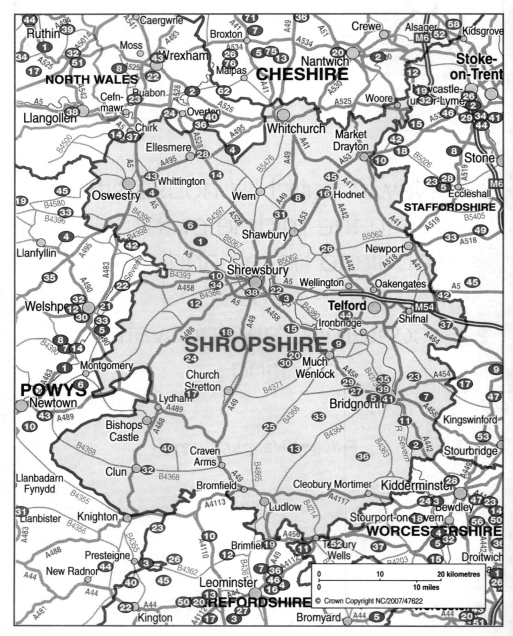

Opening Dates

January

SUNDAY 20
37 Swallow Hayes

February

SUNDAY 10
3 Attingham Park

March

TUESDAY 25
32 Radnor Cottage

SUNDAY 30
30 Preen Manor

April

SUNDAY 20
6 Brownhill House
26 Moortown
39 30 Victoria Road
41 8 Westgate Villas

May

FRIDAY 2
45 Wollerton Old Hall

SUNDAY 4
18 Holly Grove
37 Swallow Hayes

MONDAY 5
25 Millichope Park
28 Oteley

TUESDAY 6
6 Brownhill House

SUNDAY 11
14 Gate Cottage
44 Windy Ridge

FRIDAY 16
31 Preston Hall

SUNDAY 18
1 Adcote School
7 Chyknell
8 The Citadel
16 Hodnet Hall Gardens
23 Lower Hall
24 Marehay Farm

TUESDAY 20
6 Brownhill House

SUNDAY 25
36 Stottesdon Village Gardens
40 Walcot Hall

MONDAY 26
6 Brownhill House (Evening)
36 Stottesdon Village Gardens
40 Walcot Hall

TUESDAY 27
32 Radnor Cottage

THURSDAY 29
30 Preen Manor

June

SUNDAY 1
4 Bluebell Cottage
17 Holly Cottage
22 Longner Hall
34 Shoothill House
35 Stanley Hall

TUESDAY 3
6 Brownhill House

WEDNESDAY 4
12 Edge Villa

FRIDAY 6
10 Cruckfield House

SUNDAY 8
1 Adcote School
2 Applecross House
9 The Cottage
14 Gate Cottage
24 Marehay Farm
27 Morville Hall Gardens

SATURDAY 14
43 Whittington Village Gardens

SUNDAY 15
43 Whittington Village Gardens

TUESDAY 17
32 Radnor Cottage

SUNDAY 22
19 Holmcroft
21 Little Heldre

THURSDAY 26
30 Preen Manor

SUNDAY 29
13 Field House

July

WEDNESDAY 2
42 Weston Park

TUESDAY 8
6 Brownhill House

SUNDAY 13
5 Bridgwalton House
29 Poplar Cottage Farm
44 Windy Ridge

SATURDAY 19
11 Dudmaston Hall Gardens

SUNDAY 20
20 Jessamine Cottage
38 Valducci Flower & Vegetable Gardens

TUESDAY 22
6 Brownhill House
32 Radnor Cottage

THURSDAY 24
30 Preen Manor

August

SUNDAY 3
12 Edge Villa

SUNDAY 10
44 Windy Ridge

SUNDAY 17
21 Little Heldre

SUNDAY 24
20 Jessamine Cottage

September

SUNDAY 7
2 Applecross House
6 Brownhill House
44 Windy Ridge

SATURDAY 13
15 Harnage Farm

SUNDAY 14
34 Shoothill House

October

SUNDAY 5
30 Preen Manor

Gardens open to the public

3 Attingham Park
11 Dudmaston Hall Gardens
20 Jessamine Cottage
42 Weston Park
45 Wollerton Old Hall

By appointment only

33 Ruthall Manor

Also open by appointment ☎

2 Applecross House
5 Bridgwalton House
6 Brownhill House
8 The Citadel
10 Cruckfield House
12 Edge Villa
14 Gate Cottage
17 Holly Cottage
18 Holly Grove
21 Little Heldre
23 Lower Hall
24 Marehay Farm
25 Millichope Park
28 Oteley
30 Preen Manor
31 Preston Hall
32 Radnor Cottage
34 Shoothill House

37 Swallow Hayes
38 Valducci Flower & Vegetable Gardens
40 Walcot Hall
44 Windy Ridge

The Gardens

ABERNANT
See Powys.

1 ADCOTE SCHOOL
Little Ness SY4 2JY. Adcote School Educational Trust Ltd. *8m NW of Shrewsbury. Via A5, turn off NE follow signs to Little Ness.* Home-made teas. **Adm £4, chd free. Suns 18 May; 8 June (2-5).**
26 acres; fine trees incl beeches, tulip trees, oaks (American and evergreen), atlas cedars, wellingtonia etc. Rhododendrons, azaleas; landscaped garden. House (part shown) designed by Norman Shaw RA; Grade I listed building. School Fête 8 June. Gravel paths, some slopes.

2 NEW APPLECROSS HOUSE
Alveley WV15 6NB. Mary & Colin Wells, 01746 780313, mary@marywells.com. *6m S of Bridgnorth. Alveley off A442 Bridgnorth & Kidderminster rds. N from Kidderminster, turn L just after the Royal Oak PH. S from Bridgnorth, turn R after the Squirrel PH. At T-junction in front of post office turn R and follow NGS signs.* Home-made teas. **Adm £3, chd free. Suns 8 June; 7 Sept (1-5). Visitors also welcome by appt June/July only, groups of 10+, small coaches.**
2 acre garden spilt into several small areas, developed from paddocks since 1995. Features incl ponds, pergolas, vegetable garden, orchard, dovecote and collection of contemporay sculpture. Large range of trees, shrubs and herbaceous plants. Overlooks Severn Valley with view of Clee Hills. Footpath access to Severn Valley Country Park (½ m). Some gravel paths.

3 ◆ ATTINGHAM PARK
Shrewsbury SY4 4TP. The National Trust, 01743 708162, attingham@nationaltrust.org.uk. *4m SE of Shrewsbury. From M54 follow A5 to Shrewsbury then B4380 to Atcham.* **Gardens only adm £4.20, chd £2.20. For times & dates of opening, please email or tel. For NGS: Sun 10 Feb (9-4).**
Attingham Park (house not open) is a landscape park designed by Humphry Repton. There are attractive walks through the grounds and along the river which is lined with swathes of snowdrops from late January. There are also extensive walks through the woodland and deer park. Mobility buggys and wheelchairs available to loan free of charge.

BIRCH TREES
See Staffordshire & part of West Midlands.

4 BLUEBELL COTTAGE
Aston. SY11 4JH. Rob & Deborah Lewis. *1m E of Oswestry. Off A5. Signed Mile End Golf course.* Home-made teas. **Adm £3, chd free. Sun 1 June (2-5.30).**
1½ acres of lawns, specimen trees, ponds and various water features. Elevated gazebo with views of Breidden Hills. Recently created stream with oriental theme. Small bluebell wood and kitchen garden. Several seating areas to relax and enjoy the garden. New for 2008 ornamental dovecote. Unusual nearby village church also open. Some gravel paths.

BODYNFOEL HALL
See Powys.

5 NEW BRIDGWALTON HOUSE
Telegraph Lane, Morville WV16 5NP. Mary Bower, 01746 714401. *1m from Bridgnorth. Off A458 Shrewsbury to Bridgnorth, nr Morville. Signed on the day.* Home-made teas. **Adm £3.50, chd free. Sun 13 July (2-6). Also open Poplar Cottage Farm. Visitors also welcome by appt, coaches permitted.**
1¼ acres plantsmans award winning garden with many unusual trees and shrubs. Collections of daphnes and peonies with oriental design at the garden. Wonderful views.

1 THE BRODDER
See Staffordshire & part of West Midlands.

6 BROWNHILL HOUSE
Ruyton XI Towns SY4 1LR. Roger & Yoland Brown, 01939 261121, brownhill@eleventowns.co.uk, www.eleventowns.co.uk. *10m NW of Shrewsbury. On B4397. Park at Bridge Inn.* Home-made teas. **Adm £3, chd free. Suns 20 Apr; 7 Sept; Tues 6, 20 May; 3 June; 8, 22 July; (1.30-5). Evening Opening Mon 26 May (6.30-8.30). Visitors also welcome by appt May to Aug.**
Unusual and distinctive hillside garden (over 600 steps) bordering R Perry. Great variety of plants and styles from laburnum walk and formal terraces to woodland paths, plus large kitchen garden. Over 100 varieties of plants for sale, proceeds to NGS. Featured on Central Tonight TV.

CASTELL Y GWYNT
See Powys.

CHURCH TERRACE
See Powys.

7 CHYKNELL
Bridgnorth WV15 5PP. Mr & Mrs W S R Kenyon-Slaney. *5m E of Bridgnorth. Between Claverley & Worfield. Signed off A454 Wolverhampton to Bridgnorth & A458 Stourbridge to Bridgnorth.* Teas. **Adm £3, chd free. Sun 18 May (2-6).**
5 acres of magnolias, rhododendrons, azaleas, roses and herbaceous plants; interesting shrubs and fine trees in tranquil park setting. Formal structure of hedged compartments designed by Russell Page in 1951. Hungry light soil susceptible to drought.

CIL Y WENNOL
See Powys.

8 THE CITADEL
Weston-under-Redcastle SY4 5JY. Mr Beverley & Mrs Sylvia Griffiths, 01630 685204, griffiths@thecitadelweston.co.uk, www.thecitadelweston.co.uk. *12m N of Shrewsbury. On A49. At Xrds turn R for Hawkstone Park, through village of Weston-under-Redcastle, ¼ m on R beyond village.* Home-made teas. **Adm £3, chd free. Sun 18 May (2-5). Visitors also welcome by appt, May only, coaches permitted.**
Imposing castellated house (not open) stands in 4 acres. Mature garden, with fine trees, rhododendrons, azaleas, acers and camellias. Herbaceous borders; walled potager and Victorian

thatched summerhouse provide added interest. Paths meander around and over sandstone outcrop at centre. Featured in 'Shropshire Magazine', Highly commended in Shropshire Star Garden of the Year competiton.

  ♿ ✕ ⊛ 🛏 ☕ ☎

9 THE COTTAGE
2 Farley Dingle, Much Wenlock TF13 6NX. Mr & Mrs P D Wight. *2m E of Much Wenlock. On A4169 Much Wenlock to Telford rd. At the end of the dead end lane, opp the road signed Wyke. Parking is limited.* Home-made teas. **Adm £3. Sun 8 June (11-5).**
Cottage garden of 2 acres, set at the end of a small valley, enclosed by woodland. Natural stream surrounded by hostas, ferns, shrubs and perennials, meanders through the garden. The sides of the valley have been terraced to create an amphitheatre. Steps, bridges and paths abound. Children under 16yrs must be supervised. Featured in & on 'Shropshire Life', BBC Gardeners World.

✕ ⊛ ☕

10 CRUCKFIELD HOUSE
Ford SY5 9NR. Mr & Mrs G M Cobley, 01743 850222. *5m W of Shrewsbury. A458, turn L towards Shoothill.* Home-made teas. **Adm £4.50, chd £1. Fri 6 June (2-6). Visitors also welcome by appt June & July only, groups of 25 +.**
4-acre romantic S-facing garden, formally designed, informally and intensively planted with substantial variety of unusual herbaceous plants. Nick's garden, with many species trees and shrubs, surrounds a large pond with bog and moisture-loving plants. Ornamental kitchen garden with pretty outbuildings. Rose and peony walk. Courtyard fountain garden and an extensive shrubbery. Extensive clematis collection. Large rockery and lily pond.

✕ ⊛ ☕ ☎

CWM-WEEG
See Powys.

CYFIE FARM
See Powys.

DINGLE NURSERIES & GARDEN
See Powys.

11 ♦ DUDMASTON HALL GARDENS
Quatt, nr Bridgnorth WV15 6QN. The National Trust, 01746 780866, dudmaston@nationaltrust.org.uk.

4m SE of Bridgnorth. On A442, between Bridgnorth & Kidderminster. **Garden only adm £3, chd £1. Sun to Wed 1 Apr to 30 Sept. For NGS: Sat 19 July (12-6).**
9 acres with a good mixture of herbaceous borders incl large border in front of the Brew House with a beautiful back drop of 2 mature wisterias. The Lady Labouchere rose border looks and smells fantastic, rockery with lavender, erigeron and caryopteris. Wide range of large and small trees incl *Cornus kousa*. Access to flat terraced areas of garden. Other areas incl steep slopes or gravel.

  ♿ ✕ ⊛ ☕

12 EDGE VILLA
Edge, nr Yockleton SY5 9PY. Mr & Mrs W F Neil, 01743 821651, bill@billfneil.fsnet.co.uk. *6m from Shrewsbury. From A5 take either A488 signed to Bishops Castle or B4386 to Montgomery for approx 6m then follow NGS signs.* Light refreshments (June), Home-made teas (Aug). **Adm £3, chd free. Wed 4 June (10-1); Sun 3 Aug (2-5.30). Visitors also welcome by appt, groups of 10+, small coaches only.**
2 acres of newly planted garden with outstanding views of S Shropshire hills. Herbaceous borders, self-sufficent organic vegetable plot. New orchard with chickens, foxes permitting. June opening mainly plant sale. Gravel paths and grass slopes.

  ♿ ✕ ⊛ ☕ ☎

13 FIELD HOUSE
Clee St Margaret SY7 9DT. Dr & Mrs John Bell. *8m NE of Ludlow. Turning to Stoke St Milborough & Clee St Margaret, 5m from Ludlow, 10m from Bridgnorth along B4364. Through Stoke St Milborough to Clee St Margaret. Ignore R turn to Clee Village. Field House on L.* Home-made teas. **Adm £3, chd free. Sun 29 June (2-6).**
1-acre garden created since 1982 for yr-round interest. Mixed borders; rose walk; pool garden; herbaceous borders. Donkeys, sheep and ducks.

  ♿ ✕ ⊛ ☕

14 GATE COTTAGE
Cockshutt SY12 0JU. G W Nicholson & Kevin Gunnell, 01939 270606. *10m N of Shrewsbury. On A528. At Cockshutt take rd signed English Frankton. Garden 1m on R. Parking in adjacent field.* **Adm £2.50, chd 50p. Suns 11 May; 8 June (1-5). Visitors also welcome by appt.**

2 acres of informal mixed plantings of trees, shrubs, herbaceous plants of interest to flower arrangers and plantsmen. Pool, rock garden and informal pools. Large collection of hostas; old orchard with roses, incl items of unusual growth or colour. New plantings of meconopsis and arum lilies.

⊛ ☕ ☎

GLANSEVERN HALL GARDENS
See Powys.

15 HARNAGE FARM
Cound SY5 6EJ. Mr & Mrs Ken Cooke. *8m SE of Shrewsbury. On A458. Turn to Cound 1m S of Cross Houses. Harnage Farm 1m, bearing L past church.* Home-made teas. **Adm £3, chd free. Sat 13 Sept (12-5).**
1/2 -acre farmhouse garden; stocked with herbaceous plants, shrubs and climbers. Extensive views over beautiful Severn Valley. 15 min woodland walk through fields to conservation wood and Ian's wildlife pool.

  ♿ ✕ ☕

Self-sufficent organic vegetable plot . . .

HEATH HOUSE
See Staffordshire & part of West Midlands.

16 HODNET HALL GARDENS
nr Market Drayton TF9 3NN. Mr & The Hon Mrs Heber-Percy, 01630 685786 (Secretary), www.hodnethallgardens.org *5 1/2 m SW of Market Drayton. 12m NE Shrewsbury. At junction of A53 & A442.* Light refreshments & teas. **Adm £4, chd £2. Sun 18 May (12-5).**
60-acre landscaped garden with series of lakes and pools; magnificent forest trees, great variety of flowers, shrubs providing colour throughout season. Unique collection of big-game trophies in C17 tearooms. Kitchen garden. For details please see website. Partial wheelchair access, gravel and grass paths.

  ♿ ☕

17 NEW HOLLY COTTAGE
Prolley Moor, Wentnor SY9 5EH.
Julian French & Heather
Williams, 01588 650610. *7m NE*
of Bishop's Castle. From A489
take rd signed Wentnor. In Wentnor
pass The Crown on R. Take next R
signed Prolley Moor, then 1st L,
signed Adstone. Home-made teas.
Adm £3, chd free. Sun 1 June
(2-6). Visitors also welcome by
appt May to Sept. Minibus or
cars only. No coaches.
Organic garden of 2½ acres set in
beautiful countryside under the
Long Mynd. Areas incl 1 acre of
5yr old native woodland, wild
flower meadow with willow circle
and allotment area. Nearer the
house the flower garden is stocked
with herbaceous plants, trees and
shrubs with pond, trellis and old
orchard. Photograph in the 'South
Shropshire Journal'. Gravel and
grass paths.
  ♿ ❀ ☕

18 HOLLY GROVE
Church Pulverbatch SY5 8DD. Peter
& Angela Unsworth, 01743 718221.
6m S of Shrewsbury. Midway between
Stapleton & Church Pulverbatch. From
A49 follow signs to Stapleton &
Pulverbatch. Home-made teas. **Adm**
£3, chd free. Sun 4 May (2-6).
Visitors also welcome by appt.
3-acre garden set in S Shropshire
countryside. Yew and beech hedges
enclosing 'rooms', box parterres,
pleached limes, vegetable garden, rose
and herbaceous borders containing
many rare plants. New arboretum, lake
and wild flower meadows. Opportunity
to see rare White Park cattle and Soay
sheep.
♿ ❀ ❀ ☕ ☎

19 HOLMCROFT
Wyson Lane, Brimfield, nr Ludlow
SY8 4NW. Mr & Mrs Michael
Dowding,
www.anenglishcottageonline.com.
4m S of Ludlow. 6m N of Leominster.
From Ludlow or Leominster leave A49
at Brimfield sign. From Tenbury Wells
turn L when A456 meets A49, then 1st
L into Brimfield. Home-made teas.
Adm £3, chd free. Sun 22 June
(2-5.30).
¾ acre with C17 thatched cottage set
amongst a series of terraced gardens.
Herb 'partier', sunken garden,
camomile bank, gravel garden and
willow tunnel leading to long borders of
mixed planting. Kitchen garden,

woodland walk and orchard with
spectacular views. Semi finalist
'Shropshire Star' Gardener of the Year.
Garden on slope but paths allow
wheelchair access to most areas.
Hand rail added to woodland walk.
♿ ❀ ❀ ☕

Organic garden set in beautiful countryside under the Long Mynd . . .

20 ♦ JESSAMINE COTTAGE
Kenley SY5 6NS. Lee & Pamela
Wheeler, 01694 771279,
www.stmem.com/jessamine-
cottage. *6m W of Much Wenlock.*
Signed from B4371 Much Wenlock to
Church Stretton rd and from A458
Shrewsbury to Much Wenlock rd at
Harley. **Adm £3, chd £1. Weds to**
Suns & Bank Hols, 1 May - 31 Aug.
For NGS: Suns 20 July; 24 Aug (2-6).
3-acre garden. Mature wildlife pond;
large wild flower meadow; mixed island
beds; lime avenue; large kitchen
garden; parterre; stream and
woodland. Rose garden and
ornamental trees, large range of
attractive perennials and shrubs
provide all season colour.
♿ ❀ ❀ ☕

21 LITTLE HELDRE
Buttington SY21 8TF. Peter & Gillian
Stedman, 01938 570457,
p.stedman317@btinternet.com. *12m*
W of Shrewsbury. Off A458. From
Welshpool take A458 Shrewsbury rd
for 3m, turn R into Heldre Lane. From
Shrewsbury turn L past Little Chef at
Trewern into Sale Lane, follow signs.
Home-made teas. **Adm £2.50, chd**
free. Suns 22 June; 17 Aug (2-5.30).
Visitors also welcome by appt, not
suitable for coaches.
1¾ -acre garden on steep N-facing
slope. Terracing; lawns; shrubs;
herbaceous borders; pond; gunnera;
wooded dingle circular walk. Moon
gate giving extensive views to Berwyn
Mountains.
❀ ☕ ☎

22 LONGNER HALL
Atcham, Shrewsbury SY4 4TG. Mr &
Mrs R L Burton. *4m SE of*
Shrewsbury. From M54 follow A5 to
Shrewsbury, then B4380 to Atcham.

From Atcham take Uffington rd,
entrance ¼ m on L. Home-made teas.
Adm £4, chd free. Sun 1 June (2-5).
A long drive approach through
parkland designed by Humphry
Repton. Walks lined with golden yew
through extensive lawns, with views
over Severn Valley. Borders containing
roses, herbaceous and shrubs, also
ancient yew wood. Enclosed walled
garden containing mixed planting,
garden buildings, tower and game
larder. Short woodland walk around old
moat pond. Some gravel paths,
woodland walk not suitable for
wheelchairs.
♿ ❀ ☕

23 LOWER HALL
Worfield WV15 5LH. Mr & Mrs C F
Dumbell, 01746 716607. *3½ m E of*
Bridgnorth. ½ m N of A454 in village
centre. Home-made teas. **Adm £3.50,**
chd free. Sun 18 May (2-6). Visitors
also welcome by appt, during
weekdays, groups 20+, coaches
permitted.
4 acres on R Worfe. Garden developed
by present owners. Courtyard with
fountain, walled garden with old-
fashioned roses, clematis and mixed
borders. Water garden with pool,
primula island and rock garden.
Woodland garden with rare trees incl
magnolias, paper bark and Japanese
maples. Courtyard garden with gravel,
bridges to woodland garden have
slight slopes.
♿ ☕ ☎

MAESFRON HALL AND
GARDENS
See Powys.

24 MAREHAY FARM
Gatten, Ratlinghope SY5 0SJ. Stuart
& Carol Buxton, 01588 650289. *6½*
m W of Church Stretton. 6m S of
Pontesbury, 9m NNE of Bishops
Castle. 1½ m from 'The Bridges' Xrds
& the intersection of the Longden,
Pulverbatch & Bishops Castle rd and
the minor rd from Church Stretton to
the Stiperstones. Home-made teas.
Adm £2.50, chd free. Suns 18 May;
8 June (11-6). Visitors also welcome
by appt, mid May to mid July.
In 1982 a building society surveyor
reported there is no garden and at this
height (1100ft). elevation and aspect
there never will be. Since 1900 on
heavy boulder clay a 1½ acre
woodland/water garden evolved, with
primulas, hostas, iris, damp/shade
tolerant perennials. Rhododendrons,
azaleas, various conifers, trees, roses

and shrubs complementing the location. Third prize in Shropshire Star garden competition. Wheelchairs with assistance, some gravel.

 ♿ ⛶ 🛌 ☕ ☎

MILL COTTAGE
See Powys.

㉕ MILLICHOPE PARK
Munslow SY7 9HA. Mr & Mrs L Bury, 01584 841234, sarah@millichope.com. *8m NE of Craven Arms. From Ludlow (11m) turn L off B4368, 3/4 m out of Munslow.* Home-made teas. **Adm £4, chd free. Mon 5 May (2-6). Visitors also welcome by appt, week days only.** 13-acre garden with lakes, woodland walks, fine specimen trees, wild flowers and herbaceous borders, good autumn colour.

⚘ ☕ ☎

㉖ MOORTOWN
nr Wellington TF6 6JE. Mr David Bromley. *8m N of Telford. 5m N of Wellington. Take B5062 signed Moortown 1m between High Ercall & Crudgington.* **Adm £4, chd £1.60. Sun 20 Apr (2-5.30).** Approx 1-acre plantsman's garden. Here may be found the old-fashioned, the unusual and even the oddities of plant life, in mixed borders of 'controlled' confusion.

♿ ⚘ ☕

㉗ MORVILLE HALL GARDENS
nr Bridgnorth WV16 5NB. *3m W of Bridgnorth. On A458 at junction with B4368.* Home-made teas at Morville Hall. **Combined adm £5, chd £1 (share to Morville Church). Sun 8 June (2-5).** A varied and interesting group of gardens that immediately surround a beautiful Grade 1 listed mansion (house not open).

☕

THE COTTAGE
Mr & Mrs Begg
Pretty walled cottage garden with good climbers, informal vegetable area with soft fruit bushes. Good lawn and small fish pond with kettle feature.

THE DOWER HOUSE
Dr Katherine Swift
1 1/2 -acre sequence of gardens in various historical styles designed to tell the history of British gardening from medieval times to the present, incl turf maze, cloister

garden, Elizabethan knot garden, Edwardian fruit and vegetable garden, C18 canal garden, wild garden.

♿ ⚘

1 THE GATEHOUSE
Mr & Mrs Rowe
1/2 -acre walled garden comprising, formal and woodland areas with colour-filled herbaceous borders.

2 THE GATEHOUSE
Mrs G Medland
A garden in transition. Cottage garden with colourful borders.

MORVILLE HALL
Dr & Mrs J C Douglas & The National Trust
4-acre garden in fine setting, incl box parterre, mature shrub borders, pond garden, medieval stewpond and a small award-winning vineyard.

SOUTH PAVILION
Mr & Mrs B Jenkinson
Walled courtyard garden with a collection of hebes, cistus and roses, incl wall covering R.banksiae Lutea.

♿

> Here may be found the old-fashioned, the unusual and even the oddities of plant life . . .

㉘ OTELEY
Ellesmere SY12 0PB. Mr & Mrs R K Mainwaring, 01691 622514. *1m SE of Ellesmere. Entrance out of Ellesmere past Mere, opp Convent nr to A528/495 junction.* **Adm £3, chd free. Mon 5 May (2-6). Visitors also welcome by appt, May/June only, groups of 10+, coaches permitted.** 10 acres running down to Mere, incl walled kitchen garden; architectural features; many interesting trees, rhododendrons and azaleas; views across Mere to Ellesmere Church. Wheelchairs only if dry. Some steep slopes and some gravel which can be avoided.

♿ ⚘ ☕ ☎

㉙ POPLAR COTTAGE FARM
Morville, nr Bridgnorth WV16 4RS. Elizabeth & Barry Bacon. *3/4 m NW of Morville. On A458.* Teas available at Bridgwalton House. **Adm £2.50, chd free (share to Morville Church Building Trust). Sun 13 July (2-6). Also open Bridgewalton House.** 1/3 -acre flower arranger's garden with yr-round interest. Different soil textures and micro-climate allow for varied planting in a series of exciting 'rooms' - many unusual plants. Recently restored gipsy caravan to view.

♿

POWIS CASTLE GARDEN
See Powys.

㉚ PREEN MANOR
Church Preen SY6 7LQ. Mrs Ann Trevor-Jones, 01694 771207. *6m W of Much Wenlock. Signed from B4371.* Home-made teas. **Adm £3.50, chd 50p 5-16yrs. Suns 30 Mar; 5 Oct (2-5); Thurs 29 May 26 June; 24 July (2-6). Visitors also welcome by appt, June & July only, groups of 10+.** 6-acre garden on site of Cluniac monastery and Norman Shaw mansion. Kitchen, chess, water and wild gardens. Fine trees in park; woodland walks. Developed over last 25yrs with changes always in progress. Produce stall (Mar, Oct), Harvest Thanksgiving in church adjacent to garden 4.30 (Oct).

♿ ⚘ ☕ ☎

㉛ PRESTON HALL
Preston Brockhurst SY4 5QA. C C & L Corbet, 01939 220312, corbetleil@btinternet.com. *8m N of Shrewsbury. On A49.* Cream teas. **Adm £3, chd free. Fri 16 May (2.30-6). Visitors also welcome by appt, small groups, coaches permitted.** Garden around stone Cromwellian house (not open). Interesting perennials, tulips, trees and shrubs. Good walk around meadow, woodland walk, cutting garden and courtyard garden. Featured in Shropshire Star. Grass paths.

♿ ⚘ ☕ ☎

㉜ RADNOR COTTAGE
Clun SY7 0JA. Pam & David Pittwood, 01588 640451. *7m W of Craven Arms. 1m E of Clun on B4368.* Home-made teas. **Adm £2.50, chd free (share to Clun Methodist Church). Tues 25 Mar; 27 May; 17 June; 22 July (2-6). Visitors also welcome by appt April - July.** 2 acres on S-facing slope, overlooking

Clun Valley. Wide variety of garden habitats all densely planted. Incl sunny terracing with paving and dry-stone walling; alpine troughs; cottage garden borders; damp shade for white flowers and gold foliage; pond, stream and bog garden; orchard; rough grass with naturalised bulbs and wild flowers.

✖ ✿ ☕ ☎

THE ROCK HOUSE
Llanbister. See Powys.

ROSE COTTAGE
See Powys.

ROWAN
See Powys.

33 RUTHALL MANOR
Ditton Priors WV16 6TN. Mr & Mrs G T Clarke, 01746 712608. *7m SW of Bridgnorth. Ruthall Rd signed nr garage.* **Adm £2.50, chd free. Visitors welcome by appt, May to Sept - any number.**
1-acre garden with ha-ha and old horse pond planted with water and bog plants. Rare specimen trees. Designed for easy maintenance with lots of ground cover and unusual plants. New gravel art garden and dryer climate adaptions. Dogs on leads. Featured in Shropshire Gardens Revisited.

♿ ✖ ☎

34 SHOOTHILL HOUSE
Ford, Shrewsbury SY5 9NR. Colin & Jane Lloyd, 01743 850795. *5m W of Shrewsbury. From A458 turn L towards Shoothill (signed).* Home-made teas. **Adm £3, chd 50p. Suns 1 June; 14 Sept (2-5.30). Visitors also welcome by appt, mid May - early June, groups 20+.**
6-acre garden, incorporating small wood with pond, wild flower meadows, childrens' garden and several lawned areas surrounded by mixed borders. Large well maintained Victorian greenhouse in newly renovated walled kitchen garden. Mature wildlife pond surrounded by species trees and shrubs with extensive views over Welsh hills. Sculpture trail (June).

✖ ✿ ☕ ☎

42 SMITHY COTTAGE
See Staffordshire & part of West Midlands.

35 STANLEY HALL
Bridgnorth WV16 4SP. Mr & Mrs M J Thompson. *½ m N of Bridgnorth. Leave by N gate; B4373; turn R at*

Stanley Lane. Home-made teas. **Adm £3, chd 50p. Sun 1 June (2-6).**
Drive ½ m with rhododendrons, azaleas, fine trees and chain of pools.

♿ ☕

36 STOTTESDON VILLAGE GARDENS
DY14 8UE. Stottesdon Garden Committee, 01746 718405 or 718543. *Between Bridgnorth & Cleobury Mortimer. Signed from A4117, B4363 & B4364. Please park in the designated car parks. Coaches welcome by arrangement. Dogs must be on leads. Tickets available from car parks. Midwinters (1st garden from Bridgnorth direction) & Station Rd (1st garden from Ludlow direction).* **Adm £3.50, chd free. Sun 25, Mon 26 May (1-6).**
12 gardens set in the beautiful Shropshire countryside. All but one garden has wheelchair access.

♿ ✿ ☕

Packed with spring bulbs and flowers. Emerging perennials show the promise of summer . . .

37 SWALLOW HAYES
Rectory Road, Albrighton WV7 3EP. Mrs P Edwards, 01902 372624, patedwards570@hotmail.com. *7m NW of Wolverhampton. M54 exit 3. Rectory Rd to R, 1m towards Wolverhampton off A41 just past Wyevale Garden Centre.* Soup (Jan). **Adm £3, chd free. Suns 20 Jan (10-dusk); 4 May (2-5.30). Visitors also welcome by appt, all year, coaches permitted.**
2 acres planted since 1968 with emphasis on all-yr interest and ease of maintenance. National Collections of *Hamamelis* and Russell lupins. Nearly 3000 different plants, most labelled. Children's trail; hardy geraniums, trees, shrubs, herbaceous ferns, groundcover and bulbs. Some gravel paths.

♿ ✿ NCCPG ☕ ☎

TAN-Y-LLYN
See Powys.

38 VALDUCCI FLOWER & VEGETABLE GARDENS
Vicarage Road Site, Meole Brace SY3 0NR. Luigi Valducci, 07921 368968, valbros@btconnect.com. *2m W of Shrewsbury. Meole Brace Garden & Allotment Club. On A5 exit at Dobbies roundabout, direction Shrewsbury. Follow sign for Nuffield Hospital, opp hospital Stanley Lane, follow Stanley Lane until you reach Vicarage Rd. Car park on R, garden on L.* Light refreshments & teas. **Adm £3, chd free. Sun 20 July (12-5). Visitors also welcome by appt.**
1200 sq yds of gardens and allotments containing 4 greenhouses, orchard and site of Valducci National Collection of *Brugmansias* (Angel's Trumpets) with over 80 varieties. An Italian style of gardening focusing on vegetables and flowers with a European feel.

♿ ✖ ✿ NCCPG ☕

39 NEW 30 VICTORIA ROAD
Bridgnorth WV16 4LF. Mr & Mrs Parker. *A458 Bridgnorth bypass, take rd into Bridgnorth at Ludlow Rd roundabout signed town centre. At T-junction (pay & display parking B/N council offices) turn R garden on L. 8 Westgate Villas 100yds on L past Victoria Rd.* Teas at 8 Westgate Villas. **Combined with 8 Westgate Villas adm £4, chd free. Sun 20 Apr (2-5.30).**
1930's town garden facing SW. Walled formal area, lawn with herbaceous borders, quiet sitting area, pond, summerhouse and large patio with containers and hanging baskets. Packed with spring bulbs and flowers. Emerging perennials show the promise of summer. In attractive market town on R Severn with cliff railway between High and Low Town. Severn Valley steam railway and Thomas Telford church. Limited wheelchair access.

♿ ✖ ✿ ☕

40 WALCOT HALL
Lydbury North SY7 8AZ. Mr & Mrs C R W Parish, 01588 680570, helen@walcothall.co.uk, www.walcothall.co.uk. *4m SE of Bishop's Castle. B4385 Craven Arms to Bishop's Castle, turn L by Powis Arms, in Lydbury North.* Home-made teas. **Adm £3.50, chd free. Sun 25, Mon 26 May (1.30-5.30). Visitors also welcome by appt for groups of 10+, throughout the year.**
Arboretum planted by Lord Clive of

India's son. Cascades of rhododendrons, azaleas amongst specimen trees and pools. Fine views of Sir William Chambers' Clock Towers, with lake and hills beyond. Walled kitchen garden; dovecote; meat safe; ice house and mile-long lakes. Outstanding ballroom where excellent teas are served. Russian wooden church, Grotto and Fountain under construction; tin chapel. Beautiful borders and rare shrubs.

THE WERN
See Powys.

41 NEW 8 WESTGATE VILLAS
Salop Street, Bridgnorth WV16 4QX. Bill & Marilyn Hammerton. *From A458 Bridgnorth bypass, take rd into Bridgnorth at Ludlow Rd roundabout signed town centre. At T-junction (pay & display parking at B/N council offices here) turn R garden 100 yds on L just pass entrance to Victoria Rd.* Home-made teas. **Combined with 30 Victoria Way adm £4, chd free. Sun 20 Apr (2-5.30).**
Town garden having formal Victorian front garden with box hedging and water feature to compliment house. Back garden has shade border, lawn, small knot garden and orchard together with a strong oriental influence, incl Japanese style teahouse and zen garden. Bridgnorth is an attractive market town on the R Severn with cliff railway between high and low town, Severn Valley steam railway and Thomas Telford Church.

WESTLAKE FISHERIES
See Powys.

42 ◆ WESTON PARK
Weston-under-Lizard, Shifnal TF11 8LE. The Weston Park Foundation, 01952 852100, enquiries@weston-park.com. *6m E of Telford. Situated on A5 at Weston-under-Lizard. J12 M6 & J3 M54.* **House and Garden adm £7, chd £5, concessions £6, Garden only adm £4, chd £2.50, concessions £3.50. For opening dates & times please tel or email.For NGS: Wed 2 July (11-5).** Capability Brown landscaped gardens and parkland. Formal gardens restored to original C19 design, rose garden and long border together with colourful adjacent Broderie garden. New yew hedge maze and orchard in the walled garden. Head Gardener Finalist of Horticultral Week award, Professional Gardener of the Year.

WESTWINDS
See Powys.

43 ◆ WHITTINGTON VILLAGE GARDENS
nr Oswestry SY11 4EA. *2½ m NE of Oswestry. Daisy Lane & Top St, Whittington. Turn off B5009 150yds NW of church into Top St. Car parking at Whittington Castle (charge) & Top St.* Home-made teas at Greystones, Daisy Lane. **Adm £3, chd free. Sat 14, Sun 15 June (1-5).**
Opening off Daisy Lane, adjacent gardens. Cottage, featuring pots brimful of colour, an old garden being remodelled, flower arranger's designer plot. Modern family garden for leisure bordered by plant packed beds. On larger plots, kitchen gardens, mature trees and shrubs in woodland. Ponds and environmentally friendly wild flower areas. The gardens are sited close to a moated castle, built by the Normans as a welsh border fortification and recently benefitting from a lottery grant facelift.

44 WINDY RIDGE
Church Lane, Little Wenlock, Telford TF6 5BB. George & Fiona Chancellor, 01952 507675, fionachancellor@btinternet.com, www.gardenschool.co.uk. *2m S of Wellington. Follow signs for Little Wenlock from the north (junction7, M54) or east (off A5223 at Horsehay). Park at 'The Huntsman' PH in centre of village.* Home-made teas. **Adm £3.50, chd free.Suns 11 May; 13 July; 10 Aug; 7 Sept (12-5). Visitors also welcome by appt anytime, coaches permitted.**
Award-winning ⅔-acre village garden highly praised by Roy Lancaster with a strong design and exuberant planting. Surprising features, winding paths to explore and quiet corners to linger in, to appeal to all generations. 1000 species of plants (mostly labelled) with plant list available. Featured in 'Shropshire Magazine', 'Country and Border Life'. Gravel paths.

45 ◆ WOLLERTON OLD HALL
Wollerton TF9 3NA. Mr & Mrs J D Jenkins, 01630 685760, www.wollertonoldhallgarden.com. *4m SW of Market Drayton. On A53 between Hodnet & A53-A41 junction. Follow brown signs.* **Adm £5, chd £1. Fris, Suns, Good Friday to Sept. For NGS: Fri 2 May (12-5).**
4-acre garden created around C16 house (not open). Formal structure creates variety of gardens each with own colour theme and character. Planting is mainly of perennials, the large range of which results in significant collections of salvias, clematis, crocosmias and roses. Lunches provided. Featured in various publications.

WOODHILL
See Powys.

Shropshire County Volunteers

County Organiser
Chris Neil, Edge Villa, Edge, Yockleton, Shrewsbury SY5 9PY, 01743 821651, bill@billfneil.fsnet.co.uk ,

County Treasurer
Melinda Laws, 50 Sheinton Street, Much Wenlock TF13 6HU, 01952 727237, melinda@mlaws.freeserve.co.uk

Publicity
David Brown, Pelham Grove, Cound, Shrewsbury SY5 6AL, 01743 761636, pelham-grove@breathemail.net

Leaflet Coordinator
Fiona Chancellor, Windy Ridge, Little Wenlock, Telford TF6 5BB, 01952 507675, fionachancellor@btinternet.com

Assistant County Organisers
Christine Brown, Pelham Grove, Cound, Shrewsbury SY5 6AL, 01743 761636
Bill Neil, Edge Villa, Edge, Yockleton, Shrewsbury SY5 9PY, 01743 821651

SOMERSET & BRISTOL AREA

Bath & South Gloucestershire

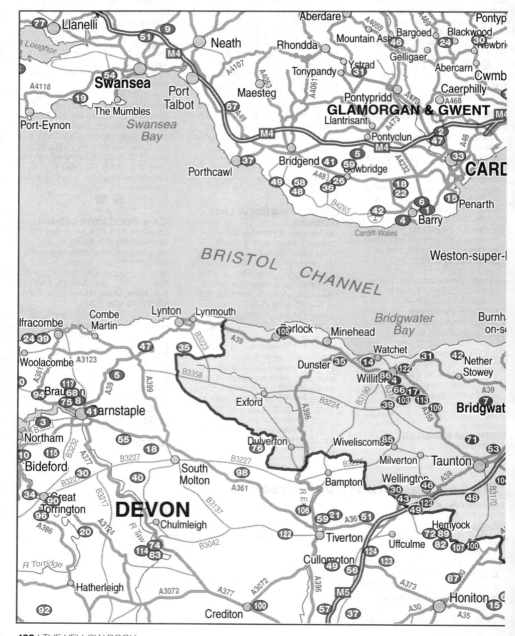

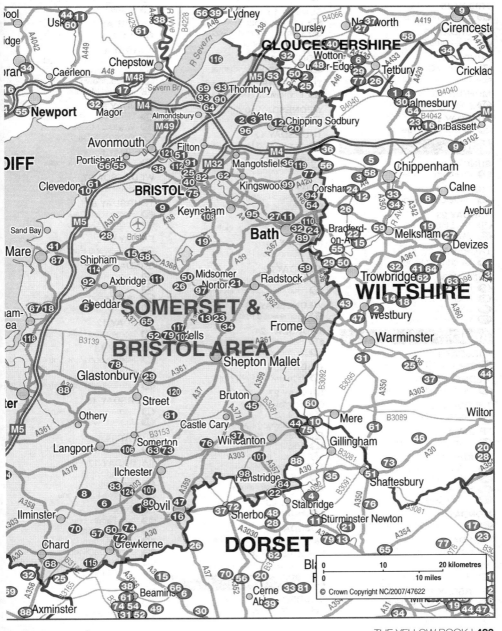

Opening Dates

February

SUNDAY 3
93 Rock House

FRIDAY 15
97 Sherborne Garden

SATURDAY 16
97 Sherborne Garden

SUNDAY 17
39 Elworthy Cottage
97 Sherborne Garden

MONDAY 18
97 Sherborne Garden

TUESDAY 19
97 Sherborne Garden

March

SUNDAY 2
97 Sherborne Garden

TUESDAY 4
53 Hestercombe Gardens

SUNDAY 23
101 The Stables
115 Wayford Manor

THURSDAY 27
39 Elworthy Cottage

SUNDAY 30
42 Fairfield
93 Rock House
95 Saltford Farm Barn
122 Wibble Gardens

April

TUESDAY 1
59 Homewood Park Hotel

WEDNESDAY 2
59 Homewood Park Hotel

THURSDAY 3
59 Homewood Park Hotel

FRIDAY 4
59 Homewood Park Hotel

SUNDAY 6
26 Coley Court & Rose Cottage
32 Crowe Hall
59 Homewood Park Hotel
101 The Stables

MONDAY 7
59 Homewood Park Hotel

TUESDAY 8
59 Homewood Park Hotel

WEDNESDAY 9
59 Homewood Park Hotel

THURSDAY 10
59 Homewood Park Hotel

FRIDAY 11
59 Homewood Park Hotel

SATURDAY 12
73 Lytes Cary Manor

SUNDAY 13
39 Elworthy Cottage
59 Homewood Park Hotel
115 Wayford Manor

MONDAY 14
59 Homewood Park Hotel

TUESDAY 15
59 Homewood Park Hotel

WEDNESDAY 16
59 Homewood Park Hotel

THURSDAY 17
59 Homewood Park Hotel

FRIDAY 18
59 Homewood Park Hotel

SUNDAY 20
14 Binham Grange Garden
49 Hangeridge Farmhouse
56 25 Hillcrest Road
59 Homewood Park Hotel

MONDAY 21
59 Homewood Park Hotel

TUESDAY 22
14 Binham Grange Garden
59 Homewood Park Hotel

WEDNESDAY 23
59 Homewood Park Hotel

THURSDAY 24
11 Bath Priory Hotel
59 Homewood Park Hotel

FRIDAY 25
59 Homewood Park Hotel

SUNDAY 27
40 Emmaus House
58 Holt Farm
59 Homewood Park Hotel
63 Kingsdon Nursery
72 Lower Severalls
74 Manor Farm
91 18 Queens Gate
114 Watcombe
120 Westbrook House

MONDAY 28
59 Homewood Park Hotel

TUESDAY 29
59 Homewood Park Hotel

WEDNESDAY 30
59 Homewood Park Hotel

May

THURSDAY 1
44 Forest Lodge

59 Homewood Park Hotel
61 Jasmine Cottage

FRIDAY 2
16 1 Braggchurch (Evening)
59 Homewood Park Hotel

SATURDAY 3
16 1 Braggchurch (Evening)

SUNDAY 4
59 Homewood Park Hotel
72 Lower Severalls
98 3 Southdown
115 Wayford Manor

MONDAY 5
59 Homewood Park Hotel
115 Wayford Manor
123 Wrangway Gardens

TUESDAY 6
59 Homewood Park Hotel

WEDNESDAY 7
59 Homewood Park Hotel

THURSDAY 8
59 Homewood Park Hotel
61 Jasmine Cottage

FRIDAY 9
59 Homewood Park Hotel

SUNDAY 11
20 Camers
31 Court House
59 Homewood Park Hotel
98 3 Southdown

MONDAY 12
59 Homewood Park Hotel

TUESDAY 13
59 Homewood Park Hotel

WEDNESDAY 14
59 Homewood Park Hotel

THURSDAY 15
59 Homewood Park Hotel
61 Jasmine Cottage

FRIDAY 16
59 Homewood Park Hotel

SATURDAY 17
68 Lift The Latch
83 Old Coat Inn
121 159 Westbury Lane

SUNDAY 18
4 Aller Farmhouse
39 Elworthy Cottage
44 Forest Lodge
56 25 Hillcrest Road
59 Homewood Park Hotel
68 Lift The Latch
72 Lower Severalls
79 Milton Lodge
83 Old Coat Inn
98 3 Southdown

101 The Stables
114 Watcombe

MONDAY 19
59 Homewood Park Hotel

TUESDAY 20
59 Homewood Park Hotel
117 Wellfield Barn

WEDNESDAY 21
59 Homewood Park Hotel

THURSDAY 22
59 Homewood Park Hotel
61 Jasmine Cottage
121 159 Westbury Lane

FRIDAY 23
59 Homewood Park Hotel

SATURDAY 24
57 Hinton St George Gardens

SUNDAY 25
50 Harptree Court
57 Hinton St George Gardens
59 Homewood Park Hotel
63 Kingsdon Nursery
115 Wayford Manor
123 Wrangway Gardens

MONDAY 26
59 Homewood Park Hotel

TUESDAY 27
59 Homewood Park Hotel

WEDNESDAY 28
59 Homewood Park Hotel

THURSDAY 29
10 Barum
39 Elworthy Cottage
59 Homewood Park Hotel
61 Jasmine Cottage

FRIDAY 30
59 Homewood Park Hotel
77 Marshfield Gardens (Evening)

SATURDAY 31
76 Maple House
77 Marshfield Gardens

June

SUNDAY 1
9 Barrow Court
32 Crowe Hall
40 Emmaus House
59 Homewood Park Hotel
76 Maple House
77 Marshfield Gardens
86 Orchard Wyndham
109 Triscombe Nurseries
113 Vellacott

MONDAY 2
59 Homewood Park Hotel

TUESDAY 3
53 Hestercombe Gardens
59 Homewood Park Hotel

WEDNESDAY 4
59 Homewood Park Hotel
114 Watcombe

THURSDAY 5
10 Barum
41 14 Eskdale Close
59 Homewood Park Hotel
61 Jasmine Cottage
70 Little Garth
113 Vellacott

FRIDAY 6
59 Homewood Park Hotel

SATURDAY 7
47 190 Goldcroft
92 Rackley House

SUNDAY 8
23 Church Farm House
25 Clifton Gardens
28 Congresbury Gardens
47 190 Goldcroft
54 Hill Lodge
59 Homewood Park Hotel
78 Meare Gardens
79 Milton Lodge
89 Prior Park Landscape Garden
92 Rackley House

MONDAY 9
47 190 Goldcroft (Evening)
59 Homewood Park Hotel

TUESDAY 10
59 Homewood Park Hotel

WEDNESDAY 11
59 Homewood Park Hotel

THURSDAY 12
10 Barum
59 Homewood Park Hotel
61 Jasmine Cottage
70 Little Garth
113 Vellacott

FRIDAY 13
16 1 Braggchurch (Evening)
46 Gardd Owen
59 Homewood Park Hotel

SATURDAY 14
16 1 Braggchurch (Evening)
36 Dyrham Park
62 28 Kensington Road (pre-book)
82 26 Northumberland Road
120 Westbrook House

SUNDAY 15
6 Barcroft Hall Gardens & Wildlife Area
34 Darkey Pang Tso Gang
36 Dyrham Park
46 Gardd Owen
59 Homewood Park Hotel
62 28 Kensington Road (pre-book)
64 Kingston
69 The Lintels
72 Lower Severalls
81 Northfield House

82 26 Northumberland Road
88 Penwood Farm
115 Wayford Manor

MONDAY 16
59 Homewood Park Hotel

TUESDAY 17
59 Homewood Park Hotel

WEDNESDAY 18
59 Homewood Park Hotel
119 West Littleton Gardens

THURSDAY 19
19 1 Bromley Villas (Evening)
39 Elworthy Cottage
59 Homewood Park Hotel
61 Jasmine Cottage
70 Little Garth
99 Special Plants
113 Vellacott

FRIDAY 20
59 Homewood Park Hotel

SATURDAY 21
62 28 Kensington Road (pre-book)
105 Stowleys

SUNDAY 22
48 Goosehill
59 Homewood Park Hotel
62 28 Kensington Road (pre-book)
80 Montacute House
88 Penwood Farm
102 Stoberry Garden
103 Stogumber Gardens

MONDAY 23
59 Homewood Park Hotel
102 Stoberry Garden

TUESDAY 24
59 Homewood Park Hotel

WEDNESDAY 25
34 Darkey Pang Tso Gang (Evening)
59 Homewood Park Hotel

THURSDAY 26
59 Homewood Park Hotel
61 Jasmine Cottage
70 Little Garth
113 Vellacott

FRIDAY 27
46 Gardd Owen
59 Homewood Park Hotel
95 Saltford Farm Barn (Evening)

SATURDAY 28
62 28 Kensington Road (pre-book)

SUNDAY 29
1 Abbey Farm
46 Gardd Owen
48 Goosehill
59 Homewood Park Hotel
62 28 Kensington Road (pre-book)
85 Olive Cottage
87 3 Palmer's Way
95 Saltford Farm Barn

113 Vellacott

MONDAY 30
1 Abbey Farm
59 Homewood Park Hotel

July

TUESDAY 1
1 Abbey Farm
59 Homewood Park Hotel

WEDNESDAY 2
59 Homewood Park Hotel

THURSDAY 3
59 Homewood Park Hotel
61 Jasmine Cottage
70 Little Garth

FRIDAY 4
24 Claverton Manor
59 Homewood Park Hotel

SATURDAY 5
21 The Chalet

SUNDAY 6
14 Binham Grange Garden
33 Daggs Allotments
43 Fernhill
59 Homewood Park Hotel
67 Laburnum Cottage

MONDAY 7
59 Homewood Park Hotel

TUESDAY 8
14 Binham Grange Garden
59 Homewood Park Hotel

WEDNESDAY 9
43 Fernhill
59 Homewood Park Hotel

THURSDAY 10
59 Homewood Park Hotel
61 Jasmine Cottage
70 Little Garth

FRIDAY 11
59 Homewood Park Hotel

SATURDAY 12
62 28 Kensington Road (pre-book)

SUNDAY 13
7 Barford Park
19 1 Bromley Villas
27 45A Combe Park
35 Dunster Castle Gardens
40 Emmaus House
49 Hangeridge Farmhouse
55 Hillcrest Gardens
56 25 Hillcrest Road
59 Homewood Park Hotel
62 28 Kensington Road (pre-book)
75 22 Mansfield Street (pre-book)
79 Milton Lodge
106 Sutton Hosey Manor
108 Tranby House

MONDAY 14
59 Homewood Park Hotel

TUESDAY 15
38 Easton-in-Gordano Gardens
59 Homewood Park Hotel
124 Yews Farm

WEDNESDAY 16
59 Homewood Park Hotel

THURSDAY 17
59 Homewood Park Hotel
61 Jasmine Cottage
70 Little Garth
99 Special Plants

FRIDAY 18
59 Homewood Park Hotel

SATURDAY 19
8 Barrington Gardens
60 Hooper's Holding
62 28 Kensington Road (pre-book)
73 Lytes Cary Manor
83 Old Coat Inn
107 Tintinhull

SUNDAY 20
18 Brent Knoll Gardens
37 Eastfield
59 Homewood Park Hotel
60 Hooper's Holding
62 28 Kensington Road (pre-book)
75 22 Mansfield Street (pre-book)
83 Old Coat Inn
87 3 Palmer's Way
118 West Huntspill Gardens

MONDAY 21
37 Eastfield
59 Homewood Park Hotel

TUESDAY 22
38 Easton-in-Gordano Gardens
59 Homewood Park Hotel

WEDNESDAY 23
59 Homewood Park Hotel

THURSDAY 24
59 Homewood Park Hotel
61 Jasmine Cottage
70 Little Garth

FRIDAY 25
59 Homewood Park Hotel

SATURDAY 26
20 Camers
62 28 Kensington Road (pre-book)

SUNDAY 27
13 Binegar Village Gardens
20 Camers
27 45A Combe Park
30 Cothay Manor Gardens
59 Homewood Park Hotel
62 28 Kensington Road (pre-book)
75 22 Mansfield Street (pre-book)

MONDAY 28
59 Homewood Park Hotel

TUESDAY 29
38 Easton-in-Gordano Gardens

59 Homewood Park Hotel

WEDNESDAY 30
59 Homewood Park Hotel

THURSDAY 31
59 Homewood Park Hotel
61 Jasmine Cottage
70 Little Garth

August

FRIDAY 1
59 Homewood Park Hotel

SATURDAY 2
75 22 Mansfield Street (pre-book)

SUNDAY 3
13 Binegar Village Gardens
29 Coombe House
43 Fernhill
59 Homewood Park Hotel
116 Wayside

MONDAY 4
59 Homewood Park Hotel

TUESDAY 5
59 Homewood Park Hotel

WEDNESDAY 6
43 Fernhill
59 Homewood Park Hotel

THURSDAY 7
56 25 Hillcrest Road
59 Homewood Park Hotel
70 Little Garth

FRIDAY 8
59 Homewood Park Hotel
71 Little Yarford Farmhouse
(Evening)

SATURDAY 9
71 Little Yarford Farmhouse

SUNDAY 10
39 Elworthy Cottage
59 Homewood Park Hotel
71 Little Yarford Farmhouse
108 Tranby House

MONDAY 11
59 Homewood Park Hotel
71 Little Yarford Farmhouse

TUESDAY 12
59 Homewood Park Hotel

WEDNESDAY 13
59 Homewood Park Hotel

THURSDAY 14
59 Homewood Park Hotel
70 Little Garth

FRIDAY 15
59 Homewood Park Hotel

SUNDAY 17
49 Hangeridge Farmhouse
59 Homewood Park Hotel

MONDAY 18
- 59 Homewood Park Hotel

TUESDAY 19
- 59 Homewood Park Hotel

WEDNESDAY 20
- 59 Homewood Park Hotel

THURSDAY 21
- 11 Bath Priory Hotel
- 59 Homewood Park Hotel
- 70 Little Garth
- 99 Special Plants

FRIDAY 22
- 59 Homewood Park Hotel

SUNDAY 24
- 59 Homewood Park Hotel
- 85 Olive Cottage

MONDAY 25
- 17 Braglands Barn
- 45 Gants Mill & Garden
- 59 Homewood Park Hotel

TUESDAY 26
- 59 Homewood Park Hotel

WEDNESDAY 27
- 59 Homewood Park Hotel

THURSDAY 28
- 39 Elworthy Cottage
- 59 Homewood Park Hotel
- 70 Little Garth

FRIDAY 29
- 59 Homewood Park Hotel

SUNDAY 31
- 59 Homewood Park Hotel
- 90 Quakers

September

MONDAY 1
- 59 Homewood Park Hotel

TUESDAY 2
- 59 Homewood Park Hotel

WEDNESDAY 3
- 59 Homewood Park Hotel

THURSDAY 4
- 59 Homewood Park Hotel
- 61 Jasmine Cottage
- 70 Little Garth

FRIDAY 5
- 59 Homewood Park Hotel

SUNDAY 7
- 59 Homewood Park Hotel
- 66 Knoll Cottage
- 122 Wibble Gardens

MONDAY 8
- 59 Homewood Park Hotel

TUESDAY 9
- 59 Homewood Park Hotel

WEDNESDAY 10
- 59 Homewood Park Hotel

THURSDAY 11
- 59 Homewood Park Hotel
- 61 Jasmine Cottage
- 70 Little Garth

FRIDAY 12
- 59 Homewood Park Hotel

SATURDAY 13
- 72 Lower Severalls

SUNDAY 14
- 12 Beechwell House
- 59 Homewood Park Hotel
- 102 Stoberry Garden
- 112 University of Bristol Botanic Garden

MONDAY 15
- 59 Homewood Park Hotel

TUESDAY 16
- 59 Homewood Park Hotel

WEDNESDAY 17
- 59 Homewood Park Hotel

THURSDAY 18
- 59 Homewood Park Hotel
- 99 Special Plants

FRIDAY 19
- 59 Homewood Park Hotel

SATURDAY 20
- 72 Lower Severalls

SUNDAY 21
- 59 Homewood Park Hotel

MONDAY 22
- 59 Homewood Park Hotel

TUESDAY 23
- 59 Homewood Park Hotel

WEDNESDAY 24
- 59 Homewood Park Hotel

THURSDAY 25
- 59 Homewood Park Hotel

FRIDAY 26
- 59 Homewood Park Hotel

SUNDAY 28
- 59 Homewood Park Hotel

MONDAY 29
- 59 Homewood Park Hotel

TUESDAY 30
- 59 Homewood Park Hotel

October

SATURDAY 4
- 73 Lytes Cary Manor

SUNDAY 5
- 58 Holt Farm

SATURDAY 18
- 68 Lift The Latch

SUNDAY 19
- 68 Lift The Latch

SUNDAY 26
- 109 Triscombe Nurseries

Gardens open to the public

- 8 Barrington Court
- 14 Binham Grange Garden
- 24 Claverton Manor
- 30 Cothay Manor Gardens
- 32 Crowe Hall
- 35 Dunster Castle Gardens
- 36 Dyrham Park
- 39 Elworthy Cottage
- 40 Emmaus House
- 44 Forest Lodge
- 45 Gants Mill & Garden
- 53 Hestercombe Gardens
- 72 Lower Severalls
- 73 Lytes Cary Manor
- 79 Milton Lodge
- 80 Montacute House
- 89 Prior Park Landscape Garden
- 97 Sherborne Garden
- 99 Special Plants
- 107 Tintinhull
- 112 University of Bristol Botanic Garden

By appointment only

- 2 Algars Manor
- 3 Algars Mill
- 5 Badgers' Acre
- 15 Bourne House
- 22 Cherry Bolberry Farm
- 51 4 Haytor Park
- 52 Henley Mill
- 65 Kites Croft
- 84 35 Old Station Gardens
- 94 St Catherines Court
- 96 Serridge House
- 104 Stoke St Mary Gardens
- 110 8 Trossachs Drive
- 111 Ubley Hill Farm House
- 124 Yews Farm

Also open by appointment ☎

- 1 Abbey Farm
- 4 Aller Farmhouse
- 8 Greenmantle, Barrington Gardens
- 12 Beechwell House
- 13 The Coach House, Binegar Village Gardens
- 18 Copse Hall, Brent Knoll Gardens
- 19 1 Bromley Villas
- 20 Camers
- 23 Church Farm House
- 27 45A Combe Park
- 28 Yeo Meads, Congresbury Gardens
- 34 Darkey Pang Tso Gang
- 43 Fernhill
- 47 190 Goldcroft

54 Hill Lodge
58 Holt Farm
60 Hooper's Holding
61 Jasmine Cottage
62 28 Kensington Road
63 Kingsdon Nursery
66 Knoll Cottage
67 Laburnum Cottage
70 Little Garth
71 Little Yarford Farmhouse
75 22 Mansfield Street
81 Northfield House
85 Olive Cottage
87 3 Palmer's Way
88 Penwood Farm
91 18 Queens Gate
92 Rackley House
93 Rock House
95 Saltford Farm Barn
98 3 Southdown
102 Stoberry Garden
113 Vellacott
114 Watcombe
115 Wayford Manor
117 Wellfield Barn
120 Westbrook House

The Gardens

1 ABBEY FARM ♿ ☎
Montacute TA156UA. Mr & Mrs G Jenkins, 01935 823572, abbeygj@dsl.pipex.com. *4m from Yeovil. Follow A3088, take slip rd to Montacute, turn L at T-junction into village. Turn R between Church & King's Arms (no through rd).* Home-made teas. **Adm £3.50, chd free. Sun 29, Mon 30 June; Tue 1 July (2-5.30). Visitors also welcome by appt.**
2¹/₂ acres of mainly walled gardens on sloping site, provide the setting for Cluniac medieval Priory gatehouse. Interesting plants incl roses, shrubs, grasses, clematis. Herbaceous borders, white garden, gravel garden. Small arboretum. Pond for wildlife - frogs, newts, dragonflies. Fine mulberry, walnut and monkey puzzle trees. Seats for resting. Gravel garden, short steep slope.
♿ ✕ ✿ ☕ ☎

2 ALGARS MANOR
Station Road, Iron Acton BS37 9TB. Dr & Mrs J M Naish, 01454 228372, johnnaish@msn.com. *9m N of Bristol. 3m W of Yate/Chipping Sodbury. Turn S off Iron Acton bypass B4059, past village green, 200yds, then over level Xing (Station Rd).* **Visitors welcome by appt for entrance to both Algars Manor and Algars Mill gardens, groups & garden clubs particularly**

welcome. **Combined adm £4, chd free.**
2 acres of woodland garden beside R Frome, mill stream, native plants mixed with collections of 60 magnolias and 70 camellias, eucalyptus and other unusual trees and shrubs. Mar/Apr camellias, magnolias; Apr/May/June rhododendrons, azaleas; Oct autumn colours. Limited wheelchair access, gravel paths, some steep slopes.
♿ ☎

3 ALGARS MILL
Station Road, Iron Acton BS37 9TD. Mr & Mrs John Wright, 01454 228373, marilyn@algarsmill.plus.com. *9m N of Bristol. 3m W of Yate/Chipping Sodbury. (For directions see Algars Manor).* **Visitors welcome by appt for entrance to both Algars Manor & Algars Mill gardens. Combined adm £4, chd free.**
2-acre woodland garden bisected by R Frome; spring bulbs, shrubs; very early spring feature (Feb-Mar) of wild Newent daffodils. 300-400yr-old mill house (not open) through which millrace still runs.
♿ ☎

Wonderful wildlife habitats, with almost 1000 trees planted . . .

4 ALLER FARMHOUSE
nr Williton TA4 4LY. Mr & Mrs Richard Chandler, 01984 633702. *7m E of Minehead, 1m S of Williton. From A358 (¹/₂ m S of Williton) by Q8 garage, through Sampford Brett, then Capton; exit to A39 Williton via St Peter's Church.* Teas. **Adm £3, chd free. Sun 18 May (2-5.30). Visitors also welcome by appt May/June only for groups of 10-25. No coaches.**
2-3 acres. Hot, dry, sunny, S-facing, surrounded by pink stone walls and sub-divided into 5 separate compartments by same. 'Cliff Garden' is old 3-sided quarry. Old magnolias, figs, Judas, etc; newer acacias; many unusual and/or tender plants. Garden now 15yrs old. Uneven paths, steps, slopes, slippery if wet.
✕ ✿ ☕ ☎

5 BADGERS' ACRE
Stone Allerton BS26 2NW. Lucy Hetherington & Jim Mathers, 01934 713159, lucyhetherington@btinternet.com. *3m SW of Cheddar. Please call for directions.* **Adm £2.50, chd free. Visitors welcome by appt 1 May to 30 Sept incl.**
1 acre, mixed planting, colour-themed beds, secret shady walk, rockery, pond and vegetable potager.
✿ ☎

6 NEW BARCROFT HALL GARDENS & WILDLIFE AREA
North St, South Petherton TA13 5DA. Mr & Mrs Brian Herrick. *N side of S Petherton. From A303 drive to centre of S Petherton, through village, R at fork with Methodist Church into North St (St James St), R into Barcroft Lane, follow signs.* **Adm £3.50, chd free (share to Local disabled and mobility challenged charities). Sun 15 June (10.30-5).**
Barcroft Hall gardens and wildlife areas were created by the present owners of the 90-acre farm estate 7 yrs ago. Wonderful wildlife habitats, with almost 1000 trees planted, coupled with formal areas, have resulted in a stunning environment. Specifically designed for reasonable disabled access. Mobility awareness day. Local produce. Some gravel paths and slopes may only be accessible by motorised mobility vehicles.
♿

7 BARFORD PARK
Spaxton TA5 1AG. Mr & Mrs Michael Stancomb. *4¹/₂ m W of Bridgwater. Midway between Enmore & Spaxton.* Cream teas. **Adm £3, chd free. Sun 13 July (2-5.30).**
10 acres incl woodland walk. Formal garden, wild garden and water garden, surrounding a Queen Anne house (not open) with park and ha-ha. Partial wheelchair access.
♿ ✿ ☕

8 NEW BARRINGTON GARDENS
Barrington TA19 0JR. *5m NE of Ilminster. In Barrington village on B3168, 100yds from entrance to Barrington Court.* **Sat 19 July (11-5). Combined adm £2.50 for Greenmantle and The Cottage, chd free, adm to Barrington**

Court £8.10, chd £3.50.
Beautiful hamstone village offering 3 quite different gardens incl NT Barrington Court Gardens.

◆ BARRINGTON COURT

Ilminster TA19 0NQ. **The National Trust, 01460 241938, barringtoncourt@nationaltrust.org.uk. Adm £8.10, chd £3.50. Mar to Oct daily (not Weds).**
Well known garden constructed in 1920 by Col Arthur Lyle from derelict farmland (the C19 cattle stalls still exist). Gertrude Jekyll suggested planting schemes for the layout. Paved paths with walled rose and iris, white and lily gardens, large kitchen garden.
&. ✗ ✿ ☕

NEW THE COTTAGE

Water Street. **Maureen & Tony Russell.** *Approx 100yds from entrance to Barrington Court.* Small cottage garden with summerhouse, ponds and vegetable garden.
✗

NEW GREENMANTLE

6 Water Street. **Colin & Jill Leppard, 01460 54434.** *Approx 250yds from entrance to Barrington Court.* **Visitors also welcome by appt some eves/w/e.**
1-acre wildlife/cottage garden, moving through large traditional herbaceous (butterfly) borders with water features, pergola and vegetable garden into orchard/coppice incorporating various wildlife habitats incl meadow, wildlife pond and living willow features. Partial wheelchair access. 2 large unfenced ponds, one deep.
&. ✿ ☕ ☎

Crammed with shrubs and perennials from around the world . . .

9 BARROW COURT

Barrow Court Lane, Barrow Gurney BS48 3RP. **Mrs Jo Collins, Organiser.** *16m NE of Weston-super-Mare & 8m SW of Bristol. On A370. Turn off onto A3130 to Barrow Gurney. Turn immed R into Barrow Court Lane.*

¹/₂ m up lane turn R into Barrow Court. Home-made teas. **Adm £3, chd free. Sun 1 June (2-6).**
Early C20 listed Italianate garden, designed by Inigo Thomas. Formal areas are set on 3 levels and incl parterres, fish pond, balustrades and gazebos. Also a small arboretum and wild spinney.
✿ ☕

10 BARUM

50 Edward Road, Clevedon BS21 7DT. **Marian & Roger Peacock, www.barum.pwp.blueyonder.co.uk.** *12m W of Bristol. M5 J20, follow signs to pier, continue N, past Walton Park Hotel, turn R at St Mary's Church. Up Channel Rd, over Xrds, turn L into Edward Rd at top.* **Adm £2.50, chd free. Thurs 29 May; 5, 12 June (2-5).**
Informal ¹/₃-acre plantsman's garden, reclaimed by the owners since 1991 from years of neglect. Now crammed with shrubs and perennials from around the world, incl tender and exotic species using the clement coastal climate and well-drained soil. The vegetable patch uses a no-tread bedding system growing several tender crops.
✗ ✿

11 BATH PRIORY HOTEL

Weston Road, Bath BA1 2XT. **Jane Moore, Head Gardener, www.thebathpriory.co.uk.** *Close to centre of Bath. From Bath centre take Upper Bristol Rd, turn R at end of Victoria Park & L into Weston Rd.* Home-made teas. **Adm £2.50, chd free. Thurs 24 Apr; 21 Aug (2-5).**
3-acre walled garden. Main garden has croquet lawn, herbaceous borders and dell with snowdrops and spring bulbs in April. Adjoining garden has summer meadow and woodland borders with specimen trees. Formal pool surrounded by roses leads to stone gazebo overlooking the vegetable garden which supplies the restaurant. Late summer colour August.
&. ✗ ✿ ☕

12 BEECHWELL HOUSE

51 Goose Green, Yate BS37 5BL. **Tim Wilmot, 01454 318350, timwilmot@blueyonder.co.uk.** *10m NE of Bristol. From centre of Yate (Shopping & Leisure Centre) or Station Rd B4060, turn N onto Church Rd. After ¹/₂ m turn L onto Greenways Rd then immed R onto continuation of Church Rd. Goose Green starts after 200yds. After 100yds take R-fork, garden 100yds on L.* Cream teas.

Adm £3, chd free. Sun 14 Sept (1-6). Visitors also welcome by appt June-Sept for groups of 10+.
Enclosed, level, subtropical garden created over last 17yrs and filled with exotic planting, incl palms (over 12 varieties), tree ferns, yuccas, agaves and succulent bed, phormiums, bamboos, bananas, aroids and other 'architectural planting'. Wildlife pond and koi pond. C16 40ft deep well. Rare plant raffle every hour.
✗ ☕ ☎

13 BINEGAR VILLAGE GARDENS

Binegar BA3 4UE. *4m NE of of Wells. On A37 Binegar (Gurney Slade), at George Inn, follow sign to Binegar 1m past PH and church to Xrds at Binegar Green. From Wells B3139, 4m turn R signed Binegar, 1m to Xrds at Binegar Green.* Cream teas. **Combined adm £4, chd free. Suns 27 July; 3 Aug (2-6).**
One of the highest villages on the Mendips with C13 church.
☕

CHURCH FARM HOUSE

Susan & Tony Griffin
(See separate entry).
&. ✗ ✿ ⊨

THE COACH HOUSE

Bennetts Lane. **James Shanahan & Richard Higgins, 01749 840973, richardhiggins@talktalk.net.** *From Green, 100yds along Bennetts Lane on R.* **Visitors also welcome by appt July, Aug only.**
Described by Carol Klein as 'a grand parkland garden'. Divided into formal flower, vegetable and water gardens, walks and lawns. Features the famous Wallemi nobilis pine and collections of fuschia and old French roses. Featured on BBC2 Open Gardens. Gravel and grass paths.
&. ✗ ✿ ☎

SPINDLE COTTAGE

Angela & Alban Bunting, www.spindlecottage.co.uk. *Binegar Green, parking on the Green*
The garden has always been a place for children to romp about. Low maintenance with 3 magical playhouses (Ruth's Cottage, Tom's Lodge and Charlotte's Post Office), built for our grandchildren and all the visiting children that come on holiday. Cottage garden flower beds, productive vegetable

plot, hedgehog house. Many places to sit under cover. Well and wildlife pond on the green. Featured in 'Country Living' and 'Somerset Life' and on BBC2 Open Gardens.

 ♿ ✖ ⊛ 🛏

⑭ NEW ◆ BINHAM GRANGE GARDEN
Old Cleeve, Minehead TA24 6HX. Stewart & Marie Thomas, 01984 640056, www.binhamgrange.co.uk. *4m E of Dunster. Take A39 for Minehead, R at Xrds after Washford to Blue Anchor, past Old Cleeve, garden on L.* **For NGS: Sun 20, Tue 22 Apr (2-5); Sun 6, Tue 8 July (2-6).**
Jacobean House set in 300 acres of landscape and gardens with extensive views of the Somerset countryside. Formal parterre, Italian-style garden, pergola, island beds, cutting and vegetable garden. Plants to excite the senses with conservation and wildlife emphasis. A garden for all seasons.

 ♿ ⊛ ☕

Willow weaving, dancing figures, tree house, swings . . .

⑮ BOURNE HOUSE
Bourne Lane, Burrington BS40 7AF. Mr & Mrs C Thomas, 01761 462494, bourne.thomas@tiscali.co.uk. *12m S of Bristol. N of Burrington. Turn off A38 signed Blagdon-Burrington; 2nd turning L.* Home-made teas. **Adm £3, chd free. Visitors welcome by appt, max 24, no coaches.**
5 acres, 2 paddocks. Stream with waterfalls and lily pond; pergola; mature trees and shrubs. Mixed borders; large area hardy cyclamen and rose bed. Spring bulbs.

 ♿ ✖ ☕ ☎

⑯ NEW 1 BRAGGCHURCH
93 Hendford Hill, Yeovil BA20 2RE. Veronica Sartin. *Walking distance of Yeovil centre. Approaching Yeovil on A30 from The Quicksilver Mail PH roundabout, go halfway down Hendford Hill, 1st driveway on R. Roadside parking at Southwoods (next R down hill) and Public Car Park at bottom of Hendford Hill.* **Evening Openings £5, chd free, wine/soft drink, cheese and biscuits, Fri 2, Sat 3 May; Fri 13, Sat 14 June (5-9).**
Old garden of undulating lawns and mature trees evolving, since May 2002, to semi-wild, nature-friendly, woodland garden with a few surprises within the new planting. Willow weaving, dancing figures, tree house, swings. Retreat.

 ✖

⑰ BRAGLANDS BARN
Stogumber TA4 3TP. Simon & Sue Youell, www.braglandsbarn.com. *4m SE of Williton. From Taunton follow A358 for 11m. Turn L at 1st sign to Stogumber. 200metres after Stogumber stn.* Light refreshments & teas. **Adm £2.50, chd free. Mon 25 Aug (11-5.30).**
2-acre garden created since 1995 on site that contains areas of waterlogged clay and well-drained sand. Herbaceous borders, shrubs and trees with many rare and unusual plants. Pond and bog garden. Planted to provide colour and interest over a long period, especially late summer. Aim of garden is to grow interesting plants in an informal setting.

 ♿ ✖ ⊛ ☕

⑱ BRENT KNOLL GARDENS
TA9 4DF. *2m N of Highbridge. Off A38 & M5 J22.* Cream teas at Copse Hall. **Combined adm £5, chd free. Sun 20 July (2-6).**
The distinctive hill of Brent Knoll, an iron age hill fort, is well worth climbing 449ft for the 360 degree view of the surrounding hills, including Glastonbury Tor and 'levels'. The lovely C13 church is renowned for its bench ends.

 ☕

BURROWS GREEN
Brent Street. Yvonne Radford
A small garden overflowing with scent and colour.

 ♿ ✖

COPSE HALL
Mrs S Boss & Mr A J Hill, 01278 760301, susan.boss@gmail.com. Visitors also welcome by appt.
The S-facing Edwardian house (not open) on the lower slopes of the Knoll sits above 3 terraces with borders and lawns below. Ha-ha, wild area and pond with Great Crested newts, crinkle crankle walled kitchen garden with heritage vegetables, kiwi fruit, feijoas and wall-trained fruit. A wood in which to walk your dog, some old trees, new wildflower area and rare breed Soay sheep. Partial wheelchair access.

 ♿ ⊛ ☎

PEN ORCHARD
Brent St. John & Wiet Harper
A busy people's garden to relax in.

 ♿ ✖

⑲ 1 BROMLEY VILLAS
Bromley Road, Stanton Drew BS39 4DE. Mr & Mrs S Whittle, 01275 331311, judith.chubb@qfruit.co.uk. *7m S of Bristol. From A37 Chelwood roundabout take A368 towards Chew Valley Lake. 2nd turning on R. Follow car park signs. Park only in designated car park. Strictly no parking on Bromley Rd.* Home-made teas. **Adm £3, chd free. Sun 13 July (2-6). Evening Opening £4.50, wine, Thur 19 June (6-9). Visitors also welcome by appt June/July only, no coaches.**
A lawnmower's nightmare! A garden maturing nicely, just like its owners. Rose arches, rills, fruit and figs, sculptured mounds, fire pit, monolith and menagerie. Just under an acre of interesting things to see. Art and plant sales.

 ✖ ⊛ ☕ ☎

⑳ CAMERS
Old Sodbury BS37 6RG. Mr & Mrs A G Denman, 01454 322430, www.camers.org. *2m E of Chipping Sodbury. Entrance in Chapel Lane off A432 at Dog Inn.* Home-made teas. **Adm £4, chd free. Sun 11 May; Sat 26, Sun 27 July (2-5.30). Visitors also welcome by appt Feb to Oct for groups of 15+.**
Elizabethan farmhouse (not open) set in 4 acres of garden and young woodland with spectacular views over Severn Vale. Garden full of surprises divided into range of formal and informal areas planted with very wide range of species to provide yr-round

interest. Parterre, topiary, Japanese garden, bog shade and prairie areas, waterfalls, white and hot gardens, woodland walks. Featured in English Garden Magazine & on BBC Radio Bristol 2007. Some steep slopes.

 ⛿ ☕ ☎

㉑ THE CHALET
52 Charlton Road, Midsomer Norton BA3 4AH. Sheila & Chris Jones. $1/2$ m from centre of Midsomer Norton. Just off A367. Past the White Post Inn towards Radstock, turn L immed after next mini roundabout into Charlton Rd. Disabled parking only at house. Home-made teas. **Adm £2, chd free.** Sat 5 July (2-5).
Covering 1 acre, garden contains lots of interest with plenty of lawns, mixed borders, vegetable garden and 80yr-old rotating cedar shingle summerhouse. Topiary is slowly becoming a feature. A quiet, relaxing garden next to a busy rd, it is shared by Orchard Lodge (52a), the next generation of the family.

 ⛿ ☕

㉒ CHERRY BOLBERRY FARM
Furge Lane, Henstridge BA8 0RN. Mrs Jenny Raymond, 01963 362177. 6m E of Sherborne. In centre of Henstridge, turn R at small Xrds signed Furge Lane. Continue straight on to farm. Home-made teas available on request. **Combined adm £3, chd free. Combined with 35 Old Station Gardens. Visitors welcome by appt June/July for individuals and groups of 10+.**
30 yr-old, owner-designed 1-acre garden planted for yr-round interest with wildlife in mind. Colour-themed island beds, shrub and herbaceous borders, unusual perennials, old roses and specimen trees. Vegetable and flower cutting garden, greenhouses, nature ponds. Wonderful extensive views.

 ⛿ ☕ ☎

㉓ NEW CHURCH FARM HOUSE
Turners Court Lane, Binegar BA3 4UA. Susan & Tony Griffin, 01749 841628, argriffin@btconnect.com. 4m NE of Wells. On A37 Binegar (Gurney Slade), at George Inn, follow sign to Binegar. 1m past PH and church to Xrds at Binegar Green, turn R, 300metres, turn R. From Wells B3139, 4m turn R signed Binegar. 1m to Xrds. Turn L, 300metres turn

R. Adm £3, chd free. Sun 8 June (11-5). Also open with Binegar Village Gardens 27 July and 3 Aug. Visitors also welcome by appt June to Sept incl.
Carol Klein said 'Wow' when she saw our colour wheel themed borders with novel plantstands in June 2007. Views to church and Mendips beyond. 2nd walled area features spring border, shrubs, trees, climbing roses. Seduced by prairie planting so bank area in development. Gravel forecourt, 2 shallow steps.

 ☎

80yr-old rotating cedar shingle summerhouse . . .

㉔ ◆ CLAVERTON MANOR
Claverton, Bath BA2 7BD. American Museum in Britain, 01225 821013, www.americanmuseum.org. 2m E of Bath. The American Museum is signed from Bath city centre and from A36 Warminster rd. Coaches must only approach via city centre up Bathwick Hill. **House and garden adm £7.50, chd £4, concessions £6.50, garden only adm £5, chd £3, concessions £4. Tue to Sun, 15 Mar to 2 Nov; Mons Bank Hols & Aug. For NGS: Fri 4 July (12-5).**
Located in AONB with stunning views across the Avon Valley, garden incl replica of George Washington's Mount Vernon garden, a Colonial Herb garden and American Arboretum. Explore a unique mixture of American botanical discoveries made 200yrs ago by Lewis and Clark or walk the Backwoods Trail through manor's upper woodland. Titanic exhibition - the ship that shook America. Wheelchair access limited to terrace, main lawn and house. Most of main garden features not accessible.

⛿ ☕

㉕ ◆ CLIFTON GARDENS
Bristol BS8 3LH. Close to Clifton Suspension Bridge between the Mansion House & Christ Church. Home-made teas. **Combined adm £3, chd free. Sun 8 June (2-5).**

☕

NEW 41 CANYNGE ROAD
John & Anne Newman
Large mature walled town garden with many interesting shrubs as well as lawn, trees and rose garden.

43 CANYNGE ROAD
Martin Appleby
Happy garden for children and birds: organic vegetables; lovely summerhouse. Each separate lawn area has a different mood.

 ☕

3 NORLAND ROAD
Mrs J C Torrens
Charming town garden filled with relaxed and varied planting, full of yr-round interest. Shrubs, small trees, bulbs and perennials. Wildlife fiendly.

11 PERCIVAL ROAD
Mr & Mrs R L Bland
Small, enclosed urban garden, most plants in containers. Large variety of individual, interesting plants. 120 tree species.

 ⛿

㉖ NEW COLEY COURT & ROSE COTTAGE
Smithams Hill, East Harptree BS40 6BY. Home-made teas at Rose Cottage, cream teas at New Manor Farm Shop, N Widcombe. **Combined adm £4, chd free.** Sun 6 Apr (2-5).

☕

COLEY COURT
Coley BS40 6AN. Mrs M J Hill. 1m E of East Harptree. From A39 at Chewton Mendip take B3114 for 2m. Well before E Harptree turn R at sign Coley and Hinton Blewett
Early Jacobean house (not open). 1-acre garden, stone walls, spring bulbs; 1-acre old mixed orchard.

 ⛿

NEW ROSE COTTAGE
Smithams Hill. Bev & Jenny Cruse. From B3114 turn into High St in East Harptree. L at Clock Tower and immed R into Middle St, continue up hill for 1m. From B3134 take East Harptree turning opp Castle of Comfort, continue for $1^1/_2$ m. Car parking in field opp cottage
1-acre hillside cottage garden with

panoramic views over the Chew Valley. Garden is bordered by stream and established mixed hedges. Wildlife area and pond in field next to car park.

27 NEW 45A COMBE PARK

Weston, Bath BA1 3NS. Stephen Brook, 01225 428288. *1¹/₂ m W of city centre. Follow signs for Royal United Hospital in Weston. Garden 10metres from main hospital entrance.* Adm £2.50, chd free. Suns 13, 27 July (1-5). Visitors also welcome by appt for individuals or groups, no coaches.

Walled town garden creatively landscaped on 3 levels with raised borders of colour-schemed perennials. Grasses, phormiums, acers and vine-covered pergola lead to fernery with large tree ferns. Pond with wooden walkway, small central lawn and secluded seating areas. Some steps.

28 CONGRESBURY GARDENS

BS49 5EX. *8m N of Weston-super-Mare. 13m S of Bristol on A370. At T-lights in Congresbury head E signed Churchill - Cheddar. From A38, take B3133 to Congresbury.* Home-made teas at Silver Mead & Yeo Mead am, Fernbank pm. Combined adm £5, chd free. Sun 8 June (10.30-5).

FERNBANK

High Street. Simon & Julia Thyer. *100yds along High St from Ship & Castle*
Informal garden of approx ¹/₃ acre, tucked away behind Victorian house (not open). Patio with hundreds of potted plants, jungle-like conservatory, kitchen garden with picturesque greenhouse and potting shed, 2 ponds, mature copper beech, small Mediterranean courtyard. Narrow paths. Free range bantams. Featured in 'The English Garden'.

MIDDLECOMBE NURSERY

Nigel J North, www.middlecombenursery. co.uk. *On the edge of Congresbury, on the Bristol side, turn to Wrington along the Wrington rd off the A370 Weston*

to Bristol rd. Garden 200yds on L
Series of gardens covering 1 acre, many different styles and features. Excellent shrub borders. Patio gardens, pond and water features, lawns, deck areas etc. Dogs on leads.

OAKSIDE

Paul Laws. *200yds along High St from Ship & Castle*
28metres x 48metres. Tropical garden packed with unusual plants. Bananas, elephant ears, daturas, cannas, bamboo, agaves, konjac acers. Various sitting areas, decking, pergolas, water features, doves.

NEW SILVER CRAIG

High Street. Pamela Clogstoun. *60 yds from Ship & Castle PH* Interesting cottage garden.

3 SILVER MEAD

Terry & Geraldine Holden. *Approx ¹/₂ m along High St from Ship & Castle, R into Silver St, 1st L into Silver Mead* Approx ¹/₃ acre manicured shrub/herbaceous borders and trees developed over past 21yrs from farmland. Two 'hot' Mediterranean-type patios, water features, pots, lavender walk. Organic vegetable plot. Uninterrupted views of Mendips. Short steep slope to main part of garden.

NEW YEO MEADS

Debbie Fortune & Mark Hayward, 01934 832904, mark.hayward@sky.com. *150yds along High St from Ship & Castle PH on L.* Visitors also welcome by appt June, July, Aug.
1¹/₄ acres, formally laid out in C17 incl 350yr-old Cedar of Lebanon tree, Atlas Blue cedar, 300+ yr-old oak, acacia, Japanese acer, 150 yr-old lime, many with large growths of mistletoe. Victorian pond with topiarised golden cypress trees set off by darker copper beech behind octagonal thatched summerhouse. Vegetable garden, orchard, herbaceous borders and hard landscaping.

29 NEW COOMBE HOUSE

Bove Town, Glastonbury BA6 8JG. Mr Colin Wells-Brown & Mr Alan Gloak, www.coombehouse.org. *¹/₂ m from town centre. Take bus from town hall car park. Bove Town top of High St.* Home-made teas. Adm £3, chd free. Sun 3 Aug (2-6).
2-acre romantic and lavishly-planted garden, incl unusual and tender plants. Dramatic scenes, pools, terraces and Abbot's retreat. Kitchen garden, orchards, nut walk and lots to see and ponder on. An English garden in a mystical town with lots of country views. Partial wheelchair access, gravel path to kitchen garden.

Dramatic scenes, pools, terraces and Abbot's retreat . . .

30 ◆ COTHAY MANOR GARDENS

Greenham, nr Wellington TA21 0JR. Mr & Mrs Alastair Robb, 01823 672283, cothaymanor@btinternet.com. *5m SW of Wellington. At M5 J26 or 27 take direction Exeter or Wellington respectively. Approx 4m take direction Greenham. After 1m follow tourist signs. In lane keep always L. Car park 1m.* Adm £4.50, chd under 12 £2.50. Weds, Thurs, Suns, Easter to end Sept incl (2-6), groups welcome. For NGS: Sun 27 July (2-6).
Few gardens are as evocatively romantic as Cothay. Laid out in 1920s and replanted in 1990s within the original framework, Cothay encompasses a rare blend of old and new. Plantsman's paradise set in 12 acres of magical gardens. Gravel paths.

31 COURT HOUSE

East Quantoxhead TA5 1EJ. Lady Luttrell. *12m W of Bridgwater. Off A39; house at end of village past duck pond.* Home-made teas in village hall. **Adm £4, chd free. Sun 11 May (2-5).** Lovely 5-acre garden; trees, shrubs, many rare and tender; herbaceous and 3-acre woodland garden. Views to sea and Quantocks.

32 ♦ CROWE HALL
Bath BA2 6AR. Mr John Barratt, 01225 310322. *1m SE of Bath. L up Widcombe Hill, off A36, leaving White Hart on R. Limited parking.* **Adm £4, chd £1. For NGS: Suns 6 Apr; 1 June (2-6).**
Large varied garden; fine trees, lawns, spring bulbs, series of enclosed gardens cascading down steep hillside. Italianate terracing and Gothic Victorian grotto contrast with park-like upper garden. Dramatic setting, with spectacular views of Bath. Lovely walks through the fields along mown grass paths.

33 DAGGS ALLOTMENTS
High Street, Thornbury BS35 2AW, www.thornburyallotments.com. *Park in free car park off Chapel Str.* Home-made teas. **Adm £3, chd free. Sun 6 July (2-5).**
Situated in historic town on edge of Severn Vale. 105 plots, all in cultivation, many organic, incl vegetables, soft fruit, herbs and flowers for cutting. Narrow, steep, grass paths between plots. Featured on BBC2 Open Gardens.

34 DARKEY PANG TSO GANG
High Street, Oakhill BA3 5BT. Chrissy & Graham Price, 01749 840795, www.darkeypang.org.uk. *3m N of Shepton Mallet. Off A367 in Oakhill High St opp converted chapel.* Home-made teas. **Adm £3, chd 50p (share to The Mendip Society). Sun 15 June (2-6). Evening Opening £4, chd 50p, wine, Wed 25 June (6.30-9). Visitors also welcome by appt.**
³/₄ -acre garden creatively designed and landscaped by owners since 1981. Crammed with trees, shrubs, herbaceous and climbers, the garden is an adventure along winding paths with a lushness of greens and leaf combinations linking wild and cultivated areas with grotto, terraces, pergola, wildlife pond and bog garden with the recently-discovered cave being a major feature.

35 ♦ DUNSTER CASTLE GARDENS
Dunster TA24 6SL. The National Trust, 01643 821314, www.nationaltrust.org.uk. *3m SE of Minehead. NT car park approached direct from A39 Minehead to Bridgwater rd, nr to A396 turning. Car park charge to non-NT members.* **House and garden adm £8.60, chd £4.20, family £20.50, garden only adm £4.80, chd £2.20, family £11.80. Opening times vary; please phone or visit website for details. For NGS: Sun 13 July (11-4.30).**
Hillside woodland garden surrounding fortified mansion, previously home to the Luttrell family for 600yrs. Terraced areas, interlinked by old carriage drives and paths, feature tender plants. National Collection of Arbutus (Strawberry Tree). Fine views over polo lawns and landscape with C18 features. Mobility vehicle available and guide with wheelchair route marked.

Roof garden . . . beds filled with tropical plants . . .

36 ♦ DYRHAM PARK
Bath SN14 8ER. The National Trust, 01179 372501, www.nationaltrust.org.uk. *12m E of Bristol. 8m N of Bath. Approached from Bath to Stroud rd (A46), 2m S of Tormarton interchange with M4 exit 18.* **House and garden adm £10, chd £5, family £25, park/garden only adm £4, chd £2, family £8.90. Park open daily; house & garden 14 Mar to 2 Nov, Fri to Tues. For NGS: Sat 14, Sun 15 June (11-5).**
Situated on W side of late C17 house. Herbaceous borders, yews clipped as buttresses, ponds and cascade, parish church set on terrace. Niches and carved urns. Long lawn to old West entrance. Restored orangery. Deer park with designated walks giving magnificent views. Steep slopes in park, cobbles in courtyard.

37 NEW EASTFIELD
Pound Lane, Yarlington, Wincanton BA9 8DQ. Lucy McAuslan-Crine. *3m W of Wincanton. A303 Wincanton exit, follow A371 to Castle Cary, Shepton Mallet, L on bend to Yarlington (2m). 2nd or 3rd R to Yarlington. At Xrds follow lane past front of Stags Head to end, entrance and parking at rear of Eastfield.* **Adm £3, chd free. Sun 20, Mon 21 July (11-5).**
¹/₄ acre made up of small gardens each with a different planting style. Mixture of tender and hardy herbaceous plants and shrubs incl olive trees, palms, agapanthus. A hint of the Mediterranean in Somerset. Ponds, roof garden, organic kitchen garden, young orchard, greenhouse, conservatory with beds filled with tropical plants. 2 unfenced ponds, steep steps to roof garden.

38 EASTON-IN-GORDANO GARDENS
BS20 0NB. *5m W of Bristol. M5 J19 Gordano Services, exit Bristol. Turn L for Easton-in-Gordano, past King's Arms PH. Park in church hall car park by football field & follow directions in car park.* Home-made teas at 36 Church Road. **Combined adm £3, chd free. Tues 15, 22, 29 July (2-5).**

36 CHURCH ROAD
Mr & Mrs I Crichton
¹/₄ -acre garden developed around ancient dewpond. Unusual secret garden incl large pond with fish, waterfall, and bridge built by local school. Herbaceous borders contain many flower arrangers' plants. Limited wheelchair access.

16 GORDANO GARDENS
Mr & Mrs Milsom
Cottage-style garden 80ft long with many pretty and unusual features incl decked area, natural pond with waterfall, grasses and herbaceous plants.

39 ♦ ELWORTHY COTTAGE
Elworthy TA4 3PX. Mike & Jenny Spiller, 01984 656427, www.elworthy-cottage.co.uk. *12m NW of Taunton. On B3188 between Wiveliscombe & Watchet.* **Adm £2.50,**

chd free. Thurs, Fris, Apr to Aug (10-4). Please phone for other times. For NGS: Sun 17 Feb; Thur 27 Mar; Sun 13 Apr; Sun 18, Thur 29 May; Thur 19 June; Sun 10, Thur 28 Aug. Suns (2-5); Thurs (10-4).

1-acre plantsman's garden and nursery in tranquil setting. Island beds, scented plants, clematis, unusual perennials and shrubs to provide yr-round interest. In spring, pulmonarias, hellebores and more than 100 varieties of snowdrops. Planted to encourage birds, bees and butterflies, lots of birdsong. Wild flower areas, decorative vegetable garden, living willow screen. Stone ex privy and pigsty feature.

✕ ❀

40 ◆ EMMAUS HOUSE
Clifton Hill, Bristol BS8 1BN. **Sisters of La Retraite, 0117 907 9950, www.emmaushouse.org.uk.** *From Clifton Downs down to Clifton Village to bottom of Regent St on R. Opp Saville Place.* **Adm £3, chd free. For NGS: Suns 27 Apr; 1 June; 13 July (11-4). Open for groups by appt (see website).**

1½ acres with Victorian walled kitchen garden, also fruit, formal herb and Zen gardens. Rose and herbaceous borders, lawns, secret garden with summerhouse. Courtyard garden with original stone watercourse. Ponds with fountains and fine views towards Dundry. Recently excavated remains of old coach house in wild garden. Partial wheelchair access only. Some sloping paths and steps.

✿ ✕ ❀ 🛏 ☕

41 NEW 14 ESKDALE CLOSE
Weston-Super-Mare BS22 8QG. Janet & Adrian Smith. *1½ m E of WSM town centre. J21 M5, 1½ m (B3440) towards WSM town centre. L at chevrons into Corondale Rd, 1st R into Garsdale Rd. Park halfway along and take footpath beside no. 37.* Home-made teas. **Adm £2,50, chd free. Thur 5 June (2-5.30).**

Interestingly-planned, natural style cottage garden with all-yr interest. Fish pond with seating areas, lawn, patio, rockery with conifers, Heidi playhouse with secrets. Wisteria archway leading to productive vegetable, herb and fruit garden.

✿ ✕ ❀ ☕

42 FAIRFIELD
nr Stogursey TA5 1PU. Lady Gass. *7m E of Williton. 11m NW of Bridgwater. From A39 Bridgwater to Minehead rd turn N; garden 1½ m W of Stogursey on Stringston rd. No coaches.* Teas. **Adm £3, chd free. Sun 30 Mar (2-5.30).**

Woodland garden with bulbs, shrubs and fine trees; paved maze. Views of Quantocks and sea.

✿ ✕ ❀ ☕

43 FERNHILL
nr Wellington TA21 0LU. Peter & Audrey Bowler, 01823 672423, www.sampfordarundel.org.uk/fernhill. *1m W of Wellington. On A38, White Ball Hill. Past Beam Bridge Hotel stay on A38 at top of hill, follow signs on L into garden & car park.* Home-made teas. **Adm £2.50, chd free.** Sun 6, Wed 9 July; Sun 3, Wed 6 Aug (2-5.30). **Visitors also welcome by appt June/July/Aug for groups of 10+, no coaches in car park.**

Mature wooded garden in approx 2 acres with rose, herbaceous, shrub and mixed borders, all unique in colour and content. Interesting octagonal pergola; alpine and bog garden with waterfalls and pools leading to shady arbour. Fine views over ha-ha to Blackdowns and Mendips.

✕ ❀ ☕ ☎

Heidi
playhouse
with secrets . . .

44 ◆ FOREST LODGE
Pen Selwood BA9 8LL. Mr & Mrs James Nelson, 01747 841283. *1½ m N of A303, 3m E of Wincanton. Leave A303 at B3081 (Wincanton to Gillingham rd), up hill to Pen Selwood, L towards church. ½ m, garden on L.* **Adm £2.50, chd free. For NGS: Thur 1, Sun 18 May (2-5).**

3-acre mature garden with many camellias and rhododendrons. Lovely views towards Blackmore Vale. Part formal with pleached hornbeam allée and rill, part water garden with lake. Unusual trees. Featured on BBC2 Open Gardens.

✕ ❀ ☕

45 ◆ GANTS MILL & GARDEN
Bruton BA10 0DB. Alison & Brian Shingler, 01749 812393, www.gantsmill.co.uk. *½ m SW of Bruton. From Bruton centre on Yeovil rd, A359, under railway bridge, 100yds uphill, fork R down Gants Mill Lane.* **Garden adm £3, chd £1. Mill & garden £5, chd £1. Suns, Bank Hols 15 May to end Sept. For NGS: Mon 25 Aug (2-5).**

¾ -acre garden. Clematis, rose arches and pergolas; streams, ponds, bog garden; brick circle, grasses in gravel; garden sculpture exhibition; riverside walk to the top weir; colour-themed planting with many iris, oriental poppies, delphiniums, day lilies, dahlias; also vegetable, soft fruit and cutting flower garden. The garden is overlooked by the historic watermill, also open on NGS day. Featured in 'Gardeners' World'.

✿ 🛏 ☕

46 NEW GARDD OWEN
16 Owen Street, Wellington TA21 8JY. Carole & Tim Lomas, 01823 664180. *From centre of Wellington follow signs to Sports Centre (B3187) for ½ m. R along Seymour St opp Dolphin PH, next L.* Home-made teas all days, ploughmans lunches 13, 27 June if ordered in advance. **Adm £2.50, chd free (share to All Saints Church, Rockwell Green). Fri 13 (12.30-4.30), Sun 15 (1.30-4.30), Fri 27 (12.30-4.30), Sun 29 June (1.30-4.30).**

Inspirational small garden comprising formal, rose and wild gardens, potager garden and pergola with a profusion of roses. Managed organically for the benefit of wildlife. Winner Best Rear Garden, Wellington in Bloom.

✕ ☕

47 190 GOLDCROFT
Yeovil BA21 4DB. Eric & Katrina Crate, 01935 475535. *Take A359 from roundabout by Yeovil College, then 1st R.* Home-made teas. **Adm £2.50, chd free. Sat 7, Sun 8 June (2-5). Evening Opening** wine, Mon 9 June (4-8). **Visitors also welcome by appt.**

¼ acre. Colour-themed shrub and herbaceous borders and island beds, rose garden, raised pond, seaside deck, fernery, hosta walk, arbour surrounded by silver bed, vegetable garden designed for the visually impaired and greenhouse. Many mature shrubs and trees and sensory features. Featured in 'The Garden'.

✗ ⊛ ☕ ☎

48 NEW GOOSEHILL

Sellicks Green TA3 7SA. Marina & Chris Lane. $3^1/_2$ m SW of Taunton. On rd between Blagdon Hill and Pitminster. Cream teas. Adm £2.50, chd free. Suns 22, 29 June (2-6).

Pretty 2-acre country garden surrounding C15 thatched house (not open) with extensive views of Blackdown and Brendon Hills. Traditional cottage garden with listed moon gate, potager, orchard, vegetable plot and exotic courtyard garden. Mature trees and hedges provide structure. Featured on BBC2 Open Gardens.

✗ ⊛ ☕

49 HANGERIDGE FARMHOUSE

Wrangway TA21 9QG. Mrs J M Chave. 2m S of Wellington. 1m off A38 bypass signed Wrangway. 1st L towards Wellington Monument over mway bridge 1st R. Home-made teas. Adm £2, chd free. Suns 20 Apr; 13 July; 17 Aug (11-5). Also open with Wrangway Gardens 5, 25 May.

Informal, relaxing, 30 yr-old family garden set under Blackdown Hills. Seats to enjoy views across Somerset landscape. Atmospheric mix of herbaceous borders, mixed rockeries and newly-created oriental garden, this lovingly-designed and still-evolving garden contains wonderful flowering shrubs, heathers, mature trees, rambling climbers and bulbs in season. Content and design belie its 1-acre size.

⏥ ✗ ⊛ ⊨ ☕

50 HARPTREE COURT

East Harptree BS40 6AA. Mr & Mrs Richard Hill & Mr & Mrs Charles Hill. 8m N of Wells. A39 Bristol rd to Chewton Mendip, then B3114 to E Harptree, gates on L. From Bath, A368 Weston-super-Mare rd to W Harptree. Cream teas. Adm £3, chd free. Sun 25 May (2-6).

Spacious garden designed when the house was built in 1797. Two ponds linked by a romantic waterfall and a stream, flanked by large trees. Herbaceous borders, lily pond and formal garden are among other features.

⏥ ⊛ ⊨ ☕

51 4 HAYTOR PARK

Bristol BS9 2LR. Mr & Mrs C J Prior, 0117 985 6582, chris_prior@blueyonder.co.uk. 3m NW of Bristol city centre. Edge of Coombe Dingle. From A4162 Inner Ring Rd between A4 Portway & A4108 Falcondale Rd, take turning into Coombe Bridge Ave, Haytor Park is 1st turning L. No parking in Haytor Park. Tea & cake. Adm £3.50, chd free. Visitors welcome by appt.

Discover an urban hideaway, packed with plants for every season. Arches and paths lead the wanderer to hidden spaces, a circle here, a pond there, is that a dragon lurking? Peace and tranquility enhanced by trickling water and lush planting at every level.

✗ ⊛ ☕ ☎

52 HENLEY MILL

Wookey BA5 1AW. Peter & Sally Gregson, 01749 676966, millcottageplants@tiscali.co.uk. 2m W of Wells. Off A371. Turn L into Henley Lane, driveway 50yds on L. Home-made teas. Adm £3, chd free. Visitors welcome by appt May to Sept, incl coaches and groups.

$2^1/_2$ acres beside R Axe. Traditional and unusual cottage plants informally planted in formal beds with roses, hydrangea borders, shady 'folly garden' and late summer borders with grasses and perennials. Ornamental kitchen garden. Rare Japanese hydrangeas.

⏥ ✗ ⊛ ☕ ☎

Listed moon gate, exotic courtyard garden . . .

53 ◆ HESTERCOMBE GARDENS

Cheddon Fitzpaine TA2 8LG. Mr P White, Hestercombe Gardens Trust, 01823 413923, www.hestercombe.com. 4m N of Taunton. Follow tourist signs. Adm £7.50, chd £3, concessions £6.95. Daily all yr (closed Xmas Day) (10-5.30). For NGS: Tues 4 Mar; 3 June (10-5.30).

Georgian landscape garden designed by Coplestone Warre Bampfylde, Victorian terrace/shrubbery and stunning Edwardian Lutyens/Jekyll formal gardens together make up 40 acres of woodland walks, temples, terraces, pergolas, lakes and

cascades. Featured in various publications and on ITV Tenth Anniversary Celebrations. Gravel paths, some steep slopes, steps.

⏥ ⊛ ☕

54 HILL LODGE

Northend, Batheaston BA1 8EN. Susan & Sydney Fremantle, 01225 852847, sydney.fremantle@homecall.co.uk. 4m NE of Bath. Turn N in Batheaston village up steep, small rd signed Northend & St Catherine. Hill Lodge $3/_4$ m on L. Parking in courtyard for disabled, frail & elderly. Home-made teas. Adm £3.50, chd free. Sun 8 June (2-5). Visitors also welcome by appt mid-May for alpines, throughout summer until late Sept (asters). Individuals or groups, no coaches.

3-acre country garden used for work experience by horticultural students because of variety of features incl stream, small wildlife lake, 2 ponds, bog garden, herbaceous borders, alpine bed, rose/clematis pergola, small cottage garden, vegetable garden, orchard, coppice and hill with trees and view. Small lake with nesting waterfowl. Plants for sale in aid of Off The Record Young Carers' Service. Some slopes.

⏥ ✗ ⊛ ☕ ☎

55 HILLCREST GARDENS

Redcliffe Bay BS20 8HN. $2^1/_2$ m from Portishead. Take Nore Rd S out of Portishead centre for $2^1/_2$ m. Past Feddon Village (old Nautical School), Hillcrest Rd is 1st L. Combined adm £3, chd free. Sun 13 July (10.30-5).

Coastal village with stunning views of Wales and the Bristol Channel. Weather permitting spectacular sunsets.

25 HILLCREST ROAD

Colin & Molly Lewis. (see separate entry).

✗

LITTLE GABLE

2 Hillcrest Road. Bill & Maureen Lloyd

Garden built virtually from scratch over 11yrs. Lawned area with pond and herbaceous border, gravel garden and small Japanese garden, all with panoramic views over the Channel. Enclosed patio area with rhododendrons and azaleas. A particular feature is the hydrangea hedge.

✗

56 25 HILLCREST ROAD
Redcliffe Bay BS20 8HN. Colin & Molly Lewis. *2¹/₂ m from Portishead. Take Nore Rd S out of Portishead centre for 2¹/₂ m. Past Feddon Village (old Nautical School). Hillcrest Rd is 1st L.* Home-made & cream teas. **Adm £2, chd free. Suns 20 Apr; 18 May; 13 July (10.30-5); Thur 7 Aug (2-6).**
Sloping garden with 3 terraces; bottom - a lawn, middle - a formal garden with central fountain and extensively planted, top - a large patio with wisteria-covered pergola and spectacular water feature. Front garden is a riot of colour.
✖ ☕

The planting scheme is luscious and exotic with vibrant colour theming . . .

57 HINTON ST GEORGE GARDENS
TA17 8SA. *3m N of Crewkerne. N of A30 Crewkerne-Chard; S of A303 Ilminster Town Rd, at roundabout signed Lopen & Merriott, then R to Hinton St George.* Home-made teas. **Combined adm £5, chd free (share to Cats Protection). Sat 24, Sun 25 May (2-5.30).**
Pretty village with thatched Hamstone houses and C15 church.
☕

NEW ARKARINGA
69 West Street. Bel Annetts. *Access through passage on L*
This long, narrow sloping garden was planned to avoid the rectangular and to provide contrast in colour, texture, shape and habit in the planting (both vertically and horizontally) yr-long. Church view enhances effect. Steep steps, no handrail. Easier exit by gate at rear.

HOOPER'S HOLDING
45 High Street. Ken & Lyn Spencer-Mills
(See separate entry).
♿

MALLARDS
Gas Lane. Captain & Mrs T Hardy
Small garden surrounding bungalow with lovely views. Mixture of shrubs and herbaceous plants in beautiful peaceful setting. Front garden only accessible to wheelchairs.

THE OLD MALT HOUSE
High Street. Lady Peyton
1¹/₂ -acre plantsman's garden with views to Mendips. Wide variety of interesting trees, shrubs and perennials. Formal pool, sculptures.
✖

58 HOLT FARM
Bath Road, Blagdon BS40 7SQ. Mr & Mrs Tim Mead, 01761 462215. *12m S of Bristol. Off A368 Weston-super-Mare to Bath rd, between Blagdon & Ubley. Entrance to Holt Farm approx ¹/₂ m outside Blagdon, on LH-side.* Home-made teas. **Adm £2.50, chd free. Suns 27 Apr; 5 Oct (2-5).** Visitors also welcome by appt.
Contemporary planting. Quirky sculptures. Bountiful bulbs. Autumnal 'fireworks'. 'Posh' vegetable patch. Great views. Sinful teas. Featured in 'GGG'.
✖ ✿ ☕ ☎

59 HOMEWOOD PARK HOTEL
Abbey Lane, Hinton Charterhouse BA2 7TB. Homewood Park Hotel, www.homewoodpark.co.uk. *6m S of Bath. Just off A36 Warminster rd, before village of Hinton Charterhouse.* **Adm £3, chd free. Sun to Fri, Apr to Sept (11-5).**
Set in 10 acres of formal and informal gardens, incl circular rose garden and large herbaceous borders, rolling lawns and cut flower garden. Also large parkland with mature trees. Bath in Bloom award winner. Gravel paths, large front lawn, gentle slopes.
♿ ⬛

60 HOOPER'S HOLDING
45 High Street, Hinton St George TA17 8SE. Ken & Lyn Spencer-Mills, 01460 76389, kenlyn@devonrex.demon.co.uk. *(see directions for Hinton St George Gardens).* Home-made teas. **Adm £2.50, chd free (share to Cats Protection). Sat 19, Sun 20 July (2-5.30).** Also opening with **Hinton St George Gardens** 24, 25 May. Visitors also welcome by appt up to mid-Aug.

¹/₃ -acre garden in colour compartments; lily pool; azaleas, rare herbaceous and shrubby plants, many exotics. Pedigree cats. Garden mosaics developing. Gravel area, help with pushing available.
♿ ☕ ☎

61 JASMINE COTTAGE
26 Channel Road, Clevedon BS21 7BY. Margaret & Michael Redgrave, 01275 871850, www. bologrew.pwp.blueyonder.co.uk. *12m W of Bristol. M5 J20. Follow signs to seafront & pier, continue N on B3124, past Walton Park Hotel, turn R at St Mary's Church. Wheelchair access at rear entrance in The Avenue.* **Adm £2.50, chd free. Every Thur, 1 May to 31 July; Thurs 4, 11 Sept (11-4).** Visitors also welcome by appt May to 11 Sept.
Mature garden with specimen trees and shrubs. Pergola walk beside colourful herbaceous border leading to extensive bed of salvias and tender perennials. Unusual climbers grown for summer display. A decorative mini potager uses salmon traps for peas, beans and sweet peas. Adjacent nursery open May to Sept. Featured in 'Western Daily Press'. RHS Recommended Garden 2008.
♿ ✖ ✿ ☎

62 28 KENSINGTON ROAD
St George, Bristol BS5 7NB. Mr Grenville Johnson & Mr Alan Elms, 0117 949 6788, www.victorianhouse-garden.pwp.blueyonder.co.uk. *2¹/₂ m E of Bristol City centre. Take A420 in direction of St George towards Kingswood & Chippenham Rd. At Bell Hill St George, turn into Kensington Rd. Entrance to garden in Cromwell Rd at side of house.* **Adm £3.50. By appt only Sats, Suns 14, 15, 21, 22, 28, 29 June; 12, 13, 19, 20, 26, 27 July (2-5).** Visitors also welcome by appt throughout June & July.
Award-winning, small courtyard town house garden on 2 decked levels with Italianate classical features incorporating temple folly ruin, exotic and S-hemisphere gardens. Woodland stumpery and wildlife pond all add to the romantic atmosphere. The planting scheme is luscious and exotic with vibrant colour theming. Max 5 adults can be accommodated. Featured on BBC Gardeners' World and in Amateur Gardening and Gardeners' World magazines. Regret due to steps wheelchairs cannot be accommodated.
✖ ☎

63 KINGSDON NURSERY
Somerton TA11 7LE. Patricia
Marrow, 01935 840232. *2m SE of
Somerton. Off B3151 Ilchester rd.
From Ilchester roundabout on A303
follow NT signs to Lytes Cary; L opp
gates, 1/2 m to Kingsdon. Drive through
village, nursery signs on L, gate.* **Adm
£2.50, chd free. Suns 27 Apr; 25
May (2-7). Visitors also welcome by
appt.**
2-acre plantsman's garden with lovely
plants to see. Large nursery. Selection
of trees, shrubs and herbaceous and
rock plants for sale. Knowledgeable
gardener to help with new or
established gardens.

♧ ⍟ ☎

64 KINGSTON
Tockington Green. BS32 4LG. John
& Carol Phillpott. *2m N of
Almondsbury. Off A38.* **Adm £1.50,
chd free. Sun 15 June (2-6).**
Compact courtyard garden with
fishpool, village well, trees, shrubs,
perennials and bedding. Featured in
BBC2 Open Gardens.

♧ ✄ ⍟

65 KITES CROFT
Westbury-sub-Mendip BA5 1HU. Dr
& Mrs W I Stanton, 01749 870328.
*5m NW of Wells. On A371 Wells to
Cheddar rd, follow signs from
Westbury Cross.* **Visitors welcome by
appt.**
2-acre sloping garden planted for
colour throughout season with fine
views to Glastonbury Tor. Wander
down winding paths to rockery where
cypress-like columnars and yuccas
lend a Mediterranean air, pass ponds
and lawn to densely-planted mixed
borders, shrubs and perennials. Fruit
trees incl figs, walnut and mulberry. In
the wood primroses, bluebells and
cyclamen thrive.

⍟ ☎

66 KNOLL COTTAGE
Stogumber TA4 3TN. Elaine & John
Leech, 01984 656689, www.knoll-
cottage.co.uk. *3m SE of Williton.
From Taunton take A358 towards
Minehead. After 11m turn L to
Stogumber. In centre of Stogumber, R
towards Williton. After 1/3 m, R up
narrow lane, follow signs for parking.*
Home-made teas. **Adm £3, chd free.
Sun 7 Sept (2-5.30). Also open with
Stogumber Gardens** 22 June.
Visitors also welcome by appt.
2-acre garden started from fields in
1998. Extensive mixed beds with

shrubs, perennials and annuals. Over
80 different roses. Woodland area incl
many different rowans, hawthorns and
birches. Pond, vegetable and fruit area.

⍟ ♭ ☕ ☎

67 LABURNUM COTTAGE
Middle Street, Brent Knoll TA9 4BT.
Catherine Weber, 01278 760594. *2m
N of Highbridge. Off M5 at J22. Follow
A38 in Bristol direction for 1/2 m, turn L
into Brent Knoll. 1m then R at junction,
1st L into Middle Str.* Cream teas.
**Adm £3, chd free. Sun 6 July
(2-5.30). Visitors also welcome by
appt.**
1/2 -acre garden, recently developed, to
display collection of over 300 varieties
of hemerocallis (daylilies) incl many
unusual forms and spider types, some
for sale. Large, sweeping borders with
mixed plantings of shrubs, perennials
and many grasses. Registered
hemerocallis display garden. Gravel
paths.

♧ ✄ ⍟ ☕ ☎

Colourful rhododendrons, azaleas and acers in spring and vivid autumn colours . . .

68 LIFT THE LATCH
Blacklands Lane, Forton, Chard
TA20 2NF. Pauline & David Wright.
*11/2 m S of Chard. Signed in Forton
village. Blacklands Lane is off B3162 at
E end of Forton. Parking at Alpine
Grove Touring Park.* Teas. **Adm £2.50,
chd free. Sat 17, Sun 18 May; Sat
18, Sun 19 Oct (2-5).**
This pretty cottage garden is bordered
by a small stream incl large wildlife
pond and raised fish pond. Wide
variety of evergreens, giving yr-round
interest. Openings timed to coincide
with particularly colourful
rhododendrons, azaleas and acers in
spring and vivid autumn colours from
many trees and shrubs such as rhus,
liquidambar and cornus. Well worth a
visit. Music from local musicians.
Featured on BBC2 Open Gardens and
in 'Amateur Gardening' and 'Sunday
Times Magazine'.

♧ ✄ ⍟ ☕

69 THE LINTELS
Littleton-on-Severn BS35 1NS. Mr &
Mrs Ernest Baker. *10m N of Bristol,
31/2 m SW of Thornbury. From old
Severn Bridge on M48 take B4461 to
Alveston. In Elberton, take 1st L to
Littleton-on-Severn. 4th house 100yds
past Field Lane.* **Adm £2, chd free.
Sun 15 June (2-5).**
Small cottage-type garden in front of
house with good variety of herbaceous
plants. Main attraction Japanese
garden at rear with waterfall, koi carp,
stream, teahouse.

70 LITTLE GARTH
Dowlish Wake TA19 0NX. Roger &
Marion Pollard, 01460 52594. *2m S
of Ilminster. Turn R off Ilminster to
Crewkerne rd at Kingstone Cross, then
L, follow Dowlish Wake sign. Turn L at
Glebe Cottage (white cottage) before
reaching church. Turn R following
signs. Speke Hall car park in front of
nearby church may be used.* **Adm
£2.50, chd free. Every Thur, 5 June
to 11 Sept (10-5.30). Visitors also
welcome by appt.**
1/2 -acre plantsman's garden for all
seasons with many interesting and
unusual perennials. Although
essentially cottage style, emphasis is
placed on the artistic arrangement of
plants, using foliage, grasses and
colour themes. Teas and plants for sale
at nearby Cider Mill. Featured in 'The
Guardian'.

⍟ ✄ ☎

**71 LITTLE YARFORD
FARMHOUSE**
Yarford, Kingston St Mary TA2 8AN.
Brian Bradley, 01823 451350,
yarford@ic24.net. *31/2 m N of
Taunton. From Taunton on Kingston St
Mary rd. At 30mph sign turn L at
Parsonage Lane. Continue 11/4 m W, to
Yarford sign. Continue 400yds. Turn R
up concrete rd. Park on L.* Cream teas
(except eve). **Adm £3.50, chd free.
Sat 9, Sun 10 Aug (2-6), Mon 11 Aug
(11-5). Evening Opening £10, wine,
music & canapés, Fri 8 Aug (6-8.30).
Visitors also welcome by appt, no
large coaches.**
Creative landscaping around C17
farmhouse (not open). Interesting
and specimen trees including
pendulous, fastigiate and
variegated cultivars, especially beech.
3 waterlily ponds, shrubs, climbers,
herbaceous and grasses. Some
slopes.

⍟ ✄ ♧ ☕ ☎

72 ◆ **LOWER SEVERALLS**
Crewkerne TA18 7NX. Mary Pring,
01460 73234,
www.lowerseveralls.co.uk. *1½ m NE
of Crewkerne. Signed off A30
Crewkerne to Yeovil rd or A356
Crewkerne to A303.* **Adm £3, chd
free. Tues, Weds, Fris, Sats Mar to
July & Sept. For NGS: Suns 27 Apr;
4, 18 May; 15 June (2-5); Sats 13, 20
Sept (10-5).**
3-acre plantsman's garden beside early
Hamstone farmhouse. Herbaceous
borders and island beds with
collections of unusual plants, shrubs
and interesting features incl dogwood
basket, wadi, herb garden. Green
roofed building. Nursery specialises in
herbs, geraniums and salvias. Featured
in 'Gardens Illustrated' and RHS
handbook.
  ♿ ✂ ❀ ☕

73 ◆ **LYTES CARY MANOR**
Kingsdon TA11 7HU. National Trust,
01458 224471,
www.nationaltrust.org.uk. *3m SE of
Somerton. Signed from Podimore
roundabout at junction of A303, A37,
take A372.* **House and garden adm
£7, chd £3.50, garden only adm £5,
chd £2.50. Sats to Weds, 15 Mar to
2 Nov (11-4.30). For NGS: Sats 12
Apr; 19 July; 4 Oct (11-4.30).**
Garden laid out in series of rooms with
many contrasts, topiary, mixed borders
and herbal border based on famous
C16 Lytes Herbal, which can be seen
in house.
  ♿ ✂ ❀ ☕

Victorian paving and pots lead to split level garden featuring scented and flowering plants . . .

74 ◆ **MANOR FARM**
Middle Chinnock TA18 7PN. Earl &
Countess Antrim. *4m SW of Yeovil.
Off A30 from Crewkerne towards
Yeovil, look for signs A356 from A303
towards Crewkerne. Follow signs to
Middle Chinnock.* Home-made teas.

Adm £5, chd free. Sun 27 Apr (2-5).
Garden of rooms, now completely
organic; incl formal areas, mixed
borders, pond garden, views across
fields to wildlife pond, herb garden,
vegetable and cutting garden, orchard
and newly-planted nuttery. Wonderful
display of spring bulbs. Exhibition of
paintings and prints. mostly accessible
to wheelchairs, gravel paths and some
areas of wood chips.
♿ ✂ ☕

75 NEW **22 MANSFIELD
STREET**
BS3 5PR. Alice Hindle, 0117
9663448 (eve),
tralela@hotmail.co.uk. *From
Redcliffe area of Bristol take A38 S
through Bedminster into West
Street. Turn L into Parson Street.
Mansfield Street is third L.* Home-
made teas. **Adm £2, chd free. By
appt only** Suns 13, 20, 27 July;
Sat 2 Aug (2-5.30). **Visitors also
welcome by appt.**
Stylish, small city garden (10metres
x 5metres). Victorian paving and
pots lead to split level garden
featuring scented and flowering
plants. Decking gives views over
gravel area surrounded by
buddleia, fuchsias and lavender,
which flows into circular lawn
flanked by cottage garden plants.
Many bees in summer. 6-8 people
at any one time. Featured on
BBC2 Open Gardens 2007. Only
accessible via steps.
☕ ☎

76 **MAPLE HOUSE**
South Barrow, Yeovil BA22 7LN. Mr
& Mrs P K Shaw & Mrs E Verrinder.
*6m SW of Castle Cary. Off A359 but
best approached from Sparkford.
Garden is 2m N of Sparkford. Follow rd
sign to South Barrow & Lovington opp
Haynes Publishers, then NGS sign.* Tea
& cake. **Adm £4, chd free. Sat 31
May; Sun 1 June (2-6).**
Gently sloping 5-acre site with fine view
to Glastonbury Tor and Mendips.
Developing garden begun in 1996,
with lake, shrubberies, lawns, mown
paths, pergola. 4-acre wild flower
meadow (Somerset Wildlife site and
private nature reserve) with mature and
recently planted hedges, small wood of
native trees and shrubs. Pond; garden
around house with alpine bed and
herbaceous borders. Conservation a
priority.
♿ ✂ ❀ ☕

77 **MARSHFIELD GARDENS**
Marshfield SN14 8LR. *7m NE of
Bath. From Bath A46 to Cold Ashton
Roundabout, turn R onto A420.
Marshfield 2m. From M4 J18, turn R
onto A46 and L at Cold Ashton
Roundabout.* Home-made light
lunches and teas at 111 High Street.
**Combined adm £4.50, chd free. Sat
31 May; Sun 1 June (1-6). Evening
Opening** £4.50, wine at Weir
Cottage, Fri 30 May (5-8).
5 gardens in large, interesting village.
Guided walks 10.30 31 May, 1 June.
Other village attractions (01225
891229 for info).
☕

MONTAGUE HOUSE
1 Old School Court. Mr & Mrs
David Dodd. *Off E end of High
Str, turn R before Old School into
Weir Lane. Opp Weir Cottage*
Started in 2006. Grass, gravel,
flower borders, box trees,
espaliered apple trees and little
lavender walk. Old dry stone walls
form 2 sides. Wonderful view
across fields. Approx 100 sq yds.
✂

NEW **4 OLD SCHOOL COURT**
Mrs Jenny Wilkinson
Small courtyard garden with
cottage-style planting showing the
use of mixed planting in a small
space. Many clematis, roses and
other climbers on walls, arches
and pergola. Narrow path and
small garden restrict visitor
numbers at any one time.
✂

WEIR COTTAGE
Weir Lane. Ian & Margaret
Jones. *Opp Old School Court*
Approx ¼ -acre walled garden
divided into terraces. S-facing,
open aspect. Lawn, borders and
vegetable garden.
❀

43 HIGH STREET
Linda & Denis Beazer. *Continue
on from Weir Cottage, entrance
from Weir Lane*
Walled garden with terraced
potager and companion planting
leading to lawned area with
shrubs and herbaceous borders
and pond.
✂

111 HIGH STREET
Joy & Mervyn Pierce. *Bristol end
of village*

Large garden and paddock, split into many areas. Pond, summerhouse, many seating places, vegetable garden, walnut tree planted by owner 48 yrs ago. Quiet, relaxing garden.

&

78 MEARE GARDENS
Meare BA6 9TY. *3m W of Glastonbury. B3151 from Glastonbury to Wedmore into Meare. New House on L, parking along St Marys Rd/Oxenpill.* Home-made teas. **Combined adm £3, chd free.** Sun 8 June (2-6).
Meare village has a long history of farming and drainage with several C14 ecclesiastical buildings.

KNIGHTS COTTAGE
Oxenpill. Mr & Mrs Turner-Welch. *Continue through village after leaving The New House. At L on leaving village*
Cottage garden, mixed plantings. Water features and courtyard area.

MEAREWAY FARM
3 Meareway. Lee & Emma Butler. *Continue past The New House, next R into Meareway. 1st house on L past new houses. Minimal parking in Meareway Lane* Interesting S-facing garden. Mixed ornamental cottage plantings with some formality. Unusual plants and integrated vegetable growing within ornamental planting schemes. New children's play area and willow house.

THE NEW HOUSE
St Mary's Road. Joan & Ashley Middleton. *Parking in St Mary's Rd, opp Great House Court Lane* Cottage garden of approx ½ acre. Attractive landscaping with interesting plants and shrubs. Ornamental koi carp pond and marginal plants.

79 ◆ MILTON LODGE
Wells BA5 3AQ. Mrs D Tudway Quilter, 01749 672168, www.miltonlodgegardens.co.uk. *½ m N of Wells. From A39 Bristol-Wells, turn N up Old Bristol Rd; car park first gate on L.* **Adm £4, chd under 14 free. Tues, Weds, Suns & Bank Hols**

Easter to 31 Oct (2-5). **For NGS:** Suns 18 May; 8 June; 13 July (2-5). Mature Grade II listed terraced garden with outstanding views of Wells Cathedral and Vale of Avalon. Mixed borders, roses, fine trees. Separate 7-acre arboretum.

80 ◆ MONTACUTE HOUSE
Montacute TA15 6XP. The National Trust, 01935 823289, www.nationaltrust.org.uk. *4m W of Yeovil. NT signs off A3088 & A303.* **House and garden adm £9.50, chd £4.50, garden only adm £5.70, chd £2.80. Daily, not Tues, Mar to Oct.** For NGS: Sun 22 June (11-5).
Magnificent Elizabethan house with contemporary garden layout. Fine stonework provides setting for informally planted mixed borders and old roses; range of garden features illustrates its long history.

& ✂ ✿

81 NORTHFIELD HOUSE
Barton Rd, Barton St David TA11 6BJ. Mr & Mrs D R Clarke, 01458 223203, donald@clarke2186.fsnet.co.uk. *4m E of Somerton. From A37 Lydford traffic lights take B3153 Somerton rd. In Keinton Mandeville, turn R into Barton Rd, 100yds before derestriction sign. From Somerton take B3153 Castle Cary rd. In Keinton Mandeville, turn L into Barton Rd, 100yds after 30mph sign. House 250yds on L immed beyond Barton St David sign.* Home-made teas. **Adm £3, chd free.** Sun 15 June (2-5). **Visitors also welcome by appt.**
2 acres of semi-formal gardens, orchard and ponds with splendid views over Somerset levels to Glastonbury Tor and Mendips. Main features are rose arbour, nepeta beds and Shona sculptures. Large pond, children should be supervised.

82 26 NORTHUMBERLAND ROAD
Redland BS6 7BB. Gwendoline Todd. *Bristol. 5 mins walk from Redland stn, close to & parallel with Cranbrook Rd.* Light refreshments & teas next door or across rd. **Adm £2, chd free. Sat 14, Sun 15 June (11-5).**
Fragrant country cottage garden in middle of city with emphasis on scent and yr-round interest. This delightful small garden is packed with a wide range of plants and climbers. Patio is

taken over by unusual plants and herbs in pots to provide constantly changing display. Front garden has been planted to give a completely different feel and has a jungle effect. Featured in Amateur Gardening magazine.

Fragrant country cottage garden in middle of city . . .

83 NEW OLD COAT INN
Coat TA12 6AR. T S & S D Wilson-Chalon. *8m N of Yeovil. 2m N of A303 Tintinhull Forts junction.* Cream teas. **Adm £2.50, chd free. Sats, Suns 17, 18 May; 19, 20 July (2-6).**
2 acres of formal, informal and woodland plantings. Herbaceous borders, rockery and scree area, mature trees, fish pond and wildlife pond with lilies and marginal plants. Productive vegetable plots and 4 greenhouses.

84 35 OLD STATION GARDENS
Henstridge, Templecombe BA8 0PU. Mary McLean, 01963 364321, marysmclean@btinternet.com. *6m E of Sherborne, 9m W of Shaftesbury on A30.* Home-made teas available on request. **Combined adm £3, chd free. Combined with Cherry Bolberry Farm. Visitors welcome by appt June/July for individuals and groups of 10+.**
Small owner-designed plantaholic's garden. Many exotics mixed with roses, clematis and herbaceous. Raised beds, pergolas, patio and pond. Floriferous and abundant planting with added spring underplanting of bulbs to give extra interest. Bonsai collection of native and exotic trees.

85 OLIVE COTTAGE
Langley Marsh, Wiveliscombe
TA4 2UJ. Mrs Frankie Constantine,
01984 624210. *1m NW of
Wiveliscombe. From Taunton take
B3227 to Wiveliscombe. Turn R at T-
lights. At Square turn R past White
Hart & continue 1m. Olive Cottage on
R before Three Horseshoes PH.*
Home-made teas. **Adm £2.50, chd
free** (share to St Margarets
Hospice). **Suns 29 June; 24 Aug
(2-6). Visitors also welcome by appt.**
An informal cottage garden of about 2/3
acre created by the owner over 30yrs.
Small pond, bog garden and new
rockery, together with shrubs,
perennials, climbers and trees create
colour and interest throughout the yr.
Productive kitchen garden and 2
greenhouses where many of the plants
are raised. Some gravel paths, 2 short
slopes.
&. ✗ ⊗ ☕ ☎

86 ORCHARD WYNDHAM
nr Williton TA4 4HH. The Trustees.
*7m SE of Minehead. 16m Taunton. In
Williton A39 Minehead rd. L opp
agricultural machines showroom
signed Bakelite Museum, follow lane
past church to lodge, long drive to
house.* **Adm £3, chd free. Sun 1 June
(2-5.30).**
Garden of historic house (not open) in
parkland setting: woods, interesting old
trees, borders, rose walk, small lake,
wild garden. Gravel paths.
✗

Swallows
nest annually in
tea room . . .

87 3 PALMER'S WAY
Hutton BS24 9QT. Mary & Peter
Beckett, 01934 815110,
macbeckett@clara.co.uk. *3m S of
Weston-super-Mare. From A370 (N or
S) follow signs to Hutton. In village turn
L at PO, then 1st L in St Mary's Rd
then 1st L. Car park at St Mary's field,
signed, 2 mins walk. Very limited
disabled parking at garden.* Home-
made teas. **Adm £2.50, chd free.
Suns 29 June; 20 July (2-6). Visitors
also welcome by appt, Weds in July
only.**

Informal tapestry of densely-packed
mixed planting with sculptures and
found objects. Unusual perennials incl
hardy geraniums, ferns, grasses,
climbers. Knot garden surrounds herbs
and Minarette fruit trees. Gravel bed
and wildlife ponds. Major re-vamp of
borders incl new trees. Enjoy your
home-made teas in the tropical
conservatory. Home-made preserves,
crafts. Some steps, grass area, limited
access when wet.
&. ✗ ⊗ ☕ ☎

88 PENWOOD FARM
Parchey, Chedzoy, nr Bridgwater
TA7 8RW. Mr & Mrs E F W Clapp,
01278 451631. *3 1/2 m E of Bridgwater.
Take A39 from Bridgwater. Bridge over
M5, turn sharp R into Chedzoy Lane.
At T-junction in village turn L. Pass
church approx 3/4 m. Penwood Farm
facing sharp LH-bend. From Stawell off
Glastonbury rd, cross bridge over
King's Sedgemoor Drain (Parchey
River). 1st house on L. Teas.* **Adm
£2.50, chd free** (share to Chedzoy
Playing Field Association). **Suns 15,
22 June (2-5). Visitors also welcome
by appt June & July only, coaches
permitted.**
Plant lover's garden of approx 3/4 acre.
Terrace, patio, pergola, gravel, rock,
water and kitchen gardens. Over 400
different varieties of rose - old, 'new'
English and modern; collections of
clematis, hosta, penstemon, shrubs
and herbaceous perennials, many
unusual plants and trees. Japanese-
style bridge over sunken lavender knot
garden bordering 2 rill ponds with
water lilies. Swallows nest annually in
tea room.
✗ ⊗ ☕ ☎

**89 ◆ PRIOR PARK LANDSCAPE
GARDEN**
Ralph Allen Drive, Bath BA2 5AH.
The National Trust, 01225 833922,
www.nationaltrust.org.uk. *1m S of
Bath. Visitors are advised to use public
transport as there is no parking at Prior
Park or nearby, except for disabled
visitors. Telephone 01225 833422 for
'How to get there' leaflet.* **Adm £5,
chd £2.80. Daily, not Tues, 1 Mar to
31 Oct (11-5.30). Sats, Suns 1 Nov
to 22 Feb 2009 (11-dusk). Last adm
1 hr before closing. For NGS: Sun 8
June (11-5.30).**
Beautiful and intimate C18 landscape
garden created by Bath entrepreneur
Ralph Allen (1693-1764) with advice
from the poet Alexander Pope and
Capability Brown. Sweeping valley with
magnificent views of the city, Palladian

bridge and lakes. The Wilderness
Project, supported by the Heritage
Lottery Fund, was completed summer
2007. The restoration involved
reinstating the Serpentine Lake,
Cascade and Cabinet to their former
glory. Featured on radio and TV and in
regional press.
✗ ☕

90 QUAKERS
Lower Hazel BS35 3QP. Mrs Mary
Bailey. *10m N of Bristol. Turn off A38
in Rudgeway, signed Lower Hazel &
Old Down. 1/4 m at bottom of hill.*
Cream teas. **Adm £2.50, chd free**
(share to St Mary's Church,
Olveston). **Sun 31 Aug (2-5.30).**
Mature 3/4 -acre garden set against
backdrop of natural woodland. Colour-
themed mixed borders of seasonal
interest. vegetable plot and extensive
climbers on house. Several changes
since 2001. 1/4 -acre 'paddock' with
large pond, trees and shrubs now
shared with chickens and ducks.
✗ ⊗ ☕

91 18 QUEENS GATE
Stoke Bishop BS9 1TZ. Sheila & Eric
White, 01179 626066,
sheilaericwhite@yahoo.co.uk. *3m
NW of Bristol. From M5 J17, follow
A4018 (Bristol West) to Westbury-on-
Trym. At village centre join Stoke Lane,
go over T-lights, past shops to T-
junction. Turn R for 500yds then L at
mini-roundabout & immed R into Druid
Stoke Ave. Access lane on R between
20 & 22. No parking/access via
Queens Gate.* Home-made teas. **Adm
£3, chd free. Sun 27 Apr (2-6).
Visitors also welcome by appt.**
All-yr garden with adjoining woodland
garden. Various design features and
numerous unusual plants and trees,
grasses and containers. Good variety
of bulbs in spring. Colour-themed
borders, pergola and small Japanese
garden. Gravel area and alterations to
other areas for ease of maintenance.
Featured in 'Gardens Monthly'. Gravel
path in woodland.
&. ✗ ⊗ ☕ ☎

92 RACKLEY HOUSE
Rackley Lane, Compton Bishop
BS26 2HJ. R & J Matthews, 01934
732311. *2m W of Axbridge. SE
Weston-super-Mare. Leave A38 at
Cross & take rd to Loxton, Bleadon.
Rackley Lane approx 1 1/2 m from
Cross; Rackley House is only house on
RH-side at end of lane.* Cream teas.
Adm £2.50, chd free. Sat 7, Sun 8

June (2-5.30). Visitors also welcome by appt.

½-acre garden on S-facing slope with light alkaline soil. Features incl iris garden, rockery and scree, small knot garden, pond and terrace. Some unusual plants and variety of cyclamen, old-fashioned roses and penstemons. Fairly steep slopes, ramps provided for some steps. Help available if required.

Many old favourites planted into gravel . . .

93 ROCK HOUSE
Elberton BS35 4AQ. Mr & Mrs John Gunnery, 01454 413225. *10m N of Bristol. 3½ m SW Thornbury. From Old Severn Bridge on M48 take B4461 to Alveston. In Elberton, take 1st turning L to Littleton-on-Severn & turn immed R.* **Adm £2.50, chd free (share to St John's Church, Elberton). Suns 3 Feb (11-4); 30 Mar (2-6). Visitors also welcome by appt.**
1-acre walled garden undergoing improvement. Pond and old yew tree, mixed borders, cottage garden plants and developing woodland.

94 NEW ST CATHERINES COURT
St Catherine BA1 8HA. James Keach & Jane Seymour, alison@allium.freeserve.co.uk or applications in writing to Garden Flat, 3 Walnut Terrace, Bath BA1 6AB. *5m NE of Bath. After A46 crosses A420 heading towards Bath take 3rd L signed St Catherine. Garden 10mins drive down this narrow lane.* Home-made teas. **Adm £5, chd free. Visitors welcome by appt only.**
Originally built in C16 with impressive terraces. Its ancient yew hedges, numerous water features, grotto and orangery contribute to its romantic atmosphere. The garden has recently been undergoing renovation and the borders have been completely replanted in a contemporary style with late summer colour and grasses. Dogs allowed on leads.

95 SALTFORD FARM BARN
565a Bath Road, Saltford BS31 3JS. Eve Hessey, 01225 873380, eve.hessey@blueyonder.co.uk. *6m W of Bath. On A4 between Bath & Bristol, Saltford Farm Barn is at Bath end of village. Parking arrangements will be signed - busy A4 not suitable for parking.* Home-made teas. **Adm £3, chd free. Suns 30 Mar; 29 June (2-5). Evening Opening £3.50, wine, Fri 27 June (6-9). Visitors also welcome by appt.**
1-acre garden with 5 main separate gardens. Ornamental vegetable garden with trained fruit trees contained within scented hedges of lavender, rosemary and box. Woodland garden with seasonal shrubs and trees underplanted with spring bulbs, hellebores, ferns, foxgloves and alpine strawberries. Garden of reflection depicting owner's life in New Zealand and England, labyrinth, meadow, orchard and Mediterranean garden. Crafts for sale. Guided tours. Gravel paths.

96 SERRIDGE HOUSE
Henfield Road, Coalpit Heath BS36 2UY. Mrs J Manning, 01454 773188. *9m N of Bristol. On A432 at Coalpit Heath T-lights (opp church), turn into Henfield Rd. R at PH, ½ m small Xrds, house with iron gates on corner.* Cream teas. **Adm £4, chd free. Visitors welcome by appt July/Aug only, groups of 10+.**
2½-acre garden with mature trees, heather and conifer beds, island beds mostly of perennials, woodland area with pond.

97 ◆ SHERBORNE GARDEN
Litton BA3 4PP. Mr & Mrs John Southwell, 01761 241220. *15m S of Bristol. 15m W of Bath, 7m N of Wells. On B3114 Litton to Harptree rd, ½ m past The Kings Arms. Car park in field.* Tea & biscuits. **Adm £3, chd free. Mons only June-Sept, groups other days by appt. For NGS: Daily Fri 15 Feb to Tue 19 Feb (11-3); Sun 2 Mar (11-4).**
4½-acre gently sloping garden of considerable horticultural interest. Small pinetum, giant grasses area, woodland garden and 3 linked ponds with bridges. Collections of hollies (100), ferns (250), Asian wild roses with hybrids and climbing species, all well labelled, hemerocallis, water lilies and unusual trees and

shrubs. The winter garden includes snowdrops and hellebores. Picnic area.

98 NEW 3 SOUTHDOWN
Milborne Port Rd, Charlton Horethorne DT9 4NQ. Pippa Hill, 01963 220367. *4½ m NE of Sherborne. From Sherborne, B3145 towards Wincanton, at Charlton Horethorne 1st R to Milborne Port Rd. From Wincanton, follow signs to Sherborne, Milborne Port Rd on L after church.* Teas. **Adm £2, chd free. Suns 4, 11, 18 May (11-5). Also open The Stables, North Cheriton 18 May. Visitors also welcome by appt.**
Long garden with meandering curves leading towards views across fields. Mixed planting using many old favourites planted into gravel and amongst shrubs with one or two rarities. Many hidden surprises, garden full of sculptures, large and small, some easier to find than others. Ceramic sculpture studio, items for sale.

99 ◆ SPECIAL PLANTS
Nr Cold Ashton SN14 8LA. Derry Watkins, 01225 891686, www.specialplants.net. *6m N of Bath on A46. From Bath on A46, turn L into Greenways Lane just before roundabout with A420.* **Adm £4, chd free. Weds July to Sept (11-5). For NGS: Thurs 19 June; 17 July; 21 Aug; 18 Sept (11-5).**
Architect-designed ¾-acre hillside garden with stunning views. Started autumn 1996. Exotic plants. Gravel gardens for borderline hardy plants. Black and white (purple and silver) garden. Vegetable garden and orchard. Hot border. Lemon and lime bank. Annual, biennial and tender plants for late summer colour. Spring-fed ponds. Bog garden. Woodland walk. Allium alley. Free list of plants in garden. Adjoining nursery, open Mar through Oct. Featured in Saturday Telegraph.

SPRINGDALE
On Devon/Somerset border. Please see Devon entry.

101 NEW THE STABLES
North Cheriton, nr Templecombe BA8 0AL. **David & Gaynor Tunbridge.** *2m S of Wincanton. Sherborne B3145 to Wincanton, R at North Cheriton, follow signs. Blandford A357 to Wincanton. Through Templecombe, L North Cheriton, follow signs. Please park with care in narrow lane or follow signs to field parking.* **Adm £2.50, chd free. Suns 23 Mar** (11-4.30); **6 Apr** (2-5); **18 May** (11-5). **Also open 3 Southdown,** Charlton Horethorne 18 May.
Hidden garden, 1/3 acre, in pretty village. Sloping site bounded by stone walls, bank to field. Trees and shrubs attractively set out to suit surroundings. Spring garden full of hellebores, ferns and early flowering plants. Patio, steps to lower lawn, shallow steps through terraced garden to main lawn and mature borders. Lovely views.
🌼

102 NEW STOBERRY GARDEN
Stoberry Park, Wells BA5 3LD. **Frances and Tim Young,** 01749 672906, www.artinthegarden.org. *1/2 m N of Wells. From Bristol - Wells on A39, L into College Rd and immed L through Stoberry Park.* Home-made teas. **Adm £3.50, chd free. Sun 22, Mon 23 June; Sun 14 Sept** (11-5). **Visitors also welcome by appt.**
With breathtaking views over Wells and the Vale of Avalon, this 6-acre family garden planted sympathetically within its landscape provides a stunning combination of vistas accented with wildlife ponds, water features, sculpture, 1 1/2 -acre walled garden, sunken garden, gazebo, potager, lime walk. Colour and interest in every season; spring bulbs, irises, roses, acer glade, salvias. Several seated areas to relax and enjoy views and garden. Featured on BBC Inside Out and in 'Somerset Life' and local press.
✂ ☎

Stunning combination of vistas accented with wildlife ponds, water features, sculpture . . .

103 STOGUMBER GARDENS
TA4 3TH. *11m NW of Taunton. On A358. Sign to Stogumber, W of Crowcombe.* Home-made teas at village hall. **Combined adm £3, chd free. Sun 22 June** (2-6).
Five delightful gardens of interest to plantsmen in lovely village at edge of Quantocks.
☕

BROOK HOUSE
Brook Street. **Dr & Mrs J Secker-Walker.** *Next to car park*
Enclosed partially-walled garden, redesigned over last 3 yrs. Terraced patio area, lawn, mixed borders leading to small bog garden by brook and meadow with recently-restored wildlife pond.
✂

BUTTS COTTAGE
Daphne & Jim Morrison
Cottage garden with old roses, old-fashioned perennials, alpines, pond, small vine house and organic fruit and vegetable garden.
✂

CRIDLANDS STEEP
Mrs A M Leitch
Large and interesting garden with cider apple orchard and wildlife pond. Hidden paths leading to secret garden.
🌼

KNOLL COTTAGE
Elaine & John Leech
(See separate entry).

POUND HOUSE
Mr & Mrs B Hibbert. *Opp car park*
Old orchard on terraced sloping site, garden started 2000. Young trees, shrub borders, herbaceous plants, rockery, organic vegetable garden and courtyard with climbing plants and herbs.
✂

104 STOKE ST MARY GARDENS
TA3 5BY. *2 1/2 m SE of Taunton. From M5 J25 take A358 S towards Ilminster. Turn 1st R after 1 1/2 m. 1st R in Henlade then 1st L signed Stoke St Mary. Car parking in village hall car park, no parking at either garden.* Teas at Tuckers Farmhouse. **Combined adm £3, chd free. Visitors welcome by appt May to Sept, groups of 10+.**
Village nestles below beautiful backdrop of Stoke Hill. The 2 gardens lie between C13 church (with stained glass windows by the renowned Patrick Reyntiens) and popular Half Moon Inn. Playground at nearby Village Hall for parents with young children. Featured in 'Amateur Gardening', 'Somerset Life' and local press.
 ☎

FYRSE COTTAGE
Miss S Crockett, 01823 442556, stepcroc@tiscali.co.uk
Secluded cottage garden with an oriental flavour. 1/2 acre of lush planting with stream, pond, pergola and lots of sculptures and Chinese pots. Birch avenue leading to 1/2 -acre wildlife area.
✂

TUCKERS FARMHOUSE
Rebecca Pow & Charles Clark, 01823 443816, rebecca@powproductions.tv
Family garden in lovely rural location. Formal/cottage-style extending to natural with wildlife. Jekyll-style border and 'busy persons' gravel/grass border. Topiary, exotic planting in courtyard and pear tree avenue. Kids cricket pitch. Fruit garden and raised bed vegetable garden developed for TV Roots and Shoots series. Gravel and Jekyll borders devised for BBC 'Gardeners' World' magazine and vegetable garden for 'Kitchen Garden' magazine.
♿ ✂

105 STOWLEYS
Bossington Lane, Porlock TA24 8HD. **Rev R L Hancock.** *NE of Porlock. Off A39. 6m W of Minehead.* Cream teas. **Adm £2, chd free. Sat 21 June** (2-6).
Medium-sized garden, approx 2 acres with magnificent views across Porlock Bay and Bristol Channel. Roses, unusual tender plants incl leptospermum, drimys and

embothrium. Open day to incl Rev Rex Hancock's 80th birthday celebrations. Watchet Town Band. Gravel paths.

106 SUTTON HOSEY MANOR
Long Sutton TA10 9NA. Roger Bramble. *2m E of Langport, on A372. Gates N of A372 at E end of Long Sutton.* Home-made teas. **Adm £3, chd £2. Sun 13 July (2.30-6).**
3 acres, of which 2 walled. Lily canal through pleached limes leading to amelanchier walk past duck pond; rose and juniper walk from Italian terrace; Judas tree avenue; *Ptelea* walk. Ornamental potager. Drive-side shrubbery. Music by players from Sinfonia of Westminster.

107 ◆ TINTINHULL
nr Yeovil BA22 8PZ. **The National Trust, 01935 823956, www.nationaltrust.org.uk.** *5m NW of Yeovil. Tintinhull village. Signs on A303, W of Ilchester.* **Adm £5.40, chd £2.80. Weds to Suns, 15 Mar to 2 Nov. For NGS: Sat 19 July.**
C17 and C18 house (not open). Famous 2-acre garden in compartments, developed 1900 to present day, influenced by Hidcote; many good and uncommon plants.

108 TRANBY HOUSE
Norton Lane, Whitchurch BS14 0BT. Jan Barkworth. *5m S of Bristol. 1/2 m S of Whitchurch.* Leave Bristol on A37 Wells Rd, through Whitchurch village, 1st turning on R signed Norton Malreward. Teas. **Adm £2.50, chd free. Suns 13 July; 10 Aug (2-5).**
1¼-acre well-established informal garden, designed and planted to encourage wildlife. Wide variety of trees, shrubs and flowers; ponds and wild flower meadow. Plant sales in aid of The Wildlife Trust.

109 TRISCOMBE NURSERIES
West Bagborough TA4 3HG. Stuart Parkman. *8m Taunton, 15m Minehead. On A358, signed between villages of W Bagborough and Crowcombe.* Teas at Triscombe Stables. **Adm £2.50, chd free. Suns 1 June (2-5.30); 26 Oct (1-4).**
Private arboretum planted since 1986 in lovely location overlooking fields up to the Quantocks (AONB & SSSI). Acers, Japanese azaleas, oak,

coccinea splendens, conifers. Parrotia, cornus chinensis and more, underplanted incl cowslips.

110 8 TROSSACHS DRIVE
Bathampton BA2 6RP. Sheila Batterbury, 01225 447864, sheila@batterbury88.fsnet.co.uk. *1m E of Bath. On A36. From Bath, 2nd R up Warminster Rd (A36) into Trossachs Drive. From Warminster, 3rd L on entering Bathampton.* **Visitors welcome by appt.**
Terraced garden with views over Bath. Winding paths, ponds and waterfalls. Unusual plants and shrubs, rockeries, bog garden, herbaceous perennials, old roses, sitting areas with fine views over the countryside. An interesting garden with the benefit of National Trust woods as backdrop. A haven for wildlife. A plantswoman's garden. Featured in 'Amateur Gardening'. Mostly accessible to wheelchairs.

111 UBLEY HILL FARM HOUSE
Ubley Drove, Blagdon BS40 7XN. Peter Gilraine, 01761 462663, peter.gilraine@btinternet.com. *2m SE of Blagdon. From A38 (20m S of Bristol) at Churchill traffic lights, turn L onto A368 to Blagdon, 2m turn R onto B3134 (Burrington Combe), proceed to top of hill, 3m. Ubley Drove on L. 1/2 m down this no-through-rd, garden at end on R.* **Adm £3, chd free. Visitors welcome by appt** May to Aug incl, **cakes and refreshments available on request.**
1-acre garden set in secluded spot on top of Mendips with far-reaching views over Severn Estuary and Chew Valley. Sheltered S-facing lawn with herbaceous borders, raised flower beds and bog garden. Sit awhile in our courtyard garden and take in the almost subtropical splendour before climbing terraced rockeries to view wildlife pond and waterfall. Wild flower meadows and mass blooming of orchids in June. A plantsman's delight. Resident artist's studio available for viewing.

112 ◆ UNIVERSITY OF BRISTOL BOTANIC GARDEN
Bristol BS9 1JB, 01173 314912, www.bris.ac.uk/Depts/BotanicGardens. *1/2 m W of Durdham Down. By car from city centre, proceed across Downs towards Stoke Bishop, crossing T-lights at edge of Downs.*

Stoke Park Rd, 1st turning R off Stoke Hill. Parking opp in Churchill Hall Car Park. **Adm £4.50, chd free. Weds, Thurs, Fris, Suns, 21 Mar to 2 Nov (10-4.30)** plus some special Sat openings. **For NGS: Sun 14 Sept (2-5).**
New Botanic Garden being developed with organic flowing network of paths which lead visitors through collections of Mediterranean flora, rare natives, useful plants (incl European and Chinese herbs) and those that illustrate plant evolution. Angiosperm Phyllogeny display illustrates latest understanding of flowering plant relationships. Tropical pool, home to Giant Amazon Waterlily. Many tropical fruit and medicine plants. Tours of botanic garden to explain how the collections have been developed and used 2.15 and 2.45. Featured on BBC1 Points West and ITV West Tonight.

Music by players from Sinfonia of Westminster . . .

113 VELLACOTT
Lawford, Crowcombe TA4 4AL. Kevin & Pat Chittenden, 01984 618249. *9m NW of Taunton. Off A358, signed Lawford.* Home-made teas. **Adm £2.50, chd free. Sun 1 June, Every Thur, 5 June to 26 June; Sun 29 June (1-5).** Visitors also welcome by appt.
1-acre cottage garden with splendid views. Mixed herbaceous and shrub borders, grasses, alpines and ponds. A collection of trees, mainly betula and sorbus grown for bark and berries. Ornamental vegetable garden and other interesting features.

114 WATCOMBE
92 Church Road, Winscombe BS25 1BP. Peter & Ann Owen, 01934 842666, peter.o@which.net. *2m NW of Axbridge. From Axbridge, A371 to A38 N. Turn R up hill then next L into Winscombe Hill. After 1m reach The Square. Pink house on L after further 150yds down hill.* Home-made teas April, cream teas May & June. **Adm £2.50, chd free (share to Alzheimer's Society). Suns 27 Apr; 18 May; Wed**

4 June (2-6). **Visitors also welcome by appt.**
³/₄ -acre mature Italianate garden with colour-themed, informally planted mixed borders. Topiary, box hedging, lime walk, pleached hornbeams, orchard, vegetable plot, 2 small formal ponds, many unusual trees and shrubs.

115 WAYFORD MANOR

Crewkerne TA18 8QG. Mr & Mrs Robin Goffe, 01460 73253. *3m SW of Crewkerne. Turning N off B3165 at Clapton; or S off A30 Chard to Crewkerne rd.* Cream teas. **Adm £3, chd £1. Suns 23 Mar; 13 Apr; Sun 4, Mon 5, Sun 25 May; Sun 15 June (2-5). Visitors also welcome by appt.**
The mainly Elizabethan manor (not open) mentioned in C17 for its 'fair and pleasant' garden was redesigned by Harold Peto in 1902. Formal terraces with yew hedges and topiary have fine views over W Dorset. Steps down between spring-fed ponds pass mature and new plantings of magnolia, rhododendron, maples, cornus and, in season, spring bulbs, cyclamen, giant echium. Primula candelabra, arum lily, gunnera around lower ponds. Featured in 'The English Garden' magazine & calendar & 'The Daily Telegraph'.

Italianate garden, undulating lawns bordered by mature shrubs . . .

116 NEW WAYSIDE

Shepperdine Road, Oldbury Naite BS35 1RJ. Peter & Belinda Orford. *4m NW of Thornbury. From A38 follow signs to Oldbury Power Station then signs to Hill & Shepperdine. R at Xrds, then L into Shepperdine Rd, 3rd L.* Light refreshments & teas. **Adm £3, chd free. Sun 3 Aug (2-5).**
²/₃ -acre country garden with ornamental pond, Mediterranean plants, Italianate garden, undulating lawns bordered by mature shrubs, collection of acers, paddock, raised beds, herb corner, 3 patios, summerhouse. Gravel paths.

117 WELLFIELD BARN

Walcombe Lane, Wells BA5 3AG. David & Virginia Nasmyth, 01749 675129. *¹/₂ m N of Wells. From A39 Bristol to Wells rd turn R at 30mph sign into Walcombe Lane. Entrance at 1st cottage on R, parking signed.* Home-made teas. **Adm £3, chd free. Tue 20 May (11-6). Visitors also welcome by appt, coaches permitted (max 29 seater).**
1¹/₂ -acre gardens, made by owners over the past 11yrs from concrete farmyard. Ha-ha, wonderful views, pond, lawn, mixed borders, grass walks and interesting young trees. Structured design integrates house with landscape. New areas under development.

118 NEW WEST HUNTSPILL GARDENS

Highbridge TA9 3SD. *1m S of Highbridge. Off M5 at J22. Follow A38 towards Bridgwater through Highbridge into Westhuntspill. R at Orchard PH into Church Rd. 1st & 2nd L, ltd parking on rd.* Home-made teas. **Combined adm £3, chd free (share to Dystonia Society). Sun 20 July (2-5.30).**
Sprawling rural village with 2 churches, village hall, village green with old pump, school and 4 PHs, one C14.

NEW JOYCE & PETES

12 Grange Road. Joyce & Pete Wrigglesworth
Small garden with much interest. 3 yrs' development from scratch incl shrubs, perennials, annuals, small pond, ferns, small vegetable patch, carnivorous plants, shingle and grass areas.

NEW PATS

3 Sunny Close. Mrs Pat Boult
Large colourful garden with herbaceous border 60ftx15ft with other mixed borders of shrubs and plants, lawn, shingle and patio areas with pots of colourful plants, raised vegetable area leading to main garden through arch.

119 WEST LITTLETON GARDENS

SN14 8JE. *8m N of Bath. M4 J18, 2nd L signed West Littleton, 1m to village. From Bath A46, R after Dyrham Park then turning signed W Littleton as*

above. Parking 50yds beyond telephone box. Home-made teas. **Combined adm £3.50, chd free. Wed 18 June (2-6).**
Attractive small, rural community of 22 houses of traditional architecture within the Badminton Estate. 2 working farms and a church notable for its C13 bell turret, one of the finest examples in Glos.

CADWELL BARN

John & Elizabeth Edwards. *¹/₂ m on Marshfield side of W Littleton*
Pleached lime walk, Italianate garden with several small enclosures.

LITTLETON HOUSE

Christopher Bell. *Opposite car park in centre of village*
Herbaceous borders set off by dry stone walls and traditional stables and cow byres. Many roses, especially climbers and ramblers.

ST JAMES'S GRANGE

Mr & Mrs David Adams. *On R just past red phone box at top of village green*
In delightful setting overlooking unusual C13 church spire. Dry stone walls support pleached lime terracing, courtyard's raised mixed borders and enclose kitchen garden. Trees, shrubs, lavender beds, rose pergola, parterre, box hedging and water. A garden with French overtones.

120 WESTBROOK HOUSE

West Bradley BA6 8LS. Keith Anderson and David Mendel, 01458 850604. *4m E of Glastonbury. From A361 at W Pennard follow signs to W Bradley (2m).* **Adm £3, chd free (share to West Bradley Church). Sun 27 Apr; Sat 14 June (11-5). Visitors also welcome by appt.**
1¹/₂ acres of formal gardens with mixed shrub/herbaceous borders; 2 acres of newly-planted orchard and meadows with spring flowers and species roses.

121 NEW 159 WESTBURY LANE

Coombe Dingle BS9 2PY. Maureen Dickens. *2m from J18 M5. L A4162/Sylvan Way, B4054/Shirehampton Rd, R to*

Westbury Lane. 1st house on R. Home-made teas. **Adm £3, chd free. Sat 17, Thur 22 May (2-5).** Gently sloping garden, newly-designed by owner. Large patio at rear, walled beds, pond and many other features. Some common and unusual plants with successional planting to give colour throughout yr. Closely planted in owner's style. From patio, garden is seen through rambler and other climber-covered wooden archways.

122 NEW WIBBLE GARDENS
Wibble Farm Nurseries, Williton TA4 4DD. Mrs Michelle Francis. *1m NE of Williton. On main A39 rd between Williton and W Quantoxhead.* Light refreshments & teas. **Adm £2.50, chd free. Suns 30 Mar; 7 Sept (11-4).**
1 acre of gardens adj to 17-acre nursery nestling at foot of Quantock Hills. Full of interesting and many rare plants. Started in 1987, a true garden to delight and inspire. Newly-planted maze.

Nurserymen available for advice. Nursery demonstrations. Slightly sloping, grass paths.

123 NEW WRANGWAY GARDENS
Wrangway, Wellington TA21 9QG. *2m SW of Wellington. 1m off A38 bypass signed Wrangway, 1st L towards Wellington monument over motorway bridge, 1st R.* Home-made teas. **Combined adm £4, chd free. Mon 5, Sun 25 May (11-5).**
2 contrasting gardens.

NEW BROOMSTAIRS
M & G Blake. *From Hangeridge Farm, continue parallel to motorway, 2nd L (signed dead-end), uphill to end of lane*
Over 4 acres of natural garden on slope overlooking Taunton Deane. Wonderful views, unusual trees and shrubs with range of rhododendrons, azaleas and

camellias. Arboretum, woodland garden and pond.

HANGERIDGE FARMHOUSE
Mrs J M Chave
(See separate entry).

124 YEWS FARM
East Street, Martock TA12 6NF. Louise & Fergus Dowding, 01935 822202. *Midway between Yeovil and Langport. Turn off main str through village at Market House, onto East Str, past PO, garden 150yds on R.* Home-made teas. **Adm £4, chd free. Tue 15 July (2-6). Visitors welcome by appt.**
1 acre of theatrical planting. Outsized plants in jungle garden incl 14ft high echium and Ferrula communis. Sculptural planting for height, shape, leaf and texture. Self-seed gravel garden, box and bay ball border, espalier apples, cloud pruning. Working organic kitchen garden feeds growing family. Hens and pigs are the compost heap, teenage cider orchard. Featured in 'English Garden' and 'Kitchen Garden'.

Bristol Area County Volunteers

County Organiser
Eileen Mantell, Rook Farm, Oldbury-on-Severn BS35 1PL, 01454 412281, eileen.richard@btopenworld.com

County Treasurer
Richard Bennett, Rook Farm, Oldbury-on-Severn, BS35 1PL, 01454 412281, eileen.richard@btopenworld.com

Publicity
Mary Popham, Apple Acre, Star, Winscombe BS34 1QF, 01934 843789, MrsMPopham@aol.com

Leaflets
Jean Damey, 2 Hawburn Close, Brislington, Bristol BS4 2PB, 0117 9775587, jddamey@hotmail.com

Assistant County Organisers
Graham Guest, The Caves, Downside Road, Backwell BS48 3DH, 01275 472393, gandsguest@btinternet.com
Margaret Jones, Weir Cottage, Weir Lane, Marshfield, Chippenham SN14 8NB, 01225 891229, weircott@3disp.co.uk
Jane Perkins, Woodland Cottage, Oldbury-on-Severn BS35 1PL, 01454 414570, jane.perkins@simtec.ltd.uk

Somerset County Volunteers

County Organiser
Patricia Davies-Gilbert, Coombe Quarry, West Monkton, Taunton TA2 8RE, 01823 412187, patriciacoombequarry@tiscali.co.uk

County Organiser Designate
Lucy Hetherington, Badgers Acre, Stone Allerton, Axbridge BS26 2NW, 01934 713159, lucyhetherington@btinternet.com

County Treasurer
David Bull, Greenfield House, Stone Allerton, Nr Axbridge BS26 2NH, 01934 712609, davidvivien@q-serve.com

Publicity
Alan Hughes, Dodhill Firs, Nailsbourne, Taunton TA2 8AT, 01823 451633, dodhill@hotmail.com

Photographer/Talks
Andrew & Sarah Wilcox, Epworth, Kingston St. Mary, Taunton TA2 8HZ, 01823 451402, epworth2@tiscali.co.uk

Assistant County Organisers
Brian & Dilly Bradley, Little Yarford Farmhouse, Kingston St Mary, Taunton TA2 8AN, 01823 451350
Lella Fountaine, 116 Wellsway, Bath BA2 4SD, 01225 334821, fountaines@tiscali.co.uk
Alison Highnam, Candleford, Fernhill, East Stour, Nr Gillingham SP8 5ND, 01747 838133
Rosemary Lee, Bay House West, Bay Hill, Ilminster TA19 6AT, 01460 54117, rosemarylee@supanet.com
Diana Sprent, Watermeadows, Clapton, Crewkerne TA18 8PU, 01460 74421, sprentmead@hotmail.com
Judith Stanford, Bowden Hill Cottage, Bowden Hill, Chilcompton, Radstock BA3 4EN, 01761 414266

STAFFORDSHIRE

& part of West Midlands

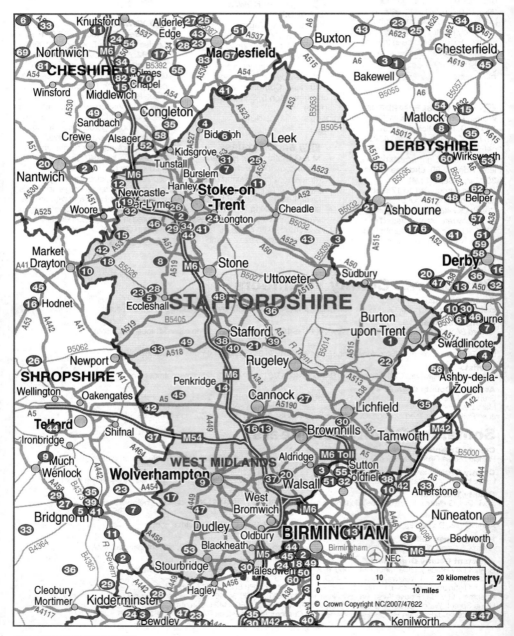

Opening Dates

March

SUNDAY 23
- 38 23 St Johns Road

SUNDAY 30
- 30 Millennium Garden

April

SUNDAY 27
- 23 Heath House

May

THURSDAY 1
- 42 Smithy Cottage

FRIDAY 2
- 38 23 St Johns Road

SUNDAY 11
- 20 Four Seasons

WEDNESDAY 14
- 1 Bankcroft Farm
- 11 Consall Hall Landscape Garden (Evening)

SATURDAY 17
- 9 43 Broad Lane

SUNDAY 18
- 3 The Beeches
- 16 Dorset House
- 20 Four Seasons
- 39 The Secret Garden

WEDNESDAY 21
- 1 Bankcroft Farm

SATURDAY 24
- 34 The Old Dairy House

SUNDAY 25
- 2 Barn House
- 34 The Old Dairy House
- 49 Yew Tree Cottage

MONDAY 26
- 42 Smithy Cottage

WEDNESDAY 28
- 1 Bankcroft Farm

THURSDAY 29
- 47 The Wombourne Wodehouse

SATURDAY 31
- 19 10 Fern Dene

June

SUNDAY 1
- 21 The Garth
- 23 Heath House

WEDNESDAY 4
- 1 Bankcroft Farm

THURSDAY 5
- 42 Smithy Cottage

FRIDAY 6
- 38 23 St Johns Road

SATURDAY 7
- 28 Lower House

SUNDAY 8
- 5 Birch Trees
- 24 High Trees
- 28 Lower House

WEDNESDAY 11
- 1 Bankcroft Farm

FRIDAY 13
- 39 The Secret Garden
- 40 Shepherds Fold Gardens (Evening)
- 48 Yarlet House

SATURDAY 14
- 18 Elvendell

SUNDAY 15
- 8 The Bowers
- 30 Millennium Garden

WEDNESDAY 18
- 1 Bankcroft Farm

SUNDAY 22
- 3 The Beeches
- 9 43 Broad Lane
- 25 The Hollies
- 32 Moss Cottage
- 46 Wilkins Pleck

SATURDAY 28
- 17 The Elms

SUNDAY 29
- 7 Bleak House (Evening)
- 21 The Garth
- 22 Grafton Cottage
- 33 The Mount
- 39 The Secret Garden

July

THURSDAY 3
- 42 Smithy Cottage

SATURDAY 5
- 5 Birch Trees

SUNDAY 6
- 6 Blackwood House Farm
- 14 4 Dene Close
- 22 Grafton Cottage
- 45 The Wickets

SATURDAY 12
- 9 43 Broad Lane
- 10 1 The Brodder

SUNDAY 13
- 10 1 The Brodder
- 24 High Trees
- 32 Moss Cottage
- 40 Shepherds Fold Gardens

SATURDAY 19
- 4 Biddulph Grange Garden
- 18 Elvendell
- 36 The Old School House

SUNDAY 20
- 7 Bleak House
- 8 The Bowers
- 23 Heath House
- 31 Moorfield
- 36 The Old School House
- 41 Silverwood
- 49 Yew Tree Cottage

SUNDAY 27
- 2 Barn House
- 3 The Beeches
- 26 6 Kendal Place
- 46 Wilkins Pleck

August

SATURDAY 2
- 9 43 Broad Lane (Evening)

SUNDAY 3
- 12 Courtwood House
- 24 High Trees
- 27 Lilac Cottage

THURSDAY 7
- 42 Smithy Cottage

FRIDAY 8
- 39 The Secret Garden

SUNDAY 10
- 16 Dorset House
- 20 Four Seasons
- 22 Grafton Cottage
- 29 Manor Cottage Garden

TUESDAY 12
- 15 Dorothy Clive Garden

SATURDAY 16
- 9 43 Broad Lane (Evening)

TUESDAY 19
- 15 Dorothy Clive Garden

SUNDAY 24
- 5 Birch Trees

MONDAY 25
- 5 Birch Trees

SATURDAY 30
- 17 The Elms

September

THURSDAY 4
- 42 Smithy Cottage

FRIDAY 19
- 38 23 St Johns Road

SATURDAY 20
- 4 Biddulph Grange Garden

SUNDAY 21
- 25 The Hollies

October

WEDNESDAY 8
⑪ Consall Hall Landscape Garden (Evening)

MONDAY 20
㊸ Stonehill Quarry Garden

MONDAY 27
㊸ Stonehill Quarry Garden

November

MONDAY 3
㊸ Stonehill Quarry Garden

MONDAY 10
㊸ Stonehill Quarry Garden

Gardens open to the public

④ Biddulph Grange Garden
⑪ Consall Hall Landscape Garden
⑮ Dorothy Clive Garden
㊹ The Trentham Estate

By appointment only

⑬ 12 Darges Lane
㉟ The Old Rectory, Clifton Campville
㊲ 15 St Johns Road

Also open by appointment ☎

② Barn House
③ The Beeches
⑤ Birch Trees
⑦ Bleak House
⑧ The Bowers
⑨ 43 Broad Lane
⑩ 1 The Brodder
⑫ Courtwood House
⑭ 4 Dene Close
⑯ Dorset House
⑰ The Elms
⑱ Elvendell
㉑ The Garth
㉒ Grafton Cottage
㉓ Heath House
㉔ High Trees
㉕ The Hollies
㉙ Manor Cottage Garden
㉚ Millennium Garden
㉛ Moorfield
㉝ The Mount
㊳ 23 St Johns Road
㊴ The Secret Garden
㊵ Shepherds Fold Gardens
㊶ Silverwood
㊷ Smithy Cottage
㊸ Stonehill Quarry Garden
㊺ The Wickets
㊻ Wilkins Pleck
㊼ The Wombourne Wodehouse
㊾ Yew Tree Cottage

The Gardens

① BANKCROFT FARM

Tatenhill DE13 9SA. Mrs Penelope Adkins. *2m SW of Burton-on-Trent. Branston Rd. Take Tatenhill Rd off A38 Burton-Branston flyover. 1m, 1st house on L approaching village. Parking on farm.* **Adm £2.50, chd free. Every Wed 14 May to 18 June (2-5).**
Lose yourself for an afternoon in our 1½ acre organic country garden. Arbour, gazebo and many other seating areas to view ponds and herbaceous borders, backed with shrubs and trees with emphasis on structure, foliage and colour. Productive fruit and vegetable gardens, wildlife areas and adjoining 12 acre native woodland walk. Picnics welcome. Winner Best Wildlife Pond, Gold for rear garden & vegetable.
🕭 ✗ ⊗ ☕

Waterfalls and camellia walk make this an oasis of peace in suburbia . . .

② BARN HOUSE

Clayton Road, Newcastle-u-Lyme ST5 4AB. Mike French, 01782 636650, frenchmike@talk21.com. *1m S of Newcastle. ½ m from exit 15 M6. L to A519 Clayton Rd to Newcastle. Straight over next roundabout. Barn House is on L after 80yds before pedestrian crossing lights. 1¼ m from Newcastle town centre S towards M6, pass the Nuffield Hospital, Barn House is 80yds on the R after pedestrian crossing lights up drive. Parking available on Sundays at the Nuffield Hospital.* **Adm £3, chd free. Suns 25 May; 27 July (1-5). Visitors also welcome by appt.**
Beautiful landscaped ¾ -acre garden created by a surgeon whilst on call for kidney transplantation. 3 ponds linked by waterfalls and camellia walk make this an oasis of peace in suburbia. 'Secret' garden with rockeries and mature specimen trees and shrubs with a potager/market garden to boot. Enforced redesigning in 2007 due to storms. Pictorial and descriptive history of the garden.
🕭 ✗ ⊗ ☕ ☎

③ THE BEECHES

Mill Street, Rocester ST14 5JX. Mr & Mrs K Sutton, 01889 590631, joy@joy50.orangehome.co.uk. *5m N of Uttoxeter. On B5030, turn R into village by JCB factory. By Red Lion PH take rd for Marston Montgomery. Garden 250yds on R.* Home-made teas. **Adm £3, chd free. Suns 18 May; 22 June; 27 July (1.30-5). Visitors also welcome by appt May to Aug.**
Stunning plant lover's garden of approx ⅔ acre, enjoying views of surrounding countryside. Formal box garden, vibrant colour-themed herbaceous borders, shrubs incl rhododendrons, azaleas (looking good in May), pools, roses, fruit trees, clematis and climbing plants yr-round garden. Cottage garden planting with a secret round every corner.
🕭 ✗ ⊗ ☕ ☎

④ ◆ BIDDULPH GRANGE GARDEN

Grange Road, Biddulph ST8 7SD. The National Trust, 01782 517999, www.nationaltrust.org.uk. *3½ m SE of Congleton. 7m N of Stoke-on-Trent off the A527. Congleton to Biddulph rd.* **Adm £5.80, chd £2.90. Wed to Sun 15 Mar to 2 Nov. For NGS: Sats 19 July; 20 Sept (11-5).**
Exciting and rare survival of high Victorian garden extensively restored since 1988. Conceived by James Bateman, the 15 acres are divided into a number of smaller gardens designed to house specimens from his extensive plant collection. An Egyptian Court, Chinese Temple and Willow Pattern bridge, pinetum and arboretum combine to make the garden a miniature tour of the world.
✗ ⊗ ☕

⑤ BIRCH TREES

Copmere End, Eccleshall, Stafford ST21 6HH. Susan & John Weston, 01785 850448. *1½ m W of Eccleshall. On B5026, turn at junction signed Copmere End. After ½ m straight* across Xrds by Star Inn. Home-made teas. **Adm £3, chd free. Sun 8 June; Sat 5 July; Sun 24, Mon 25 Aug** (1.30-5.30). Also open **Lower House** 8 June. Visitors also welcome by appt. Limited parking for private visits.

Peaceful ½ -acre country garden with views over surrounding countryside. Plant enthusiasts' garden with many rare and unusual varieties, designed with wildlife in mind. Herbaceous borders, peat bed, water features and vegetable plot. Featured in 'Staffordshire Life'.

& ✗ ✿ ☕ ☎

---

6 BLACKWOOD HOUSE FARM
Horton ST13 8QA. Anne & Adam James. *4m W of Leek. 6m N of Stoke on Trent. A53 Stoke to Leek turn off at Black Horse PH in Endon, go to T-junction, turn R into Gratton Lane. Take 4th L (approx 2½ m) signed Lask Edge, over ford up bank, farm on L.* Home-made teas. **Adm £3, chd free. Sun 6 July (2-5).**

1½ acre country cottage garden with spectacular views. Large mixed borders, rockery, natural stream and koi carp pond. Grass and gravel paths through shrubs and trees. Lovely colourful wildlife garden packed with plants.

✗ ✿ ☕

---

7 BLEAK HOUSE
Bagnall ST9 9JT. Mr & Mrs J H Beynon, 01782 534713. *4m NE of Stoke-on-Trent. A5009 to Milton Xrds, turn for Bagnall. 2m up hill past golf course to corner opp Bagnall Heights.* Home-made teas. **Adm £3, chd free. Sun 20 July (1-5). Evening Opening £4, light refreshments & wine, Sun 29 June (5-9).** Visitors also welcome by appt groups of 10+, coaches permitted.

1 acre on many levels. Natural stone quarry with jungle planting, pool and waterfall. Italianate terraces with canal, rose garden, white garden planted in Edwardian style around Edwardian house (not open), many unusual plants. Display by N Staffs bee keepers, local honey for sale and make your own candle.

✗ ✿ ☕ ☎

---

8 THE BOWERS
Church Lane, Standon, nr Eccleshall ST21 6RW. Maurice & Sheila Thacker, 01782 791244, metbowers@aol.com. *5m N of Eccleshall. Take A519 & at Cotes*

Heath turn L signed Standon. After 1m turn R at Xrds by church, into Church Lane ½ m on L. Home-made teas. **Adm £2.50, chd free. Suns 15 June; 20 July (1.30-5).** Visitors also welcome by appt June & July evenings only.

Romantic multi-roomed cottage garden set in ¾ -acre quiet rural location. Strong colour-themed borders planted with rare and unusual perennials. Over 150 clematis, height and blossom in abundance. Water feature, collections of hardy geraniums and hostas. A colourful tranquil oasis. Winner of Stone in Bloom, Front & Back Gardens & Gardener of the Year.

✗ ✿ ☕ ☎

Country garden trying to survive and stay sane against rabbits and moles . . .

---

9 43 BROAD LANE
Bradmore, Wolverhampton WV3 9BW. Bob Parker & Greg Kowalczuk, 01902 332228, roboparker@blueyonder.co.uk. *2m SW of Wolverhampton. 2m from town centre on SW side. Follow signs for Bantock House, adjacent to Bantock Park. Broad Lane is part of B4161. 200yds from Bradmore Arms T-light.* Home-made teas. **Adm £2.50, chd free. Sat 17 May; Sun 22 June; Sat 12 July (1.30-5.30). Evening Openings £3.50, light refreshments, wine, Sat 2, 16 Aug (7.30-10.30). Visitors also welcome by appt June to Aug, groups of 10+.**

Escape the hustle and bustle of busy urban surroundings and enter the secure solitude of the high walled secret garden. A magical Aladdin's cave, full of the unexpected. Candles flicker and lanterns glow in the evening. Daylight is no less enchanting, the background is green, a plantsman's garden, but different. Featured in & on various publications & TV.

☕ ☎

---

10 1 THE BRODDER
Old Springs. TF9 2PQ. Jackie Burwood, 01630 657188. *2m E of Market Drayton. On A53 Market Drayton to Newcastle under Lyme. Turn R to Almington. Through village, cottage on RH-side. Parking in signed field. Uneven sufaces.* Home-made teas. **Adm £3, chd free. Sat 12, Sun 13 July (2-5).** Visitors also welcome by appt July, limited parking, small groups (mini bus).

Pretty, plant lovers country garden trying to survive and stay sane against rabbits and moles. An ever expanding use of grasses to unite the garden with surrounding countryside. Sit in the summerhouse and enjoy the views or under the pergola and relax to the sound of running water. Featured in 'Sunday Sentinel'.

✗ ✿ ☕ ☎

---

10 CHESTNUT WAY
Repton. See Derbyshire.

---

11 ◆ CONSALL HALL LANDSCAPE GARDEN
Wetley Rocks ST9 OAG. William Podmore, 01782 749994/551947, www.consallgardens.co.uk. *7m from Stoke-on-Trent, Leek & Cheadle. A52 after Cellarhead Xrds. Turn L on to A522, after ¼ m turn R to Consall & straight on through village. Garden entrance ¾ m on R. Ample free car park.* **Adm £5, chd £1.50.** For opening times, please tel or see website. For NGS: **Evening Openings** Weds 14 May; 8 Oct (4-8).

Beautiful secluded 70-acre landscape garden. Easy access to many exceptional vistas enhanced by lakes and trees with bridges, grottoes and follies. Covered seats enabling the garden to be enjoyed in all weathers. Dogs on leads. Featured in & on various publications & TV.

& ✿ ☕

---

12 COURTWOOD HOUSE
Court Walk, Betley CW3 9DP. Mike & Edith Reeves, 01270 820715, thereeve@homecall.co.uk. *6m S of Crewe. On A531 going toward Keele & Newcastle-u-Lyme or from J16 of the M6 pick up the A531 off the A500 on the Nantwich rd. In Betley Village into courtyard by sign 'Betley Court'.* Home-made teas. **Adm £3, chd free. Sun 3 Aug (2-5.30).** Visitors also welcome by appt, max no of 25 in any one visit.

Small L-shaped, walled garden, which

---

is designed as a huge walk-through sculpture. Many creations, structures and water features, with hidden spaces and seating areas, with strong shapes and effects. Small art gallery within this secluded oasis. Display of art work - acrylic paintings. Featured in & on 'Crew Chronicle' 'Best Kept Garden' award, 'Sunday Sentinel', BBC TV.

✕ ☕ ☎

⑬ 12 DARGES LANE

Great Wyrley WS6 6LE. Mrs A Hackett, 01922 415064. *2m SE of Cannock. From A5 take A34 towards Walsall. Darges Lane is 1st turning on R (over brow of hill). House on R on corner of Cherrington Drive.* **Adm £2.50, chd 50p. Visitors welcome by appt March to Nov, no restrictions on numbers.**

¼ -acre well-stocked plantsmanís and flower arrangerís garden on two levels. Foliage plants a special feature. Mixed borders incl trees, shrubs and rare plants giving yr-round interest. Features constantly changing. National Collection of lamiums. Collection of 93 clematis. The overall effect is attractive and enticing to the plant lover.

✕ ❀ NCCPG ☎

Victorian bandstand, re-located from Illfracombe pier . . .

⑭ 4 DENE CLOSE

Penkridge ST19 5HL. David & Anne Smith, 01785 712580. *6m S of Stafford. On A449 from Stafford. At far end of Penkridge turn L into Boscomoor Lane, 2nd L into Filance Lane, 3rd R Dene Close. Please park with consideration in Filance Lane. Disabled only in Dene Close.* Home-made teas. **Adm £2.50, chd free. Sun 6 July (11-5). Visitors also welcome by appt.**

Medium-sized plant lovers' garden has been created over 37yrs. Wide variety of herbaceous perennials, foliage plants; over 60 varieties of grasses, incl miscanthus, pennisetums and bamboos. Gravelled areas and mixed borders, some colour themed, small water feature. 'Rainbow border' 54ft long with many perennials incl achilleas, hemerocallis and heleniums. Featured in 'Express & Star. Award winners- Stafford in Bloom,.

✕ ❀ ☕ ☎

⑮ ◆ DOROTHY CLIVE GARDEN

Willoughbridge, Market Drayton TF9 4EU. Willoughbridge Garden Trust, 01630 647237, www.dorothyclivegarden.co.uk. *1m SE of Bridgemere Garden World. From M6 J15 take A53, then A51 midway between Nantwich & Stone, 2m from village of Woore.* **Adm £5, chd free, 11-16 £1, concessions £4. Open daily 15 Mar to Oct. For NGS: Tues 12, 19 Aug (10-5.30).**

12 informal acres, incl superb woodland garden, alpine scree, gravel garden, fine collection of trees and spectacular flower borders. Renowned in May when woodland quarry is brilliant with rhododendrons. Creative planting over last 5yrs has produced stunning summer borders. Much to see, whatever the season.

♿ ❀ ☕

⑯ DORSET HOUSE

68 Station Street, Cheslyn Hay WS6 7EE. Mary & David Blundell, 01922 419437, david.blundell@homecall.co.uk. *2m SE of Cannock. J11 M6. A462 towards Willenhall, L at island, follow rd to next island. R into one-way system (Low St), at T-junction L into Station St. A5 Bridgetown L over M6 toll rd to island, L into Coppice Rd. At T-junction R into Station St.* Home-made teas. **Adm £3, chd free. Suns 18 May; 10 Aug (12-5). Visitors also welcome by appt May to July, groups of 10+, coaches permitted.**

Inspirational ½ -acre plantaholic's country garden giving all-yr interest. Many unique features, wealth of unusual rhododendrons, acers, shrubs and perennials, planted in mixed borders. Clematis-covered arches, intimate seating areas, hidden corners, water features, stream, all creating a haven of peace and tranquillity. Featured in 'Express & Star & 'Staffordshire Life'.

♿ ✕ ❀ ☕ ☎

⑰ NEW THE ELMS

Post Office Road, Seisdon, Wolverhampton WV5 7HA. Mr Alec Smith & Ms Susan Wilkinson, 01902 893482, a.smith365@btinternet.com. *6m W of Wolverhampton. A454 B'north rd. After Lealans Nurseries on R, turn L at Fox PH into Fox Rd. 1m T-junction. L at Seven Stars PH into Ebstree Rd. Take 2nd L into Post Office Rd (after narrow bridge). Garden on R through large walled entrance..* Home-made teas. **Adm £4.50, chd free. Sats 28 June; 30 Aug (2-5). Visitors also welcome by appt, max 25 visitors, no large coaches.**

4 acre country garden, set around large Georgian villa. Kitchen herb garden with roses, topiary and pots. Tropical style walled garden enclosing swimming pool. Variety of borders and lawns. Ha-ha leading to open lawned area with new and ancient trees. Victorian bandstand, re-located from Illfracombe pier, fully restored by present owner.

♿ ✕ ❀ ☕ ☎

⑱ ELVENDELL

4 Partridge Ride, The Burntwood, Loggerheads TF2 2QX. John & Joy Hainsworth, 01630 672269. *8m SW of Newcastle-under-Lyme. On Staffordshire-Shropshire borders. Turn off A53 Newcastle to Market Drayton rd on to Kestrel Drive nr Loggerheads Xrds & adjacent hotel.* Home-made teas. **Adm £3, chd free. Sats 14 June; 19 July (1.30-4.30). Visitors also welcome by appt June & July for groups of 10+.**

½ -acre woodland idyll. Creative hard landscaping, many unusual and exotic plants, pools, waterfalls (one in carved rock and glass), bog gardens, rhododendron, shrub and herbaceous borders. Groves of mature tree ferns.

✕ ❀ ☕ ☎

⑲ 10 FERN DENE

Madeley, Crewe CW3 9ER. Martin & Stella Clifford-Jones. *10m W of Newcastle under Lyme. Madeley is on A525 between Keele/ Woore. Enter Moss Lane next to Madeley Pool. 2nd R, Charles Cotton Drive. At end turn R then L into the Bridle Path, 1st R to Fern Dene.* Home-made teas. **Adm £3, chd free. Sat 31 May (2-5).**

Garden occupies 1 acre on sloping site with natural springs. Designed to encourage wildlife with several ponds, native plants and woodland walk. Planting incls many trees and shrubs especially acers, cornus and salix. Unusual features incl grass spiral and oriental garden. Featured on BBC2 Open Gardens.

20 NEW FOUR SEASONS
26 Buchanan Road, Walsall WS4 2EN. Tony & Marie Newton. *Adjacent to Walsall Arboretum. M6 J7 take A34 Walsall. At double island take 3rd exit A4148 (signed Wolverhampton A454) onto Ring rd. Over 2 islands, at large junction turn R A461 (signed Lichfield). At 1st island take 3rd exit Buchanan Ave, R into Buchanan Rd. Extensive parking in road or avenue.* **Adm £3, chd free (share to Walsall Cardiac Rehabilitation Trust).** Suns 11, 18 May; 10 Aug (10-6).
S-facing 1/3-acre, suburban garden, gently sloping to arboretum, some steep steps. For all seasons and age groups. 200 acers, 350 azaleas, bright clipped conifers, shrubs provide back drop for spring bulbs, perennials, summer bedding. Many 'rooms' and themes incl contrast of red, blue and yellow. Jungle, oriental pagoda, water features. Winner Walsall in Bloom & Daily Mail' National Garden Competitions'. Featured on ITV Central News.

21 THE GARTH
2 Broc Hill Way, Milford, Stafford ST17 0UB. Mr & Mrs David Wright, 01785 661182. *41/2 m SE of Stafford. A513 Stafford to Rugeley rd; at Barley Mow turn R (S) to Brocton; L after 1/2 m.* Cream teas. **Adm £2.50, chd free.** Suns 1, 29 June (2-6). **Also open The Secret Garden** 29 June. **Visitors also welcome by appt, coaches permitted.**
1/2 acre garden of many levels on Channock Chase AONB. Acid soil loving plants. Series of small gardens, water features, raised beds. Rare trees, island beds of unusual shrubs and perennials, many varieties of hosta and ferns. Ancient sandstone caves. Featured on Stoke & Stafford Radio. Winner of Stafford in Bloom.

22 GRAFTON COTTAGE
Barton-under-Needwood DE13 8AL. Margaret & Peter Hargreaves, 01283 713639, marpeter@talktalk.net. *6m N of Lichfield. Leave A38 for Catholme S of Barton, follow sign to Barton Green, 1/4 m on L.* Home-made teas. **Adm £2.50, chd free (share to Alzheimer's Research Trust).** Suns 29 June; 6 July; 10 Aug (1.30-5.30). **Visitors also welcome by appt for groups. Coaches permitted.**
Step into an idyllic English cottage garden and roam around the winding paths clothed with highly scented flowers, old fashioned roses, dianthus, sweet peas, phlox, lilies. Stately delphiniums form a backdrop to the herbaceous borders. Over 100 clematis,incl 30 from the viticella collection wander, through trellises and amongst campanula, achillea, viola and many more unusual perennials. Textured plants, artemisia, atrepex, heuchera form the basis of colour-themed borders, use of cottage garden annuals add to the tranquillity. Small vegetable plot. Featured on BBC Gardeners' World.

23 HEATH HOUSE
Offley Brook, nr Eccleshall ST21 6HA. Dr D W Eyre-Walker, 01785 280318. *3m W of Eccleshall. Take B5026 towards Woore. At Sugnall turn L, after 11/2 m turn R immed by stone garden wall. After 1m straight across Xrds.* Home-made teas. **Adm £3, chd free (share to Adbaston Church).** Suns 27 Apr; 1 June; 20 July (2-5). **Visitors also welcome by appt.**
11/2 -acre country garden of C18 miller's house in lovely valley setting, overlooking mill pool. Plantsman's garden containing many rare and unusual plants in borders, bog garden, woodland, alpine house, raised bed and shrubberies.

24 HIGH TREES
18 Drubbery Lane, nr Longton Park ST3 4BA. Peter & Pat Teggin, 01782 318453, p.teggin@btinternet.com. *5m S of Stoke-on-Trent. Off A5035, midway between Trentham Gardens & Longton. Opp Longton Park.* Cream teas. **Adm £3, chd free (share to Douglas Macmillan Hospice).** Suns 8 June; 13 July; 3 Aug (2-5). **Visitors also welcome by appt June & July, coaches permitted.**
Very pretty secluded suburban garden with coordinated design features.

Colour themed herbaceous borders planted with many unusual plants highlighting colour, texture and form for all yr interest. An ideas garden where roses intermingle with clematis, and the coolness of hostas and ferns contrast with lush summer planting. Featured in 'Staffordshire Life' & on Satellite TV.

25 THE HOLLIES
Leek Road, Cheddleton ST13 7HG. Tim & Amanda Bosson, 01538 361079, tim_bosson@hotmail.com, www.hollies-garden.co.uk. *2m S of Leek. On A520. Large NGS arrow to direct.* Cream teas (£2). **Adm £2.50, chd free.** Suns 22 June; 21 Sept (11-5). **Visitors also welcome by appt.**
On edge of village a private walled garden and a delight to see. Amanda and Tim invite you to wander around their secret oasis whilst watching their various water features. Impressive formal garden which features an array of colour surrounded by shrubs and trees. Devon Cream Teas are a speciality for this couple from Devonshire and the cream is specially sent up.

An ideas garden where roses intermingle with clematis, and the coolness of hostas . . .

26 6 KENDAL PLACE
Clayton, Newcastle-under-Lyme ST5 3QT. Joanne Barnes. *1m S of Newcastle-under-Lyme. Leave Newcastle on A519 Clayton Rd. 1st R Abbots Way, 1st L Earls Dr, 175yds, 2nd R Kendal Place. 2m from M6 J15 L onto A519 over 2 roundabouts, 1st L into Abbots Way then as above. Please park with consideration (cul-de-sac).* **Adm £2.50, chd free (share to Turning Point Staffordshire).** Sun 27 July (2-5).
Passionate about pots in small well-designed Gold Medal winning garden. A jewel box of beautiful plant treasures giving inspiration and ideas. Well tended clusters of phormiums,

grasses, ferns, ricinus, agapanthus, colourful containers and hanging baskets. Featured in & on 'Sunday Sentinel', BBC2 Open Gardens. 2 Gold, 2 Silver, 1 Bronze medals - Newcastle-under-Lyme - Britain in Bloom Residential Gardens.

✗ ✿

27 LILAC COTTAGE
Chapel Lane, Gentleshaw, nr Rugeley WS15 4ND. Mrs Sylvia Nunn, www.lilaccottagegarden.co.uk. *5m NW of Lichfield. Approx midway between Lichfield & Rugeley on A51 at Longdon, turn W into Borough Lane signed Cannock Wood & Gentleshaw. Continue 1m to T-junction. L for 1¹/₂ m to Gentleshaw. From Burntwood, A5190 head N on Rugeley Rd at Burntwood Swan island; turn L at Xrds approx ¹/₂ m past Nags Head PH, over Xrds to Gentleshaw. Parking only at Cannock Wood and Gentleshaw village hall. Roadside disabled & elderly parking only at Lilac Cottage.* **Adm £2.50, chd free. Sun 3 Aug (1.30-5).**
Plant enthusiast's 1-acre country garden with emphasis on colour-themed borders and plant associations. Wealth of unusual perennials, especially geraniums, hostas, penstemons and achilleas, interspersed with English roses, interesting trees and shrubs. Small wildlife pool, bog garden, vibrant hot border, shady walks, tranquil sunken garden, sweeping vistas. All-yr interest. Perennial plants for sale. Featured in & on 'Sunday Mecury'. BBC2 Gardening World, & local press & radio. Some gravel paths.

& ✗ ✿ ☕

28 LOWER HOUSE
Sugnall Parva, Eccleshall ST21 6NF. John & Anthea Treanor. *2m W of Eccleshall. On B5026 Loggerheads Rd turn R at sharp double bend. House ¹/₂ m on L.* Home-made teas. **Adm £3, chd free (share to Holy Trinity & St Chads Churches, Eccleshall). Sat 7, Sun 8 June (2-6). Also open Birch Trees.**
Unusual perennials and shrubs in subtle purples, pinks and cream give a gentle rhythm to this country cottage garden covering more than 1 acre with lawns, pools, orchard and vegetable garden. Colour-themed sunken garden and dry -shade planting in front C18 former farmhouse (not open). Owners strive towards all-yr interest. Featured in local press. Some gravel paths.

& ✿ ☕

29 MANOR COTTAGE GARDEN
2 Manor Cottage, Hanchurch, Stoke-on-Trent ST4 8SD. Dr & Mrs Clement, 01782 644112, darrenjclement@tiscali.co.uk. *4m S of Newcastle-under-Lyme. From J15 M6 follow A519 S towards Eccleshall. Straight on at T-lights, past Hanchurch village, under M6, 2nd R onto private rd.* Home-made teas. **Adm £2.50, chd free. Sun 10 Aug (11-5). Visitors also welcome by appt Aug only, groups max 15. no coaches.**
Welcome to 'the jungle'. This small semi-tropical garden comprises a small courtyard garden with phormiums and other architectural foliage plants. Off the courtyard the main garden, 'the jungle', incl bananas, bamboos, ferns, foxglove trees, cannas and day lilies in abundance. Small informal pond. Good end-of-season interest. Featured in 'Sentinel on Sunday'.

✗ ✿ ☕ ☎

Beautifully scented old roses, peonies, pinks and interestingly sculptured trunks of old pear trees . . .

30 MILLENNIUM GARDEN
London Road, Lichfield WS14 9RB. Carol Cooper, 01543 262544. *1m S of Lichfield. Off A38 along A5206 towards Lichfield fork ¹/₄ m before Shoulder of Mutton PH. Park in field on L.* Home-made teas. **Adm £3.50, chd free. Suns 30 Mar; 15 June (2-6). Visitors also welcome by appt.**
2 acre garden with many flower beds, host of golden daffodils in March. Millennium bridge over landscaped water garden, leading to attractive walks along rough mown paths through maturing woodland, and seasonal wild flowers, Uneven surfaces and gravel paths.

& ✗ ☕ ☎

MILLPOOL
See Cheshire & Wirral.

31 NEW MOORFIELD
Post Lane, Endon, Stoke-on-Trent ST9 9DU. Ian & June Sellers, 01782 504096. *4m W of Leek. 6m from Stoke-on-Trent A53. Turn into Station Rd over railway line, canal bridge with lights, 1st on L opp Endon Cricket Club.* Home-made teas. **Adm £3, chd free. Sun 20 July (1.30-5). Visitors also welcome by appt July & Aug, groups of 10+.**
Flower arrangers delight situated in ¹/₃ acre. This colourful garden has a variety of different styles ranging from herbaceous borders to areas with a Mediterranean feel, the garden incls many structural features such as unusual wooden tree stumps to a spacious summerhouse.

& ✿ ☕ ☎

32 NEW MOSS COTTAGE
Moss Lane, Madeley CW3 9NQ. Liz & Alan Forster. *7m W of Newcastle-under-Lyme. Madeley is on A525 between Keeley/Woore. Enter Moss Lane next to Madeley pool.* Home-made teas. **Adm £3, chd free. Sun 22 June; Sun 13 July (1.30-5).**
¹/₃ acre secluded and colourful cottage garden with mixed beds and herbaceous borders. Water features and seating areas, some planting has been done with wildlife in mind. All-yr round interest, beautifully scented old roses, peonies, pinks and interestingly sculptured trunks of old pear trees. Plant sales by www.specialperennials.com. Featured in & on 'Sunday Sentinel', BBC2 Open Gardens.

✗ ✿ ☕

33 THE MOUNT
Coton, Gnosall ST20 0EQ. Andrew & Celia Payne, 01785 822253. *8m W of Stafford. 4m E of Newport. From Stafford take A518 W towards Newport/Telford. Go through Gnosall, over canal. Garden on edge of Gnosall Village, on LH-side of A518. Parking approx 200yds signed up lane.* Home-made teas. **Adm £3, chd free. Sun 29 June (2-5.30). Visitors also welcome by appt June to Aug only.**
Evolving and colourful plantsman's garden divided into different areas covering ³/₄ -acre. Wildlife friendly with small pond and bog area, visitors will admire over 40 hostas, huge kiftsgate

rose, interesting and colourful containers combined with some exotic planting, numerous trees and many unusual perennials.

✗ ❀ ☕ ☎

㉞ THE OLD DAIRY HOUSE
Trentham Park, Stoke-on-Trent ST4 8AE. Philip & Michelle Moore. *S edge of Stoke-on-Trent. Behind Trentham Gardens on rd to Trentham Church and Trentham Park Golf Club. From A34 turn into Whitmore Rd B5038. 1st L and follow NGS signs.* Home-made teas. **Adm £3, chd free. Sat 24, Sun 25 May (2-5.30).** Grade 2 listed house (not open) designed by Sir Charles Barry forms backdrop to this 2-acre garden in peaceful parkland setting. New long border ready this year. Large seating area for relaxing teas. Gravel paths.

♿ ✗ ❀ ☕

㉟ THE OLD RECTORY, CLIFTON CAMPVILLE
B79 0AP. Martin & Margaret Browne, 01827 373533, mbrowne526@aol.com. *6m N of Tamworth. 2m W of M42 J11, in centre of Clifton Campville. Village signed off B5493 from Statfold or No Man's Heath. Entrance to garden on S side of Main St at top of hill, between bus shelter and school.* Home-made teas. **Adm £3, chd free. Visitors welcome by appt groups welcome throughout the year, visits tailored to your needs.** Tranquil 2-acre garden around historic former Rectory developed over 26yrs by the present owners. Established trees underplanted with a diverse range of plants. Enjoy a garden on an ancient site, full of colour and interest at all seasons. Paths give easy access to lawns, borders, fruit and vegetables. Small walled garden and gravel areas.

♿ ✗ ☕ ☎

㊱ THE OLD SCHOOL HOUSE
Stowe-by-Chartley, Stafford ST18 0LG. Keith & Wendy Jones. *5m S of Stone. Adjacent to village hall, 7m from Stafford A51 at Weston. A518 E towards Uttoxeter. Approx 1½ m past Amerton Farm. After approx ½ m turn R signed Stowe (Bridge Lane). L at T-junction past church & Cock Inn. 100yds on R.* Light lunches (Suns) & home-made teas. **Adm £2.50, chd free. Sat 19 (2-6), Sun 20 July (11-5).** Informal cottage-style garden of ½ acre; developed from former school yard. Mixed herbaceous borders; lawn and recycled paved sitting areas;

rockery, small pond, containers. Unexpected garden hidden from the road creating a tranquil setting within a small country village.

❀ ☕

ORCHARD HOUSE
See Cheshire & Wirral.

㊲ 15 ST JOHNS ROAD
Pleck, Walsall WS2 9TJ. Maureen & Sid Allen, 01922 442348, sidallen@blueyonder.co.uk. *2m W of Walsall. Off J10 M6. Head for Walsall on A454 Wolverhampton Rd. Turn R into Pleck Rd A4148 then 4th R into St Johns Rd.* **Adm £2.50, chd free. Visitors welcome by appt June to Aug, max of 50, coaches permitted.** Long peaceful garden, small trees, shrubs, perennials, some unusual. Tropical area, koi pond. Visit mid June for lush foliage and good leaf and colour combinations. Small Japanese style area with maples, bridge, stream, teahouse. Walk through shady area, with ferns, into gravel garden, pretty planting for wildlife at best July/Aug. Featured in 'Daily Mail' & local press.

✗ ☎

㊳ 23 ST JOHNS ROAD
Stafford ST17 9AS. Colin & Fiona Horwath, 01785 258923, fiona_horwath@yahoo.co.uk. *½ m S of Stafford Town Centre. On A449. Through entrance into private park, therefore please park considerably.* Home-made teas. **Adm £2.50, chd free. Sun 23 Mar; Fris 2 May; 6 June; 19 Sept (2-5). Visitors also welcome by appt.** Town garden with a country feel packed with interesting plants and run organically. Many bulbs, shady walk, herbaceous borders, wildlife pond and bog garden. Climbers ramble over pergolas and arches; herb garden; rockery and raised vegetable beds. Victorian-style greenhouse.

✗ ❀ ☕ ☎

Wander through the evergreen arch and there before you a fantasy for the eyes and soul . . .

㊴ NEW THE SECRET GARDEN
Little Haywood ST18 0UL. Derek Higgott & David Aston, 01889 883473. *5m SE of Stafford. A51, from Rugeley or Weston signed Little Haywood ½ m from Seven Springs. A513 Coley Lane from public house's at Back Lane, R into Coley Grove. Entrance to garden in Coley Grove.* Home-made teas. **Adm £3, chd free. Suns 18 May, 29 June; Fris 13 June, 8 Aug (11-5). Also open The Garth 29 June. Visitors also welcome by appt May to Aug.** Wander past the other cottage gardens and through the evergreen arch and there before you a fantasy for the eyes and soul. Stunning garden approx ½ -acre, created over the last 25yrs. Strong colour theme of trees and shrubs, underplanted with perennials 1000 bulbs and laced with clematis; other features incl water, laburnum and rose tunnel and unique buildings. Is this the jewel in the crown? Raised gazebo with wonderful views over untouched meadows and Cannock Chase. Hardy Plant Society sale in village hall 18 May. 1st in Village Open Gardens, Stafford in Bloom Most Enthusiastic award & 1st for Large Rural Garden.

✗ ☕ ☎

㊵ SHEPHERDS FOLD GARDENS
Wildwood, Stafford ST17 4SF, 01785 660819, alison.jordan2@byinternet. *3m S of Stafford. Follow A34 out of Stafford towards Cannock, 2nd R onto the Wildwood Estate. Follow ring rd around, Shepherds Fold is 5th turning on L. Limited parking in cul de sac. Please use as drop off & park on ring rd.* Home-made teas at no. 8, glass of wine no. 9. **Combined adm £3.50, chd free (share to Multiple Sclerosis Society). Sun 13 July (11.30-5). Evening Opening £4.50, wine, Fri 13 June (6.30-8.30). Visitors also welcome by appt for all 3 gardens.** Deceptive gardens with views over open countryside. Three very different gardens showing how similar sites can be made to look and feel individual.

☕ ☎

7 SHEPHERDS FOLD
Avril & David Tooth
W-facing plant lovers' garden with many interesting features incl

variety of unusual pots and water feature. Themed area with sun house.

8 SHEPHERDS FOLD
David & Janet Horsnall
Maturing S-facing garden on heavy clay. Variety of different areas and terraces. Plantsman's garden with magnificent roses, quiet areas with architectural plants and wide range of perennials. Area of wild flowers - under construction.

9 SHEPHERDS FOLD
Peter & Alison Jordan
S-facing garden on heavy clay soil. Informal cottage planting, interesting terraces and features, yr-round interest, unusual perennials.
✿

41 SILVERWOOD
16 Beechfield Road, Trentham ST4 8HG. Aki & Sarah Akhtar, 01782 643313, sarah.akhtar4@btinternet.com. *3m S of Stoke on Trent. From A34 Trentham Gardens roundabout take A5035 Longton Rd. After Nat West Bank take R turn into Oaktree Rd. From Longton (A50) follow A5035 into Trentham. After PH take L turn into Oaktree Rd, which becomes Beechfield Rd. Parking limited.* Home-made teas. **Adm £3, chd free (share to Breast Cancer Campaign). Sun 20 July (2-5). Visitors also welcome by appt July only.**
Small secluded garden with many interesting shrubs, perennials and trees. Souvenirs from all over the world planted for the pleasure of the owners.
 ♿ ✕ ✿ ☕ ☎

42 SMITHY COTTAGE
Mucklestone TF9 4DN. Diana Standeven, 01630 672677. *8m SW of Newcastle-under-Lyme. On B5026 between Woore A51 & Loggerheads A53 opposite Mucklestone Church.* **Adm £3, chd free. Mon 26 May; Thurs 1 May; 5 June; 3 July; 7 Aug; 4 Sept (2-5). Visitors also welcome by appt at anytime.**
An eclectic mix of rarities satisfying the most picky plantsperson in a conservation rural village. Maintained by Diana and her family. Featured in & on 'Amateur Gardening', BBC2 Open Garden & ITV Central.
✕ ✿ ☕ ☎

43 STONEHILL QUARRY GARDEN
Great Gate, Croxden, nr Uttoxeter ST10 4HF. Mrs Caroline Raymont, 01889 507202. *6m NW of Uttoxeter. A50 to Uttoxeter. Take B5030 to JCB Rocester, L to Hollington & Croxden Abbey. Third R into Keelings Lane & Croxden Abbey. At Great Gate, T-junction L to Stonehill.* Tea & Coffee. **Adm £2.50. Mons 20, 27 Oct; 3, 10 Nov (2-5). Visitors also welcome by appt March/Apr & Oct/Nov, groups of 15+.**
6-acre quarry garden incorporating numerous ornamental trees and shrubs (magnolias, acers, catalpa, Davidia, paeonias, azaleas) underplanted with unusual Asiatic and American woodlanders (lilies, trillium, erythroniums, paris, podophyllum, arisaemas, hellebores), bamboo 'jungle', rock garden, mixed borders. Spring bulbs and hellebores. Autumn colour of particular interest with new winter bark feature to give a 'zing' to dreary days. C12 Croxden Abbey ruins (adm free) 500 metres, Churnet Valley walks (2½ km). Featured in 'Gardens Illustrated'. BBC Gardens Year. NO children.
 ♿ ✕ ✿ ☕ ☎

An eclectic mix of rarities satisfying the most picky plantsperson . . .

44 ◆ THE TRENTHAM ESTATE
Stone Road, Stoke-on-Trent ST4 8AX. Michael Walker, 01782 646646, www.trentham.co.uk. *M6 J15. Well signed on roundabout, A34 with A5035.* **Adm £7, chd £6, concessions £6.50. Open daily except Christmas day 10-6.**
One of the largest garden regeneration projects in Britain, using award winning designers Tom Stuart-Smith and Piet Oudolf, who have introduced vast contemporary plantings, using over 300,000 choice perennials and bulbs. Collection of show gardens and new 7 acre garden by Piet Oudolf. Featured in & on various publications & TV.
 ♿ ✕ ✿ ☕

7 WARREN DRIVE
See Derbyshire.

45 THE WICKETS
47 Long Street, Wheaton Aston ST19 9NF. Tony & Kate Bennett, 01785 840233. *8m W of Cannock. From M6 J12 turn W towards Telford on A5; across A449 Gailey roundabout; A5 for 1½ m; turn R signed Stretton, 150yds turn L signed Wheaton Aston; 2½ m turn L; ½ m over canal bridge; garden on R. Or Bradford Arms Wheaton Aston 2m.* **Adm £2.50, chd free. Sun 6 July (1.30-5). Visitors also welcome by appt.**
⅓ -acre garden of many features, full of ideas for smaller gardens. A more open front garden is contrasted by many themed areas behind the house. Pond, dry stream, clock golf, gravel beds and many hanging baskets and containers. Popular and pleasant walks along Shropshire Union Canal just 25yds away. Featured in 'Shropshire Life'.
 ♿ ✕ ✿ ☕ ☎

46 WILKINS PLECK
off Three Mile Lane, Whitmore, nr Newcastle-under-Lyme ST5 5HN. Sheila & Chris Bissell, 01782 680351. *5m SW from Newcastle-under-Lyme. Take A53 SW from Newcastle-under-Lyme. At Whitmore turn R at Mainwaring Arms PH. Signed RH-side at Cudmore Fisheries. Please NO Dogs in car park in field at landowners request.* **Adm £4.50, chd free (share to National Society for Epilepsey). Suns 22 June; 27 July (2-5). Visitors also welcome by appt.**
5½ acres of paradise in North Staffordshire.
✕ ✿ ☕ ☎

47 THE WOMBOURNE WODEHOUSE
Wolverhampton WV5 9BW. Mr & Mrs J Phillips, 01902 892202. *4m S of Wolverhampton. Just off A449 on A463 to Sedgley.* Home-made teas. **Adm £3.50, chd free. Thur 29 May (2-5.30). Visitors also welcome by appt May, June & July.**
18-acre garden laid out in 1750. Mainly rhododendrons, herbaceous border, woodland walk, water garden and over 170 different varieties of tall bearded irises in walled kitchen garden. Partial wheelchair access.
 ♿ ✕ ✿ ☕ ☎

48 YARLET HOUSE

Stafford ST18 9SU. Mr & Mrs Nikolas Tarling. *2m S of Stone. Take A34 from Stone towards Stafford, turn L into Yarlet School and L again into car park.* **Adm £3, chd free (share to Staffordshire Wildlife Trust). Fri 13 June (1.30-4.30).**
4 acre garden with extensive lawns, walks and herbaceous borders. Water garden with rare lilies, putting course and garden chess board. Sweeping views across Trent Valley to Sandon. Yarlet School Art Display. Gravel paths.

Come and sit in our new oak timbered vinery and take tea . . .

49 YEW TREE COTTAGE

Podmores Corner, Long Lane, White Cross, Haughton ST18 9JR. Clive & Ruth Plant, 01785 282516, pottyplantz@aol.com. *4m W of Stafford. Take A518 W Haughton, turn R Station Rd (signed Ranton) 1m, then turn R at Xrds 1/4 m on R.* Home-made teas. **Adm £2.50, chd free. Suns 25 May; 20 July (2-5). Visitors also welcome by appt anytime, please ring and we will advise if worth your trip.**
Cottage garden of 1/3 acre designed by plantaholics to complement Victorian cottage. Many unusual perennials incl shade lovers such as meconopsis and arisaema. Gardeners are passionate about salvia and lathyrus. Gravel and vegetable gardens, courtyard. Come and sit in our new oak timbered vinery and take tea. Runners up Staffordshire in Bloom.

Staffordshire County Volunteers

County Organiser
Susan Weston, Birch Trees, Copmere End, Eccleshall, Stafford ST21 6HH, 01785 850448, sueweston@copmere.orangehome.co.uk

County Treasurer
Sue Jones, Church Farm Cottage, Mucklestone, Market Drayton TF9 4DN, sr.jones@mmu.ac.uk

Publicity
Bert Foden, The Cottage, Tongue Lane, Brown Edge, Stoke on Trent ST6 8UQ, 01782 513033, jeanandbert@btinternet.com

Assistant County Organisers
Pat Teggin, High Trees, 18 Drubbery Lane, Stoke-on-Trent ST3 4BA, 01782 318453, pat.teggin@btinternet.com
John Weston, Birch Trees, Copmere End, Stafford ST21 6HH, 01785 850448, sueweston@copmere.orangehome.co.uk

SUFFOLK

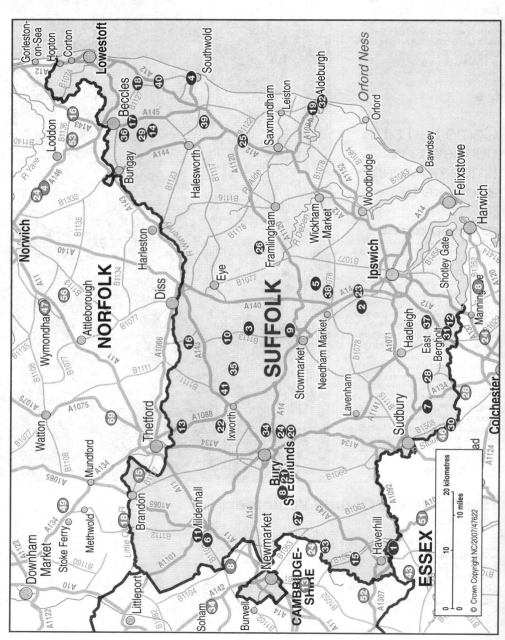

Opening Dates

February

SUNDAY 24
14 Gable House

March

SATURDAY 15
16 Green Farm House

SUNDAY 16
16 Green Farm House

April

TUESDAY 1
39 Woottens

WEDNESDAY 2
39 Woottens

THURSDAY 3
39 Woottens

SUNDAY 6
12 East Bergholt Place
15 Great Thurlow Hall
35 Walsham Gardens

TUESDAY 8
39 Woottens

WEDNESDAY 9
39 Woottens

THURSDAY 10
39 Woottens

SUNDAY 13
25 Magnolia House

TUESDAY 15
39 Woottens

WEDNESDAY 16
39 Woottens

THURSDAY 17
39 Woottens

SUNDAY 20
10 Corner Cottage

TUESDAY 22
39 Woottens

WEDNESDAY 23
39 Woottens

THURSDAY 24
39 Woottens

SATURDAY 26
2 Blakenham Woodland Garden

SUNDAY 27
2 Blakenham Woodland Garden
5 Brook Hall
12 East Bergholt Place

TUESDAY 29
39 Woottens

WEDNESDAY 30
39 Woottens

May

THURSDAY 1
39 Woottens

SUNDAY 4
1 Abbotts Hall
19 Heron House
30 Rosedale
32 Stanford House

TUESDAY 6
39 Woottens

WEDNESDAY 7
39 Woottens

THURSDAY 8
39 Woottens

TUESDAY 13
39 Woottens

WEDNESDAY 14
39 Woottens

THURSDAY 15
39 Woottens

SUNDAY 18
28 The Priory

TUESDAY 20
39 Woottens

WEDNESDAY 21
39 Woottens

THURSDAY 22
39 Woottens

SATURDAY 24
39 Woottens

SUNDAY 25
5 Brook Hall
18 Henstead Exotic Garden
22 The Kitchen Garden
39 Woottens

MONDAY 26
22 The Kitchen Garden
39 Woottens

TUESDAY 27
39 Woottens

WEDNESDAY 28
39 Woottens

THURSDAY 29
39 Woottens

FRIDAY 30
39 Woottens

SATURDAY 31
39 Woottens

June

SUNDAY 1
27 Ousden Gardens
37 Windmill Cottage

38 Woodwards

TUESDAY 3
39 Woottens

WEDNESDAY 4
39 Woottens

THURSDAY 5
39 Woottens

FRIDAY 6
39 Woottens

SATURDAY 7
36 White House Farm
39 Woottens
41 Wyken Hall

SUNDAY 8
7 The Coach House
14 Gable House
20 Home Farm House
24 The Lucy Redman School of Garden Design
31 Rosemary
39 Woottens
40 Wrentham Gardens
41 Wyken Hall

MONDAY 9
39 Woottens

TUESDAY 10
39 Woottens

WEDNESDAY 11
39 Woottens

THURSDAY 12
39 Woottens

SATURDAY 14
39 Woottens

SUNDAY 15
23 Lime Kiln House
38 Woodwards
39 Woottens

TUESDAY 17
39 Woottens

WEDNESDAY 18
39 Woottens

THURSDAY 19
39 Woottens

SATURDAY 21
39 Woottens

SUNDAY 22
26 Monksfield House
34 The Wallow
39 Woottens

TUESDAY 24
39 Woottens

WEDNESDAY 25
39 Woottens

THURSDAY 26
39 Woottens

SATURDAY 28
4 Bridge Foot Farm

SUNDAY 29
4 Bridge Foot Farm
5 Brook Hall
9 Columbine Hall

July

TUESDAY 1
39 Woottens

WEDNESDAY 2
39 Woottens

THURSDAY 3
39 Woottens

TUESDAY 8
39 Woottens

WEDNESDAY 9
39 Woottens

THURSDAY 10
39 Woottens

SATURDAY 12
39 Woottens

SUNDAY 13
29 Redisham Hall
30 Rosedale
38 Woodwards
39 Woottens

TUESDAY 15
39 Woottens

WEDNESDAY 16
39 Woottens

THURSDAY 17
39 Woottens

SATURDAY 19
21 Ickworth House Park & Gardens
39 Woottens

SUNDAY 20
3 Bresworth House
17 Hall Farm
39 Woottens

TUESDAY 22
39 Woottens

WEDNESDAY 23
39 Woottens

THURSDAY 24
39 Woottens

SATURDAY 26
39 Woottens

SUNDAY 27
8 Cobbs Hall
39 Woottens

TUESDAY 29
39 Woottens

WEDNESDAY 30
39 Woottens

THURSDAY 31
39 Woottens

August

TUESDAY 5
39 Woottens

WEDNESDAY 6
39 Woottens

THURSDAY 7
39 Woottens

TUESDAY 12
39 Woottens

WEDNESDAY 13
39 Woottens

THURSDAY 14
39 Woottens

SUNDAY 17
38 Woodwards

TUESDAY 19
39 Woottens

WEDNESDAY 20
39 Woottens

THURSDAY 21
39 Woottens

TUESDAY 26
39 Woottens

WEDNESDAY 27
39 Woottens

THURSDAY 28
39 Woottens

September

TUESDAY 2
39 Woottens

WEDNESDAY 3
39 Woottens

THURSDAY 4
39 Woottens

TUESDAY 9
39 Woottens

WEDNESDAY 10
39 Woottens

THURSDAY 11
39 Woottens

TUESDAY 16
39 Woottens

WEDNESDAY 17
39 Woottens

THURSDAY 18
39 Woottens

TUESDAY 23
39 Woottens

WEDNESDAY 24
39 Woottens

THURSDAY 25
39 Woottens

TUESDAY 30
39 Woottens

October

SUNDAY 12
12 East Bergholt Place

Gardens open to the public

2 Blakenham Woodland Garden
7 The Coach House
13 Euston Hall
21 Ickworth House Park & Gardens
23 Lime Kiln House
26 Monksfield House
38 Woodwards
39 Woottens
41 Wyken Hall

By appointment only

6 6a Church Walk
11 Crossbills
33 Thrift Farmhouse

Also open by appointment ☎

3 Bresworth House
4 Bridge Foot Farm
5 Brook Hall
10 Corner Cottage
17 Hall Farm
18 Henstead Exotic Garden
24 The Lucy Redman School of Garden Design
25 Magnolia House
27 Jonsyl, Ousden Gardens
30 Rosedale
36 White House Farm
37 Windmill Cottage
40 Mill Cottage, Wrentham Gardens

Beautiful in spring when the wisteria, laburnum and lilac are complemented by the many late flowering tulips and alliums . . .

The Gardens

1 NEW **ABBOTTS HALL**
Sturmer CB9 7XH. Mr & Mrs M
King. *20m S of Bury St Edmunds.
Sturmer Village on A1017. 1m out
of Haverhill towards Halstead.*
Home-made teas. **Adm £3, chd
free. Sun 4 May (2-5).**
Partially walled 2-acre garden
surrounding late Georgian house
(not open). Manicured lawns,
traditional herbaceous borders,
kitchen and cutting garden, small
orchard, rose garden and
woodland walk. Particularly
beautiful in spring when the
wisteria, laburnum and lilac are
complemented by the many late
flowering tulips and alliums. Some
gravel paths and slopes,
wheelchair users must be
accompanied.

2 ◆ **BLAKENHAM WOODLAND
GARDEN**
Little Blakenham IP8 4LZ. Lord
Blakenham, 07760 342817,
blakenham@btinternet.com. *4m NW
of Ipswich. Follow signs at Little
Blakenham, 1m off B1113.* **Adm £3,
chd £1.50. 1 Mar to 30 Jun. For
NGS: Sat 26, Sun 27 Apr (10-5).**
Beautiful 6-acre woodland garden with
variety of rare trees and shrubs.
Chinese rocks and a landscape
sculpture. Especially lovely in spring
with daffodils, camellias, magnolias
and bluebells followed by roses in early
summer.

3 **BRESWORTH HOUSE**
Stonham Road, Cotton IP14 4RG.
Keith & Ann Bullock, 01449 780102,
keith.bullockbres@tiscali.co.uk. *6m
N of Stowmarket. Between B1113 &
A140 close to Cotton Church.* Home-
made teas. **Adm £2.50, chd free. Sun
20 July (2-5). Visitors also welcome
by appt, individuals & groups
welcome Apr to July.**
Quiet 1-acre garden sheltered by
mature indigenous trees. Unique water
feature and recycled iron sculptures.
Interesting plants, ornamental trees
and shrubs, vegetable plot, cows
grazing next door. A tranquil rural
haven. Interesting Norman church next
door.

4 **BRIDGE FOOT FARM**
Reydon, Southwold IP18 6PS. David
& Susan Evan Jones, 01502 725293.
*A1095 on main rd into Southwold.
Follow signs to Southwold. Honey
coloured house on LH-side opp new
development before Bridge Rd and
bridge.* Home-made teas (£2.50) in
outbuildings. **Adm £2.50, chd free.
Sat 28, Sun 29 June (2-5). Visitors
also welcome by appt during June &
July.**
The garden is divided into 3 areas,
gravel paths and no grass. The front
garden is planted with perennials and
clematis. Behind the outbuildings the
area is full of climbers, geraniums etc.
Within the 'L' shape of the house,
replanted in 2007 are roses, and
clematis on arches and trellis.

5 **BROOK HALL**
Church Road, Crowfield IP6 9TG. Mr
& Mrs D S Pumfrey, 01449 711575.
*3m N of Coddenham. 1m S of
Stonham Aspal, Pettaugh A1120, 1/4 m
from Crowfield Church. Brook Hall is
reached down a farm drive.* Light
refreshments & cream teas. **Adm £3,
chd free. Suns 27 Apr; 25 May; 29
June (10.30-5). Visitors also
welcome by appt May & June;
groups of 10+, coaches permitted.**
Secluded 1 1/2 acres of mature country
garden. Hedges, walls and trees
separate diverse mixed borders.
Clematis and roses ramble at will.
Kitchen garden with raised beds and
soft fruit. Large natural pond, small
wilderness walk, and places to sit and
relax.

CHIPPENHAM PARK
See Cambridgeshire.

6 **6A CHURCH WALK**
Mildenhall IP28 7ED. Mr & Mrs D G
Reeve, 01638 715289,
j.reeve05@tiscali.co.uk. *15m W of
Bury St Edmunds. Nr church in
Mildenhall centre. From Fiveways
roundabout at Barton Mills on A11
follow signs to Mildenhall.* **Visitors
welcome by appt during May, June
& July.**
Walled garden surrounding modern
bungalow. Sunken paved area, raised
bed with pond and waterfall. Patio with
water feature, established rockery,
many herbaceous plants and shrubs
incl collection of hemerocallis.

7 ◆ **THE COACH HOUSE**
Assington CO10 5LQ. Mrs Justine
Ferrari. *5m S of Sudbury. On A134.
Turn R into Assington village. On sharp
LH-bend turn R into The Coach
House.* **Adm £3, chd free. For NGS:
Sun 8 June (2-6).**
Semi-formal 2-acre plantswoman's
garden generously planted with
herbaceous borders incl colour-
themed beds. Pond garden, potager,
woodland beds and wild flower areas.
Abundantly planted with roses and
scented plants. Free range pure-bred
hens.

A tranquil
rural haven . . .

8 **COBBS HALL**
Great Saxham IP29 5JN. Dr & Mrs R
H Soper. *4 1/2 m W of Bury St
Edmunds. A14 exit to Westley. R at
Westley Xrds. L fork at Little Saxham
signed Hargrave & Chevington. Approx
1 1/2 m to sign on R turn. Mustard-
coloured house 300yds on L.* Home-
made teas. **Adm £3, chd free. Sun 27
July (2-6).**
2 acres of lawns and borders;
ornamental trees, large fish/lily pond.
Parterre, folly, walled kitchen garden,
grass tennis court and pretty
courtyard.

9 **COLUMBINE HALL**
Stowupland IP14 4AT. Hew & Leslie
Stevenson,
www.columbinehall.co.uk. *1 1/2 m NE
of Stowmarket. Turn N off A1120 opp
Shell garage across village green, then
R at T-junction into Gipping Rd.
Garden on L just beyond derestriction
sign.* Home-made teas. **Adm £3, chd
free. Sun 29 June (2-6).**
Formal gardens, designed by George
Carter, surround moated medieval
manor house (not open). Also, outside
the moat, bog garden, Mediterranean
garden, colour-themed vegetable
garden, orchards and parkland.
Gardens developed since 1994 with
constant work-in-progress, incl
transformed farm buildings, wilderness
and eyecatchers. Some gravel paths.

10 CORNER COTTAGE
Rickinghall Road, Gislingham
IP23 8JJ. Trevor & Pauline Cox,
01449 781379. *5m W of Eye. Situated
approx 9m N of Stowmarket or approx
2½ m S of Rickinghall on B1113.* **Adm
£2.50, chd free. Sun 20 Apr (11-5).
Visitors also welcome by appt.**
Our ¾ -acre plot has 2 separate parts:
paved area with raised beds and the
main garden, developed over the last
18yrs. Trees and shrubs underplanted
with spring bulbs in beds, are linked by
meandering paths to give an open
woodland effect.
✗ ✿ ☕ ☎

See over 200 varieties of snowdrops together with cyclamen, hellebore and early flowering bulbs . . .

11 CROSSBILLS
Mildenhall IP28 7AL. David &
Yvonne Leonard, 01638 712742.
*5 mins from Mildenhall centre. From
Fiveways roundabout at Barton Mills
on A11 follow signs to Mildenhall.
Please park on industrial estate opp
house.* **Visitors welcome by appt
May & June only.**
¼ -acre partially walled garden on
edge of town the light, sandy
Breckland soil has been developed into
2 separate areas of gravel gardens.
Many varieties of cistus, lavender and
drought tolerant plants. Featured in
'The Garden' magazine.
✗ ✿ ☎

12 EAST BERGHOLT PLACE
East Bergholt CO7 6UP. Mr & Mrs
Rupert Eley. *On B1070 towards
Manningtree, 2m E of A12. Situated on
the edge of East Bergholt.* **Home-**
made teas. **Adm £3, chd free. Suns
6, 27 Apr; 12 Oct (2-5).**
20-acre garden originally laid out at the
beginning of the century by the present
owner's great grandfather. Full of many
fine trees and shrubs some of which
are rarely seen in East Anglia.

Particularly beautiful in spring when the
rhododendrons, magnolias and
camellias are in full flower, and in
autumn with newly cut topiary and
autumn colours. National Collection of
deciduous euonymus.
✗ ✿ NCCPG ☕

13 ◆ EUSTON HALL
Thetford IP242QP. His Grace The
Duke of Grafton, 01842 766366,
www.eustonhall.co.uk. *12m N of
Bury St Edmunds. 3m S of Thetford on
A1088.* **House and Garden £6, chd
£2, OAPs £5, Garden only £3, chd
£2. Thurs 19 June to 18 Sept; Suns
29 June; 13 July; 7 Sept (2.30-5).**
Terraced lawns, herbaceous borders,
rose garden, C17 pleasure grounds,
lake and watermill. C18 house open;
famous collection of paintings. C17
church; temple by William Kent. Shop
and teas.
♿ ✗ ☕

14 GABLE HOUSE
Halesworth Road, Redisham
NR34 8NE. Mr & Mrs John Foster,
01502 575298. *5m S of Beccles. From
Bungay A144 to Halesworth for 5m,
turn L at St Lawrence School, 2m to
Gable House.From A12 Blythburgh
A145 to Beccles. At Brampton X-roads
L to Station Rd. 3m on at junction is
Gable House.* Home-made teas. **Adm
£3, chd free (share to St Peters
Church, Redisham). Suns 24 Feb
(11-4); 8 June (11-5).**
1-acre garden contains a wide range of
interesting plants. In Feb visitors can
see over 200 varieties of snowdrops
together with cyclamen, hellebore and
early flowering bulbs. Wide range of
summer flowering shrubs, roses and
perennials providing colour for June
opening. Glasshouses are well stocked
with abundance of interesting plants
from alpines to tender species, many
for sale.
✗ ✿ ☕

15 GREAT THURLOW HALL
Haverhill CB9 7LF. Mr & Mrs George
Vestey. *12m S of Bury St Edmunds,
4m N of Haverhill. Great Thurlow village
on B1061 from Newmarket; 3½ m N
of junction with A143 Haverhill/Bury St
Edmunds rd.* **Adm £2.50, chd free.
Sun 6 Apr (2-5).**
River walk and trout lake with extensive
and impressive display of daffodils and
blossom. Spacious lawns, shrubberies
and roses. Walled kitchen garden.
Some gravel.
♿ ☕

**16 NEW GREEN FARM
HOUSE**
The Green, Redgrave, nr Diss
IP22 1RR. Mr & Mrs Peter Holt-
Wilson. *1m N of Botesdale. Take
A143 to Botesdale, then B1113 to
Redgrave, 1st turning L down lane
(The Green) just after (30)mph sign.
Garden 1st R. From A1066
Diss/Thetford rd, turn R in South
Lopham to Redgrave. Garden last
lane on R.* Home-made teas. **Adm
£3, chd free. Sat 15, Sun 16 Mar
(2-5).**
The garden is large and lovely in
spring with a good variety of
daffodils and snowdrops. Formal
garden, herbaceous beds and
interesting collection of trees.
Photographic Art Exhibition.
✿ ☕

17 HALL FARM
Weston, Beccles NR34 8TT. Mr &
Mrs Peter Seppings, 01502 715065,
peterseppings@pennylane.entadsl.
com. *The private garden at Winter
Flora. 1½ m S of Beccles. On A145.
The entrance is the same as for
Winter Flora, continue 300yds along
the drive to the private house.* Home-
made lunches, wine & teas. **Adm £3,
chd free. Sun 20 July (11.30-5).
Visitors also welcome by appt
mid Apr to mid Sept, coaches
permitted.**
The large photogenic pond set in
1½ acres is surrounded by primulas,
iris and rushes with several seats incl
colourful frog. Pots brimming with
tender plants are grouped on the vine-
shaded terrace whilst clematis and
roses smother the pergola. Replanting
and extra paving in the parterre has
enhanced this pretty garden. Emphasis
on easier maintenance and global
warming continues to infuence the
choice of plants. Planted in 2007 25m
white hydrangea walk, borders one
side of the parterre, foxgloves, ferns
and hellebores are shaded by the
walnut tree. Story-telling by David
Sham.
♿ ✿ ☕ ☎

**18 HENSTEAD EXOTIC
GARDEN**
Yew Cottage, Church Road,
Henstead NR34 7LD. Andrew
Brogan, 01502 743006,
absuffolk@hotmail.com. *Equal
distance between Beccles, Southwold
& Lowestoft approx 5m. 1m from A12
turning after Wrentham (signed
Henstead) very close to B1127.* Home-

made teas. **Adm £3, chd free. Sun 25 May (11-5). Visitors also welcome by appt private groups as small as 2 or 3.**

1-acre exotic garden featuring 50 large palms, 20+ bananas and 200 bamboo plants. 2 streams, 20ft tiered walkway leading to Thai style wooden covered pavilion. Mediterranean and jungle plants around 3 large ponds with fish and 'Suffolk's most exotic garden. Exotic and unusual plants for sale, teas served in tropical hardwood summerhouse - you could be in Bali!. 'Jaw droppingly impressive' - Suffolk Magazine. Featured on BBC Look East.

⑲ HERON HOUSE
Priors Hill Road, Aldeburgh IP15 5EP. Mr Jonathan Hale.
Junction of Priors Hill Rd & Park Rd. Teas at Stanford House. **Combined with Stanford House adm £4, chd free. Sun 4 May (2-5).**
2 acres with views over coastline, river and marshes. Unusual trees, herbaceous beds, shrubs and ponds with waterfall in large rock garden, stream and bog garden. Interesting attempts to grow half hardy plants in the coastal micro-climate.

☕

⑳ HOME FARM HOUSE
Rushbrooke IP30 0EP. Anita Wigan.
3m SE of Bury St Edmunds. A14 J44, proceed towards town centre, after 50yds 1st exit from roundabout then immed R. Proceed 3/4 m to T-junction, turn L, follow rd for 2m Rushbrooke Church on L, turn R into drive opp church. Home-made teas. **Adm £3, chd free. Sun 8 June (2-5). Also open The Lucy Redman School of Garden Design.**
3 acres walled garden with mixed shrubs and herbaceous borders, roses and formal lawns. 1-acre organic kitchen garden plus glasshouses with peaches, apricots, nectarines, grapes and figs etc. 5-acre parkland with moat garden, specimen trees and orchard. Small cottage garden alongside moat.

㉑ ◆ ICKWORTH HOUSE PARK & GARDENS
Horringer IP29 5QE. The National Trust, 01284 735270,
www.nationaltrust.org.uk. *2m SW of Bury St Edmunds. Ickworth is in the village of Horringer on the A143 Bury to Haverhill Rd.* **Adm £3.80, chd £1.**

Italianate Gardens Mar to Jan 11-4, park all yr 8-8. For NGS: Sat 19 July (10-4).
70 acres of garden. South gardens restored to stylised Italian landscape to reflect extraordinary design of the house. Fine orangery, agapanthus, geraniums and fatsias. North gardens informal wild flower lawns with wooded walk; the *Buxus* collection, great variety of evergreens and Victorian stumpery. New planting of cedars. The Albana Wood, a C18 feature, initially laid out by Capability Brown, incorporates a fine circular walk.

KIRTLING TOWER
See Cambridgeshire.

㉒ NEW THE KITCHEN GARDEN
Church Lane, Troston IP31 1EX. Francine Raymond, www.kitchen-garden-hens.co.uk. *8m NE of Bury St Edmunds. Troston is signed off A143 at Gt Barton & off B1088 at Honington & Ixworth. Garden is opp the church. Please park in village.* Home-made teas. **Adm £3, chd free. Sun 25, Mon 26 May (2-5).**
2/3-acre country garden, catering for family, local wildlife and flock of Buff Orpington hens. Vegetable, fruit, cutflower and herb gardens, wild areas, chicken run, perennial beds and formal yew-lined allèe. Opening in conjunction with St Mary's Church opp housing impressive wall paintings. Flower Festival at church, wild flower meadow in churchyard. Featured in & on the 'English Gardens' various publications, TV & Radio. Gravel areas, slopes, narrow paths.

㉓ ◆ LIME KILN HOUSE
Old Ipswich Road, Claydon IP6 0AD. Kathy Kalafat & Tim Young, 01473 833332,
www.limekilnroses.co.uk. *3m N of Ipswich. Off A14 J52 signed B1113 Bramford, Blakenham & Claydon, take Claydon exit from roundabout, then 1st R into Old Ipswich Rd. Garden 100 metres on L, behind large beech trees.* **Adm £3, chd £1. For garden details please see website or tel.** For NGS: Sun 15 June (11-5).
Currently under renovation. Wild romantic garden of approx 2 acres. Originally an old Suffolk farmhouse with

working lime kiln. Gardens established in 1920's following the removal of old farm buildings. In the1970/80's a famous Rosarium established by Humphrey Brooke for the preservation and conservation of old roses. Neglected in parts since his death in 1988 the roses are still magnificent in the summer months. Old roses grow in wild profusion, over pergolas, arches, walls and summerhouses, and up trees. Very old beech and lime trees, Irish yews and mulberry. Display of native British wild flowers.

2/3-acre country garden, catering for family, local wildlife and flock of Buff Orpington hens . . .

㉔ THE LUCY REDMAN SCHOOL OF GARDEN DESIGN
6 The Village, Rushbrooke IP30 0ER. Lucy Redman & Dominic Watts, 01284 386250, lucy@lucyredman.co.uk, www.lucyredman.co.uk. *3m E of Bury St Edmunds. From A14 Bury St Edmunds, E Sudbury exit, proceed towards town centre. After 50yds, 1st L exit from roundabout and immed R. 3/4 m to T-junction, turn L, follow rd for 2m. Before church turn R between white houses, past brick well, thatched house on L.* Home-made teas at Home Farm House. **Adm £2.50, chd free. Sun 8 June (2-5). Also open Home Farm House. Visitors also welcome by appt.**
Thatched cottage surrounded by 3/4 -acre quirky plantsman's family garden divided into compartments with impressive colour-coordinated borders containing many interesting combinations of unusual shrubs, roses, grasses and perennials. Grass parterre, turf tree seat, sculptures, wildlife pond, sedum roofed pavilion. Unusual bulb and rhizome garden, willow igloo and tunnel. Featured in 'Society of Garden Designers', 'English Garden' & 'Homes & Gardens' magazines. Lucy is gardening columnist for 'EADT Suffolk' magazine.

25 MAGNOLIA HOUSE
Yoxford IP17 3EP. Mr Mark Rumary, 01728 668321. *4m N of Saxmundham. Centre of Yoxford on A1120.* **Adm £2.50, chd free. Sun 13 Apr (2-5.30). Visitors also welcome by appt.**
Small, completely walled, romantic garden, tucked behind a pretty C18 village house (not open). Ingeniously designed to appear larger and planted to provide yr-round colour, scent and horticultural interest. Contains ancient mulberry, raised Moorish-style pool and newly planted Victorian flower garden. Featured in 'The English Garden'.
🍴 ⊛ ☕ ☎

26 NEW ◆ MONKSFIELD HOUSE
The Green, Monks Soham IP13 7EX. Kay & Richard Lacey, 01728 628449, www.k-plants.co.uk. *3m E of Debenham. 4m W of Framlingham. Off A1120 between Framsden & Earl Soham, drive through Ashfield cum Thorpe. Follow rd for 3m, turn R signed Monk Soham. Fork L at Y-junction, garden on L aftter ³/₄ m.* **Adm £2.50, chd free.** For NGS: **Sun 22 June (11-5).**
Young 2-acre garden formed 3yrs ago on former meadow land. Plantsman's garden comprising large herbaceous and shrub border with cottage style planting. Large natural pond. ¹/₃ -acre woodland garden with tranquil walks. Formal parterre, wild meadow with native orchids. Feature waterfall with bog and alpine planting. 4 native orchids and common broomrape in flower. Mail order plant nursery open to NGS visitors.
♿ ⊛ ☕

27 NEW OUSDEN GARDENS
CB8 8TW. *8m SE of Newmarket. From clock roundabout in Newmarket take B1063 via Cheveley, Ashley to Ousden.* Light refreshments & teas at Jonsyl. **Combined adm £3, chd free.** Sun 1 June (11-6).
Charming village with historic Norman Church. Both gardens within ¹/₂ m of Fox PH. Organic gardens, koi pond, art, garden honey for sale, ornamental breeds of chicken. Featured in EADT Suffolk Magazine.
☕

NEW JONSYL
Front Street. John & Sylvia Pettitt, 01638 500378, sylvia.pettitt@lineone.net. *Opp village hall in Front St.* **Visitors also welcome by appt Apr to Aug.**
Set amongst 7 acres of paddocks, 3 acres have been dedicated to gardens, lawns, ponds and wildlife. The remaining paddocks have resident beehives and may not be entered. Gardens incl herbaceous borders, roses, perennials and shrubs with many mature and young trees.
🍴 ⊛ ☎

NEW LITTLY WOOD HOUSE
Back Street, off Lords Lane. Colin & Maggie Wotherspoon. *Down Lords Lane from Fox PH. Park in farmyard. Turn R into Back St. Garden 3rd entrance on R* ²/₃ -acre organic garden of trees, shrubs, perennials and wild flowers in a relaxed cottage garden style. Areas of shade, vegetables, greenhouses and lawns. 4 ponds and separate wildlife area accessed by winding path.
🍴 ⊛

Charming village with historic Norman Church . . .

28 THE PRIORY
Stoke-by-Nayland CO6 4RL. Mr & Mrs H F A Engleheart. *5m SW of Hadleigh. Entrance on B1068 to Sudbury (NW of Stoke-by-Nayland).* Home-made teas. **Adm £3, chd free. Sun 18 May (2-5).**
Interesting 9-acre garden with fine views over Constable countryside; lawns sloping down to small lakes and water garden; fine trees, rhododendrons and azaleas; walled garden; mixed borders and ornamental greenhouse. Wide variety of plants; peafowl. Some gravel paths, slight slope.
♿ ⊛ ☕

29 REDISHAM HALL
Beccles NR34 8LZ. The Palgrave Brown Family. *5m S of Beccles. From A145, turn W on to Ringsfield-Bungay rd. Beccles, Halesworth or Bungay, all within 5m.* Home-made teas. **Adm £3.50, chd free. Sun 13 July (2-6).**
C18 Georgian house (not open). 5-acre garden set in 400 acres parkland and woods. Incl 2-acre walled kitchen garden (in full production) with peach house, vinery and glasshouses. Lawns, herbaceous borders, shrubberies, ponds and mature trees.
♿ 🍴 ☕

30 ROSEDALE
40 Colchester Road, Bures CO8 5AE. Mr & Mrs Colin Lorking, 01787 227619, rosedale@beeb.net. *6m SE of Sudbury. 9m NW of Colchester on B1508. As you enter the village of Bures, garden on L. From Sudbury follow signs through village towards Colchester, garden on R as you leave village.* Home-made teas. **Adm £2.50, chd free. Suns 4 May; 13 July (12-5.30). Visitors also welcome by appt.**
Approx ¹/₃ -acre plantsman's garden; many unusual plants, herbaceous borders, pond, woodland area.
🍴 ⊛ ☕ ☎

31 ROSEMARY
Rectory Hill, East Bergholt CO7 6TH. Mrs N E M Finch. *9m NE of Colchester. Turn off A12 onto B1070 to East Bergholt, 1st R Hadleigh Rd, bear L at end of rd. At junction with Village St turn R, pass Red Lion PH, post office & church. Garden 100yds down from church on L.* Home-made teas. **Adm £3, chd free. Sun 8 June (2.30-5).**
This romantic garden, which appeals particularly to artists, has been developed over 34yrs. Planted to reveal paths and vistas. Over 100 old-fashioned roses. 2 bog beds, unusual trees, good bulbs and many unusual plants. Planted for all seasons.
♿ ⊛ 🛏 ☕

SHRUBS FARM
See Essex.

32 STANFORD HOUSE
Priors Hill Road, Aldeburgh IP15 5EP. Lady Cave. *From A12 take A1094 to Aldeburgh. On approach to town go over 1st roundabout then almost immed R into Park Rd. At tennis courts on the R turn R into Priors Hill Rd.* **Combined with Heron**

House adm £4, chd free. Sun 4 May (2-5).
1½ acres of terraced garden with waterfall, water garden and wide variety of rare plants and specimen shrubs luxuriating in mild maritime climate. Beautiful views over river marsh and sea.

Beautiful views over river marsh and sea . . .

33 THRIFT FARMHOUSE
Kirtling Cowlinge CB8 9JA. Mrs Jan Oddy, 01440 783274, janoddy@yahoo.co.uk. *7m N of Newmarket. Great Bradley Rd from Kirtling - Great Bradley Rd from Cowlinge. Turn R at Xrds to Kirtling. Car parking in adjacent meadow.* **Visitors welcome by appt, Mar to Nov incl.**
Forever changing, 6 acres, attractive country cottage garden, set around thatched house (not open). Island beds, full of mixed trees, shrubs and perennials, shady woodland areas. Natural pond, orchard of mixed fruits and meadows of sheep and wild flowers.

34 THE WALLOW
Mount Road, Bury St Edmunds IP31 2QU. Linda & Mike Draper, 01284 788055, www.thewallow.co.uk. *2m E of Bury St Edmunds. Leave A14 J45 at Rougham Industrial Site, ½ m along Sow Lane to T-junction at Battlies Corner. Take L towards BSE for ½ m along Mount Rd.* Home-made teas. **Adm £2.50, chd free. Sun 22 June (2-5).**
2¼ acres of garden with wild pond, flower meadows, orchard, potager, silver birch planting with snakeshead fritillaries and herbaceous borders. Yr-round interest. Owner keen propagator, small nursery, new woodland planting. Partial wheelchair access, sloping grass, ok for pushed chairs, easy access to grassy area.

35 WALSHAM GARDENS
Walsham-le-Willows IP31 3AD. *11m E of Bury St Edmunds. From A143 to Diss take turning to village.* Home-made teas in Priory Room. **Combined adm £4, chd free** (share to St Marys Church, Walsham-le-Willows). **Sun 6 Apr (2-5).**
5 different gardens in a lovely village in the middle of Suffolk.

THE BEECHES
Grove Road. Dr A J Russell
150yr-old, 3-acre garden, which incl specimen trees, pond, potager, memorial garden, lawns and variety of beds.
Improvements to stream area.

NEW CAUSEWAY HOUSE
The Causeway. Mrs J Russell
Garden approx 1-acre, shrubs, water feature. Originally designed by Notcutts.

MALTINGS HOUSE
The Street. Mrs P D Blyth
Spring garden. Hostas, bluebells, primroses, aconites, daffodils, shrubs, laburnum, snowdrops and crocuses. Walled garden with partial wild patch under hazel trees. Croquet lawn and large vegetable area with fruit cage.

NUNN'S YARD
The Street. Steve Colby
3 acres, long term landscaping, tree and hedge planting. Areas completed are split into planting themes, statues, archways, shrubs, herbaceous, perennials and specimen trees.

THUMBIT
Badwell Road. IP31 3BT. Mrs James, 01359 259414, thumbit@tecova.com. *From A143 (Bury - Diss) to Xrds by church. Follow Badwell Ash Rd to outskirts of village ½ m.* **Visitors also welcome by appt.**
House is part of thatched C16 one-time public house (not open). Shared driveway (please do not drive in). Small informal garden with emphasis on design and plant association. Pergola, pool, topiary and potager. 500 choice plants, shrubs, roses and climbers.

36 WHITE HOUSE FARM
Ringsfield, Beccles NR34 8JU. James & Jan Barlow, 07795 170892 Head gardener, whf707@aol.com. *2m SW of Beccles. From Beccles take B1062 towards Bungay, after 1½ m turn L, signed Ringsfield. Continue for 1m passing Ringsfield Church. Garden 300yds on L over small white railed bridge.* Light refreshments & teas. **Adm £3, chd free. Sat 7 June (11-5). Visitors also welcome by appt all yr, min 4, max 16 visitors.**
Fine garden of approx 30 acres with superb views over the Waveney Valley. Formal gardens and parkland with specimen trees, copses and lawns, good deal of mixed hedging. NB Beck and 2 ponds are not fenced. Partial wheelchair access.

37 WINDMILL COTTAGE
Mill Hill, Capel St Mary IP9 2JE. Mr & Mrs G A Cox, 01473 311121. *3m SW of Ipswich. Turn off A12 at Capel St Mary. At far end of village on R after 1¼ m.* Home-made teas. **Adm £2.50, chd free. Sun 1 June (2-6). Visitors also welcome by appt.**
½ -acre plantsman's cottage-style garden. Island beds, pergolas with clematis and other climbers. Many trees and shrubs, wildlife ponds and vegetable area. Featured in & on East Anglian 'Derby Times', Suffolk BBC Radio, Suffolk SGR.

38 NEW ◆ WOODWARDS
Blacksmiths Lane, Coddenham, Ipswich IP6 9TX. Marion & Richard Kenward, 01449 760639. *7m N of Ipswich. From A140 turn onto A14, after ¼ m turn off B1078 towards Wickham Market, Coddenham is on route.* **Adm £2.50, chd free. Other times by appt. For NGS: Suns 1, 15 June; 13 July; 17 Aug (10-6).**
Award-winning, S-facing, gently sloping garden of ¾ -acre, overlooking the rolling Suffolk countryside, designed and maintained by the owners for yr round colour and interest, lots of island beds, well stocked with 1000s of shrubs and perennials, vegetable plot, numerous hanging baskets and well manicured lawns. Village gardens and Scarrcow Festival 15 June. Featured in 'East Anglian Daily Times'.

SUFFOLK

39 ◆ WOOTTENS
Blackheath Road, Wenhaston
IP19 9HD. Mr M Loftus, 01502
478258, www.woottensplants.co.uk.
*18m S of Lowestoft. On A12 & B1123,
follow signs to Wenhaston.* **Adm £1,
chd/concessions 50p. For NGS:
Every Tues, Weds, Thurs 1 Apr to 30
Sept; Iris field 24 May to 10 June;
Iris sibirica field Sats, Suns 14, 15,
21, 22 June; Hemerocallis field Sats,
Suns 12,13, 19, 20, 26, 27 July (9.30-
5).**
Small romantic garden, redesigned in
2003. Scented-leafed pelargoniums,
violas, cranesbills, lilies, salvias,
penstemons, primulas, etc. 2 acres of
bearded iris, ¼ acre of iris sibiricas, 1
acre of hemerocallis. Wheelchair users
will need assitance with access to
fields.

&♿ ⋈ ⊛

40 WRENTHAM GARDENS
NR34 7JF. *4m N of Southwold. 5m S
of Lowestoft. From A12 in centre of
Wrentham take B1127 Southwold Rd.
Small car park at junction followed by 3
laybys on L. Some parking available at
no 70.* Home-made teas at Mill
Cottage & 34 Southwold Rd.
**Combined adm £3, chd free. Sun 8
June (11-6).**
All gardens within 600yds of junction.
Spread out village along A12. Some
interesting buildings - C15 church and
Georgian Meeting House. Featured on
BBC TV - Look East.

☕

LILBOURNE
70 Southwold Road. Mr & Mrs
Richard Wood
Attractive country garden that
slopes away from the house
towards a meadow. Divided into 3
sections with interesting mixed
borders of herbaceous and
cottage plants, gravel garden and
boat seat feature.

MILL COTTAGE
34 Southwood Road. Gillian
Innes, 01502 675281. Visitors
also welcome by appt June &
early July only.
Picturesque ⅓ -acre plantsman's
garden. Mixed herbaceous,
shrubs, roses, vegetables and fruit
for a difficult site, which blends
into its rural setting. Attractive
(hidden) yard garden.

⋈ ⊛ ☎

68 SOUTHWOLD ROAD
Mrs C Reeve
Open aspect sloping down to
meadow, broken by islands of
trees, shrubs and ornamental
plants together with old favourite
cottage garden perennials. Tree-
house, accessed at own risk.
Gentle grass slopes.

&♿ ⋈ 🛏

41 ◆ WYKEN HALL
Stanton IP31 2DW. Sir Kenneth &
Lady Carlisle, 01359 250262,
www.wykenvineyards.com. *9m NE
of Bury St Edmunds. Along A143.
Follow signs to Wyken Vineyards on
A143 between Ixworth & Stanton.*
**Adm £3.50, chd free, concessions
£3. Suns to Fris 6 Apr to 1 Oct 2-6.
For NGS: Sat 7 (10-6), Sun 8 June
(2-6).**
4-acre garden much developed
recently; knot and herb garden; old-
fashioned rose garden, wild garden,
nuttery, pond, gazebo and maze;
herbaceous borders and old orchard.
Woodland walk, vineyard. Starred in
'GGG'.

&♿ ⋈ ⊛ ☕

Suffolk County Volunteers

County Organisers
East Patricia Short, Ruggs Hall, Raydon, Ipswich IP7 5LW, 01473 310416
West Jenny Reeve, 6a Church Walk, Mildenhall IP28 7ED, 01638 715289, j.reeve05@tiscali.co.uk

County Treasurers
East Geoffrey Cox, Windmill Cottage, Mill Hill, Capel St. Mary, Ipswich, Suffolk IP9 2JE, 01473 311121, gaandemcox@lineone.net
West David Reeve, 6a Church Walk, Mildenhall, Bury St. Edmunds IP28 7ED, 01638 715289, j.reeve05@tiscali.co.uk

Assistant County Organisers:
East Joan Brightwell, Bucklesham Hall, Bucklesham IP10 0AY, 01473 659263
West Lucy Redman, 6 The Village, Rushbrooke, Bury St. Edmunds IP30 0ER, 01284 386250, lucy@lucyredman.co.uk
East Hans Seiffer, Garden House Farm, Rattlesden Road, Drinkstone, Bury St Edmunds IP30 9TN, 01449 736434,
       hans.seiffer@dial.pipex.com
East Joby West, The Millstone, Friars Road, Hadleigh IP7 6DF, 01473 823154

Mark your diary with these special events in 2008

EXPLORE SECRET GARDENS DURING CHELSEA WEEK

Tue 20 May, Wed 21 May, Thur 22 May, Fri 23 May
Full day tours: £78 per person, 10% discount for groups
Advance Booking required, telephone 01932 864532 or
email pennysnellflowers@btinternet.com

Specially selected private gardens in London, Surrey and Berkshire. The tour price includes transport and lunch with wine at a popular restaurant or pub.

FROGMORE – A ROYAL GARDEN (BERKSHIRE)

Tue 3 June 10am - 5.30pm (last adm 4pm)
Garden adm £4, chd free. Advance booking recommended telephone 01483 211535
or email orders@ngs.org.uk

A unique opportunity to explore 30 acres of landscaped garden, rich in history and beauty.

FLAXBOURNE FARM – FUN AND SURPRISES (BEDFORDSHIRE)

Sun 8 June 10am - 5pm Adm £5, chd free
No booking required, come along on the day!

Bring the whole family and enjoy a plant fair and garden party and have fun in this beautiful and entertaining garden of 2 acres.

WISLEY RHS GARDEN – MUSIC IN THE GARDEN (SURREY)

Tue 19 August 6 - 9pm

Adm (incl RHS members) £7, chd under 15 free

A special opening of this famous garden, exclusively for the NGS. Enjoy music and entertainment as you explore a range of different gardens.

For further information visit www.ngs.org.uk or telephone 01483 211535

SURREY

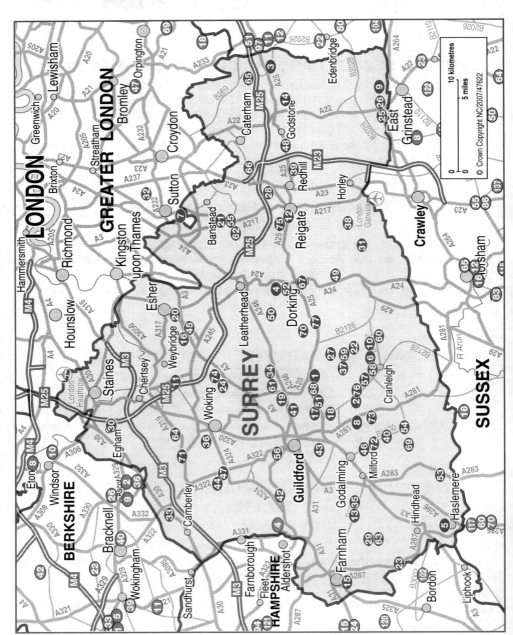

Opening Dates

February

SUNDAY 17
28 Gatton Park

WEDNESDAY 20
28 Gatton Park

March

SUNDAY 9
1 Albury Park

MONDAY 24
69 Vann

TUESDAY 25
69 Vann

WEDNESDAY 26
69 Vann

THURSDAY 27
69 Vann

FRIDAY 28
69 Vann

SATURDAY 29
69 Vann

SUNDAY 30
64 Timber Hill
69 Vann

MONDAY 31
69 Vann

April

TUESDAY 1
69 Vann

WEDNESDAY 2
69 Vann

THURSDAY 3
69 Vann

FRIDAY 4
69 Vann

SATURDAY 5
69 Vann
73 Wintershall Manor

SUNDAY 6
19 Clandon Park
69 Vann

WEDNESDAY 9
12 Caxton House

SATURDAY 12
24 Dunsborough Park

SUNDAY 13
22 Coverwood Lakes
40 Lodkin

SUNDAY 20
16 Chestnut Lodge
22 Coverwood Lakes

46 Munstead Wood
72 Winkworth Arboretum

WEDNESDAY 23
55 41 Shelvers Way

SATURDAY 26
73 Wintershall Manor

SUNDAY 27
22 Coverwood Lakes
34 Hatchlands Park
55 41 Shelvers Way
64 Timber Hill
71 Westways Farm

May

SUNDAY 4
15 Chestnut Cottage
22 Coverwood Lakes
43 Loseley Park
49 The Old Croft

MONDAY 5
49 The Old Croft
69 Vann
70 Walton Poor House

TUESDAY 6
69 Vann

WEDNESDAY 7
69 Vann

THURSDAY 8
69 Vann

FRIDAY 9
69 Vann

SATURDAY 10
69 Vann

SUNDAY 11
8 Birtley House
17 Chilworth Manor
22 Coverwood Lakes
45 Moleshill House
69 Vann

TUESDAY 13
27 Fulvens Hanger

WEDNESDAY 14
27 Fulvens Hanger
45 Moleshill House

THURSDAY 15
27 Fulvens Hanger

FRIDAY 16
27 Fulvens Hanger

SATURDAY 17
9 Braekenas
23 Crosswater Farm

SUNDAY 18
9 Braekenas
23 Crosswater Farm
33 Hall Grove School
37 Knowle Grange

46 Munstead Wood
52 Quinneys
59 Spurfold

MONDAY 19
14 Chauffeur's Flat

TUESDAY 20
14 Chauffeur's Flat

WEDNESDAY 21
14 Chauffeur's Flat

THURSDAY 22
14 Chauffeur's Flat

FRIDAY 23
14 Chauffeur's Flat
57 Smithwood House (Evening)

SATURDAY 24
14 Chauffeur's Flat
65 Titsey Place Gardens

SUNDAY 25
11 40 Byfleet Road
14 Chauffeur's Flat
44 Memoirs
49 The Old Croft

MONDAY 26
49 The Old Croft

FRIDAY 30
57 Smithwood House (Evening)

June

SUNDAY 1
69 Vann
70 Walton Poor House

MONDAY 2
30 Great Fosters
69 Vann

TUESDAY 3
30 Great Fosters
69 Vann

WEDNESDAY 4
21 The Copse Lodge (Evening)
30 Great Fosters
69 Vann

THURSDAY 5
30 Great Fosters
69 Vann

FRIDAY 6
25 Felbridge Copse (Evening)
26 Felbridge Courtyard (Evening)
69 Vann

SATURDAY 7
61 Stuart Cottage
69 Vann

SUNDAY 8
6 Barhatch Farm
21 The Copse Lodge
40 Lodkin

50 Polesden Lacey
66 Tollsworth Manor
67 6 Upper Rose Hill
69 Vann

WEDNESDAY 11
6 Barhatch Farm
58 Spring Cottage (Evening)

THURSDAY 12
58 Spring Cottage (Evening)

FRIDAY 13
58 Spring Cottage (Evening)

SATURDAY 14
24 Dunsborough Park
39 Little Priory (Evening)
65 Titsey Place Gardens
68 Vale End (Evening)

SUNDAY 15
5 Bardsey
10 Burstowe's Croft
13 Chandlers
35 Hideaway House
39 Little Priory
42 Longer End Cottage
60 Square Leg Cottage
68 Vale End

WEDNESDAY 18
10 Burstowe's Croft
60 Square Leg Cottage

THURSDAY 19
58 Spring Cottage (Evening)

FRIDAY 20
4 Ashleigh Grange (Evening)
54 The Round House (Evening)
58 Spring Cottage (Evening)

SATURDAY 21
58 Spring Cottage (Evening)
63 Tilford Cottage

SUNDAY 22
4 Ashleigh Grange
18 Chinthurst Lodge
54 The Round House
63 Tilford Cottage

MONDAY 23
14 Chauffeur's Flat

TUESDAY 24
14 Chauffeur's Flat

WEDNESDAY 25
4 Ashleigh Grange
14 Chauffeur's Flat
18 Chinthurst Lodge

THURSDAY 26
14 Chauffeur's Flat

FRIDAY 27
14 Chauffeur's Flat

SATURDAY 28
14 Chauffeur's Flat
62 35 Tadorne Road
63 Tilford Cottage

SUNDAY 29
14 Chauffeur's Flat
62 35 Tadorne Road
63 Tilford Cottage

July

FRIDAY 4
75 Woodbury Cottage (Evening)

SATURDAY 5
38 Little Mynthurst Farm
75 Woodbury Cottage

SUNDAY 6
38 Little Mynthurst Farm
75 Woodbury Cottage
77 Wotton House

SATURDAY 12
49 The Old Croft
65 Titsey Place Gardens

SUNDAY 13
21 The Copse Lodge
36 Horsell Allotments & Birch Cottage Garden
49 The Old Croft
61 Stuart Cottage
77 Wotton House

WEDNESDAY 16
21 The Copse Lodge (Evening)
68 Vale End

SATURDAY 19
20 Claremont Landscape Garden

SUNDAY 20
11 40 Byfleet Road
29 Gorse Cottage
47 19 Oak Tree Road
55 41 Shelvers Way
77 Wotton House

SATURDAY 26
2 Appletrees (Evening)

SUNDAY 27
2 Appletrees
32 72 Green Wrythe Lane
70 Walton Poor House
77 Wotton House

WEDNESDAY 30
2 Appletrees (Evening)

August

SUNDAY 3
25 Felbridge Copse
26 Felbridge Courtyard
48 Odstock

FRIDAY 8
59 Spurfold (Evening)

SATURDAY 9
7 Bethany
49 The Old Croft

SUNDAY 10
7 Bethany
41 Long Barton
49 The Old Croft

SATURDAY 16
31 Green Lane Farm
65 Titsey Place Gardens

SUNDAY 17
16 Chestnut Lodge
42 Longer End Cottage

TUESDAY 19
74 Wisley RHS Garden (Evening)

SUNDAY 24
31 Green Lane Farm

MONDAY 25
61 Stuart Cottage (Evening)

SATURDAY 30
75 Woodbury Cottage

SUNDAY 31
75 Woodbury Cottage

September

WEDNESDAY 3
75 Woodbury Cottage

SUNDAY 7
20 Claremont Landscape Garden
42 Longer End Cottage

SATURDAY 13
24 Dunsborough Park

SUNDAY 14
37 Knowle Grange

October

SUNDAY 5
1 Albury Park
34 Hatchlands Park
72 Winkworth Arboretum

SUNDAY 12
70 Walton Poor House

SUNDAY 19
22 Coverwood Lakes

February 2009

SUNDAY 15
28 Gatton Park

WEDNESDAY 18
28 Gatton Park

Gardens open to the public

19 Clandon Park
20 Claremont Landscape Garden
22 Coverwood Lakes
23 Crosswater Farm
28 Gatton Park
34 Hatchlands Park
43 Loseley Park
50 Polesden Lacey
53 Ramster
65 Titsey Place Gardens
72 Winkworth Arboretum
74 Wisley RHS Garden

By appointment only

- **3** Arden Lodge
- **51** Postford House
- **56** 67 & 69 Shepherds Lane
- **76** Woodhill Manor

Also open by appointment ☎

- **2** Appletrees
- **4** Ashleigh Grange
- **5** Bardsey
- **6** Barhatch Farm
- **13** Chandlers
- **27** Fulvens Hanger
- **31** Green Lane Farm
- **37** Knowle Grange
- **40** Lodkin
- **42** Longer End Cottage
- **45** Moleshill House
- **48** Odstock
- **54** The Round House
- **55** 41 Shelvers Way
- **57** Smithwood House
- **58** Spring Cottage
- **59** Spurfold
- **61** Stuart Cottage
- **63** Tilford Cottage
- **67** 6 Upper Rose Hill
- **68** Vale End
- **69** Vann
- **71** Westways Farm
- **75** Woodbury Cottage

The Gardens

ABBOTSMERRY BARN
See Kent.

1 ALBURY PARK
Albury GU5 9BH. Trustees of Albury Estate. *5m SE of Guildford. From A25 take A248 towards Albury for ¹/₄ m, then up New Rd, entrance to Albury Park immed on L.* Home-made teas. **Adm £3.50, chd free. Suns 9 Mar; 5 Oct (2-5).**
14-acre pleasure grounds laid out in 1670s by John Evelyn for Henry Howard, later 6th Duke of Norfolk. ¹/₄ m terraces, fine collection of trees, lake and river. Albury Park Mansion gardens also open (by kind permission of Historic House Retirement Homes Ltd. House not open). Gravel path and slight slope.
♿ ✗ ☕

23 ANGLESEY ROAD
See Hampshire.

2 APPLETREES
Stonards Brow, Shamley Green GU5 0UY. Mr & Mrs A Hodgson, 01483 898779, thodgson@uwclub.net. *5m SE of Guildford. A281 Guildford to Horsham rd, turn L at Shalford on B2128 via Wonersh to Shamley Green. Turn R before Red Lion PH, then R into Sweetwater Lane. At top of lane turn R into Stonards Brow or follow signs to car park when entering village. From Ewhurst/Cranleigh turn L at village stores, proceed down Hullbrook Lane following signs to Longacre School car park.* Cream teas. **Adm £2.50, chd free. Sun 27 July (2-6). Evening Openings £4.50, wine & cheese, Sat 26, Wed 30 July (5-8). Visitors also welcome by appt in July & Aug, for groups of 15+ for morning coffee, afternoon tea or evening wine.**
¹/₄ -acre garden with many interesting features. Several small water features incl koi pond. Summerhouse, greenhouses, raised railway sleeper beds, pergolas. Shrub and perennial borders. Patio and gravel area with several colourful containers. Raised vegetable beds; jungle beds with bananas and an elevated walkway; new secret garden and white water garden. Obelisks and clematis, all on a sandy loam soil. An ideas garden.
♿ ✥ ☕ ☎

3 ARDEN LODGE
Pastens Road, Limpsfield RH8 0RE. Mr & Mrs C Bruce-Jones, 01883 722171, chris.bruce-jones@virgin.net. *1m E of Oxted. From A25 take B269 Edenbridge Rd for 200yds. R down Brick Kiln Lane. Pastens Rd 2nd turning L, house at end of rd.* Refreshments by arrangement. **Adm £3, chd free. Visitors welcome by appt Apr to July for groups & individuals.**
2-acre garden on greensand with extensive views. Sunken garden with formal fishpond and arbour; pergola; herbaceous border; rhododendrons, azaleas and much formal and informal mixed planting with interesting trees, shrubs, roses and containers. Some gravel paths.
♿ ✗ ☕ ☎

4 ASHLEIGH GRANGE
off Chapel Lane, Westhumble RH5 6AY. Clive & Angela Gilchrist, 01306 884613, ar.gilchrist@btinternet.com. *2m N of Dorking. From A24 at Boxhill/Burford Bridge follow signs to Westhumble.*

Through village & L up drive by ruined chapel (1m from A24). Home-made teas. **Adm £3, chd free. Evening Opening £4, wine, Fri 20 June (6-8). Sun 22, Wed 25 June (2-5.30). Visitors also welcome by appt May to July.**
Sloping chalk garden on 3¹/₂ -acre site in charming rural setting with delightful views. Many areas of interest incl rockery and water feature, raised ericaceous bed, prairie-style bank, foliage plants, woodland walk and fernery. Large mixed herbaceous and shrub borders planted for dry alkaline soil and widespread interest.
♿ ✿ ☕ ☎

Fragrant herb and rose parterre bordered by lavender and box; pink, purple and white herbaceous borders . . .

5 BARDSEY
11 Derby Road, Haslemere GU27 1BS. Maggie & David Boyd, 01428 652283, maggie.boyd@tiscali.co.uk. *¹/₄ m N of Haslemere stn. Turn off B2131 (which links A287 to A286 through town) 400yds W of stn into Weydown Rd, 3rd R into Derby Rd, garden 400yds on R.* Home-made teas. **Adm £3, chd free. Sun 15 June (11-5). Visitors also welcome by appt June & July, groups of 15+ only.**
Two-acre garden on greensand and clay, separated into 4 distinct areas. Fragrant herb and rose parterre bordered by lavender and box; pink, purple and white herbaceous borders; raised vegetable beds and caged fruit garden. In lower garden several natural and temperamental ponds, planting and area of young fruit trees.
♿ ✗ ✿ ☕ ☎

6 BARHATCH FARM

Barhatch Lane, Cranleigh GU6 7NG. Mr & Mrs P M Grol, 01483 277968. *2m N of Cranleigh. A281 from Guildford, L at B2128 to Cranleigh, through village, take Ewhurst Rd for 1m, turn L into Barhatch Rd which becomes Barhatch Lane. Garden 1st on R after Cranleigh Golf & Leisure Club.* Home-made teas. **Adm £3, chd free.** Sun 8, Wed 11 June (11-5). **Visitors also welcome by appt in June only.**
6-acre garden, created by present owners, surrounding listed Tudor farmhouse (not open). Herbaceous borders and abundance of old roses, incl romantic rose tunnel. Walled pond, ornamental pond, interesting sunken Zen garden. Wild flower and allium meadow leading to yew tree walk. Partial wheelchair access.

♿ ⛶ ❀ ☕ ☎

An oasis in an urban setting . . .

BENTLEY VILLAGE GARDENS

See Hampshire.

7 BETHANY

87 Sandy Lane, South Cheam SM2 7EP. Brian & Pam West & Mr & Mrs L West. *2m W of Sutton. Approx 1m S of Cheam village, or from A217 turn into Northey Ave. At small roundabout L into Sandy Lane, then approx 100yds on L.* Home-made teas. **Adm £2.50, chd free.** Sat 9, Sun 10 Aug (1-5.30).
1/3 -acre plantsman's garden with a subtropical feel where palm trees, tree ferns, banana trees, agave and bamboo surround the wide lawn. Vibrant coloured dahlias and a large collection of cannas make this an exciting August garden. Behind pretty summerhouse is vegetable garden and greenhouses.

⛶ ❀ ☕

8 BIRTLEY HOUSE

Bramley GU5 0LB. Mr & Mrs Simon Whalley. *5m S of Guildford. From Guildford S on A281. Through Bramley look out for Birtley Courtyard on L on S-bend. Immed after, on R, entrance to*

Birtley House. Home-made teas. **Adm £4, chd free.** Sun 11 May (2-5).
48 acres of restored parkland, woods and gardens. Herbaceous and shrub borders, lake, pond, secret garden, rose garden, kitchen garden, orchard. Wide variety of trees and shrubs. Bulbs, wisteria, bluebell wood and rhododendrons in spring. Nature trail/bluebell walk approx 30mins. Some gravel paths, main features accessible; regret nature trail unsuitable for wheelchairs.

♿ ❀ ☕

BOXWOOD HOUSE

See Berkshire.

9 BRAEKENAS

West Hill Road, Dormans Park RH19 2ND. Ann & Ray Lindfield. *3m N of East Grinstead. From London on A22 turn L at T-lights in Blindley Heath - Ray Lane. In Lingfield turn R at 2nd roundabout - East Grinstead Rd. Fork L into Blackberry Lane, keep racecourse on L, turn L at bottom of hill, R into Dormans Park. Then 1st L, 1st R West Hill.* Home-made teas. **Adm £3, chd free.** Sat 17, Sun 18 May (2-6).
Created 47 yrs ago by present owners, a garden for all seasons with lovely specimen shrubs and trees, incl azaleas and camellias. Immaculate vegetable plot.

♿ ⛶ ❀ ☕

BROADHATCH HOUSE

See Hampshire.

10 BURSTOWE'S CROFT

The Green, Ewhurst GU6 7RT. Wendy & Richard Worby. *3m E of Cranleigh. Take B2127 from obelisk at E end of Cranleigh. 2m to Ewhurst village. Take 2nd R signed Horsham & Ellens Green, garden 200yds on R. Parking further 200yds at cricket green or Plough Lane.* Home-made teas. **Adm £3, chd free.** Sun 15, Wed 18 June (11-5).
Gently-sloping 1-acre informal country garden. Meander around large borders with scented shrubs, herbaceous plants, ornamental and fruit trees. Rose garden with charming rose-covered gazebo, many old-fashioned varieties. Vegetable garden and greenhouse. Gravel garden with pond. Path through mini woodland with shade-loving plants. Short walk to Square Leg Cottage, also open.

♿ ⛶ ❀ ☕

11 NEW 40 BYFLEET ROAD

Addlestone KT15 3JX. Mrs Lyn Davis & Mr J Coxe. *1 1/2 m NW of Weybridge. From M25 J11 take A317 to Addlestone, onto A318 to White Hart PH. Turn L over New Haw canal bridge. 2nd turn R into slip rd.* Home-made teas. **Adm £2.50, chd free.** Suns 25 May; 20 July (11-5).
An oasis in an urban setting. This 250ft long garden has individual rooms, each with its own interest. Herbaceous plants mingle with mature shrubs and trees. Kitchen garden and glasshouse lead to access path through majestic oaks onto canal towpath. Woodland craft furniture display, subject to weather. Gravel path.

♿ ❀ ☕

12 CAXTON HOUSE

67 West Street, Reigate RH2 9DA. Bob & Marj Bushby. *1/2 m W of Reigate. On A25 towards Dorking, approx 1/4 m W of Reigate on L. Parking on rd.* Cream teas. **Adm £3, chd free (share to Parkinson's Disease Society).** Wed 9 Apr (2-5).
Large garden with wildlife wood, 3 ponds, lots of spring planting - primroses, bulbs and large collection of hellebores.

♿ ❀ ☕

13 NEW CHANDLERS

Lower Ham Lane, Elstead GU8 6HQ. Mrs Kim Budge, 01252 703717, kim@budgeuk.freeserve.co.uk. *From A3 Milford take B3001 to Elstead. Entering village turn 2nd R signed EVTC (tennis club). From Farnham, B3001 through village, then L after tel box signed EVTC. Park on Burford Lea recreation ground. Disabled parking use Hideaway House, Lower Ham Lane (off Broomfield).* Home-made teas & wine at Hideaway House. **Combined adm with Hideaway House £3.50, chd free.** Sun 15 June (2-6). **Visitors also welcome by appt Apr to Aug, no coaches.**
Come and enjoy a stroll around this 1/2 -acre garden brimming with exciting planting combinations, many unusual shrubs, trees, grasses, perennials and bulbs. Divided into rooms incl a picturesque potager with step-over apple trees and companion planting, woodland, and mixed

borders radiating from a semi-circular slate, multi-level patio and pergola. Winner BBC Gardeners' World Formal Garden Bedding competition. Slate path at entrance, narrow woodland path.

  ♿ ☎ 🕿

CHARTS EDGE
See Kent.

CHARTWELL
See Kent.

⑭ CHAUFFEUR'S FLAT
Tandridge Lane, Tandridge RH8 9NJ. Mr & Mrs Richins. *2m E of Godstone. Turn off A25 for Tandridge. Take drive on L past church. Follow arrows to circular courtyard.* Home-made teas Sats & Suns only. **Adm £3, chd free (share to Sutton & Croydon MS Therapy Centre).** Mon 19 to Sun 25 May incl; Mon 23 to Sun 29 June incl (10-5).
Enter 1-acre tapestry of magical secret gardens with magnificent views. Touching the senses, all sure-footed visitors may explore the many surprises on this exuberant escape from reality. Imaginative use of recycled materials creates an inspired variety of ideas, while wild and specimen plants reveal an ecological haven.

🐾 ☕

⑮ CHESTNUT COTTAGE
15 Jubilee Lane, Boundstone, Farnham GU10 4SZ. Mr & Mrs David Wingent. *2½ m SW of Farnham. From A31 roundabout take A325 to Petersfield, ½ m bear L. ½ m over staggered Xrds, at mini roundabout into Sandrock Hill Rd for ½ m. R into Jubilee Lane.* Home-made teas. **Adm £2.50, chd free.** Sun 4 May (2-5.30).
½ -acre garden created by owners on different levels. Rhododendrons, azaleas, acers and conifers. Long pergola with wisteria and roses, attractive gazebo copied from the original at NT Hunting Lodge in Odiham. Peaceful setting.

🐾 ☕

⑯ CHESTNUT LODGE
Old Common Road, Cobham KT11 1BU. Mr R Sawyer. *From A3 take A245 towards Cobham bearing L at 2nd roundabout onto A307. Just after Dagenham Motors turn L into Old Common Rd, Chestnut Lodge at very end.* Home-made teas. **Adm £4, chd. Regret children under 15 not admitted.** Suns 20 Apr; 17 Aug (11-5).

Very interesting 5-acre garden offering unrivalled opportunity to enjoy fine specimen trees, wonderful wisteria, shrubs and rare and exotic plants at close quarters. Areas near house formally planted, while opposite is large naturalised pond, home to many waterfowl incl flamingos. Formal areas planted round rectangular pools are complemented by bonsai and topiary which lead to an aviary walk with many fine tropical birds. Some gravel paths.

♿ 🐾 ☕

⑰ CHILWORTH MANOR
Halfpenny Lane, Chilworth GU4 8NN. Mia & Graham Wrigley. *3½ m SE of Guildford. From centre of Chilworth village turn into Blacksmith Lane. 1st drive on R on Halfpenny Lane.* Home-made teas. **Adm £4, chd free.** Sun 11 May (11-5).
Extensive grounds of lawns and mature trees around C17/C18 manor on C11 monastic site. Substantial C18 terraced walled garden laid out by Sarah, Duchess of Marlborough, with herbaceous borders, topiary and fruit trees. Original stewponds integrated with new Japanese-themed garden and woodland garden and walk. Paddock home to alpacas. Ongoing restoration project aims to create a contemporary and practical garden sensitive to its historic context.

🐾 ☕

⑱ CHINTHURST LODGE
Wonersh Common Road, Wonersh GU5 0PR. Mr & Mrs M R Goodridge. *4m S of Guildford. From A281 at Shalford turn E onto B2128 towards Wonersh. Just after Wonersh rd sign, before village, garden on R.* Home-made teas. **Adm £3, chd free.** Sun 22, Wed 25 June (12-5.30).
1-acre yr-round enthusiast's atmospheric garden. Herbaceous borders, white garden, specimen trees and shrubs, gravel garden with water feature, small kitchen garden, fruit cage, 2 wells, ornamental ponds, millennium parterre garden, herb area.

♿ 🐾 ☕

⑲ ◆ CLANDON PARK
West Clandon GU4 7RQ. The National Trust, 01483 222482, www.nationaltrust.org.uk. *3m E of Guildford on A247. From A3 follow signs to Ripley to join A247 via B2215.* House & Garden £7.70, chd £3.90. Garden only £3.90, chd £2. Tues to Thurs & Suns 16 Mar to 2 Nov, House 11-4, Garden 11-5. For NGS: Sun 6 Apr (11-5).

Garden around the house laid out informally, apart from parterre beneath S front. To the S a mid C18 grotto. Principal front faces parkland, laid out in the style of Capability Brown around 1770. Created in 1901, Dutch garden modelled on the pond garden at Hampton Court Palace. Large bulb field looks stunning in spring.

♿ 🐾 ☕

Original stewponds integrated with new Japanese-themed garden and woodland garden and walk . . .

⑳ ◆ CLAREMONT LANDSCAPE GARDEN
Portsmouth Road, Esher KT10 9JG. The National Trust, 01372 467806, www.nationaltrust.org.uk. *1m SW of Esher. On E side of A307 (no access from A3 bypass).* **Adm £5.80, chd £2.90.** opening dates and times vary according to season; phone or see website for details. For NGS: Sat 19 July; Sun 7 Sept (10-6).
One of the earliest surviving English landscape gardens, begun by Vanbrugh and Bridgeman before 1720 and extended and naturalized by Kent and Capability Brown. Lake, island with pavilion; grotto and turf amphitheatre; viewpoints and avenues.

♿ 🐾 ☕

㉑ THE COPSE LODGE
Brighton Road, Burgh Heath KT20 6BL. Marian & Edward Wallbank. *6m S of Sutton. On A217. 200yds past T-lights at junction with Reigate Rd. Turn L into Heathside Hotel, park in hotel car park courtesy of hotel. Proceed on foot 80yds to garden. Disabled parking at garden.* Home-made teas. **Adm £3.50, chd free.** Suns 8 June; 13 July (1.30-5.30). **Evening Openings** £4.50, wine, Wed 4 June; Wed 16 July (6-9).
Very unusual 1 acre garden with architectural features and exciting

planting. Large Japanese garden abounds with acers, bamboo, wisteria and bonsai. Wander through the tea house and emerge refreshed to enjoy the contrast of exotic planting and beautiful tender specimens. New potager kitchen garden.

 ♿ ✕ ❎ ☕

22 ♦ COVERWOOD LAKES
Peaslake Road, Ewhurst GU6 7NT. The Metson Family, 01306 731101, www.coverwoodlakes.co.uk. *7m SW of Dorking. From A25 follow signs for Peaslake; garden 1/2 m beyond Peaslake.* **Adm £5, chd £2, concessions £4. For NGS: Suns 13, 20, 27 Apr; Suns 4, 11 May (2-6); Sun 19 Oct (11-4.30).**
14-acre landscaped garden in stunning position in the Surrey Hills with 4 lakes and bog garden. Extensive rhododendrons, azaleas, primulas and fine trees. 3 1/2 -acre lakeside arboretum. Marked trail through the working farm with Hereford cows and calves, sheep and horses, extensive views of the surrounding hills.

♿ ✕ ❎ ☕

23 ♦ CROSSWATER FARM
Crosswater Lane, Churt GU10 2JN. Mrs E G Millais & Family, 01252 792698, www.rhododendrons.co.uk. *6m S of Farnham, 6m NW of Haslemere. From A287 turn E into Jumps Rd 1/2 m N of Churt village centre. After 1/4 m turn acute L into Crosswater Lane & follow signs for Millais Nurseries.* Home-made teas NGS days only. **Adm £3, chd free. Daily 21 Apr to 6 June (10-5). For NGS: Sat 17, Sun 18 May (10-5).**
Idyllic 6-acre woodland garden. Plantsman's collection of rhododendrons and azaleas, incl rare species collected in the Himalayas, hybrids raised by the owners. Everything from alpine dwarfs to architectural large-leaved trees. Ponds, stream and companion plantings incl sorbus, magnolias and Japanese acers. Trial gardens of new varieties. RHS Rothschild Cup for best display of rhododendrons. Featured in 'The Telegraph'. Grass paths soft after rain.

♿ ✕ ❎ ☕

24 DUNSBOROUGH PARK
Ripley GU23 6AL. A J H Baron Sweerts de Landas Wyborgh. *6m NE of Guildford. Entrance across Ripley Green via The Milkway opp Wylie & Mar.* Home-made teas. **Adm £4, chd free. Sats 12 Apr; 14 June; 13 Sept (12-5).**

Extensive walled gardens of 6 acres redesigned by Penelope Hobhouse and Rupert Golby. Good structure with much box hedging creating many different garden rooms. Exciting long herbaceous borders with beautiful standard wisterias. Unusual 70ft ginkgo hedge and ancient mulberry tree. Atmospheric water garden recently redesigned and restored. Fabulous display of tulips in Apr with 7000 bulbs and large cut flower garden.

♿ ✕ ❎ ☕

Featuring 'celebrity plants' used at events, with hydrangeas from the Prince of Wales's wedding . . .

EDENBRIDGE HOUSE
See Kent.

ELM TREE COTTAGE
See London.

FAIRACRE
See Berkshire.

25 NEW FELBRIDGE COPSE
Woodcock Hill, Felbridge RH19 2RA. Paul & Martin Thomas-Jeffreys. *1m N of E Grinstead. From S, on A22 1/4 m N of A22/A264 junction. From N, M25 J6 8m S on A22, approx 1m S of New Chapel roundabout. Look out for yellow NGS signs, parking in field at Felbridge Courtyard.* Light refreshments, home-made teas & wine. **Adm £3, chd free. Evening Opening, wine, Fri 6 June (6-8.30). Sun 3 Aug (2-5.30). Also open Felbridge Courtyard.**
Home of the celebrated London floral designer, Paul Thomas. 2 1/4 - acre Jekyll based garden wrapped around 1916 Lutyens cottage (not open). Sunken rose garden, enclosed courtyard garden, pair of herbaceous long borders, woodland and meadow. Featuring 'celebrity plants' used at events, incl hydrangeas from the Prince of Wales's wedding. Featured in '25 Beautiful Homes'. Gravel paths.

♿ ✕ ☕

26 NEW FELBRIDGE COURTYARD
Woodcock Hill, Felbridge RH19 2QZ. Caroline & Richard Teed. *1m N of E Grinstead. From S, on A22 1/4 m N of A22/A264 junction. From N, M25 J6 8m S on A22, approx 1m S of New Chapel roundabout. Look out for yellow NGS signs, parking in field.* Light refreshments, home-made teas & wine. **Adm £3, chd free. Evening Opening, wine, Fri 6 June (6-8.30). Sun 3 Aug (2-5.30). Also open Felbridge Copse.**
2-acre garden in three parts: front gravel and formal pond with pergola; main courtyard garden with sunken circular terrace, vine, alpine bed and clipped box; rear herbaceous garden with rill and wisteria pergola. Field of native and fruit trees. Many design features. Gravel paths, sunken terrace.

♿ ✕ ☕

FROGMORE HOUSE GARDEN
See Berkshire.

FROYLE GARDENS
See Hampshire.

BROCAS FARM
See Hampshire.

27 NEW FULVENS HANGER
Fulvens, off Crest Hill, Peaslake GU5 9PG. Mr & Mrs J Price, 01306 730421. *6m E of Guildford. A25 to Shere. Turn R through village and up hill. Over railway bridge then 1st L towards Peaslake. After village sign 3rd L opp bus shelter into Crest Hill. 1st R into Fulvens, 2nd L down single track lane.* Home-made teas. **Adm £3, chd free. Tue 13 May to Fri 16 May incl (11-5). Visitors also welcome by appt.**
Exciting new 3-acre woodland garden in early stages of development. Lovely bluebell walk and many recent specimen plantings. Newly-built Huf house sits in the middle of this woodland haven and around the house find contemporary, innovative planting. Recently-dug pond gives a feeling of tranquil oasis. Featured on BBC TV Open Gardens.

♿ ✕ ❎ ☕ ☎

1¹/₂-acre floriferous garden
created from a cow paddock.
Emphasis on colour in mixed
borders, much of which is raised
from seed and cuttings each
year by the owner . . .

28 ◆ GATTON PARK
Rocky Lane, Merstham RH2 0TW.
Royal Alexandra & Albert School,
01737 649068,
www.gattonpark.com. *3m NE of
Reigate. 5 mins from M25 J8 (A217) or
from top of Reigate Hill, over M25 then
follow sign to Merstham. Entrance is
off Rocky Lane accessible from Gatton
Bottom or A23 Merstham.* Teas. **Adm
£3.50, chd free. 1st Sun of each
month Feb to Oct incl (1-5). For
NGS: Sun 17, Wed 20 Feb (12-4);
Sun 15, Wed 18 Feb 2009.**
Formerly home to the Colman family (of
mustard fame), now the grounds of the
Royal Alexandra and Albert School.
Hidden gardens within historic
Capability Brown parkland. 1910
Edwardian Japanese garden restored
for Channel 4's 'Lost Gardens'.
Dramatic 1912 Pulham rock garden,
walled gardens, lakeside trail.
Restoration of gardens ongoing and
maintained by volunteers. Ivan Hick's
children's trail behind main lake.
Massed snowdrops in Feb/Mar.
Children's rucksacks available for £10
deposit, containing binoculars and quiz
sheets. Limited wheelchair access.
&. ⊛ ☕

29 GORSE COTTAGE
Tilford GU10 2EA. A M How. *5m SE
of Farnham. Midway between Farnham
& Hindhead. Garden is opp The
Grange, approx 1¹/₂ m from Tilford
Green at Rushmoor end of village.
Rushmoor sign outside garden fence.*
**Adm £3, chd free. Sun 20 July (2-
5.30).**
Approx ³/₄ -acre plantsman's informal
garden in tranquil rural setting with
lawns, mature trees, herbaceous
borders and shrubs. Pond and stream
with moisture-loving plants.
&. ✄ ☕

30 GREAT FOSTERS
Stroude Road, Egham TW20 9UR.
The Sutcliffe Family,
www.greatfosters.co.uk. *1m S of
Egham. On A30 at T-lights opp Virginia
Water, turn down Christchurch Rd
B389. Continue over roundabout and
after railway bridge turn L at T-lights
into Stroude Rd. Great Fosters approx
³/₄ m on R.* Light refreshments & teas
(not NGS). **Adm by donation,
suggested donation £4 per person.
Mon 2 June to Thur 5 June incl (10-
5).**
Within the 50-acre estate, this
wonderful and inspiring garden has
been beautifully restored over the last
12yrs. Framed on 3 sides by a Saxon
moat, the knot garden of intricate
design has fragrant beds of flowers
and herbs and is bordered by clipped
hedges and topiary. Beyond, find the
grass amphitheatre, large lake,
wisteria-draped Japanese bridge,
sunken rose garden and tranquil lily
pond. Partial wheelchair access.
&. ✄ ⊨ ☕

31 GREEN LANE FARM
**Cudworth Lane, Newdigate
RH5 5BH. Mr & Mrs P Hall, 01306
631214.** *8m S of Dorking. On A24 turn
L at Beare Green roundabout signed
Newdigate. R at T-junction in
Newdigate, L at Church, R into
Cudworth Lane. Farm ¹/₄ m on R.*
Home-made teas. **Adm £3, chd free.
Sat 16, Sun 24 Aug (2-5). Visitors
also welcome by appt June to Aug,
groups of 15+.**
1¹/₂ -acre floriferous garden created
from a cow paddock. Emphasis on
colour in mixed borders, much of
which is raised from seed and cuttings
each yr by the owner. Many containers
brimming with colour and gravel area
with lovely grasses. Rose walk leads to
unique oak summerhouse; beautiful

gypsy vardo (caravan) restored by
owner. Farm walk circling 3 lakes.
Featured in 'BBC Homes & Antiques'.
&. ⊛ ☕ ☎

32 72 GREEN WRYTHE LANE
**Carshalton SM5 2DP. Mrs G
Cooling.** *1m E of Sutton. From
Carshalton Ponds turn N across ponds
into North St. Continue to Wrythe
Green, then 1st R into Green Wrythe
Lane.* Home-made teas. **Adm £2.50,
chd under 12 free (share to Royal
Marsden Hospital). Sun 27 July
(10.30-4.30).**
170ft x 50ft colourful cottage style
garden of various habitats, incl
herbaceous borders, woodland area,
wildlife pond. A plantaholic's delight,
worked organically: an oasis in
suburbia. Cover from the elements.
Painted pot stall.
✄ ⊛ ☕

33 HALL GROVE SCHOOL
**London Road (A30), Bagshot
GU19 5HZ. Mr & Mrs A R Graham &
Mr & Mrs P D Smithson,
www.hallgrove.co.uk.** *6m SW of
Egham. M3 to J3, follow A322 1m until
sign for Sunningdale A30, 1m E of
Bagshot, opp Long Acres garden
centre, entrance at footbridge.* Ample
car park. Home-made teas. **Adm £5,
chd free. Sun 18 May (2-5.30) Live
music at 4pm.**
Formerly small Georgian country
estate, now co-educational
preparatory school. Grade II listed
house (not open). Mature parkland with
specimen trees. Tour comprises three
contrasting private gardens within the
old estate. Historical features incl ice
house, old walled garden, heated
peach wall. Much recent development.
Lots of ideas for keen gardeners.
&. ✄ ⊛ ☕

34 ◆ HATCHLANDS PARK
**East Clandon GU4 7RT. The
National Trust, 01483 222482,
www.nationaltrust.org.uk.** *4m E of
Guildford. In East Clandon, off A246.
A3 from London, follow signs to Ripley
to join A247 & via West Clandon to
A246. From Guildford take A25 then
A246 towards Leatherhead at West
Clandon.* **House & Garden £6.60, chd
£3.30. Garden only 3.50, chd £1.80.
23 Mar to 30 Oct: Parkland daily (11-
6); House Tues, Weds, Thurs, Suns
& BH Mons (2-5). For NGS: Suns 27
Apr; 5 Oct (11-6).**
Garden and park designed by Repton
in 1800. Follow one of the park walks

to the stunning bluebell wood in spring. In autumn enjoy the changing colours on the long walk. S of the house a small parterre designed by Gertrude Jekyll in 1913 to flower in early June. House open.

35 NEW HIDEAWAY HOUSE
Lower Ham Lane, Elstead GU8 6HQ. Mr & Mrs C Burridge. *For directions see entry for Chandlers.* Home-made teas & wine. **Combined adm with Chandlers £3.50, chd free.** Sun 15 June (2-6).
3/4 -acre Italianate garden with large rolling lawn interspersed with follies, ornaments and unusual archtectural plants, designed for easy maintenance. Also incl woodland area, rockery, formal and natural pond. Many exceptional pots with annual and specimen displays. Large patio area for teas.

HOATH HOUSE
See Kent.

HOOK ROAD
See London.

36 HORSELL ALLOTMENTS & BIRCH COTTAGE GARDEN
GU21 4PN. *1 1/2 m W of Woking. From Woking follow signs to Horsell, along High St, Bullbeggars Lane at Chobham end of Village. Nearest parking by Cricketers PH, Horsell Birch. Limited parking in village.* Home-made teas at Birch Cottage. **Combined adm £3, chd free.** Sun 13 July (11-4).
'War of the Worlds' village. Church with Norman keep and a number of period properties.

BIRCH COTTAGE GARDEN
5 High Street. Celia & Mel Keenan. *Entrance on High St opp Bullbeggars Lane*
Created since 1999, smallish garden designed to reflect the 400yr-old Grade II listed cottage. Active dovecote, gravel garden, shrubs and perennials, archway with climbers through to potager, developing knot garden, courtyard with containers and hanging baskets.

HORSELL ALLOTMENTS
Bullbeggars Lane. Horsell Allotment Assn, www. windowonwoking.org.uk/ sites/haa. *Disabled parking only on site*
Large site with over 100 individual plots growing a variety of flowers, fruit and vegetables. Mixture of modern, well known, heritage and unusual vegetables, many not seen in supermarkets. Featured in 'Kitchen Garden' magazine, 'Woking Review' and 'Woking News & Mail'.

Walk the rural one-mile Bluebell Valley Unicursal Path of Life and discover its secret allegory . . .

KIMPTON HOUSE
See Hampshire.

37 KNOWLE GRANGE
Hound House Road, Shere GU5 9JH. Mr P R & Mrs M E Wood, 01483 202108. *8m S of Guildford. From Shere (off A25), through village for 3/4 m. After railway bridge, continue 1 1/2 m past Hound House on R (stone dogs on gatepost). After 100yds turn R at Knowle Grange sign, go to end of lane.* Home-made teas. **Adm £5, chd free.** Suns 18 May; 14 Sept (11-5). Visitors also welcome by appt in May, June & Sept only, for groups of 20+.
80-acre idyllic hilltop position. Extraordinary and exciting new 7-acre gardens, created from scratch since 1990 by Marie-Elizabeth Wood, blend the free romantic style with the strong architectural frame of the classical tradition. Walk the rural one-mile Bluebell Valley Unicursal Path of Life and discover its secret allegory. Deep unfenced pools, high unfenced drops.

LEYDENS
See Kent.

LITTLE LODGE
See London.

38 LITTLE MYNTHURST FARM
Norwood Hill RH6 0HR. Mr & Mrs G Chilton. *4m SW of Reigate. Take A217 towards Horley; after 2m turn R down Irons Bottom Lane (just after Sidlow Bridge). 1st R Dean Oak Lane, then L at T-junction.* Home-made teas. **Adm £3.50, chd free.** Sat 5, Sun 6 July (12-5).
The house where Lord Baden-Powell lived. 12-acre garden in lake setting around old farmhouse (not open). Walled garden, old-fashioned roses, shrubs, herbaceous. Tudor courtyard and orchard. Bird and butterfly garden. Kitchen garden with large greenhouses. Secret garden, parterre with box hedging.

39 LITTLE PRIORY
Sandy Lane, South Nutfield RH1 4EJ. Richard & Liz Ramsay. *1 1/2 m E of Redhill. From Nutfield, on A25, turn into Mid St, following sign for South Nutfield. 1st R into Sandy Lane. Follow signs to parking, approx 300yds.* Cream teas. **Adm £3, chd free (share to St Catherine's Hospice). Evening Opening £4, wine,** Sat 14 June (6-8); Sun 15 June (1-5).
So much to see: richly planted 5-acre country garden with magnificent views and a large pond to relax beside. Incl Victorian walled garden with restored greenhouses, fruit and vegetable garden, old orchard and wild flower meadow. Some steep slopes.

40 LODKIN
Lodkin Hill, Hascombe GU8 4JP. Mr & Mrs W N Bolt, 01483 208323, willibolt2@aol.com. *3m S of Godalming. Just off B2130 Godalming to Cranleigh rd, on outskirts of Hascombe; take narrow lane signed to garden.* Home-made teas. **Adm £3.50, chd & disabled free.** Suns 13 Apr; 8 June (2-5.30). Visitors also welcome by appt at any time.
Developed over 32 yrs, this garden is now well over twice its original size and incl 110ft of mainly restored Victorian glasshouses, extensive flower borders and kitchen garden. Flowering trees, shrubs, thousands of bulbs and a natural area with pond, stream and bog garden, planned to encourage wildlife. Partial wheelchair access, garden very steep in parts.

41 LONG BARTON

12 Longdown Road, Guildford GU4 8PP. Harry & Rose-Marie Stokes. *1m E of Guildford. A246 (Epsom Rd) from Guildford, after ¹/₂ m turn R into Tangier Rd. At top turn L into Warren Rd, becoming One Tree Hill. At Xrds turn sharp R into Longdown Rd, last house on R in rd.* Home-made teas. **Adm £3.50, chd free (share to St Martha on the Hill). Sun 10 Aug (10-5).**

Interesting 2-acre garden attempts to enhance the glory of its setting in the beautiful Surrey Hills. Hundreds of Japanese maples, knot garden, cyclamen lawns, pagan love temple, specimen trees, topiaries and large formal fish pond. Wrought iron, stonework and 3 water features. Many alpines. New acer plantation. Two large flat lawns interspaced between the slopes which fall 60ft from top to bottom.

42 LONGER END COTTAGE

Normandy Common Lane, Normandy GU3 2AP. Ann & John McIlwham, 01483 811858, jmcilwham@hotmail.com. *4m W of Guildford on A323. At War Memorial Xrds in Normandy turn R into Hunts Hill Rd then 1st R into Normandy Common Lane.* Home-made teas. **Adm £3, chd free (share to St Mark's Church, Wyke, 17 Aug only). Suns 15 June; 17 Aug; 7 Sept (1-6). Visitors also welcome by appt, groups of 15+.**

1¹/₂ -acre garden divided into rooms with wide variety of plants, shrubs and trees incl roses, delphiniums, tree ferns, gunnera, grasses etc. Knot garden, laburnum walk, wild flower meadow, folly and small stumpery add to the attraction of the garden. 2008 will see further additions to Longer End. Featured in 'The English Garden' and 'English Garden'/NGS Calendar. Uneven drive.

Woodland, orchard and fields with rare-breed sheep and goats, chicken and ducks . . .

43 ◆ LOSELEY PARK

Guildford GU3 1HS. Mr & Mrs M G More-Molyneux, 01483 304440, www.loseley-park.com. *4m SW of Guildford. Leave A3 at Compton S of Guildford, on B3000 for 2m. Signed. Guildford stn 2m, Godalming stn 3m.* **House & gardens £7, chd £3.50, concessions £6.50. Garden only £4, chd £2, concessions £3.50. Garden May to Sept, Tues to Suns & BH Mons (11-5); House May to Aug, Tues to Thurs, Suns & BH Mons (1-5). For NGS: Sun 4 May (11-5).**

Delightful 2¹/₂ -acre walled garden based on design by Gertrude Jekyll. Award-winning rose garden (over 1,000 bushes, mainly old-fashioned varieties), extensive herb garden, fruit/flower garden, white garden with fountains, and spectacular organic vegetable garden. Magnificent vine walk, herbaceous borders, moat walk, ancient wisteria and mulberry trees. Wild flower meadow.

LOWDER MILL

See Sussex.

44 NEW MEMOIRS

Stafford Lake, Queen's Road, Bisley GU24 9AY. Mr Ted Stephens. *Approx 6m N of Guildford. A322 Guildford to Bagshot rd to Bisley, then L into Queens Rd at T-lights after Fox PH. Follow Queens Rd for just under 1m then L into unmarked track (footpath sign) and follow NGS signs.* Home-made teas. **Adm £3.50, chd free. Sun 25 May (1-6).**

Interesting and varied 8-acre organic garden created by owners. Formal lawn and borders, stream, ponds, bog garden, kitchen garden, terrace garden, wildlife areas, woodland, orchard and fields with rare-breed sheep and goats, chicken and ducks. Small museum of gardening and agricultural tools. Hand-made jewellery sale.

45 MOLESHILL HOUSE

The Fairmile, Cobham KT11 1BG. Penny & Maurice Snell, 01932 864532, pennysnellflowers@btinternet.com, www.pennysnellflowers.co.uk. *2m NE of Esher. On A307 Esher to Cobham Rd next to free car park by A3 bridge, at entrance to Waterford Close.* Home-made teas. **Adm £3, chd free. Sun 11 May with music. Wed 14 May (2-5). Visitors also welcome by appt, groups of 10+.**

To meet the challenges of climate change, significant replanning and replanting has taken place in this romantic garden surrounding Victorian house. Short woodland path with shade-loving plants leads from dovecote to beehives. Informally planted colour-coordinated borders contrast with the strict formality of topiary box and garlanded cisterns. Mediterranean courtyard with bright colours and tender plants, conservatory, fountains, bog garden, pleached avenue of 38 Sorbus lutescens, pots and many unusual features. Garden 5 mins from Claremont Landscape Garden, Painshill Park & Wisley, also adjacent excellent dog-walking woods. Featured on BBC TV, in 'GGG' & foreign press.

46 MUNSTEAD WOOD

Heath Lane, Godalming GU7 1UN. Sir Robert & Lady Clark. *2m SE of Godalming. Take B2130 Brighton Rd towards Horsham. After 1m church on R, Heath Lane just after on L. Entrance to Munstead Wood 400yds on R. Parking on L of Heath Lane. Disabled parking available, ask at main gate.* Home-made teas. **Adm £3, chd free (share to Meeting Point, Mayfield School). Suns 20 Apr; 18 May (2-5).**

This former home of Gertrude Jekyll (designed by Edwin Lutyens) is surrounded by a 10-acre restored garden incl woodland, rivers of daffodils, paths through azaleas and rhododendrons, sunken rockery, lawns, shrubbery, rose-covered pergola, tank garden, topiary box, clematis garland, borders. Doorway in bargate wall to spring and summer gardens. Primula garden behind yew hedge. Some gravel paths.

47 **19 OAK TREE ROAD**
Knaphill GU21 2RW. Barry & Pam Gray. *5m NW of Guildford. From A3 take A322 Bagshot Rd, continue through Worplesdon, straight over at Brookwood Xrds. 1st turning on L into Oak Tree Rd (opp Sainsbury's).* Cream teas. **Adm £2.50, chd free (share to Brainwave). Sun 20 July (11-5).** Colourful front garden of informal bedding, baskets and containers featuring tender perennials and annuals grown by owners. Back garden (approx 80ft x 35ft) has lawn, patio, small pond, trees, shrubs and perennials for foliage, texture, scent and yr-round interest. 3 greenhouses, fruit trees and vegetables. No wasted space in this delightful garden. Winner Woking in Bloom and Shoot People's Garden Award. Featured in 'Garden Answers' & 'Woman's Weekly'.

✕ ☕

Through wisteria-clad pergola experience the first magnificent view of curving lawns bordered by flowering cherries . . .

48 **ODSTOCK**
Castle Square, Bletchingley RH1 4LB. Averil & John Trott, 01883 743100. *3m W of Godstone. Just off A25 in Bletchingley. At top of village nr Red Lion PH. Parking in village, no parking in Castle Square.* Home-made teas. **Adm £3, chd free. Sun 3 Aug (11-5). Visitors also welcome by appt.**
$^2/_3$ -acre plantsman's garden maintained by owners and developed for all-yr interest. Special interest in grasses and climbers, approx 80 at last count. Japanese features; dahlias. No-dig, low-maintenance vegetable garden. Children's quiz. Disabled parking by gate, short gravel path.

♿ ✕ ✿ ☕ ☎

OLD BUCKHURST
See Kent.

49 **THE OLD CROFT**
South Holmwood RH5 4NT. David & Virginia Lardner-Burke, www.lardner-burke.org.uk. *3m S of Dorking. From Dorking take A24 S for 3m. Turn L at sign to Leigh-Brockham into Mill Road. ¹/₂ m on L, 2 free car parks in NT Holmwood Common. Follow signs for 500yds along woodland walk. Disabled and elderly: for direct access tel 01306 888224.* Cream teas. **Adm £4, chd free. Suns, Bank Hol Mons 4, 5, 25, 26 May; Sats, Suns 12, 13 July; 9, 10 Aug (2-6).**
'5-acre paradise garden' (Surrey Life) encompasses many diverse areas of exquisite natural beauty. Stunning and imaginative vistas; many unusual specimen trees and shrubs, stream, lake, bog gardens, woodland, roses, amazing topiary buttress hedge, elevated 'hide', tropical bamboo maze. 'Through wisteria-clad pergola experience the first magnificent view of curving lawns bordered by flowering cherries...' (SL). Glorious colour in all seasons. Visitors return again and again.

♿ ✿ ☕

OLD THATCH
See Hampshire.

50 ◆ **POLESDEN LACEY**
Bookham RH5 6BD. The National Trust, 01372 452048, www.nationaltrust.org.uk. *1¹/₂ m S of Great Bookham. Nr Dorking, off A246 Leatherhead to Guildford rd.* **House & garden £10.50, chd £7.20. Garden only £6.50, chd £3.20. Daily 2 Jan to 23 Dec, times vary according to season. Phone or see website for details. For NGS: Sun 8 June (11-5).** 30 acres formal gardens in an exceptional setting on the North Downs; walled rose garden, winter garden, lawns; magnificent views. Regency villa dating from early 1820s, remodelled after 1906 by the Hon Mrs Ronald Greville. King George VI and Queen Elizabeth the Queen Mother spent part of their honeymoon here. No dogs in formal gardens.

♿ ✿ ☕

51 ◆ **POSTFORD HOUSE**
172 Dorking Road, Chilworth GU4 8RN. Mrs M R Litler-Jones, 01483 202657. *4m SE of Guildford. A248 Guildford to Dorking rd, garden between boundary of Chilworth and Albury.* Refreshments by arrangement. **Adm £3, chd free. Visitors welcome by appt (2-6) in May only, groups of 4+, coaches permitted.**
25 acres of woodland and formal gardens, incl rose and vegetable garden. Lovely walk along stream with rhododendrons, azaleas and established trees.

♿ ✿ ☕ ☎

52 **QUINNEYS**
Camilla Drive, Westhumble RH5 6BU. Peter & Jane Miller. *1m N of Dorking. Turn L off A24 (going N) into Westhumble St, just before Boxhill roundabout. After ¹/₄ m, pass Boxhill and Westhumble stn & go through archway into Camilla Dr. House 3rd on L. Limited parking at garden. Parking available at Boxhill stn (3 mins walk). Coming from Leatherhead (going S) on A24 turn R just after Boxhill roundabout signed Westhumble stn. Then as above.* Home-made teas. **Adm £3, chd free. Sun 18 May (2-6).** 3 acres created at the breakup of the neighbouring estate of Camilla Lacey, incorporating some of the original cedar trees. Present owners have planted a mini arboretum, and have used the concept of 'tapestry' hedges to good effect. Also incl some rare trees and shrubs, an ancient glorious wisteria, rhododendrons and azaleas in full flower. Interesting water garden. Efforts now focussed on the establishment of a 'Jekyll' herbaceous border.

♿ ✕ ✿ ☕

53 ◆ **RAMSTER**
Chiddingfold GU8 4SN. Mr & Mrs Paul Gunn, 01428 654167, www.ramsterweddings.co.uk. *1¹/₂ m S of Chiddingfold. On A283; large iron gates on R.* **Adm £5, chd under 16 free, concessions £4.50. Daily 4 Apr to 22 June (10-5) & last two weekends in Oct (11-4).** Mature woodland garden of exceptional interest with lakes, ponds and woodland walk. Outstanding collection of fine rhododendrons and azaleas in bloom in early spring with stunning varieties of camellias, magnolias and carpets of bluebells. Many rare trees and shrubs, wild flower areas, bog garden. A truly beautiful and peaceful garden.

♿ ✿ ☕

54 **THE ROUND HOUSE**
Dunsfold Road, Loxhill GU8 4BL. Mrs Sue Lawson, 01483 200375, suelaw.law@btinternet.com. *4m S of Bramley. Off A281. At Smithbrook Kilns turn R to Dunsfold. Follow to T-junction. Go R (B2130). After 2m Park*

Hatch on R, enter park, follow drive to garden. Home-made teas. **Adm £3, chd free. Sun 22 June (2-6). Evening Opening £4.50, wine, Fri 20 June (5-dusk). Visitors also welcome by appt in June & July for groups of 10+, no coaches.**
2½-acre walled Victorian garden on sloping site with far-reaching views. Continual renewal and clearance programme since 2002. Orchard with fruit trees. Mixed planted beds with annuals, perennials and roses. Former greenhouse beds used for cutting flowers. Serpentine walks, unusual statuary and ornamental fishpond. 75 metre lavender walk. Featured in 'Surrey Life'. Gravel paths, steep slopes.

SANDY SLOPES
See Hampshire.

SHALFORD HOUSE
See Sussex.

55 41 SHELVERS WAY
Tadworth KT20 5QJ. Keith & Elizabeth Lewis, 01737 210707. *6m S of Sutton off A217. 1st turning on R after Burgh Heath T-lights heading S. 400yds down Shelvers Way on L.* Home-made teas. **Adm £2.50, chd free. Wed 23, Sun 27 Apr; Sun 20 July (1.30-5). Visitors also welcome by appt May to July only for groups of 10+.**
½-acre back garden of dense and detailed planting, interesting at all seasons, starting with a mass of spring bulbs with over 100 varieties of daffodils. In one part, beds of choice perennials are interlaced by paths and backed by unusual shrubs and mature trees; in the other, cobbles and shingle support grasses and special plants for dry conditions.

56 67 & 69 SHEPHERDS LANE
Guildford GU2 9SN. Charles & Gwen Graham & Mrs J Hall, 01483 566445, charlesadgraham@btopenworld.com. *1m NW of Guildford. From A3 take A322 Worplesdon Rd. Turn L at T-lights at Emmanuel Church into Shepherds Lane. Gardens on L on brow of hill. Alternatively, via A323 Aldershot Rd and Rydes Hill Rd, Shepherds Lane 2nd on R.* **Adm £2.50, chd free. Visitors welcome by appt May to July, individuals and groups welcome.**
Enter No. 67 via fuchsia-lined alley onto patio, passing pond and gravel beds towards fern walk and white garden. Enjoy colour-themed shrub and herbaceous borders, architectural grass garden and fruit garden. Enter garden of No. 69 via rose arch to find peaceful enclosure with silver, pink and purple beds and stunning specimen trees.

Cobbles and shingle support grasses and special plants for dry conditions . . .

57 SMITHWOOD HOUSE
Smithwood Common Road, Cranleigh GU6 8QY. Barbara Rubenstein, 01483 267969, bsrubenstein@aol.com. *2m N of Cranleigh. From Cranleigh turn R at cricket ground passing Cranleigh School. 1½ m N of school and 1st house on L past Winterfold turn. From Guildford A281, 1m S of Bramley turn L onto B2128. At roundabout R then immed L into Smithwood Common Rd, 2nd house on R.* **Adm £4, chd free. Evening Openings Fris 23, 30 May (6-9). Visitors also welcome by appt 23 May to 6 June only.**
3-acre park-like garden surrounding listed Georgian farmhouse (not open) with formal and informal areas. Many mature specimen trees and shrub borders. Sculpture walk with musical theme and water features. Formal yew walk with topiary and garden temple. Natural pond with waterfall and ornamental planting and secluded seating areas. Featured on BBC TV Open Gardens.

58 SPRING COTTAGE
Smithwood Common Road, Cranleigh GU6 8QN. Mr & Mrs D E Norman, 01483 272620, norman.springcott@btinternet.com. *1m N of Cranleigh. From Cranleigh cricket ground take rd signed Cranleigh School. Garden is ¼ m N of Cranleigh School entrance. From Guildford A281, follow signs to Cranleigh. Turn L immed after roundabout into Smithwood Common Rd. Garden*

1¼ m on R. **Adm £5, chd free. Evening Openings incl wine, Wed 11, Thur 12, Fri 13 June, Thur 19, Fri 20, Sat 21 June (5-dusk). Visitors also welcome by appt in June only for groups of 12+.**
Our roses should be good in June, so come to see them and enjoy a drink whilst wandering round our 1¼ -acre garden. We have planted many young trees and are working towards less labour-intensive plantings. Hostas are a great favourite but there are many other plants concentrating on interesting colours, texture and shape of foliage.

59 SPURFOLD
Peaslake GU5 9SZ. Mr & Mrs A Barnes, 01306 730196, spurfold@btinternet.com. *8m SE of Guildford. A25 to Shere. Turn R through Shere village & up hill. Over railway bridge 1st L to Peaslake. In Peaslake turn L after village stores Radnor Rd. Approx 500yds up single track lane to car park.* Home-made teas. **Adm £3, chd free. Sun 18 May (11-5). Evening Opening £5, wine, Fri 8 Aug (5-8). Visitors also welcome by appt, groups of 12+.**
Wonderful garden set in area of outstanding natural beauty. Approx 4 acres, large herbaceous and shrub borders, formal pond with Buddha head from Cambodia, sunken gravel garden with topiary box and water feature, four terraces, beautiful lawns, mature rhododendrons and azaleas, woodland path, and gazebos. Garden contains unique collection of Indian elephants and other objets d'art. Featured on BBC TV Digging Deep.

60 SQUARE LEG COTTAGE
The Green, Ewhurst GU6 7RR. Monica & Anthony Rosenberg. *3m E of Cranleigh. Directions as Burstowe's Croft, garden opp cricket green.* Home-made teas. **Adm £2.50, chd free. Sun 15, Wed 18 June (11-5).**
Peaceful, romantic plantsperson's garden which incl fernery, scented roses, rose arbour and pond. Also a small paddock with fruit trees and pumpkin bed. Raised decorative vegetable and herb beds, and a greenhouse with a collection of pelargoniums. Lots of places to sit and have tea, and perhaps watch the cricket. Short walk to Burstowe's Croft, also open. Gravel drive.

SQUERRYES COURT
See Kent.

61 STUART COTTAGE
Ripley Road, East Clandon
GU4 7SF. Mr & Mrs J M Leader,
01483 222689. *4m E of Guildford. Off A246 or from A3 through Ripley until roundabout, turn L and continue through West Clandon until T-lights, then L onto A246. East Clandon 1st L.* Home-made teas. **Adm £3, chd free. Sat 7 June (2-5). Sun 13 July (2-6). Evening Opening with music £5, wine, Mon 25 Aug (5-8). Visitors also welcome by appt, groups of 15+.**
$1/2$ -acre partly walled garden using some traditional box shapes and hedging to offer formality in the otherwise informal garden of this C16 cottage. Wisteria and rose/clematis walks give shade to the S/W aspect while rosemary and lavender edge the brick paths. Unusual herbaceous plants vie for attention among cottage garden favourites. From decorative organic kitchen garden walk to small chequerboard orchard. Featured in 'GGG'.
&. ⊛ ☕ ☎

62 35 TADORNE ROAD
Tadworth KT20 5TF. Dr & Mrs J R Lay. *6m S of Sutton. On A217 to large roundabout, 3m N of M25 J8. Take B2220 signed Tadworth. Tadorne Rd 2nd on R.* Home-made teas. **Adm £2.50, chd free. Sat 28, Sun 29 June (2-6).**
$1/3$ -acre hedged garden with a colourful herbaceous border, shrubby island beds, rose and clematis-covered pergola leading to secluded seating area, potager-style vegetable plot, soft fruit, woodland corner, varied patio display and plant-filled conservatory.
🐾 ☕

63 TILFORD COTTAGE
Tilford Road, Tilford GU10 2BX. Mr & Mrs R Burn, 01252 795423, rodburn@tiscali.co.uk, www.tilfordcottagegarden.co.uk. *3m SE of Farnham. From Farnham stn along Tilford Rd. Tilford Cottage opp Tilford House. Parking on village green.* Light refreshments & teas. **Adm £5, chd free. Sats, Suns, 21, 22, 28, 29 June (11-4). Visitors also welcome by appt all yr for groups of 8+.**
Artist's garden with a surprise at every turn. Herb garden within yew hedging, knot garden with box and topiary, wild flower and Japanese garden with slate river. Victorian glasshouse, hosta beds, rose, apple and willow arches,

herbaceous borders and children's fairy grotto. Monet-style bridge, river walk, bog gardens and Mediterranean terrace. Many quiet areas for contemplation. Holistic treatment centre open. Art studio open and sculptures in grounds (part of Surrey Open Studios). Featured in 'The English Garden'.
&. ⊛ ☕ ☎

Herbaceous borders and children's fairy grotto. Monet-style bridge, river walk . . .

64 TIMBER HILL
Chertsey Road, Chobham
GU24 8JF. Mr & Mrs Nick Sealy. *4m N of Woking. $2^{1}/2$ m E of Chobham and $1/3$ m E of Fairoaks aerodrome on A319 (N side). $1^{1}/4$ m W of Ottershaw, J11 M25.* Lunches & home-made teas in lovely old barn. **Adm £3, chd free. Suns 30 Mar; 27 Apr (11.30-4.30).**
15 acres of field, parkland and garden incl woodland garden with magnolias, camellias and rhododendrons, spring bulbs and bluebells, according to season. Fine trees incl cherries, oaks, liquidambar and tulip tree. Shrub and groundcover borders surround house.
&. 🐾 ☕

65 ◆ TITSEY PLACE GARDENS
Titsey Hill, Oxted RH8 0SD. The Trustees of the Titsey Foundation, 01273 715359, www.titsey.org. *3m N of Oxted. A25 between Oxted & Westerham, turn L into Limpsfield Village down High St, turn L (on sharp bend) into Bluehouse Lane & R into Water Lane. Follow rd under M25 through park to walled garden car park. Brown signs from A25 at Limpsfield.* Teas in new Tearoom. **House & garden adm £6. Garden only £3.50, chd £1. Weds & Suns mid May to end Sept (1-5). For NGS: Sats 24 May; 14 June; 12 July; 16 Aug (1-5). Garden only on these days. Car park & picnic area open from 12.**

One of the largest surviving estates in Surrey. Magnificent ancestral home and gardens of the Gresham family since 1534. Walled kitchen garden restored early 1990s. Golden Jubilee rose garden. Etruscan summer house adjoining picturesque lakes and fountains. 15 acres of formal and informal gardens in idyllic setting within the M25. Regular feature in 'Country Life'.
🐾 ☕

66 TOLLSWORTH MANOR
Rook Lane, Chaldon CR3 5BQ. Carol & Gordon Gillett. *2m W of Caterham. From Caterham-on-the-Hill, take B2031 through Chaldon. 300yds out of Chaldon take concrete farm track on L. Parking in farmyard beyond house.* Home-made teas. **Adm £3, chd free (share to St Catherine's Hospice). Sun 8 June (11-5).**
Old-fashioned country garden, created from derelict site over 25yrs by present owners. Well-stocked herbaceous borders with old-fashioned roses, peonies, delphiniums. Wildlife pond and duck pond with ducks. Lovely views over surrounding farmland. Shetland pony. Friendly welcome, interesting plants for sale, lovely home-made cakes. Gravel drive & uneven paths.
&. 🐾 ⊛ ☕

TUDOR ROAD GARDENS
See London.

67 6 UPPER ROSE HILL
Dorking RH4 2EB. Peter & Julia Williams, 01306 881315, juliawill@talktalk.net. *Town centre. From roundabout at A24/A25 junction follow signs through town centre towards Horsham. Turn L (under cedar tree) after Cricketers PH by flint wall. Parking available in rd & behind Sainsbury's (5 mins walk).* Home-made teas. **Adm £2.50, chd free. Sun 8 June (11-5.30). Visitors also welcome by appt.**
$1/2$ -acre plantsman's informal terraced garden on dry sand. Surprising secluded setting with striking outlook onto St Paul's Church. Planted for yr-round interest of foliage and form; fruit and vegetables, gravel bed and alpine troughs, borders and rockeries. Range of drought-tolerant plants. Autumn colour, grasses attractive into Oct.
🐾 ⊛ ☕ ☎

68 VALE END
Chilworth Road, Albury GU5 9BE.
Mr & Mrs John Foulsham, 01483
202594,
daphne@dfoulsham.freeserve.co.uk.
*4m SE of Guildford. From Albury take
A248 W for ¹/₄ m.* Home-made teas.
**Adm £3, chd free. Evening
Opening with music £5, wine, Sat
14 June (6-8.30). Sun 15 June; Wed
16 July (2-5). Visitors also welcome
by appt.**
1-acre walled garden on many levels in
beautiful setting overlooking mill pond.
Richly diverse planting of roses,
shrubs, annuals and perennials on light
sandy soil. Clipped yew walk with
festooned rope swag, tiny courtyard,
fruit, vegetable and herb garden.
Pantiled water cascade and newly-
created gravel gardens. River and
woodland walks from the garden gate.

69 VANN
Hambledon GU8 4EF. Mrs M Caroe,
01428 683413,
www.vanngarden.co.uk. *6m S of
Godalming. A283 to Wormley. Turn L
at Hambledon. Follow yellow Vann
signs for 2m. Please do not park in rd,
park in field.* Home-made teas 5 May
only. **Adm £4.50, chd free (share to
Hambledon Village Hall). Mon 24
Mar to Sun 6 Apr incl (10-6); Mon 5
May (2-6). Tue 6 May to Sun 11 May
incl (10-6); Sun 1 June to Sun 8 June
incl (10-6). Visitors also welcome by
appt.**
English Heritage registered 4¹/₂ -acre
garden surrounding Tudor and William
and Mary house (not open) with later
changes by W D Caröe. Old cottage
garden, pergola, ¹/₄ -acre pond,
Gertrude Jekyll water garden, azaleas,
spring bulbs, woodland, mixed
borders. Fritillaria *meleagris* in Mar/Apr.
Island beds, crinkle crankle wall.
Maintained by owner with 3 days' help
per week. Seen on Bremner Bird &
Fortune. Water garden paths are not
suitable for wheelchairs, but many
others are. Deep water.

WALBURY
See Hampshire.

70 WALTON POOR HOUSE
Ranmore RH5 6SX. Nicholas & Prue
Calvert. *6m NW of Dorking. From
Dorking take rd to Ranmore, continue
for approx 4m, after Xrds in dip 1m on
L. From A246 at East Horsley go S into
Greendene, 1st L Crocknorth Rd, 1m*

on R. Home-made teas. **Adm £3, chd
free. Mon 5 May; Suns 1 June; 27
July (12-5.30); Sun 12 Oct (2-5).**
'One of the most beautiful places I've
been', said a visitor. Deeply tranquil,
almost secretive garden in N Downs
Area of Outstanding Natural Beauty.
Paths wind between 4 acres of fine
mature trees and colourful shrubs.
Pond fringed with bold foliaged plants;
hideaway dell; herb garden linked with
the well-known herb nursery. Leads to
superb walks on Downs. Relaxation
therapy! Herb talk 3pm.

71 WESTWAYS FARM
Gracious Pond Road, Chobham
GU24 8HH. Paul & Nicky Biddle,
01276 856163. *4m N of Woking. From
Chobham Church proceed over
roundabout towards Sunningdale, 1st
Xrds R into Red Lion Rd to junction
with Mincing Lane.* Home-made teas.
**Adm £2.50, chd free (share to
Chobham Floral Club). Sun 27 Apr
(10-5). Visitors also welcome by
appt.**
Open 8-acre garden surrounded by
woodlands planted in 1930s with
mature and some rare rhododendrons,
azaleas, camellias and magnolias,
underplanted with bluebells,
erythroniums, lilies and dogwood;
extensive lawns and sunken pond
garden. Working stables and
sandschool. Lovely Queen Anne
House (not open) covered with listed
*Magnolia grandiflora. Victorian design
glasshouse.* Limited wheelchair access
to woodland.

WHEATLEY HOUSE
See Hampshire.

WHISPERS
See Hampshire.

**72 ◆ WINKWORTH
ARBORETUM**
Hascombe Road, nr Godalming
GU8 4AD. The National Trust, 01483
208477, www.nationaltrust.org.uk.
*2m S of Godalming on B2130.
Coaches by written arrangement. Stn:
Godalming 3m.* **Adm £4.60, chd
£2.30, family ticket £11.50. Daily all
yr, dawn to dusk. For NGS: Suns 20
Apr; 5 Oct (11-5).**
110 acres of rolling Surrey hillside set in
a valley leading down to a reservoir
and wetland area. Planted with rare
trees and shrubs leading to impressive
displays in spring with magnolias,
azaleas and bluebells matched by the

dramatic reds, golds and browns of
maples, cherries etc during autumn.
National Collection of Sorbus. Awarded
Stephenson R Clarke Cup at RHS
Great Autumn Show for trees showing
autumnal fruits. Limited wheelchair
access.
NCCPG

**Pond fringed
with bold
foliaged
plants;
hideaway
dell . . .**

73 WINTERSHALL MANOR
Bramley GU5 0LR. Mr & Mrs Peter
Hutley. *3m S of Bramley Village. On
A281 turn R, then next R. Wintershall
Drive next on L. Bus: AV33 Guildford-
Horsham, alight Palmers Cross, 1m.*
Cream teas. **Adm £3, chd 50p (share
to Wintershall Charitable Trust).
Sats 5, 26 Apr (2-5).**
2-acre garden and 200 acres of park
and woodland. Bluebell walks in
spring, wild daffodils, rhododendrons,
specimen trees. Lakes and flight
ponds; superb views. Chapel of St
Mary, stations of Cross, Rosary Walk
and St Francis Chapel. Some gravel
paths and steep slopes.

74 ◆ WISLEY RHS GARDEN
GU23 6QB. Royal Horticultural
Society, www.rhs.org.uk. *1m NE of
Ripley. SW of London on A3 & M25
(J10). Follow signs.* **All yr, not
Christmas Day. Mon to Fri 10-6, Sat
& Sun 9-6 (Nov-Feb 4.30). For NGS:
Special Evening Opening with
music Tue 19 Aug (6-9) Adm (incl
RHS members) £7, chd under 15
free (share to RHS Wisley Garden).
Reserve table for dinner 01483
211773.**
Primary garden of the RHS and centre
of its scientific and educational
activities. Arboretum, alpine and wild
garden, rock garden, mixed borders,
model gardens, model fruit and
vegetable garden, rose garden,
orchard and trial grounds. Picnics not
allowed in the garden.

20 acres of parkland featuring Italian garden created in 1640 by George Evelyn . . . Terraced mount, classical garden temple, statuary, tortoise house (uninhabited) . . .

75 WOODBURY COTTAGE

Colley Lane, Reigate RH2 9JJ. Shirley & Bob Stoneley, 01737 244235. *1m W of Reigate. M25 J8, A217 (direction Reigate). Immed before level Xing turn R into Somers Rd, cont as Manor Rd. At very end turn R into Coppice Lane & follow signs to car park. Garden is 300yds walk from car park.* Home-made teas. **Adm £3, chd free. Evening Opening £4, wine, Fri 4 July (5-8). Sats, Suns 5, 6 July; 30, 31 Aug; Wed 3 Sept. (Sats, Wed 2-5, Suns 11-5). Visitors also welcome by appt, groups of 10+ close to opening days.**
Cottage garden of just under ¼ -acre, made and maintained by owners. Garden is stepped on slope with mixed planting, enhanced by its setting under Colley Hill. A rich diversity of plants, colour-themed, still vibrant in Sept.

🏃 ⊗ ☕ ☎

76 WOODHILL MANOR

Woodhill Lane, Shamley Green GU5 0SP, 01483 891004, stephanie@smithkingdom.com, www.woodhillmanor.com. *5m S of Guildford. Directions on application when booking visit.* Home-made teas. **Adm £4, wheelchairs £3, regret no children. Pre-booked visitors welcome by appt Wed 23, Thur 24 Apr (10.30-4.30); Weds 18 June (Artist's Day £8) & 25 June (10.30-6). Wed 13 Aug (10.30-8.30, wine). Groups of 10+, no coaches. Pre-booking for all dates essential**
Inspirational and colourful private gardens, parkland and ponds in 20 acres. Stunning views. Spring bulbs and bluebells, established formal and herbaceous beds, creative parterres, wisteria, vines, lavenders and roses. Fine mature trees (tulip tree, cedar, mulberry and monkey puzzles). Organic fruit cage. Wild flower meadow. Partial wheelchair access. Deep water, steep steps and slopes.

♿ 🏃 ⊗ ☕ ☎

77 WOTTON HOUSE

Guildford Road, Dorking RH5 6HS. Hayley Conference Centres Ltd. *3m W of Dorking. On A25 towards Guildford. Gravel driveway (signed), adjacent to Wotton Hatch PH.* Light refreshments & cream teas (not NGS). **Adm £2.50, chd free. Suns 6, 13, 20 27 July (11-4).**
20 acres of parkland featuring Italian garden created in 1640 by George Evelyn and designed by his brother John, the eminent designer and diarist. Terraced mount, classical garden temple, statuary, tortoise house (uninhabited), and grottoes. Recently restored and widely held to be the first example of an Italian-style garden in England.

🏃 🛏 ☕

Surrey County Volunteers

County Organiser
Mrs Gayle Leader, Stuart Cottage, East Clandon, Surrey GU4 7SF, 01483 222689

County Treasurer
Mr Roger Nickolds, Old Post House, East Clandon, Surrey GU4 7SE, 01483 224027, rogernickolds@hotmail.com

Publicity
Mrs Pauline Elliott, Spring Lodge, Green Lane, Ockham, Surrey GU23 6PQ, 01483 284554, pauline.elliott@tiscali.co.uk

Assistant County Organisers
Mrs Anne Barnes, Spurfold, Radnor Road, Peaslake, Guildford, Surrey GU5 9SZ, 01306 730196
Mrs Maggie Boyd, Bardsey, 11 Derby Road, Haslemere, Surrey GU27 1BS, 01428 652283
Mr Keith Lewis, 41 Shelvers Way, Tadworth, Surrey KT20 5QJ, 01737 210707
Mrs Shirley Stoneley, Woodbury Cottage, Colley Lane, Reigate, Surrey RH2 9JJ, 01737 244235
Mrs Averil Trott, Odstock, Castle Square, Bletchingley, Surrey RH1 4LB, 01883 743100

SUSSEX

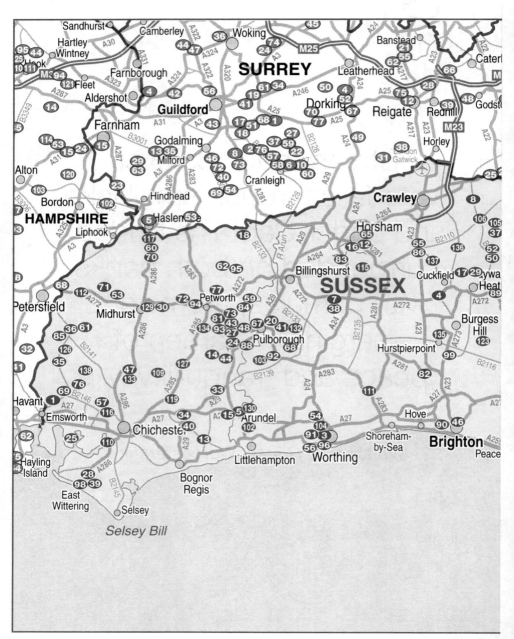

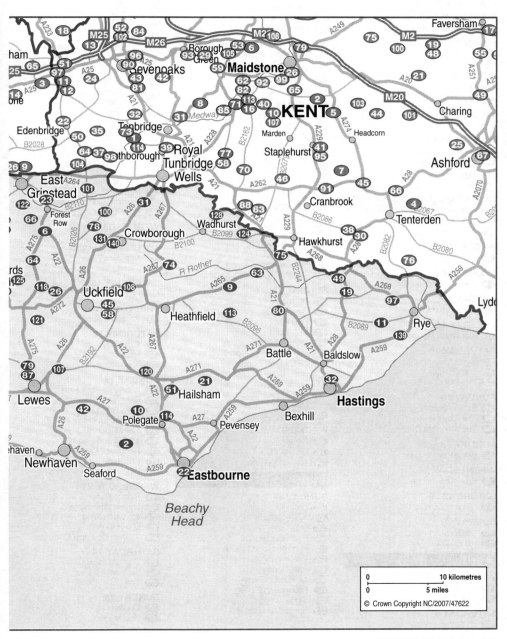

© Crown Copyright NC/2007/47622

Opening Dates

February

SUNDAY 10
76 Mitchmere Farm

THURSDAY 14
76 Mitchmere Farm

SUNDAY 17
35 Dormers
72 The Manor of Dean
76 Mitchmere Farm

SUNDAY 24
35 Dormers

TUESDAY 26
99 Pembury House

WEDNESDAY 27
34 Denmans Garden
99 Pembury House

THURSDAY 28
99 Pembury House

March

TUESDAY 4
99 Pembury House

WEDNESDAY 5
99 Pembury House

THURSDAY 6
99 Pembury House

SUNDAY 9
1 Aldsworth House

TUESDAY 11
1 Aldsworth House

SATURDAY 15
21 Butlers Farmhouse
48 The Grange
72 The Manor of Dean

SUNDAY 16
21 Butlers Farmhouse
48 The Grange
72 The Manor of Dean

SUNDAY 23
18 Bradstow Lodge

WEDNESDAY 26
18 Bradstow Lodge

SATURDAY 29
69 Lordington House

SUNDAY 30
69 Lordington House
100 Penns in the Rocks

April

WEDNESDAY 2
14 Bignor Park
78 Moorlands

SATURDAY 5
104 6 Plantation Rise

SUNDAY 6
10 Bates Green
104 6 Plantation Rise

WEDNESDAY 9
14 Bignor Park
78 Moorlands

SUNDAY 13
59 Horsebridge House

WEDNESDAY 16
14 Bignor Park
78 Moorlands

SATURDAY 19
63 King John's Lodge
72 The Manor of Dean
110 Rymans

SUNDAY 20
62 Kiln Copse Farm
63 King John's Lodge
72 The Manor of Dean
110 Rymans

WEDNESDAY 23
14 Bignor Park
78 Moorlands

SATURDAY 26
36 Down Place
112 Sandhill Farm House
129 The Walled Garden at Cowdray

SUNDAY 27
35 Dormers
36 Down Place
42 Firle Place
71 Malt House
87 Offham House
88 The Old Post Office (Evening)
96 18 Pavilion Road
108 Rose Cottage
112 Sandhill Farm House
129 The Walled Garden at Cowdray
131 Warren House

WEDNESDAY 30
14 Bignor Park
78 Moorlands
136 46 Westup Farm Cottages

May

SUNDAY 4
4 Ansty Gardens
15 4 Birch Close
16 Blue Jays
45 Framfield Grange
53 Hammerwood House
54 The Healing Garden
71 Malt House
96 18 Pavilion Road
97 Peasmarsh Place
120 Siggle Wriggle
127 Upwaltham Barns

MONDAY 5
15 4 Birch Close
71 Malt House
123 Stonehealed Farm
127 Upwaltham Barns
131 Warren House

TUESDAY 6
118 Sheffield Park Garden

WEDNESDAY 7
9 Bateman's
14 Bignor Park
43 Fittleworth House
73 Manvilles Field
78 Moorlands

SATURDAY 10
52 Ham Cottage

SUNDAY 11
26 Clinton Lodge
30 Cowdray Park Gardens
46 The Garden House
52 Ham Cottage
53 Hammerwood House
80 Mountfield Court

WEDNESDAY 14
14 Bignor Park
43 Fittleworth House
73 Manvilles Field
78 Moorlands

THURSDAY 15
60 Houndless Water

FRIDAY 16
23 Caxton Manor

SATURDAY 17
23 Caxton Manor
52 Ham Cottage
72 The Manor of Dean

SUNDAY 18
6 Ashdown Park Hotel
7 Bakers House
52 Ham Cottage
66 Legsheath Farm
72 The Manor of Dean
96 18 Pavilion Road
115 Sedgwick Park House
117 Shalford House
131 Warren House

WEDNESDAY 21
14 Bignor Park
43 Fittleworth House
73 Manvilles Field
78 Moorlands
136 46 Westup Farm Cottages

SATURDAY 24
37 Duckyls Holt
63 King John's Lodge
105 The Priest House

SUNDAY 25
28 Cookscroft
37 Duckyls Holt

47 Gardeners Cottage
55 High Beeches
56 Highdown
63 King John's Lodge
108 Rose Cottage
109 Roundhill Cottage

MONDAY 26
28 Cookscroft
37 Duckyls Holt
63 King John's Lodge
109 Roundhill Cottage
131 Warren House

WEDNESDAY 28
14 Bignor Park
43 Fittleworth House
73 Manvilles Field
78 Moorlands
121 Sparrow Hatch

THURSDAY 29
29 Copyhold Hollow
121 Sparrow Hatch

FRIDAY 30
64 Latchetts

SATURDAY 31
22 51 Carlisle Road
64 Latchetts
70 Lowder Mill
83 The Nook
101 Perryhill Farmhouse

June

SUNDAY 1
11 Beauchamps
22 51 Carlisle Road
51 Hailsham Grange
54 The Healing Garden
70 Lowder Mill
83 The Nook
87 Offham House
96 18 Pavilion Road
101 Perryhill Farmhouse
116 Sennicotts
124 Tinkers Bridge Cottage
138 Wildham

MONDAY 2
133 West Dean Gardens

WEDNESDAY 4
43 Fittleworth House
73 Manvilles Field
78 Moorlands

THURSDAY 5
17 Borde Hill Garden, Park & Woodland
102 Pindars
126 Uppark
130 Warningcamp House
138 Wildham

SATURDAY 7
58 Hobbs Barton
65 Leechpool Cottage
79 Mount Harry House & Mount Harry Lodge

85 Nyewood House
112 Sandhill Farm House

SUNDAY 8
1 Aldsworth House
26 Clinton Lodge
33 Dale Park House
50 Great Lywood Farmhouse
56 Highdown
58 Hobbs Barton
65 Leechpool Cottage
74 Mayfield Gardens
84 North Springs
85 Nyewood House
91 Palatine & Oak Grove Gardens
93 Park Lodge
103 Pine Cottage
112 Sandhill Farm House

MONDAY 9
26 Clinton Lodge
58 Hobbs Barton

TUESDAY 10
1 Aldsworth House

WEDNESDAY 11
43 Fittleworth House
56 Highdown
73 Manvilles Field
78 Moorlands

THURSDAY 12
67 Little Hill (Evening)
107 Ringmer Park
125 Town Place

FRIDAY 13
8 Bankton Cottage (Evening)

SATURDAY 14
22 51 Carlisle Road (Evening)
36 Down Place
72 The Manor of Dean
110 Rymans
139 Winchelsea's Secret Gardens

SUNDAY 15
7 Bakers House
36 Down Place
67 Little Hill
72 The Manor of Dean
94 6 Park Terrace (Day & Evening)
96 18 Pavilion Road
107 Ringmer Park
108 Rose Cottage
110 Rymans
120 Siggle Wriggle

MONDAY 16
26 Clinton Lodge

WEDNESDAY 18
2 Alfriston Clergy House
43 Fittleworth House
73 Manvilles Field
78 Moorlands
102 Pindars
127 Upwaltham Barns

THURSDAY 19
94 6 Park Terrace

107 Ringmer Park
125 Town Place
130 Warningcamp House

FRIDAY 20
50 Great Lywood Farmhouse (Evening)
64 Latchetts

SATURDAY 21
37 Duckyls Holt
64 Latchetts
89 Old Scaynes Hill House
105 The Priest House
106 Ridge House

SUNDAY 22
3 Ambrose Place Back Gardens
4 Ansty Gardens
37 Duckyls Holt
89 Old Scaynes Hill House
98 33 Peerley Road
106 Ridge House
107 Ringmer Park
125 Town Place
128 Villa Elisabetta

MONDAY 23
26 Clinton Lodge

WEDNESDAY 25
43 Fittleworth House
63 King John's Lodge (Evening)
73 Manvilles Field
78 Moorlands
121 Sparrow Hatch
136 46 Westup Farm Cottages

THURSDAY 26
121 Sparrow Hatch

FRIDAY 27
39 Earnley Grange (Evening)
95 Parsonage Farm (Day & Evening)
108 Rose Cottage (Evening)

SATURDAY 28
8 Bankton Cottage
12 4 Ben's Acre
90 64 Old Shoreham Road

SUNDAY 29
26 Clinton Lodge
125 Town Place

July

WEDNESDAY 2
43 Fittleworth House
78 Moorlands

THURSDAY 3
126 Uppark

SUNDAY 6
51 Hailsham Grange
54 The Healing Garden
75 Merriments Gardens
86 Nymans
125 Town Place
132 West Chiltington Village Gardens
140 Winsley

MONDAY 7
26 Clinton Lodge

WEDNESDAY 9
43 Fittleworth House
78 Moorlands

SATURDAY 12
8 Bankton Cottage
31 Crown House

SUNDAY 13
10 Bates Green
31 Crown House
91 Palatine & Oak Grove Gardens
117 Shalford House
125 Town Place
132 West Chiltington Village Gardens

WEDNESDAY 16
43 Fittleworth House
78 Moorlands

FRIDAY 18
64 Latchetts
111 St Mary's House & Gardens

SATURDAY 19
13 Berri Court (Evening)
39 Earnley Grange
48 The Grange
64 Latchetts
72 The Manor of Dean
111 St Mary's House & Gardens
122 Standen

SUNDAY 20
39 Earnley Grange
48 The Grange
72 The Manor of Dean
107 Ringmer Park

WEDNESDAY 23
43 Fittleworth House
78 Moorlands

THURSDAY 24
41 Ebbsworth

FRIDAY 25
41 Ebbsworth

SATURDAY 26
68 Little Wantley

SUNDAY 27
57 4 Hillside Cottages
68 Little Wantley

MONDAY 28
26 Clinton Lodge

WEDNESDAY 30
43 Fittleworth House
78 Moorlands

August

SATURDAY 2
14 Bignor Park

SUNDAY 3
14 Bignor Park

MONDAY 4
26 Clinton Lodge

WEDNESDAY 6
78 Moorlands

FRIDAY 8
52 Ham Cottage (Evening)
64 Latchetts

SATURDAY 9
21 Butlers Farmhouse
64 Latchetts
114 Sayerland House

SUNDAY 10
18 Bradstow Lodge
21 Butlers Farmhouse
62 Kiln Copse Farm
100 Penns in the Rocks
135 Westfield

WEDNESDAY 13
18 Bradstow Lodge
62 Kiln Copse Farm
78 Moorlands

SATURDAY 16
101 Perryhill Farmhouse

SUNDAY 17
72 The Manor of Dean
101 Perryhill Farmhouse

WEDNESDAY 20
78 Moorlands

THURSDAY 21
38 Durrance Manor (Evening)

SATURDAY 23
12 4 Ben's Acre

SUNDAY 24
38 Durrance Manor
69 Lordington House

MONDAY 25
69 Lordington House
81 New Barn

WEDNESDAY 27
78 Moorlands

SUNDAY 31
19 Brickwall
82 Newtimber Place

September

WEDNESDAY 3
9 Bateman's
78 Moorlands

SATURDAY 6
63 King John's Lodge
110 Rymans

SUNDAY 7
6 Ashdown Park Hotel
16 Blue Jays
63 King John's Lodge
88 The Old Post Office
95 Parsonage Farm
110 Rymans
123 Stonehealed Farm

WEDNESDAY 10
78 Moorlands
127 Upwaltham Barns

SATURDAY 13
20 Broomershill House
72 The Manor of Dean

SUNDAY 14
10 Bates Green
20 Broomershill House
72 The Manor of Dean
86 Nymans
93 Park Lodge
98 33 Peerley Road
115 Sedgwick Park House
130 Warningcamp House

WEDNESDAY 17
78 Moorlands

SATURDAY 20
75 Merriments Gardens
112 Sandhill Farm House

SUNDAY 21
107 Ringmer Park
112 Sandhill Farm House
113 Sarah Raven's Cutting Garden
117 Shalford House

WEDNESDAY 24
78 Moorlands

SUNDAY 28
42 Firle Place
55 High Beeches
94 6 Park Terrace

October

WEDNESDAY 1
14 Bignor Park
78 Moorlands

TUESDAY 7
118 Sheffield Park Garden

WEDNESDAY 8
14 Bignor Park
78 Moorlands

THURSDAY 9
60 Houndless Water

FRIDAY 10
60 Houndless Water

WEDNESDAY 15
14 Bignor Park
78 Moorlands

WEDNESDAY 22
14 Bignor Park
78 Moorlands

SUNDAY 26
97 Peasmarsh Place

WEDNESDAY 29
14 Bignor Park
78 Moorlands

November

WEDNESDAY 26
(34) Denmans Garden

February 2009

SUNDAY 8
(76) Mitchmere Farm

WEDNESDAY 11
(99) Pembury House

THURSDAY 12
(76) Mitchmere Farm
(99) Pembury House

FRIDAY 13
(99) Pembury House

SUNDAY 15
(76) Mitchmere Farm

WEDNESDAY 18
(99) Pembury House

THURSDAY 19
(99) Pembury House

FRIDAY 20
(99) Pembury House

Gardens open to the public

(2) Alfriston Clergy House
(5) Arundel Castle
(9) Bateman's
(17) Borde Hill Garden, Park & Woodland
(26) Clinton Lodge
(34) Denmans Garden
(42) Firle Place
(49) Great Dixter House & Gardens
(51) Hailsham Grange
(55) High Beeches
(56) Highdown
(63) King John's Lodge
(75) Merriments Gardens
(86) Nymans
(92) Parham Gardens
(105) The Priest House
(111) St Mary's House & Gardens
(113) Sarah Raven's Cutting Garden
(118) Sheffield Park Garden
(122) Standen
(126) Uppark
(129) The Walled Garden at Cowdray
(133) West Dean Gardens

By appointment only

(24) Champs Hill
(25) Chidmere Gardens
(27) Coates Manor
(32) Dachs Halt
(40) Eastergate House
(44) Five Oaks Cottage
(61) Kent House
(77) Moor Farm
(119) Sherburne House
(134) Westacre

Also open by appointment ☎

(7) Bakers House
(8) Bankton Cottage
(10) Bates Green
(12) 4 Ben's Acre
(15) 4 Birch Close
(18) Bradstow Lodge
(22) 51 Carlisle Road
(28) Cookscroft
(31) Crown House
(33) Dale Park House
(35) Dormers
(36) Down Place
(37) Duckyls Holt
(38) Durrance Manor
(39) Earnley Grange
(43) Fittleworth House
(46) The Garden House
(54) The Healing Garden
(57) 4 Hillside Cottages
(58) Hobbs Barton
(60) Houndless Water
(64) Latchetts
(66) Legsheath Farm
(70) Lowder Mill
(71) Malt House
(72) The Manor of Dean
(76) Mitchmere Farm
(78) Moorlands
(81) New Barn
(83) The Nook
(85) Nyewood House
(87) Offham House
(89) Old Scaynes Hill House
(90) 64 Old Shoreham Road
(91) Palatine & Oak Grove Gardens
(94) 6 Park Terrace
(97) Peasmarsh Place
(98) 33 Peerley Road
(99) Pembury House
(100) Penns in the Rocks
(101) Perryhill Farmhouse
(102) Pindars
(104) 6 Plantation Rise
(106) Ridge House
(108) Rose Cottage
(109) Roundhill Cottage
(110) Rymans
(112) Sandhill Farm House
(115) Sedgwick Park House
(120) Siggle Wriggle
(123) Stonehealed Farm
(124) Tinkers Bridge Cottage
(125) Town Place
(128) Villa Elisabeta
(136) 46 Westup Farm Cottages
(138) Wildham
(132) Palmer's Lodge, West Chiltington Village Gardens

The Gardens

ABBOTSMERRY BARN
See Kent.

① NEW ALDSWORTH HOUSE
Emsworth Common Road, Aldsworth PO10 8QT. Tom & Sarah Williams. *6m W of Chichester. From Havant follow signs to Stansted House until Emsworth Common Rd. Stay on this rd to reach Aldsworth. From Chichester take B2178; go straight on at Funtington, house 1st on R in Aldsworth (not in Emsworth). Teas (Mar) & Home-made teas (June).* **Adm £3, chd free.** *Suns, Tues 9, 11 Mar; (11-4); 8, 10 June (2-7).* 6-acre Victorian family garden being adapted to modern needs by plantaholic owners, with enthusiastic help from terriers and spaniel. Unusual trees, shrubs and perennials incl hellebores, old apple trees, magnolias, roses and 120 clematis. Great views. Carpets of spring bulbs, particularly snowdrops, crocus and daffodils. Gravel and walled gardens. Small arboretum. Stansted Garden Show 6-8 June.
  ♿ ✕ ☕

② ◆ ALFRISTON CLERGY HOUSE
Alfriston BN26 5TL. The National Trust, 01323 870001, www.nationaltrust.org.uk. *4m NE of Seaford. Just E of B2108, in Alfriston village, adjoining The Tye & St Andrew's Church. Bus: RDH 125 from Lewes, Autopoint 126 from Eastbourne & Seaford.* **Adm £3.70, chd £1.85. Mon, Wed, Thur, Sat, Sun (10-5).** *For NGS: Wed 18 June (10-5).* Enjoy the scent of roses and pinks in a tranquil setting with views across the meandering R Cuckmere. Visit this C14 thatched Wealden hall house, the first building to be acquired by the National Trust in 1896. Our gardener will be available to talk to you and welcome you to this peaceful cottage garden.
✕

Enjoy the scent of roses and pinks . . .

❸ AMBROSE PLACE BACK GARDENS
Richmond Road, Worthing BN11 1PZ. *'... a horticultural phenomenon'* Daily Telegraph. 25th Anniversary year. *Take Broadwater Rd into town centre, turn R at Town Hall T-lights into Richmond Rd. Garden entrances on L opp Library. Parking in rds.* Afternoon teas/cakes at 'Way-In Café', Worthing Tabernacle Church by £1.50 prepaid ticket only from 10 Ambrose Place or entry points. **Gardens combined adm £4, chd under 14 free. Sun 22 June (11-1 & 2-5).**
Start Tour at Ambrose Villa in Portland Rd or 1 Ambrose Place next to St Paul's Community Centre. Featured widely in press and on radio. Limited access to some gardens.

1 AMBROSE PLACE
Mrs M M Rosenberg
Traditional walled garden; shrubs, pond, climbing plants.
🏃 ✿

3 AMBROSE PLACE
Tim & Fiona Reynoldson
Delightful English cottage garden.
🏃

4 AMBROSE PLACE
Mark & Caroline Robson
Paved garden, raised herbaceous borders, lawn and flowering summer plants.
🏃

5 AMBROSE PLACE
Pat & Sue Owen
Paved town garden with raised borders, variety of flowering shrubs and herbaceous plants.
🏃 ✿

6 AMBROSE PLACE
Catherine Reeve
Lawned garden with charming colourful borders and summerhouse.
🏃 ✿

7 AMBROSE PLACE
Mark & Susan Frost
Small courtyard garden, with conservatory.
🏃

8 AMBROSE PLACE
Claire & Steve Hughes
Children's wonderland garden with colourful borders.
🏃

9 AMBROSE PLACE
Anna & Derek Irvine
Small courtyard with trough fountain leads through greenhouse to paved town garden with three further fountains and a brick rill.
🏃 ✿

10 AMBROSE PLACE
Alan & Marie Pringle
Mediterranean garden with Alhambra-inspired pond, cypress trees and lush borders.
🏃 ✿

11 AMBROSE PLACE
Mrs M Stewart
Mature garden with roses, summerhouse, flowering plants.
🏃

12 AMBROSE PLACE
Peter & Nina May
Rediscovered designer garden being brought back to life.
🏃

13 AMBROSE PLACE
Linda Gamble
Charming courtyard garden with colourful seasonal flowers.
🏃

14 AMBROSE PLACE
Andy & Lucy Marks
Paved town garden, roses, flowering shrubs, summer perennials and fig tree.
🏃

AMBROSE VILLA
Mark & Christine Potter
Victorian-style secret garden with pond, mature trees and shrubs. Flower and vegetable borders and long-established fruit-bearing vine and fig. Delightful shady areas and summerhouse.
🏃 ✿

❹ ANSTY GARDENS
Haywards Heath RH17 5AW. *3m W of Haywards Heath on A272. 1m E of A23. Start in car park signed in Ansty village.* Home-made teas at Whydown Cottage in May, Apple Tree Cottage in June. **Combined adm £4, chd free. Suns 4 May; 22 June (1.30-6).**
All four gardens are very different. You will be assured of a very warm welcome from the owners and our helpers for the day. We will be happy to answer any questions, we are all 'hands-on gardeners'.

APPLE TREE COTTAGE
Deaks Lane. Mr & Mrs G J Longfield
2-acre garden surrounds C16 cottage (not open) with mature trees, herbaceous and raised beds, rockery, fernery and vegetable garden with fruit cage. Usual and unusual plants in cottage style. Views over farmland and woodland.
🏃 ✿

LEAFIELD
Bolney Road. Mr & Mrs Paul Dupée
2¹/₂ acres. Rockery and herbaceous borders, incl many hardy geraniums, acers, eucalyptus and other unusual shrubs. Meadow and woodland areas. Exhibition of owner's contemporary watercolours of flowers. Garden game for children.
🏃 ✿

NETHERBY
Bolney Road. Mr & Mrs R Gilbert
¹/₂ -acre cottage garden, with 3 ponds and 2 Japanese bridges. Laburnum arch. Raised beds and vegetable garden.
🏃 🛏

WHYDOWN COTTAGE
Bolney Road. Mrs M Gibson & Lance Gibson
1-acre woodland garden, with water features. Many unusual trees, incl an embothrium. Fresh planting annually. Ideas for the smaller garden.
🏃 ✿

5 ◆ ARUNDEL CASTLE
Arundel BN18 9AB. Arundel Castle Trustees Ltd, 01903 882173, www.arundelcastle.org. *In the centre of Arundel, N of A27.* Castle & gardens £12, concessions £9.50, chd £7.50, family £32. Gardens only adult/chd £6.50. 21 Mar to 2 Nov Tues to Suns (10-5). Mons in Aug & Bank Hol Mons.
Home of the Duke and Duchess of Norfolk. 40 acres of grounds and garden. New for 2008: Earl's Garden based on early C17 classical designs. 2 restored Victorian glasshouses with exotic fruit and vegetables. Walled flower and kitchen gardens. Specialising in unusual tender perennials and plants for mild climates. C14 Fitzalan Chapel white garden.

The old walled kitchen garden has beds of herbaceous perennials . . .

6 ASHDOWN PARK HOTEL
Wych Cross RH18 5JR. Mr Kevin Sweet. *6m S of E Grinstead. Take A22, 3m S of Forest Row turn L at Wych Cross by garage, 1m on R. From M25 take M23 S, exit J10 on A264 to E Grinstead. Approach from S on A22, turn R at Wych Cross.* Teas (not NGS). Adm £3.50, chd free. Suns 18 May; 7 Sept (2-5).
186 acres of parkland, grounds and gardens surrounding Ashdown Park Hotel. Restoration work started in 2005 on the walled garden with the planting of herbaceous perennials, roses, lime trees, box hedging and wall-trained fruit trees. A peaceful oasis in the heart of Ashdown Forest. Woodland walks. Gravel paths, slopes, some uneven paths.

7 BAKERS HOUSE
Bakers Lane, Shipley RH13 8GJ. Mr & Mrs Mark Burrell, 01403 741215. *5m S of Horsham. Take A24 to Worthing, then A272 W, 2nd turn to Dragon's Green. L at George & Dragon PH, Bakers Lane then 300yds on L.* Home-made teas. Adm £3, chd free (share to St Mary the Virgin, Shipley). Suns 18 May; 15 June (2-6). Visitors also welcome by appt, groups of 10+ only.

Large Wealden garden, lake, laburnum tunnel, shrubs, trees, rose walks of old-fashioned roses; scented knot garden, bog gardens, lemon and olive walk. Gravel paths, partial wheelchair access.

8 BANKTON COTTAGE
Turners Hill Road, Crawley Down RH10 4EY. Robin & Rosie Lloyd, 01342 718907, rosie.lloyd@dsl.pipex.com. *4m W of East Grinstead. 2½ m E of M23 J10. On B2028 1m N of Turners Hill Xrds. Parking only on rd.* Home-made teas. Adm £3.50, chd free. Sats 28 June; 12 July (2-5.30). Evening Opening £4.50, wine, Fri 13 June (6-8.30). Visitors also welcome by appt late May to early Aug, for groups of 20+.
Almost unanimously described as a 'romantic' garden by visitors, the old walled kitchen garden has beds of herbaceous perennials, roses and clematis, box-edged lavender parterre and serpentine yew hedging. Beyond, lake, swans, bog garden and woodland. Many terracotta pots planted up.

9 ◆ BATEMAN'S
Burwash TN19 7DS. The National Trust, 01435 882302, www.nationaltrust.org.uk. *6m E of Heathfield. ½ m S of A265 on rd leading S at W end of Burwash, or N from Woods Corner (B2096).* Adm £7.20, chd £3.60. Sats to Weds 15 Mar to 2 Nov (1-4.30). For NGS: Weds 7 May; 3 Sept (11-4.30).
Home of Rudyard Kipling from 1902-1936. Kipling planted yew hedges and rose garden, as well as constructing the pear alley and pond. The mill, within the grounds, grinds local wheat into flour.

10 BATES GREEN
Arlington, nr Hailsham BN26 6SH. Carolyn & John McCutchan, 01323 485152, batesgreen@dsl.pipex.com, www.batesgreen.co.uk. *3½ m SW of Hailsham and of A22. 2m S of Michelham Priory. 2½ m N from Wilmington on A27. Bates Green on small back rd (Tyehill Road) running from Yew Tree Inn in the centre of Arlington village to Caneheath nr Old Oak Inn.* Light refreshments & home-made teas. Adm £4, chd free. Suns 6 Apr; 13 July; 14 Sept (11-5). Visitors also welcome by appt.
Plantsman's 2-acre tranquil garden

with pond and organic raised bed vegetable garden. April: woodland behind meadow carpeted in anemones; shaded areas incl narcissi, primroses, violets and pulmonaria; tulips in herbaceous borders. July: alliums, hardy geraniums, kniphofias, hemerocallis, grasses, salvias. September: peaks with cyclamen, colchicum, asters, heleniums, miscanthus, verbenas, sedums and butterflies. Featured in 'The English Garden'.

11 BEAUCHAMPS
Float Lane, Udimore, Rye TN31 6BY. Matty & Richard Holmes. *3m W of Rye. 3m E of Broad Oak Xrds. Turn S off B2089 down Float Lane ½ m.* Home-made teas. Adm £4, chd free. Sun 1 June (2-6).
Nestling in the beautiful Brede Valley, this lovely informal garden, maintained by its owners, displays a wide range of unusual herbaceous plants, shrubs and trees incl fine specimens of *Cornus controversa* 'Variegata' and *Crinodendron hookerianum*. Small orchard, kitchen garden and copse. Many home-propagated plants for sale, incl some fine irises. Featured as Garden of the Week in 'Rye & Battle Observer'. Wheelchair access not recommended after wet weather.

12 4 BEN'S ACRE
Horsham RH13 6LW. Pauline Clark, 01403 266912. *From A281 via Cowfold, R into St Leonards Rd by Long Room Restaurant into Comptons Lane. 4th R into Brambling Rd. From Dorking A24, L to A264, 2nd L B2195. Over T-lights into Harwood Rd, L at roundabout, Comptons Lane. Herons Way 5th L.* Home-made teas. Adm £2.50, chd free (share to Born Free). Sats 28 June; 23 Aug (11.30-5). Visitors also welcome by appt.
Described as a little piece of heaven, set on the edge of St Leonards Forest and Horsham riverside walk. Plant lover's garden, 100ft x 45ft, using different levels and interesting design for shape, colour and texture. Relaxed planting of verbena, grasses and many flowers, ornamental trees and shrubs for colour and foliage, box hedging and topiary for formality. Water features, ornaments and pots. Summerhouse and arbour, with other seating for relaxing and viewing. Sat 28 June Flower Festival in St Mary's Church. Featured in 'Amateur Gardening'.

13 BERRI COURT
Main Road, Yapton BN18 0EB. Mr & Mrs J C Turner. *5m SW of Arundel. A2024 Littlehampton to Chichester rd. In centre of village between Shoulder of Mutton & The Olive Branch PHs. Car park is opp T-junction next to the Free Church chapel.* **Evening Opening** £3.50, wine, Sat 19 July (6-8).
Intensely planted 2-acre garden of wide interest; trees, flowering shrubs, heathers, eucalyptus, daffodils, shrub roses, hydrangeas and lily pond.
♿ ❀

One-acre semi-wild garden with rhododendrons, spring bulbs and mixed summer borders . . .

14 BIGNOR PARK
Pulborough RH20 1HG. The Mersey Family, www.bignorpark.co.uk. *5m S of Petworth and Pulborough. Well signed from B2138. Nearest village Sutton.* Home-made teas 2, 3 Aug only. **Adm £3, chd free. Every Wed 2 Apr to 28 May (2-5); Sat 2, Sun 3 Aug (12-5); Every Wed 1 to 29 Oct (2-5).**
11 acres of garden to explore, with magnificent views of S Downs. Interesting trees, shrubs, wild flower areas with swathes of daffodils in spring. Walled flower and vegetable gardens. Plenty of seats for contemplation, and shelter if it rains. Temple, Greek pavilion, Zen pond and unusual sculptures. Surprises for children. Dogs on leads welcome. Plant Fair 30, 31 Aug (donation to NGS).
♿ ☕

15 4 BIRCH CLOSE
Arundel BN18 9HN. Elizabeth & Mike Gammon, 01903 882722, e.gammon@toucansurf.com. *1m S of Arundel. From A27/A284 roundabout at W end of Arundel take Ford Rd. After ¹/₂ m turn R into Maxwell Rd. Follow signs for ¹/₂ m.* Home-made teas. **Adm £3, chd free. Sun 4, Mon 5 May (2-5). Visitors also welcome by appt in May and June only.**

¹/₃ acre of woodland garden on edge of Arundel with woods on three sides. Wide range of mature trees and shrubs (incl silver birch, chestnut, stewartia, acer, rhododendron, viburnum and cornus alternifolia) and many hardy perennials. Particular emphasis on spring flowers (bluebells, narcissi, tulips, alliums, camassia and forget-me-nots) and clematis (over 100 incl 11 different montana). All set in a tranquil setting with secluded corners, meandering paths and plenty of seating. Featured in 'Amateur Gardening' & 'Flora' magazine.
✒ ❀ ☕ ☎

16 NEW BLUE JAYS
Chesworth Close, Horsham RH13 5AL. Stella & Mike Schofield. *From A281 (East St) L down Denne Rd ¹/₄ m, L to Chesworth Close. Garden at end of close with 4 disabled parking spaces. Other parking in Denne Rd car park; some spaces in Deene Rd, Normandy and Queensway, free on Suns.* Home-made teas. **Adm £2.50, chd free. Suns 4 May; 7 Sept (1.30-5.30).**
One-acre semi-wild garden with rhododendrons, spring bulbs and mixed summer borders. A small stream and R Arun form the boundary under tall trees. Large WW2 pill box which formed part of the Horsham defence system. Small orchard and vegetable plot. Small art show.
♿ ✒ ❀ ☕

17 ◆ BORDE HILL GARDEN, PARK & WOODLAND
Balcombe Road, Haywards Heath RH16 1XP. Borde Hill Garden Ltd, 01444 884121, www.bordehill.co.uk. *1¹/₂ m N of Haywards Heath.* **Adm £7.50, chd £4, concessions £6.50. 21 Mar to 3 Sept (10-6 or dusk if earlier). For NGS: Thur 5 June (10-6).**
Botanically rich heritage garden set in 200 acres of stunning parkland with an immense diversity of rare trees and shrubs incl magnolias, rhododendrons, azaleas (some later flowering) and camellias. Planted as garden rooms, incl a lavish rose garden, romantic Italian garden and subtropical dells. Woodland and lakeside walks with magnificent views. Featured in 'The English Garden'.
♿ ❀ ☕

18 BRADSTOW LODGE
The Drive, Ifold RH14 0TE. Ian & Elizabeth Gregory, 01403 753248, bradstow-lodge@tiscali.co.uk. *1m S of Loxwood. From A272/A281 take B2133 (Loxwood). ¹/₂ m S of Loxwood take the Plaistow rd, after 800yds turn R into The Drive (by village shop). Follow signs. Parking in The Drive only, please park considerately.* Home-made teas. **Adm £3, chd free. Suns, Weds 23, 26 Mar; 10, 13 Aug (2-5). Also open 10, 13 Aug Kiln Copse Farm. Visitors also welcome by appt.**
Plantsman's garden on Wealden clay created from a triangular plot to give different areas with wide-ranging and varied plantings from wild to formal with all-yr interest. Ponds, bog garden, recently planted knot garden, raised beds, greenhouses and vegetable areas. Many pots and containers. New small water feature for 2008. Featured in 'Amateur Gardening'.
♿ ✒ ❀ ☕ ☎

BRAEKENAS
See Surrey.

19 BRICKWALL
Rye Road, Northiam TN31 6NL. The Frewen Educational Trust Ltd. *8m NW of Rye. S end of Northiam High St at A28/B2088 junction. Rail and bus: Rye, Northiam to Hastings service.* Home-made teas. **House & garden £5. Garden only £3, chd under 16 free. Sun 31 Aug (2-5).**
Listed garden surrounding a Grade I listed Jacobean Mansion (also open) and currently housing school for dyslexic children. Gardens incl chess garden with topiary yew pieces and number of Stuart characteristics: brick walls, clipped yew and beech are particular features, also small arboretum. Some shallow steps.
♿ ❀ ☕

20 BROOMERSHILL HOUSE
Broomershill Lane, Pulborough RH20 2HZ. *1m N of Pulborough. From A283 turn up Broomershill Lane at White Horse PH, signed Murrells Nursery; garden on R after nursery. From A29 turn up Broomershill Lane, continue up hill, garden on L before nursery.* Home-made teas. **Adm £3.50, chd free. Sat 13, Sun 14 Sept (2-6).**
2-acre garden originally created by award-winning designer Fiona Lawrenson for all-yr interest. Herbaceous walk with espaliered fruit

on old brick walls; pleached hornbeams, reflective pool, summerhouse, grasses border and decorative vegetable garden. Glorious views to S Downs across meadows.

 ♿ ✂ ♨

㉑ BUTLERS FARMHOUSE
Butlers Lane, Herstmonceux BN27 1QH. Irene Eltringham-Willson, www. irenethegardener.zoomshare.com. *3m E of Hailsham. Take A271 from Hailsham, go through the village of Herstmonceux, turn R signed Church Rd then approx 1m turn R.* Teas in Mar, Cream teas in Aug. Adm Mar £3, Aug £3.50, chd free. Sat, Sun 15, 16 Mar. Sat, Sun 9, 10 Aug **with live jazz** (2-5).
Lovely rural setting for 1/2 -acre garden surrounding C16 farmhouse (not open) with views of S Downs. Pretty in spring with primroses and hellebores. Mainly herbaceous with rainbow border, small pond with dribbling frogs and Cornish-inspired beach corner. Still being restored to former glory, as shown in old photographs, but with a few quirky twists. Recent projects incl a grass corner and poison garden. Relax and listen to live jazz in the garden in August. Featured in 'Sussex Life'.

 ♿ ✂ ♨ ⊨ ♨

㉒ 51 CARLISLE ROAD
Eastbourne BN21 4JR. Mr & Mrs N Fraser-Gausden, 01323 722545, fgausden@ic24.net. *200yds inland from seafront (Wish Tower), close to Congress Theatre.* Home-made teas. Adm £3, chd free. Sat 31 May; Sun 1 June (2-5.30). **Evening Opening** £4, wine, Sat 14 June (6-8). Visitors also welcome by appt.
Walled, S-facing garden (82ft sq) with mixed beds intersected by stone paths and incl small pool. Profuse and diverse planting. Wide selection of shrubs, old roses, herbaceous plants and perennials mingle with specimen trees and climbers.

✂ ✿ ♨ ☎

㉓ CAXTON MANOR
Wall Hill, Forest Row RH18 5EG. Adele & Jules Speelman. *1m N of Forest Row, 2m S of E Grinstead. From A22 take turning to Ashurstwood, entrance on L after 1/3 m, or 1m on R from N.* Home-made teas. Adm £3.50, chd free. Fri 16, Sat 17 May (2-5).
Delightful Japanese-inspired gardens planted with mature rhododendrons,

azaleas and acers, surrounding large pond with massive rockery and waterfall, beneath the home of the late Sir Archibald McIndoe (house not open). Elizabethan-style parterre at rear of house. Featured on BBC TV Open Gardens.

✂ ✿ ♨

㉔ CHAMPS HILL
Waltham Park Road, Coldwaltham RH20 1LY. Mr & Mrs David Bowerman, 01798 831868. *3m S of Pulborough. On A29, turn R to Fittleworth into Waltham Park Rd; garden 400yds.* Home-made teas. Adm £4, chd free. Visitors welcome by appt, groups of 10+. Mar, May and Aug best for viewing, but all-yr interest.
27 acres of acid-loving plants around sand pits and woodland. Superb views. Sculptures.

 ♿ ✂ ♨ ☎

㉕ CHIDMERE GARDENS
Chidham Lane, Chidham PO18 8TD. Jackie & David Russell, 01243 572287, info@chidmeregardens.com, www.chidmeregardens.com. *6m W of Chichester at SE end of Chidham Lane by pond in village.* Home-made teas. Adm £3.50, chd free. Visitors welcome by appt.
C15 house (not open) is excitingly situated next to Chidmere Pond, so much so that the well-filled greenhouse which borders the mere feels almost like a houseboat. Divided by tall yew and hornbeam hedges, the garden has fine flowering trees, roses and well-stocked herbaceous borders. Recent projects incl wild flower meadow, alpine greenhouse, fruit and vegetable garden and orchards with over 150 varieties of apples used to produce Chidmere Farm apple juice. Featured in 'Chichester Observer'.

 ♿ ♨ ☎

㉖ ◆ CLINTON LODGE
Fletching TN22 3ST. Lady Collum, 01825 722952, www.clintonlodgegardens.co.uk. *4m NW of Uckfield. From A272 turn N at Piltdown for Fletching, 1 1/2 m.* Adm £4, chd free. For NGS: Suns 11 May; 8 June. Mons 9, 16, 23, Sun 29 June; Mons 7, 28 July; 4 Aug (2-5.30).
6-acre formal and romantic garden, overlooking parkland, with old roses, double herbaceous borders, yew hedges, pleached lime walks, copy of C17 scented herb garden, medieval-style potager, vine and rose allée, wild

flower garden. Canal garden, small knot garden and shady glade. Caroline and Georgian house, not open. Group visits by arrangement. Featured in many publications incl 'Sussex Life', 'Period Living' & 'Mid Sussex Times'.

✂ ✿ ♨

The greenhouse which borders the mere feels almost like a houseboat . . .

㉗ COATES MANOR
Fittleworth RH20 1ES. Mrs G H Thorp, 01798 865356. *3 1/2 m SW of Pulborough. Turn off B2138 signed Coates.* Adm £3.50, chd free. £5 with light refreshments, by arrangement. Visitors welcome by appt all year.
1 acre, mainly shrubs and foliage of special interest, surrounding Elizabethan house (not open). Flowing design punctuated by clipped shrubs and specimen trees. Paved walled garden with interesting perennials, clematis, scented climbers and smaller treasures. Cyclamen, nerines, amaryllis, berries and coloured foliage give late season interest.

✂ ♨ ☎

㉘ COOKSCROFT
Bookers Lane, Earnley PO20 7JG. Mr & Mrs J Williams, 01243 513671, williams.cookscroft@virgin.net, www.cookscroft.com. *6m S of Chichester. At end of Birdham Straight A286 from Chichester, take L fork to E Wittering B2198. 1m on, before sharp bend, turn L into Bookers Lane. 2nd house on L.* Home-made teas. Adm £3, chd free. Sun 25, Mon 26 May (2-6). Visitors also welcome by appt all year, coaches and groups welcome.
5-acre garden started from fields in 1988. Many trees grown from provenance seeds or liners. Collections of eucalyptus, birch, snake bark maples and unusual shrubs. 3 ponds with waterfalls. Cottage garden and Japanese garden. Interesting and developing garden, incl woodland area: what two fully-employed couples have achieved at the weekends! Featured in 'Chichester Observer'.

 ♿ ✿ ♨ ☎

29 COPYHOLD HOLLOW
Copyhold Lane, Borde Hill, Haywards Heath RH16 1XU. Frances Druce, www.copyholdhollow.co.uk. *2m N of Haywards Heath. Follow signs for Borde Hill Gardens. With BHG on L, over brow of hill and take 1st R signed Ardingly. Garden* ½ *m. Home-made teas.* **Adm £3, chd free. Thur 29 May (2-4.30).**
Enchanting N-facing 1½ -acre cottage and woodland garden, in a steep-sided hollow surrounding C16 listed house (not open) behind 1000yr-old box hedge. Mixed borders, pond and bog garden. Mature woodland enhanced with young camellias, rhododendrons, shrubs, non-native trees and bulbs. Wildlife encouraged. Rough hewn oak steps up 'Himalayan Glade'. Featured in 'The English Garden'.

30 COWDRAY PARK GARDENS
Midhurst GU29 0AY. The Viscount & Viscountess Cowdray. *1m E of Midhurst on A272. Follow A272 towards Petworth and Haywards Heath, entrance on R 200yds past Cowdray Park Golf Club. From Petworth follow A272 towards Midhurst, entrance on L after entering park through wrought iron gates.* Light refreshments & cream teas. **Adm £4, chd free. Sun 11 May (2-5).**
Avenue of wellingtonias, woodland walk; grass garden, rhododendrons, azaleas; lakes; large variety of trees and shrubs, herb parterre. Lebanon cedar 300yrs old; pleasure garden surrounded by ha-ha, themed herbaceous border; laburnum tunnel, cherry avenue and valley garden. Deep unfenced water.

31 CROWN HOUSE
Sham Farm Road, Eridge TN3 9JU. Major L Cave (Retd), 01892 864389. *3m SW of Tunbridge Wells. Signed from A26 Tunbridge Wells to Crowborough rd, approx 400yds. Buses: 29 (½ hourly service), also 225, 228 & 229. In Eridge take Rotherfield turn S (Sham Farm Rd), 1st R, house 1st on L, short walk from bus stop.* Cream teas. **Adm £4, chd free (share to MS Society). Sat 12, Sun 13 July (2-6). Visitors also welcome by appt May to Sept (not Weds). Please phone at least 1 week in advance to confirm availability.**
1½ acres with pools and fountain, rose garden and rose walk, herbaceous

borders and heather border, herb garden. Full size croquet lawn. Laid out as a series of garden rooms in the style of Gertrude Jekyll. Panoramic views of the High Weald and Eridge Park. Aerial photographs showing development of garden since 1969. Rose walk not suitable for wheelchairs.

Rough hewn oak steps up 'Himalayan Glade' . . .

32 NEW DACHS HALT
St Helens Road, Hastings TN34 2EA. Max & Lee Colton, 01424 420443. *1½ m N of town centre. From A21 take A2101 (Hastings town centre), L at roundabout, approx ½ m down St Helens Rd.* Teas by prior arrangement. **Adm £3, chd free (share to RNLI). Visitors welcome by appt spring to autumn for groups of 4+. Written confirmation will be requested for large groups.**
Designed and maintained by owners with mobility problems. Full of ideas to help the disabled, this small garden shows what can be achieved if you're determined enough. Divided into rooms by steps, paths, slopes and archways. Packed with plants and shrubs, ponds, pots and plenty of seats. Featured on BBC TV Open Gardens. Steps and sloping paths with handrails.

33 DALE PARK HOUSE
Madehurst BN18 0NP. Robert & Jane Green, 01243 814260, robertgreen@farming.co.uk. *4m W of Arundel. Take A27 E from Chichester or W from Arundel, then A29 (London) for 2m, turn L to Madehurst & follow red arrows.* Home-made teas. **Adm £3, chd free. Sun 8 June (2-5). Visitors also welcome by appt.**
Set in parkland on S Downs with magnificent views to sea. Large walled garden with 200ft herbaceous border, mixed borders and rose garden. Rose

and clematis arches, interesting collection of hostas, foliage plants and shrubs, orchard and kitchen garden.

34 ◆ DENMANS GARDEN
Denmans Lane, Fontwell BN18 0SU. Michael Neve & John Brookes, 01243 542808, www.denmans-garden.co.uk. *5m from Chichester & Arundel. Off A27, ½ m W of Fontwell roundabout.* **Adm £4.50, chd (4-14) £3, senior citizen £4.25, family £14. Open daily (9-5, or dusk if earlier), not 25, 26 Dec & 1 Jan. For NGS: Weds 27 Feb; 26 Nov (9-5).**
Nearly 4-acre garden designed for yr-round interest through use of form, colour and texture. Home of John Brookes, renowned garden designer and writer, it is a garden full of ideas to be interpreted within smaller home spaces. Award-winning café.

35 DORMERS
West Marden PO18 9ES. Mr & Mrs John Cairns, 02392 631543. *10m NW of Chichester. On B2146. In centre of village turn up hill towards Rowlands Castle.* **Adm £3, chd free. Suns 17, 24 Feb (12-4); 27 Apr (2-5). Visitors also welcome by appt May & June.**
Village garden on chalk, started from scratch in 1997. Cottage-style planting, mainly herbaceous and bulbs, hellebores in early spring. Each area with a different colour scheme, small but productive vegetable patch. Gravel paths.

36 DOWN PLACE
South Harting GU31 5PN. Mr & Mrs D M Thistleton-Smith, 01730 825374. *1m SE of South Harting. B2141 to Chichester, turn L down unmarked lane below top of hill.* Cream teas. **Adm £3, chd free (share to Friends of Harting Church). Sats, Suns 26, 27 Apr; 14, 15 June (2-6). Visitors also welcome by appt Apr to July.**
7-acre hillside, chalk garden on the N side of S Downs with fine views of surrounding countryside. Extensive herbaceous, shrubs and rose borders on different levels merge into natural wild flower meadow renowned for its collection of native orchids. Fully stocked vegetable garden and greenhouses. Spring flowers and blossom.

37 DUCKYLS HOLT
Selsfield Road, West Hoathly
RH19 4QN. Mrs Diana Hill & Miss
Sophie Hill, 01342 810282. *4m SW of
East Grinstead, 6m E of Crawley. At
Turners Hill take B2028. After 1m S
fork L to West Hoathly.* Home-made
teas. **Adm £3.50, chd free. Sat, Sun,
Mon 24, 25, 26 May; Sat 21, Sun 22
June (11-6). Opening with The
Priest House 24 May, 21 June
combined adm £4. Visitors also
welcome by appt in May & June.**
Delightful cottage garden of approx 2
acres on many different levels. Small
herb garden, colourful formal and
informal plantings, herbaceous
borders, rose border and newly-
restored formal rose garden, chickens
and runner ducks (mink and fox
permitting). Mature azaleas and
rhododendrons in season.

❀ ☕ ♿

38 DURRANCE MANOR
Smithers Hill Lane, Shipley
RH13 8PE. Gordon & Joan Lindsay,
01403 741577,
galindsay@dial.pipex.com. *7m SW
of Horsham. Take A24 to A272 (S from
Horsham, N from Worthing), then turn
W towards Billingshurst. Go 1.7m to
2nd turning on L on Smithers Hill Lane
signed to Countryman PH. Durrance
2nd on L.* Home-made teas. **Adm £3,
chd free. Evening Opening, wine,
Thur 21 Aug (5.30-8.30). Sun 24 Aug
(2-6). Visitors also welcome by appt.**
2-acre garden surrounding medieval
hall house (not open) with Horsham
stone roof. Uninterrupted views to S
Downs and Chanctonbury Ring over
ha-ha. Colourful long borders, grass
garden with complementary plants,
walled gravelled garden with exotic
planting, large pond, wild flowering
meadow and orchard, greenhouse and
vegetable garden. Featured in 'Sussex
Life'. Gravel paths.

♿ ☕ ☎

Wide range of
vegetables
grown using
new and
traditional
methods . . .

39 NEW EARNLEY GRANGE
Almodington Lane, Earnley
PO20 7JS. Mr & Mrs I J Parker,
01243 512362,
ij.parker@btconnect.com. *6m S
of Chichester. A286 take L turn to
Almodington Lane. End of lane,
sharp R-hand bend, garden on L.*
Cream teas. **Adm £3.50, chd free.
Evening Opening, wine, Fri 27
June (5-8). Sat 19, Sun 20 July
(2-5). Visitors also welcome by
appt.**
Opportunity to see a newly-planted
(2008) 4-acre garden designed by
Chelsea and Hampton Court gold
medallist Chris Beardshaw (The
Flying Gardener). Features an
English rose garden, lime walk,
long borders, Italian garden, herb
terrace and grass walks. Also an
existing Victorian walled garden
with newly-built greenhouse.
Long herbaceous borders for
all-yr interest, fruit trees and soft
fruits.

♿ ✂ ☕ ☎

40 EASTERGATE HOUSE
Church Lane, Eastergate PO20 3UT.
Michael & Jacintha Hutton, 01243
544195,
jacintha@eastergatehouse.co.uk.
*7m E of Chichester. On A27 turn R at
Fontwell roundabout onto A29. At War
Memorial turn immed into Church Lane
for approx 250yds.* **Adm £3.50, chd
free. Visitors welcome by appt all
year, groups of up to 20.**
1-acre walled and hedged garden has
herbaceous borders interplanted with
shrubs and roses, water garden and
paved potager. In spring, superb
magnolia and wisteria.

☎

41 EBBSWORTH
Nutbourne RH20 2HE. Mrs F
Lambert. *2¹⁄₂ m E of Pulborough. Take
A283 E from junction with A29 (Swan
Corner) 2m with 2 L forks signed
Nutbourne. Pass Rising Sun & follow
signs to garden.* Home-made teas.
**Adm £3, chd free. Thur 24, Fri 25
July (2-5).**
Charming, well-planted, owner-
maintained cottage garden,
surrounding old cottage (not open).
Roses and lilies, together with
herbaceous borders. Man-made
stream and ponds planted with water
plants.

✂ ☕

EDENBRIDGE HOUSE
See Kent.

**FELBRIDGE COPSE &
COURTYARD**
See Surrey.

42 ◆ FIRLE PLACE
Lewes BN8 6LP. 8th Viscount Gage,
01273 858567, www.firleplace.co.uk.
*3m E of Lewes. On A27 turn R from
Lewes & L from Eastbourne. Follow
tourist signs.* **House & garden £8, chd
£5. Garden only £4, chd £2.50. Firle
Place open Easter, Bank Hols,
Weds, Thurs & Suns June to Sept
(2-4.30). For NGS: Suns 27 Apr; 28
Sept (12-5).**
'The Pleasure Grounds'. Wild
woodland garden dating back to C16
currently undergoing renovation,
situated above Firle Place (also open)
giving far-reaching views over Firle Park
towards the Sussex Weald. Woodland
paths and avenues leading to hidden
glades, each with themed plantings.
Garden only open NGS days. Local
crafts & garden stalls. House open
from 1pm, discount for garden
visitors.

❀ ☕

43 FITTLEWORTH HOUSE
Bedham Lane, Fittleworth
RH20 1JH. Edward & Isabel
Braham, 01798 865074 Mark
Saunders. *3m SE of Petworth. Just off
A283, midway between Petworth and
Pulborough, 200yds along lane signed
Bedham.* **Adm £3, chd free. Every
Wed 7 May to 30 July (2-5). Also
open Weds May & June Manvilles
Field. Visitors also welcome by appt
Apr to Sept for groups of 4+.**
Mature 3-acre garden encompassing
wisteria-covered Georgian House (not
open). Magnificent cedar, rose garden,
rhododendrons. Lawns and mixed
borders, fountain. Working walled
kitchen garden, wide range of
vegetables grown using new and
traditional methods. Apple tunnel and
150ft-long colour borders. Large new
'Victorian' glasshouse and old potting
shed.

♿ ❀ ☎

44 FIVE OAKS COTTAGE
West Burton RH20 1HD. Jean &
Steve Jackman, 07939 272443,
jestjsck@tiscali.co.uk. *5m S of
Pulborough. From A29 4m S of
Pulborough, take B2138 signed to
Fittleworth & Petworth. Turn immed L &
L again at T-junction. 1m on the L.
Please follow these directions to avoid
coming through the village.* **Adm**

£2.50. Visitors welcome by appt. **Regret not suitable for children.** Artistic and quirky mix of unusual cultivars and self-seeding English natives. Designed to attract insects and birds. A wildlife garden, undergoing some renewal and replanting in 2008.

✖ ⊗ ☎

45 FRAMFIELD GRANGE
Framfield TN22 5PN. Mr & Mrs Jack Gore. *3m E of Uckfield. From Uckfield take B2102 to Framfield 2½ m. Continue through Framfield on B2102. The Grange is approx ¼ m E on R.* Home-made teas. **Adm £5, chd free. Sun 4 May (2-5).**
10 acres of garden with shrub borders, wild flower meadow and lakes. Woodland walks, bluebell glades. Many hybrids and species of rhododendrons and azaleas. Beautifully kept walled kitchen garden.

& ⊗ ☕

46 THE GARDEN HOUSE
5 Warleigh Road, Brighton BN1 4NT. Bridgette Saunders & Graham Lee, 01273 702840, contact@ gardenhousebrighton.co.uk. *1½ m N of sea front. 1st turning L off Ditchling Rd, heading N from sea front.* Home-made teas. **Adm £3, chd free. Sun 11 May (2-5). Visitors also welcome by appt at any time for groups of 10+.**
Tucked away in the heart of the city, this 'secret' walled garden is full of trees, shrubs, organic vegetables and herbaceous perennials, with a pond and many quirky and fun features. In Victorian times it was a market garden supplying cut flowers to Brighton's shops...now it's a delightful surprise. Featured on BBC TV Open Gardens and in 'Gardens Monthly' magazine.

✖ ⊗ ☕ ☎

47 GARDENERS COTTAGE
West Dean PO18 0RX. Jim Buckland & Sarah Wain. *6m N of Chichester. Follow signs to West Dean Gardens and park in Gardens car park. Follow signs to cottage.* Home-made teas. **Adm £3, chd free. Sun 25 May (11-5).**
Small serene and secluded theatrical retreat with strong emphasis on texture, foliage and good structure created by trees. Topiary, labyrinthine paths, interesting spaces. Separate courtyard garden with pond.

✖ ☕

Small serene and secluded theatrical retreat with strong emphasis on texture, foliage and good structure created by trees . . .

48 THE GRANGE
Fittleworth RH20 1EW. Mr & Mrs W Caldwell. *3m W of Pulborough. A283 midway Petworth-Pulborough; in Fittleworth turn S onto B2138 then turn W at Swan PH.* Home-made teas. **Adm £3, chd free. Sats, Suns 15, 16 Mar; 19, 20 July (2-5.30).**
3-acre garden gently sloping to R Rother. Walled formal area divided by yew hedges nr pretty, late C17 house (not open), with old roses, thyme lawn, small potager and orchard. Shade areas contain an increasing collection of hellebores; masses of naturalised spring bulbs. Colour-themed herbaceous and mixed borders; hot garden. Gravel paths.

& ⊗ ☕

49 ◆ GREAT DIXTER HOUSE & GARDENS
Northiam TN31 6PH. Olivia Eller/Great Dixter Charitable Trust, 01797 252878, www.greatdixter.co.uk. *8m N of Rye. ½ m NW of Northiam off A28.* **House & garden £8, chd £3.50. Garden only £6.50, chd £3. Tues to Suns & Bank Hol Mons, 21 Mar to Oct 26 (House 2-5, Garden 11-5).**
Designed by Lutyens and Nathaniel Lloyd whose son, Christopher, officiated over these gardens for 55yrs, creating one of the most experimental and constantly changing gardens of our time. Wide variety of interest from clipped topiary, wild meadow flowers, natural ponds, formal pool and the famous long border and exotic garden. A long and varied season is aimed for. Snowdrop and crocus weekends in Feb/Mar, Christmas Fair in Dec. Study days and events available all-yr. See website for details. Partial wheelchair access.

& ✖ ⊗ ☕

50 GREAT LYWOOD FARMHOUSE
Lindfield Road, Ardingly RH17 6SW. Richard & Susan Laing. *2½ m N of Haywards Heath. Take B2028 for Ardingly. 2m from centre of Lindfield, turn L down single track.* Home-made teas. **Adm £3.50, chd free. Sun 8 June (2-6). Evening Opening £5, wine, Fri 20 June (6-8).**
Approx 1½ -acre terraced garden surrounding C17 Sussex farmhouse (not open). Landscaped and planted since 1997, with views to S Downs. Featuring lawns and grass walks, mixed borders, rose garden, kitchen garden and orchard, walled garden with dovecote.

✖ ⊗ ☕

51 ◆ HAILSHAM GRANGE
Vicarage Road, Hailsham BN27 1BL. Noel Thompson Esq, 01323 844248, noel-hgrange@amserve.com. *Adjacent to church in centre of Hailsham. Turn L off Hailsham High St into Vicarage Rd, park in public car park.* **Adm £3.50, chd free. For NGS: Suns 1 June; 6 July (2-5.30).**
Formal garden designed and planted in grounds of former early C18 Vicarage (not open). Series of garden areas representing modern interpretation of C18 formality; Gothic summerhouse; pleached hedges; herbaceous borders, colour-themed romantic planting in separate garden compartments. Some gravel paths.

& ✖ ⊗ 🛏 ☕

52 HAM COTTAGE
Hammingden Lane, Highbrook, Ardingly RH17 6SR. Peter & Andrea Browne. *5m N of Haywards Heath. On B2028 1m S of Ardingly turn into Burstow Hill Lane. Signed to Highbrook, then follow NGS signs.* Home-made teas. **Adm £4, chd free. Sats, Suns, 10, 11, 17, 18 May (2-6). Evening Opening £5, wine, Fri 8 Aug (5-9).**

8 acres of undulating garden mostly created from agricultural land. Interesting variety of trees and shrubs, rhododendrons, azaleas and camellias round the pond. 2 areas of woodland, one with a drift of bluebells, the other with a sandstone outcrop, part of which forms a small amphitheatre. Stream-fed bog garden, formal garden with theme planting and vegetable garden, all created by present owners. Energy-saving devices on display: solar powered system for night-time greenhouse & house water heating; photovoltaic modules and wind turbine for lighting.

53 HAMMERWOOD HOUSE
Iping GU29 0PF. Mr & Mrs M Lakin. *3m W of Midhurst. 1m N of A272 Midhurst to Petersfield rd. Well signed.* Home-made teas. **Adm £3, chd free (share to Iping Church). Suns 4, 11 May (1-5).**
Large garden with some herbaceous planting although much admired for its rhododendrons, azaleas, acers, cornus and arboretum. ¼ m walk to wild water garden.

Profusion of colour and scent in an immaculately maintained small garden . . .

54 THE HEALING GARDEN
35 Hayling Rise, High Salvington, Worthing BN13 3AL. Ivan & Janice Mitchell, 01903 263183. *2m NW of Worthing. From Brighton/Worthing follow A27 towards Arundel past Warren Rd roundabout and Offington Corner roundabout, up Crockhurst Hill into Arundel Rd. Hayling Rise on R marked by bus shelter, no 35 on L past church. From A24 head W to Arundel at Offington Corner roundabout.* Home-made teas. **Adm £3, chd free. Suns 4 May; 1 June; 6 July (10-5). Visitors also welcome by appt May to July for small groups. Guided walk with herbalist.**

Medicinal herb garden containing over 700 different types of trees, shrubs and plants from all over the world. Many of the plants will not be found anywhere else in Sussex. Although still a young garden, there is plenty to please the senses. It looks good, it smells good, and by golly it does you good! Herbalist (owner) will be delighted to help and advise visitors about medicinal plants. Comprehensive collection of culinary herbs, incl 4 different types of bay tree. Featured in 'Sussex Life'.

55 ◆ HIGH BEECHES
Handcross RH17 6HQ. High Beeches Gardens Conservation Trust, 01444 400589, www.highbeeches.com. *5m NW of Cuckfield. On B2110, 1m E of A23 at Handcross.* **Adm £5.50, chd under 14 free. 21 Mar to 31 Oct daily (not Weds) 1-5. For NGS: Suns 25 May; 28 Sept (1-5).**
25 acres of enchanting landscaped woodland and water gardens with spring daffodils, bluebells and azalea walks, many rare and beautiful plants, wild flower meadows and glorious autumn colours. Picnic area. National Collection of Stewartia. Limited wheelchair access.
NCCPG

56 ◆ HIGHDOWN
Littlehampton Road, Goring-by-Sea BN12 6PF. Worthing Borough Council, 01903 501054, www.highdowngardens.co.uk/Highdown/. *3m W of Worthing. Off A259. Stn: Goring-by-Sea, 1m.* **Collection box. Open daily Apr to Sept (10-6), Mons to Fris Oct to Mar (10-4.30), not Christmas period. For NGS: Sun 25 May; Sun 8, Wed 11 June (10-6).**
Famous garden created by Sir Frederick Stern situated in chalk pit and downland area containing a wide collection of plants. Many plants were raised from seed brought from China by great collectors like Wilson, Farrer and Kingdon-Ward. Green Flag Award. Woodchip and grass paths and slopes, may cause problems for wheelchair users.
NCCPG

57 4 HILLSIDE COTTAGES
Downs Road, West Stoke PO18 9BL. Heather & Chris Lock, 01243 574802. *3m NW of Chichester. From A286 at Lavant, head W for 1½ m, nr Kingley Vale.* **Adm £2.50, chd free. Sun 27 July (2-5).** Visitors also

welcome by appt June, July & Aug. Garden 120ft x 27ft in established rural setting, created from scratch in 1996. Densely planted with mixed borders and shrubs, large collection of roses, clematis and fuchsias. Profusion of colour and scent in an immaculately maintained small garden.

HOATH HOUSE
See Kent.

58 HOBBS BARTON
Streele Lane, Framfield, nr Uckfield TN22 5RY. Mr & Mrs Jeremy Clark, 01825 732259, hobbsbarton@btinternet.com. *3m E of Uckfield. From Uckfield take B2102 E to Framfield, or approaching from S leave A22 at Pear Tree junction S end of Uckfield bypass. Garden signed from centres of Framfield & Buxted.* Home-made teas. **Adm £5 (Sat & Sun), £4 (Mon), chd free. Sat 7, Sun 8, Mon 9 June (2-5.30). Visitors also welcome by appt June & July only.**
In a peaceful pastoral setting, typical of rural Sussex and well removed from the noise of traffic, this is a mature garden of 2¾ acres developed by the present owners over the past 35yrs. Wide sweeping lawns lead to areas planted with many types of rose, shrubberies and herbaceous borders; numerous specimen trees incl *Metasequoia glyptostroboides*, liriodendron, giant prostrate junipers; pretty water features; part-walled vegetable and fruit garden. Developing woodland garden.

59 HORSEBRIDGE HOUSE
Fittleworth Road, Wisborough Green RH14 0HD. J R & K D Watson. *2½ m SW of Wisborough Green. From Wisborough Green take A272 towards Petworth. Turn L into Fittleworth Rd, signed Coldharbour, proceed 2m. At sign 'Beware low flying owls' turn R into Horsebridge House. From Fittleworth take Bedham Lane, 2½ m NE.* Home-made teas. **Adm £3.50, chd free. Sun 13 Apr (10.30-4.30).**
Formal garden divided into rooms centred on 1920s croquet lawn. Unusual hedging and shrub planting, spring cherry, apple and pear blossom with underplanted daffodils. Formal vegetable garden with box hedging; asparagus bed. Large play area for children under 5 with parental supervision. Featured in 'Sussex Life'.

60 HOUNDLESS WATER

Bell Vale Lane, Fernhurst GU27 3DJ. Mark & Rebecca Smith, 01428 641438. *1½ m S of Haslemere, 6m N of Midhurst. Take A286 N from Midhurst towards Haslemere, through Fernhurst. Take 2nd R after Kingsley Green into Bell Vale Lane, garden 1st on L.* Home-made teas. **Adm £3, chd free. Thur 15 May; Thur 9, Fri 10 Oct (11-3). Visitors also welcome by appt, not Aug, cars only.**
5-acre Victorian garden, gardened by current owners since 2002. Mature plantings of azaleas, rhododendrons and acid-loving trees, underplanted with bluebells. Restored listed greenhouse. Small kitchen garden and orchard. Formal borders nr house lead to stone steps to wild flower meadow.

✕ ❀ ☕ ☎

61 KENT HOUSE

East Harting GU31 5LS. Mr & Mrs David Gault, 01730 825206. *4m SE of Petersfield. On B2146 at South Harting take Elstead to Midhurst rd E for ½ m. Just W of Turkey Island, turn N up no through road for 400yds.* **Adm £3, chd free. Visitors welcome by appt Apr to Aug. Refreshments possible by arrangement.**
1½ -acre garden with fine trees, ha-ha, shade-loving plants for Apr and May, walled garden, exceptional views of the Downs from pretty Georgian house (not open). Mixed borders of unusual shrubs and herbaceous plants. Short slope up driveway.

♿ ❀ ☕ ☎

62 KILN COPSE FARM

Kirdford RH14 0JJ. Bill & Pat Shere. *4m NE of Petworth. Take A283 from Petworth then fork R signed Kirdford & Balls Cross. Through Balls Cross, over narrow bridge then 400yds on L.* Home-made teas. **Adm £3, chd free. Sun 20 Apr; Sun 10, Wed 13 Aug (12-5.30). Also open 10, 13 Aug Bradstow Lodge.**
2-acre garden on clay that has gradually evolved to blend with the natural woodland setting. Many informal mixed shrub and herbaceous borders, low-maintenance conifer border, spacious lawns, vegetable garden, pergola, ponds with bridge and stepping stones. In spring, lovely wild flowers with a beautiful woodland bluebell walk. Partial wheelchair access.

♿ ✕ ❀ ☕

KIMPTON HOUSE

See Hampshire.

63 ◆ KING JOHN'S LODGE

Sheepstreet Lane, Etchingham TN19 7AZ. Jill & Richard Cunningham, 01580 819232, www.kingjohnslodge.co.uk. *2m W of Hurst Green. A265 Burwash to Etchingham. Turn L before Etchingham Church into Church Lane which leads into Sheepstreet Lane after ½ m. L after 1m.* **Adm £3, chd free. Nursery & garden open daily 10-5.30. For NGS: Sats (2-6), Suns, Mon (11-5) 19, 20 Apr; 24, 25, 26 May; 6, 7 Sept. Evening Opening,** wine, **Wed 25 June (6-9).**
4-acre romantic garden for all seasons surrounding an historic listed house (not open). Formal garden with water features, rose walk and wild garden and pond. Rustic bridge to shaded ivy garden, large herbaceous borders, old shrub roses and secret garden. Further 4 acres of meadows, fine trees and grazing sheep. Nursery.

♿ ❀ ⛺ ☕

Artistic and quirky cottage garden, made and maintained by owners . . .

64 LATCHETTS

Freshfield Lane, Danehill RH17 7HQ. Mr & Mrs Laurence Hardy, 01825 790237, laurence@flb.uk.com. *5m NE of Haywards Heath. SW off A275. In Danehill turn into Freshfield Lane at War Memorial. 1m on R (not Latchetts Farmhouse).* Cream teas. **Adm £4, chd free. Fris, Sats: 30, 31 May; 20, 21 June; 18, 19 July; 8, 9 Aug (1.30-5.30). Visitors also welcome by appt, coaches welcome.**
Much-admired 8-acre garden of trees, ponds, fine lawns, colourful shrub, herbaceous and bedding borders, roses, water features, fruit and vegetables, vistas, terraces, arches, ha-has, unusual plants, Christian Millennium Garden, woodland walk, humour and surprise. Imaginatively designed and impeccably maintained, remarkable diversity and interest. Children's Safari Hunt. Featured in 'GGG'.

♿ ❀ ☕ ☎

65 NEW LEECHPOOL COTTAGE

Leechpool Lane, Horsham RH13 6AG. Margaret Penny. *1m N of town centre. From Horsham stn N to Harwood Rd B2195. After 2nd roundabout 2nd L Woodland Way, to Leechpool Lane. From N take by-pass A264 Roffey after T-lights. Ist R Woodland Way.* **Adm £2.50, chd free (regret not suitable for small children).** Sat 7, Sun 8 June (1-5).
Artistic and quirky cottage garden, made and maintained by owners. Many interesting features incl topiary, Italian-style courtyard, conservatory, fountains, old-fashioned climbing roses, small Japanese garden and woodland stream.

❀ ☕

66 LEGSHEATH FARM

nr Forest Row RH19 4JN. Mr & Mrs M Neal, 01342 810230, legsheath@btinternet.com. *4m S of E Grinstead. 2m W of Forest Row, 1m S of Weirwood Reservoir.* Home-made teas. **Adm £5, chd free. Sun 18 May (2-5). Visitors also welcome by appt.**
Panoramic views over Weirwood reservoir. Exciting 10-acre garden with woodland walks, water gardens and formal borders. Of particular interest, clumps of wild orchids, fine davidia, acers, eucryphia and rhododendrons. Mass planting of different species of meconopsis on the way to ponds.

❀ ☕ ☎

LEYDENS

See Kent.

67 LITTLE HILL

Hill Farm Lane, Codmore Hill, Pulborough RH20 1BW. Barbara & Derek James. *1m N of Pulborough. Hill Farm Lane off A29 by The Rose PH, garden 10th on L. Overflow parking in field before garden entrance, follow signs.* Light refreshments & teas. **Adm £3, chd free. Evening Opening,** wine, **Thur 12 June (5-7). Sun 15 June (2-5).**
4 acres of formal gardens with sunken rose garden and pond, tiered rock garden with waterfall and pond, rose and grape arbour in middle of box-hedged beds, hidden rhododendron dell. Some annuals, perennials, shrubs, trees and small orchard, vegetable plot and fruit cage. Wild flowers. Some gravel and stone paths, mostly lawn.

♿ ✕ ☕

68 LITTLE WANTLEY

Fryern Road, Storrington RH20 4BJ. Hilary Barnes. *1m W of Storrington. Follow signs to West Chiltington. Entrance approx 1m on R in Fryern Rd. Parking in field.* Home-made teas. **Adm £3.50, chd free. Sat 26, Sun 27 July (2-5.30).**
Award-winning (Daily Mail Garden of the Year 2006) naturalistic garden of approx 3$^{1}/_{2}$ acres. Wide range of plants grown in neutral/acid soil with deep mixed herbaceous borders. Secret garden reached by pergola walk. 1$^{1}/_{2}$ -acre lake excavated in 1997 with unusual cantilevered jetty and impressive marginal planting. Stumpery. Music by The Wheelwrights Brass Quintet. Deep water: children must be strictly supervised.

69 NEW LORDINGTON HOUSE

Lordington, Chichester PO18 9DX. Mr & Mrs John Hamilton. *7m W of Chichester. On W side of B2146, 1$^{1}/_{2}$ m S of Walderton, 6m S of South Harting.* Home-made teas. **Adm £3 (Mar), £4 (Aug), chd free. Sat 29, Sun 30 Mar (11-5); Sun 24, Mon 25 Aug (11-6).**
Vestigial C17 garden layout, fine house (not open). Large walled gardens, elegant topiary and commanding views. Drought-resistant borders planted in blocks of colour, serious vegetable patch, poultry. Carpet of daffodils in spring. Owner-gardeners negotiating steep learning curve. Gravel paths, uneven paving, slope to kitchen garden.

70 LOWDER MILL

Bell Vale Lane, Fernhurst, nr Haslemere GU27 3DJ. Anne & John Denning, 01428 644822. *1$^{1}/_{2}$ m S of Haslemere. 6m N of Midhurst. Follow A286 out of Midhurst towards Haslemere, through Fernhurst and take 2nd R after Kingsley Green into Bell Vale Lane. Lowder Mill approx $^{1}/_{2}$ m on R.* Home-made teas in former water mill, adjoining mill pond. **Adm £3, chd £1.50. Sat 31 May; Sun 1 June (11-5). Visitors also welcome by appt end May, early June for groups of 12+.**
Mill House and former water mill on Sussex/Surrey/Hampshire border. Set in 3 acres of gardens, courtyard, lake, ponds, orchard and kitchen garden.

The gardens had been neglected, but, redesigned by Bunny Guinness in 2002, they are being restored by the present owners, with work still ongoing. Unusual chickens, ducks and resident kingfishers.

71 MALT HOUSE

Chithurst Lane, Rogate GU31 5EZ. Mr & Mrs G Ferguson, 01730 821433. *3m W of Midhurst. From A272, 3$^{1}/_{2}$ m W of Midhurst turn N signed Chithurst then 1$^{1}/_{2}$ m, very narrow lane; or at Liphook turn off A3 onto old A3 (B2070) for 2m before turning L to Milland, then follow signs to Chithurst for 1$^{1}/_{2}$ m.* Light refreshments & teas. **Adm £3, chd free. Sun 27 Apr; Sun 4, Mon 5 May (2-6). Visitors also welcome by appt.**
6 acres; flowering shrubs incl exceptional rhododendrons and azaleas, leading to 50 acres of arboretum and lovely woodland walks plus many rare plants and trees.

Elegant topiary and commanding views . . .

72 THE MANOR OF DEAN

Pitshill, Tillington GU28 9AP. Mr & Mrs James Mitford, 07887 992349, emma@mitford.uk.com. *3m W of Petworth. On A272 from Petworth to Midhurst. Pass through Tillington village. A272 then opens up to short section of dual carriageway. Turn R at end of this section and proceed N, entrance to garden approx $^{1}/_{2}$ m.* Home-made teas. **Adm £2.50, chd free. Sats, Suns 17 Feb; 15, 16 Mar, 19, 20 Apr; 17, 18 May; 14, 15 June; 19, 20 July; 17 Aug; 13, 14 Sept (2-5). Visitors also welcome by appt.**
Approx 3 acres. Traditional English garden, herbaceous borders, a variety of early-flowering bulbs and snowdrops, spring bulbs, grass walks, walled kitchen garden with vegetables and fruit, some available for purchase. Asparagus bed. Lawns, rose garden and informal areas. Some house renovation in progress, may affect parts of the garden.

73 NEW MANVILLES FIELD

Bedham Lane, Fittleworth RH20 1JH. Mrs P Aschan. *3m SE of Petworth. Just off A283 between Petworth and Pulborough, 400yds along lane signed Bedham.* **Adm £3, chd free. Every Wed in May & June (2-5). Also open Weds in May & June Fittleworth House.**
2-acre established garden, returning to the NGS in 2008, featuring a wonderful mix of shrubs, clematis, roses and herbaceous perennials. Established trees, orchard, lawns and lovely views.

74 MAYFIELD GARDENS

TN20 6TE. *10m S of Tunbridge Wells. Exit A267 into Mayfield. At N end of village turn R at Costcutter, signed car park. Follow yellow signs to first garden, detailed map available.* Home-made teas at Warren House. **Combined adm £4, chd free. Sun 8 June (2-5.30).**
Attractive old Wealden village in conservation area dating back to Saxon times.

LAUREL COTTAGE
South Street. Barrie Martin
Cottage garden with variety of plants and shrubs and attractive view.

MAY COTTAGE
Fletching Street. Kathleen & Ian Lyle
Cottage garden. Wide variety of interesting plants, shrubs and trees, raised beds, small pond.

SUNNYBANK COTTAGE
Fletching Street. Eve & Paul Amans
S-facing informal garden with views and well-stocked feature bank with numerous specimen shrubs.

UPPERCROSS HOUSE
South Street. Mrs Rosemary Owen
Cottage garden with good views. Plenty of shrubs and plants and water feature.

NEW THE VALE
Vale Road. Jon & Sue Barnes
Informal gardens extending to
1¼ acres with outstanding
southerly views.

WARREN HOUSE
The Warren. C Lyle
2-acre family garden with good
range of shrubs, meadow and
stream. Sculptures.
⌖ ✄

75 ◆ MERRIMENTS GARDENS
Hurst Green TN19 7RA. Mr D Weeks
& Mrs P Weeks, 01580 860666,
info@merriments.co.uk. *1m N of
Hurst Green. Between Hawkhurst &
Hurst Green.* **Adm £4.50, chd £2.**
**Easter to end Sept, Mon to Sat
(10-5), Sun (10.30-5). For NGS: Sun
6 July (10.30-5); Sat 20 Sept (10-5).**
4-acre garden of richly and
imaginatively planted deep curved
borders, colour themed using a rich
mix of trees, shrubs, perennials,
grasses and many unusual annuals
which ensure an arresting display of
colour, freshness and vitality from
spring to autumn. Featured on BBC
Gardeners' World.
⌖ ❀ ☕

76 MITCHMERE FARM
Stoughton PO18 9JW. Neil & Sue
Edden, 02392 631456,
sue@mitchmere.ndo.co.uk. *5½ m
NW of Chichester. Turn off the B2146
at Walderton towards Stoughton. Farm
is ¾ m on L, ¼ m beyond the turning
to Upmarden.* **Adm £3, chd free.** Sun
10, Thur 14, Sun 17 Feb (11-4); Sun
8, Thur 12, Sun 15 Feb 2009. Visitors
also welcome by appt mid Jan to
mid Mar.
1½ -acre garden started in 1991 in
lovely downland position. Unusual
trees and shrubs, many coloured
stems or catkins growing in dry
gravel, briefly wet most years when
the Winterbourne rises and flows
through the garden. Drifts of
snowdrops and crocuses. Small
collection of special snowdrops. Small
formal kitchen garden, free-range
bantams. Wellies advisable. Local
craftspeople selling garden-related
products; Sussex Snowdrop Trust stall;
paintings by local artists. Featured in
'Country Living' & article by Anna
Pavord in 'Independent'. Gravel and
shallow steps but alternative grass
paths.
⌖ ✄ ❀ ☕ ☎

77 NEW MOOR FARM
Horsham Road, Petworth
GU28 0HD. Richard Chandler,
01798 342161,
richardandflo1@btinternet.com.
*1m E of Petworth. Off A272,
signed by cottage.* **Adm £3.50.**
Visitors welcome by appt April
to July, for coaches and groups
of 10+.
Enjoy the many pleasures of the
countryside on this arable farm
with Countryside Stewardship,
featuring wildlfe and wild flowers,
lakes and birds. Take a farm trailer
ride past bluebell woods and
wildlife (the nightingales are
abundant in April and early
summer). Learn what goes on in
arable farming today and ask the
questions you've always wanted
answered!
✄ ⌂ ☕ ☎

Take a farm
trailer ride past
bluebell woods
and wildlife (the
nightingales are
abundant in
April and early
summer) . . .

78 MOORLANDS
Friar's Gate, nr Crowborough
TN6 1XF. Dr & Mrs Steven Smith &
Dr Lucy & Mr Mark Love, 01892
652474. *2m N of Crowborough. St
Johns Rd to Friar's Gate. Or turn L off
B2188 at Friar's Gate signed Horder
Hospital.* **Adm £4, chd free.** Every
Wed 2 Apr to 29 Oct (11-5). Visitors
also welcome by appt.
4 acres set in lush valley deep in
Ashdown Forest; water garden with
ponds, streams and river; primulas,
rhododendrons, azaleas. River walk
with grasses and bamboos. Rockery
restored to original 1929 design. The
many special trees planted 28yrs ago
make this garden an arboretum.
❀ ☕ ☎

**79 MOUNT HARRY HOUSE &
MOUNT HARRY LODGE**
Ditchling Road, Offham BN7 3QW.
Lord & Lady Renton, Mr & Mrs
Stewart-Roberts. *2m N of Lewes. On
S side of Ditchling Rd B2116, ½ m W
of A275.* Home-made teas. **Adm £4,
chd free.** Sat 7 June (2-5).
2 adjoining 7-acre and 1-acre terraced
gardens on chalk. Herbaceous and
shrubbery borders, wild flower walk,
specimen trees, laburnum walks,
walled garden, dell garden,
conservatory, ornamental tree
nursery. In beautiful downland
setting.
⌖ ❀ ☕

80 MOUNTFIELD COURT
nr Robertsbridge TN32 5JP. Mr &
Mrs Simon Fraser. *3m N of Battle. On
A21 London-Hastings; ½ m from
Johns Cross.* Home-made teas. **Adm
£3.50, chd free.** Sun 11 May (2-5).
3-acre wild woodland garden;
walkways through exceptional
rhododendrons, azaleas, camellias and
other flowering shrubs; fine trees and
outstanding views. Small paved herb
garden.
☕

81 NEW BARN
Egdean, nr Petworth RH20 1JX. Mr
& Mrs Adrian Tuck, 01798 865502.
*2m SE of Petworth. ½ m S of Petworth
turn off A285 to Pulborough, at 2nd
Xrds turn R into lane. Or 1m W of
Fittleworth take L fork to Midhurst off
A283. 150yds turn L.* Home-made
teas. **Adm £3, chd free.** Mon 25 Aug
(10.30-5.30). Visitors also welcome
by appt.
Converted C18 barn (not open) with
2-acre garden in beautiful peaceful
farmland setting. Large natural pond
and stream. Owner-maintained and
planned for yr-round interest from
snowdrops, camellias, spring flowers,
masses of bluebells, azaleas, water-
irises, roses, shrubs and herbaceous
through to autumn colour. Trees
planted for flower, bark and leaf. Seats
and 2 swings. Fountain by H Bowden.
New sculpture.
⌖ ✄ ❀ ☕ ☎

82 NEWTIMBER PLACE
Newtimber BN6 9BU. Mr & Mrs
Andrew Clay, www.newtimber.co.uk.
*7m N of Brighton. From A23, take
A281 towards Henfield. Turn R at small
Xrds signed Newtimber in approx ½ m.*
Home-made teas. **Adm £3.50, chd
free.** Sun 31 Aug (2-5.30).

Beautiful C17 moated house (not open). Gardens and woods full of bulbs and wild flowers in spring. In summer, roses, herbaceous border and lawns. Moat flanked by water plants. Mature trees. Wild garden, ducks, chickens and fish. Gravel drive, humped bridges. Unfenced moat; children must be supervised.

83 THE NOOK
New Road, Southwater RH13 9AU. Les White, 01403 730401, leswhite500@btinternet.com. *2m S of Horsham at N end of Southwater. At Hop Oast roundabout on A24 S of Horsham, take rd to Southwater. Next roundabout, 2nd exit. New Rd is on R towards end of stretch of straight rd.* Light refreshments & home-made teas. **Adm £3, chd free. Sat 31 May; Sun 1 June (10-5). Visitors also welcome by appt.**
Primarily a wildlife garden. Stone, bark and decking pathways lead you around natural streams, ponds, rocks and woodpiles. Ferns, grasses, bamboos and mature trees dominate the scene, although there are contrasting areas such as Mediterranean, patio, planted walls and traditional borders. Featured on BBC Southern Counties Radio. Some deep water; children must be accompanied.

84 NORTH SPRINGS
Bedham, nr Fittleworth RH20 1JP. Mr & Mrs R Haythornthwaite. *Between Fittleworth and Wisborough Green. From Wisborough Green take A272 towards Petworth. Turn L into Fittleworth Rd signed Coldharbour. Proceed 1¹/₂ m. From Fittleworth take Bedham Lane off A283 and proceed for approx 3m NE. Limited parking.* Home-made teas. **Adm £3, chd free. Sun 8 June (12-5).**
Hillside garden with beautiful views surrounded by mixed woodland. Focus on structure with a wide range of mature trees and shrubs. Stream, pond and bog area. Abundance of roses, clematis, hostas, rhododendrons and azaleas.

85 NYEWOOD HOUSE
Nyewood, nr Rogate GU31 5JL. Mr & Mrs C J Wright, 01730 821563, suewarren@compuserve.com. *4m E of Petersfield. From A272 at Rogate take South Harting rd for 1¹/₂ m. Turn L*

at pylon towards South Downs Hotel. Nyewood House 2nd on R over cattle grid. Cream teas. **Adm £3, chd free. Sat 7, Sun 8 June (2-6). Also open 7, 8 June Sandhill Farm House. Visitors also welcome by appt April to July.**
Victorian country house garden with stunning views of S Downs. 3 acres comprising formal gardens with rose walk and arbours, pleached hornbeam, colour-themed herbaceous borders, shrub borders, lily pond and kitchen garden. Wooded area featuring wild orchids. New soft fruit area. Gravel driveway.

86 ◆ NYMANS
Handcross RH17 6EB. The National Trust, 01444 405250, www.nationaltrust.org.uk. *4m S of Crawley. On B2114 at Handcross signed off M23/A23 London-Brighton rd. Bus: 73 from Hove or Crawley & 271 from Haywards Heath.* **Adm £8, chd £4. Opening days & times vary according to season. Please phone or see website for details. For NGS: Suns 6 July; 14 Sept (10-5).**
One of the greatest C20 gardens in the country with an important collection of rare plants, set around a romantic house and ruins in the natural wooded estate. The garden design incl a pinetum, heather garden, rose garden, wisteria-clad pergola, walled garden, summer borders and massed plantings of magnolias, camellias and rhododendrons. Garden tours with NGS-sponsored Nymans Careership Student. Featured on BBC TV & Radio, and in many publications incl 'Telegraph', 'Observer', 'Mirror' and 'Country Living'.

87 OFFHAM HOUSE
Offham BN7 3QE. Mr S Goodman & Mr & Mrs P Carminger, m.carminger@talk21.com. *2m N of Lewes on A275. Cooksbridge stn ¹/₂ m.* Home-made teas. **Adm £3.50, chd free (share to Lewes Victoria Hospital League of Friends). Suns 27 Apr; 1 June (1-5). Visitors also welcome by appt 2 weeks either side of open days.**
Fountains, flowering trees, double herbaceous border, long peony bed. 1676 Queen Anne house (not open) with well-knapped flint facade. Herb garden. Walled kitchen garden with glasshouses.

Meandering through L-shaped plot . . . designed to reveal itself in stages . . .

OLD BUCKHURST
See Kent.

88 THE OLD POST OFFICE
London Road, Coldwaltham RH20 1LG. Patrick & Stephanie Fane. *2m S of Pulborough. On A29. 300yds S of St Giles' Church. Parking in Sandham Hall car park next door.* **Adm £2.50, chd free. Evening Opening, wine, Sun 27 Apr (5-7). Sun 7 Sept (2-5).**
Enthusiastic plantaholic's garden, meandering through L-shaped plot. Designed to reveal itself in stages with planting for yr-round colour, form and texture. Plants for sandy soil or special areas (bog garden, loggery) incl trees, shrubs, roses, climbers, perennials and bulbs. 2 ponds, potager, hillock with summerhouse. Unfenced ponds, small children must be supervised.

89 OLD SCAYNES HILL HOUSE
Clearwater Lane, Scaynes Hill RH17 7NF. Sue & Andy Spooner, 01444 831602. *2m E of Haywards Heath. On A272, 50yds down Sussex border path beside BP Garage shop, & opp Farmers Inn. No parking at garden (drop off only), please park considerately in village.* Home-made teas. **Adm £3, chd free (share to Court Meadow Assn). Sat 21, Sun 22 June (2-5.30). Visitors also welcome by appt June & July only for groups of 10+.**
In memory of Sarah Robinson. Entrance archway with steps leading to 1-acre natural garden on S-facing slope of predominantly heavy clay. Mature trees and shrubs with some unusual specimens. Several colourful herbaceous borders and island beds with ornamental grasses. Many roses, small wild flower meadow with orchids, woodland walk, small orchard, fruit and vegetable area, bog garden and natural-looking pond.

90 64 OLD SHOREHAM ROAD
Hove BN3 6GF. Brian & Muriel
Bailey, 01273 889247,
baileybm@ntlworld.com. *A270. On S
side between Shirley Drive & Upper
Drive.* Home-made teas. **Adm £2.50,
chd free. Sat 28 June (2-5.30).
Visitors also welcome by appt,
groups of 4+.**
12.6m by 33.6m designed and built by
owners. S-facing on chalk with
secluded terrace, conservatory,
pergola, rose arbour, bog garden,
arches, trellises, vegetable garden,
alpine beds, parterre, ponds, waterfall,
many clematis and hostas. Automatic
watering.
&. ✗ ✿ ☕ ☎

**91 NEW PALATINE & OAK
GROVE GARDENS**
Worthing BN12 6JP. Mrs Jennie
Rollings, 01903 708870,
jrollings@wsgfl.org.uk. *1m W of
Worthing.* Turn S off A259 at
roundabout onto The Boulevard,
signed Goring. Take R turn at next
roundabout into Palatine Rd.
School approx 100yds on R.
Direction to Oak Grove available at
Palatine School. **Combined adm
£3.50, chd free. Suns 8 June; 13
July (11-5). Visitors also
welcome by appt, coaches and
groups of 10+.**
Two, large, closely located, award-
winning gardens created by
teachers, volunteers and children
with special needs. One price, two
gardens. Tickets and entry at
Palatine Gardens.
&. ✿ ☕ ☎

**NEW OAK GROVE COLLEGE
GARDENS**
In contrast to Palatine, Oak Grove
College, opening for the first time
for the NGS, is an example of a
garden-in-the-making, showing
how much can be achieved in less
than 3yrs. Waterwise gardens,
large courtyard with seating area,
water feature, sculptures and
extensive planting, memorial
gardens, spiral herb garden, large
food growing area, polytunnels,
living willow and reclaimed
woodland. Gold Award SE in
Bloom Schools Competition.
Worthing in Bloom: Best School
Garden and School Project; Highly
Commended Waterwise Garden.
Contributor to Chris Beardshaw's
'Growing Schools Garden', Best
in Show at RHS Hampton Court
Flower Show.

**PALATINE SCHOOL
GARDENS**
Palatine Road, Worthing,
www.goring-by-
sea.com/palatine
This large, mature garden, with its
varied collection of plants, never
ceases to surprise visitors.
Conservation and wildlife areas
with with large and small ponds
and bog garden. Sea garden,
oriental garden, dry gardens,
thinking garden, rockeries, echium
walk, labyrinth, mosaics, picnic
areas and interesting tree
collection.

Gold Award South East in Bloom Schools Competition . . .

92 ◆ PARHAM GARDENS
Parham Park, Storrington, nr
Pulborough RH20 4HS. Home of
Lady Emma & Mr James Barnard,
01903 742021,
www.parhaminsussex.co.uk. *4m SE
of Pulborough. On A283 Pulborough-
Storrington rd.* **House & garden adm
£7.50, chd £3.50, concessions
£6.50. Garden only £5.50, chd £2.50,
concessions £4.50. 23 Mar to 28
Sept, gardens Tues to Fris, Suns &
Bank Hol Mons, house Weds, Thurs,
Suns & Bank Hol Mons. Garden
weekend 12, 13 July.**
Famous for its long tradition of
beautiful arrangements within the
house, all the flowers at Parham are
grown in its romantic walled garden.
Regimented rows contrast dramatically
with enormous herbaceous borders
overflowing with 'Edwardian opulence'!
Weird vegetables, brick and turf maze,
lake and arguably the most sensual
greenhouse in Sussex.
&. ✿ ☕

93 PARK LODGE
Bedham Lane, Fittleworth
RH20 1JH. Mark & Louise Saunders.
*3m SE of Petworth. On A283 midway
between Petworth and Pulborough on
lane signed to Bedham and
Wisborough Green, 150yds on L.* **Adm
£2.50, chd free. Suns 8 June; Sun 14
Sept (1-5).**

1/2 -acre head gardener's cottage
garden now in its 4th yr of planning
and development. New hedges of
beech and yew and rose-covered
pergola planted to create rooms
within the garden. Wildlife pond,
chickens, mixed borders,
summerhouse surrounded by
vegetables and bold display of dahlias.
Also open, walled kitchen garden and
new glasshouse of Fittleworth House
(see separate entry).
&. ✗

94 6 PARK TERRACE
Tillington, Petworth GU28 9AE. Mr &
Mrs H Bowden, 01798 343588,
isabellebowden@aol.com. *On A272,
between Midhurst & Petworth. 1m W
of Petworth, turn uphill at sign to
Tillington Village, past Horseguards PH
and church, no 6 is past village hall.
Please do not park in residents'
spaces but further up the lane.* Light
refreshments & home-made teas. **Adm
£3, chd free. Day & Evening
Opening** with wine, Sun 15 June
(11-9). Thur 19 June; Sun 28 Sept
(11-5). **Visitors also welcome by
appt. Coaches & groups up to 40
welcome.** Lunches, teas & evening
snacks by arrangement, plenty of
room to sit and eat.
Terraces under ivy, wisteria and roses.
Small ponds, aviary, archways,
topiaries, leafy tunnels and a large
dome covered in fruit trees, clematis,
jasmine and roses. Sunset terrace
with S Downs views. Raised dry
beds, herbaceous beds, lots of
shrubs, pigsty and greenhouse.
Garden designed for entertaining. It
provides lots of quiet retreats in
complete privacy, basking to the
sound of water from fountains made
by Humphrey.
✿ ☕ ☎

95 PARSONAGE FARM
Kirdford RH14 0NH. David & Victoria
Thomas. *5m NE of Petworth. Take
A283 from Petworth, fork R signed
Kirdford and Balls Cross. After approx
5m and after Kirdford village sign on L,
turn R just before T-junction to
Plaistow.* Teas & wine. **Adm £4, chd
free. Day & Evening Opening,** wine,
Fri 27 June (2-9). Sun 7 Sept (2-6).
Major garden under restoration and
development, now growing to maturity
in parts. 5 acres of formal gardens on a
grand scale, C18 walled garden,
topiary walk, pleached lime allée, tulip
tree avenue, rose borders, vegetable
garden, trained fruit, lake and turf

amphitheatre. Recent developments are the planting of an autumn shrubbery and holm oak avenue. Owner and Head Gardener available to give advice.

 ♿ ✕ ☕

96 18 PAVILION ROAD
Worthing BN14 7EF. Andrew Muggeridge & Ya-Hui Lee. *Nr Worthing main stn.* **Adm £2.50. Suns 27 Apr; 4, 18 May; 1, 15 June (1-4).** Town garden. This is a plantsman's garden: many unusual perennials, lots of grasses, many infill plants throughout the season. Sunflowers, leonotis and seasonal pots. The design is always changing, described as 'organised chaos', plenty to see. Regret not suitable for children or wheelchairs. Featured in 'The English Garden', 'Amateur Gardening', 'Sussex Life' & 'County Times'.

✕ ⚘

Croquet lawn (open for play) . . . Dahlia mania corner . . .

97 PEASMARSH PLACE
Church Lane, Peasmarsh TN31 6XE. Viscount Devonport, 01797 223398, jmcarree@hotmail.com. *3¹/₂ m NW of Rye. From A268 in Peasmarsh take Church Lane (signed Norman Church), garden 1m on R after church.* Home-made teas. **Adm £3.50, chd free. Suns 4 May; 26 Oct (2-5). Visitors also welcome by appt.**
7-acre garden surrounding Peasmarsh Place (not open). Yew-enclosed rose garden and various features with an Alice in Wonderland connection. Fine display of spring flowers and autumn colour. Contains National Collections of limes and sweet chestnuts. Large and varied arboretum mostly planted since 1976 with fine walks and outdoor sculpture.

♿ ✕ ⚘ NCCPG ☕ ☎

98 33 PEERLEY ROAD
East Wittering PO20 8PD. Paul & Trudi Harrison, 01243 673215, stixandme@aol.com. *7m S of Chichester. From A286 take B2198 to*

Bracklesham. Turn R into Stocks Lane then L at Royal British Legion into Legion Way & follow rd round to Peerley Rd halfway along. **Adm £2.50, chd free. Suns 22 June; 14 Sept (12-4). Visitors also welcome by appt.**
Small garden 65ft x 32ft, 110yds from sea. Packed full of ideas and unusual plants using every inch of space to create unusual rooms and places for adults and children to play. Specialising in unusual plants that grow well in seaside conditions. A must for any suburban gardener. Great winter interest.

✕ ⚘ ☎

99 PEMBURY HOUSE
Ditchling Road (New Road), Clayton, nr Hassocks BN6 9PH. Nick & Jane Baker, 01273 842805, www.pemburyhouse.co.uk. *6m N of Brighton. On B2112, 110 metres from A273.* Feb & Mar openings: some parking at the house, otherwise parking at village green. Light refreshments & teas. **Adm £3, chd free. Tues, Weds, Thurs: 26, 27, 28 Feb; 4, 5, 6 Mar (11-4); Weds, Thurs, Fris, 11 Feb to 20 Feb 2009** £3.50 (11-4). **Visitors also welcome by appt in February 2008 only, for groups of 15+.**
Ours is a garden where the Christmas Day flower count often exceeds 50 different types. Depending on the season, winter-flowering shrubs, hellebores and drifts of snowdrops are at their best Feb/Mar. The hellebores are a great source of joy, with each individual flower asking to be turned up and admired. Winding paths give a choice of garden walks, with views to the S Downs and countryside. Lots of seats and secret places. Wellies and winter woollies advised. Filmed by BBC Gardeners' World. Limited wheelchair access in winter.

♿ ⚘ ☕ ☎

100 PENNS IN THE ROCKS
Groombridge TN3 9PA. Lady Gibson, 01892 864244. *7m SW of Tunbridge Wells. On B2188 Groombridge to Crowborough rd just S of Plumeyfeather corner.* Home-made teas. **Adm £1. Suns 30 Mar; 10 Aug (2.30-5.30). Visitors also welcome by appt.**
Large wild garden with rocks, lake, C18 temple and old walled garden with herbaceous, roses and shrubs. House (not open) part C18. Dogs under control in park only (no shade in car park). Group visits by arrangement.

✕ ⚘ ☕ ☎

101 PERRYHILL FARMHOUSE
Hartfield TN7 4JP. John & Diana Whitmore, 01892 770266, dianawhitmore@gmail.com. *7m E of East Grinstead. Midway between E Grinstead & Tunbridge Wells. 1m N of Hartfield on B2026. Turn into unmade lane adjacent to Perryhill Nurseries.* Home-made teas. **Adm £4, chd free. Sats, Suns 31 May; 1 June; 16, 17 Aug (2-5). Visitors also welcome by appt.**
1¹/₂ acres, set below beautiful C15 hall house (not open), with stunning views of Ashdown Forest. Herbaceous and mixed borders, formal rose garden and climbing rose species, water garden, parterre, pergola. Many varieties of unusual shrubs and trees. Croquet lawn (open for play). Top and soft fruit. Productive Victorian greenhouse. Dahlia mania corner.

♿ ✕ ⚘ ☕ ☎

102 PINDARS
Lyminster, nr Arundel BN17 7QF. Mr & Mrs Clive Newman, 01903 882628, pindars@btinternet.com. *2m S of Arundel. Lyminster on A284 between A27 & A259. 1m S of A27 Pindars on L. Park beyond house in designated field.* Home-made teas. **Adm £3, chd free. Thur 5, Wed 18 June (2-5). Visitors also welcome by appt May to July only, for groups of 10-20 approx.**
Owner designed, created and maintained garden of herbaceous and shrub borders (with interesting and unusual plants), Mediterranean gravel and grasses area, new shady scree garden. Vegetable patch, rugosa hedges and trees that have matured along with their owners! Some gravel paths.

♿ ✕ ⚘ ☕ ☗ ☕ ☎

103 PINE COTTAGE
Rackham, Pulborough RH20 2EU. Rob & Glenys Rowe. *4m S of Pulborough. From Pulborough take A283 to Storrington, after 4m turn into Greatham Rd. Follow Rackham signs. From Arundel take A284 then B2139 to Storrington. After Amberley turn L into Rackham St. Please park as indicated, no roadside parking please. Garden entrance via public footpath adjacent to Rackham Old School and Rackham Woods.* Home-made teas. **Adm £3, chd free. Sun 8 June (2-5).**
The 4-acre garden has been sympathetically developed since 1995 to fit into the surrounding unspoilt landscape of the S Downs and Arun

Valley. 3 large ponds, wild flower meadows, kitchen garden and orchard. Relaxed planting with native species gives a naturalistic feel and encourages as wide a range of wildlife as possible. Organic principles are applied throughout the garden. Deep water, children must be strictly supervised.

✗ ✿ ☕

Secret gardens, wild flower meadows and crumbly gothic ruins all show to delightful effect in a garden full of surprises . . .

104 6 PLANTATION RISE
Worthing BN13 2AH. Mr & Mrs N Hall, 01903 262206, trixiehall@btinternet.com. 2m from sea front on outskirts of Worthing. A24 meets A27 at Offington roundabout. Proceed into Offington Lane. Take 1st R into The Plantation, 1st R again to Plantation Rise. Please park in The Plantation, short walk to Plantation Rise. Light refreshments & home-made teas. Adm £3, chd free. Sat 5 (10-4), Sun 6 Apr (1-5). Visitors also welcome by appt all year. Award-winning garden 70ft x 80ft lovingly landscaped by owners. Featuring pond, summerhouse, pergolas, various trees and shrubs. Perennial plants, all-yr colour. Spring bulbs and heathers. Featured in 'Daily Mail' & 'Ideal Homes'.

& ✗ ☕ ☎

105 ◆ THE PRIEST HOUSE
North Lane, West Hoathly RH19 4PP. Sussex Archaeological Society, 01342 810479, www.sussexpast.co.uk/priest. 4m SW of East Grinstead. Turn E to West Hoathly 1m S of Turners Hill at the Selsfield Common junction on B2028. 2m S turn R into North Lane. Garden ¼ m further on. House & garden adm £2, chd £1. Garden only £1, chd free. Within walking distance of Duckyls Holt. Combined adm £4, chd free. Tues to Sats & BH Mons Mar to Oct (10.30-5.30). For NGS:

Sats 24 May; 21 June (10.30-5.30). C15 timber-framed house with cottage garden. Large selection of culinary and medicinal herbs in small formal garden with mixed herbaceous borders, plus long-established yew topiary, box hedges and espalier apple trees. Small woodland garden with fernery. Adm to Priest House Museum £1 for NGS visitors.

✿

106 RIDGE HOUSE
East Street, Turners Hill RH10 4PU. Mr & Mrs Nicholas Daniels, 01342 715344. 4m SW of East Grinstead. 3m E of Crawley. On B2110, 5m SE of J10 M23. Via A264 & B2028. 30yds E of Crown PH on Turners Hill Xrds. Parking at recreation ground E of Ridge House. Home-made teas. Adm £3, chd free. Sat 21, Sun 22 June (2-6). Visitors also welcome by appt June only, groups of 10+, coaches permitted. 1-acre garden with mixed borders, Victorian greenhouse, pond, dell and productive vegetable garden. Nigel's garden gives all-yr interest and offers a quiet corner to absorb the beautiful view of the High Weald of Sussex. The garden offers interest, calm and unexpected vistas.

& ✿ ☕ ☎

107 RINGMER PARK
Ringmer, Lewes BN8 5RW. Deborah & Michael Bedford. On A26 Lewes to Uckfield rd. 1½ m NE of Lewes, 5m S of Uckfield. Home-made teas. Adm £4, chd free. Thurs, Suns 12, 15, 19, 22 June; Suns 20 July; 21 Sept (2-5). Densely-planted 6-acre garden created by the owners over the last 20yrs. A formal garden with soft edges, the emphasis is on continuous flowering from spring bulb displays through to Oct, with bold and dramatic blocks of colour. Features incl a striking hot garden, rose garden, pergola covered with roses and clematis and bordered by peonies, double herbaceous borders and much more. Outstanding views of the S Downs.

& ☕

108 ROSE COTTAGE
Hadlow Down TN22 4HJ. Ken & Heather Mines, 01825 830314, kenmines@hotmail.com. 6m NE of Uckfield. After entering village on A272, turn L (100yds) by phone box just after New Inn, follow signs. Home-made teas. Adm £3, chd free. Suns 27 Apr; 25 May; 15 June (2-5.30). Evening Opening £5, wine, Fri 27 June (6-8). Visitors also welcome by appt.

Plantsman's ⅔ -acre garden. Old-fashioned roses, exuberant planting and luxuriance within a strong design results in a garden that visitors refer to as harmonious and tranquil and which evokes memories of childhood. Self-seeding is encouraged, so a constantly-changing garden. Collection of David Newman sculptues are integral to the design, further enhanced by Victorian church stonework. Bug hunt and fact sheets for children and adults.

✗ ✿ ☕ ☎

109 ROUNDHILL COTTAGE
East Dean PO18 0JF. Mr Jeremy Adams, 01243 811447. 7m NE of Chichester. Take A286 towards Midhurst. At Singleton follow signs to Charlton/East Dean. In East Dean turn R at Star & Garter Inn, Roundhill is approx 100yds. Home-made teas. Adm £3, chd free. Sun 25, Mon 26 May (2-6). Visitors also welcome by appt. 1-acre country garden set in tranquil fold of the S Downs, designed in 1980 by Judith Adams whose inspiration came from French impressionists and continued by her daughter Louise, whose love of secret gardens, wild flower meadows and crumbly gothic ruins all show to delightful effect in a garden full of surprises. Come and enjoy.

& ✗ ☕ ☎

110 RYMANS
Apuldram PO20 7EG. Mrs Michael Gayford, 01243 783147. 1m S of Chichester. Take Witterings rd, at 1½ m SW turn R signed Dell Quay. Turn 1st R, garden ½ m on L. Home-made teas. Adm £3.50, chd free. Sats, Suns 19, 20 Apr; 14, 15 June; 6, 7 Sept (2-5). Visitors also welcome by appt. Walled and other gardens surrounding lovely C15 stone garden (not open); bulbs, flowering shrubs, roses, ponds, potager. Many unusual and rare trees and shrubs. Exhibition and sale of work by Fine Cell Work.

✿ ☕ ☎

111 ◆ ST MARY'S HOUSE & GARDENS
Bramber BN44 3WE. Mr Peter Thorogood, 01903 816205, www.stmarysbramber.co.uk. 1m E of Steyning. 10m NW of Brighton in Bramber Village off A283. Adm £3.50, chd £1. House open to public at other times; please phone or see

website for details. For NGS: Fri 18, Sat 19 July (2-5.30).
Five acres of gardens, incl charming formal topiary beds, ancient ivy-clad 'Monk's walk', large example of the prehistoric ginkgo biloba, and magnificent magnolia grandiflora around Grade I listed C15 timber-framed medieval house, once a pilgrim inn. The Victorian 'Secret' gardens also incl splendid 140ft fruit wall, rural museum, terracotta garden, the delightful Jubilee rose garden, pineapple pits and English poetry garden. Featured in 'Etc' magazine.

112 SANDHILL FARM HOUSE
Nyewood Road, Rogate GU31 5HU. Rosemary Alexander, 01730 818373, www.rosemaryalexander.co.uk, r.a.alexander@talk21.com. *4m SE of Petersfield. From A272 Xrds in Rogate, take rd S signed Nyewood/Harting. Follow rd for approx 1m over small bridge. Sandhill Farm House on R, over cattle grid.* Teas (Suns only) at The Malt House, South Harting. **Adm £3.50, chd free.** Sats, Suns 26, 27 Apr; 7, 8 June; 20, 21 Sept (2-5). Also open 7, 8 June **Nyewood House. Visitors also welcome by appt, groups of 10+.**
Front and rear gardens are broken up into garden rooms. Front garden incl small woodland area planted with early spring flowering shrubs and bulbs, white garden and hot dry terraced area. Rear garden has mirror borders, small decorative vegetable garden and 'red' border. New grit and grasses garden. Home of author and Principal of The English Gardening School.

113 ◆ SARAH RAVEN'S CUTTING GARDEN
Perch Hill Farm, Willingford Lane, Brightling TN32 5HP. Sarah Raven, 01424 838013, www.perchhill.co.uk. *7m SW of Hurst Green. From A21 Hurst Green take A265 Heathfield Rd for 6m. In Burwash turn L by church, go 3m to Xrds at top of hill. At large green triangle, R down Willingford Lane, garden 1/2 m on R.* Field parking, uneven ground. **Adm £4, chd under 14 free, concessions £3.** 26, 27 Apr; 14, 15 June; 23, 24 Aug (9.30-5). For NGS: Sun 21 Sept (10-4).
Inspirational, intensive and productive 2-acre garden with rooms full of annuals and biennials for picking. New vegetable and fruit garden. Extravagant mix of colour and

structure: salvias, cardoons, artichokes, brilliantly-coloured dahlias, zinnias, gladioli, cannas, jungly corn and banana foliage. Featured in many publications and on BBC Gardeners' World.

114 SAYERLAND HOUSE
Sayerland Lane, Polegate BN26 6QP. Penny & Kevin Jenden. *2m S of Hailsham, 1m N of Polegate. At Cophall roundabout on A27 take A22, turn L at 1st turning (100yds). Follow through Bay Tree Lane, turn sharp L into Sayerland Lane.* Home-made teas. **Adm £4, chd free.** Sat 9 Aug (2-5.30) **with live folk music.**
5-acre garden surrounding listed C15 house (not open). Several distinct garden areas. Walled garden with colour-themed herbaceous borders, enclosed rose garden, ponds, kitchen garden, wild flower areas and tropical beds. Many mature shrubs and specimen trees.

115 SEDGWICK PARK HOUSE
Horsham RH13 6QQ. John & Clare Davison, 01403 734930, simon@sedgwickpark.com, www.sedgwickpark.co.uk. *1m S of Horsham off A281. Take A281 towards Cowfold/Brighton. Hillier Garden Centre on R, then 1st R into Sedgwick Lane. After Sedgwick sign post, enter N gates of Sedgwick Park. Enter also by W gates via Broadwater Lane, from Copsale or Southwater A24.* Home-made teas. **Adm £4, chd free.** Suns 18 May; 14 July (12-5). **Visitors also welcome by appt, horticultural societies and garden clubs.**
Extensive parkland, meadows and woodland of approx 120 acres. Formal gardens originally landscaped by Harold Peto featuring 20 interlinking pools, cascades and impressive water garden known as 'The White Sea'. Large Horsham stone terraces and lawns look out onto clipped yew hedging and mature trees incl rare, 'Champion' specimen trees. Beautiful secluded rosewalk and colourful borders. Azaleas, rhododendrons and colourful walkways form superb setting for the house. Beyond finest views to S Downs, Chanctonbury Ring and Lancing College Chapel. Featured in 'W Sussex County Times'. Uneven paving, slippery when wet; unfenced ponds and swimming pool.

Wild flower meadows with orchids. Prairie-style plantation and stumpery . . .

116 SENNICOTTS
West Broyle, Chichester PO18 9AJ. Mr & Mrs James Rank. *2m NW of Chichester. From Chichester take B2178 signed Funtington for 2m. Entrance on R. Long drive, ample parking nr house. From Fishbourne turn N marked Roman Palace then straight on until T-junction. Entrance opp Salt Hill Rd.* Home-made teas. **Adm £3.50, chd free.** Sun 1 June (2-6).
Garden very much in progress. Rhododendrons, azaleas, mature trees and woodland walks. 2 lime tree walks, walled garden with working vegetable garden, lawns and greenhouses. All surrounded by small parkland. .

117 SHALFORD HOUSE
Square Drive, Kingsley Green GU27 3LW. Vernon & Hazel Ellis. *2m S of Haslemere. Just S of border with Surrey on A286. Square Drive is at brow of hill, to the E. Turn L after 0.2m and follow rd to R at bottom of hill.* Home-made teas. **Adm £3.50, chd free.** Suns 18 May; 13 July (2-5.30); 21 Sept (2-5).
10-acre garden designed and created from scratch over last 15yrs. Wonderful hilly setting with terraces, streams, ponds, waterfall, sunken garden, herbaceous borders, productive walled kitchen garden, wild flower meadows with orchids. Prairie-style plantation and stumpery merging into 7-acre woodland. Further 30-acre wood with beech, rhododendrons, bluebells, ponds, Japanese-themed area and woodland walks. Woodland trail incl children's quiz. Dogs permitted in woods only. Regional Finalist 'Country Life' Genius of Place Award.

118 ◆ **SHEFFIELD PARK GARDEN**
Sheffield Park TN22 3QX. The National Trust, 01825 790231, www.nationaltrust.org.uk. *10m S of E Grinstead. 5m NW of Uckfield; E of A275.* **Adm £7.30, chd £3.65 (see website for adm details). Open all yr; please phone or visit website for details. For NGS: Tues 6 May; 7 Oct (10.30-5.30).**
Magnificent 120 acres (40 hectares) landscaped garden laid out in C18 by Capability Brown and Humphry Repton. Further development in early yrs of this century by its owner Arthur G Soames. Centrepiece is original lakes, with many rare trees and shrubs. Beautiful at all times of the year, but noted for its spring and autumn colours. National Collection of Ghent azaleas. Mobility vehicles and wheelchairs available to hire. To pre-book phone 01825 790302.
🚻 ✕ ⊛ **NCCPG**

119 SHERBURNE HOUSE
Eartham, nr Chichester PO18 0LP. Mr & Mrs Angus Hewat, 01243 814261, anne.hewat@virgin.net. *6m NE of Chichester. Approach from A27 Chichester-Arundel rd or A285 Chichester-Petworth rd, nr centre of village, 200yds S of church.* **Adm £3.50, chd free. Visitors welcome by appt, groups and individuals, refreshments by arrangement.**
Chalk garden of approx 2 acres. Shrub and climbing roses, lime-tolerant shrubs, herbaceous, grey-leaved and foliage plants, pots, water feature, small herb garden, kitchen garden potager with octagonal pergola, fruit cage, wild flower meadow and conservatory.
🚻 ✕ ☕ ☎

120 SIGGLE WRIGGLE
Nash Street, Chiddingly/Hailsham BN27 4AA. Mr Paul Hastie, 01825 873134, siggle1@aol.com. *3m NW of Hailsham. From A22 Eastbourne to Uckfield. 1m NW of Boship roundabout turn R into Nash St, signed Gun Hill. 400yds on L opp Marigolds Farm. Please park in Nash St.* **Adm £3.75, chd free. Suns 4 May; 15 June (1-5). Visitors also welcome by appt, May to July only for groups,of 6+.**
Garden of shadows and light. 2-acre garden planted and maintained by present owner since 1996. Garden fans out from C16 cottage (not open) bedecked with old roses. Hornbeam

walk, pond, rose garden, 300ft mixed border, woodland garden, small fruit and vegetable garden, beech ave, yew roundel and rough meadow. Extensive bamboo collection. Gravel paths and some steps.
🚻 ✕ ⊛ ☕ ☎

121 SPARROW HATCH
Cornwell's Bank, nr Newick BN8 4RD. Tony & Jane Welfare. *5m E of Haywards Heath. From A272 turn R into Oxbottom Lane (signed Barcombe), 1/2 m fork L into Narrow Rd, continue to T-junction & park in Chailey Lane (no parking at house).* **Adm £2.50, chd free. Weds, Thurs 28, 29 May; 25, 26 June (2-5).**
Delightful 1/3 -acre plantsman's cottage garden, wholly designed, made and maintained by owners. Many features incl 2 ponds, formal and wildlife, herbaceous borders, shady dell, vegetables, herbs, alpines. Planned for owners' enjoyment and love of growing plants, both usual and unusual. Home propagated and grown plants for sale. Featured in 'Amateur Gardening'.
✕ ⊛

Planned for owners' enjoyment and love of growing plants, both usual and unusual . . .

122 ◆ **STANDEN**
West Hoathly Road, East Grinstead RH19 4NE. The National Trust, 01342 323029, www.nationaltrust.org.uk. *1 1/2 m S of E Grinstead. Signed from B2110 & A22 at Felbridge.* **House & garden £7.80, chd £3.90. Garden only £4.60, chd £2.30. Weds to Suns 15 Mar to 2 Nov, also Mons 21 July to 31 Aug (11-5.30). Last entry to house 4pm. For NGS: Sat 19 July (11-5.30).**
Approx 12 acres of hillside garden, divided into small compartments: notably a quarry garden, kitchen garden and bamboo garden with pool and cascades. Woodland walks and stunning views over the Medway and Ashdown Forest.
🚻 ⊛ ☕

123 STONEHEALED FARM
Streat Lane, Streat BN6 8SA. Lance & Fiona Smith, 01273 891145, afionasmith@hotmail.com. *2m SE of Burgess Hill. From Ditchling B2116, 1m E of Westmeston, turn L (N) signed Streat, 2m on R immed after railway bridge.* Home-made teas. **Adm £3.50, chd free. Mon 5 May; Sun 7 Sept (2-5.30). Visitors also welcome by appt in May & Sept for groups of 10+.**
1 1/2 acres overlooking S Downs. Contrasting areas offer many places to sit and enjoy: the sheltered courtyard terrace, hidden front garden, shady pond with serpentine bridge, secluded circle, gravelled kitchen garden, new lime walk and walnut grove, and the oak tree deck that overlooks it all. Structural planting enhances seasonal bulbs, flowering shrubs, perennials and grasses.
🚻 ✕ ⊛ ☕ ☎

124 TINKERS BRIDGE COTTAGE
Tinkers Lane, Ticehurst TN5 7LU. Mrs M A Landsberg, 01580 200272. *11m SE of Tunbridge Wells. From B2099 1/2 m W Ticehurst, turn N to Three Leg Cross for 1m, R after Bull Inn. House at bottom of hill.* **Adm £5, incl tea, chd free. Sun 1 June (2.30-5.30). Visitors also welcome by appt Apr to Sept.**
12 acres landscaped; stream garden nr house (not open) leading to herbaceous borders, wildlife meadow with ponds and woodland walks. Access over grass.
🚻 ⊛ ☕ ☎

125 TOWN PLACE
Ketches Lane, Freshfield, nr Sheffield Park RH17 7NR. Mr & Mrs A C O McGrath, 01825 790221, mcgrathsussex@hotmail.com, www.townplacegarden.org.uk. *3m E of Haywards Heath. From A275 turn W at Sheffield Green into Ketches Lane for Lindfield. 1 3/4 m on L.* Cream teas. **Adm £4, chd free. Thurs 12, 19 June. Suns 22, 29 June; 6, 13 July (2-6). Visitors also welcome by appt 8 June to 12 July only for groups of 20+, £6 per person.**
3 acres with over 600 roses, 150ft herbaceous border, walled herb garden, shrubbery, ancient hollow oak, orchard and potager. 'Green' Priory Church and Cloisters. C17 Sussex farmhouse (not open). Featured in 'Groei & Bloei' Classic English border.
🚻 ✕ ⊛ ☕ ☎

126 ◆ UPPARK
South Harting GU31 5QR. The
National Trust, 01730 825415,
www.nationaltrust.org.uk. $1^1/_2$ m S of
S Harting. 5m SE of Petersfield on
B2146. **House & garden £7.80, chd
£3.90. Garden only £3.80, chd £1.70.
Suns to Thurs 16 Mar to 30 Oct
11.30-5. For NGS: Thurs 5 June; 3
July (11.30-5).**
Intimate restored picturesque garden
nestles behind Uppark House, in
contrast to the sweeping panoramic
views to the S. Gardener leads tours at
12 and 2.30 to tell the history and
development of the site. Fine restored
mansion.
 ♿ ✗ ✿ ☕

Kitchen garden
lovingly restored
with working
Victorian
glasshouse . . .

---

127 UPWALTHAM BARNS
Upwaltham GU28 0LX. Roger & Sue
Kearsey. 6m S of Petworth. 6m N of
Chichester on A285. Light
refreshments, home-made teas &
wine. **Adm £3.50, chd free (share to
St Mary the Virgin). Sun 4, Mon 5
May; Weds 18 June; 10 Sept (11-5).**
Unique farm setting has been
transformed into a garden of many
rooms. Entrance is a tapestry of
perennial planting to set off C17 flint
barns. At the rear, walled terraced
garden redeveloped and planted in an
abundance of unusual plants.
Extensive vegetable garden. New ideas
for 2008. Roam at leisure, relax and
enjoy at every season, with lovely
views of S Downs and C12 Shepherds
Church (open to visitors).
♿ ✗ ✿ ☕

128 VILLA ELISABETTA
Cousley Wood, Wadhurst TN5 6HA.
Jim & Kathy Cooper, 07803 134720,
cooper-j9@sky.com. 6m S of
Tunbridge Wells. Off B2100 halfway
between Wadhurst and Lamberhurst.

Light refreshments & home-made teas.
Adm £3, chd free. Sun 15 July (2-5).
Visitors also welcome by appt, small
groups only, parking limited.
Garden of $1^1/_2$ acres with roses,
specimen trees and shrubs,
herbaceous and themed gardens. Yr-
round interest and lots of places to sit
and enjoy. Surprises round every
corner.
♿ ✗ ✿ ☕ ☎

**129 ◆ THE WALLED GARDEN AT
COWDRAY**
Cowdray Park, Midhurst GU29 9AL.
Jan Howard, 01730 816881,
www.walledgardencowdray.co.uk.
$1/_4$ m from centre of Midhurst. Entrance
off mini roundabout on A272 going
towards Petworth. **Adm £3.50, chd
under 12 free. All yr Mons to Fris 9-
5, Sats, Suns 10.30-5. Please phone
in advance as can be closed for
private events. For NGS: Sat 26, Sun
27 Apr (11-4).**
Unique location next to the Cowdray
ruins on the edge of Midhurst,
surrounded by the world-renowned
polo grounds and Capability Brown
parkland. The 1-acre Tudor Pleasure
Garden, restored by Jan Howard of
'Room in the Garden', features a cool
herbaceous border and hot tropical
border. Also knot, herb garden and
vegetable areas. Fruit trained on
ancient walls and beautiful
glasshouse with exotic tender plants.
Extensive displays of tulips in Apr.
Produce from The Walled Garden.
Sussex Heritage Trust Award. Featured
on BBC TV.
♿ ✗ ✿ ☕

130 WARNINGCAMP HOUSE
Warningcamp, Arundel BN18 9QY.
David & Sarah Houghton King. 2m
NE of Arundel off A27. Leaving Arundel
towards Worthing cross railway bridge,
take 1st L signed Burpham. Follow rd
for approx 1m, take 1st turn at junction
and gate faces you. Home-made teas.
**Adm £3, chd free. Thurs 5, 19 June
(10-5); Sun 14 Sept (2-5).**
Formal garden laid out in 1920s to
reflect the Victorian house first built in
1820. Incl kitchen garden and cutting
flowers, lovingly restored with working
Victorian glasshouse. Formal garden
to front of house features scented
'peony and pinks' walk, rose
garden, long borders and parterre.
Gravel paths, some uneven
surfaces.
♿ ✗ ☕

131 WARREN HOUSE
Warren Road, Crowborough
TN6 1TX. Mr & Mrs M J Hands.
$1^1/_2$ m SW of Crowborough Cross.
From Crowborough towards
Uckfield A26, 4th turning on R. 1m
down Warren Rd. From South 2nd L
after Blue Anchor. Home-made teas.
**Adm £3, chd free. Sun 27 Apr; Bank
Hol Mon 5, Sun 18, Bank Hol Mon
26 May (2-5).**
Beautiful house (not open) steeped in
history with 9-acre garden and views
over Ashdown Forest. Series of
gardens old and new, displaying
wealth of azaleas, rhododendrons,
impressive variety of trees and shrubs.
Sweeping lawns framed by delightful
walls and terraces, woodlands, ponds,
ducks.
✗ ✿ ☕

**132 WEST CHILTINGTON
VILLAGE GARDENS**
RH20 2LA. 2m E of Pulborough. 3m N
of Storrington. At Xrds in centre of
West Chiltington opp Queens Head.
**Combined adm £3.50, chd free.
Suns 6, 13 July (1.30-5.30).**
2 adjoining $1/_2$ -acre plantsman's
gardens with contrasting designs and
features.
☕

HUNTERS BARN
The Hollow. Ann & Derek Frost
Converted barn (not open). Garden
completely reshaped and
replanted in 3 different areas by
present owners. Formal area for
sitting and wild area still being
developed. Water feature.
✗

PALMER'S LODGE
Broadford Bridge Road.
Richard Hodgson, 01798
812751. Visitors also welcome
by appt in July only.
Charming $1/_2$ -acre plantsman's
garden with herbaceous and
shrub borders. Fruit and vegetable
garden, small greenhouse.
✗ ☎

133 ◆ WEST DEAN GARDENS
West Dean PO18 0QZ. Edward
James Foundation, 07795 002353,
www.westdean.org.uk. 5m N of
Chichester. On A286. **Adm £6.75, chd
£3.25, concessions £6.25. Daily Mar
to Oct (10.30-5); Weds to Suns Nov
to Feb (11-4). Closed Christmas &
New Year. For NGS: Mon 2 June
(10.30-5).**

35-acre historic garden in tranquil downland setting. 300ft long Harold Peto pergola, mixed and herbaceous borders, rustic summerhouses, redeveloped water and spring garden, specimen trees. Restored 2½-acre walled garden contains fruit collection, 13 Victorian glasshouses, apple store, large working kitchen garden, extensive plant collection. Circuit walk (2¼ m) climbs through parkland to 45-acre St Roche's Arboretum. National Collections of *Aesculus* and *liriodendron*.

&. ✗ ✪ NCCPG ☕

134 NEW **WESTACRE**
Burton Park Road, Petworth GU28 0JS. Mrs R Charles, 01798 344467. *2m S of Petworth, off A285 (Chichester rd). Turn L past garage onto Burton Rark Rd, garden ¼ m on L.* Light refreshments & home-made teas. **Adm £3.50, chd free. Visitors welcome by appt. groups of 15+.** Old gardener (Gaywood Farm, Pulborough) learns new tricks! Started from scratch but framed by old forest trees and with glimpses of the Downs, this 3yr-old garden now has a pond and bog gardens, a pergola leading to a potager, wall planting, terrace beds and raised shrub banks. Unusual plants are maturing well in much enriched poor sandy soil. Intriguing from spring to autumn.

&. ✗ ☕ ☎

Old gardener (Gaywood Farm, Pulborough) learns new tricks! Started from scratch but framed by old forest trees and with glimpses of the Downs . . .

135 NEW **WESTFIELD**
Malthouse Lane, Hurstpierpoint BN6 9JX. Phil & Cherry Radford. *Next to Hurstpierpoint College. With College cricket pitch on your L, after 200m white rocks on grass verge. Parking opposite.* Light refreshments & home-made teas. **Adm £3.50, chd free. Sun 10 Aug (2-5).** Beautiful, well-kept ¾-acre exotic/Colonial-style garden, surrounded by mature trees leading into ¾-acre woodland walk with barked paths and Treasure Hunt for children. Enjoy a touch of the Tropical!

&. ✗ ☕

136 **46 WESTUP FARM COTTAGES**
Balcombe RH17 6JJ. Chris & Sarah Cornwell, 01444 811891. *3m N of Cuckfield. ¼ m N Balcombe stn, turn L off B2036 immed before Balcombe Primary School (signed). ¾ m.* **Adm £2.50, chd free. Weds 30 Apr; 21 May; 25 June (12-5). Visitors also welcome by appt, groups of 4+, coaches welcome.** Hidden in the countryside of the High Weald, this cottage garden contains unique and traditional features, linked by intimate paths through lush and subtle planting. Featured in 'Amateur Gardening'.

✗ ✪ ☎

137 **WHITEHOUSE COTTAGE**
Staplefield Lane, Staplefield RH17 6AU. Mr Barry Gray. *5m NW of Haywards Heath. E of A23 & 2m S of Handcross. In Staplefield at Xrds by cricket pavilion take turning marked Staplefield Lane for 1m.* **Adm £2, chd free. Open daily throughout the year during daylight hours, no appointment necessary.** 4 acres of woodland with mixed shrubs, paths beside stream linked by ponds. Best in April, May and June.

138 **WILDHAM**
East Marden/Stoughton PO18 9JG. Consie & Mark Dunn, 01243 535202, consie@eastmarden.net. *4m SE of South Harting. B2141 to Chichester, turn R to East Marden, in East Marden follow signs to Stoughton, garden up track on R 1m from wishing well.* Home-made teas. **Adm £3, chd free. Sun 1, Thur 5 June (11-5). Visitors also welcome by appt.**

Very informal chalk garden on steep hill. Dripping with roses and clematis, unusual shrubs. Glorious position. God's garden with minor interference from an idle amateur. New patio with steps decorated with pots.

☕ ☎

139 **WINCHELSEA'S SECRET GARDENS**
TN36 4AB. *2m W of Rye.* Home-made teas at Cleveland House. **Combined adm £5, chd free. Sat 14 June (2-6).** Winchelsea is a beautiful medieval town, founded in 1288 by Edward I. Notable buildings incl the splendid C14 church and Court Hall. It is one of the few surviving C13 English towns where the streets are laid out in a grid system. Because of this, the gardens are hidden behind old walls. Many of the gardens open this year have lovely water features and wonderful views of the sea or across the beautiful Brede Valley. Town maps given to all visitors.

☕

AMERIQUE
Castle Street. Mr & Mrs D O'Brien
Mature garden, partly walled, extending to a wild area with herb garden to attract bees and butterflies. Old-fashioned roses - ramblers, scramblers and bush varieties abound.

&. ✗

CHAPEL PLAT
Hiham Green. Mr & Mrs R D Cooper
Small enclosed town garden.

✗

CLEVELAND HOUSE
Rookery Lane. Mr & Mrs J Jempson
This beautiful 1⅓-acre walled garden has recently undergone a huge transformation due to box blight. New semi-wild area, summerhouse and trees. Lovely views.

&. ✗

COOKS GREEN
Barrack Square. Roger & Tina Neaves
Part-walled cottage garden with far-reaching sea views.

✗

NEW **FIVE CHIMNEYS**
Mill Road. Tony & Sue Davis
Garden of approx ⅓ acre incl kitchen garden, separated from

the main lawned area by a pleached hornbeam hedge, rose garden.

 ♿ ⚘

NEW KING'S LEAP
Castle Street. Philip Kent
Large cottage-style garden comprising mixed beds, oodland border and rockery, all packed with plants for colour and interest.

 ♿ ⚘

PERITEAU HOUSE
High Street. Dr & Mrs Lawrence Youlten
Old walled garden with herbaceous borders, fountain and 300yr-old yew tree. Featured on ITV and in 'Wealden Times'. Access to garden up 4 steps, then level.

⚘

NEW RYE VIEW
The Strand. Howard Norton & David Page. *On A259*
Newly-created riverside garden with views over Pear Tree Marsh. A blend of formal and informal planting with a collection of silver plants and unusual shrubs.

 ♿ ⚘ ⊛

TRUNCHEONS
Rectory Lane. Patrick & Monica Edge-Partington
Garden with ha-ha overlooking National Trust pasture.

⚘

NEW THE WELL HOUSE
Castle Street. Alice Kenyon
Recently renovated partially walled garden using gravel as well as lawn. Existing trees to aim at all-yr interest.

⚘

Wildlife encouraged, as is seeding of colourful annuals as well as 'gifts' from the birds . . .

140 NEW WINSLEY
The Twitten, off Southview Road, Crowborough TN6 1HF. Kathryn & Robin Willig. *1m SW from Crowborough Cross. Off A26 into Southview Rd. Park here, The Twitten not suitable.* Home-made teas. **Adm £3.50, chd free (share to Friends of Crowborough Hospital). Sun 6 July (2-5).**
$1\frac{1}{3}$-acre garden with many established trees and shrubs including a fabulous eucalyptus tree. Herbaceous planting, roses, orchard with wild flowers and vegetable garden. Delightful pond area. Wildlife encouraged, as is seeding of colourful annuals as well as 'gifts' from the birds. Featured on BBC TV Open Gardens.

⚘ ⊛ ☕

Sussex County Volunteers

East & Mid Sussex
County Organiser
Rosie Lloyd, Bankton Cottage, Turners Hill Road, Crawley Down RH10 4EY, 01342 718907, rosie.lloyd@dsl.pipex.com
Sussex County Treasurer
Robin Lloyd, Bankton Cottage, Turners Hill Road, Crawley Down RH10 4EY, 01342 718907, robin.lloyd@dsl.pipex.com
Sussex Publicity
Sara Turner, 9 Terminus Avenue, Bexhill-on-Sea TN39 3LS, 01424 210716, sara.kidd@btconnect.com

West Sussex
County Organiser
Carrie McArdle, Message Cottage, Kirdford RH14 0JR, 01403 820272, carrie.mcardle@btinternet.com
Deputy County Organiser
Jane Allen, Dyers House, Pickhurst Road, Chiddingfold, Surrey GU8 4TG, 01428 683130, nicholasallen@btinternet.com
County Treasurer
Peter Edwards, Quince Cottage, The Street, Bury, Pulborough RH20 1PA, 01798 831900, peteredwards425@btinternet.com

WARWICKSHIRE

Birmingham & part of West Midlands

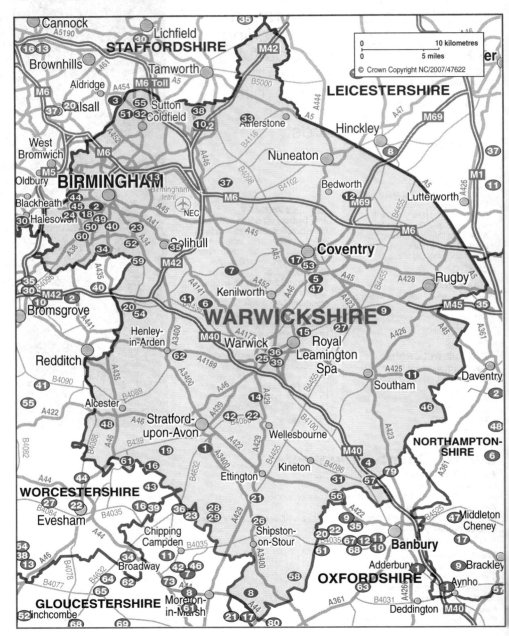

Opening Dates

February

SUNDAY 10
48 Ragley Hall Gardens

March

THURSDAY 6
62 Wootton Grange

April

THURSDAY 3
62 Wootton Grange

SUNDAY 6
15 19 Church Lane
19 Elm Close
28 Ilmington Gardens

SUNDAY 13
42 Parham Lodge

WEDNESDAY 16
24 89 Harts Green Road

SUNDAY 27
22 Greenlands
44 50 Pereira Road

WEDNESDAY 30
23 Hall Green Gardens

May

SUNDAY 4
47 The Quarry Garden

MONDAY 5
17 Earlsdon Gardens
47 The Quarry Garden

TUESDAY 6
21 The Folly Lodge

WEDNESDAY 14
24 89 Harts Green Road

THURSDAY 15
62 Wootton Grange

SATURDAY 17
54 Tanworth-in-Arden Gardens

SUNDAY 18
3 Ashover
5 Avondale Nursery
14 Cedar House
54 Tanworth-in-Arden Gardens
59 Wits End

SUNDAY 25
8 Barton House
19 Elm Close
43 Pebworth Gardens

MONDAY 26
7 Balsall Common Gardens
10 Bridge House
43 Pebworth Gardens

June

SUNDAY 1
30 Inglenook

WEDNESDAY 4
24 89 Harts Green Road

SATURDAY 7
27 Hunningham Village Gardens

SUNDAY 8
9 Bourton & Draycote Gardens
16 Dorsington Gardens
22 Greenlands
27 Hunningham Village Gardens
32 18 Ladywood Road
38 Middleton Hall

TUESDAY 10
21 The Folly Lodge

SATURDAY 14
2 Ashmead House Garden
29 Ilmington Manor

SUNDAY 15
1 Alscot Park
2 Ashmead House Garden
37 Maxstoke Castle
51 Stoneleigh House
53 Styvechale Garden Trail
58 Whichford & Ascott Gardens
60 Woodbrooke Quaker Study
   Centre

SATURDAY 21
5 Avondale Nursery
33 Latimers Rest

SUNDAY 22
5 Avondale Nursery
15 19 Church Lane
26 Honington Village Gardens
31 Ivy Lodge
33 Latimers Rest
40 Moseley Gardens South
49 Sir Johns Gardens
55 91 Tower Road
57 Warmington Village Gardens

THURSDAY 26
41 Packwood House

SATURDAY 28
59 Wits End

SUNDAY 29
23 Hall Green Gardens
34 Little Indonesia
45 Pereira Road Gardens

July

SUNDAY 6
4 Avon Dassett Gardens
13 Castle Bromwich Hall Gardens
20 Elmhurst
52 Stonor Road Gardens

WEDNESDAY 9
24 89 Harts Green Road

SATURDAY 12
35 Marie Curie Hospice Gardens

SUNDAY 13
12 Bulkington Gardens
30 Inglenook
50 The Stables Selly Park

TUESDAY 15
21 The Folly Lodge

SATURDAY 19
56 Upton House

SATURDAY 26
33 Latimers Rest

SUNDAY 27
33 Latimers Rest
34 Little Indonesia

August

SUNDAY 3
3 Ashover

SUNDAY 10
5 Avondale Nursery
59 Wits End

TUESDAY 12
21 The Folly Lodge

SUNDAY 24
42 Parham Lodge

MONDAY 25
10 Bridge House

September

WEDNESDAY 3
24 89 Harts Green Road

TUESDAY 9
21 The Folly Lodge

SUNDAY 14
5 Avondale Nursery

THURSDAY 18
6 Baddesley Clinton Hall

SATURDAY 20
25 Hill Close Gardens

October

SUNDAY 12
48 Ragley Hall Gardens

February 2009

SUNDAY 8
48 Ragley Hall Gardens

Gardens open to the public

5 Avondale Nursery

6 Baddesley Clinton Hall
11 Bridge Nursery
13 Castle Bromwich Hall Gardens
24 89 Harts Green Road
25 Hill Close Gardens
36 The Master's Garden
38 Middleton Hall
39 The Mill Garden
41 Packwood House
47 The Quarry Garden
48 Ragley Hall Gardens
56 Upton House

By appointment only

18 Edgbaston Garden Sculpture Trail
46 Priors Marston Manor Garden
61 Woodpeckers

Also open by appointment ☎

3 Ashover
8 Barton House
23 16 Burnaston Road, Hall Green Gardens
23 37 Burnaston Road, Hall Green Gardens
15 19 Church Lane
4 The Coach House, Avon Dassett Gardens
18 Edgbaston Garden Sculpture Trail
19 Elm Close
23 36 Ferndale Road, Hall Green Gardens
23 Hall Green Gardens
21 The Folly Lodge
29 Ilmington Manor
33 Latimers Rest
34 Little Indonesia
42 Parham Lodge
44 50 Pereira Road
46 Priors Marston Manor Garden
52 172 Stonor Road, Stonor Road Gardens
55 91 Tower Road
59 Wits End
61 Woodpeckers
62 Wootton Grange

The Gardens

1 🆕 **ALSCOT PARK**
Atherstone on Stour CV37 8BL.
Mr & Mrs Holman-West. *3m S of Stratford-upon-Avon. On A3400.* Home-made teas. **Adm £5, chd free. Sun 15 June (2-6).**
Unique opportunity to visit this Historic House and 6-acre garden set within stunning parkland which combines both traditional and contemporary design and includes

original walled kitchen garden, C18 orangery, modern and traditional borders and an array of magnificent trees. Coaches must be booked - 07917 030580. NCCPG plant fair. Childrens activities.
♿ ✕ ⊛ ☕

Topiary and roses on arches, in beds and as ground cover . . .

2 🆕 **ASHMEAD HOUSE GARDEN**
49 Carpenter Road, Edgbaston B15 2JP. Mrs Angela Beatson Wood. *Off A38, S from M6 J6. From A38 turn R up Lee Bank Middleway to Five Ways. 1st L, 2nd R.* Cream teas. **Adm £2.50, chd free. Sat 14; Sun 15 June (11-5).**
25 yr-old garden with a central diagonal axis surrounded by ancient Edgbaston trees, lime, ash and turkey oak. Acid soil favours camellias and azaleas. Colour-coded herbaceous beds in June, irises, topiary and roses on arches, in beds and as ground cover. Walled on 2 sides and high mounds to sit and enjoy the views. Music.
♿ ✕ ⊛ ☕

3 **ASHOVER**
25 Burnett Road, Streetly B74 3EL. Jackie & Martin Harvey, 0121 353 0547. *8m N of Birmingham. Off B4138.* Cream teas. **Adm £3, chd free. Suns 18 May; 3 Aug (1.30-5.30). Visitors also welcome by appt, May-Aug, incl coaches.**
Secluded 1/3 -acre, romantic country-style garden, profusion of mixed planting. Vibrant in May with tapestry of azaleas, tulips and complementary plants. In summer packed, colour-themed herbaceous borders, artistically planted with flowers and foliage to give maximum effect of colour, form and texture. Extended hot border a special feature. Established

pond and waterfalls, grasses and ferns. Featured in 'Gardeners' World' magazine.
✕ ⊛ ☕ ☎

4 **AVON DASSETT GARDENS**
CV47 2AE. *7m N of Banbury. From M40 J12 turn L & L again B4100. 2nd L into village. Park in village & at top of hill.* Home-made teas at Old Mill Cottage. **Combined adm £5, chd free (share to Myton Hamlet Hospice). Sun 6 July (2-6).**
Small, pretty Hornton stone village. 2 churches open for visitors.
☕

AVON COTTAGE
Mrs M J Edginton
Interesting contrasts between cottage garden, courtyard and vegetable garden.
♿

AVON HOUSE
Mrs L Dunkley
Mature garden, principally shrubs, featuring hostas.
♿

THE COACH HOUSE
Bitham Hall. Mr & Mrs G J Rice, 01295 690255. Visitors also welcome by appt, groups & coaches, all yr.
Sloping 2-acres, part of former Victorian garden overlooking Edge Hill. Walls give shelter and support to many climbers and more tender perennials and shrubs. Planted to give yr-round interest. Woodland, alpines, fruit and vegetables.
☎

HILL TOP FARM
Mrs N & Mr D Hicks
1 acre. Display of bedding plants, perennials, shrubs, conifers and heathers. Extensive kitchen garden. Greenhouses.
 ✕ ⊛

THE LIMES
Mr & Mrs B Anderson
Large ecological garden. Wide variety of roses, shrubs and trees.
♿

OLD MILL COTTAGE
Mr & Mrs M J Lewis
Conservation garden of 3/4 acre with shrubs, perennial borders and rockeries. Collection of alpines and herbs. Pond and tropical garden. Mediterranean gravel garden.
♿

THE OLD NEW HOUSE
Mr & Mrs W Allen
1-acre, formal rose garden, herbaceous borders and specimen trees.

THE OLD RECTORY
Lily Hope-Frost
2-acre mature garden with colourful terrace and wide stone steps leading to fountain and small wood, surrounding listed house (not open) mentioned in Domesday Book. Many places to sit. Entrance to church through walled garden.

ORCHARD END
Jill Burgess
1-acre garden with fruit trees, old yew and box hedging, large pond and herbaceous borders.

POPPY COTTAGE
Mr & Mrs R Butler
Newly established pretty cottage garden. Water feature and kitchen garden.

5 ◆ AVONDALE NURSERY
at Russells Nursery, Mill Hill, Baginton CV8 3AG. Mr Brian Ellis, 024 7667 3662, www.avondalenursery.co.uk. *3m S Coventry. At junction of A45/A46 take rd to Baginton, 1st L to Mill Hill. Park in Russell's Nursery.* **Adm £3, £4 on 21 & 22 June, chd free. Mon to Sat, 10-12.30, 2-5, Sun 10.30-12.30, 2-4.30. For NGS: Sun 18 May; Sat 21 June, Suns 22 June; 10 Aug; 14 Sept (11-4). Also open with Styvechale Gardens.**
Plantaholic nurseryman's garden. Formal layout for easy access, ever increasing collection of rare and unusual well labelled cottage garden plants. All yr interest, incl many geums, geraniums, shasta daisies, crocosmia, michaelmas daisies and ornamental grasses. A hidden gem on the outskirts of Coventry. Sculpture exhibition 21/22 Jun.

6 ◆ BADDESLEY CLINTON HALL
Knowle B93 0DQ. The National Trust, 01564 783294, baddesleyclinton@nationaltrust.org. uk. *7½ m NW of Warwick. ¾ m W of A4141 Warwick to Birmingham rd nr Chadwick End.* **House and Garden Adm £8.40, chd £4.20, Garden only**

Adm £4.20, chd £2.10. Wed-Sun & BH Mons 9 Feb-2 Nov, 11-5; 5 Nov-21 Dec, 11-4. For NGS: Thur 18 Sept (11-5).
Medieval moated manor house little changed since1634. Walled garden and herbaceous borders, natural areas, lakeside walk, nature trail. Gravel paths, some steep slopes around lake area.

A car or cycle is necessary in order to get round to all these gardens . . .

7 BALSALL COMMON GARDENS
CV7 7DG. *5m W of Coventry, 10m N of Warwick. 5m S of M42/M6 intersection. From T-lights at junction of A452/B4101, go E on B4101 towards Coventry for 1m. L into Hodgetts Lane.* Teas at the Scout Room, Holly Lane. **Combined adm £4, chd free (share to Balsall Village Hall). Mon 26 May (11-6).**
A variety of gardens to suit most interests. Map available at each garden. Please note that a car or cycle is necessary in order to get round to all these gardens.

NEW ALDER HOUSE
Mr & Mrs M Hawley
Mixed borders of perennials, shrubs and trees, raised pond and wildlife pond.

THE BUNGALOW
Mr & Mrs G Johnson
2 acres with mixed borders, pond and lawns, a flower arranger's garden.

THE COTTAGE
Enid & John Hinton
Developing garden with mixed borders, mature trees, wildlife pond with waterlilies and organic vegetable plot.

FIRS FARM
Mr & Mrs C Ellis
1-acre garden, courtyard with tubs, walled garden, formal garden with mixed borders and pergola supporting varieties of honeysuckle. Open grassed area with fruit and ornamental trees.

MERIGLEN
Mr & Mrs J Webb
Mixed borders of shrubs and perennials, conservatory and greenhouse.

THE PINES
Mr & Mrs C Davis
1½ -acre formal garden divided into series of ornamental areas, vegetables, fruit, herbs and apiary.

8 BARTON HOUSE
Barton-on-the-Heath GL56 0PJ. Mr & Mrs I H B Cathie, 01608 674303, cathie@bartonfarms.fsnet.co.uk. *2m W of Long Compton. 2m off A3400 Stratford-upon-Avon to Oxford rd. 1¼ m off A44 Chipping Norton to Moreton-in-Marsh rd.* Home-made teas. **Adm £5, chd £2.50. Sun 25 May (2-6). Visitors also welcome by appt.**
6½ acres with mature trees, azaleas, species and hybrid rhododendrons, magnolias, moutan tree peonies. National collection of arbutus. Japanese garden, catalpa walk, rose garden, secret garden and many rare and exotic plants. Victorian kitchen garden. Exotic garden with palms, cypresses and olive trees established 2002. Vineyard planted 2000 - free wine tasting. Manor house by Inigo Jones (not open). Other visits for groups 25+ 01608 67430.

9 BOURTON & DRAYCOTE GARDENS
Rugby CV23 9QS. *7m SE of Coventry. Between Rugby & Princethorpe, off B4453 signed Bourton.* Home-made teas at Wellington Cottage (garden not open). **Combined adm £4, chd free. Sun 8 June (2-5).**
Two small villages in one Parish. Bourton has a tracery of footpaths and interesting church, Draycote is more remote and quiet. Live music by the Bourton trombones.

FIELDGATE COTTAGE
Wendy Morris & Steve Smith
Stunning cottage garden. Small collections of clematis, hosta and pelargoniums, many containers and an inspirational shed.

  ♿ ✕ ⊛

NEW THE MANOR FARM
Mr & Mrs John Morton
Small garden started in spring 2005 being developed from lawn and rough tree area to harmonise with pools and beautiful countryside.

✕

NEW MANOR HOUSE
Mr & Mrs R J K Morton
Well established, mature family garden in an attractive setting with water filled moated area. Enclosed vegetable garden and raised beds.

✕

THE OLD PRESBYTERY
Donald & Julie Pennington
Large garden with open aspects and dry, sandy soil. A range of naturalised borders, with shrubs and trees, some formal bedding. Extensive vegetable garden with soft fruit and varied orchard.

♿ ✕

POTNEY COTTAGE
Heather & Jeremy Patton
Different areas, each with a different feel. Cottage plants, exotica, vegetable plot and pond. New area for fruit trees and relaxation.

✕

NEW ROWAN GATE
Dr & Mrs T R B Mitchell
$1/3$ -acre garden on alkaline clay running down to a stream. Varied range of trees, shrubs, roses (inc R.Filipes kiftsgate), herbaceous plants and grasses. Young topiary, grass mound, 2 pools with wildlife.

♿

An inspirational
shed . . .

10 NEW BRIDGE HOUSE
Dog Lane, Bodymoor Heath B76 9JF. Mr & Mrs J Cerone. *5m S of Tamworth. From A446 head N on A4091, R at sign into Bodymoor Heath Lane. $3/4$ m into village, R into Dog Lane.* Home-made teas.
Adm £3, chd free. Mons 26 May; 25 Aug (2-5.30).
1-acre garden surrounding converted public house divided into smaller areas with a mix of shrub borders, azalea and fuchsia, herbaceous and bedding, orchard, kitchen garden and wild flower meadow. Pergola walk, wisteria, pond and lawns.

♿ ⊛ ☕

11 ◆ BRIDGE NURSERY
Tomlow Road, Napton CV47 8HX. Christine Dakin, 01926 812737, www.bridge-nursery.co.uk. *3m E of Southam. Brown tourist sign at Napton Xrds on the A425 Southam to Daventry rd.* **Adm £2, chd free. Apr-Oct (10-4).**
This challenging 1-acre garden (clay soil, exposed position) is home to an exciting range of rare and unusual plants. Grass paths meander round well-stocked informal borders. A haven for wildlife. Features incl a large pond, bamboo grove (with panda sculptures) and willow dome. Groups welcome by appointment.

♿ ⊛

12 NEW BULKINGTON GARDENS
CV12 9LY. Mr Paul Nash. *4m N of Coventry, 2m E of Bedworth. On the B4109 from Coventry, B4029 from Bedworth.* Light refreshments & teas at 29 Hemsworth Drive & 284 Nuneaton Road. **Combined adm £4, chd free. Sun 13 July (1-6).**
8 gardens in large village. Parking, WC & maps at village centre. Maps at gardens.

☕

NEW 28 CLAREMONT CLOSE
Joyce & Roy Evans
Medium-sized garden well stocked with herbaceous, perennial and seasonal plants. Greenhouse, small kitchen garden and wildlife pond.

✕ ⊛

NEW 284 NUNEATON ROAD
Eileen & Peter Houghton
Large mature garden with many fruit and other trees. Lawns with island beds, vegetable plot, fruit cage, water cascading into large fishpond.

NEW 288 NUNEATON ROAD
Pat Corby
Ideal example of the small garden approach to a big garden with shrubs, herbaceous borders, patio with raised beds, small pond, a big country view and greenhouses with a variety of cacti and succulents.

✕ ⊛

NEW 29 HEMSWORTH DRIVE
Lynn & Paul Spencer
Larger than average rear garden with a variety of planting and water features.

NEW 290 NUNEATON ROAD
Joanne & Ian Mountford
Large landscaped garden with trees, shrubs, ponds and pet poultry.

NEW 49 COVENTRY ROAD
Paul & Janet Nash
2 mature gardens designed and planted for all year interest. Extensive variety of plants, shrubs and trees, wide range of fruit, pond.

♿ ✕

NEW 76 BARBRIDGE ROAD
Cyril & Margaret Norman
Shrubs, perennials, summer bedding, paved and scree areas, rockery and small water feature. Many hanging baskets and tubs.

♿

NEW 30 CLAREMONT CLOSE
John & Maureen Huggins
Small low maintenance garden with attractive field view.

♿

13 ◆ CASTLE BROMWICH HALL GARDENS
Chester Road. B36 9BT. Castle Bromwich Hall Gardens Trust, 0121 749 4100, www.cbhgt.org.uk. *4m E of Birmingham. 1m J5 M6 (exit N only).* **Adm £3.50, chd 50p, concessions £3. Phone or check web for details of opening days & times.** For NGS: Sun 6 July (1.30-5.30).
Restored C18 formal walled gardens provide visitors with the opportunity to see a unique collection of historic plants, shrubs, medicinal and culinary herbs and fascinating vegetable collection. Intriguing holly maze. Several fruits within the orchards and

along the paths incl apple, pear, apricot, quince, medlar, fig and cherry. Guided tours, gift shop.

14 CEDAR HOUSE
Wasperton CV35 8EB. Mr & Mrs D L Burbidge. *4m S of Warwick. On A429, turn R between Barford & Wellesbourne, entrance nr end of village on L.* Home-made teas. **Adm £3, chd free (share to St Johns Church). Sun 18 May (2-5).**
3 acres, shrubs, herbaceous borders, ornamental trees, woodland walk. Cedar trees 200-300yrs old, fish pond, swimming pool area. Grass garden. Also open Gilbert Scott Church with Pugin window. New tree plantation and a big surprise in the grass garden. Some gravel paths.

15 19 CHURCH LANE
Lillington CV32 7RG. David & Judy Hirst, 01926 422591. *1¹/₂ m NE Leamington Spa. Take A445 towards Rugby. Church Lane is on RH-side just beyond roundabout junction with B4453. Garden on corner of Hill Close. Enter via driveway in Church Lane.* **Adm £2, chd free. Suns 6 Apr; 22 June (2-5.30). Visitors also welcome by appt, Tuesdays in Mar (for hellebores), Mondays in July.**
Plantpersons' cottage style suburban garden with several aspects and areas. A rich variety of planting for yr-round interest. Narrow paths. Not suitable for the very young or infirm.

16 DORSINGTON GARDENS
CV37 8AR. *6m SW of Stratford-upon-Avon. On B439 from Stratford turn L to Welford-on-Avon, then R to Dorsington.* Light refreshments & teas. **Combined adm £5, chd free (share to St Peters Church & Air Ambulance). Sun 8 June (12-5).**
Pretty conservation area village. Maps given to all visitors. For information 01789 720581.

NEW ABERFOYLE
Mr & Mrs B Clarke
Well established cottage garden, fine trees and shrubs.

THE BARN
Mr & Mrs P Reeve
2 tier country garden with shrubs, herbaceous borders and vegetable patch.

COLLETTS FARM
Mr & Mrs D Bliss
Trees and shrubs, container flowers. Highly productive kitchen garden with fan-trained fruit.

DORSINGTON ARBORETUM
Mr F Dennis
12 acres with collection of several hundred trees from around the world leading to Udde Well Pond (ancient well) and willow walk.

NEW DORSINGTON HOUSE
Mr & Mrs I Kolodotschko
Laid out in 2006, the garden was designed in conjunction with its contemporary house for yr-round interest through use of form, colour and texture. Nearly 5 acres, it forms various areas which are extensions of the internal spaces.

2 DORSINGTON MANOR
Mr & Mrs C James
³/₄ -acre garden, relaxed and peaceful in style, full of perennials, shrubs and trees.

GLEBE COTTAGE
Mr & Mrs A Brough
Over ³/₄ acre of land reclaimed into an uncomplicated garden which, over several yrs, has developed into interesting and varied garden rooms. A surprise at each turn.

KNOWLE THATCH
Mr & Mrs P Turner
Large garden with mature trees, shrubs and herbaceous borders.

NEW MANOR FARM
Mr F Dennis
Old farmhouse garden under restoration.

MILFIELD
Mrs H Dumas
Small but beautifully planted cottage garden with a feeling of space and simplicity touched with a hint of grandeur in the form of the statuesque urns.

THE MOAT HOUSE
Mr & Mrs R Vaudry
6-acre moated garden incl orchard with wild flower meadow. Walled garden, herbaceous borders, rose and lavender beds, walled vegetable garden.

THE OLD MANOR
Mr F Dennis
3 acres with fairy walk, herb garden, ornamental fish pond, sunken water garden leading to Highfield, (Mr F Dennis) with its Mediterranean garden, container plants and bonsai collection.

THE OLD RECTORY
Mr & Mrs N Phillips
2-acre Victorian garden with mature trees incl old espalier fruit trees. Box hedges, herbaceous borders, many old roses, large pool, small wood.

SAPPHIRE HOUSE
Mrs D Sawyer
Orchard, vegetable garden, shrub beds, lawns and large walnut trees.

THE WELSHMAN'S BARN
Mr F Dennis
5 acres with Japanese garden, Oz maze, bronze sculpture garden of heroes, wild flower garden and stream.

WINDRUSH
Mrs M B Mills
An abundant natural patchwork of shrubs and perennials run riot with little interference, interspersed with distinct niches.

Hidden walks and arches . . .

⓱ EARLSDON GARDENS

CV5 6FS. *Coventry. Turn towards Coventry at A45/A429 T-lights. Take 3rd L turn into Beechwood Ave, Earlsdon Gardens.* Home-made teas at 59 The Chesils. **Combined adm £3, chd free. Mon 5 May (11-4).** Maps at all gardens. Earlsdon Festival.

3 BATES ROAD
Victor & Judith Keene
Large established garden, with lots of spring interest incl rhododendrons, azaleas, mature trees and kitchen garden.

155 BEECHWOOD AVENUE
Nigel & Jan Young
Garden with open traditional character, constantly being enhanced with interesting planting. Water feature.

59 THE CHESILS
John Marron & Richard Bantock
Herbaceous plants jostle for attention in a richly planted garden on several levels.

40 HARTINGTON CRESCENT
Viv & George Buss
Surprisingly large garden with interest for all ages, water feature and fern garden.

114 HARTINGTON CRESCENT
Liz Campbell & Denis Crowley
Large, mature, pretty garden on several levels with hidden aspects.
�

36 PROVIDENCE STREET
Rachel Culley & Steve Shiner
Large peaceful cottage garden. Water features, packed herbaceous borders, vegetable plot, yr-round interest and colour.

87 ROCHESTER ROAD
Edith Lewin
Peaceful, mature cottage garden.

54 SALISBURY AVENUE
Peter & Pam Moffit
Plantaholic's garden with a large variety of plants, clematis and small trees, some unusual.
�

⓲ EDGBASTON GARDEN SCULPTURE TRAIL

5 Farquhar Road East. B15 3RD. John Alexander-Williams, 01214 541279, johnaw@blueyonder.co.uk. *4m SW of Birmingham. Under 1m from Birmingham Botanical Gardens. Farquhar Rd East is a triangle off Farquhar Rd, between Somerset & Richmond Hill Rds in Edgbaston.* **Adm £2.50, chd £1. Visitors welcome by appt, any day, any time, all year, groups 10+ can have teas.** Town garden of $^{1}/_{3}$ -acre. Evolved over 22 yrs to provide interlinking areas of interest with hidden walks and arches designed, to create sculpture trail. Some 80 sculptures by owner provide surprise and amusement and set off very personal collection of shrubs, trees and plants. Featured in 'Amateur Gardening'.
�☎

⓳ ELM CLOSE

Binton Road, Welford-on-Avon CV37 8PT. Eric & Glenis Dyer, 01789 750793, glenisdyer@btinternet.com. *5m SW of Stratford. Off B4390. Elm Close is between Welford Garage & The Bell Inn.* Home-made teas. **Adm £3, chd free. Suns 6 Apr; 25 May (2-5). Visitors also welcome by appt for groups of 10+.** $^{2}/_{3}$ -acre packed with super plants and stocked for yr-round colour and interest. Clematis, daphnes, peonies, hostas and hellebores a particular speciality. Featured in 'Garden News' and 'Womens Weekly'. Gravel front drive.
�☎

⓴ [NEW] ELMHURST

Vicarage Hill, Tanworth-in-Arden B94 5EA. Mr & Mrs R Lockwood, 01564 742641. *Off B4101, $^{3}/_{4}$ m from village.* Home-made teas. **Adm £2.50, chd free. Sun 6 July (2-6). Also open with Tanworth-in-Arden Gardens.** $^{1}/_{2}$ -acre with wide range of plants, some unusual, for yr-round interest. Herbaceous borders, woodland area, rockery, small pond and interesting features. Bark path to gravel area.
�

㉑ THE FOLLY LODGE

Halford CV36 5DG. Mike & Susan Solomon, 01789 740183. *3m NE Shipston-on-Stour. On A429 (Fosse Way). In Halford take turning to Idlicote. Garden on R past Feldon Edge.* Home-made teas. **Adm £2.50, chd free. Tues 6 May, 10 June, 15 July, 12 Aug, 9 Sept (2-5). Visitors also welcome by appt for groups 8+.** Winding paths lead through colour-themed borders to hidden and surprising spaces. The informal planting scheme is enhanced by ceramics, sculptures and mosaics made by the owner. An artist's and plant-lover's garden described by visitors as 'a unique garden that we will remember for a long time'. Gravel paths, some steps.
�☎

GILMORTON GARDENS
See Leicestershire & Rutland.

㉒ GREENLANDS

Stratford Road, Wellesbourne CV35 9ES. Elizabeth Street. *4m E of Stratford-upon-Avon. Situated at the Loxley/Charlecote crossroads on the B4086, next to airfield.* **Adm £2.50, chd free. Suns 27 Apr, 8 June (11-5).** 1-acre with mature trees, shrubs, herbaceous borders and semi-wild areas. Winding paths and secluded garden rooms. 2 gravel gardens and tree lined vistas. Exhibition of flower paintings and sketches taken from the garden. Some gravel & bark chip paths.
�

㉓ HALL GREEN GARDENS

Birmingham B28 8SQ. *Off A34, 3m city centre, 6m from M42 J4. Take A34 towards Shirley, R at lights past station, 1st R, 1st L.* Home-made teas at Ferndale Rd & also 16 Burnaston Rd in Jun. **Combined adm £2.50 Apr, £3.50 Jun, chd free (share to Air Ambulance). Wed 30 Apr; Sun 29 June (2-6).**
☕

16 BURNASTON ROAD
Howard Hemmings & Sandra Hateley, 0121 624 1488, howard.hemmings@blueyonder. co.uk. Visitors also welcome by appt, mid-May to mid-July. S-facing formal lawn and border garden with interesting features incl an unusual log display, multi-coloured gravel, and bark covered shrub border, manicured

An unusual log display . . .

conifers, water feature and arch way leading to tranquil seating area.

37 BURNASTON ROAD
Mrs C M Wynne-Jones, 0121 608 2397. **Not open 30 Apr. Visitors also welcome by appt in June & July.**
Approx 1/8 acre, well-planted suburban garden. Interesting array of plants by experienced propagator. Patio, lawn, mixed borders and shade area. Vegetables and soft fruit.

36 FERNDALE ROAD
Mrs A A Appelbe & Mrs E A Nicholson, 0121 777 4921. **Visitors also welcome by appt, anytime.**
Large suburban florist's garden with many unusual plants giving yr-round interest. Garden divided into distinct areas, large ornamental garden with pool and waterfalls, tree and soft fruit garden and side patio.

120 RUSSELL ROAD
Mr D Worthington. **Not open 30 Apr.**
Plantsman's sub-divided garden designed by owner. Features formal raised pool, shrubs, climbers, old roses, herbaceous and container planting. Comprehensive overhaul of planting and some features in the last 2 yrs.

24 ◆ 89 HARTS GREEN ROAD
Harborne B17 9TZ. Mrs Barbara Richardson, 0121 427 5200. *3m SE of Birmingham. Off Fellows Lane-War Lane.* **Adm £2.50, chd free. For NGS: Weds 16 Apr; 14 May; 4 June, 9 July; 3 Sept (2-5).**
Wildlife-friendly split-level garden protected by mature trees. Extensively planted with unusual herbaceous perennials, shrubs and climbers incl over 80 varieties of clematis. Herbs and edible flowers border a path through the rockery and 50 varieties of Hemerocallis in July. Large display of plants in containers featuring vegetables, half hardy perennials and shade plants. Pond.

Old toll gate, ornamental stone bridge over the Stour . . .

25 ◆ HILL CLOSE GARDENS
Warwick CV34 6HF. Hill Close Gardens Trust, 01926 493339, www.hillclosegardens.com. *Town Centre. Entry from Friars St. by Bread & Meat Close. Car park by entrance next to racecourse.* **Adm £3, chd free. Fri & Sun (2-5), Sat & BH Mons (11-5), 21 Mar-26 Oct. For NGS: Sat 20 Sept (11-5).**
Restored G2* Victorian leisure gardens comprising 16 individual hedged gardens, 7 with brick summerhouses. Herbaceous borders, heritage apple and pear trees, C19 daffodils, many varieties of asters, chrysanthemums, heleniums and dahlias. Heritage vegetables incl rhubarb. NCCPG plant exchange border. Head Gardener's walk 2nd Fri in month. Designated wheelchair route.

26 HONINGTON VILLAGE GARDENS
Shipston CV36 5AA. *1 1/2 m N of Shipston-on-Stour. Take A3400 towards Stratford then turn R signed Honington. Home-made teas.* **Combined adm £4, chd free. Sun 22 June (2.15-5.30).**
C17 village, recorded in Domesday, entered by old toll gate. Ornamental stone bridge over the Stour and interesting church with C13 tower and late C17 nave after Wren.

HOLTS COTTAGE
Mr & Mrs R G Bentley
Cottage garden being restored to original layout and opening onto parkland. Interesting trees incl fruit trees and shrubs with herbaceous borders and ponds.

HONINGTON GLEBE
Mr & Mrs J C Orchard
2-acre plantsman's garden consisting of rooms planted informally with yr-round interest in contrasting foliage and texture. Old walled garden laid out with large raised lily pool and parterre filled with violas and perennials.

HONINGTON HALL
B H E Wiggin
Extensive lawns and fine mature trees with river and garden monuments. Carolean house (not open). Parish church adjoins house.

MALT HOUSE RISE
Mr & Mrs M Underhill
Small garden, well stocked with interesting established shrubs and many container plants.

THE OLD HOUSE
Mr & Mrs I F Beaumont
Small structured cottage garden formally laid out with box hedging and small fountain. Informally planted, giving an almost billowing, frothy appearance.

ORCHARD HOUSE
Mr & Mrs Monnington
Small developing garden created in recent yrs by owners with informal mixed beds and borders.

27 HUNNINGHAM VILLAGE GARDENS
CV33 9DY. *6m NE of Leamington Spa, 8m SW of Rugby, 7m S of Coventry. Just off the Fosseway-B4455, or take B4453 from Leamington through Weston-under-Wetherley and turn off R to Hunningham. Park in village.* Home-made teas at Parish Room in Church from 2. **Combined adm £3, chd free (share to Hunningham PCC). Sat 7, Sun 8 June (12.30-5.30).**
Hunningham consists of approx 70 dwellings, an interesting church and PH by the side of the R Leam. Picnic areas. Lunches and local produce at Hill Top Farm.

THE COACH HOUSE, SNOWFORD HALL FARM
Long Itchington Rd. Rudi & John Hancock
Walled country garden with quarry feature.

HUNNINGHAM CROFT
Main Street. Hazel & Paddy Taylor. *Next door to Red Lion PH*
Interesting garden with large collection of clematis, a number of

which will be in flower. New water feature. Gravel path in front garden.

&. ✕ ✿

THE MOTTE
School Lane. Margaret & Peter Green
Plant lover's garden under development, woodland and exotic borders, Mediterranean area, water garden. Conservatory for tender plants.

&.

THE OLD HALL
Main Street. Nicholas & Rona Horler
Large old garden with walled area. Listed building (not open).

THE OLDE SCHOOL HOUSE
School Lane. Lawford & Chris Hill
¹/₂ -acre of garden and paddock. Alpines, knot garden. Views over church and farmland.

&.

SNOWFORD HALL COTTAGES
Long Itchington Road. Mark Hancock
Large, isolated, rural garden with extensive raised bed vegetable plot, trees and borders. Borders planted with perennials to give yr-round colour. Large rose bed.

&. ✕

❷❽ ILMINGTON GARDENS
Shipston-on-Stour CV36 4LA. *8m S of Stratford-upon-Avon. 4m NW of Shipston-on-Stour off A3400. 3m NE of Chipping Campden.* Home-made teas in Village Hall. **Combined adm £4, chd free (share to Air Ambulance). Sun 6 Apr (2-6).**
Most attractive Cotswold village with 2 inns and Norman church. Ilmington traditional Morris dancers.

CRAB MILL
Mr & Mrs L Hodgkin
Terraced garden with dry stone walls and sunken courtyard round C18 house (not open). Daffodils, clematis, camellias. Paths through orchard with bluebells, cherry blossom and fritillaries. Steps to rose garden.

&.

FOXCOTE HILL
Mr & Mrs M Dingley
Garden developed on sloping site

on edge of village retaining most of old orchard with naturalised bulbs. Paths through orchard give views over countryside towards Edge Hill. Paved courtyard with fountain.

FOXCOTE HILL COTTAGE
Miss A Terry
Hillside garden with dry stone walls enclosing banks planted with alpines and spring bulbs.

✕

FROG ORCHARD
M Naish
Open garden surrounding an interesting modern house (not open), with trees and flowers beds, bordered on one side by a pretty little stream.

&.

THE GREY HOUSE
Mr & Mrs B Blackie
Formal lawns and beds with orchard on elevated site surrounding Georgian farmhouse, overlooking village and distant views.

✕

❷❾ ILMINGTON MANOR
Front Street. CV36 4LA. Mr & Mrs Taylor, 01608 682230, mtilmington@btinternet.com. *8m S of Stratford-upon-Avon.* **Adm £3, chd free (share to Air Ambulance). Sat 14 June (2-6). Visitors also welcome by appt.**
Hundreds of old and new roses, ornamental trees, shrubs and herbaceous borders, lily pond, topiary, orchard, fish ponds, daffodils in April. House (not open) dates from 1600. Also open with Illmington Gardens.

&. ☎

❸❶ INGLENOOK
20 Waxland Road, Halesowen B63 3DW. Ron & Anne Kerr. *¹/₄ m from Halesowen town centre. M5 J3 take A456 to Kidderminster, R at 1st island, 1st L into Dogkennel Lane. Waxland Rd 2nd L. 2 car parks in town centre, limited roadside parking.* Home-made teas. **Adm £2.50, chd free. Suns 1 June; 13 July (1-5).**
Charming garden featuring waterfalls which cascade over rocks down to ponds set within a woodland area. A path meandering through the trees brings you back to the lawn and patio. Hidden area hosts greenhouses, vegetable plots, asparagus beds and mixed borders. Enjoy panoramic views from the raised decked area with its

semi-tropical planting overlooking terraces which display a wide variety of low-growing conifers.

✕ ✿ ☕

❸❶ NEW IVY LODGE
Radway CV35 0UE. Mr Martin Dunne. *12m S of Warwick. From J12 M40 take B4451 to Kineton, B4086 S for 3m to signed turning, Radway.* **Adm £3.50, chd free. Sun 22 June (2-5).**
The garden planted in 1956 by the late Jim Russell and the current owner's mother. They incorporated a 3-acre field to make a 4-acre garden situated on the lower slopes of the Edgehill. In June the rambling roses are a wonderful sight climbing through the old fruit trees and shrubs. Grass paths wind through the wilder areas of the garden amongst the flower beds, shrubs and ornamental trees.

✕

Orchard with bluebells, cherry blossom and fritillaries . . .

❸❷ 18 LADYWOOD ROAD
Four Oaks, Sutton Coldfield B74 2SW. Ann & Ron Forrest. *2m N of Sutton Coldfield. Off A454, Four Oaks Road, nr stn.* Home-made teas. **Adm £3, chd free. Sun 8 June (1-5).**
Spacious informal garden on Four Oaks Estate. Approx 1¹/₄ acres, secluded and densely planted with roses, peonies, irises and lupins in herbaceous beds. Pond with fountain. Feature cedar tree, azaleas and rhododendrons.

&. ✿ ☕

❸❸ LATIMERS REST
Hipsley Lane, Baxterley CV9 2HS. Gerald & Christine Leedham, 01827 875526. *3m S of Atherstone on B4116. From A5 Atherstone, at island, take Merevale Lane to Baxterley. From M42 J9 take A4097 for Kingsbury. At island follow signs to Hurley & Baxterley, garden nr church.* Home-made teas. **Adm £3, chd free. Sat & Sun 21, 22 June; 26, 27 July (1-6). Visitors also welcome by appt, inc coaches.**

A garden of contrasts in beautiful Baxterley. Brilliant Austin roses star in 2 acres of lush lawns. Floral borders below stately trees. Fuchsia baskets light courtyards with water gardens, herbs and dahlias leading to Good Life veggies with melons and tomatoes and a young arboretum beyond.

  🚶 ✂ ☕ ☎

34 LITTLE INDONESIA
20 Poston Croft, Kings Heath B14 5AB. Dave & Pat McKenna, 0121 628 1397, pat_mckenna66@hotmail.com, www.littleindonesia.wordpress.com. *1½ m from Kings Heath High St. Poston Croft is 6th L off Broad Lane, which is off A435 Alcester Rd.* Home-made teas. **Adm £3, chd free. Suns 29 June; 27 July (11-4). Visitors also welcome by appt, June - Aug, groups 10+.**
A garden that is the realisation of my dreams. An amazing plant paradise with the feel of entering a jungle, even though we are in the heart of Birmingham. Planted so that it seems to go on for ever. Plants of unusual leaf shapes and textures. Bananas, cannas and grasses jostle with one another for space. A plantaholic's paradise. Featured in 'Gardeners World' Magazine, on 'BBC Gardeners' World' and Central TV. Steps down to garden, gravel paths.

✂ ☕ ☎

35 MARIE CURIE HOSPICE GARDENS
911-913 Warwick Road. B91 3ER. Marie Curie Hospice. *¼ m SE of Solihull. Car park kindly provided by Solihull School on B4025 between town & hospice. Disabled badge holders park at hospice.* Home-made teas. **Adm £2, chd free (share to Marie Curie Cancer Care). Sat 12 July (1.30-5).**
The hospice garden of tranquillity invites you to stroll down a garden path which has secluded seating areas, water features, mixed planting and climbers. The festival garden is a family garden with playhouse, seating area and water feature.

🚶 ✂ ❀ ☕

36 ◆ THE MASTER'S GARDEN
Lord Leycester Hospital. CV34 4BH. The Governors. *W end of Warwick High St, behind hospital.* **Adm £2, chd free. Apr-Sept (10-4.30).**
Restored historic walled garden hidden behind the medieval buildings of this home for retired ex-servicemen, also

open to the public. Mixed shrub and herbaceous planting with climbing roses and clematis, Norman arch, ancient Egyptian Nilometer, thatched summerhouse, gazebo, knot garden and C18 pineapple pit.

✂

Bananas, cannas and grasses jostle with one another . . .

37 MAXSTOKE CASTLE
Coleshill B46 2RD. Mr & Mrs M C Fetherston-Dilke. *2½ m E of Coleshill. E of Birmingham, on B4114. Take R turn down Castle Lane, Castle drive 1¼ m on R.* Home-made teas. **Adm £6.50, chd free, concessions £4. Sun 15 June (11-5).**
Approx 5 acres of garden and grounds with herbaceous, shrubs and trees in the immed surroundings of this C14 moated castle. Some rooms in house also open.

🚶 ✂ ❀ ☕

38 ◆ MIDDLETON HALL
Tamworth B78 2AE. Middleton Hall Trust, 01827 283095, middletonhalltrust.co.uk. *4m S of Tamworth, 2m N J9 M42. On A4091 between The Belfry & Drayton Manor.* **Adm £3, chd £1. Suns & Bank Hol Mons, Apr-Sept. For NGS: Sun 8 June (1-5).**
Two walled gardens set in 40 acres of grounds surrounding GII Middleton Hall, the C17 home of naturalists Sir Francis Willughby and John Ray. Large colour themed herbaceous borders radiating from a central pond, restored gazebo, pergola planted with roses and wisteria. Courtyard garden with raised beds. SSSI Nature Trail, craft centre, music in Hall. Gravel paths.

🚶 ❀

39 ◆ THE MILL GARDEN
55 Mill Street, Warwick CV34 4HB. Julia Measures. *Off A425 beside castle gate at the bottom of Mill St. Use St Nicholas car park.* **Adm £1.50, chd free with adult. 1 Apr to 31 Oct (9-6).**
½ -acre garden with abundance of plants, shrubs and trees beneath the walls of Warwick Castle beside the R Avon. Place of peace and beauty.

40 MOSELEY GARDENS SOUTH
Birmingham B13 9TF. *3m city centre. Halfway between Kings Heath and Moseley village. From A435 turn at the main Moseley T-lights on to St Mary's Row/Wake Green Rd. 1st R, Oxford Rd, then 1st R, School Rd. Prospect Rd is 3rd on L, Ashfield Rd is 4th on R.* **Combined adm £3.50, chd free. Sun 22 June (2-6).**

7 ASHFIELD ROAD
Hilary Bartlett & John Dring
Small garden with secluded, cottage feel. Attractive pond with rockery, waterfall and shingle bank. % plant sales in aid of Prostrate Cancer.

❀

19 PROSPECT ROAD
Mr A J White
Well planted suburban garden with plenty of colour.

65 SCHOOL ROAD
Wendy Weston
Small shady garden with patio, pergola and pond. Designed for easy maintenance.

41 ◆ PACKWOOD HOUSE
Hockley Heath B94 6AT. The National Trust, 01564 783294, packwood@nationaltrust.org.uk. *11m SE of Birmingham. 2m E of Hockley Heath.* **House and Garden Adm £7.30, chd £3.65, Garden only Adm £4.20, chd £2.10. 9 Feb-2 Nov, Wed-Sun & BH Mons, 11-5. For NGS: Thu 26 June (11-5).**
Carolean yew garden representing the Sermon on the Mount. Tudor house with tapestries, needlework and furniture of the period. Gravel paths, steps to raised terrace.

🚶 ✂ ❀

42 PARHAM LODGE
Alveston CV37 7QN. Mr & Mrs K C Edwards, 01789 268955. *2m E of Stratford-upon-Avon. Off B4086, Stratford to Wellesbourne rd.* Home-made teas. **Adm £3, chd free. Suns 13 Apr; 24 Aug (1-5). Visitors also welcome by appt.**
31-yr-old garden with a small wood, large old cedar, copper beech, hornbeams and a large pond. Sunny and shady seating areas, terraces, pots and topiary. Variety of unusual shrubs for all seasons, roses. Large island bed incl grasses, herbaceous and small orchard with many bulbs. Birds and wildlife encouraged. Small village, church worth a visit, good pub.

🚶 ❀ ☕ ☎

Lawns lead down to the lake around which you can walk amongst the trees and wildlife with stunning views . . .

43 PEBWORTH GARDENS
Stratford-upon-Avon CV37 8XZ. *9m SW of Stratford-upon-Avon. On B439 at Bidford turn L towards Honeybourne, after 3m turn L at Xrds signed Pebworth*. Home-made teas at Pebworth Village Hall. **Combined adm £4, chd free.** Sun 25, Mon 26 May (2-6).
Peaceful village with beautiful church. Some parts are very old - Shakespeare referred to 'Piping Pebworth'. A number of thatched cottages line Friday Street.

1 ELM CLOSE
Mr & Mrs G Keyte
Small cottage garden, very well stocked and with many features of interest.

ICKNIELD BARN
Sheila Davies
Very small walled cottage garden which almost becomes a part of the living room! Designed for relaxation and pottering, yet still full of interest.

IVYBANK
Mr & Mrs R Davis
1/3 -acre garden with ferns, ivies, roses and shrubs. Nursery holds National Collection of Pelargoniums and Hederas.

THE KNOLL
Mr K Wood
Cottage-style walled garden.

NEW THE MOUNT
Mr & Mrs J A Ilott
Traditional garden with heavy clay soil overlying blue lias. Large lawn with perennial borders and rose arbour at rear. Front cottage garden.

NEW PRIMROSE HILL
Richard & Margaret Holland
Split-level garden completely redesigned in 2007 and still settling in. Raised rose beds, upper and lower lawns, terrace, shrubbery, pergola, lavender borders and fish pond.

NEW WELL COTTAGE
Mrs O'Grady
Family garden wth cottage style planting, mature trees, pond, organic potager and chickens. Gravel path to front & side garden.

44 50 PEREIRA ROAD
Harborne B17 9JN. Peg Peil, 0121 427 7573. *Between Gillhurst Rd & Margaret Grove, 1/4 m from Hagley Rd or 1/2 m from Harborne High St*. Home-made teas. **Adm £2, chd free.** Sun 27 Apr (2-5). **Also open with Pereira Road Gardens. Visitors also welcome by appt.**
Plantaholic's garden with over 1000 varieties, many unusual. Large bed of plants with African connections. Many fruits, vegetables, herbs, grasses. Plant sales in aid of CAFOD.

45 PEREIRA ROAD GARDENS
Harborne B17 9JN. *Between Gillhurst Rd & Margaret Grove, 1/4 m from Hagley Rd or 1/2 m from Harborne High St*. Home-made teas at 10 Pereira Rd. **Combined adm £3, chd free.** Sun 29 June (2-5).
Bird Sanctuary also open.

10 PEREIRA ROAD
Muriel May
S aspect sloping garden with steps, shaded, mature silver birch and acid-loving shrubs, some landscaping.

14 PEREIRA ROAD
Mike Foster
Well established suburban garden with mixed herbaceous and shrub borders, small fruit and vegetable area. Wildlife friendly with 2 ponds and natural area.

50 PEREIRA ROAD
Peg Peil
(See separate entry).

55 PEREIRA ROAD
Emma Davies & Martin Commander
Sloping gravelled garden with mixed planting, grasses and small pond.

46 NEW PRIORS MARSTON MANOR GARDEN
CV47 7RH. Dr & Mrs Mark Cecil, 07758 360839, clare.will@btopenworld.com. *8m SW of Daventry. Off A361 between Daventry and Banbury at Charwelton*. **Adm £4.50, chd free.** Visitors welcome by appt. **Weekdays only, 1 Jul - 29 Aug, 10.30-4, groups and individuals.**
Greatly enhanced by present owners to relate back to a Georgian manor garden. Wonderful walled kitchen garden provides seasonal produce and cut flowers for the house. Herbaceous flower beds and a sunken terrace with water feature by William Pye. Lawns lead down to the lake around which you can walk amongst the trees and wildlife with stunning views up to the house and the new garden aviary. Some gravel paths and steep slopes.

47 NEW ♦ THE QUARRY GARDEN
Mill Hill, Baginton CV8 3AG. Russells Nurseries, www.russellsgardencentre.co.uk. *2m S Coventry centre. 1/4 m from Lunt Roman Fort, opp Old Mill PH*. Teas 4 & 5 May only. Quarry open 1 Feb-24 Dec, 10.30-4.30, adm £2. FOR NGS adm £3, chd free (quarry garden & maze). For NGS: Sun 4, Mon 5 May (11-4.30).
Stunning 6-acre quarry garden with a 35ft rock face. Ponds and rock features amongst a beautiful collection of magnolias and camellias, best in April, followed by a blaze of colour with azaleas and rhododendrons amongst oaks, crategus, birches, conifers, heathers etc. Adjacent - mixed hedge maze 45 x 45yds. Gravel paths, some steep slopes.

48 ◆ RAGLEY HALL GARDENS
Alcester B49 5NJ. Marquess & Marchioness of Hertford, 07917 425664, rossbarbour@ragleyhall.com. *2m SW of Alcester. Off A435/A46 8m from Stratford-upon-Avon.* **Adm £3, chd free. 15 Mar-2 Nov, 10-6, during school holidays and weekends.** For NGS: Suns 10 Feb, 12 Oct, 8 Feb 2009 (11-3).
24 acres of gardens, predominantly mature broadleaved trees, within which a variety of cultivated and non-cultivated areas have been blended to achieve a garden rich in both horticulture and bio-diversity. The winter garden, spring meadows and bulbs make way for summer meadows, herbaceous borders, annual bedding and rose beds to provide a rich tapestry of form, colour and contrast all yr. Some steep slopes.
&. ⋊

49 NEW SIR JOHNS GARDENS
B29 7EP, www.spca.org.uk. *S Birmingham. Off A441, nr Selly Park Tavern.* Home-made teas at 47 St Johns Road. **Combined adm £3.50, chd free. Sun 22 June (1-5.30).**
3 gardens with interesting features, created by 3 plantaholics.
☕

SECRET GARDEN
73 Sir Johns Road. Mrs Carol Dockery.
Tropical cordylines, banana, washitonia palms, rare yucca - on different levels leading to sun house with a Morroccan feel. Featured in 'Garden Monthly'.
⋊

NEW 47 SIR JOHNS ROAD
Julie & Steve Cray
150x22ft. Side has seating and shade loving plants, patio with pot plants through to lawned area with cottage garden feel, pergola over agaves and succulents, arch through to area with exotic plants.
⋊ ❀

NEW 61 ST JOHNS ROAD
Graham Allen
English suburban garden with interesting plants, scree bed, pond, patios, range of pots and shrubs.
⋊

SOUTH KILWORTH GARDENS
See Leicestershire & Rutland.

50 NEW THE STABLES SELLY PARK
B29 7JW. *2m SW Birmingham, nr. University. From A38 take Eastern Rd, R into Selly Wick Rd - which is also off A441. Park in rd.* Home-made teas at no 9. **Combined adm £3, chd free. Sun 13 July (2-6).**
4 small interesting and different S and W facing gardens leading off a secluded private driveway in a peaceful mature woodland setting (designated Nature Conservation area) all landscaped and planted from 'building sites' since 1994.
☕

NEW 9 THE STABLES
Jeff & Heather Bissenden
Front garden recently landscaped with rockery, heathers, sunny and shady areas. Walled rear contains vegetables, ornamental shrubs and woodland, patio pots and hanging baskets containing unusual geraniums.
&. ⋊ ❀

NEW 18 THE STABLES
Altaf & Shenaz Kotadia
Secluded, leafy, walled rear and side garden with attractive thatched gazebo and shrub border. Lawn and interesting patio area with built-in barbecue, climbing plants and colourful pots.
&. ⋊

NEW 3 THE STABLES
Mark & Annie Kenchington
Open plan front and secluded walled rear garden with over 150 different ornamental and flowering shrubs, trees, perennials and alpines. Lawn and patio with colourful pots and baskets, small kitchen garden with raised beds.
&. ⋊ ❀

NEW 5 THE STABLES
Francis & Kate Peart
With woodland on its SE border, this compact and partially shaded garden was designed for low maintenance, featuring terracotta fountain, pots and a small pond for wildlife.
&. ⋊

51 STONELEIGH HOUSE
17a Wentworth Road, Four Oaks Park B74 2SD. Richard & Gillian Mason. *1½ m N Sutton Coldfield on A5127. L at Four Oaks Station, 500yds on L.* Cream teas. **Adm £3, chd free. Sun 15 June (1-5).**
½ -acre, mixed beds and borders with mature trees and rhododendrons. Ornamental and wildlife pond, raised beds vegetable plot, various pots and planters. Front garden wild flower meadow.
&. ⋊ ☕

52 STONOR ROAD GARDENS
Hall Green B28 0QJ. *3m W of Solihull. From Robin Hood island on A34 take Baldwins Lane exit. Stonor Rd is 2nd L.* Home-made teas at 172 Stonor Road. **Combined adm £3.50, chd free (share to Marie Curie Cancer Care). Sun 6 July (2-5).**
4 very different gardens demonstrating the variety of design and planting that can be achieved in a modest space. Home-made preserves.
☕

152 STONOR ROAD
Mrs Hull & Mr Dale
Designed for modern living with outdoor dining area, pergola, well planted borders with interesting collection of grasses. Hanging baskets, hostas and clematis.
⋊

154 STONOR ROAD
Mrs J Seager
Small suburban garden with choice plants both in borders and containers. Large pool, with waterfall and koi carp, bordered by alpine bed. Interesting collection of bonsai, seating areas.
⋊

166 STONOR ROAD
Mrs & Mrs R Healey
Very colourful garden with well planted borders, immaculate lawn and a wealth of hanging baskets and containers. Very attractive seating areas at the bottom of the garden.
&. ⋊ ❀

172 STONOR ROAD
Mrs O Walters, 0121 745 2894. Visitors also welcome by appt, Mar to Aug, individuals or small groups.
Plantswoman's garden (approx 65ft x 24ft) with wide variety of plants, some not considered

hardy in this area. Scree, containers, shade beds, ferns, climbers, conservatory, gravel stream and small wildlife pond. Always something new.

Leads into vegetables, orchard and hens . . .

53 STYVECHALE GARDEN TRAIL
Stivichall CV3 5BE. *From A45 take B4113, Leamington Road, towards Coventry. 2nd R into Baginton Road. The Chesils is 1st L.* Light refreshments & teas at 59 The Chesils, Smithy Cottage & The Hiron. **Combined adm £3, chd free. Sun 15 June (11-6).** Maps at Avondale Nursery and St Thomas Mores Church.

AVONDALE NURSERY
Mr Brian Ellis
(See separate entry).

59 THE CHESILS
John Marron & Richard Bantock
Herbaceous plants jostle for attention in a richly planted garden on several levels.

91 THE CHESILS
Graham & Pat White
A series of rooms incl water, gravel and a wildlife garden bursting and brimming with unusual plants.

16 DELAWARE ROAD
Val & Roy Howells
A garden of interest with architectural plants such as phormiums, palms and bamboos. Peaceful seating areas with water features.

SMITHY COTTAGE
Jane & Peter Woodward
Garden constructed on different levels around early C17 cottage. Sunken garden, kitchen garden, summer house terrace, pond and perennial borders.

6 TOWNSEND CROFT
Jean & John Garrison
An herbaceous border and heathers surround decoratively paved and planted area to the front. To the back are deep colourful herbaceous borders with gazebo, water features, hidden garden and mature trees. Interesting and varied planting.

NEW 21 STAMFORD AVENUE
Jan Cooper
An impressive collection of heucheras is just one of the delights of this mature suburban garden.

NEW 2 THE HIRON
Sue & Graham Pountney
Not just a water garden, but every nook and cranny packed with fascinating plants.

54 NEW TANWORTH-IN-ARDEN GARDENS
B94 5EA. *9m S of Birmingham, between A435 & A3400. Just off B4101.* Home-made teas in all gardens, tea 50p, cream teas £4. **Combined adm £5, chd free (share to Edward's Trust). Sat 17, Sun 18 May (2-6).** Lovely village with an interesting church.

NEW ELMHURST
Vicarage Hill. Mr & Mrs Richard Lockwood
See separate entry.

NEW FAIRLAWNS
Mr & Mrs Ward
Small immaculate garden with many unusual plants.

NEW THE SPINNEY
Mr & Mrs John Palmer
1/2 -acre garden on 3 sides, many mature trees, wide variety of shrubs incl rhododendrons, azaleas, camellias and magnolias in spring. 2 water features, sculptures and many plants in pots.

NEW THE UPLANDS
Mrs Lindi Lea
1 1/2 -acre sunny mature hillside

garden arranged in 3 tiers of ascending wildness. The first mimics hot desert, leads into vegetables, orchard and hens, finishing in pasture, planned for yr-round colour.

55 NEW 91 TOWER ROAD
B75 5EQ. Heather & Gary Hawkins, 0121 323 2561, heatherhawkins@talktalk.net. *3m N Sutton Coldfield. From A5127 at Mere Green Island, turn into Mere Green Rd, L at St James, L again.* Cream teas. **Adm £2.50, chd free. Sun 22 June (1.30-5.30).** Visitors also welcome by appt, groups 10+.
163ft mature garden with curved borders and island beds, mixed shrubs and perennials thrive in this S-facing garden. Fish pond, rockery, vegetable plot and and unusual cast iron water feature all provide additional interest and an ideal garden for both restful comtemplation and hide and seek.

56 ◆ UPTON HOUSE
Banbury OX15 6HT. The National Trust, 01295 670266, www.nationaltrust.org.uk. *7m NW of Banbury. On A422, 1m S of Edgehill.* **House and Garden Adm £8.50, chd £4.20, Garden only Adm £5, chd £2.50, Groups, garden £4.25, House £6.70. Mar-Nov, 11-5 (House 1-5) Sat-Wed (7 days Easter & summer hols). For NGS: Sat 19 July (11-5).** Extensive valley gardens with elements from medieval through to 1930s. Cascading terraces of colourful borders descend to a rare kitchen garden, with pools and a bog garden in the valley below. National Collection of Asters splendid in the autumn. Wide lawns surround house famous for an internationally important collection of fine art and porcelain. Access to S lawn for views over garden only.

WALTON GARDENS
See Leicestershire & Rutland.

57 WARMINGTON VILLAGE GARDENS
OX17 1BY. *5m NW of Banbury. Off B4100.* Home-made teas at village hall. **Combined adm £4, chd free**

(share to Katherine House Hospice). **Sun 22 June (1-6).** Village map given to all visitors. Heritage trail.

3 COURT CLOSE
Mr & Mrs C J Crocker
Terraced garden with pockets of interest and lots of seating. Mixed planting for through the year colour with many aromatic plants. Water features incl spring fed well, mixed surfaces, patios with container planting.

THE GLEBE HOUSE
Mrs J Thornton
Village garden of 1/4 acre with lawns, mature trees, roses, shrubs and perennials. Interesting conifer border established 1976. Flagstone terrace with distant views over countryside.

GROVE FARM HOUSE
Richard & Kate Lister
This large garden is now taking shape after 5yrs of development. A field, which originally ran to the back door, has new paths, hedges, trees and beds - herbaceous and edible - and a knot garden.

NEW MANOR COTTAGE
Mr & Mrs P Matthews
Cottage garden with wisteria archway. Water feature, mixed borders, quiet seating areas and terraced herb garden.

THE MANOR HOUSE
Mr & Mrs G Lewis
Large garden, fruit and vegetable plot, flower beds, knot garden.

NEW OLD SCHOOL FARMHOUSE
Mr & Mrs J Deakin
1/3 -acre, under re-development. Walled garden with mixed borders, small woodland walk, grassed area with ornamental trees. 2007 planting of widened mixed border, hosta bed and small herb garden.

NEW 1 RECTORY CLOSE
Mrs J Adams
A garden that wraps around the

house with beech hedge, trees and shrubs. Floral border, pond, fruit trees and vegetable patch leading to a walled garden.

SPRINGFIELD HOUSE
Jenny & Roger Handscombe
Interesting house (1539) set in 1/2 - acre, very informal country garden.

NEW 1 THE WHEELWRIGHTS
Miss L Bunn
Very small terraced walled garden with mixed surfaces, Hornton stone retaining walls and steps. Mostly shrubs, grasses and ferns with specimen fastigiated yews and ornamental vine. No gnomes! 15 steps up to garden.

NEW 2 THE WHEELWRIGHTS
Mrs C Hunter
Very small walled garden laid to grass, paving, flower beds and containers. Tradition planting of perennials. 15 steps up to garden.

WESTERING
Mr & Mrs R Neale
Attractive 1/2 acre garden with herbaceous borders stocked with many interesting and unusual plants, vegetable plot, pond and chickens.

58 WHICHFORD & ASCOTT GARDENS
CV36 5PQ. *6m SE of Shipston on Stour. Turn E off A3400 at Long Compton for Whichford.* Teas in the Reading Room adjacent to Church. **Combined adm £4, chd free. Sun 15 June (2-6).** Enjoy a stroll around two peaceful stone villages on the edge of the Cotswolds with C13 church, pottery and inn.

ASCOTT LODGE
Charlotte Copley
Beautiful views, lawns sloping down to pond, well stocked shrub borders, courtyard garden. Many interesting plants. Gravel paths.

BROOK HOLLOW
Mr & Mrs J A Round
Terraced hillside garden with large variety of trees, shrubs and plants,

stream and water features. Competition for children. Wheelchair access to lower garden only.

THE OLD HOUSE
Whichford. Mr & Mrs T A Maher
Undulating, softly planted gardens spilling down through mature trees and shrubs to wildlife ponds. Gravel paths.

THE OLD RECTORY
Whichford. Mr & Mrs P O'Kane
Informal garden structured around ponds and streams with interesting borders.

NEW SCHOOL HOUSE
Janet Knight
1/3 acre village garden overlooking the village green. Lawns, shrub roses and herbaceous perennials.

SEPTEMBER HOUSE
Mrs J Clayton
Secluded peaceful garden, in full colour in June, with roses and other interesting plants.

THE WHICHFORD POTTERY
Mr & Mrs J B M Keeling,
www.whichfordpottery.com
Secret walled garden, unusual plants, large vegetable garden and rambling cottage garden. Adjoins the pottery and shop. Featured in ' GGG'.

WILLOUGHBY GARDENS
See Leicestershire & Rutland.

Quiet seating areas and terraced herb garden . . .

59 WITS END
59 Tanworth Lane, Shirley B90 4DQ. Sue Mansell, 0121 744 4337. *2m SW of Solihull. Take B4102 from Solihull, 2m. R at island onto A34. After next island (Sainsbury's) Tanworth Lane is 1st L off A34.* Home-made teas. **Adm £2, chd free. Sun 18 May (2-5); Sat 28 June (3-6); Sun 10 Aug (2-5).**

Visitors also welcome by appt, groups of 10+.

Peaceful and interesting all-yr-round plantaholic's cottage-style garden. Hundreds of perennials, alpines and shrubs, many new rare and unusual in various shaped beds (some colour co-ordinated) and borders. Gravel area, alpine sinks, rockery, extensive shade and small waterfall, river and bog. Millenium Wheel of sleepers and crazypaving in woodland setting. Plants in aid of Alzheimers Society. Assistance available for shallow steps.

60 WOODBROOKE QUAKER STUDY CENTRE
1046 Bristol Road, Selly Oak B29 6LJ, www.woodbrooke.org.uk. *4m SW of Birmingham. On A38 Bristol Rd, S of Selly Oak, opp Witherford Way.* Light refreshments & teas. **Adm £3, chd £1.50. Sun 15 June (2.30-5.30).** 10 acres of organically-managed garden and grounds. Grade II listed former home of George Cadbury (not open). Herbaceous and shrub borders, walled garden with herb garden, potager and cutting beds, Chinese garden, orchard, arboretum, lake and extensive woodland walks. Very fine variety of trees. Craft stalls, boating on lake. Lake not wheelchair accessible.

61 WOODPECKERS
The Bank, Marlcliff, nr Bidford-on-Avon B50 4NT. Drs Andy & Lallie Cox, 01789 773416, andrewcox@doctors.org.uk. *7m SW of Stratford-upon-Avon. Off B4085 between Bidford-on-Avon & Cleeve Prior.* **Adm £5, chd free. Visitors welcome by appt.**

Peaceful 2¹/₂ -acre plantsman's country garden designed and maintained by garden-mad owners since 1965. A garden for all seasons. Unusual plants, hidden surprises, interesting trees, colour-themed borders, potager and knot garden. Wooden sculptures of St Fiacre and The Green Man carved by the owner. Lovely garden buildings of framed green oak. Featured in 'Country Homes & Interiors' & "Daily Telegraph".

Snowdrops, hellebores, clematis, roses, grasses and alpines . . .

62 WOOTTON GRANGE
Pettiford Lane, Henley-in-Arden B95 6AH. Mrs Jean Tarmey, 01564 792592. *1m E of Henley-in-Arden. Take 1st R off A4189 Warwick Rd on to Pettiford Lane, garden is 300yds on R. From A3400 in Wootton Wawen turn by craft centre on to Pettiford Lane, garden 1m on L.* Light refreshments & teas. **Adm £2.50, chd free. Thurs 6 Mar (11-3); 3 Apr; 15 May (2-5). Visitors also welcome by appt, inc groups, all year.**
1-acre farm garden with yr-round interest surrounding early Victorian farmhouse (not open). Wide variety of unusual plants incl snowdrops, hellebores, clematis, roses, grasses and alpines. Bog garden, kitchen garden.

Warwickshire and part of the West Midlands County Volunteers

County Organiser Warwickshire
Julia Sewell, Dinsdale House, Baldwins Lane, Upper Tysoe, Warwick CV35 0TX, 01295 680234, sewelljulia@btinternet.com

County Organiser West Midlands
Jackie Harvey, Ashover, 25 Burnett Road, Streetly, Sutton Coldfield B74 3EL, 0121 353 0547

County Treasurer, Warwickshire
John Wilson, Victoria House, Farm Street, Harbury, Leamington Spa CV33 9LR, 01926 612572

County Treasurer, West Midlands
Martin Harvey, Ashover , 25 Burnett Road, Streetly, Sutton Coldfield B74 3EL, 0121 353 0547

Assistant County Organisers
Mary Lesinski, The Master's House, Lord Leycester Hospital, High Street, Warwick CV34 4BH, 01926 499918, lordlycester@btinternet.com
Peter Pashley, Millstones, Mayfield Avenue, Stratford-upon-Avon CV37 6XB, 01789 294932, peter@peterpash.mail.co.uk
Janet Neale, Westering, The Green, Warmington, Banbury OX17 1BU, 01295 690515

Mark your diary with these special events in 2008

EXPLORE SECRET GARDENS DURING CHELSEA WEEK

Tue 20 May, Wed 21 May, Thur 22 May, Fri 23 May
Full day tours: £78 per person, 10% discount for groups
Advance Booking required, telephone 01932 864532 or
email pennysnellflowers@btinternet.com

Specially selected private gardens in London, Surrey and Berkshire. The tour price includes transport and lunch with wine at a popular restaurant or pub.

FROGMORE – A ROYAL GARDEN (BERKSHIRE)

Tue 3 June 10am - 5.30pm (last adm 4pm)
Garden adm £4, chd free. Advance booking recommended telephone 01483 211535
or email orders@ngs.org.uk

A unique opportunity to explore 30 acres of landscaped garden, rich in history and beauty.

FLAXBOURNE FARM – FUN AND SURPRISES (BEDFORDSHIRE)

Sun 8 June 10am - 5pm Adm £5, chd free
No booking required, come along on the day!

Bring the whole family and enjoy a plant fair and garden party and have fun in this beautiful and entertaining garden of 2 acres.

WISLEY RHS GARDEN – MUSIC IN THE GARDEN (SURREY)

Tue 19 August 6 - 9pm

Adm (incl RHS members) £7, chd under 15 free

A special opening of this famous garden, exclusively for the NGS. Enjoy music and entertainment as you explore a range of different gardens.

For further information visit www.ngs.org.uk or telephone 01483 211535

WILTSHIRE

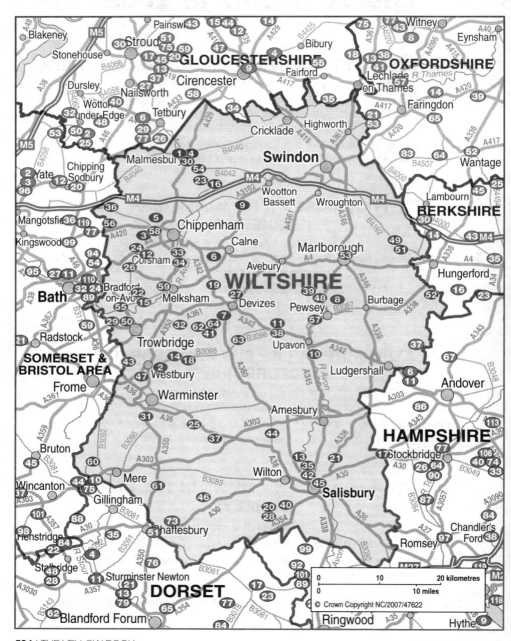

Opening Dates

February

SUNDAY 3
22 Great Chalfield Manor

SATURDAY 9
34 Lacock Abbey Gardens

SUNDAY 10
34 Lacock Abbey Gardens

SATURDAY 16
34 Lacock Abbey Gardens

SUNDAY 17
34 Lacock Abbey Gardens

March

SUNDAY 2
1 Abbey House Gardens

SUNDAY 23
36 Littleton Drew Gardens

MONDAY 24
36 Littleton Drew Gardens

SUNDAY 30
44 The Mill House

April

WEDNESDAY 2
57 Sharcott Manor

SUNDAY 6
7 Broadleas Gardens Charitable Trust
12 Corsham Court
57 Sharcott Manor

SUNDAY 13
56 Ridleys Cheer

SUNDAY 20
8 Broomsgrove Lodge
35 Little Durnford Manor
48 Oare House

SUNDAY 27
29 Iford Manor
55 Priory House

May

SUNDAY 4
61 Waterdale House

WEDNESDAY 7
19 Enfield
57 Sharcott Manor

THURSDAY 8
19 Enfield

FRIDAY 9
45 Mompesson House

SUNDAY 11
6 Bowood Rhododendron Walks
17 Downs View
41 Mansion Farm House

56 Ridleys Cheer
62 Wellaway

WEDNESDAY 14
19 Enfield

THURSDAY 15
19 Enfield

FRIDAY 16
38 Mallards

SUNDAY 18
3 Biddestone Manor
11 Conock Manor
39 Manor Farm
47 Oak Tree Cottage

WEDNESDAY 21
19 Enfield

THURSDAY 22
19 Enfield

SUNDAY 25
28 Hyde's House
36 Littleton Drew Gardens
37 Long Hall
59 32 Shurnhold

MONDAY 26
36 Littleton Drew Gardens

WEDNESDAY 28
19 Enfield

THURSDAY 29
19 Enfield

FRIDAY 30
63 Windmill Cottage

June

SUNDAY 1
9 33 Calne Road
42 Mawarden Court
55 Priory House

TUESDAY 3
9 33 Calne Road

WEDNESDAY 4
19 Enfield
57 Sharcott Manor

THURSDAY 5
19 Enfield

SATURDAY 7
14 Court Lane Farm

SUNDAY 8
10 Chisenbury Priory
12 Corsham Court
14 Court Lane Farm
16 Dauntsey Gardens
18 Edington Gardens
20 Faulstone House
21 The Grange
24 Guyers House
32 Keevil Gardens

52 The Old Rectory
54 The Pound House (Afternoon & Evening)
56 Ridleys Cheer

WEDNESDAY 11
19 Enfield

THURSDAY 12
19 Enfield
40 Manor House

FRIDAY 13
63 Windmill Cottage

SATURDAY 14
53 Poulton House

SUNDAY 15
5 Bolehyde Manor
13 The Court House
26 Hazelbury Manor Gardens
35 Little Durnford Manor
39 Manor Farm
50 The Old Malthouse
58 Sheldon Manor

WEDNESDAY 18
19 Enfield

THURSDAY 19
19 Enfield
49 The Old Farmhouse
51 The Old Mill

FRIDAY 20
38 Mallards
59 32 Shurnhold (Evening)

SATURDAY 21
23 Great Somerford Gardens

SUNDAY 22
23 Great Somerford Gardens
31 Job's Mill

WEDNESDAY 25
19 Enfield

THURSDAY 26
19 Enfield

FRIDAY 27
63 Windmill Cottage

SATURDAY 28
44 The Mill House

SUNDAY 29
44 The Mill House
46 North Cottage & Woodview Cottage (Afternoon & Evening)

July

WEDNESDAY 2
57 Sharcott Manor

SATURDAY 5
2 Beggars Knoll

SUNDAY 6
- **2** Beggars Knoll
- **4** Blicks Hill House
- **25** Hatch House
- **64** Worton Gardens

FRIDAY 11
- **38** Mallards
- **63** Windmill Cottage

SUNDAY 13
- **33** Lackham Gardens

SATURDAY 19
- **15** The Courts
- **60** Stourhead Garden

SUNDAY 20
- **17** Downs View
- **48** Oare House
- **55** Priory House

FRIDAY 25
- **63** Windmill Cottage

SATURDAY 26
- **30** 3 Ingram Street

SUNDAY 27
- **30** 3 Ingram Street

August

WEDNESDAY 6
- **57** Sharcott Manor

SUNDAY 17
- **43** The Mead Nursery

September

WEDNESDAY 3
- **57** Sharcott Manor

THURSDAY 4
- **40** Manor House

FRIDAY 5
- **40** Manor House

SUNDAY 7
- **47** Oak Tree Cottage
- **57** Sharcott Manor

SATURDAY 20
- **15** The Courts

February 2009

SUNDAY 1
- **22** Great Chalfield Manor

SATURDAY 7
- **34** Lacock Abbey Gardens

SUNDAY 8
- **34** Lacock Abbey Gardens

SATURDAY 14
- **34** Lacock Abbey Gardens

SUNDAY 15
- **34** Lacock Abbey Gardens

Gardens open to the public

- **1** Abbey House Gardens
- **6** Bowood Rhododendron Walks
- **7** Broadleas Gardens Charitable Trust
- **12** Corsham Court
- **15** The Courts
- **22** Great Chalfield Manor
- **29** Iford Manor
- **33** Lackham Gardens
- **34** Lacock Abbey Gardens
- **43** The Mead Nursery
- **44** The Mill House
- **45** Mompesson House
- **58** Sheldon Manor
- **60** Stourhead Garden
- **61** Waterdale House

By appointment only

- **27** Home Covert Gardens & Arboretum

Also open by appointment ☎

- **2** Beggars Knoll
- **3** Biddestone Manor
- **4** Blicks Hill House
- **5** Bolehyde Manor
- **10** Chisenbury Priory
- **11** Conock Manor
- **14** Court Lane Farm
- **19** Enfield
- **36** Goulters Mill Farm, Littleton Drew Gardens
- **27** Home Covert Gardens & Arboretum
- **30** 3 Ingram Street
- **38** Mallards
- **40** Manor House
- **46** North Cottage & Woodview Cottage
- **47** Oak Tree Cottage
- **50** The Old Malthouse
- **53** Poulton House
- **54** The Pound House
- **56** Ridleys Cheer
- **57** Sharcott Manor
- **59** 32 Shurnhold
- **23** Somerford House, Great Somerford Gardens
- **63** Windmill Cottage

Can't make it to Beijing? Get a taste of China in Wiltshire . . .

The Gardens

1 ♦ **ABBEY HOUSE GARDENS**
Malmesbury Town Centre
SN16 9AS. Barbara & Ian Pollard,
01666 827650,
www.abbeyhousegardens.co.uk. *5m
N of J17 M4. Beside C12 Abbey.
Parking in town centre (short stay) or
follow brown signs to long stay (via
steps to gardens).* **Adm £6.50, chd
£2.50, concessions £5.75. 21 Mar to
31 Oct inc.** For NGS: Sun 2 Mar
(11-5.30).
5 beautiful acres planted by present
owner. Over 130,000 spring bulbs
especially tulips, 'medieval' herb
garden, topiary, knot garden,
herbaceous borders, laburnum walk,
UK's largest private collection of roses
(over 2000), unique auricula theatre,
ornamental trees, rare plants, wooded
walk to river, 'monastic' fish ponds,
waterfall and fernery. Colour, peace
and contrast. Gravel paths, some
slopes.
♿ ✖ ⊗ ☕

BATH PRIORY HOTEL
See Somerset & Bristol.

2 **BEGGARS KNOLL**
Newtown, Westbury BA13 3ED.
Colin Little & Penny Stirling, 01373
823383. *1m SE of Westbury. Turn off
B3098 at White Horse Pottery, up hill
towards the White Horse for 1km.
Limited parking at end of drive.* Home-
made teas. **Adm £3, chd free. Sat 5,
Sun 6 July (2-6). Visitors also
welcome by appt.**
Can't make it to Beijing? Get a taste of
China in Wiltshire instead. Visit one of
the very few Chinese gardens in the
UK. 1-acre sloping site with 3 pavilions,
moongate, zigzag pathways, ponds - a
series of garden rooms full of rare
Chinese plants. Also podocarp and
viburnum collections, mixed borders,
large potager with chickens and
outstanding views.
✖ ⊗ ☕ ☎

3 **BIDDESTONE MANOR**
Biddestone SN14 7DJ. Mr H Astrup,
01249 713211. *5m W of Chippenham.
On A4 between Chippenham &
Corsham turn N. From A420, 5m W of
Chippenham, turn S. Car park, please
do not park on rd.* Home-made teas.
**Adm £3.50, chd free. Sun 18 May
(2-5). Visitors also welcome by appt,
for gardening groups of 10+, Thurs
afternoon or evening.**
First ever May opening! See the spring

in our peaceful 8 acres with small lake and streams, wild flowers, arboretum with grasses and bulbs, walled kitchen garden, orchard, cutting garden, beautiful shrub borders. C17 Manor House (not open) with ancient dovecote.

 ♿ ✕ ⊛ ☕ ☎

④ BLICKS HILL HOUSE
Blicks Hill, Malmesbury SN16 9HZ. Alan & Valerie Trotman, 01666 829669. *1/2 m E of Malmesbury. W of (A429) bypass, between roundabouts.* Home-made teas. **Adm £3.50, chd free. Sun 6 July (12-5.30). Visitors also welcome by appt, groups 10+.** Colourful 1-acre garden on sloping site with mature trees, created since 2004 and packed with shrubs and perennials, many rare and unusual, herbaceous border. Unique pergola leading into woodland glade. New water feature, stream and waterfall constructed in green slate. Hanging baskets, tubs and bedding plants add extra impact.

✕ ☕ ☎

⑤ BOLEHYDE MANOR
Allington SN14 6LW. The Earl & Countess Cairns, 01249 652105, amcairns@aol.com. *1 1/2 m W of Chippenham. On Bristol Rd (A420). Turn N at Allington Xrds. 1/2 m on R.* Parking in field. Home-made teas. **Adm £3.50, chd 50p (share to Kington St Michael Church on open day). Sun 15 June (2.30-6). Visitors also welcome by appt in groups.** Series of gardens around C16 manor house (not open), enclosed by walls and topiary, densely planted with many interesting shrubs and climbers, mixed rose and herbaceous beds. Inner courtyard with troughs full of tender plants, wild flower orchard, vegetable, fruit garden and greenhouse yard. Collection of tender pelargoniums, adventure tree house for children. Featured in 'GGG' & Local Press. Some steps.

 ♿ ✕ ⊛ ☕ ☎

⑥ ♦ BOWOOD RHODODENDRON WALKS
nr Chippenham SN11 9PG. The Marquis of Lansdowne, 01249 812102, www.bowood.org. *3 1/2 m SE of Chippenham. Entrance off A342 between Sandy Lane & Derry Hill villages.* **Adm £5.25, chd free, concessions £4.75. Daily, late Apr to early June.** For NGS: **Sun 11 May (11-6).**

This 60-acre woodland garden of azaleas and rhododendrons is one of the most exciting of its type in the country. From the individual flowers to the breathtaking sweep of colour formed by hundreds of shrubs, surrounded by carpets of bluebells, this is a garden not to be missed. Planting first began in 1850 and some of the earliest known hybrids feature among the collection. Bowood House and Gardens a separate attraction, 2m from Rhododendron Walks.

✕

⑦ ♦ BROADLEAS GARDENS CHARITABLE TRUST
Devizes SN10 5JQ. Lady Anne Cowdray, 01380 722035, broadleasgardens@btinternet.co.uk. *1m S of Devizes. On A360 or follow tourist signs from Long Street.* **Adm £5.50, chd £2, groups of 10+ £5. Apr to Oct Suns, Weds & Thurs.** For NGS: **Sun 6 Apr (2-6).** 9-acre garden, a sheltered dell planted with many unusual trees and shrubs. Azaleas, rhododendrons and magnolias with underplantings of trilliums, erythroniums and many others. Herbaceous borders and perennial garden full of interesting plants. Partial wheelchair access.

 ♿ ⊛

⑧ NEW BROOMSGROVE LODGE
New Mill, Pewsey SN9 5LE. Mr & Mrs Peter Robertson. *2m N of Pewsey. From A345 take B3087 Burbage Rd, after 1 1/2 m L to New Mill, through village and past canal. Park in field.* Light refreshments & teas. **Adm £3, chd free. Sun 20 Apr (2-6).** Alongside stunning views of Martinsell Hill, discover the imaginatively planted herbaceous borders and the organic raised vegetable garden. Visit the pond where you might bump into a friendly chicken, the well-stocked greenhouses and vibrantly planted pots that make every corner a surprise.

 ♿ ✕ ⊛ 🛏 ☕

⑨ 33 CALNE ROAD
Lyneham SN15 4PT. Sue & Sam Wright. *7m N of Calne. Next to RAF Lyneham entrance.* Home-made teas. **Adm £2, chd 50p. Sun 1, Tue 3 June (1-5).** Approx 3/4 -acre informal garden comprising modest collection of hostas, clematis and roses. Small kitchen garden, pond and mature orchard with bantams, chickens, geese, doves and dovecote. Green oasis surrounded by activity.

 ♿ ✕ ⊛ ☕

⑩ CHISENBURY PRIORY
East Chisenbury SN9 6AQ. Mr & Mrs John Manser, 07810 483984, john.manser@shaftesbury.co.uk. *3m SW of Pewsey. Turn E from A345 at Enford then N to E Chisenbury, main gates 1m on R.* Cream teas. **Adm £3, chd free. Sun 8 June (2-6). Visitors also welcome by appt.** Medieval Priory with Queen Anne face and early C17 rear (not open) in middle of 5-acre garden on chalk. Mature garden with fine trees within clump and flint walls, herbaceous borders, shrubs, roses. Moisture-loving plants along mill leat, carp pond, orchard and wild garden, many unusual plants.

 ♿ ✕ ⊛ ☕ ☎

CLAVERTON MANOR
See Somerset & Bristol.

CONHOLT PARK
See Hampshire.

⑪ CONOCK MANOR
Chirton SN10 3QQ. Mrs Bonar Sykes, 01380 840227. *5m SE of Devizes. Off A342.* Cream teas. **Adm £3, chd free (share to Chirton Church). Sun 18 May (2-6). Visitors also welcome by appt.** Mixed borders, flowering shrubs, extensive replanting incl new arboretum, interesting decorative brickwork with tiled water runnels to replace old borders. C18 house in Bath stone (not open). Trees of interest incl Liriodendron tulipifera, Zelkova, Catalpa and many different magnolias. Some gravel paths.

 ♿ ✕ ⊛ ☕ ☎

Visit the pond where you might bump into a friendly chicken . . .

12 ◆ CORSHAM COURT
Corsham SN13 0BZ. Mr James Methuen-Campbell, 01249 701610, www.corsham-court.co.uk. *4m W of Chippenham. S of A4.* House & garden £6.50, chd £3, concessions £5. Garden only £2.50, chd £1.50, concessions £2. Please phone or visit website for open days. For NGS: Suns 6 Apr; 8 June (2-5.30). Park and gardens laid out by Capability Brown and Repton. Large lawns with fine specimens of ornamental trees, lily pond with Indian bean trees, spring bulbs, young arboretum, C18 bath house, Elizabethan mansion with alterations. Easy gravel paths.
&. ⊛

13 THE COURT HOUSE
Lower Woodford SP4 6NQ. Mr & Mrs J G Studholme. *3m N of Salisbury. On Woodford Valley rd, parallel to A360 & A345.* Home-made teas. Adm £3, chd free. Sun 15 June (2-6).
3½-acre garden on the banks of the Avon. Herbaceous borders, waterside planting, yew hedges, rambler roses and wild flowers. Ancient site of Bishop's Palace in the time of Old Sarum.
&. ⊛ ☕

14 COURT LANE FARM
Bratton BA13 4RE. Lt Col & Mrs Anthony Hyde, 01380 830364. *2m E of Westbury. Off B3098.* Home-made teas. Adm £3, chd free. Sat 7 (2-6), Sun 8 June (12-6). Visitors also welcome by appt.
Cottage garden of 1 acre, informal, mature and full of interest with numerous rooms. Garden objects, incl rural items, shepherds hut, contemporary sculpture and pottery. Rambling and climbing roses tumble over arches and banks. 80 varieties of hardy geraniums, topiary and wildlife pond.
⚹ ⊛ ☕ ☎

15 ◆ THE COURTS
Holt BA14 6RR. The National Trust, 01225 782340, www.nationaltrust.org.uk. *2m E of Bradford-on-Avon. S of B3107 to Melksham. In Holt follow NT signs, park at village hall.* Adm £5, chd free. For NGS: Sat 19 July; Sat 20 Sept (11-5.30).
Beautifully kept but eclectic garden. Yew hedges divide garden compartments with colour themed borders and organically shaped

topiary. Water garden with 2 recently restored pools, temple, conservatory and small kitchen garden split by an apple allée, all surrounded by 3½ acres of arboretum with specimen trees. Wheelchair access map at reception.
&. ⚹ ⊛ ☕

CROWE HALL
See Somerset & Bristol.

16 DAUNTSEY GARDENS
SN15 4HW. *5m SE of Malmesbury. Approach via Dauntsey Rd from Gt Somerford, 1¼ m from Volunteer Inn.* Home-made teas at Idover House. Combined adm £5, chd free. Sun 8 June (1.30-5).
☕

THE COACH HOUSE
Col & Mrs J Seddon-Brown
Walled garden with mixed borders of herbaceous plants, shrubs, trees, climbing roses and clematis. Approach this peaceful little garden along the drive bordered by mop-head pruned crateagus prunifolia.
&. ⚹

DAUNTSEY PARK WALLED GARDEN
Miss Ann Sturgis
5-acre garden, incl 2-acre walled garden with yew topiary and box-edged gravel paths. Espaliered fruit trees and wide range of organically-grown vegetables. Rebuilt range of greenhouses. Orchard and woodland walk.
&. ⚹

IDOVER HOUSE
Mr & Mrs Christopher Jerram
Medium-sized garden in established setting with many trees incl two large wellingtonias. Spacious lawns, replanted herbaceous borders, formal rose garden, swimming pool garden, duck pond, yew hedge walk to kitchen garden and woodland garden area.
&. ⚹

THE OLD POND HOUSE
Mr & Mrs Stephen Love
A mixture of formal and informal. Fat carp, fat ducks and lean gardeners! Clipped yews, orchard, striped lawns and a footpath leading to Dauntsey Park Walled Garden.
⚹

17 DOWNS VIEW
Stockbridge Road, Lopcombe Corner SP5 1BW. Chris & Ross Walker. *7m E of Salisbury. At junction of A30 & A343. Parking 200 metres from junction, on A343.* Teas. Adm £2.50, chd free. Suns 11 May; 20 July (12-6).
Approx 40m x 30m garden designed, built and planted over the last few yrs from a grassed area. Vegetable garden and new fruit trees, decked seating spot and terrace with formal planting, sloping down to more informal part around wildlife pond.
⚹ ☕

DYRHAM PARK
See Somerset & Bristol.

Fat carp, fat ducks and lean gardeners! Clipped yews and striped lawns . . .

18 EDINGTON GARDENS
BA13 4QF. *4m NE of Westbury. On B3098 between Westbury & West Lavington. Park off B3098 in church car park or in Monastery Rd opp Monastery Garden House.* Home-made teas in Parish Hall. Combined adm £5, chd free. Sun 8 June (2-6). Village map given to all visitors.
☕

NEW BECKETTS
Mr & Mrs David Bromhead
An old 2-acre garden with varied established hedges compartmenting the garden. Borders, lawns, rose garden, vegetable and fruit garden, lake and lovely views. Some gravel, some narrow paths.
&. ⊛ ⌂

BONSHOMMES COTTAGE
Mr Michael Jones. *Through Old Vicarage garden to avoid steep steps*
¼-acre hillside garden with mixed herbaceous, roses, shrubs. Some long-established Japanese knotweed has been retained as a practical feature.

EDINGTON PRIORY
Mr & Mrs R Cooper
4-acre gardens with medieval well, walls and carp lake. Herbaceous borders, kitchen garden and extensive lawns with shrubs and roses.

THE MONASTERY GARDEN
Mr & Mrs Allanson-Bailey
2¹/₂ -acre garden with many varieties of spring bulbs and shrub roses, 3-acre additional walled garden, medieval walls of national importance.

  ♿ ✿

THE OLD VICARAGE
Mr J N d'Arcy
2-acre garden on greensand on hillside with fine views. Intensively planted with herbaceous borders, wall borders, gravel garden and shrubs. Arboretum with growing range of unusual trees. Woodland plants, bulbs and lilies, with recently introduced species from abroad. National Collection of evening primroses, with over 20 species.

  ♿ ✕ ✿ NCCPG

⑲ ENFIELD
62 Yard Lane, Netherstreet, Bromham SN15 2DT. Graham & Elizabeth Veals, 01380 859303, graham@vealsgd.freeserve.co.uk. *4m NW of Devizes. E off A342 into Yard Lane, garden ¹/₄ m on R. Limited parking.* Teas. **Adm £2.50, chd free. Every Weds & Thurs, 7 May to 26 June; (10.30-6).** Visitors also welcome by appt.
The cottage garden style of planting combines old favourites with many plants not commonly seen in gardens today. The ¹/₂ acre includes 4 separate areas and over 550 species and cultivars of herbaceous plants incl a significant collection of foxgloves in the last 2 yrs.

  ♿ ✕ ✿ ☕ ☎

⑳ FAULSTONE HOUSE
Bishopstone SP5 4BQ. Miss Freya Watkinson. *6m SW of Salisbury. Take minor rd W off A354 at Coombe Bissett, after 3m turn S into Harvest Lane 300yds E of White Hart Inn.* Teas. **Adm £2.50, chd free.** Sun 8 June (2-6).
Separate smaller gardens in large garden surrounding Old Manor House (not open). C14 Defence Tower converted to pigeon loft in C18. Many old-fashioned roses, herbaceous

plants (some unusual), vegetable garden. Meadow with river frontage set in rural surroundings, including the Faulstone herd of Belted Galloways.

  ♿ ✕ ✿ ☕

GANTS MILL & GARDEN
See Somerset & Bristol.

㉑ THE GRANGE
Winterbourne Dauntsey SP4 6ER. Mr & Mrs Rebdi. *4m NE of Salisbury on A338.* Home-made teas. **Adm £3, chd free. Sun 8 June (2-6).**
Spacious 6-acre garden with R Bourne running through. Clipped box, borders. Laburnum, rose and clematis arched walk, lily pond, vegetable and herb garden. Wild natural area. Restored C17 thatched barn open. Gravel paths.

  ♿ ✕ ✿ ☕

㉒ ♦ GREAT CHALFIELD MANOR
nr Melksham SN12 8NH. Mr & Mrs R Floyd & The National Trust, 01225 782239, patsy@greatchalfield.co.uk. *3m SW of Melksham. Take B3107 from Melksham then 1st R to Broughton Gifford. Follow sign for Atworth, turn L for 1m to Manor. Park on grass outside.* **House and Garden adm £6.40, Garden only adm £4.20. NGS day £3.50, chd free. Suns Apr to Oct (2-5). Tues to Thurs guided House tours (11-5). For NGS: Sun 3 Feb (2-4.30). Sun 1st Feb 2009.**
Garden and grounds of 7 acres laid out 1905-12 by Robert Fuller and his wife to designs by Alfred Parsons, Capt Partridge and Sir Harold Brakspear. Incl roses, daffodils, spring flowers, topiary houses, borders, terraces, gazebo, orchard, autumn border. C15 moated manor (not open) and adjoining Parish Church. Snowdrops and aconites enhance moat walk in early spring. Some gravel but also special wheelchair access.

  ♿ ✕ ✿ ✿

Possibly the oldest allotments in the country which are well used . . .

㉓ GREAT SOMERFORD GARDENS
SN15 5JB. *4m SE of Malmesbury. 4m N of M4 between J16 & J17; 2m S of B4042 Malmesbury to Wootton Bassett rd; 3m E of A429 Cirencester to Chippenham rd.* Home-made teas at The Mount House. **Combined adm £4, chd free (share to Clic Sargent). Sat 21, Sun 22 June (1-5.30).**
Medium-sized village, bordered by R Avon, with thriving community, school, pub, post office and general stores. Also has possibly the oldest allotments in the country which are well used. River walk.

  ☕

CLEMATIS
Dauntsey Road. Mr & Mrs Arthur Scott
Small but active, charming village garden created about 19yrs ago. Very well stocked herbaceous borders, shrubs, fruit trees and a pond, with small collection of approx 20 clematis.

  ✕

1 HOLLOW STREET
Bridget Smith
¹/₄ -acre, next door to Old Maltings. Lilies, penstemon and other assorted perennials.

  ✕

THE MOUNT HOUSE
Park Lane. Mr & Mrs McGrath
3-acres of lawns, herbaceous beds, shrubs, large trees, fruit and vegetables. Ancient motte area has been sympathetically replanted and meanders to the R Avon. Historic barn open.

  ♿ ✿

SOMERFORD HOUSE
West Street. Mr & Mrs Martin Jones, 01249 721249. **Visitors also welcome by appt in June & July, no coaches.**
3-acre garden developed over the last 28yrs which incorporates the original orchard and features roses, shrubs, old wisteria, perennials, rockery and pool, vegetables and soft fruit. Gravel drive.

  ♿ ✕ ☎

㉔ GUYERS HOUSE
Pickwick, Corsham SN13 0PS. Mr & Mrs Guy Hungerford. *4m SW of Chippenham. Guyers Lane signed directly off A4 opp B3109 Bradford-on-Avon turning.* Teas. **Adm £3, chd**

free. Sun 8 June (2-5.30).
6-acre garden. Herbaceous borders, yew walks, pleached hornbeam walk. Extensive lawns, ponds, walled garden, rose hoops, climbing and shrub roses, walled kitchen garden, orchard, herb garden.

 ♿ 🐱 ❁ ☕

25 HATCH HOUSE
Mill Lane, Upton Lovell BA12 0JP. Mr & Mrs Peter Akers. *6m E of Warminster. From A36 follow signs into village and Hatch House.* Cream teas. **Adm £2.50, chd free.** Sun 6 July (2-6).
1³/₄ -acre garden on the site of an old cloth mill with industrial archaeological interest. Progress has been made on the renewal of the garden and the river banks. Herbaceous border, rose garden, pebble garden and fernery.

🐱 ❁ ☕

26 HAZELBURY MANOR GARDENS
Wadswick, Box SN13 8HX. *5m SW of Chippenham, 5m NE of Bath. From A4 at Box, A365 to Melksham, at Five Ways junction L onto B3109, 1st L, drive immed on R.* Home-made teas. **Adm £4.50, chd free.** Sun 15 June (2-6).
8 acres Grade II landscaped organic gardens around C15 fortified manor (not open). Impressive yew topiary and clipped beeches around large lawn, herbaceous and mixed borders ablaze in summer, laburnum and lime walkways, rose garden, stone circle and rockery. Walled kitchen garden.

🐱 ❁ ☕

HILL LODGE
See Somerset & Bristol.

HILLTOP
See Dorset.

HODGES BARN
See Gloucestershire North & Central.

27 HOME COVERT GARDENS & ARBORETUM
Roundway SN10 2JA. Mr & Mrs John Phillips, 01380 723407. *1m N of Devizes. On minor rd signed Roundway linking A361 to A342, 1m from each main rd.* **Adm £4, chd free. Visitors welcome by appt.**
Extensive garden on greensand created out of ancient woodland since 1960. Situated below the Downs with distant views. Formal borders around the house contrast with water gardens

in the valley below. Wide range of trees, shrubs and plants grown for yr-round interest. Mar/Apr camellias, magnolias, erythroniums. May/June rhododendrons, malus, davidia, many flowering trees. July/Aug hydrangeas, eucryphias. Water gardens path very steep.

♿ ☎

HOMEWOOD PARK HOTEL
See Somerset & Bristol.

HOOKSHOUSE POTTERY
See Gloucestershire North & Central.

1³/₄-acre garden on the site of an old cloth mill with industrial archaeological interest . . .

28 HYDE'S HOUSE
Dinton SP3 5HH. Mr George Cruddas. *9m W of Salisbury. Off B3089 nr Dinton Church.* Teas. **Adm £3.50, chd free.** Sun 25 May (2-5).
3 acres of wild and formal garden in beautiful situation with series of hedged garden rooms. Numerous roses and borders. Large walled kitchen garden, herb garden and C13 dovecote (open). Charming C16/18 Grade I listed house (not open), with lovely courtyard. NT walks around park and lake.

❁ ☕

29 ◆ IFORD MANOR
nr Bradford-on-Avon BA15 2BA. Mr & Mrs Hignett, 01225 863146, www.ifordmanor.co.uk. *7m S of Bath. Off A36, brown tourist sign to Iford 1m. Or from Bradford-on-Avon or Trowbridge via Lower Westwood village (brown signs).* **Adm £4.50, chd under 10 free, concessions £4.** Easter Mon, Suns Apr & Oct; May to Sept: Tues, Weds, Thurs, Sats, Suns & Bank Hol Mons. For NGS: Sun 27 Apr (2-5).
Very romantic award-winning, Grade I listed Italianate garden famous for its tranquil beauty. Home to the

Edwardian architect and designer Harold Peto 1899-1933. The garden is characterised by steps, terraces, sculpture and magnificent rural views. House not open. Featured in 'The English Garden'. Steep steps.

☕

30 NEW 3 INGRAM STREET
Malmesbury SN16 9BX. Terry & Doreen Soule, 01666 822903, terrylsoule@aol.com. *Use Cross Hayes car park, exit to Silver Street and follow NGS signs 200metres.* Home-made teas. **Adm £3, chd free.** Sat 26, Sun 27 July (11-5). **Visitors also welcome by appt in July for groups 10+.**
Small town garden divided into sections each with their own interesting features incl herbaceous borders, many clematis, water features and a collection of prize begonias.

☕ ☎

31 JOB'S MILL
Crockerton BA12 8BB. Lady Silvy McQuiston. *1¹/₂ m S of Warminster. Down lane E of A350, S of A36 roundabout.* Home-made teas. **Adm £2.50, chd free (share to Butterfly Conservation).** Sun 22 June (2-6).
Delightful medium-sized terraced garden through which R Wylye flows. Herbaceous border and water garden.

❁ ☕

32 KEEVIL GARDENS
BA14 6NA. *6m E of Trowbridge, S of A361. All gardens within walking distance, nr E end of Main St. Park in Main St or Martins Rd.* **Combined adm £3.50, chd free.** Sun 8 June (2-6).
Quiet village with unspoiled largely C14-C18 main street lined with GI and GII listed houses and GI listed C13/C14 church of St Leonards.

EDGECOMBE COTTAGE
Madeline & Brian Webb
Thatched cottage with approx ¹/₄ acre of garden lovingly established over the last 15 yrs. Herbaceous borders, varieties of perennials, roses, pergolas and water feature.

🐱

FIELDHEAD HOUSE
Peter & Janie Dixon
Recently extended garden of former vicarage set in approx 2 acres. Contains roses, clematis

etc with kitchen garden, pond, small orchard, fine hedging and Italianate swimming pool area (viewable but not open). Gravel paths.

LONGLEAZE HOUSE
John & Olga Gower Isaac
C18 village farmhouse (not open). 1-acre garden developed over last 9yrs with shrubs, climbers, species roses, herbaceous perennials, bulbs etc. Children's pirate ship. Gravel paths.

KEMPSFORD MANOR
See Gloucestershire North & Central.

33 ◆ LACKHAM GARDENS
Lacock SN15 2NY. Wiltshire College Lackham, 01249 466800, www.lackhamcountrypark.co.uk. *4m S of Chippenham. On A350, 7m S of M4 J17, between Chippenham and National Trust village of Lacock.* **Adm £2, chd free, concessions £1.50. Open for special events commencing 15-16 Mar. For NGS: Sun 13 July (10-5).**
Large walled garden, greenhouses, lawn paths separating plots with variety of interesting shrubs, vegetables, cut flowers, bedding and fruit plants. Pleasure gardens, sensory garden, ornamental pond, mixed borders, lawns, woodland walks, laurel maze, various plant collections, NCCPG of populus. Museum of Agriculture and Rural Life incl horticultural equipment. Students won Gold and Silver Medals at shows. Featured in local press and on regional TV. Some gravel & grass paths but access to all main features.

  NCCPG

34 ◆ LACOCK ABBEY GARDENS
Chippenham SN15 2LG. The National Trust, 01249 730459, www.nationaltrust.org.uk. *3m S of Chippenham. Off A350. Follow NT signs. Use public car park just outside Abbey.* **Adm £2.80, chd free. Daily Mar to Oct (11-5.30). For NGS: Sats, Suns, 9, 10 16, 17 Feb 2008; 7, 8, 14, 15 Feb 2009.**
Victorian woodland garden with pond, botanic garden and exotic tree specimens. Display of early spring flowers with carpets of aconites, snowdrops, crocuses and daffodils. C13 Abbey with C18 Gothic additions.

35 LITTLE DURNFORD MANOR
nr Salisbury SP4 6AH. The Earl & Countess of Chichester. *3m N of Salisbury. Just beyond Stratford-sub-Castle.* **Adm £3, chd £1. Suns 20 Apr; 15 June (2-6).**
Extensive lawns with cedars, walled gardens, fruit trees, large vegetable garden, small knot and herb gardens. Terraces, borders, sunken garden, water garden, lake with islands, river walks, labyrinth walk.

36 LITTLETON DREW GARDENS
SN14 7LL. *6m W of Chippenham. Nr The Gibb PH on B4039. Car parking on rd to Littleton Drew and walk down to Goulters Mill, or drive/ walk up to Barton Cottage.* Cream teas at Goulters Mill Farm. **Combined adm £3.50, chd free. Sun & Mon 23, 24, Mar; 25, 26, May (2-5).**

BARTON COTTAGE
Littleton Drew. Beryl Willis. *Turn N off B3095, 2nd cottage on L. Park opp*
Small garden surrounding Elizabethan Cotswold cottage. Densely planted with many unusual perennials, topiary, pond with ferns and small potager incl espalier apples, standard redcurrant and gooseberries. Over 70 different clematis.

GOULTERS MILL FARM
The Gibb. Mr & Mrs Michael Harvey, 01249 782555. *Parking at top of 300yd drive, elderly/disabled at the Mill.* **Visitors also welcome by appt, all yr.**
³/₄ -acre garden in a steep sided valley bordered by the beginnings of the Bybrook, threaded through with gravel paths, punctuated with topiary and mounds of shrubs and underplanted with an eclectic mix of perennials and self-sown annuals, dahlias and salvias. Hellebores, tulips, anemones, daphne bholua, sarcocca, and lonicera fragrantissima and later a heady mix of delphiniums, eremurus, aconites and asters. Bluebell wood a must in May, in June and July the N side of the valley is alive with harebells, rock roses, vipers bugloss and blue butterflies if you are lucky. Featured in 'Beautiful Britain'. Gravel paths, steep rockery.

37 LONG HALL
Stockton BA12 0SE. Mr & Mrs N H Yeatman-Biggs. *7m SE of Warminster. S of A36, W of A303 Wylye interchange.* Cream teas. **Adm £3, chd free. Sun 25 May (2-5).**
4-acre mainly formal garden. Series of gardens within a garden with clipped yews, flowering shrubs, fine old trees, masses of spring bulbs and fine hellebore walk. C13 Hall (not open).

Harebells, rock roses, vipers bugloss and blue butterflies if you are lucky . . .

38 MALLARDS
Chirton SN10 3QX. Tim & Jenny Papé, 01380 840593, jennypape@tiscali.co.uk. *4¹/₂ m SE of Devizes. Just N of A342. Through village, garden on R.* **Adm £2.50, chd free. Fris 16 May; 20 June; 11 July (2-5). Visitors also welcome by appt May, June & July for individuals & groups. No coach access.**
1-acre hidden garden slopes gently down to the upper R Avon and is bordered by woodland on 2 sides. Colourful sunny gravel bed, herbaceous and mixed borders, woodland glade, miniature dell and waterside, all informally planted with many unusual plants and careful use of colour. Woodland walk.

39 MANOR FARM
Huish SN8 4JN. Mr & Mrs J Roberts. *3m NW of Pewsey. Huish is signed from A345 by White Hart PH in Oare. Follow lane for 1m into Huish, turn R by dead-end sign.* Home-made teas. **Adm £3, chd free. Suns 18 May; 15 June (2-5.30).**
Fine downland views surround this intriguing garden which has a surprise around every corner. Ongoing design and planting schemes create new interest each year. Wide variety of clematis and roses, pleached lime walk, woodland pond and grotto. Landscaped farmyard featuring duckpond and thatched granary. Good wheelchair access except woodland walk & pond.

40 MANOR HOUSE
Stratford Tony SP5 4AT. Mr & Mrs H Cookson, 01722 718496, lucindacookson@care4free.net. *4m SW of Salisbury. Take minor rd W off A354 at Coombe Bissett. Garden on S after 1m.* Home-made teas. **Adm £3, chd free. Thur 12 June; Thur 4, Fri 5 Sept (2-5). Visitors also welcome by appt.**
Varied 4-acre garden. Formal and informal areas, small lake fed from R Ebble, herbaceous beds with colour through to late autumn incl many salvias. Pergola covered vegetable garden, parterre garden, orchards, shrubberies, interesting mature and newly planted trees, many original contemporary features. Sitting areas to enjoy both internal and external views.
 ♿ ✕ ✿ ☕ ☎

41 NEW MANSION FARM HOUSE
Close Lane, Marston SN10 5SN. Mr & Mrs L Courth. *5m SW Devizes. From A360 Devizes to Salisbury, turn R into Potterne, through Worton signed L to Marston.* **Adm £4, chd free combined with Wellaway. Sun 11 May (2-6).**
1-acre garden on clay redesigned by owner 5yrs ago. Many new plantings, incl hedges. Mixed borders, pond, lawns, spring bulbs, many varieties of trees, yew and beech hedges and seating areas. Some gravel paths.
 ♿

42 NEW MAWARDEN COURT
Stratford Road, Stratford Castle SP1 3LL. Mr & Mrs Colin Harris. *2m WNW Salisbury. A345 from Salisbury, L at traffic lights, opp St Lawrence Church.* **Adm £5, chd free. Sun 1 June (2-5).**
Recently recreated garden, new rose garden approached through a pergola flanked by an herbaceous border. Path through line of white beam leading towards R Avon and a woodland path through a plantation of poplars.
 ♿ ✕

MAYO FARM
See Dorset.

43 ◆ THE MEAD NURSERY
Brokerswood, nr Rudge BA13 4EG. Mr & Mrs S Lewis-Dale, 01373 859990, www.themeadnursery.co.uk. *3m W*

of Westbury. E of Rudge. Follow signs for Country Park at Brokerswood. Halfway between Rudge & Country Park. **Adm £2.50, chd £2.50 inc tea & home made cake, NGS day only. Weds to Sats, Feb to mid Oct (9-5); Suns (12-5); closed Easter Sun. For NGS: Sun 17 Aug (12-5).**
1¼-acre nursery and garden giving ideas on colour and design with herbaceous borders, raised alpine beds, sink garden and bog bed. Well-drained Mediterranean-style raised bed and small wildlife pond. Nursery with extensive range of herbaceous perennials, alpines, pot-grown bulbs and grasses in peat free compost. Garden party with stalls. Featured in 'Bath Magazine'.
 ♿ ✕ ✿ ☕

44 ◆ THE MILL HOUSE
Berwick St James SP3 4TS. Diana Gifford Mead, 01722 790 331. *8m NW of Salisbury. S of A303 on B3083, S end of village.* Cream teas at Berwick St James Village Hall on 30 Mar only. **Adm £3, chd free. Mar - June. For NGS: Sun 30 Mar; Sat 28, Sun 29 June (2-6).**
Come and see R Till (SSSI) and old unspoilt water meadow (under countryside stewardship). Over 100 species of old-fashioned roses and amazing climbers in trees. Maybe water vole and dragonflies in pond. Variety of spring flowers and daffodils. 12-acres of Nature Reserve.
 ♿ ⛵ ☕

45 ◆ MOMPESSON HOUSE
The Close, Salisbury SP1 2EL. The National Trust, 01722 335659, mompessonhouse@nationaltrust.org.uk. *Enter Cathedral Close via High St Gate, Mompesson House on R.* **Garden adm £1.50, chd free. Sat to Wed, Mar to Oct, 11-5. For NGS: Fri 9 May (11-4).**
The appeal of this comparatively small

but attractive garden is the lovely setting in Salisbury Cathedral Close, with a well-known Queen Anne house. Planting as for an old English garden with raised rose and herbaceous beds around the lawn. Climbers on pergola and walls, shrubs and small lavender walk. Cake stall.
 ♿ ✕ ✿ ☕

46 NORTH COTTAGE & WOODVIEW COTTAGE
Tisbury Row, nr Tisbury SP3 6RZ. Jacqueline & Robert Baker, Diane McBride, 01747 870019. *12m W of Salisbury. From A30 turn N through Ansty, L at T-junction, towards Tisbury. From Tisbury take Ansty rd. Entrance nr junction signed Tisbury Row.* Light refreshments, teas and wine. **Adm £2.50, chd free. Afternoon & Evening Opening, wine, Sun 29 June (2-8). Visitors also welcome by appt in groups.**
Two cottage gardens divided into rooms, continuously changing and developing, incl fruit and vegetables, greenhouses and allotment. 4-acre smallholding containing orchard, ponds and coppice wood. Attractive perennial and annual planting provides colour and variety. Various water features, unique sculptures to be found round every corner, coppicing and hedge laying practised. Family made craft for sale, lace-making demonstration.
 ✕ ✿ ☕ ☎

47 OAK TREE COTTAGE
Hisomley, Dilton Marsh BA13 4DB. Chris & Pam Good, 01373 822433. *2m SW of Westbury. Signs from A36, A350 & A3098. Single track roads, park on grass inside property.* Home-made teas. **Adm £2.50, chd free. Suns 18 May; 7 Sept (2-5). Visitors also welcome by appt.**
7 yrs ago our garden, vegetable garden and orchard did not exist. Imagination, hard work and good soil have provided what you see today. The garden around the house leads to over 50 old apple varieties in the orchard - then enjoy the view as you walk to the fledgling vineyard.
 ♿ ✕ ✿ ☕ ☎

48 OARE HOUSE
Rudge Lane, nr Pewsey SN8 4JQ. Mr Henry Keswick. *2m N of Pewsey. On Marlborough Rd (A345).* Home-made teas. **Adm £3, chd free. Suns 20 Apr; 20 July (2-6).**
Fine house (not open) in large garden

> Unique sculptures to be found round every corner, coppicing and hedge laying practised . . .

with fine trees, hedges, spring flowers, woodlands, extensive lawns and kitchen garden. Partial wheelchair access, some steps and gravel paths.

 ♿ ☕

49 NEW THE OLD FARMHOUSE

Oxford Street, Ramsbury SN8 2PG. Mrs Kate Staples. *8m NE Marlborough. From A4 or B1492 head to Ramsbury, from The Bell PH take Oxford St uphill. House next to Midway Store.* Home-made teas. Adm £5, chd free (combined with The Old Mill). Thurs 19 June (2-6). Packed full of delightful plants reflecting the enthusiasm of the owner. A listed granary behind a mixed border of billowing flowers incorporating traditional cottage garden plants and new treasures with other beds, borders and climbers. Newly planted small woodland area. Short gravel approach.

♿ ✗ ❀ ☕

50 THE OLD MALTHOUSE

Lower Westwood BA15 2AG. Simon & Amanda Relph, 01225 864905, simonrelph@onetel.com. *2m SW of Bradford-on-Avon. Take B3109 S, R to Westwood at 1st Xrds after leaving Bradford-on-Avon, 300yds past The New Inn on R.* Light refreshments & teas. Adm £2.50, chd free (share to Tulsi Trust). Sun 15 June (2-5.30). Visitors also welcome by appt. 1 acre. At front, small garden with unusual water feature. To the side, long border against N-facing wall with mainly white flowering shrubs and herbaceous plants. Through the wall to 3 garden rooms: lawn surrounded by shrubs, another small lawn with semi-circular flame border facing splendid magnolia across pond, gravel courtyard with 6 island beds, 2 lily ponds and sculptured water feature enclosed by rose-covered pergola on two sides. Some gravel paths.

♿ ❀ ☕ ☎

51 THE OLD MILL

Ramsbury SN8 2PN. Mr & Mrs James Dallas. *8m NE of Marlborough. From A4 or B1492 head to Ramsbury. At The Bell PH follow sign to Hungerford. Garden behind yew hedge on R 100yds beyond The Bell.* Adm £5, chd free (combined with The Old Farmhouse). Thurs 19 June (2-6).

Garden in grounds of disused mill house on R Kennet. Mill stream, millrace and pool take up nearly $1/2$ acre of 5 acres. Side streams criss-crossed by bridges meander through mixture of wild and cultivated area. Colour-themed borders, gravelled areas full of unusual plants; an exciting blend of traditional and contemporary features, in keeping with peaceful and pretty setting. New features for 2008. Teas at Old Farmhouse.

✗ ❀

Millennium rill, willow tunnel, scented philadelphus walk and fine roses . . .

52 THE OLD RECTORY

Ham SN8 3QR. Mr & Mrs N Baring. *3m S of Hungerford. Take A338, bear L after 2½ m on minor rd signed Ham. Entrance 50yds from village green on N side of Inkpen Rd.* Teas. Adm £3.50, chd free. Sun 8 June (2-6). 4-acre garden incl wide expanse of lawn and yew-edged enclosures leading to informal area with fine old trees and some recent planting. Mixed rose and herbaceous beds around house, flowering shrubs, restored pond with new waterside plants. Separate cottage garden. Unfenced pond.

♿ ✗ ❀ ☕

53 POULTON HOUSE

Marlborough SN8 2LN. Mr & Mrs Martin Ephson, eugenia@poultonhouse.com. *½ m E of Marlborough centre. Take Ramsbury rd from The Green in Marlborough ⅓ m, large white gates on L.* Home-made teas. Adm £3, chd free. Sat 14 June (2-6). Visitors also welcome by appt in June & July, for groups 10-20 max, by e mail or in writing. Evolving 7-acre garden round fine Queen Anne manor house (not open) with interesting and mature trees set in sweeping lawns. Many different aspects, incl walled garden with topiary, sunken potager and orchard

with mown geometric patterns. Long herbaceous borders, millennium rill, willow tunnel, scented philadelphus walk and fine roses. Woodland path leads to large riverside pool surrounded by wildlife area interplanted with native trees. New vegetable garden. Very limited wheelchair access.

♿ ✗ ❀ ☕ ☎

54 THE POUND HOUSE

Little Somerford SN15 5JW. Mr & Mrs Michael Baines, 01666 823212. *2m E of Malmesbury on B4024. In village turn S, leave church on R. Car park on R before railway bridge.* Home-made teas & wine. Adm £2.50, chd free. Afternoon & Evening Opening, wine, Sun 8 June (2-7). Visitors also welcome by appt. Large garden surrounding former rectory. Mature trees, hedges and spacious lawns. Well-stocked herbaceous borders, roses, shrubs, pergola, parterre, swimming pool garden, water, ducks, chickens, alpacas and horses. Lots of places to sit!.

♿ ✗ ❀ ☕ ☎

PRIOR PARK LANDSCAPE GARDEN

See Somerset & Bristol.

55 NEW PRIORY HOUSE

Market Street, Bradford-on-Avon BA15 1LH. Mr & Mrs Tim Woodall. *Town centre. Park in town centre. Take A363 signed Bath up Market St. House 500yds.* Home-made teas. Adm £2.50, chd free. Suns 27 Apr; 1 June; 20 July (2-5.30). $3/4$ -acre town garden, mostly formal. Tulips, irises, roses and colour coordinated herbaceous borders. Knot garden in front of part Georgian House is an interpretation of the sash windows. Some steep parts.

♿ ✗ ❀ ☕

56 RIDLEYS CHEER

Mountain Bower SN14 7AJ. Mr & Mrs A J Young, 01225 891204, antonyoung@ridleyscheer.co.uk, www.ridleyscheer.co.uk. *9m WNW of Chippenham. At The Shoe, on A420 8m W of Chippenham, turn N then take 2nd L & 1st R.* Cream teas. Adm £3.50, chd free. Suns 13 Apr; 11 May; 8 June (2-6). Visitors also welcome by appt, incl groups & coaches.

1½-acre informal garden with unusual trees and shrubs, incl acers, liriodendrons, magnolias, daphnes, hellebores, hostas and euphorbias. Over 125 different rose varieties incl hybrid musks, albas, tree ramblers and species roses, planted progressively over past 36yrs. Potager, miniature box garden, 2-acre arboretum planted 1989, and 3-acre wild flower meadow.

  ♿ ✗ ⊗ ⊨ ☕ ☎

57 SHARCOTT MANOR

nr Pewsey SN9 5PA. Captain & Mrs D Armytage, 01672 563485. *1m SW of Pewsey. Via A345 from Pewsey towards Salisbury. Turn R signed Sharcott at grass triangle. 400yds up lane, garden on L over cattle-grid.* Home-made teas. **Adm £3, chd free. Wed 2 Apr (11-5), Sun 6 Apr; Weds 7 May; 4 June; 2 July; 6 Aug; 3 Sept, Sun 7 Sept (2-6). Visitors also welcome by appt at any time for groups & coaches.**
6-acre plantsman's garden on greensand with water, planted for yr-round interest. Mature trees, many climbers and tree roses. Densely-planted mixed borders of shrubs, roses and perennials with unusual plants. Woodland walk round ⅓-acre lake. Carpeted with narcissi in spring. Raised kitchen garden. Small collection of ornamental waterfowl. Featured in 'Amateur Gardening'. Gravel paths.

♿ ✗ ⊗ ☕ ☎

58 ◆ SHELDON MANOR

nr Chippenham SN14 0RG. Kenneth & Caroline Hawkins, 01249 653120, www.sheldonmanor.co.uk. *1½ m W of Chippenham. Take A420 W. 1st L signed Chippenham RFC, entrance approx ½ m on R.* **Adm £4.50, chd free. Thurs, May to Sept.** For NGS: Sun 15 June (2-4).
Wiltshire's oldest inhabited manor house with C13 porch and C15 chapel. Gardens with ancient yews, mulberry tree and profusion of old-fashioned roses blooming in May and June. BBC TV location for Jane Austen's Persuasion. Featured in 'Saturday Telegraph' & 'Sunday Times'.

59 32 SHURNHOLD

Melksham SN12 8DG. Alvin & Judith Howard, 01225 704839, bolingbroke.design@tinyworld.co. uk. *¼ m W of Melksham. On A365 nr George Ward School.* **Adm £2.50, chd free. Sun 25 May (2-5). Evening**

Opening, wine, Fri 20 June (6-9). **Visitors also welcome by appt.**
Eccentric ⅓-acre garden featuring Japanese, Roman and French styles. Incl Chinese pavilion, Gothic summerhouse, Tudor tree house, permanent tent, garden studio, fernery, rose garden, ponds, fountains and water features. Short steep drive, gravel paths.

♿ ✗ ☎

SHUTE FARM
See Dorset.

SNAPE COTTAGE PLANTSMAN'S GARDEN
See Dorset.

SPECIAL PLANTS
See Somerset & Bristol.

60 ◆ STOURHEAD GARDEN

Stourton BA12 6QD. The National Trust, 01747 841152, www.nationaltrust.org.uk. *3m NW of Mere on B3092. Follow NT signs.* House and Garden Adm £10.50, chd £5.20, Garden only Adm £6.30, chd £3.40. Garden daily all yr. House 15 Mar to 2 Nov 11.30-4.30, closed Weds & Thurs. For NGS: Sat 19 July (9-7).
One of the earliest and greatest landscape gardens in the world, creation of banker Henry Hoare in 1740s on his return from the Grand Tour, inspired by paintings of Claude and Poussin. Planted with rare trees, rhododendrons and azaleas over last 250yrs. Buggy and shuttle available.

♿ ✗

8 TROSSACHS DRIVE
See Somerset & Bristol.

61 ◆ WATERDALE HOUSE

East Knoyle SP3 6BL. Mr & Mrs Julian Seymour, 01747 830262. *8m S of Warminster. N of East Knoyle, garden signed from A350.* **Adm £3, chd free. Mar to June incl.** For NGS: Sun 4 May (2-6).
4-acre mature woodland garden with rhododendrons, azaleas, camellias, maples, magnolias, ornamental water, bog garden, herbaceous borders. Bluebell walk. New shrub border created by storm damage mixed with agapanthus, half hardy salvias and echiums.

⊗ ☕

62 NEW WELLAWAY

Close Lane, Marston SN10 5SN. Mr & Mrs P Lewis, www.flornamental.co.uk. *5m SW of Devizes. From A360, Devizes to Salisbury, R into Potterne through Worton, signed L to Marston, Lane ½ m on L.* Home-made teas. **Adm £4, chd free combined with Mansion Farm House. Sun 11 May (2-6).**
2-acre flower arranger's garden comprising herbaceous borders, orchard, vegetable garden, ornamental and wildlife ponds, lawns and naturalised areas. Planted since 1979 for yr-round interest. Shrubberies and rose garden, other areas underplanted with bulbs or ground cover. Springtime particularly colourful with daffs, tulips and hellebores.

♿ ✗ ☕

WESTON HOUSE
See Dorset.

63 WINDMILL COTTAGE

Kings Road, Market Lavington SN10 4QB. Rupert & Gill Wade, 01380 813527. *5m S of Devizes. Turn E off A360 1m N of West Lavington, 2m S of Potterne. At top of hill turn L into Kings Rd, L into Windmill Lane after 200yds. Limited parking.* **Adm £2.50, chd free. Fris 30 May; 13, 27 June; 11, 25 July (1.30-5.30). Visitors also welcome by appt late May to July, for groups 5+.**
1-acre cottage-style garden on greensand. Mixed beds and borders with long season of interest, roses on pagoda, large vegetable patch for kitchen and exhibition at local shows, polytunnel and greenhouse. Whole garden virtually pesticide free for last 12yrs. Featured on 'Radio Wiltshire'.

⊗ ☎

Over 125 different rose varieties . . . hybrid musks, albas, tree ramblers and species roses, planted progressively over past 36 years . . .

WORTON GARDENS
SN10 5SE. *3m SW of Devizes. A360 Devizes to Salisbury, turn W in Potterne or just N of West Lavington. From Seend turn S at Bell Inn, follow signs to Worton.* Teas at the Grange. **Combined adm £4, chd free.** Sun 6 July (2-6).

ASHTON HOUSE
Mrs Colin Shand
$1/2$ -acre garden in 3 sections with herbaceous borders, many shrubs and birch grove, walled courtyard, small gravel garden and raised vegetable garden. House burnt down before 2006 opening but garden being fully maintained while house is rebuilt.

BROOKFIELD HOUSE
Mr & Mrs Graham Cannon
1-acre part-walled garden with mixed borders and separate fruit and vegetable garden, rose garden and fine views.

THE GRANGE
Mr & Mrs Simon Jacobs
$1^1/2$ -acre garden in 5 sections. Box hedging, pond garden, herbaceous borders, unusual trees and walled kitchen garden. Rose garden, lawns and fine views around early C17 timber-framed house (not open).

Did you find the shepherd's hut or the 'sash window' knot garden . . . ?

Wiltshire County Volunteers

County Organisers
Mr & Mrs Sean Magee, Byams House, Willesley, Tetbury GL8 8QU, 01666 880009, sean@magees.demon.co.uk

Assistant County Organisers
Mrs David Armytage, Sharcott Manor, Pewsey SN9 5PA, 01672 563485
Mrs Robert Coate, Colts Corner, Upper Woodford, Salisbury SP4 6PA, 01722 782365
Mrs Anthony Heywood, Monkton House, Monkton Deverill, BA12 7EX, 01985 844486
Mrs Colin Shand, Brow Cottage, Seend Hill, Seend, Melksham SN12 6RU, 01380 828866

WORCESTERSHIRE

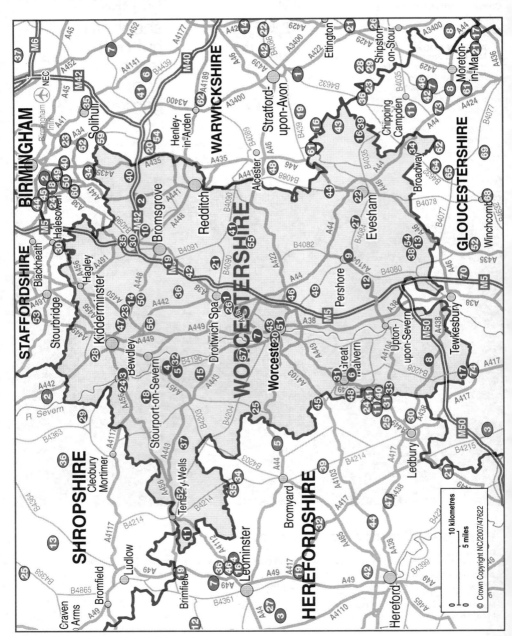

Opening Dates

February

SATURDAY 2
20 The Greyfriars

WEDNESDAY 13
14 Dial Park

THURSDAY 14
14 Dial Park

SATURDAY 16
7 Beckett Drive Gardens

March

THURSDAY 6
41 Red House Farm

WEDNESDAY 12
47 Stone House Cottage Gardens

THURSDAY 13
41 Red House Farm

THURSDAY 20
41 Red House Farm

FRIDAY 21
46 Spetchley Park Gardens

SATURDAY 22
47 Stone House Cottage Gardens

SUNDAY 23
16 Frogs Nest
39 4 Poden Cottages
56 Whitlenge Gardens

MONDAY 24
16 Frogs Nest
17 Gadfield Elm House
33 Little Malvern Court
39 4 Poden Cottages
56 Whitlenge Gardens

THURSDAY 27
41 Red House Farm

SATURDAY 29
55 White Cottage

SUNDAY 30
14 Dial Park
55 White Cottage

April

THURSDAY 3
41 Red House Farm

SUNDAY 6
27 Holland House

THURSDAY 10
41 Red House Farm
47 Stone House Cottage Gardens

SATURDAY 12
55 White Cottage

SUNDAY 13
52 Weavers & Tickners Cottages

55 White Cottage

THURSDAY 17
41 Red House Farm

SUNDAY 20
18 Gladderbrook Farm
32 Little Larford
48 Tannachie

THURSDAY 24
41 Red House Farm

SATURDAY 26
45 Shuttifield Cottage
51 The Walled Garden
55 White Cottage

SUNDAY 27
1 24 Alexander Avenue
12 1 Church Cottages
32 Little Larford
55 White Cottage

May

THURSDAY 1
41 Red House Farm

SATURDAY 3
45 Shuttifield Cottage
55 White Cottage

SUNDAY 4
18 Gladderbrook Farm
28 Honeybrook House Cottage
54 Whitcombe House
55 White Cottage
56 Whitlenge Gardens

MONDAY 5
17 Gadfield Elm House
33 Little Malvern Court
55 White Cottage
56 Whitlenge Gardens

THURSDAY 8
41 Red House Farm

WEDNESDAY 14
26 Hiraeth

THURSDAY 15
41 Red House Farm

FRIDAY 16
47 Stone House Cottage Gardens

SATURDAY 17
51 The Walled Garden
55 White Cottage

SUNDAY 18
14 Dial Park
44 St Egwins Cottage

THURSDAY 22
22 Harrells Hardy Plants Nursery Garden
41 Red House Farm

SATURDAY 24
45 Shuttifield Cottage
55 White Cottage

SUNDAY 25
5 Astley Towne House
12 1 Church Cottages
16 Frogs Nest
18 Gladderbrook Farm
24 High Bank
34 Luggers Hall
39 4 Poden Cottages
52 Weavers & Tickners Cottages
54 Whitcombe House
55 White Cottage
56 Whitlenge Gardens

MONDAY 26
16 Frogs Nest
17 Gadfield Elm House
29 Hunters End
39 4 Poden Cottages
52 Weavers & Tickners Cottages
55 White Cottage
56 Whitlenge Gardens

THURSDAY 29
22 Harrells Hardy Plants Nursery Garden
41 Red House Farm

SATURDAY 31
37 Orleton House

June

SUNDAY 1
3 The Antiquary
26 Hiraeth
35 Marlbrook Gardens
37 Orleton House
50 Tythe Barn House

WEDNESDAY 4
19 Grafton Manor

THURSDAY 5
41 Red House Farm

SATURDAY 7
43 32 Rogers Hill
45 Shuttifield Cottage
51 The Walled Garden
55 White Cottage

SUNDAY 8
1 24 Alexander Avenue
2 Alvechurch Gardens
8 Birtsmorton Court
18 Gladderbrook Farm
27 Holland House
39 4 Poden Cottages
52 Weavers & Tickners Cottages
54 Whitcombe House
57 Worlds End Nurseries

THURSDAY 12
41 Red House Farm

SATURDAY 14
31 Layton Avenue Gardens
55 White Cottage

SUNDAY 15
4 Astley Country Gardens
15 Eastgrove Cottage Garden Nursery
22 Harrells Hardy Plants Nursery Garden
28 Honeybrook House Cottage
31 Layton Avenue Gardens
39 4 Poden Cottages
48 Tannachie
55 White Cottage

WEDNESDAY 18
26 Hiraeth
47 Stone House Cottage Gardens

THURSDAY 19
40 Pump Cottage
41 Red House Farm

SATURDAY 21
40 Pump Cottage
55 White Cottage

SUNDAY 22
16 Frogs Nest
18 Gladderbrook Farm
34 Luggers Hall
39 4 Poden Cottages
44 St Egwins Cottage

TUESDAY 24
40 Pump Cottage

THURSDAY 26
22 Harrells Hardy Plants Nursery Garden
41 Red House Farm

SATURDAY 28
45 Shuttifield Cottage

SUNDAY 29
10 Burcot Grange
16 Frogs Nest
22 Harrells Hardy Plants Nursery Garden
24 High Bank
39 4 Poden Cottages

July

WEDNESDAY 2
19 Grafton Manor

THURSDAY 3
41 Red House Farm
45 Shuttifield Cottage (Evening)

SATURDAY 5
9 21 Bridge Street
23 Harvington Hall
53 Westacres
55 White Cottage

SUNDAY 6
2 Alvechurch Gardens
3 The Antiquary
9 21 Bridge Street

23 Harvington Hall
26 Hiraeth
46 Spetchley Park Gardens
53 Westacres
54 Whitcombe House
55 White Cottage

THURSDAY 10
22 Harrells Hardy Plants Nursery Garden
41 Red House Farm

SATURDAY 12
49 The Tynings (Evening)
51 The Walled Garden

SUNDAY 13
7 Beckett Drive Gardens
29 Hunters End
30 Kokopelli
57 Worlds End Nurseries

WEDNESDAY 16
47 Stone House Cottage Gardens

THURSDAY 17
41 Red House Farm

SATURDAY 19
21 Hanbury Hall
45 Shuttifield Cottage
55 White Cottage

SUNDAY 20
22 Harrells Hardy Plants Nursery Garden
35 Marlbrook Gardens
44 St Egwins Cottage
55 White Cottage

WEDNESDAY 23
26 Hiraeth

THURSDAY 24
41 Red House Farm

SATURDAY 26
37 Orleton House

SUNDAY 27
1 24 Alexander Avenue
5 Astley Towne House
37 Orleton House
49 The Tynings

THURSDAY 31
41 Red House Farm

August

SUNDAY 3
3 The Antiquary
24 High Bank
28 Honeybrook House Cottage

WEDNESDAY 6
11 Burford House Gardens

THURSDAY 7
22 Harrells Hardy Plants Nursery Garden
41 Red House Farm

SATURDAY 9
45 Shuttifield Cottage

SUNDAY 10
25 High View
26 Hiraeth
30 Kokopelli
44 St Egwins Cottage

WEDNESDAY 13
47 Stone House Cottage Gardens

THURSDAY 14
41 Red House Farm

SUNDAY 17
35 Marlbrook Gardens

THURSDAY 21
41 Red House Farm

SUNDAY 24
18 Gladderbrook Farm
56 Whitlenge Gardens

MONDAY 25
16 Frogs Nest
17 Gadfield Elm House
56 Whitlenge Gardens

THURSDAY 28
41 Red House Farm

SUNDAY 31
5 Astley Towne House
22 Harrells Hardy Plants Nursery Garden

September

THURSDAY 4
41 Red House Farm

FRIDAY 5
26 Hiraeth (Afternoon & Evening)

SATURDAY 6
35 Marlbrook Gardens (Evening)

SUNDAY 7
18 Gladderbrook Farm
28 Honeybrook House Cottage

THURSDAY 11
41 Red House Farm

SATURDAY 13
47 Stone House Cottage Gardens

SUNDAY 14
22 Harrells Hardy Plants Nursery Garden

THURSDAY 18
41 Red House Farm

THURSDAY 25
41 Red House Farm

SUNDAY 28
5 Astley Towne House

October

THURSDAY 2
41 Red House Farm

THURSDAY 9
41 Red House Farm

THURSDAY 16
41 Red House Farm

THURSDAY 23
41 Red House Farm

THURSDAY 30
41 Red House Farm

February 2009

SATURDAY 7
20 The Greyfriars

Gardens open to the public

11 Burford House Gardens
15 Eastgrove Cottage Garden Nursery
20 The Greyfriars
21 Hanbury Hall
22 Harrells Hardy Plants Nursery Garden
23 Harvington Hall
33 Little Malvern Court
41 Red House Farm
42 Riverside Gardens at Webbs of Wychbold
46 Spetchley Park Gardens
47 Stone House Cottage Gardens
55 White Cottage
56 Whitlenge Gardens
57 Worlds End Nurseries

By appointment only

6 Barnard's Green House
13 Conderton Manor
36 New House Farm
38 Overbury Court

Also open by appointment ☎

1 24 Alexander Avenue
5 Astley Towne House
9 21 Bridge Street
10 Burcot Grange
14 Dial Park
18 Gladderbrook Farm
24 High Bank
25 High View
26 Hiraeth
28 Honeybrook House Cottage
29 Hunters End
30 Kokopelli
32 Little Larford
37 Orleton House
39 4 Poden Cottages
40 Pump Cottage
43 32 Rogers Hill
44 St Egwins Cottage
45 Shuttifield Cottage
49 The Tynings
50 Tythe Barn House

53 Westacres
54 Whitcombe House
35 Oak Tree House, Marlbrook Gardens
35 24 Braces Lane, Marlbrook Gardens
35 Saranacris, Marlbrook Gardens

The Gardens

1 24 ALEXANDER AVENUE
Droitwich Spa WR9 8NH. Malley & David Terry, 01905 774907. *1m S of Droitwich. Droitwich Spa towards Worcester A38.Or from M5 J6 to Droitwich Town centre.* **Adm £3, chd free.** Suns 27 Apr; 8 June; 27 July (2-6). **Visitors also welcome by appt.** 40 x 10metres garden is a lesson in what can be done in a small space. Turning a barren patch of grass into a paradise. High hedges, clad with clematis from the 100+ varieties grown, obscure views of neighbouring houses. Borders filled with dazzling array of interesting plants, many rare. Fine collection of ferns. Alpines grow in stone troughs and gravel garden. 'A garden of immaculate artistry'. Display Viticella clematis (July). Featured in 'GGG'.

2 ALVECHURCH GARDENS
B48 7LP, 0121 445 4335. *3m N of Redditch, 3m NE of Bromsgrove. From Bromsgrove M42 J2 (Hopwood) L on A441 to next island L B4120 signed Alvechurch. From Redditch A441 to Bordesley Island on B4120 signed Alvechurch. From Birmingham, Kings Norton A441 to island at bottom of Hopwood Hill. 2nd exit signed B4120 Alvechurch.* Light refreshments & teas at The Barn, Rectory Cottage and The Baptist Church Hall. **Combined adm £5, chd free.** Suns 8 June; 6 July (1-6).
Large village - much new development but interesting core - buildings spanning medieval to Edwardian - church on hill. Approx 15 gardens of diverse character and size. Maps. Featured in various publications & on Radio WM etc.

THE BARN
John & Jill Alexander
³/₄ -acre open aspect garden with borders and island beds, variety of shrubs. Large natural pool with summerhouse and jetty.

38 BEAR HILL
Mark & Kathy Collinson
Professionally landscaped terraced garden comprising several themed areas with wide variety of colours and styles, which incl a series of arches, patios and water features.

NEW 11 BEAR HILL DRIVE
Margaret Haste. *Bear Hill Drive is located at rear of The Red Lion Inn*
This 120ft x 30ft garden was designed and planted in 2002. In 2 sections with 2 rose beds and an arch dividing them. Steps at the bottom lead to a sream.
&

1A BLYTHESWAY
John & Lorna Sage
Large front garden, bordering 2 sides of bungalow. Mixture of varieties of shrubs and herbaceous perennials, with overall effect of being a cottage garden. Small enclosed courtyard with container plants.

28 CALLOW HILL ROAD
Martin & Janet Wright
Flat rear garden designed to appear larger than it is, with curving paths, views through archways, shrub borders, herbaceous border, pond, waterfall and rockery. Front garden mix of shrubs, perennials and rockery with similar aim.
❀

THE COACH HOUSE
School Lane. Lynne Clark
Small partially walled, L-shaped garden on 2 levels overlooking church, with a feature non-varieal vine across the house. Partially raised beds with cottage plants.
❀

HILL COTTAGE
Scarfield Hill. Philip & Elisabeth Aubury
¹/₂ -acre informal garden surrounding Victorian house (not open). Planted for yr-round interest, colour, scent and to encourage wildlife. Small pool and water feature, shrub and herbaceous borders. Fruit and vegetable gardens, field meadow.

THE OLD SWAN
9 Swan Street. Ray & Norma Yarnell. *Opp The Swan PH*
Cottage garden divided between blue brick yard with lots of colour in pots. Rear garden with winding path between deep mixed borders and interesting modern features.
✖

RECTORY COTTAGE
Old Rectory Lane. Celia & Steve Hitch
Riverside garden with established trees and borders, secret garden, ducks and moorhens, bog garden to be constructed. Courtyard garden with many climbers and colourful containers. We had a mallard sitting on eggs in our hanging basket. Many visitors were concerned about how the ducklings would get out - they managed it successfully. Steep garden in areas by river.
& ✖ ⊨

SUNNYMEAD
Station Road. Anne & Andy Humphries
Wrap around informal garden with shrubs, herbaceous borders and fruit trees. Beautiful views.
&

NEW PRIMROSE COTTAGE
Callow Hill Road. Jane & Eddie Brennan
Large, sloped garden with beds of shrubs of contrasting colours interspersed with a selection of potted plants and shrubs. Summerhouse, pond with waterfall, courtyard with hanging baskets and pots.

19 RED LION STREET
Mrs E A Waters. *Access down alleyway/right of way behind Georgian terrace cottages*
Long garden. New owner 8yrs ago, cleared own and next door's site in order to re-landscape. New features added each yr incl herbaceous borders, pool and summerhouse.
✖ ✿

NEW THE SHRUBBERY
Chris & Stephanie Miall
2 acre garden with large mature trees, formal areas, rockery, pond, wooded area and paddock. Access from Bear Hill only.

29 TANYARD LANE
Kate & Peter Glover
Cottage style garden incl clematis, roses, raised vegetable beds, espalier fruit trees, sundeck, patio, swing and sunsail together with seasonal pots in a walled setting.
& ✖

31 TANYARD LANE
Peter & Eileen McHugh
Small partly walled garden, with shrubs, perennials, conifers and roses. Pots with annual colour and topiary are a feature of this fairly new garden.
&

A wonderful range of 7 gardens of great variety . . .

❸ THE ANTIQUARY
48 High Street, Bewdley DY12 2DJ. Karen Raine. *3m W of Kidderminster. (B4194) Bewdly Centre. Follow signs to garden parking in Gardener's Meadow car park by the river.* Home-made teas. **Adm £2.50, chd free. Suns 1 June; 6 July; 3 Aug (12-5).**
Hidden away behind unassuming High St. Frontage 200ft SW facing walled town house garden with 4 distinct rooms separated by wisteria pergola and jasmine arch. Herbaceous garden, pond, herb garden, developing meadow, orchard area and vegetable plot. Free-range rare breed hens add charm to this tranquil oasis. Winner - Vegetable Category & 2nd place Large Graden Category - Bewdley in Bloom.
✖ ☕

❹ ASTLEY COUNTRY GARDENS
Astley, nr Stourport-on-Severn DY13 0SG. *3m SW of Stourport-on-Severn. Take A451 out of Stourport, turn L onto B4196 for Worcester. Start at Astley Village Hall where map and descriptions of gardens are available.* Home-made teas at Astley Towne House, Little Yarhampton & Sandstone Barn. **Combined adm £5, chd free. Sun 15 June (1-6).**
A wonderful range of 7 gardens of great variety reflecting different opportunites and owners' enccentricities in peacful country settings. An entire afternoons outing.
☕

ASTLEY TOWNE HOUSE
Tim & Lesley Smith
2½ acres incl sub-tropical planting. Stumpery garden with tree ferns and woodland temple. Many features.
✿

6 ELM GROVE
Areley Kings DY13 0NT. Michael & Audrey Ecob
Good example of what can be achieved in a small area on very sandy soil. The garden is a blaze of colour and contains some most unusual plants skilfully chosen to complement each other. Complete with vegetables, greenhouse and fishpool. Featured in BBC Curious Gardens.
✖

LITTLE YARHAMPTON
Skene & Petrena Walley
Beautiful views from very spacious upper garden with a pretty walk down to a sizeable lake in a secluded valley, surrounded with a young arboretum with many different kinds of oak.
✖

NEW LONGMORE HILL FARMHOUSE
Roger & Christine Russell
½-acre garden of C17 farmhouse (not open). Small feature courtyard leading to part-walled terrace and lily pond. Mixed borders, mature shrubs, climbing roses and clematis. Vegetable garden.

POOL HOUSE
Philip Siegert & Onnagh O'Sullivan
Lawns, with flowering tulip and handkerchief trees, lead down from one of the few Strawberry Hill Gothic houses in the Midlands, to a lovely lake with large tame carp which is fed by other lakes. Walled garden with tree peonies and old-fashioned roses. Now garden organically and also home to the Pool House herd of British White Cattle.
& ✖

NEW SANDSTONE BARN
Julien & Helen Tanser. *Adjacent to Longmore Hill Farmhouse*
Good plant stall from Little Larford, tea and cakes/cream teas served in pretty walled courtyard.
✖ ✿

THE SYTCH
Stan & Hilary Kilby
Beautiful terrace with lawns leading to new water feature and views beyond. Mixed borders with productive vegetable garden, poultry and orchard. Pedigree flock of Bleu de Maine sheep.

THE WHITE HOUSE
Dunley. Tony & Linda Tidmarsh
Classical style garden divided by yew hedges, shrub borders and brick walls into separate 'rooms' around a central lawn. Variety features celebrate events in the owners family. Italian garden contains cascade made of copper, 4 pools, one incorporating the girls entrance to Tipton Boarding School. Superb climbing roses.

5 ASTLEY TOWNE HOUSE
Astley DY13 0RH. Tim & Lesley Smith, 01299 822299. *3m W of Stourport-on-Severn. On B4196 Worcester to Bewdley Road.* Home-made teas. **Adm £3.50, chd free. Suns 25 May; 27 July; 31 Aug; 28 Sept (1-5). Visitors also welcome by appt.**
2½ acres incl sub-tropical planting. Winding paths through a jungle garden incorporating bananas, palms and many other rare and exotic plants. Stumpery garden with many tree ferns and woodland temple. Tree top high safari lodge, revolving classical summerhouse and stone columns with statuary.

6 BARNARD'S GREEN HOUSE
10 Poolbrook Road, Malvern WR14 3NQ. Mr & Mrs Philip Nicholls, 01684 574446. *1m E of Malvern. At junction of B4211 & B4208.* **Adm £3, chd free. Visitors welcome by appt, April to Sept.**
Newly developed 2 acre garden with mature trees and 7 new shrub and herbaceous borders. The woodland has been replanted and incorporates a gravel garden, and stumpery. The rose garden is best in June and red garden superb in July/Aug. The vegetable garden nr the house, surrounded by roses, mixed borders. The millennium dome in the centre. 1635 half-timbered house (not open). Featured in 'Telegraph' & 'Cotswold Life'.

7 BECKETT DRIVE GARDENS
Northwick WR3 7BZ. *1½ m N of Worcester city centre. Cul-de-sac off A449 Ombersley Rd directly opp Granthams garage, 1m S of Claines roundabout on A449.* Home-made teas at 6 Beckett Drive. **Combined adm £2 (Feb),£2.50, chd free (July). Sat 16 Feb (10-2); Sun 13 July (10-4).**
Two individual but contrasting gardens both with an abundance of plants and interesting design ideas. Some winter interest for the February opening with hellebores, bulbs and structural planting in both gardens together with ideas for overwintering exotics.

5 BECKETT DRIVE
Jacki & Pete Ager
Intriguing design ideas and something of interest around every corner. Flowerbeds are stocked with shrubs, perennials and alpines in a landscaped setting. The garden incls some unexpected and surprising features. Plant sale (July).

6 BECKETT DRIVE
Guy Lymer
Eclectic mix of planting, modern sculpture and water features with lighting for each. Established shrubs for yr-round interest are complemented by exotic plants, ornamental grasses and a natural arbour.

8 BIRTSMORTON COURT
nr Malvern WR13 6JS. Mr & Mrs N G K Dawes. *7m E of Ledbury. On A438.* Home-made teas. **Adm £4, chd free. Sun 8 June (2-5.30).**
Fortified manor house (not open) dating from C12; moat; Westminster pool, laid down in Henry VII's reign at time of consecration of Westminster Abbey; large tree under which Cardinal Wolsey reputedly slept in shadow of ragged stone; white garden. Potager; topiary.

9 21 BRIDGE STREET
Pershore WR10 1AJ. Michael & Primrose Upward, 01386 556683, michaelupward@btinternet.com. *Next to Star Hotel, Bridge St. Entrance through the Star Hotel carpark. Tickets available at front door of 21 Bridge St.* **Adm £3, chd £2. Sat 5, Sun 6 July (2-6). Visitors also welcome by appt.**

Narrow garden in 2 sections of 100ft. The upper path winding through a crowded area of trees, shrubs and herbaceous plants towards the house and patio. Lower part contains alpine house, bulbs and propagating frames. 4 beds of plants, an alpine bed and 'chess board'.

Large tree under which Cardinal Wolsey reputedly slept in shadow of ragged stone . . .

10 BURCOT GRANGE
Burcot, Bromsgrove B60 1BJ. Mr & Mrs Bales, 0121445 5552, www.burcotgrange.com. *2m N of Bromsgrove. Approach Burcot village, once within village take rd called Greenhill signposted off only roundabout. Burcot Grange on L, halfway up hill.* Home-made teas. **Adm £2.50, chd free. Sun 29 June (2-5). Visitors also welcome by appt.**
5 acres of mature garden incorporating water features, many mature trees and an abundance of summer colour. Some bumpy paths.

11 ◆ BURFORD HOUSE GARDENS
Tenbury Wells WR15 8HQ. Burford Garden Company, 01584 810777, www.burford.co.uk. *1m W of Tenbury Wells. 8m from Ludlow on A456.* **Adm £3.95, chd £1. Daily Jan to Dec, except Christmas & Boxing day. For NGS: Wed 6 Aug (9-6).**
The 7 acres of Burford House gardens sweep along the banks of the picturesque R Teme. Originally designed by the late John Treasure in 1952 around early Georgian house (now containing an Interior furnishings shop), the gardens contain National Collection of clematis. Giant *Wisteria macrobotrys* 'Burford' and around 2000 other kind of plants.

CAVES FOLLY NURSERY
See Herefordshire.

12 1 CHURCH COTTAGES
Church Road, Defford WR8 9BJ.
John Taylor. *3m SW of Pershore.
A4104 Pershore to Upton rd. Turn into
Defford. Black & white cottage at side
of church. Parking in village hall car
park.* Light refreshments & teas. **Adm
£2.50, chd free. Suns 27 Apr; 25
May (11-5).**
True countryman's 1/3 -acre garden,
interesting layout. Specimen trees;
water features; vegetable garden;
aviary, poultry; cider making. Featured
in local press.

13 CONDERTON MANOR
nr Tewkesbury GL20 7PR. Mr & Mrs
W Carr, 01386 725389,
carrs@conderton.wanadoo.co.uk.
*5½ m NE of Tewkesbury. On Bredon -
Beckford rd or from A46 take Overbury
sign at Beckford turn.* **Adm £4.
Visitors welcome by appt.**
7-acre garden with magnificent views
of Cotswolds. Flowering cherries and
bulbs in spring. Formal terrace with
clipped box parterre; huge rose and
clematis arches mixed borders of roses
and herbaceous plants, bog bank and
quarry garden. Many unusual trees and
shrubs make this a garden to visit at all
seasons. Gravel areas and slopes.
Contact owners to make
arrangements for disabled WC.

14 DIAL PARK
Chaddesley Corbett DY10 4QB.
David & Olive Mason, 01562 777451,
olivemason@btinternet.com. *4½ m
from Kidderminster, 4½ m from
Bromsgrove. On A448 midway
between Kidderminster & Bromsgrove.
Limited parking at garden, or park in
village or at village hall.* Teas (Feb),
Home-made teas (March & May). **Adm
£2.50, chd free. Wed 13, Thur 14
Feb (11-4); Suns 30 Mar; 18 May (2-
5); Feb 2009. Visitors also welcome
by appt, all yr-round for groups &
individuals, coaches permitted.**
Approx 3/4 -acre garden in rural setting
in conservation area on edge of
attractive village. Large collections of
snowdrops, antique daffodil varieties
and hardy ferns. Very wide range of
plants planted for yr-round interest.
Small collection of country tools and
bygones. Featured in 'Garden News' &
'Garden Style'.

**15 ◆ EASTGROVE COTTAGE
GARDEN NURSERY**
Sankyns Green, Shrawley WR6 6LQ.
Malcolm & Carol Skinner, 01299
896389, www.eastgrove.co.uk. *8m
NW of Worcester. On rd between
Shrawley (B4196) & Great Witley
(A443). Follow brown tourist signs to
Sankyns Green.* Teas (NGS day only).
**Adm £4, chd free. Thurs to Sats 24
Apr to 19 July, 11 Sept to 9 Oct
(Thurs only). For NGS: Sun 15 June
(2-5).**
Unpretentious garden surrounded by
ancient cloud hedge and comprising
many intimate areas, winding brick
paths, great (alpine) wall of china, red
hot Lloydian area, long blue, white and
yellow border. Inspired planting invites
quiet sitting. 2 acre arboretum with
wide ride, grass and labyrinth.
Excellent nursery. Wild flowers in glade.
Old fashioned home-made teas in
orchard with tablecloths and posies.
Home-made ice cream everyday.

16 FROGS NEST
8 Stratford Road, Honeybourne,
Evesham WR11 7PP. Nina & Steve
Bullen. *6m E of Evesham. 5m N of
Broadway, 5m S of Bidford. Parking at
the Gate Inn.* Home-made teas. **Adm
£3, chd free. Suns, Mons 23, 24 Mar;
25, 26 May (11-6); Suns 22, 29 June;
Mon 25 Aug (2-6). Also open 4
Poden Cottages (not Aug).**
Well worth the journey! 2 quite different
gardens make 'Frogs Nest' a special
visit. S-facing front garden is quite
formal with herbaceous borders and
tongue-in-cheek woodland walk
complete with 'boathouse'. N-facing
back garden has ponds and all-yr
colour and interest. Garden to relax in.

Tongue-in-cheek
woodland walk
complete with
'boathouse' . . .

17 GADFIELD ELM HOUSE
Malvern Road, Staunton GL19 3PA.
Canon & Mrs John Evans. *7m W of
Tewkesbury. 12m S of Malvern. 1m
from Staunton Cross on the Malvern
Rd (B4208). 2m SE J2 M50.* Home-
made teas. **Adm £2, chd free. Mons
24 Mar; 5, 26 May; 25 Aug (2-6).**
Garden created over 25yrs from
scratch. Vistas, temples, statues,
herbaceous borders. Field walk with
view of Malverns, Bredon Hill and the
Cotswolds. Rare breed poultry.
Featured in 'The Citizen & 'The Chiltern
Echo'. Gravel paths.

18 GLADDERBROOK FARM
High Oak, Heightington DY12 2YR.
Mike & Sue Butler, 01299 879923,
sue.butler4@btinternet.com. *3m W
of Stourport-on-Severn. Take A451
from Stourport. At Dunley turn R
signed Heightington. After 2m turn R
signed High Oak follow rd for 3/4 m.
Park at High Oak Farm by kind
permission of Mr & Mrs T Sprague.
Garden 100yds down lane.* Home-
made teas. **Adm £3, chd free. Suns
20 Apr; 4, 25 May; 8, 22 June; 24
Aug; 7 Sept (12-5). Visitors also
welcome by appt also groups.**
Plantsman's 1-acre garden on heavy
clay with stunning views, developed
from a field since 2001. Unusual trees,
shrubs, perennials and grasses. 2-acre
spring wild flower meadow, developing
arboretum, small orchard, vegetable
plot, water feature and nursery with
unusual plants for sale. Stout shoes
advisable.

19 NEW GRAFTON MANOR
Grafton Lane. B61 7HA. John &
June Morris. *1½ m SW of
Bromsgrove. M5 J5 on A38 to
Bromsgrove, signed L.* **Adm £4,
chd free. Weds 4 June; 2 July
(10-4).**
The gardens are a combination of
sweeping vistas and vast trees like
Wellingtonia, Korean pines and
cedars of Lebanon, complemented
by detailed planting in borders
and corners. There is a stunning
2 acre lake and 120ft herbaceous
borders all lovingly cared for by
June & John Morris.
Plantsperson's garden. Gravel
paths and steep slope, access to
main garden.

20 ◆ THE GREYFRIARS
Friar Street, Worcester WR1 2LZ.
The National Trust, 01905 23571,
hanburyhall@nationaltrust.org.uk. *In Friar Street within the centre of Worcester. Please use city car parks.* Adm £1.50 (incl NT members), chd free. For NGS: Sat 2 Feb, 2009 Sat 7 Feb (12-4).
Delightful city garden created from the clearance of back to back housing. An archway leads through to the walled garden containing a beautiful display of spring bulbs incl snowdrops and daffodils.
🍴 ⊛ ☕

21 ◆ HANBURY HALL
School Road, Droitwich WR9 7EA.
The National Trust, 01527 821214
Neil Cook,
hanburyhall@nationaltrust.org.uk.
3m NE of Droitwich. 6m S of Bromsgrove. Signed off B4090 and B4091. House and Garden adm £7.20, chd £3.60, Garden only adm £4.80, chd £2.40. For NGS: Sat 19 July (11-5.30).
Re-creation of C18 formal garden by George London. Parterre, fruit garden and wilderness. Mushroom house, Orangery and Ice house, William and Mary style house dating from 1701. Opportunity to meet the gardeners and to see behind the scenes in the walled garden.
♿ 🍴 ⊛ ☕

22 ◆ HARRELLS HARDY PLANTS NURSERY GARDEN
Rudge Road, Evesham WR11 4JR.
Liz Nicklin & Kate Phillips, 07799 577120/07733 446606,
www.harrellshardyplants.co.uk. *¼ m from centre of Evesham. From High St turn into Queens Rd opp Catholic church. Turn R at end of Queens Rd, then L into Rudge Rd. Approx 150yds on R is a small lane to nursery gardens.* Adm £2.50, chd free. Open Suns 10-12noon, & private visits. For NGS: Thurs & Suns 22, 29 May; 15, 26, 29 June; 10, 20 July; 7, 31 Aug; 14 Sept (2-5).
Informal 1 acre garden on W-facing slope overlooking cricket ground and R Avon. Large collections of hemerocallis, grasses and hardy perennials, many unusual. Jewel bed, bog garden, prairie border, sunshine bed and 'cottage garden corner'. Featured in 'Cotswold Life Magazine'; Channel 4 'Life Begins Again' & BBC2 Gardeners World.
🍴 ⊛ ☕

23 ◆ HARVINGTON HALL
Harvington DY10 4LR. The Roman Catholic Archdiocese of Birmingham, 01562 777846,
www.harvingtonhall.com. *3m SE of Kidderminster. ½ m E of A450 Birmingham to Worcester Rd & about ½ m N of A448 from Kidderminster to Bromsgrove.* House and Garden adm £5, chd £3.50, concessions £4.30, Garden only £2, chd 50p. Wed to Sun Apr to Sept. For NGS: Sat 5, Sun 6 July (11.30-4.30).
Romantic Elizabethan moated manor house with island gardens. Small Elizabethan-style herb garden, tended by volunteers from the Hereford and Worcs Gardens Trust. The main Hall gardens are looked after by volunteers who 'adopt' a bed. Tours of the Hall, which contains secret hiding places and rare wall paintings, are also available.
♿ 🍴 ⊛ ☕

200 year-old wooden stile and oak sculptures . . .

24 ◆ HIGH BANK
Cleobury Road, Bewdley DY12 2PG.
Stuart & Ann McKie, 01299 401342.
3½ m W of Kidderminster. A456. ½ m W of Bewdley town centre on B4190 (signed Tenbury). Parking available opp garden entrance. Light refreshments & teas. Adm £2.50, chd free. Suns 25 May; 29 June; 3 Aug (11-5). Visitors also welcome by appt.
Beautiful garden approx ⅓-acre with many old and protected trees. Restored in keeping with Edwardian house (not open). Featuring original summerhouse, rhododendrons and azaleas (May). Large collection of roses, herbaceous borders, courtyard garden, pergola walk and water features. Garden is still being developed. Winners large garden category Bewdley in Bloom.
🍴 ⊛ ☕ ☎

25 NEW HIGH VIEW
Martley WR6 6PW. Mike & Carole Dunnett, 01886 821559,
mike.dunnett@virgin.net. *1m S of Martley. On B4197 between Martley & A44 at Knightwick.* Refreshments available at Admiral Rodney PH, ½ m away. Adm £3, chd free. Sun 10 Aug (11-5). Visitors also welcome by appt, June to Sept for groups of 10+.
Intriguing 2½-acre garden developed over the last 30yrs. Magnificent views over the Teme valley. The garden has many features incl patio container planting, ponds and imaginatively designed borders containing many unusual trees, shrubs and herbaceous plants selected for summer colour. Access to garden via steep slopes and steps - but the walk is well worth it.
🍴 ⊛ ☎

26 HIRAETH
30 Showell Road, Droitwich WR9 8UY. Sue & John Fletcher, 07752 717243 / 01905 778390,
jfletcher@inductotherm.co.uk. *1m S of Droitwich. On The Ridings estate. Turn off A38 roundabout into Addyes Way, 2nd R into Showell Rd, 500yds on R.* Home-made teas. Adm £2.50, chd free. Weds, Suns 14 May; 1, 18 June; 6, 23 July; 10 Aug (Wed 12-5), (Sun 2-6). Afternoon & Evening Opening Fri 5 Sept (2-8). Visitors also welcome by appt.
Traditional cottage garden at rear incorporating pool, waterfall feature, 200yr-old wooden stile and oak sculptures. Time is needed to inspect the collection of herbaceous plants, hostas, ferns and other new and unusual varieties. Front garden contains numerous trees, shrubs and ornamental barrels, rose arch, wood and metal sculptures.
🍴 ⊛ ☕ ☎

27 HOLLAND HOUSE
Main Street, Cropthorne WR10 3NB.
Mr Peter Middlemiss. *5m W of Evesham. Equidistant between Evesham and Pershore. Travel on B4084 (old A44) & take turning signed Cropthorne village centre (on R from Evesham, on L from Pershore). Follow road round to R & then Holland House car park signed to the L. Please park in the car park & not on the rd.* Home-made teas. Adm £3, chd free (share to USPG). Suns 6 Apr; 8 June (2-5).
Formal gardens laid out by Lutyens in

1904 with rose garden; thatched house dating back to C16 (not open). Lovely riverside setting with banks of early daffodils in March and roses in June.

※ ⊨ ☕

㉘ HONEYBROOK HOUSE COTTAGE
Honeybrook Lane, Kidderminster DY11 5QS. Gerald Majumdar, 01562 67939, www.cottagegarden.org.uk. *1½ m N of Kidderminster. On A442 leaving Kidderminster towards Bridgnorth, 300yds from the island at the Three Crowns & Sugar Loaf PH turn R into Honeybrook Lane.* Home-made teas. **Adm £3.50, chd free. Suns 4 May; 15 June; 3 Aug; 7 Sept (12-5). Visitors also welcome by appt, groups 10+.**
2 acre counrty garden with beautiful views. Paths lead from the cottage garden through the woodland to the sloping prairie garden, down past shade borders to the brook, wildlife pond, herbaceous borders and long tree lined walk. Developed since 2003. Featured in 'English Garden', & BBC Open Gardens.

※ ⊛ ☕ ☎

㉙ NEW HUNTERS END
Button Bridge Lane, Button Bridge DY12 3DW. Norma & Colin Page, 01299 841055, norma@normapage.wanadoo.co .uk. *6m NW of Bewdley. B4194, Button Bridge Lane ¾ m on L.* Home-made teas. **Adm £3, chd free. Mon 26 May; Sun 13 July (2-5.30). Visitors also welcome by appt groups of 10+, no coaches.**
¾ -acre garden full of horticultural and artistic surprises. Tranquil seating areas in a kaleidoscope of colour.

♿ ※ ☕ ☎

ILMINGTON MANOR
See Warwickshire & part of West Midlands.

㉚ KOKOPELLI
185 Old Birmingham Road, Marlbrook, Bromsgrove B60 1DQ. Bruce Heideman & Sue James, 0121 445 2741, private@kokopelligardens.me.uk, www.kokopelligardens.me.uk. *2m N of Bromsgrove. 1m N of M42 J1, follow B4096 signed Rednal. 1m S of M5 J4, follow A38 signed Bromsgrove,*

turn L at T-lights into Braces Lane, turn R at Old Birmingham Rd. Home-made teas. **Adm £2.50, chd free. Suns 13 July; 10 Aug (1.30-6). Visitors also welcome by appt, for goups of 10+.**
Developing organic garden with winding path leading down a gentle slope through 3 distinctly different areas finishing in large fruit and vegetable garden showcasing heritage varieties. Planting throughout the garden eclectic. Extensive use of rainwater harvesting (2 water butts!), 10 compost bins, featuring sustainable technology. Featured in & on 'Worcestershire Life', 'The Village' and BBC2 Open Gardens.

※ ⊛ ☕ ☎

㉛ NEW LAYTON AVENUE GARDENS
Malvern WR14 2ND. *7m S of Worcester, 5m NW of Upton on Severn. From Worcester approach Malvern on A449. Turn L at roundabout into Townsend Way (signed A4208 Welland). After 3 roundabouts take 2nd R (Charles Way), then 2nd L into Layton Ave. From Upton approach Malvern on A4211. Take 3rd exit at Barnards Green roundabout (Pickersleign Rd). After 1m turn R at T-lights (signed A4208) Worcester) take 2nd L, then 2nd L again.* Home-made teas. **Combined adm £2.50, chd free. Sat 14, Sun 15 June (11-4).**
Two suburban, streamside gardens.

☕

NEW 10 LAYTON AVENUE
David Ranford
Secluded and inviting this mature garden wraps its self round the house (not open). Seating areas and courtyard fispond.

♿ ※

NEW 22 LAYTON AVENUE
Brian & Jenny Bradford
Redesigned since 2006 this open aspect garden features gazebo, fishpond, borders and terraces. Close planting presents a well stocked appearance to this still maturing garden. 2 steps for access to the main garden, we will arrange for a suitable ramp. Further steps lead down to the streamside this is not accessible to wheelchairs.

♿ ※ ⊛

Tranquil seating areas in a kaleidoscope of colour . . .

㉜ LITTLE LARFORD
Scots Lane, Astley Burf DY13 0SB. Lin & Derek Walker, 01299 823270, www.littlelarfordcottage.org.uk. *3m W of Stourport-on-Severn. Take A451 from Stourport, turn L onto B4196 for Worcester. After 1m turn L signed Larford Lakes. Garden approx 1½ m further on. Access via Larford Lane or Seedgreen Lane.* Home-made teas. **Adm £3, chd free. Suns 20, 27 Apr (11-5). Visitors also welcome by appt April, early May & July. Mini buses only, no coaches. groups of 10+.**
Hillside ½ -acre garden surrounding picturesque thatched cottage (not open) in woodland setting. 'Tulip Time' - many thousands of tulips in ambitious bedding displays amongst shrub and herbaceous borders. Colourful containers and hanging baskets, cut flower and vegetable garden, glasshouse and frames. Woodland walk with numerous bird boxes and viewpoint overlooking cottage towards Severn valley. Featured on BBC's Gardeners' World, ITV's Central News, & in 'Amateur Gardening' & ''Garden Answers'.

※ ⊛ ☕ ☎

㉝ ◆ LITTLE MALVERN COURT
Little Malvern WR14 4JN. Mrs T M Berington, 01684 892988. *3m S of Malvern. On A4104 S of junction with A449.* **Adm £4.50, chd 50p. Weds & Thurs 16 Apr to 17 July. For NGS: Mons 24 Mar; 5 May (2-5).**
10 acres attached to former Benedictine Priory, magnificent views over Severn valley. Intriguing layout of garden rooms and terrace round house designed and planted in early 1980's; water garden below feeding into chain of lakes; wide variety of spring bulbs, flowering trees and shrubs. Notable collection of old-fashioned roses. Topiary hedge and fine trees.

※ ⊛ ☕

THE LONG BARN
See Herefordshire.

LONGACRE
See Herefordshire.

34 LUGGERS HALL
Springfield Lane, Broadway
WR12 7BT. Kay & Red Haslam. *5m S
of Evesham. Turn off Broadway High St
by Swan Hotel, bear L into Springfield
Lane. Luggers Hall is on the L approx
300yds along. Some parking but limited
- if possible use car parks which are
close by.* Cream teas. **Adm £3, chd
free. Suns 25 May; 22 June (2-6).**
2¹/₂ -acre formal garden originally
designed by the famous Victorian
garden artist Alfred Parsons. Features
incl rose garden; parterre; walled
garden; potager; white garden; koi
pool and herbaceous borders, all
connected by gravel paths with seating
areas. An abundance of clipped box
and yew hedging; plus Victorian hazel
walk. Children with caution due to
deep water feature. Featured in 'GGG'.
Gravel paths.
& ⊛ ⛉ ☕

35 MARLBROOK GARDENS
Bromsgrove B60 1DY. *2m N of
Bromsgrove. 1m N of M42 J1, follow
B4096 signed Rednal, turn L at Xrds
into Braces Lane. 1m S of M5 J4,
follow A38 signed Bromsgove, turn L
at T-lights into Braces Lane. Car park
available.* Home-made teas at St
Lukes Church (Suns). **Combined adm
£4.50, chd free. Suns 1 June;
20 July; 17 Aug (2-6). Evening
Opening £5, wine, Sat 6 Sept
(6.30-10).**
2008 sees us reverting to the original 3
gardens of contrasting style from
gently sloping to challenging terraces.
Known for innovation, the gardens
continued to surprise and delight over
800 visitors last year. 'Experience the
Difference' with special interest for
young gardeners in June or enjoy wine
and hot dogs on our evening opening
with all gardens open under lights in
Sept. For more details visit
www.marlbrookgardens.com or send
SAE 24 Braces Lane, Bromsgrove B60
1DY. Featured in 'Worcestershire
Living'.
⛉ ⊛ ☕

24 BRACES LANE
Lynn & Alan Nokes, 0121 445
5520, alyn.nokes@virgin.net.
Visitors also welcome by appt,
groups of 15+.
Gentle sloping garden (175ft x
38ft) landscaped into 4 rooms.
Mediterranean area with exotics,
Pond, stream and patio area
planting for sunny and shady
aspects and mature lawn and
borders incl monochrome bed.

Large vegetable garden with
raised beds and greenhouses,
seating in all areas. Featured in
'Garden News' & on BBC
Gardeners World Special.
⛉ ⊛ ☎

OAK TREE HOUSE
504 Birmingham Road. Di &
Dave Morgan, 0121 445 3595,
davidmorgan@ukonline.co.uk.
Visitors also welcome by appt,
groups of 15+.
Plantsman's cottage garden
overflowing with plants, pots and
interesting artifacts. Wildlife pond,
waterfall, alpine area, plenty of
seating, secluded patio and rear
open vista. Special interests incl
scented plants and hostas.
Hidden front garden. Featured in &
on 'Mensa Magazine', 'Garden
News' and local radio.
⛉ ⊛ ☎

SARANACRIS
28A Braces Lane. John & Janet
Morgan, 0121 445 5823,
saranacris@btinternet.com.
Visitors also welcome by appt,
groups of 15+.
Riot of colour in an unusual
terraced garden. 'Jungle style'
planting with unusual and exotic
plants set amongst mature trees,
ponds, stream and waterfalls.
Roof garden, conservatory and
glasshouse planted with gingers.
Front garden redeveloped for
2008. Featured in 'Garden News',
Worcestershire Living'.
⛉ ⊛ ☎

Roof garden, conservatory and glasshouse planted with gingers . . .

36 NEW HOUSE FARM
Elmbridge Lane, Elmbridge
WR9 0DA. Charles & Carlo Caddick,
01299 851249,
carlocaddick@hotmail.com. *2¹/₂ m N
of Droitwich Spa. From Droitwich take
A442 to Cutnall Green. Take lane opp
The Chequers PH and proceed 1m to
T-junction, turning L towards Elmbridge
Green & Elmbridge. Continue along
lane passing church and church hall.
At T-junction turn into Elmbridge Lane,*

garden on L. Home-made teas. **Adm
£2.50, chd free. Visitors welcome by
appt.**
This charming garden surrounding an
early C19 red brick house (not open),
has a wealth of mature rare trees and
shrubs under planted with unusual
bulbs and herbaceous plants. Special
feature is the 'perry wheel', ornamental
vegetable gardens. Other points of
interest incl water garden, raised hot
bed and rose garden.
⛉ ⊛ ☕ ☎

THE ORCHARDS
See Herefordshire.

37 ORLETON HOUSE
Orleton, Stanford Bridge WR6 6SU.
Jenny & John Hughes, 01584
881253, jenny@orleton.co.uk,
www.orletonhouse.co.uk. *6m E of
Tenbury Wells. 15m NW of Worcester.
A443 from Worcester for 10m then
B4203 towards Bromyard. Cross R
Teme at Stanford Bridge then next R
turn. 1m down this lane.* Light lunches
& teas. **Adm £4, chd free. Sats, Suns
31 May; 1 June; 26, 27 July (11-5).
Visitors also welcome by appt for
groups of 15+.**
4 acres of garden, adjoining paddocks
and wooded areas surround a mellow
brick C19 grade 11 listed house (not
open) amid breathtaking beauty of the
Teme Valley. Superb herbaceous
borders, walled swimming pool and
richly planted gravel terrace display an
abundance of unusual plants, shrubs
and roses providing exotic colour and
perfume from May to October.
Magnificent copper beech tree
presides over the croquet lawn whilst a
stream hurries alongside a newly built
boardwalk and tree house. Jenny's
pottery workshop will be open.
& ⛉ ⊛ ☕ ☎

38 OVERBURY COURT
nr Tewkesbury GL20 7NP. Mr & Mrs
Bruce Bossom, 01386 725111,
garden@overburyestate.co.uk. *5m
NE of Tewkesbury. Village signed off
A46.* **Adm £3. Visitors welcome by
appt.**
Georgian house 1740 (not open);
landscape garden of same date with
stream and pools; daffodil bank and
grotto. Plane trees; yew hedges;
shrubs; cut flowers; coloured foliage;
gold and silver, shrub rose borders.
Norman church adjoins garden. Some
slopes, while all the garden can be
viewed, parts are not accessible to
wheelchairs.
& ⛉ ☎

Wildlife pond with frogs and fish . . .

PEBWORTH GARDENS
See Warwickshire & part of West Midlands.

THE PICTON GARDEN
See Herefordshire.

㊟ 4 PODEN COTTAGES
Honeybourne WR11 7PS. Patrick & Dorothy Bellew, 01386 438996, pots@poden.freeserve.co.uk. *6m E of Evesham. At the Gate Inn take the Pebworth, Long Marston rd, turn R at end of the Village for Mickleton. 1m on Mickleton Rd.* Home-made teas. **Adm £3, chd free.** Suns, Mons 23, 24 Mar; 25, 26 May (11-6); Suns, 8 15, 22, 29 June (2-6). Also open **Frogs Nest** (Mar, May, 22, 29 June). Visitors also welcome by appt, groups welcome.
$^1/_3$ -acre cottage and rose garden which has been planted by the owners. Paths wind through mixed herbaceous borders. 100 different roses old and modern, shrubs, small terrace and pool. Fine views over the Cotswold Hills. All-yr colour. Small vegetable garden. Featured in 'Amateur Gardening'.
👌 ✕ ✿ ☕ ☎

㊵ PUMP COTTAGE
Hill Lane, Weatheroak B48 7EQ. Mr Barry Knee, 01564 826250, barry@knee1947.freeserve.co.uk. *3m E of Alvechurch. 1½ m from J3 M42 off N-bound c'way of A435 (signed Alvechurch). Parking in adjacent field.* Home-made teas. **Adm £3, chd free.** Thu 19, Sat 21, Tue 24 June (11-5). Visitors also welcome by appt.
C19 cottage, charming plantsman's garden, approx 1 acre, adjoining open fields. Extensively planted, cottage garden, paths meandering through rockery and water features, romantic area with trees, shrubs and roses. Large natural pool, water lilies, boardwalk, wildlife area. Planted 16yrs ago, continually being developed with new features. Featured on BBC2 'Open Gardens', & Radio Hereford & Worcester. Restricted wheelchair access, some slopes, steps and narrow paths.
👌 ✕ ☕ ☎

RAGLEY HALL GARDENS
ASee Warwickshire & part of West Midlands.

㊶ ◆ RED HOUSE FARM
Flying Horse Lane, Bradley Green B96 6QT. Mrs M M Weaver, 01527 821269, www.redhousefarmgardenandnursery.co.uk. *On B4090 Alcester to Droitwich Spa. Ignore sign to Bradley Green. Turn opp The Red Lion PH.* **Adm £2, chd free.** Daily Feb to Oct. For NGS: Every Thurs 1 Mar to 31 Oct (10-5).
Paths wind through borders planted with mature trees, shrubs, roses, climbers, herbaceous perennials and spring bulbs providing colour, scent and interest throughout the yr. Featured in GGG.
✕ ✿

㊷ ◆ RIVERSIDE GARDENS AT WEBBS OF WYCHBOLD
Wychbold, nr Droitwich WR9 0DG. Webbs of Wychbold, 01527 860000, www.webbsdirect.co.uk. *2m N of Droitwich Spa. 1m N of M5 J5 on A38. Follow tourism signs from motorway.* Adm free for NGS all yr. Open daily all yr except Easter Sun, Christmas & Boxing Day & Easter Sun. For opening times please tel or see website.
Riverside gardens occupy 2½ -acres of themed gardens incl National Collection of *Potentilla fruticosa*, colour spectrum garden, white garden, dry garden, David Austin roses, grass garden and many others under continual development. The New Wave section opened in 2004; designed by Noel Kingsbury, this area features a series of plantings of naturalised perennials for differing situations. These are both eye catching and wildlife friendly. Once established they will require minimum maintenance.
👌 ✕ ✿ **NCCPG** ☕

㊸ NEW 32 ROGERS HILL
Worcester WR3 8JQ. Mrs Susan Leeman, 01905 726945, leemanhome@tiscali.co.uk. *¾ m from city centre. From M5 J6 A449 to Worcester, B4550 Blackpole Rd onto Astwood Rd, R into Landsdown Rd, 1st L into Landsdown Walk, R into Rogers Hill. From city centre, drive through Lowesmore, follow rd up Rainbow Hill, L into Landsdown Rd, 1st L into Landsdown Walk, R into*

Rogers Hill.. Light refreshments & teas. **Adm £2.50, chd free.** Sat 7 June (1-5). Visitors also welcome by appt, June & July, max 10, no coaches.
Shady 90ft wildlife garden. Small wildlife pond with frogs and fish, tiny beach with boat. Tree ferns, bananas and border of shade loving plants under mature apple trees. Nest boxes and Cross/stitch coasters of flowers for sale. Worcester Garden Centre Special Award for All Round Achievment.
✕ ☕ ☎

㊹ ST EGWINS COTTAGE
1 Church Lane, Norton, Evesham WR11 4TL. Anne & Brian Dudley, 01386 870486. *2m N of Evesham. On B4088.* Park in St Egwins Church car park only (not in Church Lane). Home-made teas at St Egwins Church. **Adm £2.50, chd free.** Suns 18 May; 22 June; 20 July; 10 Aug (2-5). Visitors also welcome by appt, May, June & July.
C16 ½ -timbered thatched cottage (not open) in open country next to C12 church (open for teas). Mature 180ft cottage garden packed with unusual and traditional plants incl ferns, hardy geraniums, phlox, clematis, lobelia, roses and shrubs for colourful yr round interest. Lawns and winding gravel paths. Small vegetable garden and chickens. Featured in 'Gloucestershire Echo' & 'Gloucestershire Citizen'.
✕ ✿ ☕ ☎

㊺ SHUTTIFIELD COTTAGE
Birchwood, Storridge WR13 5HA. Mr & Mrs David Judge, 01886 884243. *8m W of Worcester. Turn R off A4103 opp Storridge Church to Birchwood. After 1¼ m L down steep tarmac drive. Please park on roadside but drive down if walking is difficult.* Home-made teas. **Adm £3.50, chd free.** Sats 26 Apr; 3, 24 May; 7, 28 June; 19 July; 9 Aug (1-5.30). **Evening Opening** adm £4.50, Thur 3 July (5-8). Visitors also welcome by appt.
Superb position and views. 3-acre garden with extensive herbaceous borders, primula and stump bed, many unusual trees, shrubs and perennials, colour-themed for interest throughout the year. Walks in the 20-acre wood with ponds and natural wild areas where anemones, bluebells, rhododendrons and azaleas are a particular feature in spring. Large old

rose garden with many spectacular mature climbers. Small deer park and vegetable garden.

🏃 ✿ ☕ ☎

46 ◆ SPETCHLEY PARK GARDENS
Spetchley WR5 1RS. Mr R J Berkeley, 01453 810303, www.spetchleygardens.co.uk. *2m E of Worcester. On A44, follow brown signs.* **Adm £6, chd free, concessions £5.30. Open 21 Mar to 28 Sept 11-6; Oct weekends 11-4. For NGS: Fri 21 Mar; Sun 6 July (11-5.30).**
30-acre garden containing large collection of trees; shrubs and plants, many rare and unusual. Red and fallow deer in nearby park. A wonderful display of spring bulbs, but masses of colour throughout spring and summer. Every corner of this beautiful garden reveals some new vista, some new treasure of the plant world. Featured in & on 'Berkely A Country Estate'; TV House & Country, BBC Castle in the County. Gravel paths.

♿ 🏃 ☕

STANTON GARDENS
See Gloucestershire North & Central.

47 ◆ STONE HOUSE COTTAGE GARDENS
Stone DY10 4BG. James & Louisa Arbuthnott, 01562 69902, www.shcn.co.uk. *2m SE of Kidderminster. Via A448 towards Bromsgrove, next to church, turn up drive.* **Adm £3, chd free. Weds to Sats 12 March to 13 Sept 10-5. For NGS: Wed 12, Sat 22 Mar; Thur 10 Apr; Fri 16 May; Weds 18 June; 16 July; 13, 13 Aug; Sat 13 Sept (10-5).**
Beautifully planted walled garden adorned with brick follies. The garden boasts one of the largest collections of unusual and rare plants in the counrty. Adjacent nursery. Chosen by 'Daily Telegraph' in 2007 as one of the top gardens and nurseries in the country in which to see and buy plants. Partial wheelchair access.

♿ 🏃 ✿

Picnics in old orchard, Country recipes for cakes/ biscuits on sale . . .

48 NEW TANNACHIE
Harcourt Road. WR14 4DN. Mr & Mrs R Morgan. *On western slopes of Mlavern hills. Off B4232, 1.2m N of Wyche Cutting. From great Malvern take A449 then B4218 to The Wyche. Parking at Horseshoe bend on B4232 or on Harcourt Rd.* Home-made teas. **Adm £3, chd free. Suns 20 Apr; 15 June (2-5).**
Victorian garden, approx 1½ acres currently undergoing restoration. 35 metre herbacous border, terrace with views to Hay Bluff, rock garden, rhododendron area, sunken garden, children's garden with fedge and roundhouse, woodland, vegetable and fruit garden. Magnolias, azaleas, giant redwood, deodara cedar, crinodendron hookerianum, gunnera, fig and vine.

✿ ☕

49 THE TYNINGS
Church Lane, Stoulton, nr Worcester WR7 4RE. John & Leslie Bryant, 01905 840189, john.bryant@onetel.com. *5m S of Worcester; 3m N of Pershore. On the B4084 (formerly A44) between M5 J7 & Pershore. The Tynings lies beyond the church at the extreme end of Church Lane. Ample parking.* Home-made teas. **Adm £3, chd free. Sun 27 July (2-5). Evening Opening £4, wine, Sat 12 July (6-8.30). Visitors also welcome by appt, also groups mid May to mid Aug, coaches permitted.**
Plantsman's ½ -acre garden, in a rural setting with views of Stoulton Church, generously planted with unusual shrubs and trees. Island beds, herbaceous borders and water features contain an extensive (and growing) selection of lilies, euphorbias, berberis, euonymus and ferns. Wide variety of dahlias add colour throughout summer and autumn. Tree ferns, bamboos and bog garden add to the surprises round every corner. Plants labelled. Planting list available..

🏃 ✿ ☕ ☎

50 TYTHE BARN HOUSE
Chaddesley Corbett DY10 4QB. Judy & John Berrow, 01562 777014, j.berrow@virgin.net. *4½ m from Bromsgrove; 4½ m from Kidderminster. On A448. 150yds towards Kidderminster from the turn into Chaddesley Corbett village. Limited parkin at garden. Parking in village (The Talbot) or at village hall (200*

yds). Walking difficulties park in private lane. Home-made teas. **Adm £2.50, chd free. Sun 1 June (2-5.30). Visitors also welcome by appt, groups of 10+, coaches permitted.**
Approx ¾ -acre romantic garden created in old farm rickyard, within old farm building complex in conservation area. Incl old and modern roses; herbs and herbaceous borders. Small terrace garden. Shrubs and trees together with a small vegetable plot. Lovely view of the church and surrounding countryside. 'Flower Festival in Church'.

🏃 ✿ ☕ ☎

51 THE WALLED GARDEN
6 Rose Terrace, off Fort Royal Hill, Worcester WR5 1BU. Julia & William Scott. *½ m from cathedral. Via Fort Royal Hill, off London Rd (A44). Park on first section of Rose Terrace & walk the last 20yds down track.* **Adm £2, chd free. Sats 26 Apr; 17 May; 7 June; 12 July (1-5).**
Peaceful oasis of organically grown aromatic, decorative culinary and medicinal herbs, vegetables, flowers and trees in a C19 walled kitchen garden. Whilst preserving its history the garden is continuing to change and flourish. Short demonstrations of herbal interest will be held during open days.

🏃 ✿ ☕

52 NEW WEAVERS & TICKNERS COTTAGES
Upper Rochford WR15 8SL. *2m E of Tenbury Wells. From Worcester & Martley, then via Clifton on Teme B4204, or Gt Witley to Bromyard picking up B4204 at Sapey Xrds.* Home-made teas. **Combined adm £3, chd free. Suns 13 Apr, 25 May, 8 June; Mon 26 May (12-5).**
2 interesting cottage gardens created over 9yrs from owner's propagation. Old orchard undergoing gradual replanting. Picnics in old orchard, Old Country recipes for cakes/biscuits on sale.

☕

NEW TICKNERS
Anne Wiltshire. *Garden arch links to Weavers*
Small easily maintained garden. Raised beds with colourful evergreens for winter, lavender and roses for summer - containers and climbers.

🏃

NEW WEAVERS
David & Shirley Hambelton
1/2 -acre cottage garden planted by owner from seeds and cuttings over 9yrs. Old orchard slowly being replanted. Partial wheelchair access, dogs in parking area only.

53 WESTACRES
Wolverhampton Road, Prestwood DY7 5AN. Mrs Joyce Williams, 01384 877496. *3m W of Stourbridge. A449 in between Wall Heath (2m) & Kidderminster (6m). Parking Beechwood Bonsai (next door).* Home-made teas. **Adm £2.50, chd free (share to DEBRA). Sat 5, Sun 6 July (11-5). Visitors also welcome by appt.**

3/4 -acre plant collector's garden, many unusual varieties, formal area with large koi pool. Path to woodland with acres, tree ferns and 80 varieties of hostas. Conifers Japanese style garden with bamboos and grasses.

54 WHITCOMBE HOUSE
Overbury, nr Tewkesbury GL20 7NZ. Faith & Anthony Hallett, 01386 725206, tonyhallett@nsl.eclipse.co.uk. *9m S of Evesham. 9m N of Cheltenham, 5m E of Tewkesbury. Signed Overbury take A46 at Beckford Inn or at roundabout junction of A46, A435 & B4077 take small lane signed Overbury or take Bredon rd out of Tewkesbury. In village turn up hill, garden 1st on L before village hall.* Home-made teas. **Adm £4, chd free. Suns 4, 25 May; 8 June; 6 July (2-5). Visitors also welcome by appt Apr to Sept, groups 10+, coaches welcome.**

1-acre garden framed by rose-clad cotswold dry-stone walls. Colourful planting, among self seeded wild annuals, there is a border in Whitcombe of almost everything. Large mature trees: Pseudo Acacia, weeping green beech and magnificent Indian Bean tree give shape, shade and height. Shrubberies, countless roses, fruit trees and more herbaceous raised beds are found running beside gravel paths and through under-cover way. Stream babbles over waterfalls through small lake and under Captains Bridge, surrounded on both banks with primulas, arums and marginals. Garden of peace and tranquility. Teas served under the Bean Tree complete the picture. Best garden visited in S Worcestershire: Edinburgh Botanical Society, featured in 'Gloucester Echo'.

55 ◆ WHITE COTTAGE
Stock Green, nr Inkberrow B96 6SZ. Mr & Mrs S M Bates, 01386 792414. *2m W of Inkberrow, 2m E of Upton Snodsbury. A422 Worcester to Alcester, turn at brown sign for Cottage Garden also Stock Green, 11/2 m to T-junction, turn L.* **Adm £2.50, chd free, concessions £2. Fris to Tues 21 Mar to 27 July (10-5); then by appt. For NGS: Sats, Suns 29, 30 Mar; 12, 13, 26, 27 Apr; Sats, Suns, Mons 3, 4, 5, 17, 24, 25, 26 May; Sats, Suns 7, 14, 15, 21 June; 5, 6, 19, 20 July (10-5).**

2 acres, herbaceous and shrub beds, stream and spring wild flower area, rose garden, raised woodland bed, large specialist collection of hardy geraniums and echinacea. Adjacent nursery.

56 ◆ WHITLENGE GARDENS
Whitlenge Lane, Hartlebury DY10 4HD. Mr & Mrs K J Southall, 01299 250720, www.whit-lenge.co.uk. *5m S of Kidderminster.* *Take A449 from Kidderminster towards Worcester, then A442 (signed Droitwich) over small island, 1/4 m, 1st R into Whitlenge Lane. Follow signs.* **Adm £2, chd free. Open all yr except Christmas, Mon to Sat (9-5), Sun (10-5). For NGS: Suns, Mons 23, 24 Mar; 4, 5, 25, 26 May; 24, 25 Aug (10-5).**

3 acre show garden of professional designer with over 800 varieties of trees, shrubs etc. Twisted pillar pergola, camomile lawn, waterfalls and pools. Mystic features of the Green Man, 'Sword in the Stone' and cave fernery. Walk the labyrinth and take refreshments in The Garden 'Design Studio' tearoom.

WOODPECKERS
See Warwickshire & part of West Midlands.

57 ◆ WORLDS END NURSERIES
Moseley Road, Hallow WR2 6NJ. Kristina & Robin Pearce, 01905 640977, www.worldsendgarden.co.uk. *4m NW of Worcester. At Hallow PO follow lane to Sinton Green. Ignore L turn to Wichenford, garden next on R.* **Adm £3, chd free. Adjacent nursery Tues to Sats April to Sept. For NGS: Suns 8 June (11-5); 13 July (11.30-4.30).**

3/4 -acre garden laid out to a mixture of island beds and formal planting. The garden contains many unusual herbaceous plants, grasses, ferns and over 200 varieties of hostas all clearly labelled. Newly developed rill and alpine garden with stone troughs and raised beds. Featured on BBC2 Open Gardens.

Mark your diary with these special events in 2008

EXPLORE SECRET GARDENS DURING CHELSEA WEEK

Tue 20 May, Wed 21 May, Thur 22 May, Fri 23 May
Full day tours: £78 per person, 10% discount for groups
Advance Booking required, telephone 01932 864532 or
email pennysnellflowers@btinternet.com

Specially selected private gardens in London, Surrey and Berkshire. The tour price includes transport and lunch with wine at a popular restaurant or pub.

FROGMORE – A ROYAL GARDEN (BERKSHIRE)

Tue 3 June 10am - 5.30pm (last adm 4pm)
Garden adm £4, chd free. Advance booking recommended telephone 01483 211535
or email orders@ngs.org.uk

A unique opportunity to explore 30 acres of landscaped garden, rich in history and beauty.

FLAXBOURNE FARM – FUN AND SURPRISES (BEDFORDSHIRE)

Sun 8 June 10am - 5pm Adm £5, chd free
No booking required, come along on the day!

Bring the whole family and enjoy a plant fair and garden party and have fun in this beautiful and entertaining garden of 2 acres.

WISLEY RHS GARDEN – MUSIC IN THE GARDEN (SURREY)

Tue 19 August 6 - 9pm

Adm (incl RHS members) £7, chd under 15 free

A special opening of this famous garden, exclusively for the NGS. Enjoy music and entertainment as you explore a range of different gardens.

For further information visit www.ngs.org.uk or telephone 01483 211535

YORKSHIRE

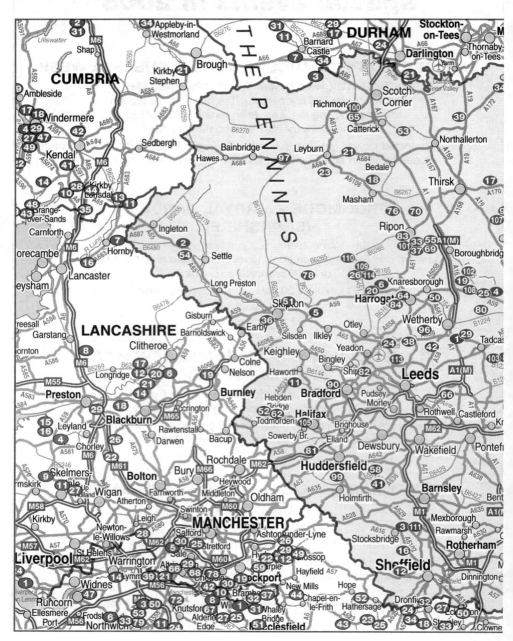

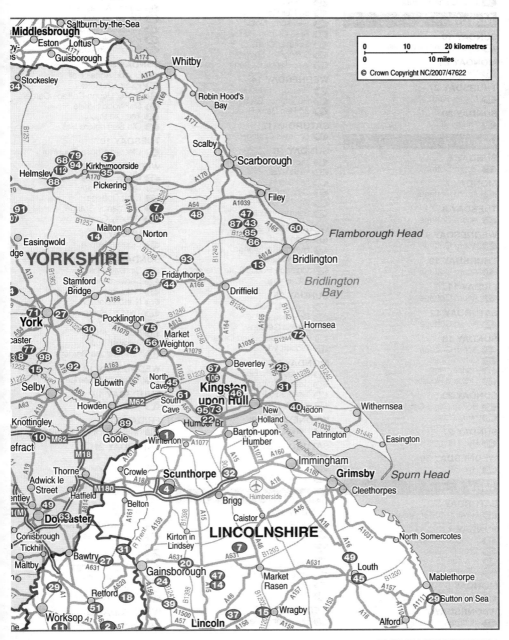

Opening Dates

February

SUNDAY 24
10 Bridge Farm House

March

SUNDAY 16
80 130 Prince Rupert Drive

MONDAY 24
111 Wortley Hall

THURSDAY 27
59 Manor Farm

SUNDAY 30
35 Friars Hill

April

SUNDAY 6
1 Acorn Cottage

MONDAY 7
1 Acorn Cottage

TUESDAY 8
1 Acorn Cottage

WEDNESDAY 9
1 Acorn Cottage

THURSDAY 10
1 Acorn Cottage

FRIDAY 11
1 Acorn Cottage

SATURDAY 12
1 Acorn Cottage

SUNDAY 13
1 Acorn Cottage
18 Clifton Castle
39 Harlsey Hall
77 Orchard House

SUNDAY 20
8 Bolton Percy Gardens
41 Highfields

SUNDAY 27
88 Rye Hill

WEDNESDAY 30
88 Rye Hill

May

SATURDAY 3
68 Nawton Tower Garden

SUNDAY 4
19 Cobble Cottage
25 Croft Cottage
68 Nawton Tower Garden
108 Whixley Gardens

MONDAY 5
68 Nawton Tower Garden

WEDNESDAY 7
47 Hunmanby Grange

SUNDAY 11
7 Blackbird Cottage
22 The Court
42 Hillbark
46 56 Hull Road
48 Jacksons Wold
84 RHS Garden Harlow Carr
95 Spinney Croft
98 Stillingfleet Lodge
109 Woodlands Cottage

WEDNESDAY 14
5 Beacon Hill House
47 Hunmanby Grange
83 24 Red Bank Road

SATURDAY 17
34 Fir Trees Cottage

SUNDAY 18
11 Brookfield
41 Highfields
66 Millrace Nursery
77 Orchard House
83 24 Red Bank Road
89 Saltmarshe Hall

WEDNESDAY 21
11 Brookfield
47 Hunmanby Grange
57 Low Askew
103 Vicarage House (Late Afternoon & Evening)

SUNDAY 25
24 Creskeld Hall
28 Dowthorpe Hall
40 Hedon Gardens
80 130 Prince Rupert Drive
110 Woodroyd

MONDAY 26
10 Bridge Farm House
19 Cobble Cottage
102 Tinkers Hollow
105 Warley House Gardens

WEDNESDAY 28
47 Hunmanby Grange

SATURDAY 31
44 Holmfield
79 Pennyholme
94 Sleightholmedale Lodge

June

SUNDAY 1
42 Hillbark
44 Holmfield
47 Hunmanby Grange
48 Jacksons Wold
49 Jasmine House
67 Molecroft Cottage
88 Rye Hill
106 26 West End

WEDNESDAY 4
47 Hunmanby Grange

FRIDAY 6
78 Parcevall Hall Gardens

SATURDAY 7
13 Burton Agnes Hall
23 Coverham Abbey
76 Old Sleningford Hall
79 Pennyholme
94 Sleightholmedale Lodge

SUNDAY 8
13 Burton Agnes Hall
30 Elvington Gardens
51 Lower Heugh Cottage Garden
73 Oakwood House
74 The Old Priory
76 Old Sleningford Hall

TUESDAY 10
17 Cleaves House (Evening)

WEDNESDAY 11
17 Cleaves House
19 Cobble Cottage
25 Croft Cottage
47 Hunmanby Grange
108 Whixley Gardens

SATURDAY 14
17 Cleaves House

SUNDAY 15
6 Birstwith Hall
27 Derwent House
43 Holly Tree Cottage
70 Norton Conyers
75 The Old Rectory
85 The Ridings
87 Rustic Cottage
92 Skipwith Hall
112 Wytherstone Gardens

WEDNESDAY 18
47 Hunmanby Grange

THURSDAY 19
2 Austwick Hall

FRIDAY 20
91 Shandy Hall (Evening)

SATURDAY 21
32 Fernleigh
99 Sunny Mount

SUNDAY 22
3 Avenue Cottage
32 Fernleigh
42 Hillbark
62 Mayroyd Mill House
65 Millgate House (Day & Evening)
72 Nutkins
89 Saltmarshe Hall
98 Stillingfleet Lodge
99 Sunny Mount
100 Swale Cottage
111 Wortley Hall

WEDNESDAY 25
47 Hunmanby Grange

FRIDAY 27
91 Shandy Hall (Evening)

SUNDAY 29
48 Jacksons Wold
58 Lower Crawshaw

July

WEDNESDAY 2
47 Hunmanby Grange
104 The Walled Garden at Scampston

SUNDAY 6
26 Dacre Banks Gardens
39 Harlsey Hall
81 2 Prospect Place
114 Yorke House

WEDNESDAY 9
47 Hunmanby Grange
88 Rye Hill

SUNDAY 13
15 Cawood Gardens
54 Lawkland Hall
59 Manor Farm
63 The Mediterranean Gardens
86 Rudston House
88 Rye Hill

WEDNESDAY 16
47 Hunmanby Grange

SATURDAY 19
94 Sleightholmedale Lodge

SUNDAY 20
12 Brookside Cottage
29 East Wing, Thorp Arch Hall
71 The Nursery
94 Sleightholmedale Lodge
112 Wytherstone Gardens
114 Yorke House

WEDNESDAY 23
36 The Grange
47 Hunmanby Grange

SUNDAY 27
43 Holly Tree Cottage
61 39 Market Place
85 The Ridings
87 Rustic Cottage
97 Stainsacre

WEDNESDAY 30
47 Hunmanby Grange

August

SUNDAY 3
53 Langton Farm
101 Thorpe Lodge

WEDNESDAY 6
36 The Grange

SATURDAY 9
60 Mansion Cottage

SUNDAY 10
4 Barley Mow

60 Mansion Cottage
63 The Mediterranean Gardens
84 RHS Garden Harlow Carr

WEDNESDAY 13
36 The Grange

THURSDAY 14
2 Austwick Hall

SUNDAY 17
66 Millrace Nursery

SUNDAY 31
20 Cold Cotes

September

SUNDAY 7
9 Boundary Cottage
16 72 Church Street
98 Stillingfleet Lodge

SUNDAY 14
58 Lower Crawshaw

SUNDAY 21
80 130 Prince Rupert Drive

Gardens open to the public

13 Burton Agnes Hall
14 Castle Howard
21 Constable Burton Hall Gardens
48 Jacksons Wold
52 Land Farm
69 Newby Hall & Gardens
70 Norton Conyers
78 Parcevall Hall Gardens
84 RHS Garden Harlow Carr
91 Shandy Hall
93 Sledmere House
98 Stillingfleet Lodge
104 The Walled Garden at Scampston
113 York Gate

By appointment only

31 Evergreens
33 Field Cottage
37 Greencroft
45 Hotham Hall
50 Kelberdale
55 Littlethorpe Manor
64 The Mews Cottage
82 The Ranch House
90 4 Shaftesbury Court
96 Spring Close Farm
107 The White House

Also open by appointment ☎

1 Acorn Cottage
2 Austwick Hall
5 Beacon Hill House
6 Birstwith Hall
7 Blackbird Cottage
9 Boundary Cottage

10 Bridge Farm House
11 Brookfield
15 9 Anson Grove, Cawood Gardens
15 21 Great Close, 9 Anson Grove, Cawood Gardens
16 72 Church Street
17 Cleaves House
19 Cobble Cottage
20 Cold Cotes
22 The Court
25 Croft Cottage
27 Derwent House
28 Dowthorpe Hall
29 East Wing, Thorp Arch Hall
32 Fernleigh
35 Friars Hill
36 The Grange
39 Harlsey Hall
40 32 Baxtergate, Hedon Gardens
43 Holly Tree Cottage
44 Holmfield
47 Hunmanby Grange
49 Jasmine House
51 Lower Heugh Cottage Garden
53 Langton Farm
58 Lower Crawshaw
60 Mansion Cottage
61 39 Market Place
62 Mayroyd Mill House
63 The Mediterranean Gardens
65 Millgate House
66 Millrace Nursery
68 Nawton Tower Garden
72 Nutkins
74 The Old Priory
75 The Old Rectory
77 Orchard House
26 Orchard House, Dacre Banks Gardens
80 130 Prince Rupert Drive
81 2 Prospect Place
85 The Ridings
86 Rudston House
88 Rye Hill
89 Saltmarshe Hall
94 Sleightholmedale Lodge
95 Spinney Croft
99 Sunny Mount
101 Thorpe Lodge
103 Vicarage House
106 26 West End
108 The Old Vicarage, Whixley Gardens
109 Woodlands Cottage
111 Wortley Hall
114 Yorke House

The Gardens

1 ACORN COTTAGE
50 Church Street, Boston Spa LS23 6DN. Mrs C M Froggatt, 01937 842519. *1m SE of Wetherby. Off A1 on A659 Church St opp Central Garage.* Home-made teas. **Adm £3 incl teas, chd free. Daily 6 Apr to 13 Apr (11-5). Visitors also welcome by appt 15 Mar to 15 April only, individuals & groups, coaches permitted.**
You are invited to come and spend peaceful time in this small well established alpine garden full of spring delights. Three generations of the family have collected the plants and bulbs, and these have recently been rearranged and the garden significantly altered for ease of maintenance and access without losing the character and uniqueness of this fine collection. Some small steps.
♿ ✂ ☕ ☎

Specimen trees, and juniper lined walk leads to jungle garden . . .

ALKBOROUGH AND BURTON STATHER GARDENS
See Lincolnshire.

ASKHAM GARDENS
See Nottinghamshire.

2 NEW AUSTWICK HALL
Town Head Lane, Austwick, nr Settle LA2 8BS. Eric Culley & Michael Pearson, 015242 51794, austwickhall@austwick.org, www.austwickhall.co.uk. *5m W of Settle. From A65 to Austwick Village. Pass Game Cock Inn on L. After Primary School turn L Town Head Lane.* Home-made teas. **Adm £2.50, chd free (share to Yorkshire Wildlife Trust). Thurs 19 June; 14 Aug (11-5). Visitors also welcome by appt.**
Historic manor house and gardens set in the dramatic limestone scenery of the Yorkshire Dales. Formal terraces with herbaceous borders are divided by lawns, gravel paths and dry stone walls. Specimen trees, and juniper lined walk leads to jungle garden. Featured in 'Yorkshire Post'.
✂ ⓒ 🛌 ☕ ☎

3 NEW AVENUE COTTAGE
Wortley Village S35 7DB. Vega Shepley & Roger England. *9m NW of Sheffield, 5m SW of Barnsley. On A629 Huddersfield - Sheffield rd in Wortley village, signed Wortley Hall & Gardens.* Teas at Wortley Hall. **Combined with Wortley Hall Gardens adm £5, chd free. Sun 22 June (12-4).**
Within the walled kitchen garden of Wortley Hall and attached to original gardeners cottage the garden overlooks the tree line of Wortley Hall Gardens. Gravelled island beds with Mediterranean style plantings are set in lawn. Areas for wildlife, large mixed shrubbery, and vegetable garden on raised beds. Garden is totally organic.
✂ ☕

4 BARLEY MOW
Moor Monkton, York YO26 8JA. Dr & Mrs Mike Ashford. *5m NW of York. Off A59.* Home-made teas. **Adm £3, chd free. Sun 10 Aug (11-6).**
This plant enthusiast's $^3/_4$ -acre garden has wide range of interesting plants both ornamental and edible. Garden peaks in July and Aug with vivid herbaceous borders and bold subtropical planting. Other features incl trellis draped with colourful climbers; formally trained apples and pears; pond, greenhouses, vegetable garden and wide range of less usual fruit. Featured in 'Garden News'. Gravel path.
♿ ✂ ⓒ ☕

5 BEACON HILL HOUSE
Langbar, nr Ilkley LS29 0EU. Mr & Mrs D H Boyle, 01943 607544. *4m NW of Ilkley. 1$^1/_4$ m SE of A59 at Bolton Bridge.* Home-made teas. **Adm £3, chd free, concessions £2.50 (share to Riding for the Disabled). Wed 14 May (1.30-6). Visitors also welcome by appt late Feb to July, please call or write to arrange.**
Fairly large garden, facing S and sheltered by woodland, on the slopes of Beamsley Beacon at 900ft above sea-level. An old fernery and big windbreak survive from original Victorian garden. Today, features of particular interest are snowdrops, early flowering rhododendrons in spring, and enormous climbing and rambling roses in July. Some unusual flowering trees and shrubs, several mixed borders, 2 ponds, which attract wildlife, small kitchen garden and cool greenhouse.
✂ ⓒ ☕ ☎

6 BIRSTWITH HALL
High Birstwith, nr Harrogate HG3 2JW. Sir James & Lady Aykroyd. *5m NW of Harrogate. Between Hampsthwaite & Birstwith villages, close to A59 Harrogate/Skipton rd.* Home-made teas. **Adm £3.50, chd free. Sun 15 June (2-5). Visitors also welcome by appt, coaches permitted. Please write.**
Large 8-acre garden nestling in secluded Yorkshire dale with formal garden and ornamental orchard, extensive lawns, picturesque stream, large pond and Victorian greenhouse.
♿ ⓒ ☕ ☎

7 BLACKBIRD COTTAGE
Scampston YO17 8NG. Mrs Hazel Hoad. *5m E of Malton. Off A64 to Scarborough through Rillington, turn L signed Scampston only. Follow signs.* Home-made teas. **Adm £2.50, chd free. Sun 11 May (10-5). Visitors also welcome by appt.**
$^1/_3$ -acre plantswoman's garden made from scratch since 1986. Great wealth of interesting plants, with shrub and herbaceous border and a new themed gravel garden. Alpines a speciality. Please visit throughout the day to ease pressure on small but inspirational garden. Plants for sale by Mrs Rona Ashworth BSc (Hort).
✂ ⓒ ☕ ☎

8 BOLTON PERCY GARDENS
YO23 7BA. *5m E of Tadcaster. 10m SW of York. Off A64 (Leeds - York).* Light lunches & teas at Bolton Percy Parish Room from 11.30. **Combined adm £3.50, chd free. Sun 20 Apr (12.30-5).**
☕

BOLTON PERCY CEMETERY
Bolton Percy All Saints
An opportunity to meet Roger Brook who gardens an acre of old village churchyard where garden plants are naturalised. Beautiful C15 church with acclaimed millennium window. Plants sale incl dicentras from National Collection. Featured in 'Garden News'.
✂ ⓒ NCCPG

WINDY RIDGE
Mr & Mrs J S Giles. *Marsh Lane* Natural cottage-style garden sloping down to the Ings, greatly influenced by Margery Fish. Wide

collection of Elizabethan and Barnhaven primroses. Paths meander through natural plantings of unusual hardy plants.

✗ ❀

⑨ BOUNDARY COTTAGE
Seaton Ross, York YO42 4NF. Roger Brook, 01759 319156, twinponds@talktalk.net. *5m SW of Pocklington. From A64 York, take Hull exit & immed B1228, approx 9m, then follow signs Seaton Ross. From M62 Howden N on B1228 approx 11m, R turn to Seaton Ross. Garden 1m before Seaton Ross. From Hull turn R 100yds before Seaton Ross.* Home-made teas. **Adm £3, chd free.** Sun 7 Sept (12-5). **Visitors also welcome by appt, groups of 10-30.**
Second opening of horticulturist Roger Brook's new ³/₄ -acre plantsmans garden, incl twin ponds, gravel borders, cactus and succulent planting, mixed and herbaceous borders, boggy plantings, acid border, rock garden, young specimen trees, unorthodox vegetables, fruit and seasonal container displays. National Collection of Dicentra. Featured in 'The Journal'.

& ✗ ❀ NCCPG ☕ ☎

⑩ BRIDGE FARM HOUSE
Long Lane, Great Heck DN14 0BE. Barbara & Richard Ferrari, 01977 661277. *6m S of Selby. 3m N of M62 (J34) A19 turn E at roundabout or Snaith onto A645, straight on at T-lights then 1st R to Great Heck. House 1st on L, park in adjacent field.* Home-made teas. **Adm £2.50, chd free.** Sun 24 Feb; Mon 26 May (12-4). **Visitors also welcome by appt.**
Large all-yr round organic garden designed and created by owners since 2002. Creatively planted with many unusual and interesting plants incl; long double borders, ponds, bog, gravel, pots, poultry, wildlife areas, vegetables, working compost heaps, trees, woodland, spring interest borders and named varieties of snowdrops and hellebores.

& ✗ ❀ ☕ ☎

⑪ BROOKFIELD
Jew Lane, Oxenhope BD22 9HS. Mrs R L Belsey, 01535 643070. *5m SW of Keighley. Take A629 towards Halifax. Fork R onto A6033 towards Haworth. Follow signs to Oxenhope. Turn L at Xrds in village. 200yds after PO fork R, Jew Lane.* Home-made teas. **Adm £3, chd free.** Sun 18, Wed

21 May (1-5). **Visitors also welcome by appt.**
1-acre, intimate garden, incl large pond with island, mallards and new apricot call ducks, white call ducks, dominoes and European pochard. Many varieties of candelabra primulas and florindaes, azaleas, rhododendrons. Unusual trees and shrubs, screes, greenhouse and conservatory. New series of island beds. Partial wheelchair access.

& ✗ ❀ ☕ ☎

⑫ BROOKSIDE COTTAGE
Brookside Bank Road, Stannington S6 6GU. Shirley Samworth. *2¹/₂ m from Sheffield city centre. M1 J36, A61 (Sheffield) to Hillsborough. Follow signs for Stannington/Dungworth.* Home-made teas. **Adm £2.50, chd free.** Sun 20 July (11-4).
Long triangular shaped garden sloping steeply away behind old cottages, overlooking fields and woodland. Steps between 3 levels lead to areas of differing interest, giving senses of both secrecy and surprise planted and arranged with artistic flair in the cottage style. Featured in & on 'Sheffield Star', 'Sheffield Telegraph' & BBC Radio Sheffield.

✗ ❀ ☕

⑬ ◆ BURTON AGNES HALL
Driffield YO25 4ND. Mrs S Cunliffe-Lister, 01262 490324, www.burton-agnes.com. *Between Driffield & Bridlington. Burton Agnes is on A614.* **House and Garden £6, chd £3, concessions £5.50, Garden only £3.50, chd £1.50, concessions £3.25** (donation to NGS). Tues 1 April to Fri 31 Oct. For NGS: Sat 7, Sun 8 June (11-5).
8 acres. Lawns with clipped yew and fountains; woodland gardens and walled garden containing potager; herbaceous and mixed borders; maze with thyme garden; jungle garden; campanula collection garden and coloured gardens containing giant games boards. Collections of hardy geraniums, clematis, penstemons and many unusual perennials. Gardeners' Fair 7, 8 June.

& ❀ ☕

⑭ ◆ CASTLE HOWARD
nr York YO60 7DA. Castle Howard Estate Ltd, 01653 648333, www.castlehoward.co.uk. *15m NE of York, 6m W of Malton. Off the A64.* **House and Garden £10.50, chd £6.50, concession £9.50, Garden only £8, chd £5, concession £7.50.**

Daily 1 Mar to 4 Nov 10-4, garden & grounds daily except 25 Dec.
Formal grounds laid out from C18 to present, incl fountains, lakes, cascades and waterfalls. Woodland garden, Ray Wood, has collection of rhododendron species and hybrids amounting to 800 varieties. Notable collection of acers, nothofagus, arbutus, styrax, magnolia and conifers. Formal rose gardens incl old, China and Bourbon roses, hybrid teas and floribunda. Ornamental vegetable garden planted in 2006.

& ❀ ☕

Coloured gardens containing giant games boards . . .

⑮ CAWOOD GARDENS
YO8 3UG. *5m N of Selby. On B1223 5m NW of Selby & 7m SE of Tadcaster. Between York & A1 on B1222.* Light Refreshments at 9 Anson Grove, home-made teas at Ash Lea. **Combined adm £5, chd free.** Sun 13 July (12-5).
An attractive, historic, riverside village. Village maps given at all gardens.

☕

9 ANSON GROVE
Tony & Brenda Finnigan, 01757 268888. **Visitors also welcome by appt, groups of 10+.**
Enjoy tranquillity in this small orientally-influenced garden with winding paths and raised areas. Although compact, imaginative design has created a garden of interest with 4 pools, water features, Zen garden, pagoda and over 30 grasses. Crafts and plants for sale.

✗ ❀ ☎

ASH LEA
Michael & Josephine Welbourn
Shrubs and fernery lead to colourful formal borders, in contrast to a relaxed atmosphere by a clear pool, leading to dining area and traditional vegetable garden edged in clipped box.

✗

21 GREAT CLOSE
David & Judy Jones, 01757 268571. Visitors also welcome by appt, groups of 10+.
All-yr interest, with mixed planting in ever-changing borders, incl vegetables, herbs, grasses and many unusual and some exotic perennials. Ponds, stream and rose walk make a colourful but relaxing garden.
✗ ✿

Cascades, wild flower meadow . . .

16 72 CHURCH STREET
Oughtibridge S35 0FW. Linda & Peter Stewart, 0114 286 3847, lindastewart@talktalk.net. *6m N of Sheffield. M1 (J36) A61 (Sheffield). Turn R at Norfolk Arms PH. In Oughtibridge follow one-way system turning L immed after zebra crossing.* Home-made teas. **Adm £2.50, chd free. Sun 7 Sept (11-4). Visitors also welcome by appt.**
Wildlife-friendly 1/3 -acre garden on N-facing slope. Informal beds providing yr-long interest have mixed plantings of trees, shrubs, phormiums, bamboos, grasses, ferns, bulbs and perennials which lead to a natural stream with a backdrop of native woodland.
✗ ✿ ☕ ☎

17 CLEAVES HOUSE
Thirlby YO7 2DQ. Margaret & Tony May, 01845 597606. *3m E of Thirsk. From A170 in Sutton under Whitestone Cliff take turning signed Felixkirk. Almost immed take rd R signed Thirlby.* Home-made teas. **Adm £3, chd free. Evening Opening , wine, Tue 10 June (6-9); Wed 11, Sat 14 June (1-5). Visitors also welcome by appt 12 to 30 June. Access for cars & minibuses. No coaches.**
Informal 2-acre garden on sloping site with beautiful views. Bold, interesting planting with many unusual trees, shrubs, roses, pond and bog area, small wood. Enthusiastically gardened and planted by the owners since 1991. Featured in 'Yorkshire Life'. Parts of garden not accessible by wheelchair, particularly if wet.
♿ ✗ ✿ ☕ ☎

18 NEW CLIFTON CASTLE
Ripon HG4 4AB. Lord & Lady Downshire. *2m N of Masham. On road to Newton-le-Willows & Richmond. Gates on L next to red telephone box.* Home-made teas. **Adm £3.50, chd free (share to Talking Space). Sun 13 Apr (2-5).**
Fine views, river walks, wooded pleasure grounds with bridges and follies. Cascades, wild flower meadow and 19C walled kitchen garden.
♿ ☕

19 COBBLE COTTAGE
Rudgate, Whixley YO26 8AL. John Hawkridge & Barry Atkinson, 01423 331419. *3m E of A1 off A59 York - Harrogate.* **Combined Sun 4 May, Wed 11 June (11.30-5) with Whixley Gardens adm £5, combined Mon 26 May (11-5) with Tinkers Hollow adm £3, chd free. Visitors also welcome by appt June & July, groups of 10+.**
Imaginatively designed, constantly changing, small cottage garden full of decorative architectural plants and old family favourites. Interesting water garden, containers and use of natural materials. Secret courtyard garden and new Japanese garden.
✗ ✿ ☎

COBWEBS
See Lincolnshire.

20 COLD COTES
Cold Cotes Road, nr Kettlesing, Harrogate HG3 2LW. Penny Jones, Ed Loft, Doreen & Joanna Russell, 01423 770937, info@coldcotes.com. *7m W of Harrogate. Off A59. After Black Bull PH turn R to Menwith Hill/Darley.* Home-made teas. **Adm £3.50, chd free. Sun 31 Aug (11-5). Visitors also welcome by appt.**
Large peaceful garden with expansive views is at ease in its rural setting. Series of discreet gardens incl formal areas around house, streamside walk and sweeping herbaceous borders inspired by the designer Piet Oudolf which are at their height in late summer, lead to a newly developed woodland garden with wonderful autumn colour. Art & Craft activities.
✗ ✿ 🛏 ☕ ☎

21 ◆ CONSTABLE BURTON HALL GARDENS
nr Leyburn DL8 5LJ. Mr Charles Wyvill, 01677 450428, www.constableburtongardens.co.uk

. 3m E of Leyburn. Constable Burton Village. On A684, 6m W of A1. **Adm £3, chd 50p, concessions £2.50. Daily 15 Mar to 28 Sept.**
Large romantic garden with terraced woodland walks. Garden trails, shrubs, roses and water garden. Display of daffodils and over 5000 tulips planted annually amongst extensive borders. Fine John Carr house (not open) set in splendour of Wensleydale countryside. Tours of house and garden possible for groups of 25+. Some gravel paths.
♿ ✿

22 THE COURT
Humber Road, North Ferriby HU14 3DW. Guy & Liz Slater, 01482 633609, guyslater@thecourt.fsworld.co.uk. *7m W of Hull. Travelling E on A63 towards Hull, follow sign for N Ferriby. Through village to Xrds with war memorial, turn R & follow rd to T-junction with Humber Rd. Turn L & immed R into unmarked cul-de-sac, last house on LH-side.* Home-made TEAS. **Adm £2.50, chd free. Sun 11 May (1-5). Also open Spinney Croft. Visitors also welcome by appt.**
Romantic, restful and secluded, informal garden with yr-round interest. Hidden seating areas and summerhouses, small pond and waterfall. 2/3 -acre garden surrounded by trees contains laburnum and wisteria tunnel which leads to well-planted shady woodland area, around tennis court. Many interesting features, courtyards and a 'pretty potty patio'.
♿ ✿ ☕ ☎

23 NEW COVERHAM ABBEY
Leyburn DL8 4RL. Mr & Mrs Nigel Corner. *A6108 to Middleham then Coverdale Road out of Middleham following signs to 'The Forbidden Corner', past pond on R. Drive at bottom of steep bank on L before Church.* **Adm £3, chd free (share to Great North Air Ambulance). Sat 7 June (2-5).**
Varied garden set within grounds of 13C Premonstratensian Abbey ruins. Knot garden and herbaceous borders. Featured in 'Country Life'.
♿ ✗ ✿ ☕

24 CRESKELD HALL
Arthington, nr Leeds LS21 1NT. J & C Stoddart-Scott. *5m E of Otley. On A659 between Pool & Harewood.* Home-made teas. **Adm £3.50, chd free. Sun 25 May (12-5).**

Historic picturesque 3¹/₂ -acre Wharfedale garden with beech avenue, mature rhododendrons and azaleas. Gravel path from terrace leads to attractive water garden with canals set amongst woodland plantings. Walled kitchen garden and flower garden. Specialist nurseries.

25 CROFT COTTAGE
Green Hammerton YO26 8AE. Alistair & Angela Taylor, 01423 330330. *6m E of Knaresborough. 3m E of A1M adjacent to A59. Entrance through orchard off old Harrogate rd.* Home-made teas. **Adm £2.50, chd free, combined with Whixley Gardens adm £5. Sun 4 May; Wed 11 June (11.30-5). Visitors also welcome by appt.**
Secluded ¹/₂ -acre cottage garden divided into a number of garden rooms. Conservatory, clipped yew, old brick, cobbles and pavers used for formal areas leading to water feature, mixed borders and orchard with wild flowers.

26 DACRE BANKS GARDENS
Nidderdale HG3 4EW. *4m SE of Pateley Bridge, 10m NW of Harrogate. On B6451. Limited wheelchair access. Parking at each garden.* Home-made teas at Low Hall & Yorke House. **Combined adm £5, chd free. Sun 6 July (11-5).**
Lovely walk between gardens along valley. Picnic area at Yorke House.

LOW HALL
Mrs P A Holliday, 01423 780230
Romantic walled garden on different levels around a C17 family home (not open) with shrubs, climbing roses, tender plants, herbaceous borders and pond garden. Mature yews and beech hedges. For B&B details please tel or see NGS website.

ORCHARD HOUSE
Dacre Banks. Mr & Mrs J T Spain, 01423 780502. Visitors also welcome by appt.
2 acres of simple natural uncontrived garden blending into beautiful surrounding countryside and providing a haven for wildlife. Shrub and perennial plantings from shade to full sun together with productive fruit and vegetables.

YORKE HOUSE
Mr Anthony & Mrs Pat Hutchinson
(See separate entry).

27 DERWENT HOUSE
59 Osbaldwick Village, Osbaldwick YO10 3NP. Dr & Mrs D G Lethem, 01904 410847, davidlethem@tiscali.co.uk. *2m E of York. On village green at Osbaldwick off A1079. Parking in old school yard opp church 15 June.* Home-made teas. **Adm £2.50, chd free. Sun 15 June (1.30-5). Visitors also welcome by appt in June.**
³/₄ -acre, attractive village garden extended in 1984 to provide new walled garden, summer house, conservatories and terraces. Rose garden, box parterres, pelargoniums, hardy geraniums and ornamental allée of apple and pears. Double herbaceous border leads to meadow with species roses and eucalyptus. Featured in 'The English Garden'.

uncontrived garden blending into beautiful surrounding countryside and providing a haven for wildlife . . .

28 DOWTHORPE HALL
Skirlaugh HU11 5AE. Mr & Mrs J Holtby, 01964 562235, john.holtby@farming.co.uk. *6m N of Hull, 8m E of Beverley. On the A165 Hull to Bridlington Rd halfway between Coniston & Skirlaugh on the RH-side travelling N. Signed at the bottom of drive which has white railings.* **Adm £5, chd free. Sun 25 May (11-5). Visitors also welcome by appt.**
3¹/₂ acres owned by professional garden designer. Kitchen garden, orchard, Mediterranean-style planting, small gravel garden and main lawn area surrounded by shrubs, beautiful mature trees and sumptuous herbaceous borders. Pond with island.

29 EAST WING, THORP ARCH HALL
Thorp Arch LS23 7AW. Fiona & Chris Royffe, 01937 843513, plantsbydesign@btinternet.com, www.eastwinggardens.info. *1m S of Wetherby. Take A659 into Boston Spa centre. Turn at HSBC over bridge to Thorp Arch, at end of Main St turn L into Thorp Arch Park & R over cattle grid.* Home-made teas. **Adm £3.50, chd free. Sun 20 July (12-5). Visitors also welcome by appt May to Sept, groups of 15+.**
³/₄ -acre surrounding East Wing of C18 John Carr house (not open). Inspiring, imaginatively developed contemporary garden in parkland setting. Striking views, dramatic combinations of plants framed by yew hedges and trained trees. Courtyards, ponds, potager, earth sculpture and dry garden, newly designed features. Photographic exhibition.

30 ELVINGTON GARDENS
nr York YO41 4HD. *8m SE of York. From A1079, immed after leaving York's outer ring rd, turn S onto B1228 for Elvington.* Light refreshments & teas at village hall. **Combined adm £3.50, chd free. Sun 8 June (12-5).**
Village Fete.

THE OLD COACH HOUSE
Church Lane. Simon & Toni Richardson
Delightful atmospheric owner-made 2-acre garden. Grass paths meander through trees and sunlit borders past summerhouse and round large pond to pergola, vegetables and meadow beyond. Enclosed flower garden with ornamental pool adjacent to house.

RED HOUSE FARM
Church Lane. Professor & Mrs E Macphail
Large country garden developed over 25yrs. Extensive mixed borders with fine collection of hardy perennials, shrubs and roses. Maturing hedges partially divide the garden, long rose pergola leads to wildlife pond and wild flower meadow. Attractive courtyard with interesting plantings and ¹/₂ -acre young wood with pond.

③① EVERGREENS
119 Main Road, Bilton HU11 4AB.
Phil & Brenda Brock, 01482 811365.
5m E of Hull. Leave city by A165. Exit
B1238. Bungalow ½ m on L opp Asda
car park entrance. **Visitors welcome**
by appt.
1 acre with mosaics and sundials,
tower, raised beds, rockeries and
landscaped pond. Japanese garden,
seaside garden, summerhouse.
Collection of dwarf conifers. 'Fun'
items. Photographs showing
development of garden, front garden
redesigned 2005.

FANSHAWE GATE HALL
See Derbyshire.

③② FERNLEIGH
9 Meadowhead Avenue, Sheffield
S8 7RT. Mr & Mrs K Littlewood,
01142 747234. *4m S of Sheffield city*
centre. A61, A6102, B6054
roundabout, exit B6054 towards
Holmesfield. 1st R Greenhill Ave, then
2nd R Meadowhead Ave. Light
refreshments & teas. **Adm £2.50, chd**
free. Sat 21, Sun 22 June (1-5).
Visitors also welcome by appt Apr
to July, groups of 10+.
Plantswomans ⅓ -acre cottage
style garden with large variety of
unusual plants set in differently
planted sections to provide all-yr
interest. Auricula theatre and paved
area for drought resistant plants in
pots. Featured in & on local press &
radio.

③③ FIELD COTTAGE
Littlethorpe Road, Ripon HG4 3LG.
Richard & Liz Tite, 01765 690996,
liz.tite@talk21.com. *1m SE of Ripon.*
Off A61 Ripon bypass follow signs to
Littlethorpe, continue straight on at
church, (Littlethorpe Rd) round sharp
LH-bend 250yds on LH-side by
derestriction sign. **Visitors welcome**
by appt, groups of 20+, coaches
permitted.
1-acre plantsman's garden with walled
garden and small pond, raised sleeper
beds and gravel garden. Perennials incl
late flowering autumn bed, vegetable
plot, Victorian-style greenhouse with
pelargoniums and extensive range of
unusual and tender plants in
containers.

③④ NEW FIR TREES
COTTAGE
Stokesley TS9 5LD. Helen &
Mark Bainbridge,
www.firtreespelargoniums.co.uk.
1m S of Stokesley. On A172
garden will be signed Pelargonium
Exhibition. **Adm £3, chd free.** Sat
17 May (10-4).
1 acre mixed shrubaceous
borders, large rockeries, spring
bulbs, species tulips, conifers,
fritillaries, erythroniums and
secluded ornamental pond.
Tranquil garden boarded by
farmland with views to Cleveland
Hill and Roseberry Topping.
Designed and maintained by
owners since 1992 with low
maintenence in mind. Chelsea
Gold Medal Pelargonium
Nursery. Exceptional cacti
collection.

③⑤ FRIARS HILL
Sinnington YO62 6SL. Mr & Mrs C J
Baldwin, 01751 432179,
friars.hill@abelgratis.co.uk. *4m W of*
Pickering. On A170. **Adm £3, chd**
free. Sun 30 Mar (1-5). **Visitors also**
welcome by appt individuals &
groups of up to 40.
1¾ -acre plantswoman's garden
containing over 2500 varieties of
perennials and bulbs, with yr-round
colour. Early interest with hellebores,
bulbs and woodland plants.
Herbaceous beds. Hostas,
delphiniums, old roses and stone
troughs.

THE GARDENS AT DOBHOLME
FISHERY
See Derbyshire.

③⑥ THE GRANGE
Carla Beck Lane, Carleton
BD23 3BU. Mr & Mrs R N Wooler,
01756 709342. *1½ m SW of Skipton.*
Turn off A56 (Skipton-Clitheroe) into
Carleton. Keep L at Swan PH,
continue through to end of village &
turn R into Carla Beck Lane. From
Skipton town centre follow A6131.
Turn R to Carleton. Cream teas. **Adm**
£3.50, chd free (share to Sue Ryder
Care Manorlands Hospice). Weds 23
July; 6, 13 Aug (1-5). Visitors also
welcome by appt in July & Aug,
groups 10+.
Now reaching maturity, a plantsman's
garden of over 4 acres of different
features restored by the owners during
the last 12 years. Large herbaceous
border with ha-ha, walled garden, rose
and clematis walk, ornamental grass
beds, water features and vegetable
beds, some unusual mature tree
specimens. New in 2007, formal
parterre garden. Some gravel paths
and slight inclines.

③⑦ GREENCROFT
Pottery Lane, Littlethorpe, nr Ripon
HG4 3LS. Mr & Mrs David Walden,
01765 602487. *1m SE of Ripon. Off*
A61 Ripon bypass, follow signs to
Littlethorpe. Turn R at church (Pottery
Lane) to Bishop Monkton for 1½ m.
On RH-side after Littlethorpe Pottery
(open). Car parking in field opp and at
Pottery. **Visitors welcome by appt**
also groups & coaches.
½ -acre informal garden made and
built by owners. Special ornamental
features incl gazebo, temple, pavilion,
stone wall with mullions, pergola and
formal pool. Long herbaceous borders
lead to circular enclosed garden
planted with late flowering perennials,
annuals and exotics. Log cabin with
shingle roof built alongside large pond.

Tranquil garden boarded by
farmland with views to
Cleveland Hill and Roseberry
Topping. . . .

GRINGLEY GARDENS
See Nottinghamshire.

39 NEW HARLSEY HALL
Northallerton DL6 2BL. Sir
Joseph & Lady Barnard, 01609
882203. *14m S of Teeside. 7m E
of Northallerton. From Northallerton
A684 N towards A19. 5m L to East
Harlsey. R at Cat & Bagpipes.
From N 14m S Teeside on A19. R
¼m N of Tontine Inn. From S 12m
N of A19. L ¼m of Tontine Inn.*
Adm £3, chd free. Suns 13 Apr; 6
July (2-5). Visitors also welcome
by appt, please tel.
5 acres of grounds incl shrubs,
herbaceous plants, climbing
roses, lonicera and clematis.
Terraced lawns down to a series of
lakes planted with cedars, acers,
gean cherries, oaks and
rhododendrons. Visit early spring
for daffodils followed by bluebells.
Many wild flowers, primroses and
violets. St Oswald's Church
containing effigy of Geoffrey de
Hotham. Limited wheelchair
access. No access to lake area.
Gravel paths.
&. ☎

40 HEDON GARDENS
HU12 8JN. *Follow A1033 from Hull,
towards Hedon..* Light refreshments &
teas at Church. Combined adm £5,
chd free (share to St Augustines
Restoration Appeal). Sun 25 May
(11-5).
Historic market town, with royal
charters dating back to C12. Present
mayor is its 660th. Town Hall open,
which contains ancient and civic silver,
incl England's oldest civic mace. St
Augustines Church 'The King of
Holderness' (open) also town
museum. Tickets (with map) on sale
at church.
☕

32 BAXTERGATE
John & Barbara Oldham, 01482
898382. Visitors also welcome
by appt for 6+ visitors.
Superb, well designed garden
made in 6yrs by former owners of
The White Cottage, Halsham.
Gravel and raised beds with many
unusual plants, minute vegetable
garden and fish pond. Featured in
'The Journal'.
☓ ❀ ☎

56 ROSLYN CRESCENT
Ernie & Monica Kendall
Small town garden for plant

enthusiasts, with yr-round interest,
featuring hostas, mini hostas,
ferns and other shade loving
plants.
☓

41 HIGHFIELDS
Manorstead, Skelmanthorpe
HD8 9DW. Julie & Tony Peckham.
*8m SE of Huddersfield. M1 (J39) A636
towards Denby Dale. Turn R in Scissett
village (B6116) to Skelmanthorpe. After
2nd Police Speed Check sign turn L
(Barrowstead), continue to top of hill.*
Adm £2, chd free. Suns 20 Apr; 18
May (2-5).
Small garden which shows creativity
within metres rather than acres! 2
ponds, gravel bed, box parterre with
obelisk water feature, arbours, arches
and vertical structures. Reopens with
new features incl alpine bed, herb bed
and raised beds to the front of the
house.
❀ ☕

Visit early spring for daffodils followed by bluebells. Many wild flowers, primroses and violets . . .

42 HILLBARK
Church Lane, Bardsey LS17 9DH.
Tim Gittins & Malcolm Simm,
www.hillbark.co.uk. *4m SW of
Wetherby. Turn W off A58 into Church
Lane, garden on L before church.*
Home-made teas. Adm £3, chd free.
Suns 11 May; 1, 22 June (11-5).
Established, award winning 1-acre
country garden. 3 S-facing levels,
distinct intimate areas; hidden corners;
surprise views. Evergreen structure
blends with formal topiary and
perennial flowers. Dramatic specimen
yew. Small ornamental ponds,
summerhouse overlooking gravel, rock
and stream gardens, large natural
pond with ducks. Marginal planting incl
bamboo, gunnera and royal fern.
Woodland approached by bridge
across stream. Large rambling roses.
Unusual ceramics.
☓ ❀ ☕

43 HOLLY TREE COTTAGE
Back Street, Burton Fleming
YO25 3PD. Susan & Philip Cross,
01262 470347,
skcross@hotmail.co.uk. *11m NE of
Driffield. 11m SW of Scarborough, 7m
NW of Bridlington. From Driffield
B1249 before Foxholes turn R to
Burton Fleming. From Scarborough
A165 R to Burton Fleming.* Home-
made teas. Combined with The
Ridings adm £5, chd free. Suns 15
June; 27 July (1-5). Visitors also
welcome by appt.
The owners' 3rd NGS garden, but
different in size and shape. Superbly
designed small garden planted with
over 100 clematis and 50 roses,
hardy geraniums, unusual plants and
shrubs in colour-themed mixed
borders. Attractive seating areas,
pergolas, water features and wildlife
areas. Featured in 'The Journal'.
❀ ☕ ☎

44 HOLMFIELD
Fridaythorpe YO25 9RZ. Susan &
Robert Nichols, 01377 236627,
susan.nichols@which.net,
www.holmfieldnurseries.co.uk. *9m
W of Driffield. From York A166
through Fridaythorpe. 1m turn R
signed Holmfield. 1st house on lane.*
Home-made teas. Adm £3, chd free.
Sat 31 May; Sun 1 June (11-5).
Visitors also welcome by appt June,
July only.
Informal 2-acre country garden on
gentle S-facing slope. Developed from
a field over last 20yrs. Large mixed
borders, octagonal gazebo. Vegetable
and fruit areas. Collection of phlomis.
Family garden with sunken trampoline,
large lawn. Adjacent nursery with
unusual perennials. Some gravel
areas.
&. ☓ ❀ ☕ ☎

45 HOTHAM HALL
Hotham YO43 4UA. Stephen &
Carolyn Martin, 01430 422054. *15m
W of Hull. Nr North Cave, J38 of M62
turn towards North Cave, follow signs
for Hotham.* Visitors welcome by
appt, groups.
C18 Grade II house (not open), stable
block and clock tower in mature
parkland setting with established
gardens. Lake with bridge over to
newly planted island (arboretum).
Garden with Victorian pond and mixed
borders. Selection of spring flowering
bulbs. Gravel paths.
&. ☎

46 **NEW** **56 HULL ROAD**
Cottingham HU16 4PU. Keith &
Mary Gregersen. *NW edge of
Hull. From Hull, Cottingham Rd &
Hill Rd (continuation), L after West
Bulls PH. From Cottingham 1/4 m
from roundabout.* Light
refreshments & teas. **Adm £2.50,
chd free. Sun 11 May (2-5).**
Immaculate well designed 1/3 -acre
suburban garden broken into
several distinct areas featuring
mature trees, mixed border, pond,
fernery, gravel garden and several
seating areas.

  🚻   ❀   ☕

Nuttery, romantic flower garden with mixed borders and pebble pool . . .

47 **HUNMANBY GRANGE**
Wold Newton YO25 3HS. Tom & Gill
Mellor, 01723 891636,
gill.mellor@btconnect.com,
www.hunmanbygrange.co.uk.
*121/2 m SE of Scarborough. Hunmanby
Grange is a farm between Wold
Newton & Hunmanby on the rd from
Burton Fleming to Fordon.* Tea (Weds),
Home-made teas (Sun). **Adm £3, chd
free. Weds 7 May to 30 July (1-5);
Sun 1 June (11-5). Visitors also
welcome by appt.**
3-acre garden created from exposed
open field, on top of Yorkshire Wolds
nr coast. Hedges and fences now
provide shelter from wind, making
series of gardens with yr-round interest
and seasonal highlights. Adjacent
nursery. Artist painting in garden and
display of work. Featured in ' Yorkshire
Today' & 'Woman & Home'.

  🚻   ❀   ☕   ☎

48 ◆ **JACKSONS WOLD**
Sherburn YO17 8QJ. Mr & Mrs
Richard Cundall, 01944 710335,
www.jacksonswoldgarden.com.
*11m E of Malton, 10m SW of
Scarborough. A64 in Sherburn. T-lights
take Weatherthorpe Rd. R fork to
Heslerton Wold.* **Adm £3, chd free.
Tues, Weds May to July.** For NGS:
Suns 11 May; 1, 29 June (12-5).

2-acre garden with stunning views of
the Vale of Pickering. Walled garden
with mixed borders, numerous old
shrub roses underplanted with unusual
perennials. Woodland paths lead to
further shrub and perennial borders.
Lime avenue with wild flower meadow.
Traditional vegetable garden with
roses, flowers and box edging framed
by Victorian greenhouse. Adjoining
nursery. Featured in 'Yorkshire Life'.

  🚻   ❀   ☕

49 **JASMINE HOUSE**
145 The Grove, Wheatley Hills,
Doncaster DN2 5SN. Ray & Anne
Breame, 01302 361470. *2m E of
Doncaster. 1m E of Doncaster Royal
Infirmary off A18. Turn R into Chestnut
Ave (Motor Save on corner).* Home-
made teas. **Adm £2, chd free (share
to Aurora Trust Fund). Sun 1 June
(1-5). Visitors also welcome by appt.**
Small enchanting garden for all
seasons with distinctive design
features, skilled planting and wide
range of unusual plants in borders and
pots. Climbers festoon archways that
lead to enclosed gardens displaying
grasses, ferns, alpines, bonsai and
tender perennials. Winner Doncaster in
Bloom.

  🚻   ❀   ☕   ☎

50 **KELBERDALE**
Wetherby Road, Knaresborough
HG5 8LN. Stan & Chris Abbott,
01423 862140,
chris@kelberdale.fsnet.co.uk. *1m S
of Knaresborough. On B6164
Wetherby rd. House on L immed after
new ring rd (A658) roundabout.*
Visitors welcome by appt **Apr to end
July, groups of 8+, coaches
welcome.**
Winner of 3 national awards, this
owner made and maintained
plantsman's garden has a bit of
everything. Full of yr round interest with
large herbaceous border, colour
themed beds, pond and bog garden,
alpine house and troughs. Vegetable
garden, wild garden with pond and
meadow.

  🚻   ❀   ☎

52 ◆ **LAND FARM**
Colden, Hebden Bridge HX7 7PJ.
Mr J Williams, 01422 842260,
www.landfarmgardens.co.uk. *8m W
of Halifax. From Halifax at Hebden
Bridge go through 2 sets T-lights. Take
turning circle to Heptonstall. Follow
signs to Colden. After 23/4 m turn R at
'no through' rd, follow signs to garden.*

**Adm £4, chd free. Weekends &
Bank Hols May to end Aug 10-5.**
6 acres incl alpine, herbaceous, formal
and newly developing woodland
garden, meconopsis varieties in June,
cardiocrinum *giganteum*in July.
Elevation 1000ft N-facing. C17 house
(not open). Art Gallery.

  🚻   ❀   ☕

53 **NEW** **LANGTON FARM**
Great Langton, Northallerton
DL7 0TA. Richard & Annabel
Fife, 01609 748446. *5m W of
Northallerton. B6271 in Great
Langton between Northallerton
and Scotch Corner.* Cream teas.
**Adm £3, chd free. Sun 3 Aug
(2-6). Visitors also welcome by
appt July to Sept.**
Riverside garden comprising
formal and informal gravel areas,
nuttery, romantic flower garden
with mixed borders and pebble
pool. Organic.

  🚻   ❀   ☎

54 **LAWKLAND HALL**
Austwick LA2 8AT. Mr & Mrs G
Bowring. *3m N of Settle. Turn S off
A65 at Austwick/Lawkland Xrds or
Giggleswick/Lawkland Xrds signed
Lawkland/Eldroth. Follow signs to
Lawkland.* Home-made teas. **Adm £3,
chd free. Sun 13 July (12.30-5.30).**
Old stone walls and established
hedges surround and divide garden of
Grade I Elizabethan hall (not open) into
smaller enclosures. Potting shed,
heather-thatched gazebo in rose
garden, summer house in kitchen
garden. Relaxed, mixed planting styles
rub shoulders with formality. Small lake
attracts wildlife incl kingfishers and
dragonflies. Plentiful seating and level
underfoot with few steps.

  🚻   ❀   🛏   ☕

55 **NEW** **LITTLETHORPE
MANOR**
HG4 3LG. Mr & Mrs J P
Thackray, john_p_thackray@
compuserve.com. *Outskirts of
Ripon by racecourse. Ripon
bypass A61. Follow Littlethorpe Rd
from Dallamires Lane roundabout
to stable block with clock tower.
Map supplied on application.*
Visitors welcome by appt **Apr to
Sept, groups of 20+, coaches
permitted.**
11 acres. Walled garden based on
cycle of seasons with box,
herbaceous, roses, gazebo.

Sunken garden with white rose parterre, herbs, brick pergola with blue and yellow borders. Terraces, formal lawns with fountain pool, hornbeam towers, box headed hornbeam drive. Parkland with lake, classical pavilion, cut flower garden. Spring bulbs. Featured in 'Country Life'. Partial wheelchair access.

🦽 🍴 ✿ ☎

56 LONDESBOROUGH CROSS
Shiptonthorpe YO43 3PA. Mr & Mrs J W Medd, www.ngs.org.uk. *2m From Market Weighton, 5m from Pocklington. A1079 Hull to York rd. Turn off in Shiptonthorpe down the side of church. Londesborough Cross is at bottom of Town St.* **Adm £3.50, chd free. For details of opening times please see website.**
In 24yrs railway goods yard transformed by owners into delightful garden with ponds, bog area, large herbaceous borders, screes and rock garden. Pergola and arches planted with clematis and good hosta collection. Woodland garden planted with large collection of hardy ferns, many rare, and plants for shade incl trilliums and meconopsis. New thatched log cabin.

🦽 🍴 ✿

57 LOW ASKEW
Cropton YO18 8ER. Mr & Mrs Martin Dawson-Brown. *5m W of Pickering. Signed to Cropton from A170. Between the villages of Cropton & Lastingham.* Home-made teas. **Adm £3, chd free. Wed 21 May (2-5).**
Designed by present owners to harmonise with the ancient and beautiful valley of the R Seven in which garden is situated. Now in its 3rd decade new plantings and ideas underway. Plants stall incl rare pelargoniums. Enchanting riverside walk.

✿ 🍵

58 LOWER CRAWSHAW
Emley, nr Huddersfield HD8 9SU. Mr & Mrs Neil Hudson, 01924 840980, janehudson42@btinternet.com. *8m E of Huddersfield. From Huddersfield turn R to Emley off A642 (Paul Lane). M1 J39 (A636) direction Denby Dale, 1m after Bretton roundabout turn R to Emley, ½ m beyond Emley village turn R (Stringer House Lane) continue for ¾ m. Car park in adjacent field.* Home-made teas. **Adm £3.50, chd free. Suns 29 June; 14 Sept (12-5).**

Visitors also welcome by appt in June & July, groups of 10+, no coaches.
3-acre garden in open country on eastern slopes of the Pennines, surrounding 1690's farmhouse (not open) with extensive range of old farm buildings. Garden created by owners since 1996. Natural stream runs through the garden, dammed on several levels and opening into 2 large ponds. Walled potager created from old barn, enclosed rose garden, orchard, and courtyard. Naturalistic planting of shrubs, trees and perennials. Featured in 'The English Garden'. Partial wheelchair access.

🦽 🍴 ✿ 🍵 ☎

51 NEW LOWER HEUGH COTTAGE GARDEN
Kirk Lane, Eastby BD23 6SH. Mr Trevor Nash, 01756 793702, nash862@btinternet.com. *2½ m NE of Skipton. Follow the A59/65 N ring rd around Skipton, turn at signs for Embasy (railway) and Eastby. In Embasy follow signs Eastby & Barden onto Kirk Lane. 6th house on R.* Home-made teas. **Adm £3, chd free. Sun 8 June (1-6). Visitors also welcome by appt anytime of year, up to 30 max.**
Visit unique Japanese 'stroll through garden' extending over almost 1 acre. Main emphasis is on conifers, acers, bamboos, grasses, heathers and wide selection of Japanese plants set within landscaped beds amid manicured lawns and beech hedges. Contains Karesansui, roji, woodland garden, springs, streams and floral rock garden. Yorkshire in Bloom Gold Medal. Partial wheelchair access.

🦽 🍵 ☎

59 MANOR FARM
Thixendale YO17 9TG. Charles & Gilda Brader, 01377 288315, www.manorfarmthixendale.co.uk. *10m SE of Malton. Unclassified rd through Birdsall, ½ m up hill, turn L at Xrds for Thixendale - 3m, 1st farm on R. 17m E of York, turn off A166 rd at the top of Garrowby Hill, follow signs for Thixendale, 4m turn into village, drive through to end, farm on L.* Teas, soup & rolls (Mar), Home-made teas (July). **Adm £3, chd free. Thur 27 Mar (11-4); Sun 13 July (10-5).**
Created since 1987 lying in a frost pocket and wind tunnel! 1-acre garden featuring pergolas, a traditional

conservatory, courtyard, alpine areas, large rocks, running water and a ruined shed which stands by a small knot garden. Lawn surrounded by mixed beds of interesting plants. Shaded area with many special hellebores. New projects recently completed.

🍴 ✿ 🛏 🍵

Visit unique Japanese 'stroll through garden' . . .

60 MANSION COTTAGE
8 Gillus Lane, Bempton YO15 1HW. Polly & Chris Myers, 01262 851404, chrismyers@tinyworld.co.uk. *2m NE of Bridlington. From Bridlington take B1255 to Flamborough. 1st L at T-lights, go up Bempton Lane, turn 1st R into Short Lane then L at T-junction. Cross railway into Bempton, Gillus Lane is L fork at church.* Delicious fresh lunches & home-made teas. **Adm £2.50, chd free. Sat 9, Sun 10 Aug (10-4). Visitors also welcome by appt, incl groups, end July to end Aug.**
Peaceful, secluded truly hidden garden with many different views. New for 2008, cutting area, 100ft mixed border, vegetable and recycling plot. Wide variety of architectural planting enhanced by water features, ponds, shady border, bog garden, scented border and patio, grasses, pergola and climbers, decks and lawns, summerhouse and late-flowering tender perennial bed.

✿ 🍵 ☎

61 39 MARKET PLACE
South Cave HU15 2BS. Lin & Paul Holland, 01430 421874. *12m W of Hull. From A63 turn N to South Cave on A1034. House on LH-side opp PO, before Xrds.* Home-made teas. **Adm £2.50, chd free. Sun 27 July (2-5). Visitors also welcome by appt.**
Small walled garden with eclectic planting. Established trees, cottage garden plants and evergreen shrubs. Rockeries, gravel fernery with grasses and water feature. Interesting stonework and lots of nooks and crannies. A few shallow steps and gravel paths.

✿ 🍵 ☎

62 MAYROYD MILL HOUSE
Mayroyd Lane, Hebden Bridge
HX7 8NS. Richard Easton & Steve
Mackay, 01422 845818. *At Hebden
Bridge (A646) follow signs to Railway
Stn. Car parking at stn.* Home-made
teas. **Adm £2.50, chd free. Sun 22
June (1-5.30). Visitors also welcome
by appt, June & Aug only, groups of
10+.**
Steep steps lead down to approx
$1/3$-acre S-facing designers' garden
with bold herbaceous and ornamental
grass plantings created for naturalistic
effect. Many rare and unusual plants;
woodland shade; bog areas and
riverbank walk. National Collection of
astrantias in full flower at time of
opening.
✖ ✿ NCCPG ☕ ☎

**63 THE MEDITERRANEAN
GARDENS**
Doncaster Road, Branton, nr
Doncaster DN3 3LT. Susan &
Michael, michaelcider@aol.com. *3m
SE of Doncaster. M18 J4 to
Armthorpe. L at roundabout through
Cantley Old Village. L at roundabout
B1396 to Branton.* Refreshments,
cream teas & wine at 'The Rooftops'
across the rd. **Adm £2.50, chd free.
Suns 13 July; 10 Aug (10-4). Visitors
also welcome by appt June to Sept,
coaches permitted.**
Enclosed within $1/4$-acre, 6 individual
Mediterranean themed gardens,
entirely designed, built and planted by
owners, are packed full of colourful
horticultural gems. Courtyard garden
with fountain and pool, organic cooks
garden with raised beds, greenhouses,
arbours, arches and resting places, all
linked by paved paths. Many baskets
and containers imaginatively planted to
compliment the different colour
schemes within the gardens. Featured
on Gardeners' World, Doncaster in
Bloom - Gold Award.
♿ ✖ ✿ ☎

64 THE MEWS COTTAGE
1 Brunswick Drive, Harrogate
HG1 2PZ. Mrs Pat Clarke, 01423
566292,
patriciamclarke@hotmail.com. *W of
Harrogate town centre. From Cornwall
Rd, N side of Valley Gardens, 1st R
(Clarence Dr), 1st L (York Rd), 1st L
(Brunswick Dr).* **Visitors welcome by
appt Apr to end Oct for groups of
2+, coaches welcome.**
Small tranquil garden on sloping site
featuring a terracotta tiled courtyard
with trompe l'oeil. A garden of special

interest to hardy planters over a long
season; recommended for an August
visit when a large collection of phlox
paniculata is in flower.
✖ ☎

65 MILLGATE HOUSE
Millgate, Richmond DL10 4JN. Tim
Culkin & Austin Lynch, 01748
823571,
oztim@millgatehouse.demon.co.uk,
www.millgatehouse.com. *Centre of
Richmond. House is located at bottom
of Market Place opp Barclays Bank.
Next to Halifax Building Soc.* **Adm
£2.50, chd £2. Day & Evening
Opening Sun 22 June (8-8). Visitors
also welcome by appt.**
SE walled town garden overlooking R
Swale. Although small, the garden is
full of character, enchantingly secluded
with plants and shrubs. Foliage plants
incl ferns and hostas. Old roses,
interesting selection of clematis, small
trees and shrubs. RHS associate
garden. Immensely stylish, national
award-winning garden.
✖ 🛏 ☎

78ft rose walk with many clematis underplanted with hostas . . .

66 MILLRACE NURSERY
84 Selby Road, Garforth LS25 1LP.
Mr & Mrs Carthy, 0113 2869233,
carol@millrace-plants.co.uk. *5m E of
Leeds. On A63 in Garforth. 1m from
M1 J46, 3m from A1.* Home-made
teas. **Adm £2.50, chd free. Suns 18
May; 17 Aug (1-5). Visitors also
welcome by appt.**
Over looking a secluded valley. Garden
developed over last 7yrs to incl large
herbaceous borders containing many
unusual perennials, shrubs and trees.
The immediate garden also incl an
ornamental pond, vegetable garden
and small woodland. The outer garden
leads through a wild flower meadow to
large bog garden and wildlife ponds.
Specialist nursery.
♿ ✿ ☕ ☎

**67 NEW MOLECROFT
COTTAGE**
Northgate, Walkington
HU17 8ST. Keith & Beverley
Reader. Teas at 18 West End.
**Adm £3, chd free. Sun 1 June
(1.30-5). Also open 26 West End.**
The quintessential English garden.
This 1-acre plot incl Yorkshire
terrace with pots and pond.
Traditional maintained lawn and
herbaceous border area with trees,
78ft rose walk with many clematis
underplanted with hostas. Hot
gravel garden, vegetable plot, wild
garden and orchard.
✖ ✿ ☕

68 NAWTON TOWER GARDEN
Nawton YO62 7TU. Douglas Ward
Trust, 01439 771218. *5m NE of
Helmsley. From A170, between
Helmsley & Nawton village, at Beadlam
turn N $2 1/2$ m to Nawton Tower.* **Adm
£1.50, chd free. Sat 3, Sun 4, Mon 5
May (2-6). Visitors also welcome by
appt spring time.**
Large garden; heathers,
rhododendrons, azaleas, shrubs,
bluebells, bulbs and trees. Featured in
'GGG'.
✿ ☎

69 ◆ NEWBY HALL & GARDENS
Ripon HG4 5AE. Mr R C Compton,
01423 322583, www.newbyhall.com.
*2m E of Ripon. Signed from A1 &
Ripon town centre.* **House and
Garden £10.20, chd £7.80,
concessions £9.20, Garden only
£7.20, chd £5.80, concessions
£6.20. 21 Mar to 28 Sept; Tues to
Sun, Bank Hols & Mons July & Aug.**
40 acres extensive gardens laid out in
1920s. Full of rare and beautiful plants.
Formal seasonal gardens, stunning
double herbaceous borders to R Ure
and National Collection holder *Cornus*.
Miniature railway and adventure
gardens for children. Sculpture Park
(June to Sept).
♿ ✖ ✿ NCCPG ☕

70 ◆ NORTON CONYERS
Wath, nr Ripon HG4 5EQ. Sir James
& Lady Graham, 01765 640333,
norton.conyers@bronco.co.uk. *4 m
N of Ripon. Take Melmerby & Wath
sign off A61 Ripon-Thirsk. Go through
villages, boundary wall. Signed entry
300metres on R.* **Adm £4, chd free.
Please tel for details. For NGS: Sun
15 June (2-5).**
Large C18 walled garden of interest to
garden historians. Interesting iron

entrance gate; herbacous borders, yew hedges and orangery with an attractive little pond in front. Small sales area specialising in unusual hardy plants, fruit in season. House, which was visited by Charlotte Brontî, is an original of Thornfield Hall in 'Jane Eyre' is closed for repairs during early summer to re-open in July.

&. ✕ ✿ ☕

71 THE NURSERY

15 Knapton Lane, Acomb YO26 5PX. Tony Chalcraft & Jane Thurlow. *2¹/₂ m W of York. Follow B1224 towards Acomb & York city centre, from A1237 York ringroad. Turn L at first mini roundabout into Beckfield Lane. Knapton Lane 2nd L after 150 metres.* Home-made teas. **Adm £2, chd free. Sun 20 July (1-5).** Attractive 1-acre organic fruit and vegetable garden behind suburban house created from previous nursery. Bush and trained fruit trees (incl 40+ varieties apples and pears), large and small greenhouses, productive vegetables grown in bed and row systems interspersed with informal ornamental plantings providing colour and habitat for wildlife.

✕ ☕

72 NEW NUTKINS

72 Rolston Road, Hornsea HU18 1UR. Alan & Janet Stirling, 01964 533721, ashornsea@aol.com. *12m NE of Beverley. On B1242 S-side of Hornsea between Freeport & golf course.* Home-made teas. **Adm £2.50, chd free. Sun 22 June (12-5). Visitors also welcome by appt.** ³/₄ -acre garden with good backbone of mature plants and trees, herbaceous borders, bog garden and recently developed woodland garden and stream-side area. Seating areas to linger and enjoy different views of the garden. Partial wheelchair access, gravel paths and steps.

&. ✕ ☕ ☎

73 OAKWOOD HOUSE

Todds Close, Tranby Lane, Swanland HU14 3NT. Judy & Mike Sketch. *8m W of Hull. M62, A63 towards Humber Bridge - Beverley A164 - L at 2nd roundabout into Swanland. Take 2nd R into Todds Close, house 1st on R.* Home-made teas. **Adm £2.50, chd free. Sun 8 June (12-5).**

Canopy of mature trees shelters an eclectic mix of plants. Good backbone of shrubs under-planted with bulbs and herbaceous plants in softly curved borders creating plenty of colour, form and texture. Several seating areas either in sun, shade or even by water.

✕ ☕

Seating areas to linger and enjoy different views of the garden . . .

74 THE OLD PRIORY

Everingham YO42 4JD. Dr J D & Mrs H J Marsden, 01430 860222, marsd13@aol.com. *15m SE of York, 5¹/₂ m from Pocklington. 2m S of the A1079 York-Hull Rd. Everingham has 3 access rds, the Old Priory is to the east of the Village. Car parking at the Village Hall opp, disabled people may be dropped off/park at the Old Priory.* Home-made teas & wine at village hall. **Adm £3, chd free. Sun 8 June (1-5). Visitors also welcome by appt. Garden best either side of opening, coaches permitted.** Country garden of 2 acres on dry sandy loam and wet peat land. Conservatory, polytunnels, walled vegetable garden. Mixed herbaceous borders drop down to bog garden where paths bridge the stream into less formal garden which leads to lake. Short woodland walk. Children enjoy the animals. Rare opportunity to view the Grade 1 listed Italianate RC church of St Mary & St Everilda. Completed 1839 (1-3).

&. ✕ ✿ ☕ ☎

75 THE OLD RECTORY

Nunburnholme YO4 1QU. Mr & Mrs M Stringer, 01759 302295. *13m SE of York. Turn off Hull-York A1079 at Hayton (between Beverley & York). Follow signs to Nunburnholme. Please park in field.* Home-made teas. **Adm £3, chd free. Sun 15 June (1.30-5). Visitors also welcome by appt.** Large very pretty informal garden with natural stream running through, chalk-loving plants. Shrubs and herbaceous beds blending into attractive surrounding countryside. Owner-maintained.

&. ✕ ☕ ☎

76 NEW OLD SLENINGFORD HALL

Mickley, nr Ripon HG4 3JD. Jane & Tom Ramsden. *5m NW of Ripon. Off A6108. After N Stainley turn L, follow signposts to Mickley. Gates on R after 1¹/₂ m opp cottage.* Home-made teas in art gallery. **Adm £3.50, chd free (share to Holyrood House Centre For Health & Pastoral Care). Sat 7, Sun 8 June (1-5).** Early C19 house (not open) and garden with original layout of interest to garden historians. Many acres with mature trees, woodland walk and Victorian fernery. Romantic lake with islands, watermill, walled kitchen garden, long herbaceous border, yew and huge beech hedges. Several plant and other garden stalls. The garden has been closed for the new herbaceous border to be planted in the walled garden, which is in the process of being re-developed.

✿ ☕

77 ORCHARD HOUSE

Appleton Roebuck, York YO23 7DD. David & Sylvia Watson, 01904 744460. *8m SW of York. 3m from A64 Bilborough Top flyover on Main St in Appleton Roebuck.* Home-made teas. **Adm £3, chd free. Suns 13 Apr; 18 May (11-5). Visitors also welcome by appt Apr & May, groups of 10+, coaches permitted.** Fascinating 1-acre garden created and maintained by owners in harmony with surrounding countryside. Brimming with unusual features and ideas. Paths of brick, cobble and grass wind through extensive colourful plants to old oak revolving summerhouse, exposed tree roots with sunken garden and grotto. Parasol bed, 'torr' with chapel of rest, lily pond, rill, stream, wildlife pond.

✕ ✿ ☕ ☎

78 ♦ PARCEVALL HALL GARDENS

Skyreholme BD23 6DE. Walsingham College, 01756 720311, www.parcevallhallgardens.co.uk. *9m N of Skipton. Signs from B6160 Bolton Abbey-Burnsall rd or off B6265 Grassington-Pateley Bridge.* **Adm £5.75, chd £2.50, concessions £4.75. Daily Good Fri 21 March to 31 Oct. For NGS: Fri 6 June (10-5).** 16 acres in Wharfedale sheltered by mixed woodland; terrace garden, rose garden, rock garden, fish ponds. Mixed borders, tender shrubs (desfontainea, crinodendron, camellias); autumn colour. Birdwatching, old apple orchard for picnics. Featured in 'The English Garden'.

79 PENNYHOLME
Fadmoor YO62 7JG. Mr & Mrs P R Wilkinson. *7m NE of Helmsley. From A170 between Kirkbymoorside & Nawton, turn N. 1/2 m before Fadmoor turn L, signed 'Sleightholmedale only' continue N up dale, across 3 cattle grids, to garden. No buses.* Home-made teas. **Adm £3, chd free.** Sats 31 May; 7 June (1-5). Also open **Sleightholmedale Lodge.**
Enchanting 10-acre country garden. Unique river and dale setting. Extensive collection of magnificent rhododendrons and azaleas in mature oak wood circular walk. Currently developing traditional rose/mixed borders, water features, wildlife garden and tree garden.

80 130 PRINCE RUPERT DRIVE
Tockwith, York YO26 7PU. Mr & Mrs B Wright, 01423 358791, anneswright@hotmail.co.uk, www.dryad-home.co.uk. *7m E of Wetherby. From B1224 Wetherby/York rd turn N to Cattal, after 1m turn R at Xrds to Tockwith. 1st turning on R in village. Please do not park in the cul-de-sac.* Home-made teas. **Adm £2.50, chd free.** Suns 16 Mar (1-4); 25 May; 21 Sept (1-5). Visitors also welcome by appt groups of 15+.
1/2-acre enthusiast's garden planted for yr-round interest from early hellebores, cyclamen and bulbs to late perennials and grasses mixed with our large fern collection, in beds connected by gravel paths. Many plants grown from seed, incl wild-collected seed. Rock and bog gardens, pond and pergola, glasshouses, shade house, kitchen garden with vegetables and trained fruit, small nursery.

81 2 PROSPECT PLACE
Outlane, Huddersfield HD3 3FL. Carol & Andy Puszkiewicz, 01422 376408, carol-puszkiewicz@talktalk.net. *5m N of Huddersfield. 1m N of M62. J24 (W) take A643 to J23 (E) follow A640 to Rochdale. Turn R immed before 40mph sign (Gosport Lane). Parking in adjacent field.* Home-made teas. **Adm**

£2.50, chd free. Sun 6 July (12-5). Visitors also welcome by appt June & July, groups of 6+.
Long intimate garden high in the Pennines (900ft). Narrow paths lead from cottage herbaceous borders and pond to shade areas and secret garden with camomile lawn, chocolate and silver borders surrounding circular bed and productive kitchen garden with trained fruit and flowers. Evolving wild area with native trees, large pond with indigenous planting, narrow stream and meadow. New for 2008 childrens garden trail.

82 NEW THE RANCH HOUSE
60 Clara Drive, Calverley, nr Leeds LS28 5QP. Preston Harrison, 0113 257 0114, preston.harrison@btinternet.com. *8m NW of Leeds. From A6120 ring rd, take A657 through Calverley. Turn R just before petrol stn. House 1/2 m on R.* Home-made teas. Visitors welcome by appt May to Aug, groups of 10+, coaches permitted.
2-acre garden created in 1998 by owner. Series of interconnecting areas separated by yew hedges are linked by grass paths. Rose and clematis arches provide a succession of harmonious plantings to the numerous herbaceous and mixed borders. Ponds; woodland garden has evolving underplanting beneath mature trees with shrubs and woodlanders creating a naturalistic atmosphere. Efficient composting system.

83 24 RED BANK ROAD
off Whitcliffe Lane, Ripon HG4 2LE. Margaret & David Rivers. *3/4 m from Ripon town centre. Follow Harrogate Rd (old A61 not bypass) turn off at Nissan showroom (Whitcliffe Lane), Red Bank Rd is 3rd on R (about 1m).* Home-made teas. **Adm £2, chd free.** Wed 14, Sun 18 May (2-5).
Plant enthusiasts' small garden recently remodelled, now planted for yr-round interest. Raised beds, rockeries and gravel contain wide variety of perennials incl species peonies (some grown from seed), alpines and shrubs chosen to be able to cope with the difficult conditions of dry sun and dry shade.

Arches covered with climbers lead to secret garden with lavender edged beds . . .

RENISHAW HALL
See Derbyshire.

84 ◆ RHS GARDEN HARLOW CARR
Harrogate HG3 1QB. Royal Horticultural Society, 01423 565418, www.rhs.org.uk/harlowcarr. *11/2 m W of Harrogate town centre. On B6162 (Harrogate - Otley).* Refreshments at Bettys Café tearooms. **Adm £6, chd £2.** Open all yr except Christmas Day, for times see website or tel. For NGS: Suns 11 May; 10 Aug (9.30-6).
One of Yorkshire's most relaxing yet inspiring locations! Highlights incl spectacular herbaceous borders, streamside garden, alpines, scented and kitchen gardens. 'Gardens Through Time', woodland and wild flower meadow. Events all yr.

85 NEW THE RIDINGS
Bridlington Road, Burton Fleming YO25 3PE. Roy & Ruth Allerston, 01262 470489. *11m NE of Driffield. 11m SE of Scarborough, 7m NW of Bridlington. From Driffield B1249 before Foxholes turn R to Burton Fleming. From Scarborough A165 R to Burton Fleming.* Home-made teas. Combined with **Holly Tree Cottage** adm £5, chd free. Suns 15 June; 27 July (1-5). Visitors also welcome by appt.
Tranquil cottage garden designed by owners in 2001 on reclaimed site. Brick pergola and arches covered with climbers lead to secret garden with lavender edged beds. Colour-themed mixed borders with old English roses. Paved terrace with water feature and farming bygones. Small vegetable plot and greenhouse.

86 RUDSTON HOUSE

Rudston, nr Driffield YO25 4UH. Mr & Mrs Simon Dawson, 01262 420400. *5m W of Bridlington. On B1253. S at Bosville Arms for approx 300yds.* Cream teas. **Adm £3.50, chd free. Sun 13 July (11-5). Visitors also welcome by appt July & Aug.**
Birthplace of authoress Winifred Holtby. Victorian farmhouse (not open) and 3 acres of exuberant garden with fine old trees, lawns, paths with clipped box hedges, conifers, shrubs, greenhouses, roses, interesting potager with named vegetable varieties, hosta beds with lilies, and short woodland walk, with pond. Plenty of seats and interesting corners and features; children love to explore. Partial wheelchair access.

  🚻 🐕 ☕ ☎

87 NEW RUSTIC COTTAGE

Front Street, Wold Newton, nr Driffield YO25 3YQ. Jan Joyce. *13m N of Driffield. From Driffield take B1249 to Foxholes (12m), take L turning signed Wold Newton. Turn L onto Front St, opp village pond, continue up hill garden on L.* Light refreshments & teas in village hall. **Adm £2, chd free. Suns 15 June; 27 July (11-4). Also open Holly Tree Cottage & The Ridings.**
Plantsman's cottage garden of much interest with many choice and unusual plants, incl old-fashioned roses, fragrant perennials and herbs grown together with wild flowers to provide habitat for birds, bees, butterflies and small mammals. It has been described as 'organised chaos'! The owner's 2nd NGS garden. Parts of village incl Rustic Cottage are in conservation area. Featured in 'The Journal'.

  🐕 🌼 ☕

88 RYE HILL

15 Station Road, Helmsley YO62 5BZ. Dr & Mrs C Briske. *Centre of Helmsley. Signed at Helmsley bridge on A170 (Thirsk-Scarborough).* Home-made teas. **Adm £2.50, chd free (share to St Catherine's Hospice). Suns, Weds 27, 30 Apr; 1 June; 9, 13 July (2-5). Visitors also welcome by appt, May, June & July. Please apply in writing.**
Plantswoman's garden designed, constructed and maintained by owners. Divided into interlinking compartments, each planted in different style: formal, woodland and cottage. Intense planting using unusual plants for yr-round colour and interest. Conservatory, well stocked with tender species, ponds and many architectural features. New projects each yr.

  🚻 🐕 🌼 ☕ ☎

89 SALTMARSHE HALL

Saltmarshe DN14 7RX. Mr & Mrs Philip Bean, 01430 430199, pmegabean.aol.com. *6m E of Goole. From Howden (M62, J37) follow signs to Howdendyke & Saltmarshe. House in park W of Saltmarshe village.* Home-made teas. **Adm £3.50, chd free. Suns 18 May; 22 June (12-5). Visitors also welcome by appt May & June.**
Large lawns, fine old trees, R Ouse and a Regency house (not open) with courtyards provide setting for shrubs, climbers, herbaceous plants and roses. Of special interest to plantsmen and garden designers are pond garden, walled garden and large herbaceous border. Approx 10 acres. Featured in 'The English Garden'.

  🚻 🐕 🌼 ☕ ☎

90 4 SHAFTESBURY COURT

Shaftesbury Avenue, Bradford West BD9 6BQ. Mrs Pam Greenwood, 01274 495307. *Between Bradford Royal Infirmary & Allerton. Follow Duckworth Lane W into Pearson Lane. Shaftesbury Avenue 3rd turn on R off Pearson Lane. Please park in Shaftesbury Avenue but not on grass verges, access to Shaftesbury Court by foot.* **Visitors welcome by appt.**
1/4 -acre plant lover's garden for all seasons especially concentrating on late summer colour, woodland plants and bulbs in spring. Narrow paths divide borders full of many rare and unusual perennials, small shrubs and bulbs for both sun and shade, the boundary walls are festooned with climbers.

  🐕 🌼 ☎

91 ◆ SHANDY HALL

Coxwold YO61 4AD. The Laurence Sterne Trust, 01347 868465, shandyhall@dial.pipex.com. *N of York. From A19, 7m from both Easingwold & Thirsk, turn E signed Coxwold.* **Adm £2.50, chd £1. Garden Suns to Fris May to Sept 11-4.30; House Weds 2-4.30, Suns 2.30-4.30 May to Sept. Groups by appt at other times. For NGS: Evening Opening Fris 20, 27 June (5.30-9).**
Home of C18 author Laurence Sterne.

2 walled gardens, 1 acre of unusual perennials interplanted with tulips and old roses in low walled beds. In old quarry, another acre of trees, shrubs, bulbs, climbers and wild flowers encouraging wildlife, incl over 130 recorded species of moths. Moth trap identification and release evenings on NGS openings. Featured on BBC Radio York, Dales Diary.

  🛆 🌼

92 NEW SKIPWITH HALL

Skipwith, Selby YO8 5SQ. Mr & Mrs C D Forbes Adam. *9m S of York, 6m N of Selby. From York A19 Selby, L in Escrick, 4m to Skipwith. From Selby A19 York, R onto A163 to Market Weighton, then L after 2m to Skipwith.* Home-made teas. **Adm £4, chd free. Sun 15 June (1-5).**
4-acre garden within walls, recreated over past 5yrs. Formal mixed borders, kitchen garden with pool, herb maze, vegetable and cutting beds, Italian garden. Courtyard, pleached trees, orchard lined by espaliers and fans, woodland with mini arboretum. Gravel paths.

  🛆 🐕 ☕

Kitchen garden with pool, herb maze, vegetable and cutting beds . . .

93 ◆ SLEDMERE HOUSE

Driffield YO25 3XG. Sir Tatton Sykes, 01377 236637, www.sledmerehouse.com. *7m W of Driffield. 17m from city of York, 10m from Beverley. Sledmere House is 35min drive from M62.* **House and Garden adm £6, chd £2, concessions £5.50, Garden only adm £4, chd £1, (RHS) concessions £3. For details of openings & times see website or tel.**
Award winning garden incl octagonal walled garden, herbaceous borders, roses, perennials, bulbs and parterre. Capability Brown landscaped park with mature beech trees and 'eyecatchers'. Sledmere Garden Show Sat 18 May, plants for sale. Yorkshire in Bloom - Gold.

  🛆 🌼 ☕

94 SLEIGHTHOLMEDALE LODGE
Fadmoor YO62 6JG. Dr & Mrs O James, 01751 431942. *6m NE of Helmsley. Parking can be limited in wet weather. Teas at* **Pennyholme**. **Adm £3, chd free. Sats 31 May; 7 June (1-5); Sat 19, Sun 20 July (2-6). Also open Pennyholme Sats 31 May; 7 June. Visitors also welcome by appt any number, anytime, no coaches.** Hillside garden, walled rose garden and herbaceous borders. Not suitable for wheelchairs.
🛏 🐕 ☕ ☎

95 NEW SPINNEY CROFT
Melton Road, North Ferriby HU14 3ES. Mrs Elaine Waldren, 01482 631910, elaine@carafax11.karoo.co.uk. *7m W of Hull. Travelling E on A63 towards Hull, follow sign for N Ferriby, straight through T-lights. Garden 2nd largish house on R, behind brick wall. Home-made teas.* **Adm £2.50, chd free. Sun 11 May (1-5). Also open The Court. Visitors also welcome by appt June & July only.**
1/2 -acre attractive, tranquil village garden. Beautiful rockery and stream with bridge, going down to lawned area. Short woodland walk leading to quiet area with breeze house at end of path. Landscaped 1993 by Peter Orme and maturing well.
♿ 🐕 ☕ ☎

96 SPRING CLOSE FARM
Gill Lane, Kearby LS22 4BS. John & Rosemary Proctor, 0113 2886310. *3m W of Wetherby. A661 from Wetherby town centre, turn L at bottom of Spofforth Hill to Sicklinghall. 1m after village turn L at Clap Gate towards Kearby.* **Visitors welcome by appt May to Sept, groups of 10+, coaches permitted. Light refreshments.**
Large mature yet evolving quiet country garden, originally an exposed site, now divided into garden rooms sheltered by clipped yew and beech hedging, with allées and tranquil water garden leading to new orchard with ha-ha and stunning views over Wharfe Valley. Underplanted roses, mulberry trees and herbaceous borders with archways to walled garden with small greenhouse, and enclosed cottage garden.
♿ 🐕 ☕ ☎

SQUIRREL LODGE
See Nottinghamshire.

97 STAINSACRE
Carperby DL8 4DD. Colin & Pat Jackson. *7m W of Leyburn. From A684 1m N of Aysgarth Falls. Light refreshments & teas at village hall.* **Adm £3.50, chd free. Sun 27 July (1-5).**
1-acre site on S-sloping hillside created by owners since 1996. Deep mixed borders and island beds with wide variety of hardy and unusual perennials. 2 small wildlife ponds and artificial stream. Open grassed area with native trees and gravel area with specimen hostas. Featured in 'WI Magazine'. Gravel and grass paths.
♿ 🐕 ☕ ☕

Beautiful rockery and stream with bridge . . .

98 ◆ STILLINGFLEET LODGE
Stewart Lane, Stillingfleet, Nr York YO19 6HP. Mr & Mrs J Cook, 01904 728506, www.stillingfleetlodgenurseries.co.uk. *6m S of York. From A19 York-Selby take B1222 towards Sherburn in Elmet.* **Adm £4, chd 5-16yrs 50p. Weds, Fris 16 Apr to 30 Sept; 1st & 3rd Sats each month 1-5. For NGS: Suns 11 May; 22 June; 7 Sept (1.30-5).**
Plantsman's garden subdivided into smaller gardens, each based on colour theme with emphasis on use of foliage plants. Wild flower meadow and natural pond. 55yds double herbaceous borders. Organic garden. New modern rill garden. Adjacent nursery.
♿ 🐕 ☕ ☕

99 NEW SUNNY MOUNT
Well Hill, Honley, Holmfirth HD9 6JF. Barry & Jenny Kellington, 01484 660783, barrykellington@aol.com. *3m S of Huddersfield, 3m N of Holmfirth. Turn to Honley off A616 (New Mill Rd), drive through village, turn R at roundabout. Garden entrance 100 metres on L. Please park in village. Light refreshments & teas.* **Adm £2.50, chd free. Sat 21, Sun 22**

June (11-5). **Visitors also welcome by appt June & July only, groups of 10+.**
The garden, designed by present owner around Georgian cottage (not open), contains an interesting range of planting, stone and mosaic paving, sheltered courtyard and summerhouse. Attractive kitchen garden, with raised vegetable beds, divided by gravel paths, central pergola, chicken run, fruit garden and pond. Art, craft and garden design exhibition.
🐕 ⚙ ☕ ☎

100 SWALE COTTAGE
Station Road, Richmond DL10 4LU. Julie Martin & Dave Dalton. *Richmond town centre. On foot, facing bottom of Market Place, turn L onto Frenchgate, then R onto Station Rd. House 1st on R.* **Adm £2.50, chd free. Sun 22 June (1-5).**
1/2 -acre urban oasis on steep site, with sweeping views and hidden corners. Several enclosed garden rooms on different levels. Mature herbaceous, rose and shrub garden with some areas of recent improvement. Magnificent yew and cedar. Organic vegetables and soft fruit, pond, orchard, adjacent paddock with sheep and hens. Some steep slopes and rough paths.
♿ 🐕 ⚙

101 THORPE LODGE
Knaresborough Road, Ripon HG4 3LU. Mr & Mrs T Jowitt, 01765 602088, jowitt@btinternet.com. *1m S of Ripon. On Ripon-Bishop Monkton-Knaresborough rd 3/4 m from Ripon bypass.* **Home-made teas. Adm £5, chd under 12 free. Sun 3 Aug (1-6). Visitors also welcome by appt groups of 20+, coaches permitted.**
Beautiful, large country garden of 12 acres with extensive colour-themed flower borders, walled rose garden, canals and fruit trees. Pleached hornbeam walk and allées leads to walks through mature woodland with vistas and ponds. Courtyard with exotic shrubs and tender plants in pots. Area for picnics.
♿ ⚙ 🛏 ☕ ☎

102 TINKERS HOLLOW
Church Field Lane, Great Ouseburn, York YO26 9SG. Heather & Eric Sugden. *Between York & Harrogate off B6265. 4m E of A1 (M) J47, (A59) towards York. Before Green Hammerton take B6265 towards*

Boroughbridge. Follow signs to Great Ouseburn. Car parking at Tinkers Hollow. **Combined with Cobble Cottage adm £3, chd free.** Mon 26 May (11-5).

Just over 1 acre, with wide range of features. Ponds connected by waterfall and small stream help extend the diverse range of plants grown. Several pergola walk-ways provide interesting and varied routes linking bog, perennial and shrub borders. By complete contrast the most distant part of the garden is left to nature with wild pond and folly to add intrigue.

  🚻 ❀

103 VICARAGE HOUSE
Kirkby Wharfe LS24 9DE. Mr & Mrs R S A Hall, 01937 835458. *1m S of Tadcaster. (A162) turn L (B1223) after 1m turn L to Kirkby Wharfe. Parking on rd.* **Adm £2.50, chd free. Refreshments** Late Afternoon - Early Evening Opening Wed 21 May (4-7.30). **Visitors also welcome by appt May & June, groups of 10+.**

Secluded 1-acre country garden surrounded by mature trees, colour-themed border, extensive herbaceous borders, raised beds. Species primulae and aquilegias. Gravel pathways.

🗡 ❀ ☕ ☎

104 ◆ THE WALLED GARDEN AT SCAMPSTON
Rillington YO17 8NG. Sir Charles & Lady Legard, 01944 759111, www.scampston.co.uk. *5m E of Malton. 1/2 m N of A64, signed Scampston only.* **House and Garden £10, chd £6, Garden only £5, chd £3, concessions £4.50. For details of openings & dates see website or tel. For NGS:** Wed 2 July (10-5).

An exciting modern garden designed by Piet Oudolf. The 4 1/2 -acre walled garden contains a series of hedged enclosures. In July the extravagant perennial meadow will be at its best. Also, many rare species, rock garden and woodland walk. Featured in 'Gardens Illustrated' & 'House & Garden'.

  🚻 🗡 ❀ ☕

105 NEW WARLEY HOUSE GARDENS
Stock Lane, Warley HX2 7RU. Dr & Mrs P J Hinton. *2m W of Halifax. From Halifax take A646 (Burnley). Turn R up Windleroyd Lane approx 1m after A58, A646 junction (King Cross). Turn L at T-junction into Stock Lane. Park on* *rd before Warley Village.* Home-made teas. **Adm £3, chd free.** Mon 26 May (1-5).

Following the demolition of original early C18 house and years of neglect the partly walled 2 1/2 -acre garden is being renovated by the present owners. Rocky path and Japanese style planting leads to lawns and lovely S-facing views over open countryside. The alpine ravine is now planted with ferns, and fine trees give structure to the developing woodland area. Drifts of groundcover, shrub and herbaceous plantings, wild flowers and heathers maintain constant seasonal interest. Featured in 'Halifax Evening Courier'. Partial wheelchair access.

  🚻 🗡 ❀

relaxing environment and splendid views over the Nidd valley . . .

106 26 WEST END
Walkington HU17 8SX. Miss Jennifer Hall, 01482 861705. *2m SW of Beverley. On the B1230, 100yds beyond Xrds in centre of village on the R.* Teas at 18 West End (nearly next door). **Adm £3, chd free.** Sun 1 June (1.30-5). **Also open Molecroft Cottage. Visitors also welcome by appt June & early July, for groups 6+.**

Exceptionally charming and interesting 1-acre cottage garden opening into old wooded gravel pit still being developed by owner. Many rare plants collected over 21yrs.

🗡 ❀ ☕ ☎

107 THE WHITE HOUSE
Husthwaite YO61 4QA. Mrs A Raper, 01347 868688. *5m S of Thirsk. Turn R off A19 signed Husthwaite. 1 1/2 m to centre of village opp parish church.* **Visitors welcome by appt.**

Come and meet the gardener, an enthusiastic plantswoman. Exchange ideas and visit a 1-acre country garden with walled garden, conservatory and gardens within the garden. Herbaceous, particularly a hot summer border and shrubs and many fascinating unusual plants. Landscaping and planting in the old orchard. A garden for all seasons.

  🚻 🗡 ❀ ☎

108 WHIXLEY GARDENS
YO26 8AR. *Between York & Harrogate. 3m E of A1(M) off A59 York-Harrogate. Signed Whixley.* Light refreshments & teas at The Old Vicarage. **Combined with Croft Cottage adm £5, chd free.** Sun 4 May; Wed 11 June (11.30-5).

☕

ASH TREE HOUSE
High Street. Mr & Mrs E P Moffitt

Well designed unusual garden of approx 1/4 -acre with extensive rockeries making full use of sloping site. Established herbaceous plants, shrubs and climbers achieve a cottage garden effect. Access only by steps.

🗡 ❀

THE BAY HOUSE
Stonegate. Mr & Mrs Jon Beckett

Densely planted courtyard garden on differing levels.

🗡

COBBLE COTTAGE
John Hawkridge & Barry Atkinson
(See separate entry).

THE OLD VICARAGE
Mr & Mrs Roger Marshall, biddymarshall@btopenworld. com. Visitors also welcome by appt March to July, groups of 20+, coaches permitted.

Delightful 3/4 -acre walled flower garden with mixed borders, unusual shrubs, climbers, roses, hardy and half-hardy perennials, bulbs and hellebores. Paths and garden structures lead to new vistas and hidden areas using the garden's natural contours.

🗡 ❀ ☎

109 WOODLANDS COTTAGE
Summerbridge, nr Harrogate HG3 4BT. Mr & Mrs Stark, 01423 780765, annstark@btinternet.com. *4m E of Pateley Bridge, 10m NW of Harrogate. On the B6165 (Ripley-Pateley Bridge) 1/2 m W of Summerbridge.* Home-made teas. **Adm £2.50, chd free.** Sun 11 May (1.30-5). **Visitors also welcome by appt, coaches permitted.**

1-acre plantswomen's garden in Nidderdale. Garden is designed to harmonise with the surrounding countryside and has several differing areas of planting with many unusual plants, natural rock outcrops, wild flower meadow, vegetable garden and formal areas. Featured in 'Yorkshire Life'. Gravel paths, some slopes.

110 NEW WOODROYD
Harefield Lane, Pateley Bridge HG3 5QE. Steve & Elaine Rice. *12m NW of Harrogate, 9m SW of Ripon. Entering Pateley Bridge from Harrogate (B6165) on B6265, turn L immed after 30mph restriction sign.* Cream teas. **Adm £2.50, chd free.** Sun 25 May (12-5).
1-acre planted in cottage garden style supported by many mature shrubs on steep W-facing sloping site. Paths, steps and terraces lead to small secret gardens and areas to sit. Small pool, pergola, arbours, and ornamental grass border, combine colourful plantings with relaxing environment and splendid views over the Nidd valley.

111 WORTLEY HALL
Wortley Village S35 7DB, 0114 2882100, info@wortleyhall.com, www.wortleyhall.com. *9m NW of Sheffield & 5m SW of Barnsley. On A629 Huddersfield - Sheffield rd in Wortley village, signed Wortley Hall & Gardens.* Light refreshments & teas. **Adm £3, chd free.** Mon 24 Mar; combined with **Avenue Cottage** adm **£5** Sun 22 June (12-4). Visitors also welcome by appt, groups 15+, can incl guided tour.
26 acres of elegant Italianate gardens set within landscaped parkland. Formal gardens with sunken garden, arbour and clipped yew balls all framed with

seasonal bedding and perennial borders leading to walled organic kitchen garden. Informal walks through pleasure grounds reveal C18/19 plantings incl 500yr old hollow oak, lake and ice house. March opening, large display of daffodils and spring woodland bulbs. Guided tours with Head Gardener 1pm and 3pm both days. Silver award - Yorkshire in Bloom.

112 WYTHERSTONE GARDENS
Pockley YO62 7TE. Lady Clarissa Collin, 01439 770012, www.wytherstonegardens.co.uk. *2m NE of Helmsley. Signed from A170.* Teas NGS days only. **Adm £3.50, chd £1 under 6 free.** Suns 15 June, 20 July (1-5).
A true plantsman's garden set in 8 acres of rolling countryside on edge of the North York Moors. The garden is divided by beech hedges, creating interlinked specialised 'feature' gardens, incl Mediterranean, ericaceous, terraced, good small arboretum (incl the most northerly Wollemia nobilis planted outside), fern garden, paeonia garden and newly planted foliage and bamboo garden. Plants not thought hardy in the north of England grow happily on Wytherstone's free draining soil. Delightful on-site nursery where all the plants are propagated from the garden.

113 ◆ YORK GATE
Back Church Lane, Adel LS16 8DW. Perennial, 0113 267 8240, www.perennial.org.uk. *5m N of Leeds centre. 2¼ m SE of Bramhope, signed from A660. Park in Church*

Lane nr church and take public footpath through churchyard & straight on to garden. **Adm £3.50, chd free, £2.50 (Sept).** Thurs, Suns & Bank Hol Mons, 23 Mar to 28 Sept (2-5), for evening opening times please see website or tel.
1-acre masterpiece and outstanding example of C20 English garden design. Within a series of inner gardens are shrubs and herbaceous borders, ponds, pinetum, dell, fern border, nut walk, white and silver borders, kitchen garden and famous herb garden with topiary. Each area has its own unique architectural features and evergreens are used to great effect throughout. Featured in 'The Independent' & 'The Guardian'.

114 YORKE HOUSE
Dacre Banks, Nidderdale HG3 4EW. Anthony & Pat Hutchinson, 01423 780456, pat@yorkehouse.co.uk, www.yorkehouse.co.uk. *4m SE of Pateley Bridge, 10m NW of Harrogate. On B6451. Car park.* Home-made teas. **Adm £3, chd free. Combined with Dacre Banks Gardens** adm **£5, 6 July.** Suns 6, 20 July (11-5). Visitors also welcome by appt June to Aug, incl coaches.
Flower arranger's 2-acre garden with colour-themed borders full of flowering and foliage plants and shrubs. Extensive water feature incl large ornamental ponds and stream. Other features incl nut walk, rose pergola, patios, gazebo, Millennium garden and wildlife area. The garden enjoys beautiful views across Nidderdale. Picnic area.

Yorkshire County Volunteers

County Organisers
N Yorks - Districts of Hambleton, Richmond, Ryedale, Scarborough & Cleveland Jane Baldwin, Riverside Farm, Sinnington, York YO62 6RY, 01751 431764, wnbaldwin@yahoo.co.uk
E Yorks Sally Bean, Saltmarshe Hall, Saltmarshe, Goole DN14 7RX, 01430 430199, pmegabean@aol.com
West & South Yorks & North Yorks District of Craven, Harrogate, Selby & York Bridget Marshall, The Old Vicarage, Whixley, York YO26 8AR, 01423 330474, biddymarshall@btopenworld.com

County Treasurer
Angela Pugh, Savage Garth, Nun Monkton, York YO26 8ER, 01423 330456, angie.pugh@btinternet.com

Publicity
Felicity Bowring, Lawkland Hall, Austwick, Lancaster LA2 8AT, 01729 823551, diss@austwick.org

County Booklet & Advertising
Tim Gittins, Hillbark, Church Lane, Bardsey, Leeds LS17 9DH, 01937 574968, timgittins@aol.com

Assistant County Organisers
Deborah Bigley, The Old Rectory, Great Langton, Northallerton DL7 0TA, 01609 748915, debsandbobbigley@aol.com
Annabel Fife, Langton Farm, Great Langton, Northallerton DL7 0TA, 01609 748446, annabelfife@fsmail.net
West & South Yorks, Jane Hudson, Lower Crawshaw, Emley, Huddersfield HD8 9SU, 01924 840980, janehudson42@btinternet.com

ng's gardens open for charity

Millpond, stream, grotto, potager and trompe l'oeil all contribute to the owner's design for surprise, concealment, scent, colour and, above all, fun. New 'scratch & sniff' herb garden with rills . . .

Mill Dene Garden, Gloucestershire

Mark your diary with these special events in 2008

EXPLORE SECRET GARDENS DURING CHELSEA WEEK

Tue 20 May, Wed 21 May, Thur 22 May, Fri 23 May
Full day tours: £78 per person, 10% discount for groups
Advance Booking required, telephone 01932 864532 or
email pennysnellflowers@btinternet.com

Specially selected private gardens in London, Surrey and Berkshire. The tour price includes transport and lunch with wine at a popular restaurant or pub.

FROGMORE – A ROYAL GARDEN (BERKSHIRE)

Tue 3 June 10am - 5.30pm (last adm 4pm)
Garden adm £4, chd free. Advance booking recommended telephone 01483 211535
or email orders@ngs.org.uk

A unique opportunity to explore 30 acres of landscaped garden, rich in history and beauty.

FLAXBOURNE FARM – FUN AND SURPRISES (BEDFORDSHIRE)

Sun 8 June 10am - 5pm Adm £5, chd free
No booking required, come along on the day!

Bring the whole family and enjoy a plant fair and garden party and have fun in this beautiful and entertaining garden of 2 acres.

WISLEY RHS GARDEN – MUSIC IN THE GARDEN (SURREY)

Tue 19 August 6 - 9pm

Adm (incl RHS members) £7, chd under 15 free

A special opening of this famous garden, exclusively for the NGS. Enjoy music and entertainment as you explore a range of different gardens.

For further information visit www.ngs.org.uk or telephone 01483 211535

WALES

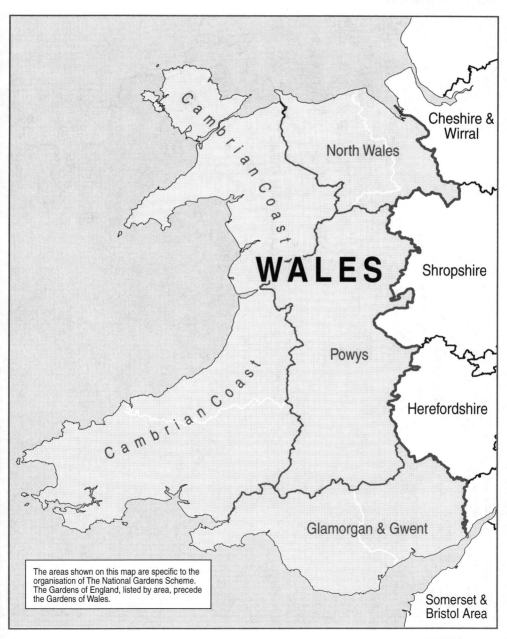

Cheshire & Wirral

North Wales

C a m b r i a n   C o a s t

WALES

Shropshire

Powys

C a m b r i a n   C o a s t

Herefordshire

Glamorgan & Gwent

The areas shown on this map are specific to the
organisation of The National Gardens Scheme.
The Gardens of England, listed by area, precede
the Gardens of Wales.

Somerset &
Bristol Area

CAMBRIAN COAST

Gwynedd, Ceredigion/Cardiganshire, Pembrokeshire & Carmarthenshire

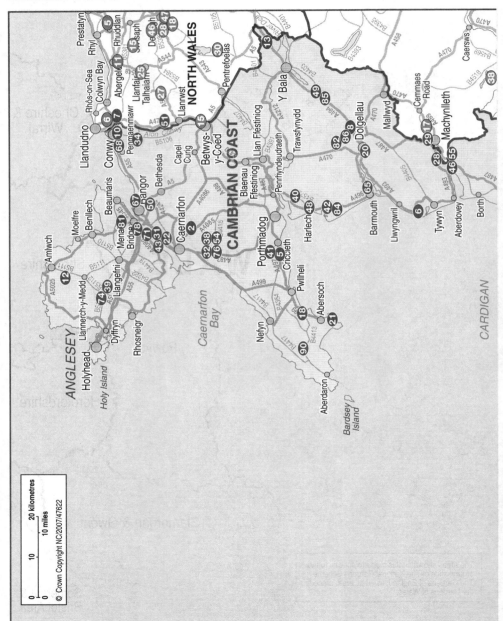

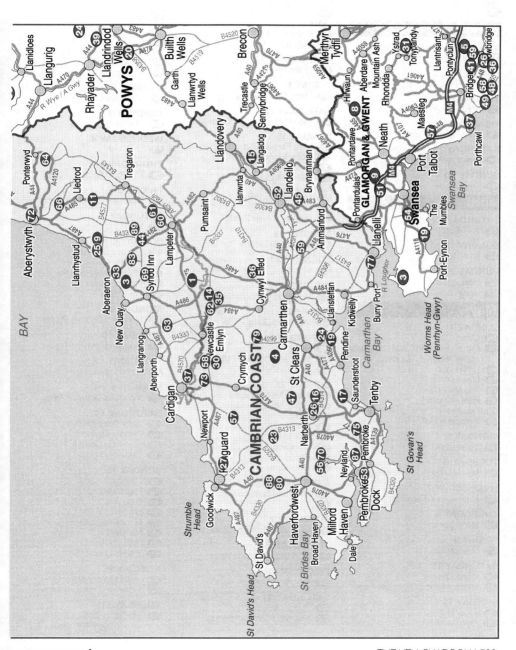

Opening Dates

February

SATURDAY 2
67 Penrhyn Castle

March

SUNDAY 9
58 Nant-yr-Eryd

FRIDAY 21
71 Plas Newydd

SUNDAY 23
5 Bont Fechan Farm

MONDAY 24
5 Bont Fechan Farm

SATURDAY 29
88 Weir Castle

SUNDAY 30
88 Weir Castle

April

SATURDAY 12
88 Weir Castle

SUNDAY 13
88 Weir Castle

SUNDAY 27
51 Maenan Hall
87 Upton Castle Gardens

May

SUNDAY 4
34 Gilfach
42 Llanbedr Spring Festival Gardens
   - Gwyl Wanwyn Llanbedr
46 Llwyncelyn
52 Maesquarre
55 The Mill House
63 Pant-yr-Holiad
75 Rosewood
80 Treffgarne Hall

MONDAY 5
52 Maesquarre

TUESDAY 6
52 Maesquarre

WEDNESDAY 7
52 Maesquarre (Evening)

THURSDAY 8
52 Maesquarre

FRIDAY 9
52 Maesquarre

SATURDAY 10
52 Maesquarre
54 Megans Wood Gwernoer Farm

SUNDAY 11
3 Arnant House
8 Bryn Gwern

20 Craig y Ffynnon
30 Ffynone
47 Llwyngarreg
54 Megans Wood Gwernoer Farm
65 Pen y Bryn
72 Plas Penglais
81 Treffos School

WEDNESDAY 14
31 Foxbrush

FRIDAY 16
45 Llwyn Cyll (Evening)

SATURDAY 17
57 Moorland Cottage Plants

SUNDAY 18
5 Bont Fechan Farm
17 Colby Woodland Garden
18 Coron
29 Felin y Ffridd
50 Llys-y-Gwynt
57 Moorland Cottage Plants
69 Perth Yr Eglwys
77 Stradey Castle Gardens

MONDAY 19
57 Moorland Cottage Plants

TUESDAY 20
57 Moorland Cottage Plants

THURSDAY 22
57 Moorland Cottage Plants

FRIDAY 23
57 Moorland Cottage Plants

SATURDAY 24
25 Dyffryn
57 Moorland Cottage Plants
88 Weir Castle

SUNDAY 25
1 Alltyrodyn Mansion
7 Bryn Eisteddfod
22 Crug Farm
25 Dyffryn
26 Dyffryn Farm
57 Moorland Cottage Plants
74 Rhyd
88 Weir Castle

MONDAY 26
57 Moorland Cottage Plants
90 Y Felin

TUESDAY 27
57 Moorland Cottage Plants

THURSDAY 29
57 Moorland Cottage Plants

FRIDAY 30
57 Moorland Cottage Plants

SATURDAY 31
10 Bunclody
57 Moorland Cottage Plants

June

SUNDAY 1
10 Bunclody
57 Moorland Cottage Plants
64 Pantyrhedyn
70 Picton Castle & Woodland Gardens
82 Ty Capel Ffrwd
84 Ty Newydd

MONDAY 2
57 Moorland Cottage Plants

TUESDAY 3
57 Moorland Cottage Plants

WEDNESDAY 4
31 Foxbrush

THURSDAY 5
57 Moorland Cottage Plants

FRIDAY 6
57 Moorland Cottage Plants

SATURDAY 7
57 Moorland Cottage Plants

SUNDAY 8
11 Bwlch y Geuffordd
16 Coed-y-Ffynnon
57 Moorland Cottage Plants
63 Pant-yr-Holiad
85 Tyn y Cefn

MONDAY 9
57 Moorland Cottage Plants

TUESDAY 10
57 Moorland Cottage Plants

THURSDAY 12
57 Moorland Cottage Plants

FRIDAY 13
57 Moorland Cottage Plants

SATURDAY 14
2 Antur Waunfawr
16 Coed-y-Ffynnon
57 Moorland Cottage Plants
79 Tradewinds

SUNDAY 15
21 Crowrach Isaf
28 Esgairweddan
34 Gilfach
44 Llanllyr
57 Moorland Cottage Plants
58 Nant-yr-Eryd
68 Pensychnant
79 Tradewinds

MONDAY 16
40 Hotel Maes-y-Neuadd
57 Moorland Cottage Plants

TUESDAY 17
57 Moorland Cottage Plants

THURSDAY 19
57 Moorland Cottage Plants

FRIDAY 20
57 Moorland Cottage Plants

SATURDAY 21
43 Llanidan Hall
57 Moorland Cottage Plants
59 The National Botanic Garden of
Wales (Evening)
88 Weir Castle

SUNDAY 22
4 Blaendwr
37 Glanhelyg
50 Llys-y-Gwynt
57 Moorland Cottage Plants
66 Penbanc
88 Weir Castle

MONDAY 23
57 Moorland Cottage Plants

TUESDAY 24
57 Moorland Cottage Plants

THURSDAY 26
57 Moorland Cottage Plants

FRIDAY 27
57 Moorland Cottage Plants

SATURDAY 28
14 Cilgwyn Bach Farm
35 Glandwr
43 Llanidan Hall
57 Moorland Cottage Plants
62 The Old Vicarage

SUNDAY 29
14 Cilgwyn Bach Farm
35 Glandwr
47 Llwyngarreg
57 Moorland Cottage Plants
60 New Hall
61 Oakmeadows at Maesyderi Farm
62 The Old Vicarage

MONDAY 30
57 Moorland Cottage Plants

July

TUESDAY 1
57 Moorland Cottage Plants

THURSDAY 3
57 Moorland Cottage Plants

FRIDAY 4
57 Moorland Cottage Plants

SATURDAY 5
57 Moorland Cottage Plants

SUNDAY 6
4 Blaendwr
13 Caerau Uchaf
33 Gerallt
57 Moorland Cottage Plants

MONDAY 7
57 Moorland Cottage Plants

TUESDAY 8
57 Moorland Cottage Plants

THURSDAY 10
57 Moorland Cottage Plants

FRIDAY 11
57 Moorland Cottage Plants

SATURDAY 12
57 Moorland Cottage Plants
88 Weir Castle

SUNDAY 13
24 Delacorse
36 Glangwili Lodges
57 Moorland Cottage Plants
70 Picton Castle & Woodland
Gardens
73 Rhosygilwen Mansion
75 Rosewood
88 Weir Castle

MONDAY 14
57 Moorland Cottage Plants

TUESDAY 15
57 Moorland Cottage Plants

WEDNESDAY 16
36 Glangwili Lodges

THURSDAY 17
57 Moorland Cottage Plants

FRIDAY 18
57 Moorland Cottage Plants

SATURDAY 19
57 Moorland Cottage Plants

SUNDAY 20
15 Cilgwyn Lodge
19 The Cors
32 Gardd y Coleg
57 Moorland Cottage Plants
74 Rhyd

MONDAY 21
57 Moorland Cottage Plants

TUESDAY 22
57 Moorland Cottage Plants

THURSDAY 24
57 Moorland Cottage Plants

FRIDAY 25
53 Mead Lodge
57 Moorland Cottage Plants
76 St John the Baptist & St George

SATURDAY 26
53 Mead Lodge
57 Moorland Cottage Plants

SUNDAY 27
53 Mead Lodge
57 Moorland Cottage Plants
83 Ty Glyn Walled Garden
86 Tyn-Twll

MONDAY 28
53 Mead Lodge
57 Moorland Cottage Plants

TUESDAY 29
57 Moorland Cottage Plants

THURSDAY 31
57 Moorland Cottage Plants

August

FRIDAY 1
57 Moorland Cottage Plants

SATURDAY 2
57 Moorland Cottage Plants

SUNDAY 3
27 Dyffryn Fernant
38 Gwyndy
57 Moorland Cottage Plants
85 Tyn y Cefn

MONDAY 4
57 Moorland Cottage Plants

TUESDAY 5
57 Moorland Cottage Plants

THURSDAY 7
57 Moorland Cottage Plants

FRIDAY 8
57 Moorland Cottage Plants

SATURDAY 9
57 Moorland Cottage Plants
88 Weir Castle

SUNDAY 10
8 Bryn Gwern
9 Bryngwyn Farm
19 The Cors (Evening)
48 Llyn Rhaeadr
57 Moorland Cottage Plants
88 Weir Castle

MONDAY 11
57 Moorland Cottage Plants
88 Weir Castle

TUESDAY 12
57 Moorland Cottage Plants

WEDNESDAY 13
26 Dyffryn Farm

THURSDAY 14
57 Moorland Cottage Plants

FRIDAY 15
57 Moorland Cottage Plants

SATURDAY 16
57 Moorland Cottage Plants

SUNDAY 17
34 Gilfach
57 Moorland Cottage Plants
82 Ty Capel Ffrwd

MONDAY 18
57 Moorland Cottage Plants

TUESDAY 19
57 Moorland Cottage Plants

THURSDAY 21
40 Hotel Maes-y-Neuadd
57 Moorland Cottage Plants

FRIDAY 22
- **57** Moorland Cottage Plants
- **79** Tradewinds (Evening)

SATURDAY 23
- **57** Moorland Cottage Plants

SUNDAY 24
- **57** Moorland Cottage Plants

MONDAY 25
- **57** Moorland Cottage Plants
- **90** Y Felin

TUESDAY 26
- **57** Moorland Cottage Plants

THURSDAY 28
- **57** Moorland Cottage Plants

FRIDAY 29
- **57** Moorland Cottage Plants

SATURDAY 30
- **57** Moorland Cottage Plants

SUNDAY 31
- **37** Glanhelyg
- **57** Moorland Cottage Plants
- **64** Pantyrhedyn

September

MONDAY 1
- **57** Moorland Cottage Plants

TUESDAY 2
- **57** Moorland Cottage Plants

THURSDAY 4
- **57** Moorland Cottage Plants

FRIDAY 5
- **57** Moorland Cottage Plants

SATURDAY 6
- **57** Moorland Cottage Plants

SUNDAY 7
- **57** Moorland Cottage Plants
- **80** Treffgarne Hall

SATURDAY 13
- **79** Tradewinds

SUNDAY 14
- **47** Llwyngarreg
- **79** Tradewinds

SUNDAY 28
- **77** Stradey Castle Gardens

February 2009

SUNDAY 8
- **67** Penrhyn Castle

Gardens open to the public

- **2** Antur Waunfawr
- **17** Colby Woodland Garden
- **22** Crug Farm
- **27** Dyffryn Fernant
- **32** Gardd y Coleg
- **40** Hotel Maes-y-Neuadd

- **59** The National Botanic Garden of Wales
- **67** Penrhyn Castle
- **68** Pensychnant
- **70** Picton Castle & Woodland Gardens
- **71** Plas Newydd
- **83** Ty Glyn Walled Garden
- **87** Upton Castle Gardens

By appointment only

- **6** Bronclydwr
- **12** Cae Newydd
- **23** Cwm Pibau
- **39** Gwyndy Bach
- **41** Kinlet
- **49** Llys Arthur
- **56** Millinford
- **78** Tan Dinas
- **89** Winllan Wildlife Garden

Also open by appointment ☎

- **3** Arnant House
- **4** Blaendwr
- **5** Bont Fechan Farm
- **7** Bryn Eisteddfod
- **8** Bryn Gwern
- **10** Bunclody
- **11** Bwlch y Geuffordd
- **13** Caerau Uchaf
- **15** Cilgwyn Lodge
- **16** Coed-y-Ffynnon
- **18** Coron
- **19** The Cors
- **24** Delacorse
- **26** Dyffryn Farm
- **29** Felin y Ffridd
- **30** Ffynone
- **31** Foxbrush
- **33** Gerallt
- **34** Gilfach
- **35** Glandwr
- **43** Llanidan Hall
- **44** Llanllyr
- **45** Llwyn Cyll
- **46** Llwyncelyn
- **47** Llwyngarreg
- **48** Llyn Rhaeadr
- **50** Llys-y-Gwynt
- **52** Maesquarre
- **54** Megans Wood Gwernoer Farm
- **60** New Hall
- **61** Oakmeadows at Maesyderi Farm
- **62** The Old Vicarage
- **73** Rhosygilwen Mansion
- **74** Rhyd
- **79** Tradewinds
- **80** Treffgarne Hall
- **82** Ty Capel Ffrwd
- **84** Ty Newydd
- **85** Tyn y Cefn
- **88** Weir Castle
- **90** Y Felin

The Gardens

1 **ALLTYRODYN MANSION**
Capel Dewi SA44 4PS. Mr & Mrs Donald Usher. *8m W of Lampeter, off A475. Take B4459 at Rhydowen to Capel Dewi. Entrance on R by South Lodge.* Cream teas. **Adm £3, chd free (share to Capel Dewi Church).** Sun 25 May (11-5).
Early C19 garden. Approx 8 acres, mostly mature woodland with many fine trees. Old walled garden. Rare stone-built gothic cold bathhouse. Early C20 lake, Dutch garden and rhododendron plantings. Garden is best in spring when rhododendrons and azaleas are in bloom. Walled garden now being used for production of organic produce.
& ✕ ⊗ ☕

2 ◆ **ANTUR WAUNFAWR**
Bryn Pistyll, Waunfawr, Caernarfon LL55 4BJ. Menna Jones, 01286 650721. *4½ m SE of Caernarfon. On A4085. Waunfawr village, turn L following signs, bear L for approx ½ m.* **Adm by donation. Open all yr.** For NGS: Sat 14 June (11-3).
Gardens and 7-acre Nature Park developed by Antur Waunfawr, a community venture providing employment opportunities for people with learning disabilities. Meadows, woodland walks, wildlife and ornamental ponds, soft fruit garden, herbaceous perennial beds. Well stocked wildlife plant nursery, greenhouses.
& ⊗ ☕

Community venture providing employment opportunities . . .

3 **ARNANT HOUSE**
Llwyncelyn SA46 0HF. Pam & Ron Maddox, 01545 580083. *On A 487, 2m S of Aberaeron. Next to Llwyncelyn Village Hall. Parking in lay-by opp house.* Light refreshments & teas. **Adm £2.50, chd free.** Sun 11 May (12-5). Visitors also welcome by appt.

Garden created in 7yrs from derelict ground. 1-acre, in Victorian style and divided into rooms and themes. Laburnum arch, wildlife ponds, rotunda and tea house. Wide, long borders full of perennial planting with a good variety of species, numerous statues and oddities to be discovered. Several different magnolias, rhododendrons in May.

 ♿ ✗ ☕ ☎

4 NEW BLAENDWR
Cwmbach, Whitland SA34 0DN. Arthur & Barbara Howells, 01994 448256, bahowells@hotmail.co.uk. *7m N of Whitland and St Clears. From St Clears town centre take Llanboidy rd through Llangynin, then keep R towards Blaenwawn; Blaendwr is approx 3m on R before Xrds. From Haverfordwest take Whitland bypass, turn L for Llanboidy. Turn R at 3rd Xrds and R again at next Xrds.* **Adm £2, chd free. Suns 22 June; 6 July (2-6). Visitors also welcome by appt.**
1/2-acre carefully casual cottage garden. Borders of healthy perennials and clematis-covered pergolas on exposed hilltop location, with charming water features, small children's garden, and plentiful plant interest. Garden designed for full wheelchair access and easy walking.

♿ ✗ ☎

5 BONT FECHAN FARM
Llanystumdwy LL52 0LS. Mr & Mrs J D Bean, 01766 522604. *2m W of Criccieth. On the A497 to Pwllheli on L of main rd.* Home-made teas. **Adm £2, chd free. Sun 23, Mon 24 Mar; Sun 18 May (11-5). Visitors also welcome by appt.**
Cottage garden with rockery, fish pond, herbaceous border, steps to river. Large variety of plants. Nicely planted tubs; good vegetable garden and poultry. Rhododendron and azaleas.

♿ ☀ ☕ ☎

6 BRONCLYDWR
Rhoslefain, Tywyn LL36 9LT. Mr & Mrs Michael Bishton, 01654 710882, michael@bronclydwr.co.uk. *5m N of Tywyn. Take A493 Dolgellau to Tywyn rd. At Rhoslefain take Tonfanau rd for about 1/2 m. Fork L along private rd to end of tarmac rd then take unmade rd to large house on edge of wood.* **Adm**

£4, chd free. **Visitors welcome by appt mid June to end July.**
1-acre unique plantsman's garden of peaceful historic farmhouse overlooking Cardigan Bay. Many unusual and tender plants are grown incl protea, puya, amicia, echiums, watsonias, arums, *Beschorneria yuccoides*, euryops, restios etc. Interesting trees, shrubs, bamboos; bog garden and wild wooded area.

✗ ⊕ ☎

Borders of healthy perennials and clematis-covered pergolas on exposed hilltop . . .

7 BRYN EISTEDDFOD
Glan Conwy LL28 5LF. Dr Michael Senior, 01492 581175. *3 1/2 m SE of Llandudno. 3m W Colwyn Bay. Up hill (Bryn-y-Maen direction) from Glan Conwy Corner where A470 joins A55.* Home-made teas. **Adm £2.50, chd 50p. Sun 25 May (2-5). Visitors also welcome by appt.**
8 acres of landscaped grounds incl mature shrubbery, arboretum, old walled 'Dutch' garden, large lawn with ha-ha. Extensive views over Conwy Valley, Snowdonia National Park, Conwy Castle, town and estuary.

♿ ⊕ ☕ ☎

8 BRYN GWERN
Llanfachreth LL40 2DH. H O & P D Nurse, 01341 450255, antique_pete@btopenworld.com. *3m NE of Dolgellau. Do not go to village of Llanfachreth, stay on A494 Bala-Dolgellau rd: 13m from Bala. Take 1st Llanfachreth turn R. From Dolgellau 4th Llanfachreth turn L, follow signs. No coach parking.* Cream teas. **Adm £3, chd free. Suns 11 May; 10 Aug (10-5). Visitors also welcome by appt.**
Wander through 2 acres of trees and shrubs, incl acers, azaleas, pieris, rhododendrons, gunnera (watch it grow!) and bulbs in spring;

hydrangeas, eucryphia, magnolias, embothriums, fuchsias and primulas during summer. Semi-wild cultivated garden, home to cats, dogs, chickens, ducks and wild birds. Eat your cream teas or just sit and become intoxicated with the smells and breathtaking views of Cader Idris. Wheelchair access to main area.

♿ ✗ ⊕ ☕ ☎

9 BRYNGWYN FARM
Llanon SY23 5LA. Philip & Gillian Morgan. *10m S of Aberystwyth on A487. Turn L at Central Hotel in Llanon. Bryngwyn is 1 1/2 m uphill on R.* Home-made teas. **Adm £2.50, chd free. Sun 10 Aug (11-5).**
1-acre S-facing cottage garden 500ft above Cardigan Bay, stocked by knowledgeable plantswoman and containing a selection of trees, shrubs, perennials, fruit and vegetables that can cope with this challenging site. Walks around large wildlife pond and broadleaf woodland planted in 2005 in adjacent fields.

♿ ✗ ⊕ ☕

10 BUNCLODY
Henryd Road, Conwy LL32 8TN. Dawn Humphreys, 01492 580930. *1 1/2 m S Conwy. Cross Conwy Bridge, L through arch onto B5106 to Gyffin (1/4 m). Henryd Rd opp corner shop. 1m, passing R turn. Garden 2nd house on R.* Light refreshments & teas. **Adm £3, chd free (share to Cruse Bereavement Care). Sat 31 May; Sun 1 June (12-4). Visitors also welcome by appt.**
Garden only 5yrs old. 3/4 acre. Distinct areas linked by curving paths and beds. Circular lawn surrounded by roses and shrubs. Gazebo with natural stream, pond and bridges. Walled garden, bog garden with boardwalk. Hot house with lotus, giant taro and bougainvillea. Packed with interest. Amazing what has been achieved in a short time.

✗ ⊕ ☕ ☎

11 BWLCH Y GEUFFORDD
Bronant SY23 4JD. Mr & Mrs J Acres, 01974 251559, gayacres@aol.com. *6m NW of Tregaron. 12m SE of Aberystwyth off A485. Take turning opp Bronant school for 1 1/2 m then turn L up a 1/2 m track.* Home-made teas. **Adm £3, chd 50p. Sun 8 June (11-6). Visitors also welcome by appt.**
1000ft high, 2-acre wildlife garden featuring lake with water lilies and a

series of pools linked by waterfalls, a number of theme gardens, from Mediterranean to woodland and from oriental to exotic jungle with hut. Plenty of sympathetic seating and large sculptures. Pond dipping for children on days by appointment but not on open day. Gravel paths but specialised wheelchair available to borrow for visitors weighing less than 10st.

Plenty of sympathetic seating and large sculptures . . .

12 CAE NEWYDD
Rhosgoch, Anglesey LL66 0BG. Hazel & Nigel Bond, 01407 831354. *3m SW of Amlwch. L immed after Amlwch Town sign on A5025 from Benllech, follow signs for leisure centre & Lastra Farm. After L turn for Lastra Farm, follow rd for approx 3m, pass through Rhosgoch, keep to main rd, follow signs for Llyn Alaw. Garden/car park on L.* Visitors welcome by appt Apr to Sept.
Started 2002 from exposed 2½ -acre S-facing field, overlooking Llyn Alaw with panoramic views of Snowdonia. Spring borders, mixed beds of interesting shrubs, grasses and perennials; large wildlife pond, meadow area with cut paths and buddleias, vegetable garden with polytunnel and chicken run. Paved area near house with raised beds and formal pond. Sheltered mature paddock garden with pond/bog area, formal herb bed and walled former pigsty providing additional shelter.

13 CAERAU UCHAF
Sarnau LL23 7LG. Mr & Mrs Toby Hickish, 01678 530493, summersgardens@tiscali.co.uk. *3m NE of Bala. From A5 N of Corwen turn L A494 to Bala. Approx 5m turn R into Sarnau, keep R up hill approx 1m. From Bala take A494 NE. After approx 3m turn L into Sarnau, keep R up hill approx 1m. Coaches strictly by appt.* Home-made teas. Adm £3, chd free. Sun 6 July (2-5). Visitors also welcome by appt.
Herbaceous borders, lawns, ornamental vegetable garden,

woodland walks - some paths rather steep. New developments every yr. Wonderful views. Tatton Park winners of RHS gold medal and best back to back garden. Gravel paths, steep slopes.

14 NEW CILGWYN BACH FARM
Heol-y-Dderwen, Pont-Tyweli, Llandysul SA44 4RP. Jean & Ian Wilson. *15m N of Carmarthen. Turn off A486 Llandysul to Newcastle Emlyn rd at Half Moon PH (300yds from Llandysul bridge). Pass Jewson's building supplies on L, garden 2nd house on L.* Cream teas. Adm £2.50, chd free. Sat 28, Sun 29 June (11-5). Also open Glandwr (³/₄ m).
1-acre garden with informally-planted raised beds, gravel walks, lawns, sculptures and old stone buildings. Small wildlife pond. Views of surrounding hills. Short walk in wild area. Best in Village, Llangeler Parish in Bloom.

15 CILGWYN LODGE
Llangadog SA19 9LH. Keith Brown & Moira Thomas, 01550 777452, keith@cilgwynlodge.co.uk. *3m NE of Llangadog village. 4m SW of Llandovery. Turn off A40 into centre of Llangadog. Bear L in front of village shop then 1st R towards Myddfai. After 2½ m pass Cilgwyn Manor on L then 1st L. Garden ¼ m on L.* Home-made teas. Adm £2.50, chd free. Sun 20 July (1-5). Visitors also welcome by appt, coaches and parties welcome.
Fascinating and much-admired 1-acre garden with something for everyone. Wide variety of herbaceous plants displayed in extensive colour-themed borders, over 250 varieties of hostas, a growing collection of clematis and many borderline hardy rare or unusual plants.Traditional vegetable and fruit garden and large waterlily pond. Featured on Wedi 3 S4C TV. One garden wheelchair-accessible, other has slopes and gravel paths.

16 COED-Y-FFYNNON
Lampeter Velfrey SA67 8UJ. Col R H Gilbertson, 01834 831396, rh.gilbertson@virgin.net. *2½ m SE of Narberth. From Penblewin roundabout on A40 follow signs to Narberth & then*

to crematorium. Straight on through Llanmill & Lampeter Velfrey. Garden ¹/₂ m on L. Adm £2.50, chd free (share to Paul Sartori Foundation). Sun 8, Sat 14 June (2-6). Visitors also welcome by appt in June & July, groups and coaches welcome.
Enthusiast's 1-acre garden with over 140 varieties of old fashioned roses. Informal planting and very naturalistic garden style with ample provision for wildlife. Roses at their best early June to early July. Relaxed rural setting, lots of rough grass; don't expect manicured lawns. Talks and guided tour available. Parking in field which may contain farm animals.

17 ◆ COLBY WOODLAND GARDEN
Amroth SA67 8PP. The National Trust, 01834 811885. *6m N of Tenby. 5m SE of Narberth. Signed by brown tourist signs on coast rd & A477.* Adm £4.20, chd £2.10, family £10.50. Open daily Apr to Oct. For NGS: Sun 18 May (10-5).
8-acre woodland garden in a secluded and tranquil valley with fine collection of rhododendrons and azaleas. Walled garden open by kind permission of Mr and Mrs A Scourfield Lewis. Some steep areas.

18 CORON
Llanbedrog LL53 7NN. Mr & Mrs B M Jones, 01758 740296. *3m SW of Pwllheli. Turn R off A499 opp Llanbedrog Village sign, before garage, up private drive.* Cream teas. Adm £3, chd free. Sun 18 May (11-5.30). Visitors also welcome by appt.
6-acre mature garden featuring Davidia involucrata, overlooking Cardigan Bay. Pathways leading through extensively planted areas with rhododendrons, embothriom, azaleas, camellias, bluebell walks, wooded slopes and rock outcrops providing shelter for tender plants, lakes and bog gardens; orchards, walled vegetable and formal garden.

19 THE CORS
Newbridge Road, Laugharne SA33 4SH. Nick Priestland, 01994 427219, nickpriestland@hotmail.com. *12m SW of Carmarthen. From Carmarthen, turn R in centre of Laugharne at The Mariners PH. At bottom of Newbridge Rd on R. Use public car parks, 5 mins walk.* Home-made teas. Adm £3, chd

free. Sun 20 July (2-6). **Evening Opening**, wine, Sun 10 Aug (6-9). **Visitors also welcome by appt.**
Approx 2½ acres set in beautiful wooded valley bordering river. Large bog garden with ponds, gunnera, bamboos and tree ferns. Exceptional, elegant plantsman's garden with unusual architectural and exotic planting incl Tetrapanax papyrifer, Blechnum chilense, chusan palms and sculptures. Many water features, children must be supervised.

♿ ✂ ✿ ☕ ☎

20 CRAIG Y FFYNNON
Ffordd y Gader, Dolgellau LL40 1RU. Jon & Shân Lea. *Take Tywyn rd from Dolgellau main sq. Park on rd by Penbryn Garage. Walk up rd signed Cader Idris. Garden entrance on L 50yds from junction.* **Adm £3, chd free (share to League of Friends Dolgellau Hospital). Sun 11 May (11-5).**
N-facing 2-acre Victorian garden set out in 1870s. Majority of garden planted with mature specimen trees, rhododendrons and azaleas predominate. More formal herbaceous borders and greenhouse enclosed by box hedges. Wildlife pond; unusual shade-loving plants and ferns. Book reading, by local authors, of their new books.

✂ ✿

21 NEW CROWRACH ISAF
LL53 7BY. Margaret & Graham Cook. *1½ m SW of Abersoch. Follow rd through Abersoch & Sarn Bach, L at sign for Bwlchtocyn for ½ m until junction and no-through rd - Cim Farm. Turn R, parking 50metres on R.* Cream teas. **Adm £2.50, chd free. Sun 15 June (11-4).**
2-acre plot incl 1 acre fenced against rabbits, developed from 2000. Incl island beds, windbreak hedges and wide range of geraniums, shrubs and herbaceous perennials. Views over Cardigan Bay and Snowdonia. Grass and gravel paths, some gentle slopes.

♿ ✂ ☕ ✿

22 ◆ CRUG FARM
Caernarfon LL55 1TU. Mr & Mrs B Wynn-Jones, 01248 670232, www.crug-farm.co.uk. *2m NE of Caernarfon. ¼ m off main A487 Caernarfon to Bangor rd. Follow signs from roundabout.* **Adm £3, chd free.** Nursery Thurs to Suns and Bank Hols 24 Feb to 30 Jun; Thurs to Sats July/Aug/Sept (10-5). For NGS: Sun 25 May (10-5).
3 acres; grounds to old country house (not open). Gardens filled with choice, unusual collections of plants. Collected by the Wynn Jones, winners of the Sir Bryner Jones Memorial Award for their contribution to horticulture. Featured on Radio 4. No wheelchair access to mound or WC.

♿ ✂ ✿ ☕

Scented walled garden, with chamomile lawn . . . extensive organic kitchen garden . . .

23 CWM PIBAU
New Moat SA63 4RE. Mrs Duncan Drew, 01437 532454. *10m NE of Haverfordwest. 3m SW of Maenclochog. Off A40, take B4313 to Maenclochog, follow signs to New Moat, pass church, then 2nd concealed drive on L, ½ m rural drive.* **Adm £3, chd free. Visitors welcome by appt.**
5-acre woodland garden surrounded by old deciduous woodland and streams. Created in 1978, contains many mature, unusual shrubs and trees from Chile, New Zealand and Europe, set on S-facing sloping hill. More conventional planting nearer house.

☎

24 DELACORSE
Laugharne SA33 4QP. Annie Hart, 01994 427728. *13m SW of Carmarthen. On A4066 from St Clears, after Cross Inn turn L signed to Ant's Hill Caravan Park, continue ½ m. Access to garden further ½ m on bumpy track with traffic controls. Parking in field. Alternatively, on foot from Laugharne, 20 mins walk along footpath up-river from Dylan Thomas Boathouse Museum.* Light refreshments & teas. **Adm £2.50, chd free (share to Stroke Association). Sun 13 July (11-5). Visitors also welcome by appt May to Sept, for groups of 10+.**
3-acre garden beside Tâf Estuary, in peaceful, beautiful landscape with fine views. Scented walled garden, with chamomile lawn; sheltered courtyard with exotics; mixed borders providing all-yr interest; lawns and informal pond areas, with living willow work, merging into woodland, reed beds and salt marsh. Extensive organic kitchen garden.

♿ ✿ ☕ ☎

25 DYFFRYN
Pennant, Llanon SY23 5PB. Mrs Jo Richards. *15m S of Aberystwyth on A487. From N through Llanon, L at Old Bakery, then 2nd L. From S through Aberarth, R uphill to Pennant, A4577. Follow signs.* Light refreshments & teas. **Adm £2.50, chd free. Sat 24, Sun 25 May (11-5).**
²⁄₃ -acre garden now 28yrs old has matured into a W Wales rainforest with many mature trees and shrubs. Rooms with paving, water features and oriental touches - bamboos and grasses. Abundant birdlife and plenty of seats in different areas. BBQ and soup. Guide dogs permitted.

♿ ✂ ✿ ☕

26 DYFFRYN FARM
Lampeter Velfrey, Narberth SA67 8UN. Dr & Mrs M J R Polson, Mr & Mrs D Bradley, 01834 861684, sally.polson@virgin.net. *3m E of Narberth. From junction of A40 & A478 follow signs for crematorium, continue down into Llanmill. Then uphill, at brow turn L at Bryn Sion Chapel Xrds (before Lampeter Velfrey). After ½ m rd turns R under railway bridge. Dyffryn Farm straight ahead, parking under bridge and immed on R.* Home-made teas. **Adm £2.50, chd free (share to Paul Sartori Foundation). Sun 25 May; Wed 13 Aug (11-4). Visitors also welcome by appt, £3 per person, coaches permitted.**
Large garden, in several areas on different levels, in 'naturalised' manner (not landscaped or contrived) using secluded valley backcloth. Highlights incl 70+ bamboos; grasses, herbaceous plants, unusual shrubs; stream, pond with island and small woodland; all in relaxed style with 'hidden' havens. Supervised children very welcome. Bric-a-brac stall.

✿ ☕ ☎

27 ◆ DYFFRYN FERNANT
Llanychaer, Fishguard SA65 9SP. Christina Shand & David Allum, 01348 811282, www.genuslocus.net. *3m E of Fishguard, then ¹/₂ m inland. A487 Fishguard to Cardigan. After approx 3m, at end of long straight hill, turn R signed Llanychaer with blue rd signs 'unsuitable for long vehicles'. After exactly ¹/₂ m is Dyffryn track, on L behind LH bend, with wooden sign.* **Adm £3.50, chd free. Opening days and times vary; please phone or visit website for details. For NGS: Sun 3 Aug (10-5).**
The just-tamed meets the decidedly wild with a touch of the tropics in this adventurous 6-acre garden, making the most of dramatic landscape. Choice plants designed to be appreciated in contrasted areas. Lush bog garden, intriguing sculptures, obelisk, jungly courtyard, fernery, large pond, new grasses garden. Featured in 'The English Garden', 'Country Homes & Interiors' and 'Gardening Which?' Starred garden in 'GGG'.

28 ESGAIRWEDDAN
Pennal SY20 9JZ. Mr & Mrs John & Annie Parry. *4m W of Machynlleth. From Machynlleth take A493 towards Aberdovey. Esgairweddan is on R between Pennal & Cwrt.* Home-made teas. **Adm £2.50, chd free. Sun 15 June (2-5).**
Small garden with 400yr-old farmhouse (not open), ³/₄ m drive from rd entrance leading through oak woodland with wonderful view of Dovey estuary.

29 FELIN Y FFRIDD
Ffriddgate SY20 8QG. Mr & Mrs J W Osselton, 01654 702548. *1m N of Machynlleth. From S, take A487 from Machynlleth to Dolgellau. After approx 1m turn R at B4404 to Llanwrin. Garden short distance on L before bridge. From N, take A487, turn L on B4404.* Cream teas. **Adm £2.50, chd free. Sun 18 May (2-5.30). Visitors also welcome by appt.**
Approx 1 acre, bordered by R Dulas. Lower garden has pond, gravel paths and old mill where woodland edge is being developed. Upper garden has grass paths, mixed borders and island beds, where conifers and viburnums contrast with colourful, scented azaleas and rhododendrons. Wide choice of home-grown plants for sale.

30 FFYNONE
Boncath SA37 0HQ. Earl & Countess Lloyd George of Dwyfor, 01239 841610. *9m SE of Cardigan. 7m W of Newcastle Emlyn. From Newcastle Emlyn take A484 to Cenarth, turn L on B4332, turn L again at Xrds just before Newchapel.* Home-made teas. **Adm £3, chd free. Sun 11 May (1-5). Visitors also welcome by appt.**
Large woodland garden designated Grade I on Cadw register of historic gardens in Wales. Lovely views, fine mature specimen trees; formal garden nr house with massive yew topiary; rhododendrons, azaleas, woodland walks. House (also Grade I) by John Nash (1793), not open. Later additions and garden terraces by F Inigo Thomas c1904. Steep paths, limited wheelchair access.

An intriguing walk with various shade plants . . .

31 FOXBRUSH
Felinheli LL56 4JZ. Mr & Mrs B S Osborne, 01248 670463. *3m SW of Bangor. On Bangor to Caernarfon rd, entering village opp Felinheli signpost.* Cream teas. **Adm £2, chd free. Weds 14 May; 4 June (3-8). Visitors also welcome by appt March to end June for 2+, coaches permitted.**
Fascinating 3-acre country garden created around winding river; ponds and small wooded area. Rare and interesting plant collections incl rhododendrons, ferns, clematis and roses; 45ft long pergola; fan-shaped knot garden. Truly a wildlife garden, planted in a very natural style following horrendous devastation caused by floods of 2004.

32 ◆ GARDD Y COLEG
Carmel LL54 7RL. Pwyllgor Pentref Carmel Village Committee. *Garden at Carmel village centre. Parking on site.* **Adm £2, chd free. For NGS: Sun 20 July (2-5).**
Approx ¹/₂ acre featuring raised beds planted with ornamental and native plants mulched with local slate. Benches and picnic area, wide pathways suitable for wheelchairs. Spectacular views. Garden created by volunteers.

33 GERALLT
Bro Allt y Graig SA46 0DU. Huw & Dilys Lewis, 01545 570 591, dilysjlewis@btinternet.com. *Off A482 Aberaeron - Lampeter rd. Turn at D & L Davies Garage. Entry at first bend where road divides. Please park at Memorial Hall on A482 in Aberaeron.* Cream teas. **Adm £3, chd free. Sun 6 July (11-5). Visitors also welcome by appt.**
Mature 1920s bungalow garden containing a large variety of shrubs, lavenders and roses such as 'Chapeau de Napoleon'. Sections include a pond-side area with gunnera and bamboo, a slate bed, woodland glade and a herb plot with a wide variety of herbs both culinary and medicinal. West Wales Herb Group demonstration. Some gravel paths, steep slopes & narrow paths.

34 GILFACH
Rowen LL32 8TS. James & Isoline Greenhalgh, 01492 650216. *4m S of Conwy. At Xrds 100yds E of Rowen S towards Llanrwst, past Rowen School on L; turn up 2nd drive on L.* Home-made teas. **Adm £2, chd free. Suns 4 May; 15 June; 17 Aug (2-5.30). Visitors also welcome by appt.**
1-acre country garden on S-facing slope with magnificent views of the R Conwy and mountains; set in 35 acres of farm and woodland. Collection of mature shrubs is added to yearly; woodland garden, herbaceous border, small scree bed and pool. Some slopes and steps but wheelchair access available to main features and viewpoints.

35 GLANDWR
Pentrecwrt, Llandysul SA44 5DA. Mrs Jo Hicks, 01559 363729. *15m N of Carmarthen, 2m S of Llandysul, 7m E of Newcastle Emlyn. On A486. At Pentrecwrt village, take minor rd opp Black Horse PH. After bridge keep L for ¹/₄ m. Glandwr is on R.* Cream teas. **Adm £2.50, chd free. Sat 28, Sun 29 June (11-5). Also open Cilgwyn Bach Farm** (³/₄ m). **Visitors also welcome by appt.**
Delightful 1-acre cottage garden, bordered by a natural stream, with colour-themed areas and rockery. Mature natural woodland provides an intriguing walk with various shade plants, ground covers, shrubs and many surprises.

36 GLANGWILI LODGES

Llanllawddog SA32 7JE. Chris & Christine Blower. *7m NE of Carmarthen. Take A485 from Carmarthen. 1/4 m after Stag & Pheasant PH in Pontarsais turn R for Llanllawddog and Brechfa. 1/2 m after Llanllawddog Chapel, rd bears sharply R, Glangwili Lodges 100yds on R.* Home-made teas. **Adm £3, chd free. Sun 13 (11-4), Wed 16 July (1-5).** 16 acres incl 1-acre walled garden, former nursery to Glangwili Mansion. Restoration initiated 6yrs ago. Borders with colourful perennials and cottage-style beds. Rockery, alpines, water features, koi pond; collections of maples and unusual trees; wild flower area. Woodland stream walks. Valley setting with superb views of Gwili Valley and Brechfa Forest.

37 GLANHELYG

Lon Helyg, Llechryd SA43 2NJ. Mike & Ann Williamson, www.glanhelyg.co.uk. *3m SE of Cardigan. From A484 Cardigan-Newcastle Emlyn, L into Lon Helyg 50yds after Llechryd sign, house at end.* Teas. **Adm £2.50, chd free. Suns 22 June; 31 Aug (12-6).** 31/2 -acre woodland, meadow and walled garden. Recently re-designed Victorian walled garden contains a large variety of plants, many semi-tender in prairie style planting. Art gallery. Gravel paths.

38 NEW GWYNDY

Y Fron LL54 7RE. David & Mary Lloyd-Evans. *6m S of Caernarfon. At Groeslon roundabout, approx 6m S of Caernarfon on A487. Follow signs for Groeslon, Carmel & Fron. After 2m at 30mph sign in Fron, turn L then immed R up track for 1/4 m. Parking next to garden at beginning of track.* Light refreshments. **Adm £2.50, chd free. Sun 3 Aug (11-5).** Exposed 11/2 -acre hillside garden (altitude 1000ft). Mainly shrubs, small trees, perennials, lawns and small vegetable garden. Totally organic with wildlife in mind. Glorious panoramic views of the Nantlle Ridge and surrounding area. Wheelchair access dependent on several previous days of dry weather as main access to garden via grass. Gently sloping.

39 GWYNDY BACH

Llandrygarn LL65 3AJ. Keith & Rosa Andrew, 01407 720651, info@keithandrew-art.com. *5m W of Llangefni. From Llangefni take B5109 towards Bodedern, cottage exactly 5m out on the L.* **Adm £2.50, chd free. Visitors welcome by appt Apr to Sept, coaches permitted.** 3/4 -acre artist's garden, set amidst rugged Anglesey landscape. Romantically planted in intimate rooms with interesting rare plants and shrubs, box and yew topiary, old roses and Japanese garden with large koi pond. National Collection of Rhapis miniature Japanese palms. Studio attached.

NCCPG

> At best in spring, although even in deep winter there is something of interest . . .

40 ◆ HOTEL MAES-Y-NEUADD

Talsarnau, nr Harlech LL47 6YA. Mr & Mrs P Jackson & Mr & Mrs P Payne, 01766 780200, maes@neuadd.com. *3m NE of Harlech. Take B4573 old Harlech rd at T-junction with A496. Hotel signed 1/4 m on L. Take small lane on L immed after sign, just before small bridge on bend. Hotel entrance & car park 1/2 m up hill, through small hamlet (tel box on L). Follow brown signs.* **Adm £2.50, chd under 12 free, concessions £2. Open daily except Christmas and New Year (10-5). For NGS: Mon 16 June; Thur 21 July (10-5).** Gardens and grounds of country house hotel, parts of which C14. Views towards Snowdon, Cardigan Bay and Lleyn Peninsula. 80 acres, meadows, woodland walks, 2 working walled gardens, unusual cultivars, cut flower borders; innovative, intensive, organic gardening methods with aesthetic appeal. Fruit and vegetables for sale. Suitable for assisted wheelchair users only. Slate & gravel paths to all vegetable gardens, gravel drive.

41 NEW KINLET

Penrallt, Llanystumdwy, Criccieth LL52 0SR. Dr William E Hughes, 01766 522596, www.mygarden.me.uk. *Off A497, 1m outside Criccieth, R into village, follow signs to Rabbit Farm. On passing church, 50yds on L is Penrallt estate of bungalows. Garden at 1st bungalow on R.* Home-made teas by prior arrangement. **Adm £3, chd free. Visitors welcome by appt all yr, max 20.** Plantsman's garden with wide range of unusual and rare plants, specialising in ferns and shade plants. Mostly on steep slope intersected by spring-lines. At best in spring, although even in deep winter there is something of interest. Detailed handout outlining plants of interest will be available. Website chronicles garden's development since 2003.

42 LLANBEDR SPRING FESTIVAL GARDENS - GWYL WANWYN LLANBEDR

LL45 2PA. *7m N of Barmouth. On A496. Signs in village. Maps and programmes in village shops.* Teas at Aber Artro Hall. **Combined adm £10 (valid 2 days), chd free. Sun 4, Mon 5 May (11-5). Gate money to NGS Sun only.** Glorious, stylish, varied spring gardens in coastal micro-climate. Festival of gardens and music. Musical events in gardens, details in Llanbedr shops and Inn. Sun 4, Mon 5 May. Group NGS ticket valid both days. Gate money to NGS Sun only.

ABER ARTRO HALL

Paul & Carolyn Morgan. *Turn R off A496 in front of Victoria Inn in Llanbedr (L if coming from Harlech). After 1m turn R at sign Cwm Nantcol & follow arrows* Arts and Crafts 1910, 5-acre garden by architect Charles Edward Bateman. Terraced borders; riverside walk; fine trees, ponds. Hillside rock and wild garden leads to ancient woodland. Kitchen garden incl fruit pergola; secret Tuscan garden; William Morris 'wallpaper' garden. Featured in 'GGG' and 'Country Life'. Partial wheelchair access, one steep slope - ask for reserved parking.

LLWYN

Mr & Mrs Rodney Payne. *Park on A496. Short walk uphill or shuttle service 11-4 on the hour* Mature 2-acre sloping garden, terrace leading down to formal lawn and pond. Mixed borders; wildlife pond, sunken garden, parterre, kitchen garden; woodland. Interesting variety of flowering trees, shrubs and plants, especially beautiful in spring.

PLAS GWYNFRYN

J D S Evans. *R off A496 in front of Victoria Inn in Llanbedr (L coming from Harlech). After $^1/_2$ m, L at sign* Spectacular 7-acre landscaped glacial rock garden. Sweeping lawns surrounded by rhododendrons, azaleas, magnolias, fine specimen trees incl taxodium, ginkgo, palms; fish pond, bamboo jungle, herbaceous borders, kitchen garden; woodland paths. Coastal and mountain scenery.

43 LLANIDAN HALL

Brynsiencyn LL61 6HJ. Mr J W Beverley, 07759 305085, beverley.family@btinternet.com. *5m E of Llanfair Pwll. From Llanfair PG (Anglesey) follow A4080 towards Brynsiencyn for 4m. Turn at/opp Groeslon PH. Continue for 1m, garden entrance on R.* Light refreshments & teas. **Adm £2.50, chd free (share to CAFOD). Sats 21, 28 June (10-4). Visitors also welcome by appt.** Walled garden of 1$^3/_4$ acres. Physic and herb gardens, ornamental vegetable garden, herbaceous borders, water features and many varieties of old roses. Sheep, ponies, rabbits and hens to see. Children must be kept under supervision. Llanidan Church will be open for viewing. Gravel paths, water features.

44 LLANLLYR

Talsarn SA48 8QB. Mr & Mrs Robert Gee, 01570 470900. *6m NW of Lampeter. On B4337 to Llanrhystud.* Home-made teas. **Adm £3.50, chd under 12 free. Sun 15 June (2-6). Visitors also welcome by appt.** Large early C19 garden on site of medieval nunnery, renovated & replanted since 1989. Large pool, bog garden, formal water garden, rose & shrub borders, gravel gardens,

laburnum arbour, allegorical labyrinth and mount, all exhibiting fine plantsmanship. Yr-round appeal, interesting & unusual plants. Gravel paths.

45 LLWYN CYLL

Trap SA19 6TR. Liz & John Smith, 01558 822398, liz-johntrap@amserve.com. *3m SE of Llandeilo. In Trap turn towards Glanaman & Llandybie (at The Cenan Arms). Llwyn Cyll is $^1/_2$ m on L adjoining Llwyn Onn. Parking limited.* **Evening Opening** £2.50, chd £1, wine, Fri 16 May (4.30-8). **Visitors also welcome by appt almost daily mid Apr to mid Sept. If possible please ring to avoid disappointment.** 3$^1/_2$ -acre country garden of yr-round interest. Abundant, colourful terraced and walled borders, orchard, vegetable garden. Sun and shade areas with sympathetic planting. A plantsman's garden with many rarities and specimen trees. Up to 40 different magnolias in the arboretum, many in flower late Apr to early June. Featured in 'Garden News'.

Breeding waterfowl with many ducklings throughout spring . . .

46 LLWYNCELYN

Glandyfi SY20 8SS. Mr & Mrs Stewart Neal, 01654 781203, joyneal@btinternet.com. *12m N of Aberystwyth. On A487 Machynlleth (5$^1/_2$ m). From Aberystwyth, turn R just before Glandyfi sign.* Home-made teas. **Adm £3.50, chd free combined with Mill House. Sun 4 May (11-6). Visitors also welcome by appt, individuals & coaches.** 8-acre woodland hillside garden/arboretum alongside Dyfi tributary. Collections of hybrid/species rhododendrons flowering Christmas-Aug. Mollis azaleas in many shades, bluebells in ancient oak wood. Rare species and hybrid hydrangeas. Large fernery, many overseas taxa added to natives. Formal garden contains terrace, parterre and potager. Large plant sale.

47 LLWYNGARREG

Llanfallteg SA34 0XH. Paul & Liz O'Neill, 01994 240717, lizpaulfarm@yahoo.co.uk. *19m W of Carmarthen. A40 W from Carmarthen, turn R at Llandewi Velfrey to Llanfallteg. Go through village, garden $^1/_2$ m further on, 2nd farm on R.* Home-made teas. **Adm £3, chd free. Suns 11 May; 29 June; 14 Sept (2-6). Visitors also welcome by appt.** 3-acre plantsman's garden with many trees. Bog garden, woodland gardens, long borders, peat beds, gravel garden, vegetable plot, several ponds. Rhododendrons, magnolias, meconopsis, acers. Primulas and massed grasses among many unusual plantings. Beautiful even in the rain! Several deep water features. Young children must be closely supervised.

48 NEW LLYN RHAEADR

Parc Bron-y-Graig, Centre of Harlech LL46 2SR. Mr D R Hewitt & Miss J Sharp, 01766 780224. *From A496 take B4573 into Harlech, take turning to main car parks S of town, L past overspill car park, garden 75yds on R.* **Adm £2.50, chd free (share to WWF). Sun 10 Aug (10-5). Visitors also welcome by appt (because of breeding waterfowl, limited to groups of 10 on conducted pm tours).** Developing 2-acre landscaped garden originally part of Bron-y-Graig (estate garden) with remaining original 6 stone seats, small lake for 20 species of waterfowl, fish pond, waterfalls, rockeries, lawns, borders, woodland, ferns, heathers and wild flowers. Views of Cardigan Bay. Breeding waterfowl with many ducklings throughout spring and summer. Car park, toilets and refreshments all within 200yds in Harlech.

49 LLYS ARTHUR

Llanuwchllyn, nr Bala LL23 7UG. Mr & Mrs E Morgan, 01678 540233. *On A494, on Dolgellau side of Llanuwchllyn, opp Penial Chapel, over bridge, 1st house on L.* **Visitors welcome by appt June to Sept, coaches and groups welcome.** Nestled in foothills of Aran range, approx 1 acre of garden with herbaceous borders, grassy paths, ponds, hidden statues, secret corners and vegetable garden. Lots of seating areas and many different plants making an interesting place for visitors morning, afternoon or evening.

🏃 ☎

50 LLYS-Y-GWYNT
Pentir Road, Llandygai LL57 4BG. **Jennifer Rickards & John Evans, 01248 353863.** *3m S of Bangor. 300yds from Llandygai roundabout at J11 of A5 & A55, just off A422. From A5 & A55 follow signs for services (Gwasanaethau) and find 'No Through Road' sign 50yds beyond. Turn R then L.* Home-made teas. **Adm £2.50, chd free. Suns 18 May; 22 June (11-4). Visitors also welcome by appt.**
Rambling 2-acre garden in harmony with and incl magnificent views of Snowdonia. Incorporating large Bronze Age cairn. Designed to wander, with paths to provide shelter and interest. The exposed site planted for wind tolerance, yr-round colour and wildlife. Pond, waterfall and N-facing rockery. Good family garden.

♿ 🏃 ⊕ ☕ ☎

51 MAENAN HALL
Maenan, Llanrwst LL26 0UL. **The Hon Mr & Mrs Christopher Mclaren.** *2m N of Llanrwst. On E side of A470, ¼ m S of Maenan Abbey Hotel.* Home-made teas. **Adm £3.50, chd £2.50. Sun 27 Apr (10.30-5.30).**
About 4 hectares of ground, some steeply sloping, with mature hardwoods; upper part has many ornamental trees, shrubs and roses, walled garden, borders and lawns, all with lovely views over Conwy valley and Snowdonia foothills. Rhododendrons, camellias, magnolias, pieris and hydrangeas predominate in woodland dell. Many of the original plants are from Bodnant. Partial wheelchair access, though not to dell. Some slopes.

♿ ⊕ ☕

Unexpected, secluded country garden, a relaxing oasis . . .

52 MAESQUARRE
Bethlehem Road, Llandeilo SA19 6YA. **Mr & Mrs Geoffrey Williams, 01558 822960.** *1½ m E of Llandeilo. From Llandeilo take A483 across R Towy. At Ffairfach mini roundabout turn L along unclassified Bethlehem Rd, garden on R after 2m. Parking nearby.* **Adm £2.50, chd free. Sun 4 May to Tue 6 May & Thur 8 May to Sat 10 May (2-6). Evening Opening,** light refreshments, Wed 7 May (5-8). **Visitors also welcome by appt.**
Spacious and peaceful garden attempting to combine the owners' interest in unusual shrubs and trees and local flora and fauna. Large closely-planted pond area, slopes of developing and maturing shrubs and trees, natural woodland, with an attractive stream flowing throughout, form the main features of the garden. Spinning demonstration on 6 May. Large pond, children must be supervised.

🏃 ⊕ ☕ ☎

53 NEW MEAD LODGE
Imble Lane, Pembroke Dock SA72 6PN. **John & Eileen Seal.** *From A4139 between Pembroke and Pembroke Dock take B4322 signed Pennar and Leisure Centre. After ½ m turn L into Imble Lane. Mead Lodge at end.* **Adm £2.50, chd free (share to Paul Sartori Foundation). Fri 25 July to Mon 28 July incl (11-5).**
Unexpected, secluded country garden, a relaxing oasis on S-facing slope overlooking the R Pembroke estuary. Varied ¾ -acre garden reflects the owners' keen interest in ferns, grasses and herbs. Incl terraces with Chinese and Mediterranean influences, colour-themed beds, small arboretum, fernery and vegetable garden. Readings of garden-related poetry and prose on some days.

⊕ ☕

54 MEGANS WOOD GWERNOER FARM
Nantlle LL54 6BB. **Mrs Black, 01286 880913.** *2m E of Penygroes. On B4418 Penygroes to Rhyd-Ddu rd, past big house on L, 1st house on R over cattle grid. Halfway between Talysarn & Nantlle.* Light refreshments & teas. **Adm £2.50, chd free. Sat 10, Sun 11 May (11-4). Visitors also**

welcome by appt in May.
3-acre woodland garden set on steep hillside. Panoramic views of the Nantlle valley and Snowdon. Woodland underplanted with over 1000 rhododendrons, azaleas and camellias. Ornamental pond and waterfall on site of mines. 2 new gardens created in 2007. The first a memorial to Megan's husband, Reg, who had the vision to see the potential for turning a waste copper mine site into the garden we see today. The second a kitchen garden with greenhouse, fruit trees, vegetables and shrubs.

🏃 ⊕ ☕ ☎

55 THE MILL HOUSE
Glandyfi SY20 8SS. **Professor & Mrs J M Pollock.** *Entrance at Llwyncelyn.* **Adm £3.50, chd free, combined with Llwyncelyn. Sun 4 May (11-6).**
Picturesque garden of a former water mill with millstream, millpond, and several waterfalls in woodland setting, about 1½ acres. Azaleas, rhododendrons and spring colour enhance waterside vistas, which have a Japanese theme.

🏃

56 MILLINFORD
Millin Cross SA62 4AL. **Drs B & A Barton, 01437 762394.** *3m E of Haverfordwest. From Haverfordwest on A40 to Carmarthen, turn R signed The Rhos, take turning to Millin. Turn R at Millin Chapel then immed L over river bridge.* **Adm £3. Visitors welcome by appt.**
Spacious, undulating and peaceful garden of 4 acres on bank of Millin Creek. Varied collection of over 125 different trees, many unusual, plus shrubs, herbaceous plants and bulbs in beautiful riverside setting. Impressive terracing and water features. Visit in spring, summer and early autumn. Two ponds, children must be supervised.

🏃 ☕ ☎

57 MOORLAND COTTAGE PLANTS
Rhyd-y-Groes, Brynberian SA41 3TT. **Jennifer & Kevin Matthews,** www.moorlandcottageplants.co.uk. *12m SW of Cardigan. 16m NE of Haverfordwest, on B4329, ¾ m downhill from cattlegrid (from Haverfordwest) and 1m uphill from signpost to Brynberian (from Cardigan).* **Adm £1.80, chd 50p (share to Paul Sartori Foundation).**

Daily (not Weds) 17 May to 7 Sept (10.30-5.30).
Country garden located at 720ft on the wild Preseli hillside. 1/2 -acre of diverse, mollusc-proof plantings linked by meandering paths. Cottage garden borders, grasses and bamboos, shady areas with ferns. Some rarities. Gardening without pesticides or fungicides encourages abundant wildlife. Adjoining nursery (open 1 Mar to 30 Sept) specialising in hardy perennials, ornamental grasses & ferns.

✕ ❀

58 NANT-YR-ERYD
Abercych, Boncath SA37 0EU. Alan & Diana Hall. *5m SE of Cardigan, 5m W of Newcastle Emlyn. Off B4332 Cenarth to Abercych, Boncath Rd. Turn N to Abercych, through village and take L fork.* **Adm £2, chd free (share to Paul Sartori Foundation). Suns 9 Mar (11-4); 15 June (11-5).**
Charming well-maintained cottage garden of 1 acre. 50 varieties of daffodils in spring. Impressive rose display (Rosa mundii, 'Abbotswood' etc) and wild flower meadow in summer. Use of attractive outbuildings for fernery. Mature and new topiary gardens.

✕ ☕

59 NEW ◆ THE NATIONAL BOTANIC GARDEN OF WALES
Llanarthne SA32 8HG, 01558 668768,
www.gardenofwales.org.uk. *10 mins from M4. M4 W to Pont Abraham, then A48 to Cross Hands, then half way between Cross Hands and Carmarthen. Follow brown signs.* **Adm £3, chd free. Open daily, not Christmas Day. Phone or see website for details. For NGS: Evening Opening with Longest Day Musical Celebration, wine, Sat 21 June (4-9).**
More than 600 acres of elegant Regency parkland is home to this stunning young garden, the centrepiece of which is the prestigious great glasshouse. Lakeside walks, informal areas to attract wildlife as well as herbaceous borders, Japanese garden and double-walled garden. New Tropical House opened in 2007. National Lottery Awards Best Environmental Project.

♿ ✕ ❀ ☕

Ponds and lakes laced with water lilies and bog plants . . . only the hardiest of plants and shrubs survive . . .

60 NEW HALL
Bettws Bledrws SA48 8NX. Maureen & Dave Allen, 01570 493188. *3m N Lampeter, 6m S Tregaron. On A485, 100yds from church.* **Adm £3.50, chd free, combined with Oakmeadows. Sun 29 June (11-5). Visitors also welcome by appt.**
Cottage garden established in 2000 from derelict ground by keen plantswoman and her husband. Well stocked herbaceous borders incl interesting trees & shrubs, water garden and koi ponds with large gunneras and bog plants. Collection of Japanese acers.

✕ ☎

61 OAKMEADOWS AT MAESYDERI FARM
SA48 8LY. Glenda Johnson, 01570 493221. *3m N of Lampeter, 6m S of Tregaron. On A485 midway betweeen Llangybi and Bettws Bledrws, opp layby.* **Home-made teas. Adm £3.50, chd free, combined with New Hall. Sun 29 June (11-5). Visitors also welcome by appt.**
Created over the last 5yrs from rough pasture and maturing well. Designed and maintained by an enthusiastic plantswoman, containing many interesting trees, an eclectic mix of shrubs, cottage garden perennials, water & bog garden. Gravel areas with raised beds, a small woodland with shade-loving plants.

✕ ❀ ☕ ☎

62 THE OLD VICARAGE
Llangeler SA44 5EU. Mr & Mrs J C Harcourt, 01559 371168. *4m E of Newcastle Emlyn. 15m N of Carmarthen on A484. From N Emlyn turn down lane on L in Llangeler before church.* **Cream teas. Adm £2.50, chd free. Sat 28, Sun 29 June (11-6). Visitors also welcome by appt, late June & July, access for 29-seater coaches.**
A garden gem created since 1993. Less than 1 acre divided into 3 areas of roses, shrubs and a semi-formal pool with an interesting collection of unusual herbaceous plants.

✕ ❀ ☕ ☎

63 PANT-YR-HOLIAD
Rhydlewis SA44 5ST. Mr & Mrs G H Taylor. *10m NE of Cardigan. From A487 take B4334 at Brynhoffnant S towards Rhydlewis, after 1m turn L, driveway 2nd L.* **Teas. Adm £3, chd £1. Suns 4 May; 8 June (2-5).**
5 acres embracing walled garden housing tender plants, alpine beds, water features, rare trees and shrubs, with further 15 acres of woodland setting. Extensive collection rhododendron species. Home of Holiad rhododendron hybrids.

✕ ❀ ☕

64 NEW PANTYRHEDYN
Ystumtuen SY23 3AE. Denise & Brian Winter. *10m E Aberystwyth. From A44 take Ystumtuen sign midway between Llywernog and Ponterwyd, 1/2 m on R park on roadside, then 200yds up track.* **Light refreshments & teas. Adm £2.50, chd free. Suns 1 June; 31 Aug (11-5).**
6-acre wildlife garden in stunning mountain situation at 1000ft. Ponds and lakes laced with water lilies and bog plants, winding grass paths through woodland, abundant wildlife and wildflowers, plenty of seating. Only the hardiest of plants and shrubs survive the very steep slopes. Not suitable for the less able.

☕

65 PEN Y BRYN
Glandwr LL42 1TG. Phil & Jenny Martin. *On A496 7m W of Dolgellau, situated on N side of Mawddach Estuary. Park in or nr layby and walk L up narrow lane.* **Cream teas. Adm £2.50, chd free (share to Hospice at Home). Sun 11 May (11-4).**
Hidden hillside garden on different levels with range of acid-loving shrubs and enhanced natural rockeries set against breathtaking panoramic views of Cader Idris and the Mawddach Estuary. S-facing with woodland walks and rock cannon. Featured in local press.

✕ ☕

66 **PENBANC**
Llanilar SY23 4NY. Enfys & David
Rennie. *Off A487, 6m SE of
Aberystwyth. From Llanfarian take
A485 signed Tregaron for 2¹/₂ m. Turn
L into lane immed after Cwmaur
Estate. Penbanc in ¹/₂ m, overlooking
river bridge. Park in field next to river.*
Home-made teas. **Adm £3, chd free.**
Sun 22 June (2-6).
¹/₂ -acre, S-facing sloping cottage
garden alongside R Ystwyth with views
over valley. Established orchards, large
vegetable garden and densely planted
herbaceous borders created in 2005,
with masses of roses, clematis,
campanula lactiflora, hardy geraniums,
grasses and shrubs. Riverside wildlife
walk.
✗ ⊕ ☕

67 ◆ **PENRHYN CASTLE**
Bangor LL57 4HN. The National
Trust, 01248 353084,
www.nationaltrust.org.uk. *3m E of
Bangor. On A5122. Buses from
Llandudno, Caernarfon, Betws-y-
Coed; alight: Grand Lodge Gate. J11
A55, signed from thereon.* **Adm £1,
chd free. Wed to Mon, 19 Mar to 2
Nov (11-5). For NGS: Sat 2 Feb
2008; Sun 8 Feb 2009 (11-3).**
Large grounds incl Victorian walled
garden; fine trees, shrubs, wild garden,
good views. Snowdrop walks. Partial
wheelchair access, some uneven
gravel/grass paths, some steps, bark
chippings.
♿ ☕

68 ◆ **PENSYCHNANT**
Sychnant Pass, nr Conwy LL32 8BJ.
Pensychnant Foundation Wardens
Julian Thompson & Anne Mynott,
01492 592595,
julian@pensychnant.fsnet.co.uk.
*2¹/₂ m W of Conwy. At top of Sychnant
Pass between Conwy &
Penmaenmawr. From Conwy turn L
into Upper Gate St by Heddlu/Police;
after 2¹/₂ m Pensychnant's drive signed
on R. From Penmaenmawr, fork R by
Mountain View PH; summit of
Sychnant Pass after walls,
Pensychnant's drive on L.* **Adm £2,
chd 50p. Open Wed to Sun, Apr to
Sept (11-5). For NGS: Sun 15 June
(11-5).**
Diverse herbaceous borders
surrounded by mature shrubs, banks
of rhododendrons, ancient and
Victorian woodlands. 12 acre
woodland walks with views of Conwy
Mountain and Sychnant. Woodland
birds. Picnic tables, archaeological trail

on mountain. A peaceful little gem.
Large Victorian gothic house (open)
with art exhibition. Partial wheelchair
access, steps and steep terrain, please
phone for advice.
♿ ✗ ⊕ ☕

Large tropical glasshouse filled with beautiful and interesting exotic species . . .

69 **PERTH YR EGLWYS**
Mydroilyn, Lampeter SA48 7QX.
Elizabeth Gould & Christopher May.
*Off A 487, 4m S of Aberaeron. Turn L
at Llanarth, signed Mydroilyn. Through
village to chapel, R to school, R again
at school, 300yds.* Home-made teas.
**Adm £3, chd free. Sun 18 May
(11-5).**
3-acre well-established arboretum and
garden with many unusual trees and
shrubs. Streamside walks, extensive
bog gardens with large areas of
candelabra primulas, pulmonarias,
irises, various ferns, bluebell banks.
Rhododendrons, azaleas, extensive
perennial borders, vegetable garden.
✗ ⊕ ☕

70 ◆ **PICTON CASTLE &
WOODLAND GARDENS**
The Rhos SA62 4AS. Picton Castle
Trust, 01437 751326,
www.pictoncastle.co.uk. *3m E of
Haverfordwest. On A40 to
Carmarthen, signed off main rd.*
**Garden £4.95, chd £2.50,
concessions £4.75. House adm
additional £1, chd 50p. Daily 1 Apr
to 30 Sept, not Mons (but open
Bank Hol Mons). For NGS: Suns 1
June; 13 July (10.30-5).**
Mature 40-acre woodland garden with
unique collection of rhododendrons
and azaleas, many bred over 41yrs,
producing hybrids of great merit and
beauty; rare and tender shrubs and
trees incl magnolia, myrtle, embothrium
and eucryphia. Wild flowers abound.
Walled garden with roses; fernery;
herbaceous and climbing plants and
large clearly-labelled collection of
herbs.
♿ ⊕ ☕

71 ◆ **PLAS NEWYDD**
Anglesey LL61 6DQ. The National
Trust, 01248 714795,
www.nationaltrust.org.uk. *2m S of
Llanfairpwll. A55 junctions 7 & 8 on
A4080.* **House and garden adm £7,
chd £3.50, garden only adm £5, chd
£2.50. Sats to Weds, 1 Mar to 29
Oct (11-5.30, house 12-4.30). For
NGS: Fri 21 Mar (11-5.30).**
Gardens with massed shrubs, fine
trees, lawns sloping down to Menai
Strait. Magnificent views to
Snowdonia. Woodland walk leading to
Marine Walk. Australasian arboretum
and wild flowers. Terrace garden with
summer display and water features.
Very good area for bird-watching and
fungi in autumn. Rhododendron
garden 1 Apr to early June only. C18
house by James Wyatt contains Rex
Whistler's largest painting; also Military
Museum.
♿ ✗ ☕

72 **PLAS PENGLAIS**
SY23 3DF. University of Wales,
Aberystwyth. *NE of Aberystwyth on
A487. Entrance alongside Penglais
Lodge, opp side of rd to University
Campus. Park on campus.* Home-
made teas. **Adm £2.50, chd free. Sun
11 May (2-5).**
Sheltered garden of Georgian Mansion
surrounded by native trees and
carpeted with bluebells. Rockery,
walled terrace, pond, extensive lawns,
rhododendrons and many unusual
specimen shrubs and trees. Remains
of old Botany Dept 'order beds'. Large
tropical glasshouse filled with beautiful
and interesting exotic species.
♿ ✗ ⊕ ☕

73 **RHOSYGILWEN MANSION**
Cilgerran, Cardigan SA43 2TW. Glen
Peters & Brenda Squires, 01239
841387, www.retreat.co.uk. *5m S of
Cardigan. From Cardigan follow A478
signed Tenby. After 6m turn L at
Rhoshill towards Cilgerran. After ¹/₄ m
turn R signed Rhosygilwen. Mansion
gates ¹/₂ m.* Light refreshments & teas
(not NGS). **Adm £3, chd free. Sun 13
July (11-5).** Visitors also welcome by
appt.
20 acres of garden in 55 acre estate.
Pretty ¹/₂ m drive through woodland
planting. Spacious lightly wooded
grounds for leisurely rambling, 1-acre
walled garden fully productive of fruit,
vegetables and flowers; authentically
restored Edwardian greenhouses,
many old and new trees, small formal
garden. Gravel paths.
♿ ✗ 🛏 ☕ ☎

74 RHYD

Trefor, Anglesey LL65 4TA. Ann & Jeff Hubble, 01407 720320, jeffh43@btinternet.com. *7m W of Llangefni. Nr Holyhead. From Bodedern 2¹/₄ m along B5109 towards Llangefni, turn L.* Home-made teas. **Adm £2.50, chd free. Suns 25 May; 20 July (11-5). Visitors also welcome by appt Apr to Sept, coaches permitted.**
5 acres of gardens, arboretum, meadows and nature reserve. Herbaceous beds, pergolas, ponds, stream, rockery, garden room and (new 2005) decking and fernery. Many species of roses, climbing and standard. Clematis and rhododendron. Wide variety of herbaceous plants especially hosta and primula. Many places to sit and ponder or watch the wildlife.
♿ ✗ ❀ ☕ ☎

75 ROSEWOOD

Redberth, nr Tenby SA70 8SA. Mr & Mrs K Treadaway. *3m SW of Kilgetty. On old A477, now bypassed, 80yds from centre of village, on W side. Coming from W, turn for Sageston and almost immed R towards Redberth. First cottage after village boundary sign. From E, turn for Redberth and continue along old A447, second cottage after village turn. Ample parking on roadside.* **Adm £2.50, chd free (share to Paul Sartori Foundation). Suns 4 May; 13 July (2-6).**
Intimate and well-maintained ¹/₄ -acre garden, cleverly designed in different areas, with abundant, colourful mixed plantings incl scattered exotic species and a National Collection of clematis (subgenus viorna) plus many other clematis in bloom all yr, but especially in summer.
✗ ❀

76 ST JOHN THE BAPTIST & ST GEORGE

Lon Batus, Carmel LL54 7AR. Bishop Abbot Demetrius. *7m SE of Caernarfon. On A487 Porthmadog Rd, at Dinas roundabout exit 1st L to Groeslon, turn L at PO for 1¹/₂ m. At village centre turn L & L again at Xrds.* Teas. **Adm £1, chd free. Fri 25 July (2-5).**
Holy community in the making under the authority of The Orthodox Catholic and Holy Synod of Malan. This is not a garden in the traditional sense but a spiritual retreat from the stresses and strains of modern life, surrounded on all sides by space and rural tranquillity. We are privileged to share a glimpse of a more contemplative life.
✗ ☕

77 NEW STRADEY CASTLE GARDENS

Llanelli SA15 4PL. Sir David Mansel Lewis. *1m NW of Llanelli town centre. Entrance approx ³/₄ m from Furnace off B4308 Furnace to Kidwelly rd.* **Adm £4, chd free. Suns 18 May; 28 Sept (2-5.30).**
Enjoy a rural oasis and stroll in the extensive grounds of the mid-C19 mansion. Formal parterre, pond and herbaceous borders enhance the immediate house surrounds. The 'Wilderness' garden, with many fine shrubs and trees, has been restored and developed within the curtilage of the former C17 house. Wheelchair access along lengthy drive and in 'Wilderness' garden. Children must be supervised.
♿ ✗ ☕

Half-acre walled garden with double rill, pergola and statuary . . .

78 TAN DINAS

Llanfairpwll, Anglesey LL61 5YL. Charles Ellis, 01248 714373, charles.ellis@tesco.net. *2m W of Menai Bridge. On main rd between Llanfairpwll & Britannia Bridge, 250yds from the Marquess of Anglesey's Column. Parking in Column car park, access via path through Column woods. Visitors, cars can unload but not park at garden.* **Adm £2, chd free. Visitors welcome by appt May, June, July.**
An interesting 1¹/₂ -acre cottage garden. Overlooked by the Marquess of Anglesey's Column, 200yds from the Menai Straits. Carefully designed and planted on 3 levels; shrubbery, large pond garden, vegetable and fruit areas, heather garden. Careful planting ensures all-yr colour. Many interesting trees and shrubs are now reaching maturity.
✗ ❀ ☎

79 TRADEWINDS

Ffynnonwen, Penybont, Carmarthen SA33 6PX. Stuart Kemp-Gee & Eve Etheridge, 01994 484744, ffynnonwen@hotmail.com. *10m NW of Carmarthen. A40 W from Carmarthen approx 4m, then turn R onto B4298 to Meidrim. In Meidrim R onto B4299 to Trelech. After approx 5¹/₂ m turn R at Tradewinds sign, then approx ¹/₂ m, next to 2nd farm.* Light refreshments & teas. **Adm £3, chd free. Sat 14, Sun 15 June; Sat 13 Sept, Sun 14 Sept (11-5). Evening Opening, wine, Fri 22 Aug (4.30-8). Visitors also welcome by appt.**
1¹/₂ -acre plantsman's garden with abundance of herbaceous perennials, shrubs and trees giving yr-round interest for the discerning gardener. Incl liquidambars, Aralia elata 'Variegata' and Trochodendron. Mixed borders, natural streams and natural pond. 2 acres being developed into an arboretum and herbaceous borders. Picturesque garden in tranquil setting.
✗ ❀ ☕ ☎

80 NEW TREFFGARNE HALL

Treffgarne, Haverfordwest SA62 5PJ. Mr & Mrs Batty, 01437 741115. *7m N of Haverfordwest, signed off A40. Proceed up through village and follow rd round sharply to L, Hall ¹/₄ m further on L.* **Adm £3, chd free (share to Paul Sartori Foundation). Suns 4 May; 7 Sept (10-4). Visitors also welcome by appt.**
4-acre garden under development since 1993. Thriving in splendid hilltop location, substantial collection of exotics incl echiums, proteas, michelias, acacias, salvias and palms in superbly landscaped ¹/₂ -acre walled garden with double rill, pergola and statuary. Broadwalk with long border, rockery and gravel garden. Several smaller planting schemes.
❀ ☕ ☎

81 TREFFOS SCHOOL

Llansadwrn, Anglesey LL59 5SL. Dr & Mrs Humphreys. *2¹/₂ m N of Menai Bridge. A5025 Amlwch/Benllech exit from the Britannia Bridge onto Anglesey. Approx 3m turn R towards Llansadwrn. Entrance to Treffos School is 200yds on LH-side.* Cream teas. **Adm £2.50, chd free. Sun 11 May (12-2.30).**

7 acres, child-friendly garden, in rural location, surrounding C17 house now run as school. Garden consists of mature woodland, underplanted with spring flowering bulbs and rhododendrons, ancient beech avenue leading down to rockery, herbaceous borders and courtyards.

 & ⚔ ❀ ☕

Hostas, lilies and meconopsis blend together in small bluebell wood . . .

82 **TY CAPEL FFRWD**
Llanfachreth LL40 2NR. Revs Mary & George Bolt, 01341 422006. *4m NE of Dolgellau, 18m SW of Bala. From A470 nr Dolgellau take A497 towards Bala. Turn L after 200yds signed Dolgellau. 1st R signed Llanfachreth, 4m. Uphill to village, L at T-junction, past war memorial on L, 1/2 m. Park nr chapel, walk 30yds downhill to garden. No parking beside cottage. From S via Trawsfynydd, go through Ganllwyd, 1st L after signpost Llanfachreth. Follow NGS signs.* Cream teas. **Adm £2.50, chd free.** **Sun 1 June; Sun 17 Aug (11-5). Visitors also welcome by appt.**
1-acre cottage garden, started from nothing, still being created. A stream, the ffrwd, runs through garden and flowers and azaleas fill the bank with colour in spring. Wide collection of plants, many unusual. Trees blend into surrounding countryside. Mature roses incl climbers. Hostas, lilies and meconopsis blend together in small bluebell wood. Fuchsias and lilies fill large pots on patio where home-made teas can be enjoyed beside stream. Some steep paths.

❀ ☕ ☎

83 ◆ **TY GLYN WALLED GARDEN**
Ciliau Aeron SA48 8DE. Ty Glyn Davis Trust, 01970 832268. *3m SW of Aberaeron. Turn off A482 Aberaeron to Lampeter at Ciliau Aeron signed to Pennant. Entrance 700metres on L.* **Adm £2.50, chd free. For NGS: Sun 27 July (11-5).**
Secluded L-shaped walled garden in beautiful woodland setting alongside R

Aeron, developed specifically for special needs children. S-facing productive terraced kitchen garden overlooks herbaceous borders, orchard and ponds with child orientated features and surprises amidst unusual shrubs and perennials. Newly planted fruit trees selected from former gardener's notebook of C19.

 & ⚔ ❀ ☎

84 **TY NEWYDD**
Dyffryn Ardudwy LL44 2DB. Guy & Margaret Lloyd, 01341 247357, guylloyd@btinternet.com. *51/2 m N of Barmouth, 41/2 m S of Harlech. A496 Barmouth to Harlech rd, 1/2 m N of Dyffryn Ardudwy, area sometimes referred to as Coed Ystumgwern. At bus shelter and phone box turn down lane towards sea, driveway 30yds on L.* Home-made teas. **Adm £2.50, chd free. Sun 1 June (10-5). Visitors also welcome by appt all yr. Access for coaches difficult.**
31/2 acres of maritime garden and pasture, diversely planted with trees and shrubs for yr-round interest. Some areas still being developed. Extensive vegetable and fruit areas. Greenhouse and polytunnel for overwintering tender subjects, propagation, spring/summer bedding and summer salads. Interesting plant sales area.

⚔ ❀ ☕ ☎

85 **NEW** ◆ **TYN Y CEFN**
Llanuwchllyn LL23 7UH. Trevor and Diane Beech, 01678 540551. *6m W of Bala. From Bala take A494 towards Dolgellau. Small lane on L approx 21/2 m from Llanuwchllyn. From Dolgellau take A494 towards Bala. Small lane on R approx 4m from turn to Drws y Nant.* Light refreshments & teas. **Adm £2.50, chd free (share to The Andrew McCartney Trust Fund (for brain tumour research). Suns 8 June; 3 Aug (12-5). Visitors also welcome by appt June to Aug incl, no access for coaches.**
1-acre very exposed sloping meadow garden at foot of the Aran with panoramic views. Features sheltered, enclosed garden for tender plants and trees. Wildlife area incl 2 ponds and developing woodland area to attract birds. Mature shrub beds and feature trees incl majestic eucalyptus. Steep slopes and unfenced ponds.

❀ ☕ ☎

86 **TYN-TWLL**
LL40 2DP. Sue & Pete Nicholls. *11/2 m NE of Llanfachreth. From Dolgellau on Bala rd (A494), 1st L to Llanfachreth opp Brithdir sign. Continue up hill, 1st R then 1st L and follow signs to Tyn Twll.* Cream teas and light refreshments. **Adm £2.50, chd free. Sun 27 July (10-5).**
Created by 2 artists, Tyn Twll is set in 21/2 acres of ancient woodland with imaginative architectural features using local materials. Traditional planting, rockeries, walled fruit and vegetable garden, short woodland walk and pond area in sheltered setting, providing a haven for wildlife. Some uneven ground and sloping slate paths.

 & ❀ ☕

87 **NEW** ◆ **UPTON CASTLE GARDENS**
Cosheston, Pembroke Dock SA72 4SE. Prue & Stephen Barlow, 01646 689996, prue@uptoncastle.com. *4m E of Pembroke Dock. 2m N of A477 between Carew and Pembroke Dock. Follow brown signs through Cosheston.* **Adm £3, chd £1.50, family £7. Tues to Suns, Apr to Oct (10-4.30), also Mons in Aug and Bank Hols. For NGS: Sun 27 Apr (10-4.30).**
35 acres of mature gardens and arboretum with many unusual camellias, magnolias, rhododendrons and other trees and shrubs incl a 50yr-old Davidia (handkerchief tree). Formal rose gardens, herbaceous borders, Victorian kitchen garden (now being restored), woodland walk to the estuary and C13 chapel. Limited wheelchair access, disabled may be dropped at ho use.

 & ☕

88 **WEIR CASTLE**
Treffgarne, Wolfscastle SA62 5LR. D J & D C Morris, 01437 741252. *On A40 between Haverfordwest and Fishguard. Approx 5m from Haverfordwest (before Wolfscastle). Just past signs for Treffgarne and Angling Centre, turn L up drive.* **Adm £2.50, chd free (share to Paul Sartori Foundation). Sats, Suns: 29, 30 Mar; 12, 13 Apr; 24, 25 May; 21, 22 June; 12, 13 July; Sat, Sun, Mon 9, 10, 11 Aug (11-5). Visitors also welcome by appt.**

(The grounds of a farmhouse, not actually a castle.) Fairly steep hillside, richly planted with well-chosen shrubs and perennials, with attractive features and lovely views. The result of flair and imagination and brilliant use of a difficult site.

89 WINLLAN WILDLIFE GARDEN
Talsarn SA48 8QE. Mr & Mrs Ian Callan, 01570 470612. *8m NNW of Lampeter. On B4342, Talsarn-Llangeitho rd.* **Adm £3, chd free. Visitors welcome by appt daily, Sun 15 June to Mon 30 June (2-5).**
6-acre wildlife garden owned by botanists happy to share their knowledge with visitors. Garden includes a large pond, small woodland, 600yds of riverbank walk and a 4-acre hay meadow with over 10,000 wild orchids incl the rare greater butterfly orchid.

4-acre hay meadow with over 10,000 wild orchids including the rare greater butterfly orchid . . .

90 Y FELIN
Aberdaron Road, Sarn Meyllteyrn, Llyn Peninsula LL53 8HF. Betty & Ian Wood, 01758 730794, d.i.wood@btinternet.com. *10m W of Pwllheli. On B4413 close to seaside villages of Abersoch, Nefyn and Aberdaron on Llyn Peninsula. Travelling W towards Aberdaron, 50yds from centre of Sarn, The Mill House Restaurant is on R. Gates to garden at far end of restaurant car park. Limited parking here after 2pm, otherwise park in village.* Home-made teas. **Adm £2.50, chd free (share to Rotary Club of Pwllheli Trust Fund). Mons 26 May; 25 Aug (12-5). Visitors also welcome by appt for groups of 10+.**
2-acre garden bounded by upper reaches of R Soch. Interesting range of habitats incl bluebell wood, ponds, streamside, herbaceous borders, shrubs and vegetables. Haven for wildlife. Old millpond and working water wheel are reminders of Y Felin's past role (since around 1541) as a water mill. Children need careful supervision in view of water features. 1st Prize Best Large Garden Attracting Wildlife NW Wales. Partial wheelchair access.

Cambrian Coast County Volunteers

Gwynedd

County Organisers
North Grace Meirion-Jones, Parc Newydd, Rhosgadfan, Caernarfon LL54 7LF, 01286 831195
South Marian Osselton, Felin y Ffridd, Friddgate, Machynlleth SY20 8QG, 01654 702548

County Treasurers
North William Hughes, Kinlet, Penrallt Estate, Llanystumdwy, Criccieth LL52 0SR, 07725 891883, william@mygarden.ws
South Michael Bishton, Bronclydwr, Rhoslefain, Tywyn LL36 9LT, 01654 710882, m.bishton@btopenworld.com

Assistant County Organisers
North Hazel Bond, Cae Newydd, Rhosgoch, Amlwch, Anglesey LL66 0BG, 01407 831354, nigel@cae-newydd.co.uk
North Janet Jones, Coron, Llanbedrog, Pwllheli LL53 7NN, 01758 740296 janetjones@hotmail.co.uk
South Hilary Nurse, Bryn Gwern, Llanfachreth, Dolgellau LL40 2DH, 01341 450255

Ceredigion/Cardiganshire

County Organiser
Joy Neal, Llwyncelyn, Glandyfi, Machynlleth SY20 8SS, 01654 781203, joyneal@btinternet.com

County Treasurer
Rodney J Dyer, Robin Hill, Coed y Garth, Furnace, Machynlleth SY20 8PG, 01654 781223, jandrdyer@btinternet.com

Assistant County Organiser
Jennifer Dyer, Robin Hill, Coed y Garth, Furnace, Machynlleth SY20 8PG, 01654 781223, jandrdyer@btinternet.com
Lisa Raw-Rees, The Old Mill, Water Street, Aberaeron SA46 0DG, 01545 570107, hywelrawrees@hotmail.com

Carmarthenshire & Pembrokeshire

County Organisers
Mrs Jill Foster, Heron Cottage, Picton Ferry, The Rhos, Haverfordwest SA62 4AR, 01437 751241
Mrs Jane Stokes, Llyshendy, Llandeilo SA19 6YA, 01558 823233, ivor.t.stokes@btopenworld.com

County Treasurer
Mrs Susan Allen, Pen y coed Farm, Whitland SA34 0LR, 01994 241269

Publicity
Mrs Jo Hammond, Ashdale, Llanmill, Narberth SA67 8UE, 01834 869140
Mrs Nicky Rogers, Hayston, Merrion, Pembroke SA71 5EA, 01646 661462, haystonhouse@btinternet.com

ngs gardens open for charity

5-acre Grade 1 listed unique garden which was buried and forgotten after World War II and rediscovered in 2000. Created around 1895, the garden contains underground grottoes, tunnels and ferneries and above ground stunning water features. You will not be disappointed . . .

Dewstow Gardens and Grottoes, Devon

GLAMORGAN & GWENT

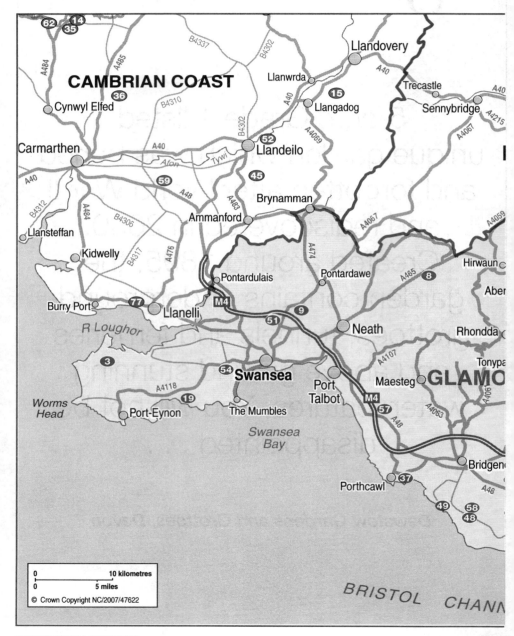

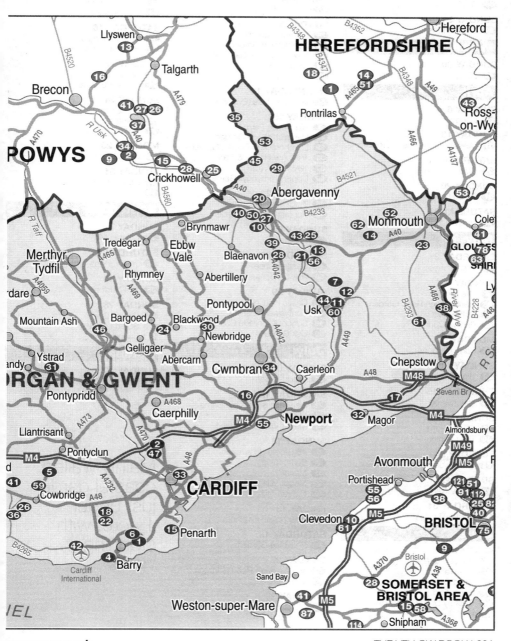

Opening Dates

February

SATURDAY 2
38 The Nurtons

SUNDAY 3
38 The Nurtons

March

SUNDAY 30
49 Slade

April

SUNDAY 6
28 Llanover

SUNDAY 13
17 Dewstow Gardens & Grottoes

SATURDAY 19
21 Glebe House

SUNDAY 20
21 Glebe House

SATURDAY 26
36 Nash Manor

May

SATURDAY 3
4 The Birches

SUNDAY 4
4 The Birches
33 Marlborough Road Gardens
39 Ochran Mill
41 Penllyn Court

MONDAY 5
1 Barry Gardens

SUNDAY 11
23 High Glanau Manor

THURSDAY 15
54 Touchwood

SUNDAY 18
38 The Nurtons
40 The Orchids

TUESDAY 20
54 Touchwood (Day & Evening)

SUNDAY 25
25 Llan-y-Nant

SATURDAY 31
56 Trostrey Lodge

June

SUNDAY 1
5 Bordervale Plants
9 Brynyrenfys
14 Coed Cefn
51 Springfield
56 Trostrey Lodge
62 Woodlands Farm

WEDNESDAY 4
44 Plas Newydd Cottage

SATURDAY 7
24 Hillcrest Bungalow

SUNDAY 8
24 Hillcrest Bungalow
26 Llanblethian Gardens
37 Newton Village Gardens
39 Ochran Mill
58 Ty Newydd

WEDNESDAY 11
61 Veddw House (Evening)

SUNDAY 15
3 Big House Farm
27 Llanfoist Village Gardens
29 Llanthony and District Gardens
55 Tredegar House & Park
57 Twyn-yr-Hydd
59 Upper Trerhyngyll Gardens

SATURDAY 21
15 77 Coleridge Avenue
42 Penmark Village Gardens

SUNDAY 22
7 Brynderi

SATURDAY 28
11 Castle House
60 Usk Gardens

SUNDAY 29
11 Castle House
46 Pontygwaith Farm
48 School & College Gardens
60 Usk Gardens

July

SUNDAY 6
20 Gardd-y-Bryn

SATURDAY 12
22 Hen Felin & Swallow Barns
31 Maendy
32 Magor Village Gardens

SUNDAY 13
6 46 Brookfield Avenue
8 Brynheulog
31 Maendy
32 Magor Village Gardens
39 Ochran Mill

FRIDAY 18
2 Beachouse (Evening)

SATURDAY 19
47 Rhiwbina Gardens

SUNDAY 27
33 Marlborough Road Gardens
53 Three Wells

TUESDAY 29
33 Marlborough Road Gardens
(Evening)

August

SUNDAY 3
1 Barry Gardens
39 Ochran Mill

SATURDAY 16
16 Croesllanfro Farm
24 Hillcrest Bungalow

SUNDAY 17
16 Croesllanfro Farm
24 Hillcrest Bungalow

SUNDAY 24
5 Bordervale Plants
12 Cefntilla
34 7 Montresor Court

MONDAY 25
12 Cefntilla

SUNDAY 31
35 Nant-y-Bedd
45 Pont Escob Mill

September

SUNDAY 7
39 Ochran Mill

SATURDAY 13
38 The Nurtons

SUNDAY 14
38 The Nurtons

SUNDAY 28
10 Castell Cwrt
50 South Lodge
52 Sunnyside

October

SUNDAY 12
17 Dewstow Gardens & Grottoes

Mainly walled coastal garden, just under 1 acre, with stunning views . . .

Gardens open to the public

- **5** Bordervale Plants
- **17** Dewstow Gardens & Grottoes
- **18** Dyffryn Gardens
- **38** The Nurtons
- **43** Penpergwm Lodge
- **54** Touchwood
- **55** Tredegar House & Park
- **57** Twyn-yr-Hydd
- **61** Veddw House

By appointment only

- **13** Clytha Park
- **19** 11 Eastcliff
- **30** Llwyn-y-Wen Farm

Also open by appointment ☎

- **1** 47 Aneurin Road, Barry Gardens
- **1** 11 Arno Road, Barry Gardens
- **2** Beachouse
- **6** 46 Brookfield Avenue
- **8** Brynheulog
- **9** Brynyrenfys
- **11** Castle House
- **15** 77 Coleridge Avenue
- **16** Croesllanfro Farm
- **23** High Glanau Manor
- **24** Hillcrest Bungalow
- **25** Stallcourt Mews, Llanblethian Gardens
- **28** Llanover
- **33** 6 Alma Road, Marlborough Road Gardens
- **39** Ochran Mill
- **46** Pontygwaith Farm
- **49** Slade
- **51** Springfield
- **52** Sunnyside

The Gardens

① BARRY GARDENS
Barry CF63 2AS. *6m SW of Cardiff. See garden entries for directions.* Home-made teas at Arno Rd & Aneurin Rd. **Combined adm £5, regret not suitable for young children. Mon 5 May; Sun 3 Aug (2-6).**
Three very different small gardens in Barry.
☕

47 ANEURIN ROAD
Dave Bryant, 01446 406667, davebryant@uk2.net. *A4050 Cardiff to Barry, take roundabout L marked Barry Docks & Sully. At 2nd roundabout turn R towards*

Barry town centre, under railway bridge and up hill towards centre. Opp YMCA turn L, then 1st R. **Visitors also welcome by appt all yr, weekends & after 6 weekdays.**
Small front garden with wide range of plants, sweet peas, dahlias, fuchsias, roses and lilies, all planted in over 300 various pots, containers and hanging baskets, which change over the seasons. 3rd place Vale of Bloom, Barry.
✗ ✿ ☎

11 ARNO ROAD
Little Coldbrook. Debbie Palmer, 01446 743642, deb.palmer@ntlworld.com. *On A4050 Cardiff to Barry, take roundabout marked Barry Docks & Sully. 2nd R into Coldbrook Rd, 2nd L into Langlands Rd, then 6th R into Norwood Cres, 1st L into Arno Rd.* **Visitors also welcome by appt.**
Plantaholic's small paradise garden. Herbaceous borders, slate scree planted with dwarf hardy geraniums. Alpine bed, ponds and fernery. Formal front garden, informally planted with perennials. Developing winter garden and late summer plants and clematis.
✗ ✿ ☎

1 NORTH WALK
Sue Hyett. *From A4050 at roundabout marked Barry & Barry College, turn L. Continue past Barry Hospital, garden by road sign for Barry College, before pedestrian crossing*
Plantsman's garden of three parts: cottage garden, hot gravel garden and difficult, unusually shaped back garden with pond designed for wildlife and mixed raised beds with oriental influences. Colourful late-flowering perennials in July and Aug.
✗ ✿

Horticultural excitement and soothing peace . . .

② BEACHOUSE
10 Clos y Bryn, Rhiwbina, Cardiff CF14 6TR. Annie Jones, 029 2065 5272, anne.c.jones@ntlworld.com. *2m N of Cardiff. From M4 J32 go S on A470. 1st L, before lights R at mini-roundabout at Deri Stores following signs for Wenallt Reservoir and Woodland (3rd L Wenallt Rd). Then 2nd L, 1st R. Disabled parking available, otherwise please use Wenallt Rd.* Light refreshments & teas. **Adm £3, chd free. Evening Opening, Fri 18 July (6-10).** Also opening with **Rhiwbina Gardens** Sat 19 July. **Visitors also welcome by appt.**
Designed in 1999 as lakeland beach with several wooden outbuildings, decks and boardwalks with views. Planted with specimen plants. Designed for all-yr interest and weather, for horticultural excitement and soothing peace. Designed by gardener/owner with MS; unusual solutions to problems encountered by the disabled. Featured in 'Garden News' and 'S Wales Echo'. Ideal for wheelchair users.
♿ ✗ ✿ ☕ ☎

③ BIG HOUSE FARM
Llanmadoc SA3 1DE. Mr & Mrs M Mead. *15m W of Swansea. M4 J47. Take A483 signed Swansea. Next roundabout R A484 signed Llanelli. 2nd roundabout L B4296 signed Gowerton. R at 1st T-lights onto B4295. 10m after Bury Green, R to Llanmadoc. Pass Britannia Inn, L at T-junction uphill past red tel box. 100 yds turn R. Honesty car park on R.* Home-made teas. **Adm £2.50, chd free. Sun 15 June (2-6).**
Mainly walled coastal garden, just under 1 acre, with stunning views. A variety of interesting plants and shrubs in mixed borders. Small Mediterranean garden and walled kitchen garden.
♿ ☕

④ THE BIRCHES
Dingle Close, Barry CF62 6QR. Paul & Peta Goodwin. *6m W of Cardiff. Into Barry from Cardiff on A4050. At 1st roundabout straight on (signed to airport), next roundabout L to Pontypridd Rd, next roundabout 2nd exit to Park Cres, next roundabout 4th exit to Park Rd. After approx ½ m bear L onto Porth Y Castell; 2nd L to Min Y Mor, 1st L Marine Drive and park. Walk 70yds down field, garden entrance through stone archway.* **Adm £3. Sat 3, Sun 4 May (2-6).**

Large coastal garden with terraces and different rooms combining hard and soft landscaping. Mediterranean retreat, palm tree area, pergola, water features. Good design, beautiful plants and easy maintenance are equally important. Described as 'stunning' by many visitors. Still developing. Adjacent nature reserve, combining woodland and wild flower meadow.

5 ◆ **BORDERVALE PLANTS**
Ystradowen, Cowbridge CF71 7SX. Mrs Claire Jenkins, 01446 774036, www.bordervale.co.uk. *8m W of Cardiff. 10 mins from M4. Take A4222 from Cowbridge. Turn R at Ystradowen postbox, then 3rd L & proceed ½ m, following brown signs. Garden on R. Parking in rd past corner. Teas 1 June only.* Adm £2.50, chd free. **Fris, Sats, Suns & Bank Hols Mar to Sept. For NGS: Suns 1 June; 24 Aug (10-5).**
Within mature woodland valley (semi-tamed), with stream and bog garden, extensive mixed borders; wild flower meadow, providing diverse wildlife habitats. Children must be supervised. The nursery specialises in unusual perennials and cottage garden plants. 10% of plant sales to NGS on NGS days. Disabled access to nursery, steep slopes in garden.

6 **46 BROOKFIELD AVENUE**
CF63 1EQ. Norah Bawn, 01446 745863. *On A4050 Cardiff to Barry, take roundabout marked Barry Docks & Sully. 2nd R into Coldbrook Rd E, 2nd R into Meadow Vale, leading to Brookfield Ave. 4th cul de sac on R. No parking in cul de sac, vehicle turning point only.* Home-made teas. Adm £2, chd free. **Sun 13 July (2-6). Visitors also welcome by appt for viewing only, no teas.**
Unusually shaped large front garden, packed with colourful trees, shrubs, perennials and annuals, designed to maximise all-yr colour and interest. Many interesting planting features incl water features and separate rooms approach. Relaxing smaller back garden with summerhouse, raised terrace, rockery, water feature and many varied plants. Background music in rear garden. Wheelchair access to front garden only.

7 **BRYNDERI**
Wainfield Lane, Gwehelog, Usk NP15 1RG. Ann & Alwyne Benson, www.brynderi.co.uk. *2m N of Usk*

towards Raglan. Follow Monmouth rd signed Gwehelog, L at Hall Inn PH onto Wainfield Lane. Parking in field 100metres from house. Home-made teas. Adm £3, chd free. **Sun 22 June (2-6).**
2 acres incl Kew fountain and pool surrounded by lawn and yews; round lawn with colour-themed borders and vine-covered arbour. Wisteria-clad pergola, knot garden, specimen tree collection in elevated area with stunning views, trained fruit trees and raised beds. New areas being developed.

8 **BRYNHEULOG**
45 Heol y Graig, Cwmgwrach, Neath SA11 5TW. Lorraine Rudd, 01639 722593. *8m W of Neath. From M4 J43 take A465 to Glyneath, then rd signed Cwmgwrach. Entering village pass Dunraven PH, turn L at school sign, approx 100yds fork L into Glannant Place. Up hill, bear sharp R, approx 200yds turn L up steep track. 2nd house on L.* Home-made teas. Adm £3, chd free. **Sun 13 July (10.30-5.30). Visitors also welcome by appt.**
As seen on BBC TV Open Gardens! Now in its second year, this keen plantswoman's hillside garden perfectly reflects the dramatic setting and surrounding natural beauty. Garden incl potager, tropical greenhouse, orchids and new rose garden. Natural Health Centre on site.

9 **BRYNYRENFYS**
30 Cefn Road, Glais, Swansea SA7 9EZ. Edith & Roy Morgan, 01792 842777, edith.morgan@tiscali.co.uk. *5m W of Neath. M4 J45, take A4067 R at 1st roundabout, then 1st R and follow yellow signs.* Home-made teas. Adm £2.50, chd free (share to Swansea Alzheimer's Society). **Sun 1 June (12-6). Also open Springfield. Visitors also welcome by appt May to Aug, coaches welcome.**
If you love plants you'll be at home here. A small surprising garden full of interest. Unusual trees, shrubs and perennials vie for attention with the panoramic view. Wildlife and weed friendly with no bedding! Seating on different levels, so stay a while, unwind and be welcome. Croeso! Two local nurseries with plants for sale and gardening advice.

10 **CASTELL CWRT**
Llanelen NP7 9LE. Lorna & John McGlynn. *1m S of Abergavenny. From Abergavenny/Llanfoist take B4269 signed Llanelen. After passing Grove Farm turn R up single track rd. Rd climbs up steeply over canal. Approx 500yds entrance to Castell Cwrt on L. Separate disabled parking available.* Home-made teas. Combined adm £5, chd free. **Sun 28 Sept (1-5). Combined with South Lodge, Llanfoist.**
Large informal family garden in rural surroundings with fine views overlooking Abergavenny. Lawns, established trees with autumn colours, shrubs and herbaceous borders. Organic kitchen and vegetable gardens. Hay meadow, family pets and livestock in fields. Children very welcome. Some gravel and grass paths.

Topiary animals and 'medieval' herb garden, all awaiting discovery by the curious visitor . . .

11 **CASTLE HOUSE**
Monmouth Road, Usk NP15 1SD. Mr & Mrs J H L Humphreys, 01291 672563, www.uskcastle.com. *200yds NE from Usk centre. Turn up lane opp fire stn off Monmouth Rd.* **Open with Usk Gardens. Combined adm £6, chd free, £9 for 2 days (share to Usk Gardens Open Days). Sat 28, Sun 29 June (10-5). Visitors also welcome by appt for groups, coach parking in Usk town. Adm £4, chd free.**
Enjoy views of the Usk valley from the enchanting, romantic ruins of Usk Castle which overlook the early C19 gardens of the Castle House below. Long, herbaceous border backed by castellated, clipped yew hedge; pond, fountain, topiary animals and 'medieval' herb garden, all awaiting discovery by the curious visitor. Fine trees. Some cobbled paths, disabled parking in stable yard.

12 CEFNTILLA

Usk NP15 1DG. Lord Raglan.
3m NE of Usk. From S, take B4235 Usk to Chepstow rd to Gwernesney & follow signs N to Cefntilla, about 1m. From N, take Chepstow rd S from Raglan & follow signs through Llandenny. Home-made teas.
Adm £3.50, chd free. Sun 24, Mon 25 Aug (12-5).
Rectangular former Jacobean garden area greatly extended in 1850s with woodland ircumambulatory. Lawns set about with good trees, shrubs, colourful herbaceous borders, fine rosebeds, topiary walk with golden and Irish yews, handsome large lily pond. A varied yet restful mix of formal and informal in about 6 acres.

13 CLYTHA PARK

Abergavenny NP7 9BW. Sir Richard Hanbury-Tenison, 01873 840085.
Half-way between Abergavenny (4m) and Raglan (4m). On B4598 (not A40).
Adm £3, chd free. Visitors welcome by appt 1 May to 30 Jun, please speak to Mrs Keiser, details & directions will be sent.
Large C18 garden around 1½ -acre lake with wide lawns and good trees. Visit the 1790 walled garden or walk around the lake on a serpentine path laid out over 250 yrs ago; a 'secret' garden at the furthest point. Some gravel paths.

14 COED CEFN

Tregaer, Monmouth NP25 4DT. Brian & Alison Willott. *2m N of Raglan. A40/A449 to Raglan junction. Take A40 to Abergavenny, follow sign to Dingestow, immed L to Tregaer. Well-signed along 1½ m lane to Coed Cefn.* Home-made teas. **Combined adm £5, chd free. Sun 1 June (2-6). Combined with Woodlands Farm.**
Garden undergoing renovation and development, round C16 house (not open), with many climbing shrubs. Planned for low maintenance and wildlife habitats. Walled kitchen garden with potager, large fruit cage, peaches, figs. Terraces with raised bed and red garden. Shrubbery and laburnum tunnel. 2 large ponds. Old orchard with rambler roses and new fruit trees.

15 77 COLERIDGE AVENUE

Penarth CF64 2SR. Diana Mead, 02920 703523. *3m SW of Cardiff. M4 J33 to Cardiff Bay. B4160 (B4055) for Penarth and Barry. At T-lights, straight across to next lights. Keep L, take 1st exit to Lower Penarth into Redlands Rd, then 4th L into Cornerswell Rd, 1st L into Coleridge Ave.* **Adm £2, chd free. Sat 21 June (11-4). Visitors also welcome by appt Sept & Oct only.**
Professional artist's imaginative solution for a small awkwardly-shaped plot comprising three distinct linked areas: cottage-style front with serpentine 'river bed' gravel and paving path; small side vegetable garden with pyramid and step-over apples, sweet peas and herbs; sheltered tiny rear garden with tender plants, restricted pear trees and frog pond. Exhibition and sale of original flower watercolours, prints and cards.

> ## Underground grottoes, tunnels and ferneries and above ground stunning water features . . .

16 CROESLLANFRO FARM

Rogerstone NP10 9GP. Barry & Liz Davies, 01633 894057, lizplants@aol.com. *3m W of Newport. From M4 J27 take B4591 to Risca. Take 2nd R, Cefn Walk (also signed 14 Locks Canal Centre). Proceed over canal bridge, continue approx ½ m to island in middle of lane. White farm gate opp. Limited parking.* Home-made teas. **Adm £3.50, chd free. Sat 16, Sun 17 Aug (2-5.30). Visitors also welcome by appt Jun to Sept.**
Large sweeping borders of mass-planted perennials fill this 1½ -acre garden, created over 28 yrs by Liz Davies, garden designer. Wide variety of plants, many unusual, concentrate on form and texture, which fill the late summer borders. Architectural features include folly, grotto and terracing. Extensive replanting for 2008.

17 NEW ♦ DEWSTOW GARDENS & GROTTOES

Caerwent, Caldicot NP26 5AH. John Harris, 01291 430444, www.dewstow.com/gardens.htm *5m W of Chepstow. From A48 Newport to Chepstow rd, L to Caerwent & Dewstow golf club. Garden next to golf club. Coaches permitted.* **Adm £5, chd free. Weds to Suns and Bank Hol Mons, 20 Mar to 12 Oct; daily from mid July to end Aug. See website for opening times. For NGS: Suns 13 Apr; 12 Oct (10.30-4).**
5-acre Grade 1 listed unique garden which was buried and forgotten after World War 11 and rediscovered in 2000. Created around 1895 by James Pulham & Sons, the garden contains underground grottoes, tunnels and ferneries and above ground stunning water features. You will not be disappointed. Wheelchair access very limited.

18 ♦ DYFFRYN GARDENS

nr Cardiff CF5 6SU. Vale of Glamorgan Council, 02920 593328, www.dyffryngardens.org.uk. *5m N of Cardiff. Exit J33 from the M4, on the A4232 signed Barry; 1st interchange 4th exit A48 signed Cowbridge. In St Nicholas village turn L, Dyffryn is signed.* **Adm Mar to Oct (Nov to Feb adm in brackets) £6.50 (£3.50), chd £2.50 (£1.50), concessions £4.50 (£2.50). Mar to Oct (10-6), Nov to Feb (11-4), closed Tues & Weds.**
Outstanding Grade I listed Edwardian garden. Formal lawns; fountains and pools; seasonal beds; trees and shrubs. Garden rooms, incl Pompeian, Paved Court and Theatre garden. Arboretum contains trees from all over the world incl 13 champion trees - one the original *Acer griseum* collected by 'Chinese' Wilson. The gardens have recently been restored to Thomas Mawson's original 1904 design with help from Heritage Lottery Fund.

19 11 EASTCLIFF

Southgate SA3 2AS. Mrs Gill James, 01792 233310. *7m SW of Swansea. Take the Swansea to Gower rd & travel 6m to Pennard. Through village of Southgate & take 2nd exit off roundabout. Garden 200yds on L.* **Adm £3, chd free. Visitors welcome by appt.**

Seaside garden, approx 1/3 acre, and developed beds for all-yr interest. Large number of white, blue-green and unusual plants such as artemesia, melianthus, euphorbia, allium and Mediterranean plants. Woodland area and gravel bed.

 ♿ ✕ ☎

20 GARDD-Y-BRYN
The Hill Education & Conference Centre, Abergavenny NP7 7RP. Coleg Gwent. *1/4 m N of town centre. From A40 in Abergavenny, follow signs to Hill College.* Cream teas. **Adm £3, chd free. Sun 6 July (2-6).**
Recently-restored Victorian walled garden on S-facing slope overlooking Abergavenny and surrounded by mature woodland. Divided into various themed gardens incl fruit, vegetables, flowers for cutting, wild garden. Unusual, interesting, trees and shrubs. Atmospheric Mediterranean garden now complete with intriguing human sundial. Wonderful new outdoor mural of Usk Valley and Sugar Loaf Mountain. Harpist performing in garden.

✕ ✿ 🛏 ☕

Small hamlet . . . fantastic community spirit but no pub, no church, no shop, no school . . .

21 GLEBE HOUSE
Llanvair Kilgeddin NP7 9BE. Mr & Mrs Murray Kerr. *Midway between Abergavenny (5m) and Usk (5m). On B4598.* Home-made teas. **Adm £3, chd free. Sat 19, Sun 20 Apr (2-6).**
1 1/2 acres with small ornamental vegetable garden and summerhouse. Colourful herbaceous borders filled with tulips, orchard, S-facing terrace and climbers. Set in picturesque Usk Valley with wonderful all-round views.

♿ ✕ ✿ ☕

22 NEW HEN FELIN & SWALLOW BARNS
CF5 6SU. *3m from Culverhouse Cross roundabout. M4 J33, A4232 to Penarth, 1st exit to Culverhouse Cross roundabout. A48, follow signs to Cowbridge. At St Nicholas turn L at T-lights down Dyffryn Lane, past Dyffryn House. R at T-junction, both houses on L. Follow signs. Parking in paddock at rear of Hen Felin.* Cream teas, cheese and wine, BBQ 12-2.30. **Combined adm £3, chd free. Sat 12 July (12-7).**
Small hamlet in the middle of rich agricultural land. Fantastic community spirit but no pub, no church, no shop, no school. Garden opening in memory of Piers Frampton, much-missed neighbour. Music, plant sales, artists corner.

☕

NEW THE BARNS
Mrs Janet Evans
10yr-old garden with packed herbaceous borders, formal and informal. Orchard, hens, riverside meadow, herb garden and lavender patio.

♿

HEN FELIN
Dyffryn. Rozanne Lord. *House at end of village on R before humpback bridge*
Beautiful cottage garden with stunning borders, wishing well, 200yr-old pig sty, secret garden, lovingly-tended vegetable patch and chickens. Mill stream running through garden. Unprotected river access, children must be supervised.

♿ ✿

23 HIGH GLANAU MANOR
Lydart, Monmouth NP25 4AD. Mr & Mrs Hilary Gerrish, 01600 860005. *4m SW of Monmouth. Situated on B4293 between Monmouth & Chepstow. Turn into 'Private Road' opp Five Trees Carp Fishery.* Home-made teas. **Adm £3, chd free. Sun 11 May (2-6). Visitors also welcome by appt.**
Listed Arts and Crafts garden laid out by H Avray Tipping in 1922. Original features incl impressive stone terraces with far-reaching views over the vale of Usk, pergola, herbaceous borders, Edwardian glasshouse, rhododendrons and azaleas.

✕ ✿ ☕ ☎

24 HILLCREST BUNGALOW
Waunborfa Road, Cefn Fforest, Blackwood NP12 3LB. Mr M O'Leary and Mr B Price, 01443 837029. *3m W of Newbridge. Follow A4048 to Blackwood town centre or A469 to Pengam T-lights, then NGS signs.* Light refreshments. **Adm £3, chd free. Sat 7, Sun 8 June; Sat 16, Sun 17 Aug (12-6). Visitors also welcome by appt Apr-Sept, incl groups of any size.**
Welcoming 1 1/3 -acre garden with fine view over valley. Profusely planted with bulbs, perennials, shrubs and trees for yr-round interest. Tulip trees, embothrium, box parterre, gazebo, herb wheel, elevated viewing terrace. Secluded places to sit and enjoy. Featured in 'Garden News'. Caerphilly County Award for Horticultural Excellence.

♿ ✕ ☕ ☎

25 LLAN-Y-NANT
Coed Morgan, Abergavenny NP7 9UR. Mrs Grace Pitchford. *4m E of Abergavenny. 4m W of Raglan. Take B4598 from Abergavenny (old Raglan rd), L at Chart House PH and follow signs.* Home-made teas. **Adm £3.50, chd free. Sun 25 May (2-6).**
3 acres of garden and woodlands. Lawns, shrub and flower beds, alpines and kitchen garden. Many comfortable sitting areas to rest a while. The garden is level and very suitable for older and disabled visitors. Small lake with ducks and other wildlife.

♿ ✕ ✿ ☕

26 NEW LLANBLETHIAN GARDENS
Cowbridge CF71 7JF. *7m E of Bridgend. From Cardiff A48 W, through Cowbridge, L up hill towards Llantwit Major. L at Cross Inn PH into Llanblethian.* Home-made teas at Hillcot House. **Adm £3.50, chd free. Sun 8 June (2-6). Also open Newton Village Gardens & Ty Newydd.**
Picturesque hillside country village, quiet and unspoilt. Adjacent to popular market town of Cowbridge.

☕

NEW HILLCOT HOUSE
Church Road. John & Andrea Clowes
New garden on exposed S-facing slope with beautiful view to open countryside. Borders offering all-yr interest. Upper and lower lawns connected by grassy slope, steps and path. Featured on BBC TV Open Gardens.

NEW STALLCOURT MEWS
Stallcourt Close. Dick & Beverly
Tonkin, 01446 772704,
beverlytonkin@btinternet.com.
Rear of Llanblethian Church.
Visitors also welcome by appt.
Front terraced courtyard garden.
Side and rear sloping garden with
60m stream (unfenced) and
ponds. Largely impulse planting
so quite varied; vegetable garden
and short woodland walk. No
wheelchair access to courtyard.

Spring bulbs
should be in
full bloom . . .
traditional
Welsh dancing,
music and a
harpist . . .

**27 LLANFOIST VILLAGE
GARDENS**
NP7 9PE. Brian Barnes,
www.llanfoist-open-gardens.co.uk.
*1m SW of Abergavenny on B4246.
Map provided with ticket. Most
gardens within easy walking distance
of the village centre. Free minibus to
others. Limited wheelchair access to
some gardens.* Coffee & teas in some
gardens, lunch in Village Hall. Adm £5,
chd 50p (share to Llanfoist Villagers
Association). Sun 15 June (10-5.30).
Make this a great day out. Visit around
15 exciting and contrasting village
gardens, both large and small, set just
below the Blorenge Mountain on the
edge of the Black Mountains. This is
our 6th annual event. Some of the
gardens are open for the 1st time,
others are back by popular demand.
We will be serving morning coffee,
cooked lunches and afternoon teas, to
keep you fortified. Canal trips between
some gardens.

28 LLANOVER
nr Abergavenny NP7 9EF. Mr & Mrs
M R Murray, 01873 880232,
elizabeth@llanover.com,
www.llanovergarden.co.uk. *4m S of
Abergavenny, 15m N of Newport. On
A4042 Abergavenny - Pontypool.*
Home-made teas. Adm £4, chd free.
Sun 6 Apr (2-5). Visitors also
welcome by appt Oct to June,
groups of 15+.
15-acre listed garden and arboretum
with lakes, streams, cascades and a
dovecote. Champion trees present incl
*Quercus alba, Aesculus californica,
Sorbus wardii, Betula costata* and
Abies concolor. The numerous
magnolias, camellias and the avenue of
spring bulbs should be in full bloom.
Traditional Welsh dancing, music
and a harpist. Gravel and grass
paths.

**29 LLANTHONY AND DISTRICT
GARDENS**
NP7 7LB. *5m N of Abergavenny. From
Abergavenny roundabout take A465 N
towards Hereford. 4.8m turn L onto
Old Hereford Rd signed Pantygelli 2m.
Myndd Ardrem ¹/₂ m on R, Mione on L.
Directions to other gardens provided.*
Home-made teas at Perthi Crwn.
Combined adm £4, chd free (share
to Llanthony and District Garden
Club). Sun 15 June (10.30-4.30).
Located in an area of outstanding
beauty within the Black Mountains
rural communities of Fforest Coal
Pit, Cwmyoy and the village of
Llanvihangel Crucorney. The garden
settings reflect the diversity of the local
landscape with views across valleys,
mountains and forests.

MIONE
Llanvihangel Crucorney. Yvonne
& John O'Neil
Established garden with wide
variety of plants. Pergola with 6
varieties of climbing roses, wildlife
pond, containers with diverse
range of planting. Several seating
areas, each with a different
atmosphere.

MYNYDD ARDREM
Llanvihangel Crucorney. Linda &
Geoff Walsh
This lovely garden was re-started
6 yrs ago within established
mature boundaries, in order to
create a romantic setting for the
Victorian house. Beautiful roses,

clematis, herbaceous borders,
shrubs, trees and a wisteria-clad
pergola. Gravel paths.

PERTH-Y-CRWN
Cwmyoy. Jim Keates
Restored farmhouse garden with
stunning views, SW aspect facing
valley and mountainside beyond.
Sunny, walled garden with fruit,
vegetables and flowers, formal
rose garden and newly-created
wild flower bank.

30 LLWYN-Y-WEN FARM
Hafodyrynys Road, Crumlin
NP11 5AX. Mrs Helen Lewy, 01495
244797, robertplewy@gmail.com.
*11m NW of Newport, 6m W of
Pontypool. M4 J28, take A467 to
Risca. 11m to Crumlin T-lights, turn R
on A472 to Pontypool. Entrance ¹/₄ m
on R. Limited parking; lay-bys on main
road.* Cream teas. Adm £5, chd free.
Visitors welcome by appt Apr to
July for parties of 10+.
2 acres of Welsh hillside with spring
creating trout pond and bog garden, at
best in May, June, July. A
plantswoman's paradise, of great
interest to those in search of the
unusual. Auriculas, primulas,
hellebores and shade and damp-loving
plants a speciality. Informal mass of
flowers in orchard setting. 12 metre-
long rockery. Additional fields with
bluebell walks in May. Featured in
'Garden News'.

31 NEW MAENDY
Llanwonno Road, Ynyshir
CF39 0AS. Margaret Lush. *5m
NW of Pontypridd. From
Pontypridd follow A4058 for
Rhondda Valleys. Take new relief rd
to Aberdare. After crossing new
bridge, turn L at Ynyshir, garden
few yds on L.* Home-made teas.
Adm £2.50, chd free (share to
Rhondda Macmillan Nurses). Sat
12, Sun 13 July (2-6).
Established garden with large trees
and shrubs, traditional borders,
box parterre, vegetable patch and
water features. Dense planting of
shady corners, summerhouse,
seating areas, unusual ornamental
displays, all set in spacious
lawns.

32 MAGOR VILLAGE GARDENS
NP26 3HT. *9m W of Chepstow. M4 J23A onto B4245 to Magor. No parking at The Hawthorns and only ltd disabled parking at Lilac Cottage, please park in Queens Gardens (signed) for The Hawthorns and village car park for Lilac Cottage.* Cream teas at The Hawthorns. **Combined adm £3.50, chd free. Sat 12, Sun 13 July (1-6).**
2 very different gardens, one formal, one quirky. Magor Marsh Wildlife Reserve also open, entrance to Marsh between village car park and Lilac Cottage.

THE HAWTHORNS
Magor NP26 3BZ. John & Rosemary Skinner. *150yds from roundabout. W side of Magor, well signed*
Formal bedding scheme with standard fuchsias, summer bedding and conifers shaped into domes and archways, perennial garden with covered walkway, water-feature and garden seat with passion flower canopy known as 'The Secret Garden' with dovecote. Plenty of seating. Partial wheelchair access.

NEW LILAC COTTAGE
Whitewall. Christine & Bernard Rowlands
³/₄ -acre cottage garden with rooms, interesting water features and sitting areas plus vegetable garden.

33 MARLBOROUGH ROAD GARDENS
Penylan, Cardiff CF23 5BD. *1¹/₂ m NE of Cardiff city centre. M4 J29, Cardiff E A48, then Llanedeyrn/Dock exit, towards Cyncoed and L down Penylan Hill. Marlborough Rd is L at T-lights at bottom of hill. Look out for NGS signs.* Light refreshments & home-made teas at all gardens. **Combined adm £4, chd free (share to Alzheimer's Society). Suns 4 May; 27 July (2-6). Evening Opening, wine, Tue 29 July (5-9).**
Victorian suburb of terraced houses with small gardens and many parks.

6 ALMA ROAD
Melvyn Rees, 02920 482200. Visitors also welcome by appt.
S-facing terraced house garden

30ft x 15ft with many species from the S and E hemispheres, incl *Dicksonia antarctica, D. squarosa* and *Sophora* in a riot of exotic foliage. Slate used as paving material with gravel infill. Decking provides a raised seating area. Featured in 'South Wales Echo'.

7 CRESSY ROAD
Victoria Thornton
Terraced house garden, 30ft x 15ft, started from scratch in 2000. A secluded haven with a delightful exotic mix of tropical, agaves, bamboos, grasses, bonsai and containerised specimen trees. Conservatory, barrel pond and fern walkway. Featured in 'South Wales Echo'.

102 MARLBOROUGH ROAD
Mrs Judith Griffiths
Come and discover a secret stone-walled garden behind a busy street. A garden of contrasts: Mediterranean-style sunny patio/shady areas. Wander through an informal mix of cottage garden plants, established shrubs and fruit trees.

34 NEW 7 MONTRESOR COURT
NP44 3HG. Mark Everson. *Southern edge of Cwmbran. From A4042 Crown roundabout, take exit to Llantarnam. Cross bridge, through T-lights and L at small roundabout. Montresor Court is 2nd L.* Light refreshments & teas. **Adm £3, chd free. Sun 24 Aug (10.30-5).**
Sheltered suburban garden full of rare exotic and unusual plants from all corners of the globe. Tree fernery leads from patio to lawn bordered by palms, bamboos and arid plants in a series of raised beds. Deck provides seating area.

35 NANT-Y-BEDD
Fforest Coal Pit NP7 7LY. Sue & Ian Mabberley. *10m NW of Abergavenny. Turn into Llanvihangel Crucorney from A465 Abergavenny/Hereford rd. L at Skirrid Inn and L at bottom. After 1m L to Fforest Coal Pit. After 2m at the junction of five roads, straight ahead to Grwyne Fawr Reservoir and Forestry Commission 'Mynydd Du'. Nant y*

Bedd 5m. **Combined adm £5, chd free. Sun 31 Aug (10.30-5). Open with Pont Escob Mill.**
2 acres high in Black Mountains with interesting mix of flowers, vegetables, fruit and trees bisected by natural stream. Managed organically, it provides produce for house. Variety of wildlife and choice of flowers is testament to the efficiency of this approach. 'An oasis in the forest'. Late summer opening for variety of vegetables. Featured on BBC2 Open Gardens. Winner Llanthony & District Wildlife Garden.

36 NASH MANOR
Cowbridge CF71 7NS. Jennifer, Eric & Guy Williams. *2m SW of Cowbridge. W along A48 passing Cowbridge. Turn L at Pentre Meyrick on B4268 signed Llysworney/Llantwit Major. Through Llysworney, Nash Manor straight ahead.* Cream teas. **Adm £3, chd free. Sat 26 Apr (2-6).**
Large garden of C16 Grade I listed manor house, gradually being reclaimed. Courtyard with wisteria and tulips. Walled garden with lily pond and spring bulbs. Many mature trees incl wonderful copper beech. Featured on BBC TV Open Gardens.

37 NEW NEWTON VILLAGE GARDENS
Porthcawl CF36 5NT. *M4 J37, then A4229 to Porthcawl. Approx 3m A4106 to Bridgend. L at 1st roundabout, 2nd L to Newton.* Home-made teas at Newton Cottage & Tyn-y-Caeau Farm, wine at The Old Orchard. **Combined adm £5, chd free. Sun 8 June (1-6). Also open Llanbleddian Gardens & Ty Newydd.**
Charming seaside village with 800yr-old Norman church, village green and friendly pubs. Gardens range from small cottage to larger gardens with wonderful herbaceous borders.

NEW CROWN HOUSE
Sarah & Tim Lewis. *Adjacent to The Green in Newton*
A family garden. One area has mature shrubs and plants and is perfect for entertaining; the other area, separated by an old wall, is a children's paradise, with fruit trees and a more relaxed feel.

NEW LLWYNRHOS
Clevis Hill. Andrew & Liz Singer
Small cottage-style garden with large mixture of plants. Paths, steps and limestone walls renovated and considerable new planting over last 3 yrs. Patio garden with herbs and summer vegetables. Plant sale in aid of Barnardos.

NEWTON COTTAGE
Newton, Porthcawl. Mr & Mrs J David
Large informal cottage garden. Mixed borders, good variety of shrubs, climbers and herbaceous plants. Newly-planted box garden. Kitchen garden.

NEW THE OLD ORCHARD
12 Newton-Nottage Road. Richard & Caroline Howe
Cottage garden with steps up to the rear gardens, populated with fruit trees, June-flowering roses, small herb garden and vegetable patch.

NEW TYN-Y-CAEAU FARM
Tyn-y-Caeau Lane. Mr & Mrs J P John. *From Newton village return to A4106 Bridgend Rd, straight over roundabout into Tyn-y-Caeau Lane, approx 1m along lane*
Three yr-old garden with herbaceous borders, vegetable garden, ponds, wild flower meadow, orchard with fruit trees and hens. Wonderful panoramic view of Bristol Channel.
♿ ⚔ ✿

38 ◆ THE NURTONS
Tintern NP6 7NX. Adrian & Elsa Wood, 01291 689253, info@thenurtons.co.uk. *7m N of Chepstow. On A466 opp Old Station.* Adm £3, chd free. Daily Easter-end Sept (11-5). For NGS: Sat 2, Sun 3 Feb; (1.30-4.30); Sun 18 May; Sat 13, Sun 14 Sept (1.30-5).
Exciting 3½-acre garden on a secluded magical & historical site with stunning views of the Wye Valley. Yr-round interest with snowdrops in winter and great colour in summer and autumn. Choice plant collections in hot Mediterranean, cool woodland and water settings. Partial wheelchair access along gravel paths.
⚔ 🛏

39 OCHRAN MILL
Llanover NP7 9HU. Elaine & David Rolfe, 01873 737809, www.ochranmill.co.uk. *3m S of Abergavenny. On A4042 midway between Llanover & Llanelen.* Adm £3, chd free. Suns 4 May; 8 June; 13 July; 3 Aug; 7 Sept (1-5). Visitors also welcome by appt.
Grade II listed water mill (not working) approx 1½-acres. A 'garden in the making' taking shape over last 6 yrs from fields. Large colour-themed herbaceous borders, bog garden, shrub borders, gravel and grasses, woodland borders incl large collection of hellebores. Large water feature and rose/clematis pergola. Field for picnics and stream to play in. Pinball and arcade collection (very popular with non-gardeners and children). Featured in 'The Guardian' and 'Glorious Gardens of Monmouthshire' and on BBC Radio 4 'Gardener of the Year Quiz'. Gravel paths, gentle slopes.
♿ ⚔ ✿ ☎

40 NEW THE ORCHIDS
Blaenavon Rd, Abergavenny NP7 9NY. Margaret Underwood. *2m from Abergavenny. From Abergavenny section of A465 Heads of the Valleys Road, take B4246 for Llanfoist or Govilon. Blaenavon Rd is between the 2 villages. Garden 200yds on L, British Waterways car park a further 30yds on R.* Home-made teas. Adm £3, chd free (share to Gwent Wildlife Trust). Sun 18 May (2-6).
Bijou garden adj to Monmouthshire and Brecon Canal with ancient beechwood as backdrop and many unusual plants and shrubs. Woodland and sculpture gardens close to canal, informal meadow areas, heather and conifer bank, pond, formal courtyards, borders and vegetables. Featured on BBC Open Gardens. Unfenced pond and canal, children must be supervised at all times.
⚔ ✿ ☕

Bijou garden adjacent to Monmouthshire and Brecon Canal . . .

41 PENLLYN COURT
nr Cowbridge CF71 7RQ. Mr & Mrs John Homfray. *17m W of Cardiff. A48 W of Cardiff towards Bridgend. Bypass Cowbridge, turn R at Pentre Meyrick, then 2nd R, Penllyn Court on L.* Home-made teas. Adm £3, chd free. Sun 4 May (2-6).
Large family garden with semi-formal walled garden, orchard with fruit trees and bulbs, stumpery, mixed plantings of shrubs and spring flowers. Vegetable garden. Gravel paths.
♿ ⚔ ✿ ☕

42 NEW PENMARK VILLAGE GARDENS
CF62 3BP. *4m W of Barry. Take B4265 from Barry to Penmark.* Light refreshments & home-made teas. Combined adm £5, chd free. Sat 21 June (11-5).
Only 12m W of Cardiff, Penmark is a quaint rural village, steeped in history with its origins dating from the Norman conquest. The gardens are all within a mile circular walk and feature a medieval 'strip', courtyard, hillside and walled gardens, stream and woodland walks. Map available.
☕

NEW THE BYRE
Cherie John
S-facing Mediterranean courtyard garden, abundantly stocked with flowering pots and specimen plants, incl Magnolia grandiflora 'Exmouth'. Gravel paths.
♿ ⚔

NEW ELDERBERRY HOUSE
Mr & Mrs P Bottrill
Nestled at the back of 'Albert Square'! A secluded garden with an eclectic mix of shrubs, perennials and quirky features. Limited wheelchair access.
♿ ⚔ ✿

NEW GILESTON HOUSE
Kath Linton
Original medieval 'strip' garden designed by current owners. Wonderfully laid out with a series of curved lawns, abundantly stocked flower beds and shrubberies presenting an ever-changing vista round each corner.
♿ ⚔ ✿

NEW **GLEN VIEW**
Mr & Mrs J & R A Board
Large garden with woodland walk, traditional rose beds, specimen trees and vegetable garden. Beautifully laid out, with secret cottage garden.
&. X

NEW **GWAL EIRTH**
Gwyn Grisley
Beautiful terraced garden created by keen gardener. Plantaholic's paradise filled with many varieties of perennials, grasses, ferns and hostas. Samples of owner's pottery displayed throughout garden.
X ⊛

NEW **PENMARK PLACE**
Mr & Mrs Andrew Radcliffe
C13 manor house with enclosed walled garden, large vegetable plot and orchard. Rose hedges, perennial beds, 100yr-old varieties of apple and pear.
&. X

NEW **SEFTON BUNGALOW**
Cynthia John
Meandering stream with specimen trees situated on the lea of a field, with panoramic views. Garden with many plants of note. Unprotected stream, children must be supervised.
&. ⊛

Old courtyard . . . now flagged and cobbled with sunny flower beds . . .

43 ◆ **PENPERGWM LODGE**
nr Abergavenny NP7 9AS. Mr & Mrs Simon Boyle, 01873 840208, www.penplants.com. *3m SE of Abergavenny, 5m W of Raglan. On B4598. Turn opp King of Prussia Inn. Entrance 150-yds on L.* **Adm £3.50, chd free. Thurs to Suns, 20 Mar to 28 Sept (2-6).**
3-acre garden with lawns, mature trees, Italianate parterre and brick-

pillared vine walk. Jubilee tower overlooks terraced ornamental garden with cascading water. S-facing terraces planted with rich profusion and vibrant colours. Special plant nursery. Some gravel paths.
&. ⊛ ⊨

44 **NEW** **PLAS NEWYDD COTTAGE**
Porthycarne Street, Usk NP15 1SA. Dr Pauline Ruth. *A449 to Usk. L at Three Salmons PH, R up Porthycarne Close opp Veterinary Hospital. Old coach house on L at top.* Home-made teas. **Adm £3, chd free (share to Alzheimer's Society). Wed 4 June (1-6). Also open with Usk Gardens 28/29 June.**
Old courtyard at front originally for coaches and horses for Georgian house next door. Now flagged and cobbled with sunny flower beds. Steeply terraced back garden to castle woods. Espalier trees, roses, shrubs and vegetables. Wide views to SW over Usk. Woodland at top. Not suitable for disabled.
⏾

45 **NEW** **PONT ESCOB MILL**
Fforest Coal Pit, Abergavenny NP7 7LS. Lord & Lady Crickhowell. *5m NNW of Abergavenny. Turn into Llanvihangel Crucorney from A465 Abergavenny/Hereford rd. L at Skirrid Inn, keep L following signs to Fforest Coal Pit. Car park at Xrds.* Home-made teas. **Combined adm £5, chd free (share to Llanthony & District Garden Club). Sun 31 Aug (10.30-5). Open with Nant y Bedd.**
³/₄ -acre garden in the heart of the Black Mountains surrounding a converted mill (not open). Acer glade, spacious lawn, mature trees and the R Grwyne Fawr making the garden boundary on one side. Colourful climbers and late summer flowering shrubs with steep stone steps to upper terraces.
X ⏾

46 **PONTYGWAITH FARM**
Edwardsville, nr Treharris CF46 5PD. Mr & Mrs R J G Pearce, 01443 411137. *2m NW of Treharris. N from Cardiff on A470. At roundabout take A4054 (old Ponytpridd to Merthyr rd),*

travel N towards Aberfan for approx 3m through Quakers Yard and Edwardsville. 1m after Edwardsville turn very sharp L by old black bus shelter, garden at bottom of hill. Light refreshments & teas. **Adm £2.50, chd free. Sun 29 June (10-6). Visitors also welcome by appt May to Aug, no coaches.**
Large garden surrounding C17 farmhouse adjacent to Trevithick's Tramway. Situated in picturesque wooded valley. Fish pond, lawns, perennial borders, lakeside walk and rose garden. Grade II listed humpback packhorse bridge in garden, spanning R Taff, featured in film Bridge of Lies. Gravel path, steep slope down to river.
&. ⊛ ☕ ☎

47 **NEW** **RHIWBINA GARDENS**
Cardiff CF14 6TR. *2m N of Cardiff city centre. M4 J32, then S on A470, then follow directions for each garden.* Light refreshments & teas at Beachouse. **Combined adm £4, chd free. Sat 19 July (2-6).**
Rhiwbina has a village atmosphere in a North Cardiff suburb.
X ⏾ ☕

BEACHOUSE
Annie Jones. *M4 J32, then S on A470. 1st L, before lights R at mini roundabout. At Deri Stores follow signs for Wenallt Reservoir and Woodland (3rd L Wennallt Rd). Then 2nd L, 1st R. Some disabled parking, otherwise use Wenallt Rd*
see separate entry.

NEW **4 CEFN-NANT**
Mrs Sylvia Fidler. *As before, then 1st L, before lights R at mini roundabout. At Deri Stores, 1st R into Heoluchaf then 1st L into Cefn-Nant*
Mature garden front and rear with a mixture of shrubs, annuals, perennials and fruit. Small pond, patio and seating areas.
X

NEW **34 KYLE CRESCENT**
Dr Robyn Phillips. *M4 J32 then A470/Manor Way towards Cardiff. Kyle Crescent on L after 3rd set of T-lights and Tesco Extra. From Cardiff, R at T-lights at Tesco Extra, R at next T-lights, 1st R, 1st L*
An urban oasis, designed to provide natural privacy, all-yr interest and a natural flow around

the garden. several seating areas in sun or shade for relaxing. Lush planting using a variety of plants, some less usual.

&. ⊛

NEW 2 WINDMILL CLOSE
Thornhill. Mr & Mrs J C Palmer. *As before, then 1st L, before lights R at mini roundabout. At Deri Stores follow signs for Wenallt Reservoir. Past Deri Inn, 1st L Heol Llanishen Fach. Then R onto Thornhill Rd, 1st L Templeton Ave, at T-junction, L onto Heol Hir, 3rd L onto Lyric Way. Park here, Windmill Close 1st R*
Small suburban garden with raised decking and patio areas overlooking pond and stream. Mix of evergreen and deciduous shrubs and perennials, especially fuchsias. Alpines and containerised plants for yr-round interest.

✗ ⊛

48 SCHOOL & COLLEGE GARDENS
St Brides Major & St Donats Castle. *See individual entries for directions.* Home-made teas at Atlantic College. **Combined adm £5 or £3.50, each garden, chd free. Sun 29 June (11-4).**
School and College approx 3m drive apart, both situated in an Area of Outstanding Natural Beauty, close to Heritage Coast. Willow weaving workshop at St Brides School.

☕

ST BRIDES C/W PRIMARY SCHOOL
Heol Yr Ysgol, St Brides Major. *4m SW of Bridgend. From M4 J35 1st exit to A473. At 3rd roundabout take 2nd exit to A48, over mini roundabout. At next roundabout 1st L to Ewenny Rd, signed Llantwit Major B4265. Continue to St Brides Major, R at Fox & Hounds, 1st L to Heol Yr Ysgol*
This school garden has been developed and maintained by the school's Gardening Club which meets weekly after school and has approx 40 members. Individual gardens within the school grounds incl: Warm Welcome Garden, Woodland, Organic Fruit and Vegetable Garden, Easter Garden, Jewish Garden, Sensory Garden, Patchwork Garden, Butterfly

Garden, Flower Diary Garden, Woven Willow Playground, Maze, Nature Reserve and Wild flower Meadow, craft willow bed. Willow weaving workshop. Wales in Bloom 2nd prize, Best Kept School in Vale of Glamorgan, National runner-up Eco School of the Year.

✗ ⊛

ST DONATS CASTLE (ATLANTIC COLLEGE)
St Donats, Llantwit Major. **United World College of the Atlantic, www.atlanticcollege.org.** *6m SW of Cowbridge, 2¼ m W of Llantwit Major. From Barry follow B4265 to Llantwit Major. Castle signed at 2nd roundabout. Continue 1m on B4265 turning L at staggered junction. At next T-junction L into St Donats village and enter grounds 2nd gate on R. From Bridgend follow B4265 to Wick and further 1m to staggered junction*
Rare surviving large-scale Tudor terraced garden attached to a predominantly medieval castle, partly restored and added to in the early C20. The 5 terraces of garden cascade down the the SW slope of ground leading from the castle to the shores of the Bristol Channel.

⊛

Early spring flowers: snowdrops, daffodils, crocus, cyclamen, bluebells . . .

49 SLADE
Southerndown CF32 0RP. **Rosamund & Peter Davies, 01656 880048, ros@sladewoodgarden.plus.com.** *5m S of Bridgend. M4 J35. Follow A473 to Bridgend. Take B4265 to St Brides Major. Turn R in St Brides Major*

for Southerndown. At Southerndown turn L opp 3 Golden Cups PH onto Beach Rd. Follow rd into Dunraven Park. Turn 1st L over cattle grid on to Slade drive. Home-made teas. **Adm £3, chd free. Sun 30 Mar (2-6). Visitors also welcome by appt, groups welcome, coaches permitted.**
Woodland garden and walk. Display of early spring flowers: snowdrops, daffodils, crocus, cyclamen, bluebells. Mature specimen trees. Herbaceous borders, terraced lawns, orchard, hens. Extensive views over Bristol Channel. Heritage Coast wardens will give guided tours of adjacent Dunraven Gardens with slide shows every ½ hr from 3pm.

✗ ⊛ ☕ ☎

50 NEW SOUTH LODGE
Merthyr Rd, Llanfoist NP7 9LR. **David & Rachel Best.** *1m SW of Abergavenny.* Home-made teas. **Combined adm £5, chd free. Sun 28 Sept (1-5). Open with Castell Cwrt.**
1½ -acre landscaped partially walled garden surrounding C19 former brewery manager's villa (not open). Enclosure with ducks, chickens and pigs, terrace with herbs, vegetable garden, fishpond and child-friendly spaces for young family visitors. Garden beside old tram road with access to Monmouthshire and Brecon Canal and Blorenge Mountain. Artist owner's prints of domestic fowl and animals for sale.

✗ ☕

51 SPRINGFIELD
176 Clasemont Road, Morriston SA6 6AJ. **Carole & Stuart Jones, 01792 773827.** *4m N of Swansea. From M4 J46 follow A48 E for 1m. From Morriston Cross take A48 W for 1m, garden on A48 50yds from entrance to Morriston Golf Club.* Home-made teas & wine. **Adm £2, chd free. Sun 1 June (2-7). Also open Brynrenfys. Visitors also welcome by appt.**
Small informal suburban garden with interesting mix of trees, shrubs, bulbs and perennials to give yr-round interest. Incl small pond and pebble pond and many containerised plants. Several seating areas give the garden a relaxed feel.

☕ ☎

52 **NEW** **SUNNYSIDE**
The Hendre NP25 5HQ. Helen &
Ralph Fergusson-Kelly, 01600
714928, helen-fk@hotmail.com.
*4m W of Monmouth. On B4233
Monmouth to Abergavenny rd.
Parking in field 50metres from
garden.* Home-made teas. **Adm
£3, chd free. Sun 28 Sept (12-5).
Visitors also welcome by appt
May to end Sept, eves & w/e for
small groups.**
Listed house (not open) on old
Rolls estate. Mature, sloping
garden of ⅓ acre with lawns, trees,
shrubs and herbaceous borders
planted with interesting perennials
and grasses for late season colour.
Designed and planted by owner.
Some gravel paths. Water feature.
Seating areas to enjoy views over
surrounding countryside.

53 **THREE WELLS**
Llanvihangel Crucorney,
Abergavenny NP7 7NR. Antony &
Verity Woodward. *8m N of
Abergavenny. Off A465 Abergavenny-
Hereford rd. At Llanvihangel Crucorney
turn downhill at Skirrid PH and 1st R
over hump-back bridge. After ⅔ m, L
by grass triangle and follow yellow
signs. 1-way system in place as very
steep, narrow single track lanes. If wet,
car park may be 15-minute walk.* Light
refreshments & home-made teas. **Adm
£3.50, chd free (share to Longtown
Mountain Rescue). Sun 27 July
(11-6).**
Highest property opening in
Monmouthshire. 6-acre smallholding in
mountain setting (reaching nearly
1600ft) on Offa's Dyke footpath in
Brecon Beacons National Park. For
anyone fit and intrepid who sees
beauty in wild places - in upland wild-
flower meadows, dry-stone walls and
mountain springs, forgotten farm
machinery in field corners and
gateways framing 70-mile views.

54 ◆ **TOUCHWOOD**
4 Clyne Valley Cottages, Killay,
Swansea SA2 7DU. Carrie Thomas,
01792 522443,
www.touchwoodplants.co.uk. *4m W
of Swansea. Take A4118 (Gower rd)
past Killay shops and over mini-
roundabout towards Gower. 2nd L
(halfway down hill) into Clyne Valley
Road, which leads to Clyne Valley
Cottages.* **Adm £2, chd free. Open
days and times vary according to**
season; phone or see website for
details. **For NGS: Thur 15 May (2-
4.30). Tue 20 May day (2-4.30) &
Evening Opening (6-8.30).**
Plantsman's intimate cottage garden,
most items grown from seed. Annuals,
biennials, perennials, bulbs, shrubs,
grasses, climbers, herbs, vegetables
and alpines. National Collection of
Aquilegia vulgaris, hybrids and cultivars
are flowering May and beginning of
June. Set in historical country park, nr
Clyne and Singleton gardens. Featured
in 'Mail on Sunday', 'Gardeners' World'
magazine and on BBC Gardeners'
World.

11-acre site
containing
gardens
designed and
constructed by
horticulture
students . . .

55 ◆ **TREDEGAR HOUSE &
PARK**
Newport NP10 8YW. Newport City
Council, 01633 815880,
anne.tame@newport.gov.uk. *2m SW
of Newport town centre. Signed from
A48 (Cardiff rd) & M4 J28.* **Adm £2.50,
chd free. For NGS: Sun 15 June
(11-5).**
Series of C18 walled formal gardens
surrounding magnificent late C17
house (also open). Early C18 orangery
garden with coloured mineral parterres.
Open on NGS day Growing Space
gardens maintained to a high standard
by staff and clients with mental
illnesses. Six separate areas incl bog
garden, ornamental pond and secret
cottage garden. Also open by appt tel
01633 810718.

56 **TROSTREY LODGE**
Bettws Newydd, Usk NP15 1JT.
Roger & Frances Pemberton. *4m W
of Raglan. 7m E of Abergavenny. Off
the old A40 (unnumbered)
Abergavenny - Raglan. 1m S of Clytha*
Gates and 1½ m N of Bettws Newydd.
Home-made teas Sun only. **Adm £3,
chd free. Sat 31 May; Sun 1 June
(12-6).**
Enjoy one of the most glorious
views in the Usk Valley. A
spectacular tulip tree, generally in
flower at this time, dominates the
approach across a Regency ha-ha;
then enter this pretty stone walled
cottage garden-cum-orchard which
is packed with abundance and
interest.

57 **NEW** ◆ **TWYN-YR-HYDD**
Margam Country Park, Margam
SA13 2TJ. Neath Port Talbot
College, 01639 648261,
robert.priddle@nptc.ac.uk. *2m W
of Pyle. M4 J38, take A48 signed
Margam Park. Pass entrance to
Park, after ½ m turn L into garden.*
**Adm £3, chd free. Daily 9.30 -
4.30, Apr to Sept. For NGS: Sun
15 June (10.30-5).**
Spread out over 11-acre site and
containing gardens designed and
constructed by horticulture
students. Incl herb, prairie,
woodland, and a vegetable garden
which incl heritage varieties.
Grounds also contain walled
garden designed by Arts and
Crafts designer Ralph Hancock.
Tours and horticultural
demonstrations by college
lecturers. Featured on HTV, Radio
Wales and in press. Prairie garden
winner of Silver Gilt Medal at Royal
Welsh Show. Limited access to
woodland garden.

58 **NEW** **TY NEWYDD**
Clementstone, Wick CF71 7PZ.
Glyn & Liz Gibson. *5m SW of
Bridgend. M4 J35, follow A473 to
Bridgend. Take B4265 to Wick.
Turn L at Star Inn into Ewenny. 1m
turn R at Stone Lodge over
sleeping policeman. 2nd farm on L.*
Home-made teas & wine. **Adm £3,
chd free. Sun 8 June (12-6). Also
open Llanbleddian Gardens &
Newton Village Gardens.**
Sloping garden with herbaceous
borders, cottage garden planting,
wildlife pond, raised vegetable
beds. Woodland walk. Featured on
BBC TV Open Gardens.

My favourite
habitat is
a damp
meadow patch
with our
native wild
flowers . . .

59 NEW UPPER TRERHYNGYLL GARDENS
Trerhyngyll, Cowbridge
CF71 7TN. *2m N of Cowbridge on A4222. 15m W of Cardiff via A48 turn L to Cowbridge. Take R turn at next T-lights and go 2m along A4222 to Trerhyngyll, signed on L.* Home-made teas at Cartrefle, wine at Gwdi-Hw Cottage, plants for sale at Rose Cottage. **Combined adm £4, chd free. Sun 15 June (2-6).**
Trerhyngyll is a peaceful countryside hamlet of some 60 dwellings, nestling in the gently folding hills of the Vale of Glamorgan. The 3 gardens are typical of the hamlet.

NEW CARTREFLE
Jill & Malcolm Roberts
Just like choosing a dessert from a trolley, I like to try a bit of everything. My favourite habitat is a damp meadow patch with our native wild flowers.

NEW GWDI-HW COTTAGE
Pat & Gerry Long
Gentle sloping lawn and herbaceous borders overlooking a water meadow. Small goldfish ponds lead to a greenhouse and vegetable garden consisting of a series of raised beds that provide self-sufficiency in seasonal vegetables.

NEW ROSE COTTAGE
Sylvia & Bryan Hole
Plantaholic's cottage garden incorporating vegetables and ornamental plants. The emphasis is on informality (self-seeding is encouraged) and all-yr interest. Its backbone is hardy perennials, shrubs and bulbs. Some gravel paths.

60 USK GARDENS
Usk Town NP15 1AF. Mrs M Evans, 01291 672466, www.usktc.fg.co.uk. *From M4 J24 take A449, proceed 8m to Usk exit. Good free parking in town. Map of gardens provided with ticket.* Refreshments in Memorial Hall, Catholic Church Hall & St Mary's. **Adm £6, chd free, £9 for 2 days (share to Usk gardens open days). Sat 28, Sun 29 June (10-5). Open with Castle House.**
20+ gardens from small cottages packed with colourful and unusual plants to large gardens with brimming herbaceous borders. Wonderful

garden around the ramparts of Usk Castle. Gardeners' market with wide selection of interesting plants. Featured in Free Press, 'South Wales Argus' & 'Abergavenny Chronicle'. Limited wheelchair access to some gardens.

61 ◆ VEDDW HOUSE
Devauden NP16 6PH. Anne Wareham & Charles Hawes, 01291 650836, www.veddw.co.uk. *5m NW of Chepstow. Off B4293. Signed from PH on the green at Devauden.* **Adm £5.50, chd £1.50. Suns & Bank Hol Mon, 1 Jun to 31 Aug (2-5). For NGS: Evening Opening, wine, Wed 11 June (5-7.30).**
A modern romantic garden: 'One of the 10 best gardens to visit this summer' Katherine Lambert, editor of Good Gardens Guide in 'The Independent'. Featured on BBC Radio Wales.

62 WOODLANDS FARM
Penrhos NP15 2LE. Craig Loane. *3m N of Raglan. At Raglan, turn off A40 towards Mitcheltroy. Almost immed, turn L for Tregaer, then Penrhos and follow NGS signs.* Home-made teas. **Combined adm £5, chd free. Sun 1 June (2-6). Open with Coed Cefn.**
An evolving garden in a hidden part of Monmouthshire with a mixture of formal modern design and wild informality, incorporating the surrounding countryside with vistas that have been built into the structure of the garden. A new orangery, terrace, water features and ornamental mound add points of interest to this unique garden. Plant sale.

Glamorgan County Volunteers
County Organiser
Rosamund Davies, Slade, Southerndown, Glamorgan CF32 0RP, 01656 880048, ros@sladewoodgarden.plus.com
County Treasurer
Peter Davies, Slade, Southerndown, Glamorgan CF32 0RP, 01656 880048, peter@daviesslade.plus.com
Assistant County Organiser
Melanie Hurst, Wolf House, Llysworney, Cowbridge, Vale of Glamorgan CF71 7NQ, 01446 773659, melanie@b-theatre.com

Gwent County Volunteers
County Organiser
Joanna Kerr, Glebe House, Llanvair Kilgeddin, Abergavenny NP7 9BE, 01873 840422, joanna@amknet.com
Assistant County Organiser
Sue Carter, St Pega's, 47 Hereford Road, Monmouth NP25 3HQ, 01600 772074, stpegas47@hotmail.co.uk

NORTH WALES

Denbighshire & Colwyn, Flintshire & Wrexham

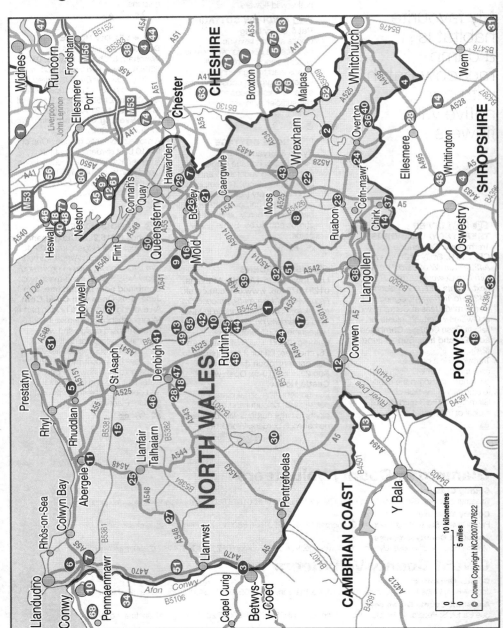

Opening Dates

February
SUNDAY 24
42 Plas Draw

March
SUNDAY 2
18 Dolhyfryd

SUNDAY 30
29 Hawarden Castle

April
SUNDAY 20
44 Ruthin Castle
50 Welsh College of Horticulture

SUNDAY 27
22 Erddig Hall

May
SATURDAY 3
17 Dibleys Nurseries

SUNDAY 4
12 Caereuni
17 Dibleys Nurseries
22 Erddig Hall

MONDAY 5
12 Caereuni
17 Dibleys Nurseries

SUNDAY 11
36 Park Cottage

SUNDAY 18
3 Beaver Grove House
8 Bryn Amma Cottage
24 The Garden House

SUNDAY 25
12 Caereuni

MONDAY 26
12 Caereuni

June
SUNDAY 1
12 Caereuni
23 Gardden Lodge

FRIDAY 6
11 33 Bryn Twr & Lynton (Evening)
39 Pen Y Ffrith Bird Gardens (Evening)

SATURDAY 7
11 33 Bryn Twr & Lynton

SUNDAY 8
4 Bettisfield Hall
11 33 Bryn Twr & Lynton
30 Isgaerwen

SUNDAY 15
15 The Cottage Garden Melin-y-Ddol

19 Dolwen
24 The Garden House
33 Llangedwyn Hall
34 Nantclwyd Hall

FRIDAY 20
28 Gwaenynog (Evening)

SUNDAY 22
28 Gwaenynog
31 Llanasa Village Gardens

SUNDAY 29
35 The Old Rectory, Llanfihangel Glyn Myfyr
37 9 The Parklands
41 Plas Ashpool
50 Welsh College of Horticulture
51 Y Graig

July
SUNDAY 6
12 Caereuni
16 The Cottage Nursing Home
49 Waen Wen

SATURDAY 12
43 Prices Lane Allotments

SUNDAY 13
24 The Garden House

SATURDAY 19
14 Chirk Castle

SUNDAY 20
26 Glan-y-Ffordd
45 Ruthin Town Gardens

SUNDAY 27
7 Broughton & Bretton Allotments
32 Llandegla Village Gardens
40 Penley Village Gardens
41 Plas Ashpool

August
SUNDAY 3
5 Bodrhyddan
12 Caereuni

SUNDAY 10
2 Bangor-on-Dee Village Gardens

TUESDAY 12
6 Bodysgallen Hall & Spa

SUNDAY 17
21 Dove Cottage

SUNDAY 24
12 Caereuni
22 Erddig Hall
36 Park Cottage

MONDAY 25
12 Caereuni

SUNDAY 31
9 Bryn Bellan

September
SUNDAY 7
12 Caereuni
13 Castanwydden
24 The Garden House

SUNDAY 21
4 Bettisfield Hall
12 Caereuni

October
SUNDAY 5
12 Caereuni
50 Welsh College of Horticulture

SUNDAY 26
12 Caereuni

Gardens open to the public
5 Bodrhyddan
14 Chirk Castle
22 Erddig Hall
24 The Garden House
39 Pen Y Ffrith Bird Gardens

By appointment only
1 Arfryn
10 Bryn Celyn
20 Donadea Lodge
25 Garthewin
27 Glog Ddu
38 Pen-y-Bryn
46 Tan y Graig
47 Trosyffordd
48 Tyddyn Bach

Also open by appointment ☎
11 33 Bryn Twr & Lynton
13 Castanwydden
18 Dolhyfryd
27 Glog Ddu
35 The Old Rectory, Llanfihangel Glyn Myfyr
41 Plas Ashpool
44 Ruthin Castle
51 Y Graig

The Gardens

1 ARFRYN
Pentrecelyn, nr Ruthin LL15 2HR. Mr & Mrs A O Davies, 01978 790475, arfrynpentrecelyn@btinternet.com. *4m S of Ruthin. On A525 Wrexham rd. At Llanfair Dyffryn Clwyd take B5429 to Graigfechan. Mold-Ruthin A494 to Llanbedr Dyffryn Clwyd turn L after*

village B5429 to Graigfechan. **Adm £2.50, chd free. Visitors welcome by appt June, July only, groups 10+.** Situated on hillside 800ft above sea level. 2-acre garden designed for yr-round interest, overlooking wonderful views. Divided into separate rooms - secret garden filled with old roses and hardy geraniums, cottage garden, wild flower bank and lawned gardens with herbaceous and shrub beds. New polytunnel garden featuring half hardy plants, trachycarpus, musa, cannas, etc.

✂ ✿ ☎

② BANGOR-ON-DEE VILLAGE GARDENS
LL13 0AT. *6m S of Wrexham. On A525 Wrexham to Whitchurch rd. Turn L signed Bangor-on-Dee. Follow signs to gardens.* Home-made teas at 17 Friars Court & Sunbank. **Combined adm £3.50, chd free. Sun 10 Aug (2-5.30).**
Picturesque village on the R Dee, beautiful church, well known basket shop and race course.

☕

17 FRIARS COURT
Mr & Mrs G P Fitton
Plantswoman's corner plot garden, contains a series of rooms with water features, arches, arbours and well stocked herbaceous borders.

✿ ✂ ✿

NEW 4 SANDOWN ROAD
Mrs Gill Williams
A garden for wildlife which incls, small pond, log-pile and planting to encourage bees, butterflies and birds. Small collection of hostas, exotics and alpines.

✿ ✂ ✿

SUNBANK
Laurels Avenue. Norman & Sylvia Jones
Approx ³/₄ -acre well cared for garden set on 3 lawned levels with wide variety of shrubs and perennials. Surrounded by mature trees and farmland with interesting water features and magnificent views over village and surrounding countryside.

✿ ✂

③ BEAVER GROVE HOUSE
Betws-y-Coed LL24 0HA. Mr J Heminsley. *¹/₂ m S of Betws-y-Coed. Opp side of R Conwy from Betws-y-Coed, one entrance drive on A470,*

200yds N of Waterloo Bridge; other entrance 800yds N of bridge on same rd. **Adm £2.50, chd 50p, OAP £1 (share to Colwyn Bay Leukaemia Research). Sun 18 May (11.30-5).**
Magic of a lost, old, unrestored garden; grass paths winding between wonderful old magnolias, azaleas and rhododendrons, leading to small arboretum. Approx 5 acres.

✿ ☕

④ BETTISFIELD HALL
Bettisfield SY13 2LB. Rev & Mrs David Butterworth. *9m SW of Whitchurch. 7m E of Ellesmere (Shropshire). 18m SE of Wrexham. Off A495 take Bettisfield/Wem rd. Garden opp historic church, St John the Baptist.* Home-made teas. **Adm £2.50, chd free. Suns 8 June; 21 Sept (2-5.30).**
On site of historic garden surrounding fortified manor house (not open). Panoramic view. Natural form gardens, sunken garden, herbs, newly established Heritage Welsh orchard. Green oak garden and furniture workshop. Blueberry and other specialist berries being grown under organic principles. 21 Sept Antique Tractor Rally, BBQ and Apple Pressing.

✿ ✿ ☕

⑤ ◆ BODRHYDDAN
Rhuddlan LL18 5SB. The Lord & Lady Langford. *1m E of Rhuddlan. From Rhuddlan take A5151 to Dyserth. Garden is on L.* Light refreshments & teas. **Adm £3, chd 50p (share to St Kentigern Hospice). Open Tues & Thurs June to Sept (2-5.30). For NGS: Sun 3 Aug (2-5.30).**
Parterre designed in 1875 by W Andrews Nesfield who also redesigned St James' Park and part of Kew Gardens. An extensive mid-Victorian shrubbery was lost through 2 World Wars and double death duties but the area has been redesigned by Lord and Lady Langford as a pond-side garden (four ponds) with a summerhouse of temple form.

✿ ☕

⑥ BODYSGALLEN HALL & SPA
nr Llandudno LL30 1RS. Historic House Hotels Ltd, www.bodysgallen.com/welcome/gardens. *2m from Llandudno. Take A55 to its intersection with A470 towards Llandudno. Proceed 1m, hotel is 1m on R.* Home-made teas. **Adm £3, chd 50p. Tue 12 Aug (2-5).**
Garden is well known for C17 box-

hedged parterre. Stone walls surround lower gardens with rose gardens and herbaceous borders. Outside walled garden is cascade over rocks. Enclosed working fruit and vegetable garden with espalier-trained fruit trees, hedging area for cut flowers with walls covered in wineberry and Chinese gooseberry. Restored Victorian woodland, walks with stunning views of Conwy and Snowdonia. Gravel paths and steep slopes.

✿ ✂ ✿ ⛺ ☕

Log-pile and planting to encourage bees, butterflies and birds . . .

⑦ BROUGHTON & BRETTON ALLOTMENTS
Main Road, Broughton CH4 0NT. Broughton & Bretton Area Allotments Association. *5m W of Chester. On A5104 (signed Penyffordd) in village of Broughton.* Home-made teas at War Memorial Institute, Main Rd. **Adm £3, chd free (share to B.I.R.D. Centre). Sun 27 July (2-6).**
Small collection of full and half sized allotment plots used by the local community to grow a mix of vegetables, flowers and soft fruit. Limited access for wheelchairs, but some plots are visible from the grass and gravel paths.

✿ ✂ ☕

⑧ BRYN AMMA COTTAGE
Frondeg, Wrexham LL14 4NB. Gillian & Roger Nock. *3m W of Wrexham. From A483 turn onto A525 towards Ruthin, after Coedpoeth Village turn L in Minera on B5426 (Minera Hall Rd), 2m turn R into unnamed lane with passing places, follow signs to field parking.* Home-made teas. **Adm £3, chd free (share to Hope House). Sun 18 May (1-5).**
Approx ¹/₂ -acre constantly evolving garden on hillside at war 900ft, nr moorland with views over Wrexham. Planted for yr-round interest, woodland slopes to stream with cataracts, flag iris, naturalised ferns and moisture-

loving plants. Lawned areas with informal borders, bluebells, perennials, rhododendrons, azaleas, ornamental trees and shrubs. Gravel paths, some moderate slopes.

  👨‍🦽 ✕ ⊛ ☕

⑨ BRYN BELLAN
Bryn Road, Gwernaffield CH7 5DE. **Gabrielle Armstrong & Trevor Ruddle.** *2m W of Mold. Leave A541 at Mold on Gwernaffield rd (Dreflan), 1/2 m after Mold derestriction signs turn R to Rhydymwyn & Llynypandy. After 200yds park in field on R.* Home-made teas. **Adm £3, chd free. Sun 31 Aug (2-5.30).**
Tranquil elegant garden transformed from wilderness in 3yrs. On 2 levels, partly walled upper garden with circular sunken lawn with majestic Sequoiadendron giganteum Wellingtonia and borders containing rhododendrons, camellias and spring flowering shrubs and bulbs. Lower garden, mainly lawn with naturalised bulb area and featuring an ornamental cutting garden with potting shed. Featured in 'English Garden', NW winner of Country Homes & Gardens 'Country Garden of the Year' Competition. Some gravel paths.

  👨‍🦽 ✕ ⊛ ☕

⑩ BRYN CELYN
Llanbedr LL15 1TT. Mrs S Rathbone, 01824 702077, skrathbone@toucansurf.com. *2m N of Ruthin. From Ruthin take A494 towards Mold. After 1 1/2 m, turn L at Griffin PH onto B5429. Proceed 1 1/2 m; garden on R.* **Adm £3, chd free. Visitors welcome by appt, from Feb to Oct, coaches welcome.**
2-acre garden with lawns surrounded by mixed borders. Walled garden with old-fashioned roses, cistus, lavender, honeysuckle, box balls and fruit trees. Gazebo and pergola leading to Mediterranean garden and woodland. Cherry trees and spring bulbs, autumn colour.

  👨‍🦽 ✕ ⊛ ☎

⑪ 33 BRYN TWR & LYNTON
Abergele LL22 8DD. Mr & Mrs Colin Knowlson & Mr & Mrs K A Knowlson, 01745 828201, apk@slaters.com. *From A55 heading W, take slip rd to Abergele. Turn L at roundabout then over T-lights; 1st L signed Llanfair T H. 3rd rd on L, No 33 is on L.* Home-made teas. **Adm £3, chd free (share to St Kentigern Hospice). Sat 7, Sun 8 June (2-5.30).**

Evening Opening £3, wine, Fri 6 June (6.30-8.30). Visitors also welcome by appt.
2 connected gardens of totally differing styles, one cottage style of planting, the other quite formal. Approx 3/4 acre in total, containing patio and pond areas; mixed herbaceous and shrub borders, many unusual plants. New features for 2008.

  ✕ ⊛ ☕

⑫ CAEREUNI
Ffordd Ty Cerrig, Godreir Gaer, nr Corwen LL21 9YA. Mr & Mrs Steve Williams. *1m N of Corwen. Take A5 to Bala. Turn R at T-lights onto A494 to Chester. 1st R after lay-by; house 1/4 m on L.* Home-made teas. **Adm £2.50, chd free. Sun 4, BH Mon 5, Sun 25, BH Mon 26 May; Sun 1 June; Sun 6 July; Suns 3, 24, BH Mon 25 Aug; Suns 7, 21 Sept; Suns 5, 26 Oct (2-5).**
Third of an acre international quirky themed fantasy garden with unique features incl; Japanese smoke water garden, old ruin, Spanish courtyard, Welsh gold mine, Chinese peace garden, woodman's lodge and jungle. Mexican chapel, 1950's petrol garage. Garden begun in 1988 now 20yrs old.

  👨‍🦽 ✕ ☕

Elemental 'white witches' garden . . .

⑬ CASTANWYDDEN
Fforddlas, Llandyrnog LL16 4LR. Mr A M Burrows, 01824 790404. *4m E of Denbigh. Take rd from Denbigh due E to Llandyrnog approx 4m. From Ruthin take B5429 due N to Llandyrnog.* Home-made teas. **Adm £2.50, chd free (share to Llangynhafal Parish Church). Sun 7 Sept (2-6). Visitors also welcome by appt.**

1 acre overflowing with unusual cottage garden plants; sunken patio garden with stone troughs; newly replanted rock garden, gravel bed with grasses; trellises covered in roses and clematis; unusual trees, wonderful colour and interest all summer, late flowering salvias, autumn cyclamen. Adjacent nursery.

  ✕ ⊛ ☕ ☎

⑭ ◆ CHIRK CASTLE
nr Wrexham LL14 5AF. The National Trust, 01691 777701, www.nationaltrust.org.uk. *7m S of Wrexham, 2m W of Chirk Village. Follow brown signs from A483 to Chirk Village. 2m W on minor rds. Follow brown signs.* Light refreshments & teas. **House and Garden adm £8.80, chd £4.40, Garden only adm £6.20, chd £3.10. For opening details please see website or tel. For NGS: Sat 19 July (10-5).**
5 1/2 -acre hilltop garden with good views over Shropshire and Cheshire. Formal garden with outstanding yew topiary. Rose garden, herbaceous borders, more informal further from the building with rare trees and shrubs, pond, thatched hawk house, ha-ha with terrace and pavilion. Lime tree avenue with daffodils and statue.

  👨‍🦽 ✕ ⊛ ☕

⑮ NEW THE COTTAGE GARDEN MELIN-Y-DDOL
Marli, Abergele LL22 9EB. Tom & Jenny Pritchard. *1 1/2 m N of Llannefydd. 3m S of Bodelwyddan. 3m S of A55 between Llannefydd & Glascoed. On R Elwy adj to Pont-y-Ddol. Entrance on S side of bridge.* Home-made teas. **Adm £2.50, chd free (share to St Mary's Church, Cefn). Sun 15 June (2-5.30).**
Many cottage garden plants in informal borders. Small bog areas, grass garden, laburnum arch, small wild flower meadow, fruit and vegetables, cut flower border. Elemental 'white witches' garden. Old mill stones from the mill are used throughout garden. Living willow structure. Hens. Riverside walk. Working cottage garden, sometimes repeat flowering sacrificed for seed production. All in magical setting. Under construction for 2008: 'Dyers' Garden' & 'Aromatherapy Garden'. Adj nursery featuring plants propagated from garden.

  ✕ ⊛ ☕

16 THE COTTAGE NURSING HOME
54 Hendy Road, Mold CH7 1QS. Mr & Mrs A G & L I Lanini. *10m W of Chester. From Mold town centre take A494 towards Ruthin. 2nd R into Hafod Park. Straight on to T-junction. Turn R onto Hendy Rd. Garden at junction of Hendy Rd & Clayton Rd.* Cream teas. **Adm £2, chd £1 (share to British Heart Foundation). Sun 6 July (2-5).**
Beautiful garden set in approx 1 acre. Well-established shrubs, herbaceous plants and abundance of colourful window boxes and tubs. Heart-shaped patio, incl water feature and pergola, with natural reclaimed stone walling.
&. ⊛ ☕

17 DIBLEYS NURSERIES
Cefn Rhydd, Llanelidan LL15 2LG. Mr & Mrs R Dibley. *7m S of Ruthin. Take A525 to Xrds by Llysfasi Agricultural College. Turn onto B5429 towards Llanelidan. After 1½ m turn L, 1m up lane on L. Brown tourist signs from A525.* Home-made teas. **Adm £3, chd free (share to ActionAid). Daily Sat 3 May to Mon 5 May (10-5).**
Large arboretum with wide selection of rare and unusual trees. There will be a lovely display of rhododendrons, magnolias, cherries and camellias. Ride through the garden on a miniature railway. ³/₄ -acre glasshouses are open to show streptocarpus and other pot plants. National Collection of *Streptocarpus.*
✗ ⊛ NCCPG ☕

18 DOLHYFRYD
yn Lawnt, Denbigh LL16 4SU. Captain & Mrs Michael Cunningham, 01745 814805, virginia@dolhyfryd.com, www.dolhyfryd.com. *1m SW of Denbigh. On B4501 to Nantglyn, from Denbigh - 1m from town centre.* Light refreshments & Home-made teas; wine. **Adm £3, chd free. Sun 2 Mar (10-4). Visitors also welcome by appt Mar-Sept. Coaches permitted. Groups 10+.**
Established garden set in small valley of R Ystrad. Acres of crocuses in late Feb/early Mar. Paths through wild flower meadows and woodland of magnificent trees, shade-loving plants and azaleas; mixed borders; walled kitchen garden - recently re-designed. Many woodland and riverside birds, incl dippers, kingfishers, grey wagtails. Many species of butterfly encouraged

by new planting. If wet, phone to visit on a sunny day. Refreshments with a Welsh flavour from local produce. Plant stall. Gravel paths.
&. ⊛ ☕ ☎

19 DOLWEN
Cefn Coch, Llanrhaeadr-ym-Mochnant SY10 0BU. Bob Yarwood & Jeny Marriott. *14m W of Oswestry. Take B4396 (or B4580 - narrow) W to Llanrhaeadr-ym-Mochnant. Turn R at W end of village opp The Plough Inn & up narrow lane for approx 1km. Garden on R.* Teas. **Adm £3, chd free. Sun 15 June (1-6). Also open Llangedwyn Hall.**
2 acres of hillside garden with pools, stream, small wood and many different types of unusual plants all backed by a stupendous mountain view.
☕

Many woodland and riverside birds, incl dippers, kingfishers, grey wagtails . . .

20 DONADEA LODGE
Babell CH8 8QD. Mr P Beaumont, 01352 720204. *7m NE of Denbigh. Turn off A541 Mold to Denbigh at Afonwen, signed Babell; T-junction turn L. A55 Chester to Conway take B5122 to Caerwys, 3rd turn on L.* **Adm £2.50, chd free. Visitors welcome by appt May, June & July (11-6), individuals, groups & coaches welcome.**
1-acre shady garden showing 25yrs of imaginative planting to enhance the magic of dappled shade, moving through different colour schemes, with each plant complementing its neighbour. Over 100 clematis, also a medlar tree over 100yrs old.
&. ✗ ☎

21 DOVE COTTAGE
Rhos Road, Penyffordd, Nr Chester CH4 0JR. Chris & Denise Wallis. *6m SW of Chester. From Chester A55 S*

exit A550 follow signs for Corwen. Turn L immed opp Penyffordd railway stn. From Wrexham A541 for Mold, R at Pontblyddyn for Chester, turn R immed opp Penyffordd railway stn. Home-made teas. **Adm £3, chd free (share to SENSE & MPS Society). Sun 17 Aug (2-5).**
Approx 1½ -acre garden, many shrubs and herbaceous plants set informally around lawns. Small kitchen garden, 2 ponds (1 wildlife), summerhouse, pergola and woodland planted area. Gravel paths, slight incline.
&. ✗ ⊛ ⊨ ☕

22 ◆ ERDDIG HALL
nr Wrexham LL13 0YT. The National Trust, 01978 355314, www.nationaltrust.org.uk. *2m S of Wrexham. Signed from A483/A5125 Oswestry rd; also from A525 Whitchurch rd.* House and Garden adm £8.80, chd £4.40, Garden only adm £5.50, chd £2.75. (Guided tours 12 and 3pm £3 only tour proceeds for NGS). For other opening details please tel or see website. For NGS: Suns 27 Apr; 4 May; 24 Aug (11-5).
Important, listed Grade 1 historic garden. Formal C18 and later Victorian design elements incl pleached lime tree avenues, trained fruit trees, wall plants and climbers, herbaceous borders, roses, herb border, annual bedding, restored glasshouse and vine house. National Collection of Ivy.
&. ✗ ⊛ NCCPG

23 GARDDEN LODGE
Gardden, Ruabon LL14 6RD. Richard & Angela Coles. *5m SW of Wrexham. Heading S on B5605 from Wrexham, through Johnstown. Turn R into Tatham Rd, past Gardden Ind. Est. Turn R after 100yds. Parking in Gardden Ind Est and Tatham Road. Short walk up lane to garden. Disabled visitor parking, limited access to garden.* Home-made teas. **Adm £2.50, chd free. Sun 1 June (2-5.30).**
Within woodland, a secluded and sheltered garden. Gardden Lodge is one of the 'lost houses of Wales' (not open) dating back to the C18, some original features remain. Specimen tulip tree in the centre surrounded by lawns and rhododendrons, with mixed herbaceous borders, terraced garden to rear. Some of the garden is on a terrace, which is not accessible to wheelchairs, but the garden can be enjoyed from ground level.
&. ⊛ ☕

24 ◆ **THE GARDEN HOUSE**
Erbistock LL13 0DL. Mr & Mrs S Wingett, 01978 781149, gardens@simonwingett.com. *5m S of Wrexham. On A528 Wrexham to Shrewsbury rd. Follow signs at Overton Bridge to Erbistock Church.* **Adm £3, chd free. Apr to Oct, Wed to Fri (11-5); Sun (2-5). For NGS: Suns 18 May; 15 June; 13 July; 7 Sept (2-5).**
Shrub and herbaceous plantings in monochromatic, analogous and complementary colour schemes. Rose pergolas, National Collection of hydrangea (over 300 species and cultivars). Sculpture Garden. Large lily pond, Victorian dovecote.
& ⊛ NCCPG ☕

25 **GARTHEWIN**
Llanfair T.H. LL22 8YR. Mr Michael Grime, 01745 720288. *6m S of Abergele & A55. From Abergele take A548 to Llanfair TH & Llanrwst. Entrance to Garthewin 250yds W of Llanfair TH on A548 to Llanrwst.* **Adm £3, chd free. Visitors welcome by appt in April, May & June.**
Valley garden with ponds and woodland areas. Much of the 8 acres have been reclaimed and redesigned providing a younger garden with a great variety of azaleas, rhododendrons and young trees, all within a framework of mature shrubs and trees. Small chapel open.
☎

26 **NEW** **GLAN-Y-FFORDD**
Bannel Lane. CH7 3AP. Ken & Ann Darlington. *1m SE of Buckley. From Wrexham A550, at Penymynydd roundabout, L onto A5118 Mold. 250yds R for Buckley over railway bridge (T-lights). Fieldgate entrance on L 200yds after The Winding House. From Mold take A5118 off Wylla roundabout through Llong, pass cement works, take 2nd L to Buckley over railway bridge. Fieldgate entrance on L 200yds after Winding House. Parking in field with access to garden. We do not recommend parking on the busy rd. Home-made teas.* **Adm £2.50, chd free. Sun 20 July (2-5).**
Established garden on S-facing slope. Mixed borders of shrubs and herbaceous plants. Vegetable garden and greenhouse.
✗ ⊛ ☕

27 **GLOG DDU**
Llangernyw, Abergele LL22 8PS. Pamela & Anthony Harris, 01745 860611, www.glogddu.blogspot.com. *1m S of Llangernyw. Through Llangernyw going S on A548. R into Uwch Afon. L after 1m at grass triangle. Follow rd, past new houses, down narrow lane. Glog Ddu is 1st house on R.* **Adm £2.50, chd free. Visitors welcome by appt 1 June to 30 Sept, max no. 20 due to restricted access.**
The result of three generations of gardening enthusiasm, a garden inspired by an Edwardian plantsman with a fascinating history. Approx 2 acres incl. rhododendrons, herbaceous borders, fledgling arboretum with rare trees, many grown from seed. The garden has been planted for yr-round interest with an emphasis on autumn colour.
✗ ⊛ ☎

28 **GWAENYNOG**
Denbigh LL16 5NU. Major & Mrs Tom Smith. *1m W of Denbigh. On A543, Lodge on L, ¼ m drive.* Home-made teas. **Adm £3, chd free (share to St James' Church, Nantglyn). Sun 22 June (2-5.30). Evening Opening £3, wine & light refreshments, Fri 20 June (6.30-8.30).**
2 acres incl the restored kitchen garden where Beatrix Potter wrote and illustrated the 'Tale of the Flopsy Bunnies'. Small exhibition of some of her work. C16 house (not open) visited by Dr Samuel Johnson during his Tour of Wales.
& ✗ ⊛ ☕

29 **HAWARDEN CASTLE**
Hawarden CH5 3B. Sir William & Lady Gladstone. *6m W of Chester. On B5125 just E of Hawarden village. Entrance via farm shop.* **Adm £3, chd £2. Sun 30 Mar (2-6).**
Large garden and picturesque ruined castle. Take care and supervise children. Dogs on short leads only.
&

30 **ISGAERWEN**
nr Pentrellyncymer LL21 9TU. Michael Williams. *10m W of Ruthin. 10m SW of Denbigh. From Ruthin take B1505 towards Cerrigydrudion, ½ m (Cross Keys PH) fork R to Bontuchel & Cyffylliog, 5m through Cyffylliog towards Clocaenog forest, 3m straight over small Xrds at edge of forest, 2m straight over Xrds at top of forest, 50yds fork R, garden ½ m.* Cream teas. **Adm £2.50, chd free. Sun 8 June (11-5).**
At 1500ft, isolated with stunning views, 2-acre garden balances the formal and informal - shrubbery, woodland copses, herbaceous and bog gardens, open spaces. The garden shows what can be grown in the wind with a short growing season. Children very welcome - games, venture.
✗ ⊛ ☕

> The garden shows what can be grown in the wind with a short growing season . . .

31 **LLANASA VILLAGE GARDENS**
CH8 9NE. *3m SE of Prestatyn. Llanasa is situated between Holywell & Prestayn, signed off A5151 by village of Trelawnyd.* Light refreshments & teas in village hall. **Combined adm £4, chd free. Sun 22 June (12-5).**
Small village in conservation area. Winner Wales in Bloom & Best Kept Village awards.
☕

NEW **GADLYS FARM HOUSE**
CH8 9LY. Dr & Mrs John Martin
Pretty lawned garden with colourful borders of shrubs and perennials. Vegetables are grown in raised beds.

GLANABER
Mr & Mrs David Roberts
1-acre garden created from pastureland dominated by rare holm oak; large duck pond, bridges, arches, footpaths create pleasant walks; spring bulbs; herbaceous and bedding plants. C18 house (not open).

GOLDEN GROVE
N R & M M J Steele-Mortimer
Attractive Edwardian terraced garden, walled on 3 sides, designed by Lady Aberconway on the site of a C17 walled garden. Recent improvements incl nuttery and retangular raised pond. Partial wheelchair access.
& ✗

THE OLD MANSE
Jill Espley
Sloping terraced garden with lawns, herbacous borders and rockery. Small wild flower section and vegetable area. Countryside view from top.

TAN Y COED
Mr & Mrs Bill Jones
The garden comprises approx 1/3 -acre of terraced deep beds growing an interesting variety of fruit, vegetables, herbs and flowers. Polytunnel, 2 green-houses and 2 perennial borders give yr-round colour, call across the road to chat to our hens.
❀

TAN Y FRON
Mr Meirion Ellis
Typical country cottage garden with outstanding splashes of brilliant colour and superb comprehensive vegetable garden.

Picturesque village surrounded by moorland . . .

㉜ LLANDEGLA VILLAGE GARDENS
LL11 3AP. *10m W of Wrexham. Off A525 at Llandegla Memorial Hall.* Cream teas at Llandegla Memorial Hall. **Combined adm £5, chd free. Sun 27 July (2-6).**
Small picturesque village surrounded by moorland. Church with interesting features. Communal garden area by river. Calor Village of Year award 2007; N Wales winner of Environment Category. Wales in Bloom, Silver Award, 2005, 2006. RHS Discretionary Award 2008 for Wales in Bloom. B&B available in village. Contact Keith Jackson.
☕

ERRW LLAN
3 Maes Teg. Mr & Mrs Keith Jackson
1/4 -acre garden made to attract wildlife. Plants grown for birds and butterflies. Trees for a variety of nesting sites. Pond to encourage frogs, toads, newts and damsel flies.

GLAN-YR-AFON
Mr & Mrs D C Ion. *Mini bus from Memorial Hall*
1-acre informal country garden surrounding this 200yr old farmhouse on 3 sides with a wide variety of features incl stream, 2 ponds, herbaceous borders, rockery and several ancient trees.
✈

OLD TY HIR FARM
Chester Road. Mr & Mrs D M Holder. *Mini bus from Memorial Hall*
Open plan garden with wide variety of trees, shrubs and many secret areas to explore.
✈

SWN Y GWYNT
Phil Clark. *Situated in Llandegla Village*
1/4 -acre plantsman's garden, shrubs and associated plants for shade.
✈

VILLAGE COTTAGE
Pat & Walt Standring
Very small country garden with lots of pots and interesting features.
✈

㉝ LLANGEDWYN HALL
Llangedwyn SY10 9JW. Mr & Mrs T M Bell. *8m W of Oswestry. On B4396 to Llanrhaeadr-ym-Mochnant about 5m W of Llynclys Xrds.* Home-made teas. **Adm £3, chd free. Sun 15 June (12-5). Also open Dolwen.**
Approx 4-acre formal terraced garden on 3 levels, designed and laid out in late C17 and early C18. Unusual herbaceous plants, sunken rose garden, small water garden, walled kitchen garden and woodland walk.
♿ ✈ ❀ ☕

㉞ NANTCLWYD HALL
Ruthin LL15 2PR. Sir Philip & Lady Isabella Naylor-Leyland. *4m S of Ruthin. Take A494 from Ruthin to Corwen. Garden is 1 1/2 m from Pwllglas on L, through stone gateway in beech hedge.* **Adm £3, chd 50p. Sun 15 June (2-6).**
Approx 3 acres of formal gardens incl Italian garden, parkland with lake and further grounds. Temples and follies by Sir Clough Williams-Ellis. Grotto by Belinda Eade. Rustic bridge over R Clwyd.
✈ ❀

㉟ THE OLD RECTORY, LLANFIHANGEL GLYN MYFYR
LL21 9UN. Mr & Mrs E T Hughes, 01490 420568, elwynthomashughes@hotmail.com. *2 1/2 m E of Cerrigydrudion. From Ruthin take B5105 SW for 12m to Llanfihangel Glyn Myfyr. Turn R just after Crown PH (follow signs). Proceed for 1/3 m, garden on L.* Home-made teas. **Adm £2.50, chd free (share to Cancer Research UK). Sun 29 June (2-5). Visitors also welcome by appt.**
17yr-old garden of approx 1 acre set in beautiful, tranquil, sheltered valley. A garden for all seasons; hellebores; abundance of spring flowers; mixed borders; water, bog, and gravel gardens; walled garden with old roses, pergola, bower and garden of meditation. Also incl garden created 12yrs ago by son which features hardy orchids and gentians.
♿ ✈ ❀ ⌂ ☕ ☎

㊱ PARK COTTAGE
Penley LL13 0LS. Dr & Mrs S J Sime. *3m E of Overton on Dee. 12m SE Wrexham. Signed from A539. Roadside parking in village involves 250yd walk to garden. Please no parking at house.* Home-made teas. **Adm £2.50, chd £1. Suns 11 May; 24 Aug (2-5).**
Relaxed garden emerging on a site of 5 acres. 3 1/2 acres developed so far. Large plant collection specialising in the hydrangea family. Ponds, grass garden, maze and many other features. New areas to see each year. Wide variety of plants from the garden for sale.
✈ ❀ ☕

㊲ 9 THE PARKLANDS
Chirk LL14 5PN. Sarah Wilkie. *10m SW of Wrexham. S from Wrexham on A483, turn R signed Chirk at Macdonald's roundabout. Through Chirk Village, turn L at St Mary's Church into Trevor Rd, park here please. Bear L then R into Shepherd's Lane, then R into The Parklands.* Home-made teas. **Adm £2.50, chd free. Sun 29 June (2-5).**
Pleasantly situated in newly built development on the edge of the village. Front garden laid to lawn, trees and shrubs. Smaller rear a garden of mixed planting, trees shrubs, perennials and climbers. Small vegetable garden. Several places to sit and enjoy the superb views over surrounding countryside.
✈ ❀ ☕

38 PEN-Y-BRYN
Llangollen LL20 8AA. Mr & Mrs R B Attenburrow, 01978 860223. *14m SW of Wrexham. Located above centre of Llangollen. Groups by appt should apply for directions.* **Visitors welcome by appt, groups of 10+.**
3-acre garden on wooded plateau overlooking town with panoramic view. On site of old hall with established trees, shrubs and rhododendrons; walled garden; water features; folly; extensive lawns and herbaceous borders. Some gravel paths.
♿ ⚔ ⊗ ☎

39 NEW ◆ PEN Y FFRITH BIRD GARDENS
Llandegla Road, Llanarmon-Yn-Ial, nr Mold CH7 4QX. David & Wendy Minshull, www.pen-y-ffrithbirdgardens.co.uk. *In between Mold, Ruthin & Wrexham. A494 Mold to Ruthin Rd turn L for Llanarmon-yn-Ial then follow brown tourist signs. A525 Wrexham to Ruthin follow brown tourist signs.* Light refreshments & teas. **Adm £3, chd free. For NGS: Evening Opening** Fri 6 June (6-9).
18 acres of beautiful woodland gardens home to a superb collection of ornamental waterfowl. Rhododendrons, azaleas, extensive hosta collection and herbaceous planting. House garden has a Japanese influence. Enjoy woodland walk to see fernery and artistically planted bog garden. Bluebell walk. Some gravel paths. some steep slopes.
♿ ⚔ ⊗ ☕

40 PENLEY VILLAGE GARDENS
LL13 0LU. *12m SE of Wrexham. On A539. In village turn L opp Maelor School if approaching from Wrexham. Follow signs to gardens.* Home-made teas at Penley Hall Stables. **Combined adm £3.50, chd free. Sun 27 July (2-5.30).**
Attractive village surrounded by farmland with thatched primary school and C16 village pub.
☕

26 OAKWOOD PARK
Eva & Phil Bassett
Young garden started in 2000. Mixed borders with trees, shrubs, perennials and annuals. Roses, clematis and other climbers on trellises. Small pond, bog area and raised borders with fruit trees, berries and vegetables.
⚔ ⊗

PENLEY HALL STABLES
Andrew & Angela Wilson
Approx 1-acre walled garden with shrubs and herbaceous plants, pools and bog garden. Created within old stable yard and surrounding land. Croquet (free tuition).
⚔

41 PLAS ASHPOOL
Llandyrnog LL16 4HP. Mrs F Bell, 01824 790612. *Half way between Bodfari & Llandyrnog on B5429; 5m outside Denbigh.* Home-made teas. **Adm £2.50, chd free. Suns 29 June; 27 July (1-6). Visitors also welcome by appt.**
Informal cottage garden set in a semi-walled plot with views of valley and Clwdyian Hills. Kitchen garden, bees, hens and ducks amongst a colourful mixture of herbaceous plants, New for 2008, a wild flower meadow in the making.
⚔ ⊗ ☕ ☎

42 PLAS DRAW
Llangynhafal LL15 1RT. Graham Holland. *4m NE of Ruthin. From Mold or Ruthin on A494 turn into B5429 at Llanbedr DC, after ½ m turn R signed Llangynhafal. Gate 1½ m on R.* Light refreshments & teas. **Adm £2.50, chd £1 (share to Llangynhafal Church). Sun 24 Feb (12.30-4).**
Four acres around 18C house (not open). Drifts of snowdrops, pools, woodland.
♿ ⚔ ☕

43 NEW PRICES LANE ALLOTMENTS
Prices Lane, Wrexham LL11 2NB. Wrexham Allotment & Leisure Gardeners Association. *1m from town centre. From A483, take exit for Wrexham Ind Estate and follow A5152 towards the town centre. Allotments signed from there.* Home-made teas. **Adm £3, chd free. Sat 12 July (11-6).**
120 plus plots, growing a good variety of flowers, fruit and vegetables. Plots for the disabled and school children. Association shop, selling a wide range of garden requisites and seeds.
♿ ⊗ ☕

44 RUTHIN CASTLE
Castle Street, Ruthin LL15 2NU. Ruthin Castle Ltd, 07834 211989, gardens_ruthincastle@hotmail.co.uk, www.ruthincastlehotel.com. *Turn L at Natwest Bank. On roundabout in centre of Ruthin.* **Adm £3. Sun 20 Apr (11-5). Visitors also welcome by appt.**
Wonderfully exciting restoration project, progressing fast, of Victorian and formal gardens. Walkways, courtyards, rose garden, dry moats and dungeons in C13 castle ruins. Lawns with rare and beautiful trees. The hotel was frequented by Edward, Prince of Wales.
⚔ ⊗ 🛏 ☎

45 RUTHIN TOWN GARDENS
LL15 1HY. *Centre of Ruthin. From St Peter's Sq, take rd to R of NatWest bank.* Home-made teas in Annies Teashop. **Combined adm £3, chd free. Sun 20 July (11-5).**
Medieval town, many historic buildings set in beautiful Vale of Clwyd. Small and charming gardens. 5 Upper Clwyd St Second in 2007 Ruthin Flower Show Town Garden Award.
⊗ ☕

ANNIES
5 Upper Clwyd Street. Mr & Mrs J P R & A Holmes. *From Ruthin Sq, go down side of Dodds Estate Agent, past bookshop to Annie's teashop. Garden through double gates by steps*
Small town garden with many different blooms. Lots of pots, very colourful. Approach via steep hill; gravel in garden area.
♿ ⊗

BERWYN
Upper Clwyd Street. Susan Evans. *100yds off St Peter's Sq*
Very pretty tiny walled town garden, all pots. A framed picture of a garden.
⚔

SIR JOHN TREVOR GARDEN
Castle Street. Stuart & Jackie Jones. *From St Peter's Sq take Corwen Rd (towards Ruthin Castle). House on L 200yds*
Small town garden. Selection of plants and shrubs and patio containers.
⚔

46 TAN Y GRAIG
Mill Lane, Llannefydd Road, Henllan LL16 5BD. Jim & Barbara Buchanan, 01745 816161. *On B5382 Denbigh to Henllan rd. Mill Lane is 100yds below Church Tower off the Llannefydd rd. Garden is top bungalow*

in Mill Lane. **Adm £2.50, chd free. Visitors welcome by appt.** Elevated 1/2 -acre garden with panoramic views over surrounding countryside, dissected by terraced walks and backed by a high limestone cliff abundant with wildlife. Large rockery, shrub and perennial beds containing over 500 varieties of plants - many unusual. Small adjacent nursery with all plants propagated from the garden.

🌿 ❀ ☎

47 TROSYFFORDD
Ystrad LL16 4RL. Miss Marion MacNicoll, 01745 812247, marionphysio@btinternet.com. *1 1/2 m W of Denbigh. From A525 Denbigh to Ruthin rd, turn R in out- skirts of Denbigh by swimming pool, on Ystrad rd signed Prion & Saron. Follow for 1 1/2 m, Trosyffordd is 2nd drive on R after 1st hill.* **Adm £3, chd free. Visitors welcome by appt April to September. Coaches permitted.** Medium-sized artists and plantsman's garden created from a field since 1940. Unusual trees grown from seed. Mixed borders with roses, herbaceous, shrubs and grasses. Colour schemes. New: small arboretum started in 2005. Teas for groups by arrangement or bring a picnic.

♿ ❀ ☎

48 TYDDYN BACH
Bontuchel, Ruthin LL15 2DG. Mr & Mrs L G Starling, 01824 710248. *4m W of Ruthin. B5105 from Ruthin, turn R at Cross Keys towards Bontuchel/Cyffylliog. Through Bontuchel, river is now on R. Turn L up narrow rd, steep hill just before bridge. House 1st on L.* **Adm £2. Visitors welcome by appt July & August.** Mainly organic, very pretty cottage garden with prolific vegetable garden. Wildlife friendly with hedges and wood pile. Greenhouse packed with plants for both pots and the garden.

🌿 ☎

49 WAEN WEN
Llandyrnog LL16 4LE. Mr & Mrs David Lloyd. *4m E of Denbigh. 3/4 m E from Llandyrnog on B5429.* Home- made teas. **Adm £2.50, chd free. Sun 6 July (2-6).** 1-acre garden with informal mixed borders surrounding farmhouse. Exciting features around every corner of farm buildings. Pond and bog area. Short walk to 10yr-old copse. Dogs may be walked in designated fields.

❀ ☕

50 NEW WELSH COLLEGE OF HORTICULTURE
Holywell Road, Northop CH7 6AA. M B Simkin (Principal), 01352 841000, info@wcoh.ac.uk, www.wcoh.ac.uk. *10m W of Chester. Leave A55 at exit to Northop. From E carry on through T-lights in village. College on R after 1/2 m. From W, R at T-lights.* Light refreshments & teas in Coffee Shop. **Adm £3, chd free. Suns 20 Apr; 29 June; 5 Oct (10-4).** Over 91 hectares of land. Developed over the past 50 yrs the picturesque surrounding provide a number of different landscaped areas. Favourites incl ornamental gardens, grass gardens, pinetum, courtyard, gold garden, winter stem bed, shrubbery, heather garden, rock gardens, and village beds.

♿ ❀ ☕

51 NEW Y GRAIG
Llandegla, Wrexham LL11 3BG. Janet Strivens, 01978 790657, strivens@liv.ac.uk. *8m SE of Ruthin. From Wrexham take A525 towards Ruthin. After approx 7m The Plough PH on L. Take lane immed on L of The Plough and follow it up the hill for 1m, carefully.* Light refreshments & teas. **Adm £2.50, chd free (share to Clwyd Guild of Spinners, Weavers & Dyers). Sun 29 June (11.30-5.30). Visitors also welcome by appt May, June, July only. No large parties.** 1/2 acre of enchanting informal hillside garden at over 1000ft beneath a limestone outcrop. Herbaceous beds full of colour, rockeries, many clematis and old roses, small ponds and water lilies. 3 acres of field with recently established woodland incl specimen trees. Vegetable garden and wonderful views over the Clwydians. Spinning demonstrations by the Clwyd Guild of Spinners, Weavers & Dyers. Some steep uneven paths, steps & gravel.

🌿 ❀ ☕ ☎

North Wales County Volunteers
Denbighshire & Colwyn

County Organiser & Leaflet Coordinator
Rhian Davey, Ffynnon Y Milgi, Llanelidan, Ruthin LL15 2TD, 01824 750507, rmdavey@f-y-m.net

County Treasurer
Elizabeth Sasse, Hendy, Trefechan Road, Afonwen, Mold CH7 5UP, 01352 720220

Publicity
Jessica Craft, Bryn Glas, Prion, Denbigh LL16 4RY, 01745 890251, jessiecraft8@aol.com

Assistant County Organiser
Sue Rathbone, Bryn Celyn, Llanbedr, Ruthin LL15 1TT, 01824 702077, skrathbone@toucansurf.com

Flintshire & Wrexham

County Organiser
Angela Wilson, Penley Hall Stables, Penley, Wrexham LL13 0LU, 01948 830439, wilsons.penley@tiscali.co.uk

County Treasurer
Peter Manuel, Tir y Fron, Ruabon, Wrexham LL14 6RW, 01978 821633

Press & Publicity Officer
Ann Rathbone, Woodfield House, Station Road, Hawarden CH5 3EG, 01244 532948
Anne Saxon, Leeswood Green Farm, Leeswood, Mold CH7 4SQ, 01352 771222, annemsaxon@yahoo.co.uk

Mark your diary with these special events in 2008

EXPLORE SECRET GARDENS DURING CHELSEA WEEK

Tue 20 May, Wed 21 May, Thur 22 May, Fri 23 May
Full day tours: £78 per person, 10% discount for groups
Advance Booking required, telephone 01932 864532 or
email pennysnellflowers@btinternet.com

Specially selected private gardens in London, Surrey and Berkshire. The tour price includes transport and lunch with wine at a popular restaurant or pub.

FROGMORE – A ROYAL GARDEN (BERKSHIRE)

Tue 3 June 10am - 5.30pm (last adm 4pm)
Garden adm £4, chd free. Advance booking recommended telephone 01483 211535 or email orders@ngs.org.uk

A unique opportunity to explore 30 acres of landscaped garden, rich in history and beauty.

FLAXBOURNE FARM – FUN AND SURPRISES (BEDFORDSHIRE)

Sun 8 June 10am - 5pm Adm £5, chd free
No booking required, come along on the day!

Bring the whole family and enjoy a plant fair and garden party and have fun in this beautiful and entertaining garden of 2 acres.

WISLEY RHS GARDEN – MUSIC IN THE GARDEN (SURREY)

Tue 19 August 6 - 9pm

Adm (incl RHS members) £7, chd under 15 free

A special opening of this famous garden, exclusively for the NGS. Enjoy music and entertainment as you explore a range of different gardens.

For further information visit www.ngs.org.uk or telephone 01483 211535

POWYS

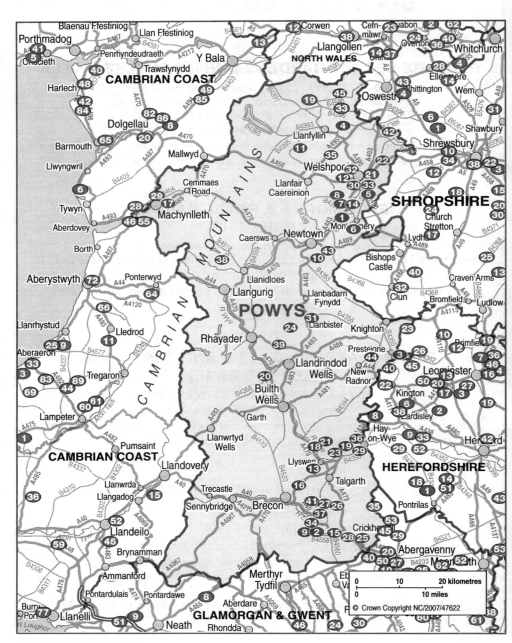

Opening Dates

March

SUNDAY 23
22 Maesfron Hall and
Gardens

April

SUNDAY 13
33 Rowan

SUNDAY 27
28 Penmyarth

May

SATURDAY 3
24 Mill Cottage
35 Tan-y-Llyn

SUNDAY 4
24 Mill Cottage
35 Tan-y-Llyn
36 Tawryn

MONDAY 5
20 Llysdinam
24 Mill Cottage
36 Tawryn

SUNDAY 11
15 Gliffaes Country House Hotel
23 Maesllwch Castle

SATURDAY 17
7 3 Church Terrace
12 Dingle Nurseries & Garden
14 Glansevern Hall Gardens

SUNDAY 18
4 Bodynfoel Hall
12 Dingle Nurseries & Garden
18 Llanstephan House

SUNDAY 25
40 The Walled Garden

MONDAY 26
11 Cyfie Farm

June

SUNDAY 1
41 The Wern

SATURDAY 7
5 Brooks Lodge
35 Tan-y-Llyn
44 Whimble Garden and Nursery
and Railsgate Barn Garden

SUNDAY 8
5 Brooks Lodge
26 Oak Cottage
29 Pen-y-Maes
31 The Rock House
35 Tan-y-Llyn

SUNDAY 15
25 The Neuadd, Llanbedr
33 Rowan

SUNDAY 22
37 Treberfydd
38 Ty Capel Deildre

SUNDAY 29
13 Felinnewydd

July

SATURDAY 5
35 Tan-y-Llyn

SUNDAY 6
35 Tan-y-Llyn

SATURDAY 12
7 3 Church Terrace
14 Glansevern Hall Gardens

SUNDAY 13
19 Llowes Gardens
34 Talybont Gardens

SATURDAY 19
30 Powis Castle Garden

August

SUNDAY 3
7 3 Church Terrace
8 Cil y Wennol

SUNDAY 10
20 Llysdinam

WEDNESDAY 13
17 Grandma's Garden

SUNDAY 31
3 The Bindery

September

MONDAY 1
3 The Bindery

SUNDAY 7
22 Maesfron Hall and Gardens
39 Vale House

SUNDAY 14
21 Lower Fferm Wen

SATURDAY 20
7 3 Church Terrace
14 Glansevern Hall Gardens

October

SATURDAY 18
12 Dingle Nurseries & Garden

SUNDAY 19
12 Dingle Nurseries & Garden

Gardens open to the public

2 Ashford House
12 Dingle Nurseries & Garden
14 Glansevern Hall Gardens
17 Grandma's Garden

30 Powis Castle Garden
44 Whimble Garden and
Nursery and Railsgate Barn
Garden

By appointment only

1 Abernant
6 Castell y Gwynt
9 Coity Mawr
10 Cwm-Weeg
16 Glyn Celyn House
27 The Old Vicarage
32 Rose Cottage
42 Westlake Fisheries
43 Westwinds
45 Woodhill

Also open by appointment ☎

4 Bodynfoel Hall
7 3 Church Terrace
11 Cyfie Farm
20 Llysdinam
22 Maesfron Hall and Gardens
24 Mill Cottage
29 Pen-y-Maes
33 Rowan
35 Tan-y-Llyn
36 Tawryn
38 Ty Capel Deildre
40 The Walled Garden

The Gardens

1 ABERNANT
Garthmyl SY15 6RZ. J A & B M
Gleave, 01686 640494,
johngleave@virgin.com. *Mid-way
between Welshpool (9m) & Newtown
(9m) on A483. 1¹/₂ m S of Garthmyl.
Approached over steep humpback
bridge, then straight ahead through
gate. No parking for coaches.* Home-
made teas. **Adm £3, chd free.**
**Visitors welcome by appt Apr, June,
July.**
Approx 2¹/₂ acres incl cherry orchard,
lawns, knot garden, roses, lavender,
rockery, containers, ornamental shrubs
and trees, specimen fern garden,
ornamental pond, potager; additional
woodland area with natural pond and
stream with walks and views of R
Severn. Several examples of archaic
sundials. Come and picnic in the
cherry orchard.
🍴 ✿ ☕ ☎

❷ ◆ ASHFORD HOUSE
Talybont-on-Usk LD3 7YR. Mrs E Anderson, 01874 676271. $6^{1}/_{2}$ m SE of Brecon. Off A40 on B4558. 1m SE of Talybont-on-Usk. **Adm £2.50, chd free. Tues, Apr to Sept (2-6).**
1-acre walled garden surrounded by woodland and wild garden approx 4 acres altogether; restored and developed since 1979. Mixed shrub and herbaceous borders; meadow garden and pond; alpine house and beds; vegetables. A relaxed plantsman's garden. Weekly openings mean visitors may enjoy a peaceful garden in its everyday state.

&. ❀

❸ NEW THE BINDERY
14 Hereford Street, Presteigne LD8 2AR. Marion and Chris Rowlatt. 6m S of Knighton. 13 m NE of Leominster. At Presteigne follow yellow signs. **Adm £3, chd free. Sun 31 Aug (11-6); Mon 1 Sept (2-6).**
Colour and contrast are the themes of this secret cottage garden. A series of small rooms have been created as a beacon for birds. The planting is informal and in high summer, berries, bamboos, grasses, crocosmia, helenium, asters and acidanthera provide movement, sunshine, colours and perfume. We have a collection of birds that don't need feeding as well as lots that do! Teas in the town. Featured in 'Hortus' and 'Country Life'.

🏵

❹ BODYNFOEL HALL
Llanfechain SY22 6XD. Trustees of Bodynfoel Estate, 01691 648486, bonnore@tiscali.co.uk. 10m N of Welshpool via A490 towards Llanfyllin. Take B4393, follow signs. Home-made teas. **Adm £3.50, chd free, concessions £2. Sun 18 May (2-6). Visitors also welcome by appt June/July only.**
Approx 5 acres of garden, woodland and ponds. Wide variety of trees, shrubs, rhododendrons and azaleas with woodland walks. Pondside planting links the 3 ponds. Mixed borders and paths surround the house, with lawns and ha-ha offering far-reaching views into Shropshire. One steep area unsuitable for wheelchairs.

&. ❀ ☕ ☎

❺ BROOKS LODGE
Leighton Park, Welshpool SY21 8LW. Geoff & Valerie Vine. 2m E of Welshpool. SE off A483 onto A490. Just after river/railway bridge, turn L signed Cilcewydd (Leighton). R onto B4388 for 100yds. L at Lodge House, continue up lane to car park. Light refreshments & teas. **Adm £3, chd free. Sat 7, Sun 8 June (1-5.30).**
$^{3}/_{4}$ -acre garden that has several distinct areas arising from natural topography of site. Incl small walled garden, herbaceous border, shrubberies, woodland garden and courtyard garden. Divided by natural pond and stream, all richly planted. Pond and stream unfenced, children must be supervised. Royal Forestry Society's Charles Ackers Redwood Grove and Pinetum few hundred yds from car park. Oldest and tallest Redwoods in Britain, enjoyable for family groups. Guided tours, by arrangement with warden David Williams, throughout the day. Display of artwork at house. Winner of 'County Times' Garden of the Year 2007. Featured in 'Shropshire Star'.

🏵 ❀ ☕

A series of small rooms have been created as a beacon for birds . . .

❻ CASTELL Y GWYNT
Montgomery SY15 6HR. Angela & Roger Hughes, 01686 668317, r.dhughes@btinternet.com. 2m S of Montgomery. Please tel for directions. Home-made teas. **Adm £3. Visitors welcome by appt for groups mid-May to Sept.**
$1^{1}/_{2}$ -acre garden at 900ft, set within 6 acres of land managed for wildlife. Native woodland corridors with mown rides surround hayfield and pool with turf-roofed summerhouse. Enclosed kitchen garden with boxed beds of vegetables, fruit and cutting flowers, greenhouse, orchard. Shrubberies, deep mixed borders and more formal areas close to house. Outstanding views of Welsh mountains.

❀ ☕ ☎

❼ 3 CHURCH TERRACE
Berriew, Welshpool SY21 8PF. Mr Jimmy Hancock, 01686 640774. 5m S of Welshpool. In village centre, behind the Church. **Adm £2, chd free. Sats 17 May; 12 July; Sun 3 Aug; Sat 20 Sept (2-6). Visitors also welcome by appt.**
$^{1}/_{4}$ -acre garden with river below. Plantsman's garden with trees, shrubs, climbers and diverse range of rare and unusual plants to create interest throughout yr; keen gardeners who feel they need something different to stimulate their garden will see what can be achieved in a small garden. 30ft x 12ft greenhouse with good range of tender, interesting plants. Visitor numbers limited due to size of garden, personal tour incl with owner, Head Gardener, Powis Castle 1972-96.

🏵 ❀ ☎

❽ CIL Y WENNOL
Berriew, Welshpool SY21 8AZ. Willie & Sue Jack. 5m SW of Welshpool. Berriew is off the A483 Welshpool to Newtown rd. By Berriew School take B4385 towards Castle Caereinion. Cil y Wennol is $^{3}/_{4}$ m along the B4385. Home-made teas. **Adm £3.50, chd free. Sun 3 Aug (2-6).**
$3^{1}/_{2}$ -acre established garden set around Tudor cottage (not open). Long curving drive leads to front garden of traditional formal cottage design with more recent influences. Rear gardens: sweeping array of new-style prairie planting, spectacular views, enclosed vegetable garden, croquet lawn. Crescent-shaped hedges, slate walls, amphitheatre steps and congruent sculptures. Steep steps/path to rear garden. Owner's open studio and exhibition of contemporary glass, metal work and sculptures.

🏵 ❀ ☕

❾ COITY MAWR
Talybont-on-Usk LD3 7YN. Mr & Mrs William Forwood, 01874 676664. 6m SE of Brecon. Leave Talybont village on B4558 towards Brecon. Approx $^{1}/_{2}$ m at pink cottages take L signed Talybont reservoir, then 1st R up to rd junction; turn L to Coity Mawr at top on R. **Adm £3, chd free. Visitors welcome by appt.**
$4^{1}/_{2}$ acres at 850ft created over 14yrs; work still in progress. Terraced with spectacular view of Black Mountains across Usk valley. Mature trees, unusual plants and shrubs; rose and water gardens; parterre; willow arbour.

&. 🏵 ❀ ☎

10 CWM-WEEG

Dolfor, Newtown SY16 4AT. Dr W Schaefer & Mr K D George, 01686 628992, wolfgang.schaefer@virgin.net. *4¹/₂ m SE of Newtown. Take A489 E from Newtown for 1¹/₂ m, turn R towards Dolfor. After 2m turn L down farm track.* Teas. **Adm £3, chd free.** **Visitors welcome by appt from mid-May to mid-Sept, inaccessible for coaches.**

2¹/₂-acre garden set within 12 acres of wild flower meadows and bluebell woodland with stream centred around C15 farmhouse (not open). Formal garden commenced in 1990s in English landscape tradition with vistas, grottos, lawns and extensive borders terraced with stone walls, translates older garden vocabulary into an innovative C21 concept. Runner up in County Times Best Garden mid-Wales. Steep paths in wood.

Spectacular views of Vyrnwy Valley and Welsh Hills . . .

11 NEW CYFIE FARM

Llanfihangel, Llanfyllin SY22 5JE. Group Captain Neil & Mrs Claire Bale, 01691 648451, info@cyfiefarm.co.uk. *6m SE of Lake Vyrnwy. B4393 from Llanfyllin. After approx 4m, L signed Llanfihangel/Dolanog B4382. After leaving Llanfihangel towards Dolanog, 1st L. 3rd farm on L.* Home-made teas. **Adm £3.50, chd free. Mon 26 May (2-5).** Visitors also welcome by appt.

1-acre hillside country garden with spectacular views of Vyrnwy Valley and Welsh Hills. Terraced formal areas with roses, mature shrubs, herbaceous borders. Walks through garden on different levels, leading to informal areas with mature trees, rhododendrons, azaleas, heathers. Stepped path to lower summerhouse where wild garden, bluebell bank views and peaceful location enjoyed.

12 ◆ DINGLE NURSERIES & GARDEN

Welshpool SY21 9JD. Mr & Mrs D Hamer, 01938 555145. *2m NW of Welshpool. Take A490 towards Llanfyllin and Guilsfield. After 1m turn L at sign for Dingle Nurseries & Garden.* **Adm £3, chd free. Open all yr (8.30-5). For NGS: Sats, Suns 17, 18 May; 18, 19 Oct.**

4-acre garden on S-facing site, sloping down to lake. Beds mostly colour themed with a huge variety of rare and unusual trees and shrubs. Set in hills of mid Wales this beautiful and well known garden attracts visitors from Britain and abroad.

FELIN Y FFRIDD
See Gwynedd.

13 NEW FELINNEWYDD

Llandefalle, nr Brecon LD3 0NE. Huw Evans-Bevan. *5¹/₂ m NE of Brecon. From Brecon follow A470 for 5¹/₂ m towards Builth Wells, turning L at Llanfilo. Garden on L after Llandefalle.* Home-made teas. **Adm £3, chd free. Sun 29 June (2-5).**

Large renovated garden surrounding impressive Victorian house. Newly-designed mixed borders and attractive organic kitchen garden. Lawns lead down to stream. Mature trees.

14 ◆ GLANSEVERN HALL GARDENS

Berriew SY21 8AH. G & M Thomas, 01686 640644, glansevern@yahoo.co.uk. *5m SW of Welshpool. On A483 at Berriew. Signposted.* **Adm £4, chd free. Thurs, Fris, Sats & Bank Hol Mons 1 May to 27 Sept (12-last entry 5). For NGS: Sats 17 May; 12 July; Sat 20 Sept (12-5).**

20-acre mature garden situated nr banks of R Severn. Centred on Glansevern Hall, a Greek Revival house dated 1801 (not open). Noted for variety of unusual tree species; much new planting; lake with island; woodland walk; large rock garden and grotto. Roses and herbaceous beds. Water garden and large walled garden, with fruit, vegetable and ornamental planting. Interesting shelters and follies. Walk down to R Severn through Folly Garden. Majority accessible to wheelchair users.

15 GLIFFAES COUNTRY HOUSE HOTEL

Crickhowell NP8 1RH. Mr & Mrs N Brabner & Mr & Mrs J C Suter. *2¹/₂ m NW of Crickhowell. 1m off A40.* Home-made teas. **Adm £3, chd free. Sun 11 May (2-5).**

Large garden; spring bulbs, azaleas and rhododendrons; ornamental pond; heathers, shrubs and ornamental trees; fine maples; superb position high above R Usk.

16 GLYN CELYN HOUSE

Felinfach, nr Brecon LD3 0TY. Mr & Mrs N Paravicini, 01874 624836. *4m NE of Brecon. On A470 east of Brecon on hill above Felinfach.* **Adm £3, chd free. Visitors welcome by appt Apr to Sept, groups of 10+ incl coaches.**

13-yr-old 7-acre sloping garden still in the making. 2 streams supply water to fountains and lake. Mixed planting within yew and hornbeam hedges. Woodland walks lead to lake and unusual grotto. Well-established trees among newly-planted shrubs and trees. Pretty kitchen garden with raised beds and rose and sweet pea covered arches. Glorious views over the Black Mountains.

17 ◆ GRANDMA'S GARDEN

Plas Dolguog Estates, Machynlleth SY20 8UJ. Diana & Richard Rhodes, 01654 703338, diana@sol-star.fsnet.co.uk. *1¹/₂ m E of Machynlleth. Turn L off A489 Machynlleth to Newtown rd. Follow brown tourist signs to Plas Dolguog Hotel.* **Adm £3.50, chd £1.50, concessions for wheelchair carers. Weds & Suns all yr (10-6). For NGS: Wed 13 Aug (10.30-6).**

Inspiration for the senses. Old and new areas, 7 sensory gardens, riverside boardwalk, stone circle, wildlife pond, willow arbour, strategic seating. Continuous new attractions. Wildlife abundant. 9 acres in which to find peace. Sculptures, poetry, arboretum. Great for children and access. Books, handmade cards, craft stall. Featured in local press. 2 short slopes require assistance for manual wheelchair users. Access statement available. Books and information available in Braille.

THE GRIGGS
See Herefordshire.

HERGEST CROFT GARDENS
See Herefordshire.

HILL HOUSE FARM
See Herefordshire.

IVY COTTAGE
See Herefordshire.

LITTLE HELDRE
Buttington. See Shropshire.

18 NEW LLANSTEPHAN HOUSE
nr Brecon LD3 0YR. Lord & Lady Milford. *10m SW of Builth Wells. Leave A470 at Llyswen onto B4350. 1st L after crossing river in Boughrood. Follow yellow signs. From Builth Wells leave A470 at Erwood Bridge. 1st L then follow signs.* Home-made teas. **Adm £3, chd free. Sun 18 May (2-5).**
Large garden with rhododendrons, azaleas, shrubs, water garden, shrub roses, walled kitchen garden, greenhouses and very fine specimen trees. Beautiful views of Wye Valley and Black Mountains.
 ♿ ☕

LLANTHONY AND DISTRICT GARDENS
See Gwent.

19 LLOWES GARDENS
nr Hay-on-Wye HR3 5JA. *3¹/₂ m W of Hay-on-Wye. On A438 between Clyro and Glasbury-on-Wye at Llowes. Follow yellow signs in village.* Light refreshments, lunches & teas at Llowes Court. **Combined adm £6, chd free. Sun 13 July (11-5).**
3 very interesting, very different gardens around the church (Celtic cross and Kilvert associations).
 ♿ ☒ ☕

LLOWES COURT
Mr & Mrs Briggs. *On L from Clyro off A438.* Home-made teas
Large low-lying garden of walled courtyards, lawns, woodland and meadows. Deep pools and stream (keep children attended) surrounding C16 house (not open). Grotto, rill, mounts, box, yew alley. Formal garden in reclaimed farmyard, rose tunnel, vegetables, roaming ducks and hens.
 ♿ ☒

2 MILL COTTAGES
Lyn & Chris Williams. *In village* Fascinating long narrow garden with a series of individual areas

imaginatively planted. Features a variety of unusual stonework, interesting collection of grasses and many hidden surprises.
♿ ☒

PLAS WYE
Geoff & Helen Hardy. *On R of A438 from Clyro*
Mature 1-acre densely planted colourful garden in a series of interconnecting areas cleverly linked over different levels. Water features, roses, laburnum arch, old apple trees and views of the Black Mountains.
 ♿ ☒

LLWYNCELYN
See Ceredigion/Cardiganshire.

Restored Victorian conservatories, tower and shell grotto . . .

20 LLYSDINAM
Newbridge-on-Wye LD1 6NB. Sir John & Lady Venables-Llewelyn & Llysdinam Charitable Trust, 01597 860190/200. *5m SW of Llandrindod Wells. Turn W off A470 at Newbridge-on-Wye; turn R immed after crossing R Wye; entrance up hill.* Home-made teas. **Adm £3, chd free. Mon 5 May; Sun 10 Aug (2-6). Visitors also welcome Mar to Oct incl, garden clubs & coaches, please tel in advance.**
Large garden. Azaleas, rhododendrons, water garden and herbaceous borders, shrubs, woodland garden, Victorian kitchen garden and greenhouses. Fine view of Wye Valley. Gravel paths.
 ♿ ☒ ☕ ☏

21 LOWER FFERM WEN
Ffynnon Gynydd, nr Glasbury-on-Wye HR3 5NG. E Curtis. *6¹/₂ m W of Hay-on-Wye. Take A438 from Glasbury. 1st L (Maesyronnen Chapel). Continue up hill to junction, turn R. Continue straight up hill for 2m. Entrance to garden on L immed before*

cattle grid. Home-made teas. **Adm £3, chd free. Sun 14 Sept (2-5).**
4-acre garden situated at over 1000ft. Natural stream and pools with willow beds and bog plantings. Mixed shrub and herbaceous borders, shrub and climbing roses. Developing orchard, spinney and specimen trees. Kitchen garden. Stunning views of Black Mountains and Brecon Beacons.
 ♿ ☒ ☕

22 NEW MAESFRON HALL AND GARDENS
Trewern, Welshpool SY21 8EA. Dr & Mrs T Owen, 01938 570600, www.maesfron.co.uk. *4m E of Welshpool. On A458 Shrewsbury to Welshpool road.* Light refreshments & teas. **Adm £3.50, chd free. Suns 23 Mar; 7 Sept (12-5). Visitors also welcome by appt all yr.**
Georgian house (not open) built in Italian villa style set in 4 acres of S-facing gardens on lower slopes of Moel-y-Golfa with panoramic views of The Long Mountain. Terraces, walled kitchen garden, tropical garden, restored Victorian conservatories, tower and shell grotto. Woodland and parkland walks with wide variety of trees. Guided tours of garden. Buttington Church open for visitors, 2m from Welshpool.
☒ ♿ ☕ ☏

23 MAESLLWCH CASTLE
Glasbury-on-Wye HR3 5LQ. Walter & Iona de Winton. *4¹/₂ m W of Hay-on-Wye. Turn L off A438 immed N of Glasbury Bridge. Through Glasbury, ¹/₂ m turn R at church.* Home-made teas. **Adm £3, chd free (share to All Saints Church, Glasbury-on-Wye). Sun 11 May (2-5).**
Medium-sized, owner-maintained garden. Exceptional views from terrace across R Wye to Black Mountains. Rhododendrons, fine trees incl C18 ginko and woodland walk to old walled garden now used for growing trees.
♿ ☕

24 MILL COTTAGE
Abbeycwmhir LD1 6PH. Mr & Mrs B D Parfitt, 01597 851935, www.abbeycwmhir.co.uk. *8m N of Llandrindod Wells. Turn L off A483 1m N of Crossgates roundabout, then 3¹/₂ m on L, signed Abbeycwmhir. Limited parking.* Tea. **Adm £2.50, chd £1. Sat 3, Sun 4, Mon 5 May (dawn till**

dusk). **Visitors also welcome by appt Sept, max 10, no coaches.**
$^1/_3$ -acre streamside garden consisting mainly of mature, rare and unusual trees and shrubs, particularly interesting to the plantsman! Rockery with numerous ericaceous plants and interesting water feature. Narrow paths and steps, not suitable for wheelchairs.

THE MILL HOUSE
ee Ceredigion/Cardiganshire.

NANT-Y-BEDD
See Gwent.

㉕ THE NEUADD, LLANBEDR
NP8 1SP. **Robin & Philippa Herbert.**
1m NE of Crickhowell. Leave Crickhowell by Llanbedr rd. At junction with Great Oak Rd bear L and continue up hill for 0.9m, garden on L. Ample parking. Home-made teas. **Adm £3, chd free. Sun 15 June (2-6).**
Garden under restoration and development. At 750ft in Brecon Beacons National Park. Decorative walled garden, sunken garden, winter garden, rock garden with pool and springs. Woodland walk and paths. Unusual plants and trees. Owner is wheelchair user but some paths are steep.

Small stream meanders, dammed to form pools teeming with wildlife . . .

㉖ OAK COTTAGE
Llangorse LD3 7UE. **Jill & Mike Jones.** *7m E of Brecon. From Brecon, L in Bwlch (from Crickhowell R) for Llangorse on B4560. In village, R at grass triangle with tree and bench, garden last in terrace of 3 on L.* Home-made teas. **Adm £3, chd free. Sun 8 June (2-6).**
Developed from 2 cottage gardens, this enchanting garden has evolved rather than been planned as new trees, shrubs and plants arrived. An eclectic collection of plants, many grown from seeds gathered from friends, on holidays and from cuttings. Fine views of surrounding hills.

㉗ THE OLD VICARAGE
Llangorse. **Major & Mrs J B Anderson,** 01874 658639. *6¹/₂ m E of Brecon on B4560, 4m off A40 at Bwlch. Park in Llangorse village and approach through churchyard.* **Adm £2.50, chd free. Visitors welcome by appt.**
Small family garden maintained by owners; interesting herbaceous and shrub borders; lawns, trees and vegetables.

㉘ PENMYARTH
Glanusk Park NP8 1LP. **Hon Mrs Legge-Bourke,** www.glanuskestate.com. *2m NW of Crickhowell. On A40. Park gates on L.* Home-made teas. **Adm £3, chd free. Sun 27 Apr (2-5).**
11-acre rose, rock and wild garden. Spring bulbs, azaleas, rhododendrons and water garden. Specimen trees, particularly oaks. Park and riverside of the Usk also open.

㉙ PEN-Y-MAES
Hay-on-Wye HR3 5PP. **Sh,n Egerton,** 01497 820423, sre@waitrose.com. *1m SW of Hay-on-Wye. On B4350 towards Brecon.* Cream teas. **Adm £3, chd free. Sun 8 June (2-5). Visitors also welcome by appt May/June/July for groups of 15+ incl coaches.**
2-acre garden incl mixed borders; young topiary; walled formal kitchen garden; shrub roses, irises, peony border, espaliered pears. Fine mulberry. Beautiful dry stone walling and mature trees. Great double view of Black Mountains and the Brecon Beacons from front garden.

㉚ ♦ POWIS CASTLE GARDEN
Welshpool SY21 8RF. **The National Trust,** 01938 551929, www.nationaltrust.org.uk. *1m S of Welshpool. Turn off A483 ³/₄ m out of Welshpool, up Red Lane for ¹/₄ m.* **House and garden adm £10.50; chd £5.25, garden only adm £7.50, chd £3.75, under 5s free. Thurs to Mons, 13 Mar to 2 Nov; Weds also July/Aug. Castle (1-5, last adm 4.15); garden (11-5.30, last adm 4.45). Earlier closing times after 25 Sept. For NGS: Sat 19 July.**
Laid out in early C18 with finest remaining examples of Italian terraces in Britain. Richly planted herbaceous borders; enormous yew hedges; lead statuary, large wild flower areas. One of the National Trust's finest gardens. National Collections of *Aralia, Laburnum.* Guided walks with NGS careership student gardeners. Featured in local press. Step-free route around garden via gravel paths. Some slopes, we recommend 2 people to push wheelchair.

㉛ THE ROCK HOUSE
Llanbister LD1 6TN. **Jude Boutle & Sue Cox.** *10m N of Llandrindod Wells. From Llandrindod Wells, turn R off A483 at Llanbister onto B4356. Go through village, past school & war memorial on L, up short hill, over cattle grid and turn immed R up track (take care). Park on track.* Home-made teas. **Adm £3, chd free. Sun 8 June (12-5).**
An acre of informal hillside garden at 1000ft, with sweeping views over Radnorshire Hills, managed using organic principles. Created over 10yrs from a rocky clay-covered field with plantings of hebes, bamboos and hardy perennials. Raised beds, bog gardens with raised walkway, dry shady borders, gravel garden and grazed bluebell meadow. Llanbister CP school will be running the plant stall. Display of children's work in tearoom following visit to Rock House garden to complete project on Spring.

㉜ NEW ROSE COTTAGE
SY21 9JE. **Peter & Frances Grassi,** 01938 553723, frances@anngardening.fsnet.co.uk. *3m N of Welshpool. 1m from Dingle Nursery, please telephone for directions.* Home-made teas. **Adm £3, chd free. Visitors welcome by appt June to Sept for groups.**
S-facing 1-acre garden set in wooded valley and bordered by farmland. Small stream meanders through site, dammed to form pools teeming with wildlife. Stylish summerhouse at pool edge, elegant fruit cage, rustic archways, bespoke chicken hut all add extra interest to informal ribbon borders, raised beds, vegetable garden and small orchard. Featured in regional press and North Mid-Wales and Border 'Living' magazine.

33 ROWAN
Leighton, Welshpool SY21 8HJ. Tinty Griffith, 01938 552197. *2m E of Welshpool. From Welshpool take B4388 (Buttington to Montgomery). At Leighton turn L after school then at church straight ahead between stone pillars. 1st on R, parking in churchyard.* Home-made teas. **Adm £3, chd free. Suns 13 Apr; 15 June (2-5). Visitors also welcome by appt May to end Aug.**
1 acre of traditional plantsman's country garden with village church as backdrop. Discrete paths meander around island beds and mixed borders with irises, roses, unusual and rare plants, trees dripping with climbers and a series of planted pools and marshy areas. Views over Montgomeryshire countryside. Slopes slippery if wet, gravel paths.

STAUNTON PARK
See Herefordshire.

Small garden of secret surprises built on a railway embankment . . .

34 NEW TALYBONT GARDENS
Talybont-on-Usk LD3 7JE. *6m SE of Brecon. Off A40 signed Talybont-on-Usk. Follow yellow signs to gardens.* Teas at Usk Inn Hotel, Station Rd. **Adm £4.50, chd free (share to Ty Hafan Children's Hospice). Sun 13 July (2-6).**
Two garden gems beautifully structured. Great use of space, colour and planting.

LONICERA
Station Road. Gareth & Eirona Davies
1/2 -acre garden of varied interest incorporating several small feature gardens. Rose garden; heather garden with conifers; herbaceous and woody perennials; colourful summer bedding displays;

window boxes, hanging baskets and patio tubs forming extensive frontage display; greenhouses.

NEW TY CAM
Harry Chapman. *Next to White Hart PH*
Small garden of secret surprises on 3 levels with steps built on a railway embankment. Attractive features incl patios, decks, pergolas, ponds and waterfalls. Many choice herbaceous plants, trees and shrubs.

35 TAN-Y-LLYN
Meifod SY22 6YB. Callum Johnston & Brenda Moor, 01938 500370, www.tanyllyn.the-nursery.co.uk. *1m SE of Meifod. From Oswestry on A495 turn L in village, cross R Vyrnwy & climb hill for 1/2 m bearing R at Y-junction.* Home-made teas. **Adm £2.50, chd free (share to Age Concern Montgomeryshire). Sats, Suns 3, 4 May; 7, 8 June; 5, 6 July (2-5). Visitors also welcome by appt.**
S-facing sheltered 3-acre garden, surrounded by small hills, fields and forest. Steeply sloping, the paths, beds and hedges have been laid out to complement the contours of the hill. Extensive collection of plants in containers, herb garden, thorn grove, pond, orchard and wilderness. Exhibitions, events and entertainments.

36 TAWRYN
6 Baskerville Court, Clyro HR3 5SS. Chris & Clive Young, 01497 821939. *1m NW of Hay-on-Wye. Leave A438 Hereford to Brecon rd at Clyro. Baskerville Court is behind church and Baskerville Arms Hotel. Please park in village.* Home-made teas. **Adm £2.50, chd free. Sun 4, Mon 5 May (11-5). Visitors also welcome by appt.**
1-acre steeply-terraced garden on an oriental theme. Come and see the Ghost Dragon and the River of Slate. Lots of new crooked paths and planting. Stunning views of the Black Mountains and Kilvert's Church. Colour all yr. Chris also gives talks with slides on the history of the NGS and it's charities suitable for WIs, garden clubs etc.

37 TREBERFYDD
Bwlch LD3 7PX. David Raikes, www.treberfydd.net. *61/2 m E of Brecon. From Crickhowell leave A40 at*
Bwlch and take B4560 then L for Penorth. From Brecon leave A40 at Llanhamlach. 21/2 m sign for Llangasty Church, entrance over cattle grid. Tel 01874 730205 or email david.raikes@btinternet.com for further directions. Home-made teas or bring your own picnic. **House and garden adm £5, garden only adm £3, chd free. Sun 22 June (1-5).**
10 acres of lawns, peaceful woodland walks, rose beds and herbaceous borders designed in 1852 by W A Nesfield for imposing Victorian Gothic house. Cedar of Lebanon 155 yrs old. Yews, holly oaks, copper beech, orchards and rockery. Wonderful position nr Llangorse Lake. Beacons nursery within walled garden. House tours 2 to 4.

38 TY CAPEL DEILDRE
Llanidloes SY18 6NX. Dr Beverley Evans-Britt, 01686 412602. *41/2 m N of Llanidloes. Go N from Llanidloes on B4518. 2m turn L on Clywedog rd, signed scenic route, 21/2 m on R by nature walk lay-by.* Light refreshments & teas. **Adm £3.50, chd £1. Sun 22 June (2-5.30). Visitors also welcome by appt.**
2-acre garden of almost 100% organic plants has been personally created on a former waste site over 30 years. A 1350ft windy location with stunning views of Llyn Clywedog. It consists of ponds surrounded by walks and marginal gardens, herbaceous borders containing many rare perennials, rose and begonia gardens and lawns. Featured on BBC1 Wales. Limited wheelchair access. Steep slopes and narrow paths.

39 VALE HOUSE
Nantmel, Rhayader LD1 6EL. Mrs Christine Loran. *6m N of Llandrindod Wells. At Crossgates take A44 to Rhayader. 3m, R at Nantmel village sign. Garden directly behind school.* Home-made teas. **Adm £3, chd free. Sun 7 Sept (2-5).**
Steeply-sloped garden is dominated by Victorian stone aqueduct and mature trees. Mainly alpines, heathers, climbing shrubs, conifers and large rockeried areas. Four ponds are linked by large steep wooden zig-zagged path. Seating areas. Art exhibition. Steep slopes suitable for motorized wheelchairs only.

40 THE WALLED GARDEN

Knill LD8 2PR. Dame Margaret Anstee, 01544 267411. *3m SW of Presteigne. On B4362 Walton-Presteigne rd. In Knill village turn R over cattle grid, keep R down drive.* Home-made teas. **Adm £3, chd free. Sun 25 May (2-6). Visitors also welcome by appt preferably Mar to Oct for garden groups/coach parties.**

4 acres: walled garden; river, bog garden and small grotto; primulas; over 100 varieties of roses, shrub, modern and climbing; peonies; mixed and herbaceous borders; many varieties of shrubs and mature trees; lovely spring garden. Nr C13 church in beautiful valley. Some narrow paths and uneven ground.

41 THE WERN

Llanfihangel Talyllyn LD3 7TE. Neil & Lucienne Bennett. *4m E of Brecon. From Brecon, leave A40 (S) at 1st exit onto B4558 to Groesffordd. Follow rd to Llanfihangel Talyllyn. Take 2nd R (no through rd) in front of converted barns to end. From Crickhowell leave A40 (N) at Bwlch. R onto B4560. At Llangorse turn L to Llanfihangel Talyllyn. Take 'no through rd' (2nd L), follow to end.* Home-made teas. **Adm £3, chd free. Sun 1 June (2-6).**

1-acre garden of unusual trees, shrubs and plants. Many young acers, rhododendrons and azaleas. Hot border with banana, cannas and tender plants. Secluded herb garden. Ornamental grass and bamboo garden leading to woodland walk crossing stream. Charming, productive fruit and vegetable garden and polytunnel surrounded by damsons and plums. No disabled access to woodland walk.

42 WESTLAKE FISHERIES

Domgay Road, Four Crosses SY22 6SJ. Lynn Mainwaring, 01691 831475. *9m N of Welshpool. Turn off A483 in Four Crosses, signed Pysgodfa Fishery. Follow brown tourist signs. Domgay Rd approx 1m.* Home-made teas. **Adm £3, chd 50p. Visitors welcome by appt all yr.**

A quiet scenic environment of 38 acres, managed organically on the R Vyrnwy with lakes and pools. 2-acre garden containing mixed borders, fish lawn, orchard, potager, herb and cutting garden, large vegetable garden (many unusual varieties grown), greenhouses and fruit cage. Birch walk and purple hazel walk lead to lake walks and wildlife area. NB Deep water, children must be accompanied by adults.

50 ◆ WESTONBURY MILL WATER GARDEN

See Herefordshire.

43 WESTWINDS

Common Road, Kerry SY16 4NY. Ray & Margaret Watson, 01686 670605, watrgo@supanet.com. *3m E of Newtown. Newtown to Churchstoke Rd (A489), turn R in village onto Common Rd, 400yds on L.* **Adm £3.50 incl cup of tea. Visitors welcome by appt May to Sept, small groups welcome.**

1/3 -acre informal garden on several levels with mixed borders, shrubs and pools. Meandering paths and steps lead through the various levels.

44 NEW ◆ WHIMBLE GARDEN AND NURSERY AND RAILSGATE BARN GARDEN

LD8 2PD. Elizabeth Taylor & R T Lancett, Bridgit Symons & Dr H Schofield. *6m W of Presteigne. B4356 N from Presteigne. After 1m, R for Discoed & Maes-Treylow, R onto B4372 to Kinnerton. From Kington take A44 N, at Walton take B4357, at Evanjob R for Kinnerton.* Light refreshments & teas in café. **Adm £3, chd free. Whimble Garden and Nursery open Thurs to Suns and Bank Hol Mons, Apr to mid-Oct (10.30-5.30). For**

NGS: Sat 7 June (10.30-5.30). Adjoining gardens. Panoramic views of Radnor Valley hills. Parterre with stunning herbaceous planting. Clematis and rose-covered metal sculpture. Paths through hay meadow to 'earthworks' and toposcope. Nuttery, vegetable and fruit gardens. Wildlife ponds. Mostly wheelchair access but grass path through meadow may be difficult.

Picnic spot overlooking stream, ponds and wetlands . . .

45 WOODHILL

Moelfre, Oswestry SY10 7QX. Janet Randell, 01691 791486, www.pco.powys.org.uk/woodhill. *9m W of Oswestry.* **Adm £3, chd 50p, disabled free (share to Woods, Hills & Tracks). Visitors welcome by appt, open all yr, short notice OK.**

6 acres. Informal garden designed with wheelchair users in mind set amidst wonderful views of the surrounding hills and mountains on the foothills of The Berwyns nr Snowdonia. Footpaths for disabled access totalling 3/4 m, young arboretum, picnic spot overlooking stream, ponds and wetlands. Sheltered arbour in more formal setting. All-yr interest: bluebell wood in spring; roses in summer; trees, shrubs and berries in autumn; scented winter shrubs. 1000 trees and shrubs planted informally. Abundant wildlife sightings.

Powys County Volunteers

County Organisers
South Shân Egerton, Pen-y-Maes, Hay-on-Wye HR3 5PP, 01497 820423, sre@waitrose.com
North Angela Hughes, Castell y Gwynt, Montgomery SY15 6HR, 01686 668317, r.dhughes@btinternet.com

County Treasurer
Elizabeth Spear, The Glyn, Berriew, Welshpool SY21 8AY, 01686 640455, eds@glj.co.uk

Publicity
North Elizabeth Spear, The Glyn, Berriew, Welshpool SY21 8AY, 01686 640455, eds@glj.co.uk

Early Openings 2009

Don't forget early planning for 2009

Gardens across the country open from late January onwards – before the new Yellow Book is published – with glorious displays of colour including hellebores, aconites, snowdrops and carpets of spring bulbs.

Cambrian Coast
8 FEBRUARY 2009
Penrhyn Castle

Cambridgeshire
01 FEBRUARY 2009
The Mill House, Grantchester

Cheshire & Wirral
17 JANUARY 2009
Ness Botanic Gardens

Cornwall
7 FEBRUARY 2009
Coombegate Cottage
15 FEBRUARY 2009
Coombegate Cottage

Devon
4 JANUARY 2009
Sherwood
11 JANUARY 2009
Sherwood
18 JANUARY 2009
Sherwood
25 JANUARY 2009
Sherwood
1 FEBRUARY 2009
Cherubeer Gardens
Little Cumbre
Sherwood
8 FEBRUARY 2009
Cherubeer Gardens
Little Cumbre
Sherwood
15 FEBRUARY 2009
Little Cumbre
Sherwood
22 FEBRUARY 2009
Little Cumbre
Sherwood

Essex
8 FEBRUARY 2009
Green Island

Gloucestershire North & Central
8 FEBRUARY 2009
Trench Hill
15 FEBRUARY 2009
Trench Hill

Hampshire
15 FEBRUARY 2009
Bramdean House
22 FEBRUARY 2009
Little Court
23 FEBRUARY 2009
Little Court
24 FEBRUARY 2009
Little Court

Herefordshire
5 FEBRUARY 2009
Ivy Croft
12 FEBRUARY 2009
Ivy Croft
26 FEBRUARY 2009
Ivy Croft

Lancashire Merseyside & Greater Manchester
15 FEBRUARY 2009
Weeping Ash
22 FEBRUARY 2009
Weeping Ash

Lincolnshire
21 FEBRUARY 2009
21 Chapel Street
22 FEBRUARY 2009
21 Chapel Street

Drifts of snowdrops, hellebores and crocus form a carpet under clipped evergreens and shrubs . . .

London
22 FEBRUARY 2009
Myddelton House Gardens

Northamptonshire
15 FEBRUARY 2009
Dolphins
22 FEBRUARY 2009
Greywalls

Surrey
15 FEBRUARY 2009
Gatton Park
18 FEBRUARY 2009
Gatton Park

Sussex
8 FEBRUARY 2009
Mitchmere Farm
11 FEBRUARY 2009
Pembury House
12 FEBRUARY 2009
Mitchmere Farm
Pembury House
13 FEBRUARY 2009
Pembury House
15 FEBRUARY 2009
Mitchmere Farm
18 FEBRUARY 2009
Pembury House
19 FEBRUARY 2009
Pembury House
20 FEBRUARY 2009
Pembury House

Warwickshire & part of West Midlands
8 FEBRUARY 2009
Ragley Hall Gardens

Wiltshire
7 FEBRUARY 2009
Lacock Abbey Gardens
8 FEBRUARY 2009
Lacock Abbey Gardens
14 FEBRUARY 2009
Lacock Abbey Gardens
15 FEBRUARY 2009
Lacock Abbey Gardens

Garden Visiting Around the World

Heading off on holiday? Whether you're planning a short trip north of the border or across the channel or a longer visit down under or to our see our North American cousins, why not visit a few of the wonderful gardens open for charity elsewhere in the world?

America

GARDEN CONSERVANCY
Publication Open Days Directory
W www.gardenconservancy.org
Visit America's very best, rarely seen private gardens. The Open Days Program is a project of The Garden Conservancy, a non-profit organisation dedicated to preserving America's gardening heritage.

Australia

AUSTRALIA'S OPEN GARDEN SCHEME
Contact Neil Robertson
E national@opengarden.org.au
W www.opengarden.org.au
More than 700 inspiring gardens drawn from every Australian State and territory including tropical gardens, arid-zone gardens as well as featuring Australia's unique flora.

Belgium

JARDINS OUVERTS DE BELGIQUE – OPEN TUINEN VAN BELGIË
Publication Catalogue of Belgian Open Gardens, published annually in March
Contact Dominique Petit-Heymans
E info@open-tuinen.be
W www.open-tuinen.be
A non-profit organisation founded in 1994. Most of the proceeds from

entry fees support charities chosen by garden owners.

France

JARDINS ET SANTÉ
E jardinsetsante@wanadoo.fr
W www.jardins-sante.org
Jardins et Santé is an association with humanitarian aims, created in 2004 by a team of volunteers. The funds raised through the opening of gardens are used to finance scientific research in the field of neurology. Contributions are also made to the development of the therapeutic role of the garden, particularly in hospitals and retirement homes. In January 2007, a research grant was presented to Dr Seegmuller to help carry out a research project on the syndrome of Epilepsy. In 2008, different projects of therapeutic gardens will be subsidised, in particular a project for autistic children and children suffering from epilepsy.

Japan

THE N.G.S. JAPAN
Contact Tamie Taniguchi
E tamieta@syd.odn.ne.jp
W www.ngs-jp.org
The N.G.S. Japan was founded in 2001. Most of the proceeds from entry fees support children's and welfare charities as nominated by

owners and Japanese garden conservation.

Netherlands

THE NEDERLANDSE TUINENSTICHTING (DUTCH GARDEN SOCIETY, NTS)
Publication Open Tuinengids, published annually in March
E info@tuinenstichting.nl
W www.tuinenstichting.nl
The Dutch Garden Society was founded in 1980 to protect and restore gardens, public parks and cemeteries.

Scotland

SCOTLAND'S GARDENS SCHEME
Publication Gardens of Scotland
Contact Paddy Scott
T 0131 226 3714
E info@sgsgardens.co.uk
W www.gardensofscotland.org
Founded in 1931, Scotland's Gardens Scheme provides visitors with the opportunity to explore some of Scotland's finest gardens. The funds raised by the owners are donated to The Queen's Nursing Institute of Scotland, The National Trust for Scotland, The Royal Fund for Gardeners' Children and Perennial – The Gardeners' Royal Benevolent Society

National Plant Collections in the NGS

Over 100 of the gardens that open for The National Gardens Scheme are custodians of National Plant Collections®, the National Council for the Conservation of Plants and Gardens (NCCPG), although this may not always be noted in the garden descriptions.

The NCCPG can be contacted at 12 Home Farm, Loseley Park, Guildford, Surrey GU3 1HS Tel: 01483 447544 Fax: 01483 458933. Website: www.nccpg.com

A

AESCULUS, LIRIODENDRON
West Dean Gardens
Sussex

AGAPANTHUS
Pine Cottage
Devon

ANEMONE (JAPANESE)
Heathlands
Hampshire

ANEMONE JAPONICA AND HELLEBORES
Broadview Gardens
Kent

ANEMONE NEMOROSA
Kingston Lacy
Dorset

AQUILEGIA VULGARIS
Touchwood
Glamorgan & Gwent

ARBUTUS
Dunster Castle Gardens
Somerset & Bristol

ARUNCUS AND FILIPENDULA
Windy Hall
Cumbria

ASTER
Upton House
Warwickshire

ASTILBE, HYDRANGEA AND POLYSTICHUM (FERNS)
Holehird Gardens
Cumbria

ASTILBE, IRIS ENSATA, TULBAGHIA
Marwood Hill
Devon

ASTRANTIA
Mayroyd Mill House
Yorkshire
Warren Hills Cottage
Leicestershire & Rutland

AUBRIETA, LAWSON CYPRESS, HARDY FUCHSIA AND SKIMMIA
University of Leicester Harold Martin Botanic Garden
Leicestershire & Rutland

B

BEARDED IRIS
Myddelton House Gardens
London

BERBERIS
Mill Hill House
Nottinghamshire

BRUGMANSIA
Valducci Flower & Vegetable Gardens
Shropshire

BRUNNERA AND OMPHALODES
Hearns House
Oxfordshire

BUDDLEJA DAVIDII AND LEUCANTHEMUM SUPERBUM (SHASTA DAISIES)
Shapcott Barton Estate
Devon

BUDDLEJA, CLEMATIS VITICELLA AND PENSTEMON
Longstock Park Water Garden
Hampshire

C

CEANOTHUS
Eccleston Square
London

CENTAUREA
Bide-a-Wee Cottage
Durham & Northumberland

CLEMATIS
Burford House Gardens
Worcestershire

CLEMATIS (SUBGENUS VIORNA)
Rosewood
Cambrian Coast

CLEMATIS VITICELLA
Hawthornes Nursery Garden
Lancashire

CLEMATIS VITICELLA CVS
Roseland House
Cornwall

COLCHICUM
Felbrigg Hall
Norfolk

CORNUS
Newby Hall & Gardens
Yorkshire

D

DIANTHUS
Dippers
Devon
Kingstone Cottages
Herefordshire

DICENTRA
Boundary Cottage
Yorkshire

E

EUCALYPTUS, PODOCARPACEAE AND ARALIACEAE
Meon Orchard
Hampshire

EUPHORBIA
University of Oxford Botanic Garden
Oxfordshire

EVENING PRIMROSES
The Old Vicarage
Wiltshire

F

FORSYTHIA
Burlingham Gardens
Norfolk

Accommodation available at NGS Gardens

We feature here a list of NGS garden owners or county volunteers who offer accommodation. We have listed them by Yellow Book county and indicated whether they offer Bed & Breakfast (**B&B**), Self-Catering (**SC**), or Hotel (**H**) accommodation. You will also find a reference to accommodation in the main directory with their garden entry, unless the property owner is a member of the county team and does not open their garden.

Bedfordshire

TOFTE MANOR
Souldrop Road, Sharnbrook
MK44 1HH
Mrs S Castleman
T 01234 781425 / 07787 155167
E enquiries@toftemanor.co.uk
W www.toftemanor.co.uk
Accommodation C17 manor house with double and single accommodation of a very high standard. Full use of study (TV), drawing room, library, labyrinth, tennis court and swimming pool. Holistic therapies available. See website for further details.
B&B

DISCLAIMER
The descriptions provided in this section have been given to the NGS by the garden owners. The NGS cannot guarantee the accuracy of the information given to us, and accepts no responsibility for any error or misrepresentation. All liability for loss, disappointment, negligence or other damage caused by reliance on the information contained in this listing, or in the event of bankruptcy or liquidation or cessation of trade of any company, individual or firm mentioned, is hereby excluded. We strongly recommend that you carefully check prices and other details when you book your accommodation. The NGS has no statutory control over the establishments or their methods of operating. The NGS cannot become involved in legal or contractual matters and cannot get involved in seeking financial recompense.

Buckinghamshire

THE OLD VICARAGE
Padbury MK18 2AH
Mr & Mrs. H. Morley-Fletcher
T 01280 813045
E belindamf@freenet.co.uk
Accommodation Twin or double bedroom with private bathroom in a Victorian house, surrounded by 2$\frac{1}{2}$ acres of garden. Breakfast comes from our organic garden, or from local sources wherever possible. Convenient for Silverstone, Stowe and Addington Manor Equestrian Centre.
B&B

Cambrian Coast

DYFFRYN FERNANT
Llanychaer, Fishguard SA65 9SP
Christina Shand
T 01348 811282
E christina.shand@virgin.net
W www.genuslocus.net
Accommodation Cosy one roomed converted barn in the heart of the garden with wood burning stove. Sleeps 4. Secluded, romantic and peaceful. Self catering.
SC

HOTEL MAES-Y-NEUADD
Talsarnau, nr Harlech LL47 6YA
Peter & Lynn Jackson & Peter Payne
T 01766 780200
E maes@neuadd.com
W www.neuadd.com
Accommodation 15 individually designed ensuite double/twin rooms. C14 manor house with bar, terrace, lounge, conservatory and highly acclaimed restaurant serving fresh, local produce and home grown fruit & vegetables. B&B from £49.
H

RHOSYGILWEN MANSION
Rhoshill SA43 2TW
Dr Glen Peters
T 01239 841387

E enquiries@retreat.co.uk
W www.retreat.co.uk
Accommodation Country mansion with 9 double/twin bedrooms, 7 en-suite, 1 also a family room. B&B per room (for 2 people) from £65, single occupancy from £35. Evening meals available by prior arrangement.
B&B

Cambridgeshire

39 FOSTER ROAD
Campaign Avenue, Sugar Way, Woodston, Peterborough PE2 9RS
Robert Marshall and Richard Handscombe
T 01733 555978
E robfmarshall@btinternet.com
Accommodation Private house, off-street parking, 20 minutes walk from city centre & station. First floor room with double bed, own bathroom with bath & shower, TV, wi-fi, tea, coffee, etc. Use of lounge. English breakfast. £30 pppn.
B&B

SOUTH FARM
Shingay-cum-Wendy
SG8 0HR
Philip Paxman
T 01223 207581
E philip@south-farm.co.uk
W www.south-farm.co.uk
Accommodation 2 self-contained apartments for 2 or 4 each. They can be self catering. Also 3 double ensuite. Dinner and lunch available. Prices from £80 per night or £70 single. Not usually available Saturdays.
B&B SC

Cornwall

BONYTHON MANOR
Cury Cross Lanes, nr Helston
TR12 7BA
Richard & Sue Nathan
T 01326 240234
E sue@bonythonmanor.co.uk
W www.bonythonmanor.co.uk

Accommodation 4 properties sleeping 10, 6, 4 and 2. All 5* accommodation with ensuite facilities and private gardens. Bookings through 'Rural Retreats' – 01386 701177. www.ruralretreats.co.uk. Cottage refs: Bonython Farmhouse – CW042, Mews Cottage – CW047, St Corantyn Cottage – CW048, Spring Water Barn – CW058.
SC

CARWINION
Mawnan Smith, Falmouth
TR11 5JA
A & J Rogers
T 01326 250258
E jane@carwinion.freeserve.co.uk
W www.carwinion.co.uk
Accommodation 1 double, 2 twin/double ensuite rooms in quiet country house set in 14 acres of valley garden. Children & dogs welcome. Rooms £80 per night. Single occ. £45. SC flat sleeps 2. Cottage sleeps 6.
B&B SC

CREED HOUSE
Creed, Grampound, Truro
TR2 4SL
Mr & Mrs William Croggon
T 01872 530372
Accommodation Georgian Rectory, 2 bedrooms with super king beds, 1 with twin beds, all with private or ensuite bathrooms. Prices £90 per night. Single occ. £60. Member of County Team.
B&B

EDNOVEAN FARM
Perranuthnoe, Penzance TR20 9LZ
Christine & Charles Taylor
T 01736 711883
E info@ednoveanfarm.co.uk
W www.ednoveanfarm.co.uk/gardens
Accommodation Granite barn above Mount's Bay, stunning views; formal parterre giving way to open terraces; Italian & gravel gardens. Four poster beds, roll top baths, and patchwork quilts. 3 ensuite rooms with private terrace. 5 diamonds.
B&B

HALLOWARREN
Carne, Manaccan, Helston
TR12 6HD
Amanda Osman
T 01326 231224
W www.stanthony.co.uk
Accommodation Victorian cottage – sleeps 2, part of period Cornish farmhouse. All seasons. Traditional barn – sleeps 5. Full central heating. Both equipped to very high standard with all linen supplied. Atmospheric

setting in woodland garden bordering stream.
SC

HIDDEN VALLEY GARDENS
Treesmill, Nr Par PL24 2TU
Patricia Howard
T 01208 873225
W www.hiddenvalleygardens.co.uk
Accommodation Comfortable B&B & SC studio accommodation in a stone barn conversion set in a 'hidden' valley with a 4 acre display garden. 2 double, 1 twin, Garden studio all have ensuite. B&B prices £24 – £27 pppn. Single occ. £32 – £35.
B&B SC

TREGOOSE
Grampound, Truro TR2 4DB
Anthony & Alison O'Connor
T 01726 882460
W www.tregoose.co.uk
Accommodation 1 double room (four poster), ensuite. 1 twin, ensuite bath with shower over. 1 double with private bath/shower. Prices from £43 per person.
Member of County Team.
B&B

TREGREHAN GARDEN COTTAGES
Par PL24 2SJ
Tom & Jo Hudson
T 01726 812438
E info@tregrehan.org
W www.tregrehan.org
Accommodation SC cottage accommodation on Cornwall's historic Tregrehan Estate situated between Fowey & Charlestown. Cottages sleep 1 to 8, short or week breaks, thoughtful hospitality within one of Cornwall's great gardens of outstanding botanical merit. Prices from £175, 4 nights for 2 people.
SC

TREWOOFE ORCHARD
Lamorna, Penzance TR19 6BW
Barbara & Dick Waterson
T 01736 810214
E trewoofe@waterson.org.uk
W www.lamorna-valley.co.uk
Accommodation 1 double ensuite, 1 twin with private bathroom (both with baths). From £80 per night per room. Reduced single rate from Oct – April inc. Three night minimum July – Sept inc. Secluded and tranquil. Non smoking. Special diets catered for.
B&B

Cumbria

BRACKENRIGG LODGE
Windy Hall Road, Bowness-on-Windermere LA23 3HY
Lynne Bush
T 015394 47770
E lynne@brackenriggs.co.uk
W www.brackenriggs.co.uk
Accommodation Ideally located, tranquil, rural 3 acre setting, home of roe deer & red squirrels. Close to the village and lake. Resident owner guarantees comfortable, clean accommodation. A real home from home. (SC – 1 apartment & 1 cottage).
SC

LAKESIDE HOTEL
Lake Windermere, Newby Bridge
Ulverston LA12 8AT
Mr N R Talbot
T 015395 30001
E sales@LakesideHotel.co.uk
W www.LakesideHotel.co.uk
Accommodation The best 4* hotel and spa on the shores of Lake Windermere – a spectacular location. Guests enjoy exclusive use of luxury Health and Leisure Spa. Bedrooms with private gardens available. (78 rooms).
H

LANGHOLME MILL
Woodgate, Lowick Green, Ulverston LA12 8ES
Mr & Mrs G Sanderson
T 01229 885215
E info@langholmemill.co.uk
Accommodation Ten minutes from Lake Coniston with stunning views, this C17 corn mill comprises 4 double bedrooms & large garden designed around the mill race featuring rhododendrons, hostas & acers. Ideal for walkers & families.
SC

LINDETH FELL COUNTRY HOUSE HOTEL
Lyth Valley Road, Bowness-on-Windermere LA23 3JP
Air Cdr & Mrs P A Kennedy
T 01539 443286
E kennedy@lindethfell.co.uk
W www.lindethfell.co.uk
Accommodation On a tree lined drive above Lake Windermere, standing in magnificent private gardens. 14 bedrooms, singles, doubles and family rooms. Price from £45 B&B. Five course dinner available. Many awards including AA Top 200 hotel and Gold Award. A 3* Country House Hotel.
H

RYDAL HALL
Rydal, Ambleside LA22 9LX
Diocese of Carlisle
T 015394 32050
E mail@rydalhall.org
W www.rydalhall.org
Accommodation Rydal Hall is a grade 2 listed house situated in the heart of the English Lake District with recently restored Thomas Mawson Gardens. A number of rooms have a wonderful view down the Rothay Valley
B&B SC

WHITBYSTEADS
Askham, Penrith CA10 2PG
Thomas and Victoria Lowther
T 01931 712284
E info@gnap.fsnet.co.uk
W www.whitbysteads.org
Accommodation Working hill farm in the Lake District National Park with beautiful views. 1 double bedroom, ensuite, 1 double & 1 twin bedroom with separate bathroom. Children, dogs & horses welcome. Full English breakfast. £40 – £50 pppn.
B&B

Derbyshire

THE CASCADES
Clatterway, Bonsall DE4 2AH
Mr & Mrs A Clements
T 01629 822464
E info@cascadesgardens.com
W www.cascadesgardens.com
Accommodation Set in a beautiful 4 acre garden within The Peak District National Park and close to Chatsworth. Cascades offers a range of luxury 5 star accommodation. Ideal for a relaxing short break or holiday.
B&B

THE RIDDINGS FARM
Kirk Ireton, Ashbourne DE6 3LB
Mr & Mrs P R Spencer
T 01335 370331
E http.members.lycos.co.uk/ivycottage
Accommodation ETC 3*. Delightful, peacefully situated barn conversion looking over Carsington Water. Spacious 2 bedroomed, accommodation, sleeps 3 – 4. Sorry no pets, no smoking. Towels, linen and electricity included. £230–£330 per week.
Member of County Team.
SC

SHATTON HALL FARM COTTAGES
Bamford, Hope Valley S33 0BG
Angela Kellie
T 01433 620635
E ahk@peakfarmholidays.co.uk

W www.peakfarmholidays.co.uk
Accommodation Three comfortable stone cottages, each with two double bedrooms, open plan living area. 4* accommodation, around listed Elizabethan farmhouse. Secluded location with good access and within easy reach of Chatsworth House and Haddon Hall.
SC

Devon

BARLEYCOTT
Blakewell, Barnstaple EX31 4ES
Les & Barbara Shapland
T 01271 375002
E lb.shapland@onetel.net
Accommodation Converted barn in a beautiful countryside garden. 1 double with ensuite bathroom. Many gardens around, including Rosemoor, to visit. Close to woodland walks, trout farm and Barnstaple 1½ miles for restaurants.
B&B

BROOK
East Cornworthy, Totnes TQ9 7HQ
Mr & Mrs P Smyth
T 01803 722424
Accommodation One twin room with private bathroom. Cottage set in lovely tranquil valley within walking distance of the River Dart and Dittisham. The garden extends to 3 acres.
See East Cornworthy Gardens for details of garden.
B&B

THE CIDER HOUSE
Buckland Abbey, Yelverton PL20 6EZ
Mrs Sarah Stone
T 01822 853285
E sarah.stone@cider-house.co.uk
W www.cider-house.co.uk
Accommodation House formerly part of Cistercian monastery of Buckland; 1 double & 1 twin room each with private bathroom, plus extra twin room if required. Minimum stay 2 nights. £80 per room per night. Cottage sleeps 5 in 3 bedrooms; sitting room with log fire, dining room, kitchen. Walled garden, use of tennis court.
Member of County Team.
B&B SC

DARTINGTON HALL
Totnes TQ9 6JE
Dartington Hall Trust
T 01803 847147
E bookings@dartingtonhall.com
W www.dartingtonhall.com
Accommodation There are 51 bedrooms within the C14 medieval courtyard, most retaining their original

character. From beamed ceilings to an etching of a C15 Spanish galleon carved onto a wall, history can be discovered all over the courtyard and gardens.
H

KINGSTON HOUSE
Staverton, Totnes TQ9 6AR
Michael & Elizabeth Corfield
T 01803 762235
E info@kingston-estate.co.uk
W www.kingston-estate.co.uk
Accommodation Kingston House, 5 Diamonds – Gold award, has 3 beautiful suites and 9 Five Star cottages. The house is set in the gardens, offering delicious food using garden produce whenever possible, excellent wine list. Price on application.
B&B SC

LITTLE ASH FARM
Fenny Bridges EX14 3BL
Sadie & Robert Reid
T 01404 850271
Accommodation En-suite family room sleeps 4. Family suite, twin and double with bathroom. Single, en-suite. All rooms have TV and tea tray. Full breakfast in large conservatory overlooking garden. From £24. Non smoking.
B&B

NORTH BORESTON FARM
Halwell, Totnes TQ9 7LD
Rob & Jan Wagstaff
T 01548 821320
E borestongarden@btinternet.com
Accommodation Converted old granary. Comfortably furnished living room and well equipped kitchen upstairs; bedroom (sleeps 2) with en-suite shower room downstairs. French windows onto own terrace. Covered parking. Ideally located for best of coast, Dartmoor and great gardens.
SC

THE OLD RECTORY
Ashford, Barnstaple EX31 4BY
Ann Burnham
T 01271 377408
E annburnham@btinternet.com
Accommodation You will enjoy your stay at the recently renovated Old Rectory. Attractive bedrooms with full ensuite. Delicious breakfasts; dinner or supper on request. The view is superb. Log fires in winter.
B&B

REGENCY HOUSE
Hemyock, Cullompton EX15 3RQ
Mrs Jenny Parsons
T 01823 680238

E jenny.parsons@btinternet.com
Accommodation Regency House is the most beautiful, spacious, Georgian rectory. Accommodation: double room, ensuite, 1 twin with private bathroom. Price £45 pppn. Dexter cattle, Jacob sheep and horses live here too. Excellent pub in Culmstock.
B&B

ST MERRYN
Higher Park Road, Braunton EX33 2 LG
Ros Bradford
T 01271 813805
E ros@st-merryn.co.uk
W www.st-merryn.co.uk
Accommodation Lovely house set in peaceful garden. 1 single/twin with private bathroom. 1 double (king-size bed) with private bathroom. 1 double (king-size bed), ensuite shower room. Minimum stay 2 nights. Strictly no smoking. Prices from £30pp.
B&B

SOUTH BANK
Southleigh, Colyton EX24 6JB
J Connor
T 01404 871251
Accommodation 1 double room (not ensuite) in sunny house with lovely views. Large garden, 3 acre field. Good walking and bird watching in quiet valleys. Near Dartmoor. Exmoor, Jurassic coast 3 miles. £20 pppn or £133 per week.
See Southleigh Gardens for details of garden.
B&B

SOUTH HEATHERCOMBE
Manaton, Newton Abbot TQ13 9XE
Mrs Julia Holden & C & M Pike Woodlands Trust
T 01647 221350
E bandb@heathercombe.com
W www.heathercombe.com
Accommodation Comfortable, well equipped accommodation in C15 Dartmoor longhouse. Twin/double ensuite bedroom & twin/double family room; whirlpool bath, TV/DVD, tea & coffee making, guest's lounge with log fire. Delicious breakfasts. Dogs welcome (kennels). From £28 pn. See Heathercombe for details of garden.
B&B

WESTCOTT BARTON
Middle Marwood, Barnstaple EX31 4EF
Howard Frank
T 01271 812842
E westcott_barton@yahoo.co.uk
W www.westcottbarton.co.uk
Accommodation Pretty bedrooms (4 double, 1 twin), all ensuite, all with

colour TV and tea/coffee making facilities. Breakfast is a movable feast and evening meals are available on request. No smoking or pets. Not suitable for children under 12 yrs. £45 per person.
B&B

WHITSTONE FARM
Whitstone Lane, Newton Abbot TQ13 9NA
Katie & Alan Bunn
T 01626 832258
E katie@whitstonefarm.co.uk
W www.whitstonefarm.co.uk
Accommodation Country house with stunning views over Dartmoor. 1 super king-sized (or twin) room, 1 king-sized room, 1 double sized room – all ensuite. Prices from £68 per night. Single occ. from £49. Come and be pampered.
B&B

WINSFORD WALLED GARDEN
Halwill Junction EX21 5XT
Aileen Birks & Michael Gilmore
T 01409 221477
E muddywellies@
winsfordwalledgarden.com
W www.winsfordwalledgarden.com
Accommodation Top quality double ensuite accommodation, located within Victorian walled summer flower garden planted in unique cottage style containing 1000's varieties. Restored Victorian greenhouses built of teak for various Bougainvillea and Hibiscus. £35 pppn & £45 for single occ.
B&B

Dorset

DOMINEYS COTTAGES
Buckland Newton, nr Dorchester DT2 7BS
Mrs W Gueterbock
T 01300 345295
E cottages@domineys.com
W www.domineys.com
Accommodation 3 delightful highly commended 2 bdrm cottages. Maintained to exceptional standards – TB4*. Enchanting gardens peacefully located in Dorset's beautiful heartland. Flower decked patios and heated summer pool. Babies & children over 5 years welcome. Regret no pets. Many NGS gardens nearby.
SC

KNOWLE FARM
Uploders, Bridport DT6 4NS
Alison & John Halliday
T 01308 485492
W www.knowlefarmbandb.com
Accommodation Welcoming, relaxing village base for the delights of West Dorset and beyond. Top quality

accommodation in C18 longhouse. Every attention to detail. Super breakfasts. Double, ensuite; twin with private bathroom. Sorry no pets, smoking or children under 12. From £35 pppn.
B&B

Durham & Northumberland

THORNLEY HOUSE
Thornley Gate, Hexham NE47 9NH
Eileen Finn
T 01434 683255
E e.finn@ukonline.co.uk
W web.ukonline.co.uk/e.finn
Accommodation Beautiful country house, 1 mile west of Allendale, near Hadrian's Wall. 3 bedrooms with facilities, TV & tea makers. 2 lounges with Steinway grand piano and plasma TV. Resident Maine Coon cats. B&B from £27 pppn – £170p.w.
B&B

Glamorgan & Gwent

BRYNDERI
Wainfield Lane, Gwehelog, Usk NP15 1RG
Ann & Alwyne Benson
T 01291 672976
E brynderi@btopenworld.com
W www.brynderi.co.uk
Accommodation Beautifully furnished single storey self – contained apartment in wing of country home. Self catering or with breakfast provided. Large lounge with French doors to private patio; double bedroom; well equipped kitchen; bathroom with towels; bathrobes and toiletries. WTB 5 star.
B&B SC

THE HILL
Pen Y Pound Rd, Abergavenny NP7 7RP
Coleg Gwent
T 01495 333777
E sam.brooks@coleggwent.ac.uk
W www.thehillabergavenny.co.uk
Accommodation The Hill offers 48 ensuite bedrooms, an executive suite and a self-contained lodge that sleeps 5. Please phone for more information and special offers.
See Gardd-y-Bryn for details of garden.
B&B SC H

LLWYN-Y-WEN FARM
Hafodyrynys Road, Crumlin NP11 5AX
Mrs H Lewy
T 01495 244797
E robert@lefray.eclipse.co.uk
W www.lefray.eclipse.co.uk
Accommodation Rooms in SC

wing of large farmhouse from £35 single and £50 double. Set in 20 acres bordering Forestry Commission land. Bluebells in May and a haven for wildlife and hundreds of birds. Picturesque walks.
B&B

THE NURTONS
Chepstow NP16 7NX
Elsa Wood
T 01291 689253
E info@thenurtons.co.uk
W www.thenurtons.co.uk
Accommodation 2 B&B suites – 1 twin with double sofa bed & 1 double, each with own private bathroom, sitting room & patio. Scenic, secluded and historical site. Organic produce. £32.50 pppn.
B&B

PENPERGWM LODGE
Abergavenny NP7 9AS
Mr & Mrs S Boyle
T 01873 840208
E boyle@penpergwm.co.uk
W www.penplants.com
Accommodation A large rambling Edwardian house in the lovely Usk valley. Pretty bedrooms have garden views, bathrooms share a corridor, breakfast and relax in the spacious and comfortable sitting room. Great walking in nearby Brecon Beacons National Park.
B&B

Gloucestershire North & Central

BANK VIEW
Victoria Road, Quenington GL7 5BP
Mr & Mrs J Moulden
T 01285 750573
E jackie.moulden@lineone.net
W www.bankviewbandb.co.uk
Accommodation 4 diamond accommodation, with 1 twin, 2 double ensuite rooms. Non smoking. Relax and unwind in the tranquil Cotswolds. Comfortable rooms look out onto beautiful scenery. Ideally based to visit Cheltenham, Oxford and Cirencester. Lovely local pubs. See Quenington Gardens for details of garden.
B&B

BERRYS PLACE FARM
Bulley Lane, Churcham, Gloucester GL2 8AS
Mr G & Mrs A Thomas
T 01452 750298
E garyjthomas@hotmail.co.uk
Accommodation Traditional farmhouse B&B with small carp lake. 6 miles west of historic Gloucester, approx 9 miles Cheltenham Spa and race course and easy reach of The

Cotswolds, Forest of Dean and Wye Valley. £35 pppn.
B&B

COOPERS COTTAGE
Wells Road, Bisley, Stroud GL6 7AG
Mr & Mrs Michael Flint
T 01452 770289
E flint_bisley@talktalk.net
Accommodation Attractive old beamed cottage, non-smoking, sleeps 2 – 4. Stands apart in owners' large, beautiful garden with lovely views. Furnished & equipped to high standard. Very quiet, good walking. Village shop & 2 pubs nearby. See Wells Cottage for details of garden.
SC

GRANGE COTTAGE
Mill Lane, Blockley, Moreton-in-Marsh GL56 9HT
Guy & Alison Heitmann
T 01386 700251
E info@grangecottagebandb.com
Accommodation 1 twin, 1 double, both ensuite. On a peaceful lane in the centre of the old part of the village. A great area for walking. See Blockley Gardens for details of garden.
B&B

KEMPSFORD MANOR
High Street, Kempsford, Fairford GL7 4EQ
Mrs Z Williamson
T 01285 810131
E ipek.williamson@tiscali.co.uk
W www.kempsfordmanor.co.uk
Accommodation C17 – 18 manor house set in peaceful gardens. Fine reception rooms. 3 – 4 double bedrooms. Price from £35 single occ. Ideal retreat. Home grown organic vegetables. Suitable for small conferences and marquee receptions. 1 mile from Wiltshire border.
B&B

Hampshire

APPLE COURT
Hordle Lane, Hordle, Lymington SO41 0HU
Charles & Angela Meads
T 01590 642130
E applecourt@btinternet.com
W www.applecourt.com
Accommodation Cottage annexe next to Apple Court. 2 bedrooms, sleeps 4. Kitchen, dining room, conservatory/lounge. Non – smoking. Regret no dogs. Beautiful location near New Forest, Lymington. From £400 per week.
B&B

WADES HOUSE
Barton Stacey, Winchester SO21 3RJ
Tony & Jenny Briscoe
T 01962 760516
E jenny.roo@btinternet.com
Accommodation Luxuriously comfortable family home. 2 double, 2 twin rooms with private facilities & lovely views over 2 acre garden. A garden lover's delight. Sitting room with TV/DVD/video and large open fire. Delicious homemade food. Dinner by arrangement. £50 pppn.
B&B

Herefordshire

ARROW COTTAGE
Weobley, Hereford HR4 8RN
David and Janet Martin
T 01544 318468
E info@arrowcottagegarden.co.uk
W www.arrowcottagegarden.co.uk
Accommodation Lovely self catering detached cottage with 3 double bedrooms, 2 reception rooms and 2 bathrooms. The cottage is available on a weekly basis (rental £350 – £550 pw). Please ring or look at our website for further details.
SC

BROBURY HOUSE
Brobury, Hereford HR3 6BS
Prof & Mrs Cartwright
T 01981 500229
E enquiries@broburyhouse.co.uk
W www.broburyhouse.co.uk
Accommodation House – B&B: Large double room, ensuite. 1 double & 1 twin large rooms each with private shower room, all with beautiful garden views. Prices from £35 pppn. Cottages – 2 spacious, recently refurbished, self catering cottages. Peak period price £440.00.
B&B SC

CAVES FOLLY NURSERY
Evendine Lane, Colwall WR13 6DY
Bridget Evans
T 01684 540631
E bridget@cavesfolly.com
W www.cavesfolly.co.uk
Accommodation Self-catering cottage on organic nursery. Idyllic setting in Malvern Hills AONB. Available to let nightly or weekly. Sleeps 6. Also self-catering B&B – choose your organic breakfast from our shop. £30 per person.
B&B SC

THE GREAT HOUSE
Dilwyn, Hereford HR4 8HX
Tom & Jane Hawksley
T 01544 318007
W www.thegreathousedilwyn.co.uk
Accommodation 3 double/twin, ensuite bathrooms. Private sunny

sitting room with door to garden. Beams, panelling, flag stone floors and enormous log fires. Price £90, single occ. £50. Dinner by arrangement from £18. Licensed. Wolsey Lodge.
B&B

HOPE END HOUSE
Hope End, Ledbury HR8 1JQ
Mr & Mrs PJ Maiden
T 01531 635890
E sharonmaiden@btinternet.com
W www.hopeendhouse.com
Accommodation Hope End House, surrounded by 100 acres of historic parkland, where once Elizabeth Barrett roamed. This romantic house has peace at its heart. Our accommodation has been awarded 5*. Our gardens tranquil and peaceful.
B&B

Hertfordshire

106 ORCHARD ROAD
Tewin, Welwyn AL6 0LZ
Linda Adams
T 01438 798147
E alannio@btinternet.com
W www.tewinvillage.co.uk
Accommodation 1 large double and 1 large twin room with private facilities, in listed C20 house, with many original features. Beautiful views over one acre garden. Peaceful country setting. Parking. Prices from £35 pppn.
B&B

WEST LODGE PARK
Cockfosters Road, Hadley Wood, Barnet EN4 0PY
Beales Hotels
T 0208 216 3900
E westlodgepark@bealeshotels.co.uk
W www.bealeshotels.co.uk
Accommodation 59 bedrooms including Superior, Executive rooms with views over our arboretum. If you are looking for something more modern, try our chestnut lodge rooms which can be found in a separate lodge in our gardens.
H

Isle of Wight

NORTHCOURT
Shorwell PO30 3JG
Mr & Mrs J Harrison
T 01983 740415
E christine@northcourt.info
W www.northcourt.info
Accommodation B&B in large C17 manor house in 15 acres of exotic gardens, on edge of the downs. 6 double/twin rooms, all ensuite. Price from £60 per room. Also wing of house for up to 14 self-catering.
B&B SC

Kent

BOYTON COURT
Sutton Valence ME17 3BY
Richard & Patricia Stileman
T 01622 844065
E richstileman@aol.com
Accommodation Country house in quiet location and surrounded by lovely garden. Close to Sissinghurst and many others. 2 double rooms (1 king-size, 1 twin) with ensuite bathrooms. Both with spectacular south facing garden and Wealden views. £90 per night. Single occ. £55.
B&B

CANTERBURY CATHEDRAL LODGE
11 The Precincts, Canterbury CT1 2EH
Dean & Chapter of Canterbury
T 01227 865212
E stay@canterbury-cathedral.org
W www.canterburycathedrallodge. org
Accommodation Ensuite double room situated within the grounds of The Cathedral offers a perfect setting for an extended visit.
B&B

3 CHAINHURST COTTAGES
Dairy Lane, Chainhurst TN12 9SU
Heather Scott
T 01622 820483 / 07729 378489
E heatherscott@waitrose.com
W www.chainhurstcottages.co.uk
Accommodation Comfortable, modern accommodation with private entrance and ensuite bathroom in quiet rural location with good local pubs. Ideal touring base for historic properties and gardens including Leeds Castle & Sissinghurst Garden. Visit Britain – 4 stars – Silver award. £37.50 pppn.
See Chainhurst Cottage Gardens for details of garden.
B&B

COTTAGE FARM
Cacketts Lane, Cudham TN14 7QG
Phil & Karen Baxter
T 01959 534048/532506
E karen@cottagefarmturkeys.co.uk
Accommodation Delightful country cottage: 1 double and 1 twin room, living room, kitchen and bathroom. Full central heating. From £350 per week self catering. B&B £35 pppn based on 2 sharing double/twin room. £45 single occ.
B&B SC

HOATH HOUSE
Chiddingstone Hoath, Edenbridge TN8 7DB
Mervyn & Jane Streatfeild
T 01342 850362
E janestreatfeild@hoath-house.freeserve.co.uk
W www.hoathhouse.co.uk
Accommodation Rambling medieval and Tudor house in extensive gardens with fine views. Convenient for Penshurst, Chartwell and Hever and recommendations for NGS openings across Kent. 2 twin rooms sharing 'Art deco' bathroom, 1 double, ensuite. Good access to London and Gatwick
Member of County Team
B&B

ROCK FARM
Nettlestead, Maidstone ME18 5HT
Mrs S E Corfe
T 01622 812244
W www.rockfarmhousebandb.co.uk
Accommodation Delightful C18 Kentish farmhouse in quiet, idyllic position on a farm with extensive views. 4 diamond B&B with 1 double and 1 twin room, both ensuite. Price £60, single occ £35.
SC

THE SALUTATION
Knightrider Street, Sandwich CT13 9EW
Mr & Mrs D Parker
T 01304 619919
E dominic@the-salutation.com
W www.the-salutation.com
Accommodation 10 bedrooms available within 3 cottages within the estate, offering exclusive and private bed and breakfast.
B&B

STOWTING HILL HOUSE
Ashford TN25 6BE
Richard & Virginia Latham
T 01303 862881
E vjlatham@hotmail.com
Accommodation 2 twins, both with bath. 1 double. A Georgian Manor house set in beautiful North Downs, with walks from our door in quiet rolling valleys and plenty of gardens to visits. Prices from £80, double & from £50, single.
Member of County Team.
B&B

WICKHAM LODGE
The Quay, High Street, Aylesford ME20 7AY
Cherith & Richard Bourne
T 01622 717267
E wickhamlodge@aol.com
W www.wickhamlodge.co.uk
Accommodation Beautifully

restored house offering every modern comfort situated on the river bank in Aylesford, one of the oldest and most picturesque villages in Kent. Cherith & Richard provide a warm and hospitable welcome for their guests.
B&B SC

Lancashire, Merseyside & Greater Manchester

MILL BARN
Goose Foot Close, Samlesbury, Bottoms, Preston PR5 0SS
Chris Mortimer
T 01245 853300
E chris@millbarn.net
Accommodation Mill Barn is a converted barn. 1 double & 1 twin room, neither ensuite. Guests are accommodated as house guests & have full access to all shared rooms – lounge, conservatory, studio etc. as well as the garden. Member of County Team.
B&B

THE RIDGES
Weavers Brow, Cont. Cowling Road, Limbrick Heath Charnock, Chorley PR6 9EB
John & Barbara Barlow
T 01257 279981
E barlow.ridges@virgin.net
W www.bedbreakfast-gardenvisits.com
Accommodation 3 bedrooms, 1 double ensuite, 1 twin & 1 single sharing a private bathroom. Second toilet in hallway. Dining room. Prices from £70 double & £40 single.
B&B

Leicestershire & Rutland

MANTON LODGE FARM
Manton, Oakham LE15 8SS
Mrs A G Burnaby-Atkins
T 01572 737269
E eba@mantonlodge.co.uk
W www.mantonlodge.co.uk
Accommodation Modernised, secluded C17 stone farmhouse set in 20 acres of grassland with stunning views over the Chater Valley.
See Manton Gardens for details of garden.
B&B SC

MEADOWSWEET LODGE
South View, Uppingham, Oakham LE15 9TU
Jane Wright
T 01572 822504
Accommodation 1 twin room with private bathroom. 2 minutes walk

from Market Place on the south slope of the town. Very sunny aspect with approx. 1 acre of garden.
See Uppingham Gardens for details of garden.
B&B

Lincolnshire

BRUNESWOLD COACH HOUSE
1A Hereward Street, Lincoln LN1 3EW
Jo & Ken Slone
T 01522 568484
E kenjo@bruneswoldcoachhouse.co.uk
W www.bruneswoldcoachhouse.co.uk
Accommodation Ground level self catering B&B accommodation within the garden of a Victorian town house in uphill Lincoln, brimming with plants and sculpture. 5 minutes walk away from the historic quarter of Lincoln. Off-road parking.
See The Coach House for details of garden.
Member of County Team.
B&B

THE OLD VICARAGE
Holbeach Hurn, Low Road, Spalding PE12 8JN
Liz Dixon-Spain
T 01406 424148
E lizds@ukonline.co.uk
W www.specialplacestostay.com
Accommodation Victorian vicarage set in 1½ acres of mature gardens. All local/home produce for breakfasts. Closed mid December – mid March. Children welcome. 2 rooms available, 1 twin/1 double.
B&B

London

38 KILLIESER AVENUE
SW2 4NT
Winkle Haworth
T 020 8671 4196
E winklehaworth@hotmail.com
W www.specialplacestostay.com
Accommodation Luxurious and stylish accommodation, 1 twin bedded room, 1 single – both with private bathroom. Price from £90. Single occ. £55. English breakfast incl.
Member of County Team.
B&B

28 OLD DEVONSHIRE ROAD
London SW12 9RB
Georgina Ivor
T 020 8673 7179
E georgina@giamanagement.com
Accommodation 1 spacious twin bedded room with private bathroom in elegant mid Victorian house. 5 minutes from Balham tube and

mainline stations; great variety of local restaurants. Price from £90. Single occ £50. English breakfast included.
B&B

Norfolk

BAGTHORPE HALL
Bagthorpe, King's Lynn PE31 6QR
Mrs Gina Morton
T 01485 578528
E enquiries@bagthorpehall.co.uk
W www.bagthorpehall.co.uk
Accommodation 2 – 3 large double bedrooms ensuite, big comfortable beds, organic and homemade breakfast. From £70 for double incl breakfast. £40 single.
B&B

BAY COTTAGE
Colby Corner, Nr Aylsham NR11 7EB
Judith & Stuart Clarke
T 01263 734574
E enchanting@btinternet.com
W www.enchantingcottages.co.uk
Accommodation Four star ETB graded country cottage with large garden. Sleeps 7 in 3 bedrooms, plus a self contained garden, oak framed annexe with wheelchair access, which sleeps 2.
See The Old Cottage for details of garden.
SC

MANOR HOUSE FARM
Wellingham, King's Lynn PE32 2TH
Robin & Elisabeth Ellis
T 01328 838227
W www.manor-house-farm.co.uk
Accommodation Award winning conversion in garden. 2 large airy double bedrooms, ensuite. Comfortable, sitting room with wood burning stove, TV and books etc plus small kitchen. Breakfast in dining room of main house. Also beautiful barn with SC for 2.
B&B SC

THE OLD RECTORY
Ridlington, North Walsham NR28 9NZ
Peter & Fiona Black
T 01692 650247
E blacks7@email.com
W www.oldrectory.northnorfolk.co.uk
Accommodation House: 1 double bedroom, ensuite; 1 double with wash basin and private bathroom. Garden room: large studio, double/twin beds, plus sofa bed, ktichen and bathroom. Prices from £50 per night. 1½ miles from East Ruston Old Vicarage Gardens
Member of County Team.
B&B SC

SALLOWFIELD COTTAGE
Wattlefield, Wymondham NR18 9PA
Caroline Musker
T 01952 605086
E caroline.musker@tesco.net
W www.sallowfieldcottage.co.uk
Accommodation One double
ensuite, one double with private
bathroom and one single with private
shower. The cottage is in a quiet
location well away from the road
surrounded by its own garden with a
large pond.
B&B

WOODLANDS FARM
Stokesby, Great Yarmouth NR29 3DX
Vivienne Fabb
T 01493 369347
E v.fabb@btinternet.com
Accommodation Convenient for
Broads, coast & Norwich. Attractive
ensuite rooms with lovely garden
views. Outdoor pool & croquet in
summer. Year round woodland walks.
Evening meals by arrangement using
home grown produce when possible.
Price £55 double, single occ. £35.
B&B

North Wales

BODYSGALLEN HALL
Llandudno LL30 1RS
Historic House Hotels Ltd.
T 01492 584466
E info@bodysgallen.com
W www.bodysgallen.com
Accommodation Standing in 200
acres of gardens and parkland,
Bodysgallen Hall provides all that is
best in country house hospitality. 33
rooms and suites, an award winning
restaurant and a health and fitness
spa are here to indulge in.
H

DOVE COTTAGE
Rhos Road, nr Chester CH4 0JR
Mr & Mrs C Wallis
T 01244 547539
E dovecottage@supanet.com
W www.visitwales.com
Accommodation Delightful C17
farmhouse. Luxurious
accommodation. 1 double room,
ensuite, 1 double room , private
shower rm. Single occ. £35 – £45,
double £50 – £60 per night.
Convenient for Chester & N Wales.
B&B

THE OLD RECTORY
Llanfihangel Glyn Myfyr,
Cerrigydrudion LL21 9UN
Mr & Mrs E T Hughes
T 01490 420568
E elwynthomashughes@hotmail.com
Accommodation Luxury rural
retreat set in idyllic garden and
countryside. 1 family room, ensuite, 1
family room with private bathroom.
Guest lounge. Price from £30 pppn.
B&B

RUTHIN CASTLE
Castle Street, Ruthin LL15 2NU
Ruthin Castle Ltd
T 01824 702664
E reservations@ruthincastle.com
W www.ruthincastle.co.uk
Accommodation A magical 62
bedroom hotel in a parkland setting ,
rich in history and character, 23 miles
from Chester. The mediaeval castle,
built by Edward 1, & owned by the
monarchy for extended periods, was
re-built in 1826. B&B from £45 pppn.
H

Northamptonshire

COTON LODGE
West Haddon Road, Guilsborough,
Northampton NN6 8QE
**Peter Hicks and Joanne de
Nobriga**
T 01604 740215
E peter@cotonlodge.co.uk
W www.cotonlodge.co.uk
Accommodation House: 1 king
sized double room & 1 twin room
both with ensuite bathrooms. Prices
from £90 per room per night.
B&B

THE OLD VICARAGE
Broad Lane, Evenley, Brackley
NN13 5SF
Philippa Heumann
T 07774 415 332
E philippaheumann@andreas-
heumann.com
Accommodation Elegant Regency
vicarage set in large attractive garden
in the picturesque village of Evenley.
Two twin bedrooms, two bathrooms.
Ideally situated for visiting gardens in
Central England – approx 5 miles
J10 M40. B&B – single £35, double
£70 per night.
Member of County Team.
B&B

STABLE COTTAGE
Kettle End, Weedon Lois, Towcester
NN12 8PW
Mr & Mrs Medlicott-Walker
T 01327 860895
E lynnmedlicott2@aol.com
Accommodation Stone built self
contained studio apartment set in
cottage garden. Furnished to high
standard. Kitchen, shower room,
conservatory and bedroom with
double and single beds. Peaceful
historic village with church and award
winning pub nearby. From £45 pppn.
See Weedon Lois Gardens for details
of garden.
B&B SC

Nottinghamshire

ASHDENE
Radley Road, Halam, Nr Southwell
NG22 8AH
David C Herbert
T 01636 812335
E david@herbert.newsurf.net
Accommodation Double, ensuite;
twin with private bathroom; 4 poster
double with shared bathroom. C15
farmhouse with resident's private
sitting room. Open fires. Double room
– £60, single occ, £40.
B&B

Oxfordshire

BROUGHTON GROUNDS FARM
North Newington, Banbury
OX15 6AW
Andrew and Margaret Taylor
T 01295 730315
E broughtongrounds@hotmail.com
W www.broughtongrounds.co.uk
Accommodation One double, one
twin and one single room in 17th
Century farmhouse, on working
mixed farm, located on the
Broughton Castle Estate. Beautiful
views and peaceful location. Prices:
£28 pppn.
B&B

BUTTSLADE HOUSE
Temple Mill Road, Sibford Gower,
Banbury OX15 5RX
Mrs Diana Thompson
T 01295 788818
E janthompson50@hotmail.com
W www.buttsladehouse.co.uk
Accommodation Sympathetically
restored stables of C17 farmhouse in
tranquil English country garden. 1
double and 1 twin bedded room with
private sitting rooms and own
bathrooms. Own bread & cakes
baked daily, seasonal fruit from
garden. SC available, please enquire.
See Sibford Gower Gardens for
details of garden.
B&B SC

GOWERS CLOSE
Sibford Gower, Banbury OX15 5RW
**Judith Hitching and John
Marshall**
T 01295 780348
E j.hitching@virgin.net
Accommodation C17 thatched
cottage has 1 double and 1 twin,
both ensuite, with low beams and log
fires, enchanting garden for
pampered guests to enjoy. Close to
Hidcote, Kiftsgate and many
Cotswold gardens. Price from £35
pppn.
See Sibford Gower Gardens for
details of garden.
B&B

SOUTH NEWINGTON HOUSE
South Newington, Banbury
OX15 4JW
Roberta & John Ainley
T 01295 721207
E rojoainley@btinternet.com
W www.southnewingtonhouse.co.uk
Accommodation Cottage annexe:
Bedroom (king-size), sitting room,
shower room & kitchen. House: 2
doubles (king-size) & 1 twin all with
private bathrooms. Prices £80 –
£100 per room per night. Single occ.
£50 – £60.
Member of County Team.
B&B SC

STAPLETON'S CHANTRY
Long Wittenham Road, North
Moreton, Didcot OX11 9AX
Dr Muir and Mrs Maggie Parker
T 01235 818900
E BedandBreakfast@
StapletonsChantry.co.uk
W www.StapletonsChantry.co.uk
Accommodation Exceptionally
comfortable and welcoming B&B in
lovely C16 family home, set in 4
acres of lovely gardens in a peaceful
and pretty village in South
Oxfordshire.
See North Moreton Gardens for
details of garden.
B&B

Powys

CYFIE FARM
Llanfihangel, Llanfyllin SY22 5JE
Neil & Claire Bale
T 01691 648451
E info@cyfiefarm.co.uk
W www.cyfiefarm.co.uk
Accommodation This beautiful,
remote, 5 star (Gold), C17 Welsh
Longhouse, boasts a magnificent
peaceful setting with stunning views.
Relax all day in your own luxurious
suite of rooms. Cordon Bleu cuisine.
Hot tub & sauna spa.
B&B SC

MILL COTTAGE
Abbeycwmhir, Llandrindod Wells
LD1 6PH
Mr & Mrs B D Parfitt
T 01597 851935
E nkmillcottage@yahoo.co.uk
W www.Abbeycwmhir.co.uk
Accommodation C18 cottage in a
peaceful village in the beautiful
Cambrian mountains. 1 double/twin
with private bathroom. 2 singles (one
with dressing room and basin).
Private bathroom. Evening meals by
arrangement. Ideal for walkers and
cyclists.
B&B

PLAS DOLGUOG HOTEL
Solstar, Dolguog Estates Felingerrig,
Machynlleth SY20 8UJ
Mr Anthony & Mrs Tina Rhodes
T 01654 702244
E res@plasdolguog.co.uk
W www.plasdolguog.co.uk
Accommodation Family run hotel,
David Bellamy Conservation Award, 9
acres including Grandma's Garden.
Family & ground floor rooms – all
individual with ensuite facilities. Cu
Og's restaurant offers panoramic
views over the Dyfi Valley &
Snowdonia National Park.
See Grandma's Garden for details of
garden.
B&B

THE WERN
Llanfihangel Talyllyn, Brecon LD3 7TE
Lucienne and Neil Bennett
T 01874 658401
E lucienne_bennett@hotmail.com
W www.bennettthewern.vispa.com
Accommodation The Wern B&B
for Horse and Rider is situated in the
Brecon Beacons National Park.
Evening meals available. The food
provided is from produce from our
gardens. Our guests have full use of
our gardens and terraces.
B&B

Shropshire

BROWNHILL HOUSE
Ruyton XI Towns, Shrewsbury
SY4 1LR
Yoland & Roger Brown
T 01939 261121
E brownhill@eleventowns.co.uk
W www.eleventowns.co.uk
Accommodation Old world
standards, modern facilities & relaxed
atmosphere. Unique 2 acre garden –
must be seen to be believed. Easy
access – Chester to Ludlow,
Snowdonia to Ironbridge and loads of
wonderful gardens. Find out all about
us on our website.
B&B

THE CITADEL
Weston-under-Redcastle, nr
Shrewsbury SY4 5JY
Beverley and Sylvia Griffiths
T 01630 685204
E griffiths@thecitadelweston.co.uk
W www.thecitadelweston.co.uk
Accommodation Luxury
accommodation in unusual red
sandstone, castellated house,
surrounded by beautiful gardens and
views across to Wales. 3 double
rooms with ensuite facilities and all
comforts. From £110 per room per
night.
B&B

MAREHAY FARM
Gatten, Pontesbury, Shrewsbury
SY5 0SJ
Carol & Stuart Buxton
T 01588 650289
Accommodation 2 ensuite rooms,
one twin, one double in one of the
last idyllic areas of England. Far from
the madding crowd and noble strife!
B&B from £27.50 per person.
B&B

Somerset & Bristol

THE BEANACRE BARN
Turners Court Lane, Binegar,
Radstock BA3 4UA
Susan & Tony Griffin
T 01749 841628
E smg@beanacrebarn.co.uk
W www.beanacrebarn.co.uk
Accommodation In the Mendip
Hills 4m north of Wells. Imaginatively
converted, beautifully furnished and
particularly spacious, beamed barn.
All modern facilities and comfort in a
traditional setting. Sleeps 2+2. Own
south-facing garden and patio.
Peaceful country retreat.
See Church Farm House for details of
garden.
SC

EMMAUS HOUSE RETREAT &
CONFERENCE CENTRE
Clifton Hill, Clifton, Bristol BS8 1BN
Sisters of La Retraite
T 0117 907 9950
E administration@emmaushouse.
org.uk
W www.emmaushouse.org.uk
Accommodation C18 listed
building in the heart of Clifton. 23
single rooms (1 designated twin, 10
convertible to twin), 7 ensuite. Prices
pppn from £40 standard to £45
ensuite. Continental breakfast. Award
winning gardens with extensive
views. Nightly 'curfew' 10.30 pm.
Latest check-in 9.00 pm.
B&B

GANTS MILL & GARDEN
Gants Mill Lane, Bruton BA10 0DB
Alison & Brian Shingler
T 01749 812393
E shingler@gantsmill.co.uk
W www.gantsmill.co.uk
Accommodation C18 farmhouse
in rural valley, by historic watermill
now generating electricity. Spacious,
comfortable, pretty, bedrooms with
lacy four-poster stargazer beds. Wide
choice of healthy and wicked
breakfasts with best local ingredients.
£35 per person per night. Vacancies
on website.
B&B

HANGERIDGE FARMHOUSE
Wrangway, Wellington TA21 9QT
Mrs J M Chave
T 01823 662339
E hangeridge@hotmail.co.uk
W www.etribes.com/hangeridge
Accommodation Situated at the foot of the Blackdown Hills within 5 mins drive from M5 (jn 25 or 26). 1 twin and 1 double room with private bathroom. B&B £23 pp per night, B&B and evening meal £28 pp per night.
B&B

HARPTREE COURT
East Harptree, Bristol BS40 6AA
Mr & Mrs Charles Hill
T 01761 221729
E location.harptree@tiscali.co.uk
W www.harptreecourt.co.uk
Accommodation 2 double rooms ensuite and 1 twin room in elegant period house surrounded by beautiful landscaped grounds. £100 B&B with afternoon tea per room per night. £65 single occ. Evening meal by arrangement. 5 Star Highly Commended.
B&B

HOMEWOOD PARK HOTEL
Abbey Lane, Hinton Charterhouse, Bath BA2 7TB
von Essen Hotels
T 01225 723731
E info@homewoodpark.co.uk
W www.homewoodpark.co.uk
Accommodation Gracious country house hotel near Bath and one of the loveliest in the West Country. 19 beautiful bedrooms, individually furnished to a high standard. B&B prices from £165.00 per room. See website for special offers.
H

KNOLL COTTAGE
Stogumber, Taunton TA4 3TN
Elaine & John Leech
T 01984 656689
E mail@knoll-cottage.co.uk
W www.knoll-cottage.co.uk
Accommodation Visit Britain 4*. Secluded rural location between the Quantocks and Exmoor. Beautiful 2 acre garden. Two ensuite bedrooms with king-sized beds in recently converted stables. Double from £50. Single from £30. Dogs welcome.
B&B

ST JAMES'S GRANGE
West Littleton, Chippenham SN14 8JE
David & Carolyn Adams
T 01225 891100
E stay@stjamesgrange.com

W www.stjamesgrange.com
Accommodation A barn conversion which looks like an old farmhouse offering 3 light and airy bedrooms with garden views. Cosy guests' sitting room. One double/twin with ensuite bathroom; one twin, one double sharing adjacent bath/shower. £55 – £65.
See West Littleton Gardens for details of garden.
B&B

SPINDLE COTTAGE
Binegar Green, Binegar, nr Bath BA3 4UE
Angela Bunting
T 01749 840497
E angela@spindlecottage.co.uk
W www.spindlecottage.co.uk
Accommodation Fairytale picturesque C17 cottage Sleeps 5, 3 bedrooms. Set in peaceful garden with summer-house, gazebo, conservatory and three magical playhouses. Within the cottage, carvings of mushrooms, spiders' webs, birds and mice. Quite magical. See Binegar Village Gardens for details of garden.
SC

WOODLAND COTTAGE
Oldbury-on-Severn BS35 1PL
Jane Perkins
T 01454 414570
E jane.perkins@simtec.ltd.uk
Accommodation 1 twin room with shared bathroom. Price £20 pppn Member of County Team.
B&B

Suffolk

THE COACH HOUSE
Assington CO10 5LQ
Mrs Justine Ferrari
T 01787 211364
E info@coachhousegreta.co.uk
W www.englishgardenbandb.co.uk
Accommodation A warm welcome awaits you in our Georgian country house. Pretty rooms, delicious local breakfast. Spend time in our 3 acre, beautiful and peaceful garden in the heart of Constable country. Price £70. Single occ. £40
B&B

GARDEN FLAT, 68 SOUTHWOLD ROAD
Wrentham, Nr Southwold NR34 7JF
Mrs Reeve
T 01502 675692
E lillylady@hotmail.co.uk
Accommodation Separately accessed self-contained flat within owner's garden. Open plan kitchen/sitting room, bathroom/power shower, spiral

staircase to twin bedroom. Private patio with seating.
See Wrentham Gardens for details of garden.
B&B SC

ROSEMARY
Rectory Hill, East Bergholt, Colchester CO7 6TH
Mrs Natalie Finch
T 01206 298241
Accommodation Situated in the heart of Constable country within easy reach of Harwich and Flatford. Garden featured on Gardener's World. 3 twin rooms – with hand basins, 1 single room. Shared bathroom. Price £29 single, £58 twin.
B&B

THRIFT FARMHOUSE
Cowlinge, Newmarket CB8 9JA
Mrs Jan Oddy
T 01440 783274
E janoddy@yahoo.co.uk
Accommodation A delightful thatched farmhouse, in tranquil 6 acres of gardens & meadows. Good local walks & bird watching. Relax in the informal atmosphere of this family home. 1 twin, 1 double in the house, 1 double ensuite in the 'piggery'. Prices from £25 – £32.
B&B

THE WALLOW
Mount Road, Bury St. Edmunds IP31 2QU
Linda & Mike Draper
T 01248 788055
E info@thewallow.co.uk
W www.thewallow.co.uk
Accommodation 2 suites comprising double bedroom, lounge and bathroom in ranch style bungalow, surrounded by countryside yet close to the town centre. Easy access to pub/restaurant via footpath/cycle track 51.
B&B

Surrey

GREAT FOSTERS
Stroude Road, Egham TW20 9UR
The Sutcliffe Family
T 01784 433822
E reservations@greatfosters.co.uk
W www.greatfosters.co.uk
Accommodation More than 4 centuries of celebrated history have enriched Great Fosters with remarkable heritage. Countless original features remain, with bedrooms varying from historic grandeur to more contemporary in style. Double/twin rooms start from £165 per night.
H

SPRING COTTAGE
Smithwood Common Road,
Cranleigh GU6 8QN
Mr & Mrs David Norman
T 01483 272620
E norman.springcott@btinternet.com
Accommodation 1st floor
accommodation in newly built barn. 1
double bedroom, bathroom, large
sitting room with TV. Lovely views
towards N and S downs. Good
walking and cycling. Enjoy garden in
all seasons. Prices from £65 per
night. Single occ. £40.
B&B SC

WOTTON HOUSE
Guildford Road, Dorking RH5 6HS
Hayley Conference Centres
T 01306 730000
E wotton@hayleycc.co.uk.
W www.hayley-conf.co.uk
Accommodation Wotton House
has 111 ensuite facilities. 91 double
rooms, 20 twins and 5 adapted for
disabled use. Each room has: Wi-Fi,
TV, Safe, tea & coffee making
facilities, hairdryers, trouser press &
iron. Dry cleaning service.
H

Sussex

BUTLERS FARMHOUSE
Butlers Lane, Flowers Green,
Herstmonceux BN27 1QH
Irene Eltringham-Willson
T 01323 833770
E irene.willson@btinternet.com
W www.irenethegardener.zoomshare.
com
Accommodation A charming C16
farmhouse in 5 acres of idyllic, quiet
countryside. Enjoy breakfast
overlooking fantastic views of the
South Downs. 2 rooms with private
bathrooms. Laze around outdoor
swimming pool. Herstmonceux and
Pevensey Castles nearby. From £75.
B&B

COPYHOLD HOLLOW
Copyhold Lane, Lindfield, Haywards
Heath RH16 1XU
Frances B G Druce
T 01444 413265
E yb@copyholdhollow.co.uk
W www.copyholdhollow.co.uk
Accommodation Guests' sitting
room with inglenook fireplace, oak
beams, cotton sheets, ensuite
bedrooms, C16 home surrounded by
countryside. Double/twin £40/£45
pppn, single £45/£55 pn. 4
Stars/Gold Award. Short break
gardening holidays.
B&B

HAILSHAM GRANGE
Hailsham BN27 1BL
Noel Thompson
T 01323 844248
E noel-hgrange@amserve.com
W www.hailshamgrange.co.uk
Accommodation Accommodation
is available in the main house (a
former vicarage circa 1700) &
adjoining Coach House. Hailsham
Grange exemplifies the classic
English style which is synonymous
with relaxed comfortable living & old
fashioned hospitality. Rates range
from £75 – £110 per room per night.
B&B

HAM COTTAGE
Highbrook, Ardingly RH17 6SR
Mr & Mrs P Browne
T 01444 892746
E aegbrowne@btinternet.com
Accommodation C18 cottage set
in 8 acres of landscaped gardens
within the heart of Sussex, providing
2 double & 1 twin room each with its
own bathroom.
B&B

KING JOHN'S LODGE
Sheepstreet Lane, Etchingham
TN19 7AZ
Jill & Richard Cunningham
T 01580 819232
E kingjohnslodge@aol.com
W www.kingjohnslodge.co.uk
Accommodation B&B in this
historic listed house surrounded by 8
acres of gardens, meadows and
newly opened propagation nursery.
All rooms ensuite. Holiday
accommodation available. Awarded 5
diamonds by SE tourist board for its
high quality.
B&B SC

LORDINGTON HOUSE
Lordington, Chichester PO18 9DX
Mr & Mrs John Hamilton
T 01243 375862
E audreyhamilton@onetel.com
Accommodation Comfortable
accommodation offered in double,
twin and single rooms with own
bath/shower. All rooms have fine
views over our AONB. Breakfast
times flexible. Packed lunches and
supper by arrangement.
B&B

MOOR FARM
Horsham Road, Petworth GU28 0HD
Richard & Flo Chandler
T 01798 342161
E richardandflo1@btinternet.com
Accommodation B&B
accommodation on large working
arable farm, well off the road,
lakeside setting, within sight of

Petworth Park. Bring your own
horse and explore the local
bridleways. Coarse fishing on site.
Good parking.
B&B

NETHERBY
Bolney Road, Ansty, Haywards Heath
RH17 5AW
Mr & Mrs Russell Gilbert
T 01444 455888
E susan@gilbert58.freeserve.co.uk
Accommodation A warm welcome
awaits you in this cosy Victorian
cottage set in ½ acre garden. Firm
beds (2 doubles, 1 twin), excellent
breakfasts and sinks in all rooms.
Rates £30 pppn. Pets by
arrangement.
See Ansty Gardens for details of
garden.
B&B

PINDARS
Lyminster Road, Lyminster, Arundel
BN17 7QF
Jocelyne & Clive Newman
T 01903 882628
E pindars@btinternet.com
W www.pindars.co.uk
Accommodation Comfortable,
friendly country house with special
emphasis on hospitality and good
food. Delicious and varied breakfasts,
imaginatively cooked. Evening meals
(usually available) with vegetables
from the prolific garden! Prices from
£60 per night.
B&B

73 SHEEPDOWN DRIVE
Petworth GU28 0BX
Mrs Angela Azis
T 01798 342269
Accommodation 2 twin with
shared bathroom. Prices from £60
per room. Single occ. £35. A short
walk from the historic town, no. 73
lies in a quiet 70s cul-de-sac and has
glorious views.
NGS Vice-President
B&B

Warwickshire & part of West Midlands

DINSDALE HOUSE
Baldwins Lane, Upper Tysoe,
Warwick CV35 0TX
Mrs Julia Sewell
T 01295 680234
E sewelljulia@btinternet.com
W www.dinsdalehouse.co.uk
Accommodation As NGS County
Organiser, Julia knows the gardens of
specific interest locally and in the
nearby Cotswolds. Large village
house with swimming pool for
guests. Close to Stratford, Warwick

and Oxford. Double/twin with ensuite. Evening meal available. Member of County Team.
B&B

SPRINGFIELD HOUSE
School Lane, Warmington, Banbury OX17 1DD
Roger & Jenny Handscombe
T 01295 690286
E jenny.handscombe@virgin.net
Accommodation C16 house with log fires and flagstone floors. 2 well appointed rooms with king or super-king beds and private bathroom. Handy for Cotswolds, Compton Verney and Shakespeare. No Smoking. From £20pppn.
See Warmington Village Gardens for details of garden.
B&B

Wiltshire

BECKETTS HOUSE
Tinhead Road, Edington, Westbury BA13 4PJ
Mrs Susan Bromhead
T 01380 830100
E sue@bromhead.org
Accommodation Attractive C17/18 listed house, in lovely village, set in 2¼ acres, tennis court, lake & superb views. Large twin bed, ensuite. Large twin bed, private bathroom. Large twin bed private shower on 2nd floor. Drawing room. Dining room.
See Edington Gardens for details of garden.
B&B

BROOMSGROVE LODGE
Broomsgrove, Pewsey SN9 5LE
Peter & Diana Robertson
T 01672 810515
E diana@broomsgrovelodge.co.uk
W www.sawdays.co.uk
Accommodation Thatched house with very comfortable twin and single accommodation. Own chickens and large vegetable garden. Close to Marlborough and the canal, with wonderful views over Pewsey Vale and Martinsell Hill.
B&B

GOULTERS MILL FARM
The Gibb, Burton, Chippenham SN14 7LL
Alison Harvey
T 01249 782555
E alison@harvey3512.freeserve.co.uk
Accommodation Delightful rooms in old mill house, all ensuite and equipped with king-sized beds. Convenient for Bristol, Bath or Cotswolds. The house is set in cottage gardens in a steep sided valley.

See Littleton Drew Gardens for details of garden.
B&B

THE MILL HOUSE
Berwick St James, Salisbury SP3 4TS
Diana Gifford Mead/ Michael Mertens
T 01722 790331
W www.millhouse.org.uk
Accommodation 4 ensuite, 2 single rooms from £55 pp single, £75, double. High quality accommodation. Very quiet, beautiful garden. Highly sourced and organic food. Part of old farm.
B&B

RIDLEYS CHEER
Mountain Bower, Chippenham SN14 7AJ
Sue & Antony Young
T 01225 891204
E sueyoung@ridleyscheer.co.uk
Accommodation 1 double with private bathroom. 1 double and 1 twin bedded room with shared bathroom. Prices from £80 per night. Single occ from £50. Dinner £30 per head.
B&B

Worcestershire

GRAFTON MANOR HOTEL
Grafton Lane, Upton Warren, Bromsgrove B61 7HA
John & June Morris
T 01527 579007
E natalie@graftonmanorhotel.co.uk
W www.graftonmanorhotel.co.uk
Accommodation Grafton Manor one time home of the Earl of Shrewsbury – now a stylish Country house hotel with nine en-suite bedrooms and an award winning restaurant.
H

HOLLAND HOUSE
Main Street, Cropthorne, Pershore WR10 3NB
Peter Middlemiss
T 01386 860330
E laycentre@hollandhouse.org
W www.hollandhouse.org
Accommodation Simple accommodation in a beautiful black and white timbered half-thatched retreat and conference centre. Advanced bookings only. Contact us to check availability and suitability.
B&B

LUGGERS HALL
Springfield Lane, Broadway WR12 7BT
Kay & Red Haslam
T 01386 852040

E luggershall@hotmail.com
W www.luggershall.com
Accommodation 2 king-size double rooms with beautiful views of gardens and 1 double room all with private ensuite bathrooms. Also self-catering in self contained apartment plus separate cottage in adjacent Cotswold village of Broadway. Prices from £65 per night.
B&B SC

RECTORY COTTAGE
Old Rectory Lane, Alvechurch, Birmingham B48 7SU
Steve & Celia Hitch
T 0121 445 4824
E celiaandsteve@reccott.freeserve.co.uk
W www.rectorycottage-alvechurch.co.uk
Accommodation Rectory Cottage is a large family home in a lovely riverside setting offering spacious and elegant bedrooms, all ensuite and overlooking the gardens. Family room, double room, twin bedded room. Easy access from Jn 2 of M42. Prices from £35 pppn.
See Alvechurch Gardens for details of garden.
B&B

WEAVERS
Rochford, Tenbury Wells WR15 8SL
Shirley Hambelton
T 01584 781767
E shirley@sigmafour.net
Accommodation Two double rooms with ensuites and country views. Walks on doorstep, enjoy our fields and old orchard. Worcester/ Hereford/Ludlow close by and several NT properties in local area. Lovely historical villages to explore. Warm & friendly welcome.
See Weavers & Tickners Cottages for details of garden.
B&B

Yorkshire

AUSTWICK HALL
Town Head Lane, Austwick, Lancaster LA2 8BS
Eric Culley and Michael Pearson
T 015242 51794
E austwickhall@austwick.org
W www.austwickhall.co.uk
Accommodation 5*, Silver Award Luxury Guest Accommodation. An Historic Manor House set in 13 acres. The four ensuite bedrooms provide spacious accommodation individually decorated and furnished with antiques. Dinner available.
B&B

Garden Index

This index lists gardens alphabetically and gives the Yellow Book county section in which they are to be found.

H

S

A catalogue record of this book is available from the British Library.

Typeset in Helvetica Neue font family.

The paper for this book conforms to Environmental Management Standard SFS-EN ISO 14001 (ed 1996)

ISBN 978-1-905942-09-1
ISSN 1365-0572
EAN 9 781905 942008